Cost Management

A Strategic Emphasis

Ninth Edition

Edward J. Blocher
University of North Carolina at Chapel Hill
Kenan-Flagler Business School

Paul E. Juras
Babson College
Accountancy and Law Divison

Steven D. Smith
Brigham Young University
Marriott School of Business

COST MANAGEMENT: A STRATEGIC EMPHASIS, NINTH EDITION

Published by McGraw Hill LLC, 1325 Avenue of the Americas, New York, NY 10121. Copyright © 2022 by McGraw Hill LLC. All rights reserved. Printed in the United States of America. Previous editions © 2019, 2016, and 2013. No part of this publication may be reproduced or distributed in any form or by any means, or stored in a database or retrieval system, without the prior written consent of McGraw Hill LLC, including, but not limited to, in any network or other electronic storage or transmission, or broadcast for distance learning.

Some ancillaries, including electronic and print components, may not be available to customers outside the United States.

This book is printed on acid-free paper.

1 2 3 4 5 6 7 8 9 LWI 24 23 22 21

ISBN 978-1-260-81471-2 (bound edition)
MHID 1-260-81471-8 (bound edition)

ISBN 978-1-264-11241-8 (loose-leaf edition)
MHID 1-264-11241-6 (loose-leaf edition)

Portfolio Manager: *Elizabeth Eisenhart*
Product Developers: *Erin Quinones/Michael McCormick*
Marketing Manager: *Lauren Schur*
Content Project Managers: *Amy Gehl/Jamie Koch*
Buyer: *Sandy Ludovissy*
Design: *Beth Blech*
Content Licensing Specialist: *Beth Cray*
Cover Image: *Shutterstock/alice-photo*
Design Elements: *©McGraw Hill Education*
Compositor: *SPi Global*

All credits appearing on page or at the end of the book are considered to be an extension of the copyright page.

Library of Congress Cataloging-in-Publication Data

Names: Blocher, Edward, author. | Juras, Paul E., author. | Smith, Steven D. (Steven Darby), author.
Title: Cost management: a strategic emphasis / Edward J. Blocher, University of North Carolina at Chapel Hill, Paul E. Juras, Boston State College, Steven Smith, Brigham Young University.
Description: Ninth edition. | New York: McGraw Hill LLC, 2021. | Includes bibliographical references and index.
Identifiers: LCCN 2020036601 | ISBN 9781260814712 (hardcover: alk. paper) | ISBN 9781264112333 (ebook)
Subjects: LCSH: Cost accounting. | Managerial accounting.
Classification: LCC HF5686.C8 B559 2021 | DDC 658.15/52—dc23 LC record available at https://lccn.loc.gov/2020036601

mheducation.com/highered

We dedicate this edition . . .

To my wife, Sandy, and our sons, Joseph
and David

Ed Blocher

To my wife, Colleen, and my children,
Stephen and Kate

Paul Juras

To my wife, Heather, and our children,
Darby, Trevor, Kelli, Finneas, and Melissa

Steve Smith

Meet the Authors

Jessica Gray Starnes/Kenan-Flagler Business
School/University of North Carolina at
Chapel Hill

Edward J. Blocher is an emeritus professor of accounting at the Kenan-Flagler Business School at the University of North Carolina at Chapel Hill. His undergraduate degree (economics) is from Rice University, his MBA from Tulane University, and his PhD from the University of Texas at Austin. Professor Blocher has presented regularly on strategic cost management at the national meetings of both the American Accounting Association (AAA) and the Institute of Management Accountants (IMA).

While he is involved in a number of accounting organizations, Professor Blocher has been most continually active in the IMA, where he has been a member of the IMA's Research Foundation. He is a certified management accountant (CMA), has taught review courses for the CMA exam, and has served on the IMA's national education committee. He has supervised or participated in the direction of several doctoral students, many of whom prepared dissertations in management accounting. Professor Blocher is also the author or coauthor of several articles in management accounting and in other areas of accounting and has served as associate editor and reviewer for a number of accounting journals. He published a 2009 article in *Issues in Accounting Education* on the topic of teaching strategic cost management.

Putting research and teaching into practice is important to Professor Blocher, who has worked closely with other firms and organizations in developing products, publications, and teaching materials. He was a member of the task force for the IMA that developed a new definition of management accounting in 2008. From 2010 to 2014, he served as a member of the joint curriculum task force of the Management Accounting Section (MAS) of the AAA and the IMA, which was charged with the responsibility of developing curriculum recommendations for accounting education. The task force has two recent publications in *Issues in Accounting Education.* Also, he has provided expert testimony and has consulted with a number of organizations regarding cost management matters.

Babson College

Paul E. Juras is the Jefferson Vander Wolk Professor of Managerial Accounting and Operational Performance and former chair of the Accountancy and Law Division at Babson College. Previously he was a professor of accountancy at Wake Forest University. He earned both his BBA and MBA at Pace University and his PhD from Syracuse University. He is a certified management accountant (CMA) and has a certified public accountant (CPA) license from New York. Professor Juras has experience in strategic management accounting. He has published articles and cases in many journals, including the *Journal of Corporate Accounting and Finance, Issues in Accounting Education, The CPA Journal,* and *Strategic Finance.* He has made numerous presentations at meetings of both the American Accounting Association (AAA) and the Institute of Management Accountants (IMA). In 2014, he received the IMA's Lybrand Gold Medal, awarded to the author(s) of the outstanding article of the year published in *Strategic Finance,* and in 2015 he received the IMA's R. Lee Brummet Award for Distinguished Accounting Educators.

Professor Juras taught managerial accounting and strategic cost management courses in the undergraduate program, the Masters of Science in Accountancy program, and the MBA program at Wake Forest University. He teaches cost management courses in the undergraduate and various graduate programs in both face-to-face and blended-learning formats at Babson College.

While he was active in CAM-I, the Consortium for Advanced Management–International, and has served in leadership roles in the Management Accounting Section of the AAA, Professor Juras dedicates most of his efforts outside the classroom to the IMA, including his role as the 2020–21 global chair of the organization. In addition, he has served as chair of the Institute of Certified Management Accountants, the organization responsible for the CMA certification; served a three-year term as chair of the IMA Research Foundation; and, for 10 years, was an associate editor of the *IMA Educational Case Journal.*

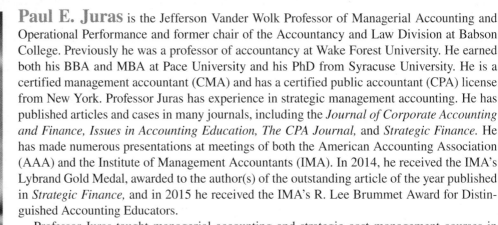

BYU Photo

Steven D. Smith is an associate professor of accountancy and the Warnick/Deloitte Fellow in the Marriott School of Business at Brigham Young University (BYU). Previously he was an assistant professor of accountancy at the University of Illinois at Urbana-Champaign. He earned BS and MACC degrees from BYU, and MS and PhD degrees from Cornell University. He is a certified management accountant (CMA). Professor Smith teaches cost and management accounting courses in the undergraduate and graduate accounting programs, as well as the executive MBA program at BYU. Professor Smith has experience working in the field of strategic cost management, including a 2016 professional development leave from BYU, during which he worked as an in-house financial planning and analysis consultant for Ortho Development Corporation, a medical device company in Salt Lake City, Utah.

Professor Smith's expertise is in the areas of management control systems, focusing on the provision of incentives and performance measurement. He has published numerous articles in prestigious academic publications such as *The Accounting Review, Review of Accounting Studies, Contemporary Accounting Research,* and *Journal of Management Accounting Research.* He has presented his research at conferences and invited presentations throughout the world, and has also published teaching cases in the *IMA Educational Case Journal* and *Strategic Finance.* Professor Smith has served in a variety of research- and teaching-focused positions in both the Management Accounting Section (MAS) of the American Accounting Association (AAA) and the Institute of Management Accountants (IMA).

The Author Team was selected to create a leading book in cost management based on leadership in teaching experience, research, commitment to learning, and a connection to the profession and practice of management accounting that provides students with up-to-date knowledge of real-world management accounting issues and practices.

Blocher/Juras/Smith

Letter to the Students:

We have written this book to help you understand the role of cost management in helping an organization succeed. Unlike many books that aim to teach you *about* accounting, we aim to show you how an important area of accounting, cost management, is *used* by managers to help organizations achieve their goals.

An important aspect of cost management in our text is the strategic focus. By *strategy,* we mean the long-term plan the organization has developed to compete successfully. Most organizations strive to achieve a competitive edge through the execution of a specific strategy. For some firms, it is low cost; for others, it might be high quality, customer service, or some unique feature or attribute of its product or service. We know in these competitive times that an organization does not succeed by being ordinary. Rather, it develops a strategy that will set it apart from competitors and ensure its attractiveness to customers and other stakeholders into the future. The role of cost management is to help management of the organization attain and maintain success through strategy implementation. Thus, for every major topic covered in our text, there is a larger issue, which is: "How does this organization compete? What type of cost management information does it need?" We do *not* cover a cost management method simply to become proficient at it. We want you to know why, when, and how the technique can be used to help the organization succeed.

An understanding of the strategic role of cost management today is so important that many senior financial managers and many CPAs—both in public and in private practice—are coming back to school to learn more about strategy, competitive analysis, and new cost management techniques. Knowing how to do the accounting alone—no matter how well you do it—is, by itself, no longer sufficient. Cost management with a strategic emphasis is one way to enhance your career and to add value to your employer, whatever type of organization it might be.

New Data Analytics in form of Applying Excel and Applying Tableau

Key Text Features that Integrate Strategy

Real-World Focus *Cost Management* provides extensive real-world examples of how cost management systems can add value to the organization. The **Real-World Focus** boxes throughout the text take real organizations and demonstrate strategy in action and the role that cost management plays in supporting the organization's strategy.

To augment this coverage, the Blocher team encourages students to further explore real-world companies through **Cost Management in Action** boxes that appear in each chapter throughout the text. This feature poses important questions that make students think critically about the relationship between cost management and organizational strategy. At the end of each chapter, the authors then supply their comments for the **Cost Management in Action** boxes.

Text Illustrations Clear and concise exhibits help illustrate basic and complicated topics throughout the book.

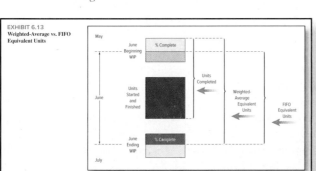

Helping Students Succeed Using *Cost Management, 9e*

Problem Material The Blocher team has taken great care to develop assignment material that effectively reinforces concepts, procedures, and strategic issues presented in each chapter. In addition, each chapter has one or more end-of-chapter assignments that focus on ethical issues or that deal with an international context or a service (i.e., nonmanufacturing) setting. The authors also include exercises and problems that relate topical coverage to the general issue of sustainability. Where appropriate, the chapters have assignments based on readings from periodicals such as *Strategic Finance, Management Accounting Quarterly, The Wall Street Journal,* and *Harvard Business Review.* These assignments link topical material in the chapter to the broader, strategic issues that organizations face. End-of-chapter assignments that embrace a distinguishing focus are identified as follows:

 Strategy   International   Service   Ethics   Sustainability

A Framework for Integrating Strategy: The Five Steps of Strategic Decision Making

The first edition of *Cost Management* introduced a five-step framework for decision making with a strategic emphasis. The framework shows that each decision starts and ends with a consideration of the organization's strategy. To extend and integrate the strategic emphasis, the ninth edition continues the tradition of including this five-step framework throughout the text. In all but a few chapters, there is a short section that uses the five-step framework to show how a consideration of the organization's strategy plays a key role in making decisions that will address the business-related problems presented in that chapter.

The Competitive Global Economic Environment Increases the Importance of Reviewing and Executing Strategy

The competitive global economic environment requires today's firms to place an even greater emphasis on the successful execution of their strategies. Moreover, increased competitive pressures may require organizations to review and modify their strategies to compete more effectively in the competitive global environment. Throughout this new edition, we also cover how economic and political forces in many countries are currently opposing certain aspects of globalization—for example, tighter immigration policies and the protection of domestic workers. We first saw this in 2016, when a referendum in the United Kingdom concerning its membership in the European Union (EU) favored separation (called Brexit, or "British Exit").

Integration of Advanced Excel Skills Development

Success in business requires the ability to use technology to extract information from quantitative data, and then to present that information in a way that helps others understand and make better decisions. Microsoft Excel has been and remains the dominant spreadsheet program for organizing, manipulating, and analyzing quantitative data. The authors of *Cost Management* have made a unique effort to integrate Excel training within the text as a complement to the material being presented. Excel instructions and hints are also presented in the end-of-chapter materials wherever spreadsheet application may be useful for students. These integrated Excel features are additional to the other Excel-focused resources of the book, as described in the paragraphs that follow.

ADDITIONAL INSTRUCTOR AND STUDENT RESOURCES

NEW Data Analytics and Visualization Assignments The ninth edition introduces additional data analytics and visualization content in *Connect.* This includes video and text instruction, assignment material, and feedback using cases developed for Tableau.

Excel Tutorials The ninth edition provides brand new, updated Excel tutorial content in each of the 20 chapters. Students can simultaneously hone their Excel skills and apply those skills to managerial topics using functions such as pivot tables, Goal Seek, and regression analysis. Tutorials are offered for each chapter in both step-by-step tutorial documents and videos, as well as in "Applying Excel" content within *Connect,* enabling instructors to more easily integrate Excel into their courses and allowing students further practice using algorithmic versions.

Excel Solution Manual For each chapter, *Cost Management* provides a solution manual in Excel form. The Excel file provides the solution to every exercise and problem in its own spreadsheet tab, with soft-coded formulas wherever computations are needed. This resource, which is unique to *Cost Management,* provides immense flexibility for instructors to (1) help students understand challenging computations, (2) easily demonstrate sensitivity of outputs to variations in inputs, (3) efficiently deploy solutions as needed, (4) resolve pesky rounding issues, and (5) facilitate additional exposure to advanced Excel functions.

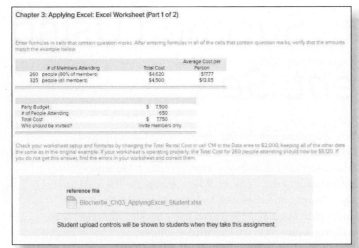

Chapter 3: Applying Excel: Excel Worksheet (Part 1 of 2)

Enter formulas in cells that contain question marks. After entering formulas in all of the cells that contain question marks, verify that the amounts match the example below.

# of Members Attending	Total Cost	Average Cost per Person
260 people (80% of members)	$4,620	$17.77
325 people (all members)	$4,500	$13.85

Party Budget	$ 7,500
# of People Attending	650
Total Cost	$ 7,750
Who should be invited?	Invite members only

Check your worksheet setup and formulas by changing the Total Rental Cost in cell C14 in the Data area to $2,000, keeping all of the other data the same as in the original example. If your worksheet is operating properly, the Total Cost for 260 people attending should now be $5,120. If you do not get this answer, find the errors in your worksheet and correct them.

reference file
Blocher8e_Ch03_ApplyingExcel_Student.xlsx

Student upload controls will be shown to students when they take this assignment.

Excel Simulations Excel Simulations, assignable in Connect, allow students to practice their Excel skills—such as basic formulas and formatting—within the context of accounting. These questions feature animated, narrated Help and Show Me tutorials (when enabled), as well as automatic feedback and grading for both students and professors. These questions differ from Applying Excel in that students work in a simulated version of Excel. *Downloading the Excel application is not required to complete Excel Simulations.*

Cases and Readings Supplement The *Cases and Readings Supplement,* available in the Instructor Library and Additional Student Resources, challenges students to think about and use cost management information in a real-world setting. Several of the cases are offered as auto-graded assignments in *Connect* in the ninth edition. The content provides critical thinking skills development as well as a basis for more comprehensive and in-depth discussions about the role of cost management in helping an organization successfully execute its strategy.

Self-Study Problems *Cost Management* provides a multifaceted self-study problem before the questions, exercises, and problems at the end of each chapter. The solution to the static version of each problem in the book is provided at the very end of the chapter. These problems are more comprehensive in nature and can be an invaluable resource for students to assess their own understanding of chapter material. The ninth edition offers algorithmic versions of the self-study problems in *Connect* in addition to the worked-through versions included in the book. Instructors can assign these now and, with the auto-grading feature, can use these as additional assessment content. Students also have access to the static book versions and tutorial videos to work on their own time and at their own pace, using the step-by-step solution to each self-study problem found in the Additional Student Resources.

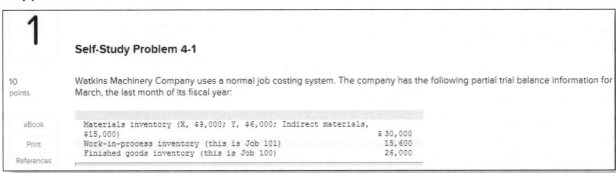

1

Self-Study Problem 4-1

10 points

eBook

Print

References

Watkins Machinery Company uses a normal job costing system. The company has the following partial trial balance information for March, the last month of its fiscal year:

```
Materials inventory (X, $9,000; Y, $6,000; Indirect materials,
  $15,000)                                              $ 30,000
Work-in-process inventory (this is Job 101)              15,600
Finished goods inventory (this is Job 100)              26,000
```

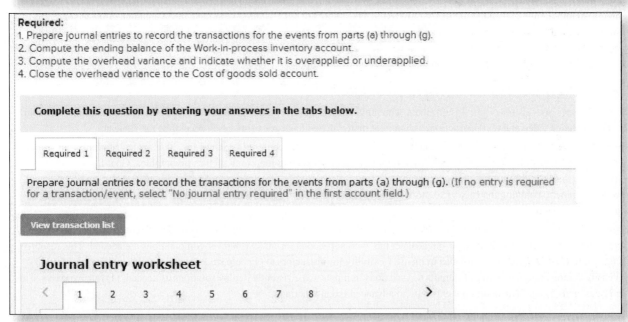

Required:
1. Prepare journal entries to record the transactions for the events from parts (a) through (g).
2. Compute the ending balance of the Work-in-process inventory account.
3. Compute the overhead variance and indicate whether it is overapplied or underapplied.
4. Close the overhead variance to the Cost of goods sold account.

Complete this question by entering your answers in the tabs below.

| Required 1 | Required 2 | Required 3 | Required 4 |

Prepare journal entries to record the transactions for the events from parts (a) through (g). (If no entry is required for a transaction/event, select "No journal entry required" in the first account field.)

View transaction list

Journal entry worksheet

< 1 2 3 4 5 6 7 8 >

Connect Library

The Connect Instructor Library is a repository for these additional resources to improve student engagement in and out of class. You can select and use any asset that enhances your lecture. Additional ancillary materials are prepared by the authors to ensure consistency and accuracy and are available in the Instructor Resources within the Connect Library and via the Additional Student Resources within the eBook. The Connect Instructor Library includes:

- Instructor's Guide and Solutions Manuals, both in PDF and Excel forms.
- Teaching notes for the Cases and Reading Supplements.
- PowerPoint lecture presentations.
- Test bank (including TestGen and Test Bank Matrices). TestGen is a complete, state-of-the-art test generator and editing application software that allows instructors to quickly and easily select test items from McGraw Hill's test bank content. The instructors can then organize, edit, and customize questions and answers to rapidly generate tests for paper or online administration.

The Additional Student Resources include:

- **Excel Tutorials.**
- **Data Analytics and Visualization Assignments.**
- **Check Figures.**
- **Self-Study Problems.**
- **PowerPoint Slides.**
- **Cases and Readings Supplement.**
- **Regression Analysis Supplement.**
- **Variance Investigation Supplement.**

Instructors: Student Success Starts with You

Tools to enhance your unique voice

Want to build your own course? No problem. Prefer to use our turnkey, prebuilt course? Easy. Want to make changes throughout the semester? Sure. And you'll save time with Connect's auto-grading too.

65%
Less Time Grading

Study made personal

Incorporate adaptive study resources like SmartBook® 2.0 into your course and help your students be better prepared in less time. Learn more about the powerful personalized learning experience available in SmartBook 2.0 at **www.mheducation.com/highered/connect/smartbook**

Affordable solutions, added value

Make technology work for you with LMS integration for single sign-on access, mobile access to the digital textbook, and reports to quickly show you how each of your students is doing. And with our Inclusive Access program you can provide all these tools at a discount to your students. Ask your McGraw Hill representative for more information.

Solutions for your challenges

A product isn't a solution. Real solutions are affordable, reliable, and come with training and ongoing support when you need it and how you want it. Visit **www. supportateverystep.com** for videos and resources both you and your students can use throughout the semester.

SUPPORT AT
every step

Students: Get Learning that Fits You

Effective tools for efficient studying

Connect is designed to make you more productive with simple, flexible, intuitive tools that maximize your study time and meet your individual learning needs. Get learning that works for you with Connect.

Study anytime, anywhere

Download the free ReadAnywhere app and access your online eBook or SmartBook 2.0 assignments when it's convenient, even if you're offline. And since the app automatically syncs with your eBook and SmartBook 2.0 assignments in Connect, all of your work is available every time you open it. Find out more at
www.mheducation.com/readanywhere

"I really liked this app—it made it easy to study when you don't have your text-book in front of you."

- Jordan Cunningham,
Eastern Washington University

Everything you need in one place

Your Connect course has everything you need—whether reading on your digital eBook or completing assignments for class, Connect makes it easy to get your work done.

Calendar: owattaphotos/Getty Images

Learning for everyone

McGraw Hill works directly with Accessibility Services Departments and faculty to meet the learning needs of all students. Please contact your Accessibility Services Office and ask them to email accessibility@mheducation.com, or visit
www.mheducation.com/about/accessibility
for more information.

Top: Jenner Images/Getty Images. Left: Hero Images/Getty Images. Right: Hero Images/Getty Images.

What's NEW about the 9th Edition

Big Data Analytics and Visualization: Applying Tableau and Applying Excel

The ninth edition of *Cost Management* introduces data analytics and visualization assignments using "Applying Tableau" in *Connect*. This includes video and text instruction, assignment material, and feedback using cases developed for both programs. These cases and assignments provide vital training and development in one of the most important emerging aspects of management: using technology to navigate and analyze large data sets and facilitating clear understanding of data insights with effective visualization tools.

New Excel Training: Videos, Documentation, and Integration

The Excel Tutorial videos and documentation for each chapter have been fully reproduced for the ninth edition, using Excel version 16. Students can simultaneously hone their Excel skills and apply those skills to managerial topics using functions such as pivot tables, charts and graphs, Goal Seek, Solver, and regression analysis. Tutorials are offered for each chapter in both step-by-step tutorial documents and videos. In addition, the book provides "Applying Excel" content within *Connect,* enabling instructors to more easily integrate Excel into their courses and allowing students further practice using algorithmic versions. As always, *Cost Management* is unique in its integration of Excel skills into both the text of the chapters and much of the end-of-chapter content.

Certified Management Accountant (CMA) Exam Preparation: Practice Problems and Essays

Cost Management: A Strategic Emphasis, 9e, also offers a large selection of recently used Certified Management Accountant (CMA) Exam problems and essay questions (with solutions) in *Connect.* These problems and essay questions are linked to the book chapters to which the topics most closely relate, and they create an even richer library of content (much of it auto-gradable) that instructors may use to build homework and other assignments. These problems also present valuable practice material for students who are interested in pursuing the CMA designation, either as students or following their formal education.

Globalization and Anti-Globalization ("Brexit")

From the first edition, the book has addressed globalization and global issues as an important feature of cost management with a strategic emphasis. Globalization appears frequently in the text and in the exercises and problems. A section in Chapter 1, under the heading The Global Business Environment, explains the new **economic nationalism** trends that oppose globalization. An example of this trend is the 2016 referendum in the United Kingdom in favor of separation from the EU (referred to as "Brexit"). Economic nationalism attempts to protect domestic workers and industries from foreign competition. It opposes globalization, free trade, and immigration. The effect of economic nationalism on the role of cost management can be significant, and we bring this up throughout the ninth edition.

Integration of Important Topics throughout the Text

Key topic areas for the course are integrated across the chapters. As previously noted, strategy is integrated throughout the text. In addition, accounting for "lean" is included in four chapters as it relates to the subject matter of that chapter. Similarly, time-driven activity-based costing (TDABC) is covered in the ABC chapter (Chapter 5) and also in the chapter on budgeting (Chapter 10). ABC appears in most of the chapters in Part Two because it has a key role in planning and decision making. Nonfinancial performance measures and the balanced scorecard (BSC) are introduced in Part One and then covered as part of the operational and management control chapters included in Parts Three and Four. Resource consumption accounting (RCA) is covered both in Chapter 5 and again in Chapter 15. The topic of capacity resource planning is covered in Chapters 10 and 15. These are just examples of the efforts the authors have made to integrate key topics throughout the text.

Enhancing Features from Prior Editions

- Significant new material has been added to *Connect* to greatly enhance the usefulness of this teaching and learning environment.

- Chapters have been revised to include up-to-date issues in cost management and discuss how accountants are dealing with these issues; examples include the COVID recession, economic nationalism (Brexit), changes in sustainability reporting practices, data analytics, the volatility of foreign exchange rates, strategic cost management, and changes in management compensation practices, among others. Because of the strategic focus of the book, we put emphasis on providing current, real-world examples in the text and in the problem material. This material is then updated for each new edition.

- End-of-chapter exercises and problems have been improved, with a strong focus on providing clarity, a clear linkage to chapter learning objectives, with varying and appropriate levels of challenge.

Mc Graw Hill connect + 🔲 proctorio

Remote Proctoring & Browser-Locking Capabilities

New remote proctoring and browser-locking capabilities, hosted by Proctorio within *Connect,* provide control of the assessment environment by enabling security options and verifying the identity of the student.

Seamlessly integrated within *Connect,* these services allow instructors to control students' assessment experience by restricting browser activity, recording students' activity, and verifying students are doing their own work.

Instant and detailed reporting gives instructors an at-a-glance view of potential academic integrity concerns, thereby avoiding personal bias and supporting evidence-based claims.

Test Builder in *Connect*

Available within *Connect,* Test Builder is a cloud-based tool that enables instructors to format tests that can be printed or administered within an LMS. Test Builder offers a modern, streamlined interface for easy content configuration that matches course needs, without requiring a download.

Test Builder allows you to:

- Access all test bank content from a particular title.
- Easily pinpoint the most relevant content through robust filtering options.
- Manipulate the order of questions or scramble questions and/or answers.
- Pin questions to a specific location within a test.
- Determine your preferred treatment of algorithmic questions.
- Choose the layout and spacing.
- Add instructions and configure default settings.

Test Builder provides a secure interface for better protection of content and allows for just-in-time updates to flow directly into assessments.

Tegrity: Lectures 24/7

Tegrity in *Connect* is a tool that makes class time available 24/7 by automatically capturing every lecture. With a simple one-click start-and-stop process, you capture all computer screens and corresponding audio in a format that is easy to search, frame by frame. Students can replay any part of any class with easy-to-use, browser-based viewing on a PC, Mac, iPod, or other mobile device. Educators know that the more students can see, hear, and experience class resources, the better they learn. In fact, studies prove it. Tegrity's unique search feature helps students efficiently find what they need, when they need it, across an entire semester of class recordings. Help turn your students' study time into learning moments immediately supported by your lecture. With Tegrity, you also increase intent listening and class participation by easing students' concerns about note-taking. Using Tegrity in *Connect* will make it more likely you will see students' faces, not the tops of their heads.

Improving Student Success with *Connect*

Production Budget – in units

Desired ending inventory (July 31)	
(The higher of 500 or 7,000 × 0.1)	700
Budgeted sales for July	+ 6,000
Total units needed for July	6,700
Beginning inventory (July 1)	
(The higher of 500 and 6,000 × 0.1)	- 600
Units to manufacture in July	6,100

Connect *End-of-Chapter Material*

Connect helps students learn more efficiently by providing feedback and practice material when they need it, where they need it. *Connect* grades homework automatically and gives immediate feedback on any questions students may have missed. The extensive assignable, gradable end-of-chapter content includes a new multitab design for easier navigation for select exercises. Significant amounts of new auto-graded *Connect* content have been added with the ninth edition, including the problem set in both static and algorithmic form, select Cases, and Applying Excel questions, along with a new algorithmic test bank.

McGraw Hill Education Customer Experience Group Contact Information

At McGraw Hill Education, we understand that getting the most from new technology can be challenging. That's why our services don't stop after you purchase our products. You can contact our Product Specialists 24 hours a day to get product training online. Or you can search the knowledge bank of Frequently Asked Questions on our support website. For Customer Support, call 800-331-5094, or visit www.mhhe.com/support. One of our Technical Support Analysts will be able to assist you in a timely fashion.

Assurance-of-Learning Ready

Many educational institutions today are focused on the notion of assurance of learning, an important element of many accreditation standards. *Cost Management: A Strategic Emphasis, 9e,* is designed specifically to support your assurance-of-learning initiatives with a simple, yet powerful, solution.

Each chapter in the book begins with a list of numbered learning objectives, which appear throughout the chapter as well as in the end-of-chapter assignments. Every Test Bank question for *Cost Management: A Strategic Emphasis* maps to a specific chapter learning objective in the textbook. Each Test Bank question also identifies topic area, level of difficulty, Bloom's Taxonomy level, and AICPA and AACSB skill area.

AACSB Statement

McGraw Hill/Irwin is a proud corporate member of AACSB International. Understanding the importance and value of AACSB accreditation, *Cost Management: A Strategic Emphasis, 9e,* recognizes the curricular guidelines detailed in the AACSB standards for business accreditation by connecting selected questions in the text and the Test Bank to the general knowledge and skill guidelines in the revised AACSB standards.

The statements contained in *Cost Management: A Strategic Emphasis* are provided only as a guide for the users of this textbook. The AACSB leaves content coverage and assessment within the purview of individual schools, the mission of the school, and the faculty. While *Cost Management: A Strategic Emphasis, 9e,* and the teaching package make no claim of any specific AACSB qualification or evaluation, we have, within the text and test bank, labeled selected questions according to the eight general knowledge and skill areas.

Enhancements for This Edition

Part One: Introduction to Strategy, Cost Management, and Cost Systems

Chapter 1: Cost Management and Strategy

- Updates to the chapter opener, all Real-World Focus items, Cost Management in Action discussion, and text references with current information
- Revision of text with updated information on economic nationalism and Brexit, business analytics, and professional certification details
- Three new problems based on current real-world trends, with clarifications and updates throughout the end-of-chapter materials and solutions

Chapter 2: Implementing Strategy: The Value Chain, the Balanced Scorecard, and the Strategy Map

- Updates to the chapter opener and all Real-World Focus items with current information
- Revision of SWOT analysis with discussion of the impact of economic nationalism on opportunities and threats
- Clarification of text on value chain and supply chain, sustainability assurance and reporting, and the Balanced Scorecard
- Three new end-of-chapter problems addressing sustainability, economic nationalism, and the Balanced Scorecard

Chapter 3: Basic Cost Management Concepts

- New Real-World Focus item discussing the impact of a cost structure decision at Caterpillar
- Updates to the Cost Management in Accounting item and the chapter's Five Steps of Strategic Decision Making section

- Clarification of language on cost behavior and cost classifications

Chapter 4: Job Costing

- Change of Thomasville Furniture example to Tomlinson Furniture, with numerous text and numerical revisions throughout the chapter
- Two new Real-World Focus items (replacing one that was dated) about the strategic relationship between price and cost
- Updates to sections on cost flows, discussing technology and the proration method for disposition of over/underapplied overhead
- Additions and revisions to end-of-chapter content for adaptability in *Connect* and to add new requirements regarding the disposition of over/underapplied overhead

Chapter 5: Activity-Based Costing and Customer Profitability Analysis

- Four new and one updated Real-World Focus items (replacing two that were dated), addressing service departments, patient profitability, and activity-based costing
- Minor revisions to end-of-chapter problems for clarity and adaptability in *Connect*

Chapter 6: Process Costing

- Revised language to improve clarity throughout the chapter
- New Real-World Focus item about spoilage in jellybean production
- Updates and minor edits throughout the end-of-chapter problems material

Chapter 7: Cost Allocation: Departments, Joint Products, and By-Products

- One new Real-World Focus item (about overhead costs and funding of

the National Institutes of Health) with updates to two others
- Clarifying language and footnote/exhibit revisions throughout
- Revisions to end-of-chapter materials and solution manual for minor errors and formatting

Part Two: Planning and Decision Making

Chapter 8: Cost Estimation

- Updated chapter opener with connection to Big Data and analytics
- Five new Real-World Focus items, addressing the importance of understanding cost structure, cost estimation challenges, the role of predictive analytics, and forecasting tools in professional football
- Minor updates and revisions to end-of-chapter materials and the solution manual

Chapter 9: Short-Term Profit Planning: Cost-Volume-Profit (CVP) Analysis

- Updated chapter opener about iHeartRadio and CVP analysis
- Two new Real-World Focus items (discussing CVP analysis for airlines and sales mix at Apple) with updates to four others
- New exhibit (9.7) with a table of expected values to help improve the discussion of dealing with uncertainty
- Minor revisions to end-of-chapter material, including a new exercise on profit planning and point of indifference

Chapter 10: Strategy and the Master Budget

- Updated chapter opener with current information about Johnson & Johnson
- Two new Real-World Focus items (discussing labor budgeting in the

video game production industry and budgeting in the nonprofit sector) with updates to three others

Chapter 11: Decision Making with a Strategic Emphasis

- Move of the appendix (about linear programming and the product mix decision) to online-only content in *Connect*
- Two new Real-World Focus items, addressing the make-or-buy decision at Apple and the keep-or-drop decision at Merck
- Minor revisions to end-of-chapter material, including replacing one problem (11-43) with a new *Connect*-adaptable problem with advanced Excel content

Chapter 12: Strategy and the Analysis of Capital Investments

- New chapter opener about Intel and capital budgeting
- Revisions to the Mendoza capital investment example to reflect MACRS 3-year depreciation, with numerous text and numerical revisions (including updated Excel screenshots) throughout
- Updates and revisions to four Real-World Focus items
- Two new problems, both available in *Connect*

Chapter 13: Cost Planning for the Product Life Cycle: Target Costing, Theory of Constraints, and Strategic Pricing

- Two new Real-World Focus items (discussing designing for the market and pricing with artificial intelligence) with updates to three others
- Appendix and associated end-of-chapter content removed

Part Three: Operational-Level Control

Chapter 14: Operational Performance Measurement: Sales, Direct Cost Variances, and the

Role of Nonfinancial Performance Measures

- Two new Real-World Focus items (discussing artificial intelligence in health care and outsourcing computing services) with removal of outdated items
- New Cost Management in Action item, discussing the limitations of (and alternatives to) standard costing systems)
- New problem about computing total price and usage variances with multiple material inputs

Chapter 15: Operational Performance Measurement: Indirect Cost Variances and Resource Capacity Management

- Minor revisions throughout for consistency, such as replacing "absorption costing" with "full costing" and "CGS" with "COGS" throughout the chapter (and the book)
- Two new Real-World Focus items (discussing employee engagement at Ameritech and nonprofit investments in technology) with updates to one other

Chapter 16: Operational Performance Measurement: Further Analysis of Productivity and Sales

- Revisions to two Real-World Focus items and the chapter opener based on current information
- Minor updates and revisions to end-of-chapter material

Chapter 17: The Management and Control of Quality

- Revisions and streamlining of chapter opener about quality in the health care sector
- Updates to two Real-World Focus items (discussing the cost of poor quality and airline quality ratings) and the Cost Management in Action item based on current information and examples
- Updates to information about the Baldrige Award and the Shingo Prize with current information

Part Four: Management-Level Control

Chapter 18: Strategic Performance Measurement: Cost Centers, Profit Centers, and the Balanced Scorecard

- Language revisions throughout the text, including replacing "uncertainty" with "controllability" and "lack of observability" with "information asymmetry" in discussion of agency theory
- New Real-World Focus item (addressing the effects of outsourcing on median pay levels at Hasbro and Mattel)
- Numerous revisions to end-of-chapter materials, including converting a number of problems to single answer format, better suited for algorithmic conversion in *Connect*

Chapter 19: Strategic Performance Measurement: Investment Centers and Transfer Pricing

- Minor revisions of text for clarity, efficiency, and accuracy, including removal of outdated financial reporting information about leases
- Updates to two Real-World Focus items with current information/ examples
- Revisions to some end-of-chapter materials to improve adaptability to algorithmic conversion in *Connect*

Chapter 20: Management Compensation, Business Analysis, and Business Valuation

- New chapter opener about CEO compensation at Bank of America
- Updates to three Real-World Focus items with current information (about SEC disclosure and say on pay, employee stock ownership at Comcast, and the S&P 500 PE ratio over time)
- Updates to end-of-chapter problems based on real-world data (e.g., Yum! Brands financials, CEO compensation), along with other adjustment from multiple-choice to single answer to better facilitate algorithmic conversion in *Connect*

Acknowledgments

Our Sincerest Thanks . . .

In writing this book, we were fortunate to have received extensive feedback from a number of accounting educators. We want to thank our colleagues for their careful and complete review of our work. The comments that we received were invaluable in helping us to shape the manuscript. We believe that this collaborative development process helped us to create a text that will truly meet the needs of today's students and instructors. We are sincerely grateful to the following individuals for their participation in the process:

Reviewers of past editions:

Wagdy Abdallah, *Seton Hall University*

Nas Ahadiat, *California State Polytechnic University–Pomona*

Margaret Andersen, *North Dakota State University*

Vidya N. Awasthi, *Seattle University*

K. R. Balachandran, *New York University*

Mohamed E. Bayou, *School of Management, University of Michigan–Dearborn*

Janice Benson, *University of Wyoming*

Jeremiah Bentley, *University of Massachusetts–Amherst*

Marvin L. Bouillon, *Iowa State University*

Kristine Brands, *Regis University*

Wayne Bremser, *Villanova University*

Wede E. Brownell, *University of Central Oklahoma*

Laurie Burney, *Baylor University*

Cathleen Burns, *Trinity University*

Tom Buttross, *Pennsylvania State–Harrisburg*

Tim Cairney, *Georgia Southern University*

Dennis Caplan, *Oregon State University*

Sandra Cereola, *James Madison University*

James A. Chiafery, *University of Massachusetts–Boston*

Bea Chiang, *The College of New Jersey*

Michele Chwastiak, *University of New Mexico–Albuquerque*

Andrew Clinton, *Central College*

Matthew Cobabe, *Virginia Tech*

Jeffrey Cohen, *Boston College*

Cheryl Corke, *Genesee Community College*

Alan B. Czyzewski, *Indiana State University*

Robert J. DePasquale, *Saint Vincent College*

Jennifer Dosch, *Metropolitan State University*

Joe Dowd, *Eastern Washington University*

Robert W. Duron, *Chadron State College*

David Eichelberger, *Austin Peay State University*

Rafik Elias, *California State University–Los Angeles*

James M. Emig, *Villanova University*

Sidney Ewer, *Missouri State University*

Karen Farmer, *Texas A&M University*

Jerry W. Ferry, *University of North Alabama*

Michael Flores, *Wichita State University*

Jay D. Forsyth, *Central Washington University*

Benjamin P. Foster, *University of Louisville*

Michael J. Gallagher, *DeSales University*

Steven Gattuso, *Canisius College*

Mike Grayson, *Jackson State University*

Ralph Greenberg, *Temple University–Philadelphia*

Olen L. Greer, *Southwest Missouri State University*

Donald C. Gribbin, *Southern Illinois University*

Sanjay Gupta, *Valdosta State University*

Matthew Haertzen, *University of Arizona*

Michael Hammond, *Missouri State University*

Betty Harper, *Middle Tennessee State University*

Jeannie Harrington, *Middle Tennessee State University*

Judith A. Harris, *Nova Southeastern University*

Syd Hasan, *George Mason University*

Haihong He, *California State University–Los Angeles*

Aleecia Hibbets, *University of Louisiana–Monroe*

James Higgins, *Holy Family University*

Jay Holmen, *University of Wisconsin–Eau Claire*

Linda Holmes, *University of Wisconsin–Whitewater*

Norma C. Holter, *Towson University*

David R. Honodel, *University of Denver*

Bambi Hora, *University of Central Oklahoma*

Todd Jensen, *California State University–Sacramento*

Sanford R. Kahn, *University of Cincinnati*

Vijay Karan, *California State University–Fullerton*

Larry N. Killough, *Virginia Polytechnic Institute and State University*

Il-Woon Kim, *University of Akron*

Mehmet C. Kocakulah, *University of Southern Indiana*

Laura Jean Kreissl, *University of Wisconsin–Parkside*

Leslie Kren, *University of Wisconsin–Milwaukee*

Sandra S. Lang, *McKendree College*

Randall E. LaSalle, *West Chester University of Pennsylvania*

Dan Law, *Gonzaga University*

Sara Leone, *University of St. Francis*

Haijin Lin, *University of Houston*

Ping Lin, *California State University–Long Beach*

Xiang Liu, *California State University–San Bernardino*

Stephen Makar, *University of Wisconsin–Oshkosh*

Joetta Malone, *Strayer University*

Man C. Maloo, *Towson University*

Linda Marquis, *Northern Kentucky University*

John McGowan, *St. Louis University*

Brian L. McGuire, *University of Southern Indiana*

Laurie B. McWhorter, *Mississippi State University*

Yaw M. Mensah, *Rutgers University*

Tammy Metze, *Milwaukee Area Technical College*

Jamshed Mistry, *Suffolk University*

Cheryl E. Mitchem, *Virginia State University*

Michael Morris, *University of Notre Dame*

Ann Murphy, *Metropolitan State College of Denver*

Richard Newmark, *University of Northern Colorado*

Jennifer Niece, *Assumption College*

Dan O'Brien, *Madison College*

Margaret O'Reilly-Allen, *Rider University*

Lisa Owens, *Clemson University*

Chei M. Paik, *George Washington University*

Frank A. Paliotta, *Northwest Christian University*

Joanne Pencak, *Castleton State College*

Hugh Pforsich, *University of Idaho*

Letitia Pleis, *Metropolitan State University of Denver*

Shirley Polejewski, *University of St. Thomas*

Kay Poston, *University of Indianapolis*

Jenice Prather-Kinsey, *University of Missouri–Columbia*

Jason T. Rasso, *University of South Carolina*

Jack Ruhl, *Western Michigan University*

Martha L. Sale, *Sam Houston State University*

Marsha Scheidt, *University of Tennessee–Chattanooga*

Stanley Self, *Kaplan University*

Dennis Shanholtzer, *Metropolitan Slate University*

Shiv Sharma, *Robert Morris University*

Kenneth P. Sinclair, *Lehigh University*

Stevenson Smith, *University of South Dakota*

John L. Stancil, *Florida Southern College*

Justin P. Stearns, *University of Illinois–Springfield*

Ronald Stoltzfus, *Eastern Mennonite University*

Ronald A. Stunda, *Birmingham–Southern College*

Steve Swirsky, *Florida A&M University*

Jerry Thorne, *North Carolina A&T State University*

Rich White, *Florida Metro University*

Many talented educators and profesionals have worked hard to create the materials for this product, and for their efforts, we are grateful. Thank you to our contributing authors and accuracy checkers who have worked diligently on this new edition:

Text, Connect, and Supplement Accuracy Checkers: Patricia Plumb; Patti Lopez; Eric Weinstein, Suffolk County Community College; Teresa Alenikov, Cerritos College
PowerPoint reviews: Helen Roybark
Excel Videos revision: Hayden Gunnell
Test Bank revision: Derek Smith
Smartbook author: Patti Lopez

Finally, we are most appreciative of the outstanding assistance and support provided by the professionals of McGraw Hill: Tim Vertovec, our BEC VP, and Elizabeth Eisenhart, our portfolio manager, for their guidance; our product developers, Erin Quinones and Michael McCormick, for their invaluable suggestions; Lauren Schur, our executive marketing manager, for her significant promotional efforts; Amy Gehl and Jamie Koch, our content project managers, for their attention to detail; and Beth Blech, for the outstanding presentation of the text.

Ed Blocher

Paul Juras

Steve Smith

Brief Contents

Contents

Introduction to Strategy, Cost Management, and Cost Systems

The objective of the first seven chapters is to introduce the strategic approach to cost management and to cover the basic concepts of cost management systems.

Chapter 1 is an introduction to cost management—how organizations plan for success through strategy, and the management accountant's role in implementing strategy. The chapter includes an introduction to the current environment of business, including contemporary management techniques and professional responsibilities.

Chapter 2 focuses on some of the principal means that organizations use to implement strategy. The chapter introduces a strategic management system known as the balanced scorecard (BSC), the strategy map, and the value chain and shows how these tools can be used to help the organization implement its strategy. These tools are foundational tools that appear throughout the text; this is why they are covered in this early chapter.

Chapter 3 defines the key terms that management accountants use to describe product cost systems and cost information for planning, decision making, and control. This terminology is important for both accountants and managers alike. The chapter also introduces the differences in management accounting among service, manufacturing, and merchandising companies.

Chapters 4, 5, 6, and 7 cover costing systems and their role in strategy implementation.

Chapter 4 provides an introduction to costing systems by defining the elements of cost and how these elements are combined to determine the cost of a product or service. There are a number of variations on this basic cost system, each of which is designed to fit a particular manufacturing or service environment. These variations are explained in Chapters 5, 6, and 7.

Chapter 5 covers a strategically important advance in product costing called activity-based costing (ABC). Rather than using the volume-based approach (explained in Chapter 4), the ABC approach incorporates the details of all the activities that are needed to provide the product or service. The result is much more accurate, and therefore more strategically useful, cost information regarding the resource demands of an organization's outputs.

Chapter 6 introduces process costing, a costing system that is applicable for firms that have relatively homogeneous products passing through similar processing steps, often in a continuous flow. Commodity-based industries are of this nature: food processing, chemical, and consumer products firms. These types of firms generally compete using a cost-leadership strategy.

Chapter 7 covers cost-allocation issues associated with costing systems—departmental cost allocation and joint cost allocation. The chapter begins with an overview of the objectives and strategic role of cost allocation and then shows how departmental costs and joint costs are allocated to products.

CHAPTER ONE

Cost Management and Strategy

After studying this chapter, you should be able to . . .

LO 1-1 Explain the use of cost management information in each of the four functions of management and in different types of organizations, with emphasis on the strategic management function.

LO 1-2 Explain the contemporary business environment and how it has influenced cost management.

LO 1-3 Explain the contemporary management techniques and how they are used in cost management to respond to the contemporary business environment.

LO 1-4 Explain the different types of competitive strategies.

LO 1-5 Describe the professional environment of the management accountant, including professional organizations and professional certifications.

LO 1-6 Understand the principles and rules of professional ethics and explain how to apply them.

deanpictures/123RF

Talk about a success story! Walmart has grown from its first discount store in 1962 to become the world's largest company, with more than $500 billion in sales. It has achieved this through clear, day-to-day attention to accomplishing its business strategy and to living up to its motto of "Save Money, Live Better." Walmart achieves success through extensive use of technology and aggressive efforts to grow the business globally. And the environment is very competitive! A key competitor, Target, with a different strategy and a different motto ("Expect More, Pay Less®") has challenged Walmart with aggressive advertising campaigns and new stores. During the 2004–2007 period, Target was outpacing Walmart in sales growth and stock price growth. This reversed in 2008, as the global economic outlook weakened for many consumers and the low-cost strategy of Walmart proved to be more successful. Since 2009, both Walmart and Target have been facing the heat of increased competition from both Amazon.com and Costco, as well as other retailers such as Dollar General. The stakes are high and the competition is fierce. Imagine yourself as a manager for one of these companies. How would you help your company be more competitive?

This book is about how managers use cost management to build a successful company, as those at Walmart and Target have done. Everyone wants to be a winner, and so it is in business and accounting. We are interested in how the management accountant can play a key role in making a firm or organization successful. Now you might be asking, "Don't we have to know what you mean by *success*?" Absolutely! A firm must define clearly what it means by success in its mission statement. Then it must develop a road map to accomplish that mission, which we call *strategy*. Briefly, strategy is a plan to achieve competitive success. In Walmart's case, the mission is to achieve customer value, and the strategy involves the extensive use of technology to reduce cost, a management structure that welcomes change, and a constant focus on customer service. For Target, the competitive focus is the promise of value through brand recognition, customer service, store location, differentiated offerings, quality, fashion, and price.

Because we are interested in how the management accountant can help a company be successful, we take a strategic approach throughout the book, beginning with an introduction to strategy in this chapter. The key idea is that success comes from developing and implementing an effective strategy aided by management accounting methods. These management accounting methods are covered in this text chapter by chapter; we include them in the text because we know they have helped companies succeed.

Management Accounting and the Role of Cost Management

Management accountants are the accounting and finance professionals who develop and use cost management information to assist in implementing the organization's strategy. **Cost management information** consists of financial information about costs and revenues and nonfinancial information about customer retention, productivity, quality, and other key success factors for the organization. **Cost management** is the development and use of cost management information.

The strategic role of the management accountant in an organization is explained in the definition of management accounting provided by the Institute of Management Accountants (IMA). Relevant additional information on the definition can be found in the IMA's Statement on Management Accounting: *Definition of Management Accounting.*[1]

> **Management accounting** is a profession that involves partnering in management decision making, devising planning and performance management systems, and providing expertise in financial reporting and control to assist management in the formulation and implementation of an organization's strategy.

Management accountants use their unique expertise (decision making, planning, performance management, and more), working with the organization's managers, to help the organization succeed in formulating and implementing its strategy. Cost management

---

cost management information

The information developed and used to implement the organization's strategy. It consists of financial information about costs and revenues and nonfinancial information about customer retention, productivity, quality, and other key success factors for the organization.

LO 1-1

Explain the use of cost management information in each of the four functions of management and in different types of organizations, with emphasis on the strategic management function.

cost management

The development and use of cost management information.

management accounting

A profession that involves partnering in management decision making, devising planning and performance management systems, and providing expertise in financial reporting and control to assist management in the formulation and implementation of an organization's strategy.

---

[1] https://www.imanet.org/insights-and-trends/statements-on-management-accounting?ssopc=1

information is developed and used within the organization's information value chain, from stage 1 through stage 5, as shown below:

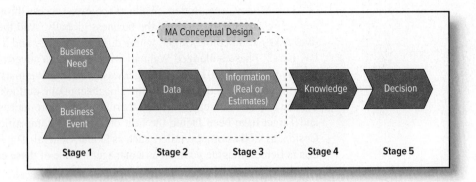

At lower stages of the value chain, management accountants gather and summarize data (stage 2) from business events (stage 1) and then transform the data to cost management information (stage 3) through analysis and use of the management accountants' expertise. At stage 4, cost management information is combined with other information about the organization's strategy and competitive environment to produce actionable knowledge. At stage 5, management accountants use this knowledge to participate with management teams in making decisions that advance the organization's strategy.

In a typical organization (illustrated in Exhibit 1.1), management accountants report to the controller, a key accounting professional in the firm. The controller, assisted by management accountants, has a wide range of responsibilities, including cost management, financial reporting, maintaining of financial information systems, and other reporting functions. The chief financial officer (CFO) has the overall responsibility for the financial function, the treasurer manages investor and creditor relationships, and the chief information officer (CIO) manages the firm's use of information technology, including computer systems and communications.

In contrast to the cost management function, the financial reporting function involves preparing financial statements for *external users* such as investors and government regulators.

EXHIBIT 1.1

A Typical Organization Chart Showing the Functions of the Controller

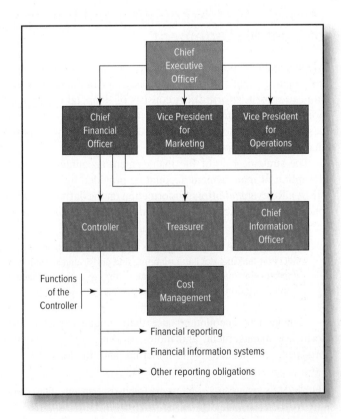

Our unique approach in this book is to demonstrate cost management from a strategic emphasis. Every cost management method we cover is linked to the firm's strategy—that is, how the method helps the firm to be successful. Why emphasize the strategic approach? Managers tell us why . . .

A recent survey of 1,500 controllers and other financial executives found that 91% of all organizations expect the controllership function to be more involved in the organization's strategy. Also, a survey of 750 chief financial officers (CFOs) conducted jointly by the Institute of Management Accountants (IMA) and the Association of Chartered Certified Accountants (ACCA) found that "the future CFO role in supporting strategic growth will be increasingly valued. Strategy formulation and execution was identified by current CFOs as the most important area in which to have experience for future CFOs." A 2014 survey of 600 financial executives by Accenture, a consulting firm, found results that confirmed the IMA/ACCA findings.

The Society of Management Accountants of Canada has developed a competency framework for certified management accountants in Canada, which has the following introduction:

Certified Management Accountants (CMAs) do more than just measure value—they create it. As the leaders in management accounting, CMAs apply a unique mix of financial expertise, strategic insight, innovative thinking and a collaborative approach to help grow successful businesses.

Sources: Daniel Butcher, "The Changing Role of the CFO," *Strategic Finance*, December 2019, pp. 21–23; Elizabeth Kennedy, "Controllers: Get Strategic!," *Strategic Finance*, May 2017, p. 13; Raef Lawson, "Become Business Partners," *Strategic Finance*, July 2016, pp. 25–31; Benjamin Kang, "Managing the Strategic Finance Gap," *Strategic Finance*, February 2014, pp. 43–48; "Future Pathways to Finance Leadership," Institute of Management Accountants and the Association of Chartered Certified Accountants, April 2014 (www.accaglobal.com/content/dam/acca/global/PDF-technical/finance-transformation/cfo-career-paths.pdf); "Building a Better Business Together: Welcome to Finance Business Partnering," The Association of International Certified Professional Accountants, 2018 (www.cgma.org/content/dam/cgma/resources/reports/downloadabledocuments/cgma-finance-business-partnering.pdf); "Competency Map of the CMA Profession," The Chartered Professional Accountants of Canada (www.cpacanada.ca/).

These financial accounting reports require compliance with certain external requirements. Cost management information is developed for use *within* the firm to facilitate management and is not needed to meet those requirements. The main focus of cost management information therefore must be *usefulness* and *timeliness;* the focus of financial reports must be *accuracy* and *compliance* with reporting requirements. However, strict adherence to accuracy can compromise the usefulness and timeliness of the information. The function of the financial information systems department is to develop and maintain the financial reporting system and related systems such as payroll, financial security systems, and tax preparation. The challenge for the controller is to reconcile these different and potentially conflicting roles.

The Four Functions of Management

The management accountant develops cost management information for the CFO, other managers, and employee teams to use to manage the firm and make the firm more competitive and successful. Cost management information is provided for each of the four major management functions: (1) strategic management, (2) planning and decision making, (3) management and operational control, and (4) preparation of financial statements. (See Exhibit 1.2.) The most important function is **strategic management,** which is the

strategic management
The development and implementation of a sustainable competitive position.

EXHIBIT 1.2
Cost Management Information Is Needed for Each of the Four Management Functions

1. **Strategic Management.** Cost management information is needed to make sound strategic decisions regarding choice of products, manufacturing methods, marketing techniques and distribution channels, customer profitability, and other long-term issues.

2. **Planning and Decision Making.** Cost management information is needed to support recurring decisions regarding replacing equipment, managing cash flow, budgeting materials purchases, scheduling production, and pricing.

3. **Management and Operational Control.** Cost management information is needed to provide a fair and effective basis for identifying inefficient operations and to reward and motivate the most effective managers.

4. **Preparation of Financial Statements.** Cost management information is needed to provide accurate accounting for inventory and other assets, in compliance with reporting requirements, for the preparation of financial reports and for use in the three other management functions.

development and implementation of a sustainable competitive position in which the firm's competitive advantage provides continued success. A strategy is a set of goals and specific action plans that, if achieved, provide the desired competitive advantage. Strategic management involves identifying and implementing these goals and action plans. Next, management is responsible for **planning and decision making,** which involve budgeting and profit planning, cash flow management, and other decisions related to the firm's operations, such as deciding when to lease or buy a facility, when to repair or replace a piece of equipment, when to change a marketing plan, and when to begin development of a new product.

The third area of responsibility, control, consists of two functions, operational control and management control. **Operational control** takes place when mid-level managers (e.g., site managers, product managers, regional managers) monitor the activities of operating-level managers and employees (e.g., production supervisors and various department heads). In contrast, **management control** is the evaluation of mid-level managers by upper-level managers (the controller or the CFO).

In the fourth function, **preparation of financial statements,** management complies with the reporting requirements of relevant groups (such as the Financial Accounting Standards Board) and relevant federal government authorities (e.g., the Internal Revenue Service and the Securities and Exchange Commission). The financial statement preparation role has recently received a renewed focus as countries throughout the world have adopted International Financial Reporting Standards (IFRS). The financial statement information also serves the other three management functions because this information is often an important part of planning and decision making, control, and strategic management.[2]

The first three management functions are covered in this text. Strategic management and the design of the costs systems upon which strategic decisions rely are covered in Part One. Part Two covers planning and decision making, Part Three covers operational control, and Part Four covers management control. Financial reporting for inventory and cost of sales is covered in Part One.

A comprehensive coverage of financial reporting is covered in courses on financial accounting, the field concerned with reporting the financial statements to investors, regulators, and other interested parties.

Strategic Management and the Strategic Emphasis in Cost Management

Effective strategic management is critical to the success of the firm or organization and is thus a pervasive theme of this book. The growing pressures of economic recession, global competition, technological innovation, and changes in business processes have made cost management much more critical and dynamic than ever before. Managers must think *competitively;* doing so requires a strategy.

Strategic thinking involves anticipating changes; products, services, and operating processes are designed to accommodate expected changes in customer demands. Flexibility is important. The ability to make fast changes is critical as a result of the demands of the new management concepts of e-commerce, speed-to-market, and flexible manufacturing. Product life cycles—the time from the introduction of a new product to its removal from the market— are expected to become shorter and shorter. Success in the recent past days or months is no longer a measure of ultimate success; the manager must be "driving" the firm by using the windshield, not the rear-view mirror.

The strategic emphasis also requires creative and integrative thinking, that is, the ability to identify and solve problems from a cross-functional view. The business functions are often identified as marketing, production, finance, and accounting/controllership. Instead of viewing a problem as a production problem, a marketing problem, or a finance and accounting problem, cross-functional teams view it from an integrative approach that combines skills from all functions simultaneously. The integrative approach is necessary in a dynamic and competitive environment. The firm's attention is focused on satisfying the customers' needs; all of the firm's resources, *from all functions,* are directed to that goal.

---

planning and decision making
Budgeting and profit planning, cash flow management, and other decisions related to operations.

operational control
The monitoring of short-term operating performance; takes place when mid-level managers monitor the activities of operating-level managers and employees.

management control
The system used by upper-level managers to evaluate the performance of mid-level managers.

preparation of financial statements
Requires management to comply with the financial reporting requirements of regulatory agencies.

[2] The professional and regulatory organizations such as the Financial Accounting Standards Board and the Securities and Exchange Commission are identified and explained at the end of this chapter.

Types of Organizations

Cost management information is useful in all organizations: business firms, governmental units, and not-for-profit organizations. Business firms are usually categorized by industry, the main categories being merchandising, manufacturing, and service. Merchandising firms purchase goods for resale. Merchandisers that sell to other merchandisers are called *wholesalers;* those selling directly to consumers are called *retailers.* Examples of merchandising firms are the large retailers, such as Walmart, Target, and Amazon.

Manufacturing firms use materials, labor, and manufacturing facilities and equipment to produce products. They sell these products to merchandising firms or to other manufacturers as materials to make other products. Examples of manufacturers are Ford, General Electric, and Cisco Systems.

Service firms provide a service to customers that offers convenience, freedom, safety, or comfort. Common services include transportation, health care, financial services (banking, insurance, accounting), personal services (physical training, hair styling), and legal services. In the United States, service industries are growing at a much faster rate than manufacturing or merchandising, in part because of the increased demand for leisure and convenience and society's increased complexity and need for information.

Governmental and not-for-profit organizations provide services, much like the firms in service industries. However, these organizations provide the services for which no direct relationship exists between the amount paid and the services provided. Instead, both the nature of these services and the customers who receive them are determined by government or philanthropic organizations. The resources are provided by governmental units and/or charities. The services provided by these organizations are often called *public goods* to indicate that no typical market exists for them. Public goods have a number of unique characteristics, such as the impracticality of limiting consumption to a single customer (clean water and police and fire protection are provided for *all* residents).

Most firms and organizations use cost management information. For example, manufacturing firms use it to manage production costs. Similarly, retail firms such as Walmart use cost management information to manage stocking, distribution, and customer service. Firms in the service industries, such as those providing financial services or other professional services, use cost management information to identify the most profitable services and to manage the costs of providing those services.

Cost management information is used in a wide variety of ways. Whatever the business, a firm must know the cost of new products or services, the cost of making improvements in existing products or services, and the cost of finding a new way to produce the products or provide the services. Cost management information is used to determine prices, to change product or service offerings to improve profitability, to update manufacturing facilities in a timely fashion, and to determine new marketing methods or distribution channels. For example, manufacturers such as Toyota study the cost implications of design options for each new product. The design study includes analysis of projected manufacturing costs as well as costs to be incurred after the product is completed, which include service and warranty costs. Service and warranty costs are often called *downstream costs* because they occur after manufacturing. By analyzing both manufacturing and downstream costs, a company is able to determine whether product enhancements might cause manufacturing and downstream costs to be out of line with expected increases in customer value and revenue for that feature.

Both large and small firms in all types of industries use cost management information. A firm's degree of reliance on cost management depends on the nature of its competitive strategy. Many firms compete on the basis of being the low-cost provider of the industry's goods or services; for these firms, cost management is critical. Other firms, such as cosmetics, fashion, and pharmaceutical firms, compete on the basis of product leadership, in which the unusual or innovative features of the product make the firm successful. For these firms, the critical management concern is maintaining product leadership through product development and marketing. The role of cost management is to support the firm's strategy by providing the information managers need to succeed in their product development and marketing efforts, such as the expected cost of adding a new product feature, the defect rate of a new part, or the reliability of a new manufacturing process.

Not-for-profit and governmental organizations also must have a strategy to accomplish their mission and satisfy their constituents. Historically, governmental units and not-for-profit agencies have tended to focus on their responsibility to spend in approved ways rather than to spend in efficient and effective ways. Increasingly, however, these types of organizations are using cost management for efficient and effective use of their financial resources.

The Contemporary Business Environment

LO 1-2

Explain the contemporary business environment and how it has influenced cost management.

Many changes in the business environment in recent years have caused significant modifications in cost management practices. The primary changes are (1) continuing growth in global competition along with the emergence of forces opposed to globalization; (2) lean manufacturing; (3) advances in information technologies, the internet, and enterprise resource management; (4) continued focus on the customer, though influenced by the growth in economic nationalism ; (5) new forms of management organization; and (6) changes in the social, political, and cultural environment of business, including the impact of climate change. The current global economic challenges (high public debt, tariffs, and concerns about immigration, among others) will surely have a significant effect on each of these six changes. It is likely there will be an even greater rate of change in each of these six areas as firms search for new ways to compete and governmental regulations adapt to the difficult economic times.

The Global Business Environment

A key development that drives the extensive changes in the contemporary business environment is the growth of international markets and trade due to the rise of economies throughout the world and the decline of trade barriers in some countries. Businesses and not-for-profit organizations, as well as consumers and regulators, are all significantly affected by the rapid growth of economic interdependence and increased competition from other countries. Here are some examples of global interdependence. The United States, Mexico, Canada Agreement (USMCA; ratified March 12, 2020) revises and replaces the North American Free Trade Agreement (NAFTA) between these three countries, the Central America Free Trade Agreement (CAFTA), the World Trade Organization (WTO), the European Union (EU), and the growing number of alliances among large multinational firms clearly indicate that the opportunities for growth and profitability lie in global markets. Most consumers benefit as low-cost, high-quality goods are traded worldwide. Managers and business owners know the importance of pursuing sales and operating activities in foreign countries, and investors benefit from the increased opportunities for investment in foreign firms.

A Force against Globalization: Economic Nationalism

The expansion of globalization has faced a strong counter-force in a number of ways since June 2016. For example, a referendum on membership in the European Union (EU) held in the United Kingdom (UK) in June 2016 resulted in a vote in favor of separating the UK from the EU (this separation is called Brexit, or "British Exit"). On January 31, 2020, the issue was resolved when the UK parliament voted to end the country's 47 years in the EU. There is an 11-month transition period (ending December 31, 2020) in which the EU and UK will determine the details of the relationships between the UK and the EU going forward. Key matters to be resolved include trading relationships between the two parties, whether there will be tariffs, quotas, or other trade limitations. Other matters to be resolved include travel between the UK and EU, customs and immigration, product safety standards, among others.

Also, there is a continuing strong worldwide growth of interest in protecting domestic workers and industries from foreign competition. Many have called this trend **economic nationalism,** which is the ideology that promotes domestic economic growth and opposes globalization, free trade, and immigration.

economic nationalism
The ideology that promotes domestic economic growth and opposes globalization, free trade, and immigration.

Economic Nationalism: Tariffs

An important element of economic nationalism is the intent to protect domestic workers and industries through tariffs. A tariff is an additional cost that importers must pay, thus increasing the cost to consumers of the imported product and making domestic products more attractive

REAL-WORLD FOCUS   Going Global: The Growing Importance of Worldwide Markets

The following table indicates the percentage of sales coming from outside the domestic market for the listed companies. Global sales have been crucial for these and many other companies. For example, while in 1970 the value of global trade was less than 30% of global gross domestic product (GDP), in 2019 that percentage had grown to 60%. (Source: World Bank)

	1993	2007	2019
General Electric	17%	50%	62%
Walmart	0.0	22	24
McDonald's	47	65	64

Sources: Company annual reports.

THE OUTLOOK FOR GLOBALIZATION AND ECONOMIC NATIONALISM

In the recent couple of years, we have seen economic nationalism strengthen in the U.S., the UK, Eastern Europe, and elsewhere in the world. Leaders of these countries have pushed for tariffs, for limiting immigration, and for ending established free trade policies. In their place, however, we have seen the growth of trading relationships in other areas of the world. For example, in 2018, Japan, Australia, Brunei, Canada, Vietnam, Singapore, Mexico, Chile, Peru, Malaysia, and New Zealand formed the Comprehensive and Progressive Agreement for Trans-Pacific Partnership (TPP), which links these 11 countries in a trading partnership. Also, in May 2019, 55 African countries joined the African Free Trade Treaty.

Sources: Michael Schuman, "Globalization Isn't Going Away," *Bloomberg Businessweek,* March 19, 2018, pp. 14–15; David Brooks, "The Revolt Against Populism," *The New York Times,* November 21, 2019.

to consumers. Tariffs have their basis in the concept of *mercantilism,* common in the 17th and 18th centuries, which measured the strength of an economy by the maximization of exports and the minimization of imports. When two or more countries adopt tariffs against each other, it is often called a "trade war."

Tariffs: Economic Uncertainty and Volatility

A typical consequence of tariffs and trade wars is increased economic uncertainty, as manufacturers and other companies try to forecast the changes in costs and prices that the trade war will cause. This uncertainty generally leads to lower or delayed investment by companies as they wait to see how the trade war develops. The uncertainty is also often associated with volatility in costs and prices that are important to the company. A good reference on the impact of uncertainty and volatility on the finance function of the company can be found in the joint publication by the Institute of Management Accountants (IMA) and the Association of Chartered Certified Accountants (ACCA): *Tomorrow's Finance Enterprise* (www.accaglobal .com/us/en/technical-activities/technical-resources-search/2014/april/tomorrows-finance-enterprise.html).[3] The conclusion of the report states: "Economic uncertainty, volatility, risk, and ambiguity are the critical challenges facing business today. This research is further evidence of the CFO's strategic business role and the need for greater alignment between business strategy and the role of the finance team, particularly the establishment of processes, systems or metrics for tracking success."

Another element of economic uncertainty that has created volatility in costs, prices, and stock values is the corona virus pandemic that started in China in late 2019 and is now (July 2020) world-wide. In addition to the human cost, the pandemic has caused severe disruption in some global supply chains as governments adopt regulations to minimize the flow of people and goods from country to country in order to halt the spread of the virus. The ultimate economic damage of the virus is difficult to estimate at this time but is expected to be very significant.

Apart from Brexit and the emergence of economic nationalism in countries around the world, it is clear that the increasing competitiveness and complexity of the global business environment means that firms need financial and nonfinancial information about competing effectively in other countries. Global business is covered in each chapter; look for the international icon next to problems involving global business. The international icon is shown in the margin opposite this paragraph.

[3] See also Michael Regan, "The Chaos Cycle," *Bloomberg Businessweek,* August 12, 2019, pp. 24–26; and Shawm Donnan, "Weaponizing Uncertainty," *Bloomberg Businessweek,* December 17, 2018, pp 34–35.

REAL-WORLD FOCUS   Manufacturing Jobs: Free Trade and Economic Nationalism

Proponents of economic nationalism want to improve the job prospects of middle- and lower-income families by reducing free trade and immigration. However, proponents of global trade say that in recent decades, trade has provided access by consumers to higher-quality and lower-price products from countries around the world. It has also sparked the growth in manufacturing in Asian countries, especially India and China. Trade agreements and reductions in tariffs have helped achieve this growth. In addition to the trade agreements and reductions in tariffs, other factors such as automation, fluctuating foreign exchange rates, and the weakening of labor unions have had an impact on manufacturing employment. Automation in manufacturing industries has caused the loss of many manufacturing jobs. The strong dollar has meant that foreign goods are less expensive in the U.S. and U.S. products are more expensive abroad (in late 2019, the dollar had appreciated by more than 20% over the euro and the UK pound since 2014). Also, the decline in labor unions in the U.S. has meant U.S. manufacturing workers have less leverage in negotiating labor contracts.

The economic impact of Brexit on the UK is expected to be approximately 40 billion pounds per year. Because the break with the European Union (EU) will mean that trade with EU countries will be more complicated, costly, and time consuming, companies such as Sony, Airbus, Citigroup, JP Morgan Chase, and Morgan Stanley are planning to move their operations out of the UK. Some UK firms have already suffered; the travel firm Thomas Cook declared bankruptcy in September 2019 and British Steel Ltd. declared bankruptcy in May 2019.

The effects in the U.S. from the economic nationalism are less clear. Tariffs have created some uncertainty but have had no clear effect as yet (July 2020) on manufacturing employment. Many experts note that the impediment to growth in manufacturing jobs is not globalization but instead is automation and the lack of a manufacturing infrastructure in the U.S. In contrast, the tariffs have created losses in certain nonmanufacturing industries, such as agriculture. Companies in the pharmaceutical, electronic manufacturing, and automobile manufacturing industries (among others) have complex global supply chains, and tariffs will alter those supply chains, perhaps moving manufacturing to other foreign countries. Note that overall the percentage of U.S. workers in manufacturing has fallen steadily since the 1940s: from a high of 40% in the 1940s to well under 10% today.

Sources: Andrew Taylor and Lisa Mascaro, "Trump, Dems in Tentative Deal on North American Trade Pact," Associated Press News, December 9, 2019 (https://newsradiowrva.radio.com/articles/national/trump-dems-in-tentative-deal-on-north-american-trade-pact); Joe Mayes, "A Costly Farewell," *Bloomberg Businessweek,* May 20, 2019, pp. 34–36; Richard Partington, "Cost of Brexit to UK Economy Running at 40 Billion Pounds per Year," *The Guardian,* February 15, 2019; Joe Mayes, "The Business Cheering Exit," *Bloomberg Businessweek,* December 9, 2019, p. 19; Ben Casselman, "Trade War Starts Changing Manufacturers in Hard-to-Reverse Ways," *The New York Times,* May 31, 2019, p. A1; Ruben Munsterman and Ellen Proper, "The Unbearable Bounty of Brexit," *Bloomberg Businessweek,* April 1, 2019, pp 34–35; Shawn Donnan and Jenny Leonard, "'Trade Wars Are Good and Easy to Win,'" *Bloomberg Businessweek,* November 18, 2019, pp. 322–36; "Blame Automation, Not Immigration," *Bloomberg Businessweek,* March 12, 2017; Dexter Roberts and Rachel Chang, "China's Robotic Revolution," *Bloomberg Businessweek,* May 1, 2017, pp. 32–34; Matt Townsend, "Can Sneaker Makers Come Home Again?," *Bloomberg Businessweek,* February 7, 2017, pp. 17–19; Michael Schuman, "Smiles Aren't Factory-Made," *Bloomberg Businessweek,* June 12, 2017, pp. 8–9.

Lean Manufacturing

To remain competitive in the face of the increased global competition, firms around the world are adopting new manufacturing technologies. These include just-in-time inventory methods to reduce the cost and waste of maintaining large levels of materials and unfinished product. Also, many firms are adopting the lean methods applied in Japanese manufacturing that have produced significant cost and quality improvements through the use of quality teams and statistical quality control. Other manufacturing changes include flexible manufacturing techniques developed to reduce setup times and allow fast turnaround of customer orders. A key competitive edge in what is called *speed-to-market* is the ability to deliver the product or service faster than the competition.

Use of Information Technology, the Internet, and Enterprise Resource Management

Perhaps the most fundamental of all business changes has been the increasing use of information technology, the internet, and other technologies such as blockchain (**www.fool.com/ investing/2018/01/10/the-basics-of-blockchain-technology-explained-in-p.aspx**) and artificial intelligence (**www.forbes.com/sites/cognitiveworld/2019/02/25/artificial-intelligence-hype-is-real/#27c54e2625fa**). This *new economy* is reflected in the rapid growth of internet-based firms; the increased use of the internet for communications, sales, and business data processing; and the use of enterprise management systems.

These technologies have fostered the growing strategic focus in cost management by reducing the time required for processing transactions and by expanding the individual manager's access to information within the firm, the industry, and the business environment around the world.

Focus on the Customer

A key element in the business environment is the need to meet high *consumer expectation* for product functionality and quality. To meet this expectation, companies have adopted shorter product life cycles, to add new features and new products as quickly as possible, thereby increasing the overall intensity of competition.

In past years, a business typically succeeded by focusing on only a relatively small number of products with limited features and by organizing production into long, low-cost, and high-volume production runs aided by assembly-line automation. The new business process focuses instead on customer satisfaction. Producing value for the customer changes the orientation of managers from low-cost production of large quantities to *quality, service, timeliness of delivery,* and the *ability to respond to the customer's desire for specific features.*

In the coming years, with the emergence of economic nationalism, the focus will move somewhat from the customer to the producer, as nations use tariffs and other means to protect local producers. Globalization offers the customer the best choice of price, quality, and functionality for products made anywhere in the world. Economic nationalism limits those choices.

Management Organization

Management organization is changing in response to the changes in technology, marketing, and manufacturing processes. Because of the focus on customer satisfaction and value, the emphasis has shifted from financial and profit-based measures of performance to customer-related, nonfinancial performance measures such as quality, time to delivery, and service. Similarly, the hierarchical command-and-control type of organization is being replaced by a more flexible organizational form that encourages teamwork and coordination among business functions. In response to these changes, cost management practices are also changing to include reports that are useful to cross-functional teams of managers. The reports reflect the multifunctional roles of these teams and include a variety of operating and financial information: product quality, unit cost, customer satisfaction, and production bottlenecks, for example. The changes in manufacturing, marketing, and management in organizations are summarized in Exhibit 1.3.

Social, Political, and Climate Change Considerations

In addition to changes in the business environment, significant changes have taken place in the social, political, and cultural environments that affect business. Although the nature and extent of these changes vary a great deal from country to country, they include a more ethnically and racially diverse workforce, changes in regulatory requirements, and a renewed sense of ethical responsibility among managers and employees.

The new business environment requires firms to be flexible and adaptable and to place greater responsibility in the hands of a more highly skilled workforce. Additionally, the changes tend to focus the firm on factors *outside* the production of its product or provision of its service to the ultimate consumer and the global society in which the consumer lives.

An example of an important political and social consideration is the emergence in the U.S. and in the EU countries of economic nationalism. Economic nationalism has fostered anti-trade and anti-immigration measures in some countries. Companies and organizations around the world are adapting to these changes.

Additionally, a worldwide concern for the effects of climate change has changed the way many manufacturers and retailers operate. A common focus now is to change to new operating methods to use less fossil fuels and to reduce the companies' impact on the environment. The topic of sustainability is covered in Chapter 2.

EXHIBIT 1.3   Comparison of Prior and Contemporary Business Environments

	Prior Business Environment	Contemporary Business Environment
Manufacturing		
Basis of competition	Economies of scale, standardization	Quality, functionality, customer satisfaction
Manufacturing process	High volume, long production runs, significant levels of in-process and finished inventory; this is called the "push" approach	Low volume, short production runs, focus on reducing inventory levels and other non-value-added activities and costs; this is called the "pull" approach
Manufacturing technology	Assembly-line automation, isolated technology applications	Robotics, flexible manufacturing systems, integrated technology applications connected by networks
Required labor skills	Machine-paced, low-level skills	Individually and team-paced, high-level skills
Emphasis on quality	Acceptance of a normal or usual amount of waste	Goal of zero defects
Marketing		
Products	Relatively few variations, long product life cycles	Large number of variations, short product life cycles
Markets	Largely domestic	Global
Management Organization		
Type of information recorded and reported	Almost exclusively financial data	Financial and operating data, the firm's strategic success factors
Management organizational structure	Hierarchical, command and control	Network-based organization forms, teamwork focus—employee has more responsibility and control, coaching rather than command and control
Management focus	Emphasis on the short term, short-term performance measures and compensation, concern for sustaining the current stock price, short tenure and high mobility of top managers	Increased emphasis on the long term, focus on critical success factors, commitment to the long-term success of the firm, including shareholder value

The Strategic Focus of Cost Management

The competitive firm incorporates the emerging and anticipated changes in the contemporary environment of business into its business planning and practices. The competitive firm is customer driven; uses advanced manufacturing and information technologies when appropriate; anticipates the effect of changes in regulatory requirements and customer tastes; and recognizes its complex social, political, and cultural environment. Guided by strategic thinking, the management accountant focuses on the factors that make the company successful rather than relying only on costs and other financial measures. We are reminded of the story of the Scottish farmer who had prize sheep to take to market. When asked why his sheep were always superior to those of his neighbors, the farmer responded, "While they're weighing their sheep, I'm fattening mine." Similarly, cost management focuses not on the measurement per se but on the *identification of measures that are critical* to the organization's success. Robert Kaplan's classification of the stages of the development of cost management systems describes this shift in focus:

> **Stage 1.** Cost management systems are basic transaction reporting systems.
>
> **Stage 2.** As they develop into the second stage, cost management systems focus on external financial reporting. The objective is reliable financial reports; accordingly, the usefulness for cost management is limited.
>
> **Stage 3.** Cost management systems track key operating data and develop more accurate and relevant cost information for decision making; cost management information is developed.
>
> **Stage 4.** Strategically relevant cost management information is an integral part of the system.

The first two stages of cost system development focus on the management accountant's measurement and reporting role, and the third stage shifts to operational control. In the fourth stage, the ultimate goal, the management accountant is an integral part of management, not a reporter but a full business partner, working on management teams to implement the firm's strategy. This requires the identification of the firm's critical success factors and the use of analytical, forward-looking decision support. **Critical success factors (CSFs)** are measures of those aspects of the firm's performance essential to its competitive advantage and, therefore, to its success. Many of these critical success factors are financial, but many are nonfinancial. The CSFs for any given firm depend on the nature of the competition it faces. The development and use of CSFs are taken up in Chapter 2.

critical success factors (CSFs)
Measures of those aspects of the firm's performance that are essential to its competitive advantage and therefore to its success.

Contemporary Management Techniques: The Management Accountant's Response to the Contemporary Business Environment

LO 1-3
Explain the contemporary management techniques and how they are used in cost management to respond to the contemporary business environment.

Management accountants, guided by a strategic focus, have responded to the six changes in the contemporary business environment with 13 methods that are useful in implementing strategy in these dynamic times. The first 6 methods focus directly on strategy implementation: the balanced scorecard and strategy map, value chain, activity-based costing and management, business analytics, target costing, and life-cycle costing. The next 7 methods help to achieve strategy implementation through a focus on process improvement: benchmarking, business process improvement, total quality management, lean accounting, the theory of constraints, sustainability, and enterprise risk management. Each of these methods is covered in one or more of the chapters of the text.

The Balanced Scorecard (BSC) and Strategy Map

Strategic information using critical success factors provides a road map for the firm to use to chart its competitive course and serves as a benchmark for competitive success. Financial measures such as profitability reflect only a partial, and frequently only a short-term, measure of the firm's progress. Without strategic information, the firm is likely to stray from its competitive course and to make strategically wrong product decisions—for example, choosing the wrong products or the wrong marketing and distribution methods.

To emphasize the importance of using strategic information, *both financial and nonfinancial,* accounting reports of a firm's performance are now often based on critical success factors in four different perspectives. One perspective is financial; the other three are nonfinancial:

1. **Financial performance.** Measures of profitability and market value, among others, as indicators of how well the firm satisfies its owners and shareholders.
2. **Customer satisfaction.** Measures of quality, service, and low cost, among others, as indicators of how well the firm satisfies its customers.
3. **Internal processes.** Measures of the efficiency and effectiveness with which the firm produces the product or service.
4. **Learning and growth.** Measures of the firm's ability to develop and utilize human resources to meet its strategic goals now and into the future.

An accounting report based on the four perspectives is called a **balanced scorecard (BSC).** The concept of balance captures the intent of broad coverage, financial and nonfinancial, of all factors that contribute to the firm's success in achieving its strategic goals. The balanced scorecard provides a basis for a more complete analysis than is possible with financial data alone. The use of the balanced scorecard is thus a critical ingredient of the overall approach that firms take to become and remain competitive. An example of a balanced scorecard is shown in Exhibit 1.4.

The **strategy map** is a diagram that links the various perspectives in a balanced scorecard. For many companies, high achievement in the learning and growth perspective contributes directly to higher achievement in the internal process perspective, which in turn causes greater achievement in the customer satisfaction perspective, which then produces the desired

balanced scorecard (BSC)
An accounting report that includes the firm's critical success factors in four areas: (1) financial performance, (2) customer satisfaction, (3) internal processes, and (4) learning and growth.

strategy map
A graphical representation of the organization's value proposition; used to depict the series of causes and effects embodied in the various perspectives of an organization's balanced scorecard.

EXHIBIT 1.4
The Balanced Scorecard:
Financial and Nonfinancial
Measures of Success

Financial Measures of Success	Nonfinancial Measures of Success
Sales growth	**Customer Satisfaction**
Earnings growth	Market share and growth in market share
Dividend growth	Customer service (e.g., based on number of complaints)
Bond and credit ratings	On-time delivery
Cash flow	Customer satisfaction (customer survey)
Increase in stock price	Brand recognition (growth in market share)
	Internal Processes
	Product quality
	Manufacturing productivity
	Cycle time (the time from receipt of a customer's order to delivery)
	Product yield and reduction in waste
	Learning and Growth
	Competence of managers (education attained)
	Morale and firmwide culture (employee survey)
	Education and training (training hours)
	Innovation (number of new products)

financial performance. The strategy map is therefore a useful means in understanding how improvement in certain critical success factors contributes to other goals and to the ultimate financial results. We cover the balanced scorecard and strategy map throughout the text, particularly in Chapters 2, 12, 18, and 20.

The Value Chain

value chain
An analytic tool firms use to identify the specific steps required to provide a product or service to the customer.

The **value chain** is an analysis tool organizations use to identify the specific steps required to provide a competitive product or service to the customer. In particular, an analysis of the firm's value chain helps management discover which steps or activities are not competitive, where costs can be reduced, or which activity should be outsourced. Also, management can use the analysis to find ways to increase value for the customer at one or more steps of the value chain. For example, companies such as General Electric, IBM, U-Haul, and Harley-Davidson have found greater overall profits by moving downstream in the value chain to place a greater emphasis on high-value services and less emphasis on lower-margin manufactured products. A key idea of value-chain analysis is that the firm should carefully study each step in its operations to determine how each step contributes to the firm's profits and competitiveness. The value chain is covered in Chapters 2, 13, and 17.

Activity-Based Costing and Management

activity analysis
The development of a detailed description of the specific activities performed in the firm's operations.

Many firms have found that they can improve planning, product costing, operational control, and management control by using **activity analysis** to develop a detailed description of the specific activities performed in the firm's operations. The activity analysis provides the basis for activity-based costing and activity-based management. Activity-based costing (ABC) is used to improve the accuracy of cost analysis by improving the tracing of costs to products or to individual customers. Activity-based management (ABM) uses activity analysis and activity-based costing to help managers improve the value of products and services and increase the organization's competitiveness. ABC and ABM are key strategic tools for many firms, especially those with complex operations or diverse products and services. ABC and ABM are explained in Chapter 5 and then applied in several of the chapters that follow.

Business Analytics

business analytics (BA)
An approach to strategy implementation in which the management accountant uses data to understand and analyze business performance.

Business analytics (BA) (also called *predictive analytics*) is an approach to strategy implementation in which the management accountant uses data to understand and analyze business performance. Business analytics often uses statistical methods such as regression or correlation analysis to predict consumer behavior, measure customer satisfaction, or develop models for setting prices, among other uses. BA is best suited for companies that have a distinctive capability that can be derived from measurable critical success factors. BA is similar to the BSC because it focuses on critical success factors; the difference is that BA uses analytical tools to develop predictive models of core business processes.

Emerging key types of BA include blockchain and artificial intelligence. Blockchain is a technology that allows all parties to a transaction to know with certainty what happened in that transaction (**www.fool.com/investing/2018/01/10/the-basics-of-blockchain-technology-explained-in-p.aspx**). Artificial intelligence seeks to build machines and software that act intelligently (**www.forbes.com/sites/cognitiveworld/2019/02/25/artificial-intelligence-hype-is-real/#52ce2b9525fa**). BA is covered in Chapter 8.

Target Costing

target costing
The desired cost for a product as determined on the basis of a given competitive price, so the product will earn a desired profit.

Target costing is a method that has resulted directly from the intensely competitive markets in many industries. **Target costing** determines the desired cost for a product on the basis of a given competitive price, such that the product will earn a desired profit. Cost is thus determined by price. The firm using target costing must often adopt strict cost reduction measures or redesign the product or manufacturing process to meet the market price and remain profitable.

Target costing forces the firm to become more competitive, and, like benchmarking, it is a common strategic form of analysis in intensely competitive industries where even small price differences attract consumers to the lower-priced product. The camera manufacturing industry is a good example of an industry where target costing is used. Camera manufacturers such as Canon know the market price for each line of camera they manufacture, so they redesign the product (add/delete features, use less expensive parts and materials) and redesign the production process to get the manufacturing cost down to the predetermined target cost. The automobile industry also uses target costing. Target costing is covered in Chapter 13.

Life-Cycle Costing

life-cycle costing
A method used to identify and monitor the costs of a product throughout its life cycle.

Life-cycle costing is a method used to identify and monitor the costs of a product throughout its life cycle. The life cycle consists of all steps from product design and purchase of materials to delivery and service of the finished product. The steps typically include (1) research and development; (2) product design, including prototyping, target costing, and testing; (3) manufacturing, inspecting, packaging, and warehousing; (4) marketing, promotion, and distribution; and (5) sales and service. Cost management has traditionally focused only on costs incurred at the third step, manufacturing. Thinking strategically, management accountants now manage the product's full life cycle of costs, including upstream (research and development, design) and downstream (marketing, sales and service) costs as well as manufacturing costs. This expanded focus means careful attention to product design because design decisions lock in most subsequent life-cycle costs. See Chapter 13 for coverage of life-cycle costing.

Benchmarking

benchmarking
A process by which a firm identifies its critical success factors, studies the best practices of other firms (or other business units within a firm) for achieving these critical success factors, and then implements improvements in the firm's processes to match or beat the performance of those competitors.

Benchmarking is a process by which a firm identifies its critical success factors, studies the best practices of other firms (or other business units within a firm) for achieving these critical success factors, and then implements improvements in the firm's processes to match or beat the performance of those competitors. Benchmarking was first implemented by Xerox Corporation in the late 1970s. Today, many firms use benchmarking. Some firms are recognized as leaders, and are therefore benchmarks, in selected areas—for example, Nordstrom in retailing, Ritz-Carlton in service, the 3M Company in manufacturing, and Apple in innovation, among others.

Benchmarking efforts are facilitated today by cooperative networks of noncompeting firms that exchange benchmarking information. For example, the International Benchmarking Clearinghouse (**www.apqc.org**) and the International Organization for Standardization (ISO) (**www.iso.org**) assist firms in strategic benchmarking.

Business Process Improvement

"Whether you think you can or whether you think you can't—you're right."

Henry Ford

Henry Ford realized that the right attitude is important to success. That belief is what continuous improvement is all about. **Business process improvement (BPI)** is a management method by which managers and workers commit to a program of continuous improvement in quality and other critical success factors. Continuous improvement is very often associated with benchmarking and total quality management as firms seek to identify other firms as models to learn how to improve their critical success factors. While BPI is an incremental method, business process reengineering (BPR) is more radical. BPR is a method for creating competitive advantage in which a firm reorganizes its operating and management functions, often with the result that positions are modified, combined, or eliminated.

business process improvement (BPI)
A management method by which managers and workers commit to a program of continuous improvement in quality and other critical success factors.

Total Quality Management

Total quality management (TQM) is a method by which management develops policies and practices to ensure that the firm's products and services exceed customers' expectations. This approach includes increased product functionality, reliability, durability, and serviceability. Cost management is used to analyze the cost consequences of different design choices and to measure and report the many aspects of quality, including, for example, production breakdowns and production defects, wasted labor or materials, the number of service calls, and the nature of complaints, warranty costs, and product recalls.

total quality management (TQM)
A method by which management develops policies and practices to ensure that the firm's products and services exceed customers' expectations.

Lean Accounting

Firms that have adopted lean manufacturing, which is one of the six key aspects of the contemporary business environment, will also typically use lean accounting. **Lean accounting** uses value streams to measure the financial benefits of a firm's progress in implementing lean manufacturing. Lean accounting places the firm's products and services into value streams, each of which is a group of related products or services. For example, a company manufacturing consumer electronics might have two groups of products (and two value streams)—digital cameras and video cameras—with several models in each group. Accounting for value streams can help the firm to better understand the impact on profitability of its lean manufacturing improvements. TQM and lean accounting are covered in Chapter 17.

lean accounting
The accounting technique that uses value streams to measure the financial benefits of a firm's progress in implementing lean manufacturing.

The Theory of Constraints

The **theory of constraints (TOC)** is a methodology that improves profitability and cycle time by identifying the bottleneck in the operation and determining the most profitable product mix given the bottleneck. TOC helps to eliminate bottlenecks—places where partially completed products tend to accumulate as they wait to be processed in the production process. In the competitive global marketplace common to most industries, the ability to be faster than competitors is often a critical success factor. Many managers argue that the focus on speed in the TOC approach is crucial. They consider speed in product development, product delivery, and manufacturing to be paramount as global competitors find ever-higher customer expectations for rapid product development and prompt delivery. TOC is covered in Chapter 13.

theory of constraints (TOC)
An analysis of operations that improves profitability and cycle time by identifying the bottleneck in the operation and determining the most profitable product mix given the bottleneck.

sustainability
The balancing of the company's short- and long-term goals in all three dimensions of performance—social, environmental, and financial.

Sustainability

Sustainability means the balancing of the organization's short- and long-term goals in all three dimensions of performance—social, environmental, and financial. We view it in the broad sense to include identifying and implementing ways to reduce cost and increase revenue as well as to maintain compliance with social and environmental regulations and expectations. This can be accomplished through technological innovation and new product development as well as commonsense measures to improve the social and environmental impacts of the company's operations. Ford Motor Company saves money through improvements in its stormwater draining system at its River Rouge, Michigan, plant; other leaders in sustainability include Toyota, Honda, McDonald's, and Walmart, among many others. The Dow Jones Sustainability Indices (**www.sustainability-indices.com/**) identify and rank companies according to their sustainability performance. Sustainability is a key topic and is covered in each chapter; a special focus on sustainability is shown in Chapter 2 in connection with the balanced scorecard. Look for the sustainability icon next to problems involving this management technique.

Enterprise Risk Management

enterprise risk management (ERM)
A framework and process that firms use to manage the risks that could negatively or positively affect the company's competitiveness and success.

Enterprise risk management (ERM) is a framework and process that organizations use to manage the risks that could negatively or positively affect the company's competitiveness and success. Risk is considered broadly to include (1) hazards such as fire or flood; (2) financial risks due to foreign currency fluctuations, commodity price fluctuations, and changes in interest rates; (3) operating risk related to customers, products, or employees; and (4) strategic risk related to top management decisions about the firm's strategy and implementation thereof. For financial service firms particularly, ERM has become a much more important topic since the passage of the Dodd-Frank Wall Street Reform and Consumer Protection Act (2010), which requires new regulations for these firms. To indicate how widely used ERM has become, a survey of more than 1,000 risk management professionals by the Risk Management Society (RIMS) found that 73% of the organizations surveyed (**https://www.rims.org/about-us/newsroom/rims-2017-enterprise-risk-management-benchmark-survey**) either had an ERM program in place or were currently implementing one. A recent survey of 100 senior finance executives by the American Productivity and Quality Center (APQC) indicates that only one in five of the executives was satisfied with their company's corporate risk management systems. So while there has been progress in risk management, there is apparently continuing room for improvement (**www.apqc.org**). The text explains the role of ERM in Chapters 10, 11, and 12.

How a Firm Succeeds: The Competitive Strategy

strategy
A plan for using resources to achieve sustainable goals within a competitive environment.

An organization succeeds by implementing a **strategy,** that is, a plan for using resources to achieve sustainable goals within a competitive environment. Finding a strategy begins with determining the purpose and long-range direction, and therefore the mission, of the company. Exhibit 1.5 lists excerpts from the mission statements of selected companies. The mission is developed into specific performance objectives, which are then implemented by specific corporate strategies, that is, specific actions to achieve the objectives that will fulfill the mission.

> "You've got to be very careful if you don't know where you are going, because you might not get there."
>
> Yogi Berra

See the Tyson Foods corporate strategy in Exhibit 1.6. Note that in Exhibit 1.5, Tyson Foods's broad mission statement is explained in terms of more specific objectives, which are in turn operationalized through specific corporate strategies.

EXHIBIT 1.5
Mission Statements of Selected Companies

Procter & Gamble (pg.com)
We believe in finding small but meaningful ways to improve lives—now and for generations to come.
Google (google.com)
To organize the world's information and make it universally accessible and useful.
Merck (merck.com)
To discover, develop and provide innovative products and services that save and improve lives around the world.
Tyson Foods (tysonfoods.com)
Sustainably feed the world with the fastest growing protein brands.

EXHIBIT 1.6
Tyson Foods Corporate Strategy
Source: Tyson Foods (tysonfoods.com).

In its Corporate Strategy Tyson will Sustainably Feed the World With the Fastest Growing Protein Brands, through the following:
- **Grow** Our business through differentiated capabilities
- **Deliver** Ongoing financial fitness through continuous improvement
- **Sustain** Our company and our world for future generations

EXHIBIT 1.7
Cost Management Focus in
Prior and Contemporary
Business Environments

	Prior Business Environment	Contemporary Business Environment
Cost management focus	Financial reporting and cost analysis; common emphasis on standardization and standard costs; the accountant as financial accounting expert and financial scorekeeper	Cost management as a tool for the development and implementation of business strategy; the accountant as business partner

EXHIBIT 1.8
Consequences of Lack of
Strategic Information

- Decision making based on intuition instead of accurate and timely information
- Lack of clarity about direction and goals
- Lack of a clear and favorable perception of the firm by customers and suppliers
- Incorrect investment decisions; choosing products, markets, or manufacturing processes inconsistent with strategic goals
- Inability to effectively benchmark competitors, resulting in lack of knowledge about more effective competitive strategies
- Failure to identify most profitable products, customers, and markets

Organizations also are using cost management to support their strategic goals. Cost management has shifted away from a focus on the stewardship role—that is, product costing and financial reporting. The new focus is on a management-facilitating role: developing cost and other information to support the management of the firm and the achievement of its strategic goals (Exhibit 1.7).

Without strategic information, the firm is likely to stray from its competitive course, to make strategically wrong manufacturing and marketing decisions or to choose the wrong products or the wrong customers. Some of the consequences of a lack of strategic information are shown in Exhibit 1.8.

Developing a Competitive Strategy

In developing a sustainable competitive position, each firm purposefully or as a result of market forces arrives at one of the two competitive strategies: cost leadership or differentiation.[4]

Cost Leadership

LO 1-4
Explain the different types of competitive strategies.

cost leadership
A competitive strategy in which a firm outperforms competitors in producing products or services at the lowest cost.

Cost leadership is a competitive strategy in which a firm outperforms competitors in producing products or services at the lowest cost. The cost leader makes sustainable profits at lower prices, thereby limiting the growth of competition in the industry through its success at reducing price and undermining the profitability of competitors, which must meet the firm's low price. The cost leader normally has a relatively large market share and tends to avoid niche or segment markets by using the price advantage to attract a large portion of the broad market. While most firms make strong efforts to reduce costs, the cost leader may focus almost exclusively on cost reduction, thereby ensuring a significant cost and price advantage in the market.

Cost advantages usually result from productivity in the manufacturing process, in distribution, or in overall administration. For example, technological innovation in the manufacturing process and labor savings from overseas production are common routes to competitive productivity. Firms known to be successful at cost leadership are typically very

[4] This section is adapted from Michael Porter, *Competitive Advantage*(The Free Press, 1985). The Porter concept of strategy is widely used. See, for example, Michael E. Porter, "The Five Forces That Shape Strategy," *Harvard Business Review,* January 2008, pp. 79–93. See also Joan Margretta, *Understanding Michael Porter* (Harvard Business Review Press, 2011).

large manufacturers, service firms, and retailers, such as Texas Instruments, Walmart, Jet-Blue, and Southwest Airlines.

A potential weakness of the cost-leadership strategy is the tendency to cut costs in a way that undermines demand for the product or service, for example, by deleting key features. The cost leader remains competitive only so long as the consumer sees that the product or service is (at least nearly) equivalent to competing products that cost somewhat more.

Differentiation

differentiation
A competitive strategy in which a firm succeeds by developing and maintaining a unique value for the product (or service) as perceived by consumers.

The **differentiation** strategy is implemented by creating a product or service that is unique in some important way, usually in regard to higher quality, better customer service, improved product features, or some type of innovation. Sometimes a differentiation strategy is called *product leadership* to refer to the innovation and features in the product. In other cases, the strategy might be called a *customer-focused* or *customer-solution* strategy, to indicate that the organization succeeds on some dimension(s) of customer service. This perception allows the firm to charge higher prices and outperform the competition in profits without reducing costs significantly. Many industries, including consumer electronics and clothing, have differentiated firms. The appeal of differentiation is especially strong for product lines for which the perception of quality and image is important, as in cosmetics, jewelry, and automobiles. Tiffany, Bentley, Rolex, Whirlpool, and BMW are good examples of firms that have a differentiation strategy.

A weakness of the differentiation strategy is the firm's tendency to undermine its strength by attempting to lower costs or by ignoring the necessity of having a continual and aggressive marketing plan to reinforce the differentiation. If the consumer begins to believe that the difference is not significant, then lower-cost rival products will appear more attractive.

Other Strategic Issues

A firm succeeds, then, by adopting and effectively implementing one of the two strategies explained earlier (and summarized in Exhibit 1.9). Recognize that although one strategy is generally dominant, a firm is most likely to work hard at process improvement throughout the firm, whether cost leader or differentiator, and on occasion to employ both of the strategies at the same time. However, a firm following both strategies is likely to succeed only if it achieves one of the strategies very well. This situation is what Michael Porter calls "getting stuck in the middle." A firm that is stuck in the middle is not able to sustain a competitive advantage. For example, giant retailer Sears has been stuck in the middle between trying to compete with Walmart on cost and price and with style-conscious Target on differentiation. The 2005 merger of Sears and Kmart has added to the confusion over the firm's direction. As evidence of the failed strategy, since the merger with Kmart, Sears has been steadily closing stores, including 142 store closures in 2018 and 20 more in 2019.

Developing a competitive strategy is the first step for a successful business. The critical next step is to implement that strategy, and this is where the management accountant comes in. The management accountant works to implement strategy as a part of the management team, by contributing the management accountant's specific expertise (cost management

EXHIBIT 1.9 Distinctive Aspects of the Two Competitive Strategies

Aspect	Cost Leadership	Differentiation
Strategic target	Broad cross section of the market	Focused section of the market
Basis of competitive advantage	Lowest cost in the industry	Unique product or service
Product line	Limited selection	Wide variety, differentiating features
Production emphasis	Lowest possible cost with high quality and essential product features	Innovation in differentiating products
Marketing emphasis	Low price	Premium price and innovative, differentiating features

methods). We cover these methods in each of the chapters as we go through the text. Our focus in each chapter, then, will be to show how the method we are covering in that chapter is used in implementing strategy. We will use the following five-step framework to show how the method demonstrated in the chapter can be used to help the organization achieve its strategy by solving a particular problem.

The Five Steps of Strategic Decision Making

The five steps for decision making with a strategic emphasis are listed next, together with a short illustration of how the steps could be used by Walmart to help the company deal with the problem of rising fuel prices that affect the cost of the firm's use of trucks to deliver products from Walmart's warehouses to its retail stores.

The first step is to determine the strategic issues surrounding the problem because the solution to any problem must fit the organization's strategy. A good decision is one that makes the organization more competitive and successful. By starting with the strategic issues, we ensure that the decision fits the organization's strategic goals.

1. **Determine the strategic issues surrounding the problem**. Fuel costs are critical to Walmart because it competes on low cost and low prices. The Walmart strategy is cost leadership. So this problem will get close management attention.
2. **Identify the alternative actions.** In one alternative, Walmart considers the use of smaller and more fuel-efficient trucks, together with a relocation of its warehouses, to reduce travel time and fuel usage. Another option would be to outsource all of Walmart's delivery needs to other trucking firms.
3. **Obtain information and conduct analyses of the alternatives.** Walmart collects relevant cost information and calculates the expected cost of each alternative and finds that the use of other truckers would provide significantly lower total fuel cost. Considering the problem strategically, Walmart projects on the one hand that it can more effectively compete with Target by providing more rapid delivery of fast-moving items to its stores, and that this could be accomplished with the use of smaller trucks. On the other hand, Walmart also knows that it competes on cost and that lower cost is critical to its success.
4. **Based on strategy and analysis, choose and implement the desired alternative.** After considering the options, Walmart chooses to develop a fleet of large, high-efficiency trucks that employ improved aerodynamics, an advanced turbine-powered hybrid engine, and electric power components (www.walmart.com).
5. **Provide an ongoing evaluation of the effectiveness of implementation in step 4.** To provide an ongoing review of delivery costs, Walmart top management instructs operational managers in the firm to present an updated review of the decision to top management once every quarter. In this way, changes in costs or strategic objectives will be reviewed on a regular basis.

REAL-WORLD FOCUS — Highly Cost-Competitive Industries: Surviving through Differentiation

Macy's Department Stores is an admired name in retailing. But the store is struggling with what the new CEO claims is a "sea of sameness." Macy's is now moving to higher-priced, trendier clothing to bolster the Macy's brand and to boost sales. In effect, Macy's is moving to a more differentiated strategy.

Much of furniture manufacturing is a very cost-competitive business. And in recent decades, furniture companies have moved manufacturing overseas in search of lower costs. Hardly any place has been affected as much as High Point, North Carolina, which in the 1940s was the location of 60% of furniture manufacturing in the U.S. Because of movement overseas, there is little left of that manufacturing dominance in High Point. To adjust to the demand for cost savings, some furniture companies in High Point have moved to more of a differentiation strategy, focusing on smaller batches of very-high-quality product. Tomlinson Company, a furniture manufacturer in High Point, is an example of this trend; the company is featured in Chapter 4.

The food industry (for foods in supermarkets) is generally regarded as largely a cost-leadership business, and recently two large companies, Kraft and Heinz, were purchased by a large investment firm. The investment firm immediately reduced costs at the combined company, resulting in significant savings. However, the Kraft Heinz brands are now suffering as a result, and a smaller competitor, General Mills, is succeeding through innovation and a focus on building brand value and sales growth. As the General Mills CEO said, "The biggest driver for long-term sustainability of a food company is organic sales growth." (Here the term *organic* does not mean organic food but growth in sales of existing brands through reinvesting in these brands, rather than by purchasing new brands.)

Sources: Suzanne Kapner, "Can This Man Save Macy's?," *The Wall Street Journal,* March 24, 2017; Kristina Leigh Painter, "As Mega-takeovers Fade in Food Industry, General Mills Strategy Emerges as Winner," *Star Tribune,* July 4, 2019 (www.startribune.com/as-mega-takeovers-fade-in-food-industry-general-mills-strategy-emerges-as-winner/512239362/); Jane Margolis, "A Town in Need of a Do-Over," *The New York Times,* July 3, 2019, p. B5.

Look for these five steps for the topics in the chapters ahead and look for the strategy icon next to problems involving strategy.

LO 1-5

Describe the professional environment of the management accountant, including professional organizations and professional certifications.

The Professional Environment of Cost Management

"Personally, I'm always ready to learn, although I do not always like being taught."

Winston Churchill

"If I had eight hours to chop down a tree, I would spend six sharpening my axe."

Abraham Lincoln

"Once you stop learning, you start dying."

Albert Einstein

Winston Churchill, the former prime minister of the United Kingdom; Abraham Lincoln, the 16th president of the United States; and Albert Einstein, theoretical physicist, understood the importance of continuous learning. Their words apply equally well to the management accountant. Management accountants must continuously improve their technical and other skills and maintain a constant high level of professionalism, integrity, and objectivity about their work. Many professional organizations, such as the Institute of Management Accountants (IMA) and the American Institute of Certified Public Accountants (AICPA), encourage their members to earn relevant professional certifications, participate in professional development programs, and continually reflect on the professional ethics they bring to their work.

Professional Organizations

The professional environment of the management accountant is influenced by two types of organizations: one that sets guidelines and regulations regarding management accounting practices and one that promotes the professionalism and competence of management accountants.

The first group of organizations includes a number of federal agencies, such as the Internal Revenue Service, which sets product costing guidelines for tax purposes, and the Federal

REAL-WORLD FOCUS   Where to Look for Information on Professional Organizations

American Institute of Certified Public Accountants (AICPA): www.aicpa.org/

Federal Trade Commission (FTC): www.ftc.gov/

Financial Executives International (FEI): www.financialexecutives .org

Institute of Internal Auditors (IIA): https://na.theiia.org/

Institute of Management Accountants (IMA): www.imanet.org

Securities and Exchange Commission (SEC): www.sec.gov/

Chartered Professional Accountants of Canada (CPA Canada) www.cpacanada.ca (Note: The Society of Management Accountants Canada and the Canadian Institute of Chartered Accountants merged in 2014 to create the Chartered Professional Accountants of Canada.)

Association of Chartered Certified Accountants (ACCA): www.accaglobal.com

The Chartered Institute of Management Accountants (CIMA, UK): www.cimaglobal.com

Consumer Financial Protection Bureau (CFPB): www.consumerfinance.gov

Federal Accounting Standards Advisory Board: www.fasab.gov

Financial Accounting Standards Board: www.fasb.org

Public Company Accounting Oversight Board: www.pcaobus.org

Trade Commission (FTC), which, to foster competitive practices and protect trade, restricts pricing practices and requires that prices in most circumstances be justified on the basis of cost. In addition, the Securities and Exchange Commission (SEC) provides guidance, rules, and regulations regarding financial reporting.

The role of the SEC has been strengthened by the Sarbanes–Oxley Act of 2002, which created the Public Company Accounting Oversight Board (PCAOB) to establish rules for "auditing, quality control, ethics, independence, and other professional standards relating to the preparation of audit reports for issuers." Of particular importance to management accountants is that the SEC, in implementing the act, now requires each public company to disclose in its annual report whether it has a code of ethics covering its chief financial executives, including high-level management accountants such as the controller.

The Dodd-Frank Wall Street Reform and Consumer Protection Act (2010) includes a variety of new regulations for the financial services industry. The act also created the Consumer Financial Protection Bureau (CFPB), the goal of which is to detect and prevent unfair lending practices. Under this act, management accountants in the financial services industry now have increased responsibilities. In May 2018, Congress acted to remove some of the Dodd-Frank rules on small and medium-sized banks, leaving only a small number of large banks subject to these rules.

In the private sector, the Financial Accounting Standards Board (FASB), an independent organization, and the AICPA supply additional guidance regarding financial reporting practices. The AICPA also provides educational opportunities in the form of newsletters, magazines, professional development seminars, and technical meetings for management accountants.

Congress established the Cost Accounting Standards Board (CASB) in 1970 (Public Law 91-379), which operates under the Office of Federal Procurement Policy "to make, promulgate, amend and rescind cost accounting standards and interpretations thereof designed to achieve uniformity and consistency in the cost accounting standards governing measurement, assignment, and allocation of cost to contracts with the United States federal government." The CASB's objective is to achieve uniformity and consistency in the cost accounting standards used by government suppliers to reduce the incidence of fraud and abuse. Twenty standards cover a broad range of issues in cost accounting.

In addition, to enhance cost accounting standards and financial reporting by federal governmental entities, Congress established in 1990 the Federal Accounting Standards Advisory Board. The FASAB publishes reports and documents on cost accounting concepts and standards that are comparable to those used in business firms.

Another group of organizations supports the growth and professionalism of management accounting practice. The Institute of Management Accountants (IMA) is the principal organization devoted primarily to management accountants in the United States. The IMA provides

Walmart and Target are two of the most successful retailers in the United States. Walmart bears the slogan "Save Money, Live Better," while Target stores say "Expect More, Pay Less." If you have shopped at either of these stores, you will likely have formed an opinion about the stores and how they compete.

Required

1. Based on your experience, explain what you think are the competitive strategies of these retailers. Are they key competitors,

targeting the same customers? Do you think each firm has adopted the most effective strategy? Why or why not?

2. While customers are pleased with Walmart's low prices, there is ongoing controversy about the firm's employment practices, including alleged discrimination against women in promotion and pay policies. What are your thoughts on the controversy? Are the ethical principles and standards of the management accountant relevant in this context?

journals, newsletters, research reports, management accounting practice reports, professional development seminars, and technical meetings that serve the broad purpose of providing continuing education opportunities for management accountants. An especially important service of the IMA is its Statements on Management Accounting and research reports, which cover a broad range of practice issues for the management accountant: management control, governance, leadership, external reporting, cost management systems, and global business. In the UK, the Chartered Institute of Management Accountants (CIMA) and the Association of Chartered Certified Accountants (ACCA) perform a similar role, as does the Chartered Professional Accountants of Canada (CPA Canada), the Spanish Management Accounting Association, the French Accounting Association, and the Institutes of Chartered Accountants in Ireland, Australia, Scotland, and India. Similar organizations are present in most other countries around the world.

In areas related to the management accounting function, Financial Executives International (FEI) provides services much like those provided by the IMA for financial managers, including controllers and treasurers.

Because one of the management control responsibilities of the management accountant is to develop effective systems to detect and prevent errors and fraud in the accounting records, the management accountant commonly has strong ties to control-oriented organizations such as the Institute of Internal Auditors (IIA). Participation in professional organizations and their professional development programs are an important way for management accountants to update their skills to meet the changing needs of their organizations.

"Even if you're on the right track, you'll get run over if you just sit there."

Will Rogers

"It is not the strongest of the species that survive, nor the most intelligent, but the one most responsive to change."

Charles Darwin

Professional Certifications

The role of professional certification programs is to provide a distinct measure of experience, training, and performance capability for the management accountant. Certification is one way in which the management accountant shows professional achievement and stature. Two types of certification are relevant for management accountants. The first is the Certificate in Management Accounting (CMA) designation administered by the Institute of Management Accountants, which is achieved by passing a qualifying exam and satisfying certain background and experience requirements. The exam has two parts: (1) financial planning, performance, and control and (2) financial decision making. Three of the six topics of part (1) [representing 55% of part (1) of the exam] are covered in this text: (a) planning, budgeting, and forecasting; (b) performance management; and (c) cost management. Three of the five topics of part (2) [representing about 50% of the content in that part of the exam] are covered in this text: (a) decision analysis, (b) investment decisions, and (c) professional ethics.[5]

The second certification is the Certified Public Accountant (CPA) designation. The CPA was updated in May 2017 to have a greater focus on the higher-order cognitive skills of analysis and evaluation, fewer multiple-choice questions but more task-based simulations. The new exam is better linked to what CPAs must do in practice, and better linked to their previous education.

Like the CMA, the CPA is earned by passing a qualifying exam and by satisfying certain background, education, and experience requirements. Unlike the CMA, which is an international designation, the CPA certificate is a professional license monitored in the United States by each state and territorial jurisdiction that has its own set of criteria. While the CPA license is critical for those accountants who practice auditing, the CMA designation is widely viewed as the most relevant for those dealing with cost management issues. In 2017 the IMA developed a new credential to supplement the CMA. The new credential, Certified in Strategy and Competitive Analysis (CSCA), will help the management accountant to achieve the career success envisioned in the definition of management accounting by focusing on the strategic role of the management accountant. The CSCA exam has three parts: (1) Strategic Analysis (25%), (2) Creating Competitive Advantage (40%), and (3) Strategy Implementation and Performance Evaluation (35%). One must be a CMA to be able to sit for the CSCA exam.

Many countries have certificates that are similar to the CPA and CMA, and many management accountants have both the CMA and the CPA certifications. In addition, the AICPA and CIMA have recently partnered to offer a credential for professional accountants called the Chartered Global Management Accountant (CGMA).

Professional Ethics

Ethics is an important aspect of the management accountant's work and profession. Professional ethics can be summed up as the commitment of the management accountant to provide a useful service for management. This commitment means that the management accountant has the competence, confidentiality, integrity, and credibility to serve management effectively. Because of its importance, ethics is covered in each chapter; look for the ethics icon next to problems involving ethics.

LO 1-6

Understand the principles and rules of professional ethics and explain how to apply them.

The IMA Statement of Ethical Professional Practice

The ethical behavior of the management accountant is guided by the Statement of Ethical Professional Practice of the Institute of Management Accountants (updated July 2017; **www.imanet.org/-/media/b6fbeeb74d964e6c9fe654c48456e61f.ashx**). The IMA Statement of Ethical Professional Practice specifies *minimum* standards of behavior that are intended to guide the management accountant and to inspire a very high overall level of professionalism. By complying with these standards, management accountants enhance their profession and facilitate the development of a trusting relationship in which managers and others can confidently rely on their work.

The IMA Statement of Ethical Professional Practice contains four main standards: (1) competence, (2) confidentiality, (3) integrity, and (4) credibility (see Exhibit 1.10). The standard of competence requires management accountants to develop and maintain the skills necessary for their area of practice and to continually reassess the adequacy of those skills as their firm grows and becomes more complex. The standard of confidentiality requires adherence to the firm's policies regarding communication of data to protect its trade secrets and other confidential information. Integrity refers to behaving in a professional manner (e.g., refraining from activities that would discredit the profession, such as unfair hiring practices) and avoiding conflicts of interest (e.g., not accepting a gift from a supplier or customer). Finally, credibility refers to the need to maintain impartial judgment (e.g., not developing

[5] The IMA has also introduced a new (2017) certification program, Certified in Strategy and Competitive Analysis (CSCA). This certificate will help the management accountant to achieve the career success envisioned in the definition of management accounting by focusing on the strategic role of the management accountant. The CSCA exam has three parts: (1) Strategic Analysis (25%), (2) Creating Competitive Advantage (40%), and (3) Strategy Implementation and Performance Evaluation (35%). One must be a CMA to be able to sit for the CSCA exam.

THE COST OF UNETHICAL BEHAVIOR
According to the Association of Certified Fraud Examiners (www.acfe.com), the typical organization loses 5% of its annual revenue to fraud. When projected on a global basis, this translates to a potential fraud of approximately $3.5 trillion worldwide.

THE REWARDS FOR DETECTING UNETHICAL BEHAVIOR
A controversial feature of the Dodd-Frank Wall Street Reform and Consumer Protection Act (2010) is a "whistleblower" provision, which provides financial rewards (up to 30% of the proceeds from a litigation settlement) for employees who report securities and other financial fraud to the SEC—a real reward for detecting fraud. This provision is in conflict with that of the Sarbanes-Oxley Act (SOX, 2002), which emphasizes internal controls and company-based "hotlines" for detecting fraud. A particular problem for management accountants is that the IMA's Statement of Ethical Professional Practice requires the management accountant, upon discovering an ethical conflict, to resolve that conflict first with the immediate supervisor, if possible, and that "communication of such problems to authorities or individuals not employed or engaged by the organization is not considered appropriate, unless you believe there is a clear violation of the law." Further complicating matters, until recently the policies of the SEC have not consistently supported this provision of the Dodd-Frank Act. However, in September 2016, the SEC brought a case against a plaintiff for retaliating against a whistleblower; the SEC now strongly supports the anti-retaliation protections in the act. Similarly, the Commodity Futures Trading Commission (CFTC) recently approved changes in its rules that strengthen anti-retaliation protections for whistleblowers.

Sources: Jason Zukerman and Matthew Stock, "CFTC Strengthens Anti-Retaliation Protections for Whistleblowers and Improves CFTC Whistleblower Award Program," *The National Law Review*, May 21, 2017; 2019 Annual Report of Dodd-Frank Whistle Blower Program. (www.sec.gov/files/sec-2019-annual%20report-whistleblower%20program.pdf).

EXHIBIT 1.10
Institute of Management Accountants Statement of Ethical Professional Practice

1. Competence
Each member has a responsibility to:
1. Maintain an appropriate level of professional leadership and expertise by enhancing knowledge and skills.
2. Perform professional duties in accordance with relevant laws, regulations, and technical standards.
3. Provide decision support information and recommendations that are accurate, clear, concise, and timely. Recognize and help manage risk.

2. Confidentiality
Each member has a responsibility to:
1. Keep information confidential except when disclosure is authorized or legally required.
2. Inform all relevant parties regarding appropriate use of confidential information. Monitor to ensure compliance.
3. Refrain from using confidential information for unethical or illegal advantage.

3. Integrity
Each member has a responsibility to:
1. Mitigate actual conflicts of interest. Regularly communicate with business associates to avoid apparent conflicts of interest. Advise all parties of any potential conflicts.
2. Refrain from engaging in any conduct that would prejudice carrying out duties ethically.
3. Abstain from engaging in or supporting any activity that might discredit the profession.
4. Contribute to a positive ethical culture and place integrity of the profession above personal interests.

4. Credibility
Each member has a responsibility to:
1. Communicate information fairly and objectively.
2. Provide all relevant information that could reasonably be expected to influence an intended user's understanding of the reports, analyses, or recommendations.
3. Report any delays or deficiencies in information, timeliness, processing, or internal controls in conformance with organization policy and/or applicable law.
4. Communicate professional limitations or other constraints that would preclude responsible judgement or successful performance of an entity.

analyses to support a decision that the management accountant knows is not correct). The guiding principles behind these standards are honesty, fairness, objectivity, and responsibility. IMA members are expected to behave in accordance with these principles and standards. The following section outlines the IMA's recommendations about how management accountants should approach ethical dilemmas.

How to Apply the Statement of Ethical Professional Practice

Handling situations in which an ethical issue arises can be very challenging and frustrating. To effectively resolve an ethical issue, it is crucial to understand the firm's business and strategy. Determining whether a particular action is ethical requires an understanding of the business context to understand the intent of the act—is it for a business purpose or is it intended to mislead or disguise fraud? An example is Sherron Watkins, an Enron Corporation employee, who is credited with bringing that firm's accounting fraud to light. She wrote a letter to the CEO that financial accounting practices at Enron did not appear to fit the firm's business or strategy.

To assist management accountants in the application of ethical practices, the IMA offers the following guidance regarding resolving ethical issues (**www.imanet.org**):

When faced with an ethical issue, the management accountant should follow the organization's established policies on the resolution of such conflict. If these policies do not resolve the ethical conflict, consider the following courses of action:

1. The resolution process could include a discussion with the member's immediate supervisor. If the supervisor appears to be involved, the issue could be presented to the next level of management.
2. IMA offers an anonymous helpline that the member may call to request how key elements of the *IMA Statement of Ethical Professional Practice* could be applied to the ethical issue.
3. The member should consider consulting his or her own attorney to learn of any legal obligations, rights, and risks concerning the issue.

Source: IMA's Statement of Ethical Professional Practice. Copyright 2017 IMA (Institute of Management Accountants). Reprinted with permission. All Rights Reserved.

Summary

The central theme of this book is that cost management information includes all the information that managers need to manage effectively to lead their firms to competitive success. Cost management information includes both financial and nonfinancial information critical to the firm's success. The specific role of cost management in the firm differs depending on the firm's competitive strategy, its type of industry and organization (manufacturing firm, service firm, merchandising firm, not-for-profit organization, or governmental organization), and the management function to which cost management is applied (the functions are strategic management, planning and decision making, management and operational control, and preparation of financial statements).

Changes in the business environment have altered the nature of competition and the types of techniques managers use to succeed in their businesses. These changes include (1) an increase in global competition (partly offset by recent developments with economic nationalism and COVID-19); (2) lean manufacturing; (3) advances in information technologies, the internet, and enterprise resource management; (4) a greater focus on the customer; (5) new forms of management organization; and (6) changes in the social, political, and cultural environment of business.

Management accountants have responded to the above six changes in the contemporary business environment with 13 methods that are useful in implementing strategy in these dynamic times. The first 6 methods focus directly on strategy implementation—the balanced scorecard and strategy map, value chain, activity-based costing and management, business analytics, target costing, and life-cycle costing. The next 7 methods focus on strategy implementation through a focus on process improvement—benchmarking, business process improvement, total quality management, lean accounting, the theory of constraints, sustainability, and enterprise risk management.

To apply new management methods effectively, it is crucial that the management accountant understand the firm's strategy. Strategy is the set of plans and policies that a firm employs to develop a sustainable competitive advantage. Using Michael Porter's framework, a firm can compete effectively either as a cost leader or through differentiation.

A variety of professional organizations support management accounting, including the Institute of Management Accountants (IMA), the American Institute of Certified Public Accountants (AICPA), and Financial Executives International (FEI), among others. Several relevant certification programs recognize competence and experience in management accounting; they include the Certified Management Accountant (CMA), the Chartered Global Management Accountant (CGMA), and the Certified Public Accountant (CPA).

The management accountant is responsible to the employer and to the public for maintaining a high standard of performance and ethical responsibility, as set forth in the IMA Statement of Ethical Professional Practice. The professional ethics standards of the management accountant include competence, confidentiality, integrity, and credibility.

Key Terms

activity analysis, *14*
balanced scorecard (BSC), *13*
benchmarking, *15*
business analytics (BA), *14*
business process improvement (BPI), *16*
cost leadership, *18*
cost management, *3*
cost management information, *3*
critical success factors (CSFs), *13*

differentiation, *19*
economic nationalism, *8*
enterprise risk management (ERM), *17*
lean accounting, *16*
life-cycle costing, *15*
management accounting, *3*
management control, *6*
operational control, *6*
planning and decision making, *6*

preparation of financial statements, *6*
strategic management, *5*
strategy, *17*
strategy map, *13*
sustainability, *16*
target costing, *15*
theory of constraints (TOC), *16*
total quality management (TQM), *16*
value chain, *14*

Comments on Cost Management in Action

A Case in Competitive Strategy: Walmart and Target

These questions are intended for open discussion and expression of differences of opinion. Here we have an outline of some thoughts on these competitive issues, combined with some of the most recent news reports.

1. Most would argue that Walmart is a cost leader because of its focus on low prices. Its operating efficiencies and persistent pursuit of low costs from its suppliers help Walmart to achieve these low prices; the slogan says it all about that firm, "Save Money, Live Better."

    Target also values low prices but competes somewhat differently. As the company website states, "our mission is . . . delivering outstanding value, continuous innovation and exceptional guest experiences by consistently fulfilling our Expect More, Pay Less® brand promise." Moreover, the Target financial report states that, for Target, the competitive focus is to offer customers "both everyday essentials and fashionable, differentiated merchandise at discounted prices." These statements point to a differentiated firm, even though low price is an element of the competition. In the recent couple of years, the two firms have adopted similar strategies regarding online sales and grocery sales, which have become very important for sales and profits at both firms. Both firms have enjoyed a strong increase in sales, profits, and stock values in recent years.

2. The controversy over Walmart's competitive and labor practices has drawn a lot of comment in the press, and opinions are divided. One line of argument would say that, as for any large business, Walmart must compete in an increasingly competitive global economy, while others might say that its values are in conflict with this type of competition. The role of the management accountant in this context is to help the firm succeed, and to do so in an ethical manner as set out in the IMA Statement of Ethical Professional Practice.

Sources: Michael A. Sainato, "Walmart Facing Gender Discrimination Lawsuits from Female Employees," *The Guardian,* February 18, 2019. See also the firms' websites: Walmart at (**www.walmart.com**) and Target at (**www.target.com**).

Self-Study Problem
(For answers, please see Solutions.)

Strategy: An Ethical Issue

Frank Sills, the CEO and founder of ENVIRO-WEAR, is facing the first big challenge of his young company. Frank began the company on the principle of environmental consciousness in the manufacture of sports and recreation wear. His idea was to develop clothing that would appeal to active people who were concerned about quality, waste in manufacturing and packaging, and the environmental impact of the manufacture of the goods they purchased. Starting with a small shop in Zebulon, North Carolina, Frank was able to develop his small business through strategic alliances with mail-order merchandisers and by effective public relations about his environmentally concerned processes. A special advantage for the young firm was Frank's knowledge of accounting and his prior experience as a CPA in a major public accounting firm and as a controller (and CMA) of a small manufacturing firm.

ENVIRO-WEAR had reached $25,000,000 in sales in its sixth year when a disastrous set of events put the firm and its prospects in a tail spin. One of the key sales managers was overheard by a news reporter telling jokes about the poor quality of the firm's clothing, and the news of it spread quickly. Also, rumors (largely unfounded) spread at the same time that the firm was not really as environmentally conscious in its manufacturing and packaging as it claimed. The result was an immediate falloff in sales, and some retailers were returning the goods.

Frank intends to fire the manager and deny publicly any association with the manager's comments, as well as to defend the firm's environmental record.

Required

1. On the basis of Porter's analysis of strategic competitive advantage, what type of competitive strategy has ENVIRO-WEAR followed? What type of strategy should it follow in the future?

2. What are the ethical issues involved in the case, and how would you resolve them?

The Student Resources section of Connect includes video tutorials for the Self-Study Problems.

Questions

1-1   Give four examples of firms you believe would be significant users of cost management information and explain why.

1-2   Give three examples of firms you believe would require somewhat unique types of cost management information because of their unique competitive strategy, and explain why.

1-3   What does the term *cost management* mean? Who in the typical firm or organization is responsible for cost management?

1-4   Name three professional cost management organizations and explain their roles and objectives.

1-5   What type of professional certification is most relevant for the management accountant and why?

1-6   List the four functions of management. Explain what type of cost management information is appropriate for each.

1-7   Which is the most important function of management? Explain why.

1-8   Identify the different types of business firms and other organizations that use cost management information, and explain how the information is used.

1-9   Name a firm or organization you know of that you are reasonably sure uses cost management and explain why it does so. Does it use cost leadership or differentiation, and why?

1-10 Many firms rely on the internet extensively. Explain how firms using cost leadership and firms using differentiation might use the internet.

1-11 The management accountant is a full business partner with management in which of the four stages of cost system development, and why?

1-12 What are some factors in the contemporary business environment that are causing changes in business firms and other organizations? How are the changes affecting the way those firms and organizations use cost management information?

1-13 Contrast past and present business environments with regard to the following aspects: basis of competition, manufacturing processes and manufacturing technology, required labor skills, emphasis on quality, number of products, number of markets, types of cost management information needed, management organizational structure, and management focus.

1-14 Name the 13 contemporary management techniques and describe each briefly.

1-15 Identify what you think is a very successful firm and explain why. How did it become successful?

1-16 Do you think there is value to the firm and to its shareholders of a strong ethical climate in the firm? Why or why not?

1-17   In recent years, the drug VIOXX was removed from the market by the pharmaceutical giant Merck & Co. The drug was used to relieve arthritis pain and was especially beneficial for patients who needed a medication that was easy on the stomach. But research reports showed there was a risk of strokes and heart attacks after taking VIOXX for 18 months. Evaluate Merck's decision on business and ethics grounds.

1-18   What would you consider to be the strategy of The Coca-Cola Company: cost leadership or differentiation? Why?

1-19   What is a commodity? Give some examples of what you consider to be commodities and explain whether you think the company making the commodity product or service is a cost leader or a differentiator and why.

1-20   Take as an example the bank where you have your account(s) and state whether you think it is a cost leader or a differentiator and why.

1-21   Consider the three broad categories of firms: manufacturers, retailers, and service firms. Give an example of a cost leader and a differentiator in each of the three categories. Do there tend to be more cost leaders relative to differentiators in one or more of these categories?

1-22   Michael Porter argues a firm cannot be at the same time a cost leader and a differentiator. Do you think a firm could be a cost leader and then become a differentiator, or vice versa?

1-23   What is the difference between strategy and planning?

Brief Exercises

[LO 1-1]   1-24   The IMA definition of management accounting states that
   a.   management accounting is the process of gathering, reporting, and analyzing information for management decision making.
   b.   management accounting is a profession that involves preparation and analysis of cost information, budgeting, and performance measurement and analysis to assist managers in decision making.
   c.   management accounting involves partnering in management decision making, planning, and performance measurement to assist in the formulation and implementation of an organization's strategy.
   d.   management accounting is a set of practices in which accountants, working within companies, help managers to make better decisions based on accurate financial information.

[LO 1-1]   1-25   Which of the following is the correct sequence in which cost management information is developed and used?
   a.   Business events, data, information, analysis, decisions
   b.   Business events, data, analysis, information, decisions
   c.   Business events, information, analysis, knowledge, decisions
   d.   Business events, data, information, knowledge, decisions

For the following multiple choice questions, 1-26 through 1-35, select the best available answer.

[LO 1-1, 1-4]   1-26   Management accounting, as defined by the IMA, uses the expertise of the management accountant to
   a.   improve quality and reduce cost.
   b.   implement a strategy of cost leadership or differentiation.
   c.   implement a tactic of customer value and shareholder value.
   d.   improve business performance and the life cycle of operations.

[LO 1-1]   1-27   The management accountants in an organization probably report directly to the
   a.   controller.
   b.   treasurer.
   c.   chief executive officer (CEO).
   d.   chief financial officer (CFO).

[LO 1-4]   1-28   Walmart, Costco, and Dollar General are retailers that probably compete on the basis of
   a.   quality and customer service.
   b.   product differentiation.
   c.   low prices.
   d.   desirable locations.

[LO 1-2]   1-29 Cost management has evolved from a focus on measurement to one of identifying those measures that are critical to the organization's success. Given this new focus, indicate which one of the following types of cost management systems cost managers are likely to be striving for.

    a. Basic transaction reporting systems

    b. A system that focuses on reliable external financial reports

    c. A system that tracks key operating data and develops accurate cost information

    d. A system in which strategically relevant cost management information is an integral part

[LO 1-3]   1-30 A management method in which managers and employees commit to a process of continuous improvement is best described as

    a. total quality management.

    b. business process improvement.

    c. lean accounting.

    d. the theory of constraints.

[LO 1-5]   1-31 Professional certifications are issued by the American Institute of Certified Public Accountants (AICPA), the Institute of Management Accountants (IMA), the Chartered Institute of Management Accountants (CIMA), and the Chartered Professional Accountants of Canada (CPA-Canada), among other professional accounting organizations. The Certificate in Management Accounting (CMA) is issued by the

    a. CIMA.

    b. IMA.

    c. CPA-Canada.

    d. AICPA.

[LO 1-6]   1-32 According to the Institute of Management Accountants Statement of Ethical Professional Practice, determining whether a particular action is ethical requires knowing

    a. whether the act is legal in your jurisdiction.

    b. the intent and the business context of the act.

    c. the amount of the fraud or theft that is involved.

    d. whether the management accountant is certified.

[LO 1-2, 1-4]   1-33 Firms that want to grow quickly in the global marketplace often employ the cost-leadership strategy because

    a. this produces favorable customs rates and import duties.

    b. manufacturers around the world adopt lean manufacturing methods to bring their costs down.

    c. this allows them to employ and benefit from enterprise management systems.

    d. there are relatively few product variations across different countries.

[LO 1-3]   1-34 The strategy map can be compared to the balanced scorecard (BSC) in that

    a. the strategy map is a subset of the BSC.

    b. the strategy map deals with the strategy component of the BSC.

    c. the strategy map provides a guide to implementing the BSC by linking the critical success factors.

    d. the strategy map and the BSC are unrelated.

[LO 1-6]   1-35 The IMA ethical standard that requires the management accountant to act with integrity

    a. requires the management accountant to mitigate actual conflicts of interest.

    b. is not a part of the IMA Statement of Ethical Professional Practice.

    c. is necessary to ensure that the management accountant's credibility is not impaired.

    d. is necessary to ensure that the management accountant does not violate confidentiality.

Exercises

[LO 1-1, 1-6]   1-36 **Strategy; Real Estate Services** As a management accountant in a small real estate services firm, you have become aware of a strategic initiative in your firm to promote its services to a new class of customers. Currently, most of your firm's customers lease space in large office buildings where they might occupy three or more floors of the building. Your firm provides maintenance, security, and cleaning services for the office space leased by these customers. The strategic initiative you have discovered is to seek out smaller firms that occupy as small a space as a few thousand square feet. You know that most of these smaller firms are now serviced in a haphazard manner, with part-time help for which turnover is very high; some of the smaller office buildings might not employ security of any kind. You expect that the demand for your company's services among firms of this smaller size will be good, but you are worried about the profitability of these new customers. In fact, although you cannot prove it with hard numbers, you are sure that this new strategy will cause big losses for your firm. You have not been consulted about this new strategy by the firm's owners because you are not viewed as part of the management decision-making team. You would like very much, however, to be more involved in the company's strategy development and decision making.

Required   What should you do or say about this new strategic initiative?

[LO 1-4]   1-37   **Strategy; Food Producer** The Yee-Haw Pickle Company in Park City, Utah, has grown in four years to supply 600 retailers nationally. The products include pickles and pickled green beans. Yee-Haw's products are unique for their unusual ingredients, such as wildflower honey used in some of their products. The owners of Yee-Haw are considering how to make the company grow. A large discount store chain with 500 stores wants to add the Yee-Haw product.

Required
1.   What type of strategy, cost leadership or differentiation, should Yee-Haw use?
2.   Should the owners accept the offer of the large discount chain?
3.   What are the key factors you considered in answering requirements 1 and 2?

[LO 1-3]   1-38   **Risk Management; Enterprise Sustainability; Lean Accounting** Jane Englehard is a feature writer for *National Business Weekly*. Her assignment is to develop a feature article on enterprise risk management. Her editor has asked her to research the available literature, including the Institute of Management Accountants Statements on Management Accounting (**www.imanet.org/insights-and-trends/statements-on-management-accounting**), and to write an informative article that would be useful to those who are not familiar with the topic.

Required
1.   What are some of the key points that Jane should integrate into her article on enterprise risk management? What are the main ideas she would want to communicate in her article?
2.   Assume that Jane's assignment is a feature article on sustainability. Answer as you did for requirement 1.
3.   Assume that Jane's assignment is a feature article on lean accounting. Answer as you did for requirement 1.

[LO 1-3]   1-39   **Contemporary Management Techniques** Tim Johnson is a news reporter and feature writer for *The Wall Street Review,* an important daily newspaper for financial managers. Tim's assignment is to develop a feature article on target costing, including interviews with chief financial officers and operating managers. Tim has a generous travel budget for research into company history, operations, and market analysis for the firms he selects for the article.

Required
1.   Tim has asked you to recommend industries and firms that would be good candidates for the article. What would you advise? Explain your recommendations.
2.   Assume that Tim's assignment is a feature article on life-cycle costing. Answer as you did for requirement 1.
3.   Assume that Tim's assignment is a feature article on the theory of constraints. Answer as you did for requirement 1.
4.   Assume that Tim's assignment is a feature article on business analytics. Answer as you did for requirement 1.

[LO 1-3]   1-40   **Balanced Scorecard** Johnson Industrial Controls Inc. (JIC) is a large manufacturer of specialized instruments used in automated manufacturing plants. JIC has grown steadily over the past several years on the strength of technological innovation in its key product lines. The firm now employs 3,500 production employees and 450 staff and management personnel in six large plants located across the United States. In the past few years, the growth of sales and profits has declined sharply because of the entrance into the market of new competitors. As part of a recent strategic planning effort, JIC identified its key competitive strengths and weaknesses. JIC's management believes that the critical strengths are in the quality of the product and that the weakness in recent years has been in customer service, particularly in meeting scheduled deliveries. The failure to meet promised delivery dates can be quite costly to JIC's customers because it is likely to delay the construction or upgrading of the customers' plants and therefore delay the customers' production and sales. JIC's management believes that the adoption of the balanced scorecard for internal reporting might help the firm become more competitive.

Required

1. Explain how the balanced scorecard might help a firm like JIC.

2. Develop a brief balanced scorecard for JIC. Give some examples of the items that might be included in each of these four parts of the scorecard: (a) customer satisfaction, (b) financial performance, (c) internal processes, and (d) learning and growth.

[LO 1-3, 1-5, 1-6]   1-41   **Banking; Strategy; Balanced Scorecard** A large U.S.-based commercial bank with global operations recently initiated a new program for recruiting recent college graduates into the financial function of the bank. These new hires will initially be involved in a variety of financial functions, including transactions processing, control, risk management, business performance reporting, new business analysis, and financial analysis. Recognizing that they are competing with many other banks for the relatively small number of qualified graduates, the bank has assigned you to develop a skills statement to be used in college recruiting as well as an in-house training program for new hires. You have some old training manuals and recruiting guides to assist you, but your boss advises you not to use them and to instead start with a fresh page. The reason for developing new materials is that the bank recently reorganized based on new management methods.

Required

1. Briefly explain 8 to 10 critical success factors for this bank. Consider how a bank of this size remains competitive and successful.

2. Develop a one-page outline of the skills statement and training program that your boss requested. Be brief and specific about the proper job description of a new employee in the finance area of the bank. What is the role of professional ethics, if any, in the job description? *Hint:* Use a balanced scorecard approach.

[LO 1-3, 1-5]   1-42   **Consulting; Balanced Scorecard** A consulting firm offering a broad range of services will soon visit your college to recruit graduates. This firm has more than 20,000 professional staff in 275 offices of 11 different countries. Most of its clients are large corporations in a variety of different industries. Because of the opportunity for the experience and travel, you are very interested in getting a job with this firm. You have an interview in two weeks, and you're planning to do some research about the firm and the job to be as well prepared as you can be for the interview.

Required   Write a brief, one-half-page statement of what you think the job description for this employer is. What skills would you need to succeed as a consultant in this firm?

[LO 1-5]   1-43   **Professional Organizations and Certification** Ian Walsh has just been hired as a management accountant for a large manufacturing firm near his hometown of Canton, Ohio. The firm manufactures a wide variety of plastic products for the automobile industry, the packaging industry, and other customers. At least initially, Ian's principal assignments have been to develop product costs for new product lines. His cost accounting professor has suggested to Ian that he begin to consider professional organizations and professional certifications that will help him in his career.

Required   Which organizations and certifications would you suggest for Ian, and why?

[LO 1-6]   1-44   **Ethics; Product Quality** HighTech Inc. manufactures computer chips and components. HighTech has just introduced a new version of its memory chip, which is far faster than the previous version. Because of high product demand for the new chip, the testing process has been thorough but hurried. As the firm's chief of operations, you discover after the chip has been on the market for a few months and is selling very well that it has a minor fault that will cause hard-to-discover failures in certain, very unusual circumstances.

Required   Now that you know of the chip's faults, what should you disclose and to whom should you disclose it?

Problems

[LO 1-2, 1-4]   1-45   **Strategy; Downsizing Luxury** Companies such as BMW, Audi, Mercedes, and Tiffany are thriving these days because they are expanding their luxury brands into more affordable product lines, thus allowing them to offer their premium branded products to a wider audience. An example is Tiffany's Heart Tag Charm, the Mercedes CLA, and the Audi A3.

Required   What type of strategy (cost leadership or differentiation) is being followed by Tiffany, BMW, Audi, and Mercedes? Comment on how effective you think this new strategy will be for these firms.

[LO 1-2]   1-46   **Current Economic Information; Use of the Internet** There are a number of sources of economic and demographic information that can assist the management accountant. The information includes financial information such as interest rates, employment, income, international trade, output of goods and services, consumer price levels, and market values of stocks and bonds. Management accountants uses this information to better understand the environment in which their firm competes. For example, when interest rates are moving up (or down) rapidly, management accountants will want to consider the effect of the interest cost changes on their analysis and recommendations regarding managing cash flow, introducing new products, improving or expanding production facilities, and so on. There are many sources for this information; one useful source is provided by the Federal Reserve Board: at **www.federalreserve.gov/apps/fof/FOFTables.aspx**.

Required Review the Federal Reserve Board statistics for gross domestic product and home mortgages statistics for the most recent years available. Comment briefly on the current state of the economy that you see in these statistics.

[LO 1-2, 1-4] **1-47 Strategy; Innovation** One common measure of a firm's efforts in innovation is the amount the firm spends on research and development and capital spending (new plant and equipment) relative to other expenditures. Based on U.S. firms in the Standard & Poor's 500 stock index, innovation measured in this way differs significantly among industries. The highest rates of innovation are in software and services, semiconductors, drugs, biotech, and technology hardware. Somewhat lower levels of innovation are seen in the food and beverage, consumer goods, household products, and automobile industries.

Required Comment on the differences observed above from a strategic point of view.

[LO 1-3] **1-48 Enterprise Risk Management** Enterprise risk management (ERM) is a management technique that provides a systematic way for companies to identify and manage the wide variety of risks in their business environment. Any one of these risks, if not properly managed, could cause the company to fail to meet its strategic goals. As an example, UnitedHealth Group (UHG; **www.unitedhealthgroup.com**) has adopted ERM to manage the risks in its business environment, which includes a variety of health care businesses, from health insurance to health care claims processing services. UHG classifies its risks into six categories (external environment, business strategies and policies, business process execution, people, analysis and reporting, and technology and data). UHG has identified four to five key risks in each of these categories.

External Environment	Business Strategies and Policies	Business Process Execution	People	Analysis and Reporting	Technology and Data
Competitor	Strategy and innovation	Operations planning	Leadership	Performance management	Technology infrastructure
Legal and regulatory	Business/product portfolio	Customer satisfaction	Skills and competencies	Budgeting and financial planning	Reliability
Catastrophic loss	Organization structure	Regulatory compliance	Communications	External reporting	System security
Medical loss/utilization trend	Organization policies	Intellectual capital	Fraud and abuse	Market intelligence	

Required Review the risks identified above and consider a company in a different industry, a manufacturer of auto parts. Identify and explain three or four ways that ERM for an auto parts manufacturer would differ from that of UnitedHealth Group.

[LO 1-4] **1-49 Strategy; Service Company** Full Frame is a family-owned company that operates five custom framing stores. Each store offers a variety of services: matting prints and mounting prints; framing photos, paintings, posters, and prints; and sales of posters and prints. About 85% of the business is the service of matting, mounting, and framing photos, prints, and paintings. The main goals of Clyde Fuller, the founder, are growth and profitability: growth now and profitability later. He sees the business as a commodity-service business in which other frame shops provide essentially the same service, and the competition is on price and quality. From his seven years in the business, he knows that any frame store's work has to be high quality or it will quickly lose customers, so he maintains quality as a necessary component of his business and uses price and customer service to succeed in competing with other shops. The strategy has worked well for Clyde as he has been able to grow from a single store seven years ago to five stores at the present time. The additional stores are managed by members of Clyde's extended family.

To achieve a competitive price, Clyde watches his costs carefully and limits the amount of profit margin that he expects from each customer transaction. He looks for only an 8% markup over the total costs of the service. This policy has meant that initially his take-home profits were not great, but the low price has enabled him to attract customers and to grow the business. Total profits have increased as the business has grown. To enhance his low-price approach, he has devised efficient techniques to provide his service, and he instructs his employees to follow his techniques to be very efficient with their time and use of materials. He also has a profit-sharing plan that rewards each store employee when cost-per-service declines at that store.

Required

1. What strategy does Clyde use in the business? Briefly explain your choice.

2. Do you think Clyde's pricing and employee-incentive policies support this strategy? Why or why not?

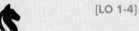

[LO 1-4]   1-50 **Strategy; Brand Value** Each year, Interbrand (a corporate strategy consultant) reports the 100 top brands in the world. The leading brands are determined from a calculation based on an analysis to determine what portion of the firm's sales and earnings can be credited to the firm's brand. For 2018, the top 10 brands were, in order:

1. Apple
2. Google
3. Amazon
4. Microsoft
5. Coca-Cola
6. Samsung
7. Toyota
8. Mercedes-Benz
9. Facebook
10. McDonald's

In addition to brand, a key measure for a company is its innovation. The Boston Consulting Group, a global consulting firm, prepares an annual survey of senior executives to rank the most innovative companies. The top 10 in 2019:

1. Google
2. Amazon
3. Apple
4. Microsoft
5. Samsung
6. Netflix
7. IBM
8. Facebook
9. Tesla
10. Adidas

Required

1. Which of the 20 firms listed would you classify as a cost leader, and which would you classify as a differentiator?

2. Explain briefly your choices in requirement 1 above.

[LO 1-4]   1-51 **Strategy; Customer Service** In its ranking of firms on the basis of customer service, global marketing information firms such as J.D. Power and media companies such as *Forbes* magazine and *USA Today* conduct independent surveys of customer satisfaction to develop a list of the top companies. The rankings below were based on ratings by *Forbes*. *Forbes* uses the American Customer Satisfaction Index (ACSI), which is a national cross-industry measure of customer satisfaction. The 2018 rankings are:

1. Chick-fil-A
2. Trader Joe's
3. Aldi
4. Amazon
5. Lexus
6. Costco
7. HEB Grocery

8. Toyota

9. Publix

10. Wegmans Food Markets

Required

1. Which of the listed firms would you classify as a cost leader and which as a differentiator?

2. Explain briefly your answer in requirement 1 above.

[LO 1-4]   1-52   **Strategy; Cost-Cutting in the Pharmaceutical Industry; Ethics** The pharmaceutical manufacturer Valeant had a business model of cost-cutting, minimizing expenditures on research, and delaying clinical trials. The model succeeded, as Valeant became one of the largest pharmaceutical companies in the world, with a market capitalization of $41 billion in 2014. In 2015 the company was investigated by the U.S. Securities and Exchange Commission (SEC) concerning drug price hikes and accounting fraud.

Required   What type of competitive strategy did Valeant employ? Is this strategy sustainable and ethical for a pharmaceutical company?

[LO 1-5]   1-53   **Different Professional Certification Programs** There are several professional certification programs that are of interest to management accountants. Each certificate is awarded based on the results of a comprehensive exam plus other education and experience requirements. Perhaps the best known is the CPA, which is administered by each of the 50 states and five other jurisdictions in the United States. The CPA certificate represents achievement of a broad knowledge of the accounting profession, including auditing, tax accounting, and governmental accounting, among others. A CPA exam revision was put in place in April 2017 to enhance the testing of higher-order skills of analysis and evaluation. Information about the CPA is available at the American Institute of Certified Public Accountants (AICPA) website (www.aicpa.org/index.htm).

In recent years, the AICPA and the CIMA have partnered to offer a certification, the Chartered Global Management Accountant (CGMA). Also, the Institute of Management Accountants (IMA; www.imanet.org/) has offered for more than 40 years a professional certification program leading to the Certificate in Management Accounting (CMA). The CMA exam has a framework similar to that of the CPA exam except that its focus is on broad business knowledge, strategy implementation, and competence in management accounting, rather than taxation and auditing.

Required   Review the AICPA and IMA websites and briefly explain how the two certification programs for the CPA and the CMA differ and which program (if any) might be most appropriate for you given your current career interests. Use specific examples that you notice in reviewing the websites.

[LO 1-5]   1-54   **Learning about Different Professional Organizations; Using the Internet** There are a number of professional organizations throughout the world that represent the interests of the management accountant professional, providing educational materials and other services to the management accountant. A partial list of some of these organizations is provided below.

Institute of Management Accounting: www.imanet.org/

Chartered Institute of Management Accountants (CIMA, UK): www.cimaglobal.com

American Institute of Certified Public Accountants: www.aicpa.org/index.htm

Financial Executives International: www.financialexecutives.org

Required   Briefly explain how the different organizations support the profession of management accounting, that is, the nature and extent of the publications they offer, educational programs, and other services. Use specific examples that you notice in reviewing the websites.

[LO 1-6]   1-55   **Ethics; Product Quality** Green Acres Inc. is a large U.S.-based multinational producer of canned fruits and vegetables. While Green Acres has a reputation of traditionally using only organic suppliers for its fruits and vegetables, it has recently experimented with produce from farmers known to have genetically modified crops. These genetically modified fruits and vegetables are often cheaper than their organic counterparts because farmers are able to achieve greater yields than with organic crops, and they have provided the firm with a way to cut its production costs. As Green Acres's chief of operations, the firm's marketing researchers have informed you that consumers continue to view Green Acres's products as organic despite the fact that Green Acres has never placed the word *organic* on its product labels. Moreover, the marketing researchers have discovered that Green Acres's sales and profits have dramatically increased in the wake of debates over the health and environmental consequences of genetically modified organisms.

Required   Now that you know of your consumers' misperception about your product, should you disclose your use of genetically modified crops to the public?

[LO 1-6]   1-56   **Ethics; Who, What, and How?; Use of Internet** Occupational fraud is defined by the Association of Certified Fraud Examiners (ACFE) as "the use of one's occupation for personal enrichment
through the deliberate misuse or misapplication of the employing organization's resources or assets."
This means that the perpetrator of the fraud steals assets from the employer, in contrast to financial
fraud in which the firm's financial statements are misrepresented. For example, the Enron fraud in
2001 is a case of financial fraud, while the theft of the company's inventory by an employee would be
occupational fraud. The ACFE's 2016 Report to the Nation on occupational fraud is shown at https://
s3-us-west-2.amazonaws.com/acfepublic/2016-report-to-the-nations.pdf. The study shows
some distinct patterns to these fraud cases.

Required   Go to the ACFE link shown above and review the study to determine the following:
1. What are the three most common behavioral indicators (red flags) of fraud?
2. Are small companies or larger companies more vulnerable to fraud, and why?
3. What was the dollar amount of the median annual loss to the companies in the ACFE's study of occupational fraud?
4. List the three top means by which occupational fraud is usually detected.
5. How important in detecting fraud is the use of "hotlines," which employees can use to report fraud?

[LO 1-6]   1-57   **Most Ethical Companies** The Ethisphere Institute (http://ethisphere.com), an organization
focused on defining and advancing corporate ethical standards and practices, prepares an annual
report that selects the most ethical global companies for that year. Ethisphere receives nominations
and selects the winners on the basis of the following criteria:

- **Ethics and Compliance Program (25%).** Program structure, oversight, and standards; training
and communication, detecting and monitoring, and enforcement.
- **Reputation, Leadership, and Innovation (20%).** A company's legal compliance, litigation, and
ethical track record.
- **Governance (10%).** The availability and quality of systems designed to ensure strong corporate
governance.
- **Corporate Citizenship and Responsibility (25%).** Performance indicators associated with sustainability, citizenship, and social responsibility.
- **Culture of Ethics (20%).** The extent to which an applicant promotes an organizational culture
that encourages ethical conduct and a commitment to compliance with the law.

There were 128 companies selected in 2019, including Hilton, IBM, Intel, Microsoft, Pepsico, Sony,
and Volvo (www.worldsmostethicalcompanies.com/honorees/).

Required   How would you use the Ethisphere report of most ethical companies, if (a) you are a business
manager, (b) you are a government regulator, or (c) you are an investor?

[LO 1-6]   1-58   **Changed Conditions and Ethical Behavior** A recent research study investigated whether the
ethical judgment of an accountant would be affected by the pattern of unethical behavior—
gradual or at a single point in time. Specifically, the following two versions of a case were presented
to accounting decision makers, both of which involved a potential misstatement of the company's financial statements: (a) a company has no unethical behavior for the first two of three years
(the financial statements are fairly presented), but in the third year the financial statements are mis-
stated, and (b) the company pushes the unethical envelope gradually over the three-year period, so
that the misstatement is there but is spread over three years.

Required   Accountants participating in the study were asked to choose in which case, (a) or (b), they
would approve the financial statements of the company. Which case do you think most participating
accountants chose, and why?

[LO 1-6]   1-59   **The Boeing 737 Max; Professional Ethics.** After two Boeing 737 MAX 8 aircraft crashed in
October 2018 and March 2019 causing 346 deaths, the plane was grounded worldwide in March
2019. The 737 Max was first entered into service in 2017, promising better performance and fuel
economy. The plane was significantly more fuel efficient than its predecessors due in part to the
use of an engine with a larger fan. However, the larger engine design also required the engines
to be located further forward and higher than previous aircraft. The new placement of engines
caused changes in the flight handling of the aircraft, so that Boeing added a new Maneuvering
Characteristics Augmentation System (MCAS) to stabilize the handling of the aircraft. It is now
believed that problems with the MCAS led to the two crashes. Boeing expected the aircraft to
return to service by the end of 2019, but on December 16, 2019, the company announced a temporary halt to the production of the aircraft. As of July 2020 it is not clear when the plane will be
returned to service.

The ongoing controversy over the 737 Max has included concerns about the relationship between the Federal Aviation Administration (FAA) and Boeing, the relationship between Boeing and various employee unions, the competitive threat from Airbus A320neo, and Boeing's financial management that focused on shareholder value.

Required

1. What is the management accountant's responsibility under the IMA Statement of Ethical Professional Practice in situations like this?

2. Why do you suppose the problems with the MCAS system were not revealed and dealt with earlier?

[LO 1-2]

1-60 **The European Union; Globalization; Strategy** The European Union (EU) is made up of 27 European countries that are bound together by trade and political agreements. The broad goal of the EU is to create an economic and political union that will foster common economic goals and political stability. The EU has achieved many of these goals over the last few decades, but concerns in recent years about immigration and economic inequality have caused problems. Starting with the July 2016 vote in the UK to leave the EU (this vote has been called Brexit), other countries (including the U.S.) have seen the growing prominence of anti-globalization efforts. Some have called this a time of "economic nationalism." These efforts have the effect of driving countries to reconsider or remove trade agreements, impose tariffs, and restrict immigration from other countries.

In recent developments: On January 15, 2020, the U.S. and China signed Phase One of a new trade deal. And the UK parliament voted on January 29, 2020, to leave the EU, reducing the number of EU countries from 28 to 27.

Required Explain briefly how you think the anti-globalization movements in the EU and the U.S. are likely to affect the work of the management accountant. What new challenges will the management accountant face? How will businesses and organizations have to change their strategies?

[LO 1-2]

1-61 **The North American Free Trade Agreement; (NAFTA, now USMCA) Globalization; Strategy** In 1992, the U.S., Mexico, and Canada agreed to enhance trade between the three countries in what is called the North American Free Trade Agreement (NAFTA). The agreement removed tariffs between the countries and had the goal of eliminating the obstacles to investments between the countries and to the movement of products and services between the countries. Opponents of NAFTA argue that it has cost many jobs in the U.S., jobs that were primarily moved to Mexico. Most economists argue that, while some jobs have been lost, the net effect of NAFTA on all three countries has been positive. Jobs have been lost in some industries and gained in others. Overall, manufacturers have used the flexibility afforded by NAFTA to strengthen the global competitiveness of their products. This is especially true for automakers, which use factories in the U.S., Canada, and Mexico to achieve the desired balance of high quality and low cost.

Some note that a problem with NAFTA is that it was written before the boom in e-commerce and as a result must be revamped to take internet sales into account. Also, some note that it is weak on labor and environmental protections, which are important to the neighboring countries. To deal with these and other issues, the three countries have agreed to a revision of NAFTA to be called the U.S.-Mexico-Canada Agreement (USMCA). As of March 2020, all three countries had ratified the treaty, which went into effect July 1, 2020. The USMCA introduces new environmental and labor standards, among other changes to the trade of agricultural and automobile products.

Required As a policy adviser to industry and professional groups of management accountants, write a brief statement that offers your thoughts on how NAFTA (now USMCA) affects trade in these three countries and how it might impact management accountants.

[LO 1-4]

1-62 **Using a Smartphone App; Strategy** Founded in the UK in 2007, Brew Dog produces a variety of craft beers and has a reputation for provocative marketing. Brew Dog has grown rapidly and in 2017 had 1,500 workers worldwide and a $12 million profit. Brew Dog promotes itself by opening Brew Dog bars located throughout the UK and also now in the U.S. Also, it has an "Equity for Punks" program, a crowdfunding effort that allows Brew Dog fans to become investors in the company; 85,000 new investors have joined the company through this program. Realizing that the craft beer business is getting more and more crowded, Brew Dog tries to distinguish itself with edgy advertising.

The craft beer industry has grown rapidly in recent decades. There are a number of small breweries, and many have successfully established themselves with a unique brand that has earned a devoted following for that brewery. However, the growth in industry sales has begun to slow in the recent few years, with a very modest increase in industry sales of only 1.5% in 2017. Thinking ahead, Brew Dog has decided to further distinguish itself by starting the "Brew Dog Network," a streaming service for smartphones priced at $4.99 per month. The Network provides hundreds of hours of videos designed to appeal to Brew Dog's customers.

Required

1. What type of strategy does Brew Dog appear to be using?

   a. Cost leadership based on rapid expansion

   b. Differentiation based on superior product

   c. Diversification based on rapid growth

   d. Differentiation based on customer satisfaction

   e. Product leadership based on innovation

2. Explain briefly your choice for strategy in part 1.

3. Do you think your answer in part 1 is the best strategy for Brew Dog? What would be a better strategy, if any? Explain briefly.

[LO 1-2]   1-63   **Comparative Advantage; Free Trade; Economic and Noneconomic Incentives** Comparative advantage is the concept in economics that states that two countries will benefit economically if the relative costs of producing two or more goods differs. The concept of comparative advantage was developed by the 19th century British economist David Ricardo, and it is used in support of free trade. A two-country, two-good example is used by Ricardo, as follows:

Hours of Work Necessary to Produce One Unit of Product		
Producing Country	**Cloth**	**Wine**
England	100	120
Portugal	90	80

Here is how it works. If England in the example has 200 hours of work available, then it can produce one unit of cloth and 5/6 unit of wine ($100 + 100 = 200$; 100 hours of wine production means $100/120 = 5/6$ of a unit of wine produced). At the same time, with 200 hours, Portugal can produce one unit of cloth and one unit of wine and have 30 hours to spare ($90 + 80 = 170 - 200 = 30$). England and Portugal will want to trade because England can make two units of cloth (with its 200 work units), and Portugal can make two units of wine ($80 \times 2 = 160$) and have 40 partial units of work to spare. The two countries can then trade to share the 40 partial units of work saved in Portugal, perhaps by allowing England some more wine and Portugal some more cloth, over time (the trade is likely to favor Portugal because of the facts of the case). The economic incentives to do this are very strong, as it is a win-win for both countries. There's more to it than that, but you get the idea.

On the other hand, we observe in practice that countries develop policies to reduce the opportunities for trade. For example, it is reported that, while membership in the European Union (EU) provides important trade advantages within the EU, English voters overwhelming supported in December 16, 2019, the Tory party, which was keen on Brexit, that is, separating from the trade agreements the country had enjoyed with the EU.

Required How do you explain the apparent inconsistency between the demonstrated economic advantages of trade and the English voters' choice to deny these benefits by supporting Brexit?

Solution to Self-Study Problem

An Ethical Problem

1. ENVIRO-WEAR's strategy to this point is best described as the differentiation strategy, wherein Frank has been able to succeed by differentiating his product as environmentally sound. This has appealed to a sufficient number of customers of sportswear, and ENVIRO-WEAR has grown accordingly. However, given the unfortunate jokes made by the sales manager and the rumors, the differentiation strategy is unlikely to continue to work because the offense of the jokes and the disclosure of some discrepancies in the manufacturing methods will undermine the appeal of environmentally sound manufacturing. Frank will have to work quickly to maintain differentiation, perhaps through a quick response that effectively shows the firm's commitment to quality and environmental issues. Failing that, Frank should quickly decide what change in strategy will be necessary for his firm to survive and continue to succeed. Frank should consider a new strategy, perhaps based on cost leadership. The cost-leadership strategy would bring Frank into competition with different types of firms, and the question for Frank would be whether his firm could successfully compete in that type of market.

2. There are a number of ethical issues in the case, which are especially important to Frank as a CMA and a CPA with previous experience in public accounting practice. Frank should try to identify and understand the different options and the ethical aspects of the consequences of those options. For example, should Frank deny all charges against the company? Should he undertake an investigation to determine what his other sales managers think (do they have the same view as the offensive sales manager)? Do the manufacturing processes of the firm really live up to the claimed quality and environmental standards? It seems the relevant ethical issue requires communicating unfavorable as well as favorable information and disclosing fully all relevant information that could reasonably be expected to influence a consumer's understanding of the situation. To mislead consumers and others would be in conflict with the professional standards Frank is very familiar with.

    Also at issue is whether it is appropriate to fire the offensive sales manager. Most would probably agree that the firing is appropriate because the sales manager has publicly put himself at odds with the strategic goals of the firm. However, others might want to consider the consequences of the firing and its fairness to the employee.

Please visit Connect to access a narrated, animated tutorial for solving this problem.

Implementing Strategy: The Value Chain, the Balanced Scorecard, and the Strategy Map

After studying this chapter, you should be able to . . .

LO 2-1 Explain how to implement a competitive strategy by using strengths-weaknesses-opportunities-threats (SWOT) analysis.

LO 2-2 Explain how to implement a competitive strategy by focusing on the execution of goals.

LO 2-3 Explain how to implement a competitive strategy using value-chain analysis.

LO 2-4 Explain how to implement a competitive strategy using the balanced scorecard and strategy map.

LO 2-5 Explain how to expand the balanced scorecard by integrating sustainability.

Jonathan Weiss/Shutterstock

Amazon typifies successful competition in the new economy far more than many firms. Some would say that Amazon invented the internet retailing business model that all other retailers are struggling to copy. Amazon understands well the strategy of developing and maintaining customer loyalty, which is the key to success in retail e-business, and implements it effectively. Amazon's stock price has more than doubled since we wrote about it in the last edition of the text!

The reason for the success: Amazon has a loyal and growing customer base because of its reliable service and low cost. Recently, it has been cited as a major factor in the bankruptcies of Borders and Circuit City. Amazon also presents a competitive threat to Walmart, OfficeMax, and other retailers. The reason: Shoppers find the same product at lower prices and enjoy the convenience of online shopping. Amazon avoids the costs to maintain retail facilities such as the Walmart stores. On the other hand, Amazon does require shipping costs on some orders. To be competitive, Walmart has been aggressively pushing online sales with very positive results and moving aggressively into grocery items. In response, Amazon is targeting the Walmart customer base, for example, by offering online grocery sales (including delivery) to food stamp recipients. This is the first time that the U.S. Department of Agriculture's Supplemental Nutrition Assistance Program (SNAP) has accepted online payment for groceries. Also, Amazon is buying other grocery chains (Whole Foods Market was purchased in June 2017) to improve its competitive position relative to Walmart. Walmart is also building its online brand; in June 2017 Walmart purchased Jet.com, an important e-commerce company. Whatever the future holds, Amazon succeeds by adapting its strategy to the competitive environment. The implementation of this strategy is critical. Success follows not just the development of a strategy, but the implementation of an effective strategy. The management accountant's role is to assist management in the development and implementation of strategy, as set forth in the IMA definition of management accounting. Robert S. Kaplan and David Norton explain this role of the management accountant in their book *The Execution Premium: Linking Strategy to Operations for Competitive Advantage* (Harvard Business School Publishing Company, 2008). This chapter covers the key tools in strategy implementation: (1) SWOT analysis, (2) a focus on execution, (3) value-chain analysis, and (4) the balanced scorecard and the strategy map.

The chapter concludes with an introduction to sustainability, which we present as an extension of the balanced scorecard. Amazon is one of the many companies with a growing and important emphasis on sustainability; currently, their sustainability performance is about on par with their peer companies. The value chain, balanced scorecard, and strategy map are foundational concepts that will appear again throughout the remaining chapters.

"Someone's sitting in the shade today because someone planted a tree a long time ago."

Warren Buffett

LO 2-1

Explain how to implement a competitive strategy by using strengths-weaknesses-opportunities-threats (SWOT) analysis.

Strengths-Weaknesses-Opportunities-Threats (SWOT) Analysis

One of the first steps in implementing strategy is to identify the critical success factors that the firm must focus on to be successful. **SWOT analysis** is a systematic procedure for identifying a firm's critical success factors: its *internal* strengths and weaknesses and its *external* opportunities and threats. Strengths are skills and resources that the firm has more abundantly than other firms. Skills or competencies that the firm employs especially well are called **core competencies.** The concept of core competencies is important because it points to areas of significant competitive advantage for the firm; core competencies can be used as the building blocks of the firm's overall strategy. In contrast, weaknesses represent a lack of important skills or competencies relative to the presence of those resources in competing firms.

Strengths and weaknesses are most easily identified by looking inside the firm at its specific resources:

SWOT analysis

A systematic procedure for identifying a firm's critical success factors: its internal strengths and weaknesses and its external opportunities and threats.

core competencies

Skills or competencies that the firm employs especially well.

- **Product lines.** Are the firm's products and services innovative? Are the product and service offerings too wide or too narrow? Are there important and distinctive technological advances?
- **Management.** What is the level of experience and competence?

- **Research and development.** Is the firm ahead of or behind competitors? What is the outlook for important new products and services?
- **Operations.** How competitive, flexible, productive, and technologically advanced are the current operations? What plans are there for improvements in facilities and processes?
- **Marketing.** How effective is the overall marketing approach, including promotion, selling, and advertising?
- **Strategy.** How clearly defined, communicated, and effectively implemented is the strategy?

Opportunities and threats are identified by looking outside the firm. Opportunities are important favorable situations in the firm's environment. Demographic trends, changes in regulatory matters, and technological changes in the industry might provide significant advantages or disadvantages for the firm. For example, the gradual aging of the U.S. population represents an advantage for firms that specialize in products and services for older people. In contrast, threats are major unfavorable situations in the firm's environment. These might include the entrance of new competitors or competing products, unfavorable changes in government regulations, and technological change that is unfavorable to the firm.

Opportunities and threats can be identified most easily by analyzing the industry and the firm's competitors:[1]

- **Barriers to entry.** Do certain factors, such as capital requirements, economies of scale, product differentiation, and access to selected distribution channels, protect the firm from newcomers? Do other factors, including the cost of buyer switching or government regulations and licensing restrictions, restrict competition?
- **Intensity of rivalry among competitors.** Intense rivalry can be the result of high entry barriers, specialized assets (and therefore limited flexibility for a firm in the industry), rapid product innovation, slow growth in total market demand, or significant overcapacity in the industry. The imposition of a tariff by another country in the pursuit of economic nationalism could be another example of a rivalry of this type; for example, the recent tariff placed by China on U.S. agricultural products is a clear threat to U.S. agriculture. We should consider how intense the overall industry rivalry facing the firm is and what the sources of this rivalry are.
- **Pressure from substitute products.** Will the presence of readily substitutable products increase the intensity level of the firm's competition?
- **Bargaining power of customers.** The greater the bargaining power of the firm's customers, the greater the level of competition facing the firm. The bargaining power of customers is likely higher if switching costs are relatively low and if the products are not differentiated.
- **Bargaining power of suppliers.** The greater the bargaining power of a firm's suppliers, the greater the overall level of competition facing the firm. The bargaining power of suppliers is higher when a few large firms dominate the group of suppliers and when these suppliers have other good outlets for their products. An important footnote to this particular threat/opportunity is that the process of globalization and automation over recent decades has dramatically reduced the bargaining power of workers, those who supply labor for the organization.

SWOT analysis guides the strategic analysis by focusing attention on the strengths, weaknesses, opportunities, and threats critical to the company's success. By carefully identifying the critical success factors in this way, executives and managers can discover differences in viewpoints. For example, what some managers might view as a strength, others might view as a weakness. SWOT analysis therefore also serves as a means for obtaining greater understanding and perhaps consensus among managers regarding the factors that are crucial to the firm's success.

A final step in the SWOT analysis is to identify quantitative measures for the critical success factors (CSFs). Critical success factors are sometimes called *value propositions,* that is, the CSF represents the critical process in the firm that delivers value to the customer. At this final step, the firm converts, for example, the CSF of customer service to a quantitative measure, such as the number of customer complaints or a customer satisfaction score.

[1] The five forces of industry competition are adapted from Michael E. Porter, "The Five Competitive Forces That Shape Strategy," *Harvard Business Review,* January 2008, pp. 79–93.

REAL-WORLD FOCUS   Globalization, Strategy, and Exchange Rates: The Euro

Since January 1999, the euro has been used as the common currency of most European Union (EU) countries. For the first 20 months following its introduction, the euro steadily lost about 25% of its value relative to the U.S. dollar. Due to changing economic circumstances, the euro began to rise in early 2002, and in August 2008 it had risen to $1.59. It then fell to a value of $1.26 in March 2009 due, in part, to falling oil prices and recession pressures in the EU during the fall of 2008. The euro remained fairly steady at that level from 2008 through July 2014. Since then, the euro has fallen dramatically against the dollar ($1.11 in May 2017 and $1.10 in November 2019); it is suggested that the reason could be that the eurozone economy remains under pressure and because of low interest rates at the European Central Bank.

The constant change of the value of the euro relative to the dollar creates three types of strategic issues for U.S. and European firms.* One is the effect on import and export opportunities. In the past few years, the rising dollar has helped EU exporters increase sales to the U.S.; products made in the EU are relatively cheaper for buyers in the U.S. For the same reasons, U.S. exports suffer with a strong dollar. In contrast to the relationship of the dollar and the euro, the dollar has fallen by more than 10% versus the Chinese currency in recent years.

The second strategic issue is that the changing euro causes fluctuations in investment opportunities, so U.S. firms have an opportunity to make strategically beneficial investments in euro countries when the euro falls against the dollar, and vice versa when the dollar falls. A third issue is that fluctuations in foreign exchange rates can significantly affect income on the financial statements of global companies; for example, the 2016 annual report for McDonald's shows the company lost more than $690 million, or approximately 3% of total sales (15% of net income), due to a decline in the currencies of the foreign countries where the company operates. In sum, companies with a significant global component to their business must plan strategically for dealing with the effects on their business of changing exchange rates.

* The Economic and Monetary Union (EMU) of Europe has 27 member countries, 19 of which have adopted the European currency, the euro. When the UK vote favoring Brexit (UK departure from the EU) took place in the summer of 2016, the value of the pound relative to the U.S. dollar fell by 10%, and in May 2020 it was 19% lower than the pre-Brexit level. The pound fell due to the uncertainly about the UK economy following the Brexit vote. Current and historical values for the exchange rate for the euro or the pound versus the U.S. dollar and for exchange rates of other currencies are available on the Federal Reserve website: **www.federalreserve.gov/releases/H10/hist/**.

Sources: Daniel Kruger, "Euro Falls Amid Talk of New ECB Bank Loans," *The Wall Street Journal,* February 15, 2019; Neil Irwin, "Waging a Currency War Holds Big Risks for the U.S.," *The New York Times,* August 8, 2019, p B3; Mark Mishler, "Currency Turmoil, Price, and Profit in Global Markets," *Journal of Accountancy,* March 2017, pp. 50–55; see also Neil Irwin, "How a Strong Dollar Creates Trouble Elsewhere," *The New York Times,* March 17, 2015, p. B1; Chesley Dulaney, "Fewer Forecasters Predict Rising Dollar," *The Wall Street Journal,* April 19, 2017, p. B18.

Identifying critical processes and developing measures for the CSFs involves a careful study of the firm's processes. Product development, manufacturing, marketing, management, and financial functions are investigated to determine in which specific ways these functions contribute to the firm's success. The objective at this step is to determine the quantitative measures that will allow the firm to monitor its progress toward achieving its strategic goals. Exhibit 2.1 lists sample CSFs and ways in which they might be measured.

Execution

"I'm convinced that about half of what separates the successful entrepreneurs from the nonsuccessful ones is pure perseverance. It is so hard."

Steve Jobs

"Coming up with an idea is the least important part of creating something great. The execution and delivery are what's key."

Sergey Brin, co-founder of Google

LO 2-2

Explain how to implement a competitive strategy by focusing on the execution of goals.

Steve Jobs, entrepreneur and leader of Apple, was known to emphasize the important role of managers in executing the organization's strategy. That is, a focus on the process of execution is critical to developing and implementing a successful strategy. Sergey Brin has similar advice derived from his firm's success—focus on execution.

Robert Kaplan and David Norton point out in their important book *The Execution Premium: Linking Strategy to Operations for Competitive Advantage* (Harvard Business School Publishing, 2008) that the successful organization must have a deliberate system to implement

EXHIBIT 2.1 **Measuring Critical Success Factors**

Critical Success Factor	How to Measure the CSF
Financial Factors	
• Profitability	Earnings from operations, earnings trend
• Liquidity	Cash flow, trend in cash flow, interest coverage, asset turnover, inventory turnover, receivables turnover
• Sales	Level of sales in critical product groups, sales trend, percentage of sales from new products, sales forecast accuracy
• Market value	Share price
Customer Factors	
• Customer satisfaction	Customer returns and complaints, customer survey
• Dealer and distributor	Coverage and strength of dealer and distributor channel relationships—e.g., number of dealers per state or region
• Marketing and selling	Trends in sales performance, training, market research activities measured in hours or dollars
• Timeliness of delivery	On-time delivery performance, time from order to customer receipt
• Quality	Customer complaints, warranty expense
Internal Processes	
• Quality	Number of defects, number of returns, customer survey, amount of scrap, amount of rework, field service reports, warranty claims, vendor quality defects
• Productivity	Cycle time (from materials to finished product); labor efficiency; machine efficiency; amount of waste, rework, and scrap
• Flexibility	Setup time, cycle time
• Equipment readiness	Downtime, operator experience, machine capacity, maintenance activities
• Safety	Number of accidents, effects of accidents
Learning and Growth	
• Product innovation	Number of design changes, number of new patents or copyrights, skills of research and development staff
• Timeliness of new product	Number of days over or under the announced ship date
• Skill development	Number of training hours, amount of skill performance improvement
• Employee morale	Employee turnover, number of complaints, employee survey
• Competence	Rate of turnover, training, experience, adaptability, financial and operating performance measures
Other	
• Governmental and community relations	Number of violations, community service activities

strategy. Kaplan and Norton suggest a six-stage system for implementing strategy that involves developing a strategy, planning the strategy, aligning the firm with the strategy, planning operations, monitoring and learning from operations, and then testing and adapting the strategy. The main point is that success will not happen without special effort in implementation. A key resource in this process is the balanced scorecard, together with strategy maps, which are covered later in the chapter and throughout the book.

To begin, effective execution requires a concise statement of strategy that is clearly communicated within the organization. It requires a business process approach to management, in which the CSFs are clearly identified, communicated, and acted upon. It means aligning strategy with action, or as the saying goes, "plan your work and then work your plan."

The nature of the types of CSFs that the manager executes depends, of course, on the type of strategy. For cost leadership firms, the CSFs are likely to relate to operational performance and quality, while differentiated firms are more likely to focus on the customer or innovation. Exhibit 2.2 summarizes the differences between the two types of competition, the nature of the required skills and resources, and the focus of efforts in execution. Also, while most topics we cover in the text are applicable to executing strategy for both cost leadership and differentiated firms, the topics in Part Three (Operational-Level Control) are particularly relevant

EXHIBIT 2.2 **Effects of Competitive Strategy on Required Resources and Execution**

Strategy	Required Resources	Execution
Cost leadership	• Substantial capital investment and access to capital • Process engineering skills • Intense supervision of labor • Products designed for ease of manufacturing	• Tight cost control • Frequent, detailed control reports • Structured organization and policies • Incentives based on meeting strict quantitative targets
Differentiation	• Strong marketing capability • Product engineering • Corporate reputation for quality or technological leadership • Long tradition in the industry or unique skills drawn from other businesses	• Strong coordination among functions: research, product development, manufacturing, and marketing

for the cost leadership firm, while those in Part Two (Planning and Decision Making) and Part Four (Management-Level Control) are useful for both types of firms.

Looking more closely at differentiated firms, the key CSFs and execution issues are in marketing and product development—developing customer loyalty and brand recognition, emphasizing superior and unique products, and developing and using detailed and timely information about customer needs and behavior. This is where the marketing and product development functions within the firm provide leadership, and the management accountants support these efforts by gathering, analyzing, and reporting the relevant information. Firms that excel in the execution of these functions include Coca-Cola, Microsoft, and IBM, which have been among the top 10 global brands for the last 10 years.

Both cost leadership and differentiation firms also can improve on execution through benchmarking and total quality improvement. The Malcolm Baldrige National Quality Award program (U.S. Department of Commerce; **www.nist.gov/baldrige/**) sets forth improvement criteria and awards firms that excel on these criteria. The criteria include a wide variety of business functions, including leadership; strategy; customers; measurement, analysis, and knowledge management; workforce; operations; and results. Another resource for benchmarking is the International Organization for Standardization, a network of national standards institutes from 163 countries (**www.iso.org**).

Value-Chain Analysis

LO 2-3

Explain how to implement a competitive strategy using value-chain analysis.

Because execution is so important in implementing strategy, managers must know how the firm's strategy and its CSFs are implemented *in each and every phase of the firm's operations.* In other words, managers must implement their firm's strategy at the detail level of operations. This sequence of activities must include all the steps necessary to satisfy customers. Value-chain analysis is a means to reach this detail level of analysis.

value-chain analysis

A strategic analysis tool used to identify where value to customers can be increased or costs reduced, and to better understand the firm's linkages with suppliers, customers, and other firms in the industry.

Value-chain analysis is a strategic analysis tool used to better understand the firm's competitive advantage; to identify where value to customers can be increased or costs reduced; and to better understand the firm's linkages with suppliers, customers, and other firms in the industry. The activities include all steps necessary to provide a competitive product or service to the customer. For a manufacturer, this starts with product development and new product testing, then materials purchases and manufacturing, and finally sales and service. For a service firm, the activities begin with the concept of the service and its design, purpose, and demand and then move to the set of activities that provide the service to create a satisfied customer. Although the value chains are sometimes more difficult to describe for a service firm or a not-for-profit organization, the approach is applied in all types of organizations. An organization might break its operations into dozens or hundreds of activities; in this chapter, it is sufficient to limit the analysis to no more than six to eight activities.

The term *value chain* is used because each activity is intended to add value to the product or service for the customer. Management can better understand the firm's competitive advantage and strategy by separating its operations according to activity. If the firm succeeds by cost leadership, for example, management should determine whether each individual activity in the value chain is consistent with that overall strategy. A careful consideration of each activity should also identify those activities in which the firm is most and least competitive.

The value chain can be thought of as three main phases, in sequence: (1) upstream, (2) operations, and (3) downstream. The *upstream phase* includes product development and the firm's linkages with suppliers; *operations* refers to the manufacturing operations or, for a retailer or service firm, the operations involved in providing the product or service; the *downstream phase* refers to linkages with customers, including delivery, service, and other related activities. Some have referred to the analysis of the upstream phase as *supply chain management* and to the analysis of the downstream phase as *customer relationship management.* Still others see the terms *value chain* and *supply chain* as essentially equivalent.

The determination of which part or parts of the value chain an organization should occupy is a strategic analysis based on the consideration of comparative advantage for the individual firm, that is, where the firm can best provide value to the ultimate consumer at the lowest possible cost. For example, some firms in the computer manufacturing industry focus on the manufacture of chips (Texas Instruments), while others primarily manufacture processors (Intel), hard drives (Seagate), or monitors (Acer). Some manufacturers (Hewlett-Packard) combine purchased and manufactured components to manufacture the complete printer or computer; others (Dell) depend primarily on purchased components. Apple contracts out all manufacturing except for the Macintosh to other companies. Samsung does its own manufacturing. In the sport-shoe industry, Reebok manufactures its shoes (in China, India, and Israel) and sells them to large retailers; Nike concentrates on design, sales, and promotion, contracting out all manufacturing. In effect, each firm establishes itself in one or more parts of the value chain on the basis of a strategic analysis of its competitive advantage. Because of the disruptive effects of COVID-19, economic nationalism and Brexit in recent years, it is likely that multinational companies will need to focus even more closely and frequently on value chain analysis—to identify the ways that tariffs, economic nationalism, and COVID-19 might impact the company's value chain.

Another example in the computer industry is Microsoft, which has expanded its business to focus on downstream services, particularly cloud computing services. The downstream services, services for customers who may have already purchased Microsoft's products (software, laptop, or other product), can greatly expand the customer's use of those products. These downstream services are often more profitable than the company's product sales.

Value-chain analysis has two steps:

Step 1. *Identify the value-chain activities.* The organization identifies the specific **value activities** that firms in the industry must perform in the processes of designing, manufacturing, and providing customer service. For example, see the value chain for the computer manufacturing industry in Exhibit 2.3.

value activities
Firms in an industry perform activities to design, manufacture, and provide customer service.

EXHIBIT 2.3 **Value Chain for the Computer Manufacturing Industry**

Step in the Value Chain	Activities	Expected Output of Activities
Step 1: Design	Performing research and development	Completed product design
Step 2: Materials acquisition	Purchasing, receiving, and stocking	Various parts and materials
Step 3: Materials assembled into components	Converting materials into components and parts used to manufacture the computer	Desired components and parts
Step 4: Intermediate assembly	Converting, assembling, finishing, testing, and grading	Boards, higher-level components
Step 5: Computer manufacturing	Final assembling, packaging, and shipping the final product	Completed computers
Step 6: Wholesaling, warehousing, and distribution	Moving products to retail locations and warehouses, as needed	Rail, truck, and air shipments
Step 7: Retail sales	Making retail sales	Cash receipts
Step 8: Customer service	Processing returns, inquiries, and repairs	Serviced and restocked computers

Using Value-Chain Analysis: Going Downstream
Where the Profits Are

Many manufacturers of expensive equipment and autos also usually have a finance unit. The finance unit is a downstream activity that provides the customer access to the needed funds, once the purchasing decision has been made. In some firms, the finance unit is the most profitable part of the overall business.

Finance Unit Profit as a % of Total Profit						
	2004	2007	2010	2013	2016	2019
Ford Motor	103%*	*	42%	25%	37%	71%
Deere	22	19	20	15	27	17
Caterpillar	19	13	10	14	20	7

*In 2004, Ford's finance unit earnings exceeded total company earnings because of losses in the automotive segment. In 2007 the finance unit earned $1.2 billion, while the company lost $5 billion. All information is taken from company annual reports.

The development of a value chain depends on the type of industry. For example, the focus in a service industry is on operations and on advertising and promotion rather than on materials and manufacturing. An example of a service industry value chain is shown in Self-Study Problem 1 at the end of the chapter.

Step 2. *Develop a competitive advantage by reducing cost or adding value.* In this step, the firm determines the nature of its current and potential competitive advantage by studying the value activities and cost drivers identified earlier. In doing so, the firm must consider the following:

1. **Identify competitive advantage (cost leadership or differentiation).** The analysis of value activities can help management better understand the firm's strategic competitive advantage and its proper positioning in the overall industry value chain. For example, IBM, Boeing, General Electric, and other firms have increased emphasis on services for their customers, as many of these services are more profitable than the sale of their basic products.

2. **Identify opportunities for added value.** The analysis of value activities can help identify activities in which the firm can add significant value for the customer. For example, food-processing plants and packaging plants are now commonly located near their largest customers to provide faster and cheaper delivery. Similarly, large retailers such as Walmart use computer-based technology to coordinate with suppliers to efficiently and quickly restock each of their stores. In banking, ATMs (automated teller machines) provide improved customer service and reduce processing costs. Banks have developed online computer technologies to further enhance customer service and to provide an additional opportunity to reduce processing costs.

3. **Identify opportunities for reduced cost.** A study of its value activities can help a firm determine those parts of the value chain for which it is *not* competitive. For example, firms in the electronics business, such as Flextronics International and Sanmina-Sci, have become large suppliers of parts and subassemblies for computer manufacturers and other electronics manufacturers such as Hewlett-Packard, Sony, Apple, and Microsoft, among others. The brand-name manufacturers have found that outsourcing some of the manufacturing to firms such as Flextronics reduces total cost and can improve speed, quality, and competitiveness.

Value-Chain Analysis in Computer Manufacturing

The computer industry provides an opportunity to show value-chain analysis in action. To illustrate, we will refer to the Computer Intelligence Company (CIC), which manufactures high-quality, high-feature computers for small businesses. CIC has an excellent reputation for customer service, product innovation, and quality. CIC is able to compete with the larger manufacturers of computers because it designs the product specially for each customer and has superior service. CIC has a growing list of customers who are willing to pay a small premium for these advantages. The manufacturing process consists primarily of assembling

EXHIBIT 2.4 **Value-Chain Analysis for CIC, a Manufacturing Company**

Value Activity	Current Operations	Decisions: Manufacture Components and/or Contract Out Marketing, Distributing, and Servicing Functions
Acquiring materials	CIC is not involved at this step in the value chain.	CIC is not involved at this step in the value chain.
Manufacturing computer chips and other parts	CIC is not involved at this step in the value chain; the cost of these parts is $200 to CIC.	CIC is not involved at this step in the value chain; the cost of these parts is $200 to CIC.
Manufacturing components, some of which CIC can make	CIC purchases $300 of parts for each unit.	CIC manufactures these parts for $190 per unit plus monthly costs of $55,000.
Assembling	CIC's costs are $250.	CIC's costs are $250.
Marketing, distributing, and servicing	CIC's costs are $175,000 per month.	CIC contracts out servicing to JBM Enterprises for $130 per unit sold.

components purchased from various electronics firms plus a small amount of metalworking and finishing. The assembly operations cost $250 per unit. The purchased parts cost CIC $500, of which $300 is for parts that CIC could manufacture in its existing facility for $190 in materials for each unit plus an investment in labor and equipment that would cost $55,000 per month. CIC is considering whether to make or continue to buy these parts.

CIC can contract out the marketing, distributing, and servicing of its units to another firm, JBM Enterprises. This would save CIC $175,000 in monthly materials and labor costs. The cost of the contract would be $130 per machine sold for the average of 600 units sold per month. CIC uses value-chain analysis to study the effect of these decisions on its strategy and costs. The analysis for CIC is summarized in Exhibit 2.4.

The Five Steps of Strategic Decision Making for CIC Manufacturing

1. **Determine the strategic issues surrounding the problem.** CIC competes as a differentiator based on customer service, product innovation, features, and reliability; customers pay more for the product as a result.

2. **Identify the alternative actions.** CIC faces two decisions, the first of which is whether to make or buy certain parts, which CIC currently buys for $300 but could manufacture for $190 per unit plus an additional $55,000 monthly cost.

The second decision is whether to continue marketing, distributing, and servicing its products or to outsource that set of activities to JBM Enterprises for $130 per unit sold and save $175,000 per month in materials and labor costs.

3. **Obtain information and conduct analyses of the alternatives.** First decision: CIC calculates that the monthly cost to buy the part is $180,000 (= 600 × $300) while the monthly cost to manufacture the part is only $169,000 (= [600 × $190] + $55,000); thus, making the part saves $11,000 per month.

Second decision: CIC calculates that the monthly cost of the contract with JBM Enterprises would be $78,000 (= 600 × $130) per month. This is a $97,000 savings over the in-house cost of $175,000 per month.

4. **Based on strategy and analysis, choose and implement the desired alternative.** First decision: As a differentiator based on product quality and innovation, CIC considers the importance of the quality of the part in question and decides to manufacture the part. Note that while this would save CIC $11,000 per month, the key reason for the decision is to control the quality of the part and thereby improve overall quality and to support the firm's differentiation strategy. Note, however, that if CIC believes that the supplier can provide the part at a higher level of quality than can CIC, the decision is reversed; it is now better to continue to buy, even if the costs are higher, in order to support quality, a critical success factor.

Second decision: As a differentiator based on customer service, CIC considers the continued high level of service from in-house personnel as critical to the company's success and continues to maintain these personnel, even if it means the loss of monthly savings of $97,000.

5. **Provide an ongoing evaluation of the effectiveness of implementation in step 4.** CIC management realizes that the quality of the product and customer service is critical to the company's success. So, CIC will continue to review the quality of product and service provided internally. If the quality of the part purchased outside or the service provided internally is inferior, then a change would be desirable.

The Balanced Scorecard and Strategy Map

LO 2-4

Explain how to implement a competitive strategy using the balanced scorecard and strategy map.

The balanced scorecard (BSC) and strategy map, introduced in Chapter 1, are key tools for the implementation of strategy. The BSC implements strategy by providing a comprehensive performance measurement tool that reflects the measures critical for the success of the firm's strategy and thereby provides a means for aligning the performance measurement in the firm to the firm's strategy. Thus, managers and employees within the firm have the awareness of the firm's CSFs (through the balanced scorecard) and an incentive to achieve these CSFs in moving the firm forward to its strategic goals. The strategy map is also used to implement strategy, but in contrast to the focus on performance measurement in the BSC, the main role of the strategy map is to develop and communicate strategy throughout the organization. The strategy map links the perspectives of the BSC in a causal framework that shows systematically how the organization can succeed by achieving specific critical success factors in the learning and growth perspective, thereby leading to desired performance in internal processes, and then to desired performance in the customer perspective, and finally to the ultimate goal—financial performance and, for a public firm, shareholder value. In sum, the BSC provides the structure of performance measures and the strategy map provides the road map the firm can use to execute the strategy.

The Balanced Scorecard (BSC)

Prior to the wide use of the BSC in the late 1990s, firms tended to focus only on financial measures of performance, and as a result, some of their critical nonfinancial measures were not sufficiently monitored and achieved. In effect, the BSC enables the firm to employ a strategy-centered performance measurement system, one that focuses managers' attention on critical success factors and rewards them for achieving these critical factors.

Now a rapidly increasing number of firms, not-for-profit organizations, and governmental units use the BSC to assist them in implementing strategy. As noted in Chapter 1, the balanced scorecard consists of four perspectives, or groupings of critical success factors: (1) the *financial perspective* includes financial performance measures such as operating income and cash flow; (2) the *customer perspective* includes measures of customer satisfaction; (3) the *internal process perspective* includes measures of productivity and speed, among others; and (4) *learning and growth* includes such measures as employee training hours and the number of new patents or new products.

Benefits of the BSC

The BSC provides five key potential benefits:

- A means for tracking progress toward achievement of strategic goals.
- A means for implementing strategy by drawing managers' attention to strategically relevant critical success factors and rewarding them for achievement of these factors.
- A framework firms can use to achieve a desired organizational change in strategy, by drawing attention to and rewarding achievement on factors that are part of a new strategy. The BSC makes the nature and direction of the desired change clear to all.
- A fair and objective basis for firms to use in determining each manager's compensation and advancement.
- A framework that coordinates efforts within the firm to achieve critical success factors. The BSC enables managers to see how their activity contributes to the success of others and motivates teamwork.

Implementing the BSC

To be implemented effectively, the balanced scorecard should:

- Have the strong support of top management.
- Accurately reflect the organization's strategy.
- Communicate the organization's strategy clearly to all managers and employees, who understand and accept the scorecard.
- Have a process that reviews and modifies the scorecard as the organization's strategy and resources change. For example, many global firms are likely to see their global supply chains significantly affected by COVID-19 and by the recent trend to economic nationalism (tariffs, changes in or withdrawal from trade agreements, . . .). These effects will likely require modification of the BSC. For example, a company that moves to locate production of a component from one country to another will want to address the effect of that change on enterprise risk—the change in foreign currency risk, the change in financial and operational risks, and so on.
- Be linked to reward and compensation systems; managers and employees have clear incentives linked to the scorecard.
- Include processes for ensuring the accuracy and reliability of the information in the scorecard.
- Ensure that the relevant portions of the scorecard are readily accessible to those responsible for the measures and that the information is also secure, available only to those authorized to have the information.
- Require those managers involved in the implementation of the BSC to also be involved in the selection of the scorecard measures.
- Be framed as a strategy map with all of the linkages among perspectives. See the following section on the strategy map.

Because of its emphasis on performance measurement, we will again cover the BSC when we cover operational-level control (Part Three) and management-level control (Part Four) in later chapters.

The Balanced Scorecard Reflects Strategy

The BSC can be viewed as a two-way street. Because it is designed to help implement strategy, it also should reflect strategy. One should be able to infer a firm's strategy by a careful study of the firm's BSC. For example, consider the BSC of an electronics manufacturer shown in Exhibit 2.5. Does this firm follow a cost leadership strategy or a differentiation strategy?

Exhibit 2.5 shows that the electronics firm places the customer perspective at the top of the scorecard. Also, while price is mentioned, note that the emphasis is on customer satisfaction, through quality, innovation, and service. A strong theme through the entire scorecard is the importance of innovation and new products. This firm succeeds through differentiation based on quality and innovation, and the scorecard reflects that. Cost control is mentioned in the innovation perspective, but as supportive of the differentiation strategy, rather than in conflict with it. Note also the inclusion of an "employees and community" perspective that reflects this firm's strategic emphasis and desire to achieve in these areas.

Timing, Cause-and-Effect, and Leading Measures in the BSC

Another look at the BSC for the electronics company in Exhibit 2.5 will reveal that some of the measures are likely to be taken daily or weekly (sales or number of defects) and some monthly or less frequently (cash flow, operating profit). So, the BSC is not a single document that is presented on a given weekly or monthly cycle, but the measures will be updated on their appropriate time line. Also, some of these measures are known to have a cause-and-effect relationship with other measures. For example, improved quality should increase sales and customer satisfaction. So, some measures are in effect "leading indicators" of what will happen to other measures in later periods. The insights to be gained from understanding these cause-and-effect relationships are captured in the strategy map.

REAL-WORLD FOCUS | The Balanced Scorecard and Strategy Map in Strategy Execution

Robert S. Kaplan and David P. Norton, who introduced the balanced scorecard (BSC), have recently pointed out the key role of the BSC and the strategy map in strategy execution and change management. Kaplan and Norton identify six stages of a closed-loop system managers should use to develop and implement strategy:

Stage 1: Develop the strategy (mission, values, and vision).

Stage 2: Translate the strategy (using critical success factors and the strategy map).

Stage 3: Align the organization (board of directors, employees, etc.).

Stage 4: Plan operations (budgeting, process improvement, etc.).

Stage 5: Monitor and learn (strategy and operating reviews).

Stage 6: Test and adapt (profitability analysis, statistical analysis, etc.).

Key elements of the six-stage system are the strategic plan, the operating plans, and the focus on execution using the strategy map in stage 2 and the execution/validation of the strategy in stages 5 and 6. Kaplan and Norton urge that the links in the strategy map should be validated with statistical analysis to identify the CSFs that best predict process performance and customer value-added. Statistical analysis of this type is covered in Chapter 8.

Source: Robert S. Kaplan and David P. Norton, "The Future of the Balanced Scorecard," *CGMA Magazine,* January 31, 2012. See also Robert S. Kaplan and David P. Norton, *The Execution Premium: Linking Strategy to Operations for Competitive Advantage* (Harvard Business School Publishing Company, 2008).

EXHIBIT 2.5 The Balanced Scorecard for an Electronics Company

	Measures
Customer Perspective	
Quality	Number of defects, delivered product quality
Price	Low price relative to competitive market price, sales volume
Delivery	Number of on-time deliveries
Shipments	Sales growth, number of customers that make up 90% of shipments
New products	Number of new products, percentage of sales from new products
Support	Response time, customer satisfaction surveys
Internal Capabilities	
Efficiency of manufacturing	Manufacturing cost, output per hour, rate of increase in use of automation
New product introduction	Rate of new product introductions
New product success	New products' sales, number of orders
Innovation	
Technology leadership	Product performance compared to competition, number of new products with patented technology
Cost leadership	Manufacturing cost as a percentage of sales, rate of decrease in cost of quality
Market leadership	Market share in all major markets
Research and development	Number of new products, number of patents
Financial Perspective	
Sales	Annual growth in sales and profits
Cost of sales	Gross margin percentage
Profitability	Operating profit
Liquidity	Cash flows
Employees and Community Perspective	
Competitive benefits and salaries	Salaries compared to norm in local area
Opportunity	Individual contribution, personal satisfaction in job
Citizenship	Company contributions to community and the institutions that support the environment

Source: Chee W. How, Kamal M. Haddad, and James W. Williamson, "Applying the Balanced Scorecard to Small Companies," Management Accounting, August 1997, pp. 21–27.

The Strategy Map

While the electronics company in Exhibit 2.5 placed the customer perspective at the top of the BSC to show its priority, it is also possible to create a strategy map by linking the perspectives in the order they contribute to the overall success of the firm. A strategy map is a cause-and-effect diagram of the relationships among the BSC perspectives. Managers use it to show how the achievement of goals in each perspective affect the achievement of goals in other perspectives, and finally the overall success of the firm.

For most firms, the ultimate goal is stated in financial performance, and for public firms in particular, in shareholder value. So, the financial perspective of the BSC is the target in the strategy map. The other BSC perspectives contribute to financial performance in a predictable, cause-and-effect way. For many firms, the learning and growth perspective is the base upon which the firm's success is built. The reason is that learning and growth—resulting in great products and great employees—drive performance in the internal processes perspective and also the customer perspective. Similarly, great performance in the internal processes perspective drives performance in the customer perspective; better operations mean more satisfied customers. Finally, satisfied customers lead directly to improved financial performance.

An Illustration of the Strategy Map: The Martin & Carlson Co.

To illustrate how the strategy map and the balanced scorecard can be used to implement strategy, consider Martin & Carlson Co., a manufacturer of high-end furniture. Janet Martin and Jack Carlson, both highly skilled in woodworking, started a small business in Graham, North Carolina, in 1990 to produce handmade furniture. First customers were friends and acquaintances; because of the very high quality and distinctive style of their furniture, the list of customers grew quickly, and Jack and Janet moved into a larger space and hired and trained additional woodworking employees. At present, the company has grown to become a nationally recognized manufacturer with annual sales of $200 million. Because of their distinctive brand, Jack and Janet have never experienced price competition, but in recent years, the costs of the commodities they require have risen sharply, and it has become more difficult to maintain their profitable growth. A consultant has been called in to help them assess their strategy going forward.

The assessment began with the consideration of the firm's mission and strategy. Owning a privately held business, Janet and Jack felt that their strategy should reflect their personal values as well as the need to provide a successful business. The consultant took them through the sequence of steps. First, determine the mission of the company and its competitive strategy (see Chapter 1 for coverage of mission and strategy). Second, use SWOT analysis and value-chain analysis to further develop the strategy. Third, determine a balanced scorecard and strategy map for the company, which requires identifying and linking goals, management techniques, and critical success factors.

In the first step, Jack and Janet chose their firm's mission, which they based on personal values that they knew were shared by their employees: "To be the highest-rated brand in crafted furniture." The strategy then followed: "To differentiate the firm based on innovation, style, quality, and customer service (with an emphasis on short lead time, the time from receipt of an order to delivery of the customer's order)." They chose as the firm's tagline, "To delight with our product, and impress with our speed."

The second step (SWOT and value chain) provided further insights, which are reflected in the BSC and strategy map. The third step was to develop the strategy map, shown in Exhibit 2.6. The financial goals are revenue growth, cost reduction, and increased return on investment (which would be achieved by the revenue growth and cost reduction). Similarly, goals were set for the other three perspectives of the BSC, being careful to ensure that the goals were consistent with the firm's mission and strategy. Note how the goals are linked to show the causal relationships among the goals. For example, improved customer satisfaction (a customer goal) should positively affect revenue growth (a financial goal). The strategy map is a key tool for Janet and Jack to better understand their road to success and, importantly, a way to communicate to their employees where and how the firm needs to perform to achieve the firm's strategy and mission.

The next step was to determine how to achieve and measure these goals. The techniques, shown in the middle column of Exhibit 2.7, are the contemporary management techniques covered in Chapter 1. They are tried and true tools for achieving the goals. The final step was to determine the measures that, when achieved, would show progress toward reaching the desired goals. For brevity, we show a small number of measures here, though in practice there may be 100 or more measures. These measures are what constitute the BSC for

EXHIBIT 2.6   A Strategy Map for Martin & Carlson Co.

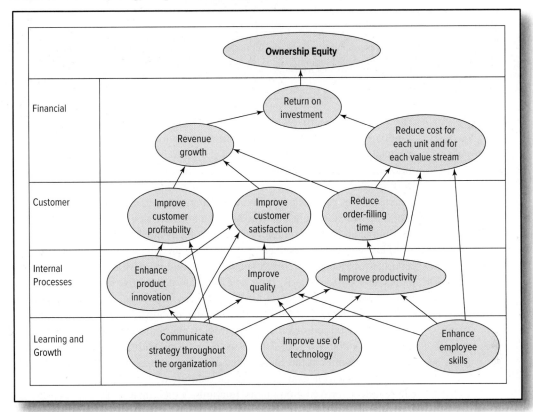

EXHIBIT 2.7 Goals, Techniques, and Measures for Martin & Carlson's Balanced Scorecard

	Goals	Techniques	Balanced Scorecard: Measures
Financial	• Increase profitability • Grow revenue • Reduce cost for each unit and each value stream		• Return on investment • Percentage increase in sales, by product line • Cost per unit, by product line
Customer satisfaction	• Improve customer profitability • Improve customer satisfaction • Reduce order-filling time	• Activity-based costing used to determine the profitability of customers and distribution channels (Ch. 5) • Theory of constraints and lean manufacturing (Ch. 13)	• Customer profitability by distribution channel and customer groups • Survey customer satisfaction • Lead time, the time between when the order is received and delivered
Internal processes	• Enhance product innovation • Improve quality • Improve productivity	• Target costing (Ch. 13) • Total quality management (Ch. 17) • Lean accounting, business process improvement (Ch. 17)	• Number of profitable new products or product features • Number of defects detected • Inventory level, process speed
Learning and growth	• Communicate strategy throughout the organization • Improve use of technology • Enhance employee skills	• Strategy map and balanced scorecard (Ch. 2) • Business analytics, enterprise risk management (Ch. 8)	• Percentage of employees trained on the firm's strategy map • Number of business risks discovered and analyzed • Training hours in skill development

Martin & Carlson Co. Janet and Jack now have the tools they need to understand their strategy, to communicate it to employees, and to measure performance and strategic success. What would happen if they had not developed these strategic tools? The answer is shown in Exhibit 1.8.

Sustainability: Expanding the Balanced Scorecard

> "Sustainability was really about taking out waste. It is often less expensive to make the product sustainable."
>
> *Lee Scott, former CEO of Walmart*

LO 2-5

Explain how to expand the balanced scorecard by integrating sustainability.

The growing concerns worldwide about climate change, volatile gasoline prices, high commodity prices, and corporate social and environmental responsibility have created new expectations that organizations adopt the triple bottom line—social, economic, and environmental performance (or "people, planet, and profits"). The triple bottom line has come to be known as *sustainability*—that is, the balancing of short- and long-term goals in all three dimensions of performance. Economic performance is measured in traditional ways, while social performance relates to the health and safety of employees and other stakeholders. The environmental dimension refers to the impact of the firm's operations on the environment.

Many companies manage sustainability in a strategic manner, through sustainability reports to shareholders. Some, such as Nike and Ford Motor Co., integrate sustainability into their balanced scorecards, both as a separate perspective and as additional measures in the internal process, customer, or learning and growth perspectives. Business analytics firms such as IBM, Oracle, and SAS Institute offer sustainability scorecard software.

The balanced scorecard and the strategy map introduced in the previous section and illustrated in Exhibit 2.6 can also be used in sustainability reporting and analysis. Exhibit 2.8 shows an example of the causal links of a strategy map for a BSC that includes sustainability measures. Note, for example, that the exhibit suggests that improved employee satisfaction can lead to improved community relations, which then leads to improved sustainability performance and sustainability ratings and thus to improved perceptions of the company by customers.

Indicators of the Concern about Sustainability

The concern for sustainability has many dimensions. One is climate change; this dimension views sustainability as a "green issue." Others concern labor, health, and safety issues in organizations around the world, and these issues would place sustainability as a part of enterprise risk management. Note the landmark Paris Climate Agreement, which was negotiated by 195 countries and adopted by consensus in December 2015. The goal of the agreement is to lower planet-warming emission enough to ensure that the atmospheric temperature would not rise by more than 3.6°F (2°C). As of December 2019, all negotiating countries have signed the accord and 147 of these have ratified it; the number of ratifying countries was sufficient that the agreement became effective on November 4, 2016. On June 1, 2017, President Trump chose to withdraw the U.S. from the Paris Agreement; the U.S. is the only country not in the climate agreement (**www.newsweek.com/ trump-paris-climate-agreement-syria-703765**).

Corporations are under pressure from regulators and shareholders to adopt sustainable practices. Being rated on sustainability—for example, by the Dow Jones Sustainability Index (**https://us.spindices.com/**)—places additional pressure on companies. Some companies, including Home Depot, Nike, Procter & Gamble, Starbucks, Nissan, Toyota, and Walmart, have adopted sustainability to improve profits. As a result of these developments, recent surveys show that the majority of chief executives see sustainability as playing a key role in their corporate strategy.[2]

---

[2] For example, Laura Palmerio and Delphine Gibassier, "Your Company's Next Leader on Climate is . . . The CFO," *Harvard Business Review,* January 28, 2020; Jill M. D'Aquila, "The Current State of Sustainability Reporting," *The CPA Journal,* July 2018 (**www.cpajournal.com/2018/07/30/the-current-state-of-sustainability-reporting/**); Jack Ewing, "Can a Company Be Virtuous and Profitable?," *The New York Times,* November 17, 2019; Curtis C. Vershoor, "Sustainability as a Strategy," *Strategic Finance,* November 2014, pp. 13–14; Marc J. Epstein and Adriana Rejc Buhovac, "A New Day for Sustainability," *Strategic Finance,* July 2014, pp. 25–33; Tamara Bekefi and Marc J. Epstein, "21st Century Sustainability,"*Strategic Finance,* November 2016, pp. 29–37; as well as information on the SASB by Jean Rogers, "The Next Frontier," *Strategic Finance,* June 2016, pp. 29–37.

EXHIBIT 2.8 A Strategy Map for Sustainability Reporting and Analysis

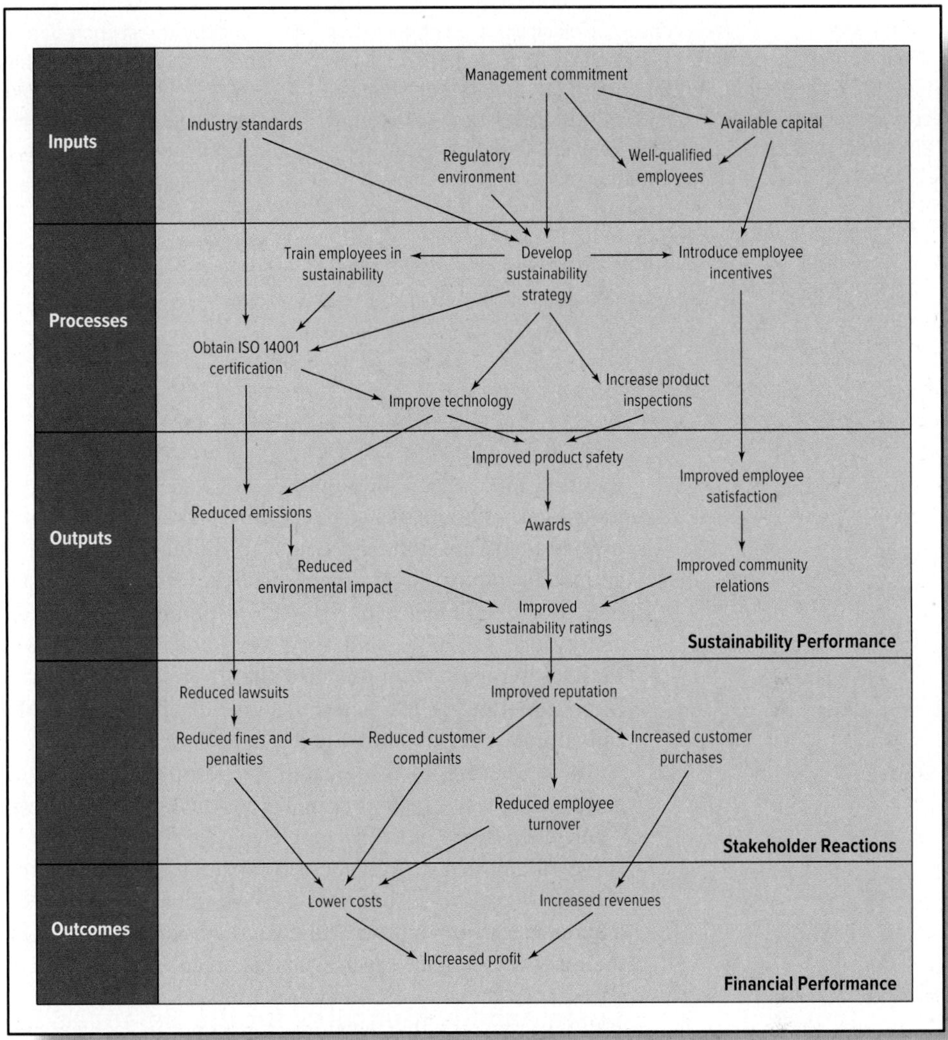

Companies are also self-reporting their progress on sustainability by using the framework of the Global Reporting Initiative (**www.globalreporting.org/Pages/default. aspx**), a pioneer in sustainability reporting since the late 1990s. Many firms, including, for example, 3M, Starbucks, Walmart, General Mills, and McDonald's, produce the Global Responsibility Report set out by the Global Reporting Initiative (GRI) framework. An alternative framework for reporting standards is provided by the Sustainability Accounting Standards Board (**www.sasb.org/**), which provides industry-specific guidance on preparing sustainability reports based on environmental, social, and governance (ESG) factors. The Sustainability Accounting Standards Board (SASB) standards and guidance are aimed at improving the quality of sustainability information that is available to investors.

How Companies Have Responded

A study of the Standard & Poor's 500 companies by the Governance and Accountability Institute (**www.ga-institute.com**) found that 92% of these companies in 2019 had produced reports on their sustainability efforts, in contrast to 82% in 2016, 72% in 2013, and 20% in 2011. So, reporting on sustainability is up; investment in sustainability is up as well.

Samsung, the South Korean consumer electronics giant, includes six main components in its smartphones: (1) display and touch-screen, (2) memory chip, (3) processor, (4) camera, (5) wireless electronics, and (6) battery. Samsung manufactures a wide range of electronic products in addition to the smartphone, including televisions, monitors, tablets, cameras, and a variety of chips.

Required

1. What strategy (cost leadership or differentiation) do you think Samsung uses and why?

2. Consider the six components of Samsung's smartphones listed above. Which do you think are manufactured by Samsung? Which components do you think are purchased from other manufacturers? That is, how much does Samsung rely on its own manufacturing in the value chain for its smartphones?

3. Apple has a very similar set of components for its smartphones. How similar do you think the two firms' value chains are likely to be?

A 2014 McKinsey & Company survey of more than 3,300 CEOs on sustainability reported that 38% of these CEOs felt that sustainability should be a "top 3" priority for their firm. The reasons sustainability was a high priority include (1) to align the company's strategy, mission, and goals; (2) to build, maintain, or improve corporate reputation; and (3) to improve operational efficiency and lower costs. In terms of the improvement in operational efficiency, 64% of the respondents said their companies were able to reduce energy use and 63% said they were able to reduce waste, thereby reducing cost. The McKinsey report recommended that in the years ahead, firms should extend the product life cycle—that is, use better design and optimization of manufacturing to facilitate multiple cycles of disassembly and reuse.

As the demand for sustainability reporting has grown, so also has the demand for sustainability assurance, the ability to add verification and credibility to the assurance reports. The Conference Board recently completed a survey of 57 large U.S. and European companies. The survey found that 65% of these companies are currently employing some type of assurance service to test the accuracy of their sustainability reports, and half of those were using the assurance services of one of the Big Four CPA firms. Most of those surveyed expected that their use of assurance services in this regard was likely to increase.[3]

Sustainability Measures for the Balanced Scorecard

Sustainability indicators (ESGs) are the measures in the sustainability perspective of the balanced scorecard. As noted above, ESGs have three components: environmental, social, and corporate governance. The World Resources Institute (WRI, www.wri.org) is a global research organization that works to sustain natural resources and to provide guidance for organizations that want to develop ESGs. The WRI provides useful categories for environmental and social ESGs that can help the management accountant develop the sustainability perspective of the BSC. The environmental component of ESGs is defined in three categories by the WRI:

1. Operational indicators measure potential stresses to the environment; for example, fossil fuel use, toxic and nontoxic waste, and pollutants.

2. Management indicators measure efforts to reduce environmental effects; for example, hours of environmental training.

3. Environmental condition indicators measure environmental quality; for example, ambient air pollution concentrations.

---

[3] McKinsey & Company, "Sustainability's Strategic Worth: McKinsey Global Survey Results," July 2014 (www.mckinsey.com/business-functions/sustainability-and-resource-productivity/our-insights/sustainabilitys-strategic-worth-mckinsey-global-survey-results). See also Thomas Singer, "Sustainability Matters: Sustainability Assurance Services," The Conference Board, November 2019. This Conference Board survey report is summarized in Ken Tysiac, "Demand for Sustainability Assurance Is Growing," *Journal of Accountancy,* November 12, 2019 (www.journalofaccountancy.com/news/2019/nov/demand-sustainability-assurance-growing-201922207.html).

REAL-WORLD FOCUS Sustainability and Decision Making at Patagonia

Patagonia, maker of clothing and gear for the outdoors enthusiast, is known for its focus on environmental issues in its manufacturing and company strategy. As an example of its commitment to the environment, the company studies the environmental impact of planned new products. One new product, a wool shirt, would be made from wool from New Zealand, processed in a factory in Japan, sewn in Los Angeles, and then packaged in Reno for distribution to retail locations worldwide. Patagonia figured the following would be the impact on the environment for a single shirt:

Miles traveled	16,280
Pounds of carbon emitted	47
Waste generated (oz)	9 (for a 7-oz shirt)
Energy consumption (megajoules)	89 (This is enough electric power for an average household for 20 hours)

Patagonia verdict: not sustainable. The product was not produced.

Sources: www.Patagonia.com; Brad Wieners, "Patagonia: For Climbing Everest, Diving the Great Barrier Reef and Saving the Planet on a Veer Run," *Bloomberg Businessweek,* October 7, 2016, pp. 54–59 (www.scribd.com/article/326753770/Patagonia-For-Climbing-Everest-Diving-The-Great-Barrier-Reef-And-Saving-The-Planet-On-A-Beer-Run); about Patagonia's activism, KIm Bhasin, "Rose Marcario: CEO of Patagonia, Inc.," *Bloomberg Businessweek,* December 18, 2018, p. 76; Patagonia's search for eco-friendly products is explained by Diane Cardwell, "Bottom Line: Earth," *The New York Times,* July 31, 2014, p. B1. Also, Patagonia's venture into the food business with Patagonia Provisions is described by Brad Wieners in "Haute Cuisine Patagonia Wants to Use Its Food Line to Teach the World to Feed Itself," *Bloomberg Businessweek,* October 10, 2016, pp. 54–59; in this article, Yvon Chouinard (Patagonia's founder) was critical of companies he said were "greenwashing," that is, they were satisfied with only making easy, low-cost efforts at sustainability, and not taking the harder, more costly sustainability projects. Note that other apparel and shoe manufacturers, including Puma, Nike, and Gap, and others are striving to reduce the environmental impact of their production.

The social component of ESGs includes the following three categories:

1. Working conditions indicators that measure worker safety and opportunity; for example, training hours and number of injuries.
2. Community involvement indicators that measure the firm's outreach to the local and broader community; for example, employee volunteering and participation in Habitat for Humanity.
3. Philanthropy indicators that measure the direct contribution by the firm and its employees to charitable organizations, for example, cash donations.

As a further indication of the increasing interest in sustainability measures, a nonprofit organization, B Lab, provides an independent certification of sustainability based on a company's performance in meeting measures of social and environmental performance, accountability, and transparency. While the B Lab certification has no legal standing, it provides a benchmark for assessing a company's sustainability performance. Over 2,000 companies worldwide currently have B Lab certification, and several thousand are pursuing the certification (**www.bcorporation.net/what-are-b-corps**).

The role of the management accountant, in developing the sustainability perspective of the BSC, is to make these ESGs an integral part of management decision making, not only for regulatory compliance but also for product design, purchasing, strategic planning, and other management functions.[4] As for the other perspectives of the BSC, there are a number of implementation issues with the sustainability perspective, including measurement problems and confidentiality issues.

---

[4] See, for example, Curtis C. Verschoor, "Should Sustainability Reporting Be Integrated?," *Strategic Finance,* December 2011, pp. 13–15; Janet Butler, Sandra Henderson, and Cecily Raiborn, "Sustainability and the Balanced Scorecard: Integrating Green Measures into Business Reporting," *Management Accounting Quarterly,* Winter 2011, pp. 1–10; "Apples, Oranges and Outliers," *The Wall Street Journal,* June 4, 2013. Also, with goals similar to that of the Global Reporting Initiative, the Sustainability Accounting Standards Board (www.SASB.org) was formed in 2011 to develop and disseminate standards for reporting on sustainability.

Summary

This chapter has discussed the four cost management resources for implementing strategy: SWOT analysis, a focus on execution, value-chain analysis, and the balanced scorecard and the strategy map. The first, SWOT analysis, helps management to implement strategy by providing a system and structure in which to identify the organization's critical success factors. The second, execution, is a management focus on making priorities and achieving these CSFs. The third, value-chain analysis, helps management to implement strategy by breaking the organization down into a sequence of value-providing activities; management can identify the CSFs at each step in the value chain and ask the question, How do we add value at this step in the value chain? The final step, the balanced scorecard and strategy map, provides a means to collect, report, and analyze the CSFs; the BSC helps management to measure progress toward strategic goals and to align employees' performance efforts, incentives, and rewards with these strategy goals.

An important supplement to the balanced scorecard and the strategy map is the organization's performance in the area of sustainability. Because of climate change, increases in commodity prices, and other factors, expectations for corporate social and environmental responsibility have increased significantly in recent years.

Key Terms

core competencies, *41*

SWOT analysis, *41*

value activities, *46*

value-chain analysis, *45*

Comments on Cost Management in Action

The two firms, Apple and Samsung, are keen competitors over patent rights, tablets, and phones. But perhaps the most visible competition is in the smartphone market. Each firm has a different approach to the competition.

1. Most would argue that Samsung is a differentiated firm, based on its product innovation. The fact that Apple and Samsung have been engaged in a lengthy patent war over smartphone technology suggests this is the case. (In 2011, Apple sued Samsung over patent infringement regarding its iPhone. Apple won that suit, and was awarded damages, but in December 2016 the U.S. Supreme Court reversed the decision of the earlier trial and sent the case back to the appeals court to reconsider the damage award. The two phone giants on June 27, 2018 agreed to drop and settle their remaining claims.)

2. As the article cited below ("Inside Samsung Phone: Samsung Parts") suggests, Samsung manufactures much of its own phones, so the value chain is internally integrated. Key parts purchased outside Samsung include the Gorilla Glass display made by Corning and some of the chips, which are made by Fujitsu Ltd., a Japanese company. Overall, Samsung has a high level of reliance on an integrated manufacturing process, involving most of the parts in the phone.

3. Unlike Samsung, Apple outsources all manufacturing to firms such as Flextronics and purchases all of the parts of its phones from other electronics manufacturers. Apple's approach to the value chain is to focus on the upstream phases of creative design and development and the downstream phases of marketing and customer service, with its Apple stores. In contrast, Samsung places a much greater emphasis on the manufacturing phase.

Note: Similar to Samsung, the Chinese company Lenovo, a manufacturer of computers, relies on in-house manufacturing. Lenovo's strategy is an integrated manufacturing process similar to that of Samsung. Most of the components of Lenovo computers and peripherals are manufactured by Lenovo.

Sources: Regarding the Apple vs. Samsung patent case, see: (https://www.theverge.com/2018/6/27/17510908/apple-samsung-settle-patent-battle-over-copying-iphone). See also Arik Hesseldahl, "Inside Samsung Phone: Samsung Parts," *The Wall Street Journal,* May 9, 2013, p. B6; Arik Hasseldahl, "What's Inside the iPad Mini," *The Wall Street Journal,* November 5, 2012, p. B5; Loretta Chao, "As Rivals Outsource, Lenovo Keeps Production In-House," *The Wall Street Journal,* July 9, 2013, p. A12.

Self-Study Problems

(For answers, please see Solutions.)

1. Value-Chain Analysis

The Waynesboro Bulls are a Class AA baseball team and farm club for the Atlanta Braves. The Bulls's league consists of eight teams that are all located within a 150-mile radius of Waynesboro. The Bulls ranked sixth of eight last year but have high hopes for the coming season in part because of the acquisition at the end of the last season of a great new pitcher, Wing Powers. Wing had the second-best ERA last season. Wing is also a popular player, seen frequently in the community, using his humor and occasionally outrageous behavior to develop a local fan club called the "Wingers." None of the other players comes close to Wing in popularity. Head Coach Bud Brown, a 15-year veteran of the Bulls, is optimistic for the coming season, noting the team's luck has "got to change." The Bulls have had only two winning seasons in the last 10 years. The Waynesboro baseball park is somewhat typical of AA parks, though somewhat older and a bit smaller. It serves a variety of soda, beer, and nachos to its fans on game days. Also in a 150-mile radius of Waynesboro are three NASCAR venues, two outdoor concert venues, 12 colleges with competitive sports teams, one major league football team, and one major league basketball team. There is no major league baseball team.

Jack Smith, a consultant for the Waynesboro Bulls, has been asked to complete a value-chain analysis of the franchise with a particular focus on a comparison with a nearby competing team, the Durham Buffaloes. Jack has been able to collect selected cost data as follows for each of the six steps in the value chain. Single-ticket prices range from $4.50 to $8.00, and average paying attendance is approximately 2,200 for Waynesboro and 3,400 for Durham.

Average Cost per Person at Scheduled Games

Waynesboro Bulls	Activities in the Value Chain	Durham Buffaloes
$0.45	Advertising and general promotion expenses	$0.50
0.28	Ticket sales: At local sporting goods stores and the ballpark	0.25
0.65	Ballpark operations	0.80
0.23	Management compensation	0.18
0.95	Players' salaries	1.05
0.20	Game-day operations: security, special entertainment, and game-day promotions	0.65
$2.76	Total cost	$3.43

Required   Analyze the value chain to help Jack better understand the nature of the competition between the Bulls and the Buffaloes and to identify opportunities for adding value and/or reducing cost at each activity.

2. SWOT Analysis

Required   Refer to the information in Self-Study Problem 1 regarding the Waynesboro Bulls. Prepare a SWOT analysis for the Bulls.

3. The Balanced Scorecard

Required   Refer to the information in Self-Study Problem 1 regarding the Waynesboro Bulls. Prepare a balanced scorecard for the Bulls.

The Student Resources section of Connect includes video tutorials for the Self-Study Problems.

Questions

2-1   Identify and explain the two types of competitive strategy.

2-2   Identify three or four well-known firms that succeed through cost leadership.

2-3   Identify three or four well-known firms that succeed through product differentiation.

2-4   How are the four strategic resources—SWOT analysis, execution, the value chain, and the balanced scorecard—linked in a comprehensive strategic analysis?

2-5   What is a strategy map and how is it used?

2-6   What is SWOT analysis? For what is it used?

2-7   What is the role of the management accountant regarding nonfinancial performance measures such as delivery speed and customer satisfaction?

2-8   What is a critical success factor? What is its role in strategic management and in cost management?

2-9   Identify four or five potential critical success factors for a manufacturer of industrial chemicals.

2-10 Identify four or five potential critical success factors for a large savings and loan institution.

2-11 Identify four or five potential critical success factors for a small chain of retail jewelry stores.

2-12 Identify four or five potential critical success factors for a large retail discount store that features a broad range of consumer merchandise.

2-13 Identify four or five potential critical success factors for an auto-repair shop.

2-14 What is a balanced scorecard? What is its primary objective?

2-15 Contrast using the balanced scorecard with using only financial measures of success.

2-16 What is sustainability, and what does it mean for a business?

2-17 Explain the uses of value-chain analysis.

2-18 Think of an example of a firm that succeeds on cost leadership and give some examples of its strengths and weaknesses that would be included in a SWOT analysis.

2-19 Think of an example of a firm that succeeds on differentiation and give some examples of its strengths and weaknesses that would be included in a SWOT analysis.

2-20 What industries do you think are most suited for value-chain analysis and why?

2-21 How would you explain the relationship between value-chain analysis and the use of the balanced scorecard for a firm that uses both? Use a hospital as an example.

2-22 Suppose you are the CEO of a large firm in a service business and you think that by acquiring a certain competing firm, you can generate growth and profits at a greater rate for the combined firm. You have asked some financial analysts to study the proposed acquisition/merger. Do you think value-chain analysis would be useful to them? Why or why not?

2-23 Consider Question 2-22 again. How would your answer differ if the firm were a manufacturer?

2-24 What are some of the key issues to consider in effectively implementing a balanced scorecard?

2-25 How many measures are usually on the balanced scorecard?

2-26 a. Consider a commodity business such as building materials, many types of food products, and many types of electronics products. A good example of a commodity is gasoline. Are these companies likely to compete on cost leadership or differentiation? Why?

   b. Consider professional service firms such as law firms, accounting firms, and medical practices. Are these firms likely to compete on cost leadership or differentiation? Why?

2-27 Many would argue that the TV manufacturing business has become largely a commodity business, and competition is based on price, with many good brands offered at low prices at retailers such as Walmart. The manufacturers of TVs are said to have a barrier to entry from other potential competitors because the existing manufacturers (LG, Sony, Samsung, etc.) have spent huge sums to develop their brands and manufacturing facilities. In recent years, there has been a large growth in the number of contract manufacturers (such as Flextronics) that manufacture TVs for the large firms. How does this affect the competition within the industry? Are there now new opportunities for smaller manufacturers of TVs?

Brief Exercises

For the following multiple choice questions, 2-28 through 2-39, select the best available answer.

[LO 2-1] 2-28 SWOT analysis is a useful tool for
   a. evaluating the performance of an organization.
   b. identifying the organization's critical success factors.
   c. developing the organization's strategy map.
   d. developing the organization's value chain.

[LO 2-2] 2-29 The following strategy implementation technique can be particularly enhanced by using benchmarking, as, for example, participating in the Malcolm Baldrige National Quality Award program:
   a. the value chain.
   b. the balanced scorecard (BSC).
   c. the strategy map.
   d. execution.

[LO 2-4] 2-30 The balanced scorecard is related to the strategy map in a way similar to how
   a. the value chain is related to product differentiation.
   b. SWOT analysis is related to execution.
   c. the organization's key activities are related to the value chain.
   d. sustainability can be related to financial reporting.

[LO 2-5]   2-31   A company taking a strategic and customer-centered point of view can best address sustainability, a concern for environmental and social as well as economic performance, through

    a. annual financial reporting to the Securities and Exchange Commission.

    b. the use of a sustainability perspective in the balanced scorecard.

    c. reporting violations of a company's human resources policy to the proper authorities.

    d. lobbying in Congress for stronger environmental regulations.

[LO 2-4]   2-32   The implementation of the balanced scorecard (BSC) can involve all of the following *except*

    a. the strong support of top management.

    b. a strategy of differentiation (as opposed to one of cost leadership).

    c. a link to reward and compensation systems.

    d. an accurate reflection of the organization's strategy.

[LO 2-4]   2-33   What does it mean for the balanced scorecard to "reflect strategy"?

    a. One should be able to infer an organization's strategy from the balanced scorecard.

    b. The management accountant develops the balanced scorecard prior to developing a strategy.

    c. The balanced scorecard is one of the key methods for implementing strategy.

    d. One cannot have an effective strategy without an effective balanced scorecard.

[LO 2-1]   2-34   Opportunities and threats in strengths-weaknesses-opportunities-threats (SWOT) analysis can be identified most readily by

    a. using value-chain analysis.

    b. analyzing the industry and the organization's competitors.

    c. analyzing the organization's critical success factors.

    d. using the strategy map.

[LO 2-3]   2-35   Which of the following statements about the value chain is correct?

    a. The two phases of the activities of the value chain are the upstream activities and the downstream activities.

    b. A company need not operate in all activities of the value chain.

    c. There are usually six to eight activities in the value chain.

    d. The value chain is intended for manufacturers.

[LO 2-1]   2-36   As opposed to identifying opportunities and threats, identifying a company's strengths and weaknesses in SWOT analysis can involve all but which of the following?

    a. Careful analysis of the company's sustainability statement

    b. Analysis of the company's code of ethics

    c. Evaluation of the company's operations, strategy, and management competence

    d. Review of the company's industry and competitive environment

[LO 2-1]   2-37   The required resources for implementing a cost leadership strategy include which of the following?

    a. Strong marketing capability

    b. Substantial capital investment and access to capital

    c. Effective product engineering and innovative design

    d. Reputation for high ethical standards

[LO 2-5]   2-38   The World Resources Institute (WRI) is an organization that

    a. provides guidance for developing and benchmarking an organization's value chain.

    b. provides resources for organizations that intend to expand globally

    c. provides guidance for organizations that want to develop indicators (ESGs) of the environmental component of sustainability.

    d. assists companies in understanding the changing environment of financial and material resources worldwide.

[LO 2-3]   2-39   Which of the following is an important method for implementing strategy?

    a. Sustainability

    b. Value-chain analysis

    c. Cost leadership

    d. Differentiation

Exercises

[LO 2-1, 2-2, 2-3, 2-4]   **2-40   Strategy; Execution**   Joel Deaine, CEO of Deaine Enterprises Inc. (DEI), is considering a special offer to manufacture a new line of women's clothing for a large department store chain. DEI has specialized in designer women's clothing sold in small, upscale retail clothing stores throughout the country. To protect the very elite brand image, DEI has not sold clothing to large department stores. The current offer, however, might be too good to turn down. The department store is willing to commit to a large order, which would be very profitable to DEI, and the order would be renewed automatically for two more years, presumably to continue after that point.

Required

1. Determine Joel's competitive strategy (cost leadership or differentiation) and use this strategy to analyze the choice Joel faces.

2. Explain two of the implementation tools covered in this chapter that Joel can use to implement his strategy.

[LO 2-3]   **2-41   Value Chain; Currency Fluctuations**   In 2011–2013, Brazil's economy was flourishing in many dimensions, except for a significant and worsening trade deficit with China in 2011–2012. The root of the problem was that the value of the Brazilian currency (the real) had increased by 10% relative to the Chinese currency (the yuan) over the prior year. The increased value of the real meant that Chinese imports were relatively cheap and Brazilian exports were relatively expensive in currency fluctuation terms.

In contrast to the above, the value of the real fell 120% relative to the yuan from January 2012 to January 2016. From January 2016 to June 2017, the real rose approximately 30% from its low in January 2016. The two currencies have been relatively stable since June 2017.

Required   Briefly explain how you would expect the currency fluctuation issues facing Brazil to affect the value chains of Brazilian companies.

[LO 2-3, 2-4]   **2-42   Value Chain; Strategy Map; Role in Corporate Alliances**   A recent report of the consulting firm McKinsey & Company indicates that about one-half of all corporate alliances fail. These alliances are partnerships in which two corporations jointly participate in one or more of the activities in the industry value chain. A good example, provided by Robert S. Kaplan and David P. Norton (creators of the balanced scorecard and strategy map), is the alliance between the European pharmaceutical compan, Solvay and U.S.-based Quintiles, a company that specializes in the conduct of clinical trials for testing potential new drugs. Solvay's strategy is to employ its research-driven organization to develop and market new drugs. One of the steps in Solvay's value chain is to complete the testing required by the U.S. Food and Drug Administration. Rather than divert its operations from research, Solvay has partnered with Quintiles. Realizing that they both benefit from the success and growth of Solvay's products, the two companies have developed a joint strategy map and identified the critical drivers for the joint success of the alliance.

Required   Considering the Solvay–Quintiles collaboration, we know that about 50% of such alliances fail. Explain briefly how you think the strategy map and value-chain analysis can help this alliance to succeed.

[LO 2-3, 2-4, 2-5]   **2-43   Value Chain; Sustainability**   One way the value chain can be helpful is to provide a basis for a company to determine the full cost of its product or service over the entire value chain. Often companies tend to focus only on manufacturing costs and ignore the upstream (design, testing, etc.) and downstream (marketing, distribution, etc.) costs of the product or service. Full value-chain analysis of this type is useful to the consumer as well as the manufacturer. For example, a product might be inexpensive to buy, but the operating costs may be higher than expected. Consider, for example, the case of the company CleanTech, which provides a cleaning service to owners of large storage tanks that often contain hazardous liquids such as fuel oil or toxic chemicals. CleanTech is considering the purchase of a new system for cleaning tanks that is somewhat more expensive than its current equipment, but one that could reduce both operating costs and the amount of environmentally harmful waste product that must be disposed of after the cleaning process is complete.

Required

1. What is the role of the value chain in CleanTech's purchase decision?

2. In its analysis, how should CleanTech include the disposal of the environmentally harmful waste product?

3. Consider how CleanTech might use a balanced scorecard with a sustainability perspective and what the measures in this sustainability scorecard might include. Give two or three examples of possible sustainability measures.

[LO 2-5]   2-44   **Strategy; Sustainability**   Seventh Generation Inc. (SGI) manufactures environmentally friendly cleaning products, including laundry detergent, soap, and all-purpose cleaners. Prior to 2008, SGI would not do business with Walmart because of the perception of a poor environmental record at the large retailer. In 2008, SGI realized that, despite the perception of Walmart's environmental record, it was important to partner with the big retailer in order to have the largest possible impact on consumers—to bring environmentally friendly products into the mainstream. In August 2010, the partnership was arranged and SGI's products started to appear in Walmart's stores. While most cleaning products sold at Walmart are offered at a lower price than SGI's products, the difference is not significant, and the Walmart prices compare well to SGI product prices at supermarkets where these products are also sold.

Required   Is this partnership a good strategy for (a) Walmart or (b) Seventh Generation Inc.? Explain why or why not.

[LO 2-5]   2-45   **Ethics; Sustainability**   Like me, perhaps you love a good cup of coffee. Suppose that you do, and you have the following information about the company that makes the coffee you are considering. You are selecting a one-pound bag of coffee, and you can choose to pay anywhere from $5 to $15 for the bag of coffee. In each of these cases, we mean ethical standards to refer to business practices and labor relations; an example of an unethical business practice would be price-fixing, and an example of unethical labor relations would be discrimination in hiring practices.

Required   Report the dollar figure asked for in each part of the four cases, and for each case, explain briefly your rationale for the price differences.

Case A: How much would you pay for the bag of coffee if (a) you know with certainty the company has high ethical standards, (b) you know with certainty the company has low ethical standards, and (c) you do not know anything about the company's ethical standards?

Case B: Similar to Case A, except that you only know what the company says about its ethical standards; however, you have for some time had high expectations that the company has high standards. How much would you pay for the bag of coffee if (a) you now find out with certainty the company has high ethical standards or (b) you now find out with certainty the company has low ethical standards?

Case C: Same as Case B, except that you have for some time had low expectations that the company has high ethical standards. How much would you pay for the bag of coffee if (a) you now find out with certainty the company has high ethical standards or (b) you now find out with certainty the company has low ethical standards?

Now suppose that with your cup of coffee you like to relax in a comfortable all-cotton shirt. You have the option to purchase a 100% organic cotton shirt, a 50% organic shirt, a 25% organic shirt, or a totally nonorganic shirt. Organic production is more environmentally safe, using no toxic dyes and no harmful cleaning or processing materials.

Case D: What price would you pay for the cotton shirt, from a low of $15 to a high of $30?

a. For the 100% organic shirt
b. For the 50% organic shirt
c. For the 25% organic shirt
d. For the nonorganic shirt
e. How much would you pay if you had no idea how much organic content was in the shirt?

Problems

[LO 2-2, 2-4]   2-46   **Strategy; Balanced Scorecard: Health Care**   Consumers, employers, and governments at all levels are very concerned about the rising costs of health care. As a result, health care systems nationwide are experiencing an ongoing demand to improve the efficiency of their operations. The health care industry faces significant challenges due to changing patient needs, reduced reimbursement, and the fierce competitive environment. The industry is experiencing consolidations through systemwide mergers and acquisitions as a way to reduce operating costs. Patients and payors are demanding a one-stop shopping approach. While improving operations is necessary, the quality of the health care delivered must not be jeopardized. The Medical University of Greenbelt is feeling the impact of the increasing penetration of its market by managed care companies. As a result, management has been asked to develop a strategic plan to ensure that its funding sources will continue to meet the demands of its patients.

Because it is an academic medical center, the Medical University of Greenbelt's mission encompasses three components: clinical care, education, and research. Management must consider these competing objectives in the proposed plan.

Required

1. What should the Medical University of Greenbelt's strategy emphasize?

2. Do you think a value-chain analysis or a balanced scorecard could help ensure the success of the Medical University of Greenbelt? How could these methods be used to help Greenbelt?

3. Determine three or four critical success factors for each of the four areas within the balanced scorecard.

[LO 2-2]   2-47   **Strategic Positioning**   Fowler's Farm is a 1,000-acre dairy and tobacco farm located in southern Virginia. Jack Fowler, the owner, has been farming since 1982. He initially purchased 235 acres and has made the following purchases since then: 300 acres in 1985, 150 acres in 1988, dairy equipment and buildings worth $350,000 in 1988, and 315 acres in 1998. The cost of farmland has inflated over the years so that, although Jack has a total investment of $1,850,000, the land's current market value is $2,650,000. The current net book value of his buildings and equipment is $300,000, with an estimated replacement cost of $1,250,000. Current price pressures on farm commodities have affected Fowler's Farm as well as others across the country. Jack has watched as many of his neighbors either have quit farming or have been consolidated into larger, more profitable farms.

Fowler's Farm consists of three different operating segments: dairy farming, tobacco, and corn and other crops intended for livestock feed. The dairy farm consists of 198 milk-producing cows that are grazed on 250 acres of farmland. The crop farm consists of the remaining acreage that covers several types of terrain and has several types of soil. Some of the land is high and hilly, some of it is low and claylike, and the rest is humus-rich soil. Jack determines the fertilizer mix for the type of soil and type of crop to be planted by rules of thumb based on his experience.

The farm equipment used consists of automated milking equipment, six tractors, two tandem-axle grain bed trucks, and numerous discs, plows, wagons, and assorted tractor and hand tools. The farm has three equipment storage barns, an equipment maintenance shed, and a 90,000-bushel grain elevator/drier. The equipment and buildings have an estimated market value of $1,500,000.

Jack employs five full-time farmhands, a mechanic, and a bookkeeper and has contracted part-time accounting/tax assistance with a local CPA. All employees are salaried; the farmhands and the bookkeeper make $25,000 a year, and the mechanic makes $32,000 annually. The CPA contract costs $15,000 a year.

In the most recent year, the farm produced 256,000 gallons of raw milk, 23,000 bushels of tobacco, and 75,300 bushels of corn. Jack sells the tobacco by contract and auction at the end of the harvest. The revenue this year was $1,345,000, providing Jack a net income after taxes of $233,500.

Jack's daughter Kelly has just returned from college. She knows that the farm is a good business but believes that the use of proper operating procedures and cost management systems could increase profitability and improve efficiency, allowing her father to have more leisure time. She also knows that her father has always run the farm from his experience and rules of thumb and is wary of scientific concepts and management principles. For example, he has little understanding of the accounting procedures of the farm, has not participated in the process, and has adopted few, if any, methods to maintain control over inventories and equipment. He has trusted his employees to maintain the farm appropriately without using any accounting or operating procedures over inventories or equipment, preventive maintenance schedules, or scientific application of crop rotation or livestock management.

Required

1. What is the competitive strategy for Fowler's Farm?

   a. Cost leadership because of increased competition

   b. Differentiation because of innovation in the farming industry

   c. Differentiation because of unique products at Fowler's Farm

   d. Cost leadership because of cost pressures in the industry

2. Explain briefly your choice for the competitive strategy for Fowler's Farm in requirement 1.

[LO 2-1]   2-48   **SWOT Analysis**

Required   Develop a SWOT analysis for Fowler's Farm based on Problem 2-47. The analysis should include two to three items in each category: strengths, weaknesses, opportunities, and threats.

[LO 2-3]   2-49 **Value-Chain Analysis**

Required   Develop a value chain of six to nine activities for Fowler's Farm based on Problem 2-47.

[LO 2-4]   2-50 **The Balanced Scorecard**

Required   Develop a balanced scorecard with three or more groups of CSFs for Fowler's Farm based on Problem 2-47. Explain your choice of groups and identify four to five CSFs in each group. Make sure that your CSFs are quantitative and can be measured.

[LO 2-2]   2-51 **Strategic Positioning**   Tartan Corporation has been manufacturing high-quality home lighting systems for more than 100 years. The company's first products in the 1920s—the Classic line—were high-quality floor lamps and table lamps made of the highest quality materials with features that other manufacturers did not attempt: multiple switches, adjustable heights, and stained glass. In the 1950s and 1960s, the company introduced a number of new products that were in demand at the time, including track lighting and lava lamps, which became the company's Modern line. A new customer style emerged in the 1960s and 1970s, which resulted in another new line of products, Contemporary. It was followed in more recent years by two new product lines, Margaret Stewart and Western. In developing and marketing the new styles, the company took advantage of the favorable reputation of the Classic line, which was the foundation of the favorable image of the company overall and which also helped in the sales of the new lines.

Jess Jones, the company's chief financial officer, had become concerned about the performance of some of the product lines in recent years. Although total sales were growing at an acceptable rate, approximately 10% per year, the sales mix was changing significantly, as shown in the following product line sales report. Jess was particularly concerned about the Classic line because of its sharp drop in sales and its high costs. Because of the high level of craftsmanship required for the Classic line, it always had higher-than-average costs for labor and materials. Furthermore, attracting and retaining the highly skilled workers necessary for this product line was becoming more and more difficult. The workers in the Classic line in 2019 were likely to be older and very loyal employees who were paid well because of their skill and seniority. These workers displayed the highest level of workmanship in the company and, some would argue, in the entire industry. Few newer employees seemed eager to learn the skills required in this product line.

Moreover, manufacturing capacity was experiencing an increasing strain. The sharper-than-expected increase in sales for the Western styles had created a backlog of orders for them, and plant managers had been scrambling to find the plant capacity to meet the demand. Some plant supervisors suggested shutting down the Classic line to make capacity for the Western line. Some managers of the Margaret Stewart line argued the same thing. However, eliminating the Classic line would make obsolete about $233,000 worth of materials inventory that is used only in the manufacture of Classic line products.

Tom Richter, the firm's sales manager, acknowledged that sales of the Classic line were more and more difficult to find and that demand for the new styles was increasing. He also noted that the sales of these products reflected significant regional differences. The Western line was popular in the South and the West, and the Contemporary, Modern, and Stewart styles were popular nationally. The Classic line tended to have strong support only in the northeast states. In some sales districts in these states, Classic sales represented a relatively high proportion of total sales.

Kelly Arnold, the firm's CEO, is aware of these concerns and has decided to set up a task force to consider the firm's options and strategy in regard to these problems.

Product Line Sales Report

	Classic	Contemporary	Margaret Stewart	Modern	Western
2020	20%	33%	5%	40%	2%
2021	16	35	11	34	4
2022	14	33	14	33	6
2023	9	31	18	31	11

Required

1. What is the competitive strategy for Tartan Corporation?
   a. Cost leadership because of increased competition
   b. Differentiation because of innovation
   c. Differentiation because of unique products and high quality
   d. Cost leadership because of cost pressures in the industry

2. What recommendation would you make to the task force?
    a. Delete the Classic line for the cost savings.
    b. Continue the Classic line because it supports the company's strategy.
    c. Delete the Classic line because of its poor sales performance.
    d. Continue the Classic line to save costs.
3. Briefly explain your answers to requirements 1 and 2.

[LO 2-1]   2-52 **SWOT Analysis**

Required   Develop a SWOT analysis for Tartan Corporation based on Problem 2-51. The analysis should include two to three items in each category: strengths, weaknesses, opportunities, and threats.

[LO 2-3]   2-53 **Value-Chain Analysis**

Required   Develop a value chain of six to eight items for Tartan Corporation based on Problem 2-51. Why would the value chain be useful to a firm like Tartan?

[LO 2-4]   2-54 **The Balanced Scorecard**

Required   Develop a balanced scorecard with three or more groups of CSFs for Tartan Corporation based on Problem 2-51. Explain your choice of groups and identify four to five CSFs in each group. Make sure that your CSFs are quantitative and can be measured.

[2-2, 2-4]   2-55 **Strategy Map**

Required   Based on your analysis of Tartan Corporation in Problems 2-51 through 2-54, create a strategy map for the company.

[LO 2-2, 2-4]   2-56 **Balanced Scorecard; Strategy Map**   The following are critical success factors for Dell Inc.:
    • Product manufacturing time
    • Customer perception of order-taking convenience and accuracy
    • Revenue growth
    • Selling expense to sales ratio
    • Number of new manufacturing processes developed
    • Order processing time
    • Materials inventory
    • Training dollars per employee
    • Number of emerging technologies evaluated
    • Customer retention
    • Manufacturing defects
    • Number of new manufacturing processes under development
    • Customer satisfaction with speed of service
    • Gross margin
    • Operating cost ratio

Required
1. Using the four BSC perspectives (learning and growth, internal processes, customer satisfaction, and financial), sort these CSFs into the appropriate perspective.
2. Create a simple strategy map for Dell.

[LO 2-2]   2-57 **Strategic Analysis**   Consider the following companies, each of which is your consulting client:
    1. Performance Bicycles, a company that supplies bicycles, parts, and bicycling equipment and clothing from its website
    2. The Oxford Omni, a downtown hotel that primarily serves convention and business travelers
    3. The Orange County Public Health Clinic, which is supported by tax revenues of Orange County and public donations
    4. The Harley-Davidson motorcycle company
    5. The Merck pharmaceutical company
    6. St. Sebastian's College, a small, private liberal arts college

Required   Determine each client's competitive strategy and related critical success factors.

[LO 2-2, 2-3, 2-4]　2-58　**Strategic Analysis; the Balanced Scorecard; Value-Chain Analysis: The Packaging Industry**
Dana Packaging Company is a large producer of paper and coated-paper containers with sales world-wide. The market for Dana's products has become very competitive in recent years because of the entrance of two large European competitors. In response, Dana has decided to enter new markets where the price competition is less severe. The new markets are principally the high end of the packaging business for products that require more technological sophistication and better materials. Food and consumer products companies use these more advanced products to enhance the appeal of their high-end products. In particular, sturdier, more colorful, more attractive, and better-sealing packaging has some appeal in the gourmet food business, especially in coffees, baked goods, and some dairy products. As a consequence of the shift, Dana has had to reorient its factory to produce the smaller batches of product associated with this new line of business. This change has required additional training for plant personnel and some upgrading of factory equipment to reduce setup time.

Dana's manufacturing process begins with pulp paper, which it produces in its own mills around the world. Some of the pulp material is purchased from recycling operators when price and availability are favorable. The pulp paper is then converted into paperboard, which is produced at Dana's own plants or purchased at times from outside vendors. In most cases, the paperboard plants are located near the pulp mills. At this point in the manufacturing process, the paperboard might be coated with a plastic material, a special embossing, or some other feature. This process is done at separate plants owned by Dana. On occasion, but infrequently, when Dana's plants are very busy, the coating and embossing process is outsourced to other manufacturers. The final step in the process is filling the containers with the food product or consumer product. This step is done exclusively at Dana-owned plants. Dana has tried to maintain a high reputation for the quality of the filling process, stressing safety, cleanliness, and low cost to its customers.

Required

1. What is the *new* competitive strategy for Dana Packaging Company?
   a. Cost leadership because of increased competition
   b. Differentiation because of niche markets
   c. Differentiation because of high technology and high quality
   d. Cost leadership because of cost pressures in the industry
2. Briefly explain your reasoning for the choice in requirement 1.
3. Develop a value chain for Dana. What are the opportunities for cost reduction and/or value enhancement from using value-chain analysis?
4. Dana's management is considering the use of a balanced scorecard for the firm. For each of the four perspectives within the balanced scorecard, list two or three examples of measurable critical success factors that should be included.

[LO 2-2, 2-4]　2-59　**Strategy Requirements under the Malcolm Baldrige National Quality Award Program**　The Malcolm Baldrige National Quality Award program was established by the U.S. Congress in 1987 to promote quality awareness and to enhance the competitiveness of U.S. businesses. The program is under the National Institute of Standards and Technology (NIST), a nonregulatory federal agency within the Commerce Department. The program has seven categories of performance criteria, including leadership, strategic planning, customer focus, measurement and analysis and knowledge management, workforce focus, operations focus, and results. The last category, results, includes five parts: customer-focused results, leadership and governance, workforce focus, financial markets, and product and process. Recipients of the prestigious Malcolm Baldrige National Quality Award are recognized annually for the firms' achievements in meeting these performance criteria.

Required　Go to the NIST website that shows the Baldrige Program's Criteria for Performance Excellence (**www.nist.gov/system/files/documents/2018/12/14/2019-2020-criteria-commentary-bnp.pdf**) and review the performance criteria. Comment on the degree to which the program stresses strategy development and strategy implementation.

[LO 2-3]　2-60　**Economic Nationalism; Strategy; Global; Value Chain**　The trend of economic nationalism (e.g., Brexit) that is affecting many countries around the world promotes keeping manufacturing jobs in the local country. As management accountants, we are concerned about how this trend will affect companies, particularly global companies, as they strive to adapt their strategy and value chain to the new economic nationalism. Three companies that are relevant in this matter are Harley-Davidson (**www.harley-davidson.com**), a manufacturer of motorcycles; GAM Enterprises Inc. (**www.gamweb.com/**), a manufacturer of precision parts used in automation in a variety of industries; and Mobile Outfitters (**www.moutfitters.com/**), a company that manufacturers screen protectors for the Apple iPhone.

Harley-Davidson (HD) has recently decided to open a manufacturing plant in Thailand to serve the growing market for its bikes in the Asian countries. HD has faced criticism for moving manufacturing jobs offshore, but HD asserts that it has little choice given the very high 60% tariff for motorcycle imports that is common in these Asian countries. Locating in Thailand would not only reduce tariffs into Thailand, but also reduce tariffs to the countries that are in a trading partnership with Thailand, the Association of Southeast Asian Nations (ASEAN). The ASEAN countries include Brunei, Cambodia, Indonesia, Laos, Malaysia, Myanmar, Philippines, Singapore, Thailand, and Vietnam.

GAM Enterprises Inc. is an Illinois-based manufacturer serving other industries that are using automation to improve the efficiency in their processes. GAM began moving its operations in Germany back to the U.S. in 2014. The reason was that GAM needed to be closer to its customers in the U.S. This was a resource for its current customers and also provided a way to attract new customers in the U.S.

Mobile Outfitters (MO) is a U.S.-based company that produces anti-glare and screen protectors for the Apple iPhone. MO has not been able to find a U.S. manufacturer that will meet its desired specifications, and as a result has outsourced some of its product to a firm overseas.

Required   For each of the three companies above—Harley-Davidson, GAM Enterprises, and Mobile Outfitters—answer each of the following questions:
1. Which competitive strategy (cost leadership or differentiation) do you think the company is using and why? Would the company's decision to relocate manufacturing into or out of the U.S. affect this strategy?
2. How would the relocation of manufacturing facilities to different countries affect the company's value chain?

[LO 2-2]   2-61 **Strategy; Critical Success Factors: Martial Arts Training**   Martial Arts of Cincinnati (MAC) provides karate training and practice services in three locations in Cincinnati, Ohio. MAC is known for its quality of training and has grown rapidly in recent years due to its solid reputation and the growing interest in martial arts, particularly karate. George Moody, the owner of MAC, is a retired police officer who has been training and teaching martial arts for almost 20 years. He has a plan to grow his business to 10 locations in the Cincinnati area in the coming 5 to 10 years. George thinks that by careful attention to customer service and by choosing his locations wisely, he can achieve this goal. He plans to locate his new studios in strip malls where rental costs are relatively low. This way he can keep his prices down, perhaps lower than other competitors, and thereby attract more customers.

George has developed a list of indicators that he uses to manage the business. The indicators are targeted to George's two key concerns—sales growth and teacher performance.

Sales Indicators (The first four indicators are obtained on a daily basis, while the last is obtained weekly.)

Number of introductory lessons
Number of new students
Number of students attending classes
Total number of enrolled students
Class size by teacher and age group

Teacher Performance Indicators (for each teacher; data collected on a monthly basis)

Number of classes taught
Average number of students per class
Average retention percentage
Student progress in martial arts skills

Required
1. How would you describe George's competitive strategy?
2. George has listed some of his CSFs. Critically review these indicators, and explain which CSFs you would add or change, and why.

[LO 2-2, 2-4]   2-62 **Balanced Scorecard; Strategy: Food Ingredients Company**   The balanced scorecard for a small food ingredients company is shown below. The information is based on an actual company, and detailed information about its operations and strategy is confidential. You may assume that the firm's products and services are used by a diverse set of customers, including different types of food processors (Kraft Heinz, Unilever, Nestle, etc.), restaurant chains, bakeries, supermarkets, and the like. The company is located in a large city.

BALANCED SCORECARD FOR A FOOD INGREDIENTS COMPANY

Goals	Scorecard Measures
Financial Perspective	
Capture an increasing share of industry growth	Company growth versus industry growth
Secure the base business while remaining the preferred supplier to our customers	Volume trend by line of business; revenue trend by line of business; gross margin
Expand aggressively in global markets	Ratio of North American sales to international sales
Commercialize a continuous stream of profitable new ingredients and services	Percentage of sales from products launched within the past five years; gross profit from new products
Customer Satisfaction	
Become the lowest-cost supplier	Total cost of using our products and services relative to total cost of using competitive products and services
Tailor products to meet local needs, and expand those products and services that meet customers' needs better than competitors	Percentage of products in R&D pipeline that are being test-marketed by our customers
Customer satisfaction	Customer survey
Internal Perspective	
Maintain lowest cost base in the industry	Our total costs relative to number one competitor; inventory turnover; plant utilization
Maintain consistent, predictable production processes	First-pass success rate
Continue to improve distribution efficiency	Percentage of perfect orders
Build capability to screen and identify profitable customers	Change in customer profitability
Integrate acquisitions and alliances efficiently	Revenues per acquired company and allied company
Learning and Growth Perspective	
Link the overall strategy to reward and recognition system	Net income per dollar of variable pay
Foster a culture that supports innovation and growth	Annual preparedness assessment; quarterly report

Required Based on the information provided, determine what you think is the competitive strategy of the company. Does the balanced scorecard shown above reflect this strategy? Why or why not?

[LO 2-2, 2-3] 2-63 **Value-Chain Analysis** Sheldon Radio manufactures yacht radios, navigational equipment, and depth-sounding and related equipment from a small plant near New Bern, North Carolina. One of Sheldon's most popular products, making up 40% of its revenues and 35% of its profits, is a marine radio, model VF4500, that is installed on many of the new large boats produced in the United States. Production and sales average 500 units per month. Sheldon has achieved its success in the market through excellent customer service and product reliability. The manufacturing process consists primarily of the assembly of components purchased from various electronics firms plus a small amount of metalworking and finishing. The assembly operations cost $110 per unit. The purchased parts cost Sheldon $250, of which $130 is for parts that Sheldon could manufacture in its existing facility for $80 in materials for each unit plus an investment in labor and equipment that would cost $35,000 per month.

Sheldon is considering outsourcing the marketing, distributing, and servicing for its units to another North Carolina firm, Brashear Enterprises. This would save Sheldon $125,000 in monthly materials and labor costs. The cost of the contract would be $105 per radio.

Required
1. Prepare a value-chain analysis for Sheldon to assist in deciding whether to purchase or manufacture the parts and whether to contract out the marketing, distributing, and servicing of the units.
2. Should Sheldon (a) continue to purchase the parts or manufacture them and (b) continue to provide the marketing, distributing, and servicing or outsource these activities to Brashear? Explain your answer.

[LO 2-2, 2-3] 2-64 **Value Chain: Harley-Davidson** Harley-Davidson, Inc. (HD) is one of the most recognized brands worldwide. The motorcycle manufacturer has one of the most loyal owner groups of any company. Unfortunately, the firm's success has come at a price. Harley has a reputation that drives some customers away and a "this is for a different generation" effect on some potential younger customers. Other potential customers are simply intimidated by the idea of riding a 500+ pound Harley-Davidson. To deal with these concerns and to try to encourage new owners, HD developed the Riding Academy program in which anyone who could pass the Motorcycle Safety Foundation's written test and driving test would be eligible for instructions on how to ride a Harley (**https://www.harley-davidson .com/us/en/learn-to-ride/new-rider.html**). The instructions are provided by local dealers. Another new program at HD is intended to attract women (between 2008 and 2010, the industry sales had dropped 40%, while at the same time the number of women who own motorcycles had doubled). HD has introduced a new bike, the Street 500, which has a lower seat height, sells for a lower price, and, at 492 pounds, is lighter than the most Harleys.

Required   Where do these two new programs fit in the Harley-Davidson value chain? From a value chain perspective, how do these programs support the firm's strategy?

[LO 2-2, 2-3]   2-65   **The Balanced Scorecard; Economic Nationalism; Strategy**   McDonald's is a global (100 countries) fast-food chain with more than 36,000 restaurants worldwide and global sales of $107 billion in 2018 (includes both company-owned and franchisee sales). McDonald's is one of the most successful companies, with stock values increasing steadily to an all-time high of over $221 in August 2019. A new Velocity Growth Plan, adopted in 2017, is a customer-centric strategy designed to drive guest count growth by retaining existing customers, regaining customers who visit less often, and converting casual to committed customers.

(Source: Company website)

Required
1. What is McDonald's competitive strategy (cost leadership or differentiation)? Briefly explain your answer.
2. Would McDonald's benefit from the use of a balanced scorecard? Why or why not? What would be some of the critical success factors in McDonald's balanced scorecard?
3. As a global company, McDonald's is subject to the risk of foreign currency fluctuations and the effect of tariffs in response to economic nationalism. Explain how changes in foreign currency exchange rates and tariffs could affect the company. How has the trend to economic nationalism in the UK (Brexit), the U.S., and elsewhere affected the company's position on currency fluctuations?

[LO 2-3]   2-66   **Value Chain; Global**   A factory owner in Bangladesh, Tipu Munshi, manufactures clothing for Walmart and other retailers around the world. One of Tipu's products is a pair of jeans sold to Asda, a Walmart subsidiary in Britain, which sells the jeans for US$22.12. Asda Stores Ltd. is the third-largest retailer in the UK, focusing on food, clothing, and general merchandise. Tipu completes each set of jeans at an average cost for materials, labor, and other factory costs, plus $0.26 profit, for a total of $7.29 each to Asda. The jeans are then shipped to Asda by Li & Fung, a Hong Kong company, for $4.33 per pair. Finally, Asda adds an additional $10.50 of cost and profit, thus arriving at the selling price of $22.12 per pair of jeans.

Required   Identify the value chain for the Asda jeans. As a manager at Asda, explain how you would use the value chain to improve the competitiveness and profitability of the business.

[LO 2-3]   2-67   **Value Chain: Multiple Industries**   Generally, the value chains involved in providing a given product or service can be from multiple industries that can be interconnected in complex ways. One example is the auto industry, where the primary consumer, the purchaser of an auto, is served by many different industries. The following figure shows five industries that support the auto purchaser directly: the manufacturer of the auto, the bank or financial institution that finances the loan for the car buyer, the insurance company, auto repair, and, at some point, a company that purchases the car and resells it. The arrows show the links of service in this multiple-industry value chain.

The value chain for the manufacturer is shown in the center column, and the steps in the chain are shown as design, purchase of materials, purchase of components (brake systems, seats, dashboard, carpeting, etc.), assembly, and delivery to the auto dealer. On the right-hand side of the figure, we show one of the suppliers of components for the auto manufacturer: an auto parts manufacturer that provides brake systems. This manufacturer also requires supplies from other companies, which in turn require parts or materials from other companies. So there are two or more levels, or "tiers," to the supply chain for the manufacturer. A thorough understanding of the value chain for the auto industry requires consideration of the full complexity of all the different suppliers and industries involved.

Note that particularly for global companies, the impact of economic nationalism and tariffs should be considered in evaluating the company's value chain. Tariffs and other tools of economic nationalism typically disrupt the company's global supply chain, often increasing costs and reducing lead times, etc.

Required   Using the following figure as a guide, create a multiple-industry value chain for a boat manufacturer, including financing, repair, used boat sales, and parts suppliers.

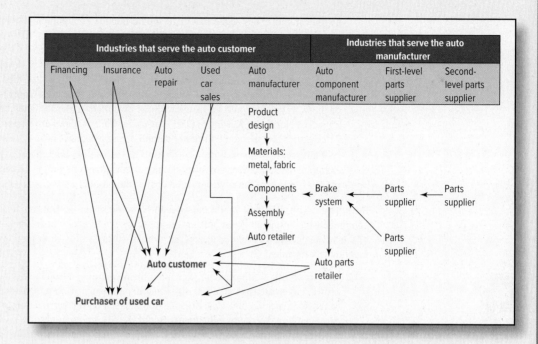

[LO 2-3] 2-68 **Follow-up to Problem 2-67; Value Chain for Financing Auto Purchases**

Required Consider the comprehensive value chain in Problem 2-67 and complete a value chain for the financing portion of the value chain only. Use a value chain with four to six steps, beginning with the application for a loan by the car buyer and ending with the car buyer completing the loan and purchase.

[LO 2-1] 2-69 **Foreign Currency Exchange Rates** The website links shown below provide historical information on the exchange rates of currencies used throughout the world. Review the changes in exchange rates for the last few years, using either of the two following sources: **www.federalreserve.gov/releases/H10/hist/** and **www.xe.com/ucc/**.

Required

1. Which Asian countries have experienced changing exchange rates relative to the U.S. dollar in recent years, and what are the implications of this trend for global companies such as General Motors?

2. Most European countries now use the euro as the currency for international exchange. Study the recent trends in the euro and determine the implications of this trend for global companies such as Walmart.

3. Which North American countries (other than the U.S.) have experienced changing exchange rates relative to the U.S. dollar in recent years, and what are the implications of this trend for global companies such as Ford Motor Company?

[LO 2-3] 2-70 **Value Chain; Innovation** To complete this assignment, read the article by Noah P. Barsky and Anthony H. Catanach Jr. titled "Every Manager Can Be an Innovator" (*Strategic Finance*, August 2011, pp. 22–29). The article provides a comprehensive discussion of how companies can use the value chain as a tool to help guide their efforts to provide ongoing innovation in their companies. The article is available at **http://imsl2.com/tools/barsky2/BARSKY_MgrInnov.pdf**.

Required

1. Explain briefly the difference between disruptive and sustaining innovation.
2. What are the five activities in the value chain depicted in the article?
3. What is the role of strategy in looking for innovation in each of the activities in the value chain?
4. Describe an example of an opportunity for innovation in market analysis.
5. Describe an example of an opportunity for innovation in product development and design.
6. Describe an example of an opportunity for innovation in sales and marketing.
7. Describe an example of an opportunity for innovation in procurement, production, and distribution.
8. Describe an example of an opportunity for innovation in after-sale customer service.

[LO 2-5] 2-71 **Measuring the Impact of Sustainability Efforts** Some economists and financial executives are beginning to consider the possibility of reporting sustainability costs and benefits in a more comprehensive manner. The Nobel Prize–winning economist Joseph Stiglitz and other economists have suggested that nations move beyond the traditional gross domestic product (GDP) measures of a nation's output. They argue that GDP should include environmental assets and liabilities. For example, the marshlands in many parts of the United States are key to aquatic life, plant life, erosion control, and storm protection, providing billions of dollars of value. So development on these marshlands should be balanced against those values that would be lost in development. An example is the development of the wetlands of southern Louisiana. As a result of this development, New Orleans and southern Louisiana are now much more vulnerable to storms. Some have estimated that the value of those wetlands would be in the trillions of dollars if the wetlands had been there to reduce the impact of Hurricane Katrina in 2005. Australia, Canada, Germany, Japan, and Mexico are among the 24 countries that use some form of "natural capital accounting."

Individual companies are also looking at the use of this type of sustainability accounting. For example, the sportswear company Puma has considered including on each product tag the estimated monetary value of the environmental cost of the production of the product.

Required   List what you would consider to be some of the advantages and disadvantages of the more comprehensive sustainability reporting proposed by some economists for governments. What are some of the advantages and disadvantages of the type of sustainability reporting being considered by Puma for individual companies?

[LO 2-4, 2-5]   **2-72   Sustainability**   As noted in the chapter, the demand for sustainability reporting has grown, and this growth has created a demand for sustainability assurance, the ability to add verification and credibility to the assurance reports. One organization focused on the verification of sustainability reports is the Sustainability Accounting Standards Board (SASB, www.sasb.org/), which has recently developed a Conceptual Framework that provides a list of criteria for management accountants to use in evaluating the measures used in sustainability reporting. These criteria are discussed in a recent article in the *CPA Journal:* Jill M. D'Aguila, "The Current State of Sustainability Reporting," *The CPA Journal,* July 2018 (www.cpajournal.com/2018/07/30/the-current-state-of-sustainability-reporting/).

Required:

1. Which three of the criteria in the following list are **not** SASB criteria?
   a. Fair representation: Metrics should accurately describe performance related to the disclosure topic.
   b. Useful: Metrics should help companies manage operations and help investors perform financial analysis.
   c. Applicable: Metrics should be based on definitions applicable to most companies within an industry.
   d. Valid: Metrics should correctly be related to the underlying sustainability issue.
   e. Comparable: Metrics should provide both quantitative and qualitative information. The quantitative data will facilitate benchmarking within an industry, and the qualitative information will facilitate comparisons.
   f. Complete: Metrics should provide sufficient information to interpret performance relative to sustainability.
   g. Comprehensive: Metrics should comprehensively reflect the theoretical foundation of the desired measure.
   h. Verifiable: Metrics should support effective internal controls to verify data and provide assurance.
   i. Aligned: Metrics should be based on those already used by companies.
   j. Neutral: Metrics should be unbiased and provide objective disclosure of performance.
   k. Distributive: Metrics should provide a range of data within an industry or across industries to allow users to differentiate performance.
   l. Scientific: Metrics should be based on appropriate scientific study.

2. The *CPA Journal* article cited above notes there are challenges to the development of widely adopted standards for sustainability reporting. What do you think are the key challenges, and why? Which of the providers of sustainability standards is most appropriate for U.S. investors, and why?

[LO 2-3]   **2-73   Economic Nationalism; Strategy; Global; Value Chain**   The trend of economic nationalism (e.g., Brexit and tariffs) that is affecting many countries around the world promotes keeping manufacturing jobs in the local country. As management accountants, we are concerned about how this trend will affect companies, particularly global companies, as they strive to adapt their strategy and their global supply chain to the new economic nationalism. Two industries that are relevant in this matter are the textile industry and the pharmaceutical industry.

The Textile Industry. Some companies in the textile industry (where production of raw materials has been moving abroad for decades) have noticed that along with the reduction of raw material production in the U.S., there has been a loss in the number of engineers and managers who are able to direct textile production. In India, China, and Pakistan, on the other hand, a large number of students are graduating with the skills necessary to deal with the production of fabric.

The Pharmaceutical Industry. The upstream activities of research and development for new drugs is a key competitive factor in the industry. However, the downstream activity of drug manufacturing, especially for generics, is more mundane, and has generally been located in the lowest-cost countries.

Required For each of the two industries above, textiles and pharmaceuticals, answer each of the following questions:

1. Which competitive strategy (cost leadership or differentiation) do you think most companies in each of these industries are using, and why? Would the decision by a company in the industry to relocate manufacturing into or out of the U.S. affect this strategy?

2. How would the relocation of manufacturing facilities to different countries affect a company's value chain in each of these industries?

[LO 2-5] **2-74 Sustainability** The great news for those concerned about climate change and sustainability is that the cost of renewable energy ("green power") is quickly decreasing. The result is that many companies, particularly larger companies, are making significant long-term investments in renewable energy, which they expect will bring their companies lower costs and help to make the companies more profitable and competitive. So there is a strong business case for sustainability for these companies. Typically the renewable energy is in the form of wind or solar power. Examples include Walmart, Apple, and Target.

Required Recent studies have shown that the investment in renewable energy has grown the fastest for the largest companies due to their economic leverage and scale of operations. Now there is concern that the growth in use of renewable energy might level off because of the obstacle of getting smaller companies to participate. As a management accountant in a smaller company, how would you seek to bridge the gap to participate in renewable energy, along with the larger firms?

[LO 2-4] **2-75 Balanced Scorecard** This chapter introduced the Balanced Scorecard (BSC) and showed applications in organizations that were using the BSC for planning and for strategy implementation. Another important use for the BSC is to evaluate mid-level and higher-level managers who are responsible for implementing the organization's strategy. The BSC is useful in this context because, by being a part of managers' performance evaluation, it focuses the managers' attention on the critical success factors that top management has determined to be strategic and have therefore entered into the BSC. This application of the BSC is covered in Chapter 18. Chapter 20 shows how the BSC can be used for evaluating the organization as a whole.

Another key way to use the BSC for mid-level managers is to use it in hiring and evaluating lower-level employees. For example, when interviewing applicants for a job, the mid-level manager could use a BSC to enumerate the desired skills for the position, and because the BSC requires measurable critical success factors, the task of selecting the best applicant will be simplified.

Required

1. Consider the use of the BSC by mid-level managers in hiring and evaluating employees who report to them. Which of the following would most likely be true for this application of the BSC?

    a. Increase in employee loyalty among the employees hired and evaluated in this way.

    b. Decrease in individual bias in selecting and evaluating employees.

    c. Decrease in the time required to complete the selection and evaluation of employees.

    d. Increase in the number of appropriate applicants for the position.

2. Explain briefly why you chose your response in part 1 above.

[LO 2-3] **2-76 Economic Nationalism; Global; Value Chain** The term *global supply chain* is often used to describe the complex set of interrelated activities and relationships that global companies use to source their needed material, labor, and equipment; to produce the product and service; and to deliver that product or service to the ultimate consumer. In the current time of economic nationalism with its focus on tariffs and other restrictions on movement of people and product, these global companies are facing disruptions of their current supply chains. These disruptions are discussed in the article "Tracking the Forces Threatening the World's Hottest Economies," by Tom Orlik, Scott Johnson, and Alex Tanzi in *Bloomberg Businessweek,* November 4, 2019, pp. 19–24 (www.bloomberg.com/graphics/2019-new-economy-drivers-and-disrupters/).

Required

1. According to Orlik, Johnson, and Tanzi, the four disrupters are (select the best answer below):

    a. Increase in the labor force, policies that increase productivity, inflation, openness to trade.

    b. Decrease in the labor force, inflation, automation, protectionism.

    c. Populist regimes, automation, climate change, protectionism.

    d. Expansion of capital stock, automation, climate change, diversity.

    e. Populist regimes, labor force, uncertainty, low productivity.

2. Tariffs have an important effect on the global supply chain. Tariffs are a cost to the seller that is usually passed on ultimately to

    a. The merchandiser.

    b. The retailer.

    c. The consumer.

    d. The country imposing the tariff.

    e. The purchaser in the country that imposed the tariff.

3. What do you consider to be the most important positive and negative impacts of tariffs on global supply chains? Explain briefly.

Solutions to Self-Study Problems

1. Value-Chain Analysis

The cost figures Jack has assembled suggest that the two teams' operations are generally quite similar, as expected in AA baseball. However, an important difference is the amount the Durham team spends on game-day operations, which is more than three times that of the Waynesboro Bulls. That difference has, in part, built a loyal set of fans in Durham, where gate receipts average more than twice those of Waynesboro ($28,500 versus $12,350). The Buffaloes appear to have found an effective way to compete by drawing attendance to special game-day events and promotions.

To begin to compete more effectively and profitably, Waynesboro might consider additional value-added services, such as game-day activities similar to those offered in Durham. Waynesboro's costs per person are somewhat lower than Durham's, but its cost savings are probably not enough to offset the loss in revenues.

On the cost side, the comparison with Durham shows little immediate promise for cost reduction; Waynesboro spends, on average, less than Durham in every category except ticket sales and management compensation. Perhaps this also indicates that instead of reducing costs, Waynesboro should spend *more* on fan development. The next step in Jack's analysis might be to survey Waynesboro fans to determine the level of satisfaction and to identify desired services that are not currently provided.

2. SWOT Analysis

The SWOT analysis for the Waynesboro Bulls might look as follows:

Strengths:

- Not much local competition for baseball; note that the 150-mile radius is probably irrelevant anyway as the Bulls's customers are local (within 20 miles); the main issue is local competition
- Wing, the new pitcher; an opportunity for more wins and increased fan interest

Weaknesses:

- Lots of losing records, which hinders fan interest
- Not much to offer by way of game-day promotions and special attractions
- What appears to be a lackluster team and coaching staff

Opportunities:

- More new players like Wing, especially those who can create some fan excitement
- New coach
- Improve the baseball park; add some improvements, such as better parking, seats, etc.
- Increase the quality and variety of food and beverages beyond soda, beer, and nachos
- Lower the ticket prices; offer free tickets to those who have attended a certain number of games
- Offer special promotions, in which groups (employees of a given company, those over 65, etc.) get a free or low-price admission

Threats:

- Only the closest of the other venues (NASCAR, outdoor concerts, etc.) would be a threat to this basically local audience
- Wing could be recruited into the majors

3. The Balanced Scorecard

While the key to growth and profitability is probably increasing fan interest, this will probably come about most directly through improvements in operations and personnel. Here is a partial list of examples.

Operations (at the Bulls's park and on travel days):

- Cleanliness of park and restrooms as measured by a survey of fans or regular review by management
- Parking, problems measured by number of complaints
- Timeliness and comfort for players and coaching staff on away days; player and staff survey

Personnel (coaching staff and players):

- Players' performance statistics
- Average player salary (benchmark to other teams)
- Average coaching staff salaries
- Average player age
- Player satisfaction as measured by multiple-question survey

Customers (the ticket-buying fans):

- Survey of customer satisfaction
- Number of paying customers to number of free admissions

Financial:

- Ticket sales revenue
- Food and beverage revenue
- Other revenue (parking, etc.)
- Ballpark maintenance cost, by category
- Travel costs for away games

Please visit Connect to access a narrated, animated tutorial for solving this problem.

CHAPTER THREE

Basic Cost Management Concepts

After studying this chapter, you should be able to . . .

LO 3-1 Recognize the strategic role of basic cost management concepts.

LO 3-2 Explain the cost driver concepts at the activity, volume, structural, and executional levels.

LO 3-3 Explain the cost concepts used in product and service costing.

LO 3-4 Demonstrate how costs flow through the accounts and prepare and interpret an income statement for both a manufacturing and a merchandising company.

LO 3-1

Recognize the strategic role of basic cost management concepts.

Irrespective of their competitive strategy, managers of successful firms must understand their firm's costs and need to apply cost management effectively. In doing so, they need to understand the key concepts and terms of cost management. We begin with an example that illustrates the importance of understanding the complexity of a firm's operations—the number and diversity of its products, production processes and locations, distribution networks, and types of customers. Complexity on any of these dimensions will have consequences for costs, and the management accountant has developed the necessary vocabulary to identify and describe these effects.

A good example of a firm that deals effectively with complexity is Procter & Gamble Inc. (P&G), one of the world's leading consumer products companies, maker of such well-known products as Tide detergent and Crest toothpaste. P&G has achieved success through

Jonathan Weiss/Shutterstock

product excellence and continuous improvement. One key area of continuous improvement is the firm's emphasis on cost reduction through product and process simplification.

As the company faces projections of slower growth, the need to control costs may intensify. In 2016 the CEO committed to a program that would cut $10 billion of costs over five years. To accomplish this, P&G evaluates the influence of products and process complexity on overall costs, a concept we study in this chapter.

Historically, P&G has had as many as 50 different varieties of some of its brands, including different size containers and flavors. In addition to variety, the number of trade promotions, discounts, rebates, and coupons that affected P&G's net price were complex. The high complexity in products and pricing increased manufacturing costs, inventory holding costs, selling and distribution costs, customer service costs, administrative and accounting costs, and other operating costs. Over time, P&G reduced its product variety significantly, cut thousands of jobs, and experienced improved overall sales and profits. While P&G has improved its supply chain—the process of managing its suppliers—to reduce supply chain cost and improve product quality and product innovation, P&G and its peers also are contending with higher costs for raw-material inputs such as petroleum and paper pulp, as well as surging transportation costs. Overall, what P&G is attempting to accomplish is effective management of its sales and costs through careful attention to its brand strategy and a reduction in product complexity.[1]

Costs, Cost Drivers, Cost Objects, and Cost Assignment

LO 3-2

Explain the cost driver concepts at the activity, volume, structural, and executional levels.

cost

Incurred when a resource is used for some purpose.

cost pools

The meaningful groups into which costs are collected.

cost driver

A factor that causes or relates to a change in the total cost of an activity.

cost object

Any product, service, customer, activity, or organizational unit to which costs are accumulated for some management purpose.

value stream

A group of related products; useful for preparing profitability reports as part of lean accounting; all the activities required to create customer value for a family of products or services.

A critical step in achieving a competitive advantage is to identify the key costs and the drivers of those costs within the company or organization. In P&G's case, product complexity is one of those key cost drivers.

A company incurs a **cost** when it uses a resource for some purpose. For example, a company producing kitchen appliances incurs the costs of certain resources, the costs of materials (such as sheet metal and bolts for the enclosure), costs of manufacturing labor, and other costs. Often costs are assigned into meaningful groups called **cost pools**. Costs can be grouped in many different ways, including by type of cost (labor costs in one pool, material costs in another), by source (department 1, department 2), or by responsibility (manager 1, manager 2). For example, an assembly department or a product engineering department might be treated as a cost pool.

A **cost driver** is any factor that has the effect of changing the amount of total cost. For a firm that competes on the basis of cost leadership, management of the key cost drivers is essential. For example, to achieve its low-cost leadership in manufacturing, P&G carefully watches the design and manufacturing factors that drive the costs of its products. It makes design improvements when necessary, and the manufacturing plants are designed and automated for the highest production efficiency. For firms that are not cost leaders, the management of cost drivers may not be so critical, but attention to the key cost drivers contributes directly to the firm's success. For example, because an important cost driver for retailers is loss and damage to merchandise, most retailers establish careful procedures for handling, displaying, and storing their merchandise.

A **cost object** is any product, service, customer, activity, or organizational unit to which costs are assigned. Products, services, and customers are generally cost objects; manufacturing departments are considered either cost pools or cost objects, depending on whether management's main focus is on the costs for the products or the costs for the manufacturing departments. The concept of cost objects is a broad concept. It includes products, groups of products (called **value streams**), services, projects, and departments; it can also apply to customers or vendors, among many other possibilities. Cost objects play a key role in decision making, performance measurement, and strategy implementation, as well as financial statement preparation and tax preparation.

[1] Sharon Terlep, "P&G Mystery: Its Cost-Cut Details Are Still Awaited," *The Wall Street Journal,* April 25, 2016, p. B3; Aaron Back, "EXCHANGE—Heard on the Street: Betting on Procter's Recovery Still a Gamble—A Few Good Months Does Not a Recovery make," *The Wall Street Journal,*Eastern ed., October 20, 2018; Aisha Al-Muslim, "P&G Moves to Streamline Its Structure; CEO David Taylor Appoints Six Unit Chiefs with Oversight of Both Products and Sales," *The Wall Street Journal (Online),*November 9, 2018.

Cost Assignment and Cost Allocation: Direct and Indirect Costs

cost assignment
The process of assigning costs to cost pools or from cost pools to cost objects.

Cost assignment is the process of assigning resource costs to cost pools and then from cost pools to cost objects. There are two types of assignment—direct tracing and allocation. Direct tracing is used for assigning direct costs, and allocation is used for indirect costs. Any cost is either a direct or indirect cost, relative to the cost pool or cost object. A **direct cost** can be conveniently and economically traced directly to a cost pool or a cost object. For example, the cost of materials required for a particular product is a direct cost because it can be traced directly to the product.

direct cost
A cost that can be conveniently and economically traced directly to a cost pool or a cost object.

In a manufacturing company, the direct materials cost is accumulated in cost pools (manufacturing departments) and then traced to each product manufactured, which is the cost object. Similarly, an airline's cost of ingredients for a passenger's beverage is a direct cost that can be traced to each passenger. For a direct cost, the cost driver is the number of units of that object—for example, the number of cartons of Tide produced by P&G or the number of passengers on Flight 617 for Delta Air Lines. Total direct cost increases directly in proportion to the number of cartons or passengers.

indirect cost
A cost that is not conveniently or economically traceable to a specific cost pool or cost object.

In contrast, there is no convenient or economical way to trace an **indirect cost** from the cost to the cost pool or from the cost pool to the cost object. The cost of supervising manufacturing employees and the cost of handling materials are good examples of costs that generally cannot be traced to individual products and therefore are considered indirect costs. Similarly, the cost of fueling an aircraft is an indirect cost when the cost object is the airline passenger because the aircraft's use of fuel cannot be traced directly to that passenger. In contrast, if the cost object for the airline is the flight, the cost of fuel is a direct cost that can be traced directly to the aircraft's use of fuel for that flight.

Because indirect costs cannot be easily traced to a single cost pool or cost object, the assignment of indirect costs is made by using cost drivers. For example, if the cost driver for materials handling cost is the number of parts, the total cost of materials handling can be assigned to each product on the basis of each product's number of parts relative to the total number of parts in all products. The result is that costs are assigned to the cost pool or cost object that caused the cost in a manner that is fairly representative of the way the cost is incurred. For example, a product with a large number of parts should bear a larger portion of the cost of materials handling than a product with fewer parts. Similarly, a department with a large number of employees should bear a larger portion of the cost of supervision provided for all departments.

cost allocation
The process of assigning indirect costs to cost pools and cost objects.

The assignment of indirect costs to cost pools and cost objects is called **cost allocation**, a form of cost assignment in which direct tracing is not economically feasible, so cost drivers are used instead. The cost drivers used to allocate or assign these costs to cost objects are often called **allocation bases**. The relationships between costs, cost pools, cost objects, and cost drivers in appliance manufacturing are illustrated in Exhibit 3.1 and Exhibit 3.2. This simplified example includes two cost objects (dishwasher and washing machine), two cost pools (assembly department and packing department), and five cost resources (electric motor,

allocation bases
The cost drivers used to allocate or assign costs to cost objects.

EXHIBIT 3.1

Relationships between Costs, Cost Pools, and Cost Objects in Appliance Manufacturing

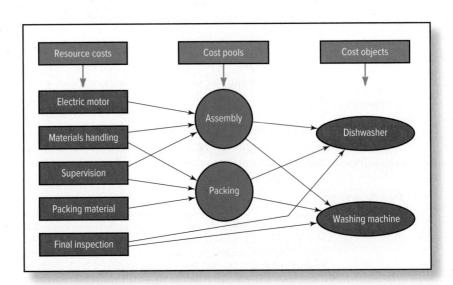

EXHIBIT 3.2
Selected Examples of Costs, Cost Pools, Cost Objects, and Cost Drivers in Appliance Manufacturing

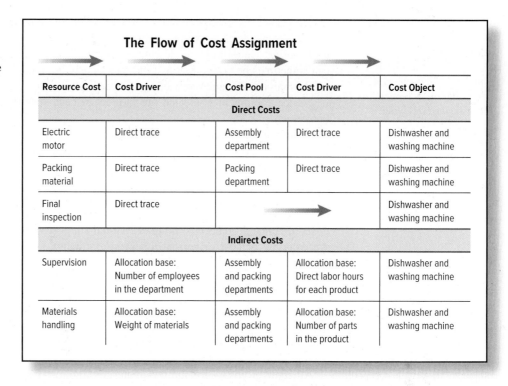

	The Flow of Cost Assignment			
Resource Cost	Cost Driver	Cost Pool	Cost Driver	Cost Object
Direct Costs				
Electric motor	Direct trace	Assembly department	Direct trace	Dishwasher and washing machine
Packing material	Direct trace	Packing department	Direct trace	Dishwasher and washing machine
Final inspection	Direct trace		→	Dishwasher and washing machine
Indirect Costs				
Supervision	Allocation base: Number of employees in the department	Assembly and packing departments	Allocation base: Direct labor hours for each product	Dishwasher and washing machine
Materials handling	Allocation base: Weight of materials	Assembly and packing departments	Allocation base: Number of parts in the product	Dishwasher and washing machine

materials handling, supervision, packing material, and final inspection). The electric motor is traced to the assembly department and from there directly to the two products, assuming for simplicity that the same motor is used in both appliances. Similarly, the packing material is traced directly to the packing department and from there directly to the two products. Each finished product, dishwasher or washing machine, is inspected, so the cost of final inspection is traced directly to each of the two products. The two indirect costs, supervision and materials handling, are allocated to the two cost pools (assembly and packing departments) and are then allocated from the cost pools to the products, as shown in Exhibit 3.2).

Exhibit 3.2 illustrates the differences between direct and indirect costs and the different types of cost drivers for each. The direct costs—electric motor, packing material, and final inspection—are traced directly to the final cost objects, the dishwasher and washing machine. In contrast, the indirect costs cannot be traced directly to the products and instead are allocated to the products using a cost driver. The details of the allocation of indirect costs are not explained here but are covered in Chapters 4, 5, and 7.

Direct and Indirect Materials Costs

direct materials cost
The cost of the materials in the product and a reasonable allowance for scrap and defective units.

Direct materials cost includes the cost of materials in the product or other cost object (less purchase discounts but including freight and related charges) and usually a reasonable allowance for scrap and defective units (e.g., if a part is stamped from strip steel, the material lost in the stamping is ordinarily included as part of the product's direct materials).

On the other hand, the cost of materials used in manufacturing that are not part of the finished product is **indirect materials cost**. Examples include supplies used by manufacturing employees, such as rags and small tools, or materials required by the machines, such as lubricant. For convenience and economic feasibility (cost versus benefit), direct materials that are a very small part of materials cost, such as glue and nails, are often not traced to each product but are included instead in indirect materials.

indirect materials cost
The cost of materials used in manufacturing that are not part of the product or are not easily or economically traceable to the finished product; a component of total manufacturing overhead.

Direct and Indirect Labor Costs

direct labor cost
The labor used to manufacture the product or to provide the service.

Direct labor cost includes the labor used to manufacture the product or to provide the service plus some portion of non-value-added time that is normal and unavoidable, such as coffee breaks and personal time. Other types of nonproductive labor that are discretionary and planned, such as downtime, payroll taxes, fringe benefits (vacation, etc.), and training, might be treated as indirect labor.

indirect labor cost
Labor costs associated with production that are not considered direct labor. Examples include supervision, quality control, inspection, purchasing and receiving, and other labor-related manufacturing support costs; a component of total manufacturing overhead.

Indirect labor costs are labor costs associated with production, but are not direct labor. Examples include supervision, quality control, inspection, purchasing and receiving, materials handling, janitorial labor, downtime, training, and cleanup. Note that an element of labor can sometimes be both direct and indirect, depending on the cost object; for example, labor for the maintenance and repair of equipment might be direct to the manufacturing department where the equipment is located but indirect to each specific product manufactured in that department.

Although these examples of direct and indirect costs are from a manufacturing setting, the concepts also apply to service companies. For example, in a restaurant where the cost object is each meal served, the food and food preparation costs are direct costs for each meal served, but the costs of purchasing, handling, and storing food items are indirect costs. Similarly, in professional services firms such as law firms or accounting firms, the professional labor and materials costs for providing client services are direct costs, but the costs of research materials, nonprofessional support staff, and training are indirect costs. An example of cost drivers at a service company, Pennsylvania Blue Shield, is shown in Exhibit 3.3.

Other Indirect Costs

In addition to labor and materials, other types of indirect costs are necessary to manufacture the product or provide the service. They include the costs of facilities, the equipment used to manufacture the product or provide the service, and any other support equipment, such as that used for materials handling.

overhead
All the indirect costs commonly combined into a single cost pool; called factory overhead in a manufacturing firm.

All indirect costs—for indirect materials, indirect labor, and other indirect items—are commonly combined into a single cost pool called **overhead**. In a manufacturing firm, it is called **factory overhead**.

factory overhead
All the indirect manufacturing costs commonly combined into a single cost pool in a manufacturing firm.

The three types of costs—direct materials, direct labor, and factory overhead—are sometimes combined for simplicity and convenience. Direct materials and direct labor are sometimes considered together and called **prime costs**. Similarly, direct labor and overhead are often combined into a single amount called **conversion cost**. The labor component of total manufacturing costs for many firms that have highly automated operations is relatively low, and these firms often choose to place their strategic focus on materials and facilities/overhead costs by combining labor costs with overhead.

prime costs
The sum of direct materials and direct labor.

conversion cost
Direct labor and factory overhead combined into a single amount.

Cost Drivers and Cost Behavior

Cost drivers provide two important roles for the management accountant: (1) enabling the assignment of costs to cost objects, as we saw in the earlier discussion and in Exhibits 3.2 and 3.3, and (2) explaining cost behavior—that is, the change in the total amount of a cost associated with changes in the level of a cost driver. Generally, an increase in a cost driver will cause

EXHIBIT 3.3
Resource Costs, Cost Pools, Cost Objects, and Cost Drivers at Pennsylvania Blue Shield

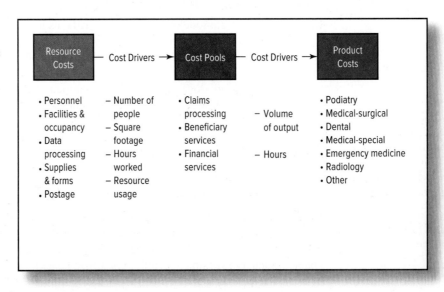

an increase in total cost. Occasionally, the relationship is inverse—for example, assume the cost driver is temperature, measured in degrees; then in the colder times of the year, increases in this cost driver will decrease total heating cost. Cost drivers can facilitate both cost assignment and cost behavior analysis at the same time. Most firms, especially those following the cost leadership strategy, use cost management to maintain or improve their competitive position. Cost management requires a good understanding of how the total cost of a cost object changes as the cost drivers change. In the remainder of this section, we focus on the cost behavior role.

The four types of cost drivers are activity-based, volume-based, structural, and executional. Activity-based cost drivers are developed at a detailed level of operations and are associated with a given manufacturing activity (or activity in providing a service), such as machine setup, product inspection, materials handling, or packaging. In contrast, volume-based cost drivers are developed at an aggregate level and relate to the amount produced or quantity of service provided. Structural and executional cost drivers involve strategic and operational decisions that affect the relationship between these cost drivers and total cost.

Activity-Based Cost Drivers

Activity-based cost drivers are those factors that cause or contribute to the changes in an activity. The drivers are identified by using activity analysis—a detailed description of the specific activities performed in the firm's operations. The activity analysis includes each step in manufacturing the product or in providing the service. For each activity, a cost driver is determined to explain how the costs incurred for that activity change. Example activities and possible cost drivers for a bank are illustrated in Exhibit 3.4. The total cost to the bank is affected by changes in the cost drivers for each activity.

The detailed description of the firm's activities helps the firm achieve its strategic objectives by enabling it to develop more accurate costs for its products and services. The activity analysis also helps improve operational and management control in the firm because performance at the detailed activity level can be monitored and evaluated, for example, by (1) identifying which activities are contributing value to the customer and which are not and (2) focusing attention on those activities that are most costly or that differ from expectations. Activity-based costing and activity-based management are explained in Chapter 5.

Volume-Based Cost Drivers

Many types of costs are volume-based, that is, the cost driver is the amount produced or quantity of service provided. Management accountants commonly call this volume, or volume of output, or simply output. Good examples of volume-based costs are direct materials cost and hourly direct labor cost—these costs increase with each unit of the volume of output. Note that the three cost drivers—the output of complete units, the quantity (in pounds, etc.) of direct materials, and the hours of direct labor—are all volume-based cost drivers and are proportional to each other.

The total of a volume-based cost increases at the rate of increase in volume, and over short ranges of output, the relationship is approximately linear. Over a very broad range of

EXHIBIT 3.4
Bank Activities and Cost Drivers

Activity	Possible Cost Drivers
Provide ATM service	Number of ATM transactions, number of customers
Provide cashier service	Number of customers
Open and close customer accounts	Number of accounts opened or closed
Advise customers on banking services	Number of customers
Prepare applications for new loans	Number of loan applications prepared
Process loan applications	Number of loan applications processed
Prepare approved loans and disburse funds	Number of loans approved
Mail customer statements	Number of accounts by customer type and size

EXHIBIT 3.5
Total Cost over a Wide Range of Output

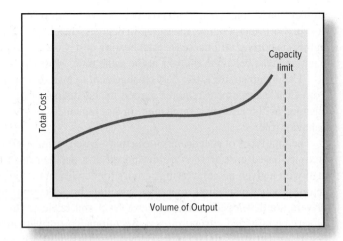

output, say, from output of zero up to plant capacity and beyond, the relationship between volume of output and cost tends to be nonlinear. As illustrated in Exhibit 3.5, at low values for the cost driver, costs increase at a decreasing rate, due in part to factors such as more efficient use of resources and higher productivity through learning. The pattern of increasing costs at a decreasing rate is often referred to as *increasing marginal productivity,* which means that the inputs are used more productively or more efficiently as manufacturing output increases.

At higher levels of the cost driver, costs begin to increase at an increasing rate, due in part to inefficiency associated with operating nearer to the limit of capacity because less-efficient resources are now being used, overtime may be required, and so on. This cost behavior at the higher levels of the cost driver is often referred to as the *law of diminishing marginal productivity.*

The nonlinear cost relationships depicted in Exhibit 3.5 present some difficulties in estimating costs and in calculating total costs because relatively simple, linear relationships cannot be used. Fortunately, we are often interested in only a relatively small range of activity for the cost driver. For example, we might know in a certain instance that a volume-based cost driver will fall somewhere between 3,500 and 3,600 units of product output. We observe that within this range, the total cost curve is approximately linear. The range of the cost driver in which the actual value of the cost driver is expected to fall and for which the relationship to total cost is assumed to be approximately linear is called the **relevant range**. Outside of this range, the relationship assumed may have to be altered.

relevant range
The range of the cost driver in which the actual value of the cost driver is expected to fall, and for which the relationship between the cost and the cost driver is assumed to be approximately linear.

EXHIBIT 3.6   Total Cost and the Relevant Range

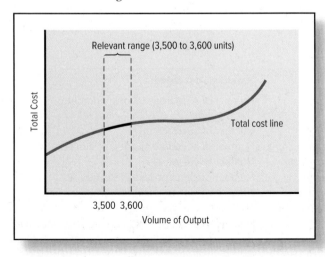

EXHIBIT 3.7   Linear Approximation for Actual Cost Behavior within the Relevant Range

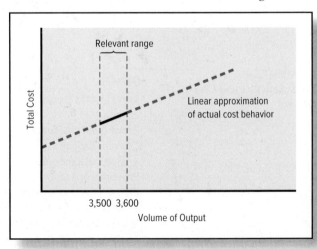

This simplification process is illustrated in Exhibit 3.6 and Exhibit 3.7. Exhibit 3.6 shows the curved actual total cost line and the relevant range of 3,500 to 3,600 units; Exhibit 3.7 shows the linear approximation of actual total cost; within the relevant range, the behavior of total cost approximates that shown in Exhibit 3.6. Note that the cost line above 3,600 and below 3,500 in Exhibit 3.7 is a dotted line to indicate that this portion of the line is not used to approximate total cost because it is outside the relevant range. Chapter 8 explains the methods management accountants use for estimating total cost.

Fixed and Variable Costs

variable cost
A cost that changes in total in response to changes in one or more cost drivers.

fixed cost
The portion of the total cost that, within the relevant range, does not change with a change in the quantity of a designated cost driver.

Total cost is made up of variable costs and fixed costs. A **variable cost** is a cost that changes in total in response to changes in one or more cost drivers. While the cost driver can be activity-based or volume-based, typically management accountants in practice use the term *variable costs* in connection with volume-based cost drivers. A common example of variable costs is the cost of direct materials. In contrast, a **fixed cost** is that portion of the total cost that, within the relevant range, does not change with the volume of a designated cost driver. *Total* fixed costs and *unit* variable costs are expected to remain approximately constant within the relevant range. Fixed cost is illustrated as the horizontal dashed line at $3,000 in Exhibit 3.8. Variable cost is $1 per unit, total cost is the upward-sloping line, and total variable cost is the difference between total cost and fixed cost. Total cost of $6,500 at 3,500 units is made up of fixed cost ($3,000) plus total variable cost (3,500 × $1 − $3,500); similarly, total cost at 3,600 units is $6,600 ($3,000 fixed cost plus 3,600 × $1 − $3,600 variable cost).

Fixed costs include many indirect costs, especially facility costs (depreciation, rent, insurance, taxes on the plant building), production supervisors' salaries, and other manufacturing

EXHIBIT 3.8
Total Cost, Total Variable Cost, and Fixed Cost

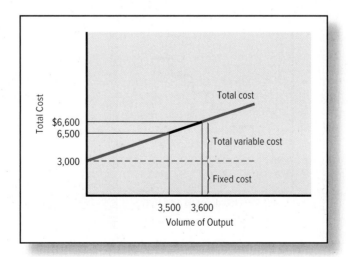

support costs that do not change with the number of units produced. However, some indirect costs that are not traceable to a cost object are nevertheless variable because they change with the number of units produced. An example is lubricant for machines. The term **mixed cost** is used to refer to total cost that, within the relevant range, includes costs for both variable and fixed components, as illustrated by the total cost line in Exhibit 3.8.

mixed cost
A cost that, within the relevant range, includes both variable and fixed cost components.

The determination of whether a cost is variable depends on the nature of the cost object. In manufacturing firms, the cost object is typically the product. In service firms, however, the cost object is often difficult to define because the service can have a number of qualitative as well as quantitative dimensions. Let's develop cost objects for one type of service firm, a hospital, which could use a number of measures of output including the number of patients served, the number successfully treated, and so on. However, a common approach in hospitals is to use the number of patient-days because this measure most closely matches the way the hospital incurs costs.

It has sometimes been said that all costs are variable in the long run; that is, with enough time, any cost can be changed. While it is true that many fixed costs do change over time (e.g., the cost of rent might increase from year to year), that does not mean these costs are variable. A variable cost is a cost for which *total costs change in proportion with changes in the volume of output.* Fixed costs are defined for a period of time rather than in relation to volume of output, and it is assumed that fixed costs will not change during this period of time, which is usually taken to be a year. For example, rent is a fixed cost that is normally the same amount *per year* and does not vary with volume. Strategically, especially for a cost leader type of firm, the important point is that both fixed and variable costs can be managed, but variable costs are managed in the very short term, as each unit is produced, while fixed costs are managed over a period of time. Some fixed costs cannot be changed for a relatively long period of time (e.g., depreciation on the factory building), while others can be changed more quickly (e.g., equipment with a one-year lease).

To summarize, when we want to understand the cost behavior of a certain cost object, we have to consider the following three questions: (1) What is the cost driver (or cost drivers if there are two or more) for this cost object? (2) What is the relevant range of the cost driver for which we are developing the cost estimate? (3) What time horizon (usually one year) are we using for fixed costs?

Step Costs

step cost
A cost that varies with the cost driver, but in discrete steps within the relevant range; also called *semi-fixed cost.*

A cost is said to be a **step cost** when it varies with the cost driver within the relevant range, but does so in steps, as shown in Exhibit 3.9. Step costs are characteristic of certain clerical tasks, such as order filling and claims processing. For example, if a warehouse clerk can fill 100 orders in a day, 10 clerks will be needed to process approximately 1,000 orders; as demand exceeds 1,000 orders, an 11th clerk must be added. The steps correspond to specific levels of the cost driver for which an additional clerk is required; in

EXHIBIT 3.9
A Step Cost

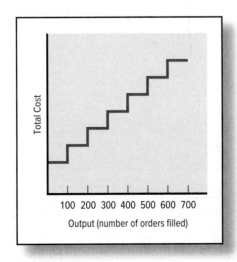

EXHIBIT 3.10
Illustration of Fixed Cost, Variable Cost, and Total Cost per Unit

	Fixed Cost		Variable Cost		Total Cost	
Units of output	10,000	20,000	10,000	20,000	10,000	20,000
Per unit	$10	$5	$8	$8	$18	$13
Total	$100,000	$100,000	$80,000	$160,000	$180,000	$260,000

EXHIBIT 3.11
Average Variable Cost and Average Fixed Cost

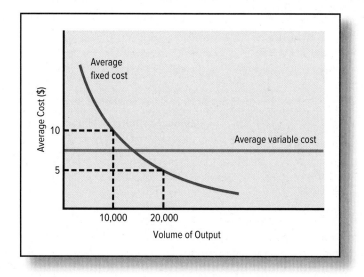

effect, each step corresponds to one additional clerk. The steps will be relatively narrow if clerks are added for relatively small increases in the cost driver; the steps will be wider for large increases.

Unit Cost

unit cost
The total cost (materials, labor, and overhead) divided by the number of units of output.

average cost
The total cost of resources consumed (materials, labor, and overhead) divided by the units of output.

Unit cost (or average cost) is the total cost of resources consumed (materials, labor, and overhead) divided by the number of units of output. While average unit cost is a useful concept in setting prices and in evaluating product profitability, it can be subject to some misleading interpretations. To properly interpret total average unit cost, we must distinguish *unit variable* costs, which do not change as output changes, from *unit fixed costs,* which do change as output changes. See Exhibit 3.10. For example, an automobile driver's cost per mile is likely lower for a person who drives a car 20,000 miles/year than it is for a person who drives a car only 5,000 miles/year because the fixed costs for the person driving 20,000 miles are spread over more miles. An increase in volume does not increase total cost by the amount of the increase in volume multiplied by total unit cost. Rather, total cost increases by the increase in volume multiplied by the unit variable cost. These relationships are illustrated graphically in Exhibit 3.11.

Capacity vs. Usage of Costs

It is important to distinguish between costs that provide capacity *for* operations (e.g., plant building and equipment) and costs that are consumed *during* operations (e.g., direct materials). The former are fixed costs, while the latter are variable costs. In practice, the management accountant uses care in making the distinctions because sometimes fixed capacity-type costs are treated as variable costs. For example, compare the cost of two types of direct labor employees who work in the assembly of a product—one is a salaried worker who is paid by the month, and another is a worker paid by the hour. The former is a fixed cost of capacity, while the latter is a variable cost. Both workers might be direct labor because they work in product assembly, but if volume of output falls and the salaried worker is idle, the total cost of that worker's labor does not change, while the total cost of labor would fall for a wage worker who has fewer hours. On the other hand, effective managers try to schedule production and

In mid-2019 China placed a tariff on U.S. soybeans. China buys more soybeans than any other country on Earth, and a large portion of U.S. soybeans had been sold to China. Now those farmers are having a tougher time selling their crop. While finding other markets is an option, the cost of production is important to know when considering what price needs to be charged. The following data provide the cost of soybean production in Illinois, which is in the U.S. heartland. This type of data is used to analyze the cost competitiveness of soybean production in the U.S.

Required

1. What can you learn from the information below about the cost of the U.S. soybean production?

2. Critically evaluate the cost information.

Source: http://corn.agronomy.wisc.edu/AA/A025.aspx, accessed August 8, 2019; https://www.usatoday.com/story/money/2019/05/30/tariffs-pause-chinas-purchases-american-soybeans-report-says/1284336001/, accessed August 9, 2019. (Refer to Comments on Cost Management in Action at the end of the chapter.)

Cost per Acre and per Bushel of Soybeans			
	Illinois Northern	Illinois Central	Illinios Southern
Variable costs (per acre)			
Seed	$ 66	$ 63	$ 64
Fertilizers	32	37	40
Pesticides	36	46	50
Drying operations	0	1	0
Fuel, lube, and electricity	69	57	68
Total variable costs	203	204	222
Overhead costs (per acre)			
Hired labor	$ 43	$ 51	59
Buildings	11	13	14
Storage	4	5	4
Machine depreciation	54	53	68
Nonland interest	43	43	46
Farm overhead	47	45	51
Total fixed costs	202	210	242
Total production cost (per acre)	**$ 405**	**$ 414**	**$ 464**
Total cost per bushel			
Average yield per acre	67	65	59
Variable costs	$ 3.03	$ 3.14	$ 3.76
Fixed costs	3.01	3.23	4.10
Total costs per bushel	**$ 6.04**	**$ 6.37**	**$ 7.86**

labor carefully by using part-time help and by other means so that no workers are idle; then, all assembly work can be considered a direct and variable cost. When idle time is present, some management accountants measure the cost of the unused capacity. Note that the cost of unused capacity would potentially apply to many types of fixed costs.

Structural and Executional Cost Drivers

Structural and executional cost drivers are used to facilitate strategic decision making. **Structural cost drivers** are strategic in nature because they involve decisions that have long-term effects on the firm's total costs. Here are four examples of decisions involving structural cost drivers.

structural cost drivers
Strategic plans and decisions that have a long-term effect with regard to issues such as scale, experience, technology, and complexity.

1. **Scale.** Larger firms have lower overall costs as a result of economies of scale. For example, a retail firm such as Walmart or Target must determine how many new stores to open in a given year to achieve its strategic objectives and compete effectively as a retailer.

2. **Experience.** Firms having employees with greater manufacturing and sales experience will likely have lower development, manufacturing, and distribution costs. For example, a manufacturer such as Hewlett-Packard uses existing manufacturing methods as much as possible for new products to reduce the time and cost necessary for workers to become proficient at manufacturing the new product.

REAL-WORLD FOCUS   Cost Behavior Is Not Just a Business Concept

PERSONAL EXPENSES EXHIBIT COST BEHAVIOR

Cost behavior is a part of everyday life. If, for example, you own a car, you probably pay an annual fee for your registration, which is fixed for the year because it does not change based on the miles you expect to drive. However, you expect to may more for gas the more miles you drive, making it a variable cost. Utilities are another example. The table below shows the data that one of the authors pulled from six recent electric bills.

Kilowatts Used	Charge
109	$ 18.82
117	$ 19.55
132	$ 21.42
155	$ 23.82
190	$ 27.75
280	$ 35.33
297	$ 37.81

If you plot the data, you see there is both a fixed and a variable component. This same type of analysis could be used for commuting costs, and other aspects of your daily life.

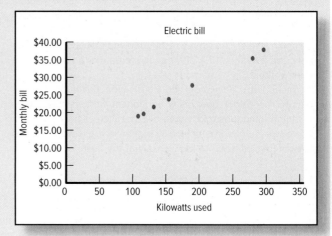

3. **Technology.** New technologies can reduce design, manufacturing, distribution, and customer service costs significantly. For example, manufacturers such as Procter & Gamble use computer technology to monitor the quantities of their products that their customers (typically, large retailers) have on hand so that they can promptly restock these products as needed.

4. **Complexity.** How many different products does the firm have? As noted in the opening discussion regarding Procter & Gamble, firms with many products have higher costs of scheduling and managing the production process, as well as the upstream costs of product development and the downstream costs of distribution and service. To further illustrate the focus on reduced complexity, in 2014 P&G indicated it would drop more than half its brands.

Strategic analyses using structural cost drivers help the firm improve its competitive position. These analyses include value-chain analysis and activity-based management. Value-chain analysis can help the firm assess the long-term consequences of its current or planned commitment to a structural cost driver. For example, the growth in size and capability of parts manufacturers for automakers should cause the automakers to reassess whether they should outsource the manufacture of certain parts that they are currently manufacturing. Activity-based management is covered in Chapter 5.

executional cost drivers

Factors that the firm can manage in the short term to reduce costs such as workforce involvement, design of the production process, and supplier relationships.

Executional cost drivers are factors the firm can manage in short-term, operational decision making to reduce costs. Here are three examples of executional cost drivers:

1. **Workforce empowerment.** Are the employees dedicated to continual improvement and quality? This workforce commitment will lower costs. Firms with strong employee relationships, such as Federal Express, can reduce operating costs significantly.

2. **Design of the production process.** Is the production process efficient? Speeding up the flow of product through the firm can reduce costs. Innovators in manufacturing technology, such as Hewlett-Packard and General Electric, can reduce manufacturing costs significantly.

3. **Supplier relationships.** Can the cost, quality, or delivery of materials and purchased parts be improved to reduce overall costs? Walmart and Toyota, among other firms, maintain a low-cost advantage partially through agreements with their suppliers to provide products or parts that meet the companies' explicit requirements as to their quality, timeliness of delivery, and other features.

REAL-WORLD FOCUS   The Changing Structure of Labor
Costs in a Gig Economy

Evidence from EY's Contingent Workforce Study shows that organizations are using contingent workers to bolster their capabilities and increase flexibility by hiring temp workers instead of permanent employees. These contingent workers help employers control labor costs and respond to the peaks and troughs in demand that come with seasonal trends. How common is this? The survey results showed that U.S. employers have, on average, 17% of their workforce made up of contingent workers.

Technology advances and automation have led companies to reconsider how many permanent workers they need, meaning temp jobs (gigs) have become increasingly common. Of course, turnover is obviously higher with gig workers, and the companies need to look closely at the costs of hiring and training a constant inflow of gig workers. Cost issues aside, companies must also consider whether contingent workers are as motivated as permanent employees. The survey responses indicated that 65% of the respondents would work differently if they were a permanent employee, and 20% of those said they would work longer hours. And do not forget, when a gig worker completes a task, his or her knowledge and experience leave, and organizations may be losing valuable institutional knowledge.

Source: "How the Gig Economy Is Changing the Workforce," https://www.ey.com/en_gl/tax/how-the-gig-economy-is-changing-the-workforce, accessed August 9, 2019; Christopher Mims, "In a Tight Labor Market, Gig Workers Get Harder to Please; Companies Like Uber, Lyft, Postmates and Instacart Could Run Out of Manpower as High Turnover Plagues the Side-Hustle Economy," *The Wall Street Journal (Online)*, May 4, 2019.

Plant managers study executional cost drivers to find ways to reduce costs. Such studies are done as a part of operational-level control, which is covered in Part Three of the text.

The Five Steps of Strategic Decision Making for Procter & Gamble

We can see how focus on cost drivers can affect P&G's success by considering the five steps of strategic decision making.

1. **Determine the strategic issues surrounding the problem.** P&G had spent many years expanding it brands. As economic conditions changed, top management needed to decide the best path to success in the future.

2. **Identify the alternative actions.** While growth may be desirable, it cannot come at the expense of profitability. Management had to decide whether to continue with a strategy that focused on expansion or pursue a path of putting increased emphasis on a much smaller level of brand offerings.

3. **Obtain information and conduct analyses of the alternatives.** The information indicated to management that the company might be able to cut billions of dollars from overhead and cost of goods sold. Management believed there would be additional savings in marketing costs.

4. **Based on strategy and analysis, choose and implement the desired alternative.** In 2014, former P&G CEO A. G. Lafley announced that the company would drop as many as 100 underperforming brands and narrow its focus to as few as 70 to 80 of its brands. In late 2018, the company announced it would change its management structure by reducing the number of business units from 10 down to six, thereby further reducing complexity.

5. **Provide an ongoing evaluation of the effectiveness of implementation in step 4.** In 2016, several of P&G's major brands still lagged behind the competition. Then-CEO David Taylor announced a new round of cost-cutting efforts, which included trying to squeeze cost savings out of its supply chain. As part of this cost-cutting, 3,000 jobs were cut globally in the fiscal year ended June 2018.[2]

---

[2] Sharon Terlep, "P&G Mystery: Its Cost-Cut Details Are Still Awaited," *The Wall Street Journal*, April 25, 2016, p. B3; Serena Ng, "P&G to Shed More Than Half Its Brands," *The Wall Street Journal*, August 1, 2014 (https://www.wsj.com/articles/procter-gamble-posts-higher-profit-on-cost-cutting-1406892304); Aisha Al-Muslim, "P&G Moves to Streamline Its Structure; CEO David Taylor Appoints Six Unit Chiefs with Oversight of Both Products and Sales," *The Wall Street Journal (Online)*, November 9, 2018.

Cost Concepts for Product and Service Costing

LO 3-3

Explain the cost concepts used in product and service costing.

Accurate information about the cost of products and services is important in each management function: strategic management, planning and decision making, management and operational control, and financial statement preparation. Cost accounting systems differ significantly between manufacturing firms that make products and merchandising firms that resell those products. Merchandising firms include both retailers, which sell the final product to the consumer, and wholesalers, which distribute the product to retailers. Service firms often have little or no inventory, so their costing systems are relatively simple. Costing systems are introduced here and covered in detail in the remaining chapters of Part One of the text. First, we have to define product and period costs.

Product Costs and Period Costs

cost of goods sold
The cost of the product transferred to the income statement when inventory is sold.

Product inventory for both manufacturing and merchandising firms is treated as an asset on their balance sheets. As long as the inventory has market value, it is considered an asset until the inventory is sold; then the cost of the inventory is transferred to the income statement as **cost of goods sold**. To understand product costs for a manufacturer, it is helpful to consider the value chain. The value chain of a manufacturer begins with the upstream activities of design, product development, and new product testing, and then moves to manufacturing, followed by the downstream activities of distribution, sales, and customer service. The costs of the upstream and downstream activities are *not* product costs.

product costs
Only the costs necessary to complete the product (direct materials, direct labor, and factory overhead).

Product costs for a manufacturing firm include *only* the costs necessary to complete the product at the manufacturing step in the value chain:

1. **Direct materials.** The materials used to manufacture the product, which become a physical part of it.
2. **Direct labor.** The labor used to manufacture the product.
3. **Factory overhead.** The indirect costs for materials, labor, and facilities used to support the manufacturing process.

Product costs for a merchandising firm include the cost to purchase the product plus the transportation costs paid by the retailer or wholesaler to get the product to the location from which it will be sold or distributed.

period costs
All nonproduct expenditures for managing the firm and selling the product; also referred to as *selling, general, and administrative (SG&A) expenses.*

All other costs for managing the firm and selling the product are not product costs. They are expensed in the period in which they are incurred; for that reason, they are also called **period costs**. Period costs (nonproduct costs) include the selling, general, and administrative costs that are necessary for the management of the company but are *not* involved directly or indirectly in the manufacturing process (or, for a retailer, in the purchase of the products for resale). Advertising costs, research and development costs, data processing costs, and executive and staff salaries are good examples of period costs. In a manufacturing or a merchandising firm, period costs are also sometimes referred to as *operating expenses* or *selling and administrative expenses.* In a service firm, these costs are often referred to as *operating*

EXHIBIT 3.12
Furniture Manufacturing Costs: Variable/Fixed, Direct/ Indirect, and Product/Period Costs

The following case illustration of a furniture manufacturer is used to provide examples of costs for each cost concept: variable/fixed, direct/indirect, and product/period. The furniture manufacturer has organized its manufacturing by product line: dining table sets, upholstered chairs, sofas, bedroom furniture, end tables, and outdoor furniture. Each product line has its own manufacturing team, although much of the equipment in the plant is shared among product lines (e.g., multiple product lines use the table saws). The company owns its retail sales outlets, each of which offers all of the firm's products. The cost object in this illustration is the *product line* called dining table sets (*not* each dining set produced).

Variable/Fixed, Direct/Indirect, and Product/Period Costs
for the Product Line, Dining Table Sets

	Product Cost		Period (Nonproduct) Cost
	Direct	**Indirect**	
Variable	Wood and fabric	Power for table saws	Sales commissions
Fixed	Salary of manufacturing supervisor for dining table sets product line	Depreciation on table saws used for all product lines	Insurance and depreciation on company-owned sales outlets

Note: This illustration is based on the *cost object,* the *product line* for dining table sets. The examples would not change if we had chosen instead to have the cost object be each *individual manufactured set* except that the manufacturing supervisor's salary would no longer be a direct fixed product cost. It would become an *indirect* fixed product cost because the salary can be traced to the product line but not to each table set manufactured.

expenses. Note that period costs may also include certain nonoperating expenses like interest. Exhibit 3.12 summarizes the previous sections with an illustration showing examples of variable and fixed, direct and indirect, and product and period costs for a furniture manufacturer. It is important to note that the three classification schemes are independent of each other. For example, knowing that a cost is variable does not tell you anything about whether it is a direct or indirect cost or whether it is a period or product cost.

Manufacturing and Merchandising Costing

LO 3-4

Demonstrate how costs flow through the accounts and prepare and interpret an income statement for both a manufacturing and a merchandising company.

The cost flows in manufacturing, retail, and service firms are illustrated in Exhibits 3.13, 3.14, 3.15A, and 3.15B. The left-hand side of Exhibit 3.13 presents a graphic representation of the flow of costs for a manufacturing company. The first step of the manufacturing process is to purchase materials. The second step involves adding the three cost elements—materials used, labor, and overhead—to work-in-process. In the third step, as production is completed, the production costs that have been accumulating in the Work-in-Process Inventory account are transferred to the Finished Goods Inventory account and from there to the Cost of Goods Sold account when the products are sold.

In the merchandising company, shown on the right-hand side of Exhibit 3.13, the process is somewhat simpler. The merchandising company purchases merchandise and places the merchandise in the Merchandise Inventory account. When sold, it is transferred to the Cost of Goods Sold account. The merchandising and manufacturing companies in Exhibit 3.13 are shown side by side to emphasize the difference that the merchandising company purchases inventory while the manufacturing company manufactures inventory using materials, labor, and overhead.

Manufacturing companies use three inventory accounts: (1) **Materials Inventory**, which contains the cost of the supply of materials to be used in the manufacturing process; (2) **Work-in-Process Inventory**, which contains all costs put into the manufacture of products that are started but not complete at the financial statement date; and (3) **Finished Goods Inventory**, which contains the cost of goods that are ready for sale. Each account has its own beginning and ending inventory balance.

An inventory formula relates the inventory accounts, as follows:

$$\text{Beginning inventory} + \text{Cost added} = \text{Cost transferred out} + \text{Ending inventory}$$

Materials Inventory
Cost of the supply of materials used in the manufacturing process or to provide the service.

Work-in-Process Inventory
An inventory account that contains all costs put into the manufacture of products that are started but not complete at the financial statement date.

Finished Goods Inventory
The cost of goods that are ready for sale.

EXHIBIT 3.13
Cost Flows in Manufacturing and Merchandising Firms
Note: In Chapter 4 there will be a more detailed discussion of the cost flows, including the possibility of some materials and labor being treated as part of overhead.

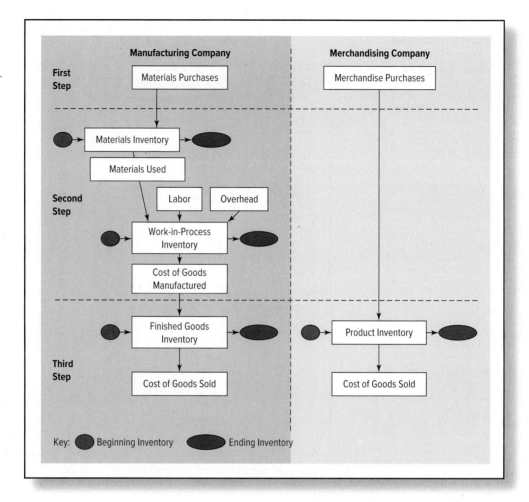

The terms *cost added* and *cost transferred out* have different meanings, depending on which inventory account is being considered:

Inventory Account	Cost Added	Cost Transferred Out
Materials Inventory	Purchase of materials	Cost of materials used in production
Work-in-Process Inventory	1. Cost of direct materials used 2. Direct labor cost 3. Overhead cost	Cost of goods manufactured
Finished Goods Inventory	Cost of goods manufactured	Cost of goods sold

The inventory formula is a useful concept to show how direct materials, direct labor, and overhead costs flow into Work-in-Process Inventory, then into Finished Goods Inventory, and finally into Cost of Goods Sold. Exhibit 3.14 illustrates the effects of the cost flows on the accounts involved when the manufacturing company converts materials into finished products and then sells them and when the merchandising company sells merchandise inventory.

The illustration in Exhibit 3.14 shows the accounts for a manufacturing company that begins the period with $10 in Materials Inventory, $10 in Work-in-Process Inventory, and $20 in Finished Goods Inventory. During the period, it purchases $70 of direct materials, uses $75 of direct materials and $80 of direct labor, and spends $100 for factory overhead. The sum of direct materials used, direct labor, and overhead ($255 − $75 + $80 + $100) is called **total manufacturing cost** for the period. Also during the period, $215 of goods are completed and transferred from the Work-in-Process Inventory account to the Finished Goods Inventory account, and $210 of goods are sold. These events leave ending inventories of $5 in the Materials Inventory account,

total manufacturing cost
The sum of materials used, labor, and overhead for the period.

EXHIBIT 3.14
Account Relationships for Manufacturing and Merchandising Companies

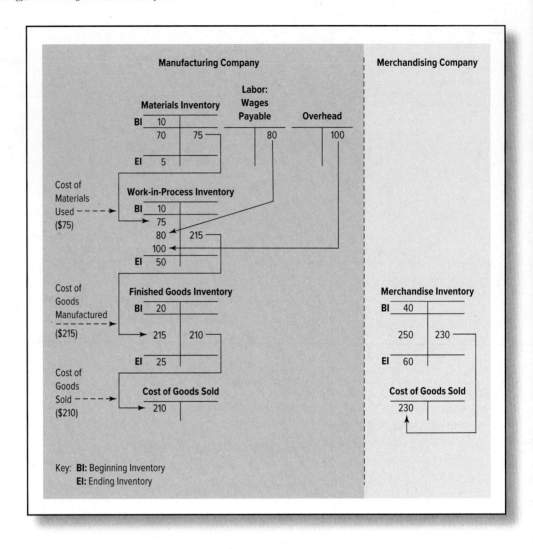

$50 in the Work-in-Process Inventory account, and $25 in the Finished Goods Inventory account. The merchandising company purchased merchandise of $250 and had cost of sales of $230, and its Merchandise Inventory account increases from $40 to $60.

Exhibit 3.15A shows how the accounting relationships are represented in the income statements for the two types of companies. Note that the manufacturing company requires a two-part calculation for cost of goods sold. The first part combines the cost flows affecting the Work-in-Process Inventory account to determine the amount of **cost of goods manufactured**, that is, the cost of the goods finished and transferred out of the Work-in-Process Inventory account during a specified period. The second part combines the cost flows for the Finished Goods Inventory account to determine the amount of the cost of the goods sold and operating income, assuming $50 of selling and administrative expense for the manufacturing firm and $40 of operating expense for the merchandising firm. Operating expenses for a merchandising company include all the nonproduct costs—facilities cost, advertising, staffing, and so on.

Exhibit 3.15B shows the relatively simple income statement for a service firm with $300 in sales, $10 in materials costs, $90 in labor costs, and $100 in other operating expenses for an operating income of $100. Exhibit 3.15 provides an introduction to cost flows in the three types of firms. The process is shown in greater detail in Chapter 4.

cost of goods manufactured
The cost of goods that were finished and transferred out of the Work-in-Process Inventory account during a given period.

Attributes of Cost Information

Accuracy

The experienced decision maker does not use accounting information without considering the potential for inaccuracy. Inaccurate data can mislead the user, resulting in potentially costly mistakes. A primary way to ensure accurate data for decision making is to design and monitor

EXHIBIT 3.15A Income Statements for Manufacturing and Merchandising Companies

MANUFACTURING INC.		
Statement of Cost of Goods Manufactured		
For the Year Ended December 31, 2022		
Materials		
Beginning Materials Inventory	$10	
Materials Purchases	70	
Materials Available	80	
Less: Ending Materials Inventory	5	
Materials Used		$ 75
Direct Labor		80
Factory Overhead		100
Total Manufacturing Costs to account for		255
Add: Beginning Work-in-Process Inventory		10
Total Manufacturing Costs		265
Less: Ending Work-in-Process Inventory		50
Cost of Goods Manufactured		$215

(No need for a Cost of Goods Manufactured Statement for Merchandising Inc.)

MANUFACTURING INC.		
Income Statement for the Year Ended December 31, 2022		
Sales		$300
Cost of Goods Sold		
Beginning Finished Goods Inventory	$ 20	
Cost of Goods Manufactured	215	
Cost of Goods Available for Sale	235	
Less: Ending Finished Goods Inventory	25	210
Gross Margin		90
Selling and Administrative Expenses		50
Operating Income		$ 40

MERCHANDISING INC.		
Income Statement for the Year Ended December 31, 2022		
Sales		$300
Cost of Goods Sold		
Beginning Merchandise Inventory	$40	
Purchases	250	
Cost of Goods Available for Sale	290	
Less: Ending Merchandise Inventory	60	230
Gross Margin		$ 70
Operating Expenses		40
Operating Income		$ 30

EXHIBIT 3.15B
Income Statement
for a Service Firm

SERVICE INC.		
Income Statement		
For the Year Ended December 31, 2022		
Sales		$300
Operating Expenses		
Materials	$ 10	
Labor	90	
Other Operating Expenses	100	200
Operating Income		$100

internal accounting controls
A set of policies and procedures that restrict and guide activities in the processing of financial data with the objective of preventing or detecting errors and fraudulent acts.

an effective system of internal accounting controls. The system of **internal accounting controls** is a set of policies and procedures that restrict and guide activities in the processing of financial data with the objective of preventing or detecting errors and fraud. The emphasis on effective internal controls has increased significantly in recent years in response to Securities and Exchange Commission (SEC) requirements imposed by the Sarbanes–Oxley Act of 2002.

Timeliness

Cost management information must be available to the decision maker in a timely manner to facilitate effective decision making. The cost of delay can be significant in many decisions, such as in filling rush orders that may be lost if the necessary information is not timely. The cost of identifying quality defects early in a manufacturing process can be far less than the cost of resources wasted when a defect is detected later in the process.

Cost and Value of Cost Management Information

Thinking of cost management information as having a certain cost and value emphasizes that the management accountant is an information specialist, very much like other financial professionals, such as tax advisers, financial planners, and consultants. The management accountant provides an information service that has both a preparation cost and a value to the user. The preparation costs for cost management information should be controlled, as should any other service provided within the firm. These preparation costs are likely influenced by the desired accuracy, timeliness, and level of aggregation; when increased accuracy, timeliness, and detail are desired, the preparation costs are higher.

perpetual inventory system
A method that updates the finished goods inventory account for each purchase or sales transaction.

periodic inventory system
A method that involves a count of inventory at the end of each accounting period to determine the ending balance in inventory.

Periodic and Perpetual Inventory Systems

Most large retailers and manufacturers use a point-of-sale or transaction-based computer system for recording sales and changes in inventory. In these systems, each sale updates the amount in the inventory account, so that the inventory balance is always current. This is called the **perpetual inventory system**. Another method, called the **periodic inventory system**, involves a count of inventory at the end of each accounting period to determine the ending balance in inventory. Often a company will use both methods. The perpetual system keeps the accounts current and the periodic system detects the amount of lost, stolen, obsolete, or damaged inventory that must be written off at the end of the accounting period. Because our focus in this text is on the flow of costs, it is not necessary to know whether the system is a periodic or perpetual system.

Summary

There are several important concepts for the management accountant that Chapter 3 presents in two groups: (1) cost objects, cost drivers, cost pools, and cost assignment and (2) product and service costing for the preparation of financial statements.

The first group of concepts includes the four types of cost drivers: activity-based, volume-based, structural, and executional. Activity-based cost drivers are at the detail level of operations: equipment setup, materials handling, and clerical or other tasks. In contrast, volume-based cost drivers are at the aggregate level: usually the number of units produced. Structural cost drivers involve plans and decisions having long-term effects; executional cost drivers have short-term effects.

The most important volume-based concepts are variable costs, which change according to a change in the level of output, and fixed costs, which do not. Direct costs are defined as costs that can be conveniently and easily traced directly to a cost object, in contrast to indirect costs, which cannot. Also, the classification of a cost within each of the cost concepts is independent of each other, which means direct costs can be either fixed or variable, and the same is true for indirect costs.

The important concepts in product costing are product costs, which are the costs of direct materials, direct labor, and indirect manufacturing (called *overhead*) required for the product and production process. Nonproduct costs (also called *period costs*) are the selling, administrative, and other costs not involved in manufacturing. The inventory formula is used to determine the cost of materials used in production, the cost of goods manufactured, and the cost of goods sold for a given period.

Key Terms

allocation bases, *78*	direct materials cost, *79*	period costs, *89*
average cost, *85*	executional cost drivers, *87*	periodic inventory system, *94*
conversion cost, *80*	factory overhead, *80*	perpetual inventory system, *94*
cost, *77*	Finished Goods Inventory, *90*	prime costs, *80*
cost allocation, *78*	fixed cost, *83*	product costs, *89*
cost assignment, *78*	indirect cost, *78*	relevant range, *82*
cost driver, *77*	indirect labor cost, *80*	step cost, *84*
cost object, *77*	indirect materials cost, *79*	structural cost drivers, *86*
cost of goods manufactured, *92*	internal accounting	total manufacturing cost, *91*
cost of goods sold, *89*	controls, *93*	unit cost, *85*
cost pools, *77*	Materials Inventory, *90*	value stream, *77*
direct cost, *78*	mixed cost, *84*	variable cost, *83*
direct labor cost, *79*	overhead, *80*	Work-in-Process Inventory, *90*

Comments on Cost Management in Action

Cost per Bushel of Soybeans in the United States

The data are taken from a 2018 survey of farmers in Illinios with more than 500 acres of productive soil. The data can be viewed at the following website: **https://www.agprofessional.com/article/2018-corn-input-cost-bushel-lowest-10-years-2019-jump**

1. Of particular value here is that the report distinguishes variable and allocated fixed costs, which is not common in reports of this type. The distinction gives the reader an opportunity to better understand how production costs behave within this sector of the farming industry and across farmers growing the same crops. A wide number of observations are possible. In particular, we see significant difference in fertilizer and pesticide costs, but not much difference in the cost of seed. Do the differences in cost of pesticides and fertilizer indicate that some farmers have superior land use practices? Maybe there are differences in the quality of the soil, or, perhaps, there is some other explanation.

   While the figures clearly show that the southern region has a total cost per acre disadvantage compared to the other two regions, the cost per bushel is significantly higher due to lower yield per acre. Again, we would have to investigate further to understand why this is the case. Maybe the higher cost per acre for fertilizer and pesticide in that region holds a clue to the reason for lower yield.

2. A number of potential questions arise about the way the data have been collected and presented. Here are some ideas to start with. First, what about the size of the farm? Should this affect the allocated fixed cost-per-acre calculations as fixed costs are driven in part by the number of acres farmed, but also by the fact that certain pieces of equipment are necessary for a farm of any size? Farm equipment might be more of a step cost than a fixed cost. If this is the case, the relatively lower equipment cost per acre might simply be due to the fact that farm sizes are larger in the north and central regions than in the southern region.

Self-Study Problem

(For answers, please see Solution.)

The following data pertain to Spartan Products Company:

Sales revenue	$1,000,000
Materials Inventory, Jan. 1	20,000
Direct labor—wages	350,000
Depreciation expense—plant and equipment	80,000
Indirect labor—wages	5,000
Heat, light, and power—plant	12,000
Supervisor's salary—plant	40,000
Finished Goods Inventory, Jan. 1	35,000
Work-in-Process Inventory, Dec. 31	25,000
Supplies—administrative office	6,000
Property taxes—plant	13,000
Finished Goods Inventory, Dec. 31	40,000
Materials Inventory, Dec. 31	30,000
Sales representatives' salaries	190,000
Work-in-Process Inventory, Jan. 1	35,000
Materials purchases	100,000
Supplies—plant	4,000
Depreciation—administrative office	30,000

Required   Prepare a statement of cost of goods manufactured and an income statement for Spartan Products Company for the year ended December 31, similar to the one in Exhibit 3.15A.

The Student Resources section of Connect includes video tutorials for the Self-Study Problems.

Questions

3-1   What is the difference between cost allocation and cost assignment?

3-2   Distinguish between direct and indirect costs and give several examples of each.

3-3   Are all direct costs variable? Explain.

3-4   Are all fixed costs indirect? Explain.

3-5   Define *cost driver*.

3-6   What is the difference between variable and fixed costs?

3-7   Explain step costs and give an example.

3-8   Define *relevant range* and explain its use.

3-9   What are conversion costs? What are prime costs?

3-10 What does the term *unit cost* mean?

3-11 Why might the term *average cost* be misleading?

3-12 How do total variable costs, total fixed costs, average variable costs, and average fixed costs react to changes in the cost driver?

3-13 Distinguish between product costs and period costs.

3-14 Explain the difference between cost of goods sold and cost of goods manufactured.

3-15 What are the three types of inventory in a manufacturing firm?

3-16 Cost management information should be timely and accurate. Which of these attributes is most important? Why?

3-17 Provide an example of an executional cost driver.

3-18 Provide an example of a structural cost driver.

3-19 Provide an example of an indirect materials cost.

3-20 Provide an example of an indirect labor cost.

Brief Exercises

[LO 3-2]   3-21 Direct materials are

	Manufacturing Cost	Prime Cost	Conversion Cost
a.	Yes	Yes	Yes
b.	No	Yes	No
c.	Yes	Yes	No
d.	No	No	No

[LO 3-2]   3-22 Which of the following costs would be included in manufacturing overhead for a computer manufacturer?
   a. The cost of the USB port hardware
   b. The wages paid to hardware assemblers
   c. The cost of the circuit boards
   d. Depreciation on assembly machinery

[LO 3-2]   3-23 Which of the following is true regarding period and product costs?
   a. Factory lease is a period cost, and sales commissions are a product cost.
   b. Factory lease is a product cost, and sales commissions are a product cost.
   c. Factory lease is a period cost, and sales commissions are a period cost.
   d. Factory lease is a product cost, and sales commissions are a period cost.

[LO 3-2]   3-24 Which of the following statements is *incorrect* regarding manufacturing overhead?
   a. Manufacturing overhead is an indirect cost to units or products.
   b. Manufacturing overhead includes both fixed and variable costs.
   c. Actual overhead costs are used in the cost accounting process.
   d. Actual overhead costs tend to remain relatively constant over various output levels.

[LO 3-2]   3-25 Direct labor costs are
   a. nonmanufacturing costs.
   b. period costs.
   c. conversion costs.
   d. overhead costs.

[LO 3-4]   3-26 Womble Inc. has beginning inventory of $200 and an ending inventory of $400 for a given period in which it purchased $13,400 worth of materials. What is the dollar amount of materials used in this period?

[LO 3-4]   3-27 Jordan Sports Inc. has labor costs and overhead totaling $2.6 million during a given period. The company purchased $10.5 million of materials during the period and used $10 million of this amount. What is the amount of total manufacturing cost for the period?

[LO 3-4]   3-28 Lucas Diving Supplies Company, in its first year of business, had labor costs of $66,000, overhead costs of $98,000, materials purchases of $22,000, and ending Materials and Work-in-Process Inventories of $1,000 and $2,000, respectively. What is the amount of cost of goods manufactured in the first year of operations?

[LO 3-4] 3-29 If a merchandising company has a beginning inventory of $400,000 and an ending inventory of $200,000, and the company purchased $1,600,000 of inventory during the month, what is the company's cost of goods sold?

[LO 3-4] 3-30 The Walden Manufacturing Corp. has office support salaries of $4,000, factory supplies of $1,000, indirect labor of $6,000, direct materials of $16,000, advertising expense of $2,500, office expense of $14,000, and direct labor of $20,000. What is the total period cost?

Exercises

[LO 3-1] 3-31 **Fares and Fees in the Airline Industry** Navigating the various websites for low fares, avoiding fees for checked bags and priority seating, and finding the right flight schedule can be a real challenge for the average airline passenger. The complexity of options and sources for purchasing a ticket have expanded significantly in recent years. And the outlook for the future is far more complex, as new search sites (Google, Hipmunk, etc.) become available and some airlines seek more control over where and how tickets on their flights are purchased. According to Forrester Research, an independent research company, the airlines want passengers to buy tickets based on value and not on low prices. They do not want passengers to comparison shop. One major airline even announced that it wanted to deliver fare information directly to customers and to bypass search systems such as Expedia or Travelocity.

Required
1. Explain why you think competition in the airline industry is a cost leadership or a differentiation type of competition.
2. Provide an example or two of how you think the complexity of fares and fees in the airline industry affects the sales and costs of the airlines.

[LO 3-1] 3-32 **Complexity of Operations and the Effect on Cost** In the mid-1990s, a large consumer goods manufacturer moved its customer-based department and specialty stores to mass merchandising in a variety of retail stores, large and small. The strategic change required it to increase significantly the complexity of its operations—the number of products, prices, discounts, patterns, colors, and sizes. After noticing the firm's expense beginning to rise, the company hired a consultant to study the firm's cost structure. The findings were as follows:

- As many as 10 different vendors provided certain purchased items.
- Of the firm's customers after the strategic shift, 98% were responsible for only 7% of total sales volume.
- The wide variety of prices, discounts, and promotional programs added complexity to the accounts receivable collection process because of increased disputes over pricing and customer balances.
- Seventy-five percent of the company sales involved products with five or more color combinations.
- Customer demands for fast delivery of new orders had caused a shift in manufacturing to smaller batch sizes and more frequent equipment setups. Thus, total setup-related costs increased.

Required What would you advise the company to do?

[LO 3-2, 3-3] 3-33 **Classification of Costs** The following are the costs incurred by a printing company:
1. Print machine setup costs
2. Cost of complexity due to the number and variety of products
3. Costs to train new printing staff in the use and safety features of the equipment
4. Ink
5. Customer service costs
6. Paper
7. Redesign of the print process to improve efficiency
8. Machine operation labor
9. Order taking
10. Purchasing and stocking paper and other supplies

Required
1. Identify the above costs as (a) activity-based costs, (b) volume-based costs, (c) structural costs, or (d) executional costs.
2. Identify each cost as either a product cost or a period cost.
3. Identify which, if any, of these costs has a potential harmful environmental impact.

[LO 3-2, 3-3]   3-34   **Classification of Costs**   The following costs were taken from the accounting records of the Barnwell Manufacturing Company:

1. State income taxes
2. Insurance on the manufacturing facilities
3. Supplies used in manufacturing
4. Wages for employees in the assembly department
5. Wages for employees who deliver the product to customers
6. Interest on notes payable
7. Materials used in the production process
8. Rent for the sales outlet in Sacramento
9. Electricity for all manufacturing equipment as a group
10. Depreciation expense on delivery trucks
11. Wages for the sales staff
12. Factory supervisors' salaries
13. Company president's salary
14. Advertising expense

Required   Classify each item as either a product cost or a period cost. Also, classify all product costs as direct or indirect, assuming that the cost object is each unit of product manufactured.

[LO 3-2, 3-3]   3-35   **Classification of Costs**   Following is a list of costs from Oakland Company, a furniture manufacturer:

1. Wood used in chairs
2. Salaries of inspectors
3. Lubricant used in machinery
4. Factory rent
5. Wages of assembly workers
6. Factory workers' compensation insurance
7. Sandpaper
8. Fabric used for upholstery
9. Property taxes on manufacturing plant
10. Depreciation on machinery

Required   Classify each cost as direct or indirect assuming that the cost object is each item manufactured. Also indicate whether each cost is a variable or fixed cost.

[LO 3-2]   3-36   **Classification of Costs**   The following is a list of costs from the accounting records of Sunshine Pool Management Inc. Each of Sunshine's 77 customers is a swim club. Sunshine maintains each customer's pool by providing lifeguards, supplies, cleaning, and repairs.

1. Lifesaving supplies
2. Salaries of Sunshine's managers
3. Pool chemicals
4. Sunshine's office rental expense
5. Wages of lifeguards
6. Workers' compensation insurance
7. Training for lifeguards
8. pH testing supplies
9. Office expense, including bookkeeping and clerical
10. Depreciation on cleaning and testing equipment

Required   Classify each item as direct or indirect assuming that the cost objects are each of the 77 swim clubs.

[LO 3-2]   3-37   **Activity Levels and Cost Drivers**   Zeller Manufacturing Company produces four lines of high-quality lighting fixtures in a single manufacturing plant. Products are built to specific customer specifications. All products are made-to-order. Management of the plant lists the following as the key activities at the plant:

1. Product design
2. Product testing

3. Developing marketing plan for new products

4. Purchasing, receiving, and inspecting materials for production

5. Manufacturing labor

6. Setups for machine

7. Product inspection, done for each product before packaging for shipment

8. Packaging and shipping

9. Sales calls for new orders from existing customers

10. Processing customer orders

11. Maintenance of plant and equipment

12. Plant security

Required Identify a cost object and a cost driver for each activity.

[LO 3-2] **3-38 Application of the Direct Cost Concept in the Fashion Industry** Jane Wilson is the production manager for a company that produces high-fashion designer clothing for women. The product is made in small batches that are presold to high-end retailers, based on specific orders. Jane manages the flow of small batches of product through the company's design/production shop in New York. The materials and labor for each batch are purchased and scheduled well in advance of the time of production. The materials are unique to the job, and the employees assigned to the job will work on it until the job is done. The company has found that dedicating specific employees to each batch improves employee satisfaction and, most important, product quality.

Required Apply what you have just learned about the direct cost concept and explain its specific application with regard to this unique firm.

[LO 3-2] **3-39 Manufacturing Direct Labor: Fixed or Variable?** To retain skilled employees instead of letting them go when demand falls, Lincoln Electric trains employees for other tasks in the company. The Cleveland-based manufacturer of welding and cutting parts has integrated the approach in all its operations so that it can guarantee employment for all employees who have been with the company for 3 or more years. This policy has worked for more than 60 years. Other companies such as Nestlé and Apex Precision Technology accomplish the same goal of keeping their employees as demand fluctuates by using part-time arrangements with the employees.

Required Discuss whether manufacturing labor should be considered a fixed or a variable cost at these companies.

[LO 3-2] **3-40 Average and Total Costs** The Accounting Club wants to have a party for its members. The cost of renting space is $1,500, and the cost of refreshments will be $15 per person.

Required

1. What is the total cost if 100 people attend? What is the average cost?

2. What is the total cost if 200 people attend? What is the average cost?

3. Explain why average total cost differs with changes in total attendance.

[LO 3-1, 3-2] **3-41 Classification of Costs** Jan Holliday Dance Studios is a chain of 45 wholly owned dance studios that offer private lessons in ballroom dancing. The studios are located in various cities throughout the southern and southeastern states. Holliday offers a set of 12 private lessons; students may pay for the lessons one at a time, but each student is required to enroll for at least a 12-lesson plan. The 20-, 40-, and 100-lesson plans offer savings. Each dance instructor is paid a small salary plus a commission based on the number of dance lessons provided.

Required

1. Holliday's owner is interested in a strategic analysis of the business. The owner wants to understand why overall profitability has declined slightly in the most recent year while other studios in the area seem to be doing well. What is the proper cost object to begin this analysis? Explain your choice.

2. For each of the following cost elements, indicate whether the cost should be classified as (a) direct, (b) indirect, (c) variable, and (d) fixed with respect to the cost object you selected in requirement 1. In some cases, two or more classifications may apply.

   1. Each dancing instructor's salary

   2. Manager's salary

   3. Music tapes used in instruction

   4. Utilities for the studio

   5. Part-time studio receptionist

6. Planning and development materials sent from the home office
7. Free lessons given by each studio as a promotion
8. Regional TV and radio advertisements placed several times a year

[LO 3-2]   3-42 **Relevant Range**   PhotoGraphicImages Inc. (PGI) is an international supplier of graphic and photo images that are used in the publishing business and by a variety of firms that need graphic images for their annual reports, sales brochures, and other documents. PGI purchases the rights to these images from other sources, including photographers, publishers, and graphic artists. PGI then pays the provider of the image a royalty based on the number of times the image will be used (e.g., the number of sales brochures that will be printed with that image). PGI operates in 16 countries, with small marketing and customer service offices located in each country. PGI's operating headquarters is located in Austin, Texas, where company management is located as well as a significant portion of the computer operations that are the backbone of the company's operations. Because of increased demand, PGI has just opened an operations center in Paris. All European- and UK-area business is now handled out of Paris, while the rest of the world's demand is handled out of Austin. The company foresees that it may be necessary to locate another operations center in China if Asian demand continues to grow.

The computer operations at each of the operating locations consist of both large and small computer servers where the images are stored, the company website is maintained, and the business records are kept. There is capacity at each location to increase the number of servers as demand increases, though the capacity for expansion is limited in the current facility in Austin.

Required
1. Assuming PGI's output volume is measured by the number of customer orders, provide some examples of the volume-based costs of this company.
2. How does the relevant range apply within this company?
3. How does the growth of PGI globally affect the firm's total costs (consider also foreign currency fluctuations)?

[LO 3-2]   3-43 **Fixed; Variable; Mixed Costs**   Adams Manufacturing's five manufacturing departments had the following operating and cost information for the two most recent months of activity:

	May	June
Units produced	10,000	20,000
Costs in each department		
Department A	$10,000	$10,000
Department B	25,000	50,000
Department C	35,000	45,000
Department D	18,000	30,000
Department E	22,000	44,000

Required   Identify whether the cost in each department is fixed, variable, or mixed.

[LO 3-2]   3-44 **Fixed; Variable; Mixed Costs**   Habib Manufacturing has five manufacturing departments and the following operating and cost information for the two most recent months of activity:

	April	May
Units produced	4,000	6,000
Costs in each department:		
Department 1	$16,000	$18,000
Department 2	16,000	26,000
Department 3	20,000	20,000
Department 4	32,000	48,000
Department 5	16,000	24,000

Required   Identify whether the cost in each department is fixed, variable, or mixed.

[LO 3-1, 3-2]   3-45 **Strategy; Variable and Fixed Costs**   Zipcar (www.zipcar.com) is a car-sharing club founded in Cambridge, Massachusetts, in 1999. The club members pay an annual fee and then have the opportunity to rent from a pool of available cars for a fixed hourly or daily rate. Zipcar is located largely in select metropolitan areas such as Boston, San Francisco, and Washington, D.C. Members, called "Zipsters," make reservations for a car on the Zipcar website and then use an access card to open the vehicle. The vehicle has a "home base" parking spot where the driver picks up and returns the vehicle. The club—which operates in more than 500 cities and towns, at more than 600 college campuses, and at 50 airports—has grown to more than 1 million members since its initial public offering in April 2011.

The Zipcar website provides details on membership and mentions a $7.00 monthly membership fee. A car can be rented for an hourly or daily rate. While the actual rate can vary, a car can be rented for about $9.00 per hour, which includes 20 free miles, or for a $73 daily rate, which includes 180 free miles per day, and a charge of $0.45 per mile for each mile over 180.

Required

1. Assume you will take a two-day trip to visit some friends over the weekend and you will drive 400 miles. What is the total cost of this trip?

2. You are trying to estimate your monthly spending on your Zipcar membership. You plan to make four weekly trips to run errands like grocery shopping, going to the pharmacy, etc. Each trip will take about two hours and be about 15 miles. You will also take a trip over a three-day weekend to visit your family and expect the trip will cover a total of 450 miles. How much do you expect your Zipcar costs to be for the coming month?

3. What are some of the car-related fixed and variable costs for Zipcar,

4. What are some of the competitive advantages and challenges of the Zipcar concept?

[LO 3-4] 3-46 **Flow of Product Costs** Billy Bob's Manufacturing had the following data for the fiscal year ended December 31.

Direct Materials Inventory, January 1	$ 30,000
Direct materials purchases	350,000
Direct materials used	345,000
Fixed factory overhead	480,000
Total factory overhead	560,000
Total manufacturing costs	1,085,000
Work-in-Process Inventory, January 1	42,000
Work-in-Process Inventory, December 31	45,000
Finished Goods Inventory, January 1	36,000
Goods available for sale	1,076,000
Cost of goods sold	1,043,000

Required Calculate the following costs:

1. Direct Materials Inventory on December 31.

2. Direct labor costs for the year.

3. Variable factory overhead costs for the year.

4. Cost of goods manufactured for the year.

5. Finished Goods Inventory on December 31.

[LO 3-2] 3-47 **Interpreting Average Cost** The American Institute of Certified Public Accountants (AICPA) and the Hackett Group, a consulting firm, partnered to study the trends in the nature of, and amount spent on, the accounting function in corporations. A key finding was that the world's best accounting departments were able to function effectively at relatively low cost; these departments' total costs were only about 1% of their firm's total revenues. In contrast, less efficient accounting departments required, on the average, 1.4% of total revenue, 40% higher than the best results. The world-class accounting departments were also faster in preparing regular financial reports (less than two days for the best departments, compared to five to eight days for the others). The study also found that larger firms spent less on accounting:

	Finance Cost as a Percentage of Total Revenue
Manufacturing Firms	
Firms with less than $1 billion in revenues	1.6%
$1 billion to $5 billion	1.4
More than $5 billion	1
Service Firms	
Less than $1 billion in revenues	2.1%
More than $1 billion	1.6

Required Prepare a brief critical review of these research results. What questions would you have for the researchers who presented these results?

[LO 3-2] 3-48 **Average Cost** Company A has 50% of its total variable manufacturing cost in labor and the other 50% in fuel. Company B has 80% of its total variable manufacturing cost in labor and the remainder in fuel. Suppose in a given year labor costs rise 5% and fuel costs rise 10%.

Required Which company has the higher percentage increase in total variable cost?

[LO 3-2]   3-49   **Classification of Costs; Customer Profitability**   Pet Partner is a small company that provides pet boarding, grooming, and minor medical services for dogs and cats. The company has been successful for its first three years because of its careful attention to customer expectations. The staff know the names of each customer's pet, their food preferences, and their individual preferences. The company is now studying the profitability of the business, using each customer as a cost object. In the business, there are a number of costs:

1. Staff salaries
2. Rent on office and work space used by the company
3. Licenses and fees
4. Supplies, grooming supplies, and related items
5. Medications
6. General legal fees
7. Accounting services provided part time by practicing accountant
8. Pet food
9. Utilities for office and work space
10. Fire insurance for office, work space, and its contents
11. Liability insurance for the company business

Required
1. For each cost category, indicate whether it is direct or indirect relative to the company's cost object.
2. Describe how Pet Partner could use the information in requirement 1 to assess the profitability of each customer.

[LO 3-2, 3-3]   3-50   **Classification of Costs**   Papa's Pizza Heaven serves take-out pizza from three locations in Columbus, Maryland. Papa's considers each pizza delivered (even if the order is for two or more pizzas) as the cost object for the company. The company incurs the following costs:

1. Food costs, including pizza dough, olive oil, tomato sauce, mozzarella cheese, mushrooms, bell peppers, Italian sausage, chopped fresh basil, pesto, pepperoni, onions, and ham
2. Salaries for drivers
3. Salaries for telephone operators
4. Salaries for cooks
5. Insurance for drivers
6. Utilities (e.g., water and electricity)
7. Advertising
8. Discount coupons offered in local newspapers to attract customers
9. Food handling licenses, inspections, and fees
10. Accounting and payroll services
11. Cooking supplies
12. Cleaning supplies
13. Mortgage payments on the three locations owned by Papa's Pizza Heaven
14. Insurance on facilities

Required
1. For each cost item, indicate whether it is fixed or variable relative to the cost object.
2. For each cost item, indicate whether it is a product or a period cost.
3. Which of the above costs could have potentially harmful environmental effects, and why?

[LO 3-2, 3-3]   3-51   **Classification of Costs**   Speedy Auto Service provides oil changes, tire repair/replacement, and minor repairs from 12 different locations in Wadesborough, Pennsylvania. The technicians who replace the oil and parts (mostly windshield wipers, air filters, and the like) are paid for an eight-hour day, irrespective of the number of customers in a given day. The cost object for Speedy is each customer visit. The cost elements for Speedy include:

1. Technicians who change the oil and replace parts
2. Parts
3. Purchase of oil and tires
4. Supplies, rags, cleanup equipment
5. Tools

6. Rental of each location

7. Advertising

8. Utilities

9. Licenses and fees

10. Employee training—10 hours at time of hiring and 2 hours per month thereafter

11. Security service to watch the locations during closing hours

12. Online software system for managing sales, costs, and financial reports, including tax returns and employee payroll

13. Disposal of waste oil and used tires

Required

1. For each cost item, indicate whether it is fixed or variable relative to the cost object.

2. For each cost item, indicate whether it is a product or a period cost.

3. Which of the above costs could have potentially harmful environmental effects? Why?

Problems

[LO 3-2] 3-52 **Executional Cost Drivers: Internet Retailer**   Assume that you are a consultant for a start-up internet retailer, Bikers.com, which provides a variety of bicycle parts and accessories in a convenient and effective customer service approach. The firm operates from an office building and nearby warehouse located in Danville, Virginia. Currently, the firm has 10 permanent administrative staff; 6 customer service representatives who respond to customer inquiries; and 12 employees who pick, pack, and ship customer orders. All orders are placed over the firm's website. A toll-free telephone number is available for customer service. The firm's sales increased at about 20% per year in the last two years, a decline from the 50% rate in its first three years of operation. Management is concerned that the decline will delay the firm's first expected profit, which had been projected to occur in the next two years. The firm is privately held and has been financed with a combination of bank loans, personal investments of top managers, and venture capital funding.

Required   What specific executional cost drivers are important in this business? How should the firm use them to improve its sales rate?

[LO 3-2] 3-53 **Structural Cost Drivers**

Case A: Food Fare is a small chain of restaurants that has developed a loyal customer base by providing fast-food items with more choices (e.g., how the hamburger should be cooked, self-serve toppings) and a more comfortable atmosphere. The menu has a small number of popular items, including several different hamburgers, grilled chicken sandwiches, and salads. Recently, to broaden its appeal, Food Fare added barbecue, seafood, and steak to its menu.

Case B: Gilman Heating and Air Conditioning Inc. provides a broad range of services to commercial and residential customers, including installation and repair of several different brands of heating and air-conditioning systems. Gilman has a fleet of 28 trucks, each operated by one or more service technicians, depending on the size of a job. A recurrent problem for Gilman has been coordinating the service teams during the day to determine the status of a job and the need for parts not kept in the service vehicle, as well as to identify which team to send on emergency calls. Gilman's service area is spread over an urban/rural area of approximately 50 square miles. The company has developed cost and price sheets so that the service technicians accurately and consistently price the service work they perform.

Required   For each case, identify the important structural cost drivers for the company and the related strategic issues that it should address to be competitive.

[LO 3-4] 3-54 **Cost of Goods Manufactured and Sold** Cornelius Company produces women's clothing. During the year, the company incurred the following costs:

Factory rent	$380,000
Direct labor	300,000
Utilities—factory	38,000
Purchases of direct materials	555,000
Indirect materials	66,000
Indirect labor	60,000

Inventories for the year were as follows:

	January 1	December 31
Materials	$25,000	$40,000
Work-in-Process	45,000	40,000
Finished Goods	135,000	75,000

Required

1. Prepare a statement of cost of goods manufactured.
2. Calculate cost of goods sold.

[LO 3-4] 3-55 **Cost of Goods Manufactured;** Income Statement The following data pertain to Babor Company for the fiscal year ended December 31:

	Prior December 31	Current December 31
Purchases of materials		$165,000
Direct labor		114,000
Indirect labor		45,000
Factory insurance		8,000
Depreciation—factory		33,000
Repairs and maintenance—factory		11,000
Marketing expenses		144,000
General and administrative expenses		86,000
Materials Inventory	$23,000	55,000
Work-in-Process Inventory	13,000	16,000
Finished Goods Inventory	17,000	24,000

Sales in the current year were $625,000.

Required Prepare a schedule of cost of goods manufactured and an income statement for the current year for Babor Company similar to those in Exhibit 3.15A.

[LO 3-4] 3-56 **Cost of Goods Manufactured; Income Statement** Consider the following information for Huntersville Inc. for the fiscal year ended December 31.

Depreciation expense—administrative office	$ 32,000
Depreciation expense—plant and equipment	86,000
Direct labor—wages	487,000
Materials Inventory, Dec. 31	26,000
Materials Inventory, Jan. 1	19,000
Direct materials purchases	155,000
Finished Goods Inventory, Dec. 31	38,000
Finished Goods Inventory, Jan. 1	15,000
Heat, light, and power—plant	44,000
Indirect labor	25,000
Property taxes—plant	34,000
Sales representatives' salaries	145,000
Sales revenue	1,495,000
Factory supervisor's salary	66,000
Supplies—administrative office	16,000
Supplies—plant	29,000
Work-in-Process Inventory, Dec. 31	9,000
Work-in-Process Inventory, Jan. 1	23,000

Required Prepare a statement of cost of goods manufactured and an income statement for Huntersville for the year ended December 31, similar to those in Exhibit 3.15A.

[LO 3-4] 3-57 **Cost of Goods Manufactured; Income Statement** Consider the following information for Fair Wind Yachts Inc., a manufacturer of sailboat rigging, blocks, and cordage.

Advertising expenses	$ 150,000
Depreciation expense—administrative office	75,000
Depreciation expense—plant and equipment	320,000
Depreciation expense—delivery trucks	45,000
Materials Inventory, beginning	16,000
Materials Inventory, ending	18,000
Direct materials purchases	410,000
Direct labor	512,000
Indirect labor	269,000
Finished Goods Inventory, beginning	55,000
Finished Goods Inventory, ending	43,000
Insurance on plant	32,000
Heat and light for plant	22,000
Repairs on plant building	36,000
Supervisor's salary—plant	98,000
Supplies—plant	132,000
Supplies—administrative office	78,000
Work-in-Process Inventory, beginning	31,000
Work-in-Process Inventory, ending	39,000
Sales representatives' salaries	325,000
Sales revenue	2,885,000

Required   Prepare a statement of cost of goods manufactured and an income statement for Fair Wind Yachts for the year ended December 31, similar to those in Exhibit 3.15A.

[LO 3-4]   3-58   **Cost of Goods Manufactured; Income Statement**   Norton Industries, a manufacturer of cable for the heavy construction industry, closes its books and prepares financial statements at the end of each month. The statement of cost of goods sold for April follows:

NORTON INDUSTRIES
Statement of Cost of Goods Sold
For the Month Ended April 30
($000 omitted)

Finished Goods Inventory, March 31	$ 50
Cost of goods manufactured	790
Cost of goods available for sale	$840
Less: Finished Goods Inventory, April 30	247
Cost of goods sold	$593

Additional Information

- Of the utilities, 80% relates to manufacturing the cable; the remaining 20% relates to the sales and administrative functions.
- All rent is for the office building.
- Property taxes are assessed on the manufacturing plant.
- Of the insurance, 60% is related to manufacturing the cable; the remaining 40% is related to the sales and administrative functions.
- Depreciation expense includes the following:

Manufacturing plant	$20,000
Manufacturing equipment	30,000
Office equipment	4,000
	$54,000

- The company manufactured 7,825 tons of cable during May.
- The inventory balances at May 31, follow:
  - Materials Inventory $23,000
  - Work-in-Process Inventory $220,000
  - Finished Goods Inventory $175,000

NORTON INDUSTRIES
Preclosing Account Balances
May 31
($000 omitted)

Cash and marketable securities	$ 54
Accounts and notes receivable	210
Direct Materials Inventory (April 30)	28
Work-in-Process Inventory (April 30)	150
Finished Goods Inventory (April 30)	247
Property, plant, and equipment (net)	1,140
Accounts, notes, and taxes payable	70
Bonds payable	582
Paid-in capital	100
Retained earnings	930
Sales	1,488
Sales discounts	20
Other revenue	2
Purchases of direct materials	510
Direct labor	260
Indirect factory labor	90
Office salaries	122
Sales salaries	42
Utilities	135
Rent	9
Property tax	60
Insurance	20
Depreciation	54
Interest expense	6
Freight-in for materials purchases	15

Required   Based on Exhibit 3.15A, prepare the following:
1. Statement of cost of goods manufactured for Norton Industries for May.
2. Income statement for Norton Industries for May.

   (CMA Adapted)

Solution to Self-Study Problem

SPARTAN PRODUCTS COMPANY
Statement of Cost of Goods Manufactured
For the Year Ended December 31

Direct materials		
Materials Inventory, Jan. 1	$ 20,000	
Purchases of materials	100,000	
Total materials available	$120,000	
Less: Materials Inventory, Dec. 31	30,000	
Direct materials used		$ 90,000
Direct labor		350,000
Factory overhead		
Depreciation expense—plant and equipment	80,000	
Indirect labor—wages	5,000	
Heat, light, and power—plant	12,000	
Supervisor's salary—plant	40,000	
Property taxes—plant	13,000	
Supplies—plant	4,000	
Total factory overhead		154,000
Total manufacturing costs		$594,000
Add: Beginning Work-in-Process Inventory, Jan. 1		35,000
Total manufacturing costs to account for		$629,000
Less: Ending Work-in-Process Inventory, Dec. 31		25,000
Cost of goods manufactured		$604,000

SPARTAN PRODUCTS COMPANY
Income Statement
For the Year Ended December 31

Sales revenue		$1,000,000
Cost of goods sold		
Finished Goods Inventory, Jan. 1	$ 35,000	
Cost of goods manufactured	604,000	
Total goods available for sale	$639,000	
Finished Goods Inventory, Dec. 31	40,000	
Cost of goods sold		599,000
Gross margin		$ 401,000
Selling and administrative expenses		
Sales representatives' salaries	$190,000	
Supplies—administrative office	6,000	
Depreciation expense—administrative office	30,000	
Total selling and administrative expenses		226,000
Operating income		$ 175,000

Please visit Connect to access a narrated, animated tutorial for solving this problem.

CHAPTER FOUR

Job Costing

After studying this chapter, you should be able to . . .

LO 4-1 Explain the types of costing systems.

LO 4-2 Explain the strategic role of costing.

LO 4-3 Explain the flow of costs in a job costing system.

LO 4-4 Explain the application of factory overhead costs in a job costing system.

LO 4-5 Calculate underapplied and overapplied overhead and show how it is accounted for.

LO 4-6 Apply job costing to a service industry.

LO 4-7 Explain an operation costing system.

LO 4-8 Explain how to handle spoilage, rework, and scrap in a job costing system (appendix).

Determining the accurate cost of a product or service plays a critical role in the success of firms in most industries. For example, McIver & Smith Fabricators Inc. of Houston, Texas (**www.mciversmith.com**), uses a product costing system to estimate costs and to charge customers for the production of pressure vessels, towers, and columns for the oil and petrochemical industry. The product costing method it uses provides a competitive edge by providing accurate cost information in a form that customers can easily understand. Similarly, Ben Hur Construction of St. Louis, Missouri (**www.benhurconstruction.com**), uses

Huntstock/Getty Images

job costing with a real-time labor and materials reporting system to provide the ability to account for materials and labor accurately at any point in the production process—important for managing the process of the job and for improving customer service. What these and many other companies have found is that a simple yet accurate method for determining product cost is crucial to their competitive success. Another example is home construction and remodeling, where product costing plays a key role in cost estimating and pricing the work (**www.homeadvisor.com/cost/additions-and-remodels/remodel-multiple-rooms/ #:~:text=Home%20Renovation%20Cost%20Estimator%20by,costs%20an%20 average%20of%20%2475%2C000%2B**).

McIver & Smith Fabricators, Ben Hur Construction, and most home builders use a type of product costing called *job costing,* which is explained in this chapter. Job costing is just one option available, and the following section explains all the different choices a management accountant must make in selecting a cost system.

Costing Systems

LO 4-1

Explain the types of costing systems.

costing

The process of accumulating, classifying, and assigning direct materials, direct labor, and factory overhead costs to products, services, or projects.

Costing is the process of accumulating, classifying, and assigning direct materials, direct labor, and factory overhead costs to cost objects, which most commonly are products, services, or projects.

In developing the particular costing system to fit a specific firm, the management accountant must make three choices, one for each of the three following characteristics of costing methods: (1) the cost accumulation method—job costing or process costing; (2) the cost measurement method—actual, normal, or standard costing; and (3) the overhead application method—volume-based or activity-based. Each product costing system will reflect these three choices. For example, a company may choose to use job costing, normal costing, and activity-based costing because that combination of choices best fits the firm's operations and strategic goals. Another firm might be better served by a product costing system based on process costing, standard costing, and volume-based costing.

The choice of a particular system depends on the nature of the industry and the product or service; the firm's strategy and management information needs; and the costs and benefits of acquiring, designing, modifying, and operating a particular system. We discuss three choices next.

Cost Accumulation: Job or Process Costing?

Costs can be accumulated by tracing costs to a specific product or service or by accumulating costs at the department level and then allocating these costs from the departments to the products or services. The first type is called *job costing* and the latter is *process costing.* In a job costing system, the jobs consist of individual products or batches of products or services. A job costing system is appropriate when most costs incurred for the job can be readily identified with a specific product, batch of products, customer order, contract, or project. Types of companies that use job costing include those in construction, printing, special equipment manufacturing, shipbuilding, custom furniture manufacturing, professional services, medical services, advertising agencies, and others. Examples of companies that could use job costing systems include Paramount Pictures (**www.paramount.com**), Jiffy Lube International (**www.jiffylube.com**), and Accenture (**www.accenture.com**). In job costing, the job might consist of a single product or multiple products in a batch. For example, a batch might consist of 20 units of a product planned for distribution to a warehouse for future sale. Alternatively, a job could consist of the quantity of products ordered by a particular customer. The first approach is often called the *push* method because it fills the warehouse, while the latter is called the *pull* method because it is based on direct customer demand. The significance of the difference between these methods will be a recurring topic in later chapters.

In contrast, process costing is likely to be found in a firm that primarily produces homogeneous products or services. These firms often have continuous mass production. In this case, it is economically impractical to trace most costs to individual products. Industries where process costing is common include the chemical industry, bottling companies, plastics, food products, and paper products. Examples of companies using process costing systems include The Coca-Cola Company (**www.coca-cola.com**) and International Paper (**www. internationalpaper.com**). This chapter describes job costing systems and operation costing,

Caterpillar is one of the world's leading manufacturers of construction and mining equipment and makes some of the world's most complex vehicles. Weighing in at more than 1 million pounds, its 797 model is one of the biggest and most complex mining trucks ever made. In fact, the truck is so large and complex that once the pieces are manufactured, they are delivered to the jobsite for assembly. *Popular Mechanics* has a website with a time-lapse video showing the production and assembly of one of these trucks:

www.popularmechanics.com/cars/trucks/a15908/cat-797-mining-truck-assembly/

Required

After watching the video, consider how well a job costing system would match up with Caterpillar's manufacturing operation for the Caterpillar 797. Also, identify some possible impacts of tariffs on steel and other materials that are used by Caterpillar in its production sites in the United States.

a variation of job costing. Chapter 6 explains process costing systems, and Chapter 7 covers a variation of process costing in which there is joint processing of multiple products.

Cost Measurement: Actual, Normal, or Standard Costing?

Costs in either a job or process costing system can be measured in their actual, normal, or standard amount. An actual costing system uses actual costs incurred for all product costs, including direct materials, direct labor, and factory overhead.

A normal costing system uses actual costs for direct materials and direct labor, and normal costs for factory overhead. Normal costing involves estimating a portion of overhead to be assigned to each product as it is produced. A normal costing system provides a timely estimate of the cost of producing each product or job.

A standard costing system uses standard costs and quantities for all three types of manufacturing costs: direct materials, direct labor, and factory overhead. Standard costs are expected costs the firm should attain. Standard costing systems provide a basis for cost control, performance evaluation, and process improvement. This chapter explains actual costing and normal costing systems; Chapters 14 and 15 explain standard costing systems. The different cost measurement systems are summarized in Exhibit 4.1.

Overhead Application under Normal Costing: Volume-Based or Activity-Based?

Volume-based product costing systems allocate overhead to products or jobs using only volume-based cost drivers, such as units produced. This approach relies heavily on the assumption that each product uses the same amounts of overhead because each product is charged the same amount. Many accountants argue that instead of assigning overhead equally to each unit, the overhead in each product should be proportional to the direct labor hours needed to manufacture that unit because more labor time also means increased overhead costs for equipment, supervision, and other facilities costs. The recognition that every unit may not use identical levels of overhead resources is a first step in improving the allocation process, but allocation using a single volume-based driver (e.g., direct labor hours) may not be sufficiently accurate to capture the differences in overhead consumption. As a result, a firm might adopt an activity-based approach to overhead allocation.

Activity-based costing (ABC) systems allocate factory overhead costs to products using cause-and-effect criteria with multiple cost drivers. ABC systems use both volume-based and non-volume-based cost drivers to more accurately allocate factory overhead costs to products based on resource consumption during various activities. Chapter 5 explains ABC systems.

EXHIBIT 4.1
Cost Measurement Systems

Costing System	Types of Cost Used for		
	Direct Materials	Direct Labor	Factory Overhead
Actual costing	Actual cost	Actual cost	Actual cost
Normal costing	Actual cost	Actual cost	Estimated overhead cost (using predetermined rate[s])
Standard costing	Standard cost	Standard cost	Standard cost

In addition to actually manufacturing specialized products, tool and die manufacturers like Dekalb Tool & Die Inc. (www.dekalbtool.com) offer a variety of design, repair, and maintenance services to meet their customers' specific needs. Companies within this industry have highly knowledgeable and skilled staff and state-of-the-art equipment. There is one additional component needed to provide their services: the raw materials. Within the tool-and-die industry, these materials are

known as tool steel. The volume of tool steel produced by U.S. steelmakers is relatively low compared to the demand. Because most of their raw material is imported, duties on these tool steel imports would adversely affect U.S. tool-and-die manufacturers and potentially increase costs throughout the supply chains they support.

Sources: www.dekalbtool.com; http://americanmachinist.com/news/tool-and-die-makers-warn-against-tool-steel-import-duties.

The Strategic Role of Costing

LO 4-2

Explain the strategic role of costing.

To compete successfully, firms need accurate cost information, regardless of their competitive strategies. This is even more likely to be true for cost leadership firms that rely on a high level of manufacturing efficiency and quality to succeed. Effective management of manufacturing costs requires timely and accurate cost information. Getting this information requires that the firm choose a cost system that is a good match for its competitive strategy. For example, a cost leadership firm that produces a commodity product is also likely to be in a process industry, such as food or chemical processing, or assembly-line manufacturing. Thus, process costing systems are likely to be a good fit. Because accurate costs are important, such firms are likely to use activity-based costing, which is more accurate than the volume-based method for overhead assignment. And finally, this type of firm is likely to choose a standard costing system to provide the cost targets and regular reports on meeting these targets. In sum, the commodity/cost leadership type of firm might very well use a cost system that combines elements of process costing (Chapter 6), activity-based costing (Chapter 5), and standard costing (Chapters 14 and 15).

Many firms' competitive environments are changing rapidly, especially in the increasingly global economy. To provide useful information, a costing system must keep up with the constantly changing environment. To be competitive, the firm needs accurate cost information—for product pricing, profitability analysis of individual products, profitability analysis of individual customers, evaluation of management performance, and refinement of strategic goals.

Job Costing: The Cost Flows

LO 4-3

Explain the flow of costs in a job costing system.

job costing
A product costing system that accumulates and assigns costs to specific jobs, customers, projects, or contracts.

job cost sheet
A cost sheet that records and summarizes the costs of direct materials, direct labor, and factory overhead for a particular job.

Job costing is a costing system that accumulates costs and assigns them to specific jobs, customers, projects, or contracts. The basic supporting document (usually in electronic form) in a job costing system is the **job cost sheet.** It records and summarizes the costs of direct materials, direct labor, and factory overhead for a particular job.

An example of a job cost sheet for Tomlinson Companies of High Point, North Carolina, with disguised information, is shown in Exhibit 4.2. Tomlinson Companies (https://www.tomlinsoncompanies.com/home) manufactures furniture with a unique focus on design and innovation, based on the work of several furniture designers. The furniture is designed for the highest level of style and function and can be available in custom-made sizes and fabrics. The company introduced such concepts as "Furniture by the Inch," "As You Like It," and "Form and Fashion." The job cost sheet in Exhibit 4.2 shows the direct materials, direct labor, and overhead required for the production of a batch of 10 sofas; the sofa is called the K.C. Sofa in the Tomlinson catalog. The example is presented in the form of a common database program to emphasize that job costing is typically done by a database software system that collects all relevant job cost data and then prepares a variety of reports, such as the job cost sheet, reports of cost by department, listing of jobs by customer, and many others, including the firm's financial statements and tax return. Database software systems are used because of the large amounts of data that manufacturing firms such as Tomlinson must maintain and

REAL-WORLD FOCUS　A Strategic Relationship between Price and Cost

You are probably familiar with the Apple iPhone, but did you know that Apple licenses some of the key technology that allows the phones to send and receive data from Qualcomm? It is part of Qualcomm's strategy and business model to generate revenue from its portfolio of more than 130,000 patents. In this situation, Qualcomm charges royalties as high as 5 percent of the average selling price of a phone. In 2017 the average retail price of an iPhone was $699, and the average cost of materials was $236, so the 5% royalty on the retail price of the phone could translate into a significant percentage of the cost

of materials. As it turns out, in 2017 Apple filed a lawsuit in California asking that the technology licenses be offered at a much lower price. In early 2019 the two companies settled before a trial could start. While the exact terms of their agreement are not public, Qualcomm expected the settlement would translate into around $2.5 billion of extra revenue.

Source: Max Chafkin and Ian King, "The Billion-Dollar War Over an $18 Part," *Bloomberg Businessweek,* October 9, 2017, pp. 52–57; David Clark and Daisuke Wakabayashi, "Qualcomm vs. Apple Is Settled, Worldwide," *The New York Times,* April 17, 2019, pp. B1–B4.

use for a variety of purposes, such as the reports listed above. Often, the software system is designed specifically for the industry. However, the system used by a company like Tomlinson could be any of a variety of the software systems available today.

Tomlinson Companies

EXHIBIT 4.2
Job Cost Sheet

Tomlinson Companies

Tomlinson Companies
Job Cost Sheet

Product	2255 K.C. Sofa	Job Number	351
Date Begun	June 6	Quantity	10
Date Complete	June 30	Unit Cost	$1,686.62

Department	Total Direct Materials Cost	Total Direct Labor Cost	Total Factory Overhead	Total Cost	Unit Materials Cost
Fabric	$ 456.00	$ —			$ 45.60
Frame Building	4,664.40	238.95			466.44
Spring-up	346.97	217.80			34.70
Sanding	—	—			—
Finishing	110.00	20.00			11.00
Fabrication	63.48	70.00			6.35
Cutting	323.19	117.50			32.32
Sewing	3.02	1,170.00			0.30
Cushion/Foam	2,123.28	136.24			212.33
Upholstery	46.48	535.50			4.65
Outsiding	100.71	239.40			10.07
Skirt	—	—			—
Final Assembly	16.20	18.00			1.62
Inspection	16.32	7.80			1.63
Packing and Shipping	2,222.40	—			222.24
Total	$10,492.45	$2,771.19	$3,602.55	$16,866.19	$1,049.25

A job cost sheet includes all three cost elements (direct materials, direct labor, overhead) as well as other detailed data required by management. The job cost sheet follows the product as it goes through the production process; all costs are recorded on the sheet as direct materials and direct labor are added. On completion of production, the overhead is added based usually on a certain dollar amount per labor hour, as shown in Exhibit 4.2. The total of all costs recorded on the job cost sheet is the total cost of the job.

Direct and Indirect Materials Costs

As part of the preparation for the job, Tomlinson purchases materials that are needed for the job. These purchases include both direct materials (lumber, fabric, and other direct materials) and indirect materials (glue, nails, and other indirect materials). The purchase of materials, for $2,400, is illustrated with the following journal entry:

| (1) | Materials Inventory | 2,400 | |
| | Accounts Payable | | 2,400 |

The purchase of materials is based off the production levels and the *bill of materials* for each product. The bill of materials is a detailed listing of all the materials needed for a given job. An example of a bill of materials used by the Packing Department of Tomlinson for the manufacture of the sofa is shown in Exhibit 4.3. The purchased materials are used as Tomlinson produces the job. Once production is to begin, the various production departments will refer to the bill of materials for the job and then use a **materials requisition** to request the materials needed for production. The actual materials requisition may be done through online data entry, or might be in the form of a source document. No matter the form, the materials requisition indicates the specific job charged with the materials used. An example of a materials requisition for Tomlinson is shown in in Exhibit 4.4. This example shows part of the total of $463 materials required for the job in the Packing Department. The material is a sofa carton for a cost of $19.99 per carton, or 10 × $19.99 = $199.90 for the job shown in Exhibit 4.2.

According to the job cost sheet, Tomlinson's packing department used a total of $2,222.40 in direct materials for Job 351. These costs are charged to Work-in-Process Inventory until the job is completed, as shown in the following entry:

| (2) | Work-in-Process Inventory | 2,222.40 | |
| | Materials Inventory | | 2,222.40 |

Indirect materials are treated as part of the total factory overhead cost. Typical indirect materials are glue, nails, and factory supplies. The journal entry to record the use of indirect materials of $50 is:

| (3) | Factory Overhead | 50 | |
| | Materials Inventory | | 50 |

materials requisition
An online data entry or a source document used to request the release of materials into the production process.

REAL-WORLD FOCUS   U.S. Furniture Manufacturing Is Making a Comeback

There are advantages to being close to the customer. In an environment where customers are used to near-instant gratification, waiting two months for a piece of furniture to be delivered from overseas can seem like an eternity. Consequently, companies like Crate & Barrel are expanding furniture manufacturing in the U.S. Of course, satisfying the customers is not the only reason for the resurgence of U.S. furniture manufacturing. It was tariffs that accelerated the opening of a fourth upholstered furniture factory by Williams-Sonoma this year.

Source: Ruth Simon, "The U.S. Furniture Industry Is Back—but There Aren't Enough Workers," *The Wall Street Journal*, December 4, 2019, https://www.wsj.com/articles/the-u-s-furniture-industry-is-backbut-there-arent-enough-workers-11575504528?mod=business_lead_pos10.

EXHIBIT 4.3

Bill of Materials for Packing Department for the K.C. Sofa at Tomlinson Companies

Tomlinson Companies

COST SHEET   PACKING

Style #   Tomlinsons - 2255 K.C. Sofa   Date 4/12/2012 (updated 10/2/19)

Packing Materials

	Cardboard					
Part	**Description**		**UOM**	**QTY**	**$PU**	**TOTAL**
1001	#2 Chair Carton Top	38 × 34 × 48¼	ea		9.9642	$ —
1002	#2 Chair Tray	37½ × 33½ × 7	ea		3.0756	$ —
1003	#3 Chair Carton	29 × 29 × 44	ea		7.7497	$ —
1004	#3 Chair Tray	28½ × 27½ × 5	ea		2.5166	$ —
1006	#4 California Chair Carton	48 × 48 × 45	ea		14.5577	$ —
1007	#4 California Chair Tray	47½ × 47½ × 5	ea		4.6902	$ —
1010	#3313 Sofa Carton	86 × 45 × 36	ea		22.2181	$ —
1011	#3313 Sofa Tray	85½ × 44½ × 7	ea		7.2315	$ —
1012	#3313 Sofa FOL Inserts	45⅝ × 3¾ × 12	ea	4	2.2160	$ 8.86
1013	California Sofa Carton	112 × 46 × 37	ea	1	19.9918	$ 19.99
1015	California Ottoman Carton		ea		11.5896	$ —
1016	California Ottoman Tray		ea		5.5223	$ —
1024	Leg Pads 10 x 10		ea		0.2843	$ —
1038	#154 Small California Carton 95 × 45 × 40		ea		19.6306	$ —
1039	#154 Small California Tray		ea		6.3877	$ —
10CalSofaTray	California Sofa Tray	112 × 46½ × 7	ea	1	7.4154	$ 7.42
10NewTray	California Sofa New Tray 106 × 56 × 7				10.4640	$ —
10ShockWatch	#S-5158 Shockwave Impact Indicator			1	2.5000	$ 2.50
	Shrink Wrap					
1004 Bag	#4 Shrink Bag	113 × 68			4.2870	$ —
1019	#1 Sofa Shrink Wrap	147 × 68		1	6.1600	$ 6.16
1020	#2 Chair Shrink Bag	68 × 78			3.2080	$ —
	Fabric Drapes					
1025	White Furniture Drapes 60 × 180			1	1.3700	$ 1.37
					TOTAL MATERIALS	$ 46.30

EXHIBIT 4.4

Materials Requisition

Tomlinson Companies

Materials Requisition   No. P-4204

Job Number	351	Date	30-Jun
Department	Packing	Received by	Tom Chan
Authorized by	Juanita Perez	Issued by	Rashad Gold

Item Number	Description	Quantity	Unit Cost	Total Cost
1013	California Sofa Carton 112 × 46 × 37	10	$19.99	$199.90

Direct and Indirect Labor Costs

time ticket

A sheet showing the time an employee worked on each job, the pay rate, and the total cost chargeable to each job.

Direct labor costs are recorded on the job cost sheet by means of a time ticket (an online data entry or source document) prepared for each employee. A **time ticket,** usually part of a costing software system, shows the amount of time an employee worked on each job, the pay rate, and the total direct labor cost chargeable to each job. Analysis of the time tickets provides information for assigning direct labor costs to individual jobs. The total cost of the $1,170 direct labor incurred in Tomlinson's Sewing Department for Job 351 is recorded by the following journal entry:

| (4) | Work-in-Process Inventory | 1,170 | |
| | Accrued Payroll | | 1,170 |

Indirect labor costs are treated as part of the total factory overhead cost. Indirect labor includes items such as salaries or wages for supervisors, inspectors, and production warehouse clerks. The following is a journal entry to record the $100 indirect labor cost incurred:

| (5) | Factory Overhead | 100 | |
| | Accrued Payroll | | 100 |

Note that in entries (3) and (5), the actual factory overhead is being accumulated in an account called Factory Overhead and is not assigned to any particular job at this point.

A Note About Technology

The exhibits give the appearance that the various forms would be in a hard-copy format. In most organizations, the tracking of the cost flows occurs in a paperless environment. Tomlinson, for example, may be able to order materials from its suppliers by merely entering a few key strokes. Barcode or RFID technology could allow for tracking the receipt of materials and also for tracking the release of materials to a specific job. Similarly, employees could use a card reader or a keyboard, or maybe some biometric scanning device, to log in and record the time worked on a specific task or job. The use of technology allows a tremendous amount of data to be captured, stored, and later analyzed to help managers better understand and control costs.

Factory Overhead Costs

overhead application

A process of allocating overhead costs to cost objects.

Overhead application is a process of allocating factory overhead costs to cost objects. In this chapter, the cost objects are jobs. Allocation is necessary because overhead costs are not traceable to individual jobs. The two approaches to allocating overhead costs covered in this chapter are actual costing and normal costing. A third approach, standard costing, is covered in Chapters 14 and 15.

Actual Costing

actual costing system

A costing process that uses actual costs incurred for direct materials, direct labor, and factory overhead.

An **actual costing system** uses actual costs incurred for direct materials and direct labor and records actual factory overhead for the jobs.

actual factory overhead

Costs incurred in an accounting period for indirect materials, indirect labor, and other indirect production costs, including factory rent, insurance, property tax, depreciation, repairs and maintenance, power, light, heat, and employer payroll taxes for factory personnel.

Actual factory overhead costs are incurred each month for indirect materials, indirect labor, and other indirect factory costs, including factory rent, insurance, property tax, depreciation, repairs and maintenance, power, light, heat, and employer payroll taxes for factory personnel. Different firms use terms such as *manufacturing overhead, indirect manufacturing cost, production overhead,* or simply *overhead* in referring to factory overhead.

Generally, the total amount of actual overhead costs is not known until the end of the accounting period when total expenses are determined. Thus, in an actual costing system, all job costs are recorded at the end of the accounting period. Revenues from all jobs and the actual expenses for direct materials, direct labor, and overhead are used to calculate overall profitability at that time. Using actual costing, the company does not know the cost or the profitability of each job when it is completed during the period; this can be determined only at the end of the period, when the company knows the actual combined cost and profitability of all the jobs combined. For management and control purposes, most companies, like

Steece Machine Tools Inc. has a monthly total actual fixed factory overhead of $60,000 and actual variable manufacturing costs per unit of $10 for one of its several products. The firm produced a total of 50,000 units in January but only 10,000 units in February because it had a large inventory of unsold products at the end of January. The unit costs would be as follows if actual costing were used to determine the manufacturing cost per unit:

Month	Production Units	Variable Cost per Unit	Fixed Cost per Unit	Total Unit Cost
January	50,000	$10	$60,000 ÷ 50,000 = $1.20	$11.20
February	10,000	10	$60,000 ÷ 10,000 = 6.00	16.00

This fluctuation in unit cost arises under actual costing because total fixed costs do not change, so unit costs change as volume changes. These changes are not desirable for cost estimation, budgeting, pricing, or product profitability analysis. Predetermined overhead rates, used in normal costing, are easy to apply and reduce monthly fluctuations in job costs caused by changes in the production volume and/or overhead costs throughout the year.

Tomlinson, need to know the cost and profitability of each job as it is completed, so they use normal rather than actual costing.

Normal Costing

normal costing system
A costing process that uses actual costs for direct materials and direct labor and applies factory overhead to various jobs using a predetermined application rate.

In practice, many firms adopt a **normal costing system** that uses actual costs for direct materials and direct labor and applies factory overhead to jobs by adding to the job an estimated amount of overhead in the job by using a predetermined rate.

Normal costing avoids the fluctuations in cost per unit under actual costing resulting from changes in the month-to-month volume of units produced and changes in overhead costs from month to month. The fluctuations in unit cost under actual costing are illustrated in Exhibit 4.5. Using a predetermined *annual* factory overhead rate normalizes overhead cost fluctuations, hence, the term *normal costing*.

The Application of Factory Overhead in Normal Costing

LO 4-4
Explain the application of factory overhead costs in a job costing system.

predetermined factory overhead rate
An estimated rate used to apply factory overhead cost to a cost object.

factory overhead applied
The amount of overhead assigned to a cost object using a predetermined factory overhead rate.

The **predetermined factory overhead rate** is an estimated rate used to apply factory overhead cost to a specific cost object or job. The amount of overhead applied to a job using a predetermined factory overhead rate is called **factory overhead applied.**

The predetermined overhead rate is so-called because it is determined from estimates of overhead costs and cost drivers for the upcoming operating period, usually the coming fiscal year. To obtain the predetermined overhead rate, use these four steps:

1. Estimate total factory overhead costs for the planned production for the upcoming operating period, usually a year. This value will become the numerator amount.
2. Select the most appropriate cost driver(s) for applying the factory overhead costs.
3. Estimate the total amount of the chosen cost driver(s) for the upcoming operating period. This value will become the denominator amount.
4. Divide the estimated factory overhead costs by the estimated amount of the chosen cost driver(s) to obtain the predetermined overhead rate.

Cost Drivers for Factory Overhead Application

The cost driver selected for applying a predetermined overhead rate (step 2 above) can be either a volume- or activity-based cost driver. This chapter explains the use of volume-based cost drivers, and Chapter 5 explains activity-based cost drivers.

Direct labor hours, direct labor costs, and machine hours are among the most frequently used volume-based cost drivers for applying factory overhead. The proper bases or cost drivers for a labor-intensive firm are probably direct labor hours, direct labor costs, or some labor-related measure. In contrast, if factory overhead costs are predominantly related to the equipment operation, the proper cost driver is probably machine hours or a related measure.

REAL-WORLD FOCUS   3-D Printing and Overhead Allocation

Companies are jumping on the 3-D printing bandwagon in a big way. In late 2016, General Electric agreed to buy two European 3-D printing machine manufacturers at a total combined cost of more than $1 billion. Back in the U.S., the company built a 3-D printing factory in Alabama. The cost was $50 million. The plant is expected to have more than 50 printing machines. Among other things, the technology is being used to produce fuel nozzles for its new commercial jet engines. Because it would be fairly easy to track how long it takes a 3-D printer to make one unit, it would make sense to allocate the overhead costs related to the machines on the basis of machine time.

Source: Ted Mann, "Industrial Firms Embrace 3-D," *The Wall Street Journal,* November 12, 2016, p. B4.

Surveys of practice show that direct labor (hours or dollars) and machine hours are the most commonly used cost drivers for overhead application. Ideally, however, the selection of an allocation base should be based on a cause-and-effect relationship.

Applying Factory Overhead Costs

The predetermined overhead rate usually is calculated at the beginning of the year and is used throughout the year.

$$\text{Predetermined factory overhead rate} = \frac{\text{Estimated total factory overhead amount for the year}}{\text{Estimated total amount of cost driver for the year}}$$

For applying manufacturing overhead, Tomlinson Companies uses a predetermined factory overhead rate of 130% of direct labor cost. Let's assume that Tomlinson has the following budgeted (i.e., estimated) and actual data.

Budgeted annual overhead for planned production for all departments	$375,000
Budgeted annual direct labor costs for all departments	288,450
Actual direct labor costs for Job 351 for all departments (from Exhibit 4.2)	2,771.19

Thus, the predetermined overhead rate is

$$\frac{\text{Budgeted factory overhead}}{\text{Budgeted direct laborrcosts}} = \frac{\$375,000}{\$288,450} = 130\% \text{ of direct labor cost}$$

Thus, for the K.C Sofa in Exhibit 4.2, total labor costs for the batch of sofas of $2,771.19 multiplied times the rate of 130% provides total factory overhead of $1.3 \times \$2,771.19 = \$3,602.55$, as shown in Exhibit 4.2. This amount would be recorded using the following journal entry:

(6)	Work-in-Process Inventory	3,602.55	
	Factory Overhead		3,602.55

The preceding entry moves the allocated overhead out of the Factory Overhead account and assigns it to a particular job. This approach is called the *plantwide method of normal costing* because total overhead for all departments is used to determine the overhead rate. An alternative approach is to determine the overhead rate for each production department. While not used by Tomlinson, the departmental approach makes use of more detailed information. Details of the departmental overhead rates are explained in the next section.

Departmental Overhead Rates

When the production departments in the plant are very similar as to the amount of overhead in each department and the usage of cost drivers in the departments, then the use of a plantwide rate (one rate for all production departments taken as a whole) is appropriate. In many cases, however, the various production departments differ significantly in the amount of cost or cost drivers. While we can see from Exhibit 4.2 that Tomlinson has 15 departments, let's make things a little easier by assuming the company has only three production departments (A, B, and C) and that the total overhead costs, direct labor costs in the three departments, and the direct labor within each department used for Job 351 are as shown below.

	Department A	Department B	Department C	Total
Overhead	$154,000	$121,000	$100,000	$375,000
Direct labor costs	110,000	93,050	85,400	288,450
Labor for Job 351	1,091.00	900.00	780.19	2,771.19

Note that the total overhead of $375,000, total direct labor costs of $288,450, and direct labor of $2,771.19 for Job 351 are the same as in our earlier calculations for the plantwide rate.

Using Tomlinson's departmental approach, the rates are calculated as follows:

Overhead Rate for Department A

$154,000 ÷ $110,000 of direct labor cost = 140% of direct labor cost
Overhead for Job 351 = $1,091.00 × 140% = $1,527.40

Overhead Rate for Department B

$121,000 ÷ $93,050 of direct labor cost = 130% of direct labor cost
Overhead for Job 351 = $900.00 × 130% = $1,170.00

Overhead Rate for Department C

$100,000 ÷ $85,400 of direct labor cost = 117% of direct labor cost
Overhead for Job 351 = $780.19 × 117% = $912.82

Using Tomlinson's plantwide approach, the overhead applied to Job 351 is $3,602.55, as shown in Exhibit 4.2. The amount applied using the departmental rates shown above would be $1,527.40 + $1,170.00 + $912.82 = $3,610.22.

The amount of $3,610.22 differs by only $7.67 from the amount determined by the plantwide rate approach, a very small difference. This means that for Job 351 the plantwide rate and the departmental rate have a similar total cost, but that will not always be the case. When the usage of resources in the three departments differs significantly from one job to another, then the departmental approach is considered to be more appropriate and accurate because job cost is based on the actual usage of the different departments, not an overall average. However, as illustrated with Job 351, it is possible that the cost of some jobs might not differ much when a plantwide approach is used rather than a departmental approach.

Disposition of Underapplied and Overapplied Overhead

LO 4-5
Calculate underapplied and overapplied overhead and show how it is accounted for.

overapplied overhead
The excess of applied overhead over actual factory overhead cost for a period.

underapplied overhead
The amount by which actual factory overhead exceeds the factory overhead applied for a given accounting period.

Using a predetermined factory overhead rate to apply overhead cost to products can cause total overhead applied to the units produced to exceed the actual overhead incurred in periods when production is higher than expected. Alternatively, applied overhead might exceed actual overhead incurred if the amount actually incurred is less than the estimated amount. **Overapplied overhead** is the amount of factory overhead applied that exceeds the actual factory overhead cost incurred.

On the other hand, it is possible that applied overhead will be less than the incurred amount of overhead, due either to the fact that the actual amount of incurred overhead was greater than expected and/or the actual production level was smaller than expected. **Underapplied overhead** is the amount by which actual factory overhead exceeds factory overhead applied. If the predetermined overhead rate has been determined carefully, and if actual production is similar to expected production, the overapplied or underapplied difference should be small.

What do we do with the difference between factory overhead applied and the actual amount of overhead incurred? Because actual production costs should be reported in the period they were incurred, total product costs at the end of the accounting period should be based on actual rather than applied overhead.

Underapplied or overapplied overhead can be disposed of in two ways:

1. Adjust the Cost of Goods Sold account.
2. Adjust the production costs of the period; that is, allocate (often called "prorate") the underapplied or overapplied overhead among the ending balances of Work-in-Process Inventory, Finished Goods Inventory, and Cost of Goods Sold.

When the amount of underapplied or overapplied overhead is not significant, it generally is adjusted to Cost of Goods Sold because all product costs eventually become cost of good sold. On the other hand, if the amount is significant, it is often prorated to Work-in-Process Inventory, Finished Goods Inventory, and Cost of Goods Sold. While addressed here, the proration method is also explained in Chapter 15.

Adjustment to Cost of Goods Sold

Suppose that Tomlinson applied $378,000 of overhead but found at the end of the year that the actual total amount of overhead incurred was $383,000. The $5,000 difference represents underapplied overhead. The appropriate adjusting entry to the Cost of Goods Sold account is:

(7)	Cost of Goods Sold	5,000	
	Factory Overhead		5,000
	To record the disposition of underapplied overhead		

At the time of the adjusting entry, the Factory Overhead account had a debit balance of $5,000; the applied amount was credited to the account for $378,000 and the incurred amount was debited for $383,000, leaving a debit balance of $5,000. The entry removes this debit balance and transfers it to Cost of Goods Sold, which causes the account balance to increase.

Proration Approach

If management believes the amount of overapplied or underapplied overhead represents a material amount, then proration of the amount to Work-in-Process Inventory, Finished Goods Inventory, and Cost of Goods Sold is the preferred method of disposal.

For illustrative purposes, assume the ending balances (before adjustment) were $50,000 of Work-in-Process Inventory, $150,000 of Finished Goods Inventory, and $800,000 of Cost of Goods Sold. The table below shows the computation of relative amounts, the assignment of the underapplied overhead, and the adjusted balances of each account.

Account	Unadjusted Balance	Relative Balance	Amount of Adjustment	Adjusted Ending Balance
Work-in-Process	$ 50,000	5%	$ 250	$ 50,250
Finished Goods	150,000	15%	750	150,750
Cost of Goods Sold	800,000	80%	4,000	804,000
Total	$1,000,000	100%	$ 5,000	$1,005,000

(7)	Work-in-Process	250	
	Finished Goods	750	
	Cost of Goods Sold	4,000	
	Factory Overhead		5,000
	To record the disposition of underapplied overhead		

No matter which method is used (adjust cost of goods sold or prorate), underapplied or overapplied overhead is usually adjusted only at the end of a year. Nothing needs to be done during the year because the predetermined factory overhead rate is based on annual figures. A variance is expected between the actual overhead incurred and the amount applied in a particular month or quarter because of seasonal fluctuations in the firm's operating cycle. Furthermore, underapplied factory overhead in one month is likely to be offset by an overapplied amount in another month (and vice versa).

Potential Errors in Overhead Application

The application of overhead is a critical step in costing, and because it is based on estimates, it is subject to potential errors in determining the cost of a product or service. There are three types of potential errors:

1. **Aggregation error.** This costing error arises when, for example, a single plantwide rate is used instead of departmental rates. The departmental rates are more accurate when the departments differ significantly in the amount of cost or the amount of the cost drivers. ABC costing, which we explain in Chapter 5, also addresses aggregation errors.

2. **Specification error.** This error arises when the wrong cost driver is used in the application rate. For example, in a plant where labor costs are relatively small and machine costs are relatively large, a rate based on machine hours is a better choice for overhead application than one based on labor hours.

3. **Measurement error.** This is a common type of error that arises when the amounts used for estimated cost drivers or estimated overhead are incorrect. Measurement error is a combination of estimation error and potential error in calculating the cost driver and overhead amounts.

The management accountant should use care to develop a cost system that minimizes these potential errors. At the same time, the management accountant must balance the cost of improving the accuracy of the cost system with the benefits of improved accuracy.

Job Costing in Service Industries; Project Costing

LO 4-6

Apply job costing to a service industry.

Job costing is used extensively in service industries such as advertising agencies, hospitals, and repair shops, as well as consulting, architecture, accounting, and law firms. Instead of using the term *job,* accounting and consulting firms use the term *client* or *project,* hospitals and law firms use the term *case,* and advertising agencies use the term *contract* or *project.* Many firms use the term *project costing* to indicate the use of job costing in service industries. Project costing is also used to track the costs and progress of nonrecurring tasks that take place within companies—for example, projects to develop a new marketing plan or to improve operating efficiency, projects to implement a new strategic direction for the company, or projects to introduce a new software system. These projects also have the characteristics that are suitable for job costing.

Job costing in service industries uses recording procedures and accounts similar to those illustrated earlier in this chapter except for direct materials involved (there could be none or an insignificant amount). The primary focus is on direct labor. The overhead costs are usually applied to jobs based on direct labor cost.

Suppose the law firm Sandings and Midgett, LLP provides legal services to a wide range of clients in the Chicago area. The firm has two main costs: (1) compensation for professional staff and (2) all other costs, which include support staff, facilities costs, and other costs. The costs of professional staff are considered direct costs for the purposes of billing clients and assessing the profitability of each client job; all other costs are considered overhead. The firm determines an overhead rate for client billing based on the number of professional staff hours used for the job. Professional staff are paid $150 per hour and their time is billed at $250 per hour. The firm estimates the following total costs for the coming year:

Estimated cost of professional staff	$ 6,000,000 (40,000 hours of staff time)
Estimated other costs (overhead)	5,000,000
Total estimated costs	$11,000,000

Suppose Abby Johnson became a new client of the firm that year and that the job for Abby required 100 hours of professional staff time. The cost to be billed to Abby for the job is determined in three steps.

1. Determine the overhead rate:

$$\frac{\text{Estimated total overhead}}{\text{Estimated total hours}} = \frac{\$5,000,000}{40,000} = \$125 \text{ per hour}$$

2. Determine applied overhead for the job:

$$100 \text{ hours for the Abby Johnson job} \times \$125 \text{ per hour} = \$12,500$$

3. Determine the total billing for the job:

Total billing for professional staff ($250 per hour × 100)	$25,000
Total overhead applied to the job ($125 per hour × 100)	12,500
Total billing for the Abby Johnson job	$37,500

The job cost of the Abby Johnson job can be determined in a similar manner, by replacing the billing rate of $250 per hour with the cost of compensation for professional staff, $150 per hour:

Total cost for professional staff ($150 per hour × 100)	$15,000
Total overhead applied to the job	12,500
Total cost for the Abby Johnson job	$27,500

The profit on the Abby Johnson job is $37,500 − $27,500 = $10,000.

The preceding costing can also be adapted to account for differences in billing rates for different levels of professional staff (partners, associates) and for differences in overhead rates for different professional staff levels, if desired. For example, (1) if partners are billed at $350 and associates are billed at $150; (2) if $2,000,000 of the $5,000,000 total overhead could be attributed to partners and $3,000,000 could be attributed to associates in the law firm; (3) if 10,000 of the 40,000 annual hours of professional time were partner hours and 30,000 were for associates; and (4) if 10 of the 100 hours of professional time for the Abby Johnson job were partner hours and the remaining 90 hours were associates' time, then the following could be calculated for billing purposes:

1. Determine the overhead rates:

$$\text{Partners: } \$2,000,000 \div 10,000 = \$200 \text{ per hour}$$
$$\text{Associates: } \$3,000,000 \div 30,000 = \$100 \text{ per hour}$$

2. Determine applied overhead:

$$\text{Partners: } 10 \times \$200 = \$2,000$$
$$\text{Associates: } 90 \times \$100 = \$9,000$$

3. Determine total billing for the job:

Partners:	
Professional time: $350 per hour × 10	$ 3,500
Overhead: $200 per hour × 10	2,000
Associates:	
Professional time: $150 per hour × 90	13,500
Overhead: $100 per hour × 90	9,000
Total billing for the Abby Johnson job	$28,000

The job cost of the Abby Johnson job can be determined in a similar manner, by replacing the billing rates of $350 and $150 per hour with the cost of compensation for professional staff. If we assume that of the $6,000,000 compensation cost, one-half is attributed to partners and the other one-half is attributed to associates, then the cost rate for a partner is $300 (= $3,000,000 ÷ 10,000 hours) and the cost rate for an associate is $100 (= $3,000,000 ÷ 30,000 hours). The job cost determination is:

Partners:	
Professional time: $300 per hour × 10	$ 3,000
Overhead: $200 per hour × 10	2,000
Associates:	
Professional time: $100 per hour × 90	9,000
Overhead: $100 per hour × 90	9,000
Total cost for the Abby Johnson job	$23,000

The profit for the Abby Johnson job is $28,000 − $23,000 = $5,000.

The differences between the two billing statements and the two job costs are significant; the second approach based on partner and associate time is more accurate and, therefore, likely to be more fair and appropriate. The second approach reflects the fact that most of the professional hours for the Abby Johnson job were for associates, who have lower billing rates and costs. The difference between the two approaches is very much like the difference between the plantwide and departmental overhead rates explained earlier.

Operation Costing

operation costing
A hybrid costing system that uses job costing to assign direct materials costs to jobs and process costing to assign conversion costs to products or services.

Operation costing is a hybrid costing system that uses a job costing approach to assign direct materials costs to jobs and a process costing approach to assign conversion costs to products or services. As a reminder, conversion costs include the cost of direct labor and factory overhead. The topic is discussed more fully in Chapter 3.

Manufacturing operations whose conversion activities are very similar across several product lines, but whose direct materials used in the various products differ significantly, use operation costing. After direct labor and factory overhead costs have been accumulated by operations or departments, these costs are then assigned to products. On the other hand, direct materials costs are accumulated by jobs or batches, and job costing assigns these costs to products or services.

Industries suitable for applying operation costing include food processing, textiles, shoes, furniture, metalworking, jewelry, and electronic equipment. For example, a glass manufacturing company that makes multiple products from a basic clear glass would be a potential user of operation costing.

Suppose that Irvine Glass Company manufactures two types of glass: clear glass and tinted glass. Department 1 produces clear glass sheets, some of which are sold as finished goods. Others are transferred to Department 2, which adds metallic oxides to clear glass sheets to form tinted glass sheets, which are then sold as finished goods. The company uses operation costing and combines direct labor and overhead into a single account called Conversion Costs.

Irvine Glass Company finished two jobs: Job A produced 10,000 sheets of clear glass and Job B produced 5,000 sheets of tinted glass. Manufacturing operations and costs applied to these products follow.

Direct materials		
Job A (10,000 clear glass sheets)		$400,000
Job B (5,000 tinted glass sheets)		
Materials for clear glass sheets in Department 1	$200,000	
Materials added to clear glass sheets in Department 2	100,000	300,000
Total direct materials		$700,000
Conversion costs		
Department 1		$180,000
Department 2		50,000
Total conversion costs		$230,000
Total costs		$930,000

Notice in this table that operation costing identifies direct materials by job; in contrast, it identifies conversion costs with each of the two production departments.

The product cost for each type of glass sheet is computed as follows:

	Clear Glass	Tinted Glass
Direct materials		
Job A ($400,000 ÷ 10,000)	$40	
Job B ($300,000 ÷ 5,000)		$60
Conversion: Department 1 ($180,000 ÷ 15,000)	12	12
Conversion: Department 2 ($50,000 ÷ 5,000)		10
Total product cost per sheet	$52	$82

Notice in this table that each glass sheet receives the same dollar amount of conversion costs in Department 1 because this operation is identical for the two products. Total product costs are calculated as follows:

Clear glass sheets ($52 per sheet × 10,000)	$520,000
Tinted glass sheets ($82 per sheet × 5,000)	410,000
Total	$930,000

The following journal entries record Irvine Glass Company's flow of costs. Department 1 makes the first entry by recording the requisition of direct materials when Job A enters production:

| (1) | Work-in-Process Inventory—Department 1 | 400,000 | |
| | Materials Inventory | | 400,000 |

Department 1 makes the following entry to record the requisition of direct materials when Job B enters production:

| (2) | Work-in-Process Inventory—Department 1 | 200,000 | |
| | Materials Inventory | | 200,000 |

Conversion costs are applied in Department 1 with the following journal entry:

| (3) | Work-in-Process Inventory—Department 1 | 180,000 | |
| | Conversion Costs | | 180,000 |

The following entry records the transfer of completed clear glass sheets to Finished Goods:

(4)	Finished Goods Inventory	520,000	
	Work-in-Process Inventory—Department 1		520,000
	Direct materials of $400,000 + Conversion ($12 per sheet × 10,000) = $520,000		

The following entry records the transfer of partially completed clear glass sheets to Department 2 for completion as tinted glass:

(5)	Work-in-Process Inventory—Department 2	260,000	
	Work-in-Process Inventory—Department 1		260,000
	Direct materials of $200,000 + Conversion ($12 × 5,000) = $260,000		

The following entry records the requisition of materials by Department 2 when Job B enters production:

| (6) | Work-in-Process Inventory—Department 2 | 100,000 | |
| | Materials Inventory | | 100,000 |

Conversion costs are applied in Department 2 with the following journal entry:

| (7) | Work-in-Process Inventory—Department 2 | 50,000 | |
| | Conversion Costs | | 50,000 |

The completed tinted glass sheets are transferred to Finished Goods:

(8)	Finished Goods Inventory	410,000	
	Work-in-Process Inventory—Department 2		410,000
	Department 2 Work-in-Process $260,000 + Direct materials for tinted glass of $100,000 + Conversion ($10 × 5,000) = $410,000		

Summary

Product costing is the process of accumulating, classifying, and assigning direct materials, direct labor, and factory overhead costs to products or services. Product costing provides useful cost information for both manufacturing and nonmanufacturing companies. Accurate cost information helps a company make better decisions and compete more effectively.

Several different product costing systems are available and can be classified on three dimensions: (1) cost accumulation method—job or processing costing systems; (2) cost measurement method—actual, normal, or standard costing systems; and (3) overhead application method—volume- or activity-based costing systems. The choice of a particular system depends on the nature of the industry and the product or service; the firm's strategy and its management information needs; and the costs and benefits to acquire, design, modify, and operate a particular system.

Job costing uses several accounts to control the product cost flows. Direct materials costs are debited to the Materials Inventory account at time of purchase and debited to the Work-in-Process Inventory account when a production department requests materials. Direct labor costs are debited to the Work-in-Process Inventory account when they are incurred. Actual factory overhead costs are debited to the Factory Overhead account when they are incurred. Factory overhead applied using the predetermined factory overhead rate in normal costing is debited to the Work-in-Process Inventory account and credited to the Factory Overhead account. When a job is complete, the cost of goods manufactured is transferred from the Work-in-Process Inventory account to the Finished Goods Inventory account.

The predetermined factory overhead rate is an estimated factory overhead rate used to apply factory overhead cost to a specific job. The application of a predetermined overhead rate has four steps: (1) estimate factory overhead costs for an upcoming operating period, usually a year; (2) select the most appropriate cost driver for charging the factory overhead costs; (3) estimate the total amount of the chosen cost driver for the upcoming operating period; and (4) divide the estimated factory overhead costs by the estimated amount of the chosen cost driver to obtain the predetermined factory overhead rate.

The difference between the actual factory overhead cost and the amount of the factory overhead applied is the overhead variance; it is either underapplied or overapplied. It can be disposed of in two ways: (1) adjust the Cost of Goods Sold account or (2) prorate the difference among the Work-in-Process Inventory, the Finished Goods Inventory, and the Cost of Goods Sold accounts.

Job costing is used extensively in service industries such as advertising agencies; construction companies; hospitals; repair shops; and consulting, architecture, accounting, and law firms.

Operation costing is used when most of the plant's products have a similar conversion cycle, but materials costs may differ significantly between jobs. In this case, direct materials costs are traced to jobs, while conversion costs are traced to departments and then to jobs.

Appendix

LO 4-8

Explain how to handle spoilage, rework, and scrap in a job costing system.

spoilage
An unacceptable unit that is discarded or sold for disposal value.

rework
The additional work that must be done to make a nonconforming good acceptable so that it can be sold in regular channels.

scrap
Materials left over from the manufacture of a product that have little or no value.

Spoilage, Rework, and Scrap in Job Costing

In today's manufacturing environment, firms adopt various quality-improvement programs to reduce spoilage, rework, and scrap. **Spoilage** refers to unacceptable units that are discarded or sold for disposal value. **Rework** is the additional work performed to make nonconforming goods into good units that can be sold in regular channels. **Scrap** is the material left over from the manufacture of the product; it has little or no value.

SPOILAGE

The two types of spoilage are normal and abnormal. **Normal spoilage** occurs under normal operating conditions; it is uncontrollable in the short term and is considered a normal part of production and product cost. That is, the cost of spoiled unit costs is absorbed by the cost of good units produced. **Abnormal spoilage** is an excess over the amount of normal spoilage expected under normal operating conditions; it is charged as a loss to operations in the period detected.

Normal spoilage is of two types: (1) specific normal spoilage, which is particular to a given job and is not due to factors related to other jobs, and (2) common normal spoilage, which is due to factors that affect two or more jobs, such as a machine malfunction that affected parts used in several jobs. Normal spoilage that is specific to a job is treated as a cost of that job so that, in effect, the cost of spoilage is spread over the cost of the good units in the job. Normal spoilage that is common to two or more jobs is charged to factory overhead and, in this way,

normal spoilage
An unacceptable unit that occurs under efficient operating conditions; spoilage that is inherent in the manufacturing process.

abnormal spoilage
Waste in excess of what is expected to occur under normal operating conditions.

affects the costs of all jobs. Abnormal spoilage is charged to a special account, such as Loss from Abnormal Spoilage, so that management attention can be given to spoilage of this type and because product cost should not include abnormal elements such as abnormal spoilage.

Suppose a furniture manufacturer spoiled 1 sofa from an order of 100 sofas (Job #1233) because of stains and tears in the fabric and that the spoilage was normal and particular to this job. At the time the spoilage was detected, a total of $500 had been incurred in the manufacture of the sofa. Suppose further that the spoiled sofa could be disposed of—sold as-is for $100—then the net cost of the spoilage is now $500 – $100 = $400. This means that $400 of work-in-process cost for the spoiled sofa will be spread over the remaining 99 sofas. The accounting treatment would be as follows:

Inventory of Spoiled Sofas for Sale	100	
Work-in-Process		100

Note that while the main Work-in-Process account is being credited for the cost of the spoiled sofa, there would be supporting details that note that Job #1233 is the specific job that would be credited for this cost of spoilage.

Suppose the same information as above, except that the spoiled sofa described was spoiled by a hard-to-detect malfunction in a fabric-cutting machine that was also involved in other jobs in the plant and had affected other jobs. This change means the spoilage is now considered common normal spoilage, and the accounting treatment is:

Inventory of Spoiled Sofas for Sale	100	
Factory Overhead	400	
Work-in-Process		500

Finally, assume again the same information as above except that the malfunction in the fabric-cutting machine is due to controllable operator error, meaning it is not part of normal operations and is now considered to be abnormal spoilage. The accounting treatment is now:

Inventory of Spoiled Sofas for Sale	100	
Loss from Abnormal Spoilage	400	
Work-in-Process		500

REWORK

There are three types of rework: (1) rework on normal defective units for a particular job, (2) rework on normal defective units common with all jobs, and (3) rework on abnormal defective units not falling within the normal range. The cost of rework units is charged to one of three accounts depending on its nature. Normal rework for a particular job is charged to the Work-in-Process account and also the specific job's subsidiary account or job cost sheet. Normal rework common to all jobs is charged to the Factory Overhead account, and abnormal rework is charged to the Loss from Abnormal Rework account.

SCRAP

Scrap can be classified according to its application to a specific job or whether it is common to all jobs. Suppose that the furniture manufacturer above incurred and sold the scrap materials from Job #1233 for $75 cash and sold the scrap common to all jobs for $200 cash. The proper journal entries follow:

Cash	75	
Work-in-Process		75
Cash	200	
Factory Overhead		200

The entry above reduces Work-in-Process, and the $75 would also be subtracted from the Job #1233 in the subsidiary account or job cost sheet. The $200 is being credited to the overhead account as a reduction to be shared by all production during the period.

Key Terms

abnormal spoilage, *124*
actual costing system, *115*
actual factory overhead, *115*
costing, *109*
factory overhead applied, *116*
job cost sheet, *111*
job costing, *111*

materials requisition, *113*
normal costing
　system, *116*
normal spoilage, *124*
operation costing, *122*
overapplied overhead, *118*
overhead application, *115*

predetermined factory overhead
　rate, *116*
rework, *124*
scrap, *124*
spoilage, *124*
time ticket, *115*
underapplied overhead, *118*

Comments on Cost Management in Action

Is Job Costing a Match for Caterpillar's Manufacturing Process?

As the video begins, you see an assembly line. As such, you might get the impression this production environment is a likely candidate for process costing. This might be true if the 797 model was being mass-produced. However, even with time-lapse photography, you can get a feel for the level of complexity associated with the manufacturing process. The time and intensity of the work being performed on each of the various components probably means that it is easy to trace many of the costs directly to each individual 797 produced. Later in the video, the support for using a job costing system becomes stronger as the actual assembly of the vehicle takes place at the customer's jobsite. There is no question that the cost of the resources devoted to onsite assembly could be cost-effectively traced to a specific job.

With respect to tariffs, in 2018 Caterpillar reported an increase in cost of sales of 11 percent, due, in large part, to tariffs on steel and aluminum imports. The cost pressures did not let up in 2019, when the company reported paying tariffs of $70 million in just the second quarter of the year. To respond to the increased costs, Caterpillar redesigned some of its machines to reduce the number of parts needed, thereby reducing overall manufacturing costs.

Sources: https://www.foxbusiness.com/financials/caterpillar-misses-profit-estimates-after-warnings-on-trump-tariffs; https://www.supplychaindive.com/news/caterpillar-tariffs-manufacturing-costs-economy/559471/ (both accessed December 11, 2019).

Self-Study Problem
(For answers, please see Solution.)

Journal Entries and Accounting for Overhead

Watkins Machinery Company uses a normal job costing system. The company has the following partial trial balance information for March, the last month of its fiscal year:

Materials Inventory (X, $3,000; Y, $2,000; Indirect materials, $5,000)	$10,000
Work-in-Process Inventory (this is Job 101)	6,000
Finished Goods Inventory (this is Job 100)	10,000

These transactions relate to the month of March:

a. Purchased direct materials and indirect materials with the following summary of receiving reports:

Material X	$10,000
Material Y	10,000
Indirect materials	5,000
Total	$25,000

b. Issued direct materials and indirect materials with this summary of requisitions:

	Job 101	Job 102	Total
Material X	$5,000	$3,000	$ 8,000
Material Y	4,000	3,000	7,000
Subtotal	$9,000	$6,000	$15,000
Indirect materials			8,000
Total			$23,000

c.   Factory labor incurred is summarized by these time tickets:

Job 101	$ 12,000
Job 102	8,000
Indirect labor	5,000
Total	$25,000

d.   Factory utilities, factory depreciation, and factory insurance incurred are summarized as follows:

Utilities	$ 500
Depreciation	15,000
Insurance	2,500
Total	$18,000

e.   Factory overhead costs were applied to jobs at the predetermined rate of $15 per machine hour. Job 101 incurred 1,200 machine hours; Job 102 used 800 machine hours.

f.   Job 101 was completed; Job 102 was still in process at the end of March.

g.   Job 100 and Job 101 were shipped to customers during March. Both jobs had gross margins of 20% based on manufacturing cost.

h.   The company closed the overapplied or underapplied overhead to the Cost of Goods Sold account at the end of March.

Required

1.   Prepare journal entries to record the transactions for the events from parts (a) through (h).

2.   Compute the ending balance of the Work-in-Process Inventory account.

3.   Compute the overhead variance and indicate whether it is overapplied or underapplied.

4.   Close the overhead variance to the Cost of Goods Sold account.

The Student Resources section of Connect includes video tutorials for the Self-Study Problems.

Questions

4-1   What is the strategic role of a costing system?

4-2   Identify the three characteristics of costing systems.

4-3   Distinguish between job costing and process costing.

4-4   Explain when companies are likely to use a job costing system or a process costing system. Provide examples.

4-5   Which costing system is extensively used in the service industry for hospitals, law firms, or accounting firms? Explain why.

4-6   What document is prepared to accumulate costs for each separate job in a job costing system? What types of costs are recorded in the document?

4-7   Explain how predetermined factory overhead rates are computed and why they are used to apply factory overhead to units of products instead of actual overhead costs.

4-8   What is the role of materials requisitions in a job costing system? Time tickets? Bills of materials?

4-9   What does the following statement mean? "Accounting for overhead involves an important cost-benefit issue." Why is that issue important?

4-10   Describe the flow of costs through a job costing system from materials through finished product.

4-11   What do *underapplied overhead* and *overapplied overhead* mean? How are these amounts disposed of at the end of a period?

4-12   Why would a manufacturing firm switch from direct labor hours to machine hours as the cost driver for factory overhead application?

4-13   Explain why overhead might be overapplied in a given period.

4-14   Distinguish between an actual costing system and a normal costing system. What are the components of actual manufacturing costs and the components of normal manufacturing costs?

4-15   What is the best way to choose an appropriate cost driver or cost drivers when applying factory overhead?

4-16   What is the difference between normal and abnormal spoilage?

4-17   How is job costing in a service firm different from job costing in a manufacturer?

Brief Exercises

[LO 4-3, 4-4] 4-18 A small consulting firm has an overhead rate of 200% of direct labor charged to each job. The materials cost (including travel and other direct costs) for a particular job is $10,000, and the direct labor is $20,000. What is the total job cost for this job?

[LO 4-4] 4-19 Nieto Machine Shop budgeted 4,000 labor hours and 8,000 machine hours used in May. Total budgeted overhead for May is $80,000. What is the overhead rate using labor hours and also using machine hours? Which would you pick and why?

[LO 4-4] 4-20 If the overhead rate is $10 per machine hour and there are 20 labor hours, 16 machine hours, and two personnel on the job, how much overhead should be applied to the job?

[LO 4-4] 4-21 Some firms pool overhead into a single plantwide overhead pool, while others accumulate overhead costs into manufacturing departments, each of which has an overhead cost pool and overhead cost application rate. Which approach is likely to provide more accurate cost numbers for cost estimating, pricing, and performance evaluation?

[LO 4-4] 4-22 Assume the following for White Top Inc. for the current fiscal year. White Top applies overhead on the basis of units produced.

Budgeted overhead	$200,000
Actual overhead	$222,000
Actual labor hours	15,000
Actual number of units sold	43,000
Underapplied overhead	$ 20,000
Budgeted production (units)	50,000

Required How many units were produced in the current fiscal year?

[LO 4-4] 4-23 Assume the following for Round Top Inc. for the current fiscal year. Round Top applies overhead on the basis of units produced.

Budgeted overhead	$350,000
Actual overhead	$360,000
Actual labor hours	22,000
Actual number of units sold	650,000
Overapplied overhead	$ 30,000
Budgeted production (units)	700,000

Required How many units were produced in the current fiscal year?

[LO 4-4] 4-24 Use the following information from BSJ Industries to determine the predetermined overhead rate based on direct labor costs.

Direct labor hours	50,000
Average hourly pay rate	$16.00
Manufacturing overhead	$1,400,000

[LO 4-4] 4-25 For the current year BSJ Industries estimated overhead would be $1,400,000 and there would be 70,000 machine hours. Using machines hours as the allocation base, how much overhead would be assigned to each of the jobs listed below?

Job	Machine Hours
246	5,200
247	4,000

[LO 4-5] 4-26 Assume that actual overhead is $613,000 in a given year, the overhead rate is $10 per unit, 60,000 units were sold, and 59,000 units were produced. For the end of the year, is overhead underapplied or overapplied? By how much?

[LO 4-5] 4-27 If the end-of-period balance for Cost of Goods Sold is $90,000 and underapplied overhead is $10,000, what is the ending balance in the Cost of Goods Sold account after adjusting for the underapplied overhead?

[LO 4-5] 4-28 When overhead is overapplied, is the balance of Cost of Goods Sold, before adjustment, too low or too high? Why?

Exercises

[LO 4-1, 4-2]   4-29 **Choice of Costing System**

Required   The following is a list of websites for a number of companies. Briefly describe each company and indicate whether it is more likely to use job costing or process costing. Explain why in each case. Also explain why you think each company (a) is or is not a global company and (b) has significant environmental issues in its operations.

1. New Century Software Inc. at www.newcenturysoftware.com.
2. FedEx Office at www.fedex.com.
3. Martin Marietta at www.martinmarietta.com.
4. Paramount Pictures at www.paramount.com.
5. Coca-Cola at www.coca-cola.com.

[LO 4-1, 4-2]   4-30 **Choice of Costing System**

Required   The following is a list of websites for a number of companies. Briefly describe each company and indicate whether it is more likely to use job costing or process costing. Explain why in each case. Also explain why you think each company (a) is or is not a global company and (b) has significant environmental issues in its operations.

1. Zurich Insurance Group at www.zurich.com.
2. Reichhold Chemical Co. at www.reichhold.com.
3. Nestlé S.A. at www.nestle.com.
4. Evian at www.evian.com.

[LO 4-3, 4-4, 4-5]   4-31 **Cost Flows; Applying Overhead** Erkens Company uses a job costing system with normal costing and applies factory overhead on the basis of machine hours. At the beginning of the year, management estimated that the company would incur $1,980,000 of factory overhead costs and use 66,000 machine hours.

Erkens Company recorded the following events during the month of April:

a. Purchased 180,000 pounds of materials on account; the cost was $5.00 per pound.
b. Issued 120,000 pounds of materials to production, of which 15,000 pounds were used as indirect materials.
c. Incurred direct labor costs of $240,000 and $40,000 of indirect labor costs.
d. Recorded depreciation on equipment for the month, $75,700.
e. Recorded insurance costs for the manufacturing property, $3,500.
f. Paid $8,500 cash for utilities and other miscellaneous items for the manufacturing plant.
g. Completed Job H11 costing $7,500 and Job G28 costing $77,000 during the month and transferred them to the Finished Goods Inventory account.
h. Shipped Job G28 to the customer during the month. The job was invoiced at 35% above cost.
i. Used 7,700 machine hours during April.

Required

1. Compute Erkens Company's predetermined overhead rate for the year.
2. Prepare journal entries to record the events that occurred during April.
3. Compute the amount of overapplied or underapplied overhead and prepare a journal entry to close overapplied or underapplied overhead into Cost of Goods Sold on April 30.

[LO 4-4, 4-5]   4-32 **Application of Overhead** Alles Company uses a job costing system that applies factory overhead on the basis of direct labor dollars. No job was in process on February 1. During the month of February, the company worked on these three jobs:

	Job Number		
	B10	**C44**	**G15**
Direct labor ($8/hour)	$34,000	?	$10,000
Direct materials	42,000	61,000	?
Overhead applied	?	20,750	6,000

During the month, the company completed and transferred Job B10 to the Finished Goods Inventory at the cost of $148,650 at the end of the month. Actual factory overhead costs during the month totaled $38,500.

Required

1. What is the predetermined factory overhead rate?

2. Compute the amount of underapplied or overapplied overhead for February.

[LO 4-3, 4-4, 4-5] 4-33 **Job Costing** Johnson Inc. is a job-order manufacturing company that uses a predetermined overhead rate based on direct labor hours to apply overhead to individual jobs. For the current year, estimated direct labor hours are 95,000 and estimated factory overhead is $617,500. The following information is for September of the current year. Job A was completed during September, and Job B was started but not finished.

September 1, Inventories	
Materials Inventory	$ 7,500
Work-in-Process Inventory (All Job A)	31,200
Finished Goods Inventory	67,000
Material purchases	104,000
Direct materials requisitioned	
Job A	65,000
Job B	33,500
Direct labor hours	
Job A	4,200
Job B	3,500
Labor costs incurred	
Direct labor ($8.50/hour)	$ 65,450
Indirect labor	13,500
Supervisory salaries	6,000
Rental costs	
Factory	7,000
Administrative offices	1,800
Total equipment depreciation costs	
Factory	7,500
Administrative offices	1,600
Indirect materials used	12,000

Required

1. What is the total cost of Job A?

2. What is the total factory overhead applied during September?

3. What is the overapplied or underapplied overhead for September?

[LO 4-3, 4-4, 4-6] 4-34 **Application of Overhead** Whitley Construction Company is in the home remodeling business. Whitley has three teams of highly skilled employees, each of whom has multiple skills involving carpentry, painting, and other home remodeling activities. Each team is led by an experienced employee who coordinates the work done on each job. As the needs of different jobs change, some team members may be shifted to other teams for short periods of time. Whitley uses a job costing system to determine job costs and to serve as a basis for bidding and pricing the jobs. Direct materials and direct labor are easily traced to each job using Whitley's cost tracking software. Overhead consists of the purchase and maintenance of construction equipment, some supervisory labor, the cost of bidding for new customers, and administrative costs. Whitley uses an annual overhead rate based on direct labor hours.

Whitley has recently completed work for three clients: Harrison, Barnes, and Tyler. The cost data for each of the three jobs are summarized below:

Job	Direct Materials	Direct Labor Hours	Direct Labor Cost
Harrison	$ 6,753	45	$15,367
Barnes	13,229	88	22,184
Tyler	42,338	133	49,654

Budgeted direct materials cost and direct labor cost for the year are estimated at $450,000 and $600,000, respectively. Direct labor hours are budgeted at 22,500 hours, and total overhead is budgeted at $495,000.

Required

1. Calculate the total cost of each of the three jobs.

2. Suppose that for the entire year, Whitley used 23,800 labor hours and total actual overhead was $525,000. What is the amount of underapplied or overapplied overhead?

3. Whitley's business is very seasonal, with summer being the period of high activity and winter the low period. How would seasonality potentially affect the job costing at the company?

4. What are some of the potential sustainability issues for Whitley?

5. Whitley has chosen direct labor hours as the cost-driver base for applying overhead. What are some alternative cost drivers, and how would you choose among them?

[LO 4-4, 4-5] 4-35 **Application of Overhead** Tomek Company uses a job costing system that applies factory overhead on the basis of direct labor hours. The company's factory overhead budget for the current year included the following estimates:

Budgeted total factory overhead	$568,000
Budgeted total direct labor hours	71,000

At the end of the year, the company shows these results:

Actual factory overhead	$582,250
Actual direct labor hours	71,500

Required

1. Compute the firm's predetermined factory overhead rate for the current year.

2. Calculate the amount of overapplied or underapplied overhead.

3. Prepare a journal entry to transfer the underapplied or overapplied overhead to the Cost of Goods Sold account.

[LO 4-4, 4-6] 4-36 **Application of Overhead** Norton Associates is an advertising agency in Austin, Texas. The company's controller estimated that it would incur $325,000 in overhead costs for the current year. Because the overhead costs of each project change in direct proportion to the amount of direct professional hours incurred, the controller decided that overhead should be applied on the basis of professional hours. The controller estimated 25,000 professional hours for the year. During October, Norton incurred the following costs to make a 20-second TV commercial for Central Texas Bank:

Direct materials	$32,000
Direct professional hours ($50/hour)	1,200

The industry customarily bills customers at 150% of total cost.

Required

1. Compute the predetermined overhead rate.

2. What is the total amount of the bill that Norton will send Central Texas Bank?

[LO 4-4, 4-6] 4-37 **Application of Overhead** Progressive Painting Company (PPC) is a successful company in commercial and residential painting. PPC has a variety of jobs: new construction, repair and repainting of existing structures, and restoration of very old buildings and homes. The company is known for the quality and reliability of its work, and customers expect to pay a little more for those benefits. One of the company's core values is sustainability, and it insists on using the most environmentally friendly paints and materials in its work; it has refused jobs where the client required a more environmentally harmful paint than PPC thought was appropriate for the application. The company's commitment to sustainability has lost PPC some jobs, but it has also attracted a loyal and growing customer base.

The company uses job costing and applies overhead on the basis of direct labor hours. Overhead for the company consists of painting equipment, trucks, supervisory labor, supplies, and administrative operating costs. The total budgeted costs for the year are shown below:

	Budgeted Data
Direct materials	$2,900,000
Direct labor hours	33,500
Direct labor dollars	$750,000
Gallons of paint	20,000
Total overhead	$360,125

PPC has just completed two jobs:

Job	Direct Materials	Gallons of Paint	Direct Labor Hours	Direct Labor Cost
Prevette	$3,800	24	42	$ 855
Harmon	4,600	38	66	1,366

Required

1. Determine the total cost of each job assuming that jobs include both direct and general operating costs (operating overhead).

2. The Prevette job required oil-based paint, and the cleanup after the job required the use of chemicals that, after use, had to be disposed of in an environmentally appropriate way. In contrast, the Harmon job required water-based paint, and the job cleanup was very quick and simple and involved no harmful chemicals. Does the job costing in requirement 1 of this question capture the difference between the two jobs in regard to the types of paint used? Do you think the costing system should capture this difference, if any, and if so, how do you think the costing system should be changed?

[LO 4-8]   4-38   **Spoilage and Scrap (Appendix)** Lexan Textile Company's Job X12 had one of its 20 units spoiled. The cost incurred on the unit was $600. It was specific normal spoilage with an estimated disposal price of $300 for the spoiled unit. Job Y34 had common normal spoilage with the estimated cost of $400 from the general production process failure and abnormal spoilage of $200. The company also incurred scrap due to Job Y34 and sold it for $80. It also sold the scrap common to all jobs for $120 cash in May.

Required

1. Make the necessary journal entries to record normal and abnormal spoilage costs.

2. Make the necessary journal entries to record both types of scrap sold.

Problems

[LO 4-2, 4-4]   4-39   **Overhead Rates** Ennis Inc. (EI; www.ennis.com) is a Texas-based machine-intensive printing company that produces business forms. The resources demanded by a specific job depend on the type and amount of paper used and the composition and the construction of the business form. All jobs are constrained by the time necessary on a press and on a collator capable of producing forms at the required size.

EI uses job costing for pricing and bidding decisions. EI uses a separate factory overhead rate for each machine. Costs of machine operator, support personnel, and supplies are identified directly with presses and collators. Other factory overhead costs—including insurance, supervision, and office salaries—are allocated to machines based on their processing capacity (the cost driver is the number of feet of business forms per minute) weighted by the maximum paper width and complexity (the cost driver is the number of colors and other features) that they are capable of handling.

When EI receives a request for a bid on a particular job, the company uses computer software to determine direct materials costs based on the type and quantity of paper. Then, it identifies the least expensive press and collator that are capable of handling the specifications for the business form ordered. The third step is to estimate the total press and collator processing costs by using specific cost-driver rates per machine time multiplied by the estimated processing time. The bid price is calculated by adding a standard markup to the total press, collator, and direct materials costs. A higher markup is used for rush jobs and jobs requiring special features.

Required   Discuss the strengths and weaknesses of the EI costing system and its strategic implications.

[LO 4-4]   4-40   **Plantwide vs. Departmental Overhead Rate** Rose Bach was recently hired as controller of Empco Inc., a sheet metal manufacturer. Empco has been in the sheet metal business for many years and is currently investigating ways to modernize its manufacturing process. At the first staff meeting Rose attended, Bob Kelley, chief engineer, presented a proposal for automating the drilling department. He recommended that Empco purchase two robots that could replace the eight direct labor workers in the department. The cost savings outlined in Bob's proposal included eliminating direct labor cost and reducing factory overhead cost to zero in the drilling department because Empco charges factory overhead on the basis of direct labor dollars using a plantwide rate.

Empco's president was puzzled by Kelley's explanation of cost savings, believing it made no sense. Rose agreed, explaining that as firms become more automated, they should rethink their factory overhead systems. The president then asked her to look into the matter and prepare a report for the next staff meeting.

Required

1. Describe the shortcomings of Empco's current system for applying overhead.
2. Explain the misconceptions in Bob Kelley's statement that the factory overhead cost in the drilling department would be reduced to zero if the automation proposal were implemented.
3. How would you improve the allocation of overhead costs?

[LO 4-4]   4-41 **Plantwide vs. Departmental Overhead Rate** Ryan Corporation manufactures auto steering systems. Prime cost and machine time estimates for one unit of the product for the year follow:

Direct materials	$200
Direct labor ($12/hour)	$300
Machine hours	20

This product requires 15 hours of direct labor in Department A and 10 hours in Department B. Also, it requires 5 machine hours in Department A and 15 machine hours in Department B. Using output as the activity, the factory overhead costs estimated in these two departments follow:

	A	B
Variable cost	$150,000	$ 80,000
Fixed cost	94,000	163,000

Management expects the firm to produce 1,000 units during the year.

Required

1. Assume that factory overhead was applied on the basis of direct labor hours. Compute the predetermined plantwide factory overhead rate.
2. If factory overhead were applied on the basis of machine hours, what would be the plantwide overhead rate?
3. If the company produced 1,000 units during the year, what was the total amount of applied factory overhead in each department in requirements 1 and 2?
4. If you were asked to evaluate the performance of each department manager, which allocation basis (cost driver) would you use? Why?
5. Compute the departmental overhead rate and amount of applied overhead for Department A using direct labor hours as the allocation base and for Department B using machine hours as the allocation base.

[LO 4-3, 4-4, 4-5]   4-42 **Cost Flows and Application of Overhead** Work-in-Process Inventory for Carston Inc. at the beginning of the year was a single job, Job T114:

Job #	Direct Materials	Direct Labor	Overhead	Total
T114	$31,500	$16,250	$28,750	$76,500

The company's budgeted costs for the year are as follows:

Budgeted overhead	
Variable	
Indirect materials	$ 68,000
Indirect labor	56,000
Employee benefits	28,000
Fixed	
Supervision	13,000
Depreciation	15,000
Total	$180,000
Budgeted direct labor dollars	$ 90,000
Rate per direct labor dollar	200.00%

The company's actual costs incurred during the year are as follows:

| | Incurred by Jobs | | | |
Job #	Materials	Labor	Other	Total
T114	$ 2,000	$10,000	$ —	$ 12,000
T119	24,000	18,000	—	42,000
T133	8,000	34,000	—	42,000
T136	1,000	16,000	—	17,000
	$35,000	$78,000		$113,000
Overhead				
Indirect materials and supplies	60,000	—	—	60,000
Indirect labor	—	50,000	—	50,000
Employee benefits	—	—	33,000	33,000
Depreciation	—	—	15,000	15,000
Supervision	—	12,000	—	12,000
Total	$60,000	$62,000	$48,000	$170,000

Required

1. What was the actual factory overhead for Carston Inc. for the year?
2. What was overapplied or underapplied overhead for the year?
3. Job T114 was the only job completed and sold in the year. What amount was included in the Cost of Goods Sold account for this job?
4. What was the amount of Work-in-Process Inventory at the end of the year?

[LO 4-3, 4-4, 4-5]   4-43   **Cost Flows; Application of Overhead** Dream Makers is a small manufacturer of gold and platinum jewelry. It uses a job costing system that applies overhead on the basis of direct labor hours. Budgeted factory overhead for the year was $455,600, and management budgeted 33,500 direct labor-hours. The company had no Materials, Work-in-Process, or Finished Goods Inventory at the beginning of April. These transactions were recorded during April:

a. April insurance cost for the manufacturing property and equipment was $1,800. The premium had been paid in January.

b. Recorded $1,025 depreciation on an administrative asset.

c. Purchased 21 pounds of high-grade polishing materials at $16 per pound (indirect materials).

d. Paid factory utility bill, $6,510, in cash.

e. Incurred 4,000 hours and paid payroll costs of $160,000. Of this amount, 1,000 hours and $20,000 were indirect labor costs.

f. Incurred and paid other factory overhead costs, $6,270.

g. Purchased $24,500 of materials. Direct materials included unpolished semiprecious stones and gold. Indirect materials included supplies and polishing materials.

h. Requisitioned $18,500 of direct materials and $1,600 of indirect materials from Materials Inventory.

i. Incurred miscellaneous selling and administrative expenses, $5,660.

j. Incurred $3,505 depreciation on manufacturing equipment for April.

k. Paid advertising expenses in cash, $2,650.

l. Applied factory overhead to production on the basis of direct labor hours.

m. Completed goods costing $64,000 during the month.

n. Made sales on account in April, $57,410. The Cost of Goods Sold was $47,860.

Required

1. Compute the firm's predetermined factory overhead rate for the year.
2. Prepare journal entries to record the April events.
3. Calculate the amount of overapplied or underapplied overhead on April 30.
4. Prepare a schedule of Cost of Goods Manufactured and a schedule of Cost of Goods Sold.
5. Compute the amount of overapplied or underapplied overhead that should be prorated to Work-in-Process, Finished Goods, and Cost of Goods Sold.
6. Using the results from requirements 4 and 5, prepare the income statement for April. Comment on whether closing the entire amount to Cost of Goods Sold would have been appropriate in this case.

[LO 4-3, 4-4, 4-5] 4-44 **Application of Overhead** The following information applies to the O'Donnell Company for March production. There are only two jobs (X and Y) in production in March.

a. Purchased direct materials and indirect materials with the following summary of receiving reports:

Material A	$16,000
Material B	12,000
Indirect materials	3,000
Total	$31,000

b. Issued direct materials and indirect materials with this summary of requisitions:

	Job X	Job Y	Total
Material A	$ 8,000	$16,000	$24,000
Material B	3,000	8,000	11,000
Subtotal	$11,000	$24,000	$35,000
Indirect materials			39,000
Total			$74,000

c. Factory labor incurred is summarized by these time tickets:

Job X	$22,000
Job Y	15,000
Indirect labor	28,000
Total	$65,000

d. Factory utilities, factory depreciation, and factory insurance incurred is summarized as follows:

Utilities	$ 3,000
Depreciation	18,000
Insurance	2,500
Total	$23,500

e. Factory overhead costs were applied to jobs at the predetermined rate of $46 per machine hour. Job X incurred 1,100 machine hours; Job Y used 800 machine hours.

f. Job X was completed; Job Y was still in process at the end of March.

The company closed the overapplied or underapplied overhead to the Cost of Goods Sold account at the end of March.

Required

1. Calculate the total manufacturing cost for Job X and Job Y for March.
2. Calculate the amount of overapplied or underapplied overhead and state whether the Cost of Goods Sold account will be increased or decreased by the adjustment.

[LO 4-3, 4-4, 4-5] 4-45 **Application of Overhead** The following information is for Punta Company for July:

a. Factory overhead costs were applied to jobs at the predetermined rate of $42.50 per labor hour. Job S incurred 6,175 labor hours; Job T used 4,275 labor hours.

b. Job S was shipped to customers during July.

c. Job T was still in process at the end of July.

d. The overapplied or underapplied overhead to the Cost of Goods Sold account was closed at the end of July.

e. Factory utilities, factory depreciation, and factory insurance incurred are summarized as follows:

Utilities	$14,250
Depreciation	45,000
Insurance	18,000
Total	$77,250

f. Direct materials and indirect materials used are as follows:

	Job S	Job T	Total
Material A	$28,500	$ 71,250	$ 99,750
Material B	12,000	35,000	47,000
Subtotal	$40,500	$106,250	$146,750
Indirect materials			211,000
Total			$357,750

g. Direct labor incurred for the two jobs and indirect labor are as follows:

Job S	$ 55,500
Job T	45,000
Indirect labor	133,000
Total	$233,500

Required

1. Calculate the total manufacturing cost for Job S and Job T for July.
2. Calculate the amount of overapplied or underapplied overhead and state whether the Cost of Goods Sold account will be increased or decreased by the adjustment.

[LO 4-3, 4-4, 4-5] 4-46 **Cost Flows; Application of Overhead** Mooresville Corporation manufactures reproductions of eighteenth-century, classical-style furniture. It uses a job costing system that applies factory overhead on the basis of direct labor hours. Budgeted factory overhead for the year was $1,261,500, and management budgeted 87,000 direct labor hours. Mooresville had no Materials, Work-in-Process, or Finished Goods Inventory at the beginning of August. These transactions were recorded during August:

a. Purchased 5,000 square feet of oak on account at $26 per square foot.
b. Purchased 50 gallons of glue on account at $36 per gallon (indirect material).
c. Requisitioned 3,500 square feet of oak and 31 gallons of glue for production.
d. Incurred and paid payroll costs of $187,900. Of this amount, $46,000 were indirect labor costs; direct labor personnel earned $22 per hour.
e. Paid factory utility bill, $15,230 in cash.
f. August's insurance cost for the manufacturing property and equipment was $3,500. The premium had been paid in March.
g. Incurred $8,500 depreciation on manufacturing equipment for August.
h. Recorded $2,400 depreciation on an administrative asset.
i. Paid advertising expenses in cash, $5,500.
j. Incurred and paid other factory overhead costs, $13,500.
k. Incurred miscellaneous selling and administrative expenses, $13,250.
l. Applied factory overhead to production on the basis of direct labor hours.
m. Produced completed goods costing $146,000 during the month.
n. Sales on account in August were $135,000. The Cost of Goods Sold was $112,000.

Required

1. Compute the firm's predetermined factory overhead rate for the year.
2. Prepare journal entries to record the August events. Letter your entries from a to n.
3. Calculate the amount of overapplied or underapplied overhead to be closed to the Cost of Goods Sold account on August 31.
4. Prepare a schedule of Cost of Goods Manufactured and Cost of Goods Sold.
5. Compute the amount of overapplied or underapplied overhead that should be prorated to Work-in-Process, Finished Goods and Cost of Goods Sold
6. Using the results from requirements 4 and 5, prepare the income statement for August. Comment on whether closing the entire amount of overapplied or underapplied overhead to Cost of Goods Sold would have been appropriate in this case.

[LO 4-3, 4-4, 4-6] 4-47 **Application of Overhead** The Meyers CPA firm has the following overhead budget for the year:

Overhead	
Indirect materials	$ 300,000
Indirect labor	1,600,000
Depreciation—Building	293,000
Depreciation—Furniture	25,000
Utilities	285,000
Insurance	34,000
Property taxes	48,000
Other expenses	135,000
Total	$2,720,000

The firm estimates total direct labor cost for the year to be $1,700,000. The firm uses direct labor cost as the cost driver to apply overhead to clients.

During January, the firm worked for many clients; data for two of them follow:

Gargus account	
Direct labor	$2,500
Feller account	
Direct labor	$8,500

Required
1. Compute the firm's predetermined overhead rate.
2. Compute the amount of overhead to be charged to the Gargus and Feller accounts using the predetermined overhead rate calculated in requirement 1.
3. Compute total job cost for the Gargus account and the Feller account.

[LO 4-3, 4-4] 4-48 **Job Cost; Cost Flows; Application of Overhead; Spreadsheet Application; Pivot Tables in Excel (see Excel tutorial on text website)** Decker Screw Manufacturing Company produces special screws made to customer specifications. During June, the following data pertained to these costs:

Summary of Direct Materials Requisitions

Department Number	Job Number	Requisition Number	Quantity	Cost per Hour
1	2906	B9766	4,550	$ 1.34
2	2907	B9767	110	22.18
1	2908	B9768	1,000	9.00
1	2906	B9769	4,430	1.35
2	2908	B9770	23	48.00

Summary of Direct Labor Time Tickets

Department Number	Job Number	Ticket Number	Hours	Cost per Unit
1	2906	1056-1168	1,102	$6.50
2	2907	2121-2130	136	8.88
1	2908	1169-1189	151	6.50
2	2908	2131-1239	32	8.88
1	2906	1190-1239	810	6.50

Summary of Factory Overhead Application Rates

Department Number	Basis of Application Rates
1	$3 per direct labor hour
2	150% of direct labor cost

Decker had no beginning Work-in-Process Inventory for June. Of the jobs begun in June, Job 2906 was completed and sold on account for $30,000, Job 2907 was completed but not sold, and Job 2908 was still in process.

Required

1. Calculate the direct materials, direct labor, factory overhead, and total costs for each job started in June.

2. Perform the same calculations as in requirement 1, but assume that the direct labor rate per hour increased by 10% in Department 1 and 25% in Department 2.

3. Perform the same calculations as in requirement 1, except use pivot tables in Excel to arrive at the answer. The Excel Tutorial for Chapter 4, in Connect, explains how to use pivot tables and provides information on an Excel add-in called Power Pivot.

4. Perform the same calculations as in requirement 2, except use pivot tables in Excel to arrive at the answer.

[LO 4-3, 4-4, 4-5]   4-49 **Application of Overhead; Cost Flows** Haughton Company uses a job costing system for its production costs and a predetermined factory overhead rate based on direct labor costs to apply factory overhead to all jobs. During the month of July, the firm processed three jobs: X13, X14, and X15, of which X13 was started in June.

Inventories	July 1	July 31
Direct Materials	$ 36,500	?
Work-in-Process	41,000	?
Finished Goods	0	0
Cost of Goods Sold	$?	
Direct materials purchased in July	55,000	
Materials issued to production:		
X13	16,380	
X14	24,220	
X15	14,000	
Factory labor hours used ($30/hour):		
X13	3,500	
X14	2,800	
X15	1,600	
Indirect labor	6,900	
Other factory overhead costs incurred:		
Rent	$131,500	
Utilities	180,600	
Repairs and maintenance	188,500	
Depreciation	131,100	
Other	56,000	

As of July 31, Job X13 was sold and Jobs X14 and X15 were still in process. Total factory overhead applied in July was $900,600.

Required

1. Compute the predetermined factory overhead rate.

2. Compute the amount of the Direct Materials account at the end of July.

3. Compute the actual factory overhead cost incurred during the month of July.

4. Compute the ending balance of the Work-in-Process Inventory account for July.

5. Prepare the Statement of Cost of Goods Manufactured for July.

6. Compute the amount of overapplied or underapplied overhead.

7. What is the cost per unit of Job X13 if it has a total of 100 units?

8. Prepare the Statement of Cost of Goods Sold for July.

[LO 4-4]   4-50 **Application of Overhead; Ethics** Aero Systems is a manufacturer of airplane parts and engines for a variety of military and commercial aircraft. All of Aero System's government contracts are priced on a cost-plus basis, while nongovernment jobs are not. It has two production departments. Department A is machine-intensive; Department B is labor-intensive. Aero Systems has adopted a traditional plantwide rate using a direct labor hour–based overhead allocation system. The company recently conducted a pilot study using a departmental overhead rate costing system. This system used two overhead allocation bases: machine hours for Department A and direct labor hours for Department B. The study showed that the system, which will be more accurate and timely, will assign lower costs to the government jobs and higher costs to the company's nongovernmental jobs. Apparently, the current (less accurate) direct labor–based costing system has overcosted government jobs and under-costed private business jobs. On hearing of this, top management has decided to scrap the plans for adopting the new departmental overhead rate costing system because government jobs constitute 40% of Aero Systems's business and the new system will reduce the price and thus the profit for this part of its business.

Required   As the management accountant participating in this pilot study project, what is your responsi-bility when you hear of top management's decision to cancel the plans to implement the new departmental overhead rate costing system? What would you do?

[LO 4-7] 4-51 **Operation Costing** Brian Canning Co., which sells canned corn, uses an operation costing system. Cans of corn are classified as either sweet or regular, depending on the type of corn used. Both types of corn go through the separating and cleaning operations, but only regular corn goes through the creaming operation. During January, two batches of corn were canned from start to finish. Batch X consisted of 800 pounds of sweet corn, and Batch Y consisted of 700 pounds of regular corn. The company had no beginning or ending Work-in-Process Inventory. The following cost information is for the month of January:

	Batch	Cost	Batch Size
Raw sweet corn	X	$ 5,200	800 lbs
Raw regular corn	Y	2,450*	700 lbs
Separating department costs		1,500	
Cleaning department costs		900	
Creaming department costs		210	

*Includes $300 for cream.

Required
1. Compute the unit cost for sweet corn and regular corn.
2. Record appropriate journal entries.

[LO 4-8] 4-52 **Spoilage, Rework, and Scrap (Appendix)** Richport Company manufactures products that often require specification changes or modifications to meet customer needs. Consequently, Richport employs a job costing system for its operations.

Although the specification changes and modifications are commonplace, Richport has been able to establish a normal spoilage rate of 2.5% of total units produced (before spoilage is identified). The company recognizes normal spoilage during the budgeting process and classifies it as a component of factory overhead. Thus, the predetermined overhead rate used to apply factory overhead costs to jobs includes an allowance for net spoilage cost for normal spoilage. If spoilage on a job exceeds the normal rate, it is considered abnormal and must be analyzed. The cause of the spoilage must then be submitted to management.

Randa Duncan, one of Richport's inspection managers, has been reviewing the output of Job N1192-122 that was recently completed. A total of 122,000 units had been started for the job, and 5,000 units were rejected at final inspection, meaning that the job yielded 117,000 good units.

Randa noted that 900 of the first units produced were rejected due to a very unusual design defect that was corrected immediately; no more units were rejected for this reason.

Randa was unable to identify a pattern for the remaining 4,100 rejected units. They can be sold at a salvage value of $7 per unit.

The total costs accumulated for all 122,000 units of Job N1192-122 follow. Although the job is completed, all of these costs are still in the Work-in-Process Inventory account (i.e., the cost of the completed job has not been transferred to the Finished Goods Inventory account).

Direct materials	$2,196,000
Direct labor	1,830,000
Applied factory overhead	2,928,000
Total cost of job	$6,954,000

Required
1. Explain the distinction between normal and abnormal spoilage.
2. Distinguish among spoiled units, rework units, and scrap.
3. Review the results and costs for Job N1192-122:
   a. Determine the normal input required to yield 117,000 good units.
   b. Prepare an analysis separating the spoiled units into normal and abnormal spoilage.
   c. Prepare the appropriate journal entries to account for Job N1192-122.

Solution to Self-Study Problem

Journal Entries and Accounting for Overhead

1. Journal entries:

(a)	Materials Inventory	25,000	
	Accounts Payable		25,000
	To record the purchase of direct materials and indirect materials.		
(b)	Work-in-Process Inventory	15,000	
	Factory Overhead	8,000	
	Materials Inventory		23,000
	To record direct and indirect materials issued.		
(c)	Work-in-Process Inventory	20,000	
	Factory Overhead	5,000	
	Accrued Payroll		25,000
	To record factory labor incurred.		
(d)	Factory Overhead	18,000	
	Utilities Payable		500
	Accumulated Depreciation—Factory		15,000
	Prepaid Insurance		2,500
	To record actual overhead costs incurred, including factory utilities, depreciation, and insurance.		
(e)	Work-in-Process Inventory	30,000	
	Factory Overhead		30,000
	To record the application of factory overhead to jobs.		

Summary of factory overhead applied

Job 101 ($15 per machine hour × 1,200 hours)	$18,000
Job 102 ($15 per machine hour × 800 hours)	12,000
Total	$30,000

(f)	Finished Goods Inventory	45,000	
	Work-in-Process Inventory		45,000
	To record the completion of Job 101.		

Total manufacturing cost for Job 101

Beginning inventory	$ 6,000
Direct materials added	9,000
Direct labor incurred	12,000
Factory overhead applied	18,000
Total	$45,000

(g)	Accounts Receivable	66,000	
	Sales		66,000
	To record the total sales revenue of Jobs 100 and 101.		
	Cost of Goods Sold	55,000	
	Finished Goods Inventory		55,000
	To record the total cost of goods sold.		

Summary of the total cost in shipping orders

Job 100	$10,000
Job 101	45,000
Total	$55,000

Sales = $55,000 × 120% = $66,000

2. Ending balance of the Work-in-Process Inventory account for Job 102:

Direct materials (X, $3,000; Y, $3,000)	$ 6,000
Direct labor	8,000
Factory overhead applied (800 machine hours × $15)	12,000
Total ending balance	$26,000

3. Factory overhead variance:

Actual factory overhead		
Indirect materials	$ 8,000	
Indirect labor	5,000	
Utilities	500	
Depreciation	15,000	
Insurance	2,500	$31,000
Less: Applied factory overhead		30,000
Underapplied factory overhead		$ 1,000

4. To record the disposition of underapplied factory overhead by closing the Factory Overhead account to the Cost of Goods Sold account:

(h)	Cost of Goods Sold	1,000	
	Factory Overhead		1,000

Please visit Connect to access a narrated, animated tutorial for solving this problem.

CHAPTER FIVE

Activity-Based Costing and Customer Profitability Analysis

After studying this chapter, you should be able to . . .

LO 5-1 Explain the strategic role of activity-based costing (ABC).

LO 5-2 Describe activity-based costing, the steps in developing an ABC system, and the benefits of an ABC system.

LO 5-3 Determine product costs under both the volume-based method and the activity-based method and contrast the two.

LO 5-4 Explain activity-based management (ABM).

LO 5-5 Describe how ABC/M is used in organizations.

LO 5-6 Use an activity-based approach to analyze customer profitability.

LO 5-7 Identify key factors for successful ABC/M implementation.

"Beware of little expenses. A small leak will sink a great ship."

Benjamin Franklin

SERGEI PRIMAKOV/Shutterstock

This chapter has a lot to do with implementing the spirit of Benjamin Franklin's observation—in cost management terms—that it really does matter how accurately you calculate a cost. Why? Consider Whitewood Industries (**www.whitewoodfurniture.com**), a North Carolina–based furniture manufacturer. The company uses Parawood as the primary raw material in much of the furniture it produces. Because Parawood is a secondary product of a rubber tree, it is expensive, but it is also considered an environmentally friendly product, which has helped increase the popularity of Whitewood's products. A quick look at its product offerings reveals hundreds of items, with varying levels of intricacy. If the company does not accurately determine the costs of making each of the different types of products, it runs the risk of incorrectly determining the profitability of each product type. The result could be increasing sales but declining profits and no clear understanding why.

Having a difficult time determining which of its products is most profitable is just one risk of inaccurate cost information. Perhaps the company keeps losing competitive bids for products and services and does not understand why. The lack of understanding of the use of resources and the assignment of related costs could put a company at a competitive disadvantage. Improved cost accuracy helps a company or organization to develop and to execute its strategy by providing accurate information about the cost of its products and services, the cost of serving its customers, the cost of dealing with its suppliers, and the cost of supporting business processes within the company.

The Strategic Role of Activity-Based Costing

LO 5-1

Explain the strategic role of activity-based costing (ABC).

Activity-based costing (ABC) is a method for improving the accuracy of cost determination. While ABC is a relatively recent innovation in cost accounting, it has been adopted by companies in varying industries and within government and not-for-profit organizations. Here is a quick example of how it works and why it is important. Suppose you and two friends (Joe and Al) go out for dinner. You each order a personal-size pizza, and Al suggests ordering a plate of appetizers for the table. You and Joe figure you will have a bite or two of the appetizers, so you agree. Dinner is great, but at the end Al is still hungry, so he orders another plate of appetizers, but this time, eats all of it. When it is time for the check, Al suggests the three of you split the cost of the meal equally. Is this fair? Perhaps Al should offer to pay more for the two appetizer plates. The individual pizzas are direct costs for each of you so that an equal share is fair, but while the appetizer plates were intended to be shared equally, it turns out that Al consumed most of them.

There are similar examples in manufacturing. Suppose you, Joe, and Al are also product managers at a plant that manufactures furniture. There are three product lines. Al is in charge of sofa manufacturing, Joe handles dining room tables and chairs, and you are in charge of bedroom furniture. The direct materials and labor costs are traced directly to each product line. Also, there are indirect manufacturing costs (overhead) that are associated with activities that cannot be traced to a single product, including materials acquisition, materials storage and handling, product inspection, manufacturing supervision, job scheduling, equipment maintenance, and fabric cutting. What if the company decides to charge each of the three product managers a "fair share" of the total indirect cost using the proportion of units produced in a manager's area relative to the total units produced? This approach is described in Chapter 4 and is commonly referred to as *volume-based costing*. Note that whether the proportions used are based on units of product, direct labor hours, or machine hours, each of these is volume-based.

But if, as is often the case, the usage of these activities is not proportional to the number of units produced, then some managers will be overcharged and others undercharged under the volume-based approach. For example, suppose Al insists on more frequent inspections of his production; then he should be charged a higher proportion of overhead (inspection) than that based on units alone. Moreover, why should you pay any portion of fabric cutting if your bedroom furniture does not require fabric?

Another consideration is that the volume-based method provides little incentive for the manager to control indirect costs. Unfortunately, the only way you could reduce your share of the indirect costs is to reduce your units produced (or hope that Joe and/or Al increases production)—not much of an incentive. On reflection, the approach that charges indirect costs to products based on units produced does not provide very accurate product costs and certainly does not provide the appropriate incentives for managing the indirect costs. One solution is to use activity-based costing to charge these indirect costs to the products, using detailed information on the activities that make up the indirect costs—inspection, fabric cutting, and materials handling. This chapter shows how to do it.

Role of Volume-Based Costing

Volume-based costing can be a good strategic choice for some firms. It is generally appropriate when common costs are relatively small or when activities supporting the production of the product or service are relatively homogeneous across different product lines. This may be the case, for example, for a firm that manufactures a limited range of paper products or a firm that produces a narrow range of agricultural products. Similarly, a professional service firm (law firm, accounting firm, etc.) may not need ABC because labor costs for the professional staff are the largest cost of the firm, and labor is also easily traced to clients (the cost object). For firms other than these, the ABC approach may be preferred to avoid the distortions from overcosting or undercosting that may occur using a volume-based approach.

Activity-Based Costing

To develop a costing system, we need to understand relationships among resources, activities, and products or services. Resources are used to perform activities, and products or services are a result of activities. Many of the resources used in an operation can be traced to individual products or services and identified as direct materials or direct labor costs. Most overhead costs relate only indirectly to final products or services. A costing system identifies costs with activities that consume resources and assigns resource costs to cost objects—such as products, services, or intermediate cost pools based on activities performed for the cost objects.

Resources, Activities, Resource Consumption Cost Drivers, and Activity Consumption Cost Drivers

Before discussing activity-based costing, several important terms must be understood: *activity, resource, cost driver, resource consumption cost driver,* and *activity consumption cost driver.*

An **activity** is a specific task, action, or unit of work done. An activity can be a single action or an aggregation of several actions. For example, moving inventory from workstation A to workstation B is an activity that may require only one action. Production setup is an activity that may include several actions. Activities are often listed in what is called an *activity dictionary.* An illustration of key activities in a firm's internal supply chain is shown by the Supply Chain Council in what is called the SCOR® (Supply Chain Operations Reference) on the Council's website (**www.apics.org/apics-for-business/products-and-services/apics-scc-frameworks/scor/**).

A **resource** is an economic element needed or consumed in performing activities. Labor and supplies, for example, are resources needed or used in performing manufacturing activities.

A **cost driver** is a factor that causes or relates to a change in the total cost of an activity. Because cost drivers cause or relate to cost changes, measured or quantified amounts of cost drivers are excellent bases for assigning resource costs to activities and for assigning the cost of activities to cost objects.

A cost driver is either a *resource consumption cost driver* or an *activity consumption cost driver.* A **resource consumption cost driver** is some measure of the frequency and intensity of demand placed on a resource by an activity. It is the basis for assigning resource costs to a particular activity or cost pool. Examples of resource consumption cost drivers are the number of items in a purchase or sales order, changes in product design, and square feet of occupied space.

activity
A specific task, action, or unit of work done.

resource
An economic element needed or consumed to perform activities.

cost driver
A factor that causes or relates to a change in the total cost of an activity.

resource consumption cost driver
A measure of the frequency and intensity of demand placed on a resource by an activity.

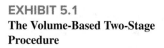

activity consumption cost driver
A measure of the demand placed on the resources by products, services, or customers.

An **activity consumption cost driver** is a measure of the demand placed on the resources by products, services, or customers. It is used to assign activity cost pool costs to cost objects. Examples of activity consumption cost drivers are the number of machine hours in the manufacturing of product X or the number of batches used to manufacture product Y.

What Is Activity-Based Costing?

activity-based costing (ABC)
A costing approach that assigns resource costs to cost objects based on activities performed for the cost objects.

Activity-based costing (ABC) is a costing approach that assigns resource costs to cost objects such as products, services, or customers based on activities performed for the cost objects. The premise of this costing approach is that a firm's products or services are the result of activities, and activities require resources, which have costs. Costs of resources are assigned to activities based on the activities that use or consume resources (resource consumption drivers), and costs of activities are assigned to cost objects based on activities performed for the cost objects (activity consumption drivers). ABC recognizes the causal or direct relationships between resource costs, cost drivers, activities, and cost objects in assigning costs to activities and then to cost objects.

ABC assigns factory overhead costs to cost objects such as products or services by identifying the resources and activities as well as their costs and amounts needed to produce output. Using resource consumption cost drivers, a firm determines the resource costs consumed by activities, calculates the cost of a unit of activity, and then assigns the cost of an activity to cost objects by multiplying the cost of each activity by the amount of the activity consumed by each of the cost objects.

The Two-Stage Cost Assignment Procedure

two-stage cost assignment
A procedure that assigns a firm's resource costs to cost pools and then to cost objects.

A **two-stage cost assignment** procedure assigns resource costs, such as factory overhead costs, to activity cost pools and then to cost objects to determine the amount of resource costs for each of the cost objects. Volume-based costing systems assign factory overhead costs first to plant or departmental cost pools and second to products or services (see Exhibit 5.1). In the first stage of volume-based costing, the factory overhead costs are combined into a single plant cost pool or several departmental cost pools. This approach is convenient and simple because many accounting systems in use today accumulate cost information by department, which is easily aggregated to the plant level. In the second stage, a volume-based rate is then used to apply overhead to each of the cost objects. The volume-based approach is used in Chapter 4 in job costing. A strictly volume-based cost assignment procedure, however, is likely to distort product or service costs. This is true especially in the second stage where the

EXHIBIT 5.1
The Volume-Based Two-Stage Procedure

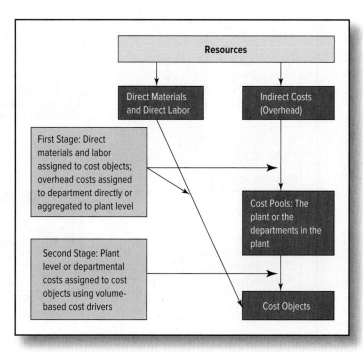

The world of sustainability reporting is evolving as it grows in significance, and management needs to be prepared. For many organizations, a sustainability framework of social, environmental, and economic performance offers an opportunity to create value for a variety of stakeholders. The challenge is for managers to understand the interrelationships between the inputs and processes and the outputs and outcomes of investments in sustainability. Developing an understanding of the inputs and processes of sustainability allows management to see how both financial and sustainability performance can be improved—and to think about opportunities for doing so.

Investments in sustainability initiatives can result in financial payoffs, such as reduced operating costs, increased revenues, lower capital costs, and, perhaps, stock market premiums. Some of the payoffs are operational in nature, such as process innovation, reduced cycle times, increased learning, and employee satisfaction. Identifying the resources needed and the full range of a sustainability initiative's impact is an important step toward better management decision making. As noted by Epstein and Buhovac, "Once identified, the impact of these costs on the company's activities, processes, products, and services can be analyzed using available tools. A number of companies, such as Sony Ericsson and Bristol-Myers Squibb, have begun the transition to improved social and environmental cost accounting in two ways: by clarifying their understanding of internal social and environmental costs through activity-based costing (ABC) and by placing a value on significant external costs through life-cycle costing (LCC) or other approaches."

Source: Marc Epstein and Adriana Rejc Buhovac, "A New Day for Sustainability," *Strategic Finance*, July 2014, pp. 25–33.

volume-based costing system uses a cost driver such as direct labor hours or output units to assign factory overhead costs. Because all products or services do not usually consume factory overhead resources in proportion to the volume-based measure the firm uses to assign factory overhead costs, a volume-based system often leads to inaccurate measures for the costs of support activities in its operations. This distortion becomes more serious when the firm manufactures a diverse mix of products with differences in volumes, sizes, or complexities and a substantial portion of the allocated costs are not related to output volume.

ABC systems differ from volume-based costing systems by linking uses of resources to activities and linking activity costs to products, services, or customers (see Exhibit 5.2). The first stage assigns factory overhead costs to activities by using appropriate resource consumption cost drivers. The second stage assigns the costs of activities to cost objects using appropriate activity consumption cost drivers that measure the demands cost objects have for the activities. By using cost drivers in both the first- and second-stage cost assignments,

EXHIBIT 5.2
The Activity-Based Two-Stage Procedure

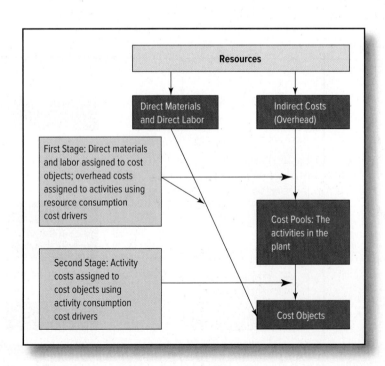

activity-based costing systems provide more accurate measures of product or service costs for the cost of activities that are not proportional to the volume of outputs produced.

In summary, ABC systems differ from volume-based costing systems in two ways. First, the ABC system defines cost pools as activities rather than production plant or department cost centers. Second, the cost drivers that the ABC system uses to assign activity costs to cost objects are drivers based on an activity or activities performed for the cost object. The volume-based approach uses a volume-based cost driver that often bears little or no relationship to the consumption of resources by the cost objects.

Steps in Developing an Activity-Based Costing System

Developing an activity-based costing system entails three steps: (1) identifying resource costs and activities, (2) assigning resource costs to activities, and (3) assigning activity costs to cost objects. Steps 1 and 2 constitute stage 1 from Exhibit 5.2, and step 3 is equivalent to stage 2 from that exhibit.

Step 1: Identify Resource Costs and Activities

Most firms record resource costs in specific accounts in the accounting system. These accounts are often based upon the underlying function of the resources that are included, such as purchasing, marketing, and office supplies. The first step in the ABC process is to determine which of the resources in each of the accounts is consumed by the identified activities. The costs of the resources consumed for a particular activity may be only a small part of the costs in a particular account. For example, a single factory supplies account may include the cost of resources consumed by several different manufacturing operations. Also, the resources to perform an activity may come from several accounts. For example, order fulfillment might require resources from warehousing, shipping, and billing accounts.

An activity analysis identifies the work performed to carry out a firm's operations. It includes gathering data from existing documents and records, as well as collecting additional data using questionnaires, observations, or interviews of key personnel. Questions that ABC project team members typically ask employees or managers in gathering activity data include the following:

- What work or activities do you do?
- How much time do you spend performing these activities?
- What resources are required to perform these activities?
- What value does the activity have for the product, service, customer, or organization?

With the help of industrial engineers and management accountants, the team also collects activity data by observing the work performed and making a list of all the activities involved.

Levels of Activities

To identify resource costs for various activities, a firm classifies all activities according to the way in which the activities consume resources.

unit-level activity
An activity performed for each unit of the cost object.

1. A **unit-level activity** is performed for each individual unit of product or service of the firm. Consider the activity of inserting a component. This activity is required for each unit produced, so the activity level varies in direct proportion to the quantity of the cost object produced. As a result, unit-level activities are said to be volume-based. The resource consumption driver and the activity consumption driver are likely to be the same for unit-level activities.

batch-level activity
An activity performed for each batch of products or services.

2. A **batch-level activity** is performed for each batch, or group, of products or services. Examples of batch-level activities are setting up machines, placing purchase orders, scheduling production, conducting inspections by batch, handling materials by batch, and expediting production.

product-level activity
An activity performed to support the production of a specific type of product or service.

3. A **product-level activity** supports the production of a specific type of product or service. Examples of product-level activities include designing products, purchasing parts required for products, and engaging in engineering changes to modify products.

facility-level activity
An activity performed to support operations in general (that is, an activity not related to volume of output, number of batches produced, or the support of individual products).

4. A **facility-level activity** supports operations in general. These activities are not caused by products or customer service needs and cannot be traced to individual units, batches, or products. Examples of facility-level activities include providing security for the plant, performing maintenance of general-purpose machines, and incurring factory property taxes and insurance. Some firms refer to these activities as business- or infrastructure-sustaining activities.

Note that a unit-level activity can always be traced to a batch (one of the units in the batch), a batch-level activity can always be traced to a product (one batch of this particular product), and a product-level activity can usually be traced to a manufacturing facility, but the reverse is not possible.

Step 2: Assign Resource Costs to Activities

Activities drive the consumption of resources, so the next step is to use resource consumption drivers to assign resource costs to activities. A firm should choose resource consumption cost drivers based on cause-and-effect relationships. Typical resource consumption cost drivers include the number of (1) labor hours for labor-intensive activities, (2) employees for payroll-related activities, (3) setups for batch-related activities, (4) moves for materials-handling activities, (5) machine hours for machine repair and maintenance, and (6) square feet for general maintenance and cleaning activities.

Ideally, the cost of resources is directly traced or assigned to activities, which requires measuring the actual usage of resources by an activity. For example, power used to operate a machine can be traced directly to that machine's operation by reading the meter attached to the machine. When direct tracing is not available, department managers and supervisors need to estimate the amount or percentage of time (or effort) employees spend on each identified activity. Exhibit 5.3 illustrates resources and resource consumption drivers for factory overhead costs at one of AT&T's plants.

Step 3: Assign Activity Costs to Cost Objects

The final step is to assign costs of activities to items of interest, generically called cost objects, based on the appropriate activity consumption cost drivers. The cost objects are the outputs resulting from the firm's activities and, typically, are products or services; however, customers, projects, and even business units can be cost objects. For example, the cost objects of an insurance company may be individual insurance policies sold to customers, claims processed, types of policies offered, insurance agents, or divisions of the company.

Benefits of Activity-Based Costing

Since the 1980s, an increasing number of firms have adopted an activity-based costing system. As previously noted, many firms found ABC reduced the distortions that resulted from using a volume-based system. ABC clearly shows the effect of differences in activities and changes in products or services on costs. Among the major benefits of activity-based costing that many firms have experienced from the improved information are:

1. **Better profitability measures.** ABC provides more accurate and informative product costs, leading to more accurate product and customer profitability measurements.
2. **Better decision making.** ABC provides more accurate measurements of activity-driving costs, helping managers to improve product and process value by making better product design decisions and better customer support decisions and fostering value-enhancement projects.

EXHIBIT 5.3
Resource and Resource Consumption Cost Drivers at an AT&T Plant

Resource	Resource Consumption Cost Driver
Personnel	Number of workers
Storeroom	Number of items picked for an order
Engineers	Time worked
Materials management	Time worked
Accounting	Time worked
Research and development	Number of new codes developed
Utilities	Square-footage

3. **Process improvement.** The ABC system provides the information necessary to identify areas where process improvement is needed.

4. **Improved planning.** Improved product costs lead to better estimates of costs for budgeting and planning.

5. **Identification of the cost of unused capacity.** Because many firms have seasonal and cyclical fluctuations in sales and production, there are times when plant capacity is supplied but not used. This can mean that costs are *incurred* for activities at the batch, product, and facility levels but are *not used.* ABC systems provide better information to identify the cost of unused capacity and maintain a separate accounting for this cost. For example, if a plant manager decides to add capacity in expectation of future increases in sales and production, then the cost of that additional capacity should not be charged to current production but charged as a lump sum in the plant's costs. Overall, the goal is to manage capacity levels to reduce the cost of underutilization of capacity and to price products and services properly. The topic of idle capacity is discussed further in another section of this chapter

Each of these benefits can contribute significantly to a company's competitiveness by helping the company make better decisions and implement its strategy.

A Comparison of Volume-Based and Activity-Based Costing

The following example, which focuses on step 3 of the ABC method, contrasts a volume-based costing system using only direct labor hours as the cost driver with an activity-based costing system that uses both volume-based and activity-based cost drivers.

Haymarket BioTech Inc. (HBT) produces and sells two secure communications systems, AW(Anywhere) and SZ (SecureZone). AW uses satellite technology and allows customers to communicate anywhere on the earth. SZ uses similar technology but only allows communication between two parties that are within 10 miles of each other. HBT's customers are governmental and corporate customers for which these products are critical; the customers rely on HBT's ability to quickly adapt its products to threats from devices that would compromise the security of the products. SZ has been successful for nearly 10 years and has undergone a number of improvements in this time; sales are expected to continue to grow at 8–10% per year. AW, a more recent product, has also been successful, but demand has not been as strong and sales growth is expected to be 3–5% per year. Because of the higher profitability of the AW system (see Exhibit 5.4), HBT is considering an extensive advertising campaign to boost sales of AW and is making plans for reallocating manufacturing facilities from SZ to AW to make this possible. HBT has the following operating data for the two products:

	AW	SZ
Production volume	5,000	20,000
Selling price	$400.00	$200.00
Unit direct materials and labor	$200.00	$ 80.00
Direct labor hours	25,000	75,000
Direct labor hours per unit	5	3.75

Volume-Based Costing

The volume-based costing system assigns factory overhead (FOH) based on direct labor hours (DLH). The firm has total budgeted FOH of $2,000,000. Because the firm budgeted 100,000 direct labor hours for the year, the FOH rate is $20 per direct labor hour:

Total FOH		$2,000,000
Total DLH	25,000 + 75,000 =	100,000
FOH rate per DLH		$ 20.00

The firm uses 25,000 direct labor hours to manufacture 5,000 units of AW, so the FOH assigned to AW is $500,000 in total and $100 per unit:

Total FOH assigned to AW	$20 × 25,000 = $500,000
Number of units of AW	5,000
FOH per unit of AW	$ 100.00

The FOH for SZ is $1,500,000 in total and $75 per unit as the firm spent 75,000 direct labor hours to manufacture 20,000 units of SZ:

Total FOH assigned to SZ	$20 × 75,000 = $1,500,000
Number of units of SZ	20,000
FOH per unit of SZ	$ 75.00

Exhibit 5.4 shows a product profitability analysis using the firm's volume-based costing system.

EXHIBIT 5.4
Product Profitability Analysis under Volume-Based Costing

	AW	SZ
Unit selling price	$400	$200
Unit manufacturing cost:		
Direct materials and labor	$200	$80
Factory overhead	100	75
Cost per unit	300	155
Gross margin	$100	$ 45
Gross margin %	25%	22.5%

Activity-Based Costing

To be able to assign activity costs to cost objects, HBT identified the following activities, budgeted costs, and activity consumption cost drivers in steps 1 and 2 of the ABC method.

Activity	Budgeted Cost	Activity Consumption Cost Driver
Engineering	$ 125,000	Engineering hours
Setups	300,000	Number of setups
Machine operation	1,500,000	Machine hours
Packing orders	75,000	Number of packing orders
Total	$2,000,000	

HBT also gathered the following operating data pertaining to each of its products:

	AW	SZ	Total
Engineering hours	500	750	1,250
Number of setups	200	100	300
Machine hours	50,000	100,000	150,000
Number of packing orders	5,000	10,000	15,000

Using the preceding data, the cost driver rate for each activity consumption cost driver is calculated as follows:

(1) Activity	(2) Budgeted Cost	(3) Budgeted Activity Consumption	(4) = (2) ÷ (3) Activity Consumption Rate
Engineering	$ 125,000	1,250 hours	$ 100 per hour
Setups	300,000	300 setups	1,000 per setup
Machine operations	1,500,000	150,000 machine hours	10 per hour
Packing orders	75,000	15,000 orders	5 per order

Factory overhead costs are assigned to both products by these calculations:

AW (5,000 units)

(1) Activity	(2) Activity Consumption Rate	(3) Activity Consumption	(4) = (2) × (3) Total Overhead	(5) Overhead per Unit
Engineering	$ 100	500 hours	$ 50,000	$ 10
Setups	1,000	200 setups	200,000	40
Machine operations	10	50,000 hours	500,000	100
Packing orders	5	5,000 orders	25,000	5
Overhead cost per unit			$775,000	$155

SZ (20,000 units)

(1) Activity	(2) Activity Consumption Rate	(3) Activity Consumption	(4) = (2) × (3) Total Overhead	(5) Overhead per Unit
Engineering	$ 100	750 hours	$ 75,000	$ 3.75
Setups	1,000	100 setups	100,000	5.00
Machine operations	10	100,000 hours	1,000,000	50.00
Packing orders	5	10,000 orders	50,000	2.50
Overhead cost per unit			$1,225,000	$61.25

Exhibit 5.5 presents a product profitability analysis under the ABC system, and Exhibit 5.6 compares product costs and profit margins under the two costing systems. The comparison shows that the volume-based product costing system significantly undercosts AW and overcosts SZ when considering the consumption of the activities and related overhead cost of resources of the two products. This overcosting/undercosting is sometimes called *cross-subsidization.* Often, the cross-subsidization is in the direction of undercosting the low-volume products (as for AW) and overcosting the high-volume products (as for SZ) using the volume-based approach. The reason is that the non-volume-based ABC costs are averaged over a larger number of units for high-volume products, thus bringing the costs of these products down, and vice versa, for the low-volume products.

For a short additional example, assume that product A is produced in a batch of 10 units, while product B is produced in a batch of 100 units, and that batch-level costs are $100 per batch. The ABC method would calculate the cost per unit of batch costs as $100 ÷ 10 = $10 per unit for the low-volume batch and $100 ÷ 100 = $1 per unit for the high-volume batch. In contrast, the volume-based method would calculate the cost of two batches and spread this equally to the 110 units produced: $200 ÷ 110 = $1.82 per unit. Using the volume-based method, the high-volume product is overcosted ($1.82 vs. $1), and the low-volume product is

EXHIBIT 5.5
Product Profitability Analysis under the ABC Costing System

	AW		SZ	
Unit selling price		$400.00		$200.00
Unit manufacturing cost				
Direct materials and labor		$200.00		$80.00
Factory overhead				
Engineering	$ 10.00		$ 3.75	
Setups	40.00		5.00	
Machine running	100.00		50.00	
Packing	5.00	155.00	2.50	61.25
Cost per unit		355.00		141.25
Gross margin		$ 45.00		$ 58.75
Gross margin %		11.25%		29.38%

EXHIBIT 5.6
**Comparison of Alternative
Costing Approaches**

	AW	SZ
Unit overhead cost		
Volume-based	$100.00	$75.00
Activity-based	155.00	61.25
Difference	($ 55.00)	$13.75
Gross margin		
Volume-based	$100.00	$45.00
Activity-based	45.00	58.75
Difference	($ 55.00)	$13.75
Gross margin %		
Volume-based	25%	22.5%
Activity-based	11.25%	29.38%

undercosted ($1.82 vs. $10). Distorted or inaccurate product costing can lead to inappropriate inventory valuations, unrealistic pricing, ineffective resource allocations, misplaced strategic focus, misidentified critical success factors, and lost competitive advantage.

The Five Steps of Strategic Decision Making for Haymarket BioTech Inc.

We can see how inaccurate costs under the volume-based method can affect HBT's success by considering the five steps of strategic decision making.

1. **Determine the strategic issues surrounding the problem.** HBT, the maker of AW and SZ, competes on product leadership (differentiation) as its customers rely on the ability of these products to provide secure communications. Because innovation is a key customer-buying criterion, HBT must take a long-term focus on developing innovations that meet expected future customer expectations and implement these innovations into successful, profitable products.

2. **Identify the alternative actions.** HBT is considering an advertising campaign and real-location of manufacturing facilities to favor the AW product line.

3. **Obtain information and conduct analyses of the alternatives.** The information available to HBT under the volume-based costing system shows a unit margin of $100 for AW and $45 for SZ, while the ABC-based costing system shows unit margins for AW and SZ of $45 and $58.75, respectively. As the ABC system provides more comprehensive and accurate cost information, HBT should rely on the latter figures, which show that on a unit basis the SZ product is more profitable.

4. **Based on strategy and analysis, choose and implement the desired alternative.** Considering the ABC cost information and the higher margins for SZ relative to AW, the plans to promote AW and reallocate manufacturing facilities from SZ to AW are not consistent with HBT's long-term growth and profitability. The firm's best advantage for future growth and profitability would be to put resources behind SZ rather than AW.

5. **Provide an ongoing evaluation of the effectiveness of implementation in step 4.** HBT should continue to review the ABC-based costs and profit margins of existing and new products, together with long-term projections of sales and customer expectations for these products, to choose the products with the best advantage for long-term growth and profitability.

Calculating the Cost of Idle Capacity in ABC

The ABC application illustrated earlier uses activity-consumption rates based on total budgeted activity costs and budgeted activity consumption. Because budgets are plans, budgeted activity costs are the planned level of spending for the planned output level, and budgeted activity consumption is based on planned usage. The ABC costs assigned to cost objects are,

idle capacity
The difference between the available capacity and the planned level of utilization.

idle capacity cost
The economic value of resources not utilized to produce products or provide services.

therefore, based on planned levels of spending and capacity usage. However, there are often differences between the capacity available and the planned level of capacity utilization, leaving **idle capacity.** There may be an economic value to the resources not used to produce products or provide services, which is known as the **idle capacity cost.** Perhaps the unused capacity can be used by other business units in the firm to expand their operations, or, alternatively, the excess capacity can be sold or leased. Information on excess capacity allows the firm to manage and reduce these costs when appropriate. What we want to know is the cost of maintaining idle or excess capacity.

A straightforward adaptation of the ABC method provides the desired additional information—the cost of capacity. Once the cost of capacity is known, the cost of idle capacity can be determined.

The underlying theory is that when cost allocation rates are estimated in conjunction with an ABC system, the denominator volume level should be consistent with the numerator (resource spending). That is, the numerator represents the dollar amount of resource cost for a given activity. The denominator should logically be measured as the amount of capacity provided by the level of spending indicated in the numerator. For example, suppose (for simplicity) that of the four activities for HBT, we consider only the engineering activity. Engineering cost for HBT is budgeted at $125,000 as currently shown, but suppose that instead of a budgeted activity consumption of 1,250 hours, HBT were to use the practical capacity of the engineering staff, which is 1,500 hours. Practical capacity is the capacity available with the current resources of people, equipment, and facilities—the reasonable level of output if the resource is fully utilized. Using practical capacity, the activity consumption rate would be $83.33 per engineering hour ($125,000 ÷ 1,500). If only 1,250 of the 1,500 hours were used, as shown in the example, then the overhead cost charged to AW and SZ would be reduced because of the lower rate ($83.33 instead of the original rate of $100). AW overhead would be reduced by $8,335.00 (500 hours × $16.67) and SZ overhead would be reduced by $12,502.50 (750 hours × $16.67). The total reduction for the two products, $20,837.50 ($8,335.00 + $12,502.50), is the cost of idle capacity. The cost of idle capacity can also be calculated directly by taking the hours of unused capacity, 250 hours (1,500 − 1,250), and multiplying by the $83.33 activity consumption rate for engineering.

Determining the cost of used and idle capacity is a strategically important feature of ABC because it helps managers plan the short- and longer-term use of the available operating resources. Also, the cost of capacity plays a central role in two methods that extend the basic ABC model; these are resource consumption accounting and time-driven activity-based costing. Both methods are explained at the end of the chapter.[1]

---

[1] Generally accepted accounting principles (FASB ASC 330-10-30) for "Inventory Costs" require the costs associated with an abnormally low production level to be treated as a period cost and not assigned to product. The authoritative accounting literature notes that some variation in production level from period to period is expected and that these variances should not affect the accounting for inventory, but when in the accountant's judgment the amount of expense is for an abnormally low production level, then the amount should be separated from inventory costs, as we have done in the above example, and charged against current income.

REAL-WORLD FOCUS   Process Analysis Reaps Benefits

Caterpillar is the world's largest construction equipment manufacturer and ranked No. 65 on the Fortune 500 list in 2018. The company has been using ABC in its factories for a few decades, and the effectiveness of the methodology comes from the fact that each manufacturing activity can be costed using normalized rates. The company then applied ABC and ABM to the Marketing & Product Support Division, a group that specializes in product support and aftermarket activities. The ABC process was used to provide cost information and measurement data, but simply costing the various support processes was not the end goal. Rather, the division now had information to aid in understanding how changes made to processes would impact cost, and allowed the move toward ABM. Within the division the low- and non-value-adding activities were identified, and the activity analysis done for ABC helped quantify the cost reductions.

Source: David G. DeFreitas, John W. Gillett, Ross L. Fink, and Whitney Cox, "Getting Lean and Mean at Caterpillar with ABM," *Strategic Finance*, January 2013, pp. 24–33.

Activity-Based Management

LO 5-4

Explain activity-based management (ABM).

Benefits of activity-based costing systems are not limited to improved assignment of product costs. The information from the ABC system can also help management increase both the value customers receive and the profits to the firm through the use of activity-based management.

What Is Activity-Based Management?

activity-based management (ABM)

Uses activity analysis and activity-based costing to help managers identify the value of activities and to make strategic performance management decisions—adding and deleting products, adjusting process capacities, adjusting prices, removing costs and complexities, and more.

Activity-based management (ABM) manages resources and activities to improve the value of products or services to customers and increase the firm's competitiveness and profitability. ABM draws on ABC as its major source of information and focuses on the efficiency and effectiveness of key business processes and activities. Using ABM, management can identify ways to improve operations, reduce costs, or increase value to customers, all of which can enhance the firm's competitiveness.

ABM applications can be classified into two categories: operational ABM and strategic ABM. Operational ABM enhances operational efficiency and asset utilization and lowers costs; its focuses are on doing things right and performing activities more efficiently. Operational ABM applications use management techniques such as activity analysis, business process improvement, total quality management, and performance measurement.

Strategic ABM focuses on choosing appropriate activities for the operation, eliminating nonessential activities, and selecting the most profitable customers. Strategic ABM applications use management techniques such as process design, customer profitability analysis, and value-chain analysis, all of which can alter the demand for activities and increase profitability through improved activity efficiency.

Exhibit 5.7 illustrates questions that strategic and operational ABC/ABM (ABC/M) can help to answer and the tools that are used. Some of the key tools of ABC/M are activity analysis; activity-based costing; performance measurement (covered in Chapters 18 and 19); and several contemporary management techniques explained in Chapter 1—benchmarking, total quality management, business process improvement, and others. Another technique, value-added analysis, is explained here.

EXHIBIT 5.7
The Role of ABC/M Tools

Critical Questions	ABC/M Tools
What do we do?	Activity analysis
How much does it cost?	Activity-based costing
How well do we do it?	Performance measurement, including the balanced scorecard
How can we do it better?	Benchmarking, total quality management, business process improvement, and business analytics

REAL-WORLD FOCUS ABC and ABM in Health Care

In a world where rising health care costs are a common phenomenon, there is an increasing need for health care providers to properly measure and manage costs. ABC is a tool that can help health care organizations better measure and manage these costs and obtain better outcomes at lower costs. Of course, cost reductions cannot come at the expense of patient safety and quality of care. A key point, therefore, is to understand the difference between the outcomes for a patient and the process of providing care. Improvements in process that lower costs while maintaining or improving the quality of outcomes is the goal. In the highly data-driven environment of health care, ABC has a role. ABC results can help quantify the costs and potential savings because the time-driver approach enables providers to determine the cost of treating a patient's condition over the longitudinal cycle of care. The application of the ABC process also means the providers will have to analyze their processes, and using ABM, non-value-added activities can be identified and potentially be removed.

Source: Robert S. Kaplan, Michael E. Porter, and Mark L. Frigo, "Managing Healthcare Costs and Value," *Strategic Finance*, January 2017, pp. 25–33.

Activity Analysis

To be competitive, a firm must assess each of its activities based on its need by the product or customer, its efficiency, and its value content. Ideally, a firm performs an activity for one of the following reasons:

• It is required to meet the specification of the product or service or satisfy customer demand.
• It is required to sustain the organization.
• It is deemed beneficial to the firm.

Examples of activities required to sustain the organization are providing plant security and compliance with government regulations. Although these activities have no direct effect on the product or service or customer satisfaction, they cannot be eliminated. Examples of discretionary activities deemed beneficial to the firm include a holiday party and free coffee. Exhibit 5.8 depicts an activity analysis. Some activities, however, may not adequately meet any of the preceding criteria, making them candidates for elimination.

EXHIBIT 5.8
Example of an Activity Analysis

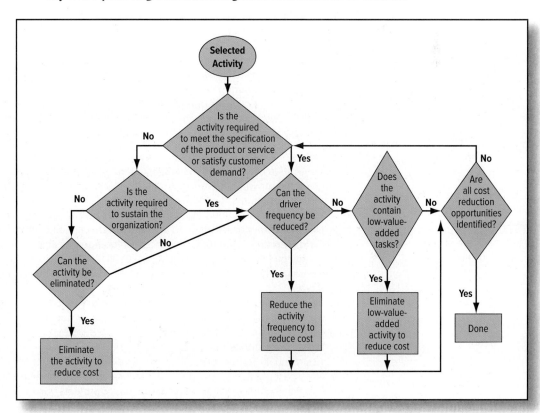

Value-Added Analysis

Eliminating activities that add little or no value to customers reduces resource consumption and allows the firm to focus on activities that increase customer satisfaction. Knowing the values of activities allows employees to see how work really serves customers and which activities may have little value to the ultimate customers and should be eliminated or reduced. In order to ensure that no activities are missed in the value-added analysis, management may want to prepare a **process map.** The process map is a diagram that identifies each step that is currently involved in making a product or providing a service. Development of the process map should include input from those currently involved in providing the product or service.

A **high-value-added activity** increases significantly the value of the product or service to the customers. Removal of a high-value-added activity decreases perceptibly the value of the product or service to the customer. Inserting a flange into a part, pouring molten metal into a mold, and preparing a field for planting are examples of high-value-added activities, as are designing, processing, and delivering products and services. Exhibit 5.9 illustrates high-value-added activities of a television news broadcasting firm. The exhibit also includes examples of low-value-added activities.

A **low-value-added activity** consumes time, resources, or space but adds little in regard to satisfying customer needs. If eliminated, customer value or satisfaction decreases imperceptibly or remains unchanged. Moving parts between processes, waiting time, repairing, and rework are examples of low-value-added activities.

Reduction or elimination of low-value-added activities reduces cost. *Low-value-added activities* are those that:

- Can be eliminated without affecting the form, fit, or function of the product or service.
- Begin with prefix "re" (such as rework or returned goods).
- Result in waste and add little or no value to the product or service.
- Are duplicated in another department or add unnecessary steps to the business process.
- Produce an unnecessary or unwanted output.

Additional examples of high- and low-value-adding activities are shown in Exhibit 5.10.

process map
A diagram that identifies each step in making a product or providing a service.

high-value-added activity
Something that, in the eyes of the consumer, adds value to a product or service.

low-value-added activity
Consumes time, resources, or space but adds little in regard to satisfying customer needs.

EXHIBIT 5.9

Television News Broadcasting Firm's High-Value-Added and Low-Value-Added Activities

Even in today's environment of increased use of social media and the internet, millions of viewers each day watch television news broadcasts. The news organizations need to be cost-effective in gathering and presenting the news, and ABM can help. Remembering that a *high-value-added activity* is one that, if eliminated, would affect the accuracy and effectiveness of the newscast and decrease total viewers as well as ratings for that time slot, let's look at a way to potentially classify various activities.

1. Activities that augment accuracy
   - Verification of story sources and acquired information—this is increasingly important given the growing presence of fake news, including deep fakes.
2. Activities that augment effectiveness
   - Efficient electronic journalism to ensure effective taped segments.
   - Newscast story order planned so that viewers can follow from one story to the next.
   - Field crew time used to access the best footage possible.
   - Meaningful news story writing.
   - Contents of the newscast planned so that viewers get the best possible package of stories.

A *low-value-added activity* is one that, if eliminated, would not affect the accuracy and effectiveness of the newscast. The activity contributes nothing to the quest for viewer retention and improved ratings.
   - Developing stories not used in a newscast.
   - Assigning more than one person to develop each facet of the same news story.
   - Newscast not completed on time because of one or more inefficient processes.
   - Too many employees on a particular shift or project.

REAL-WORLD FOCUS   The Cost of Complexity and the Role of ABC: LEGO and GM

In The LEGO Group and General Motors, the strong influence of the design staff created a proliferation of products that created additional complexity and costs without improving profits.

GM found that car models that sold less than 2,000 units were unprofitable. Even if the vehicle shared most parts with other vehicles, there were incremental costs of engineering, sales, brochures, owner manuals, and the like. So GM (as well as Ford and Chrysler) is simplifying its model lineups.

In The LEGO Group, one of the world's largest toy manufacturers, the concern arose when sales were increasing but profits were falling. This is a common sign of a company that could use ABC costing to identify those products that might have sales growth but are unprofitable. LEGO found that it, like GM, had become a design-driven company, and there was a proliferation of products, including media content like *The Lego*

Movie. The solution for LEGO was to place more emphasis on costs and to reduce the number of products and color variety; this was accomplished in part by requiring closer coordination between operations and design.

The cost of complexity as illustrated in the preceding examples is a key reason that ABC costing can play a strategic role for these firms—it provides a way to accurately determine the cost of product variety and other operating complexities so the firm can identify the most profitable products and operations.

Source: Kaj Grichnik and Conrad Winkler, *Make or Break: How Manufacturers Can Leap from Decline to Revitalization* (New York: McGraw-Hill, 2008), pp. 52–56; Sharon Terlep and Neal E. Boudette, "Unpopular Models Slow Down GM," *The Wall Street Journal,* September 9, 2008, p. B1; Ben Bold, "Lego: How Can the Business Ditch the 'Complexity' and Hit the Reset Button?," *PR Week,* September 6, 2017, **www.prweek.com/article/1443883/lego-business-ditch-complexity-hit-reset-button.**

EXHIBIT 5.10

A Classification of High-Value-Added and Low-Value-Added Activities

Activity	High-Value-Added	Low-Value-Added
Designing product	X	
Setting up		X
Waiting		X
Moving		X
Processing	X	
Reworking		X
Repairing		X
Storing		X
Inspecting		X
Delivering product	X	

Real-World Activity-Based Costing/Management Applications

LO 5-5

Describe how ABC/M is used in organizations.

Activity-based costing/management (ABC/M) applications are quite common in all sectors of the economy, including not-for-profits and governmental organizations.

One example of ABC/M in government is the U.S. Patent and Trademark Office (PTO), which uses ABC to better understand its cost structure. The PTO is not taxpayer supported; rather, it relies on user fees, and the volume of applications has been rising, making the determination of accurate costs and the setting of appropriate user fees for its different services critical. The ABC model at the PTO used 29 activities and the cost objects included utility patents, design patents, plant patents, reissues, reexaminations, trademarks, and appeals. One finding of the ABC/M implementation was that the cost of trademark processing was higher than expected.[2]

There are many other examples because the U.S. federal government encourages the use of ABC within its various units. In 1990, three officials responsible for federal financial reporting established the Federal Accounting Standards Advisory Board (FASAB) as a federal advisory committee (**www.fasab.gov**). The officials were the Secretary of the Treasury, the Director of the Office of Management and Budget, and the Comptroller General of the United States. They created FASAB to develop accounting standards and principles for the U.S. government. *FASAB Standard Number 4,* "Managerial Cost Accounting Concepts and Standards for the Federal Government," explains the advantages of ABC for use in governmental units.

---

[2] For additional examples, see Gary Cokins, *Activity-Based Cost Management in Government* (Management Concepts Inc., 2001).

Like many organizations, health care providers are facing increasing pressure to deliver their services more cost-effectively. What makes this situation more pressing for health care providers is the transition toward a value-based payment environment. A recent study conducted by the HFMA and IMA indicated a resurgence of interest in ABC, with the potential for ABC to provide useful information for process improvement frequently cited as an expectation. This process improvement information can be critical as hospital and other health care providers seek to identify the mix of patient types and volumes that can be treated while maintaining enough profitability to sustain their mission. In other words, the ABC process allows for the determination of the cost of treating different types of patients, and those costs can be compared to the reimbursements to help managers understand which patient services are profitable, which are unprofitable, and how each type of service should be managed.

Sources: Gary Cokins and Christie Scanlon, "Measuring and Managing Patient Profitability," *HFMA*, April 2017, pp. 35–44; Raef Lawson, "Costing Practices in Healthcare Organizations: A Look at Adoption of ABC," *HFMA*, December 5, 2017, **www.hfma.org/topics/article/57198.html**.

Customer Profitability Analysis

LO 5-6

Use an activity-based approach to analyze customer profitability.

"The customer is the most important part of the assembly line."

W. Edwards Deming

customer profitability analysis

Identifies customer service activities, cost drivers, and the profitability of each individual customer or customer group.

ABC/M is best known for its application in computing product costs, but firms also find it useful in determining the cost of serving customers and as a basis for evaluating the profitability of a specific customer or group of customers. Why is this important? Most managers agree that 80% of their profits come from the top 20% of their customers, and most important, the bottom 20% of their customers are unprofitable! For example, to better compete with Walmart, Best Buy worked hard to attract profitable customers (it calls them *angels*) and equally hard to discourage the unprofitable customers (the *devils*) who are price shopping and looking for discounts and promotions and comparing prices to Walmart. Best Buy studied demographic and sales data for each store location to identify angels and devils.[3]

Customer profitability analysis identifies customer service activities and cost drivers and determines the profitability of each customer or customer group. Here, customer service includes all activities required to complete the sale and satisfy the customer, including advertising, sales calls, delivery, billing, collections, service calls, inquiries, and other forms of customer service. Customer profitability analysis allows managers to:

- Identify most profitable customers.
- Manage each customer's costs-to-serve.
- Introduce profitable new products and services.
- Discontinue unprofitable products, services, or customers.
- Shift a customer's purchase mix toward higher-margin products and service lines.
- Offer discounts to gain more volume with low costs-to-serve customers.
- Choose types of after-sale services to provide.

A good understanding of the profitability of a firm's current and potential customers can help firms improve overall profits and become more competitive. This begins with an analysis of the cost to serve the customer.

---

[3] Gary McWilliams, "Analyzing Customers, Best Buy Decides Not All Are Welcome," *The Wall Street Journal*, November 8, 2004, p. 1; Jaclyne Badal, "A Reality Check for the Sales Staff," *The Wall Street Journal*, October 16, 2006, p. B3.

Customer Cost Analysis

Not all customers require similar activities either before or after the sale. Examples of customer-specific activities include:

- Order processing costs.
- Billing, collection, and payment processing costs.
- Accounts receivable and carrying costs.
- Customer service and support costs.
- Selling and marketing costs.

customer cost analysis
Identifies cost activities and cost drivers related to servicing customers.

Customer cost analysis is the process of identifying the activities and cost drivers related to servicing customers. Traditionally, these costs are hidden in the customer support, marketing, and sales function. ABC/M can help managers to understand their costs to serve customers.

Different activities often have different cost drivers. Based on the activities and cost drivers involved in services performed to acquire and complete a transaction, customer costs can be classified into the following categories:

- **Customer unit-level cost**—resources consumed for each unit sold to a customer. Examples include sales commissions based on the number of units sold or sales dollars, shipping cost when the freight charge is based on the number of units shipped, and cost of restocking each returned unit.
- **Customer batch-level cost**—resources consumed for each sales transaction. Examples include order-processing costs, invoicing costs, and recording of sales returns and allowances every time a return or allowance is granted.
- **Customer-sustaining cost**—resources consumed to service a customer regardless of the number of units or batches sold. Examples are salespersons' travel costs to visit customers, monthly statement processing costs, and collection costs for late payments.
- **Distribution-channel cost**—resources consumed in each distribution channel the firm uses to service customers. Examples are operating costs of regional warehouses that serve major customers and centralized distribution centers that serve small retail outlets.
- **Sales-sustaining cost**—resources consumed to sustain sales and service activities that cannot be traced to an individual unit, batch, customer, or distribution channel. Examples are general corporate expenditures for sales activities and the salary, fringe benefits, and bonus of the general sales manager.

Exhibit 5.11 shows customer-related activities, cost drivers and their rates, and the cost category of each of the activities of Winsome Office Supply. These activities are based on the results of a careful study of the firm's selling, administrative, and general expenditures, as well as customer transactions for the last three years. Exhibit 5.12 shows the detailed customer-related activities that Winsome experiences as part of its sales to the firm's three major customers: GereCo., HomeServ Inc., and Advance Tek.

EXHIBIT 5.11
Customer-Related Activity, Cost Driver, Cost Rate, and Cost Category: Winsome Office Supply

Activity	Cost Driver and Rate	Cost Category
Order taking	$30 per order	Customer batch-level
Order processing	$20 per order, and	Customer batch-level
	$1 per item	Customer unit-level
Delivery	$100 per trip, and	Customer batch-level
	$1 per mile	Customer batch-level
Expedited order taking, processing, and delivery	$800 per order	Customer batch-level
Customer visit	$200 per visit	Customer-sustaining
Monthly billing:		
First statement	$5 per statement	Customer-sustaining
Subsequent reminder	$25 per notice	Customer-sustaining
Sales returns	$100 per occurrence	Customer batch-level
Restocking	$5 per item returned	Customer unit-level

EXHIBIT 5.12
Customer-Related Activity for Selected Customers: Winsome Office Supply

	GereCo.	HomeServ Inc.	Advance Tek
Net sales	$463,917	$477,600	$472,576
Number of orders and deliveries	2	20	80
Average number of items per order	400	38	8
Delivery miles	10	15	20
Number of expedited orders	0	0	5
Number of visits by salesperson	1	2	5
Sales returns			
Number of requests	2	1	10
Average units per return	3	4	2
Billing reminder	0	0	2

Both customer activity costs, cost categories, and their cost drivers illustrated in Exhibit 5.11 and the detailed customer-related activities reported in Exhibit 5.12 provide the basis for analyzing customer costs. Exhibit 5.13 shows customer cost analyses for Winsome's three customers.

As illustrated in Exhibits 5.12 and 5.13, while these three customers purchased nearly equal amounts from Winsome, the costs to serve these customers ranged from $1,555 to $20,395. The costs to service these customers differ because they do not place similar demands on the service-related resources of the firm.

Customer Profitability Analysis

Customer profitability analysis combines customer revenues and customer cost analyses to assess customer profitability and helps identify actions to improve customer profitability. Exhibit 5.14 illustrates customer profitability analysis for Winsome.

The reasons that the 11.6% profit margin of GereCo. is lower than the 18.5% profit margin of HomeServ relate to sales activities. Winsome granted GereCo. much more favorable sales terms than the terms granted to HomeServ. GereCo. also had a high amount of sales returns and allowances; it returned twice as often as HomeServ did.

Although Advance Tek had the highest total sales, it generated the lowest profit, in both dollars and as a percentage, of the three customers. Winsome should be concerned about Advance Tek's high returns and its frequency of orders and number of expedited orders. Winsome needs to look into the reasons for these high levels of activity because it may

EXHIBIT 5.13
Customer Cost Analysis: Winsome Office Supply

	GereCo.	HomeServ Inc.	Advance Tek
Customer unit-level cost			
Order processing	400 × 2 × $1 = $800	38 × 20 × $1 = $760	8 × 80 × $1 = $640
Restocking	2 × 3 × $5 = 30	1 × 4 × $5 = 20	10 × 2 × $5 = 100
Customer batch-level cost			
Order taking	2 × $30 = 60	20 × $30 = 600	80 × $30 = 2,400
Order processing	2 × $20 = 40	20 × $20 = 400	80 × $20 = 1,600
Delivery			
Trips	2 × $100 = 200	20 × $100 = 2,000	80 × $100 = 8,000
Miles	10 × 2 × $1 = 20	15 × 20 × $1 = 300	20 × 80 × $1 = 1,600
Expedited orders	—	—	$800 × 5 = 4,000
Sales returns	2 × $100 = 200	1 × $100 = 100	10 × $100 = 1,000
Customer-sustaining costs			
Sales visits	1 × $200 = 200	2 × $200 = 400	5 × $200 = 1,000
Monthly billings	1 × $5 = 5	1 × $5 = 5	1 × $5 = 5
Subsequent reminders	—	—	2 × $25 = 50
Sales-sustaining costs	—	—	—
Total	$1,555	$4,585	$20,395

In late 2016, FedEx found its quarterly profits were being squeezed by the costs of handling peak holiday volumes. Its expenses were outpacing its revenue, which led to a decline in operating profits. The company started asking some of the e-commerce customers for higher prices and was willing to drop those retailers that would not pay up.

FedEx is not alone. Imagine the driver of a United Parcel Service (UPS) truck delivering a bottle of bleach to a customer in rural Oklahoma. This is not a unique occurrence. E-commerce has shifted consumer buying patterns. Rural small-town residents are more costly to serve because they are so spread out, yet these very same people are going online and finding everyday products such as dog food and fruit snacks at prices lower than in the local supermarket. These customers are further lured by the offer of free shipping, and the retailers may end up losing money on these sales.

Required

What are some of the factors management should consider in light of these declining margins?

Sources: Paul Ziorro and Ezequiel Minaya, "FedEx Toughens Stance on Retailers," *The Wall Street Journal,* December 21, 2016, p. B3; Laura Stevens, "Online Shopping Upends Small-Town Retail," *The Wall Street Journal,* September 12, 2016, p. B1.

EXHIBIT 5.14
Customer Profitability Analysis: Winsome Office Supply

	GereCo.	HomeServ Inc.	Advance Tek
Total sales	$500,000	$480,000	$540,000
Less: Sales discounts	25,000	—	27,000
Net invoice amount	$475,000	$480,000	$513,000
Less: Sales returns and allowances	4,750	2,400	30,780
Less: Cash discounts	6,333	—	9,644
Net sales	$463,917	$477,600	$472,576
Cost of goods sold	408,620	384,720	432,014
Gross margin	$ 55,297	$ 92,880	$ 40,562
Customer costs			
Order processing	$ 800	$ 760	$640
Restocking	30	20	100
Order taking	60	600	2,400
Order processing	40	400	1,600
Delivery			
Trips	200	2,000	8,000
Miles	20	300	1,600
Expedited orders	—	—	4,000
Sales returns	200	100	1,000
Sales visits	200	400	1,000
Monthly billings	5	5	5
Subsequent reminders	—	—	50
Total customer costs	$ 1,555	$ 4,585	$ 20,395
Net customer profit	$ 53,742	$ 88,295	$ 20,167

potentially lose this customer. Late payments also add to the cost to serve Advance Tek; they might indicate Advance Tek's dissatisfaction with Winsome's sales and services or a weak financial condition.

Customer profitability analysis provides valuable information for the assessment of customer value. In addition, firms must weigh other relevant factors before determining the action appropriate for each customer. The following are among these relevant factors:

- Growth potential of the customer, the customer's industry, and its cross-selling potential.
- Possible reactions of the customer to changes in sales terms or services.
- Importance of having the firm as a customer for future sales references, especially when the customer could play a pivotal role in bringing in additional business.

REAL-WORLD FOCUS   Customer Metrics and Their Impact on Financial Performance

Sunil Gupta and Valerie Zeithaml have summarized the research that examines the relationship between a variety of customer metrics and profitability. They have integrated this large amount of knowledge into the following generalizations, which they argue are supported by the research. These generalizations are important because they help us to understand the role of customer lifetime value (CLV).

1. Improvement in customer satisfaction has a significant and positive impact on firms' financial performance—shown by many studies.

2. The link between customer satisfaction and profitability is asymmetric and nonlinear—an increase in satisfaction has less of a positive effect on profitability than the negative effect of declines in satisfaction; increases in satisfaction have a greater-than-linear effect on profits.

3. The strength of the satisfaction-profitability link varies across industries as well as across firms within an industry.

4. There is a strong positive relationship between customer satisfaction and customer retention.

5. While customer satisfaction and service quality are strongly correlated with behavioral intentions, behavioral intentions imperfectly predict actual (buying) behavior.

6. The relationship between observable and unobservable metrics is nonlinear—as the relationship between satisfaction and profitability is nonlinear, so is the relationship between satisfaction and repurchase intention (an unobservable).

7. Marketing decisions based on customer metrics, such as CLV, improve a firm's financial performance.

8. Customer retention is one of the key drivers of CLV and firm profitability.

Source: Sunil Gupta and Valerie Zeithaml, "Customer Metrics and Their Impact on Financial Performance," *Marketing Science,* November–December 2006, pp. 718–39.

Customer Lifetime Value

customer lifetime value (CLV)
The net present value of estimated future profits from a given customer; in practice, a firm is likely to estimate this value over the next three to five years.

Exhibit 5.14 shows how to determine the profitability of a customer at a given point in time. Many companies now see the importance of looking at the long-term value of the customer, the expected contribution to profit during the full period the company retains the customer. This concept is called **customer lifetime value (CLV),** and it is calculated as the net present value of estimated future profits from the customer for a specified time, which may be three to five years. Present value is used because the profits from the customer are expected to occur over a number of years. To provide a more comprehensive and strategically relevant measure of the value of the customer, CLV takes into account the company's expectations about the future potential growth in profits for a customer. The following example illustrates the calculation of CLV. Assume MidTown Medical Clinic purchases medical supplies from Johnson Medical Supply Company. Johnson calculates the CLV of the medical clinic by projecting profits from the clinic. Suppose the forecast is for $20,000 profit per year for the next three years. Further, suppose Johnson uses a discount rate of 6% (the relevant discount factor is 2.673 from the present value Table 2 at the end of Chapter 12), then

$$CLV = \$53{,}460 = \$20{,}000 \times 2.673$$

CLV can be used to measure the value of a customer or group of customers and to determine how marketing and support services should be allocated to these customers to improve the firm's overall profitability. Because there is a significant level of judgment involved in estimating the variables in the calculation, it is also important to compare different calculations of CLV made with different assumptions about profit forecasts and discount rates.

Implementation Issues and Extensions

"If you want to make enemies, try to change something."

Woodrow Wilson

LO 5-7

Identify key factors for successful ABC/M implementation.

A successful ABC/M implementation requires close cooperation among management accountants, engineers, and manufacturing and operating managers. They need to act as a team in identifying activities, cost drivers, and requisite information, both financial and nonfinancial.

Following are the processes found in many successful implementations of ABC/M:

Implementation Process	Why This Leads to Success
Involve management and employees in creating an ABC system	Allows them to become familiar with ABC/M. They could then be more willing to implement the system because they feel included and share in ownership of the new system.
Use ABC/M on a job that will succeed	Shows how and why the process works. Successfully completing one job enables individuals to see the benefits of ABC/M more clearly.
Keep the initial ABC/M design simple	Avoids overwhelming users and holds costs down; also reduces implementation time.

Extensions of the ABC model are becoming more common. We discuss three of these below: multistage ABC, resource consumption accounting (RCA), and time-driven activity-based costing (TDABC). All three respond directly to the inherent complexity of resource and activity cost assignments in actual applications, noted as one of the implementation issues above. The latter two take a resource-focused approach to ABC.

Multistage Activity-Based Costing

In practice, you may find some activities are intermediate cost objects for other activities while others are assigned directly to cost objects. To capture and calculate accurately the costs for this situation, some firms use multistage activity-based costing rather than two-stage ABC described earlier in the chapter. In **multistage ABC,** resource costs are assigned to certain activities that, in turn, are assigned to other activities before being assigned to the final cost objects. The process is similar to the allocation of service department costs to producing departments, which is described in Chapter 7. Exhibit 5.15 illustrates such a case. The activity labeled "support activities" provides service to other activities later in the value chain—product/service activities, customer activities, and facility-level activities. The exhibit illustrates how a total of $70 of resource costs are assigned in multistage ABC costing. After multistage allocations, $25 is assigned to products, $20 is assigned to customer-related activities, and $25 is assigned to facility-level costs (computer equipment and software, buildings, and other equipment, etc.).

Resource Consumption Accounting (RCA)

Resource consumption accounting (RCA) is integration of principles derived from the German costing system Grenzplankostenrechnung (GPK) and ABC. On the RCA Institute website (www.rcainstitute.org), RCA is formally defined as "a dynamic, fully integrated, principle-based, and comprehensive management accounting approach that provides

multistage ABC
The assignment of resource costs to certain activities that, in turn, are assigned to other activities before being assigned to the final cost objects.

resource consumption accounting (RCA)
A comprehensive and fully integrated management accounting approach that provides management with decision support information based on an operational view of the organization.

EXHIBIT 5.15
Multistage Activity Cost Flows

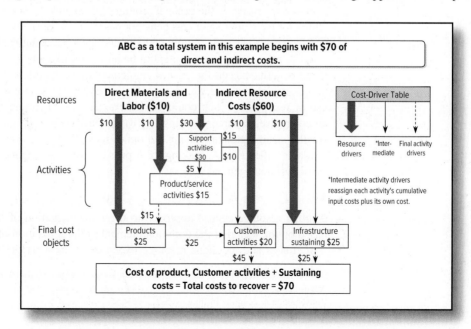

REAL-WORLD FOCUS   Time-Driven Activity-Based Costing in the Service Sector

The existing cost measurement systems within many health care provider settings are inadequate to meet the information demands within the evolving health care sector. Better cost measurement and cost management systems are needed to respond to the value-based focus being imposed upon health care providers. In response to these challenges, more than two dozen leading health care provider organizations have conducted pilot projects using time-driven activity-based costing (TDABC) to improve value. The process involves mapping the activities and measuring the costs of the underlying resources involved in treating specific medical conditions over a complete episode of care. The benefit comes as health care organizations can more accurately determine the cost of providing care for these medical conditions. With a growing emphasis on outcomes-based measurements of performance in the health care sector, the measurement of outcomes in combination with

the TDABC data, a measurement of inputs, will help improve measurements of value. As an example, a pilot project at the Cleveland Clinic has been used to simultaneously evaluate its current costing systems and also experiment with the TDABC approach. Through process mapping and calculating the labor capacity cost rates for its heart and vascular services, leaders within the organization gained insights into process steps that could be consolidated, reduced, or performed with lower-cost resources. They were also able to clearly identify the cost of unused capacity.

Sources: Robert S. Kaplan, "Improving Value with TDABC," *Healthcare Financial Management,* June 2014, pp. 77–83; Christopher Donovan, Mike Hopkins, Benjamin Kimmel, Stephanie Koberna, and Kerry Montie, "How Cleveland Clinic Used TDABC to Improve Value," *Healthcare Financial Management,* June 2014, pp. 84–88.

managers with decision support information for enterprise optimization."[4] Like ABC, RCA uses an activity/process view but integrates marginal costs and a detailed resource consumption analysis to generate information for decision support. Another notable feature of RCA is that depreciation expense is based on an estimated replacement cost for the asset rather than historical acquisition cost.

RCA's emphasis is on being able to attribute costs, both fixed and proportional, to cost objects for decision support, and there are three foundational concepts for RCA:

- The view of resources—resources are the suppliers of capacity, meaning that capacity is a function of the resources available.
- The quantity-based model—an operational view of the organization based on the concept that there is a causal relationship that can be expressed in terms of input and output units.
- Cost behavior—the characteristics of the cost are inherent to the underlying resource and the consumption of those resources by value-creating operations.

The RCA approach relies heavily on the concept of an attributable cost, which is a concept of attaching costs to a cost object only when causality exists. This concept helps ensure that decisions are not made on the basis of arbitrary allocations. Understanding and modeling causality allows for the modeling of cost behavior based on responsiveness, which is the level of correlation between a particular output quantity and the input quantity needed to produce the output.

RCA offers tremendous potential benefits, but like any system, management must decide if the benefits exceed the cost of implementation. Additionally, the collection, storage, and processing of the underlying data for an effective RCA implementation requires its own use of resources, which could be quite extensive. For large organizations, this may mean an enterprise resource planning (ERP) system needs to be in place. However, medium and smaller-sized organizations are not out of luck. There is an open source application for RCA available called ROSA, making RCA possible for those organizations that have less sophisticated cost management systems.

Time-Driven Activity-Based Costing (TDABC)

Another resource-centric approach to the implementation of large ABC costing systems is based on the idea that the common element in the utilization of activities is the unit of time. ABC traces and reassigns resource expenses to the activities that consume them and then

---

[4] In RCA, resource cost pools are called cost centers. Useful references for RCA include Kip Krumwiede and Augustin Suessmair, "Getting Down to Specifics on RCA," *Strategic Finance,* June 2007; and the Resource Consumption Accounting Institute website, **www.rcainstitute.org**.

time-driven activity-based costing (TDABC)
The assignment of resource costs directly to cost objects using the cost per time unit of supplying the resource, rather than first assigning costs to activities and then from activities to cost objects.

further reassigns them proportionately to the final cost objects based on the quantity of each activity's cost driver. When a substantial amount of the cost of a company's activities are in a highly repetitive process, the cost assignment can be based on the average time required for each activity. **Time-driven activity-based costing (TDABC)** assigns resource costs directly to cost objects using the cost per time unit of supplying the resource, rather than first assigning costs to activities and then from activities to cost objects.[5]

TDABC provides a direct way to measure idle capacity. To illustrate, assume there is a credit card processing facility and one of its activities is validation of mailing addresses. Traditional ABC would first pool the costs associated with the various activities of the facility and then select cost drivers to come up with costs per activity. The cost of activities associated with validating mailing addresses would be assigned to the cost object "mailing list validation" and that pool of costs would be divided by the number of validations to determine a cost per validation. Assume there were 10,000 validations for the year and the ABC rate was $9 per validation.

In contrast, TDABC considers the standard time for each validation, which we assume is 17 minutes. TDABC computes the cost per minute of the resources performing the work activity. In this example, we assume that two clerical workers, each paid $45,000 annually, work only on validations. TDABC calculates the total cost as $45,000 × 2 employees = $90,000; then TDABC calculates the total time available for the activity. Assuming each employee has 30 productive hours per week and actually works 50 weeks per year, the time available is 2 employees × 50 weeks × 30 hours per week × 60 minutes per hour = 180,000 minutes. The TDABC rate is $90,000 ÷ 180,000 minutes = $0.50 per minute. The cost of a validation can now be estimated to be 17 minutes × $0.50 per minute = $8.50 per validation.

TDABC can then calculate the idle capacity cost by determining the activity cost and netting it from the total expense. In this example the TDABC activity cost is calculated as $85,000 (i.e., 17 minutes × 10,000 validations × $.50 per minute). This means that $5,000 (or 10,000 minutes at $.50 per minute) of unused capacity is potentially available to be used for other work.

TDABC can be expanded to include complexities in the activity, in what is called a time equation. For example, we assume the time to validate an address is significantly increased for an international address—each requires an additional 22 minutes. Then the time equation can be determined as follows:

Time to validate address = 17 minutes + 22 minutes (if it is an international address)

The determination of the cost per minute is done in the same manner, but with the addition of the expected time for international addresses.

---

[5] Robert S. Kaplan and Steven R. Anderson, *Time-Driven Activity-Based Costing* (Boston: Harvard Business School Press, 2007).

A difference between TDABC and ABC is that TDABC is capacity-sensitive and computes a standard activity cost using standard rates, meaning activity driver rates remain constant. In contrast, ABC might not include capacity, as in the HBT case presented earlier. ABC computes the activity cost each period, and therefore, the final cost object's unit cost may fluctuate each period. TDABC requires an upfront investment to measure activity times and to continuously maintain them.

Note that traditional ABC may use amount of time for an activity. For example, setup time might be used rather than number of setups. Of course, it will be necessary to determine budgeted time for the activity and the actual time for each setup. Note, however, that this approach to ABC is still different from TDABC; TDABC uses the time to drive costs directly from resources to cost objects—there is no assignment of resource costs to activities and then from activities to cost objects.

The following is an example illustrating the use of time as a driver. Consider that the three activities—machine setup, inspection, and packaging—require an average of 80 minutes, 15 minutes, and 20 minutes, respectively. Under ABC, the activity consumption cost drivers for these activities are based on the total activity cost divided by the number of minutes available for that activity. For example, if the total cost of setup is $50,000, and there is a capacity of 1,250 minutes of setup time, then the activity rate is $50,000 ÷ 1,250 = $40 per minute. This approach can improve the ABC application because actual time is used to assign costs. For example, if setup time for a special customer order requires an additional 15 minutes, the assigned setup cost would be based on $40 per minute times the total time of 95 minutes: 95 minutes × $40 = $3,800.

A disadvantage of TDABC is its reliance on the accuracy of the time estimates; also, the effort to determine these time estimates could be very time-consuming and costly. Some activities are not time-driven and should not be included in a comprehensive TDABC; for example, in a chemical company, the cost of the setup and cleanup activities involves significant indirect materials costs, apart from the cost of the time involved. However, these materials costs could be included in a modified TDABC, where pounds of materials could be used rather than minutes of setup or cleanup; this is then a combination of time- and pounds-driven ABC. Finally, because of its distinction of resources and activities, traditional ABC can, in some cases, provide a better framework for identifying opportunities for cost savings, while TDABC can provide a better framework for identifying unused capacity.

Summary

Many companies have replaced their volume-based costing systems with activity-based costing systems for more accurate product costing and better decision making.

Volume-based costing systems use a volume-based overhead rate, either a single rate for the entire plant or departmental rates. These volume-based overhead rates typically use measures such as direct labor hours, machine hours, or direct labor costs for all products or services, even if the firm has diverse products, manufacturing processes, and volumes. For firms with more than one product or process, these overhead rates often generate inaccurate and significantly distorted product costs.

Activity-based costing systems recognize that products and services consume indirect costs in a manner that follows the usage of activities rather than the volume of output. ABC costing improves on costing accuracy because it identifies the detail-level activities that cause the consumption of resources. ABC costing assigns these activity-based costs to the products or services using activity-consumption cost drivers, rather than volume-based cost drivers.

Activity-based management manages resource costs and activities to improve the value of products or services to the customer by reducing product cost and/or increasing value-adding activities.

Customer profitability analysis and customer lifetime value are methods, enabled by activity-based costing, that provide important tools for determining the profitability of product lines, customer groups, or individual customers.

Multistage ABC, resource consumption accounting (RCA), and time-driven ABC (TDABC) are additional tools that have been developed in recognition of the complexity of cost relationships in many organizations.

Key Terms

activity, *144*
activity-based costing
(ABC), *145*
activity-based management
(ABM), *154*
activity consumption cost
driver, *145*
batch-level activity, *147*
cost driver, *144*
customer cost analysis, *159*

customer lifetime value
(CLV), *162*
customer profitability analysis, *158*
facility-level activity, *148*
high-value-added activity, *156*
idle capacity, *153*
idle capacity cost, *153*
low-value-added activity, *156*
multistage ABC, *163*
process map, *156*

product-level activity, *147*
resource, *144*
resource consumption
accounting (RCA), *163*
resource consumption cost
driver, *144*
time-driven activity-based
costing (TDABC), *165*
two-stage cost assignment, *145*
unit-level activity, *147*

Comments on Cost Management in Action

Admittedly, the answer to this question requires some guesswork. However, from the perspective of making deliveries, we can be sure that as the drive gets longer and deliveries per mile become fewer, the cost per delivery increases. If the retailer offers free shipping to remain competitive with other sellers, the customer will not be absorbing this increased cost. The retailers risk losing the customers if there is a delivery charge, but is it worth it to keep a customer that places money-losing orders? Also, retailers cannot simply seek price concessions from the delivery companies if the retailers are selling to customers who are more expensive to reach to make deliveries. Keep in mind, the customer did not decide how far the product would have to travel to be delivered. The retailers decide where to store the inventory prior to delivery. If a distribution center is close to the customer, the travel distance will be less.

Conversely, shipping companies like FedEx and UPS are in the business of delivering packages, so they cannot simply raise prices to cover the increased delivery costs it risks losing to those customers. Consider what happens to a delivery company if Amazon suddenly decides to start making its own deliveries because the cost of outsourcing that function becomes too high.

Perhaps there is room for cooperation. Both retailers and delivery companies can use business analytics. By sharing data, the retailers and delivery companies might be able to plan more cost-effective delivery routes. Perhaps there could be cooperation in the development and placement of distribution centers. Retailers might also be able to gauge the long-term buying patterns of customers to determine whether the company generates a profit from all the customer's orders, even if money is lost on a single order.

Self-Study Problem

(For answers, please see Solution.)

Volume-Based Costing versus ABC

Carter Company manufactures two products, Deluxe and Regular, and uses a traditional two-stage cost allocation system. The first stage assigns all factory overhead costs to two production departments, A and B, based on machine hours. The second stage uses direct labor hours to allocate overhead to individual products.

For the current year, the firm budgeted $1,000,000 total factory overhead cost. The $1,000,000 was for the planned levels of machine and direct labor hours shown in the following table:

	Production Department A	Production Department B
Machine hours	4,000	16,000
Direct labor hours	20,000	10,000

The following information relates to the firm's operations for the month of January:

	Deluxe	Regular
Units produced and sold	200	800
Unit cost of direct materials	$100	$ 50
Hourly direct labor wage rate	$ 25	$ 20
Direct labor hours in Department A per unit	2	2
Direct labor hours in Department B per unit	1	1

Carter Company is considering implementing an activity-based costing system. Its management accountant has collected the following information for activity cost analysis for the current year:

Activity	Budgeted Overhead	Cost Driver	Budgeted Quantity	Driver Consumption Deluxe	Regular
Materials movement	$ 7,000	Number of production runs	350	15	20
Machine setups	400,000	Number of setups	500	25	50
Inspections	588,000	Number of units	19,600	200	800
Shipment	5,000	Number of shipments	250	50	100
	$1,000,000				

Required

1. Calculate the unit cost for each of the two products under the existing volume-based costing system.
2. Calculate the overhead per unit of the cost driver under the proposed ABC system.
3. Calculate the unit cost for each of the two products if the proposed ABC system is adopted.

The Student Resources section of Connect includes video tutorials for the Self-Study Problems.

Questions

5-1   "Undercosting a product increases the profit from the product and benefits the firm." Do you agree? Why?

5-2   Firms sell products with high costs at high prices. High selling prices increase revenues and profits. Why then should managers worry about product overcosting?

5-3   Explain why a costing system that uses a volume-based rate is likely to produce distorted product costs.

5-4   What is activity-based costing, and how can it improve an organization's costing system?

5-5   Identify the general levels of cost hierarchy in activity-based costing systems.

5-6   Briefly describe the first- and second-stage procedures in assigning costs to products when using an activity-based costing system.

5-7   What type of company can benefit from an activity-based costing system?

5-8   What are unit-level activities? Give two examples of unit-level activities.

5-9   What are batch-level activities? Give two examples of batch-level activities.

5-10   What are product-level activities? Give two examples of product-level activities.

5-11   What are facility-level activities? Give two examples of facility-level activities.

5-12   Why do product costing systems using a single, volume-based cost driver tend to overcost high-volume products? Will there be any undesirable strategic effects from such product cost distortion?

5-13   What is activity-based management?

5-14   How can activity-based costing and management be used in service organizations?

5-15   Identify opportunities afforded by performing a customer profitability analysis.

Brief Exercises

[LO 5-3]   5-16   Tasty Beverage Co. produces soft drinks, specializing in fruit drinks. Tasty produces 5,000 cans of product per batch. Setup cost for each batch is $50 and each drink costs $0.10 to produce. What is the total cost per batch? How much would it cost to fill an order for 100,000 cans?

[LO 5-3]   5-17   Montross Lumber processes wood to be shipped to construction companies. In order to keep its products uniform, Montross conducts inspections on 20% of the boards produced. Inspections cost the company $10 per hour and it takes 1 minute to inspect each board. How much would it cost to fill an order for 30,000 boards?

[LO 5-3]   5-18   Orange Inc. grows and ships cabbage. It costs Orange $5 to put together each package for shipment and $0.10 to clean and process each vegetable. How much more does it cost to produce an order for 60 heads of cabbage than an order of 50 heads?

[LO 5-3]   5-19   Williams Performance Co. manufactures sports cars. After making a sale, the salesperson sends the car to be detailed before the customer takes it home. Detailing the car takes 30 minutes at a cost of

$15 per hour for direct labor and $5 per car for materials. If the company is open 5 days per week and sells an average of five cars per day, what is the average cost per 5-day week for detailing cars?

[LO 5-3] 5-20 Stackhouse Computing produces high-performance desktop computers. Labor cost data show that the company spent $1,000,000 for 5,000 computers produced, and each computer requires 2 technician hours and 5 hours of direct labor. Direct labor is paid $10 per hour by the company. What is the cost of 1 technician hour?

[LO 5-3] 5-21 Haywood Printing is processing a job with the following activity rates:

Activity	Cost Driver	Driver Rate
Direct labor	Number of hours	$8.00
Copying	Number of copies	$0.05

If this job requires 5 hours for 1,000 copies, what is the activity-based cost of the job?

[LO 5-3] 5-22 Locke Data Processing reported expenses of $5 million for labor, of which $3 million was for data analysis and $2 million was for data entry. Locke recorded 30,000 hours of data analysis and 100,000 hours of data entry. What are the activity-based rates for each type of direct labor?

[LO 5-3] 5-23 The materials handling charge for ABC Corp. is $0.50 per pound of finished product. What is the materials handling charge for a job that produced 10,000 units at a weight of 6 pounds per unit?

Exercises

Note regarding rounding errors: Many of the exercises and problems in this chapter require a series of calculations. Rounding errors can accumulate and affect totals unless each calculation is carried to a recommended four or more digits after the decimal point. If you are using a calculator, make sure all your calculations are done to 4 or more digits after the decimal. To avoid rounding errors entirely, use a spreadsheet package like Excel to set up and solve these problems.

[LO 5-1] 5-24 **Role of Activity-Based Costing in Implementing Strategy** Laurent Products is a manufacturer of plastic packaging products with plants located throughout Europe and customers worldwide. During the past 10 years, Laurent Products has successfully developed a line of packaging materials and a unique bagging system that present an important opportunity to increase the productivity of checkout counters in grocery stores. The plastic bags manufactured by Laurent are produced in several sizes and different plastic film colors and may have attractive multicolor printed designs on one or both sides to meet the specification of a particular grocery store. The advantages provided by the Laurent bagging system include the lower cost of bags and labor at the checkout counter as well as improved customer service. The system has contributed to significant growth in Laurent's sales in recent years.

Laurent's success in the grocery chain market has attracted an increasing number of competitors into the market. While the company has been very successful in bringing out a series of new product types with innovative labor-saving features for the grocery stores, Laurent's competitors have eventually been able to develop quite similar products. The result has been increased competition with a substantial reduction in Laurent's prices.

As a result of the increased competition in the grocery chain market, Laurent is planning to begin to focus on the small independent grocery stores that purchase bags from large wholesale distributors. The potential sales for this wholesaler segment is about the same size as the grocery chain market but includes a much larger number of independent store customers.

Investments in manufacturing equipment in recent years have been to support two principal objectives: to increase capacity and to reduce costs. The cost reduction initiatives principally concerned material costs and reduced processing times. Over the years, Laurent has chosen to invest in machines that are similar to existing equipment in order to capitalize on the fact that the process is relatively simple and that products can, with relatively few exceptions, be processed on any machine in the plant. The only major restriction is the number of colors that a machine can accommodate on a single pass. Future investment proposals now being considered are based on this rationale.

Required What are the key strategic issues facing Laurent, and how can ABC costing assist in resolving these issues?

[LO 5-2] 5-25 **Activity Levels and Cost Drivers** Shroeder Machine Shop has the following activities:
a. Machine operation
b. Machine setup
c. Production scheduling
d. Materials receiving

    e. Research and development

    f. Machine maintenance

    g. Product design

    h. Parts administration

    i. Final inspection of a sample of products

    j. Materials handling

Required

1. Classify each of the activities as a unit-level, batch-level, product-level, or facility-level activity.

2. Identify a potential cost driver for each activity in requirement 1.

[LO 5-2]   5-26 **Activity Levels and Cost Drivers** Steve's Slop Shop, a small hamburger shop, has identified the resources used in its operations (assume each customer's order is a batch for this example):

    a. Bread

    b. Hourly workers that cook hamburgers

    c. Store rent

    d. Ground beef

    e. Catsup

    f. Advertising for Triple-Burger special

    g. Salary for the store managers

    h. Utilities

    i. $1-off-coupon for each order

    j. Bag for each order

Required

1. Classify its costs as unit-level, batch-level, product-level, or facility-level costs.

2. Suggest a possible cost driver for each of the above items.

[LO 5-2, 5-3]   5-27 **Activity-Based Costing in the Fashion Apparel Industry** Fleet Street Inc., a manufacturer of high-fashion clothing for women, is located in South London in the UK. Its product line consists of trousers (45%), skirts (35%), dresses (15%), and other (5%). Fleet Street has been using a volume-based rate to assign overhead to each product; the rate it uses is £2.25 per unit produced. The results for the trousers line, using the volume-based approach, are as follows:

Number of units produced	10,000
Price (all figures in £)	£ 20.525
Total revenue	205,250
Direct materials	33,750
Direct labor	112,500
Overhead (volume-based)	22,500
Total product cost	168,750
Nonmanufacturing expenses	31,500
Total cost	200,250
Profit margin for trousers	5,000

Recently, Fleet Street conducted a further analysis of the trousers line of product, using ABC. In the study, eight activities were identified, and direct labor was assigned to the activities. The total conversion cost (labor and overhead) for the eight activities, after allocation to the trousers line, is as follows:

Pattern cutting	£22,000
Grading	19,000
Lay planning	18,500
Sewing	21,000
Finishing	14,300
Inspection	6,500
Boxing up	3,500
Storage	7,000

Required

1. Determine the profit margin for the trousers line using ABC

2. Comment on the difference in comparison to the volume-based calculations.

[LO 5-2, 5-3] 5-28 **Activity-Based Costing** Hakara Company has been using direct labor costs as the basis for assigning overhead to its many products. Under this allocation system, product A has been assigned overhead of $10.80 per unit, while product B has been assigned $3.60 per unit. Management feels that an ABC system will provide a more accurate allocation of the overhead costs and has collected the following cost pool and cost driver information:

Cost Pools	Activity Costs	Cost Drivers	Activity Driver Consumption
Machine setup	$360,000	Setup hours	4,000
Materials handling	100,000	Pounds of materials	20,000
Electric power	40,000	Kilowatt-hours	40,000

The following cost information pertains to the production of A and B, just two of Hakara's many products:

	A	B
Number of units produced	4,000	20,000
Direct materials cost	$42,000	$54,000
Direct labor cost	$24,000	$40,000
Number of setup hours	400	200
Pounds of materials used	1,000	3,000
Kilowatt-hours	2,000	4,000

Required

1. Use activity-based costing to determine a unit cost for each product.

2. Comment on management's belief that the ABC system will generate an overhead allocation that is more accurate than the volume-based system currently in use.

[LO 5-3] 5-29 **ABC and Job Costing Working with Unknowns** North Company designs and manufactures machines that facilitate DNA sequencing. Depending on the intended purpose of each machine and its functions, each machine is likely to be unique. The job costing system in its Norfolk plant has five activity cost pools, in addition to direct materials and direct labor. Job TPY–2306 requires 1,000 printed-circuit boards. The cost per board that passes the final inspection is $240. On average, only 50% of the completed units pass the final inspection. The prime costs per completed board include $25 for direct materials and $5 for direct labor. Information pertaining to manufacturing overhead for printed-circuit boards follows:

Activity	Cost Driver	Activity Driver Rate	Activity Consumption per Board	Factory Overhead per Board
Axial insertion	Number of axial insertions	$0.20	30	$ A?
Hardware insertion	Number of hardware insertions	2.00	B?	37.00
Hand load	Boothroyd time	C?	5	35.50
Masking	Number of points masked	0.12	100	D?
Final test	Test time	E?	10	6.00

Required Fill in the unknowns identified as A through E.

[LO 5-4] 5-30 **High-Value-Added and Low-Value-Added Activities** The Lindex General Hospital has determined the activities of a nurse, including the following:

a. Report for duty and review patient charts

b. Visit each patient and take her/his temperature

c. Update patients' records

   d. Coordinate lab and radiology works

   e. Wait for the attending physician to arrive

   f. Accompany attending physician

   g. Explain treatments to patients

   h. Call kitchen to have the wrong meal tray replaced

   i. Perform CPR

   Required Classify each item as a high-value-added or a low-value-added activity.

[LO 5-5] 5-31 **Applications of ABC/M in Government** Activity-based costing is used widely within the U.S. government. One example is the Department of Agriculture's Animal and Plant Health Inspection Service (APHIS). APHIS helps to protect U.S. agriculture from exotic pests and diseases, to minimize wildlife/agriculture conflicts, and to protect the welfare of animals used for research or sold wholesale for pets. APHIS performs its services for a variety of users, some of whom pay a user fee. ABC was adopted to provide an accurate basis for determining these fees, and also for analysis of the effectiveness and efficiency of its programs in meeting the service's overall goals. Other examples of ABC use are noted in the text, including the U.S. Postal Service and the U.S. Patent and Trademark Office.

   Required

   1. Identify an example or two of a governmental entity that you think could benefit from the application of ABC/M, and explain why.

   2. Identify some of the resources, activities, and cost drivers you would expect to see in this application.

[LO 5-1, 5-2, 5-3, 5-5] 5-32 **Product-Line Profitability; ABC** Supermart Food Stores (SFS) has experienced net operating losses in its frozen food products line in the last few periods. Management believes that the store can improve its profitability if SFS discontinues frozen foods. The operating results from the most recent period are:

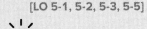

	Frozen Foods	Baked Goods	Fresh Produce
Sales	$120,000	$91,000	$158,175
Cost of goods sold	105,000	67,000	110,000

   SFS estimates that store support expenses, in total, are approximately 20% of revenues.

   The controller says that not every sales dollar requires or uses the same amount of store support activities. A preliminary analysis reveals store support activities for these three product lines are:

Activity (cost driver)	Frozen Foods	Baked Goods	Fresh Produce
Order processing (number of purchase orders)	10	45	100
Receiving (number of deliveries)	12	55	120
Shelf-stocking (number of hours per delivery)	2	0.5	4
Customer support (total units sold)	30,000	40,000	86,000

   The controller estimates activity-cost rates for each activity as follows:

Order processing	$80 per purchase order
Receiving	110 per delivery
Shelf-stocking	15.25 per hour
Customer support	0.21 per item

   Required

   1. Prepare a product-line profitability report for SFS under the current costing system.

   2. Prepare a product-line profitability report for SFS using the ABC information the controller provides.

   3. What new insights does the ABC system in requirement 2 provide to SFS managers?

   4. It is not clear what level of measure of activity was used to determine the activity-cost rates above. Comment on the impact of using the expected driver consumption versus the practical capacity of the driver when computing the activity-cost rates.

[LO 5-3, 5-5] 5-33 **Product-Line Profitability Analysis** Studemeir Paint & Floors (SPF) is a retail store specializing in home improvement. The store has experienced net operating losses in its Other Flooring Products line during the last few periods. SPF's management team thinks that the store will improve its profitability if it stops carrying the Other Flooring Products line. The operating results from the most recent period are:

	Paint and Paint Supplies	Carpet	Other Flooring Products
Sales	$295,000	$214,900	$167,900
Cost of goods sold	165,000	150,000	135,250

SPF estimates that store operating expenses are approximately 24% of revenues.

Harish Rana, SPF's controller, states that while every sale has one purchase order, not every sales dollar requires or uses the same amount of store support activities. He conducts a preliminary investigation and his results and analysis are as follows:

Activity (cost driver)	Paint and Paint Supplies	Carpet	Other Flooring Products
Order processing (number of purchase orders)	425	150	100
Receiving (number of deliveries)	50	120	60
Customer support (hours required per sale)	0.50	8.0	0.75

Harish estimates activity-cost rates for each activity as follows:

Order processing	$140 per purchase order
Receiving	180 per delivery
Customer support	18 per hour

Required
1. Prepare a product-line profitability report for SPF under the current costing system.
2. Prepare a product-line profitability report for SPF using the ABC information the controller provides.
3. What new insights does the ABC system in requirement 2 provide to SPF managers?

[LO 5-1, 5-6] 5-34 **Customer Profitability Analysis; Luxury Hotel Industry** The luxury hotel chain Ritz-Carlton introduced a system called "Mystique" that collects information about its customers from employees and staff at the hotel. The information is used to personalize the services provided to each guest. For example, a bottle of the guest's favorite type of wine would be placed in the room without the guest having to request it. Similarly, the type of fruit a guest prefers will be waiting in the room on arrival. The information is available throughout the Ritz system so that when the guest checks into any Ritz-Carlton hotel, the special treatment is available. Other hotel chains such as Hilton and Hyatt have similar programs.

Required
1. How do these information-gathering programs help the hotels become more competitive? What is the strategic role of these programs?
2. Do you see a role for activity-based costing for these firms, as it relates to their information gathering and customer service?
3. What ethical issues, if any, do you see in the information-gathering systems?

[LO 5-6] 5-35 **Customer Profitability Analysis** Colleen Company has gathered the following data pertaining to activities it performed for two of its major customers.

	Jerry, Inc.	Kate Co.
Number of orders	5	30
Units per order	1,000	200
Sales returns:		
Number of returns	2	5
Total units returned	40	175
Number of sales calls	12	4

Colleen Company sells its products at $200 per unit. The firm's gross margin ratio is 25%. Both Jerry and Kate pay their accounts promptly and no accounts receivable is over 30 days. After using business analytics software to carefully analyze the operating data for the past 30 months, the firm has determined the following activity costs:

Activity	Cost Driver and Rate
Sales calls	$1,000 per visit
Order processing	300 per order
Deliveries	500 per order
Sales returns	100 per return and $5 per unit returned
Sales salary	100,000 per month

Required

1. Using customers as the cost objects, classify the activity costs into cost categories (unit-level, batch-level, etc.) and compute the total cost for Colleen Company to service Jerry, Inc. and Kate Co.

2. Compare the profitability of these two customers. (Ignore the cost of funds.)

[LO 5-6] 5-36 **Customer Profitability Analysis** Garner Industries manufactures precision tools. The firm uses an activity-based costing system. CEO Deb Garner is very proud of the accuracy of the system in determining product costs. She noticed that since the installment of the ABC system 10 years earlier, the firm had become much more competitive in all aspects of the business and earned an increasing amount of profits every year.

In the last two years, the firm sold 1 million units to 4,100 customers each year. The manufacturing cost is $600 per unit. In addition, Garner has determined that the order-filling cost is $100.50 per unit. The $784.56 selling price per unit includes 12% markup to cover administrative costs and profits.

The order-filling cost per unit is determined based on the firm's costs for order-filling activities. Order-filling capacity can be added in blocks of 60 orders. Each block costs $60,000. In addition, the firm incurs $1,500 order-filling costs per order.

Garner serves two types of customers, designated as PC (Preferred Customer) and SC (Small Customer). Each of the 100 PCs buys, on average, 5,000 units in two orders. The firm also sells 500,000 units to 4,000 SCs. On average, each SC buys 125 units in 10 orders. Ed Cheap, a buyer for one PC, complains about the high price he is paying. Cheap claims that he has been offered a price of $700 per unit and threatens to take his business elsewhere. Garner does not give in because the $700 price Cheap demands is below cost. Besides, she has recently raised the price to SC to $800 per unit and experienced no decline in orders.

Required

1. Demonstrate how Garner arrives at the $100.50 order-filling cost per unit.

2. What would be the amount of loss (profit) per unit if Garner sells to Cheap at $700 per unit?

3. What is the amount of loss (profit) per unit at the $800 selling price per unit for units sold to SC?

[LO 5-7] 5-37 **TDABC in Banking** Second Republic Bank is a lending company that operates in the Southeastern United States. Current economic conditions have kept lending rates low, which limits the revenue potential for Second Republic. The bank manager, Vivian Caldwell is concerned about understanding and then controlling costs, and she decided to try out time-driven ABC. As a pilot, she decided to focus on understanding the cost of taking a customer's loan application. Vivian knew that it took longer to collect applicant information for a mortgage than it did for other types of loans, like auto loans or unsecured loans, but did not know the cost differences, so she collected the following information from a regional branch office.

Type of Loan	Average Time to Collect Applicant's Information
Mortgage	60 minutes
Auto	30 minutes
Unsecured	20 minutes

There are two loan application specialists, each earning $55,000 per year. Vivian determined that fringe benefits average 30% of salary and that the office support costs for an employee (computer, office space, etc.) in that regional branch averaged $5,300 per employee. Factoring in time off for vacations, time spent on training, and other required tasks, each of the application specialists had 1,600 hours available to collect applicant information.

Required

1. Determine the cost per hour available to collect loan applicant information.

2. Determine the average TDABC cost of collecting applicant information for each of the three types of loans.

Problems

[LO 5-1, 5-3]   5-38 **Activity-Based Costing; Value Chain Analysis** Drilling Company uses activity-based costing and provides this information:

Manufacturing Activity	Cost Driver	Driver Rate
Materials handling	Number of parts	$0.60
Machinery	Number of machine hours	51.00
Assembly	Number of parts	2.85
Inspection	Number of finished units	30.00

Drilling has just completed 80 units of a component for a customer. Each unit required 100 parts and 3 machine hours. The prime cost is $1,300 per finished unit. All other manufacturing costs are classified as manufacturing overhead.

Required
1. Compute the total manufacturing costs and the unit costs of the 80 units just completed using ABC costing.
2. In addition to the manufacturing costs, the firm has determined that the total cost of upstream activities, including research and development and product design, is $180 per unit. The total cost of downstream activities, such as distribution, marketing, and customer service, is $300 per unit. Compute the full product cost per unit, including upstream, manufacturing, and downstream activities. Also compute the relative proportion of each main cost category. What are the strategic implications of this new cost result?
3. Explain to Drilling Company the usefulness of calculating the total cost of the value chain and of knowing costs of different value-creating activities.

[LO 5-1, 5-3]   5-39 **Resource and Activity-Based Cost Drivers** EyeGuard Equipment Inc. (EEI) manufactures protective eyewear for use in commercial and home applications. The product is also used by hunters, home woodworking hobbyists, and in other applications. The firm has two main product lines—the highest-quality product is called Safe-T, and a low-cost, value version is called Safe-V. Information on the factory conversion costs for EEI is as follows:

	Factory Costs
Salaries	$850,000
Supplies	150,000
Factory expense	550,000
Total	$1,550,000

EEI uses ABC to determine the unit costs of its products. The firm uses resource consumption cost drivers based on rough estimates of the amount that each activity consumes, as shown below. EEI has four activities: job setup, assembly, inspecting and finishing, and packaging.

	Setup	Assembly	Inspecting and Finishing	Packaging	Total
Salaries	15%	55%	20%	10%	100%
Supplies	20	60	20		100
Factory expense		80	20		100

The activity cost drivers for the two products are summarized below.

Activities	Activity Driver
Setup	Batch
Assembly	Units
Inspect and finishing	Finishing hours
Packaging	Packing hours

	Safe-V	Safe-T
Batches	250	600
Units	60,000	72,000
Finishing hours, per unit	0.2	0.3
Packaging hours, per unit	0.1	0.15
Materials per unit	$ 3.50	$ 6.00

Required

1. Determine the amount of the cost pool for each of the four activities.
2. Determine the activity-driver rates for assigning factory costs to the two products.
3. Determine the activity-based unit cost for each of the products.
4. What is the strategic role of the information obtained in requirement 3?
5. The quantities of resource consumption cost drivers used were based on rough estimates. Under what conditions would you recommend that more accurate cost driver data be collected?

[LO 5-1, 5-3, 5-6]   5-40   **Activity-Based Costing; Customer Group Cost Analysis** Franklin Furniture Inc. (FFI) manufactures bedroom furniture in sets (a set includes a dresser, two queen-size beds, and one bedside table) for use in motels and hotels. FFI has three customer groups, which it calls the value, quality, and luxury groups. The value products are targeted to low-price motels that are looking for simple furniture, while the luxury furniture is targeted to the very best hotels. The quality line is attractive to a variety of hotels and motels that appreciate the combination of quality and value. Currently there has been a small increase in the quality and value lines, and an appreciable increase in demand in the luxury line, reflecting cyclical changes in the marketplace. Luxury hotels are now in more demand for business travel, while a few years ago, the value segment was the most popular for business travelers. FFI wants to be able to respond to the increased demand with increased production but worries about the increased production cost and about price setting as its mix of customers and production changes. FFI has used a volume-based overhead allocation rate based on direct labor hours for some time. Direct labor cost is $15 per hour.

	Budgeted Cost	Cost Driver
Materials handling	$349,600	Number of parts
Product scheduling	160,000	Number of production orders
Setup labor	216,000	Number of setups
Automated machinery	1,750,000	Machine hours
Finishing	619,500	Direct labor hours
Pack and ship	290,400	Number of orders shipped
	$3,385,500	
General, selling, and adm. costs	$5,000,000	

The budgeted production data for the three product lines follow.

Product Lines	Value	Quality	Luxury
Sets produced	15,000	5,000	600
Price	$ 650	$ 900	$1,200
Direct materials cost per set	$ 80	$50	$ 110
Number of parts per set	30	50	120
Direct labor hours per set	4	5	7
Machine hours per set	3	7	15
Production orders	50	70	200
Production setups	20	50	50
Orders shipped	1,000	2,000	300
Number of inspections	2	6	14

Required

1. Determine the cost per set and the total production cost of each of the three customer groups using activity-based costing.
2. Determine the production cost for each of the three customer groups using FFI's current volume-based approach.
3. Compare the two approaches and discuss the strategic and competitive issues of using each of the two methods.

4. The activity usage data given in the problem reflects current usage of the various cost drivers to manufacture the firm's product lines. Suppose you are given the following information regarding the firm's practical capacity for each of these activities, as follows:

Cost Driver	Practical Capacity
Number of parts	990,000
Number of production orders	800
Number of setups	200
Machine hours	100,000
Direct labor hours	123,900
Number of orders shipped	5,000

Compute the new activity rates using practical capacity and comment on how you would use this additional information for costing the firm's products and assisting in strategic planning.

[LO 5-1, 5-3] 5-41 **Volume-Based Costing versus ABC** Eastern Chemical Company produces three products. The operating results of the current year are:

Product	Sales Quantity	Target Price	Actual Price	Difference
A	1,000	$285.00	$286.00	$ 1.00
B	5,000	297.60	255.60	(42.00)
C	500	202.50	310.00	$107.50

The firm sets the target price of each product at 150% of the product's total manufacturing cost. It appears that the firm was able to sell Product C at a much higher price than the target price of the product and lost money on Product B. Tom Watson, CEO, wants to promote Product C much more aggressively and phase out Product B. He believes that the information suggests that Product C has the greatest potential among the firm's three products because the actual selling price of Product C was almost 50% higher than the target price, while the firm was forced to sell Product B at a price below the target price.

Both the budgeted and actual factory overhead for the current year are $510,000. The actual units sold for each product also are the same as the budgeted units. The firm uses direct labor dollars to assign manufacturing overhead costs. The direct materials and direct labor costs per unit for each product are:

	Product A	Product B	Product C
Direct materials	$50.00	$114.40	$65.00
Direct labor	20.00	12.00	10.00
Total prime cost	$70.00	$126.40	$75.00

The controller noticed that not all products consumed factory overhead similarly. Upon further investigation, she identified the following usage of factory overhead during the year:

	Product A	Product B	Product C	Total Overhead
Number of setups	2	5	3	$ 9,000
Weight of direct materials (pounds)	400	250	350	110,000
Waste and hazardous disposals	25	45	30	250,000
Quality inspections	30	35	35	75,000
Utilities (machine hours)	2,000	7,000	1,000	66,000
Total				$510,000

Required

1. Determine the manufacturing cost per unit for each of the products using the volume-based method.

2. What are the least profitable and the most profitable products under both the current and the ABC systems?

3. What is the new target price for each product based on 150% of the new costs under the ABC system? Compare this price with the actual selling price.

4. Comment on the result from a competitive and strategic perspective. As a manager of Eastern Chemical, describe what actions you would take based on the information provided by the activity-based unit costs.

[LO 5-2, 5-3] 5-42 **Volume-Based Costing versus ABC** Coffee Bean Inc. (CBI) processes and distributes a variety of coffee. CBI buys coffee beans from around the world and roasts, blends, and packages them for resale. Currently, the firm offers 15 coffees to gourmet shops in 1-pound bags. The major cost is direct materials; however, a substantial amount of factory overhead is incurred in the predominantly automated roasting and packing process. The company uses relatively little direct labor.

Some of the coffees are very popular and sell in large volumes; a few of the newer brands have very low volumes. CBI prices its coffee at full product cost, including allocated overhead, plus a markup of 30%. If its prices for certain coffees are significantly higher than the market, CBI lowers its prices. The company competes primarily on the quality of its products, but customers are price conscious as well.

Data for the current budget include factory overhead of $3,000,000, which has been allocated on the basis of each product's direct labor cost. The budgeted direct labor cost for the current year totals $600,000. The firm budgeted $6,000,000 for purchase and use of direct materials (mostly coffee beans).

The budgeted direct costs for 1-pound bags of two of the company's many products are as follows:

	Mona Loa	Malaysian
Direct materials	$4.20	$3.20
Direct labor	0.30	0.30

CBI's controller, Mona Clin, believes that its current product costing system could be providing misleading cost information. She has developed this analysis of the current year's budgeted factory overhead costs:

Activity	Cost Driver	Budgeted Driver Consumption	Budgeted Cost
Purchasing	Purchase orders	1,158	$ 579,000
Materials handling	Setups	1,800	720,000
Quality control	Batches	720	144,000
Roasting	Roasting hours	96,100	961,000
Blending	Blending hours	33,600	336,000
Packaging	Packaging hours	26,000	260,000
Total factory overhead cost			$3,000,000

Data regarding the current year's production of just two of its lines, Mona Loa and Malaysian, follow. There is no beginning or ending direct materials inventory for either of these coffees.

	Mona Loa	Malaysian
Budgeted sales	100,000 pounds	2,000 pounds
Batch size	10,000 pounds	500 pounds
Setups	3 per batch	3 per batch
Purchase order size	25,000 pounds	500 pounds
Roasting time	1 hour per 100 pounds	1 hour per 100 pounds
Blending time	0.5 hour per 100 pounds	0.5 hour per 100 pounds
Packaging time	0.1 hour per 100 pounds	0.1 hour per 100 pounds

Required
1. Using Coffee Bean Inc.'s current product costing system,
   a. Determine the company's predetermined overhead rate using direct labor cost as the single cost driver.
   b. Determine the full product costs and selling prices of one pound of Mona Loa coffee and one pound of Malaysian coffee.
2. Using an activity-based costing approach, develop a new product cost for 1 pound of Mona Loa coffee and 1 pound of Malaysian coffee. Allocate all overhead costs to the 100,000 pounds of Mona Loa and the 2,000 pounds of Malaysian. Compare the results with those in requirement 1.
3. What are the implications of the activity-based costing system with respect to CBI's pricing and product mix strategies? How does ABC add to CBI's competitive advantage?

(CMA Adapted)

[LO 5-1, 5-3, 5-4]   5-43 **Cost of Idle Capacity (Continuation of Problem 5-42)** Use the same information as above for Coffee Bean Inc. (CBI) except assume now that Mona Loa and Malaysian are the only two products at CBI. Also, now include the following additional information about the practical capacity Coffee Bean has in each of its activities. For example, currently Coffee Bean has total practical capacity for processing 1,400 purchase orders, 2,400 setups, etc. These are the levels of activity work that are sustainable.

Activity	Practical Capacity
Purchasing	1,400
Materials handling	2,400
Quality control	1,200
Roasting	100,000
Blending	36,000
Packaging	30,000

Required

1. Determine the activity rates based on practical capacity and the cost of idle capacity for each activity.

2. Explain the strategic role of the information you developed in requirement 1.

3. Assume the same information used in requirements 1 and 2, but now assume also that the cost in the purchasing activity consists entirely of the cost of 8 employees; the cost in materials handling consists entirely of the cost of 20 employees; the cost of quality control consists entirely of the cost of 4 employees; the cost of roasting and blending consists entirely of the costs of machines—10 roasting machines and 10 blending machines; and the cost of packaging consists entirely of the cost of 3 employees. Based on this additional information, what can you now advise management about the utilization of capacity?

[LO 5-2, 5-3]   5-44 **Activity-Based Costing** Miami Valley Architects Inc. provides a wide range of engineering and architectural consulting services through its three branch offices in Columbus, Cincinnati, and Dayton, Ohio. The company allocates resources and bonuses to the three branches based on the net income of the period. The results of the firm's performance for the most recent year follows ($ in thousands):

	Columbus	Cincinnati	Dayton	Total
Sales	$1,500	$1,419	$1,067	$3,986
Less: Direct labor	382	317	317	1,016
Direct materials	281	421	185	887
Overhead	710	589	589	1,888
Net income	$ 127	$ 92	$ (24)	$ 195

Miami Valley accumulates overhead items in one overhead pool and allocates it to the branches based on direct labor dollars. For this year, the predetermined overhead rate was $1.859 for every direct labor dollar incurred by an office. The overhead pool includes rent, depreciation, and taxes, regardless of which office incurred the expense. Some branch managers complain that the overhead allocation method forces them to absorb a portion of the overhead incurred by the other offices.

Management is concerned with the recent operating results. During a review of overhead expenses, management noticed that many overhead items were clearly not correlated to the movement in direct labor dollars as previously assumed. Management decided that applying overhead based on activity-based costing and direct tracing wherever possible should provide a more accurate picture of the profitability of each branch.

An analysis of the overhead revealed that the following dollars for rent, utilities, depreciation, and taxes could be traced directly to the office that incurred the overhead ($ in thousands):

	Columbus	Cincinnati	Dayton	Total
Direct overhead	$180	$270	$177	$627

Activity pools and their corresponding cost drivers were determined from the accounting records and staff surveys as follows:

General administration	$409,000
Project costing	48,000
Accounts payable/receiving	139,000
Accounts receivable	47,000
Payroll/Mail sort and delivery	30,000
Personnel recruiting	38,000
Employee insurance processing	14,000
Proposals	139,000
Sales meetings/Sales aids	202,000
Shipping	24,000
Ordering	48,000
Duplicating costs	46,000
Blueprinting	77,000
	$1,261,000

	Amount of Cost Driver Use by Location		
Cost Driver	**Columbus**	**Cincinnati**	**Dayton**
Direct labor cost	$ 382,413	$ 317,086	$317,188
Timesheet entries	6,000	3,800	3,500
Vendor invoices	1,020	850	400
Client invoices	588	444	96
Employees	23	26	18
New hires	8	4	7
Insurance claims filed	230	260	180
Proposals	200	250	60
Contracted sales	1,824,439	1,399,617	571,208
Projects shipped	99	124	30
Purchase orders	135	110	80
Copies duplicated	162,500	146,250	65,000
Blueprints	39,000	31,200	16,000

Required (Round all answers to thousands)

1. What overhead costs should be assigned to each branch based on ABC concepts? (Round values to two decimal places)
2. What is the contribution of each branch before subtracting the results obtained in requirement 1?
3. What is the profitability of each branch office using ABC?
4. Evaluate the concerns of management regarding the volume-based cost technique currently used.

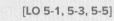

[LO 5-1, 5-3, 5-5] 5-45 **Volume-Based Costing versus ABC** ADA Pharmaceutical Company produces three drugs— Diomycin, Homycin, and Addolin—belonging to the analgesic (painkiller) family of medication. Since its inception four years ago, ADA has used a direct labor hour-based system to assign manufacturing overhead costs to products.

Eme Weissman, the president of ADA Pharmaceutical, has just read about activity-based costing in a trade journal. With some curiosity and interest, she asked her financial controller, Takedo Simon, to examine differences in product costs between the firm's current costing and activity-based costing systems.

ADA has the following budget information for the year:

	Diomycin	Homycin	Addolin
Cost of direct materials	$ 205,000	$265,000	$258,000
Cost of direct labor	250,000	234,000	263,000
Number of direct labor hours	7,200	6,800	2,000
Number of capsules	1,000,000	500,000	300,000

ADA has identified the following activities and cost drivers and has assigned them a total overhead cost of $200,000.

Activity	Cost Driver	Budgeted Overhead Cost	Budgeted Cost Driver Volume
Machine setup	Setup hours	$16,000	1,600
Plant management	Number of workers	36,000	1,200
Supervision of direct labor	Direct labor hours	46,000	16,000
Quality inspection	Inspection hours	50,400	1,050
Order expediting	Customers served	51,600	645
Total overhead		$200,000	

Takedo selected the cost drivers with the following justifications:

SETUP HOURS: The cost driver of setup hours is used because the same product takes about the same amount of setup time regardless of size of batch. For different products, however, the setup time varies.

NUMBER OF WORKERS: Plant management includes plant maintenance and corresponding managerial duties that make production possible. This activity depends on the number of workers. The more workers involved, the higher the cost.

DIRECT LABOR HOURS: Supervisors spend their time supervising production. The amount of time they spend on each product is proportional to the direct labor hours worked.

INSPECTION HOURS: Inspection involves testing a number of units in a batch. The time varies for different products but is the same for all similar products.

NUMBER OF CUSTOMERS SERVED: The need to expedite production increases as the number of customers served by the company increases. Thus, the number of customers served by ADA is a good measure of expediting production orders.

Takedo gathered the following information about the cost driver volume for each product:

	Diomycin	Homycin	Addolin
Setup hours	200	600	800
Number of workers	200	400	600
Direct labor hours	7,200	6,800	2,000
Inspection hours	150	200	700
Customers served	45	100	500

Required (Round all answers to thousands)
1. Use the firm's current direct labor hour-based costing system to calculate the unit cost of each product.
2. Use the activity-based costing system to calculate the unit cost of each product.
3. The two costing systems provide different results; give several reasons for this. Why might these differences be strategically important to ADA Pharmaceutical? How does ABC add to ADA's competitive advantage?
4. How and why may firms in the pharmaceutical industry use ABC? What is the strategic advantage?

[LO 5-3, 5-7] 5-46 **Time-Driven Activity-Based Costing (TDABC) in a Call Center** Market Makers Inc. (MMI) provides a range of services to its retail clients—customer service for inquiries, order taking, credit checking for new customers, and a variety of related services. Auto Supermarket (AS) is a large auto dealer that provides financing for the autos and trucks that it sells. AS has approached MMI to manage the inquiries that come in regarding these loans. AS is not satisfied with the performance of the call center it currently uses for handling inquiries on these loans and is considering a change to MMI. MMI has been asked to estimate the cost of providing the service for the coming year.

There are two types of loans at AS, one for autos and SUVs and another for light trucks. The loans for auto and truck buyers typically have different types of customers and loan terms, so the nature and volume of the inquiries are expected to differ. MMI would use its own call center to handle the AS engagement. The MMI call center's annual costs are as follows:

Call center costs	
Salaries	$4,223,555
Utilities	2,487,446
Leasing of facilities	1,985,513
Other expenses	819,036
Total	$9,515,550

MMI's call center is staffed 12 hours per day with 60 call staff always available. Each staff member has a paid 10-minute break for each hour worked, and an unpaid 1-hour break for a lunch/dinner during each 12-hour shift. Thus, the call center has 12,045,000 minutes (11 hr × 50 min × 60 staff × 365 days) available for calls during the year.

AS and MMI work together to estimate the number of calls and time required for each call, based on AS's prior experience with its current call center.

Inquiries	Total Calls Answered	Average Number of Minutes/Call	Total Time (minutes)
Inquire re: rates and terms			
Autos	80,000	6	480,000
Trucks	32,000	7	224,000
Inquire re: loan application status			
Autos	45,000	5	225,000
Trucks	6,750	11	74,250
Inquire re: payment status			
Autos	39,000	3	117,000
Trucks	12,000	4	48,000
Inquire re: other matters			
Autos	29,000	11	319,000
Trucks	8,500	15	127,500
			1,614,750

Required

1. Determine the amount that MMI should propose to charge AS for the coming year using TDABC, assuming MMI desires a profit of 25% of incurred cost.

2. Suppose that AS wants the proposal broken down by type of loan (auto, truck). What would the proposal look like now?

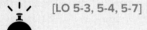 [LO 5-3, 5-4, 5-7] 5-47 **TDABC; Idle Capacity (Continuation of Problem 5-46)** Suppose that in addition to the call center engagement outlined earlier, MMI also provides the following annual service to 10 other clients:

	Total Calls Answered	Average Number of Minutes/Call
Platinum Regional Bank	234,000	6.0
Healthwise Software Inc.	66,788	5.0
Johnson Manufacturing	122,665	4.0
Lesco Online Shopping	233,756	6.0
Babcock Insurance Service	55,455	5.5
Garcia Electric Supply and Service	38,956	3.4
Gilbert's Online Garden Supplies	145,902	4.5
Financial Planning Services Inc.	68,993	11.0
Porter's Camera and Optical	198,440	5.5
Jordan Auto World Inc.	965,887	3.5

Required

1. What is the level of idle capacity at MMI, **not** assuming that AS becomes a customer? What are the implications for the operating and marketing strategies at MMI?

2. Assume that AS comes back to MMI with a revised proposal. The revised proposal includes call center activity as described in Problem 5-46, but in addition, AS wants MMI to provide error-checking services for those who apply for loans at AS. MMI would use some of the call center staff, after appropriate training, to complete the processing of the credit checks. AS expects the following service to be needed:

Processing Credit Checks	Requests	Minutes/Request
Auto	45,600	7
Truck	12,500	12

What would be the idle capacity with the revised proposal? What would be the cost of the idle capacity?

 [LO 5-3, 5-5, 5-7] 5-48 **Personnel Planning; TDABC** Recent competitive pressures have caused National Insurance Company to examine policies regarding personnel planning. As a start, the company has decided to experiment with and develop a time-driven ABC model for its claims processing center.

A study of this support center indicates the following three primary activities: remote processing of customer claims, 0.5 hour; onsite processing of customer claims, 1.0 hour; and updating/maintaining customer records, 0.2 hour. Onsite processing is required for larger claims, while remote processing is done for smaller claims. (For onsite processing, assume—for simplicity—that the claims processors use their own automobiles.) All claims will require that the customers' records be updated.

The claims processing center currently employs three full-time employees. Total annual cost of the center (salaries, depreciation, utilities, etc.) is estimated at $255,000. The net amount of available personnel time per year for this department is approximately 5,000 hours.

Required

1. Why are service organizations, such as the present example, particularly well-suited to apply activity-based costing for cost and resource planning purposes?

2. What estimates are needed to implement a time-driven activity-based costing (TDABC) model? In this regard, what is the budgeted resource cost rate for the present example?

3. Assume that the budgeted number of offsite (i.e., remote) claims is 1,900 for the year. What is the budgeted claims-processing support cost to serve this subset of customers? (Show calculation.)

4. Assume that the budgeted number of onsite (i.e., large) claims for the coming year is 2,900. What is the budgeted claims-processing support cost for this subset of customers? (Show calculation.)

5. Assume now that the customer mix reflected in requirements 2 and 3 were to change as follows: number of remote cases, 2,700; number of onsite claims, 2,000. How much labor processing time would be needed to service this revised level of service demand? What support cost would be budgeted for each class of customer?

6. In response to the projected shift in customer mix reflected above in requirement 5, why might the company not experience an immediate financial improvement? Put another way, will National's resource spending necessarily decrease in response to the shift in customer demand?

7. Finally, why might proponents of ABC (both traditional and time-driven) recommend the use of practical capacity when calculating cost rates for planning purposes?

[LO 5-1, 5-6]   5-49 **Customer Profitability Analysis** Ellie Mosk, CEO of X-Space Industries, decided to expand the company's product offering beyond the core model rocket business. After investigation, she decided to set up a separate division to design and manufacture products for the drone market. Several companies were interested in having X-Space develop these drones, and financial results, to date, have been encouraging. Revenue was $4 million, gross margins have been running about 40%, and the customer sales and support costs were $1 million. However, there is a growing concern that some customers require a disproportionate share of the sales and support resources, and the true profitability of the customers is unknown. Data were collected to support an analysis of customer profitability:

Activity	Cost Driver	Total Cost
Sales visits	Sales visit days	$486,000
Product modifications	Number of modifications	260,000
Phone calls	Number of minutes	92,000
E-mail/Electronic communications	Number of communications	162,000
		$1,000,000

Customer	Revenue	Gross Profit	Visit Days	Modifications	Phone Minutes	Electronic Communications
A	$ 400,000	$ 150,000	15	15	1,030	625
B	500,000	200,000	25	15	1,120	875
C	600,000	230,000	40	40	1,370	1,000
D	1,000,000	420,000	90	60	1,720	2,000
E	1,500,000	590,000	100	70	2,120	2,250
Totals	$4,000,000	$1,590,000	270	200	7,360	6,750

Required

1. Management felt the easiest way to allocate the sales and support costs was based on the total revenue. Using total revenue as the allocation base, determine the profitability of each of the five customers.

2. Management felt that because the data revealed some customers require a disproportionate share of sales and support resources, activity-based costing should be used to determine customer profitability. Use ABC to prepare a customer profitability analysis.

3. Compare the results from requirements 1 and 2 above. What are some strategic implications for management?

[LO 5-2, 5-7]   **5-50 Ethics; Cost System Selection** Aero Dynamics manufactures airplane parts and engines for a variety of military and civilian aircraft. The company is the sole provider of rocket engines for the U.S. military. The price is set at full cost plus a 5% markup.

Aero Dynamics's current cost system is a direct labor hour-based overhead allocation system. Recently, the company conducted a pilot study on the feasibility of using an activity-based costing system. The study shows that the new ABC system, while more accurate and timely, will result in the assignment of lower costs to the rocket engines and higher costs to the company's other products. Apparently, the current direct labor-based costing system overcosts the rocket engines and undercosts the other products. On hearing of this, top management has decided to scrap the plans to adopt the ABC system because its rocket engine business with the military is significant and the reduced cost would lower the price and, thus, the profit for this part of Aero Dynamics's business.

Required As the management accountant participating in this ABC pilot study project, what is your responsibility when you learn that top management has decided to cancel the plans for the ABC system? Can you ignore your professional ethics code in this case? What would you do?

[LO 5-1, 5-7]   **5-51 Research Assignment; Environmental Sustainability Cost Management** Environmental sustainability is not only a potential competitive advantage to an organization, but might also be a regulatory requirement. The creation of business processes to support environmental sustainability requires the expenditure of resources, and management is faced with evaluating the costs and benefits of such efforts. Chartered Professional Accountants of Canada in cooperation with the Consortium for Advanced Management International (CAM-I) offers guidance on using ABC/M to help make better decisions regarding managing the costs of environmental sustainability. Read their guidance and then answer the following questions. The guidance can be found at **www.cpacanada.ca/en/business-and-accounting-resources/management-accounting/cost-management/publications/environmental-sustainability-a-two-part-series/environmental-sustainability-guidance**.

Required
1. What is the purpose of environmental sustainability cost accounting, and why is it important?
2. How can ABC/M help support the analysis of an organization's greenhouse gases (GHGs)?
3. What are some of the characteristics that help determine how well prepared an organization is to begin using ABC/M to monitor and evaluate GHG emissions?

Solution to Self-Study Problem

Volume-Based Costing versus ABC

1. Volume-based costing system:

Stage 1 Allocation: Machine Hours
Total overhead allocated to Department A
$1,000,000 × (4,000 ÷ 20,000) = $200,000
Total overhead allocated to Department B
$1,000,000 × (16,000 ÷ 20,000) = $800,000

Stage 2 Allocation: Labor Hours	Per Unit Cost	
	Deluxe	**Regular**
Overhead allocated to		
Department A		
($200,000 ÷ 20,000) × 2 =	$ 20	
($200,000 ÷ 20,000) × 2 =		$ 20
Department B		
($800,000 ÷ 10,000) × 1 =	80	
($800,000 ÷ 10,000) × 1 =		80
Total	$100	$100

Product cost per unit:

	Deluxe	Regular
Direct materials	$100	$ 50
Direct labor		
$25 \times (2 + 1) =$	75	
$20 \times (2 + 1) =$		60
Factory overhead	100	100
Unit cost	$275	$210

2. Budgeted overhead rates for cost drivers:

Cost Driver	Budgeted Overhead	Budgeted Cost Driver Quantity	Budgeted Overhead Rate
Number of production runs	$7,000	350	$20 per run
Number of setups	400,000	500	800 per setup
Number of units	588,000	19,600	30 per unit
Number of shipments	5,000	250	20 per shipment
	$1,000,000		

3. ABC system:

	Deluxe	Regular
Overhead allocated to		
Materials movement		
$20 \times 15 =$	$ 300	
$20 \times 20 =$		$ 400
Machine setups		
$800 \times 25 =$	20,000	
$800 \times 50 =$		40,000
Inspections		
$30 \times 200 =$	6,000	
$30 \times 800 =$		24,000
Shipments		
$20 \times 50 =$	1,000	
$20 \times 100 =$		2,000
Total	$ 27,300	$66,400
Units	200	800
Overhead cost per unit	$ 136.50	$ 83
Product cost per unit		
Direct materials	$ 100	$ 50
Direct labor	75	60
Factory overhead	136.50	83
Unit cost	$ 311.50	$ 193

Note that the volume-based costing system overcosts the high-volume Regular product and undercosts the low-volume Deluxe product.

Please visit Connect to access a narrated, animated tutorial for solving this problem.

CHAPTER SIX

Process Costing

The Coca-Cola Company (**www.coca-colacompany.com**) is the world's leading manufacturer, marketer, and distributor of soft drink concentrates, syrups, and soft drinks. Coca-Cola's strategy focuses on differentiation.

Coca-Cola's differentiation strategy is apparent in its positioning. It positions itself as a unique and special product with a young, fresh image equal to none in the soft drink segment; it is a permanent reminder of classic values, of American culture inside and outside the country, and of all things American: entertainment, sports, and youth. Furthermore, its brand

monticello/Shutterstock

REAL-WORLD FOCUS   Putting Pepsi in the Can and Potato Chips in the Bag

PepsiCo is the parent company of such brands as Fritos, Quaker Oats, Gatorade, and, of course, Pepsi. All of its products can be produced and packaged in large volumes, making the production environment suitable for process costing. Sometimes it helps to see these things for yourself. Here are links to

two videos—one for filling Pepsi cans and the other for making potato chips.

Pepsi cans: www.youtube.com/watch?v=fuL-wVpMfjY
Lay's Potato Chips: www.youtube.com/watch?v=ws_K9Cxs-uE

is recognized in practically every country in the world. Its exclusive formula makes it unique, but a unique formula is not enough. In 2017, then chief operating officer James Quincy was quoted as saying, "The company needs to be bigger than its core brand." With four consecutive years of revenue decline, the company also needs to keep a close eye on its costs.

Coca-Cola uses process costing to track product costs (direct materials, direct labor, and factory overhead costs) incurred in three major processes: (1) concentrate and syrup manufacturing, (2) blending, and (3) packaging. During the first process, mixing water with sugar, colorings, and other ingredients produces concentrates, and adding sweeteners and water to the concentrates produces syrups. In the second process, pure carbon dioxide is added to the blend of syrups and water to produce the beverage. In the third process, a filler injects a precise amount of the blended beverage into plastic bottles or cans, and a metal crown or plastic closure seals the package.

Process costing is a product costing system that accumulates costs according to processes or departments and assigns them to a large number of nearly identical products. The typical firm that uses process costing employs a standardized production process to manufacture homogeneous products. Process costing provides information for managers to analyze product and customer profitability and to make pricing, product-mix, and process improvement decisions.

In today's globally competitive environment, managers must know product costs to be able to make good decisions. Imagine a large corporation's top manager trying to decide whether to discontinue a product without knowing what it costs. Managers need cost information for setting goals; forming strategy; developing long- and short-term plans; and control, performance measurement, and decision-making purposes. For example, Milliken & Company (**www.milliken.com**) uses an activity-based costing type of process costing to help managers focus on the actual costs in each process and to reduce non-value-added work in each process.

Characteristics of Process Costing Systems

LO 6-1

Identify the types of organizations for which a process costing system best supports the organization's competitive strategy.

Firms having homogeneous products that pass through a series of similar processes or departments use process costing. These firms usually engage in continuous mass production of a few similar products. Manufacturing costs are accumulated in each process. The management accountant uses a production cost report to track production quantity and cost information for each department. Unit product cost is calculated by dividing process costs in each department by the number of equivalent units produced during the period.

The process costing system is used in many industries such as chemicals, oil refining, textiles, paints, flour, canning, rubber, steel, glass, food processing, mining, electronics, plastics, drugs, paper, lumber, leather goods, metal products, and sporting goods. Process costing can also be used by service organizations with homogeneous services and repetitive processes such as mail sorting by a courier. Companies using process costing include Coca-Cola and International Paper (**www.internationalpaper.com**).

As noted earlier, the process costing system supports the strategy of process-intensive organizations by providing the department-focused cost information that supports strategy development, decision making, and performance evaluation in these organizations. For example, many process-driven firms compete on the basis of cost leadership because of their high-volume, low-price competitive environment. Organizations such as Process Industry

LO 6-2

Explain and calculate equivalent units.

Practices (PIP; **www.pip.org/**) are a consortium of member companies that share information and work together to reduce cost, improve quality, and improve product in their industries, thus supporting their competitive strategy.

Equivalent Units

A manufacturing firm typically has partially complete units (Work-in-Process) at the end of an accounting period. Under the job costing system, these partially complete units are not difficult to account for because job costs are available on job cost sheets.

In a process costing system, however, product costs for partially complete units are not readily available. Because the focus in cost accounting has shifted from jobs to processes or departments, the interest is in the unit cost of performing a certain *process* for a given period. The goal is to find the combined unit cost of all units processed in that period, including those that are partially complete at *either* the beginning or the end of the accounting period. Note that by *partially complete,* we mean partially complete for that department; a unit could be complete for a given department but still be in the Work-in-Process Inventory for a department that follows in the sequence of manufacturing processes.

With both complete and partially complete units, we need a way to measure the proper amount of production work performed during a period. An equivalent unit is the measure commonly used.

Equivalent units are the number of the same or similar complete units that could have been produced given the amount of work actually performed on both complete and partially complete units. Equivalent units are not the same as physical units. For example, suppose in a given month a chemical company had in process 30,000 gallons of a chemical, of which 20,000 gallons were complete at the end of the month but the remaining 10,000 gallons were only 50% complete. The equivalent units would be 25,000 gallons [20,000 + (10,000 × 50%)]. The percentage of completion is usually measured by percentage of total cost that has already been incurred in the production of the product.

The equivalent units should be calculated separately for direct materials, direct labor, and factory overhead when the proportion of the total work performed on the units in the Work-in-Process Inventories is not always the same for each cost element. Partially complete units are often complete for direct materials but incomplete for direct labor and factory overhead. Examples include chemical or brewing processes that add direct materials at the beginning but are not complete until the completion of processing, which can extend over hours or days.

Conversion Costs

Because overhead is often applied on the basis of direct labor hours, and because of the relatively small direct labor content in most process industries, factory overhead and direct labor costs are often combined and called *conversion costs* for the purpose of computing equivalent units of production. Linking these two cost elements is practical because direct labor cost is not a significant cost element in these process industries. This linkage is also appropriate for industries in which the direct labor and factory overhead components are incurred in nearly direct proportion to each other, even if the direct labor component was significant.

Many manufacturing operations incur conversion costs uniformly throughout production. The equivalent units of conversion costs are therefore the result of multiplying the percentage of work that is complete during the period by the number of units on which work is partially complete. For example, for 1,000 units estimated to be 30% complete in the ending Work-in-Process Inventory, the equivalent units of conversion for the period are 300 (30% × 1,000 units).

Firms using non-labor-based cost drivers (such as machine hours or the number of setups) for factory overhead costs may find that calculating separate equivalent units of production for factory overhead and direct labor costs is more appropriate. The level of significance of the direct labor costs is likely to be the main determinant of whether a separation of the costs is appropriate.

Direct Materials

Direct materials can be added at discrete points or continuously during production. If the materials are added uniformly, the proportion used for computing equivalent units of direct materials is the same as the proportion for conversion costs, and a separate calculation of

equivalent units
The number of units that could have been produced given the amount of work actually performed and quantity of other production inputs used for both complete and partially complete units; used in conjunction with process costing.

the Direct Materials per equivalent would not be necessary. There could simply be a single calculation of the cost per equivalent unit for the combined production costs. However, if the materials are added all at once, the proportion used in the computation depends on whether the point in the process where the materials are added has been reached.

Exhibit 6.1 illustrates the determination of equivalent units in direct materials for ending Work-in-Process (WIP) Inventory. The example assumes that ending WIP Inventory has 1,500 product units that are 60% complete for conversion. Exhibit 6.1 has four direct materials–adding cases: (1) Materials are added gradually throughout the process (in this case, we assume that materials are added at the same rate as conversion cost), (2) all materials are added at the beginning of the process, (3) all materials are added at the 40% point (because ending WIP is 60% complete for conversion, with materials added at the 40% point, ending WIP is thus complete for materials), and (4) all materials are added at the end of the process. Note that the equivalent units of materials in ending WIP Inventory would be 900 (1,500 × 0.6) equivalent units under case (1). The equivalent units for all four cases are shown in Exhibit 6.1.

Flow of Costs in Process Costing

In process costing, costs flow through different processes or departments. Exhibit 6.2 is a model of direct materials, direct labor, and factory overhead cost flows in a two-department process costing system. Note four key points in this exhibit. First, a separate Work-in-Process Inventory account is used to record costs of each production department. Second, when Department A finishes its work, the costs of the goods completed are transferred to Department B's Work-in-Process Inventory account for further work. After this further work, the costs of goods completed are then transferred to the Finished Goods Inventory account. Third, direct materials, direct labor, and factory overhead costs can be entered directly into

EXHIBIT 6.1 Equivalent Units for Direct Materials in Work-in-Process Ending Inventory: Four Possible Cases

| | | | Equivalent Units in Ending Work-in-Process Inventory for Direct Materials | | | |
Type of Inventory	Physical Units Partially Complete	Percentage of Completion for Conversion	Case 1 Direct Materials Added Gradually	Case 2 All Direct Materials Added at the Beginning	Case 3 All Direct Materials Added at the 40% Point	Case 4 All Direct Materials Added at the End
Ending Work-in-Process Inventory	1,500	60%	1,500 × 60% = 900	1,500 × 100% = 1,500	1,500 × 100% = 1,500	0

EXHIBIT 6.2 Flow of Costs for Two Departments in Process Costing

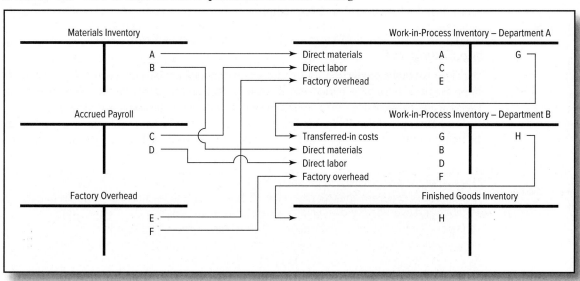

either production department's Work-in-Process Inventory account, not just that of the first department. Finally, starting with the second department (Department B), an additional cost element, *transferred-in costs,* appears. These are costs of the goods completed in the prior department and transferred into this department during the period.

Steps in Process Costing (The Production Cost Report)

LO 6-3

Describe the five steps in process costing.

The key document in a typical process costing system is the production cost report, prepared at the end of each period for each production process or department. The **production cost report** summarizes the number of physical units and equivalent units of a department, the costs incurred during the period, and the costs assigned to both units completed (and transferred out) and ending Work-in-Process Inventories. The preparation of a production cost report includes five steps (summarized in Exhibit 6.3).

Step 1: Analyze the Physical Flow of Production Units

production cost report
A report that summarizes the physical units and equivalent units of a department, the costs incurred during the period, and the costs assigned to units completed and to units in ending Work-in-Process Inventories.

The first step determines the number of units on hand in beginning Work-in-Process, the number of units started into production (or received from a prior department), the number of units completed, and the number of units in ending Work-in-Process Inventory.

The analysis of physical units includes accounting for both input and output units. *Input units* include beginning Work-in-Process Inventory and all units that enter a production department during an accounting period. *Output units* include units that are complete and transferred out from a production department and units in the ending Work-in-Process Inventory.

Step 2: Calculate Equivalent Units for Each Manufacturing Cost Element

The purpose of calculating equivalent units of production for each manufacturing cost element (direct materials, direct labor, and factory overhead) is to measure the total work expended on production during an accounting period. The partially complete physical units are converted into the equivalent number of whole units.

Step 3: Determine Total Costs for Each Manufacturing Cost Element

The total manufacturing costs for each cost element (direct materials, direct labor, and overhead) include the current costs incurred and the prior period costs of the units in Work-in-Process beginning inventory. The amount of these costs is obtained from material requisitions, labor time cards, and factory overhead allocation. The total manufacturing cost for each cost element is also called *total costs to account for.* The total cost determined in step 3 must agree with the total cost assigned in step 5.

Step 4: Compute Cost per Equivalent Unit for Each Manufacturing Cost Element

The purpose of computing cost per equivalent unit of production is to have a proper product costing for income determination and other management needs for an accounting period, which includes both complete and incomplete units.

Step 5: Assign Total Manufacturing Costs to Units Completed and Ending WIP

The objective of the production cost report is to assign total manufacturing costs incurred to the units completed during the period and the units that are still in process at the end of the period. The total costs assigned in step 5 should equal the total costs to be accounted for in step 3.

Companies generally divide the five-step production cost report into three parts: (1) production quantity information, (2) unit cost determination, and (3) cost assignment. The first

EXHIBIT 6.3
Five Steps in Process Costing

1. Analyze the physical flow of production units.
2. Calculate equivalent units for each manufacturing cost element (direct materials, direct labor, and overhead or direct materials and conversion costs).
3. Determine total costs for each manufacturing cost element from step 2.
4. Compute cost per equivalent unit for each manufacturing cost element from step 2.
5. Assign total manufacturing costs to units completed and ending Work-in-Process (WIP).

Many process industries such as paper manufacturing, chemical production, oil refining, and steel processing create environmentally sensitive waste products. Many of these firms use a sustainability scorecard as explained in Chapter 2. A critical cost management goal for these firms is to find cost-effective means to manage these waste products. Not long ago, for example, a steel plating facility in the United States needed to redesign its plant to meet U.S. environmental standards. The firm sought bids from environmental engineering firms for the redesign work. The average bid was $800,000, each requiring a significant rebuilding of the plant and extensive downtime at the plant. To avoid the cost and disruption of such a plant redesign, the company used cost management methods based in part on process cost information to develop a plan to reduce cost within the plant's current facilities. The plan involved several

changes in operations, including new ways to handle materials used in production, changes in product mix and scheduling, segregating wastewater flows, and treating some wastes within the plant rather than off site. The cost of the plan was less than 25% of the cost of the plant redesign, and it also was projected to have lower operating costs. Moreover, the plan offered a better integration of day-to-day decision making with environmental compliance, in comparison to the redesign plan of the consulting environmental engineers.

Required

Can you think of other examples of how a process industry could save money and also improve environmental sustainability?

(Refer to Comments on Cost Management in Action at the end of the chapter.)

part includes step 1, analyze the flow of physical units, and step 2, calculate equivalent units. The second part includes step 3, determine total costs to account for, and step 4, compute equivalent unit cost. The third part is step 5, assign total manufacturing costs (total costs accounted for).

Process Costing Methods

weighted-average method
A method for calculating unit cost under process costing that includes all costs, both those incurred during the current period and those incurred in the prior period that are shown as the beginning Work-in-Process Inventory of the current period.

FIFO method
A process costing method for calculating the current period's unit cost that includes only costs incurred and work performed during the current period.

The two methods used to prepare the departmental production cost report when the firm uses process costing are the weighted-average method and the first-in, first-out (FIFO) method. The **weighted-average method** includes all costs in calculating the unit cost, including both costs incurred during the current period and costs incurred in the prior period that are shown as the beginning Work-in-Process Inventory of the current period. In this method, prior period costs and current period costs are averaged—hence the name, *weighted average*. The **FIFO method** includes only costs incurred and work performed during the current period in calculating the unit cost. FIFO considers the beginning inventory as a batch of goods separate from the goods started and completed within the current period. FIFO assumes that the first work done is to complete the beginning Work-in-Process Inventory. Thus, all beginning Work-in-Process Inventories are assumed to be completed before the end of the current period.

Illustration of Process Costing

To illustrate these two process costing methods, assume that Naftel Toy Company has two production departments, molding and finishing. The molding department places a direct material (plastic vinyl) into production at the beginning of the process. Direct labor and factory overhead costs are incurred gradually throughout the process with different proportions.

Exhibit 6.4 summarizes the molding department's units and costs during June.

Weighted-Average Method

LO 6-4

Demonstrate the weighted-average method of process costing.

The weighted-average method makes no distinction between the cost incurred prior to the current period and the cost incurred during the current period. As long as a cost is on the current period's cost sheet for a production department, it is treated as any other cost regardless of when it was incurred. Consequently, the weighted average cost per equivalent unit includes costs incurred both during the current period and in the prior period that carry over into this period through beginning Work-in-Process Inventory. We use the five-step procedure to assign direct materials, direct labor, and factory overhead costs to the cost object, the molding department, for the month of June.

Step 1: Analyze the Physical Flow of Production Units

The first step is to analyze the flow of all units through production. Exhibit 6.5 presents the procedures for this step.

EXHIBIT 6.4
Basic Data for Naftel Toy Company—Molding Department

Work-in-Process Inventory, June 1	10,000 units
Direct materials: 100% complete	$10,000
Direct labor: 30% complete	1,060
Factory overhead: 40% complete	1,620
Beginning Work-in-Process Inventory	$12,680
Units started during June	40,000 units
Units completed during June and transferred out of the molding department	44,000 units
Work-in-Process Inventory, June 30	6,000 units
Direct materials: 100% complete	
Direct labor: 50% complete	
Factory overhead: 60% complete	
Costs added during June	
Direct materials	$44,000
Direct labor	22,440
Factory overhead	43,600
Total costs added during June	$110,040

EXHIBIT 6.5
Step 1: Analyze the Physical Flow of Units—Molding Department

Input	Physical Units
Work-in-Process Inventory, June 1	10,000
Units started during June	40,000
Total units to account for	50,000
Output	
Units completed and transferred out during June	44,000
Work-in-Process Inventory, June 30	6,000
Total units accounted for	50,000

The two sections in Exhibit 6.5 show the two aspects of physical units flowing through production, *input units* and *output units.* This procedure ensures that all units in production are accounted for. Input units include all units that enter a production department during an accounting period or that entered during the prior period but were incomplete at the beginning of the period. These units come from two sources: (1) beginning Work-in-Process Inventory started in a previous period that was partially complete at the end of the preceding period, which is 10,000 units in our example, and (2) work started or received in the current period, which is 40,000 units in our example. The sum of these two sources, 50,000 units, is referred to as the **units to account for,** which is the sum of beginning inventory units and the number of units started during the period.

Output units include those that have been completed and transferred out and those not yet complete at the end of a period. These units can be in one of two categories: units that were completed, which is 44,000 in our example, or in the ending Work-in-Process Inventory. The sum of these two categories (50,000 in this example) is referred to as the **units accounted for.** Note that units accounted for should match the number of units to account for.

The primary purpose of this first step is to ensure that all units in production are accounted for before we compute the number of equivalent units of production for each production element.

units to account for
The sum of the beginning inventory units and the number of units started during the period.

units accounted for
The sum of the units transferred out and ending inventory units.

Step 2: Calculate Equivalent Units for Each Manufacturing Cost Element

The second step in the process costing procedure is to calculate the number of equivalent units of production activity for direct materials, direct labor, and factory overhead, or for direct

EXHIBIT 6.6
Step 2: Calculate Equivalent Units—Molding Department: Weighted-Average Method

	Physical Units	Completion Percentage	EQUIVALENT UNITS Direct Materials	Direct Labor	Factory Overhead
Work-in-Process, June 1	10,000				
Direct materials		100%			
Direct labor		30			
Factory overhead		40			
Units started	40,000				
Units to account for	50,000				
Units completed	44,000	100%	44,000	44,000	44,000
Work-in-Process, June 30	6,000				
Direct materials		100%	6,000		
Direct labor		50		3,000	
Factory overhead		60			3,600
Units accounted for	50,000				
Total equivalent units			50,000	47,000	47,600

materials and conversion costs. A table of equivalent units, presented in Exhibit 6.6, is based on the table of physical units prepared in step 1 (Exhibit 6.5).

The weighted-average method computes the total equivalent units produced to date. The number of units in production in the current period for each manufacturing production element includes both (1) the units from previous periods that are still in production at the beginning of the current period and (2) the units placed into production in the current period.

In Exhibit 6.6, 44,000 physical units were completed and transferred out of the molding department. These units were 100% complete. Thus, they represent 44,000 equivalent units for direct materials, direct labor, and factory overhead. Note that the 44,000 units include 10,000 units placed into production prior to June and completed in June and 34,000 units (44,000 units − 10,000 units) started and completed in June.

The 6,000 units in ending Work-in-Process Inventory are complete with respect to direct materials because direct materials are added at the beginning of the process. Thus, they represent 6,000 equivalent units of direct materials. However, they are only 50% and 60% complete for direct labor and factory overhead, respectively. Therefore, ending Work-in-Process Inventory represents 3,000 equivalent units of direct labor (6,000 physical units × 50% complete) and 3,600 equivalent units of factory overhead (6,000 physical units × 60% complete).

From Exhibit 6.6, we calculate the total number of equivalent units for each cost element as follows:

$$\begin{array}{l} \text{Completed and transferred out units} \\ + \underline{\text{Ending Work-in-Process equivalent units}} \\ = \text{Total equivalent units of production} \end{array}$$

Combining completed units and ending Work-in-Process equivalent units, the equivalent units of production for the molding department under the weighted-average method are 50,000 units of direct materials, 47,000 units of direct labor, and 47,600 units of factory overhead.

Step 3: Determine Total Costs for Each Manufacturing Cost Element

The third step determines the amount spent in both the beginning Work-in-Process Inventory and current production for direct materials, direct labor, and factory overhead.

Exhibit 6.7 summarizes the total manufacturing costs to account for. As given in our example data, total manufacturing costs ($122,720) consist of the beginning Work-in-Process Inventory balance, $12,680, plus the costs added during June, $110,040.

EXHIBIT 6.7
Step 3: Determine Total Costs—Molding Department

Beginning Work-in-Process Inventory		
Direct materials	$10,000	
Direct labor	1,060	
Factory overhead	1,620	
Total		$ 12,680
Costs added during June		
Direct materials	$44,000	
Direct labor	22,440	
Factory overhead	43,600	
Total costs added		110,040
Total costs to account for		$122,720

EXHIBIT 6.8
Step 4: Compute Cost per Equivalent Unit—Molding Department: Weighted-Average Method

	Direct Materials	Direct Labor	Factory Overhead	Total
Costs (from Exhibit 6.7)				
Work-in-Process, June 1	$10,000	$ 1,060	$ 1,620	$ 12,680
Costs added during June	44,000	22,440	43,600	110,040
Total costs to account for	$54,000	$23,500	$45,220	$122,720
Divide by equivalent units				
(from Exhibit 6.6)	50,000	47,000	47,600	
Equivalent unit costs	$ 1.08	+ $ 0.50	+ $ 0.95	= $ 2.53

Step 4: Compute Cost per Equivalent Unit

For the fourth step in the process costing procedure, we compute the equivalent unit costs of production for direct materials, direct labor, and factory overhead; see Exhibit 6.8. The cost per equivalent unit for direct materials ($1.08) is computed by dividing the total direct materials cost ($54,000), including the cost of the beginning Work-in-Process ($10,000) and the cost added during June ($44,000), by the total equivalent units (50,000). Similar procedures are used for direct labor and factory overhead costs. The total equivalent unit cost of $2.53 can be determined by adding the unit direct materials cost of $1.08, the unit direct labor cost of $0.50, and the unit factory overhead cost of $0.95.

Step 5: Assign Total Manufacturing Costs to Units Completed and Ending WIP

The final step of the process costing procedure is to assign total manufacturing costs to units completed and to units in the ending Work-in-Process Inventory. Exhibit 6.9 summarizes the cost assignment. Note that output and equivalent unit information come directly from Exhibit 6.6; unit costs come from Exhibit 6.8. Also, note that the total costs accounted for in this step ($122,720) equal the total costs to account for in step 3 (Exhibit 6.7).

Production Cost Report

Steps 1 through 5 provide all of the information needed to prepare a production cost report for the molding department for June. This report is shown in Exhibit 6.10.

EXHIBIT 6.9
Step 5: Assign Total Manufacturing Costs—Molding Department: Weighted-Average Method

	Completed and Transferred Out	Ending Work-in-Process	Total
Goods completed and	$111,320		$111,320
transferred out (44,000 × $2.53)			
Ending Work-in-Process:			
Direct materials (6,000 × $1.08)		$ 6,480	6,480
Direct labor (3,000 × $0.50)		1,500	1,500
Factory overhead (3,600 × $0.95)		3,420	3,420
Total costs accounted for	$111,320	$11,400	$122,720

EXHIBIT 6.10 Production Cost Report for June—Molding Department: Weighted-Average Method

	Production Quantity Information				
	Step 1: Analyze Flow of Physical Units		**Step 2: Calculate Equivalent Units**		
	Physical Units	**Completion Percentage**	**Direct Materials**	**Direct Labor**	**Factory Overhead**
Input					
Work-in-Process, June 1	10,000				
Direct materials		100%			
Direct labor		30			
Factory overhead		40			
Units started	40,000				
Units to account for	50,000				
Output					
Units completed	44,000	100%	44,000	44,000	44,000
Work-in-Process, June 30	6,000				
Direct materials		100%	6,000		
Direct labor		50		3,000	
Factory overhead		60			3,600
Units accounted for	50,000				
Total equivalent units			50,000	47,000	47,600

	Unit Cost Determination			
Step 3: Determine Total Costs	**Direct Materials**	**Direct Labor**	**Factory Overhead**	**Total**
Work-in-Process, June 1	$10,000	$1,060	$ 1,620	$ 12,680
Costs added during June	44,000	22,440	43,600	110,040
Total costs to account for	$54,000	$23,500	$45,220	**$122,720**
Step 4: Compute Cost per Equivalent Unit				
Divide by equivalent units	50,000	47,000	47,600	
Equivalent unit costs	$ 1.08	$ 0.50	$ 0.95	$ 2.53

	Cost Assignment		
Step 5: Assign Total Manufacturing Costs	**Completed and Transferred Out**	**Ending Work-in-Process**	**Total**
Goods completed and transferred out (44,000 × $2.53)	$111,320		$111,320
Ending Work-in-Process			
Direct materials (6,000 × $1.08)		$ 6,480	6,480
Direct labor (3,000 × $0.50)		1,500	1,500
Factory overhead (3,600 × $0.95)		3,420	3,420
Total costs accounted for	$111,320	$11,400	$122,720

First-In, First-Out (FIFO) Method

LO 6-5

Demonstrate the FIFO method of process costing.

Another way to account for inventory in a process costing application is the first-in, first-out (FIFO) method, which assumes that the first units to enter a production process are the first units to be completed and transferred out.

Our illustration of the FIFO method of process costing again uses Naftel Toy Company's molding department data (see Exhibit 6.4). Unlike the weighted-average method, the FIFO method does not combine beginning inventory costs with current costs when computing equivalent unit costs. While the costs from each period are treated separately, we still follow the same five steps as in the weighted-average method in determining product costs.

EXHIBIT 6.11
Step 2: Calculate Equivalent Units—Molding Department: FIFO Method—Alternative A

	Physical Units	Completion Percentage	Equivalent Units		
			Direct Materials	Direct Labor	Factory Overhead
Input					
Work-in-Process, June 1	10,000				
Direct materials		100%	10,000		
Direct labor		30		3,000	
Factory overhead		40			4,000
Units started	40,000				
Units to account for	50,000				
Output					
Units completed	44,000	100%	44,000	44,000	44,000
Work-in-Process, June 30	6,000				
Direct materials		100%	6,000		
Direct labor		50		3,000	
Factory overhead		60			3,600
Units accounted for	50,000				
Total equivalent units (weighted-average method)			50,000	47,000	47,600
Less equivalent units in June 1 Work-in-Process			(10,000)	(3,000)	(4,000)
Equivalent units for work done in June only (FIFO method)			40,000	44,000	43,600

Step 1: Analyze the Physical Flow of Production Units

The physical flow of production units is unaffected by the process costing method used. Therefore, step 1 for the FIFO method is the same as the weighted-average method in Exhibit 6.5.

Step 2: Calculate Equivalent Units for Each Manufacturing Cost Element

The FIFO method considers the beginning inventory as a batch of goods separate from the goods started and completed within the same period. The equivalent units in the beginning Work-in-Process—work done in the prior period—are not counted as part of the FIFO method equivalent units. Only the equivalent units of the beginning Work-in-Process to be completed this period are counted.

Two equivalent, alternative procedures are used to calculate equivalent units of production under the FIFO method.

Step 2, Alternative A

One way to calculate FIFO equivalent units is to subtract the equivalent units in beginning Work-in-Process from the weighted-average equivalent units to obtain the FIFO method equivalent units, as shown in the last three rows of Exhibit 6.11. The 10,000 physical units in June 1 Work-in-Process have 100% of direct materials, so these units have 10,000 equivalent units of direct materials prior to the current period. However, these units are only 30% and 40% complete for direct labor and factory overhead, respectively, so they contribute only 3,000 equivalent units of direct labor (10,000 × 30%) and 4,000 equivalent units of factory overhead (10,000 × 40%) prior to the current period.

To calculate the total number of FIFO equivalent units, the following equation is used for each cost element:

> Completed and transferred out units
> + Ending Work-in-Process equivalent units
> = Weighted-average equivalent units
> − Beginning Work-in-Process equivalent units
> = FIFO equivalent units of work done during this period

Exhibit 6.11 shows that Naftel Toy Company must account for a total of 50,000 units. Of these, 44,000 units are complete and 6,000 units are ending Work-in-Process Inventory that is 100% complete for direct materials. The total equivalent units for the period for direct materials under the weighted-average method is 50,000. Of the 44,000 units completed during the period, 10,000 were in the beginning Work-in-Process Inventory. These 10,000 units already had all direct materials added in the prior period. Subtracting 10,000 units from the 50,000 total equivalent units for the period, the FIFO equivalent units for work done only in June for direct materials is 40,000 units. Following the same procedure, equivalent units of production for the molding department using the FIFO method are 44,000 units of direct labor and 43,600 units of factory overhead.

The difference between the weighted-average method and the FIFO method is that under the weighted-average method, the equivalent units of production completed prior to the current period are not subtracted from the total completed units, so equivalent units under the weighted-average method are always as large or larger than those under the FIFO method.

Step 2, Alternative B

An alternative way to determine the equivalent units using the FIFO method is to add equivalent units of work performed in the current period for each of the three components: (1) equivalent units added to complete the beginning Work-in-Process Inventory, (2) units started and completed during the period, and (3) equivalent units of the ending Work-in-Process Inventory. Exhibit 6.12 presents the FIFO equivalent units computation using this second alternative procedure. Notice that under the FIFO method, the equivalent units in the beginning Work-in-Process Inventory from last month's work effort are not added to equivalent units of work performed this month.

For example, the 10,000 units of beginning Work-in-Process Inventory were 30% complete for direct labor. Naftel Toy Company completed the beginning Work-in-Process Inventory by adding the remaining 70% of the direct labor and 60% of the overhead during the current period to complete production. In addition, the firm started another 40,000 units in production during the period. Of these 40,000 units, the firm started and completed production of 34,000, and the remaining 6,000 were still in the manufacturing process at the end of the period.

EXHIBIT 6.12 Step 2: Calculate Equivalent Units—Molding Department: FIFO Method—Alternative B

	Physical Units	Completion Percentage	Equivalent Units (FIFO) Direct Materials	Equivalent Units (FIFO) Direct Labor	Equivalent Units (FIFO) Factory Overhead
Input					
Work-in-Process, June 1	10,000				
Direct materials		100%	10,000		
Direct labor		30		3,000	
Factory overhead		40			4,000
Units started	40,000				
Units to account for	50,000				
Output					
Completed and transferred out from Work-in-Process, June 1	10,000				
Direct materials 10,000 × (1 − 100%)			0		
Direct labor 10,000 × (1 − 30%)				7,000	
Factory overhead 10,000 × (1 − 40%)					6,000
Started and completed (44,000 − 10,000)	34,000	100%	34,000	34,000	34,000
Work-in-Process, June 30	6,000				
Direct materials		100%	6,000		
Direct labor		50		3,000	
Factory overhead		60			3,600
Units accounted for	50,000				
Equivalent units of work for June (FIFO method)			40,000	44,000	43,600

EXHIBIT 6.13
Weighted-Average vs. FIFO Equivalent Units

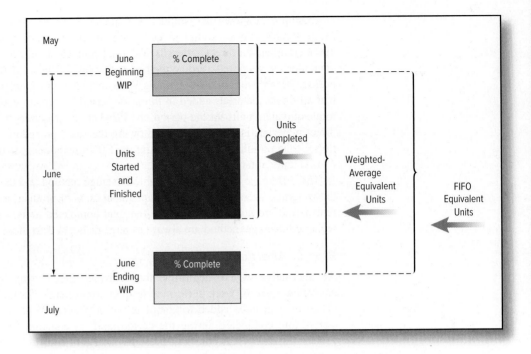

The firm has completed only 50% of the total direct labor in ending Work-in-Process Inventory, or an equivalent of 3,000 units. To summarize the direct labor used during the period, the firm used an equivalent of 7,000 units of direct labor to complete the beginning Work-in-Process Inventory on hand, started and completed 34,000 units, and used an equivalent of 3,000 units to complete 50% of the 6,000 units of ending Work-in-Process Inventory. The total direct labor of the period is equivalent to production of 44,000 FIFO units. Exhibit 6.13 graphically illustrates the difference between weighted-average and FIFO equivalent units.

Step 3: Determine Total Costs for Each Manufacturing Cost Element

The total costs incurred to manufacture product units are unaffected by the process costing method used. Therefore, step 3 is the same as the weighted-average method in Exhibit 6.7. It shows that Naftel Toy Company's molding department has $122,720 total manufacturing costs to account for.

Step 4: Compute Cost per Equivalent Unit for Each Manufacturing Cost Element

Under the FIFO method, equivalent unit costs are calculated by dividing the costs added during the current period by the equivalent units for work completed only during the current period. No cost in the beginning Work-in-Process Inventory is included in determining equivalent unit costs for cost elements. Exhibit 6.14 presents the calculations. The equivalent unit cost for direct materials ($1.10) is computed by dividing the direct materials cost added during June ($44,000) by the equivalent units for work done in June only (40,000). Similar

EXHIBIT 6.14
Step 4: Compute Cost per Equivalent Unit—Molding Department: FIFO Method

	Direct Materials		Direct Labor		Factory Overhead		Total
Costs (from Exhibit 6.7)							
Work-in-Process, June 1							$ 12,680
Costs added during June	$44,000		$22,440		$43,600		110,040
Total costs to account for							$122,720
Divide by equivalent units							
(from Exhibit 6.11)	40,000		44,000		43,600		
Equivalent unit costs	$ 1.10	+	$ 0.51	+	$ 1.00	=	$ 2.61

procedures are used for direct labor and factory overhead costs. Notice that the total equivalent unit cost of $2.61 is determined by adding the unit direct materials cost of $1.10, the unit direct labor cost of $0.51, and the unit factory overhead cost of $1.00.

Step 5: Assign Total Manufacturing Costs to Units Completed and Ending WIP

The final step of the process costing procedure is to assign total manufacturing costs to units completed and to units in the ending Work-in-Process Inventory. As for the weighted-average method, the FIFO method assigns the total costs of a period to the units completed and the units still in process at the end of the period. Unlike the weighted-average method, however, the FIFO method accounts separately for current and prior period costs.

The manufacturing process for units in the beginning Work-in-Process overlaps two periods. Thus, units completed from beginning Work-in-Process Inventory incurred costs prior to the current period as well as during the current period. This fact makes the assignment of total manufacturing costs to units completed during a period a two-part process. In the first part, the total manufacturing cost for units completed from beginning Work-in-Process is determined. In the second part, the total manufacturing costs for units started and completed during the manufacturing process in the current period are calculated.

Step 5, Part A: Total Cost of Units Completed from Beginning Work-in-Process Inventory

To determine the total manufacturing costs for the units completed from beginning WIP, the firm adds the manufacturing costs assigned to these units during the current period to the costs of the beginning Work-in-Process Inventory ($12,680).

The costs assigned to the 10,000 units of the beginning Work-in-Process Inventory that were completed and transferred out during the current period are calculated as follows:

Work-in-Process Inventory, June 1, 10,000 units	$12,680
Costs added during June to complete the beginning WIP Inventory	
Direct labor 7,000 equivalent units × $0.51 per equivalent unit	3,570
Factory overhead 6,000 equivalent units × $1.00 per equivalent unit	6,000
Total assigned to units from June 1 beginning inventory	$22,250

Step 5, Part B: Total Cost Units Started and Completed

The production cost of units started and completed in the current period can be computed by multiplying the number of units started and completed by the total cost per equivalent unit of the period.

The number of units started and completed in the period is the difference between the units completed and the number of units in beginning Work-in-Process Inventory. In the molding department example, we compute the number of units started and completed as follows:

Units completed − Units in beginning Work-in-Process Inventory = Units started and completed
44,000 units − 10,000 units = 34,000 units

Then the cost assigned to units started and completed is

34,000 units × $2.61 = $88,740

The total costs transferred out are the sum of the total cost from the beginning inventory and the total cost for units started and completed; that is,

$22,250 + $88,740 = $110,990

Ending Work-in-Process Inventory

The cost assigned under FIFO to ending Work-in-Process units is derived by multiplying the current period's cost per equivalent unit of each manufacturing cost element by the equivalent units of the ending Work-in-Process Inventory.

EXHIBIT 6.15
Step 5: Assign Total
Manufacturing Costs—
Molding Department: FIFO
Method

	Completed and Transferred Out	Ending Work-in-Process	Total
Goods completed and transferred out			
Beginning Work-in-Process	$ 12,680		$ 12,680
Current cost to complete			
Direct materials	0		0
Direct labor (7,000 × $0.51)	3,570		3,570
Factory overhead (6,000 × $1.00)	6,000		6,000
Total for beginning inventory	$ 22,250		$ 22,250
Started and completed	88,740		88,740
(34,000 × $2.61)			
Total costs transferred out	$110,990		$110,990
Ending Work-in-Process			
Direct materials (6,000 × $1.10)		$ 6,600	$ 6,600
Direct labor (3,000 × $0.51)		1,530	1,530
Factory overhead (3,600 × $1.00)		3,600	3,600
Total costs accounted for	$110,990	$ 11,730	$122,720

The cost of the 6,000 units in ending Work-in-Process Inventory of the molding department is computed as follows:

Direct materials, 6,000 equivalent units × $1.10/equivalent unit	$ 6,600
Direct labor, 3,000 equivalent units × $0.51/equivalent unit	1,530
Factory overhead, 3,600 equivalent units × $1.00/equivalent unit	3,600
Total ending WIP Inventory	$11,730

Exhibit 6.15 shows that the sum of the costs assigned to goods transferred out and in ending Work-in-Process Inventory equals the total costs accounted for of $122,720.

Production Cost Report

Steps 1 through 5 provide all of the information needed to prepare a production cost report for the molding department for June (Exhibit 6.16).

Comparison of Weighted-Average and FIFO Methods

Both the weighted-average and the FIFO methods produce the same total costs accounted for (compare Exhibits 6.10 and 6.16). The key difference between the two methods is the handling of partially completed beginning Work-in-Process Inventory units. The FIFO method separates the units in the beginning inventory from the units started and completed during the period. In contrast, the weighted-average method makes no separate treatment of the units in the beginning Work-in-Process Inventory. Thus, there is likely going to be a difference between the cost of goods completed under the weighted-average and FIFO methods. Similarly, there is likely to be a difference between ending Work-in-Process Inventory under the two methods. The exceptions would be when unit costs are constant across both the prior and current periods or when there is no beginning inventory.

The weighted-average method generally is easier to use because the calculations are simpler. This method is most appropriate when Work-in-Process Inventory is relatively small or when direct materials prices and conversion costs are stable. The FIFO method is most appropriate when direct materials prices, conversion costs, or inventory levels fluctuate significantly.

Some firms prefer the FIFO method over the weighted-average method for purposes of cost control and performance evaluation because the cost per equivalent unit under FIFO represents the cost for the current period's efforts only. Firms often evaluate department managers' performance on only current period costs without mixing in the effects of performance during different periods. Under the weighted-average method, the costs of the prior period and the current period are mixed, and deviations in performance in the current period could be concealed by interperiod variations in unit costs.

EXHIBIT 6.16
Production Cost Report for June—Molding Department: FIFO Method

	Step 1: Analyze Flow of Physical Units		Step 2: Calculate Equivalent Units		
	Physical Units	Completion Percentage	Direct Materials	Direct Labor	Factory Overhead
Input					
Work-in-Process, June 1	10,000				
Direct materials		100%	10,000		
Direct labor		30		3,000	
Factory overhead		40			4,000
Units started	40,000				
Units to account for	50,000				
Output					
Units completed	44,000	100%	44,000	44,000	44,000
Work-in-Process, June 30	6,000				
Direct materials		100%	6,000		
Direct labor		50		3,000	
Factory overhead		60			3,600
Units accounted for	50,000				
Total weighted-average equivalent units			50,000	47,000	47,600
Less: equivalent units in June 1 Work-in-Process			(10,000)	(3,000)	(4,000)
Equivalent units for FIFO method			40,000	44,000	43,600

Step 3: Determine Total Costs	Direct Materials	Direct Labor	Factory Overhead	Total
Work-in-Process, June 1				$ 12,680
Costs added during June	$44,000	$22,440	$43,600	110,040
Total costs to account for	$44,000	$22,440	$43,600	$122,720

Step 4: Compute Cost per Equivalent Unit				
Divide by equivalent units (from step 2)	40,000	44,000	43,600	
Equivalent unit costs	$ 1.10	$ 0.51	$ 1.00	$ 2.61

Step 5: Assign Total Manufacturing Costs	Completed and Transferred Out	Ending Work-in-Process	Total
Goods completed and transferred out			
Beginning Work-in-Process	$ 12,680		$ 12,680
Current cost to complete			
Direct labor (7,000 × $0.51)	3,570		3,570
Factory overhead (6,000 × $1.00)	6,000		6,000
Total for beginning inventory	$ 22,250		$ 22,250
Started and completed (34,000 × $2.61)	88,740		88,740
Total costs transferred out	$110,990		$110,990
Ending Work-in-Process			
Direct materials (6,000 × $1.10)		$ 6,600	$ 6,600
Direct labor (3,000 × $0.51)		1,530	1,530
Factory overhead (3,600 × $1.00)		3,600	3,600
Total costs accounted for	$110,990	$ 11,730	$122,720

Process Costing with Multiple Departments

Most manufacturing firms have multiple departments or use several processes that require a number of steps. As the product passes from one department to another, the cost passes from department to department. The costs from the prior department are called *transferred-in costs* or *prior department costs*. This section explains the concept of transferred-in costs and describes the weighted-average and FIFO methods of process costing for firms with multiple departments.

Transferred-in Costs

transferred-in costs
The costs of work performed in the earlier departments that are transferred into the present department.

Transferred-in costs are costs of work performed in the earlier departments that are transferred into the present department. Including these costs is a necessary part of process costing because we treat each department as a separate entity, and each department's production cost report includes all costs added to the product up to that point. If transferred-in costs were not included, each completed unit transferred out of a department would include only the value of the work performed by that department. It might help to think of transferred-in costs as similar to the direct materials introduced at the beginning of the production process. The equivalent units of production of transferred-in costs can be computed in the same manner as direct materials that are added at the beginning of a process. The difference between the direct materials cost and the transferred-in cost is that the former comes from the storeroom while the latter comes from another production department.

The equivalent units of the transferred-in cost for ending Work-in-Process Inventory is always assumed to be the same as the number of units in ending Work-in-Process Inventory. Because all units in process are complete for the prior departments' costs, by definition the number of equivalent units transferred in is the same as the number of physical units transferred in.

Suppose that Naftel Toy Company's molding department transfers its production units to the finishing department. In the finishing department, direct materials are added at the end of the process. Conversion costs (direct labor and factory overhead) are applied evenly throughout the finishing department's process. The finishing department uses direct labor cost as the cost driver to apply factory overhead costs.

Data for the finishing department for June are shown in Exhibit 6.17.

Weighted-Average Method

Follow the five-step procedure as we illustrate the weighted-average method for process costing with multiple departments.

EXHIBIT 6.17
Basic Data for Naftel Toy Company—Finishing Department

Work-in-Process, June 1	14,000 units
Transferred-in: 100% complete	$ 34,250
Direct materials: 0% complete*	0
Conversion: 50% complete	7,000
Beginning Work-in-Process Inventory	$ 41,250
Units transferred in during June	44,000 units
Transferred-in costs during June	
Weighted-average method (from Exhibit 6.10)	$111,320
FIFO method (from Exhibit 6.15)	110,990
Units completed	50,000 units
Work-in-Process, June 30	8,000 units
Transferred-in: 100% complete	
Direct materials: 0% complete	
Conversion: 50% complete	
Costs added by the finishing dept. during June	
Direct materials	$ 25,000
Conversion	47,000

*Materials are added at the *end* of the process.

REAL-WORLD FOCUS Process Costing in Practice at the U.S. Department of Agriculture (USDA)

The USDA's accounting guidance manuals discuss the different types of costing systems, including activity-based costing and process costing. One example is their publication *Product Costing Guide for Wood Dimension and Component Manufacturers.* Within this document the USDA indicates process costing is preferred when large masses of homogeneous products are produced, such as chemicals, paper, and glass. Survey results within this report indicate that the respondents use the costing information for target costing, calculating life cycle costs and in make or buy decisions.

Sources: Based on information in U.S. Department of Agriculture website (https://www.fs.fed.us/nrs/pubs/gtr/gtr_nrs140.pdf). Activity-based process costing is covered in Chapter 5. Target costing and life cycle costing are covered in Chapter 13 and the make or buy decision is covered in Chapter 11.

Steps 1 and 2: Analyze Flow of Physical Units and Calculate Equivalent Units

The first step is to analyze the flow of the physical units in production. The second step is to calculate equivalent units. Exhibit 6.18 summarizes the analysis of the flow of physical units and calculation of equivalent units. Note that because overhead is charged to the product based on direct labor cost in the finishing department, direct labor and overhead are combined into a single element, *conversion.*

The 8,000 units in ending Work-in-Process Inventory are 100% complete with respect to transferred-in costs because they were 100% complete in the preceding department. There is no direct materials component because materials are added at the end of the finishing process. Because ending Work-in-Process Inventory is only 50% complete with respect to conversion costs, ending Work-in-Process Inventory represents 4,000 equivalent units of conversion costs (8,000 physical units × 50% complete).

As Exhibit 6.18 shows, the total number of equivalent units is calculated as follows:

Completed units
\+ Ending Work-in-Process equivalent units
= Total equivalent units of production

That is, under the weighted-average method, the equivalent units of production for the finishing department include 58,000 units transferred in, 50,000 units of direct materials, and 54,000 units of conversion.

EXHIBIT 6.18
Steps 1 and 2: Analyze Physical Flow of Units and Calculate Equivalent Units—Finishing Department: Weighted-Average Method

	Step 1		Step 2		
			Equivalent Units		
	Physical Units	Completion Percentage	Transferred-in	Direct Materials	Conversion
Input					
Work-in-Process, June 1	14,000				
Transferred-in		100%			
Direct materials		0			
Conversion		50			
Transferred-in	44,000	100%			
Units to account for	58,000				
Output					
Units completed	50,000	100%	50,000	50,000	50,000
Work-in-Process, June 30	8,000				
Transferred-in		100%	8,000		
Direct materials		0			
Conversion		50			4,000
Units accounted for	58,000				
Total equivalent units			58,000	50,000	54,000

EXHIBIT 6.19
Steps 3 and 4: Determine Total
Costs and Compute Cost per
Equivalent Unit—Finishing
Department: Weighted-
Average Method

Step 3	Transferred-in	Direct Materials	Conversion	Total
Work-in-Process, June 1	$ 34,250	$ 0	$ 7,000	$ 41,250
Costs added during June	111,320	25,000	47,000	183,320
Total costs to account for	$145,570	$ 25,000	$54,000	$ 224,570

Step 4				
Divide by equivalent units (from Exhibit 6.18)	58,000	50,000	54,000	
Equivalent unit costs	$ 2.5098 +	$ 0.50 +	$ 1.00 =	$ 4.0098

Steps 3 and 4: Determine Total Costs and Compute Unit Costs

The third step is to determine the total manufacturing costs to account for, and the fourth step is to compute equivalent unit costs for transferred-in, direct materials, and conversion costs.

Exhibit 6.19 summarizes the total manufacturing costs to account for and unit costs for all cost components. Total manufacturing costs to account for ($224,570) consist of the beginning Work-in-Process Inventory balance, $41,250, plus the current costs added during June, $183,320 ($111,320 + $25,000 + $47,000).

The equivalent unit cost for units transferred in ($2.5098) is computed by dividing the total transferred-in cost ($145,570), including the cost of beginning work-in-process ($34,250) and the cost added during June ($111,320), by the total equivalent units transferred in (58,000). Similar procedures are used for direct materials and conversion costs.

Step 5: Assign Total Manufacturing Costs to Completed Units and Ending WIP

The final step of the process costing procedure is to assign total manufacturing costs to units completed and to units in ending Work-in-Process Inventory. Exhibit 6.20 summarizes the cost assignment schedule with $224,568 total costs in step 5.

Cost Reconciliation

The small difference between the total cost accounted for in step 5 and the total cost in step 3 is due to a very small rounding error. *Many of the problems in this chapter require a series of calculations. Rounding errors can accumulate and affect the total unless each calculation is carried out to a recommended four or more digits after the decimal point. If you are using a calculator, make sure all your calculations are done to 4 or more digits after the decimal. To avoid rounding errors entirely, use a spreadsheet package like Excel to set up and solve these problems.*

The FIFO Method

Now we illustrate the FIFO method of process costing for multiple departments using data from the Naftel Toy Company's finishing department.

Steps 1 and 2: Analyze Flow of Physical Units and Calculate Equivalent Units

Exhibit 6.21 summarizes the physical flow of units and equivalent units of production for the finishing department.

The physical flow of product units is unaffected by the process costing method used. Therefore, step 1 is the same as with the weighted-average method.

EXHIBIT 6.20
Step 5: Assign Total
Manufacturing Costs—
Finishing Department:
Weighted-Average Method

Step 5	Completed and Transferred Out	Ending Work-in-Process	Total
Goods completed and transferred out (50,000 × $4.0098)	$200,490		$200,490
Ending Work-in-Process			
Transferred-in (8,000 × $2.5098)		$20,078	20,078
Conversion (4,000 × $1.00)		4,000	4,000
Total costs accounted for	$200,490	$24,078	$224,568

EXHIBIT 6.21
Steps 1 and 2: Analyze Flow of Physical Units and Calculate Equivalent Units—Finishing Department: FIFO Method

	Step 1		Step 2		
			Equivalent Units		
	Physical Units	Completion Percentage	Transferred -in	Direct Materials	Conversion
Input					
Work-in-Process, June 1	14,000				
Transferred-in		100%	14,000		
Direct materials		0		0	
Conversion		50			7,000
Transferred-in	44,000	100%			
Units to account for	58,000				
Output					
Units completed	50,000	100%	50,000	50,000	50,000
Work-in-Process, June 30	8,000				
Transferred-in		100%	8,000		
Direct materials		0		0	
Conversion		50			4,000
Units accounted for	58,000				
Total equivalent units (weighted-average method)			58,000	50,000	54,000
Less: equivalent units in June 1 Work-in-Process			(14,000)	(0)	(7,000)
Equivalent units for work done in June only (FIFO method)			44,000	50,000	47,000

The 14,000 physical units in the June 1 Work-in-Process Inventory have 100% of transferred-in costs, so they represent 14,000 equivalent units of transferred-in work. Because the direct materials are added at the end of the process in the finishing department, zero equivalent units of direct materials for Work-in-Process Inventory are on hand on June 1. The beginning Work-in-Process Inventory is only 50% complete with respect to conversion, so this department has 7,000 equivalent units of conversion costs (14,000 × 50%).

As Exhibit 6.21 indicates, the total number of equivalent units is calculated as follows:

> Completed units
> + Ending Work-in-Process equivalent units
> − Beginning Work-in-Process equivalent units
> = Equivalent units of work completed during this period (FIFO)

That is, equivalent units of production for the finishing department using the FIFO method are 44,000 transferred-in units, 50,000 direct materials units, and 47,000 conversion units.

Steps 3 and 4: Determine Total Costs to Account for and Compute Unit Costs

Exhibit 6.22 shows the computation of total costs to account for and equivalent unit costs for the finishing department.

The beginning Work-in-Process Inventory has a cost of $41,250. The $182,990 total costs added during June include $110,990 transferred-in costs from the molding department, $25,000 direct materials costs, and $47,000 conversion costs incurred in the finishing department, as shown in Exhibit 6.22.

The equivalent unit cost for transferred-in units ($2.5225) is computed by dividing the transferred-in cost during June ($110,990) by the equivalent units for work completed only in June (44,000). Similar procedures are used for direct materials and conversion costs. Notice that the costs of beginning inventory are excluded from this calculation. Under FIFO, the calculations use only current costs added in June.

EXHIBIT 6.22
Steps 3 and 4: Determine Total Costs to Account for and Compute Unit Costs—Finishing Department: FIFO Method

Step 3	Transferred-in	Direct Materials	Conversion	Total
Work-in-Process, June 1				$ 41,250
Costs added during June*	$110,990	$25,000	$47,000	182,990
Total costs to account for				$224,240
Step 4				
Divide by equivalent units (from Exhibit 6.21)	44,000	50,000	47,000	
Equivalent unit costs	$ 2.5225 +	$ 0.50 +	$ 1.00 =	$ 4.0225

*Note: The transferred-in cost of $110,990 is taken from the FIFO report of the molding department, Exhibit 6.16.

Step 5: Assign Total Manufacturing Costs

The final step of the process costing procedure is to assign total manufacturing costs to units completed and to units in the ending Work-in-Process Inventory. Exhibit 6.23 summarizes the cost assignment schedule.

The total manufacturing cost associated with the 14,000 units of beginning Work-in-Process Inventory is calculated as follows:

Work-in-Process, June 1, 14,000 units	$41,250
Costs added during June to complete the beginning inventory:	
Direct materials (14,000 equivalent units × $0.50)	7,000
Conversion costs (7,000 equivalent units × $1.00)	7,000
Total for beginning inventory	$55,250

The costs assigned to the 36,000 units started and completed during June are calculated as follows:

$$36,000 \text{ units} \times \$4.0225 = \$144,810$$

The total costs for units completed are the sum of the total costs from beginning inventory and the total costs for units started and completed, that is,

$$\$55,250 + \$144,810 = \$200,060$$

The cost of the finishing department's 8,000 units in ending Work-in-Process Inventory is computed as follows:

Transferred-in: 8,000 equivalent units × $2.5225	$20,180
Conversion: 4,000 equivalent units × $1.00	4,000
Total ending Work-in-Process Inventory	$24,180

EXHIBIT 6.23
Step 5: Assign Total Costs—Finishing Department: FIFO Method

	Completed and Transferred Out	Ending Work-in-Process	Total
Goods completed and transferred out			
Beginning Work-in-Process	$ 41,250		$ 41,250
Current cost to complete			
Direct materials (14,000 × $0.50)	7,000		7,000
Conversion (7,000 × $1.00)	7,000		7,000
Total from beginning WIP Inventory	$ 55,250		$ 55,250
Started and completed (36,000 × $4.0225)	144,810		144,810
Total costs completed and transferred out	$200,060		$200,060
Ending Work-in-Process			
Transferred-in (8,000 × $2.5225)		$20,180	20,180
Conversion costs (4,000 × $1.00)		4,000	4,000
Total costs accounted for	$200,060	$24,180	$224,240

In Exhibit 6.23, the sum of the costs assigned to goods completed and to ending Work-in-Process Inventory is $224,240. Note that the amount of total costs accounted for in step 5 should equal the total costs to account for in step 3 (as shown in Exhibit 6.22).

Journal Entries for Process Costing

LO 6-7
Prepare journal entries to record the flow of costs in a process costing system.

Process costing uses the same general ledger manufacturing accounts as job costing explained in Chapter 4. However, instead of assigning product costs to specific jobs, we accumulate costs in production departments. Each department has a separate Work-in-Process Inventory account. These journal entries for Naftel Toy Company use the weighted-average method data from steps 3 and 5 of both Exhibit 6.10 (molding department) and Exhibits 6.19 and 6.20 (finishing department). Assume that 50% of the conversion costs in the finishing department are direct labor ($47,000 × 50% = $23,500).

The following direct materials were requisitioned and used:

(1)	Work-in-Process Inventory—Molding Department	44,000	
	Work-in-Process Inventory—Finishing Department	25,000	
	Materials Inventory		69,000
	To record direct materials costs added during June.		

The direct labor incurred follows:

(2)	Work-in-Process Inventory—Molding Department	22,440	
	Work-in-Process Inventory—Finishing Department	23,500	
	Accrued Payroll		45,940
	To record direct labor costs incurred during June.		

Factory overhead applied is as follows:

(3)	Work-in-Process Inventory—Molding Department	43,600	
	Work-in-Process Inventory—Finishing Department	23,500	
	Factory Overhead		67,100
	To record the application of factory overhead to departments.		

Transferred-in costs from the molding department are as follows (using weighted-average):

(4)	Work-in-Process Inventory—Finishing Department	111,320	
	Work-in-Process Inventory—Molding Department		111,320
	To record the weighted-average cost of goods completed in the molding department and transferred out to the finishing department.		

Product units finished are as follows (using weighted-average):

(5)	Finished Goods Inventory	200,490	
	Work-in-Process Inventory—Finishing Department		200,490
	To record the weighted-average cost of goods completed in the finishing department.		

Implementation and Enhancement of Process Costing

Activity-Based Costing and the Theory of Constraints

LO 6-8
Explain how process costing systems are implemented and enhanced in practice.

Process costing systems are appropriate where there are one or a few homogeneous products, as in many process industries such as chemical or paper manufacturing. The goal of the costing system is to account for production costs in the cost of Work-in-Process units and finished products in the production cost report. There is little need for cost information to identify the cost of *different products* or *different customer jobs* because there are only one or a few products and they all go through the same processing and thus have the same unit cost. But sometimes the process-based manufacturer has very different products going through different processes, making the process costing system by itself inadequate. For example, Reichhold, Inc. (**www.reichhold.com**), a manufacturer of industrial chemicals, adhesives, and other products, is a process company that uses process costing, but it has adapted the system to include activity-based costing because of its product variety. While most of its products go through similar processing steps (cleaning, reacting, filtration, and blending), some products require much more time in some steps than other products. For example, one Reichhold product requires careful cleanup of the vat where it is processed because even very small quantities of the chemical can contaminate other products that are later processed in the vat. So, activity-based costing is used to properly charge the extra cleanup costs to this product.[1] Activity-based costing is an important enhancement to process costing when product and process variety arises. For example, companies that produce products in a wide range of batch sizes (i.e., for both large- and small-volume customers) generally require ABC costing to properly identify the cost of the smaller batches; smaller batches tend to be undercosted in the volume-based methods (see Chapter 5).

Similarly, process costing information is not intended to help the firm determine the most profitable product mix or to identify the most profitable use of the plant. These questions require analyses that utilize the products' contribution margins and the location of production constraints in the plant. To determine the most profitable product mix, the process firm would use the contribution methods explained in Chapter 11 and the theory of constraints method explained in Chapter 13. For example, Reichhold could use the theory of constraints to identify the process that is a bottleneck in the manufacture of its products. After determining which process (such as cleaning or reacting) is the bottleneck, Reichhold could adjust production schedules to most profitably use this process.

Just-in-Time Systems and Backflush Costing

Firms use the just-in-time (JIT) method to minimize inventory and improve quality by carefully coordinating the receipt of materials and the delivery of product with the manufacturing processes in the plant. The goal is to have little or no Direct Materials, Work-in-Process, or Finished Goods Inventory in the plant. This saves costs that arise from holding inventory, including the risk of damage, theft, loss, or failure to find a customer for the finished product. Because inventory is minimal in an effective JIT system, there is no need for a system such as process costing to determine equivalent units and to account for production costs in Work-in-Process and Finished Goods. Simpler methods such as **backflush costing** can be used instead. These methods charge current production costs (using standard unit costs) directly to finished goods inventory, without accounting for the flows in and out of the Work-in-Process account, or directly to Cost of Goods Sold without accounting for the flows in and out of WIP or Finished Goods. Any difference between these standard unit costs and actual costs is typically very small and is charged to cost of goods sold at the end of the year. If there are a material number of units in WIP or Finished Goods at the end of the period, costs would have to be pulled back out of Cost of Goods Sold and put into the appropriate inventory accounts. Failure to do so would mean the company was not in compliance with generally accepted accounting principles (because the material amount of inventory is not valued and placed on the balance sheet). As you can imagine, the backflush method is reasonable and convenient for a JIT production environment.

A brief illustration of backflush costing follows. Assume that a company has the following information for a given month of activity:

backflush costing
A method that charges current production costs (using standard costs) directly to Finished Goods Inventory without accounting for the flows in and out of Work-in-Process, or directly to Cost of Goods Sold without accounting for the flows in and out of WIP or Finished Goods.

Purchase of direct materials	$100,000
Actual cost of direct materials used	$92,000
Conversion cost incurred	$145,000
Direct materials standard cost	$5 per unit
Conversion cost at standard	$8 per unit
Total standard cost	$13 per unit
Units produced	18,000 units
Units sold	17,000 units

[1] Edward Blocher, Betty Wrong, and Christopher T. McKittrick, "Making Bottom-Up ABC Work at Reichhold, Inc.," *Strategic Finance,* April 2002, pp. 51–55.

The cost of production using the backflush method is $13 \times 18,000 = \$234,000$, of which $90,000 (\$5 \times 18,000)$ is direct materials and $144,000 (\$8 \times 18,000)$ is conversion. The following journal entries show how the costs are applied and cost of goods sold is determined using the following five steps:

1. Direct Materials is increased for the actual cost of direct materials purchases, $100,000.
2. The Conversion Cost account is increased for the actual amount of conversion costs incurred, $145,000.
3. Finished Goods are shown at the standard cost for 18,000 units completed, $234,000; this includes $90,000 of direct materials cost and $144,000 of applied conversion cost.
4. Cost of Goods Sold are shown for sales of 17,000 units, $221,000 ($17,000 \times \$13$).
5. At the end of the accounting period, the difference ($1,000) between incurred ($145,000) and applied ($144,000) conversion costs is closed to the Cost of Goods Sold account. Also, the $2,000 difference between the actual usage of materials ($92,000) and the standard ($90,000) is closed to Cost of Goods Sold.

(1)	Direct Materials	100,000	
	Accounts Payable, Cash.		100,000
(2)	Conversion Cost Incurred	145,000	
	Wages Payable, Other Accounts		145,000
(3)	Finished Goods	234,000	
	Materials inventory (for actual usage)		90,000
	Conversion Cost Applied		144,000
(4)	Cost of Goods Sold	221,000	
	Finished Goods		221,000
(5a)	Conversion Cost Applied	144,000	
	Cost of Goods Sold	1,000	
	Conversion Cost Incurred		145,000
(5b)	Cost of Goods Sold	2,000	
	Materials Inventory		2,000

The final amount for cost of goods sold is therefore $221,000 + \$1,000 + \$2,000 = \$224,000$. The above presents a simple approach that is used when Work-in-Process is negligible. The use of standard costs means that product costs can be quickly and conveniently calculated for both production and sales; the differences between actual and standard costs are usually small and are closed to Cost of Goods Sold at the end of the period. A full explanation of standard costs and standard cost variances is provided in Chapters 14 and 15.

Normal and Standard Process Costing

Process cost reports illustrated in this chapter have taken a normal costing approach, that is, direct labor and direct materials are added to product at actual cost and overhead is determined and applied to product using a predetermined overhead rate. Normal costing is explained and illustrated in Chapter 4. An alternative approach is standard costing, in which all three cost elements—direct materials, direct labor, and overhead—are added to product at a standard cost rather than actual cost. A key advantage of the standard cost approach is that it can provide a means for evaluating performance. When direct labor or direct materials costs are rising (or falling), a standard cost approach provides a basis with which to measure and analyze the cost changes. This can help management identify and respond promptly to unexpected changes in labor or materials costs. It is particularly helpful when materials or labor costs are changing rapidly.

Both job costing (covered in Chapter 4) and process costing (covered in this chapter) can be applied using either the normal costing or the standard costing approach. Similarly, a process costing system can be either a traditional or an activity-based system. In the case of Reichhold, Inc. described earlier, the company uses an activity-based version of process costing. So, a process costing system could be either weighted-average or FIFO, and then either traditional or activity-based, and then either normal or standard. The result is that there are many possible combinations of the methods: normal/ABC process costing using the weighted-average method; normal/ABC process costing using the FIFO method; normal/ traditional process costing using the weighted-average method; and so on. For simplicity and brevity, Chapters 4 and 6 are based on normal costing only, activity-based costing is covered in Chapter 5, and standard costing is presented in Chapters 14 and 15.[2]

Summary

Process costing is a product costing system that accumulates costs in processing departments and allocates them to all units processed during the period, including both completed and partially completed units. It is used by firms producing homogeneous products on a continuous basis to assign manufacturing costs to units in production during the period. Firms that use process costing include paint, chemical, oil-refining, and food-processing companies.

Process costing systems provide information so managers can make strategic decisions regarding products and customers, manufacturing methods, pricing options, overhead allocation methods, and other issues.

Equivalent units are the number of the same or similar completed units that could have been produced given the amount of work actually performed on both complete and partially completed units.

The key document in a typical process costing system is the production cost report that summarizes the physical units and equivalent units of a production department, the costs incurred during the period, and the costs assigned to goods both completed and transferred out as well as to ending Work-in-Process Inventory. The preparation of a production cost report includes five steps: (1) analyze physical units, (2) calculate equivalent units, (3) determine total costs to account for, (4) compute unit costs, and (5) assign total manufacturing costs.

The two methods of preparing the departmental production cost report in process costing are the weighted-average method and the first-in, first-out (FIFO) method. When calculating unit costs, the weighted-average method includes costs incurred in both current and prior periods that are shown as the beginning Work-in-Process Inventory of this period. The FIFO method includes only costs incurred during the current period in calculating unit costs.

Most manufacturing firms have several departments or use processes that require several steps. As the product passes from one department to another, the costs from the prior department are transferred-in costs or prior department costs. Process costing with multiple departments should include the transferred-in costs as the fourth cost element in addition to direct materials, direct labor, and factory overhead costs.

[2] Jennifer Dosch and Joel Wilson explain the advantages of applying the standard costing approach to process costing and comment on its application in three companies in "Process Costing and Management Accounting in Today's Business Environment," *Strategic Finance,* August 2010, pp. 37–43.

Appendix

LO 6-9

Account for spoilage in process costing.

Spoilage in Process Costing

In this appendix, we explain the two types of spoilage in process costing—normal and abnormal. *Normal spoilage* occurs under normal operating conditions. It is uncontrollable in the short term and is considered a part of product cost. That is, the costs of lost units are absorbed by the good units produced. *Abnormal spoilage* exceeds expected losses under efficient operating conditions and is charged as a loss to operations in the period detected.

Two approaches are used to account for normal spoilage in process costing systems. The first approach is to count the number of normal spoiled units, prepare a separate equivalent unit computation with the cost per unit of the spoiled goods, and then allocate the cost to the good units produced. The second approach is to omit the spoiled units in computing the equivalent units of production; the spoilage cost is thus included as part of total manufacturing costs. The first approach provides more accurate product costs because it separately computes the costs associated with normal spoilage and attaches those costs to only the good units produced. The second approach is less accurate because it spreads the costs of normal spoilage over all units—good completed units, units in ending Work-in-Process Inventory, and abnormal spoiled units. This appendix discusses only the first approach.

Consider Weatherly Company, which has the following data for the current period:

	Units	Cost
Beginning Work-in-Process Inventory	2,000	
Direct materials (100% complete)		$100,000
Conversion costs (75% complete)		80,000
Units started in the period	8,000	
Costs incurred during the period		
Direct materials		300,000
Conversion costs		405,000
Ending Work-in-Process Inventory	2,000	
Direct materials (100% complete)		
Conversion costs (80% complete)		
Completed and transferred out (good units produced)	7,000	
Normal spoilage (10% of good units produced)	700	
Abnormal spoilage	300	

All costs of the spoiled units that were incurred up to the inspection point need to be reassigned. If, as in this situation, inspection of all products takes place at the completion point, the unit cost of spoilage is the total cost per equivalent unit. If the inspection point is earlier, then the cost of spoilage is adjusted accordingly by computing the number of equivalent spoiled units.

Using the five-step procedure described in the chapter, we need only add normal spoilage and abnormal spoilage components in our calculations.

Step 1. Analyze Physical Flow of Production Units

With 7,000 good production units completed in May, the normal spoiled units total 700 (7,000 × 10%). Abnormal spoilage is 300 spoiled units.

Step 2. Calculate Equivalent Units

Equivalent units for spoilage are calculated in the same way as good units. Normal and abnormal spoiled units are included in the calculation of equivalent units. Because the company inspects all products at the completion point, the same amount of work is performed on each completed good unit and each spoiled unit.

Step 3. Determine Total Costs

These costs include all costs in the beginning Work-in-Process Inventory and all costs added during the period. The detail of this step is the same as for the process costing procedure without spoilage.

EXHIBIT 6A.1
Weatherly Company's
Production Cost Report:
Weighted-Average Method

Production Quantity Information				
		Step 1: Analyze Flow of Physical Units	Step 2: Calculate Equivalent Units	
	Physical Units	Completion Percentage	Direct Materials	Conversion
Input				
Work-in-Process, May 1	2,000			
Direct materials		100%		
Conversion		75		
Units started	8,000			
Units to account for	10,000			
Output				
Units completed	7,000	100%	7,000	7,000
Normal spoilage (10%)	700		700	700
Abnormal spoilage	300		300	300
Work-in-Process, May 31	2,000			
Direct materials		100%	2,000	
Conversion		80		1,600
Units accounted for				
Total equivalent units	10,000		10,000	9,600

Unit Cost Determination			
Step 3: Determine Total Costs	**Direct Materials**	**Conversion**	**Total**
Work-in-Process, May 1	$100,000	$ 80,000	$ 180,000
Costs added during May	300,000	405,000	705,000
Total costs to account for	$400,000	$ 485,000	$ 885,000
Step 4: Compute Cost per Equivalent Unit			
Divide by equivalent units	10,000	9,600	
Equivalent unit costs	$ 40.00	$ 50.5208	$ 90.5208

Cost Assignment			
Step 5: Assign Total Manufacturing Costs	**Completed and Transferred Out**	**Ending Work-in-Process**	**Total**
Goods completed and transferred out [(Good units 7,000 + Normal spoilage 700) × $90.5208]	$697,010		$697,010
Abnormal spoilage (300 × $90.5208)			27,156
Work-in-Process, May 31 Direct materials (2,000 × $40.00)		$80,000	80,000
Conversion (1,600 × $50.5208)		80,833	80,833
Total costs accounted for	$697,010	$160,833	$884,999*

* The $1.00 difference between the costs to account for and the costs accounted for is due to rounding.

Step 4. Compute Cost per Equivalent Unit

The detail of this step is the same as for the process costing procedure without any spoilage.

Step 5. Assign Total Manufacturing Costs to Units Completed, Ending WIP, and Abnormal Spoilage

Exhibit 6A.1 summarizes the five-step procedure for the weighted-average process costing method, including both normal and abnormal spoilage. Exhibit 6A.2 is the production cost report under the FIFO process costing method.

EXHIBIT 6A.2
Weatherly Company's
Production Cost Report: FIFO
Method

Production Quantity Information				
	Step 1: Analyze Flow of Physical Units		Step 2: Calculate Equivalent Units	
	Physical Units	Completion Percentage	Direct Materials	Conversion
Input				
Work-in-Process, May 1	2,000			
Direct materials		100%	2,000	
Conversion		75		1,500
Units started in May	8,000			
Units to account for	10,000			
Output				
Units completed	7,000		7,000	7,000
Normal spoilage	700		700	700
Abnormal spoilage	300		300	300
Work-in-Process, May 31	2,000			
Direct materials		100	2,000	
Conversion	—	80		1,600
Total accounted for	10,000		—	—
Total equivalent units (weighted average)			10,000	9,600
Less equivalent units in May 1 Work-in-Process			(2,000)	(1,500)
Equivalent units for work done in May (FIFO)			8,000	8,100

Unit Cost Determination			
Step 3: Determine Total Costs	Direct Materials	Conversion Costs	Total
Work-in-Process			
Beginning inventory	$ 100,000	$80,000	$ 180,000
Costs added during the month	300,000	405,000	705,000
Total costs to account for	$ 400,000	$485,000	**$885,000**
Step 4: Compute Cost per Equivalent Unit			
Divide current period costs by equivalent units	($300,000 ÷ 8,000) =	($405,000 ÷ 8,100) =	
Equivalent unit costs	$ 37.50	$ 50.00	$ 87.50

Cost Assignment			
Step 5: Assign Total Manufacturing Costs	Completed and Transferred Out	Ending Work-in-Process	Total
Goods completed and transferred out (7,000)	$180,000		$180,000
Beginning Work-in-Process			
Current cost to complete			
Conversion (500 × $50)	25,000		25,000
Total from beginning Work-in-Process	$205,000		$205,000
Units started and completed (5,000 × $87.50)	437,500		437,500
Normal spoilage (700 × $87.50)	61,250		61,250
Total costs transferred out	$703,750		$703,750
Abnormal spoilage (300 × $87.50)			26,250
Work-in-Process, May 31 (2,000)			
Direct Materials (2,000 × $37.50)		$ 75,000	75,000
Conversion (1,600 × $50)	—	80,000	80,000
Total costs accounted for	$703,750	$155,000	**$885,000**

REAL-WORLD FOCUS   Spoilage or By-Product

Jelly Belly (www.jellybelly.com/) is a maker of jelly beans. It is a continuous production process that can take between one and two weeks to complete. There are various departments that make up the production process, from forming the centers right through to packaging. Along the way, it is not uncommon for a jelly bean to be misshapen, too big, or too small. These jelly beans, which the company calls a Belly Flop, are defective in that they cannot be sold through regular retail channels. If these items are simply disposed of, they would be considered normal spoilage and the cost of the defects would be absorbed by the jelly beans that pass inspection. If, however, there is a market for these defective units, they could be classified as a by-product, which is a topic covered in Chapter 7.

Source: www.youtube.com/watch?v=6MW3q1a_Los accessed November 22, 2019.

Key Terms

backflush costing, *208*
equivalent units, *188*
FIFO method, *191*
production cost report, *190*
transferred-in costs, *202*
units accounted for, *192*
units to account for, *192*
weighted-average method, *191*

Comments on Cost Management in Action

Achieving sustainability requires a carefully planned and executed policy for reducing the firm's environmental and social footprint. This could be measured in a number of ways, such as the amount of waste products, workplace injuries, carbon and sulfur emissions, and other social and environmental indicators.

The European Union (EU) has taken steps to promote sustainability in process-oriented firms. On July 18, 2012, the EU formed a nonprofit association called SPIRE (Sustainable Process Industry through Resource and Energy Efficiency), which has the mission to "ensure the development of enabling technologies and best practices along all the stages of large scale existing value chain productions that will contribute to a resource efficient process industry" (www.spire2030.eu/). The association has over 130 member companies and process industry stakeholders throughout Europe. To take these goals further, in July 2014 the EU adopted a proposal to boost recycling in the member states. The program is called the "European Union Circular Economy Programme" (http://europa.eu/rapid/press-release_IP-14-763_en.htm). The Circular Economy Programme's goals are to reduce municipal waste by 70% by 2025 and to reduce packaging waste by 80% by the year 2030.

While companies like American Electric Power (www.aepsustainability.com/), one of the largest electric utilities in the United States, are reducing carbon dioxide emissions by reducing their coal-fueled generation capacity, another option is to look in to the supply chain to see where opportunities for cooperation can help. For example, Ford is using military-grade aluminum from Alcoa (www.alcoa.com) to produce trucks that are sturdy yet lighter, saving carbon dioxide emissions. AKSteel (www.AKsteel.com) produces high-efficiency electrical steel that improves the energy efficiency of transformers used by utility companies. Finally, 3M (www.3m.com/Sustainability) makes an environmentally friendly immersion fluid that helps cool data centers, cutting the need for electricity.

Sources: See www.eu-nited.net/cms/upload/SPIRE_-_Sustainable_Process_Industry_October_2011.pdf; Business Roundtable, *Create—Grow—Sustain: People and Technology at Work* (2016), http://businessroundtable.org/sites/default/files/BRT%202016%20Sustainability%20Report.2016.04.23_0.pdf.

Self-Study Problems
(For answers, please see Solutions.)

1. Weighted-Average Method versus FIFO Method

Smith Electronic Company's chip-mounting production department had 300 units of unfinished product, each 40% completed on September 30. During October of the same year, this department put another 900 units into production, completed 1,000 units, and transferred them to the next production department. At the end of October, 200 units of unfinished product, 70% completed, were recorded in the ending Work-in-Process Inventory. Smith Electronic introduces all direct materials when the production process is 50% complete. Direct labor and factory overhead (i.e., conversion) costs are added uniformly throughout the process.

Following is a summary of production costs incurred during October:

	Direct Materials	Conversion Costs
Beginning Work-in-Process		$2,202
Costs added in October	$9,600	6,120
Total costs	$9,600	$8,322

Required

1. Calculate each of the following amounts using weighted-average process costing:
   a. Equivalent units of direct materials and conversion.
   b. Equivalent unit costs of direct materials and conversion.
   c. Cost of goods completed and transferred out during the period.
   d. Cost of Work-in-Process Inventory at the end of the period.
2. Prepare a production cost report for October using the weighted-average method.
3. Repeat requirement 1 using the FIFO method.
4. Repeat requirement 2 using the FIFO method.

2. Weighted-Average Method versus FIFO Method with Transferred-in Cost

Reed Company has two departments, a machining department and a finishing department. The following information relates to the finishing department: Work-in-Process, November 1, was 10 units, 40% completed, consisting of $100 transferred-in costs, $80 direct materials costs, and $52 conversion costs. Production completed for November totaled 82 units; Work-in-Process, November 30, is 8 units, 50% completed. All finishing department direct materials are introduced at the start of the process; conversion costs are incurred uniformly throughout the process. Transferred-in costs from the machining department during November were $800; costs of direct materials added were $720; conversion costs incurred were $861. Following is the summary data of Reed Company's finishing department:

Work-in-Process, November 1, 10 units	
Transferred-in: 100% complete	$ 100
Direct materials: 100% complete	80
Conversion: 40% complete	52
Total costs	$ 232
Units transferred in from machining department during November	80 units
Units completed during November and transferred out to Finished Goods Inventory	82 units
Work-in-Process, November 30	8 units
Transferred-in: 100% complete	
Direct materials: 100% complete	
Conversion: 50% complete	
Costs incurred during November	
Transferred-in	$ 800
Direct materials	720
Conversion	861
Total current costs	$2,381

Required

1. Prepare a production cost report for November using the weighted-average method.
2. Prepare a production cost report for November using the FIFO method.

The Student Resources section of Connect includes video tutorials for the Self-Study Problems.

Questions

6-1 What are the typical characteristics of a company that should use a process costing system?

6-2 List three types of industries that would likely use process costing.

6-3 Explain the primary differences between job costing and process costing.

6-4 What does the term *equivalent units* mean?

6-5 How is the equivalent unit calculation affected when direct materials are added at the beginning of the process rather than uniformly throughout the process?

6-6 What is a production cost report? What are the five key steps in preparing a production cost report?

6-7 What is the distinction between equivalent units under the FIFO method and equivalent units under the weighted-average method?

6-8 Identify the conditions under which the weighted-average method of process costing is inappropriate.

6-9 Specify the advantage of the weighted-average method of process costing in contrast to the FIFO method.

6-10   From the standpoint of cost control, why is the FIFO method superior to the weighted-average method? Is it possible to monitor cost trends using the weighted-average method?

6-11   What are transferred-in costs?

6-12   Suppose that manufacturing is performed in sequential production departments. Prepare a journal entry to show a transfer of partially completed units from the first department to the second department. Assume the amount of costs transferred is $50,000.

6-13   Under the weighted-average method, all units transferred out are treated the same way. How does this differ from the FIFO method of handling units transferred out?

6-14   Under the FIFO method, only current period costs and work are included in equivalent unit costs and equivalent units computation. Under the weighted-average method, what assumptions are made when unit costs and equivalent units are computed?

6-15   What is the main difference between journal entries in process costing and in job costing?

6-16   How do the cost flows in backflush costing systems differ from those in traditional costing systems?

6-17   Explain activity-based process costing.

Brief Exercises

Fill in the missing amount for each of the Exercises 6-18 through 6-21.

[LO 6-4, 6-5]   6-18

Work-in-Process Inventory, February 1	80,000 units
Work-in-Process Inventory, February 28	?
Units started during February	60,000
Units completed and transferred during February	75,000

[LO 6-4, 6-5]   6-19

Work-in-Process Inventory, June 1	?
Work-in-Process Inventory, June 30	55,000 gallons
Units started during June	75,000 gallons
Units completed and transferred during June	83,000 gallons

[LO 6-4, 6-5]   6-20

Work-in-Process Inventory, September 1	5,500 tons
Work-in-Process Inventory, September 30	3,400 tons
Units started during September	?
Units completed and transferred during September	7,300 tons

[LO 6-4, 6-5]   6-21

Work-in-Process Inventory, November 1	45,000 units
Work-in-Process Inventory, November 30	23,000 units
Units started during November	57,000 units
Units completed and transferred during November	?

[LO 6-2, 6-4, 6-5]   6-22   Beginning Work-in-Process is 2,000 units; 44,000 units completed, and ending Work-in-Process is 3,000 units, which are 100% complete for direct materials and 50% complete for conversion costs. The beginning WIP Inventory is 100% complete for direct materials and 50% complete for conversion.

Required

1.   What are the equivalent units for materials and conversion using the weighted-average method?

2.   What are the equivalent units for materials and conversion using the FIFO method?

[LO 6-4]   6-23   Weighted-average costs per equivalent unit are $2 for direct materials and $3 for conversion. There are no transferred-in costs and no spoilage. What is the cost of goods completed and transferred out if 10,000 units are completed and 1,000 units are in ending inventory?

[LO 6-9]   6-24   Abnormal spoilage was 100 units and normal spoilage is 400 units. Beginning Work-in-Process Inventory consisted of 5,000 units; 20,000 units were started; and 22,000 units were completed this period. How many units were in ending Work-in-Process?

[LO 6-9]   6-25   The abnormal spoilage is 300 units and the cost per equivalent unit is $2 for direct materials and $3 for conversion. The inspection point is at the end of processing. There are 600 units in ending Work-in-Process and normal spoilage is 200 units. What is the cost of spoilage shown separately on the cost report?

[LO 6-6]   6-26   There is no spoilage, the beginning WIP Inventory is 6,000 units, and the ending WIP Inventory is 4,000 units for the second department in a two-department process. What is the number of units transferred in to the second department if good output of the second department is 35,000 units?

Exercises

[LO 6-1]

6-27 Process Costing in Process Industries Process costing is a good fit for companies in process industries in which costs are more easily traced to production departments than to individual products. The products are generally produced on a continuous, mass production basis. Process industries often involve the production of a commodity product, and the companies in these industries usually have a small number of relatively homogeneous products.

Required   Give some examples of companies that would use process costing, and explain why.

[LO 6-1, 6-2, 6-4]

Note regarding rounding errors: Many of the exercises and problems in this chapter require a series of calculations. Rounding errors can accumulate and affect totals unless each calculation is carried to a recommended four or more digits after the decimal point. If you are using a calculator, make sure all your calculations are done to 4 or more digits after the decimal. To avoid rounding errors entirely, use a spreadsheet package like Excel to set up and solve these problems.

6-28 Equivalent Units; Weighted-Average Method Washington State Fisheries, Inc. processes salmon for various distributors. Two departments, processing and packaging, are involved. Data relating to tons of salmon sent to the processing department during May follow:

		Percentage Completed	
	Tons of Salmon	Direct Materials	Conversion
Work-in-Process Inventory, May 1	1,000	80%	70%
Work-in-Process Inventory, May 31	2,000	50	30
Started processing during May	7,000		

Required

1. Calculate the number of tons completed and transferred out during the month.
2. Calculate the number of equivalent units for both direct materials and conversion for the month of May, assuming that the company uses the weighted-average method.
3. How would your answer in requirement 2 change if the percentage of completion in ending inventory were as follows: direct materials 30%, conversion 40%?
4. Explain briefly why process costing is appropriate in the fish-processing industry.

[LO 6-1]

6-29 Process Costing in Sugar Manufacturing The food-processing industry, like most process industries, is a common user of process costing. Consider, for example, the sugar manufacturing industry. The processes in sugar manufacturing can differ depending on the agricultural product used to produce sugar. When sugar cane is used, the sequence of processes looks something like this:

First: Cane shredding The sugar cane is shredded into small pieces to facilitate its movement through the milling machine.

Second: Milling The shredded cane is crushed between the rollers in the milling machine to produce the cane juice.

Third: Heating and adding lime In this step, the cane juice is heated to concentrate the juice, and lime is added to reduce acidity.

Fourth: Clarifying Impure elements are removed from the juice.

Fifth: Evaporating and separating Here the juice is heated, vacuum is applied, and the liquid is centrifuged to remove the molasses and to produce what is called raw sugar.

Sixth: Crystallizing The raw sugar is melted and carbon-filtered to produce the refined sugar.

Seventh: Drying The refined sugar is dried and made ready for packaging.

Due to the nature of the seven processes, there is a relatively large amount of Work-in-Process Inventory at any point in time. Also, sugar cane and raw sugar commodity prices can be stable for a period of time, but there are periods of high volatility caused by, for example, India's mandate in 2007 to develop ethanol fuel or the supply/demand imbalance in 1980 that sent prices up. Also, government price supports, import restrictions, and quotas affect the price of sugar cane. For example, as part of its development policy, the European Union (EU) in recent years paid above-market rates for sugar from a number of African, Caribbean, and Pacific countries, many of them former colonies of European countries.

Required

1. Are firms that produce sugar likely to incur transferred-in costs? Why or why not?
2. Should a sugar producer use the FIFO or the weighted-average method for the process cost report? Explain your answer.
3. Identify and explain any sustainability issues for the production of sugar.
4. Identify and interpret the significance of any global issues for the production of sugar.

[LO 6-2, 6-4]   6-30   **Equivalent Units; Weighted-Average Method** Northern Washington Lumber Company grows, harvests, and processes timber for use as building lumber. The following data pertain to the company's sawmill:

Work-in-Process Inventory, January 1 (direct materials: 60%, conversion: 40%)	30,000 units
Work-in-Process Inventory, December 31 (direct materials: 70%, conversion: 60%)	15,000 units

During the year, the company started 180,000 units in production.

Required   Prepare a physical flow schedule and compute the number of equivalent units of both direct materials and conversion for the year, using the weighted-average method.

[LO 6-2, 6-4, 6-5]   6-31   **Equivalent Units; Weighted-Average and FIFO Methods** Murray Chemical Company refines a variety of petrochemical products. These data are from the firm's Houston plant:

Work-in-Process Inventory, September 1	4,000,000 gallons
Direct materials	50% completed
Conversion	20% completed
Units started in process during September	4,850,000 gallons
Work-in-Process Inventory, September 30	2,400,000 gallons
Direct materials	40% completed
Conversion	60% completed

Required   Compute the equivalent units of direct materials and conversion for the month of September. Use both the weighted-average and the FIFO methods.

[LO 6-2, 6-4, 6-5]   6-32   **Equivalent Units; Weighted-Average and FIFO Methods** Holly Company has the following information for December 1 to December 31. All direct materials are 100% complete.

Work-in-Process			
Beginning balance December 200 units, 20% complete for conversion	$25,000	Completed 800 units and transferred to Finished Goods Inventory	$131,182
Direct materials	54,000		
Direct labor	34,000		
Factory overhead			
Property taxes	6,000		
Depreciation	32,000		
Utilities	18,000		
Indirect labor	4,000		
Ending balance December 31, 300 units, 40% complete	30,818		

Required

1. Calculate equivalent units using the weighted-average and FIFO methods.

2. Use the given information to determine whether Holly Company is using the FIFO or weighted-average method. The beginning balance of Work-in-Process (WIP) consists of $11,000 of direct materials and $14,000 of conversion costs.

[LO 6-2, 6-4]   6-33   **Equivalent Units; Weighted-Average Equivalent Unit Cost** Perrette Motor Company rebuilds automobile engines that have been damaged or are in need of extensive repair. The rebuilt engine has a 100,000-mile warranty and is purchased by auto shops, large motor pools in companies and governmental units, and some individual auto owners. The plant in Dayton, Ohio, specializes in the Ford V6 engine. Approximately 600 to 800 engines are rebuilt each month, and the costs of the plant are assigned to monthly production using weighted-average process costing. The current month began with a Work-in-Process Inventory of 100 engines, which were 50% complete for direct materials and 50% complete for conversion costs. The direct materials cost in beginning Work-in-Process was

$50,000, while the conversion cost was $60,000. A total of 500 engines were completed and shipped out during the month, and total direct materials cost of $550,000 and conversion cost of $640,000 were incurred during the month. The ending Work-in-Process of 200 units was 50% complete for direct materials and 30% complete for conversion costs.

Required   Compute the cost per equivalent unit for direct materials and conversion for the month.

[LO 6-2, 6-3, 6-4, 6-5]   6-34   **Equivalent Units; Weighted-Average and FIFO Equivalent Unit Cost** Pablo Company calculates the cost for an equivalent unit of production using process costing.

Work-in-Process Inventory, June 1: 30,000 units	
Direct materials: 100% complete	$ 60,000
Conversion: 40% complete	25,000
Balance in Work-in-Process, June 1	$ 85,000
Units started during June	70,000
Units completed and transferred out	70,000
Work-in-Process Inventory, June 30	30,000
Direct materials: 100% complete	
Conversion: 80% complete	
Costs incurred during June	
Direct materials	$122,500
Conversion costs	
Direct labor	119,720
Applied overhead	179,580
Total conversion costs	$299,300

Required

1. Compute the costs per equivalent unit for both the weighted-average and FIFO methods.

2. Explain the difference between the FIFO and weighted-average equivalent unit costs.

 [LO 6-2, 6-3, 6-5]   6-35   **FIFO Method** Taxes R Us (TRU), an income tax preparation firm, uses the FIFO method of process costing for its monthly reports. TRU has no materials cost in the preparation of the returns. The following shows its March information:

Returns in process, March 1 (30% complete)	100
Returns started in March	1,600
Returns in process, March 31 (90% complete)	200
Labor and overhead costs for returns in process, March 1	$ 2,500
Labor and overhead costs incurred in March	$173,250

Required   Calculate the following amounts for conversion costs using the FIFO method:

1. Number of equivalent units (tax returns).

2. Cost per equivalent unit.

3. Cost of completed tax returns for the month of March.

4. Cost of tax returns in process as of March 31.

Problems

[LO 6-2, 6-4]   6-36   **Weighted-Average Method** McElroy, Inc. produces a single model of a popular cell phone in large quantities. A single cell phone moves through two departments, assembly and testing. The manufacturing costs in the assembly department during March follow:

Direct materials	$187,500
Conversion costs	163,800
	$351,300

The assembly department has no beginning Work-in-Process Inventory. During the month, it started 30,000 cell phones, but only 26,000 were fully completed and transferred to the testing department. All parts had been made and placed in the remaining 4,000 cell phones, but only 50% of the conversion had been completed. The company uses the weighted-average method of process costing to accumulate product costs.

Required

1. Compute the equivalent units and costs per equivalent unit for March in the assembly department.
2. Compute the cost of units completed and transferred to the testing department.
3. Compute the cost of the ending Work-in-Process.

[LO 6-2, 6-4]   6-37 **Weighted-Average Method** Weatherly Lumber Company processes wood pulp for manufacturing various paper products. The company employs a process costing system for its manufacturing operations. All direct materials are added at the beginning of the process, and conversion costs are incurred uniformly throughout the process. This is the company's production schedule for May:

	Tons of Pulp	Percentage Completed Materials	Conversion
Work-in-Process Inventory, May 1	5,000	100%	50%
Started during May	15,000		
Units to account for	20,000		
Units from beginning Work-in-Process, which were completed and transferred out during May	5,000		
Started and completed during May	12,000		
Work-in-Process Inventory, May 31	3,000	100%	50%
Total units accounted for	20,000		

The following cost data are available:

Work-in-Process Inventory, May 1	
Direct materials	$ 94,000
Conversion	133,120
Costs incurred during May	
Direct materials	229,800
Conversion	376,000

Required

1. Calculate the equivalent units of direct materials and conversion during May. Use the weighted-average method.
2. Calculate the cost per equivalent unit for both direct materials and conversion during May. Use the weighted-average method.

[LO 6-2, 6-5]   6-38 **FIFO Method** Refer to the information in Problem 6-37.
Required   Complete Problem 6-37 using the FIFO method.

[LO 6-2, 6-3, 6-4]   6-39 **Weighted-Average Method** Arsenio Company manufactures a single product that goes through two processes, mixing and cooking. The following data pertain to the mixing department for August:

Work-in-Process Inventory, August 1	
Conversion: 80% complete	34,000 units
Work-in-Process Inventory, August 31	
Conversion: 50% complete	30,000 units
Units started	66,000
Units completed and transferred out	?
Costs	
Work-in-Process Inventory, August 1	
Material X	$ 64,800
Material Y	88,100
Conversion	119,880
Costs added during August	
Material X	152,700
Material Y	135,900
Conversion	305,120

Material X is added at the beginning of work in the mixing department. Material Y is also added in the mixing department, but not until units are 60% complete with regard to conversion. Conversion costs are incurred uniformly during the process. The company uses the weighted-average cost method.

Required

1. Calculate the equivalent units of material X, material Y, and conversion for the mixing department.
2. Calculate the cost per equivalent unit for material X, material Y, and conversion.
3. Calculate the cost of units transferred out.
4. Calculate the cost of the ending Work-in-Process Inventory.

[LO 6-2, 6-3, 6-4]   6-40   **Weighted-Average Method** The T. L. Lin Company manufactures a variety of natural fabrics for the clothing industry in a suburb of Shanghai. The following data in Chinese currency called *yuan* pertain to the month of October.

Work-in-Process Inventory, October 1	50,000 units
Direct materials: 60% complete	55,440 yuan
Conversion: 30% complete	54,425 yuan
Costs incurred during October	
Direct materials	820,400 yuan
Conversion	1,350,600 yuan

During October, 200,000 units were completed and transferred out. At the end of the month, 30,000 units (direct materials 80% and conversion 50% complete) remain in Work-in-Process Inventory.

Required   Calculate each of the following amounts using weighted-average process costing.

1. Equivalent units of direct materials and conversion.
2. Costs per equivalent unit for direct materials and conversion.
3. Cost of goods completed and transferred out during October.
4. Cost of the Work-in-Process Inventory at October 31.
5. Check the most recent issue of *The Wall Street Journal* or go to www.federalreserve.gov/releases/ H10/hist/ to learn the exchange rate between the U.S. dollar and the Chinese yuan.

[LO 6-2, 6-4, 6-6, 6-7]   6-41   **Weighted-Average Method; Transferred-in Costs** McCallum Tool Company has two departments, assembly and finishing. The assembly department takes purchased parts and assembles the final product. The finishing department performs testing, adds other materials, and packages the product. Direct materials are added at the end of the process in the finishing department. The following summarizes the finishing department's operations for the month of July.

	Number of Units
Work-in-Process, July 1, 50% complete for conversion costs	4,000
Transferred in during July	28,000
Completed during July	27,000
Work-in-Process, July 31, 50% complete for conversion costs	5,000

	Costs
Work-in-Process, July 1 (transferred-in costs, $50,000; conversion costs, $30,125)	$ 80,125
Transferred in from assembly department during July	150,000
Direct materials added during July	60,750
Conversion added during July	110,000
Total to account for	$400,875

Required   Calculate each of the following amounts for the finishing department using the weighted-average process costing method, and then prepare the requested journal entries.

1. Equivalent units of transferred-in, direct materials, and conversion.
2. Equivalent unit costs for transferred-in costs, direct materials, and conversion.
3. Cost of goods completed and transferred out during July.

4. Cost of Work-in-Process Inventory at July 31.

5. Show the journal entries for direct materials, direct labor, overhead, and finished product for July, assuming that direct labor is 50% of conversion cost.

[LO 6-2, 6-3, 6-4]   6-42 **Reconditioning Service; Weighted-Average Method** Golf World, Inc. (GWI) sells products and services for the sport of golf. One of its key business units specializes in the repair and reconditioning of golf carts. GWI enters into contracts with a number of golf clubs throughout the U.S. in which the clubs send their carts to GWI for a complete reconditioning: motor, frame repair where necessary, and replacement of seat covers and canvas tops. The clubs usually will cycle 10–15% of their carts through this process each year. Because GWI's business has been growing steadily, it is very important to complete the reconditioning of the carts within a budgeted time and cost. The firm uses weighted-average process costing to keep track of the costs incurred in the reconditioning process.

GWI's golf cart repair and reconditioning unit has the following information for the month of November, in which 1,200 carts were started for reconditioning:

Beginning WIP: 150 units, 50% complete for materials ($16,600) and 30% complete for conversion ($20,150)

Current costs:
Direct Materials: $200,000
Conversion: $385,000 (conversion costs for GWI usually average about $250 to $320 per unit, based on an average of 1,000–1,300 units completed each month)
Ending WIP: 300 units, 30% complete for direct materials and 20% complete for conversion

Required
1. Complete the production cost report for the month of November.
2. GWI is scheduled to start another batch of 1,500 carts for reconditioning in December. Comment on the information the cost report contains regarding planning for December's work.

[LO 6-2, 6-3, 6-4]   6-43 **Weighted-Average Method** Alvis Construction Supply Company has a department that manufactures wood trusses (wood frames used in the construction industry). The following information is for the production of these trusses for the month of February:

Work-in-Process Inventory, February 1	4,000 trusses
Direct materials: 100% complete	$10,480
Conversion: 20% complete	$15,258
Units started during February	18,000 trusses
Units completed during February and transferred out	17,000 trusses
Work-in-Process Inventory, February 29	
Direct materials: 100% complete	
Conversion cost: 40% complete	
Costs incurred during February	
Direct materials	$ 59,040
Conversion	$ 92,092

Required   Using the weighted-average method, calculate the following:
1. a. Costs per equivalent unit.
    b. Cost of goods completed and transferred out.
    c. Costs remaining in the Work-in-Process Inventory account.
2. Assume that you are the company's controller. The production department's February equivalent unit cost is higher than expected. If the manager of the first department asks you to do him a favor by increasing the ending inventory completion percentage from 40 to 60% to lower the unit costs, what should you do? How much would unit cost be affected by this request?

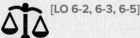

[LO 6-2, 6-3, 6-5]   6-44 **FIFO Method** Refer to the information in Problem 6-43.

Required   Repeat Problem 6-43 using the FIFO method.

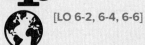

[LO 6-2, 6-4, 6-6]   6-45 **Weighted-Average Method; Transferred-in Costs** Sanyo Corporation manufactures a popular model of business calculators in a suburb of Seoul, South Korea. The production process goes through two departments: assembly and testing. The following information (in thousands of South Korean currency, the *won*) pertains to the testing department for the month of July.

Work-in-Process Inventory, July 1		6,000 units
Transferred-in costs	57,800 won	(100% complete)
Costs added in July		
Direct materials	23,400 won	(100% complete)
Conversion	23,360 won	(80% complete)

During the month of July, 15,000 units were transferred in from the assembly department at the cost of 141,700 won, and the testing department added costs of 201,820 won, as follows:

Direct materials	92,520 won
Conversion	109,300 won

During the month, 18,000 units were completed and transferred to the warehouse. At July 31, the completion percentage of Work-in-Process was as follows:

Direct materials	90%
Conversion	60%

Required

1. Prepare the production cost report of the testing department for the month of July using weighted-average process costing.

2. Check the most recent issue of *The Wall Street Journal* or **www.federalreserve.gov/releases/H10/hist/** to learn the exchange rate between the U.S. dollar and the South Korean won.

[LO 6-2, 6-5, 6-6]   **6-46   FIFO Method; Two Departments** Bhatti Company produces plastic photo frames. Two departments, molding and finishing, are involved in the manufacturing. The molding department fills the molds with hot liquid plastic that is left to cool and then opens them. The finishing department removes the plastic frame from the mold and strips the edges of the frames of extra plastic.

The following information is available for the month of January:

	January 1		January 31	
Work-in-Process Inventory	**Quantity (pounds)**	**Cost**	**Quantity (pounds)**	**Cost**
Molding department	None	—	None	—
Finishing department	5,000	$15,000	2,000	?

The WIP Inventory in the finishing department is estimated to be 40% complete for conversion both at the beginning and end of January. Costs of production for January follow:

Costs of Production	**Direct Materials**	**Conversion**
Molding department	$450,000	$90,000
Finishing department	—	80,290

The molding department started 50,000 pounds of product in January. The firm uses the FIFO method of process costing.

Required

1. Prepare a production cost report for the molding department.

2. Prepare a production cost report for the finishing department.

[LO 6-2, 6-4, 6-6]   **6-47   Weighted-Average Method; Two Departments** BDB Company manufactures its one product by a process that requires two departments. The production starts in Department A and is completed in Department B. Direct materials are added at the beginning of the process in Department A. Additional direct materials are added when the process is 50% complete in Department B. Conversion costs are incurred proportionally throughout the production processes in both departments.

On April 1, Department A had 500 units in Work-in-Process estimated to be 30% complete for conversion; Department B had 300 units in Work-in-Process estimated to be 40% complete for conversion. During April, Department A started 2,000 units and completed 2,100 units; Department B completed 2,000 units. The ending Work-in-Process Inventory on April 30 in Department A is estimated to be 50% complete for conversion, and the ending Work-in-Process Inventory in Department B is estimated to be 70% complete for conversion.

The cost sheet for Department A shows that the units in the beginning Work-in-Process Inventory had $2,750 in direct materials costs and $1,494 in conversion costs. The production costs incurred in April were $18,000 for direct materials and $21,000 for conversion. Department B's beginning Work-in-Process Inventory on April 1 was $6,100, of which $4,200 was transferred-in costs; it incurred $37,920 in direct materials costs and $24,434 in conversion costs in April.

BDB Company uses the weighted-average method for Departments A and B.

Required
1. Prepare a production cost report for Department A.
2. Prepare a production cost report for Department B.

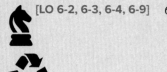

[LO 6-2, 6-3, 6-4, 6-9]   6-48   Weighted-Average Process Costing; Spoilage (Appendix) Carson Paint Company, which manufactures quality paint to sell at premium prices, uses a single production department. Production begins by blending the various chemicals that are added at the beginning of the process and ends by filling the paint cans. The gallon cans are then transferred to the shipping department for crating and shipment. Direct labor and overhead are added continuously throughout the process. Factory overhead is applied at the rate of $3 per direct labor dollar. The company combines direct labor and overhead in computing product cost.

Prior to May, when a change in the manufacturing process was implemented, Work-in-Process Inventories were insignificant. The changed manufacturing process, which has resulted in increased equipment capacity, allows increased production but also results in considerable amounts of Work-in-Process Inventory. Also, the company had 1,000 spoiled gallons in May—one-half of which was normal spoilage and the rest abnormal spoilage. The product is inspected at the end of the production process.

These data relate to actual production during the month of May:

	Costs
Work-in-Process Inventory, May 1	
Direct materials	$ 58,750
Direct labor	10,500
May costs added:	
Direct materials	346,050
Direct labor	46,295

	Units
Work-in-Process Inventory, May 1 (30% complete)	2,000
Sent to shipping department	24,500
Started in May	30,000
Work-in-Process Inventory, May 31 (80% complete)	6,500

Required
1. Prepare a production cost report for May using the weighted-average method.
2. Was the change in the manufacturing process to increase capacity an appropriate strategic move for the company? Why or why not?
3. How does the change in the manufacturing process potentially affect the company's sustainability performance?

(CMA Adapted)

[LO 6-2, 6-4, 6-6, 6-9]   6-49   Weighted-Average Method; Transferred-in Costs; Spoilage (Appendix) APCO Company manufactures various lines of bicycles. Because of the high volume of each line, the company employs a process costing system using the weighted-average method. Bicycle parts are manufactured in the molding department and then are consolidated into a single bike unit in the molding department and transferred to the assembly department, where they are assembled. After assembly, the bicycle is sent to the packing department. Annual cost and production figures for the assembly department are presented in the schedules below.

Defective bicycles are identified at the inspection point when the assembly labor process is 70% complete; all assembly materials have been added at this point. The normal rejection rate for defective bicycles is 5% of the bicycles reaching the inspection point. Any defective bicycles above the 5% quota are considered to be abnormal. All defective bikes are removed from the production process and destroyed.

Assembly Department Cost Data

	Transferred in from Molding Department	Assembly Materials	Assembly Conversion	Total Cost of Bike through Assembly
Prior period costs	$ 82,200	$ 6,660	$ 11,930	$ 100,790
Current period costs	1,237,800	96,840	236,590	1,571,230
Total costs	$1,320,000	$103,500	$248,520	$1,672,020

Assembly Department Production Data

		Percentage Complete		
	Bicycles	Transferred in	Assembly Materials	Assembly Conversion
Beginning inventory	3,000	100%	100%	80%
Transferred in from molding during year	45,000	100	—	—
Transferred out to packing during year	40,000	100	100	100
Ending inventory	4,000	100	50	20

Required

1. Compute the number of defective, or spoiled, bikes that are considered to be
   a. normal spoilage.
   b. abnormal spoilage.
2. Compute the equivalent units of production for the year for
   a. bicycles transferred in from the molding department.
   b. bicycles produced with regard to assembly materials.
   c. bicycles produced with regard to assembly conversion.
3. Compute the cost per equivalent unit for the fully assembled bike.
4. Compute the amount of the total production cost of $1,672,020 that will be associated with the following items:
   a. normal spoiled units.
   b. good units completed in the assembly department.
   c. abnormal spoiled units.
   d. ending Work-in-Process Inventory in the assembly department.
5. Describe how to present the applicable dollar amounts for the following items in the financial statements:
   a. normal spoilage units.
   b. abnormal spoilage units.
   c. completed units transferred to the packing department.
   (CMA Adapted)

[LO 6-2, 6-3, 6-4, 6-8] 6-50 **Process Costing and Activity-Based Costing** Beaumont Specialty Chemicals (BSC) is a manufacturer of specialty chemicals sold to manufacturers, hospitals, and other users. BSC produces about 1 million gallons of its main product, BSC-22, each month. The data for BSC-22 for July follow. The chemical direct materials are added at the beginning of processing.

Beginning Work-in-Process Inventory (60% complete for conversion; direct materials $55,000, conversion $7,250)	200,000 gallons
Units started	1,200,000 gallons
Units completed and transferred out	900,000 gallons
Ending Work-in-Process Inventory (50% complete for conversion)	500,000 gallons
Current manufacturing costs for BSC-22	
Materials	$183,000
Conversion	79,000

Each month BSC averages 100 batches of BSC-22 with approximately 12,000 gallons per batch, though some batches are as large as 50,000 gallons or more, and some are as small as a few hundred gallons. The pattern of customer orders is that large orders come in at all times of the month, while small orders tend to cluster around the last few days of the month. The small orders are due to salespersons trying to meet monthly sales quotas and the buying patterns of smaller customers who want their shipments early in the following month. As a result, in the average month, three-fourths of the total orders are started in the last few days of the month, and most are not completed until early in the following month. For example, in July, 100 batches were in process, and 70 were still in the ending Work-in-Process Inventory at the end of the month. Ted Brown, plant controller for BSC, thinks that the current costing method, using weighted-average process costing, underestimates the cost of the ending Work-in-Process Inventory as well as the cost of smaller jobs.

Required
1. Prepare the production cost report using the weighted-average method.
2. Assume that $28,500 of the $79,000 current conversion costs and $3,700 of the $7,250 beginning WIP conversion costs could be traced to batch-related activities such as equipment setup. Further, assume that these batch-related costs are all incurred when the batch is started. Ted has asked you to prepare an alternate production cost report that separates the batch-related costs from total conversion costs. How do the results differ from the method in requirement 1? Is Ted right about underestimating the cost of ending WIP Inventory?

[LO 6-2, 6-3, 6-4, 6-5]   6-51 **Weighted-Average Method, FIFO Method, and Rising Prices** Healthy Selections Cereals, Inc. (HSC) is a large food-processing company specializing in whole-grain, high-energy, low-calorie, and low-fat cereals that appeal to the health-conscious consumer. HSC has a premium image in the market, and most of its customers are loyal and willing to pay a bit extra to get the healthy choice that HSC offers. HSC's cereals are made in a series of processes that begin with sorting, cleaning, preparing, and inspecting the direct materials (grains, nuts, and other ingredients). The materials are then mixed and processed for consistency, cooked, given a final inspection, and packaged. All materials are added only at the beginning of the first process. The inspections in the first and final processes are made at the end of those respective processes, so all direct materials and conversion costs are lost for any defective units detected at the inspection point. The company uses weighted-average process costing and accounts for all waste as normal spoilage. Currently, commodity prices are rising sharply, affecting the costs of many of the ingredients in HSC's products. The CFO, noting the sharp rise in the cost of the company's direct materials, has considered using the FIFO method. The following data are for the first process for the current month. All output is measured in pounds.

Beginning WIP	14,000 pounds, 25% complete for conversion
Ending WIP	12,000 pounds, 40% complete for conversion
Normal spoilage	1,000 pounds
Pounds added this month	33,000 pounds

The cost information for the first process is as follows:

	Direct Materials	Conversion	Total
Beginning WIP	$3,325	$ 3,380	$ 6,705
Current costs	66,000	104,000	170,000

Required
1. Prepare a production cost report for the first process using the weighted-average method.
2. Prepare a production cost report for the first process using the FIFO method.
3. Explain which of the two methods you would recommend to the CFO, considering the firm's competitive environment.

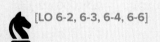

[LO 6-2, 6-3, 6-4, 6-6]   6-52 **Weighted-Average Method; Two Departments** Benoit Chemical Company (BCC) produces a variety of specialty chemicals used in the pharmaceutical industry and construction industry. BCC spends almost 20% of its net revenues on research, product development, and customer development to achieve its reputation as a high-quality producer of chemicals, a reliable supplier, and a great provider of customer service. BCC has a small number of large customers, each of which typically has one or more large orders being processed at BCC at any given point in time. These orders are typically completed over 1 to 3 months or longer. BCC uses job costing to keep track of total job costs over the duration of each order and process costing to keep track of monthly costs, department by department. The processing departments include mixing, reacting (in which chemicals are heated and sometimes vacuum is applied), cleaning, inspecting, and packaging. Much of the total product cost is accumulated in the first two processes, mixing and reacting. The following information is for activity and costs in the first two departments during the current month.

The mixing department started 74,000 gallons this month. No spoilage is measured in the mixing department, but a careful measurement of the loss of material in reacting is taken after the completion of the reacting process. No materials are added in the reacting process. The number of gallons lost (spoilage) is considered normal spoilage and none of the costs of the spoiled units can be recovered. BCC uses the weighted-average method for process costing.

Percentage completion for conversion costs is 60% in the mixing department for both beginning and ending inventory. The percentage completion for conversion costs for the reacting department for beginning and ending inventory is 30% and 40%, respectively.

Work-in-Process for the two departments is as follows.

	Mixing Department (gallons)	Reacting Department (gallons)
Beginning Work-in-Process units	28,000	16,500
Ending Work-in-Process units	26,000	18,250
Normal spoilage (lost gallons)	0	2,250

Costs in the mixing department:

	Materials	Conversion
Beginning Work-in-Process	$ 56,480	$282,400
Current costs	288,484	989,466

Transferred-in beginning Work-in-Process costs are $242,171, and conversion costs in the reacting department are as follows:

	Conversion
Beginning Work-in-Process	$412,510
Current costs	1,245,320
	$1,657,830

Required

1. Prepare the production cost report for the mixing department.
2. Prepare the production cost report for the reacting department.
3. What comments and observations do you have about the two departments' production cost reports?
4. What is BCC's competitive strategy? Explain whether or not you think the company's costing system supports this strategy.

[LO 6-8] 6-53 **Backflush Costing** Blue Water Sails, Inc. (BWS) manufactures sailcloth used by sailmakers that produce sails for sailboats. BWS's sailcloth is the conventional polyester-based sail material and is used widely in recreational boating. Sailmakers throughout the world use BWS's sailcloth. The manufacture of sailcloth has a small number of processes, and BWS integrates them carefully so that there is very little Work-in-Process Inventory. The product is measured in yards of cloth, which is prepared in rolls 42 inches wide. Because it has little Work-in-Process Inventory, BWS also uses backflush accounting to simplify the accounting for its operations. BWS has the following information for the most recent accounting period. The beginning inventory of polyester fiber was $42,000, and the ending inventory was $53,000.

Polyester fiber purchased	$710,000
Conversion cost incurred	$1,350,000
Direct materials standard cost	$4.50 per yard of cloth
Conversion standard cost	$8.50 per yard of cloth
Units produced and sold	155,000 yards of cloth

Required

1. Show the entries for manufacturing costs incurred or applied, completion of 155,000 yards of product, and the closing entries.
2. Under what conditions is backflush costing used in practice?

Solutions to Self-Study Problems

1. Weighted-Average Method versus FIFO Method

1. Weighted-average method

    a. Equivalent units

Direct materials: 1,000 + (200 × 100%)	1,200
Conversion: 1,000 + (200 × 70%)	1,140

    b. Cost per equivalent unit

Direct materials: ($9,600/1,200)	$ 8.00
Conversion: ($2,202 + $6,120)/1,140	7.30
Total unit costs: $8.00 + $7.30	$ 15.30

    c. Cost of goods completed and transferred out: $15.30 × 1,000 $15,300

    d. Cost of Work-in-Process, 10/31

Direct materials: $8 × 200 × 100%	$ 1,600
Conversion: $7.30 × 200 × 70%	1,022
Total: $1,600 + $1,022	$ 2,622

2. Weighted-average method production cost report

SMITH ELECTRONIC COMPANY
Chip-Mounting Production Department
Weighted-Average Production Cost Report

Production Quantity Information

	Step 1: Analyze Flow of Physical Units		Step 2: Calculate Equivalent Units	
	Physical Units	Completion Percentage	Direct Materials	Conversion
Input				
Beginning Work-in-Process				
Inventory	300			
Direct materials		0		
Conversion		40		
Started this period	900			
Total to account for	1,200			
Output				
Completed	1,000	100	1,000	1,000
Ending Work-in-Process				
Inventory	200			
Completion percentage				
Direct materials		100	200	
Conversion		70		140
Total accounted for	1,200			
Total work done to date				
(Total equivalent units)			1,200	1,140

Unit Cost Determination

Step 3: Determine Costs to Account for	Total Direct Materials	Conversion Costs	Total
Beginning Work-in-Process Inventory		$2,202	$ 2,202
Current costs	$9,600	6,120	15,720
Total costs to account for	$9,600	$8,322	$17,922

Step 4: Compute Unit Costs			
Cost per equivalent unit	($9,600 ÷ 1,200) =	($8,322 ÷ 1,140) =	
	$ 8.00	$ 7.30	$ 15.30

(Continued)

Cost Assignment

Step 5: Assign Total Manufacturing Costs	Completed and Transferred Out	Ending Work-in-Process	Total
Units completed and transferred out (1,000 × $15.30)	$15,300		$15,300
Ending Work-in-Process (200)			
Materials (200 × $8)		$1,600	1,600
Conversion (140 × $7.30)	—	1,022	1,022
Total costs accounted for	$15,300	$2,622	$17,922

3. FIFO method

   a. Equivalent units

Direct materials: (300 × 100%) + (1,000 − 300) + (200 × 100%)	1,200
or 1,000 + (200 × 100%) − (300 × 0%)	1,200
Conversion: [300 × (1 − 40%)] + (1,000 − 300) + (200 × 70%)	1,020
or 1,000 + (200 × 70%) − (300 × 40%)	1,020

   b. Cost per equivalent unit

Direct materials: $9,600 ÷ 1,200	$	8
Conversion: $6,120 ÷ 1,020		6
Total unit costs	$	14

   c. Cost of goods completed and transferred out from beginning Work-in-Process Inventory:

Direct materials: $0 + $8 × 300 × (100%)	$ 2,400
Conversion: $2,202 + $6 × 300 × (60%)	3,282
Total	$ 5,682
Started and completed: $14 × (1,000 − 300)	9,800
Total cost of goods completed: $5,682 + $9,800	$15,482

   d. Cost of Work-in-Process, 10/31

Direct materials: $8 × 200 × 100%	$ 1,600
Conversion: $6 × 200 × 70%	840
Total	$ 2,440

4. FIFO method production cost report

SMITH ELECTRONIC COMPANY
Chip-Mounting Production Department
FIFO Production Cost Report

Production Quantity Information

	Step 1: Analyze Flow of Physical Units	Step 2: Calculate Equivalent Units	
	Physical Units	Direct Materials	Conversion Costs
Input			
Beginning Work-in-Process Inventory	300		
Completion percentage			
Direct materials 0%		0	
Conversion 40%			120
Started this period	900		
Total units to account for	1,200		

(Continued)

Output			
Completed	1,000	1,000	1,000
Ending Work-in-Process Inventory	200		
Completion percentage			
Direct materials 100%		200	
Conversion 70%			140
Total units accounted for	1,200	1,200	1,140
Total work performed to date			
Beginning Work-in-Process Inventory	300	0	(120)
Total work performed this period (FIFO equivalent units)		1,200	1,020

Unit Cost Determination

Step 3: Determine Total Costs to Account for Flow	Direct Materials	Conversion Costs	Total
Beginning Work-in-Process Inventory		$2,202	$ 2,202
Current cost	$ 9,600	6,120	15,720
Total costs to account for	$ 9,600	$8,322	$17,922

Step 4: Compute Unit Costs	($9,600 ÷ 1,200) =	($6,120 ÷ 1,020) =	
Cost per equivalent unit	$8	$6	$14

Cost Assignment

Step 5: Assign Total Manufacturing Costs	Completed and Transferred Out	Ending Work-in-Process	Total
Units completed and transferred out (1,000)			
Beginning Work-in-Process	$ 2,202		$ 2,202
Current cost to complete			
Materials (300 × $8)	2,400		2,400
Conversion (180 × $6)	1,080		1,080
Total from beginning Work-in-Process	$ 5,682		$ 5,682
Units started and finished (700 × $14)	9,800		9,800
Total cost completed and transferred out	$15,482		$15,482
Ending Work-in-Process (2,000)			
Materials (200 × $8)		$1,600	1,600
Conversion (140 × $6)	—	840	840
Total costs accounted for	$15,482	$2,440	$17,922

2. Weighted-Average Method versus FIFO Method with Transferred-In Cost

1. Weighted-average method

REED COMPANY
Finishing Department
Weighted-Average Production Cost Report

Production Quantity Information

	Step 1: Analyze Flow of Physical Units		Step 2: Calculate Equivalent Units	
	Physical Units	Transferred in	Direct Materials	Conversion Costs
Input				
Work-in-Process, November 1 (40% complete)	10			
Started this month	80			
Total units to account for	90			
Output				
Completed	82	82	82	82
Work-in-Process, November 30 50% complete	8	8	8	4
Total accounted for	90			
Total work done to date		90	90	86

Unit Cost Determination

Step 3: Determine Total Costs to Account for	Transferred-in	Direct Materials	Conversion	Total
Work-in-Process, November 1	$100	$ 80	$ 52	$ 232
Current costs	800	720	861	2,381
Total costs to account for	$900	$800	$913	$2,613
Step 4: Compute Unit Costs	($900 ÷ 90) =	($800 ÷ 90) =	($913 ÷ 86) =	
Cost per unit	$10.00	$8.89	$10.62	$29.51

Cost Assignment

Step 5: Assign Total Manufacturing Costs	Completed and Transferred out	Ending Work-in-Process	Total
Units completed and transferred out (82 × $29.51)	$2,420		$2,420
Ending Work-in-Process (8)			
Transferred-in (8 × $10)		$ 80	80
Materials (8 × $8.89)		71	71
Conversion (4 × $10.62)		42	42
Total costs accounted for	$2,420	$193	$2,613

2. FIFO method

REED COMPANY
Finishing Department
FIFO Production Cost Report

Production Quantity Information

	Step 1: Analyze Flow of Physical Units		Step 2: Calculate Equivalent Units	
	Physical Units	Transferred in	Direct Materials	Conversion Costs
Input				
Work-in-Process, November 1	10 (40%)			
Started this month	80			
Total units to account for	90			
Output				
Completed	82	82	82	82
Work-in-Process, November 30	8 (50%)	8	8	4
Total accounted for	90			
Total work done to date		90	90	86
Work-in-Process, November 1		(10)	(10)	(4)
Total work done this month—				
FIFO equivalent units		80	80	82

Unit Cost Determination

Step 3: Determine Total Costs to Account for	Transferred in	Direct Materials	Conversion	Costs Total
Work-in-Process, November 1				$ 232
Current costs	$800	$720	$861	2,381
Total costs to account for				$2,613
Step 4: Compute Unit Costs	($800 ÷ 80) =	($720 ÷ 80) =	($861 ÷ 82) =	
Cost per unit	$10.00	$9.00	$10.50	$29.50

Cost Assignment

Step 5: Assign Total Manufacturing Costs	Completed and Transferred out	Ending Work-in-Process	Total
Units completed and transferred out (82)			
Beginning Work-in-Process	$ 232		$ 232
Current cost to complete conversion (6 × $10.50)	63		63
Total from beginning Work-in-Process	$ 295		$ 295
Units started and finished (72 × $29.50)	2,124		2,124
Total cost completed and transferred out	$2,419		$2,419
Ending Work-in-Process (8)			
Transferred-in (8 × $10)		$ 80	80
Materials (8 × $9)		72	72
Conversion (4 × 10.50)		42	42
Total costs accounted for	$2,419	$194	$2,613

Please visit Connect to access a narrated, animated tutorial for solving this problem.

CHAPTER SEVEN

Cost Allocation: Departments, Joint Products, and By-Products

After studying this chapter, you should be able to . . .

LO 7-1   Identify the strategic role and objectives of cost allocation.

LO 7-2   Explain the ethical issues of cost allocation.

LO 7-3   Use the three phases of departmental cost allocation.

LO 7-4   Explain the implementation issues of the different departmental cost allocation methods.

LO 7-5   Explain the use of cost allocation in service firms.

LO 7-6   Use the three joint product costing methods.

LO 7-7   Use the four by-product costing methods (appendix).

In keeping with their firms' mission of continual improvement in their products and services, General Electric (GE) and many other firms, such as Ford Motor Company, Johnson & Johnson, IBM, and Marriott, have sought improved methods of providing administrative services within their firms. These administrative services are often called *shared services* because they are shared among the company's departments that directly add value, which

Shutterstock/Carsten Reisinger

233

REAL-WORLD FOCUS   Direct Streaming: Content Is Not the Only Cost

Companies such as Hulu, Netflix, and HBO are in a heated competition to provide direct streaming of video content. AT&T entered the fray with its acquisition of DIRECTV in 2015. For these internet-TV providers, content is key in attracting and retaining customers, but so is price. In 2016, AT&T offered 100 channels for $35 per month. However, this $35 price might barely cover the cost of the content. In order to be profitable,

the price must also cover the shared service costs from such support departments as customer service, marketing, and data transport and storage. The cost of these services was estimated to be $3 per month for each subscriber, meaning the margins from the DIRECTV subscribers could be negative.

Source: Miriam Gottfried, "No Joy in At&T's Low-Price Plan," *The Wall Street Journal*, November 7, 2016, p. C6.

---

joint costs

The cost of resources employed jointly in the production of two or more outputs; the cost cannot be directly assigned to any one of those outputs. Assignment is made through one or more consistent allocation procedures.

service department

A unit of the organization that performs one or more support tasks for production (also known as operating) departments.

are called operating or production departments. Shared services generally include such transaction-processing services as payroll processing, claims processing, human resources, and many accounting services, among others. The firms above, among others, have studied the cost to provide the services and have been alarmed at the relatively high costs. According to the Association for Image and Information Management, the average cost of processing a single invoice averaged as much as $12.90.[1] Some firms have chosen to outsource these services or to have the operating departments provide the services locally, while others are centralizing these services to reduce cost; provide a high and standardized level of service quality; and provide a single base of technology for easy use, communication, and future modification.

With the growth of these centralized services, the need for effective methods to allocate the shared costs to the operating departments has also increased (we hereafter refer to these shared costs as joint costs). Because these **joint costs** are incurred in a service department— that is, a shared facility, manufacturing process, or service—the cost of the resources consumed cannot be directly assigned to any one unit of output, giving rise to a need for some type of allocation. A **service department** is a unit of the organization that performs one or more support tasks for production departments by supplying engineering services, information technology, quality control, human resources management, or some other service to the production departments. The production departments assemble and finish the products. The service department costs are allocated to the production departments, and then the costs of the production departments are allocated to the products. The methods used to allocate these joint costs to production departments and to the manufactured products are explained in this chapter. While manufacturing examples are most often used in this chapter, note that the allocation methods are also used in service firms. An example later in the chapter shows a service firm, a community bank, in which the production departments are the "operations" and "marketing" departments.

There are two types of joint costs covered in this chapter: (1) the costs of production departments and service departments shared by two or more different products and (2) the joint manufacturing costs for products that are not separately identifiable until some later point in the manufacturing process. An example of the latter is the cost of refining crude oil (the joint cost) into individual products: gasoline, heating oil, and other petroleum products.

While the allocations may not affect the firm's profit as a whole, the method or methods of allocation used can have a significant impact on the profitability of the departments or projects receiving the allocated costs. Therefore, we take a strategic perspective when evaluating the allocation methods by asking key strategic questions. How do these allocation methods affect the behavior of those in the production departments and the service departments? Does the service department add value, or should its work be outsourced? The answers to these and other questions can have a significant impact on a firm's competitiveness and success.

---

[1] SAP Concur Team, "Uncovering the Hidden Costs and Business Opportunities in Invoice Processing," August 16, 2018, **https://www.concur.com/newsroom/article/uncovering-hidden-costs-business-opportunities-in-invoice** (accessed Sept 30, 2019).

The Strategic Role and Objectives of Cost Allocation

LO 7-1

Identify the strategic role and objectives of cost allocation.

The strategic role of cost allocation has four objectives:

1. Determine *accurate departmental and product costs* as a basis for the evaluation of the cost efficiency of departments and the profitability of different products, financial reporting, and tax compliance.
2. *Motivate* managers to exert a high level of effort to achieve the goals of top management.
3. Provide the right *incentive* for managers to make decisions that are consistent with the goals of top management.
4. *Fairly determine the rewards* earned by the managers for their effort and skill and for the effectiveness of their decision making.

The first and most important objective requires the cost allocation method to be sufficiently accurate to support effective management decision making about products and departments. The cost allocation methods must also comply with the financial reporting standards of the Financial Accounting Standards Board (FASB) and the Internal Revenue Service. The management accountant recognizes that the desired cost allocation method might differ for the three functions: cost management, financial reporting, and tax compliance.

The second objective, motivating managers, means that to be effective, the cost allocation (when it is later used as part of performance evaluation and compensation) must reward department managers for reducing costs as desired. A key motivation issue is whether the manager *controls* the allocated cost. For example, when a department's cost allocation for equipment maintenance is based on the number of the department's machine breakdowns, the manager has an incentive to reduce breakdowns and therefore reduce the maintenance costs. On the other hand, when the cost of maintenance is allocated on the basis of a department's square feet of floor space, the manager—who cannot affect the amount of floor space—is not motivated.

The third objective, providing the incentive for decision making, is achieved when cost allocation effectively provides the incentives for the individual manager to act autonomously in a manner that is consistent with top management's goals. For example, a major advantage of cost allocation methods is that they draw managers' attention to shared facilities. The cost allocation provides an incentive for individual and joint efforts to manage these costs and encourages managers to use these facilities to improve the performance of their units.

The fourth objective, fairness, is met when the cost allocation is clear and consistently applied in determining the manager's performance evaluation and compensation. The most clear and unbiased basis for cost allocation exists when a *cause-and-effect relationship* can be determined. For example, consider cost allocation for a manufacturing service department, such as a plant maintenance department. The allocation of maintenance costs on the basis of the number of equipment breakdowns is more unbiased and fair than an allocation based on square feet, the number of products produced, or labor costs in the department. The reason is that a cause-and-effect relationship exists between maintenance costs and the number of breakdowns. Square feet or labor costs, however, do not have a clear relationship to maintenance costs.

In some situations, cause-and-effect bases are not available and alternative concepts of fairness are used. One such concept is *ability-to-bear,* which is commonly employed with bases related to size, such as total sales, total assets, or the profitability of the user departments. Other concepts of fairness are based on equity perceived in the circumstance, such as *benefit received,* which often is measured in a nonquantitative way. For example, the cost of a firm's computer services might be allocated largely or entirely to the research and development department because the computer is more critical to this department's functioning and this department uses it more than other departments.

The Ethical Issues of Cost Allocation

LO 7-2

Explain the ethical issues of cost allocation.

A number of ethical issues are important in cost allocation. First, ethical issues arise when costs are allocated to products or services that are produced for both a competitive market and a public agency or government department. Although government agencies very often purchase on a cost-plus basis, products sold competitively are subject to price competition. The incentive in these situations is for the manufacturer, using cost allocation methods, to shift costs from the competitive products to the cost-plus products.

A second ethical issue in implementing cost allocation methods is the equity or fair share issue that arises when a governmental unit reimburses the costs of a private institution or when it provides a service for a fee to the public. In both cases, cost allocation methods are used to determine the proper price or reimbursement amount. Although no single measure of equity exists in these cases, the objectives of cost allocation identified at the beginning of the chapter are a useful guide.

A third important ethical issue is the effect of the chosen allocation method on the costs of products or services sold to or from foreign subsidiaries. The cost allocation method usually affects the costs of products traded internationally and therefore the amount of taxes paid in the domestic and the foreign countries. Firms can reduce their worldwide tax liability by increasing the costs of products or services purchased in high-tax countries or in countries where the firm does not have favorable tax treatment. For this reason, international tax authorities closely watch the cost allocation methods used by multinational firms.[2]

Cost Allocation to Service and Production Departments

LO 7-3

Use the three phases of departmental cost allocation.

The preceding chapters on job costing (Chapter 4), activity-based costing (Chapter 5), and process costing (Chapter 6) provide a useful context for introducing cost allocation. Chapter 4 illustrated how overhead costs could be allocated to products in a single step, using a single overhead cost pool and single overhead rate in what we called the *volume-based approach.* Chapter 4 then showed an enhancement of the volume-based approach in which overhead was allocated to products in two steps, first to departments and then to products, in what we called the *departmental approach.* The two-step departmental approach is an improvement over the single-step, volume-based approach because it takes into account differences in costs incurred in the different departments and differences in consumption of the departments' resources by the products, thus leading to more accurate product costs.

The *activity-based approach,* explained in Chapter 5, follows a two-step approach like the departmental approach, with the difference being that it assigns costs at a much more detailed level—that of the operating activity rather than the department. Because of the greater level of detail, the activity-based approach captures more accurately the usage of resources by the different products; therefore, it provides more accurate product costs. Because of the increased accuracy, the activity-based approach is generally preferred. However, the activity-based approach is not preferred in all situations, such as those in which the company has homogeneous products and processes. Then the departmental approach is preferred because it is simpler and less costly, and it produces results comparable to the activity-based approach. Also, there are some organizations that are required by law or regulation to use the departmental approach for cost reporting and cost reimbursement; a health care provider affected by the U.S. Medicare law is one such example. These three types of overhead allocation are illustrated in Exhibit 7.1.

This chapter introduces an extended and improved version of the two-step departmental method explained in Chapter 4. The departmental cost allocation method described in this chapter is more detailed and accurate. Unlike the two-step approach, the approach in this chapter distinguishes between production and service departments. Instead of two steps only, the approach explained below has three steps (or "phases"): (1) trace, rather than allocate, all direct manufacturing costs and allocate manufacturing overhead costs to both the service departments and the production departments; (2) allocate the service department costs to the production departments; and, finally, (3) allocate the production department costs to the products.[3] The three phases are illustrated in Exhibit 7.2.

---

[2] See J. Barker, K. Asare, and S. Brickman, "Transfer Pricing as a Vehicle in Corporate Tax Avoidance," *Journal of Applied Business Research (JABR)* 33, no. 1 (2017), pp. 9–16. Taxation issues in transfer pricing are covered in Chapter 19.

[3] We use the word *phase* instead of *steps* in the remainder of the chapter because one of the allocation methods we will cover is called the *step method,* and we want to avoid creating confusion by using the word *step* in two different ways.

EXHIBIT 7.1
Three Types of Overhead Allocation

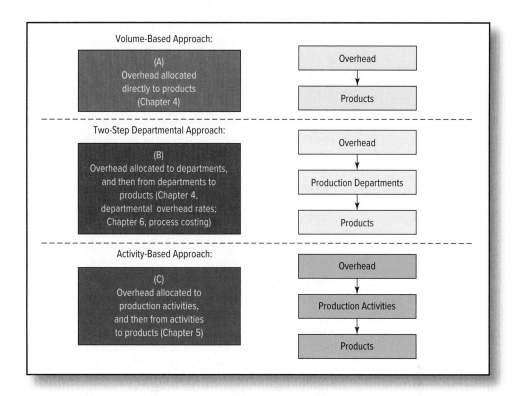

EXHIBIT 7.2   The Three Phases in Departmental Cost Allocation

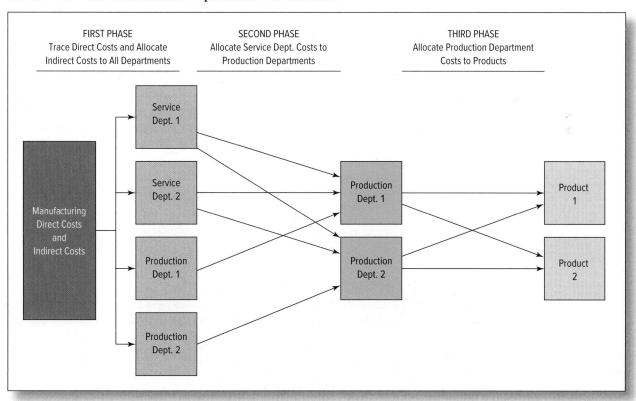

Direct manufacturing costs are wages and materials that can be directly linked or traced to a department; for example, direct materials and direct labor costs would be traced to the production departments where they are used. Direct labor and materials used in a service department would be traced to that service department. Indirect costs, such as indirect materials, indirect labor, and other costs that cannot be easily and economically traced to a department are allocated by means of a predetermined cost driver to the departments that use those resources. For example, the indirect labor cost of the plant supervisor who oversees all production and support departments would be allocated to all departments, while the indirect labor for inspection of the output of the two production departments would be allocated only to those two production departments.

The cost drivers commonly used in departmental cost allocation include labor hours, machine hours, head count (number of personnel in the department), and square feet of space in the department, among others. For example, the cost of the plant supervisor might be allocated to all departments based on the proportion of total labor hours in the departments. The cost of the inspection in the production departments might be allocated based on the number of units of output in those two departments. In practice, a variety of cost drivers are used; the goal is to use a cost driver such that the cost allocation reflects the usage of the resource in the departments.

First Phase: Trace Direct Costs and Allocate Indirect Costs to All Departments

The first phase in the departmental allocation approach traces the direct costs and allocates the indirect manufacturing costs in the plant to each service and production department.

For the first-phase allocation, see the information for Beary Company in Exhibit 7.3. Beary manufactures two products and has two manufacturing departments and two service departments. As shown in Exhibit 7.3, $36,000 of direct costs can be traced to each department, and an indirect cost of $30,000 ($25,000 labor and $5,000 materials) is common to all departments but cannot be traced directly to any department. Beary uses labor hours for allocating indirect labor cost and machine hours for allocating indirect materials cost.

The first-phase allocation for Beary Company is shown in Exhibit 7.4. Total direct costs of $36,000 are traced to the four departments, and the overhead costs are allocated using labor hours (for indirect labor) and machine hours (for indirect materials). The exhibit presents the allocation base for labor hour and machine hour usage as a percentage of total usage. The $25,000 of indirect labor is allocated to the four departments using the labor hours allocation base. For example, the amount of indirect labor allocated to service department 1 is $3,750 (service department 1's share of total indirect labor, or 15% × $25,000). The allocations of indirect labor costs to the other departments are made in the same way. Similarly, the $5,000 of indirect materials cost is allocated to the four departments using machine hours. The amount of indirect materials allocated to service department 1 is $500 (10% × $5,000). The total direct costs and allocated indirect costs shared among the four departments is $66,000, the same as total cost from Exhibit 7.3:

Service department 1	$5,850
Service department 2	8,250
Production department 1	24,750
Production department 2	27,150
Total	$66,000

Allocation in Second and Third Phases

The second phase allocates service department costs to the production departments. This is the most complex of the allocation phases because services can flow back and forth between

EXHIBIT 7.3
Data for Beary Company

	Service Department 1	Service Department 2	Production Department 1	Production Department 2	Total Hours	Total Amount
Labor hours	1,800	1,200	3,600	5,400	12,000	
Machine hours	320	160	1,120	1,600	3,200	
Direct costs	$1,600	$5,500	$15,500	$13,400		$36,000
Indirect labor			Not traceable			25,000
Indirect materials			Not traceable			5,000
						$66,000

EXHIBIT 7.4   Departmental Allocation, First Phase: Beary Company

Departmental Allocation Bases	All Departments				
	Service Department 1	Service Department 2	Production Department 1	Production Department 2	Total
Labor hours	1,800	1,200	3,600	5,400	12,000
Percent	15%	10%	30%	45%	100%
Machine hours	320	160	1,120	1,600	3,200
Percent	10%	5%	35%	50%	100%
First Phase: Trace Direct Costs and Allocate Indirect Costs to All Departments					
Direct costs	$1,600	$5,500	$15,500	$13,400	$36,000
Allocate indirect costs to departments:					
Indirect labor cost	3,750	2,500	7,500	11,250	25,000
	= 15% × $25,000	= 10% × $25,000	= 30% × $25,000	= 45% × $25,000	
Indirect materials cost	500	250	1,750	2,500	5,000
	= 10% × $5,000	= 5% × $5,000	= 35% × $5,000	= 50% × $5,000	
Totals for all departments	$5,850	$8,250	$24,750	$27,150	$66,000

reciprocal flows
The flow of services back and forth between service departments.

the service departments. These are often called **reciprocal flows**, which represent the flow of services back and forth between service departments.

The percentage of service relationships is commonly determined by reference to labor hours, units processed, or some other allocation base that best reflects the service provided in the departments. Assume that at Beary Company, the service flow percentages for each service department are determined according to the labor hours used for services provided to the other service department and to the production departments. Beary's first service department spends 40% of its labor time serving service department 2 (this is a "reciprocal flow") and 30% serving each of the two production departments. Also assume service department 2 serves service department 1 10% of the time, the first production department 30% of the time, and the second production department 60% of the time. The service department relationships for Beary Company are summarized in Exhibit 7.5.

Management accountants can choose among three common methods to allocate costs for the second phase: (1) the direct method, (2) the step method, and (3) the reciprocal method.

The Direct Method

direct method
Service department cost allocation accomplished by using the service flows *only to production departments* and determining each production department's share of that service.

The **direct method** of departmental cost allocation is the simplest of the three methods because it ignores the reciprocal flows. The cost allocation is accomplished by using the service flows *only to production departments* and determining each production department's share of that service. For example, for service department 1, the share of time for each production department is 50% of the total production department service, determined as follows (from Exhibit 7.5).

For service department 1:

Net service to both production departments from service department 1:
  30% + 30% = 60%
Production department 1's share: 30% ÷ 60% = <u>50%</u>
Production department 2's share: 30% ÷ 60% = <u>50%</u>

EXHIBIT 7.5
Reciprocal Relationships in Beary Company

From	To			
	Service Department 1	Service Department 2	Production Department 1	Production Department 2
Service department 1	—	40%	30%	30%
Service department 2	10%	—	30	60

For service department 2 (note that we use four significant digits after the decimal in order to reduce rounding error):

Net service to both production departments from service department 2:
30% + 60% = 90%
Production department 1's share: 30% ÷ 90% = 33.3333%
Production department 2's share: 60% ÷ 90% = 66.6667%

These percentage shares are used to allocate the costs from service departments to production departments, as shown in the second-phase section at the top of Exhibit 7.6. In that panel, for example, $5,850 of service department 1's costs are allocated equally to the production departments, so that each production department is responsible for $2,925, or 50%, of the costs. The $8,250 of service department 2's costs are allocated as follows: 33.3333%, or $2,750, to production department 1 and 66.6667%, or $5,500, to production department 2. Total costs in production departments 1 and 2 at the end of the second phase allocations are $30,425 and $35,575, respectively.

The third and final phase is much like the first phase. The allocation from production departments to products typically is based on the number of labor hours or machine hours used in the production departments that produce the products. For Beary Company, costs are allocated from production department 1 to products 1 and 2 on the basis of labor hours. Costs are allocated from production department 2 to products 1 and 2 on the basis of machine hours. See the third-phase panel of Exhibit 7.6. Assume that the production of product 1 requires 1,800 labor hours of production and that department 1's total labor time is 3,600 hours; thus,

EXHIBIT 7.6   Departmental Allocation, Second and Third Phases, Using the Direct Method: Beary Company

Second Phase: Allocate Service Department Costs to Production Departments Using the Direct Method				
Direct Method		**Production Department 1**	**Production Department 2**	**Total**
Service department 1	Service percent to producing dept.	30%	30%	
	Allocation percent per direct method	50% = 30 ÷ (30 + 30)	50% = 30 ÷ (30 + 30)	
	Allocation amount	**$ 2,925**	**$ 2,925**	**$ 5,850**
		= 50% × $5,850	= 50% × $5,850	
Service department 2	Service percent to producing dept.	30%	60%	
	Allocation percent per direct method	33.3333%	66.6667%	
		= 30 ÷ (30 + 60)	= 60 ÷ (30 + 60)	
	Allocation amount	**2,750**	**5,500**	**8,250**
		= 33.3333% × $8,250	= 66.6667% × $8,250	
Plus: First-phase allocation		**24,750**	**27,150**	**51,900**
Totals for production departments		**$30,425**	**$35,575**	**$66,000**

Third Phase: Allocate Production Department Costs to Products			
1. Allocation Base	**Product 1**	**Product 2**	
Base: Labor hours			
Hours	1,800	1,800	3,600
Percent	50%	50%	
Base: Machine hours			
Hours	400	1,200	1,600
Percent	25%	75%	
2. Cost Allocation to Products			
Production department 1 (labor hours basis)	**$15,212.50**	**$15,212.50**	
	= 50% × $30,425	= 50% × $30,425	
Production department 2 (machine hours basis)	**8,893.75**	**26,681.25**	
	= 25% × $35,575	= 75% × $35,575	
Totals for each product	**$24,106.25**	**$41,893.75**	**$66,000**

---

product 1 is allocated 50% (1,800 ÷ 3,600) of the total costs in production department 1. Similarly, assume that product 1 requires 400 of the 1,600 machine hours used in production department 2, and thus is allocated 25% (400 ÷ 1,600) of the costs of production department 2. Product 2's costs are determined in a similar manner, as shown in Exhibit 7.6. The total cost of $66,000 is allocated as $24,106.25 to product 1 and $41,893.75 to product 2.

The Step Method

step method
A cost allocation method that uses a sequence of steps in allocating service department costs to production departments.

The second method to allocate service department costs is the **step method**, so-called because it uses a sequence of steps in allocating service department costs to production departments. In the first step, one service department is selected to be allocated fully, that is, to allocate its costs to the other service departments as well as to each production department. The department to be allocated first usually is chosen because it provides the highest percentage of service to other service departments. At Beary Company, service department 1 provides more service (40%), and it goes first in the allocation. Service department 2 is allocated only to the production departments, in the same manner as the direct method. Overall, this means that the step method may provide more accurate allocations because one of the reciprocal flows between the two service departments (the one in the first step) is considered in the allocation—unlike the direct method, which ignores all reciprocal flows.

The first phase of the step method (tracing direct costs and initial allocation of indirect costs) is the same as for the direct method as shown in Exhibit 7.4. However, in the second phase (Exhibit 7.7), service department 1, which is in the first step, is allocated to service department 2 and the two production departments. The allocation to service department 2 is $2,340 (40% × $5,850). The allocations for the two production departments are determined in a similar manner. Then, in the second step, service department 2 is allocated to the two production departments in the same manner as the direct method in Exhibit 7.6. The only difference is that the total cost in service department 2 ($10,590) now includes the original cost in service department 2 ($8,250) plus the cost allocated from service department 1 in the first step ($2,340).

The third phase of the step method is completed in the same manner as for the direct method in Exhibit 7.6. Using the step method, the total cost allocated to product 1 is $24,008.75 and the total cost allocated to product 2 is $41,991.25, for a total of $66,000.

The Reciprocal Method

reciprocal method
A cost allocation method that considers all reciprocal flows between service departments through the use of simultaneous equations.

The **reciprocal method** is the preferred of the three methods because, unlike the others, it considers *all* reciprocal flows among the service departments. This is accomplished by using simultaneous equations; the reciprocal flows are simultaneously determined in a system of equations.

COST MANAGEMENT IN ACTION

Health Care Providers Allocate Costs for Medicare Reimbursement

Since the advent of Medicare in 1966 to cover medical expenses of individuals who are aged, blind, and disabled, health care providers have been required to use cost allocation methods to receive reimbursement from the federal government for services covered by Medicare. The costs of health care service activities are allocated to the patient revenue-generating services. Some examples of service activities and patient revenue-generating services in a hospital are shown in the accompanying table.

Which of the three allocation methods (direct, step, or reciprocal) would you recommend a hospital use in determining its cost of revenue-generating services for Medicare purposes? Explain your choice briefly.

(Refer to Comments on Cost Management in Action at the end of the chapter.)

Patient Revenue-Generating Services

Intensive care unit	Laboratory
Psychiatric care	Radiology
Coronary care	Emergency room
Surgery	Pharmacy
Anesthesia	

Service Activities

Dietary	Operation of hospital
Laundry and linen	Administrative and general
Admissions	Housekeeping
Social services	
Nursing administration	

EXHIBIT 7.7   Departmental Allocation, Second and Third Phases, Using the Step Method: Beary Company

Second Phase: Allocate Service Department Costs to Production Departments: Using the Step Method

	Service Department 2	Production Department 1	Production Department 2	Total
First Step				
Service department 1				
Service percent	40%	30%	30%	
Amount	$2,340	$1,755	$1,755	$ 5,850
	= 40% × $5,850	= 30% × $5,850	= 30% × $5,850	
Second Step				
Service department 2				
Service percent		30%	60%	
Allocation percent per direct method		33.3333	66.6667	
Amount	10,590	3,530	7,060	8,250
	= $8,250	= 33.3333%	= 66.6667%	(= 3,530
	+ $2,340	× $10,590	× $10,590	+ 7,060 − 2,340)
Plus: First-phase allocation		24,750	27,150	51,900
Totals for production departments		$30,035	$35,965	$66,000

Third Phase: Allocate Production Department Costs to Products

1. Allocation Base	Product 1	Product 2	
Labor hours			
Hours	1,800	1,800	3,600
Percent	50%	50%	
Machine hours			
Hours	400	1,200	1,600
Percent	25%	75%	
2. Cost Allocation to Products			
Production department 1 (labor hours basis)	$15,017.50	$15,017.50	
	= 50% × $30,035	= 50% × $30,035	
Production department 2 (machine hours basis)	8,991.25	26,973.75	
	= 25% × $35,965	= 75% × $35,965	
Totals for each product	$24,008.75	$41,991.25	$66,000

An equation for each service department represents the cost to be allocated, consisting of the first-phase allocation costs plus the cost allocated from the other department. For Beary Company, the equation for service department 1 is as follows, using the symbol S1 to represent service department 1 costs and the symbol S2 to represent costs in service department 2.

Allocated S1 Costs = Initial allocation + Cost allocated from S2
$$S1 = \$5,850 + (10\% \times S2)$$

Similarly, the equation for the second service department is as follows:

Allocated S2 Costs = Initial allocation + Cost allocated from S1
$$S2 = \$8,250 + (40\% \times S1)$$

These two equations can be solved for S1 and S2 by substituting the second equation into the first as follows:

$$S1 = \$5,850 + 10\% \times [\$8,250 + (40\% \times S1)]$$
$$S1 = \$6,953.125$$

And substituting S1 back into the second equation:

$$S2 = \$11,031.25$$

These values for S1 and S2 are allocated to the producing departments using the percentage service amounts for each department. We illustrate the process for Beary Company in Exhibit 7.8. Note that because the reciprocal method has considered all reciprocal service department

EXHIBIT 7.8 Departmental Allocation, Second and Third Phases, Using the Reciprocal Method: Beary Company

Second Phase: Allocate Service Department Costs to Production Departments: Using the Reciprocal Method
First: Solve the simultaneous equations for service department 1 and service department 2 (see Exhibit 7.9):

Amount allocated from service department 1	$6,953.125	
Amount allocated from service department 2	$11,031.25	

	Production Department 1	Production Department 2	Total
Second: Allocate to producing departments			
Service department 1			
Service percent	30%	30%	
Allocated amount	**$ 2,086**	**$ 2,086**	**$ 4,172**
	= 30% × $6,953.125	= 30% × $6,953.125	
Service department 2			
Service percent	30%	60%	
Allocated amount	**3,309**	**6,619**	**9,928**
	= 30% × $11,031.25	= 60% × $11,031.25	
Plus: Costs allocated in first phase	24,750	27,150	51,900
Totals for production departments	**$30,145**	**$35,855**	**$66,000**

	Product 1	Product 2	
Third Phase: Allocate Production Department Costs to Products			
1. Allocation Base			
Labor Hours	1,800	1,800	3,600
Percent	50%	50%	
Machine hours			
Hours	400	1,200	1,600
Percent	25%	75%	
2. Cost Allocation to Products			
Production department 1 (labor hours basis)	**$15,072.50**	**$15,072.50**	
	= 50% × $30,145	= 50% × $30,145	
Production department 2 (machine hours basis)	**8,963.75**	**26,891.25**	
	= 25% × $35,855	= 75% × $35,855	
Totals for each product	**$24,036.25**	**$41,963.75**	**$66,000**

activities, the allocation in the second phase is based on the actual service percentages for each production department. For example, production department 1, which receives 30% of service department 1's work, is allocated 30% of service department 1's cost, $2,086 (30% × $6,953.13). The allocation of service department 2's cost to production departments is done in a similar manner.

A simple and accurate way to calculate the reciprocal costs for S1 and S2 is to use the Solver function in Excel. Exhibit 7.9A illustrates how to use Solver for this purpose. Exhibit 7.9B provides a screenshot of the completed Solver solution for the Beary Company example.

The third-phase analysis in Exhibit 7.8 is done in the same manner as in Exhibits 7.6 and 7.7. The total cost allocated to product 1 is $24,036.25 and the total cost allocated to product 2 is $41,963.75.

Implementation Issues

LO 7-4

Explain the implementation issues of the different departmental cost allocation methods.

The key implementation issue is the choice of the most accurate allocation method. Briefly review Exhibits 7.6, 7.7, and 7.8. Note that although total costs are the same ($66,000), the amounts allocated to the two products vary. Although these amounts do not vary greatly for Beary Company, wide variations can occur in practice. When significant differences exist, a management accountant should consider the value of the reciprocal method, which is more complete and accurate than the others because it fully considers the reciprocal flows between service departments.

Three additional issues to consider when implementing the departmental allocation approach are (1) disincentive effects when the allocation base is unrelated to usage, (2) disincentive effects when the allocation base is actual usage, and (3) disincentive effects when allocated costs exceed external purchase cost.

Disincentive Effects When the Allocation Base Is Unrelated to Usage

Determining an appropriate allocation base and the percentage amount for service provided by the service departments is often difficult. For example, using labor hours could be inappropriate in an automated plant where labor is a small part of total cost. Similarly, square feet of floor space could be inappropriate for allocating certain costs when a great deal of idle space exists. Furthermore, the use of square feet of floor space can have undesirable motivational consequences. For example, if we are allocating plantwide maintenance costs to production departments using floor space as a base, a department has inadequate incentive to limit its use of maintenance. Because the actual use of maintenance is unrelated to floor space, if a given department increases its use of maintenance, then the other departments pay for the increase as well, as illustrated in Exhibit 7.10. Here, department A increases its use of maintenance from 50 to 80 maintenance requests (panel 3 in Exhibit 7.10), while department B's usage stays the same. The effect of department A's increased usage (when allocation is based on square feet) is that department B pays one-half of the increased cost ($60,000), which is likely to be perceived as unfair and therefore a disincentive for department B. In contrast, using the number of requests as a base allocates to department A the full cost of its increased usage of maintenance ($60,000), while department B's allocated cost remains the same.

Disincentive Effects When the Allocation Base Is Actual Usage

When the cost allocation base is determined from actual usage, disincentives can arise because the usage of the resource by one department will affect the cost allocation to other departments, as illustrated in Exhibit 7.11. We continue with the same example as Exhibit 7.10 except we now assume that the cost to be allocated is made up of $100,000 fixed cost and $1,000 variable cost per maintenance request. Panel 2 shows that the amount of cost allocated will be the same for both departments if the usage is the same. Panels 3 and 4 illustrate how the cost allocation changes if the usage of one of the departments changes. If the usage in department A increases (panel 3) while department B's usage remains the same, then department B has an unexpected reduction in allocated cost from $100,000 to $88,462. The reason is that the fixed costs per maintenance request are now smaller due to the increase in total maintenance requests. Department A is unlikely to see this allocation as fair. In contrast, panel 4 shows the outcome if department A reduces it usage of maintenance, while department B again maintains the same level of usage. Now department B's allocated cost increases from

EXHIBIT 7.9A **Solving for the Reciprocal Allocation Method Using the Solver Function in Microsoft Excel**

Solving reciprocal departmental allocation problems can become tedious if three or more service departments are involved. In this case, we suggest the use of software programs such as the Solver tool in Excel. The following screenshot illustrates how the Solver tool can be used to solve the Beary Company example in the text. The column for "Allocated Cost" in the spreadsheet contains the cost in each service department, while the columns for "Service Rates to" contain the reciprocal service rates. The column for "Initial Allocation to" contains the product of the "Allocated Cost" and "Service Rates" columns, using cell-based formulas. Cells E7 and F7 contain the formula-based sums of these columns. After selecting "Solver" at the far right of the Data menu, the dialog box shown in the screenshot below appears and must be completed as shown. For example, the cell E7 must be set to a value of $5,850 (the cost of the first service department). Make sure to select the "Value of" button. Also, the "By Changing Variable Cells" is B5:B6; select Add and then enter the constraint F7 = 8250. Then, select "Make Unconstrained Variables Non-Negative" and for "Select a Solving Method," choose Simplex LP. When the dialog box is complete, select Solve, and the solution will appear in cells B5 and B6 (overwriting the amounts originally entered in the Allocated Cost column). The solution is $6,953.125 in cell B5 and $11,031.25 in cell B6. The solution is shown in Exhibit 7.9B.

Solver Dialog Box

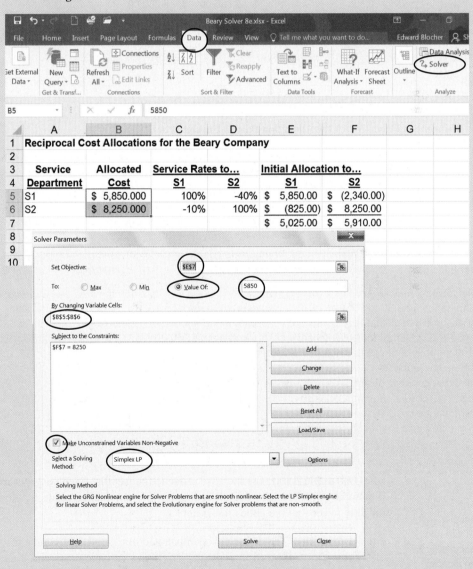

Microsoft Excel

EXHIBIT 7.9B   **Solver Solution for the Beary Company Example**

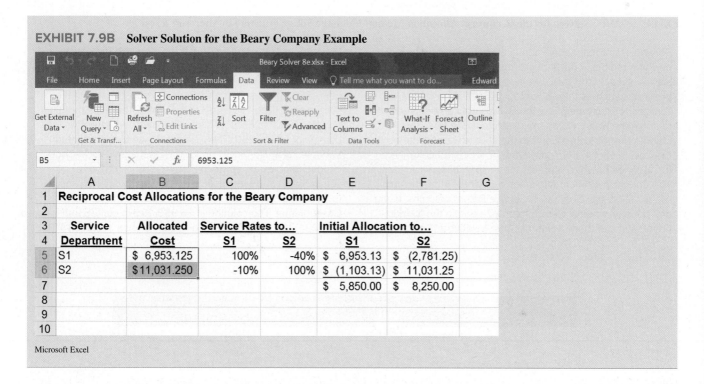

Microsoft Excel

EXHIBIT 7.10   **Disincentive Effects When the Allocation Base Is Unrelated to Usage**

	Department A	Department B	Total Maintenance Cost
Panel 1: Basic information			
Square feet of floor space	5,000	5,000	
Average number of maintenance requests	50	50	
Total maintenance costs			$200,000
Panel 2: Maintenance cost allocation in an average month using square feet of floor space or number of requests:			
Allocated maintenance cost	$100,000	$100,000	$200,000
Panel 3: Here we consider maintenance cost allocation based on square feet for a month when department A increases usage of maintenance from 50 to 80 maintenance requests, while department B's usage remains the same at 50 requests. For simplicity, assume that maintenance costs are variable with the number of maintenance requests, or $2,000 per request [$200,000 ÷ (50 + 50)], so that total maintenance costs increase to $260,000 [$2,000 × (50 + 80)]. The allocation based on square feet and number of requests is compared below:			
Number of maintenance requests	80	50	
Allocation of maintenance costs based on square feet	$130,000	$130,000	$260,000
Allocation of maintenance costs based on number of maintenance requests	$2,000 × 80 = $160,000	$2,000 × 50 = $100,000	$260,000

dual allocation

A cost allocation method that separates fixed and variable costs and traces variable service department costs to the user departments; fixed costs are allocated based on either equal shares among departments or a predetermined budgeted proportion.

$100,000 to $112,500. The increase is due to the fact that fixed costs per maintenance request is now larger due to the overall reduction in maintenance requests. Now department B is unlikely to see that the allocation is fair.

Dual Allocation   The disincentives illustrated in Exhibit 7.11 can be resolved by using dual allocation. **Dual allocation** separates fixed and variable costs and traces variable costs to the departments based on actual usage; fixed costs are allocated based on either an equal share among departments or a predetermined budgeted proportion. Exhibit 7.12 illustrates how dual allocation works. Again, panels 1 and 2 follow the example from Exhibit 7.11. Panel 3 illustrates dual allocation in which fixed costs are equally shared among the departments. The reason for the equal-share approach is that each department pays in effect a fee for the

EXHIBIT 7.11   Disincentive Effects When the Allocation Base Is Actual Usage

	Department A	Department B	Total Maintenance Cost
Panel 1: Basic information			
Actual number of maintenance requests	50	50	
Total maintenance costs			$200,000

Panel 2: Assume that maintenance costs are $100,000 fixed costs and $1,000 variable costs per request. The allocation base is $2,000 per request; $100,000 + [(50 + 50) × $1,000] = $200,000; $200,000 ÷ 100 = $2,000 per request.

	Department A	Department B	Total Maintenance Cost
Allocated maintenance costs:	$100,000	$100,000	
	= $2,000 × 50	= $2,000 × 50	$200,000

Panel 3: Department A increases its usage to 80 requests, while department B continues to use 50 requests, for a total of 130 requests. Now total maintenance costs = $100,000 fixed costs plus $1,000 × 130 requests = $230,000; $230,000 ÷ 130 = $1,769.23 per request.

	Department A	Department B	Total Maintenance Cost
Allocated maintenance costs			
based on requests:	$1,769.23 × 80	$1,769.23 × 50	
	= $141,538	= $88,462	$230,000

The outcome is that, while department B has not changed its usage of maintenance, its allocated costs have decreased and department A's allocation has increased, but not at the rate of the increase in number of requests. Department B benefits from the fact that increased usage of maintenance reduces the per-request charge from $2,000 to $1,769.23—variable costs are the same per request, but the $100,000 fixed cost is allocated over more requests. The result may not be satisfying to department A, which sees department B benefit from department A's increased usage.

Panel 4: Similar to panel 3, except that department A **reduces** its usage of maintenance to 30 requests, for a total of 80 requests for the two departments. Now total maintenance costs = $100,000 + $1,000 × (30 + 50) = $180,000; $180,000 ÷ 80 = $2,250 per request.

	Department A	Department B	Total Maintenance Cost
Allocated maintenance costs			
based on requests:	$2,250 × 30	$2,250 × 50	
	= $67,500	= $112,500	$180,000

The outcome is that, while department B has not changed its usage of maintenance, its allocated costs have increased and department A's allocation has decreased, but not at the rate of the decrease in number of requests. Department B suffers from the fact that decreased usage of maintenance in department A increases the per-request charge from $2,000 to $2,250. While department B has not changed its usage, its cost increases because of department A's decreased usage.

right to receive future services from the maintenance department, irrespective of the amount of service to be used. This concept is similar to the minimum monthly charge on a checking account or for a utility bill. Note that the effect of separating the fixed and variable costs is that department A pays for its increased usage, measured at variable cost, and department B's allocated cost does not change—a result that is likely to be satisfactory to both departments.

Panel 4 of Exhibit 7.12 illustrates the dual allocation method when fixed costs are allocated on the basis of a predetermined budget. This approach is used when usage differs significantly between departments and over time; the rationale is that the allocation of fixed costs should reflect the long-term average usage by each department. In this example, we assume that the long-term rate of usage is 60% for department A and 40% for department B.

Disincentive Effects When Allocated Costs Exceed External Purchase Cost

Another limitation of the three departmental allocation methods is that sometimes they can allocate a higher cost for the service than the department would pay were it to purchase the service from an outside supplier. Should the department pay more for a service internally than an outside vendor would charge? To motivate managers to be efficient and for fairness, the allocation should be based on the cost of obtaining the service outside the firm. Consider the data in Exhibit 7.13 for a firm with four departments that share a common data processing service costing $1,000. Data processing costs are allocated using direct labor hours in each department as shown in columns (B), (C), and (D) of Exhibit 7.13. The data processing service can also be obtained from an outside firm at the cost shown in column (E).

EXHIBIT 7.12   Dual Allocation

	Department A	Department B	Total Maintenance Cost
Panel 1: Basic information			
Actual number of maintenance requests	50	50	
Total maintenance costs			$200,000

Panel 2: Assume that maintenance costs are mixed: $100,000 fixed and $1,000 variable per request. The allocation base is $2,000 per request; $100,000 + (50 + 50) × $1,000 = $200,000; $200,000 ÷ 100 = $2,000 per request.

Allocated maintenance costs:	$100,000	$100,000	$200,000
	= $2,000 × 50	= $2,000 × 50	

Panel 3 (Dual allocation; fixed costs shared equally): Department A increases its usage to 80 requests, while department B continues to use 50 requests. Now total maintenance costs = $100,000 fixed costs plus $1,000 × 130 requests = $230,000. This method allocates fixed costs equally between the departments and variable cost based on usage.

Allocated maintenance cost:	$50,000 + ($1,000 × 80)	$50,000 + ($1,000 × 50)	$230,000
	= $130,000	= $100,000	

The outcome is that department B's cost has not changed and department A's increase is in proportion to its increased usage. The result should be satisfying to both department A and department B.

Panel 4 (Dual allocation; budget-based allocation of fixed costs): Assume, as in panel 3, that department A increases its usage to 80 requests, while department B continues to use 50 requests. Now total maintenance costs = $100,000 fixed costs plus $1,000 × 130 requests = $230,000. Budget-based allocation uses a predetermined budgeted amount of usage to allocate the fixed costs; in this example, we budget 60 requests for department A and 40 requests for department B. Thus, fixed costs are allocated $60,000 to department A and $40,000 to department B.

Allocated maintenance costs:	$60,000 + ($1,000 × 80)	$40,000 + ($1,000 × 50)	$230,000
	= $140,000	= $90,000	

This outcome could be preferred to that of panel 3 if the actual usage of the department were to fluctuate from period to period, but the long-term average usage of the resources by department A and department B is 60% and 40%, respectively.

The direct labor hours allocation base in this example penalizes department D, which can obtain the service outside the firm for $80 less than the inside cost ($200 − $120), perhaps because of the simplified nature of the requirements in department D. In contrast, department B can obtain the service outside only at a much higher price ($600 vs. $400 inside), perhaps because of the specialized nature of its data processing requirements. In this case, the allocation based on the *outside price* [column (G) in Exhibit 7.13] is fair to both departments B and D. It is a better reflection of the competitive cost of the service. The question of whether, and under what conditions, the department should be allowed to purchase outside the firm is a different issue, which is addressed in the coverage of management control in Chapters 18 and 19.

EXHIBIT 7.13   Cost Allocation Using External Prices

(A) User Department	(B) Direct Labor Hours	(C) Direct Labor Hours Allocation Base	(D) Cost Allocation Based on Direct Labor Hours	(E) Outside Price	(F) Allocation Base for Outside Price	(G) Allocation Based on Outside Price
A	3,000	30% (3,000 ÷ 10,000)	$ 300 (30% × $1,000)	$ 360	30% (360 ÷ 1,200)	$ 300 (30% × $1,000)
B	4,000	40% (4,000 ÷ 10,000)	400 (40% × $1,000)	600	50% (600 ÷ 1,200)	500 (50% × $1,000)
C	1,000	10% (1,000 ÷ 10,000)	100 (10% × $1,000)	120	10% (120 ÷ 1,200)	100 (10% × $1,000)
D	2,000	20% (2,000 ÷ 10,000)	200 (20% × $1,000)	120	10% (120 ÷ 1,200)	100 (10% × $1,000)
Total	10,000		$1,000	$1,200		$1,000

Cost Allocation in Service Industries

The concepts presented in this chapter apply equally well to manufacturing, service, or not-for-profit organizations that incur joint costs. For example, financial institutions such as commercial banks also use cost allocation. To illustrate, we use the Community General Bank (CGB), which provides a variety of banking services, including deposit accounts, mortgage loans, installment loans, investment services, and other services. Currently, CGB is analyzing the profitability of its mortgage loan unit, which has two main businesses, commercial construction loans and residential loans. An important part of the analysis of these loan businesses is determining how to trace or allocate costs to the two businesses.

The cost allocation begins by identifying which departments directly support the two loan businesses, the loan operations department and the marketing department. The *operations department* handles the processing of loan applications, safekeeping of appropriate documents, billing, and maintaining accounts for both commercial and residential loans. The *marketing department* provides direct advertising, promotions, and customer service for both types of loans. The operations and marketing departments in this illustration are comparable to the production departments in the Beary Company example used earlier in the chapter.

Other departments support the operations and marketing departments. Two important support departments are the administrative services department and the accounting department. The administrative services department provides legal and technical support. The accounting department provides financial services, including regular financial reports and the maintenance of customer records. The administrative services and accounting departments provide services to each other as well as to the operations and marketing departments, as illustrated in Exhibit 7.14. Each of the four departments has labor and certain supplies costs that can be traced directly to the departments. In addition, CGB's human resources and computer services departments provide services to all four departments. In this example, human resources and computer services are assumed to be part of the larger set of services that CGB provides to all of its business units; the mortgage loan unit is only one of these. Thus, human resources and computer services can be compared to the use of indirect labor and indirect materials in the Beary Company example earlier in the chapter; the accounting and administrative services departments provide service only to the loan unit and are comparable to the service departments used in the Beary Company example.

To summarize, the mortgage loan unit in CGB has two service departments (accounting and administrative services), two operating departments (marketing and operations), and two products (commercial loans and residential loans). The costs in the mortgage loan unit consist of $1,560,000 labor costs and $33,000 supplies costs, which can be traced directly to the two service departments and the two operations departments. In addition, there are indirect costs of $80,000 human resources costs and $66,000 computer services costs that must be allocated to the two service and two operations departments.

CGB uses the step method to allocate costs from support departments to the loan businesses. See the step method in Exhibit 7.15, which follows the same approach as for Beary Company in Exhibits 7.4 and 7.7. The top of Exhibit 7.15 shows the allocation bases that CGB uses to allocate human resources costs and computer services costs to each department. The allocation base for human resources costs is the number of employees, or the head count, in each department, and the allocation of computer services costs is based on the number of computers in each department. The number of employees and the number of computers in each department are given.

EXHIBIT 7.14
Reciprocal Relationships in Community General Bank

	To			
From	**Accounting Department**	**Administrative Services Department**	**Operations Department**	**Marketing Department**
Accounting department (service)	—	25%	35%	40%
Administrative services department (service)	20%	—	40%	40%

EXHIBIT 7.15 Cost Allocation at Community General Bank, Using the Step Method

Departmental Allocation Bases	Accounting	Administrative Services	Operations	Marketing		Total
Human resources						
Head count	80	100	160	60		400
Percent	20%	25%	40%	15%		100%
Computer services						
Number of computers	60	60	150	30		300
Percent	20%	20%	50%	10%		100%

First Phase: Trace Direct Costs and Allocate Indirect Costs to Departments

Direct costs (given)						
Labor	$ 221,000	$ 339,500	$ 554,500	$ 445,000		$1,560,000
Supplies	3,500	8,800	4,200	16,500		33,000
Indirect costs						
Human resources	16,000	20,000	32,000	12,000 (e.g., $12,000 = 15% × $80,000)		80,000
Computer services	13,200	13,200	33,000	6,600 (e.g., $ 6,600 = 10% × $66,000)		66,000
Totals for all departments	**$253,700**	**$381,500**	**$623,700**	**$480,100**		**$1,739,000**

Second Phase: Allocate Service Department Costs to Operations and Marketing, Using the Step Method

First step

Accounting department	Service percent	25%	35%	40%	
	Amount	**$63,425**	**$88,795**	**$101,480** (e.g., $101,480 = 40% × $253,700)	

Second step

Administrative services	Service percent		40%	40%	
	Allocation percent (per direct method)		50%	50%	
					[e.g., $222,462.50 =
	Amount		$ 222,462.50	$ 222,462.50	50% × ($381,500 + $63,425)]
Totals for operating departments			**$934,957.50**	**$804,042.50**	**$1,739,000**

Third Phase: Allocate Operations and Marketing Costs to Commercial and Residential Loan Businesses

	Commercial Loans	Residential Loans	
Base: Number of banking transactions	15,000	10,000	25,000
Percent	60%	40%	
Number of loans	900	3,600	4,500
Percent	20%	80%	
Operations (number of transactions basis) [e.g., $934,957.50 × 60% = $560,974.50]	$560,974.50	$ 373,983	
Marketing (number of loans basis) [e.g., $804,042.50 × 20% = $160,808.50]	160,808.50	643,234	
Totals for commercial and residential loans	$ **721,783**	**$1,017,217**	**$1,739,000**

The first phase of the allocation in Exhibit 7.15 traces the totals of $1,560,000 of labor and $33,000 for supplies costs to each department and allocates the human resources costs ($80,000) and computer services costs ($66,000) using the allocation bases head count and number of computers, respectively. The result is that the total cost of $1,739,000 is allocated as follows:

Accounting department	$ 253,700
Administrative services department	381,500
Operations department	623,700
Marketing department	480,100
Total cost	$1,739,000

In the second phase, the accounting and administrative services department costs are allocated to the operations and marketing departments using the step method and the service

REAL-WORLD FOCUS   Overhead Is a Part of University Research

In 2017 President Trump proposed a budget that cut the funding of the National Institutes of Health. Congress rejected that proposal and actually approved an increase in the funding. Why the difference? Both houses of Congress rejected the president's proposal to slash the amount of funds available for overhead—the indirect costs of research. These overhead costs are real and include such items as upkeep of laboratories and the cost of internet and data storage, and let us not forget the cost of federal regulatory compliance protecting human subjects of clinical research.

Source: Robert Pear, "Rejecting Trump Cuts, Congress Acts to Increase N.I.H Funds," *The New York Times*, September 12, 2017, p. A19.

EXHIBIT 7.16

Profitability Analysis of Commercial and Residential Loans for Community General Bank

	Commercial Loans	Residential Loans
Revenues	$2,755,455	$2,998,465
Less expenses		
Cost of funds	1,200,736	1,387,432
Allocated operating costs (Exhibit 7.15)	721,783	1,017,217
Operating profit	$ 832,936	$ 593,816
Key ratios		
Operating profit/revenue	30.2286%	19.8040%
Cost of funds/revenue	43.5767%	46.2714%

percentages in Exhibit 7.14. The accounting department goes first because it has a higher percentage service to the administrative services department (25%) than the service percentage from administrative services to accounting (20%). The result is that the $1,739,000 of total cost is now allocated to the operations department ($934,957.50) and the marketing department ($804,042.50).

In the third and final phase, the costs from the operations and marketing departments are allocated to the two businesses, commercial and residential loans. The base that CGB uses to allocate operations department costs is the number of banking transactions handled within operations (15,000 for commercial loans and 10,000 for residential loans); to allocate marketing costs, CGB uses the number of loans of either type (900 commercial loans and 3,600 residential loans). The result of the final allocation is that the total cost of $1,739,000 is allocated to the commercial loans department ($721,783) and the residential loans department ($1,017,217), as illustrated for the third phase in Exhibit 7.15.

Cost allocation provides CGB a basis for evaluating the cost and profitability of its services. By taking the allocated operating costs just determined, the cost of funds provided, and the revenue produced by both commercial and residential loans, a profitability analysis of commercial and residential loans can be completed. Assume that the commercial and residential loan businesses have revenues of $2,755,455 and $2,998,465, respectively, and direct cost of funds of $1,200,736 and $1,387,432, respectively.

The profitability analysis in Exhibit 7.16 shows that the relatively high allocated operating costs of the residential loan unit are an important factor in its overall poor performance (only 19.8% operating profit to revenue in contrast to more than 30% for the commercial loan unit). In contrast, the cost of funds appears to be comparable for both types of loans (43.58% of revenues for commercial loans and 46.27% of revenues for residential loans). The analysis indicates that the bank should investigate the profitability of residential loans and, in particular, the cost of operations and marketing for these loans.

Joint Product Costing

LO 7-6

Use the three joint product costing methods.

Many manufacturing plants yield more than one product from a joint manufacturing process. For example, the petroleum industry processes crude oil into multiple products: gasoline, kerosene, fuel oils, and residual heavy oils. Similarly, the semiconductor industry processes silicon wafers into a variety of computer memory chips with different speeds, temperature tolerances, and life expectancies. Other industries that yield joint products include lumber production, food processing, soap making, grain milling, dairy farming, and fishing.

A **joint production process** is one that yields multiple outputs from a common resource input. **Joint products** are products from a joint production process that have relatively substantial sales values. Products whose total sales values are minor in comparison to the sales value of the joint products are classified as **by-products.**

Joint products and by-products both start their manufacturing life as part of the same direct materials. Until a certain point in the production process, no distinction can be made between the products. The point in a joint production process at which individual products can be separately identified for the first time is called the **split-off point.** Thereafter, separate production processes can be applied to the individual products. At the split-off point, joint products or by-products might be salable or require further processing to be salable, depending on their nature.

Joint costs include all manufacturing costs incurred prior to the split-off point (including direct materials, direct labor, and factory overhead). For financial reporting purposes, these costs are allocated among the joint products. Additional costs incurred after the split-off point that can be identified directly with individual products are called **separable processing costs.**

Other outputs of joint production include scrap, waste, spoilage, and rework. Scrap is the residue from a production process that has little or no recovery value. Waste, such as chemical waste, is a residual material that has no recovery value and must be disposed of by the firm as required. In addition to waste and scrap, some products do not meet quality standards and can be reworked for resale. See the appendix to Chapter 4 for more coverage of spoilage, rework, and scrap.

Methods for Allocating Joint Costs to Joint Products

Joint costs are most frequently allocated to joint products using (1) the physical measure, (2) the sales value at split-off, (3) the net realizable value, and (4) the constant gross margin percentage methods.

The Physical Measure Method

The **physical measure method,** naturally enough, uses a physical measure such as pounds, gallons, yards, or units produced at the split-off point to allocate the joint costs to joint products. The first step is to select the proper physical measure as the basis for allocation. We can use units of input or units of output. For example, if we are costing tuna products, the production of 100 pounds of tuna into quarter-pound cans would have an input measure of 100 pounds and an output measure of 400 cans. When units of output are used, this also is called the **average cost method.** Assume that Johnson Seafood produces tuna filets and canned tuna for distribution to restaurants and supermarkets in the southeastern United States. The cost of 14,000 pounds of raw, unprocessed tuna plus the direct labor and overhead for cutting and processing the tuna into filets and canned tuna is the joint cost of the process. The flow of production is illustrated in Exhibit 7.17.

joint production process
A process that yields multiple outputs from a common resource input.

joint products
Products from the same production process that have relatively substantial sales values.

by-products
Products in a joint production process whose total sales values are minor in comparison with the total sales value of all the joint products.

split-off point
The point in a joint production process where products with individual identities emerge.

separable processing costs
In a joint production process, costs incurred after the split-off point that are traceable to individual products.

physical measure method
A method that uses a physical measure such as pounds, gallons, yards, or units of volume produced at the split-off point to allocate the joint costs to joint products.

average cost method
A method that uses units of output to allocate costs to products.

EXHIBIT 7.17
Flow of Production for Two Joint Products

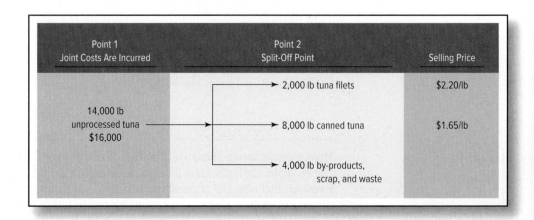

EXHIBIT 7.18
Physical Measure Method

Product	Physical Measure	Proportion	Allocation of Joint Costs	Cost per Pound
Tuna filets	2,000 lb	0.20	$16,000 × 20% = $ 3,200	$1.60
Canned tuna	8,000 lb	0.80	16,000 × 80% = 12,800	1.60
Total	10,000 lb	1.00	$16,000	

The production process starts at point 1. A total $16,000 joint cost ($7,000 direct materials, $5,000 direct labor, and $4,000 overhead) is incurred. Point 2 is the split-off point where two joint products are separated: 2,000 pounds of tuna filets and 8,000 pounds of canned tuna. Using the physical unit method, none of the joint costs are allocated to the remaining 4,000 pounds of by-product, scrap, and waste. (However, look to the appendix to the chapter to see how to account for by-products using a different method.) If we use a physical measure method, the joint cost of $16,000 is allocated as shown in Exhibit 7.18.

Based on the physical measure method (pounds in this example), when the joint products reach the split-off point, we can compute the relationship of each of the joint products to the sum of the total units. The amount of the joint cost allocated to the products is the average cost per pound of the total joint cost, that is, $1.60 per pound.

The physical measure used to determine the relative weights for allocating the joint cost should be the measure of the products at the *split-off point,* not the measure when the production of the products is complete. Thus, the relevant measure in the example is the 2,000 pounds of filets and 8,000 pounds of canned tuna.

The production costs per pound for both products follow:

Filets   **$1.60 per pound = $3,200 ÷ 2,000 pounds**
Canned tuna   **$1.60 per pound = $12,800 ÷ 8,000 pounds**

Advantages and Limitations Among the advantages of the physical measure method are that (1) it is easy to use and (2) the criterion for the allocation of the joint costs is objective. This method, however, ignores the revenue-producing capability of individual products that can vary widely among the joint products and have no relationship at all to any physical measure. Each product can also have a unique physical measure (gallons for one, pounds for another), and, hence, the physical measure method might not be applicable. The following method addresses these limitations.

The Sales Value at Split-Off Method

sales value at split-off method
A method that allocates joint costs to joint products on the basis of their relative sales values at the split-off point. Also known as the relative sales value method

The sales value at split-off method is an alternative and widely used method. The **sales value at split-off method** (or, more simply, relative sales value method) allocates joint costs to joint products on the basis of their relative sales values at the split-off point. This method can be used only when joint products can be sold at the split-off point. If we assume that Johnson can sell a pound of filets for $2.20 and a pound of canned tuna for $1.65 and that Johnson has produced 2,000 pounds of filets and 8,000 pounds of canned tuna, the $16,000 joint costs should be allocated between the products as shown in Exhibit 7.19.

The first step in the sales value method (Exhibit 7.19) is to compute the total sales value of the joint products at the split-off point. Note that the sales value is the sales price multiplied by the number of production units, *not the actual number of sales units.* Determining the proportion of the sales value of each joint product to the total sales value is the second step. The final operation allocates the total joint cost among the joint products based on those proportions.

EXHIBIT 7.19
Sales Value at Split-Off Method

Product	Units	Price per Unit	Sales Value	Proportion	Allocation of Joint Cost	Cost per Pound
Filets	2,000 lb	$2.20	$ 4,400	0.25	$16,000 × 25% = $ 4,000	$2.00
Canned tuna	8,000 lb	1.65	13,200	0.75	16,000 × 75% = 12,000	1.50
Total			$17,600	1.00	$16,000	

JOINT COSTS OF PUBLIC EDUCATION AND FUND-RAISING IN CHARITIES

Most large charities incur costs of fund-raising and public education/outreach as part of their mission. The charities also have programs they support with funds they have raised. For program evaluation and for regulatory reporting requirements, the charities must then allocate some portion of their joint costs of public education and fund-raising to the charities' programs. The practice of allocating public education/fund-raising costs is viewed as reasonable in this context—as, for example, in the case of a charity that describes the symptoms of a disease and explains the actions the individual should take if those symptoms occur. These costs can be allocated to the related programs of the charity. The cost allocation is important because it affects the total amounts the charity shows for fund-raising versus program delivery. The relationship between these costs is important because some governmental regulations restrict the "administrative cost ratio" to some maximum amount, and the relationship is also important for donors who would like to see most of their donations going to programs rather than fund-raising.

Sources: U.S. Office of Management and Budget, Circular No. A-122, "Cost Principles for Non-Profit Organizations," www.whitehouse.gov/sites/whitehouse.gov/files/omb/circulars/A122/a122_2004.pdf, accessed November 20, 2019; Joseph J. Cruitt, "How NFPs Should Allocate Joint Costs," *Journal of Accountancy,* October 2014, pp. 39–42.

In the Johnson Seafood example, the sales values of filets and canned tuna are $4,400 and $13,200, respectively, a total of $17,600. The proportion of the individual sales values of the products to the total sales value are 0.25 ($4,400 ÷ $17,600) for filets and 0.75 ($13,200 ÷ $17,600) for canned tuna. The allocated costs are $4,000 to filets and $12,000 to canned tuna. The production costs per pound for both products are calculated as follows:

Filets   **$2.00 per pound = $4,000 ÷ 2,000**
Canned tuna   **$1.50 per pound = $12,000 ÷ 8,000**

Note that filets have a higher unit cost under the sales value at split-off method than under the physical measure method. The reason is that filets have a higher relative sales value. If the sales prices are estimated accurately and no separable processing costs are involved, the sales value at split-off method generates the same gross margin percentage for both filets and canned tuna, as shown in Exhibit 7.20.

Advantages and Limitations The advantages of the sales value at split-off method are that it (1) is easy to calculate and (2) is allocated according to each product's revenues. This method is superior to the physical measure method because it allocates the joint costs in proportion to the products' ability to absorb these costs. This is an application of the ability-to-bear concept of fairness included in the objectives of cost allocation at the beginning of the chapter.

One limitation of the sales value at split-off method is that market prices for some industries change constantly. Also, the sales price at split-off might not be available because separable processing is necessary before the product can be sold.

The Net Realizable Value Method

net realizable value (NRV)
The estimated sales value of the product at the split-off point; determined by subtracting the separable processing and selling costs beyond the split-off point from the ultimate sales value of the product.

Not all joint products can be sold at the split-off point; some require additional processing before the product can be sold. Thus, there is no market price to attach to some products at the split-off point. In these cases, the concept of net realizable value is used. The **net realizable value (NRV)** of a product is the *ultimate net sales value* that is estimated at the split-off point; it is determined by subtracting the separable processing and selling costs beyond the split-off point from the estimated ultimate sales value for that product.

$$NRV = \text{Estimated ultimate sales value} - \text{Separable processing and selling costs}$$

EXHIBIT 7.20
Product-Line Profitability for Sales Value at Split-Off Method

	Tuna Filets	Canned Tuna
Sales	$2.20 × 2,000 = $4,400	$1.65 × 8,000 = $13,200
Cost of goods sold	$2.00 × 2,000 = 4,000	$1.50 × 8,000 = 12,000
Gross margin	$ 400	$ 1,200
Gross margin percent	9.09%	9.09%

EXHIBIT 7.21 **Flow of Production for Three Joint Products**

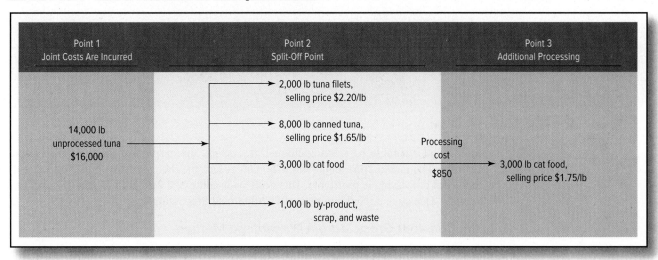

In the Johnson Seafood example, assume that in addition to filets and canned tuna, the firm processes cat food from raw, unprocessed tuna. Assume also that, at the split-off point, 14,000 pounds of tuna yield 2,000 pounds of filets and 8,000 pounds of canned tuna, as before. However, now assume that an additional 3,000 pounds of cat food are also produced. The remaining 1,000 pounds are scrap, waste, and by-products. For cat food, the tuna must be processed further for sale to pet food distributors. The separable processing cost is $850 for minerals and other supplements that are important for cat nutrition but that add no weight to the product. The pet food distributors buy the prepared cat food from Johnson at $1.75 per pound and package it into 5.5-ounce cans for sale to pet stores and supermarkets. Exhibit 7.21 is a diagram of this situation.

Exhibit 7.22 shows the joint cost allocation calculation using the net realizable value method.

If Johnson Seafood sold all of the products it produced during the period, its gross margin amounts for the products would be as shown in Exhibit 7.23. Note that the gross margin percentage is lower for cat food than for filets because of the separable processing cost of $850.

Advantages and Limitations The NRV method is superior to the physical measure method because, like the sales value at split-off method, it produces an allocation that yields a predictable, comparable level of profitability among the products. The physical measure method might provide misleading guidance to top management regarding product profitability.

The Decision to Sell before or after Additional Processing An important decision for management to make in regard to separable costs is whether the company should incur the separable costs and process the product further, as illustrated here for cat food at Johnson Seafood. Will the separable costs increase or decrease profits? The key to making this decision is to ignore the joint costs and focus instead on only the separable costs and the increase in sales value. The joint costs are not relevant for the decision because these costs will not differ between the option to sell at the split-off point or to sell after additional processing. In this example, the cat food has no sales value as scrap or waste, if not processed further, and the additional processing cost of $850 provides increased revenue of 3,000 × $1.75 = $5,250;

EXHIBIT 7.22 **Joint Cost Allocation Using the Net Realizable Value Method**

Product	Pounds	Price	Sales Value	Separable Processing	Net Realizable Value	Percent of NRV	Allocation of Joint Costs	Total Cost	Cost per Pound
Filets	2,000	$2.20	$ 4,400	—	$ 4,400	20%	$ 3,200	$ 3,200	$1.60
Canned tuna	8,000	1.65	13,200	—	13,200	60	9,600	9,600	1.20
Cat food	3,000	1.75	5,250	$850	4,400	20	3,200	4,050	1.35
Total	13,000		$22,850	$850	$22,000	100%	$16,000	$16,850	

EXHIBIT 7.23   **Product-Line Profitability for Net Realizable Value Method**

	Tuna Filets	Canned Tuna	Cat Food
Sales	$2.20 × 2,000 = $4,400	$1.65 × 8,000 = $13,200	$1.75 × 3,000 = $5,250
Cost of goods sold	$1.60 × 2,000 = 3,200	$1.20 × 8,000 = 9,600	$1.35 × 3,000 = 4,050
Gross margin	$1,200	$ 3,600	$1,200
Gross margin percent	27.27%	27.27%	22.86%

without the separable cost and additional processing, this portion of the tuna material has no value. The increased revenue of $5,250 far exceeds the increased cost of $850 so that the additional processing is profitable. This decision is addressed further in Chapter 11 under the heading "Decisions to Sell before or after Additional Processing."

The Constant Gross Margin Percentage Method

Sometimes it is desirable that the company have joint products with constant or equal gross margin percentages. If separable costs for the joint products are zero or negligible, then the NRV method described earlier will produce a joint cost allocation that results in equal or nearly equal gross margin percentages (gross margin ÷ total sales) for all joint products. When separable costs are significant and an important goal of the allocation is to achieve an allocation that results in the same gross margin percentage for all joint products, then a variation of the NRV method is used. The constant gross margin percentage method determines an allocation of joint costs so that, after allocation, all joint products have the same gross margin percentage.

The method for achieving constant gross margin percentages for joint products is illustrated in Exhibit 7.24 for Johnson Seafood. Part 1 of the exhibit assembles the necessary

EXHIBIT 7.24   **Joint Cost Allocation Using the Constant Gross Margin Percentage Method**

	Filets	Canned Tuna	Cat Food	Total
1. Summarize Basic Data				
Price (after additional processing)	$ 2.20	$ 1.65	$ 1.75	
Pounds produced	2,000	8,000	3,000	**13,000**
Total separable processing cost	—	—	850	**850**
Total joint cost				**$16,000**
2. Determine Gross Margin Percent for Total Sales				
Final sales value of production	$ 4,400	$ 13,200	$ 5,250	$ 22,850
Less: Separable costs				850
Less: Joint cost				16,000
Gross margin				$ 6,000
Gross margin percent		($6,000 ÷ $22,850 =)		**26.2582%**
3. Allocate Joint Cost; Determine Total Product Cost				
Final sales value of production for each product	$ 4,400	$ 13,200	$ 5,250	$ 22,850
Less: Gross margin for each product, at 26.2582% (rounded to nearest dollar)	1,155	3,466	1,379	6,000
Less: Separable costs	—	—	850	850
= **Allocated joint cost** (= final sales value less allocated gross margin less separable costs)	3,245	9,734	3,021	16,000
Total cost (= allocated joint cost + separable cost)	$ 3,245	$ 9,734	$ 3,871	$ 16,850
Total cost per unit	$ 1.6223	$ 1.2167	$ 1.2905	
4. Calculation of Gross Margin				
Sales	$ 4,400	$ 13,200	$ 5,250	$ 22,850
Cost of goods sold	3,245	9,734	3,871	16,850
Gross margin	$ 1,155	$ 3,466	$ 1,379	$ 6,000
Gross margin percent (some small differences due to rounding)	**26.2500%**	**26.2575%**	**26.2667%**	**26.2582%**

information. Part 2 determines the companywide gross margin percentage (in this case, 26.2582%). Part 3 determines the amount of joint cost allocation as the residual: revenue less separable costs less the desired gross margin amount for each product at 26.2582% of total gross margin. Part 4 completes the method by showing the calculation of the gross margin and gross margin percentage.

Summary

This chapter introduces the objectives, concepts, and methods of cost allocation. There are two main cost allocation applications—departmental cost allocation and joint product costing. Most important, the objectives and methods for cost allocation are determined based on the firm's strategy. Cost allocation is concerned with strategy in four key ways: (1) to determine accurate departmental and product/service costs as a basis for evaluating each department's cost efficiency and the profitability of different products, (2) to motivate managers to work hard, (3) to provide the proper incentive for managers to achieve the firm's goals, and (4) to provide a fair basis for rewarding managers for their effort.

Ethical issues often arise in cost allocation when managers must choose between alternative allocation methods. The manager must choose between methods that might decrease the cost of one product, customer, or business unit at the expense of increased costs for another product, customer, or unit.

Departmental cost allocation is performed in three phases: (1) trace all direct costs and allocate indirect costs to service and production departments, (2) allocate service department costs to production departments, and (3) allocate production department costs to products. The second phase is the most complex. Service department costs can be allocated to production departments using three methods—the direct method, the step method, or the reciprocal method. The three methods differ in the way they include service flows among service departments. The direct method ignores these flows, the step method includes some of them, and the reciprocal method includes all. For this reason, the reciprocal method is preferred.

A number of implementation issues arise when applying cost allocation methods, including the strategic and ethical issues of the cost allocation. It is also important to allocate variable and fixed costs separately (in a process called *dual allocation*), to use budgeted rather than actual amounts in the allocation, and to consider alternative allocation methods when the result of an allocation to a department is a cost that is greater than what the department would pay to purchase the service from an outside entity.

The need for joint product costing arises when two or more products are made simultaneously in a given manufacturing process. The four methods for costing joint products are the (1) physical measure method, (2) sales value at split-off method, (3) net realizable value method, and (4) constant gross margin percentage method. The physical measure method is the simplest to use but also has a significant disadvantage. Because the allocation ignores sales value, the gross margins of joint products determined using the physical measure method can differ in significant and unreasonable ways. In contrast, the sales value at split-off and net realizable value methods tend to result in similar gross margins among the joint products. The sales value at split-off method is used when sales value at split-off is known; otherwise, the net realizable value is used.

Appendix

By-Product Costing

LO 7-7
Use the four by-product costing methods.

A by-product is a product of relatively small sales value that is produced simultaneously with one or more joint products. Two approaches are used for by-product costing: (1) the asset recognition approach and (2) the revenue approach. The main difference between these approaches lies in whether they assign an inventoriable value to by-products at the split-off point. The asset recognition approach records by-products as inventory at net realizable values; the by-product is therefore recognized as inventory when the by-product is produced. In contrast, the revenue approach does not assign values to the by-products in the period of production but recognizes by-product revenue in the period sold.

EXHIBIT 7A.1
A Summary of By-Product Costing Methods

	Where in Income Statement	
When Recognized	**As Other Income**	**As a Deduction of Manufacturing Cost**
At time of production (asset recognition methods)	Other income at time of production	Net realizable value method; reduction in joint product cost at time of production
At time of sale (revenue methods)	Other income at time of sale	Reduction in cost of joint products at time of sale

Each of the two approaches contains two alternative methods, depending on the way in which by-products are reported in the income statement. The two asset recognition methods are:

Net Realizable Value Method. This method shows the net realizable value of by-products on the balance sheet as inventory and on the income statement as a deduction from the total manufacturing cost of the joint products. This is done in the *period in which the by-product is produced.*

Other Income at Production Point Method. This method shows the net realizable value of by-products on the income statement as other income or other sales revenue. This is done in the *period in which the by-product is produced.*

The two revenue methods are:

Other Income at Selling Point Method. This method shows the net sales revenue from a by-product sold *at time of sale* on the income statement as other income or other sales revenue.

Manufacturing Cost Reduction at Selling Point Method. This method shows the net sales revenue from a by-product sold *at time of sale* on the income statement as a reduction of total manufacturing cost.

In Exhibit 7A.1, we summarize the four major by-product costing methods.

ASSET RECOGNITION METHODS

We refer back to Exhibit 7.21 to illustrate the asset recognition methods. Assume that Johnson Seafood believes that it can make additional profit by taking a portion of the 1,000 pounds of scrap and waste in each batch of unprocessed tuna (see Exhibit 7.21) and reprocessing it to produce a high-quality garden fertilizer. However, the selling price of the fertilizer is expected to be relatively low, 50 cents per pound. Moreover, additional, separable processing and selling costs of 30 cents per pound would be necessary for preparing, packaging, and distributing the product. Because the sales value of fertilizer is relatively low, the firm decides to treat tuna filets, canned tuna, and cat food as joint products and fertilizer as a by-product. Suppose that Johnson sold all production of filets, canned tuna, and cat food, but sold only 400 of the 500 pounds of the fertilizer produced. Exhibit 7A.2 shows the flow of production for the three joint products and one by-product.

From Exhibit 7.22, recall that the total sales value of filets, canned tuna, and cat food is $22,850 ($4,400 + $13,200 + $5,250) and the total cost of the goods sold is $16,850 ($3,200 + $9,600 + $4,050). The net realizable value (NRV) of the 500 pounds of fertilizer produced is

$$NRV = \text{Sales Values} - \text{Separable processing and selling costs}$$
$$= (\$0.50 \times 500) - (\$0.30 \times 500)$$
$$= \$100$$

Johnson's accounting for the by-product using the asset recognition methods (the net realizable value method and the other income at production point method) appears in Exhibit 7A.3.

EXHIBIT 7A.2

Flow of Production for Three Joint Products and One By-Product

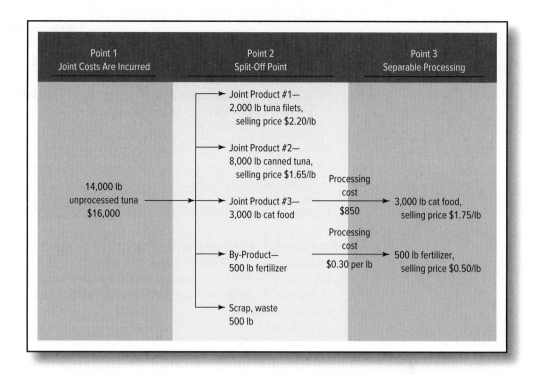

EXHIBIT 7A.3

By-Product Costing—Asset Recognition Methods (at time of production)

	Net Realizable Value Method	Other Income at Production Method
Sale of joint products (Exhibit 7.22)	$22,850	$22,850
Cost of joint products sold (Exhibit 7.22)	$16,850	$16,850
Less net realizable value of by-product	(100)	—
Cost of goods sold	$16,750	$16,850
Gross margin	$ 6,100	$ 6,000
Other income at production	—	100
Income before tax	$ 6,100	$ 6,100

Asset recognition methods are justified on the basis of the financial accounting concepts of asset recognition, matching, and materiality. By-products are *recognized* as assets with probable future economic benefits because a market exists for them. Asset recognition methods also have the preferred effect of *matching* the value of the by-product with its manufacturing cost; when the by-product is sold, its inventory cost is shown as the cost of sales. If the net realizable value of a by-product is *material* (i.e., it will have a significant effect on inventory or profit), the asset recognition methods should be used because of the matching concept.

When using the net realizable value approach to the asset recognition method, the value of the by-product is treated as a reduction to the joint costs and the inventory of the by-product is carried at its net realizable value. Also under the asset recognition method, when using the other income at production approach, the by-product is recorded in inventory at its net realizable value and there is an increase in other income at the time of production. In either case, when the by-product is sold, there is no effect on the income because the by-product is sold at its carrying cost.

REVENUE METHODS

Revenue methods recognize by-products at the time of sale. Exhibit 7A.4 illustrates the two methods. Note that Exhibit 7A.4 shows the 400 pounds of by-product sold, not the 500 pounds of by-product produced.

EXHIBIT 7A.4
By-Product Costing—
Revenue Recognition
Methods (at time of sale)

	Other Income at Selling Point Method	Manufacturing Cost Reduction Method
Sale of joint products	$22,850	$22,850
Cost of goods sold		
Cost of joint products sold	$16,850	$16,850
Less net sales revenue of by-product sold		
($0.50 − $0.30) × 400	—	(80)
Cost of goods sold	$16,850	$16,770
Gross margin	$ 6,000	$ 6,080
Other income (by-product)	80	—
Income before tax	$ 6,080	$ 6,080

Revenue methods are justified on the financial accounting concepts of revenue realization, materiality, and cost benefit. These methods are consistent with the argument that by-product net revenue should be recorded at the time of sale because this is the *point at which revenue is realized*. Revenue methods are also appropriate when the value of the by-product is *not material* in amount.

Key Terms

average cost method, *252*
by-products, *252*
direct method, *239*
dual allocation, *246*
joint costs, *234*
joint production process, *252*

joint products, *252*
net realizable value (NRV), *254*
physical measure method, *252*
reciprocal flows, *239*
reciprocal method, *241*

sales value at split-off method, *253*
separable processing costs, *252*
service department, *234*
split-off point, *252*
step method, *241*

Comments on Cost Management in Action

Health Care Providers Allocate Costs for Medicare Reimbursement

The direct method of the departmental approach to cost allocation explained in this chapter has never been permitted for Medicare cost reports. The method most likely to be used is the step method, which must be performed under Medicare guidelines and audited by a private intermediary (e.g., Blue Cross Blue Shield). A hospital chooses the order in which the step method occurs and the allocation bases (e.g., square feet, pounds of laundry, time spent, number of meals served). The order of the step method and the choice of allocation base are widely recognized as having a significant effect on allocated costs. Hospitals naturally choose methods that favor them in cost reimbursement. Many consultants, authors, and policymakers have called for improved guidance regarding the allocation of costs for Medicare reimbursement. Some have argued that because software tools are readily available to allocate costs using the reciprocal method, Medicare should require this more accurate method. Providers are allowed to adopt other allocation methods, but only upon approval. One method described in the government's cost accounting standards for Medicare and Medicaid Services is the double-apportionment method, which is a move toward the reciprocal approach.

Another disincentive issue for Medicare reimbursement has also been getting some attention. When a doctor administers a drug, the doctor is reimbursed under Medicare for 106% of the drug's cost. The additional 6% is for the doctor's service. The problem arises when two different drugs are available for the same treatment and one costs far more than the other. The doctor's incentive is to use the more expensive drug because the service fee will be higher. By 2015, the high-priced drugs represented almost two-thirds of the more than $33 billion of Medicare Part D catastrophic coverage.

Sources: Marianne L. Muise and Bonnie A. Amoia, "Step Up to the Step-Down Method," *Healthcare Financial Management*, May 2006, pp. 72–77; William N. Zelman, Michael J. McCue, and Noah Glick, *Financial Management of Health Care Organizations*, 3rd Ed. (New York: Wiley, 2009); "How to Rein in Medicare's Runaway Costs," *Bloomberg Businessweek*, May 21, 2014, p. 10; Office of the Inspector General, "High-Price Drugs Are Increasing Federal Payments for Medicare Part D Catastrophic Coverage," January 2017, https://oig.hhs.gov/oei/reports/oei-02-16-00270.pdf. Also, the relevant guidance on Medicare costing is provided by the Centers for Medicare and Medicaid Services, a U.S. federal agency to administer Medicare and Medicaid (www.cms.gov/). Medicare cost report information can be found at https://www.cms.gov/Research-Statistics-Data-and-Systems/Downloadable-Public-Use-Files/Cost-Reports. Government cost accounting standards for the Centers for Medicare & Medicaid Services can be found at www.gpo.gov/fdsys/pkg/CFR-2003-title42-vol2/pdf/CFR-2003-title42-vol2-sec413-24.pdf.

Self-Study Problem

(For answers, please see Solution.)

Joint Product Costing

Northern Company processes 100 gallons of raw materials into 75 gallons of product GS-50 and 25 gallons of GS-80. GS-50 is further processed into 50 gallons of product GS-505 at a cost of $5,000, and GS-80 is processed into 50 gallons of product GS-805 at a cost of $2,000. Exhibit 1 depicts this manufacturing flow.

EXHIBIT 1
Joint Cost Flows for Northern Company

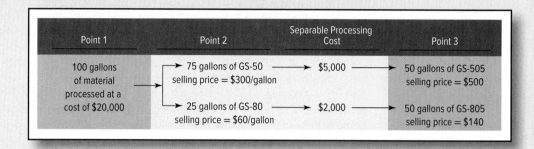

The production process starts at point 1. A total of $20,000 in joint manufacturing costs are incurred in reaching point 2. Point 2 is the split-off point of the process that manufactures GS-50 and GS-80. At this point, GS-50 can be sold for $300 a gallon, and GS-80 can be sold for $60 a gallon. The process is completed at point 3—products GS-505 and GS-805 have a sales price of $500 a gallon and $140 a gallon, respectively.

Required Allocate the joint product costs and then compute the cost per unit using each of the following methods: (1) physical measure, (2) sales value at split-off, and (3) net realizable value.

The Student Resources section of Connect includes video tutorials for the Self-Study Problems.

Questions

7-1   What are the four objectives in the strategic role of cost allocation? Explain each briefly.

7-2   Explain the difference between joint products and by-products.

7-3   What does the term *reciprocal* mean in the context of departmental cost allocation?

7-4   What are the three methods of departmental cost allocation? Explain how they differ, which is the most preferred, and why.

7-5   What are the three phases of the departmental allocation approach? What happens at each phase?

7-6   Give two or three examples of the use of cost allocation in service industries and not-for-profit organizations.

7-7   What are the four methods used in by-product costing, and how do they differ? Which is the preferred method and why?

7-8   What are the limitations of joint product and departmental cost allocation?

7-9   What are the implementation issues of departmental cost allocation?

7-10   What are some of the ethical issues of cost allocation?

Brief Exercises

Brief Exercises 7-11 through 7-14 involve departmental cost allocation with two service departments and two production departments. Use the following information for these four exercises:

Department	Cost	Percentage Service Provided to			
		S1	S2	P1	P2
Service 1 (S1)	$ 30,000	0%	30%	35%	35%
Service 2 (S2)	20,000	20	0	20	60
Production 1 (P1)	100,000				
Production 2 (P2)	150,000				

[LO 7-3]   7-11   What is the amount of service department cost allocated to P1 and P2 using the direct method?

[LO 7-3]   7-12   What is the total cost in P1 and P2 after allocation using the direct method?

[LO 7-3]   7-13   What is the total cost in P1 and P2 and what is the amount of service department cost allocated to P1 and P2 using the step method with S1 going first?

[LO 7-3]   7-14   How does your answer to 7-11 change if the cost in P1 is changed from $100,000 to $120,000?

Brief Exercises 7-15 and 7-16 require the following information:

Department	Cost	Percentage Service Provided to			
		S1	S2	P1	P2
Service 1 (S1)	$112,000	0%	40%	40%	20%
Service 2 (S2)	44,000	20	0	40	40
Production 1 (P1)	345,000				
Production 2 (P2)	216,000				
Total	$717,000				

[LO 7-3]   7-15 What percentage of S1's costs is allocated to P1 and to P2 under the direct method?

[LO 7-3]   7-16 What percentage of S2's costs is allocated to P1 and to P2 under the direct method?

Brief Exercises 7-17 through 7-20 require the following information about a joint production process for three products, with a total joint production cost of $100,000. There are no separable processing costs for any of the three products.

Product	Sales Value at Split-Off	Units at Split-Off
1	$130,000	240
2	50,000	960
3	20,000	1,200
	$200,000	2,400

[LO 7-6]   7-17 What percentage of joint cost is allocated to each of the three products using the sales value at split-off method?

[LO 7-6]   7-18 What percentage of joint cost is allocated to each of the three products using the physical units method?

[LO 7-6, 7-7]   7-19 Assume that the total sales value at the split-off point for product 1 is $50,000 instead of $130,000 and the sales value of product 3 is $2,000 instead of $20,000. Assume also that, because of its relatively low sales value, the firm treats product 3 as a by-product and uses the net realizable value method for accounting for by-products. What amount of joint cost would be allocated to the products using the sales value at split-off method?

[LO 7-6]   7-20 Assume the same as in Brief Exercise 7-19 except that product 3 is treated as a joint product. What amount of joint costs would be allocated to the three products using the relative sales value method?

Exercises

[LO 7-1]   7-21 **Cost Allocation; General Concepts** An organization's service and administrative costs can be substantial, and some or all of these costs usually are allocated to cost objects. Thus, the allocation of service and administrative costs can have a significant impact on product cost and pricing, asset valuation, and segment profitability.

Required   When service costs are allocated, they are grouped into cost pools and then allocated to departments according to some allocation base.

1. Compare and contrast the benefit-received basis and the cause-and-effect basis for cost allocation.

2. Explain what the ability-to-bear criterion means in selecting an allocation base.

(CMA Adapted)

[LO 7-1, LO 7-7]   7-22 **By-Products and Decision Making; Strategy** Lowman Gourmet Products produces a wide variety of gourmet coffees (sold in pounds of roasted beans), jams, jellies, and condiments such as spicy mustard sauce. The firm has a reputation as a high-quality source of these products. Lowman sells the products through a mail-order catalog that is revised twice a year. Joe, the president, is interested in developing a new line of products to complement the coffees. The manufacture of the jams and jellies presently produces an excess of fruit liquid that is not used in these products. The firm is now selling excess liquid to other firms as flavoring for canned fruit products. Joe is planning to refine the liquid and add other ingredients to it to produce a coffee-flavoring product instead of selling the liquid. He figures that the cost of producing the jams and jellies, and therefore the fruit liquid, is irrelevant; the only relevant concern is the cost of the additional ingredients, processing, and packaging.

Required   How would you evaluate the financial and strategic issues facing Joe in regard to his plan to develop this new line of coffee-flavoring products?

[LO 7-1, 7-7]   7-23 **By-Products; Sustainability** The effects of the Great Recession of 2007–2009 on the construction industry led to a decline in demand for paper products and increased demand for reduced carbon emissions to minimize global warming effects. As a result, significant changes have taken place in the harvesting and processing of wood products. The demand for lumber for construction has decreased, and the demand for alternative fuels has increased. The result is that the timber industry in the southeastern states and some western states has begun to emphasize the production of a timber by-product, wood pellets. The wood pellets are made from the waste of the sawmill process; that is, the tree-tops and the knotty or crooked limbs are processed into finger-sized pellets. These wood pellets are increasingly being used to replace coal in power generation plants. This is particularly true in some European countries that have taken stronger steps to produce green energy. The pellets are considered a sustainable source of energy because the trees that produce the pellets are replaced by other trees, and the growth of trees removes carbon emissions from the atmosphere; some environmentalists would argue, therefore, that the use of pellets is carbon-neutral, certainly more so than the use of coal. Coal is one-third the cost of wood pellets, but strict emissions requirements in the European Union (EU) are causing power plants in the EU to shift to wood pellets.

Required
1. Should wood pellets be accounted for as a by-product or a joint product for the timber industry? Explain briefly.
2. Assess the sustainability issue for the production of wood pellets. What are the advantages and disadvantages of the use of wood pellets in power generation as a replacement for coal?
3. Most of the current demand for wood pellets is from EU countries. Would your answers to requirements 1 and 2 differ if the wood pellets were used domestically instead of shipped to the EU for use there?

[LO 7-1, 7-2, 7-5]   7-24 **Cost Allocation and Taxation at Nonprofit Organizations** Nonprofit organizations are exempt from federal income tax except for income from any activities that are unrelated to the nonprofit's charitable purpose. An example is the use of a laboratory for both tax-exempt basic medical research and testing a taxable product for commercial pharmaceutical firms. A concern in these cases is that tax-exempt nonprofit organizations will be able to compete unfairly with for-profit firms because of their tax-exempt status. The key argument is that common costs for the nonprofit's exempt and business activities will be used to "subsidize" the for-profit business (in this case, the taxable product testing).

Required   How would cost allocation play a role in affecting the operating results of a nonprofit organization that has both business and charitable activities?

[LO 7-1, 7-3]   7-25 **Selection of an Allocation Base** Great Ape Glassworks manufactures glass used for the screens on smartphones. It has two producing departments, P1 and P2, and only one service department, S1. The company is able to track overhead to the various departments but wants to allocate the service department costs to the producing departments. However, the company is not sure which of the multiple allocation bases should be selected. The data it collected appear in the table below:

Department	Overhead Assigned	P1	P2
P1	$150,000		
P2	250,000		
S1	74,000		
Potential allocation base		P1	P2
Employee headcount		60	20
Space used (in square feet)		2,000	6,000
Productive capacity (in units)		50,000	75,000
3-year average percentage of S1 output used		60%	40%

Required
1. Determine the total estimated overhead cost for each of the producing departments after allocating the cost of the service department:
   a. Using employee headcount as the allocation base.
   b. Using occupied space as the allocation base.
   c. Using productive capacity as the allocation base.
   d. Using the 3-year average use as the allocation base.
2. Which of the four proposed allocation bases would you recommend and why?

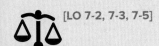

[LO 7-2, 7-3, 7-5]   7-26   **Cost Allocation in Health Care** Cost allocation is often the centerpiece of conflict that is resolved in court cases. The litigation usually involves the dispute over how costs are allocated to a product or product line that is of interest to the plaintiff. This is particularly an issue when a company produces some products or services for a price-competitive market while other products or services are produced for a governmental unit on a cost-plus or reimbursement basis.

Nursing Care Inc., or NCI, operates both a small nursing home and a retirement home. There is a single kitchen used to provide meals to both the nursing home and retirement home, meaning labor costs and utilities costs of the kitchen are shared by the two homes. There is also a centralized cleaning department that provides the cleaning services for both homes as well as the kitchen. The nursing home serves only indigent patients who are on Medicaid. The state Department of Health and Family Services (DHFS) reimburses NCI at Medicaid-approved cost reimbursement rates. The Medicaid reimbursement rates are based on cost information supplied by NCI. The relevant cost and allocation data for the most recent year appear in the following table:

	Annual Operating Cost
Cleaning department	$ 90,000
Central kitchen	$120,000

Allocation Base	Kitchen	Nursing Home	Retirement Home
Square feet of space	1,000	2,000	3,000
Number of residents	—	6	4

Required

1. Management of NCI currently allocates the kitchen and cleaning department costs based on the number of residents in each home. Determine the amount of service department costs assigned to each of the homes using this allocation base. Round percentages to two decimal places in your calculations.

2. DHFS auditors believe the step method of allocation should be used by first assigning cleaning costs based on square feet and then kitchen costs based on number of residents. Determine the amount of service department costs assigned to each of the homes using this allocation method.

3. Provide some comments as to why NCI might prefer its selected allocation method over the one supported by DHFS. Are there ethical implications related to the decision?

[LO 7-2, 7-5]   7-27   **Cost Allocation; Cost Shifting** In the last several years, airlines have succeeded in boosting profits by adding fees for previously free services such as in-flight snacks and meals, checked baggage, priority boarding, and other services. These fees have caused some shifts in customer behavior, as more airline passengers bring their own snacks on the airline and pack a smaller bag that is acceptable for "carry-on." By using carry-on luggage, the airline customer can save $25 or more in baggage-checking fees. This situation has resulted in a cost shifting for passengers, airlines, and airport security. As the number of checked bags decreases, the cost of baggage handling for the airlines decreases (and revenues increase for those bags that are checked). In contrast, the costs and delays in security checkpoints increase as security personnel must check additional carry-on bags, causing delays for passengers and the need for additional security personnel to handle the increased number of carry-on bags. Transportation Security Administration (TSA) officials explain that there has been a "huge" increase in the number of carry-on bags. In response, the Department of Homeland Security has adopted an increase in the passenger security fee each passenger pays for each flight from $2.50 in 2011 to $5.60 effective July 21, 2014. Alternatively, as suggested by the U.S. Travel Association, TSA could simply require each airline to include one free checked bag as part of the ticket price. The airline industry has objected to this fee increase on the grounds that it "diminishes customer choice and competitive differentiation among carriers."

Required

1. Explain the nature of the cost-shifting taking place currently in the airline industry.

2. What are the ethical issues, if any, in this case?

3. Explain how you think airlines compete, on cost leadership or differentiation, and explain whether the current "fees for services" approach is or is not consistent with the airlines' strategy.

[LO 7-3, 7-5]   7-28   **Departmental Cost Allocation** HomeLife Life Insurance Company has two service departments (actuarial and premium rating) and two production departments (advertising and sales). The distribution of each service department's efforts (in percentages) to the other departments is shown in the following table:

	To			
From	**Actuarial**	**Premium Rating**	**Advertising**	**Sales**
Actuarial	—	80%	10%	10%
Premium	20%	—	20	60

The direct operating costs of the departments (including both variable and fixed costs) are:

Actuarial	$80,000
Premium rating	15,000
Advertising	60,000
Sales	40,000

Required

1. Determine the total costs of the advertising and sales departments after using the direct method of allocation.

2. Determine the total costs of the advertising and sales departments after using the step method of allocation.

3. Determine the total costs of the advertising and sales departments after using the reciprocal method of allocation.

[LO 7-3]   7-29   **Departmental Cost Allocation** Robinson Products Company has two service departments (S1 and S2) and two production departments (P1 and P2). The distribution of each service department's efforts (in percentages) to the other departments is:

	To			
From	**S1**	**S2**	**P1**	**P2**
S1	—	10%	20%	?%
S2	10%	—	?	30

The direct operating costs of the departments (including both variable and fixed costs) are:

S1	$180,000
S2	60,000
P1	50,000
P2	120,000

Required

1. Determine the total cost of P1 and P2 using the direct method.

2. Determine the total cost of P1 and P2 using the step method.

3. Determine the total cost of P1 and P2 using the reciprocal method.

[LO 7-5, 7-6]   7-30   **Joint Products; Blood Donation** Donation of blood through the American Red Cross and other organizations is an important way to maintain the blood supplies that are critical to patient treatment in hospitals.

Three blood products are produced from blood received from donors: (1) red cells, used primarily in surgery; (2) platelets, used to prevent spontaneous bleeding in leukemia patients; and (3) plasma, used after further processing, for the treatment of protein deficiency. The joint cost of producing the three products consists of the blood collection costs, the safety testing costs, and further processing in a laboratory to split off the three joint products. Commonly, the joint costs are allocated to the three products on the basis of physical units produced. The National Blood Authority (NBA) in the UK observed the unfavorable effect of this approach in that the cost of each blood product could change significantly from time to time, as the demand for the products varied; the demand for the platelets was particularly volatile. In response, the NBA decided to allocate all joint costs to red cells, on the basis, in part, that plasma was routinely discarded to minimize the risk of Creutzfeldt-Jakob disease.

Required What are the advantages and disadvantages of the allocation approach proposed by the NBA? What allocation method would you suggest as an alternative, if any?

[LO 7-6]   7-31   **Joint Products** Tango Company produces joint products M, N, and T from a joint process. This information concerns a batch produced in April at a joint cost of $120,000:

| | Units Produced | After Split-Off | |
Product	and Sold	Total Separable Costs	Total Final Sales Value
M	10,000	$10,000	$160,000
N	4,000	10,000	140,000
T	5,000	5,000	25,000

Required   How much of the joint cost should be allocated to each joint product using the net realizable value method?

[LO 7-6]   7-32   **Joint Products** Arkansas Corporation manufactures liquid chemicals A and B from a joint process. It allocates joint costs on the basis of sales value at split-off. Processing 5,000 gallons of product A and 1,000 gallons of product B to the split-off point costs $5,600. The sales value at split-off is $2 per gallon for product A and $30 per gallon for product B. Product B requires additional separable processing beyond the split-off point at a cost of $2.50 per gallon before it can be sold at a price of $34 per gallon.

Required   What is the company's cost to produce 1,000 gallons of product B?

[LO 7-6, 7-7]   7-33   **Joint and By-Product Costing (Appendix)** Webster Company produces 25,000 units of product A, 20,000 units of product B, and 10,000 units of product C from the same manufacturing process at a cost of $340,000. A and B are joint products, and C is regarded as a by-product. The unit selling prices of the products are $30 for A, $25 for B, and $1 for C. None of the products requires separable processing. Of the units produced, Webster Company sells 18,000 units of A, 19,000 units of B, and 10,000 units of C. The firm uses the net realizable value method to allocate joint costs and by-product costs. Assume no beginning inventory.

Required
1. What is the value of the ending inventory of product A?
2. What is the value of the ending inventory of product B?

Problems

[LO 7-1, 7-3]   7-34   **Departmental Cost Allocation; Outsourcing** Marin Company produces two software products (Cloud-X and Cloud-Y) in two separate departments (A and B). These products are highly regarded network maintenance programs. Cloud-X is used for small networks and Cloud-Y is used for large networks. Marin is known for the quality of its products and its ability to meet dates promised for software upgrades.

Department A produces Cloud-X, and department B produces Cloud-Y. The production departments are supported by two support departments, systems design and programming services. The sources and uses of the support department time are summarized as follows:

Note regarding rounding errors: Many of the problems in this chapter require a series of calculations. Rounding errors can accumulate and affect totals unless each calculation is carried to a recommended four or more digits after the decimal point. If you are using a calculator, make sure all your calculations are done to 4 or more digits after the decimal. To avoid rounding errors entirely, use a spreadsheet package like Excel to set up and solve these problems.

| | | To | | | Total |
From	Design	Programming	Department A	Department B	Labor Hours
Design	—	5,000	1,000	9,000	15,000
Programming	400	—	600	1,000	2,000

The costs in the two service departments are as follows:

	Design	Programming
Labor and materials (all variable)	$50,000	$36,000
Depreciation and other fixed costs	40,000	4,000
Total	$90,000	$40,000

Required
1. Determine the total support costs allocated to each of the producing departments using (a) the direct method, (b) the step method (design department goes first), and (c) the reciprocal method.
2. The company is considering outsourcing programming services to DDB Services Inc. for $25 per hour. Should Marin do this?

[LO 7-3] **7-35 Departmental Cost Allocation** Logan Products has two production departments—assembly and finishing. These are supported by two service departments—sourcing (purchasing and handling of materials and human resources) and operations (work scheduling, supervision, and inspection). Logan has the following labor hours devoted by each of the service departments to the other departments.

	Total Labor Hours Used by Departments			
	Sourcing	**Operations**	**Assembly**	**Finishing**
Sourcing	—	20,000	40,000	60,000
Operations	10,000	—	60,000	50,000

The costs incurred in the plant are as follows:

Departments	Departmental Costs
Sourcing	$ 165,000
Operations	205,000
Assembly	410,000
Finishing	255,000
Total	$1,035,000

Required Use four decimal places (e.g., 33.3333%) in your calculation of percentages.
1. What are the costs allocated to the two production departments using (a) the direct method; (b) the step method, when the sourcing department that provides the greatest percentage of services to other service departments goes first, and (c) the reciprocal method?
2. What are the total costs in the production departments after allocation?

[LO 7-3, 7-4] **7-36 Departmental Cost Allocation; Outsourcing** McKeoun Enterprises is a large machine tool company now experiencing alarming increases in maintenance expense in each of its four production departments. Maintenance costs are currently allocated to the production departments on the basis of direct labor hours incurred in the production department. To provide pressure for the production departments to use less maintenance, and to provide an incentive for the maintenance department to become more efficient, McKeoun has decided to investigate new methods of allocating maintenance costs. One suggestion now being evaluated is a form of outsourcing. The producing departments could purchase maintenance service from an outside supplier. That is, they could choose either to use an outside supplier of maintenance or to be charged an amount based on their use of direct labor hours. The following table shows the direct labor hours in each department, the allocation of maintenance cost based on labor hours, and the cost to purchase the equivalent level of maintenance service from an outside maintenance provider.

Production Department	Direct Labor Hours Allocation Base (percent)	Cost Allocation Based on Direct Labor Hours	Outside Price
A	20%	$ 90,000	$115,000
B	30	135,000	92,000
C	10	45,000	69,000
D	40	180,000	184,000
Total	100%	$450,000	$460,000

Required Use four or more decimal places (e.g., 33.3333%) in your calculations.
1. As a first step in moving to the outsourcing approach, McKeoun is considering an allocation based on the price of the outside maintenance supplier for each department. Calculate the cost allocations on this basis and compare them to the current direct labor hours basis.
2. If McKeoun follows the proposed plan, what is likely to happen to the use of internally provided maintenance compared to externally provided maintenance? How will each department manager be motivated to increase or decrease the use of maintenance? What will be the overall effect of going to the new plan?

[LO 7-3, 7-5] **7-37 Departmental Cost Allocation** Barfield Corporation prepares business plans and marketing analyses for start-up companies in the Cleveland area. Barfield has been very successful in recent years in providing effective service to a growing number of clients. The company provides its service from a single office building in Cleveland and is organized into two main client-service groups: one for market research and the other for financial analysis. The two groups have budgeted annual costs of $1,250,000 and $1,750,000, respectively. In addition, Barfield has a support staff that is organized into two main functions: one for clerical, facilities, and logistical support (called the CFL group) and another for computer-related support. The CFL group has budgeted annual costs of $210,000, while the annual costs of the computer group are $600,000.

Tom Brady, CFO of Barfield, plans to prepare a departmental cost allocation for his four groups, and he assembles the following information:

Percentage of estimated dollars of work and time by CFL group:

> 10%—service to the computer group
> 15%—service to market research
> 75%—service to financial analysis

Percentage of estimated dollars of work and time by the computer group:

> 20%—service to the CFL group
> 40%—service to market research
> 40%—service to financial analysis

Required   Use four decimal places (e.g., 33.3333%) in your calculations. Determine the total cost in the financial analysis and market research groups, after departmental allocation, using (a) the direct method, (b) the step method when the sourcing department that provides the greatest percentage of services to other service departments goes first, and (c) the reciprocal method.

[LO 7-3]   7-38 **Departmental Cost Allocation** Solexx Corporation allocates its service department overhead costs to producing departments. This information is for the month of June:

	Service Departments	
	Maintenance	**Utilities**
Overhead costs incurred	$115,000	$65,000
Service provided to departments		
Maintenance	—	15%
Utilities	25%	—
Producing—A	25	40
Producing—B	50	45
Totals	100%	100%

Required   Use four decimal places (e.g., 33.3333%) in your calculations. What is the amount of maintenance and utilities department costs distributed to producing departments A and B for June using (1) the direct method, (2) the step method (maintenance department first), and (3) the reciprocal method?

[LO 7-3, 7-4, 7-5]   7-39 **Departmental Cost Allocation** Data Performance, a computer software consulting company, has three major functional areas: computer programming, information systems consulting, and software training. Carol Bingham, a pricing analyst, has been asked to develop total costs for the functional areas. These costs will be used as a guide in pricing a new contract. In computing these costs, Carol is considering three different methods of the departmental allocation approach to allocate overhead costs: the direct method, the step method, and the reciprocal method. She assembled the following data from the two service departments, information systems and facilities:

	Service Departments		Production Departments			
	Information Systems	**Facilities**	**Computer Programming**	**Information Systems Consulting**	**Software Training**	**Total**
Budgeted overhead (base)	$80,000	$40,000	$160,000	$190,000	$125,000	$595,000
Information Systems (computer hours)		600	1,200	300	900	3,000
Facilities (square feet)	240		960	600	600	2,400

Required   Use four decimal places (e.g., 33.3333%) in your calculations.

1. Using computer usage time as the allocation base for the information systems department and square feet of floor space as the application base for the facilities department, apply overhead from these service departments to the production departments, using these three methods:

    a. Direct method.

    b. Step method (both for the information systems department going first and for the facilities department going first).

    c. Reciprocal method.

2. Rather than allocate costs based on computer and floor space usage, how might Data Performance better assign the information systems department's costs?

(CMA Adapted)

[LO 7-3, 7-5]

7-40 Departmental Cost Allocation; Not-for-Profit The Fleming Foundation is a charitable organization founded by Gaylord Fleming and Sandy Fleming. The Flemings intended for the charity to provide programs in health care for older persons, particularly those in poverty. The two main program divisions of the foundation are mental health and housing for elderly individuals. In addition to these programs, the foundation also provides health care educational programs and has a significant fund-raising effort to help the foundation grow and accomplish the goals of the founders. The foundation is organized into two operating departments—education and program management. These departments are supported by two service departments—information technology (IT) and administration. To summarize, there are four departments (two service departments and two operating departments) and two programs (mental health and housing for older adults). The service department costs are allocated to the operating departments, and then the operating department costs are allocated to the programs.

There are $512,000 of costs directly traceable to each of the four departments. An additional $65,000 of indirect costs is shared among the four departments—$50,000 of which is allocated to the departments based on labor hours and $15,000 of which is allocated to the departments based on the number of personnel (head count) in the departments.

The cost, labor hours, and head count in these departments in the most recent year are as follows:

Departments	Direct Cost	Labor Hours	Head Count
Information technology	$100,000	2,000	2
Administration	122,000	6,000	3
Education	100,000	4,000	3
Program management	190,000	4,000	4
	$512,000		

IT serves education, administration, and program management 20%, 20%, and 60% of its time, respectively. Administration serves education, IT, and program management 30%, 10%, and 60% of its time, respectively.

The costs of the two operating departments (education and program management) are allocated to the two programs (mental health and housing) as follows: The costs in Education are allocated on the basis of labor hours in the programs, while the costs in program management are allocated using the head count used in the two programs. The following table shows the labor hours and head count consumption by the two programs:

	Labor Hours	Head Count
Mental health	2,000	1
Housing	2,000	3
Labor hours in education	4,000	
Head count in program management		4

Required   Use four decimal places (e.g., 33.3333%) in your calculations. Determine the costs allocated to the mental health and housing programs using the (a) direct method, (b) the step method (assuming that IT goes first), and (c) the reciprocal method.

[LO 7-3, 7-5]

7-41 Departmental Cost Allocation; Service Company Comprehensive Insurance Company has two product lines: health insurance and auto insurance. The two product lines are served by three operating departments, which are necessary for providing the two types of products: claims processing, administration, and sales. These three operating departments are supported by two departments:

information technology and operations. The support provided by information technology and operations to the other departments is shown below:

	Support Departments		Operating Departments		
	Information Technology	Operations	Claims Processing	Administration	Sales
Information technology	—	20%	20%	40%	20%
Operations	10%	—	10	50	30

The total costs incurred in the five departments are:

Information technology	$ 600,000
Operations	1,800,000
Claims processing	450,000
Administration	850,000
Sales	650,000
Total costs	$4,350,000

Required   Use four decimal places (e.g., 33.3333%) in your calculations. Determine the total costs in each of the three operating departments, after departmental allocations, using (a) the direct method, (b) the step method (first for information technology going first in the allocation and then for operations going first), and (c) the reciprocal method.

[LO 7-6]   **7-42 Joint Products** Choi Company manufactures two skin care lotions, Smooth Skin and Silken Skin, from a joint process. The joint costs incurred are $420,000 for a standard production run that generates 180,000 pints of Smooth Skin and 120,000 pints of Silken Skin. Smooth Skin sells for $2.40 per pint, while Silken Skin sells for $3.90 per pint.

Required
1. Assuming that both products are sold at the split-off point, how much of the joint cost of each production run is allocated to Smooth Skin using the relative sales value method?
2. If no separable costs are incurred after the split-off point, how much of the joint cost of each production run is allocated to Silken Skin using the physical measure method?
3. If separable processing costs beyond the split-off point are $1.40 per pint for Smooth Skin and $0.90 per pint for Silken Skin, how much of the joint cost of each production run is allocated to Silken Skin using a net realizable value method?
4. If separable processing costs beyond the split-off point are $1.40 per pint for Smooth Skin and $0.90 per pint for Silken Skin, how much of the joint cost of each production run is allocated to Smooth Skin using a physical measure method?
   (CMA Adapted)

[LO 7-6]   **7-43 Joint Products** Northwest Building Products (NBP) manufactures two lumber products from a joint milling process: residential building lumber (RBL) and commercial building lumber (CBL). A standard production run incurs joint costs of $450,000 and results in 80,000 units of RBL and 120,000 units of CBL. Each RBL sells for $10 per unit and each CBL sells for $12 per unit.

Required
1. Assuming that no further processing occurs after the split-off point, how much of the joint costs are allocated to commercial lumber (CBL) on a physical measure method basis?
2. If no further processing occurs after the split-off point, how much of the joint cost is allocated to the residential lumber (RBL) using a sales value at split-off method?
3. Assume that the CBL is not marketable at split-off but must be planed and sized at a cost of $300,000 per production run. During this process, 10,000 units are unavoidably lost and have no value. The remaining units of CBL are salable at $14 per unit. The RBL, although salable immediately at the split-off point, is coated with a tarlike preservative that costs $200,000 per production run. The RBL is then sold for $12 each. Using the net realizable value basis, how much of the completion costs should be assigned to each unit of CBL?

4. Based on information in requirement 3, should NBP choose to process RBL beyond split-off?

   a. Yes because it can charge a higher price for the residential lumber after the additional processing.

   b. Yes because total revenue for the residential lumber exceeds the incremental cost of the additional processing.

   c. No because the increase in sales revenue is less than the extra processing costs.

   d. No because additional processing results in an unavoidable loss of 10,000 units of CBL.

   (CMA Adapted)

[LO 7-6]   7-44 **Joint Products** The Bean Company provides fresh coffee beans for restaurants, hotels, and other food service companies. Bean offers three types of coffee beans: Premium, Gourmet, and Quality. Each of the three coffees is produced in a joint process in which beans are cleaned and sorted. The sorting process is the split-off point in this joint process, and the output is the three types of beans. The beans can be sold at the split-off point or processed further, with different types of roasting and additional sorting. The additional processing requires additional, separable processing costs, as shown next. Separable processing requires no special facilities, and the production costs of further processing are entirely variable and traceable to the products involved. Last year all three products were processed beyond split-off. Joint production costs for the year were $90,000,000. Sales values and costs needed to evaluate Bean's production policy follow:

	Premium	Gourmet	Quality	Total
Pounds produced	10,000,000	12,000,000	2,000,000	24,000,000
Separable processing cost	$9,000,000	$7,000,000	$5,000,000	$21,000,000
Pounds sold	10,000,000	12,000,000	2,000,000	24,000,000
Total joint cost				$90,000,000
Sales price/pound (after additional processing)	$7.00	5.00	$2.00	
Sales price at split-off	5.00	4.00	1.00	

Required

1. Determine last year's unit cost and unit gross profit for each product assuming Bean allocates joint production costs using the physical measure method.

2. Determine unit cost and unit gross profit for each product if Bean allocates joint costs using the sales value at split-off method.

3. Which of Bean's products should be processed further?

	Process further?		
	Premium	Gourmet	Quality
a.	Yes	Yes	Yes
b.	Yes	Yes	No
c.	No	No	Yes
d.	No	No	No

[LO 7-6]   7-45 **Joint Products** Johnston Adhesives Company makes three widely used industrial adhesives: A101, A204, and B216. Sales and production information for each of the three adhesives are shown in the following table. Most of Johnston's customers ask for a special blend of the three products, which improves heat-resistance. The additional separable processing requires additional time and materials, and the price is increased accordingly, as shown in the table. Assume that Johnston produces only for specific customer orders, so there is no beginning or ending inventory. Assume also that all of Johnston's customers requested the heat-resistant version of the products so that all production required additional separable processing. Total joint cost for the three products is $3,500,000.

	A101	A204	B216
Gallons sold	175,000	135,000	115,000
Final sales price per gallon	$ 14	$ 10	$ 12
Price at split-off	10	5	10
Separable processing cost	$550,000	$125,000	$625,000

Required

1. Using four decimal points in your computations, calculate the unit product cost and total gross margin for each of the three product lines using the following methods: (a) physical measure method, (b) sales value at split-off method, (c) the net realizable value method, and (d) the constant gross margin percentage method.

2. Which of the four methods listed in requirement 1 do you think would be preferred in this case? Why?

[LO 7-6, 7-7]   7-46 **Joint Products; By-Products (Appendix)** Multiproduct Corporation is a chemical manufacturer that produces two main products (Pepco–1 and Repke–3) and a by-product (SE–5) from a joint process. If Multiproduct had the proper facilities, it could process SE-5 further into a main product. The ratio of output quantities to input quantity of direct materials used in the joint process remains consistent with the processing conditions and activity level.

Multiproduct currently uses the physical measure method of allocating joint costs to the main products. The by-product is inventoried at its net realizable value, which is used to reduce the joint production costs before they are allocated to the main products.

Jim Simpson, Multiproduct's controller, wants to implement the sales value at split-off method of joint cost allocation. He believes that inventory costs should be based on each product's ability to contribute to the recovery of joint production costs. Multiproduct uses an asset recognition approach in accounting for by-products.

Data regarding Multiproduct's operations for November are presented in the following report. The joint costs of production totaled $2,640,000 for November.

	Main Products		
	Pepco–1	**Repke–3**	**By-ProductSE–5**
November sales in gallons	800,000	700,000	200,000
November production in gallons	900,000	720,000	240,000
Sales price per gallon at split-off point	$2.00	$1.50	$0.55*
Separable costs after split-off	$1,000,000	$420,000	—
Final sales price per gallon	$5.00	$4.00	—

*****Selling costs of 5 cents per gallon are incurred to sell the by-product.**

Required

1. Describe the sales value at split-off method and explain how it would accomplish Jim's objective.

2. Assuming Multiproduct adopts the sales value at split-off method for internal reporting purposes, calculate the allocation of the joint production costs for November.

3. Multiproduct plans to expand its production facilities to further process SE-5 into a main product. Determine the allocation of the joint production costs for November if SE-5 were considered a main product rather than a by-product.

(CMA Adapted)

[LO 7-2, 7-6, 7-7]   7-47 **Joint Products; By-Products (Appendix)** Quality Chemical manufactures three chemicals for industrial and retail customers. The largest-volume product, S-210, is a sweetener used in the preparation of processed foods; the second, H-35, is used in the manufacture of commercial and household cleaning agents; and the third, J-23, is a by-product that can be used in the manufacture of pesticides. The by-product is inventoried at its net realizable value, which is used to reduce the joint production costs before they are allocated to the main products using the net realizable value method. Data regarding Quality Chemical's operations for the month of July follow. During this month, Quality Chemical incurred joint production costs of $1,400,000 in the manufacture of its three products.

	S-210	H-35	J-23	Total
July sales in gallons	600,000	225,000	20,000	845,000
July production in gallons	660,000	225,000	30,000	915,000
Sales price per gallon at split-off	$ 3.25	$ 4.00	$ 0.70	
Separable processing costs	$1,233,000	$525,000		
Sales price per gallon after separable processing	$ 5.85	$ 6.25	$ —	

Required

1. Determine Quality Chemical's allocation of joint production costs and the total manufacturing costs for each product for the month of July. Be sure to present appropriate supporting calculations.

2. Prepare an analysis showing what happens if H-35 is processed further.

   a. What is profit or loss per gallon after further processing?

   b. Based on the results of part (a), should Quality Chemical sell H-35 at the split-off point or process it further?

3. As a production supervisor for Quality Chemical, you have learned that small quantities of the critical chemical compound in J-23 might be present in S-210. What should you do?

   (CMA Adapted)

[LO 7-6, 7-7]   7-48 **Joint Products; By-Products (Appendix)** The Marshall Company has a joint production process that produces two joint products and a by-product. The joint products are Ying and Yang, and the by-product is Bit. Marshall accounts for the costs of its products using the net realizable value method. The two joint products are processed beyond the split-off point, incurring separable processing costs. There is a $1,000 disposal cost for the by-product. A summary of a recent month's activity at Marshall is shown below:

	Ying	Yang	Bit
Units sold	50,000	40,000	10,000
Units produced	50,000	40,000	10,000
Separable processing costs—variable	$140,000	$42,000	$ —
Separable processing costs—fixed	$ 10,000	$ 8,000	$ —
Sales price	$ 6.00	$ 12.50	$ 1.60

Total joint costs for Marshall in the recent month are $265,000, of which $115,000 is a variable cost.

Required

1. Calculate the manufacturing cost per unit for each of the three products.

2. Calculate the total gross margin for each product.

[LO 7-1, 7-6]   7-49 **Joint Products** Yonica Petroleum is a global manufacturer of specialty chemicals that are made from the waste products of the petroleum industry. Yonica in effect recycles a good portion of the waste from the refineries used by large oil companies. The specialty chemicals are used as cleaning solvents and lubricants in industrial applications. Yonica has three products—Y64, G22, and X17—and total joint production costs of $356,000. Yonica plans to process all three products beyond the split-off point in order to be able to sell the products at the higher price after separable processing.

	Y64	G22	X17
Gallons produced and sold	22,000	45,500	18,000
Sales price at split-off point	$ 2.24	$ 2.88	$ 0.44
Separable processing costs	$65,500	$34,250	$55,400
Sales price after separable processing	$ 10.50	$ 6.75	$ 4.22
Number of customers	22	3	46

Required

1. Calculate the product cost of each of the three products using the following methods: (a) physical measure method, (b) sales value at split-off method, and (c) net realizable value method.

2. Which of the three methods listed in requirement 1 do you think would be preferred in this case? Why?

3. While Yonica chose to process all three products beyond the split-off point, do you think this is the correct decision? Which products, if any, do you think should have been processed beyond the split-off point, and why?

4. Because Yonica is involved in the recycling of waste chemicals, it is able to purchase its materials at greatly reduced cost. However, its manufacturing costs are slightly higher than some of its competitors because of the relatively high cost of recycling. Yonica plans to bring these recycling costs down in the next 18 months. Yonica has been able to compete successfully by maintaining lower margins than its competitors and because some of its customers are willing to pay more for a product that has been manufactured from recycled material. Comment on Yonica's strategy and whether you think it will continue to be successful.

5. What are some of the global issues that Yonica should consider in effectively executing its strategy?

6. What should Yonica do, if anything, to improve the overall effect of its operations on the environment?

[LO 7-2, 7-4, 7-6]   7-50   **Joint Cost Allocation: Managerial Incentives** Cameron Manufacturing produces auto parts for auto manufacturers and parts wholesalers. The business is very competitive, and productivity measures are used throughout its eight manufacturing plants. Jill Owens, the manufacturing vice president, explains to her plant managers the importance of reducing cycle time, improving throughput, and reducing waste. One type of waste she keeps close track of is waste due to accidents and injuries on the job. Jill believes that a safe workplace also contributes to productivity. A reduction in accidents and injuries can also lead to a reduction in the insurance the firm pays to cover its liability in these incidents. The premium for this insurance coverage is a single policy and is a joint cost shared by all eight plants. One of the plant managers, Mike Griffin, notes that the current procedure for allocating the cost of insurance, which is based on total plant output, does not provide plant managers with the desired incentive to reduce accidents. It just means that the larger plants get charged more. Mike suggests that the insurance cost should be charged to the plants based on the number of manufacturing personnel in each plant.

Required   What do you think of Mike's suggestion? What alternative would you suggest, if any, for allocating the cost of insurance to the plants?

Solution to Self-Study Problem

Joint Product Costing

(1) The Physical Measure Method If we use a physical measure method, the joint cost of $20,000 is allocated as shown in Exhibit 1.

The production costs per gallon for both products are the same:

$$\text{Product GS-50: } \$15,000 \div 75 = \$200$$
$$\text{Product GS-80: } \$5,000 \div 25 = \$200$$

EXHIBIT 1
Physical Measure Method

Product	Physical Measure	Proportion	Allocation of Joint Cost
GS-50	75 gallons	75%	$20,000 × 75% = $15,000
GS-80	25 gallons	25	20,000 × 25% = 5,000
	100 gallons	100%	$20,000

(2) The Sales Value at Split-Off Method If Northern Company could sell the GS-50 and GS-80 at the split-off point, then the $20,000 joint cost should be allocated among the products as shown in Exhibit 2.

EXHIBIT 2
Sales Value at Split-Off Method

Product	Units	Price	Sales Value	Proportion	Allocation of Joint Cost
GS-50	75	$300	$22,500	93.75%	$20,000 × 93.75% = $18,750
GS-80	25	60	1,500	6.25	20,000 × 6.25% = 1,250
Total			$24,000	100%	$20,000

Note that whether or not any of the gallons are sold at the split-off point is irrelevant, as the allocation is based on units produced. The production costs per gallon for both products are calculated as follows:

$$\text{Product GS-50: } \$18,750 \div 75 = \$250$$
$$\text{Product GS-80: } \$1,250 \div 25 = \$50$$

(3) The Net Realizable Value Method The net realizable values of GS-50 and GS-80 are $20,000 and $5,000, respectively, as shown in Exhibit 3. The allocated costs are $16,000 to GS-50 and $4,000 to GS-80.

EXHIBIT 3   Net Realizable Value Method

Product	Units	Price	Sales Value	Separable Processing	Net Realizable Value	Percent of NRV	Allocation of Joint Cost
GS-50	50	$500	$25,000	$5,000	$20,000	80%	$20,000 × 80% = $16,000
GS-80	50	140	7,000	2,000	5,000	20	20,000 × 20% = 4,000
Total	100		$32,000	$7,000	$25,000	100%	$20,000

The costs per gallon for products GS-505 and GS-805 are calculated as follows:

$$\text{Product GS-505: } (\$16,000 + \$5,000) \div 50 = \$420$$
$$\text{Product GS-805: } (\$4,000 + \$2,000) \div 50 = \$120$$

Please visit Connect to access a narrated, animated tutorial for solving this problem.

PART TWO

Planning and Decision Making

The objective of these six chapters is to show how cost management information can be used strategically to support management planning and decision making. A key idea that ties these chapters together is that planning and decision making require a good understanding of cost drivers—that is, the activities or transactions that cause changes in costs—both from a short-term and a long-term perspective. There are both volume-based cost drivers (explained in Chapter 4) and activity-based cost drivers (explained in Chapter 5); both types of cost drivers are important in planning and decision making.

Because of this importance, the first chapter in this part, Chapter 8, is about cost estimation—how cost estimation equations are used to predict costs using cost drivers. We cover both statistical and nonstatistical approaches to cost estimation equations. This foundational material is followed by a discussion of a short-run profit-planning tool, cost-volume-profit analysis, in Chapter 9.

Chapter 10 explains the master budget, which is one of the key planning tools that management accountants develop for their organizations. The master budget is often referred to as the most commonly used tool in management accounting for coordinating operations and for providing a set of financial targets to guide management. In Chapter 10, linkages are made to topics covered earlier in the text—for example, budgeting for sustainability, preparation of activity-based budgets, and the impact of time-based activity-based costing on budgeting systems.

Chapter 11 shows how the management accountant uses cost calculations and a strategic understanding of the competitive context of an organization to address decisions such as whether to make or buy a component of a manufactured product or service, when to add features to a product, and when to accept one-time orders from customers. In each of these decisions, competitive context is crucial. For example, suppose that a company competes on the basis of *cost leadership* and is looking for ways to reduce manufacturing costs. The management accountant determines that it is cheaper to make rather than buy a part in the product; independently, the plant engineer figures out how to do away with the part while retaining the product's functionality. This accountant's analysis is flawed because it does not consider that the company can become more competitive by a redesign of the product.

Chapter 12 covers the topic of allocating capital (funds) to long-term projects—that is, those investments that require substantial amounts of capital and that provide financial returns over an extended period of time. As such, we extend the framework covered in Chapter 11 to include the analysis of decisions that have a long-term effect on the organization. The tools for decision making in this context incorporate the time value of money and are called *discounted cash flow (DCF)* decision models. The chapter shows how to deal with uncertainty in capital budgeting, including the use of a real options approach.

Chapter 13 applies the concepts of the value chain and life-cycle analysis as cost-planning and cost-reduction tools. The value chain begins with the idea for a product or service; this is followed by market research, testing sample products, manufacturing, and, finally, sales and customer service. The chapter comprises four main parts: target costing at the front end of the value chain, the theory of constraints for the operational portion of the value chain, life-cycle costing for the full value chain, and strategic pricing.

Cost Estimation

> "You can't connect the dots looking forward; you can only connect them looking backward. So you have to trust that the dots will somehow connect in your future."
>
> *Steve Jobs*

Steve Jobs seems to be telling us that we have to look to the past to try to plan for the future, and his quote relates directly to the process of cost estimation. Cost estimation information is critical in cost planning and decision making—for example, planning a new product or plant expansion, analyzing product or customer profitability, or developing a new manufacturing and marketing strategy. One of the best ways to estimate costs is based upon historical data and past experience.

SimplyDay/Shutterstock

While companies have access to increasingly large data sets, those data must be analyzed to reveal patterns, trends, and associations. A basic requirement for cost-effective planning is to create *accurate cost estimates,* but this requirement is just the beginning. The ability to interpret the results of an estimate, to understand the underlying assumptions and limitations of a chosen estimation method, and to make recommendations based on the estimates are all critical to the planning process. This chapter not only describes methods that can be used to develop accurate estimates, it also addresses the benefits and limitations of those methods.

An example where cost estimation is particularly important is the construction industry. Large construction projects are often obtained on the basis of competitive bids. The contractors who bid on these projects must have accurate cost estimation methods to win their share of the bids and to be profitable. Cost estimation methods for contractors develop detailed analyses of the material and labor costs that are directly traceable to the project, as well as projections of the indirect costs, preferably using activity analysis as described in Chapter 5. Fluctuations in the global markets may make the cost of construction materials and other commodities used in the construction process difficult to estimate, but failure to properly estimate costs can have significant implications. For example, Westinghouse Electric Company declared bankruptcy in 2017 due, in part, to cost overruns.

Strategic Role of Cost Estimation

LO 8-1

Explain the strategic role of cost estimation.

> We first survey the plot, then draw the model;
> And when we see the figure of the house,
> Then we must rate the cost of the erection;
> Which, if we find outweighs ability,
> What do we then but draw anew the model.
>
> **—William Shakespeare,** Henry IV, part 2, act 1

As Shakespeare understood, a critical starting point for strategic management is having accurate cost estimates. The strategic approach is forward looking, and thus cost estimation is an essential element of it. **Cost estimation** is the development of a well-defined relationship between a cost object and its cost drivers for the purpose of predicting the cost.

cost estimation

The development of a well-defined relationship between a cost object and its cost drivers for the purpose of predicting the cost.

Cost estimation facilitates strategic management in three important ways. First, it helps predict future costs using previously identified activity-based, volume-based, structural, and executional cost drivers. Second, cost estimation helps identify the key cost drivers for a cost object. Third, the cost drivers and cost-estimating relationships are useful in planning and decision making; these are the two key topics of this part of the text.

Using Cost Estimation to Predict Future Costs

Strategic management requires accurate cost estimates for many applications, including these:

1. **To facilitate strategy development and implementation.** Cost estimates are particularly important for firms competing on the basis of cost leadership. Cost estimates guide management in determining which management techniques the firm should employ to succeed in its chosen strategy. Recent surveys of chief financial officers indicated that forecasting skills like cost estimation are essential to a company's success.[1] With the economic disruption of COVID-19 that began in March 2020, it is especially important for management accountants to understand and to apply effective forecasting techniques—for projecting sales, interest rates, and operational data—to refine and perhaps provide a means for change in the organization's strategy.

2. **To facilitate planning and decision making.** Cost estimates provide a critically important input for effective planning and decision making. Cost management's role in planning and decision making is covered in Chapters 9, 10, 11, and 12.

3. **To facilitate target costing and pricing.** Cost estimates are an integral part of target costing and pricing. Management uses cost estimates of different product designs as part of

---

[1] Ramona Dzinkowski, "Greater Challenges for CFOs in 2019," *Strategic Finance,* February 2019; "Topping the CFO's Agenda: Security, Analytics and Customer Service," *Protiviti,* https://www.protiviti.com/US-en/insights/finance-priorities-survey (accessed January 10, 2020). See also "CFOs Respond to the COVID-19 Pandemic," Daniel Butcher, *Strategic Finance,* May 2020.

REAL-WORLD FOCUS   A Changing Cost Structure at Amazon

You've probably all heard of the company Amazon. The company is certainly well known for quick delivery of orders and the attractiveness of its Amazon Prime membership program, which offers free 2-day shipping. But what does it take for an online retailer to make such quick deliveries?

Well, in October 2016 it was reported that opening new warehouses is one of Amazon's secrets, but expansion comes at a cost. They opened 23 warehouses in the third quarter of the year, after opening only three in the first six months of the year. Also, shipping costs in total went up 43% in the third quarter of 2016. Amazon is leasing planes to carry the goods and buying truck and trailers to build out its own logistics operation. Its operating margin for the quarter was a mere 1.8%.

If all Amazon sold was digital content, then warehouses, planes, and trucks wouldn't be necessary. However, they sell quite a few tangible goods, and those items must be stored and shipped. Amazon could contract with such organizations as FedEx or UPS to handle the deliveries, but they have decided to start to perform much of the delivery function themselves. These strategic decisions impact the cost structure of an organization, and create a need to be able to understand the underlying cost structure to remain competitive.

Source: Laura Stevens, "Amazon Takes Hit as Costs Surge—Results Disappoint as Retail Giant Invests Heavily on Warehouses, Trimming Delivery Times," *The Wall Street Journal*, Eastern edition, October 28, 2016, p. B1.

the process of selecting the particular design that provides the best value to the customer while reducing manufacturing and other costs. Target costing and pricing are covered in Chapter 13.

4. **To facilitate effective performance measurement, evaluation, and compensation.** Cost estimates play a key role in determining costs in business units, which affect division managers' financial performance and opportunity for promotion and compensation and the ability to attract capital investment to their divisions. Accurate cost estimates play a crucial role in performance measurement, which is covered in Chapters 14, 15, 16, 17, 18, 19, and 20.

Cost Estimation for Different Types of Cost Drivers

The cost estimation methods explained in this chapter can be used for any of the four types of cost drivers: activity-based, volume-based, structural, and executional. The relationships between costs and activity-based or volume-based cost drivers often are best fit by the linear cost estimation methods explained in this chapter because these relationships are at least approximately linear within the relevant range of the firm's operations.

Structural cost drivers involve plans and decisions that have a long-term and, therefore, strategic impact on the firm. Such decisions include manufacturing experience, scale and scope of product offering, product or production technology, and product or production complexity. Technology and complexity issues often lead management to use activity-based costing and linear estimation methods. In contrast, experience and scale often require nonlinear methods. As a cost driver, experience represents the reduction in unit cost due to learning. The effect on total costs of experience is nonlinear; that is, costs decrease with increased manufacturing experience. The learning effect is explained in the appendix to the chapter. Similarly, the relationship among the structural cost driver, scale, and total cost is nonlinear. The scale of the product offering refers to the quantity of similar goods manufactured, while the scope refers to the variety of products offered. Cost could increase more or less rapidly than the increase in the volume of the product produced. For example, the manufacture of 2,000 units could be less than twice the cost of producing 1,000 of the same type units. However, when referring to scope, a 22-inch industrial valve may require more than twice the cost of an 11-inch valve.

Using Cost Estimation to Identify Cost Drivers

Often the most practical way to identify cost drivers is to rely on the judgment of product designers, engineers, and manufacturing personnel. Those who are most knowledgeable about the product and production processes have the most useful information on cost drivers. Cost estimation sometimes plays a discovery role and at other times a collaborative role to validate and confirm the judgments of the designers and engineers. For example, Hewlett-Packard uses cost estimation to confirm the usefulness of cost drivers selected by teams of engineers and production personnel.

Six Steps of Cost Estimation

The six steps of cost estimation are (1) define the cost object for which the related costs are to be estimated, (2) determine the cost drivers, (3) collect consistent and accurate data on the cost object and the cost drivers, (4) graph the data, (5) select and employ an appropriate estimation method, and (6) evaluate the accuracy of the cost estimate.

Step 1: Define the Cost Object

Although it might seem elementary, defining the particular cost to be estimated requires care. For example, if the goal is to estimate product costs to improve product pricing, the relevant cost objects are the products manufactured in the plant. In contrast, if the goal is to reward managers for reducing cost, the most appropriate cost objects are the individual manufacturing departments in the plant because costs are most directly controllable by department managers.

Step 2: Determine the Cost Drivers

Cost drivers are the causal factors used in the estimation of the cost. Some examples of estimated costs and their related cost drivers follow:

Cost to Be Estimated	Cost Driver
Fuel expense for a delivery truck	Miles driven
Heating expense for a building	Temperature outside the building
Maintenance cost in a manufacturing plant	Machine hours, direct labor hours
Product design cost	Number of design elements, design changes

Identifying cost drivers is the most important step in developing the cost estimate. A number of relevant drivers might exist, yet some might not be immediately obvious. Fuel expense for a large delivery truck, for example, might be primarily a function of miles traveled, but it is also affected by the average weight delivered, the number of hours of operation, and the delivery area's terrain.

Step 3: Collect Consistent and Accurate Data

Once the cost drivers have been selected, the next logical step is collecting data on the cost object and cost drivers. The data must be consistent and accurate. *Consistent* means that each period of data is calculated using the same accounting basis (e.g., all periods use accrual accounting rather than cash-basis accounting) and all transactions are properly recorded in the period in which they occurred. For example, using biweekly data for some variables and monthly data for other variables causes errors in estimates. Similarly, mismatch between periods occurs when data for one variable are based on the calendar month while data for another variable are based on four consecutive weekly periods that do not match the calendar month. Difficulties also arise when supplies purchased during the month are used instead of supplies consumed.

The period used in cost estimation can vary from daily to weekly or annually. If the period is too short, the chance of mismatch between variables increases because of recording lags. On the other hand, if the period is too long, important short-term relationships in the data might be averaged out, and the estimate will not be as accurate. Moreover, a longer period reduces the number of data points available to improve the accuracy of the estimate. Management accountants must use business judgment to decide which time period best satisfies the objective of accurate estimation.

The accuracy of the data also depends on the source. Sometimes data developed within the firm are very reliable, as a result of management policies and procedures to ensure accuracy. External sources of data, including governmental sources, trade and industry publications, and other sources, have varying degrees of accuracy. The choice of cost drivers requires trade-offs between the relevance of the drivers and the consistency and accuracy of the data.

Step 4: Graph the Data

The objective of graphing data is to identify unusual patterns. The existence of outliers and any shift or nonlinearity in the data must be given special attention in developing the

REAL-WORLD FOCUS   Variable Costs in the Airline Industry

Estimating cost behavior can be quite a challenge. Take the airline industry is an example. There is no question that the more miles a plane flies, the more fuel it will use. In fact, a graph of miles flown versus gallons consumed would be an upward-sloping line that resembles the traditional graph of variable cost. However, the relationship between miles flown and total cost of fuel may not be anywhere close to a straight line. The underlying problem is a fluctuation in the cost per barrel of fuel.

One way to exercise some control over the total cost of fuel consumed would be through the use of fuel hedging, but

following the start of COVID-19 in March 2020 the focus of forecasting for the airlines has shifted from cost efficiency to survival. The airlines now forecast the amount and location of air traffic going forward, in order to properly manage employment decisions and aircraft readiness.

Source: Doug Cameron and Alison Sider, "Airlines Raise Ticket Prices as Fuel Costs Surge," The *Wall Street Journal,* June 7, 2018, p. A1; "Airline Unions Seek Another $32 Billion Coronavirus Bailout," *New York Post* June 26, 2020; https://nypost.com/2020/06/26/airline-unions-seek-another-32b-coronavirus-bailout/, accessed June 27, 2020.

estimate. For example, downtime to install new equipment can cause unusual production data for that week; such data should probably be excluded when developing a cost estimate for periods without equipment installations. Any unusual occurrences can be detected by studying a graph.

Step 5: Select and Employ the Estimation Method

The high-low method and regression analysis, the two estimation methods presented in the next section of the chapter, differ in their ability to provide superior accuracy in cost estimation. The management accountant chooses the method with the best accuracy/cost trade-off for the estimation objectives.

Step 6: Assess the Accuracy of the Cost Estimate

A critical final step in cost estimation is to consider the potential for error when the estimate is prepared. This involves considering the completeness and appropriateness of cost drivers selected in step 2, the consistency and accuracy of data selected in step 3, the study of the graphs in step 4, and the precision of the method selected in step 5.

A common approach for assessing the accuracy of an estimation method is to compare the estimates to the actual results over time. For example, suppose that a company predicts annual overhead costs each year. At the end of the year, it is then possible to calculate an estimation error, which is the difference between the estimated value and the actual value. Over time, these errors are collected and evaluated. One measure of cost estimation accuracy is the **mean absolute percentage error (MAPE).** MAPE is calculated by taking the absolute value of each error and then averaging those errors. Another way to assess accuracy is to use the statistical measures produced by regression analysis, as explained next.

mean absolute percentage error (MAPE)
A measure of cost-estimation accuracy, calculated as the mean (average) absolute percentage prediction error.

Cost Estimation Methods

The two estimation methods we will study in this chapter are the high-low method and regression analysis. The high-low method is the least accurate but is the easiest to understand and apply. Regression analysis is the most accurate but has greater computational complexity and requires more expertise to properly interpret the results. In choosing the best estimation method, management accountants seek a balance between the level of accuracy desired and any limitations on cost, time, effort, and expertise.

LO 8-3
Use the high-low and regression analysis methods of cost estimation.

An Illustration of Cost Estimation

To illustrate the two methods, we use the example of a management accountant, Julia Garcia, who is developing cost estimates of maintenance costs for a manufacturing plant. Garcia has the following data on maintenance costs:

	January	February	March	April	May	June	July
Maintenance costs ($)	22,843	22,510	22,706	23,032	22,413	22,935	23,175

To start, Garcia graphs the data (Exhibit 8.1) and observes that maintenance costs are increasing, although not steadily. Based only on a visual study of the graph, she also predicts that maintenance costs will be between $22,500 and $23,500 in the coming month, August. Because this prediction is rough and she wants to improve its accuracy, she turns to the cost estimation methods, beginning with the high-low method.

High-Low Method

high-low method
A method using algebra to determine a *unique* cost estimation line between representative high and low points in a given data set.

The **high-low method** uses algebra to determine a unique estimation line between representative high and low points in the data. The high-low method accomplishes two important objectives for Garcia. First, it is based on a unique cost line rather than a rough estimate based on a view of the graph. Second, it permits her to add information that might be useful in predicting maintenance costs. For example, she knows that total maintenance costs are likely to include both variable and fixed costs. The fixed-cost portion is the planned maintenance that is performed regardless of the plant's volume of activity. Also, a part of the maintenance costs varies with the number of operating hours; more operating hours mean more wear on the machines and thus more maintenance costs. She now wants to try to predict the total maintenance costs. After considering some possible cost drivers, Garcia collected the additional operating-hours information as follows:

	January	February	March	April	May	June	July
Total operating hours	3,451	3,325	3,383	3,615	3,423	3,410	3,500
Maintenance costs ($)	22,843	22,510	22,706	23,032	22,413	22,935	23,175

To use the high-low method, Garcia enters the data into a graph, as shown in Exhibit 8.2; note that operating hours (a measure of activity) are on the horizontal axis, and each data

EXHIBIT 8.1
Graph of Maintenance Costs

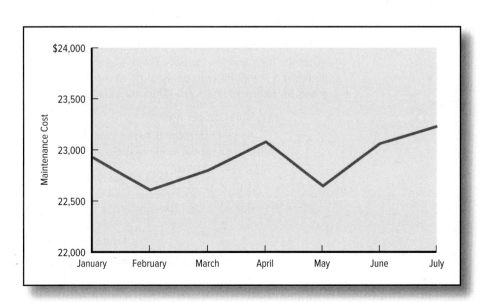

EXHIBIT 8.2
Julia Garcia's Data on Maintenance Cost and Hours

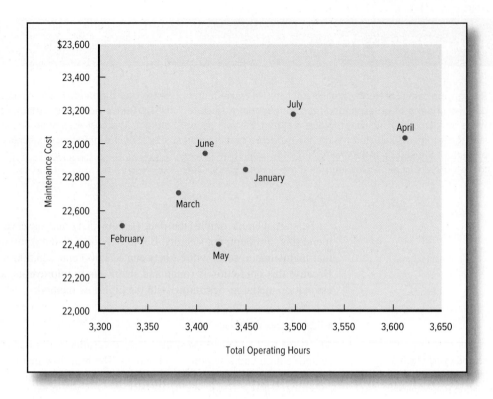

point is the location of the cost and the selected activity measure (operating hours) for a particular month. Julia then selects two points from the data, one representative of the lower activity points and the other representative of the higher activity points. Often these can be simply the lowest and highest points in the data. However, if either the highest or lowest point is not representative of the general relationship, a biased estimation can result. Both points must be representative of the data around them.

The high-low estimate is represented as follows:

$$Y = a + (b \times X)$$

where: Y = the value of the estimated maintenance cost

   a = the intercept, a fixed quantity that represents the value of Y when X = zero

   b = the slope of the line, an estimate of the unit variable cost per unit of activity on the X-axis

   X = the cost driver, the number of operating hours of operation for the plant

To obtain the high and low points, Garcia draws a freehand line through the data to help select the high and low activity points (try this yourself in Exhibit 8.2). She then chooses a high and a low point reasonably close to the freehand line. Suppose that she has chosen the points for February and April. Then she calculates the value for b as

   b = Variable cost per hour

   $$= \frac{\text{Difference between } \textit{costs} \text{ for high and low activity points}}{\text{Difference for the value of the } \textit{cost driver} \text{ for the high and low activity points}}$$

   $$b = \frac{\$23{,}032 - \$22{,}510}{3{,}615 - 3{,}325} = \$1.80 \text{ per hour}$$

Next, the value for a (the fixed quantity) can be calculated using either February or April data:

Using April Data

$$a = Y - (b \times X) = \$23{,}032 - (\$1.80 \times 3{,}615) = \$16{,}525$$

Using February data gives the same value for *a* because fixed costs are the same at both levels of operating hours; only total variable costs for the two levels differ:

Using February Data

$$a = Y - (b \times X) = \$22{,}510 - (\$1.80 \times 3{,}325) = \$16{,}525$$

So the estimation equation using the high-low method is

$$Y = \$16{,}525 + (\$1.80 \times X)$$

This equation can be used to estimate maintenance costs for August. Suppose that 3,600 operating hours are expected in August. Then maintenance costs are estimated as follows:

$$\text{Maintenance costs for August} = \$16{,}525 + (\$1.80 \times 3{,}600)$$
$$= \$23{,}005$$

Recall our discussion of the relevant range in Chapter 3. The data used to obtain the above cost equation were operating hours in the range of 3,325 to 3,615 hours, which is the relevant range for this equation. Thus, the management accountant is careful to rely only on predictions for which the operating hours fall between 3,325 and 3,615 hours. Because the operating hours for August (3,600 hours) fall in the relevant range, the estimate of $23,005 is useful.[2]

An additional consideration when using the the high-low method is the preparation and study of a graph of the data. Without the data graph, it would be difficult to determine whether the high and low points are representative of all the data points. The study of the data graph also ensures that if outliers and nonlinearity are present in the data, the management accountant will be able to identify them in the graph. (Outliers are explained in the discussion that follows; nonlinearity is explained in the final section of this chapter, titled "Implementation Problems: Nonlinearity.") The existence of outliers and nonlinearity can increase the difficulty of deriving an accurate prediction model. A study of the data graph is important for both the high-low and regression methods, but it may be the case that the analysis of the data graph is omitted by those using regression, presumably due to the additional information that comes from regression analysis without the study of the graph. For this reason, when considering a set of data with a potential outlier or other nonlinearity, a regression analysis that does not include the data graph could be inferior to any analysis that does include the data graph.

Regression Analysis

Regression analysis is a statistical method for obtaining the unique cost-estimating equation that best fits a set of data points. Regression analysis fits the data by *minimizing the sum of the squares* of the estimation errors. Each error is the distance measured from the regression line to one of the data points. Because regression analysis systematically minimizes the squared estimation errors in this way, it is sometimes called **least squares regression**. This approach is one reason regression analysis is regarded as more accurate than the high-low method.

Like the high-low method, regression analysis has two types of variables. The **dependent variable** is the cost to be estimated, which, in step 1 of the six-step process, is called the cost object.[3] The **independent variable** is the cost driver used to estimate the value of the dependent variable. Unlike the high-low method, regression analysis can include more than one independent variable in the analysis. When one independent variable is used, the analysis is called a **simple linear regression**. When two or more independent variables are used, it is called **multiple linear regression**.

---

regression analysis
A statistical method for obtaining the unique cost-estimating equation that best fits a set of data points.

least squares regression
A cost-estimation method in which the variable and fixed cost coefficients are found by minimizing the sum of the squares of the estimation errors.

dependent variable
In cost estimation, the cost to be estimated.

independent variable
A cost driver used to estimate the value of the dependent variable.

simple linear regression
Used to describe regression applications having a single independent variable.

multiple linear regression
Used to describe regression applications having two or more independent variables.

---

[2] The relevant range concept also requires caution in interpreting the value of *a*, $16,525, because this value applies when the operating hours are zero, a level far from the relevant range. Thus, while $16,525 is useful for predicting future costs (and the predicted cost of $23,005 is useful), one should not interpret $16,525 as the value of fixed cost.
[3] Although the dependent variable is a cost in most of the cases we consider, the dependent variable also could be a revenue or some other type of financial or operating data such as labor hours, cash flow, or a measure of product quality.

The regression equation has both an intercept and a slope term, much like the high-low method. In addition, the amount of the estimation error is included in the simple regression estimate, which is

$$Y = a + (b \times X) + e$$

where: Y = the amount of the *dependent variable*, the cost to be estimated

a = a *fixed quantity*, also called the intercept or constant term, which represents the amount of Y when $X = 0$

b = the *unit variable cost*, also called the *coefficient* of the independent variable, that is, the increase in Y (cost object) for each unit increase in X (cost driver)

X = the value for the *independent variable*, the cost driver for the cost to be estimated; there may be one or more cost drivers

e = the *estimation error*, which is the amount by which the regression prediction $(y = a + b \times X)$ differs from the data point

To illustrate the regression method, the following table and Exhibit 8.3A show three months of data on supplies expense and units of output. (To simplify the presentation, only three data points are used; applications of regression usually make use of many more data points.) The management accountant's task is to estimate supplies expense for month 4, in which the production level is expected to be 125 units.

Month	Supplies Expense (Y)	Units of Output (X)
1	$250	50 units
2	310	100
3	325	150
4	?	125

The regression for the data is determined by a statistical procedure that finds the unique line through the three data points that minimizes the sum of the squared error distances. The regression line (see Exhibit 8.3B) is[4]

$$Y = \$220 + \$0.75X$$

Thus, the estimated value for supplies expense in month 4 is

$$Y = \$220 + (\$0.75 \times 125) = \$313.75$$

Regression analysis gives management accountants an objective, statistically precise method to estimate supplies expense. Its principal advantage is a unique estimate that produces the least estimation error for the data. On the other hand, because the errors are squared to find the best-fitting line, the regression analysis can be influenced strongly by data points that seem to fall far outside of the pattern formed by the rest of the data. Such data points are called **outliers** and, in the presence of outliers, the estimation line is not representative of most of the data. Such a situation is illustrated in Exhibit 8.4. To prevent this type of distortion, management accountants should prepare a graph of the data prior to using regression and determine whether any outliers are present. Each outlier is reviewed to determine whether it is due to a data-recording error, normal operating condition, or unique and nonrecurring event. Guided by the objective of developing a linear equation that is most representative of the data, the accountant then decides whether to correct the data, include all data as recorded, or remove the outlier.

outliers
Unusual data points that strongly influence a regression analysis.

---

[4] The derivation of the intercept ($220) and coefficient ($0.75) for this regression line is done in Excel or other software, as illustrated later in this chapter. For those looking for advanced coverage of regression analysis, there is a Regression Analysis Online Supplement in *Connect*. This online supplement covers some of the common modeling problems in using regression analysis, such as nonlinearity, nonconstant variance, and other modeling issues. The online supplement also includes a brief discussion of how to detect and resolve these modeling issues.

EXHIBIT 8.3A   **Supplies Expense Data for Regression Application**

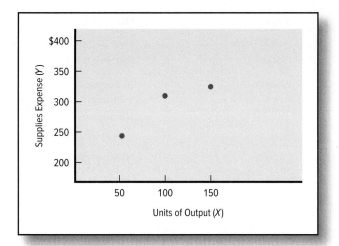

EXHIBIT 8.3B   **The Regression Line for Supplies Expense with Units of Output as the Cost Driver**

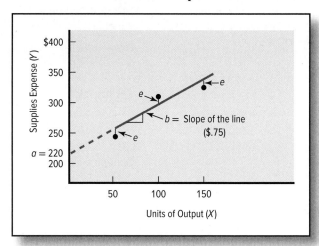

EXHIBIT 8.4
The Effect of Outliers on Regression

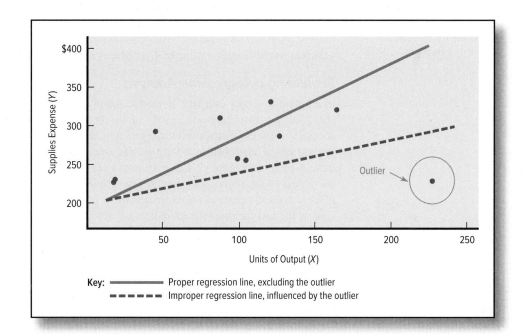

Choosing the Dependent Variable

Development of a regression analysis begins with step 1, the choice of the cost object, which is the dependent variable. The dependent variable might be at a very aggregate level, such as total maintenance costs for the entire firm, or at a less aggregated level, such as maintenance costs for each plant or department. The choice of aggregation level depends on the objectives for the cost estimation, data availability and reliability, and cost/benefit considerations. When a high level of accuracy is desired, a less aggregated level of analysis is preferred.

Choosing the Independent Variable(s)

The second step is to identify the independent variables, which are the cost drivers. Management accountants consider all financial, operating, and other economic data that might be relevant for estimating the dependent variable. The goal is to choose variables that (1) change when the dependent variable changes, that is, there is a predictive relationship (correlation) between the dependent and independent variables, and (2) do not duplicate other independent

EXHIBIT 8.5
Selected Independent Variables and Dependent Variables for Costs in a Retail Store

Selected Dependent Variables	Independent Variables	
	Financial Data	**Operating Data**
Labor expense	Wage rates	Hours worked
	Sales	Number of employees
Utilities expense	Sales	Average daily temperature
		Number of hours store is open
General expenses: office supplies, cleaning, security, and repairs	Sales Total expenses Net fixed assets	Number of employees

variables. As an example, Exhibit 8.5 presents some dependent and independent variables that might be appropriate for the study of costs in a retail store.

Most often the data in a regression analysis are numerical amounts in dollars or units. Another type of variable, called a **dummy variable**, represents the presence or absence of a condition. For example, dummy variables can be used to indicate seasonality. If the management accountant is estimating costs of production, and if production is always high in March, a dummy variable with a value of 1 for March and 0 for the other months could be used.

Evaluating a Regression Analysis

In addition to a cost estimate, if we use readily available software, then regression analysis also provides quantitative measures of its precision and reliability. *Precision* refers to the accuracy of the estimates from the regression, and *reliability* indicates whether the regression reflects actual relationships among the variables; that is, is the regression model likely to continue to predict accurately? These measures can aid management accountants in assessing the usefulness of the regression. Four key (and related) measures are explained here. These and other statistical measures are explained more fully in a regression analysis supplement available on the text website (see footnote 4).

1. *R*-squared, also called the *coefficient of determination.*
2. The *t*-value.
3. The standard error of the estimate (SE), also called the standard error of the regression.
4. The *p*-value.

R-squared, the *t*-values, and the *p*-values are used to measure the reliability of the regression; the standard error is a useful measure of the precision, or accuracy, of the regression and allows for the determination of confidence intervals around the point estimates.

R-squared is a number between zero and 1 and often is described as a measure of the explanatory power of the regression; that is, the degree to which changes in the dependent variable can be explained by changes in the independent variable(s). The higher the *R*-squared, the more reliable the regression model is for cost estimation. When viewed graphically, regressions with high *R*-squared show the data points lying near the regression line; in low *R*-squared regressions, the data points are scattered, as demonstrated in Exhibit 8.6A (high *R*-squared) and 8.6B (low *R*-squared).[5]

Each **t-value** (also known as t-stat or t-statistic) for the various independent variables is a measure of the reliability of that independent variable. *Reliability* is the degree to which an

dummy variable
Used in a regression model to represent the presence or absence of a condition.

R-squared
A number between zero and one. Often it is described as a measure of the explanatory power of the regression; that is, the degree to which changes in the dependent variable can be explained by changes in the independent variable.

t-value
A measure of the reliability of each of the independent variables.

[5] The square root of *R*-squared, or simply *R,* is called the *correlation coefficient* and is interpreted in the same manner as *R*-squared. The correlation coefficient is a number between −1 and +1; a value near zero is interpreted as a lack of relationship between the independent and dependent variables. When *R* is positive, the relationship is direct; that is, when one variable increases, so does the other. When *R* is negative, the relationship is inverse; that is, when one variable increases, the other decreases.

EXHIBIT 8.6A   Regression with High *R*-Squared

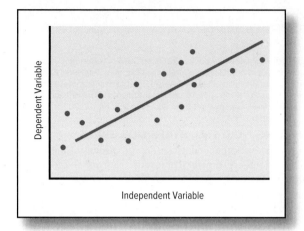

EXHIBIT 8.6B   Regression with Low *R*-Squared

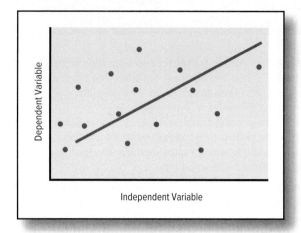

multicollinearity
The condition when two or more independent variables are highly correlated with each other.

correlation
Present when a given variable tends to change predictably in the same or opposite direction for a given change in the other, correlated variable.

standard error of the estimate (SE)
A measure of the dispersion of the actual observations around the regression line; as such it provides a measure of the accuracy of the regression's estimates.

confidence interval (CI)
When using regression analysis to estimate costs, the CI refers to a range around the regression line within which the management accountant can be confident the actual value of the predicted cost will likely fall.

independent variable has a valid, stable, long-term relationship with the dependent variable. A relatively small *t*-value (generally, the *t*-value should be more than 2) indicates little or no relationship between the independent and dependent variables. In a multiple regression model, a variable with a low *t*-value should be removed from the regression to simplify the model and to lead to more accurate cost estimates.[6]

When two or more independent variables exist, the presence of a low *t*-value for one or more of these variables is a possible signal of **multicollinearity,** which means that two or more independent variables are highly correlated with each other. As suggested by the name, independent variables are supposed to be independent of each other, not correlated. **Correlation** among variables means that a given variable tends to change predictably in the same (or opposite) direction of a given change in the other variable. Because a common trend tends to affect many types of financial data, accounting and operating data are often highly correlated; thus, management accountants must give special consideration to the possible impact of multicollinearity on their regression models.

The effect of multicollinearity is that the regression estimates of the coefficients for the independent variables are unreliable. The cost estimates of the regression will be reliable, but the value of the coefficient could not be reliably interpreted as the per-unit cost driver for the related independent variable. For example, if the independent variable is labor hours, the coefficient for this variable does not give a reliable estimate of the labor cost per hour when multicollinearity is present.

The **standard error of the estimate (SE)** is a measure of the dispersion of the actual observations around the regression line, and as such it provides a measure of the accuracy of the regression's estimate. The SE can be used to determine a range around the regression estimate in which the unknown actual value for the estimate can reasonably be expected to fall. This range is called a **confidence interval (CI)** and is used to measure the accuracy of the prediction at any point for the independent variable.

The computation of the confidence interval is straightforward. The 67% confidence interval is determined by taking the regression line and identifying a range that is a 1 standard-error (SE) distance on either side of the regression line; a 95% confidence interval would be determined by 2 standard-error distances. Confidence intervals are useful tools for management accountants to describe the degree of precision obtained from the regression prediction. To illustrate, if the regression prediction is $4,500 and the SE is $500, then the 67% confidence interval is $4,500 +/– $500; one can be 67% confident that the unknown true value of the

[6] The *t*-value can be a positive or negative number, just as the correlation coefficient (see footnote 5) can be positive or negative. A positive *t*-value means that the relationship between the dependent and independent variables is direct (when one variable increases, the other variable increases), while a negative *t*-value indicates an inverse relationship (when one variable increases, the other variable decreases).

dependent variable lies between $4,000 and $5,000. An equivalent interpretation is to say that there is a 67% probability that the unknown true value of the dependent variable lies between $4,000 and $5,000. The confidence interval for 95% would be $4,500 +/– (2 × $500), a range of $3,500 to $5,500.

Because it is used to measure a confidence interval, the SE must be interpreted by its relationship to the average size of the dependent variable. If the SE is small relative to the dependent variable, the precision of the regression can be assessed as relatively good. How small the SE value must be for a favorable precision evaluation is a matter of judgment, but a threshold of approximately 5 to 10% of the average of the dependent variable can be used.

p-value

Measures the risk that a particular independent variable has only a chance relationship to the dependent variable.

Each **p-value** of the various independent variable measures the risk that a particular independent variable has only a chance relationship to the dependent variable and there is no significant relationship. A small p-value (small risk) is desirable; a p-value of .05 or less is often used as a guide in practice. The R-squared, t-values, SE, and p-values are illustrated in the following example and are shown in the Excel spreadsheet for this example (see Exhibit 8.8 later in this section). Note that the t-values greater than 2 have low p-values. Also, there is a p-value for the regression as a whole, which is labeled "Significance F" in Exhibit 8.8. As for the p-values for each independent variable, the significance of F should be less than approximately .05 for a reliable regression.

An Example: Using Regression to Estimate Maintenance Costs

We continue the case developed earlier, Julia Garcia's estimation of maintenance costs. Following the six steps outlined in the first section of the chapter, Garcia defined the cost object and the relevant cost driver as maintenance costs and operating hours, respectively. She also collected and graphed the data (Exhibit 8.2). The next step is to solve the regression using regression software such as Excel with the following findings (Y represents maintenance cost and X represents operating hours):

$$Y = \$15,851.5 + (\$2.018 \times X)$$

The construction industry uses cost estimation extensively, and in many cases, a project cost is estimated directly based on projected labor hours, materials, and other elements of the project. However, given a growing global concern over environmental sustainability, estimating the solid waste coming from construction and demolition is increasingly important at more than a local level. Investment in urbanization projects in developing countries is growing, meaning the related construction and demolition waste is also growing. Regression was used to estimate the demolition waste generation rates in urbanization projects in India.

Required

How might the information that comes from a regression analysis estimating waste generation rates be used by management of a company, and, at a higher level, the government of a country?

(Refer to Comments on Cost Management in Action at the end of the chapter.)

Garcia expects approximately 3,600 operating hours in August, so the amount of maintenance costs for August is estimated to be

$$Y = \$15,851.5 + (\$2.018 \times 3,600) = \$23,117$$

The statistical measures are:

$$R\text{-squared} = .462$$
$$t\text{-value} = 2.07 \qquad (p = .09)$$
$$\text{Standard error of the estimate} = \$221.71$$

Garcia notes that R-squared is less than 0.5, the t-value is greater than 2.0, and the SE is approximately 1% of the mean of the dependent variable ($221.71 \div 23,117$). The SE value is very good. However, because the t-value is marginally greater than 2 (and has a weak p-value of .09) and because R-squared is low, Garcia asks her accounting assistant, Jan, to review the regression.

Jan looks at the regression and the related graphs and notices immediately that in May, maintenance costs dropped significantly in relation to the modest drop in operating hours. Based on her extensive knowledge and experience, Garcia believes that the drop in May was due to the unusually poor economic conditions that month; thus, output was reduced and operating hours and maintenance fell accordingly. Recalling that dummy variables can be used to adjust for isolated variations and seasonal or other patterns, Jan suggests that Garcia run the regression again with a dummy variable having a value of 1 in May and a value of 0 otherwise (the symbol D represents the dummy variable). The new regression result is as follows:

$$Y = \$16,475.5 + (\$1.854 \times X) - (\$408.719 \times D)$$

The coefficients in the revised equation indicate that the poor performance in May reduced estimated costs by $408.638 and that each operating hour increases maintenance cost by $1.856. With the revised regression, the estimate of maintenance costs for August is as follows (assuming no unusual unfavorable event in August, and thus $D = 0$):

$$\begin{aligned} Y &= \$16,475.5 + (\$1.854 \times 3,600) - (\$408.719 \times 0) \\ &= \$23,150 \end{aligned}$$

The statistical measures are as follows:

R-squared $= .773$

t-values:

Hours: 2.61 $\qquad (p = .06)$
Dummy variable: -2.34 $(p = .08)$
Standard error of the estimate (SE) $= \$161.24$

Garcia observes that the inclusion of the dummy variable improves R-squared, the t-values, the p-values, and the SE. For this reason, she relies on the estimate from the latter regression.

EXHIBIT 8.7

Indirect Costs, Direct Labor Hours, and Machine Hours for WinDoor Inc.

Date	Total Indirect Costs	Direct Labor Hours	Machine Hours
June 2021	$274,500	26,940	2,009
July	320,000	35,690	3,057
August	323,200	32,580	3,523
September	219,900	24,580	1,856
October	232,100	19,950	2,168
November	342,300	34,330	3,056
December	427,800	43,180	3,848
January 2022	231,000	21,290	1,999
February	257,300	28,430	2,290
March	248,700	24,660	1,894
April	248,400	27,870	2,134
May	338,400	31,940	3,145

A Second Example: Using Excel for Regression Analysis

Companies have access to more data than ever before, and the cost of storing these data is declining. When the access to data is combined with the improved analytics tools like Tableau or Microsoft's Excel and Power BI, regression becomes much more cost-effective to use. Consider a new example. Suppose that WinDoor Inc. is developing a regression cost equation for the indirect costs in its plant. WinDoor manufactures windows and doors used in home construction; both products are made in standard and custom sizes. Occasionally, a very large order substantially increases the direct and indirect costs in a given month. The indirect costs primarily consist of supplies, quality control and testing, overtime, and other indirect labor. Regression is used to budget indirect costs for the coming year, primarily for cash management purposes. The management accountant, Charlotte Williams, knows from prior years that, while correlated, both direct labor hours and machine hours in the plant are good independent variables for estimating indirect costs. She gathers the data in Exhibit 8.7 for the most recent 12 months.

Exhibit 8.8 shows both the regression data and the dialog box used to produce the regression results shown in the exhibit. Note that the independent variables (*X* Range) and dependent variable (*Y* Range) are entered into the dialog box. Labels are used in the top row of each column of data. The output is presented in the cells to the right and below the selected cell, E1. The dialog

EXHIBIT 8.8 Excel Regression Results for WinDoor Data, Showing Regression Dialog Box

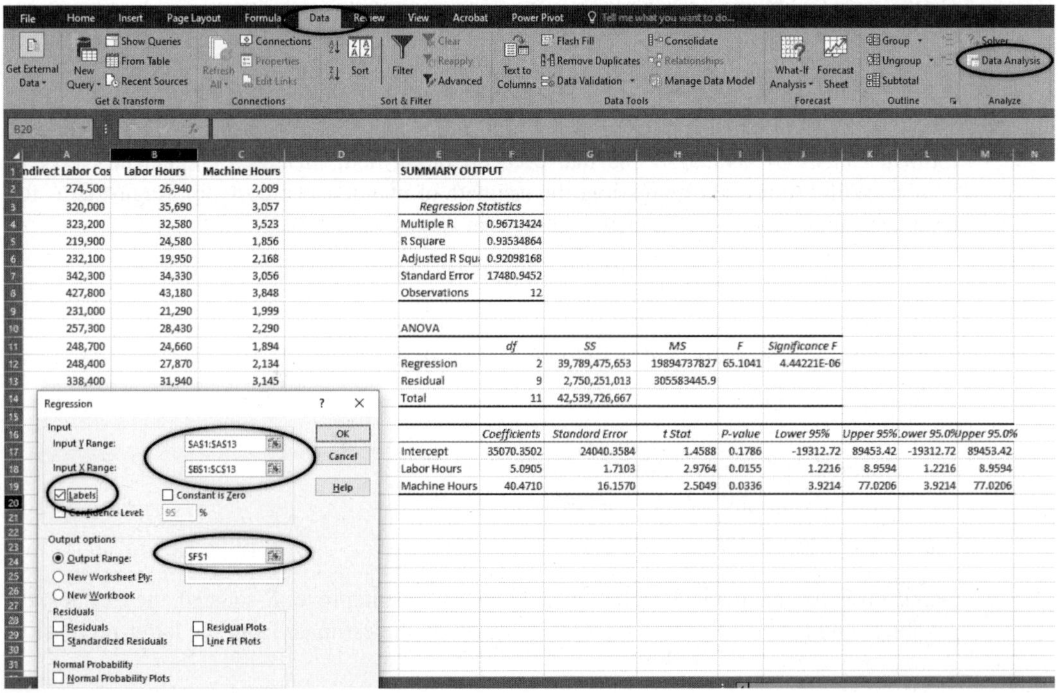

Source: Microsoft Excel

box is accessed by choosing **Data Analysis** at the right end of the ribbon under the Data tab in Excel. If Data Analysis is not on the ribbon, then it needs to be installed by clicking the **File** tab at the top left of the Excel spreadsheet and then clicking Excel Options. In the next screen, click Add-ins on the left of the screen and then choose Analysis ToolPak, which contains a number of statistical methods, including regression. The location of Data Analysis and the key data entry in the regression dialog box are marked on the spreadsheet in Exhibit 8.8.

Williams develops the regression for these data using Excel. To use Excel, she selects the Regression option from the Data/Data Analysis tab, then selects the X and Y ranges for the independent and dependent variables, and obtains the regression results in Exhibit 8.8 (where L represents direct labor hours and M represents machine hours):

$$Y = \$35{,}070.35 + (\$5.091 \times L) + (\$40.471 \times M)$$

The statistical measures follow:

R-squared $= .9353$

t-values:
    Direct labor hours: 2.976 ($p = .016$)
    Machine hours: 2.505 ($p = .034$)

Standard error of the estimate (SE) $= \$17{,}481$

The p-values for the independent variables are below .05, but because direct labor hours and machine hours may be highly correlated, multicollinearity may exist in this model. However, the regression satisfies our statistical criteria: R-squared is relatively high, the t-values are above 2.0, and the SE is only about 6% of the average indirect costs. Thus, WinDoor can use the estimate with a reasonable degree of confidence.

The WinDoor example is an application of multiple linear regression because it involves two or more independent variables. In contrast, the original Julia Garcia example, which used a single independent variable, operating hours, is an application of simple linear regression.

Illustration of the Use of Regression Analysis in the Gaming Industry

Harrah's owns many large casinos throughout the world, but particularly in Las Vegas, where it operates Flamingo Las Vegas, Planet Hollywood Las Vegas, and Paris Las Vegas. Harrah's competes in a business that is very focused on customer satisfaction and customer loyalty. To be more competitive, Harrah's uses regression analysis to predict customer satisfaction. The approach is used by many other companies, including UPS and Google. The five-step model below explains how and why Harrah's uses regression analysis.

The Five Steps of Strategic Decision Making for Harrah's

1. **Determine the strategic issues surrounding the problem.** Because it operates in a very customer-focused business, Harrah's strategy is to develop and maintain customer loyalty (a differentiation strategy) and to improve customer profitability.

2. **Identify the alternative actions.** Harrah's knows that its customers have a "pain point," the amount of gaming losses at which the customer leaves the casino. The casinos have customer service representatives, called "luck ambassadors," who are responsible for maintaining customer satisfaction and, in particular, for making sure the customer does not reach the pain point.

3. **Obtain information and conduct analyses of the alternatives.** To obtain information about the pain points of individual customers, Harrah's began a "Total Rewards" program that involved a swipeable electronic card that provides certain rewards to customers but also provides data on the customers gaming in the casino. Harrah's uses this information together with other information provided by the Rewards customers to develop a regression analysis to predict the individual customer's pain point.

4. **Based on strategy and analysis, choose and implement the desired alternative.** Harrah's has implemented the regression-based system so that when a given customer is gaming in the casino (Harrah's computer system lets it know real-time what the customer is gaming

and the gains or losses for that day), the customer service representatives can be alerted when the customer is approaching his or her predicted pain point and can be dispatched to urge that customer to take a break and perhaps enjoy a free meal at Harrah's expense.

5. **Provide an ongoing evaluation of the effectiveness of implementation in step 4.** Harrah's system requires continuous updating for new customers and changes in customer behavior, so that the regression analyses can be kept current.

Time-Series and Cross-Sectional Regression

time-series regression
The application of regression analysis to predict future amounts, using prior periods' data.

The two examples used in this chapter, the Julia Garcia case and the WinDoor Inc. case, are both examples of what is called *time-series regression.* **Time-series regression** is the application of regression analysis to predict future amounts, using a prior period's data. In contrast, **cross-sectional regression** estimates costs for a particular cost object based on information on other cost objects and variables, where the information for all variables is taken from the same period of time. For an example of cross-sectional regression, suppose a residential home builder uses regression to estimate the cost of constructing a new home, and the builder knows that the main cost driver for building cost is the size of the home, in square feet of floor space. The builder develops a regression model using the cost of homes built previously that year as the dependent variable and the size in square feet of these homes as the independent variable. The regression equation that the builder develops is then used to predict the cost of homes to be built, based on the expected size of the new home in square feet. All of the statistical measures of reliability and precision explained above apply equally to both types of regression.

cross-sectional regression
A method of cost estimation for a particular cost object based on information on other cost objects and variables, where the information for all variables is taken from the same period of time.

Implementation Problems: Nonlinearity

LO 8-4
Explain the implementation issues of the cost estimation methods.

The cost estimation methods considered thus far in this chapter, the high-low method and regression analysis, have assumed a linear relationship between the variables. However, the linear regression estimates are unreliable when the data relationships are nonlinear. Nonlinearity most often happens because of certain time-series patterns to the data such as trend and/or seasonality, an outlier in the data, or data shift. The high-low method cannot be adapted for nonlinearity, but regression analysis can be adapted for nonlinear relationships. The following explains a few of the ways regression can be adapted to a variety of nonlinear situations. Also, an example of a nonlinear regression is shown in Self-Study Problem 4 at the end of the chapter.

1. **Trend and/or seasonality.** A common characteristic of accounting data is a significant trend that results from changing prices and/or seasonality. When trend or seasonality is present, a linear regression is not a good fit to the data, and the management accountant should use a method to deseasonalize or to detrend a variable. The most common methods to do this follow:

- Use of a price index. A price index can be used to adjust the values of each variable to some common time period. Price index data are generally obtained from outside sources.

REAL-WORLD FOCUS   Be Careful about Interpretations: A Time-Series Look at NFL Passing Leaders

The graphs contain the passing yards of the NFL passing leader from 1932 to 2019. The first graph shows just the raw data, and the second graph has a trend line generated by Excel using simple regression. The forecast shows the passing leader is likely to be close to 6,000 yards in the near future. However, one must use common sense when interpreting time-series data. It may not be safe to assume that the mere passage of time is going to lead to increasing passing yardage. In this case, there have been rules changes in the NFL that favor quarterbacks and receivers, and this could have led to a shift in strategy towards an offense that favors the pass. Perhaps the benefits from those changes have been fully realized and the trend upward will not continue.

Spreadsheet tools like Excel have built-in functions that can be used to create forecasts from time-series data. In Excel that tool is called Forecast Sheet. Using that tool, the upper and lower bounds for the 95% confidence level are 3,611 and 6,049, respectively. That is quite a large range and, perhaps, indicates that the simple passage of time is not a good predictor of results.

Source: https://en.wikipedia.org/wiki/List_of_National_Football_League_annual_passing_yards_leaders; Mark Glassman, "The 6,000-Yard Season," *Bloomberg Businessweek*, September 11, 2017, p. 67.

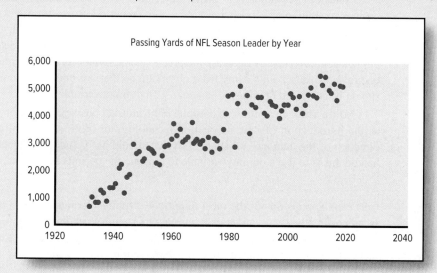

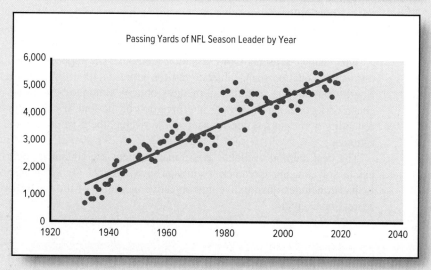

trend variable
A variable in a regression model that takes on values of 1, 2, 3, . . . for each period in sequence.

- Use of a trend variable. A **trend variable** takes on values of 1, 2, 3, . . . for each period in a sequence.
- Replacement of the original values of each of the variables with the first differences. First difference for each variable is the difference between each value and the succeeding value in the time series.

EXHIBIT 8.9
**Adjusting for Trend and
Seasonality Using First
Difference or a Price Index**

| | | Price Index Adjustment | |
| | | --- | --- |
Supplies Expense	First Difference	Price Index for Supplies Expense	Supplies Expense Adjusted for Price Index
$250	—	1.00	$250/1.00 = $250
310	$60	1.08	310/1.08 = 287
325	15	1.12	325/1.12 = 290

The index approach and the first difference approach are shown in Exhibit 8.9 using the supplies expense data from Exhibit 8.3.

Trend is present in virtually all financial time-series data used in management accounting because of inflation and growth in the economy. Thus, it is a pervasive issue in the proper development of a regression analysis.

2. **Outliers.** As mentioned earlier, when an error in the data or an unusual or nonrecurring business condition affects operations for a given period, the result might be a data point that is far from the others, an outlier. One must be careful to not conclude that every unusual data point is an outlier. It takes business judgment to make this important determination because outliers can significantly decrease the precision and reliability of an estimate. If it is clear that one or more data points came from observations that are unusual or nonrecurring, the data should be corrected or adjusted (using, e.g., a dummy variable).

3. **Data Shift.** In contrast to outliers, if the unusual business condition is long lasting, such as the introduction of new production technology or other permanent change, the average direction of the data has a distinct shift that should be included in the estimate. One way to handle this is to use a dummy variable to indicate the periods before and after the shift.

Summary

Cost estimation is one of the most important activities the management accountant performs in supporting the firm's strategy. It has an important role in developing a competitive position as well as in planning and decision making; target costing and pricing; and effective performance measurement, evaluation, and compensation.

To use cost estimation effectively, the management accountant develops and evaluates a cost-estimating model in six steps: (1) define the cost object, (2) determine the cost drivers, (3) collect consistent and accurate data, (4) graph the data, (5) select and apply a cost estimation method, and (6) evaluate the accuracy of the cost estimate.

This chapter presents two estimation methods. The high-low method develops a unique estimation equation using algebra and the representative low and high points in the data. Regression analysis, a statistical method, obtains a unique best-fitting line for the data. The chapter's focus is on the proper interpretation of the four key measures of the precision and reliability of the regression: R-squared, the t-value, the p-value, and the standard error of the estimate.

The best method available to the management accountant is regression analysis, which can be solved using spreadsheet software such as Excel. An advantage of regression analysis is that it includes quantitative and objective measures of the reliability and precision of the regression estimate.

Appendix

LO 8-5

Use learning curves in cost estimation when learning is present.

Learning Curve Analysis

One prominent example of nonlinear cost behavior is a cost influenced by learning. When an activity has a certain labor component and repetition of the same activity or operation makes the labor more productive, the task is completed more quickly with the same or a higher level of quality. Learning can occur in a wide variety of ways, from the individual level as new employees gain experience, to the aggregate level in which a group of employees experiences improvement in productivity. We consider the latter instance in this appendix.

REAL-WORLD FOCUS   Applications of Learning Curves

Learning curve analysis is commonly used to improve cost estimates in situations when learning is likely to occur.

SURVEY OF THE USE OF LEARNING CURVES

A survey of 787 management accountants and members of the Chartered Institute of Management Accountants (UK) employed in more than 20 different industries has shown that learning curves are applied most often in manufacturing firms. Also, these firms tend to use learning curves in planning and budgeting, topics we cover in Chapters 9, 10, 11, and 12.

Source: Grahame Steven, "The Learning Curve: The Key to Future Management?," *The Chartered Institute of Management Accountants, Research Executive Summary Series* 6, no. 12 (2010).

LEARNING HELPS INCREASE OUTPUT

Airplanes are complex products, and it takes time to smooth out the production process. European-based Airbus Group seems to be making progress. In December 2015, the company produced 79 aircraft, which was an improvement over the 75 produced the prior December. Production for the entire 2015 year was above the 2014 level and marked the 13th year in a row of higher output. Part of this continuous increase in production is getting through the learning curve associated with the introduction of a new model of plane.

Source: Robert Wall, "Airbus Tackles Its Procrastination Woes—Plane Maker Looks for Ways to Avoid the December Rush to Meet Jet-Delivery Targets," *The Wall Street Journal,* Europe edition, May 25, 2016, p. B1.

COMPLEXITY CAN UNDERMINE THE LEARNING CURVE

The learning curve effect comes from experience with performing a task. As noted in this chapter, the learning curve effect is well documented in the World War II aircraft industry. In modern times that learning curve effect might be undermined by complexity. The U.S. Military Joint Fighter program was developed in the 1990s as a program in which one company would produce three different versions of the same aircraft, one for the Navy, one for the Marine Corps, and one for the Air Force. The belief was that, despite the advanced technology of the planes, the large volume of production would allow the jets to be produced at a cost equal to the older planes that would be replaced. The complexity of trying to meet the needs of three distinctly different users was one of the significant factors that led to production delays and cost overruns.

Source: Valerie Insinna, "Inside America's Dysfunctional Trillion-Dollar Fighter-Jet Program" *The New York Times Magazine,* August 21, 2019, www.nytimes.com/2019/08/21/magazine/f35-joint-strike-fighter-program.html.

Costs are affected by learning in a wide variety of contexts, especially in large-scale production settings, such as the manufacture of airplanes and ships. In each case, we can model the expected improvement in productivity and use this information in the estimation of future costs. A **learning curve analysis** is a systematic method for estimating costs when learning is present.

One of the first well-documented applications of learning curves occurred in the World War II aircraft industry. Studies showed that the total time to manufacture two airplanes declined by approximately 20% of the total time without learning. In other words, the average

learning curve analysis
A systematic method for estimating costs when learning is present.

EXHIBIT 8A.1
Average Cost with Learning

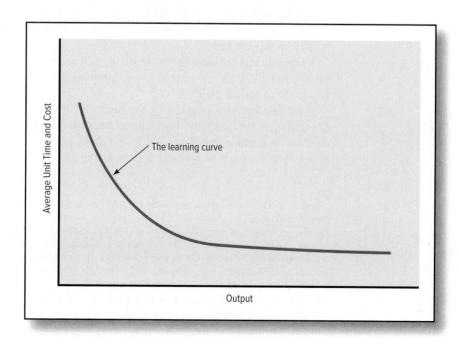

EXHIBIT 8A.2
SofTech Inc.'s Learning Curve
for Z-Base

Output (multiples of 500 lines)	Cumulative Average Time (coding for 500 lines)	Total Time
1 = 500 lines	100 hours	100 hours
2 = 1,000 lines	100 × .8 = 80 hours	80 × 2 = 160 hours
4 = 2,000 lines	80 × .8 = 64 hours	64 × 4 = 256 hours
8 = 4,000 lines	64 × .8 = 51.2 hours	51.2 × 8 = 409.6 hours

learning rate
The percentage by which
average time (or total time) falls
from previous levels as output
doubles.

per-unit time to build the first two units was 80% of the time for the first unit. For example, if the time to build the first unit is 20 hours, the *average* time to build the first two units is 16 hours (20 × 0.8), or a total of 32 hours (16 × 2) for two units. Without learning, it would take 40 hours (20 × 2). The **learning rate** is the percentage by which average time (or total time) falls from previous levels *as output doubles*. In this example, the rate is 80%. The average unit cost behavior of the learning curve is illustrated in Exhibit 8A.1. Note from the exhibit that the effect of learning is nonlinear; learning curve analysis is an example of nonlinear cost estimation.

Additional evidence of the practical importance of learning curves is the common reference to start-up costs in corporate annual reports and the financial press. A commonly accepted business principle is that new products and production processes have a period of low productivity followed by increasing productivity. Thereafter, the rate of improvement in productivity tends to decline over time until it reaches some equilibrium level where it remains relatively stable until another change in the product line or production process occurs.[7]

EXAMPLE: LEARNING CURVES IN SOFTWARE DEVELOPMENT

SofTech Inc. is a vendor of software for financial analysts. SofTech's development staff recently changed its development language, T-Base, to a new language, Z-Base, which permits faster development and provides certain object-oriented programming benefits. Now SofTech is calculating the learning time needed for its programmers to come up to speed in the new language. These estimates are important because programming costs have increased 10% to $65 per hour in the past year and are expected to rise as quickly in the coming years. For purposes of this analysis, SofTech estimates the learning rate for Z-Base to be 80% and the initial time for coding 500 lines of good code in Z-Base to be 100 hours. The time and related cost required for developing the first 4,000-line application in Z-Base can be determined by using the learning curve; see Exhibit 8A.2. Note in this exhibit that the learning rate is applied to multiple (or batch) lines of code. The reason is that, unlike WWII aircraft manufacturing, where application of the learning rate to units makes sense, the application of a learning rate to a line of code is impractical. For many of the repetitive labor tasks encountered today, the application by batch makes more sense, so we use batches in this example.

Learning rates are obtained by reviewing and analyzing historical data. The methods vary from the simple high-low method to regression analysis based on fitting a nonlinear relationship to the historical data.[8]

Note also that a learning rate of 1 is equivalent to no learning. A learning rate of .5 is best interpreted as the maximum learning rate because the total time for actual production equals the time for a single unit. Thus, the learning rate is always a number greater than .5 and less than 1. Actual case studies reveal that the learning rate most often falls near .8.

[7] As in the World War II airplane production example, the common learning rate is approximately 80%. Two conventional models are used in learning curve analysis. One measures learning on the basis of average unit cost, the other on the basis of marginal cost. Both models are conceptually and mathematically similar, although the average cost model tends to lead to lower unit costs. The average cost model is the more common, and for clarity and simplicity, it is the only model we present here. For a full explanation and comparison of the two models, see J. Chen and R. Manes, "Distinguishing the Two Forms of the Constant Percentage Learning Curve Model," *Contemporary Accounting Research,* Spring 1985, pp. 242–252.

[8] For coverage of different learning models and Excel applications, see the following case and teaching note: "Instructional Case: Estimating Learning Curve Functions for Managerial Planning, Control, and Decision Making," by David E. Stout and Paul E. Juras, *Issues in Accounting Education,* May 2009, pp. 195–217.

WHAT DECISIONS ARE INFLUENCED BY LEARNING?

Because the productivity of labor is a vital aspect of any production process, learning curve analysis can be an important way to improve the quality of a wide range of decisions. For example, when product prices are based in part on costs, learning curves could be used to determine a life-cycle plan for pricing a new product. Moreover, learning curves would be helpful in these areas:

1. **Cost-volume-profit analysis (Chapter 9).** The learning curve can cause average unit costs to decrease over a given time period, meaning the determination of a breakeven point might be significantly influenced by the presence of learning. Failing to consider learning causes overstatement of the actual number of units required for breakeven.

2. **Budgeting production levels and labor needs (Chapter 10).** Another useful application of learning curves is the development of the annual or quarterly production plan and related labor-requirements budget. When the activity or operation is affected by learning, the production and labor budgets should be adjusted accordingly.

3. **The make-or-buy decision (Chapter 11).** When the cost to make a part is affected by learning, the analysis can be used to more accurately reflect the total cost over time of the make option.

4. **Capital budgeting (Chapter 12).** Learning curves capture cost behavior more accurately over the life of the capital investment by including the expected improvements in labor productivity due to learning.

5. **Preparation of bids for production contracts, target costing, and life-cycle costing (Chapter 13).** Learning curves play an important role in ensuring that the contract cost estimates are accurate over the life of the contract.

6. **Development of standard product costs (Chapters 14 and 15).** When learning occurs, standard costs change over time, and the appropriate labor costs must be adjusted on a timely basis.

7. **Management control (Chapters 18 and 19).** The use of learning curves is important in properly evaluating managers when costs are affected by learning. The evaluation should recognize the pattern of relatively higher costs at the early phase of the product life cycle.

THE GENERAL FORM OF THE LEARNING MODEL

The learning rate is usually based on an assumed doubling of output as illustrated above, but other assumptions are possible. The general form of the learning model used most often in management applications is as follows:

$$Y = aX^b$$

where: Y = the cumulative average time per unit when producing X units

a = the time required for the first unit of output

X = cumulative output

b = the learning index

The learning rate is Y/a, and the learning index (b) can be determined from the learning rate using an algebraic approach.[9] This form of the learning model is very general and will allow consideration of other learning assumptions, in addition to the doubling-of-output base commonly used.

---

[9] To determine the learning rate (b) for a given learning rate, first develop a linear expression for the general model by taking either the log (base 10) or the natural log (ln) of both sides of the equation. Using the natural log we have

$$\ln(Y) = \ln(a) + b \times \ln(X)$$

so that:

$$b = \frac{\ln(\text{learning rate})}{\ln(\text{increase in output}/100)}$$

Thus, if we consider the changes in Y/a as X increases, the index b simplifies to the ratio of the learning rate to the rate of increase in output, or

$$b = \frac{\ln(\text{learning rate})}{\ln(2)}$$

For example, to calculate the learning index for the doubling-output assumption (200%), we use:

$$b = \frac{\ln(Y) - \ln(a)}{\ln(X)} = \frac{\ln(Y/a)}{\ln(X)}$$

And, for a learning rate of 80%, the learning index is therefore $\ln(.8)/\ln(2) = -.3219$. The index is negative because average unit labor time decreases with increasing output.

LIMITATIONS OF LEARNING CURVE ANALYSIS

Although learning curve analysis can significantly enhance the ability to predict costs when learning occurs, three inherent limitations and problems are associated with the use of this method.

The first and key limitation of using learning curves is that the approach is most appropriate for labor-intensive contexts that involve repetitive tasks performed for long production runs for which repeated trials improve performance, or learning. When the production process is designed to maximize flexibility and minimize setup times for manufacturing machinery (using robotics and computer controls as many manufacturers now do), the manufacturing setting requires relatively little repetitive labor and, consequently, relatively little opportunity for learning.

A second limitation is that the learning rate is assumed to be constant (average labor time decreases at a fixed rate as output doubles). In actual applications, the decline in labor time might not be constant. For example, the learning rate could be 80% for the first 20,000 units, 90% for the next 35,000 units, and 95% thereafter. Such differences indicate the need to update projections based on the observed progression of learning.

Third, a carefully estimated learning curve might be unreliable because the observed change in productivity in the data used to fit the model was actually associated with factors other than learning. For example, the increase in productivity might have been due to a change in labor mix, a change in product mix, or some combination of other related factors. In such cases, the learning model is unreliable and produces inaccurate estimates of labor time and cost.

Regression Analysis Supplement (online)

The Regression Analysis Supplement is available in Connect. This supplement provides advanced coverage of regression analysis. The advanced coverage is not required for any of the exercises or problems at the end of Chapter 8. While the text provides comprehensive and in-depth coverage of regression analysis, some instructors and students can pursue an advanced coverage of regression analysis through the use of this supplement. The exercises and problems in the text do not require this advanced coverage, but those exercises and problems that deal with regression analysis could be addressed at an advanced level using the content provided in this online supplement.

Key Terms

confidence interval (CI), *287*
correlation, *287*
cost estimation, *277*
cross-sectional regression, *292*
dependent variable, *283*
dummy variable, *286*
high-low method, *281*
independent variable, *283*
learning curve analysis, *295*

learning rate, *296*
least squares regression, *283*
mean absolute percentage error (MAPE), *280*
multicollinearity, *287*
multiple linear regression, *283*
outliers, *284*
p-value, *288*
regression analysis, *283*

R-squared, *286*
simple linear regression, *283*
standard error of the estimate (SE), *287*
time-series regression, *292*
trend variable, *293*
t-value, *286*

Comments on Cost Management in Action

Using Regression to Estimate Construction Costs

The regression model can be used by the construction contractor to estimate the construction demolition waste generated from a single project cost to build in the estimated cost of waste disposal into a bid. However, from an environmental impact perspective, studies indicate that demolition waste generation in Shanghai, China, has been as high as 842 kg per person per year. That is about 1,860 pounds per person per year. The government of a locality (or entire country) might use this information as the basis for regulatory reform of the construction industry. The resulting estimates could also be used to determine the need for infrastructural improvements or additional capacity to handle the waste.

Source: V. G. Ram and Satyanarayana Kalidindi, "Estimation of Construction and Demolition Waste Using Waste Generation Rates in Chennai, India," *Waste Management & Research: The Journal of the International Solid Wastes and Public Cleansing Association* 35, no. 6 (June 2017), pp. 610–617.

Self-Study Problems

(For answers, please see Solutions.)

1. Using the High-Low Method

Hector's Delivery Service uses four small vans and six pickup trucks to deliver small packages in the Charlotte, North Carolina, metropolitan area. Hector spends a considerable amount of money on the gas, oil, and regular maintenance of his vehicles, which is done at a variety of service stations and repair shops. To budget his vehicle expenses for the coming year, he gathers data on his expenses and number of deliveries for each month of the current year:

	Total Vehicle Expenses	Total Deliveries
January	$145,329	5,882
February	133,245	5,567
March	123,245	5,166
April	164,295	6,621
May	163,937	6,433
June	176,229	6,681
July	180,553	7,182
August	177,293	6,577
September	155,389	5,942
October	150,832	5,622
November	152,993	5,599
December	201,783	7,433

Required   Use the high-low estimation method to determine the relationship between the number of deliveries and the costs of maintaining the vehicles.

2. Using Regression Analysis

George Harder is the plant manager at one of Imperial Foods Company's processing plants. George is concerned about the increase in plant overhead costs in recent months. He has collected data on overhead costs for the past 24 months and has decided to use regression to study the factors influencing these costs. He has also collected data on direct materials cost, direct labor hours, and machine hours as potential independent variables to use in predicting overhead.

George performed two regression analyses on these data, with the following results:

	Regression 1 (materials cost and labor hours)	Regression 2 (materials cost, labor hours, and machine hours)
R-squared	.65	.58
Standard error	$12,554	$13,793
Standard error as a percent of the average dependent variable	12%	14%
t-values:		
Direct materials	2.0	−1.6
Labor hours	4.5	3.8
Machine hours		1.4

Required   Which of the two regressions is better and why?

3. Using Both High-Low and Regression

John Meeks Company is a medium-sized manufacturing company with plants in three small mid-Atlantic towns. The company makes plastic parts for automobiles and trucks, primarily door panels, exterior trim, and related items. The parts have an average cost of $5 to $20. The company has a steady demand for its products from both domestic and foreign automakers and has experienced growth in sales averaging between 10 and 20% over the last 8 to 10 years.

Currently, management is reviewing the incidence of scrap and waste in the manufacturing process at one of its plants. Meeks defines scrap or waste as any defective unit that is rejected for lack of functionality or another aspect of quality. The plants have a number of different inspection points, and failure or rejection can occur at any inspection point. The number of defective units is listed in the following table; management estimates the cost of this waste in direct labor and direct materials is approximately $10 per unit.

An unfavorable trend appears to exist with regard to defects, and management has asked you to investigate and estimate the defective units in the coming months. A first step in your investigation is to identify the cost drivers of defective parts, to understand what causes them, and to provide a basis on which to estimate future defects. For this purpose, you have obtained these recent data on the units produced, the units shipped, and the cost of sales since these numbers for the past 2 years are easily available and relatively reliable on a monthly basis:

	Units Produced (000s)	Cost of Sales (000s)	Units Shipped (000s)	Defective Units
January Year 1	55	$ 689	50	856
February	58	737	53	1,335
March	69	886	64	1,610
April	61	768	56	1,405
May	65	828	60	1,511
June	69	878	64	1,600
July	75	962	70	1,570
August	81	1,052	76	1,910
September	70	1,104	80	2,011
October	79	1,224	89	2,230
November	82	1,261	92	2,300
December	70	1,020	74	1,849
January Year 2	67	850	62	1,549
February	72	916	67	1,669
March	85	1,107	80	2,012
April	75	968	70	1,756
May	81	1,037	76	1,889
June	85	1,103	80	1,650
July	92	1,208	87	2,187
August	100	1,310	95	2,387
September	91	1,380	101	2,514
October	101	1,536	111	2,787
November	105	1,580	115	2,310
December	88	1,270	92	2,311

Required Use the high-low method and regression analysis to estimate the defective units in the coming months and to determine which method provides the best fit for this purpose.

4. Nonlinear Regression and Learning Curves

This self-study problem illustrates how nonlinear regression can be used to estimate the learning rate, given information on output levels and average processing times. To illustrate, we reproduce in the following the cumulative output (X) and the cumulative average time per unit (Y) for the SofTech Inc. illustration in Exhibit 8A.2. Using regression analysis, we now show that these learning curve data are consistent with the general learning model. The general form of the learning model is $Y = aX^b$, where $a =$ the time required for the first unit and $b =$ the learning index. Using a logarithmic transformation for Y, the general learning model can be shown in the equivalent log-linear form (see footnote 9 for an explanation of the learning index, the learning rate, and the other elements of the learning model): $\log(Y) = \log(a) + b \times \log(X)$. The logarithmic transformation is available in Excel in "Insert Function" under the Formulas tab.

The exhibit that follows shows that the X and Y values have been transformed (using log, base 10), and the results of a regression on log X and log Y are shown in the two right-hand columns. Note that the regression R-squared is 1.0 because the data fit perfectly an 80% learning curve; the values for Y were calculated using the 80% rate. Also, note that the learning index ($b = -.321928$) is the learning index for a model with an 80% learning rate, as shown in footnote 9.

The value of Y can now be determined for any value of X using the general model. First, we determine the value of the intercept, a. Because the log-transformed model, $\log(Y) = \log(a) + b \times \log(X)$, has $\log(a)$ as the intercept term, the value of $\log(a)$ is obtained from the regression results shown below—that is, $\log(a) = 2.8688743$. And because $\log(a) = 2.8688743$, the value of a can be determined as follows: $a = 10^{2.8688743} = 739.39$. The value for $10^{2.8688743} = 739.39$ is determined using the Power function in Excel, which is located in "Insert Function" under the Formulas tab. Thus, for example, the value of Y for $X = 1,500$ is determined as follows:

$$Y = 739.39 \times 1,500^{-.321928} = 70.2$$

Log-Linear Regression of Learning Curve Data (from Exhibit 8A.2)

X	Y	LogX	LogY
500	100	2.69897	2
1000	80	3	1.90309
2000	64	3.30103	1.80618
4000	51.2	3.60206	1.70927

Regression Statistics	
Multiple R	1
R-squared	1
Adj R-squared	1
Standard error	1.677E-16
Observations	4

ANOVA

	df
Regression	1
Residual	2
Total	3

	Coefficients
Intercept	2.8688743
LogX	−0.321928

Required Suppose that Virilli Inc., a manufacturer of high-end furniture, has the following data for one of its products, where X is cumulative output and Y is average unit time:

X	Y
10	45
18	40
25	38
43	32
55	30
70	25
93	22
110	20

1. Using log-linear regression, determine the general linear model for Virilli. Specifically, determine the values of a and b in the model $Y = aX^b$.
2. Using the model you developed in requirement 1, project the value of Y if output (X) is increased to 133.

The Student Resources section of Connect includes video tutorials for the Self-Study Problems.

Questions

8-1 Define *cost estimation* and explain its purpose.

8-2 Explain the strategic role of cost estimation.

8-3 List the two methods of cost estimation. Explain the advantages and disadvantages of each.

8-4 Explain the implementation problems in cost estimation.

8-5 What are the six steps in cost estimation? Which one is the most important? Why?

8-6 Contrast the use of regression analysis and the high-low method to estimate costs.

8-7 How can cost estimation be used in activity-based costing?

8-8 Explain how to choose the dependent and independent variables in regression analysis used for cost estimation.

8-9 What are nonlinear cost relationships? Give two examples.

8-10 List four advantages of regression analysis.

8-11 Explain what a dummy variable is and how it is used in regression analysis.

8-12 How do we know when high correlation exists? Is high correlation the same as cause and effect?

8-13 What does the coefficient of determination (R-squared) measure?

8-14 Carter Dry Cleaning has developed two regression analyses for cost estimation. The accounting manager has presented statistical measures for both of these regressions. Regression A has an R-squared value of .53 and a t-value of 1.08. Regression B has an R-squared of .89 and a t-value of 2.17. What do these statistical measures indicate about the regressions? Which regression should Carter Dry Cleaning use for cost estimation?

Brief Exercises

[LO 8-3] 8-15 Wallace Heating is attempting to estimate its costs of manufacturing heating ducts for the coming year using the high-low method. The cost driver is number of labor hours. Wallace determines that the high and low costs are $25,830 and $18,414, respectively, and the values for the cost driver are 3,495 and 1,958 hours, respectively. What is the variable cost per hour?

[LO 8-3] 8-16 Williams Inc. produces fluorescent light bulbs for commercial use. The accounting manager is attempting to estimate the total cost for the next quarter using the high-low method. He has compiled data and found the high and low costs are $10,000 and $6,000, respectively, and the associated cost drivers are 7,000 and 3,000 packs, respectively. What is the value for b (the variable cost per unit)? What is the value for a (the fixed quantity)?

[LO 8-2] 8-17 Grant Healthcare produces latex gloves for hospitals. Grant is forecasting costs for future production. The dependent variable is labor expense. List some possible independent variables for a regression analysis of financial data.

[LO 8-3, 8-4] 8-18 Smith Glass Co. produces industrial glass. Smith forecasts inspection costs using the high-low method and has compiled the following data from prior results:

	2018	2019	2020	2021	2022
Total operating hours	5,683	3,197	4,105	5,056	3,586
Inspection costs ($)	50,457	46,835	53,227	49,734	43,649

Looking solely at the data in the table, which two years should Smith select for the high-low method of analysis? Would you consider using different points and why?

[LO 8-3] 8-19 Johnson Plastics Inc. produces cases for CDs. The accounting manager has performed a regression analysis to determine future production costs. The regression estimate is $5,000, with an R-squared of .9, a t-value of 2.5, and a standard error (SE) of $400. Within what interval would she be reasonably (67%) confident that the actual values will fall?

[LO 8-3] 8-20 Peppers Lockdown produces keys for homes and cars. As Peppers planned for next year's production, the company decided to implement a high-low system to forecast future costs. With total production of 2,500,000 keys at a total cost of $10,000 in 2021, and total production of 3,000,000 keys at a total cost of $20,000 in 2022, what is the variable cost per key?

[LO 8-3] 8-21 Power Drink Inc. produces sports drinks. The accounting manager has decided to implement a high-low costing system to predict future materials handling costs. She has provided you with the following table of costs for the last five years. Looking solely at the data in the table, which two years should Smith select for the high-low method analysis? Using the data from those selected years, use the high-low method to estimate the variable cost per unit. If you were to graph the data, would you select the same two data points for your calculations?

	2018	2019	2020	2021	2022
Production hours	100,000	138,679	98,843	203,515	188,352
Handling cost ($)	456,557	498,672	507,284	601,489	544,314

[LO 8-3] 8-22 Jamison Construction has implemented a cost estimation system using regression analysis. The variable cost per hour of labor is $35 and the fixed cost was determined to be $125,000. If Jamison projects it will be working 200,000 hours in the coming year, what is the projected total cost?

[LO 8-3] 8-23 Curry Rubber manufactures rubber bands for retail companies. The accounting manager has performed a regression analysis of past data. You notice that the formula has an R-squared of .6, a t-value of 2.3, and a standard error of the estimate of $200,000. The estimate for next quarter costs is $2,584,072. What do these statistics tell you about the reliability and precision of his regression analysis?

[LO 8-3] 8-24 Miller Landscaping is attempting to estimate costs for future projects. Miller has compiled data and decided to use the high-low costing method. The low value is $250,000 for 5,000 hours, and the high value is $400,000 for 8,000 hours. What is the variable cost per hour?

[LO 8-3] 8-25 Sanders Bears produces stuffed animals. Sanders is in the process of implementing a cost forecasting system using the high-low method. The variable cost per animal is $2 and the high and low costs used are $80,000 for 30,000 animals and $40,000 for 10,000 animals. What is the value of the fixed cost for the cost estimating equation?

[LO 8-3] 8-26 Recently, Walmart offered a wireless data contract based on bandwidth used, with a minimum monthly charge of $45 for up to 5 gigabytes (GB) of use. Additional GB can be purchased at the following rates: $12 for an additional 1 GB, $30 for an additional 3 GB, and $40 for a capacity of 10 GB. What is the cost for a user who is expecting to use 9 GB?

Exercises

[LO 8-1] 8-27 **Estimating Costs in an Uncertain Environment** Many companies face increasingly unpredictable costs and revenues as the recession affects demand for products and the costs of materials and labor for these products. Revenues and costs have fluctuated significantly in recent years for such cost elements as fuel, labor, commodities (agricultural commodities, metals, etc.), interest, and rent expense, among others. Dealing with the increased fluctuations requires cost estimation methods that are more sophisticated and more frequently updated. The result is that companies are including in their cost estimation additional independent variables. Moreover, these companies are updating their estimation models more frequently. For example, Southwest Airlines updates its revenue prediction model on a daily basis.

Required Consider Southwest Airlines and the following six key areas of cost for the company. Which of these costs do you think the airline must update most frequently?
1. Flight crew.
2. Fuel costs.
3. Maintenance spending.
4. Advertising spending.
5. Aircraft ownership costs.

[LO 8-1] 8-28 **Regression Analysis** Data mining, or the use of large amounts of consumer data to predict buying patterns, is widely used in certain industries to help companies select the most profitable products and services, set prices, and increase consumer demand for their products and services. Hotels, supermarkets, airlines, credit card companies, and casinos (note the example about Harrah's in the chapter) commonly use this approach, sometimes with the help of "loyalty cards" that the customer uses at checkout. Regression analysis and other analytics are then applied to the data to help the company predict buying patterns.

Required
1. What is the strategic role of data mining?
2. What, if any, ethical issues are of potential concern when a company uses data mining?

[LO 8-2] 8-29 **Cost Classification** Match each cost to the appropriate cost behavior pattern shown in graphs (a) through (l). Any graph can fit two or more patterns.
1. The cost of lumber used to manufacture wooden kitchen tables.
2. The cost of order fillers in a warehouse. When demand increases significantly, the number of order fillers is increased, and when demand falls off significantly, the number is decreased.
3. The salary of the plant's quality control inspector, who inspects each batch of products.
4. The cost of water and sewer service to the manufacturing plant. The local municipality charges a fixed rate per gallon for usage up to 10,000 gallons and a higher charge per gallon for usage above that point.
5. The cost of an internet connection of $23 per month.
6. The cost of an internet connection of $10 per month plus $2 per hour of usage above 10 hours.

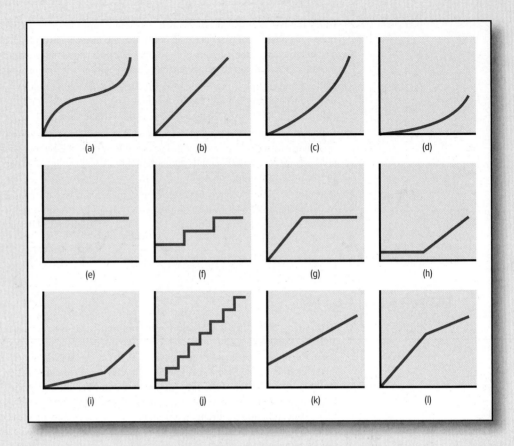

7. The cost to make copies of a given document at a printing shop, where the per-copy charge is reduced for customers who make more than 100 copies of the document.

8. The per-kilowatt-hour charge for usage above 5,000 kilowatt-hours that is increased by the local electric utility to discourage excess usage and to level demand, especially in peak load times.

9. Monthly rent of a clothing store in the SunnyVale Mall that pays a fixed rental charge of $1,000 per month plus 2% of gross sales receipts.

10. Monthly rent of a shoe store in the SunnyVale Mall that pays 6% of gross sales receipts, up to a maximum of $3,000 per month as a rental charge.

[LO 8-2]   8-30 **Cost Relationships**   ChimneySweep provides cleaning services for residential chimneys and fire-places. The cleaning service requires $35 in variable costs for cleaning materials. The fixed costs of labor, the company's truck, and administrative support are $165,000 per year. ChimneySweep averages 100 service calls per month.

Required   What is the average cost per cleaning service call?

[LO 8-2]   8-31 **Cost Relationships**   The following costs are for Optical View Inc., a contact lens manufacturer:

Output in Units	Fixed Costs	Variable Costs	Total Costs
250	$4,750	$7,500	$12,250
300	4,750	9,000	13,750
350	4,750	10,500	15,250
400	4,750	12,000	16,750

Required
1. Calculate and graph total costs, total variable cost, and total fixed cost.
2. For each level of output, calculate the per-unit total cost, per-unit variable cost, and per-unit fixed cost.
3. Using the results from requirement 2, graph the per-unit total cost, per-unit variable cost, and per-unit fixed cost, and discuss the behavior of the per-unit costs over the given output levels.

[LO 8-2] 8-32 **Cost Estimation; Average Cost** Chloe's Cafe bakes croissants that it sells to local restaurants and grocery stores. The average costs to bake the croissants are $0.55 for 2,500 and $0.50 for 5,000.

Required If the total cost function for croissants is linear, what will be the average cost to bake 4,200?

[LO 8-3] 8-33 **Cost Estimation Using High-Low; Graphs** Lawson Advertising Agency is trying to persuade Kansas City Sailboards Company to spend more on advertising. The agency's argument is that a constant and strong positive relationship exists between advertising and sales in the sailboard industry. Sue Lawson presents these data taken from industry data for stores similar in size and market share to Kansas City Sailboards:

Advertising Expense	Annual Sales
$2,500	$ 96,000
3,000	110,000
3,500	124,000
4,000	138,000
4,500	143,000
5,000	147,000
5,500	150,000

Required

1. Use the high-low method to estimate the relationship between increased advertising and sales.
2. Graph annual sales and advertising expense.
3. Do the data prove Sue's point?

[LO 8-3] 8-34 **Analysis of Regression Results** Wang Manufacturing uses regression analysis to predict manufacturing overhead costs based on direct labor hours and/or machine hours and has developed the three following regression equations:

	Regression 1	Regression 2	Regression 3
SE	33,844	45,383	31,044
R-squared	0.55	0.35	0.58
t-values:			
Direct labor hours	2.3		1.9
Machine hours		1.1	0.8

Required Which regression would you choose and why?

[LO 8-2, 8-3] 8-35 **Cost Estimation; High-Low Method; MAPE** Horton Manufacturing Inc. produces blinds and other window treatments for residential homes and offices. The owner is concerned about the maintenance costs for the production machinery because maintenance costs for the previous fiscal year were higher than he expected. The owner has asked you to assist in estimating future maintenance costs to better predict the firm's profitability. Together, you have determined that the best cost driver for maintenance costs is machine hours. The data from the previous fiscal year for maintenance costs and machine hours follow:

Month	Maintenance Costs	Machine Hours
1	$2,625	1,499
2	2,670	1,590
3	2,720	1,605
4	2,822	1,655
5	2,855	1,775
6	3,005	1,880
7	2,865	1,785
8	2,905	1,805
9	2,780	1,695
10	2,570	1,410
11	2,590	1,550
12	2,890	1,425

Required (Round all unit costs to two decimal places)
1. Use the high-low method to estimate the fixed and variable portions for maintenance costs.
2. Graph the data points to check for possible outliers and determine whether the points selected in requirement 1 are representative of the data.
3. Calculate the mean absolute percentage error (MAPE) for the cost equation you developed in requirement 1.

[LO 8-3] 8-36 **Cost Estimation; High-Low Method; MAPE** Ethan Manufacturing Inc. produces floor mats for automobiles. The owner, Joseph Ethan, has asked you to assist in estimating maintenance costs. Together, you and Joseph determine that the single best cost driver for maintenance costs is machine hours. These data are from the previous fiscal year for maintenance costs and machine hours:

Month	Maintenance Costs	Machine Hours
1	$2,600	1,690
2	2,760	1,770
3	2,910	1,850
4	3,020	1,870
5	3,100	1,900
6	3,070	1,880
7	3,010	1,860
8	2,850	1,840
9	2,620	1,700
10	2,220	1,100
11	2,230	1,300
12	2,450	1,590

Required
1. What is the cost equation for maintenance costs using the high-low method?
2. Calculate the mean absolute percentage error (MAPE) for the cost equation you developed in requirement 1.

[LO 8-5] 8-37 **The Gompertz Equation; Learning Curves** The concept of learning curves has broad application in business, medicine, and many other fields. For example, the Gompertz equation is a mathematical model that can be used to predict the number of deaths at a certain age. The Gompertz equation is very similar in form to that of the learning curve, except that *e*, the base of the natural logarithm, is used and there is a positive rather than a negative exponent in the equation. When used to predict death rates, the Gompertz equation is as follows:

$$M(x) = A\,e^{Gx}$$

where

$M(x)$	=	the number of deaths in a population of 100,000 of those at age x; $M(x)$ is often called the *mortality rate*
A	=	the initial mortality rate at age 0
G	=	the exponential rate of increase in mortality for an increase in age, x
e	=	a mathematical constant, the base of the natural logarithm, which equals approximately 2.718281828

In this context, the Gompertz equation is used to estimate the number of deaths at a given age. The equation was estimated using nonlinear regression based on 2002 U.S. census data, and the following estimated equation was derived (for ages 25 through 90). The regression had a very good fit, with an R-squared of 0.97:

$$M(x) = 8.84\,e^{.08x}$$

Required
1. Use the exponential function on your calculator or the EXP function in Excel to determine the mortality rate of any age you choose between 25 and 90.
2. Think of an application or two for which an exponential equation like the Gompertz equation could be used in cost estimation.

[LO 8-3]   8-38 **Regression and Utility Rates; Sustainability**   For several years, many utilities have employed regression analysis to forecast monthly utility usage by residential customers using weather forecasts, the number of holidays, the number of days in the month, and other factors. For example, the Connecticut Department of Public Utility Control (CDPUC) has determined that regression, properly used, can accurately predict natural gas usage. Most public gas utilities serving Connecticut have reported levels of accuracy from 4% to 10% using regression. One company, Dominion Natural Gas Company of Ohio, uses this approach not to forecast, but to explain to customers why their natural gas bills have gone up or down compared to the prior month and to the same month of the prior year. The bill shows total MCF (thousand cubic feet of natural gas) used by the customer for that month and why the total MCF usage has changed, based on three factors:

1. Change in temperature. Each degree increase in temperature causes an increase in the number of MCFs consumed. The relationship between the change in temperature and the usage of MCF is not linear, but the monthly bill shows the average change in temperature for the month and the increase or decrease in MCF related to that change.
2. Number of billing days in the period.
3. The residual—the change in usage by the customer that is not attributable to temperature or the number of days in the billing period.

A customer of Dominion has used 13.7 MCF in December and is charged $12.50 per MCF for a total bill that month of $171.25. The following data are available to compare the current month's weather and billing period to the prior month and to the same month last year:

Usage Factors	Current Month vs. Last Month	Current Month vs. Last December
Weather	3 degrees cooler; +2.5 MCF	8 degrees warmer; −3.5 MCF
Number of billing days	5 more days; +0.5 MCF	1 less day; −0.1 MCF
Customer-controlled usage	+0.9 MCF per billing period	−1.8 MCF per billing period

Required
1. Determine the amount of difference in the customer's bill from the prior month and from the current month last year.
2. How does Dominion's billing system affect environmental sustainability?

[LO 8-3]   8-39 **Interpreting Regression Results**   Recent research into the cost of various medical procedures has shown the impact of certain complications encountered in surgery on the total cost of a patient's stay in the hospital. The researchers used regression analysis and found the following results:

Total cost for patient = Constant, plus

$a \times$ Length of stay (measured in days), plus
$b \times$ Presence of one or more complications (= 1 if true, 0 if false), plus
$c \times$ Use of a laparoscope (= 1 if true, 0 if false)

where a, b, c are coefficients of the regression model. The laparoscope is an instrument somewhat like a miniature telescope with a fiber-optic system that brings light into the abdomen. It is about as big around as a fountain pen and twice as long.

The research, based on 57 patients, showed the following regression results:
R-squared: 53%
Constant term: $3,719

Coefficients and t-values for independent variables:

	Length of Stay	Complications	Laparoscope
Coefficient	$861	$1,986	$908
t-value	10.76	4.89	2.54

Required

1. What is the estimated cost for a patient whose surgery has complications and who stays in the hospital 2 days, and whose surgery requires a laparoscope?

2. Which, if any, dummy variables are used in this regression?

3. Comment on the statistical measures for the model.

[LO 8-3]   8-40 **Interperting Regression Results (Continuation of Exercise 8-39)**   The following table shows additional regression results presented by the researchers in the study described in Exercise 8-39. There are two regressions. The right-hand column shows the results for all patients, including those treated with laparoscopic surgery. The left-hand column shows the results for the sample of patients who were treated without the laparoscopic surgery.

	Nonlaparoscopic Patients Only	All Patients
Coefficients for Independent Variables		
Regression intercept	$8,043	$3,719
Length of stay		
Coefficient*	Not significant	861
Standard error for the coefficient	Not applicable	80
Number of complications		
Coefficient	3,393	1,986
Standard error for the coefficient	1,239	406
Laparoscopic		
Coefficient	Not applicable	908
Standard error for the coefficient	Not applicable	358
R-squared	0.11	0.53

*All independent variables are significant at the level of $p = .05$ (and t-value >2) except for the length of stay variable in the nonlaparoscopic condition. Also, the t-value for each independent variable can be calculated by dividing the coefficient of the variable by the standard error for the coefficient of that variable.

Required

1. Which of the two regressions has the better reliability in estimating costs? Why?

2. Calculate the t-value for each of the independent variables, and interpret the values of each coefficient and the t-values for each independent variable.

[LO 8-3]   8-41 **Cost Estimation; High-Low Method**   Albedo Inc. manufactures high-end replacement telescope lenses for amateur and professional astronomers who are seeking to upgrade the performance of their telescopes. You have just become employed as a staff accountant at Albedo, and Jordan Coleman, the controller, has asked you to help with maintenance cost estimation for the lens manufacturing process. You review the manufacturing process and decide that the best cost driver for maintenance costs is machine hours. The data below are from the previous fiscal year for maintenance costs and machine hours:

Month	Maintenance Costs	Machine Hours
1	$3,210	2,750
2	4,650	3,900
3	5,175	4,050
4	3,350	2,690
5	3,100	2,500
6	2,950	2,580
7	2,900	2,300
8	2,900	2,500
9	4,120	3,160
10	4,350	3,325
11	3,500	2,780
12	3,775	3,000

Required

1. What is the cost equation for maintenance costs using the high-low method?

2. Graph the data and comment on whether or not there are potential outliers.

Problems

[LO 8-2, LO 8-3, 8-4]

8-42 **Cost Estimation; High-Low and Regression Methods**   The Mac Davis Company specializes in the purchase, renovation, and resale of older homes. Mac employs several carpenters and painters to do the work for him. It is essential for him to have accurate cost estimates so he can determine total renovation costs before he purchases a piece of property. If estimated renovation costs plus the purchase price of a house are higher than the house's estimated resale value, it is not a worthwhile investment.

Mac has been using the home's interior square feet for his exterior paint cost estimations. Recently he decided to include the number of external openings—the total number of doors and windows in a house—as a cost driver. Their cost is significant because they require time-consuming preparatory work and careful brushwork. The rest of the house usually is painted either by rollers or spray guns, which are relatively efficient ways to apply paint to a large area. Mac has kept careful records of these exterior painting costs on his last 12 jobs:

House	Square Feet	External Openings	Costs
1	2,500	13	$2,810
2	3,010	15	3,742
3	2,800	12	3,100
4	2,850	12	3,150
5	4,600	19	4,700
6	2,700	13	3,225
7	2,600	11	2,920
8	2,550	11	2,836
9	2,600	10	3,242
10	3,700	16	4,112
11	2,650	13	3,210
12	3,550	16	3,965

Required

1. Using the high-low cost estimation technique and square feet as the independent variable, determine the cost of painting a 3,300-square-foot house with 14 external openings. Also determine the cost for a 2,400-square-foot house with 8 external openings.

2. Repeat requirement 1, but use number of external openings as the independent variable.

3. Plot the cost data against square feet and against openings. Which variable is a better cost driver? Why?

4. Create a multiple regression model for predicting cost based on openings and square feet. Comment on the statistical reliability and precision of this model.

5. What are the sustainability issues for this company, and what is the role of cost estimation in this regard?

[LO 8-3]

8-43 **Cost Estimation; Machine Replacement; Ethics**   Hardison Inc. manufactures glass for office buildings in Florida. As a result of age and wear, a critical machine in the production process has begun to produce quality defects. Hardison is considering replacing the old machine with a new machine, either brand A or brand B. The manufacturer has provided Hardison with the following data on the costs of operation of each machine brand at various levels of output:

Output (square yards)	Brand A Estimated Total Costs	Brand B Estimated Total Costs
2,000	$ 97,000	$120,000
4,000	125,000	160,000
8,000	180,000	200,000
16,000	225,000	260,000
32,000	280,000	300,000
64,000	438,000	368,000

Required

1. Graph the data for the two brands of machines.

2. Use the high-low method to determine the cost equation for each brand of machine and use the results to calculate the costs of operating each machine if Hardison's output is expected to be 25,000 square yards.

3. Using the high-low equations from requirement 2, calculate the costs of operating each machine if Hardison's output is expected to be 40,000 square yards and then for expected output of 60,000 square yards.

4. If Hardison's output is expected to be 40,000 square yards, which machine should it purchase? At 25,000 and at 60,000 square yards? Is the high-low method useful here? Why or why not?

5. As a cost analyst at Hardison, you have been assigned to complete requirement 1. A production supervisor comes to you to say that the nature of the defect in the product for the current machine is really very difficult to detect and that most customers will not notice it, so he questions replacing the machine. He suggests that you modify your calculations to justify keeping this machine to keep things the way they are and save the company some money. What do you say?

6. Assume that machine A is manufactured in Germany and machine B is manufactured in Canada. As a U.S.-based firm, what considerations are important to Hardison, in addition to those already mentioned in your answer to requirement 1?

[LO 8-3]   8-44   **Cost Estimation; High-Low Method**   Horizon BP in Antelope Park, Alaska, has noticed that utility bills are substantially higher when the average monthly temperature is colder. The only thing in the shop that uses natural gas is the furnace. Because of prevailing low temperatures, the furnace is used every month of the year (though less in the summer months and very little in August). Everything else in the shop runs on electricity, and electricity use is fairly constant throughout the year.

For a year, Horizon has been recording the average daily temperature and the cost of its monthly utility bills for natural gas and electricity.

	Average Temperature	Utility Cost
January	31°F	$760
February	41	629
March	43	543
April	44	410
May	46	275
June	50	233
July	53	220
August	60	210
September	50	305
October	40	530
November	30	750
December	10	870

Required

1. Use the high-low method to estimate utility cost for the upcoming months of January and February. The forecast for January is a near record average temperature of 58°F; temperatures in February are expected to average 40°F.

2. Use simple regression to estimate the cost formula for utility costs.

[LO 8-3, 8-4]   8-45   **Regression Analysis**   Pilot Shop is a catalog business providing a wide variety of aviation products to pilots throughout the world. Maynard Shephard, the recently hired assistant controller, has been asked to develop a cost function to forecast shipping costs. The previous assistant controller had forecast shipping department costs each year by plotting cost data against direct labor hours for the most recent 12 months and visually fitting a straight line through the points. The results were not satisfactory.

After discussions with the shipping department personnel, Maynard decided that shipping costs could be more closely related to the number of cartons shipped. He based his conclusion on the fact that 10 months ago, the shipping department added some automated equipment. Furthermore, he believes that using linear regression analysis will improve the forecasts of shipping costs. Cost data for the shipping department have been accumulated for the last 25 weeks. He ran two regression analyses of the data, one using direct labor hours, and one using the number of cartons shipped. The information from the two linear regressions follows:

	Regression 1	Regression 2
Equation	SC = 804.3 + 15.68DL	SC = 642.9 + 3.92NCS
R-squared	.365	.729
Standard error of the estimate	26.52	18.84
t-value	1.89	3.46

where

SC = Total shipping department costs
DL = Total direct labor hours
NCS = Number of cartons shipped

Required

1. Identify which cost function (regression 1 or regression 2) Pilot Shop should adopt for forecasting total shipping department costs and explain why.

2. If Pilot Shop projects that 600 cartons will be shipped in the coming week, calculate the total shipping department costs using the regression you selected in requirement 1.

3. Explain two or three important limitations of the regression you selected in requirement 1, and identify one or two ways to address the limitations. Specifically include in your discussion the effect, if any, of the global nature of Pilot Shop's business.

(CMA Adapted)

[LO 8-3] 8-46 **Analysis of Regression Results** The Maple Creek Amphitheater is an outdoor pavilion that presents musical performers throughout a six-month season, from late spring to early fall. Maple Creek presents a diverse venue of artists in a set of approximately 40 events each season. In order to better project its costs and expected attendance, Maple Creek uses regression analysis to project expected ticket sales for upcoming events for each performer. The regression results shown below are derived from the three most recent seasons. The dependent variable for Maple Creek is the number of paying ticket-holders for each event, and the five independent variables are:

1. Whether this particular performer appeared at Maple Creek previously (a dummy variable, 0 if no and 1 if yes).

2. The spending on advertising targeted to the performer's appearance.

3. The performer's local sales of CDs in the most recent year prior to his or her appearance.

4. The number of television appearances for the performer in the most recent year.

5. The number of other public performances by the performer in the recent year.

The regression results are:

Independent Variables	Results
Regression intercept	1,224
Attendance at prior concert	
Coefficient	3,445
t-value	4.11
Spending on advertising	
Coefficient	0.113
t-value	1.88
Performer's CD sales	
Coefficient	0.00044
t-value	1.22
Television appearances	
Coefficient	898
t-value	2.4
Other public performances	
Coefficient	1,233
t-value	1.3
R-squared	0.58
Standard error of the estimate	8,335

Required

1. Management did not evaluate the results of the regression and simply decided to use the preceding regression for planing purposes. Use the regression to determine what attendance would be predicted for a performer who had appeared at Maple Creek previously, had six other public performances but no TV appearances, had local CD sales of $10 million, and for whom Maple Creek planned to spend $35,000 on advertising?

2. Evaluate the precision and reliability of the regression results shown earlier. What changes, if any, do you propose for the regression? Which variables should be deleted and which do you think should be added? Why?

[LO 8-1, LO 8-3] 8-47 **Correlation Analysis** Packaging Products International (PPI) is a large manufacturer of packaging materials for supermarkets and other retail applications; the packages are used by customers to carry away their purchases. PPI has succeeded for many years by providing a high-quality product and superior customer service. Recently, additional competitors have entered the market, both local and foreign, and PPI is finding that it must increasingly compete on price. PPI's strategy for dealing with the increased competition is to market its products to smaller retailers that would appreciate the firm's quality and service, as well as the firm's ability to customize the product—for example, adding different designs and colors to the packaging material. Until recently, the firm determined product costs based on simple averages of direct materials purchases, plant labor, and overhead. The firm's management is now interested in improving the accuracy of its cost information. As a start, Chris Atkins, the management accountant, obtains the following sample of data (Table 1) showing the machine number, the order size (quantity, in thousands), the machine setup time (in average hours per unit; setup time also includes cleanup time after the order is run), run time (the average hours per unit to produce the order), and a measure of the complexity of the order based on a subjective rating where 1 = less complex and 2 = more complex (complexity relates to the number and type of images and colors printed on the packaging material).

Chris wants to run some regression analyses to better understand these data and, as a first step, obtains a correlation analysis that shows the simple correlation between each of the variables in Table 1. The results are shown in Table 2. Chris understands that each of the correlation numbers in Table 2 is equivalent to the R-squared for a simple linear regression between the variables, as follows: (correlation between two variables)^2 = the R-squared for simple regression analysis between these two variables. To illustrate, note that the correlation between machine number and order size = $-.07005$. The R-squared for the regression between these two variables (with either as the dependent variable) is $(-.07005)^2 = .0049$. Chris also recalls that a negative correlation means that the two variables are inversely related—when one increases, the other decreases.

Table 1   Plant Data for PPI

Machine Number	Order Size	Per Unit		Order Complexity
		Setup Time	Run Time	
2	1,220	0.0023	0.0290	1
2	489	0.0001	0.0434	1
2	480	0.0063	0.0419	2
4	180	0.0158	0.0400	3
4	2,160	0.0022	0.0355	1
4	1,377	0.0023	0.0405	1
4	420	0.0042	0.0400	2
4	540	0.0026	0.0413	1
4	360	0.0030	0.0411	2
4	1,080	0.0111	0.0376	2
4	300	0.0037	0.0430	1
4	2,400	0.0080	0.0345	2
4	81	0.0045	0.0407	2
8	1,350	0.0022	0.0299	1
8	120	0.0017	0.0433	1
8	120	0.0041	0.0417	2
8	2,260	0.0054	0.0340	2
8	240	0.0045	0.0425	1
8	60	0.0050	0.0467	2

Table 2   Correlation Results for PPI's Plant Data

	Number	Order Size	Complexity	Setup Time	Run Time
Number	1				
Order size	−0.07005	1			
Complexity	−0.01714	−0.14071	1		
Setup time	−0.06786	−0.01052	0.79184	1	
Runtime	0.08663	−0.73279	0.11588	−0.01959	1

Note: Correlations with absolute value > .4 are statistically significant at $p < .10$; correlations with absolute value > .5 are statistically significant at $p < .05$.

Required

1. Analyze the findings in Table 2 to assess how, if at all, order size and complexity affect setup time and run time. What other findings in Table 2 are of particular interest?

2. How can your analysis in requirement 1 help PPI become more competitive?

[LO 8-1, LO 8-3]   8-48   **Regression Analysis**   United States Motors Inc. (USMI) manufactures automobiles and light trucks and distributes them for sale to consumers through franchised retail outlets. As part of the franchise agreement, dealerships must provide monthly financial statements following the USMI accounting procedures manual. USMI has developed the following financial profile of an average dealership that sells 1,500 new vehicles annually:

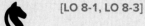

AVERAGE DEALERSHIP FINANCIAL PROFILE
Composite Income Statement

Sales	$30,000,000
Cost of goods sold	24,750,000
Gross profit	$ 5,250,000
Operating costs	
Variable	862,500
Mixed	2,300,000
Fixed	1,854,000
Operating income	$ 233,500

USMI is considering a major expansion of its dealership network. The vice president of marketing has asked Jack Snyder, corporate controller, to develop some measure of the risk associated with the addition of these franchises. Jack estimates that 90% of the mixed costs shown are variable for purposes of this analysis. He also suggests performing regression analyses on the various components of the mixed costs to more definitively determine their variability.

Required

1. Calculate the composite dealership profit if 2,000 units are sold.

2. Assume that regression analyses were performed on the separate components of the mixed costs and that a coefficient of determination value of .60 was determined as applicable to aggregate mixed costs over the relevant range.

    a. Define the term *relevant range*.

    b. Explain the significance of an *R*-squared value of .60 to USMI's analysis.

    c. Describe the limitations that may exist in applying the composite-based relationships to specific new dealerships that have been proposed.

    d. Define the *standard error of the estimate*.

3. The regression equation that Jack Snyder developed to project annual sales of a dealership has an *R*-squared of 60% and a standard error of the estimate of $4,500,000. If the projected annual sales for a dealership total $28,500,000, determine the approximate 95% confidence interval for Jack's prediction of sales. (*Hint:* The 95% confidence interval uses 2 standard errors in determining the interval.)

4. What is the strategic role of regression analysis for USMI?

(CMA Adapted)

[LO 8-3]   8-49   **Cost Estimation; High-Low Method; Regression Analysis**   Lexon Inc. is a large manufacturer of affordable DVD players. Management recently became aware of rising expenses resulting from returns of malfunctioning products. As a starting point for further analysis, Paige Jennings, the controller, wants to test different forecasting methods and then use the best one to forecast quarterly expenses for 2022. The relevant quarterly data for the previous three years follow:

2019 Quarter	Return Expenses	2020 Quarter	Return Expenses	2021 Quarter	Return Expenses
1	$12,500	1	$12,900	1	$13,300
2	11,600	2	12,100	2	12,300
3	11,300	3	11,700	3	12,100
4	13,700	4	14,000	4	14,600

The result of a simple regression analysis using all 12 data points yielded an intercept of $11,868.18 and a coefficient for the independent variable of $124.13. ($R$-squared $= 0.19$, SE $= 978.74.)

Required

1. Plot the data in the order of the dates.

2. Looking at the graph you prepared for requirement 1, select two representative data points and calculate the quarterly forecast for 2022 using the high-low method.

3. Calculate the quarterly forecasts for 2022 using the results of a regression analysis. Evaluate the results of the regression analysis and make appropriate changes to improve the model.

4. Use the Forecast Sheet tool in Excel to create the the quarterly forecast for 2022 and compare the results to those obtained from the regression results in requirement 3.

5. How does your analysis of costs change if Lexon manufactures its products in multiple global production facilities to serve the global market?

[LO 8-3]   8-50   **Time-Series Regression; Applicants for MBA Programs**   Business schools have commonly observed that when job opportunities are down, those interested in business seek to enter MBA programs. To test this hypothesis, we decided to look at the number of applicants for MBA programs and to compare that to the unemployment rate. The applications data are from the Graduate Management Admission Council (**www.gmac.com/**), while the unemployment data are taken from the website of the U.S. Bureau of Labor Statistics (**www.bls.gov/data/home.htm**). We have data for both the total unemployment rate and the rate for college graduates 25 years of age or older. The data for 2000 through 2019 are shown here:

	Unemployment Rate for College Grads (%)	Total Unemployment Rate (%)	Percentage of Schools Reporting an Increase in Full-Time MBA Applicants (%)
2000	1.6%	4.0%	63%
2001	2.2	4.6	65
2002	2.9	5.8	84
2003	3.1	6.0	35
2004	2.7	5.5	16
2005	2.3	5.1	20
2006	2.0	4.6	68
2007	2.1	5.0	64
2008	2.3	7.3	80
2009	4.6	9.9	64
2010	4.7	9.3	41
2011	4.3	8.5	28
2012	4.0	7.9	43
2013	3.7	6.7	50
2014	3.1	5.6	61
2015	2.6	5.0	57
2016	2.5	4.7	43
2017	2.1	3.9	32
2018	2.1	3.7	40
2019	2.0	3.3	40

Required

1. State whether you expect the relationship to be positive or negative (inverse).

2. Use regression analysis on the above data to determine whether there is a relationship between the unemployment rate and the number of applicants to MBA programs. Use both measures of unemployment and see if there is a difference in your results.

[LO 8-5]   8-51   **Learning Curves** The Air Force Museum Foundation has commissioned the purchase of 16 Four F Sixes, pre–World War II aircraft. They will be built completely from scratch to the exact specifications used for the originals. As further authentication, the aircraft will be made using the technology and manufacturing processes available when the originals were built. Each of the 16 airplanes will be flown to Air Force and aviation museums throughout the country for exhibition. Aviation enthusiasts can also visit the production facility to see exactly how such aircraft were built in 1938.

Soren Industries wants to bid on the aircraft contract and asked for and received certain cost information about the Four F Sixes from the Air Force. The information includes some of the old cost data from the builders of the original aircraft. The available information is for the total accumulated time as the 1st, 8th, and 32nd aircrafts, respectively, were completed. The data reflect a learning rate of 90%.

Output	Total Hours
1	250
8	1,458
32	4,724

Required

1. If Soren Industries expects that the manufacturing time and learning rate will be the same as it was in 1938, how many hours will it take to build the 16 aircraft for the Air Force Museum Foundation? Assume also that the learning that took place in the 1930s is no longer applicable, and that learning begins anew at 250 hours for the first unit.

2. What is the role of learning curves in Soren Industries's business for contracts such as this?

[LO 8-5]   8-52 **Learning Curves**   Hat Tricks Company (HTC) is a Buffalo, New York, manufacturer of hats and gloves. Recently, the company purchased a new machine to aid in producing the hat product lines. Production efficiency on the new machine increases with the workforce experience. It has been shown that as cumulative output on the new machine increases, average labor time per unit decreases up to the production of at least 3,200 units. As HTC's cumulative output doubles from a base of 100 units produced, the cumulative average labor time per unit declines by a learning rate of 80%.

HTC has developed a new style of men's hat to be produced on the new machine. One hundred of these hats can be produced in a total of 40 labor hours. All other direct costs to produce each hat are $12 per hat, excluding direct labor cost. Direct labor cost per hour is $25. Fixed costs are $8,000 per month, and HTC has the capacity to produce 3,200 hats per month.

Required   HTC plans to set the selling price for the new men's hat at 200% of direct production cost. If the company is planning to sell 100 hats, what is the selling price? If the plan is to sell 800 hats, what should be the selling price?

[LO 8-1, 8-5]   8-53 **Learning Curves**   Ellington Company manufactures a line of motorbikes and dirt bikes under the trade name CrossCountry. The company has been in business for almost 20 years and has maintained a profitable share of the recreational vehicle market due to its reputation for high-quality products. In addition, Ellington's engineering department has kept the company in the forefront by incorporating the latest technology in the CrossCountry bikes. Most subassembly work for the bikes is subcontracted to reliable vendors. However, the final assembly and inspection of all products is performed at Ellington's plant.

Ellington recently developed a new braking system for the CrossCountry Model-500 dirt bike. Because of the company's current availability of production capacity, Jim Walsh, production manager, recommended that the first lot of the new braking system be manufactured in-house rather than by subcontractors. This 50-unit production run has now been completed. The cumulative average labor hours per unit for the braking system was 50 hours. Ellington's experience with similar products indicates that a learning curve of 80% is applicable and that the learning factor can be expected to extend only through the fourth production run (50 per batch) for a total of 200 units.

Ellington's direct labor cost is $16.00 per direct labor hour. Its management must decide whether to continue producing the braking system in its own plant or to subcontract this work. Joyce Lane, Ellington's purchasing agent, has received a proposal from MACQ, a company specializing in component assembly. MACQ has done work in the past for Ellington and has proved to be a high-quality and reliable vendor. The terms of MACQ's proposal are negotiable, and before beginning discussions with them, Joyce has decided to conduct some relevant financial analysis.

Required

1. Ellington Company has an immediate requirement for a total of 1,000 units of the braking system. Determine the company's future direct labor costs to produce the required braking system units if it manufactures the units in-house.

2. A consultant has advised Joyce that the learning rate for this application might be closer to 75%. What is the effect on projected costs of using a 75% learning rate as opposed to an 80% learning rate?

3. What conditions in a manufacturing plant, if present, would offset the potential benefits of the learning curve? What is the strategic role of learning curve analysis for Ellington Company?

(CMA Adapted)

[LO 8-3, 8-4]   8-54 **Cross-Sectional Regression; Analysis of Rankings (See also Problem 8-55)**   *Bloomberg Businessweek* magazine periodically publishes a ranking of the Top Companies: Best Places to Work. The ranking gives employers, employees, and potential employees a snapshot of the overall achievements these companies have made in creating a productive and rewarding work environment. The ranking considers a number of factors (we will call these independent variables), including surveys of career service directors at U.S. colleges, surveys of the organizations themselves (on pay, benefits, and training programs, etc.), and surveys of undergraduate students. The survey data are used to create a ranking for each independent variable of the top companies. Past rankings and survey data for the top 25 organizations are shown next:

Organization/Industry	Rank	Employer Survey	Student Survey	Career Service Director Survey	Average Pay
Deloitte & Touche/accounting	1	1	8	1	55
Ernst & Young/accounting	2	6	3	6	50
PricewaterhouseCoopers/ accounting	3	22	5	2	50
KPMG/accounting	4	17	11	5	50
U.S. State Department/government	5	12	2	24	60
Goldman Sachs/investment banking	6	3	13	16	60
Teach for America/nonprofit; government	7	24	6	7	35
Target/retail	8	19	18	3	45
JPMorgan/investment banking	9	13	12	17	60
IBM/technology	10	11	17	13	60
Accenture/consulting	11	5	38	15	60
General Mills/consumer products	12	3	33	28	60
Abbott Laboratories/health	13	2	44	36	55
Walt Disney/hospitality	14	60	1	8	40
Enterprise Rent-A-Car/ transportation	15	28	51	4	35
General Electric/manufacturing	16	19	16	9	55
Phillip Morris/consumer products	17	8	50	19	55
Microsoft/technology	18	28	9	34	75
Prudential/insurance	19	9	55	37	50
Intel/technology	20	14	23	63	60
Aflac/insurance	21	9	55	62	50
Verizon Communications/utilities	22	15	37	49	40
Central Intelligence Agency (CIA)/ government	23	45	7	29	45
Raytheon/manufacturing	24	23	39	19	60
Nestlé/consumer products	25	20	31	44	50

Required

1. Using regression analysis, develop a regression model to predict company rank based on the four independent variables—employer survey rank, student survey rank, career service director rank, and average pay. Determine which, if any, of these four independent variables are significantly correlated with the overall ranking. Which is the strongest and which is the weakest independent variable, and why?

2. What are some of the limitations of the analysis you have completed in requirement 1?

[LO 8-3, 8-4]   8-55   **Cross-Sectional Regression; Rankings (See also Problem 8-54)**   *Fortune* magazine prepares an annual report of Best Companies (http://fortune.com/best-companies/) that ranks companies for workplace environment. The top 15 companies that provided selected data in the 2019 ranking are shown below, together with some basic data about the companies. *Fortune* magazine's ranking is based upon surveys of employees in the participating firms. Survey questions focus on attitudes about management, job satisfaction, and their experiences of trust and reaching their potential as part of the organization, no matter who they are or what they do.

Organization/Industry	Survey Rank*	Number of Employees	% Minority	Number of Openings
Hilton/hospitality	1	62,403	69	6,492
Salesforce/information technology	2	21,783	35	6,621
Wegmans Food Markets/retail grocery	3	48,808	24	2,000

(Continued)

Workday/information technology	4	7,962	43	1,330
Kimpton Hotels & Restaurants/ hospitality	5	8,813	55	630
Cisco/information technology	6	37,352	45	2,814
Edward Jones/financial services	7	45,085	7	4,166
Ultimate Software/information technology	8	5,274	43	1,000
Texas Health Resources/health care	9	22,055	84	944
Stryker/manufacturing & production	11	19,232	26	1,590
Publix Super Markets/retail grocery	12	200,000	43	7,000
Quicken Loans/financial services	14	15,307	31	724
Baird/financial services	16	3,472	8	140
JM Family Enterprises/manufacturing & production	17	4,188	35	129
Kimley-Horn/professional services	18	3,541	18	419

* Firms ranked 10, 13, and 15 did not report the requested employment data.

Required Use regression analysis to analyze the rankings and to determine if the rankings are related to the number of employees, new jobs (hires) in the past year, or number of job openings. What insights about the characteristics of the best companies do these data provide?

[LO 8-3] 8-56 **Cost Estimation; Regression Analysis** Plantcity is a large nursery and retail store specializing in house and garden plants and supplies. Jean Raouth, the assistant manager, is in the process of budgeting monthly supplies expense for 2022. She assumes that in some way supplies expense is related to sales, either in units or in dollars. She has collected these data for sales and supplies expenses for June 2019 through December 2021 and has estimated sales for 2022:

Date	Supplies Expense	Sales (units)	Sales (dollars)
June 2019	$2,745	354	$20,090
July	3,200	436	21,900
August	3,232	525	28,780
September	2,199	145	18,560
October	2,321	199	21,680
November	3,432	543	21,520
December	4,278	1,189	24,630
January 2020	2,310	212	19,990
February	2,573	284	21,900
March	2,487	246	18,940
April	2,484	278	21,340
May	3,384	498	32,100
June	2,945	424	28,500
July	2,758	312	22,650
August	3,394	485	24,350
September	2,254	188	18,930
October	2,763	276	22,320
November	3,245	489	30,040
December	4,576	1,045	33,090
January 2021	2,103	104	21,950
February	2,056	167	20,450
March	3,874	298	23,010
April	2,784	398	23,450
May	2,345	187	18,150
June	2,912	334	20,940
July	2,093	264	19,340
August	2,873	333	20,540
September	2,563	143	19,770

(Continued)

Date	Supplies Expense	Sales (units)	Sales (dollars)
October	2,384	245	18,570
November	2,476	232	21,890
December	3,364	1,122	34,330
January 2022 (estimated)		180	$16,000
February		230	20,000
March		190	19,000
April		450	24,000
May		350	23,000
June		350	23,000
July		450	25,000
August		550	30,000
September		300	25,000
October		300	25,000
November		450	32,000
December		950	39,000

Required

1. Develop the regression that Jean should use based on these data. Evaluate the reliability and precision of the regression you have chosen. (*Hint:* Graph the data and look for patterns.)

2. What are the predicted monthly figures for supplies expense for 2022?

[LO 8-3, 8-4]   8-57 **Cross-Sectional Regression Analysis**   WasteTec is a large construction company that specializes in the construction of large wastewater treatment plants and recycling plants. A major cost driver in either type of facility is the capacity of the plant. For example, the capacity of a recycling plant is measured by the number of tons of water per day (TPD) that the plant can process. These plants can vary in size from a few hundred TPD to as many as several thousand TPD. Regression analysis is a useful method to estimate the cost of a new plant by using a regression equation developed from prior plant construction projects. The dependent variable of the regression is the actual construction costs of each project, while the independent variable is the TPD for the plant. Below is a sample of some recent projects and the related construction costs (in thousands):

	TPD	Costs
Commerce, CA	360	$ 59,369
Hudson Falls, NY	400	77,013
Layton, UT	420	50,405
Oxford Township, NJ	450	75,779
Savannah, GA	500	87,439
Poughkeepsie, NY	506	57,463
Panama City, FL	510	60,730
Ronkonkoma, NY	518	84,457
Okahuma, FL	528	88,119
Spokane, WA	800	152,902
Arlington, VA	975	127,021
Camden, NJ	1,050	163,395
York, PA	1,344	139,302
Bridgeport, CT	2,250	344,852
Chester, PA	2,688	448,073

Required

1. Develop a regression model to predict the cost of a proposed new plant in Babylon, New York, which will have a required capacity of 750 TPD. What is the predicted cost for the Babylon plant?

2. Evaluate the precision and reliability of the regression you have developed. How could it be improved?

3. How would you incorporate sustainability issues in the analysis you have completed in requirements 1 and 2?

[LO 8-2]   8-58 **Developing a Regression Model**   Electric IQ is a software company that develops systems for managing electricity use. The company has been successful, reaching $25 million in sales after its fourth year of operations. Now the company is considering a new product line that would focus on the newly developing renewable energy sources such as wind power. To examine the potential for this new product line, the company developed a model to forecast the demand for renewable energy.

In identifying the independent variables for its forecasting model, the company decided to identify the key drivers of demand for renewable energy. The drivers were identified on two levels. The first-level drivers (social opinion and political action) contributed directly to the demand for renewable energy, while the second-level drivers contributed to the first-level drivers and, therefore, indirectly contributed to the demand for renewable energy. For example, the reporting on climate change, the technical viability of the renewable energy, and the cost of renewable energy influenced social opinion, which in turn influenced the demand for renewable energy. The drivers identified initially by Electric IQ are as follows:

Level 1 Drivers	Level 1 and Level 2 Drivers	
	Social Opinion	**Political Action**
Level 2 Drivers	Climate change data	Governmental subsidies
	Technical viability	Regulations
	Cost	Tax benefits

Required Assume that you are advising Electric IQ on developing a regression model for forecasting the demand for renewable energy. Discuss how you would measure the dependent and independent variables.

[LO 8-3] 8-59 **High-Low; Analysis of Regression Results** Regression analysis is commonly used to estimate costs. However, the usefulness of the results depends upon the quality of the data.

Fletcher Inc. is a local delivery company. The employees handle deliveries for a variety of companies that have developed apps that allow customers to place orders for food, beverages, packages, etc. The controller of Fletcher would like to come up with an estimate of the cost behavior for the delivery costs. Fifteen months of data were collected, and the data appear below.

Using the high-low method, the controller did a quick calculation and estimated the variable and fixed portions of the delivery costs. A new employee in the accounting department, however, suggested that regression would give a much better estimate of the costs.

Observation	Delivery Costs	Number of Deliveries
1	$148,620	11,540
2	150,980	12,180
3	199,200	16,560
4	143,100	11,685
5	203,695	16,685
6	183,065	14,875
7	156,390	13,010
8	193,440	13,010
9	189,330	15,555
10	151,200	11,970
11	158,445	12,630
12	188,085	15,300
13	182,320	14,580
14	144,520	11,980
15	155,680	13,000

Required
1. Using the given data, determine the estimated cost equation for delivery costs using the high-low method.
2. Using the data available, determine the estimated cost equation for the delivery costs using regression.
3. Graph the data to determine if any adjustments should be made to the regression analysis done in requirement 2.
4. Recompute the estimated cost equation for the delivery costs after making any adjustments to the data as a result of your analysis in requirement 3. What can you conclude about the various cost equations?

[LO 8-3] 8-60 **Cost Estimating for Defense Contracting; Using the Internet** Companies that do business with the U.S. Department of Defense (e.g., The Boeing Company, Lockheed Martin Corporation, General Electric, Northrop Grumman, and General Dynamics) typically develop large multiyear proposals for large-scale, defense-related projects. A key aspect of developing a successful proposal for the Department of Defense is to use proper cost estimation methods.

Required

1. Review the information at the site of the International Society of Parametric Analysis (ISPA) (**www.galorath.com/images/uploads/ISPA_PEH_4th_ed_Final.pdf**), which sets out proper estimation methods for proposals to the Department of Defense. Look especially at Chapter 3 of the ISPA's handbook. In 100 words or less, describe the cost estimation methods suggested in this document for use in developing proposals for the Defense Department. What are some examples of how cost estimation is used by defense contractors such as Boeing?

2. Review Figure 3.6 in the ISPA handbook and compare it to the related information found in this chapter. You might also consider looking at the information in the Regression Analysis Supplement on the course website (especially Exhibit S.7).

Solutions to Self-Study Problems

1. Using the High-Low Method

Begin by graphing the data to determine whether there are any unusual (i.e., seasonal) patterns or outliers, as shown in Exhibit 1.

An inspection of the graph shows no unusual patterns, so the low point (March) and the high point (December) are representative of the data and the high-low estimate can be determined as follows:

To determine the slope of the line (unit variable cost):

$$\frac{(201,783 - 123,245)}{(7,433 - 5,166)} = \$34.644 \text{ per delivery}$$

To determine the intercept:

$$\text{Using December: } \$201,783 - (7,433 \times \$34.644) = -\$55,726$$
$$\text{Using March: } \quad \$123,245 - (5,166 \times \$34.644) = -\$55,726$$

The estimation equation is

$$\text{Vehicle costs } = -\$55,726 + (\$34.644 \times \text{Number of deliveries})$$

Note that the intercept is a negative number, which simply means that the relevant range of 5,166 to 7,433 deliveries is so far from the zero point (where the intercept is) that the intercept cannot be properly interpreted as a fixed cost. The estimation equation therefore is useful only within the relevant range of approximately 5,000 to 7,500 deliveries and should not be used to estimate costs outside that range.

EXHIBIT 1
Plot of Data for Hector's Delivery Service

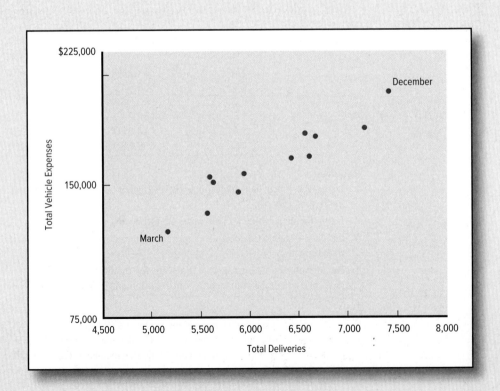

2. Using Regression Analysis

All relevant criteria favor the first regression based on higher *R*-squared and *t*-values and lower standard error. Moreover, the sign on the direct materials cost variable in regression 2 is negative, which is difficult to explain. This variable should have a direct relationship with overhead; thus, the sign of the variable should be positive. The reason for the improvement of regression 1 over regression 2 might be that machine hours are highly correlated with either direct materials costs, direct labor hours, or both, thus causing multicollinearity. By using regression 1, George excludes machine hours as an independent variable, thereby reducing or removing the multicollinearity.

3. Using Both High-Low and Regression

Begin by graphing the data for the number of defective units, as shown in Exhibit 2. The objective is to identify any unusual patterns that must be considered in developing an estimate.

Exhibit 2 shows that the number of defective units varies considerably from month to month and that a steady increase has occurred over the past two years. Knowing that the production level also has been increasing (as measured by either cost of sales, units produced, or units shipped), we now want to determine whether the relationship between defects and production level (Exhibit 3) has changed.

We begin with units produced as the independent variable because it should have the most direct relationship with defects; the other independent variables can be tried later. The second graph (Exhibit 3) makes clear that a relationship exists between units produced and the number of defects.

The next step is to quantify this relationship with the high-low method and regression analysis. We begin with the high-low analysis. For Exhibit 3, we identify Year 1 and Year 2 as representative low and high periods, respectively. Others may decide that other data points are more representative of the low and high periods, which is an inherent problem with the high-low method.

We calculate the high-low estimate as follows (these two points are not the absolute lowest and highest points, but they produce a line that is representative of the data):

$$\text{Slope} = (2{,}311 - 1{,}335) \div (88 - 58) = 32.533$$

And

$$\text{Intercept} = 2{,}311 - (32.533 \times 88) = 1{,}335 - (32.533 \times 58) = -552$$

Thus, the estimation equation is

$$\text{Number of defects} = -552 + (32.533 \times \text{Units produced})$$

The high-low estimate is subject to the limitations of subjectivity in the choice of high and low points and because it uses only those two data points to develop the estimate. Regression is performed to provide a more precise estimate. Thus, the next step is to obtain a regression analysis from the previous data and to assess the precision and reliability of the regression estimate. The regression can be completed with a

EXHIBIT 2
**Defective Units from
January Year 1 to
December Year 2**

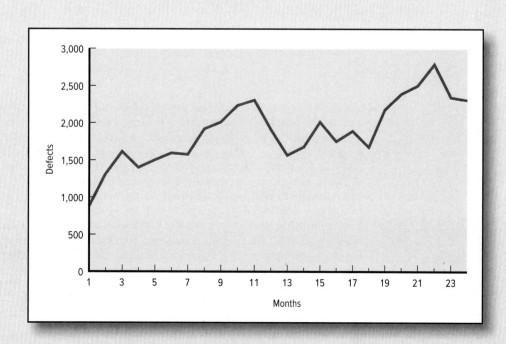

EXHIBIT 3
Defective Units vs. Production Level

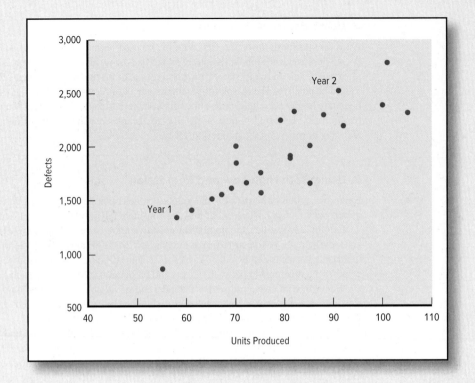

EXHIBIT 4
Regressions for the Number of Defects

Intercept	Coefficient of Independent Variable	t-Value for Independent Variable	R-Squared	Standard Error of the Estimate (SE)
Regression 1				
103.20			.883	161
	−38.974 (units shipped)	−.44		
	−2.849 (units produced)	−.38		
	4.702 (cost of sales)	.72		
Regression 2				
92.24			.881	158
	−2.230 (units produced)	−.309		
	1.837 (cost of sales)	4.54		
Regression 3				
43.95			.881	155
	1.720 (cost of sales)	12.77		

spreadsheet program or any of a number of available software packages. The results for three regression analyses are presented in Exhibit 4. The dependent variable in each case is the number of defective units.

Regression 1 has the following independent variables: cost of sales, units shipped, and units produced. R-squared and SE are OK, but we observe that all three t-values are less than 2.0, indicating unreliable independent variables. Because it is possible there could be correlation among these variables and because of the low t-values, we suspect multicollinearity may exist in this regression. To reduce the effect of multi-collinearity, we try regression 2, which removes the variable units shipped because that variable is likely to be least associated with defective units and has among the lowest of the t-values. R-squared for regression 2 is essentially the same as for regression 1, although SE improves very slightly, and the t-value for cost of sales is now OK. The results of regression 3, with the cost of sales variable only, show that SE and the t-value improve again while R-squared is unchanged. Because it has the best SE and t-values, and a very good R-squared, the third regression is the best choice.

4. Nonlinear Regression and Learning Curves

1. The regression solution for the Virilli case is shown below. The value of $b = -0.3394$, and the value of $a = 10^{2.02881} = 106.86$. The regression measures look good, as the R-squared is relatively high at .947 and the t-value for the coefficient, b, is -10.35. Overall these measures indicate that the regression has a good fit.

2. The value for Y when $X = 133$ is determined as follows:

$$Y = 106.86 \times 133^{-0.3394} = 20.33$$

X	Y	LogX	LogY
10	45	1	1.653213
18	40	1.255273	1.602060
25	38	1.397940	1.579784
43	32	1.633468	1.505150
55	30	1.740363	1.477121
70	25	1.845098	1.397940
93	22	1.968483	1.342423
110	20	2.041393	1.301030

Regression Statistics	
Multiple R	0.97313
R-squared	0.94698
Standard error	0.03162
Observations	8

	Coefficient	Standard Error	t-Stat
Intercept	2.02881	0.053959	37.59928
LogX	−0.3394	0.032782	−10.3522

Please visit Connect to access a narrated, animated tutorial for solving this problem.

CHAPTER NINE

Short-Term Profit Planning: Cost-Volume-Profit (CVP) Analysis

After studying this chapter, you should be able to . . .

LO 9-1   Explain CVP analysis, the CVP model, and the strategic role of CVP analysis.

LO 9-2   Apply CVP analysis for breakeven planning.

LO 9-3   Apply CVP analysis for profit planning.

LO 9-4   Apply CVP analysis for activity-based costing.

LO 9-5   Explain different approaches for dealing with risk and uncertainty in CVP analysis.

LO 9-6   Adapt CVP analysis for multiple products/services.

LO 9-7   Apply CVP analysis in not-for-profit organizations.

LO 9-8   Identify the assumptions and limitations of CVP analysis.

natmac stock/Shutterstock

For some companies, just about each product or service is new and different. This is true for iHeartMedia Inc. (**www.iheartmedia.com/**), a leading global media and entertainment company. Many readers may be familiar with the company's iHeartRadio service that provides more than 100 million registered users access to iHeartMedia's more than 850 radio

324

stations, millions of custom stations, and a variety of podcast offerings. Streaming of content is not their only service. iHeartMedia also presents world-class events spanning all genres of music. Each of the thousands of events it promotes offers a new opportunity to be profitable, but careful planning is necessary to achieve success. A key part of this planning for iHeart-Media is to use cost-volume-profit (CVP) analysis, the topic of this chapter. CVP analysis can be used to project estimated profits for each live event, given the company's projections about attendance; that is, CVP analysis shows the relationship between volume of attendance and the event's related costs and profits.

Some music events are planned on a fixed-fee basis; that is, the entertainer is paid a fixed amount for the performance that is not tied to attendance. Other events are planned so that the entertainer receives a payment based on attendance. The fixed-fee arrangement is somewhat riskier for iHeartMedia because the company then bears the risk of low attendance and therefore low profits or losses; of course, the upside is that if attendance is high, the company does well. In contrast, the entertainer paid on the basis of attendance shares some of the risk.

iHeartMedia uses projected ticket sales and CVP analysis to carefully project costs and profits and to plan levels of advertising and other expenses. This type of short-term profit planning is critical for any organization's overall success and profitability.

Cost-Volume-Profit Analysis

LO 9-1

Explain CVP analysis, the CVP model, and the strategic role of CVP analysis.

cost-volume-profit (CVP) analysis
A short-term profit-planning model; a method for analyzing how various operating decisions and marketing decisions will affect short-term profit.

Cost-volume-profit (CVP) analysis is a method for analyzing how various operating and marketing decisions affect short-term profit based on an understanding of the relationship between variable costs, fixed costs, unit selling price, and the output level (i.e., volume). CVP analysis has many applications:

- Setting prices for products and services.
- Determining the short-term cost or profit implications of many decisions.
- Deciding whether to introduce a new product or service.
- Determining the desirability of replacing a piece of equipment (or other fixed asset).
- Determining the breakeven point (i.e., volume level, Q, at which operating income = $0).
- Deciding whether to make or buy a given product or service.
- Determining the best product mix.
- Performing strategic "what-if" analyses.

CVP analysis is based on an explicit model of the relationships among the five factors that combine to determine the amount of short-term operating profit: variable cost per unit, total fixed costs, sales volume, selling price per unit, and sales mix.[1] The CVP model is

$$\text{Operating profit} = \text{Sales} - \text{Total costs}$$

where operating profit is profit exclusive of unusual or nonrecurring items and is *before* tax.[2] When there are no unusual or nonrecurring items, operating profit is simply before-tax income, π_B. Because we will be looking at how costs and sales vary with volume, it is important to distinguish variable and fixed costs and to show the above equation in the equivalent form below:

$$\text{Operating profit} = \text{Sales} - \text{Variable costs} - \text{Fixed costs}$$

---

[1] Sales mix, by definition, is relevant to the multiproduct (or multiservice) firm. We consider this context later in the chapter.

[2] In addition, note that *operating profit* is defined as profit before the deduction of financing costs. Thus, in the basic CVP model, we exclude fixed *financing* costs (i.e., interest expense). The extension of formulas presented in this chapter to include fixed interest expense are presented in T. Zivney and J. Goebel, "The Relationship between the Breakeven Point and Degrees of Leverage," *Journal of Financial Education* 11 (2013), pp. 122–126. For simplicity, in this chapter we use the terms *operating profit* and *pretax profit*, π_B, synonymously. Further, *fixed costs* (*F*) will be taken to mean "fixed operating costs."

The concept of breaking even relates to reporting zero operating income. This could be true for the company as a whole or for a specific product or venture.

ADJUSTING PRICES TO BREAK EVEN

Container ships move more than 95 percent of the world's manufactured goods. Slowing global trade and oversupply of shipping capacity has put downward pressure on the rates shipping companies can charge. Late last year, the freight rate, which is the price charged, averaged less than $700 per container, but the breakeven price is $1,400. Shipping companies are losing money because the $700 price barely covers the cost of the fuel to run the ship. Because of the carrying capacity of a ship, the company cannot simply add more volume, and it is difficult to cut any costs out of running a ship between two

ports, so that leaves price as the mechanism to try to reach profitability.

IT'S ALL ABOUT VOLUME

The New Zealand-based company RocketWerkz released one of the first virtual reality video games. The developers were hopeful that the game would break even, or maybe even turn a profit—it didn't. After spending nearly $650,000 on creating the game, RocketWerkz set a $20 price. It was the volume that ultimately determined whether the product would break even. The company sold enough games to cover only about 60 percent of the creation costs, meaning RocketWerkz lost money.

Sources: Costas Paris, "Taiwan Aids Shipping Firms," *The Wall Street Journal*, November 17, 2016, p. B4; Sarah E. Needleman, "Pricey VR Headsets Are Slow to Catch On," *The Wall Street Journal*, February 15, 2017, p. B4.

Now, replacing sales with the number of units sold times the selling price per unit, and replacing variable costs with the number of units sold times the variable cost per unit, the CVP model is

$$\text{Operating profit} = (\text{Units sold} \times \text{Selling price per unit})$$
$$- (\text{Units sold} \times \text{Variable cost per unit}) - \text{Fixed costs}$$

For convenience, the CVP model is typically shown in notational form, as follows:

$$\pi_B = (p \times Q) - (v \times Q) - F$$

where
- Q = Units sold (i.e., sales volume)
- p = Selling price per unit
- F = Total fixed costs
- v = Variable cost per unit
- π_B = Operating profit (i.e., profit before tax and before financing costs)

Contribution Margin and Contribution Income Statement

Effective use of the CVP model requires an understanding of three additional concepts: the contribution margin, the contribution margin ratio, and the contribution income statement. Contribution margin can be defined either on a per-unit basis or in total. The **contribution margin per unit** is the difference between the selling price per unit (p) and the variable cost per unit (v):

$$p - v = \text{Contribution margin per unit}$$

contribution margin per unit
The difference between the selling price per unit (p) and the variable cost per unit (v); a measure of the change in operating profit for each unit change in sales.

The contribution margin per unit measures the change in operating profit for each unit change in sales. If, for example, sales are expected to increase by 100 units, operating profit should increase by 100 times the contribution margin per unit. Conversely, if sales are expected to decrease by 100 units, the operating profit would decrease by 100 times the unit contribution margin. The **total contribution margin** is the contribution margin per unit multiplied by the number of units sold, Q.

total contribution margin
The contribution margin per unit, ($p - v$), multiplied by the number of units sold, Q.

For example, assume that Household Furnishings Inc. (HFI), a manufacturer of home furnishings, is interested in developing a new product, a wooden gaming table, that would be priced at $75 and would have variable costs of $35 per unit. Assume also that the new product will have no effect on sales of existing products. The investment would require new fixed costs of $5,000 per month ($60,000/yr). HFI expects sales of 2,400 units in the first year (2022) and 2,600 units in the second year (2023). These data for HFI are summarized in Exhibit 9.1.

The contribution margin per unit would be $40 ($75 – $35). If HFI expects to sell 2,400 of the new tables in 2022, it would expect total contribution margin in 2022 to increase by

EXHIBIT 9.1
Data for Household Furnishings Inc. (HFI): Gaming Table

	Per Unit	2022	2023
Fixed costs (per year)		$60,000	$60,000
Selling price	$75		
Variable cost	35		
Planned production		2,400 units	2,600 units
Planned sales volume		2,400 units	2,600 units

$96,000 ($40 × 2,400) and operating profit to increase by $36,000 ($96,000 – $60,000 fixed cost). In 2023, operating profit would be expected to increase because of a 200-unit increase in sales, from 2,400 to 2,600 units. Because estimated fixed costs are the same in both years, the projected increase in operating profit from 2022 to 2023 is equal to the change in total contribution margin from 2022 to 2023, that is, contribution margin per unit of $40 times the increase in units sold (200), or $8,000. These results are shown in Exhibit 9.2.

contribution margin ratio
The ratio of the contribution margin per unit to the selling price per unit, $(p - v) \div p$.

A measure of the profit contribution per sales dollar is the **contribution margin ratio,** which is the ratio of the contribution margin per unit to the selling price per unit, $(p - v) \div p$. The contribution margin ratio for HFI's gaming table is 53.33 percent = ($75 – $35) ÷ $75. This ratio identifies the projected increase (or decrease) in operating profit caused by a given increase (or decrease) in sales *dollars.* What is the effect on operating profit of an increase of $15,000 in sales from 2022 to 2023? We can quickly calculate that from 2022 to 2023 estimated operating profit is expected to increase by $8,000 ($15,000 × 0.5333).

contribution income statement
In a contribution income statement, variable costs are subtracted from sales to get total contribution margin, from which fixed costs are subtracted, to yield the amount of operating profit for the period.

A useful way to show the information developed in CVP analysis is to use the contribution income statement. The **contribution income statement** puts the focus on cost behavior because it separates fixed costs and variable costs. In contrast, the conventional income statement, as we used in prior chapters, puts the focus on cost type—product cost and nonproduct cost. In the contribution income statement, variable costs are subtracted from sales to get total contribution margin; fixed costs are then subtracted from total contribution margin to yield the amount of operating profit for the period. In the conventional income statement product costs are subtracted from sales to get gross margin. From gross margin, total operating expenses (fixed plus variable) are deducted to yield the amount of operating profit for the period. Exhibit 9.2 shows the contribution income statement for HFI's gaming tables. Note that the sales increase of 200 units and $15,000 is expected to produce an $8,000 increase in operating profit, as predicted by the contribution margin per unit ($40) and the contribution margin ratio (0.5333). It is not possible to predict the change in operating profit from a given change in sales with a conventional income statement because the conventional income statement does not separate total costs into fixed and variable components.

Strategic Role of CVP Analysis

"Whenever you see a successful business, someone once made a courageous decision."

Peter Drucker

There is no question that starting and running a successful business requires courage, the courage to make difficult decisions. These decisions are not made based strictly on intuition. Rather, there are tools within CVP analysis and strategic analysis that can aid the decision-making

EXHIBIT 9.2 **Contribution Income Statements for HFI's Proposed Gaming Table**

	2022		2023			
	Amount	Percent	Amount	Percent	Change	Notes
Sales	$180,000	100.00%	$195,000	100.00%	$15,000	
Variable costs	84,000	46.67	91,000	46.67	7,000	
Total contribution margin	$ 96,000	53.33%	$104,000	53.33%	$ 8,000	53.33% is the contribution margin ratio
Fixed costs	60,000		60,000		0	
Operating profit	$ 36,000		$ 44,000		$ 8,000	$8,000 = 0.5333 × $15,000

REAL-WORLD FOCUS Cost-Volume-Profit for an Airline

In the middle of 2018, Delta projected that revenue would be up 5 percent over the prior year for each passenger mile flown, but revenue is only one element of the cost-volume-profit relationship. The year 2018 was also a year when many airlines agreed to increase wages and benefits as part of a labor contract. More importantly, however, could be the impact of higher fuel costs that hit the airlines. The surge in fuel costs resulted in U.S. carriers planning to trim capacity and raise the price per seat in order to improve the profit outlook. Improving the profit outlook, however, does not translate into improving profits. Spirit Airlines reported that its increase in passenger revenue

was more than offset by the surge in costs, much of which were rising fuel costs.

We can't forget about another factor in the volume part of cost-volume-profit analysis—demand. Geopolitics and international trade tensions could hurt the demand for business travel. Also, passengers may seek alternative forms of transportation if increased ticket prices make air travel less desirable.

Source: Doug Cameron and Alison Sider, "Airlines Raise Ticket Prices as Fuel Costs Surge," *The Wall Street Journal*, June 7, 2018, p. A1; Andrew Tangel and Alison Sider, "Airlines Hurt by Fuel Costs," *The Wall Street Journal*, July 27, 2018, p. B5.

EXHIBIT 9.3
Strategic Questions That Can Be Addressed by CVP Analysis

1. What is the expected profit from a given change in sales volume for existing products, and is that change in sales volume sufficient to support strategic objectives?
2. Is the decision to add a new customer or product profitable, and is it consistent with the organization's competitive strategy?
3. Given the organization's strategy and future expectations for sales volume, is it best for the company to manufacture a certain part in-house or to purchase the part from another vendor?
4. Given the organization's strategy and future expectations for sales volume, should the organization invest in future expansion?

process. CVP analysis can help a firm execute its strategy by providing an understanding of how changes in its volume of sales affect costs and profits. Many firms, especially cost leadership firms, compete by increasing volume (often through lower prices) to achieve lower total cost per unit. This reduction in costs is achieved principally by spreading fixed costs over more units of output. CVP analysis provides a means to predict the effect of sales growth on operating profit. It also shows the risks in increasing fixed costs if volumes fall.

Some of the strategic questions that can be addressed through CVP analysis are presented in Exhibit 9.3. Note that CVP analysis also has a role in strategic positioning. A firm that has chosen to compete on cost leadership needs CVP analysis primarily at the manufacturing stage of the cost life cycle. The role of CVP analysis here is to identify the most cost-effective manufacturing methods, including automation, outsourcing, and total quality management. Whether manufacturing, retail, or service, a firm following the differentiation strategy needs CVP analysis in the early phases of the cost life cycle to assess the profitability of new products or services and the desirability of new features for existing products and services. In effect, CVP analysis can assist in target costing.

CVP Analysis for Breakeven Planning

LO 9-2

Apply CVP analysis for breakeven planning.

The starting point in many business plans is to determine the **breakeven point**, the point at which total revenue equals total costs so that operating profit is zero. This point can be determined by inserting into the organization's CVP model known (or assumed) values for unit variable cost (v), selling price per unit (p), and total fixed costs (F); setting desired before-tax profit (π_B) equal to zero; and then solving for Q. We can also determine the breakeven point in terms of sales dollars, Y (where $Y = Q \times p$).

breakeven point
The point at which total revenues equal total costs so that operating profit is zero.

Breakeven in Units, Q

Using information from Exhibit 9.2, the operating profit equation for HFI's sale of gaming tables is

$$\text{Operating profit} = \text{Sales} - \text{Variable costs} - \text{Fixed costs}$$
$$\pi_B = (p \times Q) - (v \times Q) - F$$
$$= (\$75 \times Q) - (\$35 \times Q) - \$5,000/\text{month}$$

Setting $\pi_B = 0$, we find that the breakeven point is $Q = 125$ gaming tables per month (1,500 units per year):

$$0 = [(\$75 - \$35) \times Q] - \$5{,}000/\text{month}$$
$$\$40 \times Q = \$5{,}000/\text{month}$$
$$Q = \$5{,}000/\text{month} \div \$40/\text{unit}$$
$$Q = 125 \text{ units/month}$$

For this example, the contribution margin per table sold = \$40. Therefore, at sales of 125 units, the operating profit is zero; at 126 units, the operating profit is \$40; at 127 units, the operating profit is $2 \times \$40 = \$80$; and so on. Using the contribution margin per unit gives us a quick way to estimate the change in operating profit for a change in the number of units sold. For example, at the 128-unit level, estimated operating profit (π_B) would be \$120, as follows:

Sales (128 units × \$75)	\$9,600
Variable costs (128 × \$35)	4,480
Contribution margin	\$5,120
Fixed costs per month	5,000
Operating profit (π_B)	\$ 120

Breakeven in Dollars

We can solve for the breakeven point expressed in sales dollars either indirectly—by multiplying breakeven units by the selling price per unit, p—or directly—by using the equation method in a revised form, where Y is the breakeven point in *sales dollars*. This model is equivalent to the model used for breakeven in units, except that Q is replaced by $Y \div p$ (i.e., sales in dollars divided by selling price per unit = quantity; $Y \div p = Q$), as follows:

$$\text{Operating profit} = \text{Sales} - \text{Variable costs} - \text{Fixed costs}$$
$$0 = (p \times Q) - (v \times Q) - F$$
$$0 = [(p - v) \times (Y \div p)] - F$$
$$0 = [((p - v) \div p) \times Y] - F$$

The quantity $(p - v) \div p$ is the contribution margin ratio. Thus, to break even, the firm would have to generate enough sales dollars, Y, to generate sufficient contribution margin ($Y \times$ the contribution margin ratio) to cover the fixed costs, F.

Continuing with the HFI data in Exhibit 9.2, for 2022 we have total annual variable costs (\$84,000), total annual sales (\$180,000), and total monthly fixed costs (\$5,000). Given this information, we can obtain the contribution margin ratio, $(p - v) \div p = 0.5333$ (\$40 ÷ \$75), and then solve for breakeven in dollars per month, as follows:[3]

$$0 = (0.5333 \times Y) - \$5{,}000/\text{month}^{3}$$
$$\$5{,}000/\text{month} = 0.5333 \times Y$$
$$\$9{,}375/\text{month} = Y$$

Shortcut Formulas

A convenient method for calculating the breakeven point in units is to use the profit equation in its equivalent algebraic form (derived by solving the model for Q and noting that at breakeven, $\pi_B = 0$):

$$Q = \text{Fixed costs} \div \text{Contribution margin per unit}$$
$$= F \div (p - v)$$
$$= \$5{,}000 \div (\$75 - \$35)/\text{unit} = 125 \text{ units/month}$$

---

[3] Note in the equations that sales dollars of \$9,375 per month (Y) equal the breakeven point in units, 125, times the selling price per unit, \$75. In short, $Y = p \times Q$.

The contribution margin method can also be used to obtain breakeven in dollars, using the contribution margin ratio (by solving $Y = F + [(v/p) \times Y]$), as follows:

$$Y = \frac{F}{(p - v)/p}$$

where

$$(p - v)/p = \text{the contribution margin ratio}$$

As noted above, the contribution margin ratio is 0.5333. Therefore,

$$Y = \$5,000 \div 0.5333 = \$9,375/\text{month}$$

CVP Graph and the Profit-Volume Graph

CVP graph
A diagrammatic representation (expressed in units) of how revenues and total costs change over different levels of sales volume.

Breakeven analysis is illustrated graphically in Exhibit 9.4. It shows the CVP graph at the top and the profit-volume graph beneath. The **CVP graph** is a diagram illustrating how the levels of revenues and total costs change over different levels of sales volume as expressed in units. Note in the CVP graph that at sales levels lower than 125 units per month, the revenue line falls below the total cost line, resulting in losses. In contrast, all points above the 125-unit level show a profit. Note that the slope of the total revenue line equals the selling price per unit, p ($75 in our example), while the slope of the total cost line equals the slope of the variable cost line. The slope of the variable cost line is the variable cost per unit, v ($35 in our example). The variable cost line is not shown in the exhibit.

profit-volume graph
Illustrates how the level of operating profit changes over different levels of sales volume, Q.

The **profit-volume graph** in the lower portion of the exhibit illustrates how the level of operating profit changes over different levels of sales volume, expressed in units. At a sales volume of 125 units per month, operating profit is zero. For sales volumes greater than 125 units per month operating profit is positive. The slope of the profit-volume line is the contribution margin per unit, $p - v$; therefore, the profit-volume graph can be used to observe directly how total contribution margin and operating profit change as the sales volume (expressed in units) changes. As illustrated by the profit-volume graph, the breakeven point can be expressed as the volume level that produces just enough contribution margin to cover fixed costs, F.

REAL-WORLD FOCUS   Cost Planning: Own Your Own Wheels?

With Uber recently completing its 10 billionth trip and Lyft completing its one billionth trip, ride-sharing is certainly popular. For those who live in a large urban area, participating in a car-share program (e.g., **www.zipcar.com**), having a car subscription, or simply using a ride-sharing service such as Uber (**www.uber. com/**) or Lyft (**www.lyft.com/**) may make more sense than owning a car. For a small annual fee, the car-sharing program provides a rental car that can be used for shopping excursions, travel to the regional airport, and so on. The subscription model gives the individual access to a vehicle on a regular schedule for a fixed price. In either case, the savings over car ownership can be very significant. The ride-sharing approach requires no annual fees but might have a higher cost per ride than when using car sharing or the subscription model.

Alternatives to car ownership include more than car- and ride-sharing, and in 2019 Lyft even ran a Ditch Your Car program offering passengers transportation credit to give up their cars for a defined 30-day period. The profit-planning model discussed in this chapter can be used to address the relative financial attractiveness of the available options. For example, in terms of the car-share options, one could determine the "cost indifference point"—that is, the number of rental hours per year that would yield identical total costs for each of the other options. Similarly, a "cost indifference point," expressed in number of shared rides, could be calculated and used to help determine whether complete reliance on ride-sharing makes economic sense. Other factors, strategic and nonfinancial matters, are likely to affect the decision as well.

Sources: Shivani Vora, "Test-Driving Car-Share Services," *The Wall Street Journal*, June 11, 2009, p. D2; Tim Higgins, "The End of Car Ownership: Ride Sharing and Self-Driving Vehicles Are Going to Redefine Our Relationship with Cars; Auto Makers and Startups Are Already Gearing Up for the Change," *The Wall Street Journal*, June 21, 2017, p. R1; Harry Campbell, "Should You Ditch Your Car for Uber and Lyft? We Try the Ride-Hailing Life," *Motor Trend*, February 11, 2019, **www.motortrend.com/news/should-you-ditch-your-car-to-rely-on-uber-and-lyft/**, accessed January 18, 2020.

EXHIBIT 9.4
The CVP Graph and the Profit-Volume Graph

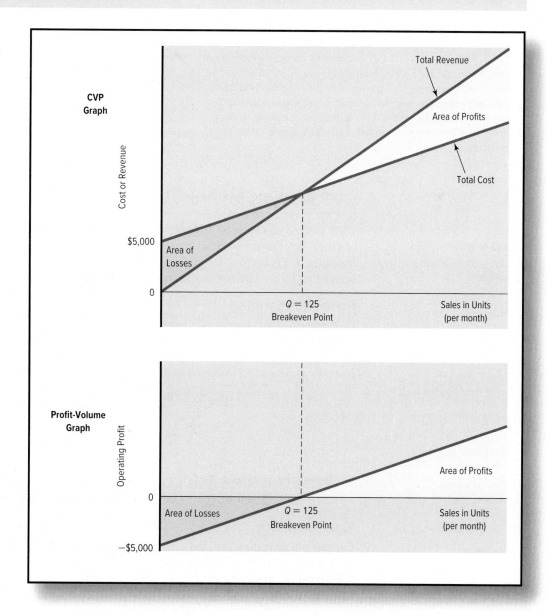

REAL-WORLD FOCUS   Changing Cost Structure at Amazon

Amazon started out as an online seller of books. Acting primarily as an intermediary between the seller and buyer, Amazon had a very low level of fixed costs. Amazon has grown over the years, and its offerings have expanded beyond just books. As part of its growth, this e-commerce giant has seen a change in its cost structure over time.

ORDER-FULFILLMENT PROCESSES: HUMAN VS. MACHINE

How do large, online retailers, such as Crate & Barrel and Amazon.com, meet seasonal demand: temporary workers or automated technology (such as robots)? Crate & Barrel reports that in one of its warehouses, robots have largely replaced human employees in the order-fulfillment process. Rather than having employees amble about the warehouse to pick items from shelves, these machines carry item-stocked shelves to employees who are then able to complete customer orders. The company reports that the use of machines during the busy holiday season enables it to reduce human labor to about half of what it would otherwise be.

Meanwhile, Amazon.com takes an alternative approach to filling customer orders. At its distribution centers, employees walk 18 to 20 miles a day down aisles lined with shelves, filling library-style carts with the latest orders and carrying items back to packing stations. Nationwide, Amazon.com significantly expands employee hiring during the busy holiday season. In short, it makes more extensive use of humans rather than machines.

Which cost-structure choice to use—increased variable costs or increased fixed cost (associated with the use of robots)—is the subject of debate among those in the e-commerce industry. Thus far, Amazon.com has eschewed the use of automated technology at its order-fulfillment centers, aside from systems that came with acquisitions such as Diapers.com.

Kiva Systems Inc., the company that makes the machines used by Crate & Barrel and other large U.S. retailers (such as Staples Inc. and Gap Inc.), is testing the idea of seasonal leases of robotic systems, an arrangement that would reduce both the short-term fixed cost and the risk of obsolescence for companies taking advantage of this option.

BRICK-AND-MORTAR BOOKSTORES

While it started out as a purely online retailer of books, Amazon has moved into the brick-and-mortar world of selling books. In February 2017, Amazon opened its first Amazon Books store in Massachusetts. Amazon describes the store as a physical extension of its e-commerce business. Descriptions aside, this transition to physical retail locations comes with the related fixed and variable costs of any other retailer with a physical presence, and certainly is a move away from its purely online roots.

Source: Geoffrey A. Fowler, "Holiday Help: People vs. Robots," *The Wall Street Journal,* December 19, 2010 (accessed at https://online.wsj.com/news/articles/SB10001424052748704073804576023613748146944); Kyle Scott Clauss, "Amazon's Brick-and-Mortar Bookstore in Dedham Opens This Week," *Boston Magazine,* February 27, 2017, https://www.boston-magazine.com/news/2017/02/27/amazon-dedham-bookstore-opens/, accessed January 18, 2020.

CVP Analysis for Profit Planning

LO 9-3

Apply CVP analysis for profit planning.

CVP analysis can be used to determine the level of sales needed to achieve a desired level of profit, determined on either a pretax or an after-tax basis. As indicated by the following examples, CVP analysis for profit planning involves revenue planning, cost planning, and accounting for the effect of income taxes (when planning for the desired profit *after* taxes).

Revenue Planning

CVP analysis assists managers in revenue planning—that is, determining the revenue required to achieve a desired profit level. For example, if HFI's management wants to know the sales volume necessary to achieve a pretax (i.e., operating) profit of $48,000, we substitute $60,000 for fixed costs ($F$) per year and $48,000 for desired pretax profit (π_B) and then solve for Q, as follows:

$$Q = \frac{F + \pi_B}{p - v}$$

$$Q = \frac{\$60,000 + \$48,000}{(\$75 - \$35)/\text{unit}} = 2,700 \text{ units/year}$$

The solution in sales dollars, Y, is

$$Y = p \times Q = \$75/\text{unit} \times 2,700 \text{ units/year} = \$202,500/\text{year}$$

Cost Planning

For cost-planning decisions, the manager assumes that the sales volume and the desired profit are known but wants to find the value of the required variable cost per unit (v) or the total fixed costs (F) to achieve the desired operating profit at the assumed sales volume, Q. Three examples follow.

Trade-Offs between Fixed and Variable Costs—Example One (One Machine)

CVP analysis can be used to determine the most cost-effective trade-off between different types of costs. To continue with the HFI example, assume sales of 2,700 units per year. Management is now considering the purchase of a new machine that will reduce variable cost per unit but also increase total fixed costs (F) by $2,250 per month. How much must the variable cost per unit (v) fall to maintain the current level of operating profit, assuming that sales volume and all other factors remain the same?

Q = 2,700 units F = $5,000 + $2,250 = $7,250/month ($87,000/year)

p = $75/unit π_B = $48,000/year

v = an unknown (previously $35)

Now, instead of solving for Q (which is given as 2,700 units), we solve for v, as follows:

$$Q = \frac{F + \pi_B}{p - v}$$

$$p - v = \frac{F + \pi_B}{Q}$$

$$v = p - \frac{F + \pi_B}{Q}$$

$$v = \$75 - [(\$87,000 + \$48,000) \div 2,700] = \$25$$

In effect, for sales and profits to remain unchanged with the increase in fixed costs, variable cost per unit (v) must fall from $35 to $25.

The above calculations can be obtained directly using Goal Seek under the Data/What-If Analysis tab in Excel (as circled in Exhibit 9.5). Note that the information for the HFI case is entered in the spreadsheet, and profit is calculated for the current variable cost per unit of $35 using the following formula in cell B8: "=B3 * (B4 – B5) – B6." The Goal Seek dialog box is shown in Exhibit 9.5. To achieve the desired operating profit of $48,000 by changing unit variable cost, we set Goal Seek to change cell B8, operating profit, to $48,000 by changing cell B5, unit variable cost. Selecting OK will enter the correct value for unit variable cost, $25, in cell B5.

Trade-Offs between Fixed and Variable Costs—Example Two (Two Machines)

A common management decision is choosing the right equipment for the work to be done. Assume, as in the preceding example, that management is considering the purchase of a new machine and has the choice between two machines. For example, one machine might have a relatively high purchase cost but lower projected operating costs compared to an alternative machine. So, the decision is whether to choose a cost structure characterized by (1) high fixed costs and low unit variable cost (the high-fixed-cost option) or (2) relatively low fixed costs and higher unit

EXHIBIT 9.5 Using Goal Seek in CVP Analysis

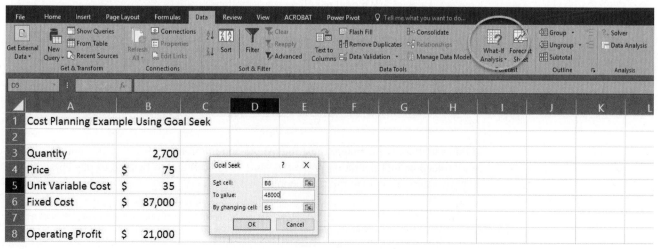

Source: Microsoft Excel

variable costs (the low-fixed-cost option). As sales volume increases, the high-fixed-cost option will be increasingly attractive because it brings a reduction in total variable costs. Breakeven analysis can help to find the sales level at which management would be indifferent between the two options (called the *indifference point*), with sales greater than this level favoring the high-fixed-cost option and sales less than this level favoring the low-fixed-cost option.

Example two assumes that HFI can choose between two machines, either of which will complete the same operation with the same quality, but with different fixed and variable costs. Machine A has fixed costs of $5,000 per year and a variable operating cost per unit of $10, while machine B has fixed costs of $15,000 per year and a variable operating cost per unit of $5. To find the indifference point, where the low-fixed-cost (machine A) and high-fixed-cost (machine B) options have the same total costs, we set the cost equations for each option equal and solve for sales quantity, Q, as follows:

$$\text{Cost of machine A} = \text{Cost of machine B}$$
$$\$5,000 + (\$10 \times Q) = \$15,000 + (\$5 \times Q)$$
$$Q = \$10,000 \div \$5 = 2,000 \text{ units per year}$$

If HFI is operating at more than 2,000 units per year, then machine B should be chosen; if it is operating at below 2,000 units per year, then machine A should be chosen.[4] For example, at 3,000 units, the total cost of machine A is $5,000 + ($10 \times 3,000) = $35,000 per year, while the cost of machine B is $15,000 + ($5 \times 3,000) = $30,000. Thus, the advantage goes to machine B at this sales level. At a level of 2,000 units per year, HFI would be indifferent between the two options.

Sales Commissions and Salaries—Example Three

Another cost-planning use of CVP analysis is to determine the most cost-effective means to manage selling costs. To illustrate, HFI management is reviewing sales salaries and commissions and finds that $1,000 of the monthly $5,000 fixed cost is for sales salaries and that $7.50 of the $35.00 variable cost per unit is a 10 percent sales commission. Suppose HFI management is considering a $450 increase in salaries with an expected reduction in the commission rate. By how much must management reduce the commission rate to keep profits the same, assuming that sales volume and all other factors remain unchanged?

With the proposed changes in variable and fixed costs to accommodate the new salaries and commission plan, fixed costs increase by $450 per month and variable costs decrease as a result of the decrease in the commission rate, r:

$$v = (\text{Commision rate} \times \text{Sales price per unit})$$
$$+ \text{ Other noncommission-based variable costs per unit}$$
$$v = (r \times \$75) + \$27.50 \text{ (i.e., } \$35.00 - \$7.50)$$

And

$$F = \text{Current monthly fixed costs} + \text{Increase in monthly salary}$$
$$F = \$5,000 + \$450 = \$5,450 \text{ per month, or } \$65,400 \text{ per year}$$

Now, we use the CVP model to solve for v, as follows:

$$Q = \frac{F + \pi_B}{p - v}$$
$$v = p - \frac{F + \pi_B}{Q}$$

and substituting for v and F, with $\pi_B = \$48,000$ and $Q = 2,700$ as before:

$$(r \times \$75) + \$27.50 = \$75 - [(\$65,400 + \$48,000) \div 2,700]$$
$$r = 0.0733$$

In this situation, the manager must reduce the commission rate from 10 percent to 7.33 percent to keep annual operating profit the same ($48,000) and to be able to pay an additional monthly salary of $450 to the salespeople.

[4] These conclusions ignore the risk preferences of the decision makers (i.e., they assume that decision makers are risk-neutral). Decision makers who are risk-averse may not be indifferent between the two decision alternatives if expected volume is approximately 2,000 units per year. To minimize potential loss, these individuals might choose the machine with relatively lower fixed costs.

REAL-WORLD FOCUS   Analysis of Social Security Retirement Benefits

By using data from the U.S. Social Security Administration (**www.ssa.gov**), a person thinking about retiring can develop a breakeven model to determine when to apply for benefits. For example, if an individual is choosing between retiring at age 70 versus age 66, how long will it take for the total of the larger payments associated with the former to add up to the total that would have been received by applying earlier? The following website can be used to answer this question: **www.socialsecurity.gov/pubs/EN-05-10147.pdf**. A person

deciding whether to retire at the age of 66 or at 70 can use the analysis in the following graph. This analysis shows that retirees who survive beyond the breakeven age of 82 would receive greater lifetime benefits by waiting to file until age 70. This breakeven age is an average and can vary depending on inflation, tax rates, and an individual's investment returns. After taking these factors into consideration when retiring at the age of 66 or 70, the breakeven age could be when the filers reach their late 80s or early 90s.

Total Cumulative Retirement Benefits at Different Ages

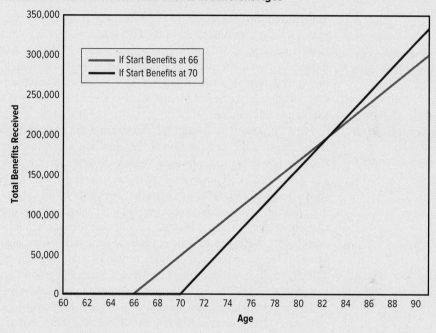

Source: Dan Caplinger, "Is Social Security Breakeven Analysis Fundamentally Flawed?," April 25, 2016 (accessed at **www.fool.com/retirement/general/2016/04/25/is-social-security-breakeven-analysis-fundamentall.aspx**).

Including Income Taxes in CVP Analysis

A manager's decisions about costs and prices usually must include some consideration of income tax effects. Let's assume that in the case of HFI, the desired level of *after-tax* profit is $48,000. If we assume that the effective income tax rate for HFI is 20 percent, then to achieve the desired annual *after-tax* profit, π_A, of $48,000, the company must generate before-tax profits (π_B) of at least $60,000 [$48,000 ÷ (1 − 0.2)]. Thus, when taxes are considered, the CVP model is as follows, where the income tax rate is t:

$$Q = \frac{F + \dfrac{\pi_A}{(1 - t)}}{(p - v)}$$

or

$$Q = \frac{\$60,000 + [\$48,000 \div (1 - 0.2)]}{\$75 - \$35} = 3{,}000 \text{ units per year}$$

This amount is an increase of 300 units over the 2,700 units required for reaching a pretax profit target of $48,000.

Airlines need a certain "passenger load factor" to break even on their flights. The moment a decision is made to fly a plane, the costs of the fuel and landing charges are fixed. If an insufficient number of paying passengers are on the plane, the contribution margin will be less than the fixed costs, resulting in a reduction in operating income. One option is to offer more amenities, which add costs, to attract passengers. Some budget airlines choose to have low prices, in the hope that the resulting volume will generate positive contribution margin to defray their fixed costs. Lately, however, some of the biggest airlines in the United States and Europe (e.g.,

American Airlines, www.aa.com) have begun offering ultra-cheap economy tickets on the same flights that offer expanded amenities for those buying premium business class seating.

Required

Develop a rationale for a company like American Airlines to try to capture both the economy- and premium-minded passengers on the same flights.

(Refer to Comments on Cost Management in Action at the end of the chapter.)

CVP Analysis for Activity-Based Costing

LO 9-4

Apply CVP analysis for activity-based costing.

activity-based costing (ABC)
A costing approach that assigns resource costs to cost objects based on activities performed for the cost objects.

The conventional approach to CVP analysis is to define output in terms of volume (i.e., physical units), as illustrated in the HFI example thus far. An alternative is to use **activity-based costing (ABC)** for constructing the CVP model. ABC identifies cost drivers for indirect cost *activities,* such as machine setup, materials handling, inspection, and engineering. In contrast, in constructing the CVP model, the volume-based approach combines the costs of these activities and treats them as fixed costs because these costs do not vary in the short run with volume.

Here's how activity-based CVP differs from the traditional volume-based approach. Recall from Chapter 5 the classification of activities into four levels: unit, batch, product, and facility. Unit-level costs are volume-based, so they are treated in the same manner under volume-based and ABC-based CVP analysis. Traditional volume-based CVP classifies the other three levels (batch, product, and facility) as costs that do not vary with volume—that is, as fixed costs. However, batch-level costs and product-level costs change with the number of batches or the number of product changes, and ABC-based CVP takes these possibilities into account. Facilities-level costs (e.g., plant expansion) are not avoidable in a short-term planning horizon; these costs take years to change, so facilities costs are treated as fixed costs under both volume-based and ABC-based CVP. In sum, two activity cost levels, batch and product levels, are modeled as costs that can change in ABC-based CVP analysis but not in volume-based CVP analysis.

In contrast to a facilities-level cost, a product-level cost (e.g., a change in product design or features) has a shorter planning period because these changes can be incorporated into the manufacturing process in several months or a small number of years. However, if the planning period is a year or less, as has been the common assumption in this text, then product-level costs will normally not be considered as a cost that can change in either ABC-based or volume-based CVP.

Many batch-level costs (product setup, inspection, purchasing, etc.) can be changed in the short term, so batch-level costs can be considered in a short-term planning horizon. Our example below uses batch-level costs to illustrate ABC-based CVP analysis. Note that these costs are normally considered to be fixed costs in volume-based CVP because these costs do not vary directly with volume.

Now, return to the HFI example from Exhibit 9.1 except we assume that HFI is currently making 3,000 tables. Suppose that the cost accounting staff at HFI has been able to assign approximately $10,000 of the $60,000 of fixed costs to batch-level activities such as machine setup and inspection. This estimate was made based upon results when the firm was operating at 100 batches per year. These costs can be traced directly to each batch, although not to each unit of output. The staff has also learned that this year's production of 3,000 units is to be produced in batches of 30 units, so 100 batches will be produced again this year. We assume that batch-level costs increase in proportion to an increase in the number of batches produced during the year; that is, they increase at the rate of $100 per batch ($10,000 ÷ 100). This assumption says, in effect, that the ABC rate of $100 per batch is a variable cost relative to the cost driver, number of batches.

The activity-based CVP model for the present context is developed as follows:

First, we define new terms for fixed cost: $F = F^{VB} + F^{AB}$,

where

F^{VB} = the portion of short-term fixed costs that does not vary with the activity cost driver, $50,000 (i.e., $60,000 − $10,000)

F^{AB} = the portion of short-term fixed costs ($10,000) that *does* vary with the activity cost driver

Second, we define the following terms:

F^{AB} = the cost per batch for the activity-based cost driver, $10,000 ÷ 100 = $100 per batch

b = the number of units in a batch, 30 in our example (i.e., 3,000 ÷ 100)

$F^{AB} ÷ b$ = the cost per unit of product for batch-related costs for batch size b
    = $3.333 ($100.00 ÷ 30)

Third, the CVP model under ABC is

$$Q = \frac{F^{VB} + \pi_B}{p - v - \left(F^{AB} ÷ b\right)}$$

where π_B = $48,000 (assumed).

Fourth, substituting data from the HFI example into the above equation, we have:

$$Q = \frac{\$50,000 + \$48,000}{\$75 - \$35 - (\$100 ÷ 30)} = 2,673 \text{ units}$$

$$= 89.1 \text{ batches } (2,673 ÷ 30)$$

This method assumes that we hold batch size, *b,* constant and vary the number of batches as the total volume changes. The number of batches must be a whole number, however. In this case, 90 batches are required for the 2,673 units: 89 batches of 30 units each (89 × 30 = 2,670 units) plus one additional batch. The formula to calculate an exact CVP point using 90 batches is as follows, where the total batch-related costs for 90 batches is 90 × $100/per batch = $9,000:

$$Q = \frac{\$50,000 + \$9,000 + \$48,000}{\$75 - \$35} = 2,675 \text{ units}$$

In sum, to achieve the above output goal, the company would produce 89 full batches (30 units/batch, or 2,670 units) plus a batch of 5 units (2,675 − 2,670). At 2,675 units, the total contribution margin of $107,000 (2,675 units × $40/unit) equals total fixed costs plus the target profit, $107,000 (i.e., $50,000 + $9,000 + $48,000).

The solution for the ABC model is slightly lower than the solution determined under the volume-based model (2,675 units vs. 2,700 units) because the ABC method allows for lower total batch-level costs. Instead of a fixed batch-level cost of $10,000 under the volume-based approach, the ABC method allows the batch-level costs to decrease (or increase) as the number of batches decreases (or increases); in this case, batch-level costs decreased from $10,000 to $9,000.

To illustrate the effect of batch size on the solution, suppose that production is scheduled in smaller batches of 20 units and that batch-related costs continue to be $100 per batch. How many units must now be produced and sold to earn a pretax operating profit of $48,000? The answer is 2,800 units and 140 batches, as shown below. Note that the cost of batch-level activities has now increased substantially, from $10,000 for 100 batches to $14,000 for 140 batches because of the smaller batch size.

$$Q = (\$50,000 + \$48,000) ÷ [\$75 - \$35 - (\$100 ÷ 20)]$$

$$= \$98,000 ÷ \$35/\text{unit}$$

$$= 2,800 \text{ units}$$

or

$$= 140 \text{ batches } (2,800 ÷ 20) \text{ of 20 units each}$$

We also could determine this from the following equation, using $14,000 for total batch-level costs:

$$Q = \frac{\$50,000 + \$14,000 + \$48,000}{\$75 - \$35} = 2,800 \text{ units}$$

Notice that the number of units to achieve the desired operating profit increases when the batch size is decreased. This is due directly to the increase in the total batch-level costs as batch size is decreased. CVP analysis based on ABC can provide a more comprehensive analysis of the relationships among volume, costs, and profits by considering batch-level costs.[5]

Dealing with Uncertainty

LO 9-5
Explain different approaches for dealing with risk and uncertainty in CVP analysis.

Thus far, we have treated all inputs to the CVP model (e.g., selling price per unit, p) as being known with certainty. As such, the basic CVP model is said to be *deterministic* in nature. Business managers know, however, that the inputs to the CVP planning model are, at best, estimates of future values.

In the decision literature, the term *uncertainty* means that a number of different values can exist for one or more of the variables in a decision model. In this section, we present two broad methods for dealing with the issue of uncertainty as applied to the CVP modeling process: sensitivity analysis and measures of operating risk.

We first discuss **sensitivity analysis**, which is the name for a variety of methods that examine how an amount (e.g., operating profit, π_B) changes if factors involved in predicting that amount (e.g., sales volume, Q) change. We discuss two separate approaches to sensitivity analysis: basic "what-if" analysis and construction of decision tables/decision trees. CVP analysis becomes an important strategic tool when managers use it to determine the sensitivity of profits to possible changes in costs, selling price, or sales volume. If these items change significantly, the firm's strategy might also have to change. For example, if there is a risk that sales levels will fall below projected levels, management might consider reducing planned investments in fixed costs (i.e., capacity-related investments).

We conclude this section by discussing two metrics commonly associated with CVP analysis: (1) margin of safety (MOS), including the MOS ratio, and (2) the degree of operating leverage (DOL).

sensitivity analysis
The name for a variety of methods that examine how an amount changes if factors involved in predicting that amount change.

What-If Analysis

what-if analysis
The calculation of an amount given different levels of a factor that influences that amount.

What-if analysis is the calculation of an amount given different levels of a factor that influences that amount. What-if analysis is a common approach to sensitivity analysis when uncertainty is present. The results of a simple what-if analysis can be presented in a data table prepared in Excel, similar to the one presented in Exhibit 9.6. In this exhibit, we examine the sensitivity of operating profit (the variable of interest) to changes in v (the variable cost per unit), holding the other factors in the CVP model constant. That is, we hold constant the number of units sold, total fixed costs for the year, and the selling price per unit and examine how operating profit changes in response to changes in the variable cost per unit.

Of course, more complicated tables can be prepared to reflect each combined result of allowing multiple variables to change. For example, we could prepare a table that shows required volume, Q, to break even under different combinations of total fixed costs and variable cost per unit, holding selling price per unit constant. The resulting table would have

EXHIBIT 9.6
What-If Sensitivity Analysis for HFI Inc. Using a Data Table

Units Sold	Variable Cost per Unit	Fixed Costs	Selling Price per Unit	Operating Profit
1,500	$30	$60,000	$75	$ 7,500
1,500	35	60,000	75	—
1,500	40	60,000	75	−7,500
1,500	45	60,000	75	−15,000

[5] See the discussion of CVP analysis for activity-based costing in Robert C. Kee, "Implementing Cost-Volume-Profit Analysis Using an Activity-Based Costing System," *Advances in Management Accounting* 10 (2001), pp. 77–94.

$m \times n$ combinations or results cells, where m = the number of variable-cost-per-unit alternatives and n = number of fixed-cost values being examined. Thus, if we were considering four different levels of fixed costs, F, and three different levels of variable cost per unit, v, the resulting table would have $4 \times 3 = 12$ combinations or results cells in our spreadsheet. (By contrast, Exhibit 9.6 has only four results cells—operating profit under four different values of variable cost per unit and a single fixed-costs value.)

Decision Tables/Decision Trees/Expected Value Analysis

The discussion thus far has not included probabilities in the analysis. One way to do this is to construct so-called decision tables (or decision trees) that include the following elements: a set of managerial *actions* or decisions (e.g., choice of cost structure), a set of *events* (e.g., level of demand for the company's product), and a set of *outcomes* (i.e., the financial consequence of various combinations of actions and events). Probabilities can be incorporated into the analysis by estimating a probability for each possible event. As you know from basic statistics, a probability is nothing more than the chance or likelihood that a given event will occur. The set of all possible events that could occur is referred to as a probability distribution. Collectively, the sum of these probabilities must equal 100 percent.

Consider HFI and its plan to sell 2,400 units in 2022 at a price of $75. Keeping the variable costs at $35 per unit and expected fixed costs at $60,000, the expected profit is $36,000. Management is quite confident in this expected outcome but at least wants to consider raising the price to $80 and wants to determine if this is a good option with respect to improving profitability. Management recognizes that raising prices will most likely reduce demand and wants to determine an expected value of this option.

The preceding information can be summarized in what is called a *decision table* (or *decision tree*). From the decision table, we can calculate the *expected value* of each action (decision alternative). Again, you probably recall from statistics that an expected value is defined as the weighted average of all possible outcomes associated with each decision alternative. The weights in this calculation are equal to the outcome probabilities. The set of expected values (one for each decision alternative) along with additional information contained in the decision table can help guide the decision choice. Exhibit 9.7 contains the results with four different expected demand levels and the probability of each outcome. The expected operating profit from the price change is $36,300, which is compared to the expected profit of $36,000 from keeping the price at $75. Looking just at the numbers, it seems that the company can be $300 more profitable by raising the price to $80. However, management should also consider other qualitative and strategic factors before taking an action that may yield only $300 of extra profit.

Margin of Safety (MOS)

margin of safety (MOS)
The amount of planned (or actual) sales above the breakeven point.

The **margin of safety (MOS)** is the amount of planned (or actual) sales above the breakeven point, measured in units or in dollars:

$$\text{MOS} = \text{Planned (or actual) sales} - \text{Breakeven sales}$$

Returning to the HFI example, the planned level of sales in 2022 is 2,400 units per year; because the breakeven quantity is 1,500 units, the margin of safety is

$$\text{MOS in units} = 2,400 - 1,500 = 900 \text{ units}$$

or

$$\text{MOS in sales dollars} = 900 \times \$75 = \$67,500$$

EXHIBIT 9.7
Decision Table with Expected Values

Expected Demand at $80 Price	Projected Operating Profit	Probability of Outcome	Expected Value
2,300 units	$43,500	5%	$2,175
2,200 units	39,000	50	19,500
2,100 units	34,500	25	8,625
2,000 units	30,000	20	6,000
Total expected value			$36,300

Using the selling price of $75 per unit, we know planned revenue is $180,000 and breakeven revenue is $112,500, so we also have

$$\text{MOS in sales dollars} = \$180,000 - \$112,500 = \$67,500$$

The margin of safety can also be expressed in ratio form, that is, as a percentage of planned sales or revenue:

$$\text{MOS ratio} = \text{MOS} \div \text{Planned sales}$$
$$= 900 \div 2,400 = 0.375$$

or

$$\text{MOS ratio} = \text{MOS} \div \text{Planned revenue}$$
$$= \$67,500 \div \$180,000 = 0.375$$

What this means is that, with everything else held constant, sales volume could fall from the planned level by 37.5 percent before losses start occurring.

margin of safety (MOS) ratio
The margin of safety (in units or in dollars) divided by breakeven sales (in units or in dollars).

The **margin of safety (MOS) ratio** is a useful measure for comparing the risk of two or more alternative products (or decision alternatives). The product with a relatively low MOS ratio is the riskier of the two products and therefore usually requires more of management's attention.

Operating Leverage

operating leverage
The extent of fixed costs in an organization's cost structure.

In physics, we refer to a lever as anything that can be used to multiply force. In profit planning, we use a similar term, **operating leverage,** to refer to the extent to which the cost structure of an organization has fixed versus variable costs. The higher the relative amount of fixed costs, the higher the operating leverage, and therefore the greater the sensitivity of operating income to changes in sales volume. As such, operating leverage is used as a multiplier. We demonstrate these concepts with the following example.

Consider two firms: One has relatively high fixed costs and relatively low variable costs per unit (a highly automated firm); the other has relatively low fixed costs and relatively high unit variable costs (a labor-intensive firm). Sample data for two such firms are shown in Exhibit 9.8.

These two situations are compared in Exhibit 9.9A (relatively high fixed costs) and Exhibit 9.9B (relatively low fixed costs). Note that the breakeven point is the same in each case, 50,000 units. However, if we examine for each firm the profit at 25,000 units above breakeven or the loss at 25,000 units below breakeven, a strong contrast emerges. For the firm with relatively high fixed costs (Exhibit 9.9A), the loss at 25,000 units is relatively large, $250,000, while the profit at 75,000 units is also relatively large, $250,000. In contrast, when fixed costs are low (Exhibit 9.9B), the loss at 25,000 units is only $75,000 and the profit at 75,000 units is only $75,000.

Sometimes showing the results of a sensitivity analysis in the form of a graph is useful. To illustrate, using the data from Exhibit 9.8 we might solve for different combinations of unit variable cost that would make us indifferent between the automated factory and the labor-intensive factory, holding sales volume, selling price per unit, and total fixed costs constant.

We generate a series of "indifference points" by expressing the unit variable cost of one alternative in terms of the unit variable cost of the other alternative. For example, letting $Y =$ the unit variable cost for the automated factory and $X =$ the unit variable cost for the labor-intensive factory, we have:

$$\text{Total cost of automated factory} = \text{Total cost of labor-intensive factory}$$
$$\$500,000 + (Y \times 50,000) = \$150,000 + (X \times 50,000)$$
$$Y = X - 7$$

EXHIBIT 9.8
Contrasting Data for Automated vs. Labor-Intensive Firms

	Automated: High Fixed Costs	Labor-Intensive: Low Fixed Costs
Fixed costs/year	$500,000	$150,000
Variable cost/unit	2	9
Selling price/unit	12	12
Contribution margin/unit	10	3

EXHIBIT 9.9A
CVP Graph for a Firm with Relatively High Fixed Costs

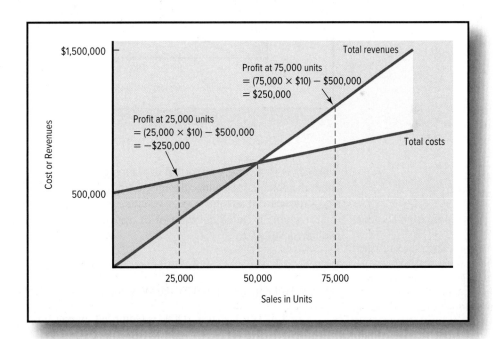

The sensitivity graph for these data appears in Exhibit 9.9C. For unit variable cost combinations above the indifference line, the labor-intensive factory is preferable; the automated factory option is preferable for unit variable cost combinations below the line.

A firm with high fixed costs (i.e., with high operating leverage) is riskier because profit is very strongly affected by the level of sales. As shown in Exhibit 9.9A, high profits are earned beyond breakeven, but high losses result from falling below breakeven. In this context, CVP

EXHIBIT 9.9B
CVP Graph for a Firm with Relatively Low Fixed Costs

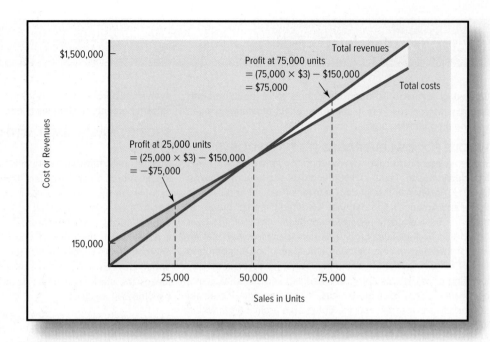

EXHIBIT 9.9C
Sensitivity Graph: Asset-Choice Decision

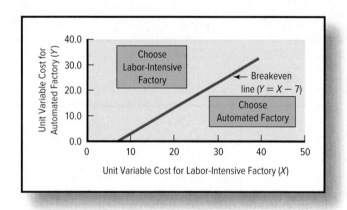

analysis is particularly important in planning the use of new manufacturing technologies that have the potential to change the relationship between fixed and variable costs.

A measure, at any given sales volume, of the sensitivity of operating income to changes in sales volume is called the **degree of operating leverage (DOL).** DOL is defined, at each volume level, Q, as[6]

degree of operating leverage (DOL)

A measure, at any level of sales volume, of the sensitivity of operating profit to changes in volume; defined as the ratio of contribution margin to operating profit at any output level, Q.

$$\text{Contribution margin} \div \text{Operating profit}$$

For the HFI data (Exhibit 9.2), the DOL for 2022 and $Q = 2,400$ units is as follows:

$$\text{DOL} = \text{Contribution margin} \div \text{Operating profit}$$
$$= \$96,000 \div \$36,000 = 2.667$$

From this volume level (i.e., $Q = 2,400$ units), operating profit would increase by 2.667 percent for each percentage change in sales volume. For example, a sales increase of 10 percent

---

[6] Zivney and Goebel (2013) (see footnote 2) show that DOL can be written as $Q/(Q–B/E)$, where B/E equals the breakeven point in terms of volume, Q. One advantage of this formulation is that it demonstrates the general point that DOL is highest at volume levels close to the breakeven point (which causes the denominator in the above expression to be small). Further, the above expression can be recast as breakeven point, $B/E = Q \times (\text{DOL} – 1)/\text{DOL}$, which shows that with no operating leverage (i.e., $\text{DOL} = 1.00$), the breakeven point $= 0$.

would result in a 26.67 percent (= 10 × 2.667%) change in operating profit (assuming everything else is held constant).

The degree of operating leverage is not a constant value, and each firm chooses its cost structure (relative mix of fixed and variable costs), which impacts the resulting degree of operating leverage. That cost structure should be consistent with the firm's competitive strategy. For example, a firm with a dominant position in its market might choose a high-fixed-costs structure, thereby raising the level of leverage to exploit its advantage. In contrast, a weaker firm might choose the less risky low-fixed-costs, low-leverage strategy.

The Five Steps of Strategic Decision Making for CVP Analysis

Here is an example to illustrate strategic decision making in CVP analysis. Russ Talmadge operates a real estate service business that provides rental management services, real estate appraisals, and a variety of other services. Russ is successful because of his knowledge and experience and the reliability of his service, which has gained him the trust of his customers, many of whom have been with him for several years. One of the key items in his office is a printer that prints copies of photos from his digital camera. The photos are used in appraisals and in other services. His printer was relatively inexpensive to buy ($99), but the ink cartridges are expensive—depending on the capacity of the cartridge, the cost is from $37.50 for a capacity of 500 copies to $80 for a capacity of 2,000 copies. Russ prints about 1,000 photos a month. He takes the following five steps to determine the best cartridge to buy for his printer.

1. **Determine the strategic issues surrounding the problem.** Russ's business is based on his knowledge and reliable service. The photos that are a part of his service must also be produced reliably (no printer jams or delays getting the photo to the customer) and be of high print quality.

2. **Identify the alternative actions.** Russ can purchase the high-capacity cartridge (2,000 copies) or the low-capacity cartridge (500 copies) for his printer. The high-capacity cartridge will cost 4 cents per copy ($80 ÷ 2,000), while the low-capacity cartridge will cost 7.5 cents per copy ($37.50 ÷ 500). Another option is to buy a new printer for $150 that has a cartridge costing $60 (capacity of 2,000 copies; 3 cents per copy).

3. **Obtain information and conduct an analysis of the decision alternatives.**

Option One: Retain current printer The high-capacity cartridge will cost $40 per month (1,000 copies at 4 cents per copy) and the low-capacity cartridge will cost $75 per month (1,000 copies at 7.5 cents per copy). The purchase cost of the printer can be ignored because it is a sunk cost; therefore, the high-capacity cartridge will always be the low-cost option.

Option Two: Buy new printer The indifference point for the new printer (assuming Russ is using the high-capacity cartridge on his current printer) would be 15,000 copies [$150 ÷ (4 cents − 3 cents)], or 15 months of usage.

4. **Based on Strategy and Analysis, Choose and Implement the Desired Alternative.**

Option One The choice of cartridge has no effect on the quality or reliability of the printer, so the choice can be made on the basis of lower cost, and in this case, the high-capacity cartridge is preferred. Also, the high-capacity cartridge would mean less frequent cartridge replacement and, therefore, less chance of a potential delay when a photo is needed quickly.

Option Two Russ would achieve breakeven on the new printer in 15 months, not a particularly long period given the number of years he has been in business. And the addition of a new printer would give him a "backup" if one of them should fail.

However, looking at a *Consumer Reports* study of printers, Russ finds that the $150 printer does not have as high a reliability or quality rating as does his current printer. Considering the importance of quality and reliability in his business, Russ chooses option one with the high-capacity cartridge.

5. **Provide an ongoing evaluation of the effectiveness of implementation in step 4.** Russ continues to review the available printers. If he determines a way to reduce the need for photos, he may be able to reduce costs substantially. He may also be able to obtain the cartridges at a lower cost from a new supplier.

CVP Analysis with Two or More Products/Services

sales mix
The relative proportion in which a company's products (or services) are sold.

weighted-average contribution margin per unit
An average per-unit contribution margin based on an assumed sales mix determined on the basis of physical units (not sales dollars).

weighted-average contribution margin ratio
An average contribution margin ratio for a given sales mix based on sales dollars (not units).

We have shown earlier how to develop a CVP model for a single product. Commonly, however, a company produces or sells two or more products/services. If the multiproduct (or multiservice) company can reasonably allocate fixed costs to each product (and if there are no demand interdependencies across products/services), then the company can construct a series of CVP models—one for each product/service.

In the absence of this, and if we are willing to assume that the company's products/services are sold in a particular **sales mix** and that this mix remains constant as total volume changes, then we can build a single CVP model for profit-planning purposes. One approach is to calculate and use something called the **weighted-average contribution margin per unit,** which is determined on the basis of the contribution margin per unit for a given product weighted by the sales mix percentage for that product. Sales mix percentages for the purposes of this calculation are based on relative *physical units* (not sales dollars) for the individual products.

Assume, for example, that a company sells two products, A and B, with corresponding per-unit contribution margins of $1 and $4. If the assumed sales mix is 50:50 (one unit of A sold for each unit of B sold), then the weighted-average contribution margin per unit would be $2.50 (i.e., [$1 × 50%] + [$4 × 50%]). If, on the other hand, the sales mix shifted to 25:75, then the weighted-average contribution margin per unit would increase to $3.25 (i.e., $1× 25% + 4 × 75%).

Of course, sales mix can also be defined on the basis of relative *sales dollars*. Such information can be used to calculate a **weighted-average contribution margin ratio,** which is determined on the basis of the contribution margin ratios of the individual products weighted by sales mix, as determined on the basis of relative sales dollars (not physical units). The weighted-average contribution margin ratio can then be used for breakeven and profit planning for sales volume expressed in dollars (Y) rather than units (Q).

In the two-product example presented earlier, assume that the sales mix based on physical units is 50:50 (as before). In addition to the assumed per-unit contribution margins ($1 and $4 for A and B, respectively), assume that the unit selling prices are $4 and $6, respectively. In this situation, the weighted-average contribution margin ratio is 50 percent, as follows:

$$(25\% \times 0.4) + (66.667\% \times 0.6) = 50\%$$

If the sales mix were to shift (as before) to 25:75, then, for every unit sold at $4, three would be sold for $6, for a combined revenue of $22 for the four units. The weighted-average contribution margin ratio would increase to 59.1 percent, as follows:

$$[25\% \times (\$4 \div \$22)] + [66.667\% \times (\$18 \div \$22)] = 59.1\%$$

EXHIBIT 9.10
Sales and Cost Data for
Windbreakers Inc.

	Calm	Windy	Gale	Total
Last period's sales	$750,000	$600,000	$150,000	$1,500,000
Percent of sales dollars	50%	40%	10%	100%
Last period's sales volume (units)	25,000	18,750	3,750	47,500
Percent of sales volume	52.63%	39.47%	7.90%	100%
Selling price per unit	$ 30	$ 32	$ 40	
Variable cost per unit	24	24	36	
Contribution margin per unit	$ 6	$ 8	$ 4	
Contribution margin ratio	20%	25%	10%	

Multiproduct Profit Planning Using the Weighted-Average Contribution Margin Ratio

To illustrate the development of a CVP model for a multiproduct firm, based on the weighted-average contribution margin ratio, we use the example of Windbreakers Inc., which sells lightweight sport/recreational jackets. Windbreakers has three products, Calm, Windy, and Gale. Relevant information for these products is presented in Exhibit 9.10. The total fixed costs for the period are expected to be $168,000, and we assume that Windbreakers's sales mix will remain constant as volume changes. As indicated in Exhibit 9.10, sales mix in dollars is 50, 40, and 10 percent, respectively, for the three products. We use sales mix in dollars here to be consistent: The contribution margin ratio determines the breakeven quantities in dollars, so we use sales mix in dollars in the calculation.

From the information in Exhibit 9.10, we can calculate the weighted-average contribution margin ratio as follows:

$$(50\% \times 0.2) + (40\% \times 0.25) + (10\% \times 0.1) = 21\%, \text{ or } 0.21$$

The breakeven point *in dollars* for all three products can be calculated as follows:

$$Y = \$168,000 \div 0.21 = \$800,000$$

This means that, at the assumed sales mix (based on relative sales *dollars* last year), total sales of $800,000 must be generated for Windbreakers to break even. The sales for each product at the overall breakeven point are as follows:

For Calm	50% × $800,000	= $400,000	($400,000 ÷ $30 =13,334 jackets)
For Windy	40% × $800,000	= 320,000	($320,000 ÷ $32 = 10,000 jackets)
For Gale	10% × $800,000	= 80,000	($80,000 ÷ $40 = 2,000 jackets)
Total		$800,000	

The sale of jackets in the assumed sales mix produces exactly the breakeven contribution margin of $168,000:

$$\$6(13,334) + \$8(10,000) + \$4(2,000) = \$168,000$$

Multiproduct Profit Planning Using the Weighted-Average Contribution Margin per Unit

From the information in Exhibit 9.10, we can calculate the weighted-average contribution margin per unit as follows:

$$0.5263(\$6.00) + 0.3947(\$8.00) + 0.0790(\$4.00) = \$6.63 \text{ (rounded)}$$

Thus, the breakeven point, at the sales mix reflected in Exhibit 9.10 based on *physical units,* is calculated as follows:

$$Q = \$168,000 \div \$6.63 \text{ per unit} = 25,334 \text{ (rounded)}$$

The total breakeven units of 25,334 can be broken down by product, as follows:

For Calm	0.5263 × 25,334	= 13,334 jackets
For Windy	0.3947 × 25,334	= 10,000 jackets
For Gale	0.0790 × 25,334	= 2,000 jackets
Total		= 25,334 jackets

Note that we could have arrived at the same breakeven numbers for each product by dividing the breakeven point in sales dollars ($400,000, $320,000, and $80,000) by their respective selling prices per unit ($30, $32, and $40). As well, we see that the weighted-average selling price per unit, $31.58 [(0.5263 × $30) + (0.3947 × $32) + (0.079 × $40)], times the total breakeven volume of 25,334 jackets equals the breakeven point in sales dollars determined previously. Finally, note that although the above examples pertain to determining the breakeven point for a multiproduct firm, the analysis is completely general and pertains to profit planning in general. As such, the same basic formulas used in the single-product case discussed earlier in the chapter can be used in the multiproduct case, once we have estimated either the weighted-average contribution margin per unit or the weighted-average contribution margin ratio.

Value Stream Accounting and CVP Analysis

When families of products are grouped into value streams in lean accounting, there is an opportunity to use CVP for the product group rather than for a single product or for multiple products. For example, families of products (or value streams) for a consumer electronics company might include one value stream for speaker systems (all the different types of speakers the company sells), one for DVD players, and additional value streams for other product groups. The use of value streams simplifies the construction of the CVP model. Lean accounting is covered in Chapter 17.

CVP Analysis for Not-for-Profit Organizations

LO 9-7

Apply CVP analysis in not-for-profit organizations.

Not-for-profit (NFP) organizations can also use CVP analysis. To illustrate, consider a family support agency, Orange County Family Support Center (OCFS), that provides training in a classroom setting for struggling young families. The training sessions cover health care for children, financial planning, and other issues; each session involves some handout materials (books, sample medications, etc.), and a paid instructor. OCFS receives financial support from the county, whose funding is falling because of a recession in the local economy. As a result, the county commissioners have set an across-the-board budget cut of 5 percent for the new fiscal year. The center's funding was $735,000 last year and is projected to be approximately $700,000 next year. OCFS's director figures that variable costs (including handout publications, medications, other materials, and some administrative costs) are $10 per visit per family for the almost 300 families who take courses at the center. All other costs are fixed, including salaries for the teachers, record-keeping costs, and facilities costs. How will the budget cut affect the level of service the center provides if we assume fixed costs cannot be changed in the short term?

To answer this question, we must determine the center's activity with the associated fixed and variable costs. OCFS uses the number of family-sessions—that is, the total number of times any family attends any session. The director estimates 13,500 family-sessions last year and also that unit variable cost is constant at $10 per family-session in the range of 10,000 to 14,000 family-sessions per year; total variable costs were therefore $135,000 ($10 × 13,500). We determine total fixed costs for last year as follows:

$$\text{Funding} = \text{Total costs}$$
$$= \text{Total fixed costs} + \text{Total variable costs}$$
$$\$735,000 = \text{Total fixed costs} + \$135,000$$
$$\text{Total fixed costs} = \$600,000$$

Now the director can analyze the effect of the budget change on the center's service levels. At the $700,000 budget level expected for next year, the activity level is approximately 10,000 family-sessions: total costs of $700,000 less fixed costs of $600,000 leaves variable costs of $100,000; thus, $100,000 ÷ $10 per family-session = 10,000 family-sessions. The director can now see that the approximate 5 percent cut in the budget is expected to result in an approximate 26 percent drop in family-sessions [26% = (13,500 − 10,000) ÷ 13,500].

Assumptions and Limitations of Conventional CVP Analysis

Linearity, the Relevant Range, and Step Costs

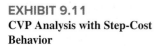

LO 9-8

Identify the assumptions and limitations of CVP analysis.

The conventional (or basic) CVP model assumes that revenues and total costs are linear over the relevant range of activity. As we indicated in Chapter 3, many cost functions are nonlinear in nature when considered over the entire range of possible output levels. However, as also stated in Chapter 3, the linearity assumption becomes defensible in many cases if we confine our analysis to the relevant range of output. Within this range, the assumption of linear cost (and revenue) functions is generally thought to yield acceptable approximations. Thus, the caution for the manager is to remember that the calculations performed within the context of a traditional CVP model should not be used outside the relevant range of activity.

Another modeling-related consideration relates to what are called step costs. As illustrated in Exhibit 9.11, the step-cost behavior under examination may make an approximation via a relevant range unworkable. Although CVP analysis can be done, it becomes somewhat more

EXHIBIT 9.11
CVP Analysis with Step-Cost Behavior

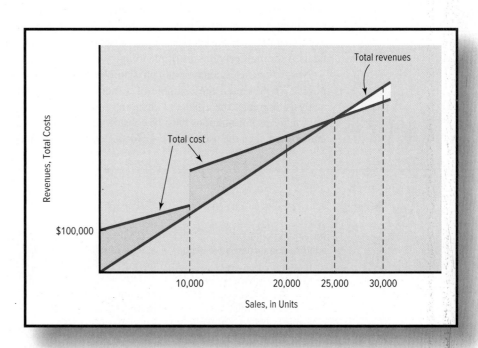

cumbersome. Exhibit 9.11 illustrates a situation with a selling price per unit of $18, a variable cost per unit of $10, initial fixed costs of $100,000, and an incremental fixed cost of another $100,000 when output exceeds 10,000 units. The additional fixed costs provide capacity for up to 20,000 additional units. A CVP analysis in this situation requires that the manager determine the breakeven point for each range (below and above the point at 10,000 units). For these data, the analysis shows an infeasible result for the initial capacity of 10,000 units:

$$Q = F \div (p - v) = \$100,000 \div (\$18 - \$10)$$
$$= 12,500 \text{ units, which is greater than the available capacity}$$

However, the breakeven point can be obtained for the upper range as follows:

$$Q = F \div (p - v) = \$200,000 \div (\$18 - \$10) = 25,000 \text{ units}$$

Summary

This chapter deals with the development of a model representing an organization's short-term profit structure. As such, the model (which we refer to as a CVP model) contains the five factors that combine to determine short-term profitability: variable cost per unit, selling price per unit, total fixed costs, sales volume, and sales mix.

Breakeven planning (a component of CVP analysis) determines the output level at which operating profit is zero. Breakeven analysis is used in planning and budgeting to assess the desirability of current and potential products and services. CVP analysis is also used in revenue planning to determine the sales volume needed to achieve a desired level of operating profit by adding desired profit to the breakeven equation. In cost planning, CVP analysis is used to find the required reduction in costs to meet desired profits or to find the required change in fixed costs for a given change in variable cost per unit (or vice versa).

The basic CVP model can be expanded and made consistent with the traditional activity-based costing (ABC) model discussed in Chapter 5. Specifically, we expanded the CVP model to include batch-level costs, which under a traditional CVP model are treated as part of short-term fixed costs.

Risk and uncertainty in CVP analysis are addressed through the use of two measures (margin of safety and degree of operating leverage) as well as through sensitivity analysis. In terms of the latter, we discussed simple what-if analysis, the preparation of decision tables and decision trees, and expected value analysis.

With two or more products or services, we typically construct a CVP model by assuming that the products (or services) are sold in a predefined mix and determined on the basis of either physical units or sales dollars associated with the individual products. The assumption of a sales mix allows us to calculate and use weighted averages for the contribution margin per unit and the contribution margin ratio. Alternatively, we can use the assumed sales mix to construct a sales basket of items. In this case, all amounts (e.g., contribution margin) are expressed on a per-basket basis. Otherwise, the formulas used in the single-product case can be used for multiproduct profit planning.

Not-for-profit organizations can also construct and use a CVP model for planning purposes. We presented the example of a municipal family support agency's use of breakeven analysis to predict the effects of changing funding levels on the agency's operations.

A number of limitations must be considered in using breakeven analysis. If these assumptions are violated, then the use of more sophisticated profit-planning models should be considered.

Key Terms

activity-based costing (ABC), *336*
breakeven point, *328*
contribution income statement, *327*
contribution margin per unit, *326*
contribution margin ratio, *327*
cost-volume-profit (CVP) analysis, *325*

CVP graph, *330*
degree of operating leverage (DOL), *342*
margin of safety (MOS), *339*
margin of safety (MOS) ratio, *340*
operating leverage, *340*
profit-volume graph, *330*
sales mix, *344*

sensitivity analysis, *338*
total contribution margin, *326*
weighted-average contribution margin per unit, *344*
weighted-average contribution margin ratio, *344*
what-if analysis, *338*

Comments on Cost Management in Action

Managing Profitability under Different Cost Structures

Companies like American Airlines began offering super-low fares as a way to fend off the increasing competition from discount airlines such as Southwest Airlines and European company Ryanair Holdings. The ability to fill seats at a low cost is what makes this approach attractive. Charging a super-low price and then adding à la carte pricing for such amenities as preboarding seat selection and getting space for carry-on bags potentially provides an additional revenue stream from the à la carte services while filling seats with price-sensitive passengers who might have flown with a competitor.

However, a low-cost provider option may be infeasible for the large airlines like American because of the structural cost drivers that are in place. These structural costs come from the hub-and-spoke approach to routes and schedules, as well as labor agreements that are in place. Therefore, it makes sense to try to attract the luxury-minded customers who are willing to pay a high price for the amenities offered with the premium-priced seats. An example of the luxury is Delta's plans to add business-class suites on some flights. These suites are, effectively, small cabins that have fully reclining seats and can be closed off from others. Filling the front of the plane with premium-price passengers and then filling the seats in the back with budget-minded passengers creates a sales mix that can turn a flight into a money maker rather than a money loser.

Sources: Robert Wall, "Airlines Step Up Class Warfare—Carriers Upgrade Perks for Premium Customers, While Cutting Amenities for Low-Fare Seats," *The Wall Street Journal,* April 24, 2017, p. B1; Robert Wall, "New Breed of Airline Upends World Travel," *The Wall Street Journal,* March 18, 2017, p. A1.

Self-Study Problem

(For answers, please see Solution.)

The following data refer to a single product, the TECHWHIZ, made by the Markdata Computer Company:

Sales price = $5,595
Direct materials cost (including purchased components) = $899
Direct labor cost = $233
Facilities costs (for a highly automated plant; mainly includes rent, insurance, taxes, and depreciation) = $2,352,000 per year

Required

1. What is the contribution margin per unit?
2. What is the breakeven point, in units and in dollars?
3. What is the required level of sales (in units) if the company plans to increase facilities costs by 5% (to improve product quality and appearance) and has a desired before-tax profit (π_B) of $200,000?
4. If the company's income tax rate is 22%, what unit sales are necessary to achieve an after-tax profit (π_A) of $150,000?

The Student Resources section of Connect includes video tutorials for the Self-Study Problems.

Questions

9-1   What is the underlying relationship depicted in a CVP analysis?

9-2   What is the contribution margin ratio, and how is it used?

9-3   What are the basic assumptions of CVP analysis?

9-4   Why do management accountants use sensitivity analysis?

9-5   What type of risk does sensitivity analysis address?

9-6   Why does the issue of income taxes not affect the calculation of the breakeven point?

9-7   What is the margin of safety (MOS), and for what is it used?

9-8   What is operating leverage, and for what is it used?

9-9   Define *degree of operating leverage (DOL).* How is DOL measured?

9-10 How is CVP analysis used to calculate the breakeven point for multiple products?

Brief Exercises

[LO 9-1]   9-11   Doughton Bearings produces ball bearings for industrial equipment. In evaluating the financial data from the previous year, the management accountant has determined that the company's selling price per unit is $25, while the variable cost per unit is $18. What is the contribution margin per unit?

[LO 9-1]   9-12   Felton Paper produces paper for textbooks. Felton plans to produce 500,000 cases of paper next quarter to sell at a price of $100 per case. The variable cost per case, including both manufacturing and selling costs, is $80. What is the total contribution margin for next quarter?

[LO 9-2]   9-13   Ford Tops manufactures hats for baseball teams. Ford has fixed costs of $175,000 per quarter and sells each hat for $20. If the variable cost per hat is $10, how many hats must Ford sell each quarter to break even?

[LO 9-2]   9-14   The Cobb Clinic treats walk-in patients for various illnesses. The management accountant has estimated that the clinic has $5,000 in monthly fixed costs in addition to a $20 cost per patient visit. If the charge is $30 per visit, how many visits per month does the clinic need to break even?

[LO 9-2]   9-15   Oxicon Inc. manufactures several different types of candy for various retail stores. The accounting manager has requested that you determine the sales dollars required to break even for next quarter based on past financial data. Your research tells you that the total variable costs will be $500,000, total sales will be $750,000, and fixed costs will be $75,000. What is the breakeven point in sales dollars?

[LO 9-3]   9-16   Williams & Williams Co. produces plastic spray bottles and wants to earn a before-tax profit of $200,000 next quarter. Variable cost is $0.50 per bottle, fixed costs are $400,000, and the selling price is $1 per bottle. How many bottles must the company sell to meet its profit goal?

[LO 9-1]   9-17   Scott Power produces batteries. The company has determined its contribution margin to be $8 per battery and its contribution margin ratio to be 0.4. What is the effect on profits of the sale of one additional battery? Of one additional dollar of sales?

[LO 9-3]   9-18   ABC Audio sells headphones and would like to earn an after-tax profit of $400 every week. Each set of headphones incurs variable cost of $5 and sells for $10. Rent and other fixed costs are $200 per week; the income tax rate is 20%. How many headphones must ABC sell per week to meet its profit goal?

[LO 9-5]   9-19   Franklin Cards sells greeting cards for $2 each and plans to sell 100,000 cards every quarter. The management accountant has determined the company must sell 80,000 cards every quarter to break even. What is the margin of safety (MOS) in both units and sales dollars?

[LO 9-5]   9-20   May Clothing is a retail men's clothing store. May's variable cost is $20 per shirt, and the sales price is $40 per shirt. May plans to sell 400,000 shirts for the year and, at this level, would generate a before-tax profit of $2,500,000. What is the degree of operating leverage (DOL) at this volume level?

Exercises

[LO 9-2, 9-3]   9-21   **Breakeven Planning; Profit Planning**   Connelly Inc., a manufacturer of quality electric ice cream makers, has experienced a steady growth in sales over the past few years. Because her business has grown, Jan DeJaney, the president, believes she needs an aggressive advertising campaign next year to maintain the company's growth. To prepare for the growth, the accountant prepared the following data for the current year:

Variable costs per ice cream maker	
Direct labor	$ 13.50
Direct materials	14.50
Variable overhead	6.00
Total variable costs	$ 34.00
Fixed costs	
Manufacturing	$ 82,500
Selling	42,000
Administrative	356,000
Total fixed costs	$480,500
Selling price per unit	$ 67.00
Expected sales (units)	30,000

Required

1. If the costs and sales price remain the same, what is the projected operating profit for the coming year?

2. What is the breakeven point in units for the coming year? (Round your answer up to the nearest whole number.)

3. Jan has set the sales target for 35,000 ice cream makers, which she thinks she can achieve by an additional fixed selling expense of $200,000 for advertising. All other costs remain as per the data in the above table. What will be the operating profit if the additional $200,000 is spent on advertising and sales rise to 35,000 units?

4. What will be the new breakeven point if the additional $200,000 is spent on advertising? (Prepare a contribution income statement to support your answer.) What is the percentage change in both fixed costs and the breakeven point? What general point is illustrated by this comparison?

5. If the additional $200,000 is spent for advertising in the next year, what is the sales level (in units) needed to equal the current year's operating profit at 30,000 units?

[LO 9-1, 9-3]   9-22   **Cost Planning; Machine Replacement**   Vista Company manufactures electronic equipment. It currently purchases the special switches used in each of its products from an outside supplier. The supplier charges Vista $2 per switch. Vista's CEO is considering purchasing either machine A or machine B so the company can manufacture its own switches. The projected data are as follows:

	Machine A	Machine B
Annual fixed costs	$135,000	$204,000
Variable cost per switch	0.65	0.30

Required

1. For each machine, what is the minimum number of switches that Vista must make annually for total costs to equal outside purchase cost?
2. What volume level would produce the same total costs regardless of the machine purchased?
3. What is the most profitable alternative for producing 200,000 switches per year?
4. Which of the two decision alternatives would you recommend? Why?

[LO 9-3]   9-23   **Structuring Sales Commissions**   Questar Electronics, a producer of a wide range of consumer products, is facing increasing competitive pressures from foreign producers. In response, Questar is reexamining its overall management control system, including the way the company compensates members of its sales force, who currently earn a 10% commission on sales. Below are highly condensed data for two representative products that Questar sells:

	Alpha	Omega
Selling price per unit	$100	$125
Variable manufacturing cost per unit	80	110
Manufacturing contribution margin	$ 20	$ 15

Required

1. What is the contribution margin for each product?
2. Which of the company's products will likely be more aggressively promoted by the company's salespeople? Why?
3. Can you suggest an alternative incentive plan, one that would better align employee and corporate interests (i.e., one that would motivate more goal-congruent behavior)?

[LO 9-3]   9-24   **Cost Planning; The Cost of an MBA; Time Value of Money**   The motivation for getting the MBA degree has many aspects—the prestige, greater opportunity for promotion, change of occupation, and increase in pay. To focus just on this last motivation, suppose that you are interested in getting an MBA and are studying the various programs in the United States. You want to balance the costs of getting the degree against the future benefits in increase of pay. You have information on the cost of two MBA programs, which includes the costs of tuition, living expenses, and forgone pre-MBA salary for the two years you are in the MBA program. School A has an average cost of $100,000, and school B, a far more prestigious school at which you think your grades would qualify you to be a successful applicant, has a cost of $250,000.

Required   Assume that you have a 10-year planning horizon, that the difference in pay for a job after both schools would remain the same for all 10 years, and the relevant cost of borrowing is 6%. Based on increase in pay only, how great would the increase for a job after leaving school B have to be relative to school A for you to be indifferent between the two schools? (*Hint:* The present value factor for an annuity of 10 years at 6% is in Table 2 at the end of Chapter 12 and equals 7.360.)

9-3, 9-5]   9-25   **Cost Planning; Compensating Sales Staff**   The Jurassic Classics has four employees on its sales team and uses a compensation that provides each person with a base salary of $40,000 per year and the opportunity to earn commission on sales. The current commission is 5% of gross sales, and sales for the most recent period were $2,500,0000. Management is considering making a change to the compensation system and wants to evaluate two possible alternatives: going to a strictly commission-based compensation system and going to purely salary-based compensation. The strictly commission-based method would eliminate the salary but raise the commission to 11% of sales. If the purely salary-based approach is adopted, the salary for each person would rise to $70,000 and the commission would be eliminated.

Required

1. Compute the total compensation of the sales team for all three options at $2,000,000, $2,500,000, and $3,000,000 of total sales.

2. What sales level would make management indifferent between the current compensation structure and the strictly commission-based structure? What is the point of indifference between the current structure and the pure salary-based structure?

3. What are some important factors that should be considered before making the decision?

[LO 9-2, 9-3]   9-26   **The Role of Income Taxes**   For the most recent year, Triad Company had fixed costs of $240,000 and variable costs of 75% of total sales revenue, earned $70,000 of net income after taxes, and had an income tax rate of 35%.

Required   Calculate the following:

1. Before-tax income.

2. Total contribution margin.

3. Total sales.

4. Breakeven point in dollar sales.

[LO 9-2, 9-3]   9-27   **CVP Analysis with Income Taxes**   Cohen Company produces and sells socks. Variable cost is $6 per pair, and fixed costs for the year total $75,000. The selling price is $10 per pair.

Required   Calculate the following:

1. The breakeven point in units.

2. The breakeven point in sales dollars.

3. The units required to make a before-tax profit of $40,000.

4. The sales dollars required to make a before-tax profit of $35,000.

5. The sales, in units and in dollars, required to make an after-tax profit of $25,000 given a tax rate of 30%.

[LO 9-1, 9-2, 9-3]   9-28   **Cost Planning; High-End Printers**   Companies that have a high demand for making copies, both color and black and white, often choose to lease a high-end printer that provides fast and reliable service at a reasonable cost. The lease is usually for 3 to 5 years, and the cost to the user is $0.01 per page for black-and-white copies and typically $0.10 per page for color copies. These are the terms of your current 3-year lease contract with Ricoh Company, which is up for renewal this month; the lease terms are expected to be the same for the next 3 years, if renewed.

Hewlett-Packard Company (HP) developed an innovative printer that can reduce the cost of color copies. The printer measures exactly how much color is used in a color copy so that the price of the copy can be determined by the amount of color used rather than a fixed price per page. The cost could be as low as $0.075 per page for a color copy. HP calls this a "flexible-pricing" approach. Assume for this example that the cost of the leased printer (3-year lease) is only the per-page charge—the initial lease cost is negligible, and the service costs would not differ between the HP printer and the printer you are using now.

Your company is an advertising agency, Tanner and Jones LLC, and the quality of the color copies is critical to your business success. The ability to rely on the printer at any time is also very important because some customer requests require urgent attention. You believe that the Ricoh and HP printers are of the same reliability, but you have not had experience with the HP printer to be sure of the copy quality. The demonstration of the HP printer has shown as good or better copy quality, but you have not had 3 years' experience with it to know what it would be like day-to-day.

Required

1. Assume that your company is considering the lease of one of these HP printers, and you expect that the average price for a color copy for your company would be $0.075 because you would carefully prioritize color copy jobs and reduce the number of copies requiring a large amount of color. You expect that training your copy center staff to properly use the new printer would cost about $12,400 for materials and lost work time. What is the breakeven number of color copies per year that would make you indifferent between the new HP printer and your current printer?

2. As in requirement 1, assume you expect that your per-copy cost for color copies with the HP printer will be $0.075, the training costs are $12,400, and you expect to make 200,000 copies per year for the next 3 years. In your negotiations with Ricoh concerning the new lease and the cost of color copies, what price would you bargain for?

3. Consider your choice between the printers within the context of the competitive and business environment of Tanner and Jones. What are the issues you should consider in addition to the cost of copies?

[LO 9-5]   9-29   **Margin of Safety**   Harold McWilliams owns and manages a general merchandise store in a rural area of Virginia. Harold sells appliances, clothing, auto parts, and farming equipment, among a wide variety of other types of merchandise. Because of normal seasonal and cyclical fluctuations in the local economy, he knows that his business will also have these fluctuations, and he is planning to use CVP analysis to help him understand how he can expect his profits to change with these fluctuations. Harold has the following information for his most recent year. Cost of goods sold represents the cost paid for the merchandise he sells, while operating costs represent rent, insurance, and salaries, which are entirely fixed.

Sales	$650,000
Cost of merchandise sold	422,500
Contribution margin	227,500
Operating costs	105,000
Operating profit	$122,500

Required
1. What is Harold's margin of safety (MOS) in dollars? What is the margin of safety (MOS) ratio?
2. Of what managerial significance are the measures calculated in requirement 1?
3. What is Harold's margin of safety (in dollars) and operating profit if sales should fall to $500,000?

[LO 9-5]   9-30   **Degree of Operating Leverage**   The following sales and cost data (in thousands) are for two companies in the transportation industry:

	Company A		Company B	
	Amount	Percent of Sales	Amount	Percent of Sales
Sales	$100,000	100%	$100,000	100%
Variable costs	50,000	50	30,000	30
Contribution margin	$ 50,000	50%	$ 70,000	70%
Fixed costs	15,000		40,000	
Operating profit	$ 35,000		$ 30,000	

Required
1. Calculate the degree of operating leverage (DOL) for each company. If sales increase from the present level, which company benefits more? How do you know?
2. Assume that sales rise 10% in the next year but that everything else remains constant. Calculate the percentage increase in profit for each company. Are the results what you expected? Explain.
3. In what sense is DOL a measure of risk?

[LO 9-5]   9-31   **CVP Analysis and Margin of Safety**

Units sold	1,000
Price	$ 10
Sales	$10,000
Variable manufacturing costs	4,000
Fixed manufacturing costs	2,000
Variable selling costs	1,000
Fixed administrative costs	1,000

Required   Using the data provided, compute the margin of safety and margin of safety ratio.

[LO 9-5]   9-32   **Degree of Operating Leverage (DOL)**   TastyKreme and Krispy Kake are both producers of baked goods, but each has followed a different production strategy. The differences in their strategies resulted in differences in their cost structure, as shown in the following table:

	TastyKreme	Krispy Kake
Estimated sales in units	20,000	15,000
Unit price	6.00	8.00
Variable cost per unit	3.00	3.00
Total fixed costs	$30,000	$45,000

Required

1. Compute the operating income and degree of operating leverage for each company.

2. Assuming sales volume for each company will decline by 10% and that their cost structures will not change, compute the percentage and dollar amount of the change in operating income for each company.

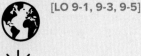

[LO 9-1, 9-3, 9-5]   9-33 **Cost Structure of Retailers; the Internet; Operating Leverage**   Today's retailers are finding that online sales and service are a necessary ingredient of their overall marketing and selling strategy because of increased competition. In certain retail sectors, consumers are moving to the internet in large numbers for convenience and selection. Unfortunately, the investment in resources, both equipment and labor, can be huge. Some studies show that less than a third of online retailers are profitable on internet sales. As a result, some new consulting firms, software firms, and service providers have begun to provide e-commerce solutions for retailers.

Required

1. How does a consulting firm, service provider, or software firm help a retailer reduce costs and become more competitive for internet sales? What is the role of operating leverage in the retailer's decision to outsource online sales and service?

2. Cost structure is not the only thing management should be concerned about when moving into online sales. What role, if any, does globalization play in a retailer's efforts to compete for internet sales?

[LO 9-3, 9-5]   9-34 **Contribution Income Statements Using Excel; Sensitivity Analysis; Goal Seek**

Required

1. Using the data from 2022 in Exhibit 9.1, create an Excel spreadsheet to provide a sensitivity analysis of the effect on operating profit of potential changes in demand for HFI Inc., ranging from a 20 percent decrease to a 20 percent increase. Use Exhibits 9.2 and 9.6 as a guide. Assume that two-thirds of fixed costs are manufacturing related; the remaining one-third are selling-related. The variable manufacturing cost per unit is $30, while the variable selling cost per unit is $5. (*Hint:* Calculate the DOL for 2022 at a sales volume of 2,400 units. How does this figure help you interpret your sensitivity analysis results?)

2. Using the spreadsheet you created, compute the new operating profit assuming a 10% decrease in demand.

3. Use the Goal Seek tool within Excel to determine the sales price per unit that would allow HFI to earn an operating profit of $100,000, assuming that all the other cost information is the same as in Exhibit 9.1. Use Exhibit 9.5 as a guide.

[LO 9-2, 9-3, 9-5]   9-35 **CVP Analysis**   Lawn Master Company, a manufacturer of riding lawn mowers, has a projected income for the coming year as follows:

Sales		$46,000,000
Operating expenses:		
Variable expenses	$32,200,000	
Fixed expenses	7,500,000	
Total expenses		39,700,000
Operating profit		$ 6,300,000

Required

1. Determine the breakeven point in sales dollars.

2. Determine the required sales in dollars to earn a before-tax profit of $8,000,000.

3. What is the breakeven point in sales dollars if the variable expenses increase by 12%?

[LO 9-6]   9-36 **Multiple Product CVP Analysis**   Smith Company can produce two types of carpet cleaners, Brighter and Cleaner. Data on these two products are as follows:

	Brighter	Cleaner
Sales volume in units	400	600
Unit sales price	$750	$1,000
Unit variable cost	300	450

The number of machine hours to produce one unit of Brighter is 1, while the number of machine hours for each unit of Cleaner is 2. Total fixed costs for the manufacture of both products are $265,200.

Required

1. Determine the breakeven point in total units for Smith Company, based on the assumption that the sales mix (on the basis of relative sales volume in units) stays constant. Use the weighted-average contribution margin approach. Round the number of units up to the next whole number.

2. At this breakeven level, how many units of each product must be sold? Be sure to round up to the next whole number.

3. What is the overall breakeven point in sales dollars? (Use both an indirect approach, based on your answer to requirement 2, and a direct approach, based on the weighted-average contribution margin ratio and the assumption that sales mix based on relative sales dollars stays constant.)

4. Of what potential managerial value is the information related to machine-hour consumption of the two products?

Problems

[LO 9-1, 9-2, 9-3] 9-37 **CVP Analysis; Strategy** Bubba's Western Wear is a western hat retailer in Lubbock, Texas. Although Bubba's carries numerous styles of western hats, each hat has approximately the same price and purchase cost, as shown in the following table. Sales personnel receive a commission to encourage them to be more aggressive in their sales efforts. Currently, the Lubbock economy is really humming, and sales growth at Bubba's has been great. The business is very competitive, however, and Bubba, the owner, has relied on his knowledgeable and courteous staff to attract and retain customers who otherwise might go to other western wear stores. Because of the rapid growth in sales, Bubba is also finding the management of certain aspects of the business more difficult, such as restocking inventory and hiring and training new salespeople.

Sales price	$ 80.00
Per unit variable expenses	
Purchase cost	43.50
Sales commissions	11.50
Total per unit variable costs	$ 55.00
Total annual fixed expenses	
Advertising	$ 98,500
Rent	146,500
Salaries	255,000
Total fixed expenses	$500,000

Required

1. Calculate the annual breakeven point, both in terms of units and in terms of sales dollars.

2. If Bubba's sells 22,000 hats, what is its before-tax income or loss? Support your answer by constructing a contribution income statement.

3. If Bubba's sells 32,000 hats, what is its margin of safety (MOS) and MOS ratio? Of what interpretive value are these two measures?

4. Bubba is considering the elimination of sales commissions completely and increasing salaries by $157,000 annually. What would be the new breakeven point in units? What would be the before-tax income or loss if 22,000 hats are sold with the new salary plan?

5. Identify and discuss the strategic and ethical issues in the decision to eliminate sales commissions (see requirement 4). How do these strategic concerns affect Bubba's decision?

[LO 9-3, 9-6] 9-38 **Profit-Planning; Multiple Products** Most businesses sell several products at varying prices. The products often have different unit variable costs. Thus, the total profit and the breakeven point depend on the proportions in which the products are sold. Sales mix is the relative contribution of sales among various products sold by a firm. Assume that the sales of Jordan Inc. for a typical year are as follows:

Product	Units Sold	Sales Mix
A	18,000	80%
B	4,500	20
Total	22,500	100%

Assume the following unit selling prices and unit variable costs:

Product	Selling Price	Variable Cost	Contribution Margin
A	$ 80	$ 65	$15
B	140	100	40

Fixed costs are $400,000 per year. Assume that the sales mix, expressed in terms of relative physical units sold, is constant as sales volume changes.

Required

1. Determine the breakeven point in total units and, for this breakeven point, calculate the number of units of A and B that must be sold. Use the weighted-average contribution margin approach and round the solution up to the next whole number.

2. Use the Goal Seek function in Excel to determine the overall breakeven point (in units) for the company.

3. Determine the overall breakeven point in terms of sales dollars based on the weighted-average contribution margin ratio (CMR). (*Hint:* The weights for calculating the weighted-average CMR are based on relative sales dollars, not units, of the two products.) Break down the total sales dollars breakeven point into sales dollars for product A and sales dollars for product B.

4. Explain the following statement: "For the multiproduct firm, there is no breakeven point independent of the sales-mix assumption."

5. Assume the original facts except that now fixed costs are expected to be $40,000 higher than originally planned. How does this expected increase in fixed costs affect the breakeven point in units? How does the percentage change in the breakeven point compare to the percentage increase in fixed costs? What general conclusion might you draw on the basis of these calculations?

[LO 9-3, 9-5]   9-39   **CVP Analysis; Profit Planning**   Horton Manufacturing Inc. (HMI) is suffering from the effects of increased local and global competition for its main product, a lawn mower that is sold in discount stores throughout the United States. The following table shows the results of HMI's operations for the most recent year:

Sales (12,500 units @ $84)	$1,050,000
Variable costs (12,500 @ $63)	787,500
Contribution margin	$ 262,500
Fixed costs	296,100
Operating profit (loss)	($ 33,600)

Required

1. Compute HMI's breakeven point in both units and dollars. Also, compute the contribution margin ratio. (Round the number of units up to the next whole number.)

2. What would be the required sales, in units and in dollars, to generate a pretax profit of $30,000? (Round the number of units up to the next whole number)

3. Assume an income tax rate of 40%. What would be the required sales volume, in both units and dollars, to generate an after-tax profit of $30,000? (Round the number of units up to the next whole number.)

4. Prepare a contribution income statement as a check for your calculations in requirement 3.

5. The manager believes that a $60,000 increase in advertising would result in approximately a $200,000 increase in annual sales. If the manager is right, what will be the effect on the company's operating profit or loss?

6. Refer to the original data. The vice president in charge of sales feels that a 10% reduction in price in combination with a $40,000 increase in advertising will cause unit sales to increases by 25%. What effect would this strategy have on operating profit (loss)?

7. Refer to the original data. During the year, HMI saved $5 of unit variable cost per lawn mower by buying from a different manufacturer. However, changing the plant machinery to accommodate the new part means an additional $50,000 in fixed costs per year. Was this a wise change? Why or why not?

[LO 9-3, 9-7]   9-40   **CVP Analysis**   General Hospital's Cardiac Diagnostic Screening Center (CDSC) is contemplating purchasing a blood gas analysis machine at a cost of $960,000. Useful life for this machine is 10 years. The screening center currently serves 3,000 patients per year, 40 percent of whom need blood gases analysis data as part of their diagnostic tests. The blood samples are presently sent to a private laboratory that charges $200 per sample. In-house variable cost is estimated to be $125 per sample if CDSC purchases the analysis machine.

Required

1. Determine the indifference point between purchasing the machine or using the private laboratory.

2. Use the Goal Seek function in Excel to determine the indifference point calculated in requirement 1.

3. Determine how many additional patients would be needed so that CDSC would be indifferent between purchasing the analysis machine and the $200 lab charge.

4. Assuming the current service level of 3,000 patients per year with 40 percent requiring blood gases testing, how much would the private laboratory have to charge per sample to make CDSC indifferent between purchasing the analysis machine and using the private laboratory's services?

5. What other considerations are relevant to this decision?

[LO 9-2, 9-3]　9-41　**CVP Analysis in a Professional Service Firm**　Leary and O'Donnell, a local CPA firm, has been asked to bid on a contract to perform audits for three counties in its home state. Because existing staff are fully scheduled, if the firm is awarded the contract, it must hire one new staff member at a salary of $52,000 to handle the additional workload. The managing partner is convinced that obtaining the contract will lead to additional new clients from the respective counties. Expected new work (excluding the three counties) is 750 hours at an average billing rate of $90.00 per hour. Other information follows about the firm's current annual revenues and costs:

Firm volume in hours (normal)	30,750
Fixed costs	$ 575,000
Variable cost	$ 35.00/hr

Should the firm win the contract, the audits of the three counties will require 950 hours of expected work.

Required

1. If the managing partner's expectations are correct, what is the lowest bid the firm can submit and still expect to increase annual net income? What would be the hourly billing rate for the county audit jobs just to break even on all the new business?

2. If the contract is obtained at a price of $44,000, what is the minimum number of hours of new business in addition to the county work that must be obtained for the firm to break even on total new business? What is the margin of safety (MOS) regarding the county audit job proposal?

[LO 9-5, 9-6]　9-42　**CVP Analysis; Sensitivity Analysis; Multiple Products**　GoGo Juice is a combination gas station and convenience store located at a busy intersection. Recently, a national chain opened a similar store only a block away; consequently, sales have decreased for GoGo. In an effort to reclaim lost sales, GoGo has implemented a promotional effort; for every $10 purchase at GoGo, the customer receives a $1 coupon that can be redeemed toward the purchase of gasoline. The average gasoline customer purchases 15 gallons of gasoline at $2.50 per gallon. The results of an average month, prior to this coupon promotion, are shown below.

Not included in the information presented below is the monthly cost of printing the coupons, which is estimated to be $500. Coupons are issued on the basis of total purchases regardless of whether the purchases are paid in cash or paid by redeeming coupons. Assume that coupons are distributed to customers for 75 percent of the total sales. Also assume that all coupons distributed are used to purchase gasoline.

	Sales	Cost of Sales (per unit or % of retail)
Gasoline	$100,000	$1.875 per gallon
Food and beverages	60,000	60%
Other products	40,000	50%

	Other Costs
Labor—station attendants	$10,000
Labor—supervision	2,500
Rent, power, supplies, and other	40,000
Depreciation (pumps, computers, counters, fixtures, and building)	7,500

Required (Round final dollar amounts to whole dollars)

1. If GoGo Juice implements the promotional coupon effort, calculate the profit (loss) before tax if the sales volume remains constant and the coupons are used to purchase gasoline. Assume the sales mix remains constant. Prepare a contribution income statement to support your answer.

2. Calculate the breakeven sales (in dollars) for GoGo Juice if the promotional effort is implemented. Assume that the product mix remains constant. Use the weighted-average contribution margin ratio approach to generate your answer. (*Hint:* Sales mix for this purpose is defined on the basis of relative sales dollars, not units.)

3. Based on the assumed sales mix (determined on the basis of relative sales dollars, not units), determine the composition of total breakeven sales dollars across the three product lines: gas, food and beverages, and other products.

4. Disregarding your responses to requirements 1 and 2, assume the weighted-average contribution margin ratio, after implementation of the coupon program, is 35 percent. Calculate the before-tax profit (loss) for GoGo Juice, assuming sales increase 20 percent due to the new program. Assume that the sales mix in terms of relative sales dollars remains constant.

5. GoGo Juice is considering using sensitivity analysis in combination with cost-volume-profit (CVP) analysis. Discuss this plan. Include in your discussion at least three factors that make sensitivity analysis prevalent in decision making.

6. Provide a brief description of the methods that can be used to deal with uncertainty.

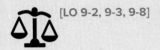

[LO 9-2, 9-3, 9-8]   9-43   **CVP Analysis; Commissions; Ethics**   Lionel Corporation manufactures pharmaceutical products sold through a network of sales agents in the United States and Canada. The agents are currently paid an 18% commission on sales; that percentage was used when Lionel prepared the following budgeted income statement for the fiscal year ending June 30, 2022:

Lionel Corporation		
Budgeted Income Statement		
For the Year Ending June 30, 2022		
($000 omitted)		
Sales		$28,500
Cost of goods sold		
Variable	$ 12,825	
Fixed	3,500	16,325
Gross profit		$12,175
Selling and administrative costs		
Commissions	$ 5,130	
Fixed advertising cost	800	
Fixed administrative cost	2,150	8,080
Operating income		$ 4,095
Fixed interest cost		705
Income before income taxes		$ 3,390
Income taxes (30%)		1,017
Net income		$ 2,373

Since the completion of the income statement, Lionel has learned that its sales agents are requiring a 5% increase in their commission rate (to 23%) for the upcoming year. As a result, Lionel's president has decided to investigate the possibility of hiring its own sales staff in place of the network of sales agents and has asked Alan Chen, Lionel's controller, to gather information on the costs associated with this change.

Alan estimates that Lionel must hire eight salespeople to cover the current market area, at an average annual payroll cost for each employee of $80,000, including fringe benefits expense. Travel and entertainment expenses are expected to total $600,000 for the year, and the annual cost of hiring a sales manager and sales secretary will be $150,000. In addition to their salaries, the eight salespeople will each earn commissions at the rate of 10% of sales. The president believes that Lionel also should increase its advertising budget by $500,000 if the eight salespeople are hired.

Required
1. Determine Lionel's breakeven point in sales dollars for the fiscal year ending June 30, 2022, if the company hires its own salesforce and increases its advertising costs. Prove this by constructing a contribution income statement.

2. If Lionel continues to sell through its network of sales agents and pays the higher commission rate, determine the estimated volume in sales dollars that would be required to generate the operating profit as projected in the budgeted income statement.

3. Describe the general assumptions underlying breakeven analysis that may limit its usefulness.

4. What is the indifference point in sales for the firm to either accept the agents' demand or adopt the proposed change? Which plan is better for the firm? Why?

5. What are the ethical issues, if any, that Alan should consider?

(CMA Adapted)

[LO 9-2, 9-5]   9-44   **CVP Analysis; Uncertainty; Sensitivity Analysis**   Don Carson and two colleagues are considering opening a law office in a large metropolitan area to make inexpensive legal services available to people who cannot otherwise afford these services. They intend to provide easy access for their clients by having the office open 360 days per year, 16 hours each day from 7:00 a.m. to 11:00 p.m. A lawyer, paralegal, legal secretary, and clerk-receptionist would staff the office for each of the two 8-hour shifts.

To determine the feasibility of the project, Don hired a marketing consultant to assist with market projections. The consultant's results show that if the firm spends $500,000 on advertising the first year, the number of new clients expected each day would have the following probability distribution:

Number of New Clients per Day	Probability
10	0.10
20	0.30
40	0.40
60	0.20

Don and his associates believe these numbers to be reasonable and are prepared to spend the $500,000 on advertising. Other pertinent information about the operation of the office follows.

The only charge to each new client would be $30 for an initial consultation. The firm will accept on a contingency basis all cases that warrant further legal work, with the firm earning 30 percent of any favorable settlements or judgments. Don estimates that 20% of new client consultations will result in favorable settlements or judgments averaging $15,000 each. He does not expect repeat clients during the first year of operations.

The hourly wages for the staff are projected to be $185 for the lawyer, $50 for the paralegal, $30 for the legal secretary, and $20 for the clerk-receptionist. Fringe benefits expense will be 40% of the wages paid. A total of 400 hours of overtime is expected for the year; this will be divided equally between the legal secretary and the clerk-receptionist positions. Overtime will be paid at one and one-half times the regular wage, and the fringe benefit expense will apply to the full wages.

Don has located 6,000 square feet of suitable office space that rents for $48 per square foot annually. Associated expenses will be $22,000 for property insurance and $32,000 for utilities. The group must purchase malpractice insurance expected to cost $180,000 annually.

The initial investment in office equipment will be $60,000; this equipment has an estimated useful life of 4 years. The cost of office supplies has been estimated to be $10 per expected new client consultation.

Required

1. Determine how many new clients must visit the law office that Don and his colleagues are considering for the venture to break even in the first year of operations. (For purposes of this calculation, treat all labor costs as fixed with respect to number of new clients.)

2. Using the probability information provided by the marketing consultant, determine whether it is feasible for the law office to achieve breakeven operations. Specifically, calculate and interpret the expected value of new clients for year 1, based on the probability data given above.

3. Explain how Don and his associates could use sensitivity analysis to assist in this analysis.

(CMA Adapted)

[LO 9-1, 9-2, 9-3]   9-45 **CVP Analysis; Strategy; Critical Success Factors**   Garner Strategy Institute (GSI) presents executive-level training seminars nationally. Eastern University (EU) has approached GSI to present 40 one-week seminars during 2022. This activity level represents the maximum number of seminars that GSI is capable of presenting annually. GSI staff would present the week-long seminars in various cities throughout the United States and Canada.

Terry Garner, GSI's president, is evaluating three financial options for the revenues from Eastern: accept a flat fee for each seminar, receive a percentage of Eastern's profit before tax from the seminars, and form a joint venture to share costs and profits.

Estimated costs for the 2022 seminar schedule follow:

	Garner Strategy Institute	Eastern University
Fixed costs for the year:		
Salaries and benefits	$200,000	N/A*
Facilities	48,000	N/A*
Travel and hotel	0	$210,000
Other	70,000	N/A*
Total fixed costs	$318,000	$210,000
Variable cost per participant:		
Supplies and materials	0	$47
Marketing	0	18
Other site costs	0	35

*Eastern's fixed costs are excluded because the amounts are not considered relevant for this decision (i.e., they will be incurred whether or not the seminars are presented). Eastern does not include these costs when calculating the profit before tax for the seminars.

EU plans to charge $1,200 per participant for each one-week seminar. It will pay all variable marketing, site, and materials costs.

Required

1. Assume that the seminars are handled as a joint venture by GSI and EU to pool costs and revenues.

   a. Determine the total number of seminar participants needed to break even on the total costs for this joint venture.

   b. Assume that the joint venture has an effective income tax rate of 30%. How many seminar participants must the joint venture enroll to earn an after-tax income of $169,400?

2. Assume that GSI and EU do not form a joint venture but that GSI is an independent contractor for EU. EU offers two payment options to GSI: a flat fee of $9,500 for each seminar or a fee of 40% of EU's profit before taxes from the seminars. Compute the minimum number of participants needed for GSI to prefer the 40% fee option over the flat fee. (Round your answer up to the nearest whole number.) Show supporting computations.

3. What are the strategic and implementation issues for GSI to consider in deciding whether to enter into the joint venture?

(CMA Adapted)

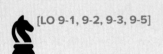

[LO 9-1, 9-2, 9-3, 9-5]   9-46 **CVP Analysis; Strategy; Uncertainty**   Computer Graphics (CG) is a small manufacturer of electronic products for computers with graphics capabilities. The company has succeeded by being very innovative in product design. As a spin-off of a large electronics manufacturer (ElecTech), CG management has extensive experience in both marketing and manufacturing in the electronics industry. A long list of equity investors is betting that the firm will really take off because of the growth of specialized graphics software and the increased demand for computers with enhanced graphics capability. A number of market analysts say, however, that the market for the firm's products is somewhat risky, as it is for many high-tech start-ups, because of the number of new competitors entering the market and CG's unproven technology.

CG's main product is a circuit board (CB3668) used in computers with enhanced graphics capabilities. Prices vary depending on the terms of sale and the size of the purchase; the average price for the CB3668 is $100. If the firm is successful, it might be able to raise prices, but it also might have to reduce the price because of increased competition. The firm expects to sell 150,000 units in the coming year, and sales are expected to increase in the following years. The future for CG looks very bright indeed, but the company is new and has not developed a strong financial base. Cash flow management is a critical feature of the firm's financial management, and top management must watch cash flow numbers closely.

At present, CG is manufacturing the CB3668 in a plant leased from ElecTech using some equipment purchased from ElecTech. CG manufactures about 70 percent of the parts in this circuit board.

CG management is considering a significant reengineering project to significantly change the plant and manufacturing process. The project's objective is to increase the number of purchased parts (to about 55%) and to reduce the complexity of the manufacturing process. This would also permit CG to remove some leased equipment and to sell some of the most expensive equipment in the plant.

The per-unit manufacturing costs for 150,000 units of CB3668 follow:

	Current Manufacturing Costs	Proposed Manufacturing Costs
Materials and purchased parts	$ 6.00	$ 15.00
Direct labor	12.50	13.75
Variable overhead	25.00	30.00
Fixed overhead	40.00	20.00
Manufacturing information for CB3668:		
Number of setups	3,000	2,300
Batch size	50	50
Cost per setup	$ 300	$ 300
Machine hours	88,000	55,000

General, selling, and administrative costs are $10 variable cost per unit and $1,250,000 fixed; these costs are not expected to differ for either the current or the proposed manufacturing plan.

Required

1. Compute the contribution margin per unit and the breakeven point in units for CB3668, both before and after the proposed reengineering project. Assume all setup costs are included in fixed overhead.

2. Determine the number of sales units at which CG would be indifferent as to the current manufacturing plan or the proposed plan.

3. Use Goal Seek in Excel to confirm your answer to requirement 2.

4. Briefly comment on CG's strategy.

5. Should CG undertake the proposed reengineering plan? Support your answer with sensitivity analysis and a discussion of short-term and long-term considerations.

[LO 9-2, 9-4]   9-47 **CVP Analysis; ABC Costing**   Using the information in Problem 9-46, complete the following:

Required

1. Compute the breakeven point in units for both the current and the proposed manufacturing plans, assuming that total setup costs vary with the number of batches and that the batch size is fixed (other than for the last batch, in most cases). Assume that setup costs are the only costs that vary with the number of batches.

2. As a check on your calculations in requirement 1, prepare a contribution income statement at the exact breakeven point for both the current plan and the proposed plan.

3. Compare your solution in requirement 2 to that for Problem 9-46 and interpret the difference.

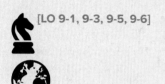

[LO 9-1, 9-3, 9-5, 9-6]   9-48 **Multiple Product CVP Analysis; Sensitivity Analysis**   Hartford Publishing Company (HPC) specializes in international business news publications. Its principal product is *HPC-Monthly,* which is mailed to subscribers the first week of each month. A weekly version, called *HPC-Weekly,* is also available to subscribers over the web at a higher cost. Sixty percent of HPC's subscribers are non-domestic customers. The company experienced a fast growth in subscribers in its first few years of operation, but sales have begun to slow in recent years as new competitors have entered the market. HPC has the following cost structure and sales revenue for its subscription operations on a yearly basis. All costs and all subscription fees are in U.S. dollars.

Fixed Costs	
$378,000 per year	
Variable Costs	
Mailing	$0.70 per issue
Commission	3.50 per subscription
Administrative	2.00 per subscription
Sales Mix Information (based on number of subscriptions)	
HPC-Weekly	25%
HPC-Monthly	75%
Selling Price	
HPC-Weekly	$52 per subscription
HPC-Monthly	20 per subscription

Required   Use the above data to determine the following:

1. Contribution margin per unit for weekly and for monthly subscriptions.

2. Contribution margin ratio for weekly and for monthly subscriptions.

3. a. HPC's breakeven point in sales units and sales dollars. Use the weighted-average contribution margin approach and show calculations. (*Hint:* When calculating the weighted-average contribution margin per unit, the weights in the calculation are based on relative units sold. When calculating the weighted-average contribution margin ratio, the weights are based on relative sales dollars, not units, of the individual products.)

    b. At the overall breakeven point in units, what is the breakeven amount (in units) for each individual product?

    c. What is the breakeven amount (in sales dollars) for each product?

4. Explain the following quote: "For the multiproduct (or multiservice) firm, there is no breakeven point independent of the sales-mix assumption."

5. Prepare a data table for the breakeven volume and percentage change in the breakeven point from the base case (requirement 3) for 1% absolute changes in sales mix for *HPC-Weekly* over the range 20% to 30%.

6. What sales level (in total units) at the assumed sales mix is required to reach a before-tax profit of $75,000?

7. Given the assumed sales mix and an average tax rate of 30%, what sales volume (in total units) is required to generate an after-tax profit, π_A, equal to 10% of sales dollars?

8. What are the critical success factors for HPC? For its domestic subscribers? For its international subscribers?

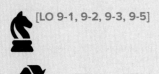

[LO 9-1, 9-2, 9-3, 9-5]   **9-49   CVP Analysis; Strategy; Sensitivity Analysis; Sustainability**   SolarFlex is a small but very innovative manufacturer of cutting-edge solar panels. A significant portion of the company's success is due to technologically superior product design. SolarFlex has invented a flexible photovoltaic panel that utilizes solar energy much more efficiently than traditional panels. Due to its flexible properties, SolarFlex's panels are also very resistant to weathering and the normal wear and tear associated with traditional panels. This has made SolarFlex panels especially popular among certain green-minded companies and individual consumers. SolarFlex's management team is made up of a number of high-profile executives who have extensive experience in the energy industry. Many equity investors and analysts believe the firm is poised to experience exponential growth in the coming years because of the growing popularity of environmentally friendly products and green engineering. However, a number of key industry experts warn that the market for SolarFlex's new technology is much riskier than many believe. They point out that the market is always risky for high-tech start-ups, especially those with new and unproven technology.

The regular price for SolarFlex's main product, the Flex 1000 panel, is $600. The firm expects to sell 380,000 units in the coming year, and sales are expected to increase during the following years.

Right now SolarFlex produces its Flex 1000 panel at a small factory it recently purchased and uses some equipment it purchased from a leading industry manufacturer. The rest of the equipment is on lease. Currently, SolarFlex manufactures about 62% of the parts in its photovoltaic panels.

SolarFlex's management team has decided that it must reconfigure its manufacturing process in order to remain competitive. The team decides to implement a plan to increase the number of purchased parts (to about 82%) and reduce the complexity of the manufacturing process. This would allow SolarFlex to remove the leased equipment and raise some cash by selling some of the purchased equipment currently used in the plant.

The per-unit manufacturing cost for 380,000 units of Flex 1000 follows:

	Current Manufacturing Costs	Proposed Manufacturing Costs
Materials and purchased parts	$180.00	$195.00
Direct labor	55.00	62.50
Variable overhead	70.00	80.00
Fixed overhead	90.00	55.00

General, selling, and administrative variable costs are $25 per unit, and total fixed costs are $2,050,000; these costs are not expected to differ for either the current or the proposed manufacturing plan.

Required

1. Compute the contribution margin per unit and the breakeven point in units for the Flex 1000 panel, both before and after the proposed reengineering project.

2. Determine the number of sales units at which SolarFlex would be indifferent between the current manufacturing plan and the proposed plan.

3. Explain briefly (a) SolarFlex's strategy and (b) if SolarFlex should undertake the proposed reengineering plan. Support your answer with a sensitivity analysis and a discussion of both short-term and long-term considerations. Your sensitivity analysis should show the amount of projected operating income under each plan as volume goes from 0 units to 900,000 units per year, in increments of 100,000 units.

4. Using the results obtained from the sensitivity analysis conducted in requirement 3, construct (in a single graph) the profit-volume equation for each of the two decision alternatives.

5. Calculate and interpret the degree of operating leverage (DOL) for each decision alternative at $Q = 400,000$ units and at $Q = 600,000$ units.

[LO 9-1, 9-2, 9-3, 9-5]   **9-50   CVP Analysis; Sustainability; Uncertainty;**   With the volatility of gasoline prices in recent years, consumers have moved to high miles-per-gallon (mpg) vehicles, in particular hybrid autos that rely on a battery as well as a gasoline engine for even greater mpg. The new vehicles save money on gas, but also reduce the motorist's "carbon footprint" in an environment of global warming. To encourage the purchase of fuel-efficient vehicles such as hybrids, the government may provide incentives, including income-tax credits, which represent dollar-for-dollar reductions in the income tax liability of the individual in the year of purchase. As both a cost conscious and an environmentally conscious consumer, you are currently evaluating whether to purchase a hybrid vehicle. Assume that you have narrowed your decision down to two choices: a gasoline-powered vehicle or its equivalent hybrid (e.g., Honda Accord vs. Accord hybrid). Relevant information regarding each of these two vehicles is as follows:

Auto	Cost	Tax Credit	Mpg
Gasoline model	$27,000	n/a	30.0
Hybrid model	38,000	$4,000	40.0

Assume, further, that you plan to keep your auto for five years and that, based on recent experience, will likely drive the car 20,000 miles per year (100,000 miles in total).

Required

1. Generate a cost function for each decision alternative, where the dependent variable, Y, is "lifetime cost" and the independent variable, X, is "lifetime miles driven."

2. Calculate the breakeven price for gas (per gallon) between the gasoline-powered model and the hybrid model.

3. Prepare a graph for lifetime cost (Y) for each of the two autos as a function of price per gallon of gas (X), based on 100,000 lifetime miles for each auto. Use the following values of X (price per gallon of gas) to generate each cost function: $2.50, $2.75, $3.00, $3.25, $3.50, $3.75, $4.00, $4.25, $4.50, and $4.75. Properly label each graph, including the points of intersection. What can you conclude based on the graph you prepared?

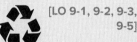

[LO 9-1, 9-2, 9-3, 9-5]

9-51 **CVP Analysis; Sustainability; Uncertainty; Decision Tables (Refer to information in Problem 9-50)**

Required

1. The information in Problem 9-50 presents a decision problem similar to the choice of cost structure (variable vs. fixed) discussed in the chapter. Here, the issue is whether to pay an upfront premium (extra fixed cost) for the hybrid model in exchange for lower variable costs over the life of the vehicle. In a typical CVP model, we are able, at any output level (X), to calculate a measure of profit sensitivity, which we call the degree of operating leverage (DOL). In the present context, which involves only costs for each vehicle over a five-year period, we cannot calculate DOL, but we might calculate an analogous measure: the ratio of percentage change in lifetime cost to percentage change in miles. Refer to this as a pseudo-DOL. Calculate this pseudo measure for each decision alternative, from a base of 100,000 lifetime miles. To calculate the percentage change figures, use 105,000 miles. What information is conveyed in the two measures you calculated?

2. The preceding calculations give you some of the information you need to make your decision. However, being the inquisitive type, you want more information. For example, you are wondering whether, in the present context (i.e., decision choice), the price of gas (per gallon) has much of an impact on the financial consequence regarding the choice of automobile. To explore this issue further, you decide to construct a decision table. As pointed out in the text, a decision table discloses combinations of actions (here, choice of automobile) and events (here, lifetime miles driven and mpg performance of each auto). Prepare a decision table that discloses the breakeven point in gas price for 90,000 miles, 100,000 miles, and 110,000 miles for each of five situations regarding the difference in initial cost (after rebate) between the gasoline-powered model and the hybrid model. Construct your table based on the following initial cost differences between the two: $5,000, $6,000, $7,000 (the base case, based on original data), $8,000, and $9,000. [*Hint:* With five different initial cost differences and three alternatives for lifetime miles driven, your decision table should disclose 15 (i.e., 5 × 3) breakeven points in terms of price per gallon of gas.] Interpret a couple of points from the decision table you constructed.

3. The following probabilities (p) apply to the set of possible events (price of gas, per gallon) listed in requirement 3 for Problem 9-50: 0.05, 0.07, 0.08, 0.10, 0.12, 0.18, 0.15, 0.12, 0.10, and 0.03. Your decision consists of one of two actions: buy the hybrid model or buy the gasoline-powered model. Given this set of probabilities and events, calculate the expected value of the lifetime cost associated with each action (decision choice) under the assumption that lifetime miles driven = 100,000. For each action, the expected value of lifetime cost, $E(a_i)$, is the weighted average of outcomes (lifetime costs), where the weights for each outcome are the outcome's probability.

4. It is certainly possible that, in some scenarios, the lifetime cost of each of the two decision alternatives is very close, even indistinguishable. But even if there are significant differences in the financial result, other factors may sway a decision. What nonfinancial factors and other quantitative factors (beyond those considered earlier) might be relevant to your decision? Explain.

Solution to Self-Study Problem

1. Contribution margin per unit = $5,595 – $899 – $233 = $4,463

2. Breakeven

    In units:

    $$Q = (F + \pi_B) \div (p - v)$$
    $$Q = \$2,352,000 \div \$4,463 = 527 \text{ units}$$

    In dollars:

    $$p \times Q = \$5,595 \times 527 = \$2,948,565$$

    Or

    $$p \times Q = \frac{F + \pi_B}{(p - v) \div p} = \frac{\$2,352,000}{0.797676} = \$2,948,565$$

3. New level of facilities costs = $2,352,000(1 + 0.05) = $2,469,600

    Let the required sales volume, in units, equal Q. Then,

    $$Q = (F + \pi_B) \div (p - v)$$
    $$Q = (\$2,469,600 + \$200,000) \div \$4,463$$
    $$= 598.2 \text{ units, which we could round up to the next whole unit}$$

4. Incorporate an income tax rate of 22% and desired after-tax profit (π_A) of $150,000:

    $$Q = \{\$2,352,000 + [\$150,000 \div (1 - 0.22)]\} \div \$4,463$$
    $$= 570.1 \text{ units, which we could round up to the next whole unit}$$

Please visit Connect to access a narrated, animated tutorial for solving this problem.

CHAPTER TEN

Strategy and the Master Budget

Johnson & Johnson (J&J), one of the largest manufacturers of health care products in the world, was started by the Johnson brothers in 1887 as a small manufacturer of health and well-being related products. Today, it has more than 135,000 employees and more than 260 operating companies in 60 countries. J&J sells its products in more than 175 countries. Surveys conducted over the years by *Bloomberg Businessweek, Forbes, Fortune,* and other business journals repeatedly rank J&J as one of the most innovative, well-managed, and most admired firms in the world.

Alexander Tolstykh/Shutterstock

How does J&J do it? It relies on a comprehensive formal planning, budgeting, and control system in formulating and implementing strategy, coordinating and monitoring operations, and reviewing and evaluating performance. Every January, each operating unit reviews and revises its 5- and 10-year plans from the previous year and prepares the budget for the coming year as well as a two-year plan. The budgeting process is not completed until the approval of the profit plan in December.

J&J is not unique. Growth and long-term profitability are results of a well-formulated strategy with good planning and implementation of the strategy. Firms need to plan for success. Budgeting is a common tool that organizations use for planning and controlling what they must do to serve their customers and succeed in the marketplace. This chapter provides a detailed discussion of the budgeting process and both the role and limitations of this process in the overall management of an organization.

Role of Budgets

LO 10-1

Describe the role of budgets in the overall management process.

> "In preparing for battle I have always found that plans are useless, but planning is indispensable."
>
> *Dwight D. Eisenhower, 34th president of the United States*

budget
A detailed plan for the acquisition and use of financial and other resources over a specified period of time—for example, a year, a month, or a quarter.

budgeting
The process of preparing one or more budgets.

While running a business is not the same as an army going in to battle, the idea of battling the competition does share some of the aspects of going to war. In both settings, the leaders must plan, but they must also be ready to react to unforeseen changes to the competitive landscape and environment. A **budget** is a detailed plan for the acquisition and use of financial and other resources over a specified period of time—for example, a year, month, or quarter—in order to accomplish the organization's objectives. A budget includes both financial and nonfinancial aspects of planned operations and projects. The budget for a period is both a guideline for operations and a projection of the operating results for the budgeted period. The process of preparing one or more budgets is called **budgeting.**

Budget preparations allow management time to anticipate and develop strategies for dealing with problems the organization might face in the coming periods. This extra time enables the organization to minimize the adverse effects that anticipated problems could have on operations. Budgets can help managers identify current and potential bottlenecks in operations. Critical resources can then be acquired to ease any bottlenecks and prevent such bottlenecks from becoming obstacles to attaining budgetary goals.

Budgets also serve as a mechanism through which top management communicates expectations throughout the entire organization. An integrated set of budgets allows each subunit to see how that subunit fits into the overall plan for the period covered by the budget. The manufacturing division knows, for example, that it needs to complete the production of so many units of a given product before a certain date if the marketing division schedules the delivery of that product to customers for various dates.

A budget can also be a motivating device. With the expected activities and operating results clearly delineated in the budget, employees know what is expected of them; this in turn can motivate employees to work to attain the budgeted goals. To enhance the role of the budget as a motivating device, many organizations have employees participate in the budgeting process, thus helping employees embrace the budget as their own.

Completion of a budget for all units of an organization facilitates the coordination of activities across subunits within the organization. For example, budgets show the effect of sales volumes on required purchases of materials, production levels, the level of administrative support needed, and the level and type of sales support and customer-service support required for the budgetary period. In short, coordination across functional areas of the organization (sales, production, purchasing, etc.) is an important managerial responsibility. Budgeting is a tool that can be used to help achieve the requisite level of coordination of organizational activities.

Budgets also provide authority to acquire and use resources. The authorization function of budgets is especially important for government and not-for-profit (NFP) organizations because budgeted amounts, sometimes referred to as *appropriations,* often serve as both approval of activities and a ceiling for expenditures.

At the end of an operating period, the budget for the period can serve as a basis for assessing performance by reporting and interpreting variances between actual and budgeted spending and operating results. The budget represents the specific results expected of the firm's divisions and employees for the period. For control purposes, actual performance can be compared to expected performance as reflected in the set of budgets prepared by the organization.[1]

Strategy and the Master Budget

Importance of Strategy in Budgeting

An organization's strategy is the path it chooses for attaining its long-term goals and its stated mission. The importance of strategy in planning and budgeting cannot be overemphasized. Too often, organizations view the budget for the coming period as a continuation of the budget for the current period with, at best, a scant attempt to link the budget to their strategy. The objective is to build a resource plan to achieve the organization's strategic goals and objectives. Therefore, a budget should start with a careful review and study of the organization's strategic plan and the resources needed to achieve that plan. Ignoring the strategic plan can result in not adequately funding the projects and initiatives that are critical to achieving long-term success.

Strategic Goals and Long-Term Objectives

long-range plan
A plan that identifies actions required during the five- to seven-year period covered by the plan to attain the organization's strategic goals.

Strategy provides the framework within which a long-range plan for the organization is developed. A **long-range plan** identifies required actions over a five- to seven-year period to attain the strategic goal(s) specified by the organization.

capital budgeting
A process of identifying, evaluating, selecting, and controlling an organization's capital investments (i.e., its long-term projects and programs).

Long-range planning often entails **capital budgeting,** which is a process for evaluating, selecting, and financing major projects and programs such as purchases of new equipment, construction of a new factory, and addition of new products. Capital budgets are prepared to bring an organization's capabilities into line with the needs of its long-range plan and long-term sales forecast. An organization's capacity is a result of capital investments made in prior budgeting periods.[2]

strategic budget expenditures
Planned spending on projects and initiatives that lead to long-term value and competitive advantage.

The strategic goals and objectives of the organization are, ultimately, accomplished through a focused set of initiatives and projects. Put another way, it is this set of initiatives and projects that creates value for the organization. As such, it is important that the organization's annual budgeting process give prominence to a particular class of capital budgeting expenditures: **strategic budget expenditures,** including those related to *sustainability.* Because such expenditures lead to long-term value creation and competitive advantage, it is important that they be clearly identified and, to the extent possible, protected.

---

[1] Analysis of actual versus budgeted results is the essence of the traditional model of financial control and is covered in Chapters 14, 15, and 16.

[2] Capital budgeting is the subject of Chapter 12.

EXHIBIT 10.1

The Relationships among Strategic Goals, Long-Term Objectives, the Master Budget, Operations, and Controls

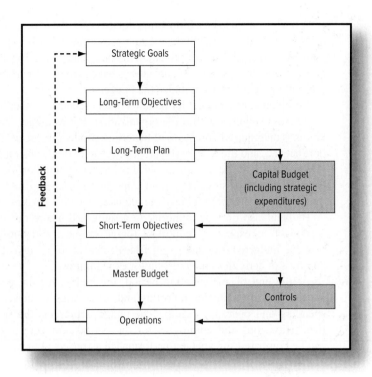

Short-Term Objectives and the Master Budget

master budget

An aggregation of all subunit budgets into an integrated plan of action for the budget period.

operating budgets

Plans for all phases of operation, including production, purchasing, personnel, and marketing budgets.

financial budgets

Budgets that identify and relate to sources and uses of funds for planned operations and capital expenditures.

Short-term objectives are goals for the coming period, which can be a month, a quarter, a year, or any length of time desired by the organization for planning purposes. These objectives serve as the basis for preparing the **master budget** for a period. The master budget is an aggregation of all subunit budgets into an integrated plan of action for the budget period. The culmination of the master budgeting process is the production of a set of budgeted (pro forma) financial statements (income statement, balance sheet, and statement of cash flows).

The master budget comprises both operating budgets and financial budgets. **Operating budgets** are plans that identify resources needed to implement strategic projects and to carry out budgeted activities such as sales and customer service, production, purchasing, marketing, and research and development, as well as the acquisition of these resources. For a manufacturer, operating budgets include production, purchasing, personnel, and marketing budgets. The set of operating budgets culminates in a budgeted income statement. **Financial budgets** identify sources and uses of funds for planned capital expenditures and for the budgeted level of operations for the upcoming period. Financial budgets include the cash budget, budgeted statement of cash flows, the budgeted balance sheet, and the capital expenditures (including strategic expenditures) budget.

Exhibit 10.1 illustrates the relationships among strategic goals, long-term objectives and plans, short-term goals, operations, and controls for an organization. By *controls,* we mean the set of procedures used to monitor the progress of the organization in terms of accomplishing its stated goals and objectives and implementing corrective action(s) if needed.[3]

The Budgeting Process

LO 10-3

Outline the budgeting process.

The traditional budgeting process can range from the informal simple processes small firms use to the lengthy procedures large firms or governments employ. Indeed, the budgeting process for large organizations may span months from start to final approval. The process usually includes the formation of a budget committee; determination of the budget period;

---

[3] The topic of control is addressed in Parts 3 and 4 of the text. Operational-level control is the subject of Part 3 (Chapters 14 through 17, inclusive), while management-level control is covered in Part 4 (Chapters 18 through 20, inclusive).

specification of budget guidelines (including the preparation of initial budget proposals); budget negotiation, review, and approval; and budget revision.

Budget Committee

The budget committee oversees all budget matters and often is the highest authority in an organization for all matters related to the budget. The committee sets and approves the overall budget goals for all major business units, coordinates budget preparation, resolves conflicts and differences that may arise during budget preparation, approves the final budget, monitors operations as the year unfolds, and reviews the operating results at the end of the period.

Budget Period

A budget usually is prepared for a set time, most commonly for the fiscal year with subperiod budgets for each of the constituent quarters or months. However, in practice, firms seldom have budgets for only one year. The budgets for the years beyond the coming year, however, usually contain only essential operating data. For example, J&J may have only skeleton budgets for its 5- and 10-year budgets. Having a long-term budget in parallel with the master budget allows alignment of strategic goals and short-term operations.

Budget Guidelines

In a traditional budgeting process the budget committee is responsible for providing initial budget guidelines that set the tone for the budget and govern its preparation. The committee issues budget guidelines after careful consideration of the general outlook of the economy and the market; the organization's strategic goals, long-term plan, strategic projects, and the expected operating results of the current period; specific corporate decisions or policies (such as mandates for downsizing, reengineering, pollution control, and special promotions); and short-term objectives. Each responsibility center (or subunit) (e.g., department, division, or region) prepares its initial budget proposal based on the budget-preparation guidelines of the organization.

Negotiation, Review, and Approval

The executives of budget units examine initial budget proposals. The examination includes determining adherence to the budget guidelines and verifying that the budget goals can be reasonably attained and are in line with the goals of the immediately higher organizational unit.

As subunits within the organization complete their budgets, the budgets go through successively higher levels of the organization until they reach the top level, at which point the combined unit budgets become the organization's budget. After a final review, the budget committee gives its approval. The CEO then approves the entire budget, which eventually is submitted to the board of directors for approval.

Revision

Procedures for budgetary revisions vary among organizations. For organizations that allow budget revisions only under special circumstances, obtaining approval to modify a budget can be difficult. Not all events, however, unfold as predicted in a budget. Strictly implementing a budget as prescribed, even when the actual events differ significantly from those expected, certainly is not a desirable behavior. In such cases, managers should be encouraged not to rely on the budget as the absolute guideline in operations.

The strategic role of budgeting for a hypothetical company, Kerry Window Systems Inc., is discussed next. This is followed by a detailed example that illustrates the steps involved in preparing a master budget for this company.

Comprehensive Budgeting Example: Kerry Window Systems Inc.

Kerry Window Systems Inc. (KWS) manufactures and sells upscale aluminum-framed windows that are priced somewhat higher than the vinyl-framed windows sold by competitors. To compete in this portion of the market, KWS stresses manufacturing quality and offers the final customer a comprehensive warranty against defects. Many view KWS as having among the best window products available.

With winter heating costs going up, there has been strong demand for quality windows, especially for older homes. Also, many families who are finding it more difficult to move up to a larger home as they had planned are remodeling or adding rooms to their existing homes, thus increasing demand for KWS's window units. The result of these economic forces is that KWS is growing very fast. Another factor affecting KWS is that the business is very seasonal because the building and remodeling season is limited to those months with good weather. Thus, KWS's manufacturing process is year-round, but its sales are seasonal. As the company grows, this means negative cash flows at certain times of the year. KWS management is particularly concerned about maintaining its product lines, and this must be done in a business environment in which available credit is hard to find, a consequence of the mortgage loan losses at many financial institutions in recent years. The owners of this business have committed to using a comprehensive budgeting system to facilitate planning and decision making for KWS. A discussion of the five steps the company will take to implement its budgeting model follows.

The Five Steps of Strategic Decision Making for Kerry Window Systems Inc.

1. **Determine the strategic issues surrounding the problem.** KWS operates in an industry that is very competitive and seasonal. Cash flow management is a common issue in the industry, particularly for fast-growing companies. Cost-cutting measures would damage the KWS brand at this stage of the company's growth, so the company depends on financing from a variety of sources.

2. **Identify the alternative actions.** The company can raise financing through additional short- or long-term debt or the sale of stock.

3. **Obtain information and analyze each decision alternative.** The company's stock price has remained steady in the prior several months, reflecting in part the market's overall concern for the industry and uncertainty about the degree of success that will be achieved by KWS's recent growth. The availability for debt is limited by the current poor conditions in the banking industry.

4. **Based on strategy and analysis, choose and implement the desired alternative.** KWS is in a difficult situation regarding cash flow management. The use of the master budget, paying particular attention to the cash budget, is crucial for the company's continued success. Forecasting sales and costs, using the tools explained in Chapter 8, is also particularly important for the company. With accurate budgets, the company thinks it will be able to more effectively project cash needs and have a plan in place for providing the needed financing when necessary.

5. **Provide an ongoing evaluation of the effectiveness of implementation in step 4.** As the company matures and its growth rate slows, and as conditions in the banking industry change, the focus on financing can shift to other issues, such as advancing and protecting the company's competitive position in the market, improving profitability, and developing effective operational-level and management-level control systems.

In the next section of this chapter, we provide an overview of the master budgeting process for a one-year period for KWS.

Master Budget

LO 10-4

Prepare a master budget and explain the interrelationships among its supporting schedules.

As noted earlier, a master budget is a comprehensive budget for a specific period. The master budget consists of a capital budget and a set of interrelated operating and financial budgets. Exhibit 10.2 delineates the relationships among components of a master budget for a hypothetical manufacturing firm, such as KWS.

Sales Budget

sales budget

A schedule showing forecasted sales, in units and dollars, for an upcoming period.

The **sales budget** shows forecasted sales, in units and dollars, for an upcoming period. Because of its effect on other budgets, the sales budget is sometimes referred to as the cornerstone of the entire master budget.

The starting point in preparing a sales budget is the sales forecast. An inaccurate sales forecast can render the entire budget a futile exercise and, when inaccurate, can impose costly expenses on the firm as well as its suppliers.

EXHIBIT 10.2
The Master Budget for a Manufacturer

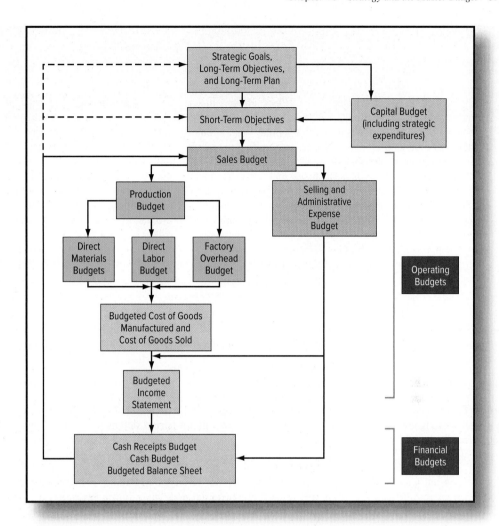

Sales forecasting by its nature is, in part, subjective. To reduce subjectivity in forecasts, many firms generate more than one independent sales forecast before preparing the sales budget for the period. The following factors should be considered in sales forecasting:

- Current sales levels and sales trends of the past few years.
- General economic and industry conditions.
- Competitors' actions and operating plans.
- Pricing policies.
- Credit policies.
- Advertising and promotional activities.
- The level of unfilled back orders.

Due to the seasonal nature of its business, Kerry Window Systems Inc. (KWS) has a March 31 fiscal year-end. Budgets for the coming year are prepared during the months of January through March. Exhibit 10.3 illustrates the sales budget for KWS for the first quarter of the

EXHIBIT 10.3
Sales Budget

KERRY WINDOW SYSTEMS INC. Sales Budget For the Quarter Ended June 30, 2022				
	April	**May**	**June**	**Quarter**
Sales in units	20,000	25,000	35,000	80,000
Selling price per unit	× $30	× $30	× $30	× $30
Gross sales revenue	**$600,000**	**$750,000**	**$1,050,000**	**$2,400,000**

REAL-WORLD FOCUS   The Importance of an Accurate Sales Forecast to the Master Budgeting Process

In the fall of 2010, in anticipation of "Black Friday," major manufacturers of LCD and LED TVs (e.g., Sony and Samsung) scrambled to cut retail prices in the U.S. market in an attempt to stave off a buildup of inventory of unsold units. To prop up sales, manufacturers also included free extras, such as Blu-ray DVD players and 3-D glasses, to make their products more attractive to consumers. This inventory buildup was directly affected by overly aggressive production plans (budgets), which in turn were affected by overly optimistic sales forecasts. At the time, TV manufacturers were anticipating a healthier U.S. economy and a willingness of consumers to "open their purse strings" for high-end electronics, including TV sets. However,

the sluggish economy resulted in just the opposite: reduced demand for premium sets with advanced features. Further pressure on demand for premium TVs resulted from the fact that as of 2010, almost half of all households in the United States had at least one flat-screen TV; newer gadgets such as Apple's iPad tablet computer exacerbated the situation. This example highlights the critical nature of the sales forecast in terms of the master budgeting process and the importance of incorporating broader economic factors into the sales forecasting process.

Source: M. Bustillo, "TV Bargains Come Early This Year," *The Wall Street Journal,* November 10, 2010 (available at http://online.wsj.com/news/articles/SB10001424052748703585004575604651652044256).

2022 fiscal year. KWS forecasts a selling price of $30 per unit. The next step is for KWS to prepare its manufacturing budgets for the quarter.

Manufacturing Budgets
Production Budget

production budget
A budget showing planned output (production) for an upcoming period.

A **production budget** shows planned production for a given period. For manufacturers, planned production in a given period depends on the following three factors: budgeted sales, the desired ending inventory (in units), and the units of Finished Goods Inventory on hand at the beginning of the period, as described by the following equation:

$$\begin{array}{cccc} \text{Budgeted} & \text{Budgeted} & \text{Desired ending} & \text{Beginning} \\ \text{production} = & \text{sales} & + \text{ inventory} & - \text{ inventory} \\ \text{(in units)} & \text{(in units)} & \text{(in units)} & \text{(in units)} \end{array}$$

To illustrate, KWS expects to have 5,000 units on hand at the beginning of the quarter, April 1. The firm's policy is to have on hand at the end of each month inventory equal to 30 percent of the following month's predicted sales (in units). KWS expects its total sales in May 2022 to be 25,000 units. The desired ending inventory on April 30, therefore, is 7,500 units, as shown in step 1. Step 2 shows that 22,500 units should be scheduled for production in April.

Step 1. Determine the desired ending inventory (April 30):

Expected sales in May	25,000 units
× Desired percentage of next month's sales to be on hand on April 30	× 30%
Desired ending inventory (April 30)	7,500 units

Step 2. Calculate budgeted production for April:

Budgeted sales for April (from Exhibit 10.3)	20,000 units
+ Desired ending inventory (April 30)	+ 7,500 units
Total number of units needed in April	27,500 units
− Beginning inventory (April 1)	− 5,000 units
Budgeted production for April	22,500 units

Exhibit 10.4 shows KWS's production budget for the first quarter of the year. This budget is based on the sales budget (Exhibit 10.3) and the expected sales in July (40,000, assumed).

Most of the quarterly amounts are simply the sums of the appropriate monthly figures. For example, in Exhibit 10.3, the budgeted sales for the quarter, 80,000 units, is the sum of the budgeted sales in April (20,000 units), May (25,000 units), and June (35,000 units). The desired ending inventory of the quarter, however, is the desired ending inventory of June—the

EXHIBIT 10.4
Production Budget

KERRY WINDOW SYSTEMS INC.				
Production Budget				
For the Quarter Ended June 30, 2022				
	April	**May**	**June**	**Quarter**
Budgeted sales (units)	20,000	25,000	35,000	80,000
Add: Desired ending inventory				
of finished units	7,500	10,500	**12,000***	**12,000**
Total units needed	27,500	35,500	47,000	92,000
Less: Beginning inventory				
of finished units	5,000†	7,500	10,500	5,000
Budgeted production (units)	**22,500**	**28,000**	**36,500**	**87,000**

*Assumed, based on anticipated July sales of 40,000 units (i.e., 12,000 units = 30% × 40,000 units).
†Assumed.

end of the quarter—not the sum of the desired ending amount in each of the three months in the quarter. The amount of beginning inventory for the quarter is the beginning inventory of the first month of the quarter. These two amounts refer to specific times in the quarter, not the amount for the entire three-month period.

Before finalizing a production budget, the production manager reviews the feasibility of the budgeted production in view of the available facilities and other activities scheduled for the same period. In the event that budgeted production exceeds the maximum capacity available, management needs to either revise the budgeted sales level or find alternatives to satisfy the demand. If the available capacity exceeds the budgeted production level, the budget allows management ample time to find alternative uses of the idle capacity or to schedule other activities such as preventive maintenance and trial runs of new production processes.

The sales budget for the quarter shows that KWS expects increasing sales. When sales vary over periods, management can either change the production level as needed, as KWS did, or choose to maintain a stable production level and schedule the entire quarter's production evenly at 29,000 units per month.

Direct Materials Usage Budget and Direct Materials Purchases Budget

direct materials usage budget
A plan that shows the amount and budgeted cost of direct materials required for planned production.

The information in the production budget becomes the basis for preparing several manufacturing-related budgets. One is the **direct materials usage budget** (Exhibit 10.5), which shows the amount and budgeted cost of direct materials required for budgeted production. The last line of the production budget (Exhibit 10.4) shows the number of units of the product that KWS plans to manufacture in April: 22,500 units. This amount is reflected in line 1 of Exhibit 10.5, KWS's direct materials usage budget. Assume that the product specification requires three pounds of aluminum alloy for each unit of the product, which is entered into line 2 of Exhibit 10.5. Therefore, KWS needs a total of 67,500 pounds of aluminum (line 3) to produce the 22,500 units budgeted in April. The remainder of the direct materials usage budget (Exhibit 10.5, part B) identifies the cost of direct materials for the budget period, which can be completed only after KWS prepares the direct materials purchases budget for the month (Exhibit 10.6). Finally, assume that KWS uses a FIFO (first-in, first-out) cost-flow assumption.

direct materials purchases budget
A budget that shows the physical amount and cost of planned purchases of direct materials.

A **direct materials purchases budget** shows the amount of direct materials, such as raw materials or component parts, to be purchased during the period (in both units and cost) to meet the production and ending materials inventory requirements. A direct materials purchases budget starts with the amount of direct materials needed in production for the current period, which was determined in line 3 of Exhibit 10.5. As indicated in Exhibit 10.6, KWS needs 67,500, 84,000, and 109,500 pounds of aluminum alloy to meet its production needs for April, May, and June, respectively.

The company's policy is to have in ending materials inventory each period an amount equal to 10 percent of the next period's production needs (line 2 of Exhibit 10.6). Line 3 of

EXHIBIT 10.5   **Direct Materials Usage Budget**

KERRY WINDOW SYSTEMS INC.
Direct Materials Usage Budget
For the Quarter Ended June 30, 2022

Line	Item	April	May	June	Quarter	Calculation
A.	**Production Requirements**					
1.	Budgeted production	22,500	28,000	36,500	87,000	*
2.	Pounds of aluminum alloy for one unit of product	× 3	× 3	× 3	× 3	
3.	**Total pounds of aluminum alloy needed in production**	**67,500**	**84,000**	**109,500**	**261,000**	
B.	**Cost of Direct Materials**					
4.	Pounds of aluminum alloy from beginning inventory	7,000	8,400	10,950	7,000	
5.	Cost per pound (FIFO basis)	× $ 2.40	× $ 2.45	× $ 2.50	× $ 2.40	
6.	Total costs of aluminum alloy, beginning inventory	$ 16,800	$ 20,580	$ 27,375	$ 16,800	(4) × (5)
7.	Total costs of aluminum alloy purchases	+ 168,805	+ 216,375	+ 284,310	+ 669,490	†
8.	Total costs of aluminum alloy available	$185,605	$236,955	$311,685	$686,290	(6) + (7)
9.	Desired ending inventory of aluminum alloy, in units	8,400	10,950	10,800‡	10,800	†
10.	Cost per unit (FIFO basis)	× $ 2.45	× $ 2.50	× $ 2.60	× $ 2.60	†
11.	Aluminum alloy, ending inventory	$ 20,580	$ 27,375	$ 28,080	$ 28,080	(9) × (10)
12.	**Total costs of aluminum alloy used in production**	**$165,025**	**$209,580**	**$283,605**	**$658,210**	**(8) – (11)**

* = Exhibit 10.4 (Production Budget).
† = Exhibit 10.6 (Direct Materials Purchases Budget).
‡ = Assumed.

Exhibit 10.5 shows that KWS needs 84,000 pounds of aluminum alloy for the budgeted production in May. Thus, KWS needs to maintain 8,400 pounds of aluminum alloy on hand at the end of April (10% of 84,000), as shown in line 2 of Exhibit 10.6. (Assume that direct materials pounds needed for production in July = 108,000.) The sum of lines 1 and 2 (Exhibit 10.6) is the total amount of direct materials needed for April, 75,900 pounds.

EXHIBIT 10.6   **Direct Materials Purchases Budget**

KERRY WINDOW SYSTEMS INC.
Direct Materials Purchases Budget
For the Quarter Ended June 30, 2022

Line	Item	April	May	June	Quarter
1.	Total direct materials needed in production (from part A of Exhibit 10.5) (in lbs.)	67,500	84,000	109,500	261,000
2.	Add: Desired direct materials ending inventory (in lbs.)	+ 8,400	+ 10,950	+ 10,800*	+ 10,800
3.	Total direct materials needed (in lbs.)	75,900	94,950	120,300	271,800
4.	Less: Direct materials beginning inventory	− 7,000	− 8,400	− 10,950	− 7,000
5.	**Total direct materials purchases (lbs.)**	**68,900**	**86,550**	**109,350**	**264,800**
6.	Purchase price per pound	× $ 2.45	× $ 2.50	× $ 2.60	
7.	**Total costs of direct materials purchases**	**$168,805**	**$216,375**	**$284,310**	**$ 669,490†**

*Assumed, based on estimated production in July.
† $669,490 = $168,805 + $216,375 + $284,310.

KWS expects to have 7,000 pounds of aluminum alloy on hand at the beginning of April (March's ending inventory). Subtracting the quantity expected to be on hand on April 1 from the total amount needed for April, we see that KWS must purchase 68,900 pounds in April (line 5 of Exhibit 10.6) to meet the expected needs in April. These steps summarize the calculations in Exhibit 10.6:

Total amount of direct materials needed in production during the month	Line 1
+ Required direct materials inventory at the end of the month	+ Line 2
= Total direct materials needed for the month	= Line 3
− Direct materials on hand at the beginning of the month	− Line 4
= Direct materials to be purchased during the month	= Line 5

KWS's purchasing department estimates the cost of aluminum alloy to be $2.45 per pound in April. Thus, the total costs for the 68,900 pounds to be purchased in April are $168,805, as shown in line 7 of Exhibit 10.6.

At the beginning of April, assume that KWS has on hand 7,000 pounds of aluminum alloy. At a cost of $2.40 per pound, the total costs of the beginning inventory are $16,800 (Exhibit 10.5, line 6). Adding the purchase cost of $168,805 in April (line 7 of Exhibit 10.6), the total costs of the direct materials available in April are $185,605 (line 8 of Exhibit 10.5). Under FIFO, KWS's cost of ending inventory in April is priced at the most recent purchase price paid, which is $2.45 per pound, or $20,580 (line 11 of Exhibit 10.5). Subtracting the cost of ending inventory, $20,580, from the total costs of direct materials available, $185,605 (line 8 of Exhibit 10.5), the total costs of direct materials to be used in April is $165,025 (line 12 of Exhibit 10.5).

Following the same procedure, KWS completes the direct materials purchases budgets for May and June. June's direct materials ending inventory of 10,800 pounds is based on the 36,000 units to be manufactured in July (3 pounds per unit × 36,000 (assumed units) = 108,000 pounds and 10% × 108,000 = 10,800 pounds).

Direct Labor Budget

To prepare the direct labor budget, KWS would take information from its production budget. Each firm needs a requisite number of employees with the required skills to carry out production activity, as budgeted. The direct labor budget enables the personnel department to plan for the hiring and repositioning of employees, if need be. A good labor budget helps the firm avoid emergency hiring, prevent labor shortages, and reduce or eliminate the need to lay off workers.

Some firms have stable employment policies or labor contracts that prevent them from hiring and laying off employees in direct proportion to their production needs. A direct labor budget enables the firm to identify circumstances when it can either reschedule production or plan temporary employee reassignments to perform other tasks.

manufacturing cells
A set of machines, typically laid out in the form of a semicircle, needed to produce a particular product or part.

Other organizations use what are called **manufacturing cells** (sets of machines laid out in the form of a semicircle) to produce a particular product or part. Organizations that use cellular manufacturing systems can use the direct labor budget to plan for maintenance, minor repairs, installation, testing, learning and growth, or other activities.

A company usually prepares a direct labor budget for each type (or class) of labor; for instance, KWS has both skilled and semiskilled factory workers. On average, the production process is expected to use 0.5 hour of semiskilled labor and 0.2 hour of skilled labor for each unit produced. The planned hourly wages are $8 and $12 for semiskilled and skilled laborers, respectively. Exhibit 10.7 illustrates the direct labor budget for the first quarter of 2022.

Factory Overhead Budget

A factory overhead budget includes all production costs other than direct materials and direct labor. Some firms, such as KWS, separate factory overhead into variable and fixed costs. Exhibit 10.8 shows KWS's factory overhead budget for the first quarter of the year. Note that variable overhead cost is assumed to be related to the number of direct labor hours (DLHs) worked.

REAL-WORLD FOCUS   Budgeting Labor Costs in the Workplace of the Future

Imagine a company with only 81 employees creating a video-game that attracted over 29 million players in just two years. That is just what Psyonix Inc. was able to accomplish. But that does not mean that only 81 people worked on the project—far from it. Over one-third of those working on the hit game "Rocket League" were contractors, and Psyonix is not alone it is use of nonemployees. Nearly 70 contracting firms are included in the credits of Square Enix Co.'s game "Final Fantasy XV." This approach to content development can be called just-in-time production, where people are contracted to help on a project,

with the contract ending as soon as the project is complete. Such a project-based approach to work may represent the workplace of the future, and budgeting the direct costs of labor would occur at the project level, where there is a small core of in-house employees and outside workers are hired for only a specific portion of a project's cycle.

Source: Lauren Weber, "For Videogame Makers, Hiring Is a Last Resort—Staffers Do the Most Critical Jobs While Outside Labor Comes and Goes," *The Wall Street Journal,* April 11, 2017, p. A1.

Cost of Goods Manufactured and Cost of Goods Sold Budgets

The cost of goods manufactured budget and the cost of goods sold budget are prepared next. Exhibits 10.4 through 10.8 provide the data needed to complete these budgets for each of the months and for the quarter. Exhibit 10.9 shows a combined cost of goods manufactured and cost of goods sold budget for the first quarter of 2022 for KWS. The company's finished goods inventory on April 1 shows a per-unit cost of $18.

Information from the cost of goods manufactured budget and the cost of goods sold budget for a period appear in two other budgets for the same period. The budgeted income statement uses the cost of goods sold figure to determine the gross margin for the period, and the balance sheet includes the finished goods ending inventory in total assets. These two pro forma financial statements are discussed later.

merchandise purchases budget
A budget that shows the amount (and cost) of merchandise a firm plans to purchase during the budget period.

Merchandise Purchases Budget

A merchandising firm does not have a production budget; instead, it prepares a merchandise purchases budget. A firm's **merchandise purchases budget** shows the amount and cost of merchandise it needs to purchase during the budget period. The basic format of a merchandise

EXHIBIT 10.7 **Direct Labor Budget**

Line		April	May	June	Quarter
	KERRY WINDOW SYSTEMS INC. **Direct Labor Budget** **For the Quarter Ended June 30, 2022**				
	Semiskilled Labor				
1.	Budgeted production (Exhibit 10.4)	22,500	28,000	36,500	87,000
2.	Semiskilled direct labor hours per unit	× 0.5	× 0.5	× 0.5	× 0.5
3.	Total semiskilled direct labor hours needed	11,250	14,000	18,250	43,500
4.	Hourly wage rate of semiskilled labor	× $ 8	× $ 8	× $ 8	× $ 8
5.	Total wages for semiskilled labor	$ 90,000	$ 112,000	$ 146,000	$ 348,000
	Skilled Labor				
6.	Budgeted production (Exhibit 10.4)	22,500	28,000	36,500	87,000
7.	Skilled direct labor hours per unit	× 0.2	× 0.2	× 0.2	× 0.2
8.	Total skilled direct labor hours needed	4,500	5,600	7,300	17,400
9.	Hourly wage for skilled labor	× $ 12	× $ 12	× $ 12	× $ 12
10.	Total wages for skilled labor	$ 54,000	$ 67,200	$ 87,600	$ 208,800
11.	**Total costs for direct labor (5 + 10)**	**$144,000**	**$179,200**	**$233,600**	**$556,800**
12.	Total direct labor hours (3 + 8)	15,750	19,600	25,550	60,900

EXHIBIT 10.8 **Factory Overhead Budget**

KERRY WINDOW SYSTEMS INC.
Factory Overhead Budget
For the Quarter Ended June 30, 2022

	Rate per Direct Labor Hour	April	May	June	Quarter
Total direct labor hours (Exhibit 10.7)		15,750	19,600	25,550	60,900
Variable factory overhead:					
Supplies	$ 0.12	$ 100,890	$100,352	$ 100,066	$ 100,308
Indirect labor	1.00	15,750	19,600	25,550	60,900
Fringe benefits	3.00	47,250	58,800	76,650	182,700
Power	0.20	3,150	3,920	5,110	12,180
Maintenance	0.08	1,260	1,568	2,044	4,872
Total variable factory overhead	$ 4.40	$ 69,300	$ 86,240	$ 112,420	$ 267,960
Fixed factory overhead:					
Depreciation		$ 30,000	$ 30,000	$ 40,000†	$ 100,000
Factory insurance		2,500	2,500	2,500	7,500
Property taxes		900	900	900	2,700
Supervision		8,900	8,900	8,900	26,700
Power		1,250	1,250	1,250	3,750
Maintenance		750	750	750	2,250
Total fixed factory overhead		$ 44,300	$ 44,300	$ 54,300	$ 142,900
Total factory overhead		$ 113,600	$130,540	$ 166,720	$ 410,860
Less: Depreciation		30,000	30,000	40,000	100,000
Cash disbursements for factory overhead		$ 83,600	$100,540	$ 126,720	$ 310,860

†KWS purchased equipment in January for $200,000, to be delivered and installed at the end of May (see item 5 under the Cash Budget subheading). Exhibit 10.8 includes one month of depreciation expense for this asset (June).

EXHIBIT 10.9
Cost of Goods Manufactured and Cost of Goods Sold Budget

KERRY WINDOW SYSTEMS INC.
Cost of Goods Manufactured and Cost of Goods Sold Budget
For the Quarter Ended June 30, 2022

	April	May	June	Quarter
Direct materials (line 12, Exhibit 10.5)	$165,025	$209,580	$283,605	$658,210
Direct labor (line 11, Exhibit 10.7)	144,000	179,200	166,720	556,800
Total factory overhead (Exhibit 10.8)	113,600	130,540	166,720	410,860
Total cost of goods manufactured	$422,625	$519,320	$683,925	$1,625,870
Finished goods beginning inventory	90,000*	140,875	194,745	90,000
Total cost of goods available for sale	$512,625	$660,195	$878,670	$1,715,870
Finished goods ending inventory†	140,875	194,745	224,852	224,852
Cost of goods sold	$371,750	$465,450	$653,818	$1,491,018

* Finished goods begining inventory, April 1, 5,000 units (Exhibit 10.4) at $18 per unit.
† Computations for cost per unit and finished goods ending inventory (FIFO basis):

Cost of goods manufactured	$422,625	$519,320	$683,925
Budgeted production (Exhibit 10.4, last line)	÷ 22,500	÷ 28,000	÷ 36,500
Manufacturing cost per unit	$18.7833	$18.5471	$18.7377
Desired ending inventory (Exhibit 10.4, line 2)	× 7,500	× 10,500	× 12,000
Finished goods ending inventory, FIFO basis	$140,875	$194,745	$224,852

purchases budget is the same as the production budget. However, instead of required production, the merchandise purchases budget provides the number of units required for *purchases* for the budget period. The number of required units is then multiplied by the cost per unit to calculate the purchases cost for the budget period.

EXHIBIT 10.10 Selling and Administrative Expense Budget

KERRY WINDOW SYSTEMS INC.
Selling and Administrative Expense Budget
For the Quarter Ended June 30, 2022

	April	May	June	Quarter
Selling expenses				
Variable selling expenses:				
Sales commissions (given)	$ 30,000	$ 37,500	$ 52,500	$ 120,000
Delivery expense (given)	2,000	2,500	3,500	8,000
Bad debts expense (allowance method)*	9,000	11,250	15,750	36,000
Total variable selling expenses	$ 41,000	$ 51,250	$ 71,750	$ 164,000
Fixed selling expenses:				
Sales salaries (given)	$ 8,000	$ 8,000	$ 8,000	$ 24,000
Advertising (given)	50,000	50,000	50,000	150,000
Delivery expense (given)	6,000	6,000	6,000	18,000
Depreciation (given)	20,000	20,000	20,000	60,000
Total fixed selling expenses	$ 84,000	$ 84,000	$ 84,000	$ 252,000
Total selling expenses	$ 125,000	$ 135,250	$ 155,750	$ 416,000
Administrative expenses (all fixed)				
Administrative salaries	$ 25,000	$ 25,000	$ 25,000	$ 75,000
Accounting and data processing	12,000	12,000	12,000	36,000
Depreciation	7,000	7,000	7,000	21,000
Other administrative expenses	6,000	6,000	6,000	18,000
Total administrative expenses	$ 50,000	$ 50,000	$ 50,000	$ 150,000
Total selling and administrative expenses	**$175,000**	**$185,250**	**$205,750**	**$566,000**
Less: Noncash expenses (bad debts expense and depreciation)	$ 36,000	$ 38,250	$ 42,750	$ 117,000
Cash disbursements for selling and administrative expenses	**$139,000**	**$147,000**	**$163,000**	**$449,000**

*Estimated bad debts = gross sales in a month × 30% × 5%:

Gross sales revenue (Exhibit 10.3)	$600,000	$750,000	$1,050,000	$2,400,000
Percent credit sales in a month	30%	30%	30%	30%
Estimated percent of credit sales that are uncollectible	5%	5%	5%	5%
Estimated bad debts expense	$9,000	$11,250	$15,750	$36,000

Selling and Administrative Expense Budget

The selling and administrative expense budget is then prepared. As indicated in Exhibit 10.10, this budget can be broken down into fixed and variable components of total selling and administrative expenses.

Note that we have subdivided the total selling and administrative expense budget into *total expenses* (for income statement purposes) and *total cash expenses* (for preparing the cash budget for the period). Noncash expenses for KWS include estimated bad debts expense (assumed equal to 5 percent of sales made on open account) plus depreciation expense. Thus, in April total budgeted noncash expenses amount to $36,000, as follows: estimated bad debts expense, $9,000; depreciation expense—selling, $20,000; and depreciation expense—administrative, $7,000.

Cash Receipts (Collections) Budget

The cash receipts budget provides details regarding anticipated collections of cash from operations for an upcoming period. Cash receipts from investing and financing activities are shown elsewhere on the cash budget. KWS has three different sources of cash receipts from operations: (1) cash sales, (2) bank credit card sales, and (3) collection of credit sales (i.e., sales made by the company on "open account").

Past history indicates that, on average, cash plus bank credit card sales for KWS represent 70 percent of gross sales revenue; the balance each month is credit sales to customers on open account. KWS estimates that the breakdown between cash and bank credit card sales is

EXHIBIT 10.11 Cash Receipts Budget—Operating Activities

Sales Data	March	April	May	June	Quarter (April–June)
Cash and bank credit card sales (70% of total sales)	$315,000	$420,000	$525,000	$735,000	$1,680,000
Credit sales (30% of total sales)	135,000	180,000	225,000	315,000	720,000
Gross sales revenue (Exhibit 10.3)	$450,000	$600,000	$750,000	$1,050,000	$2,400,000
Cash received from cash sales					
(60% of cash and bank credit card sales)		$252,000	$315,000	$441,000	$1,008,000
Cash received from bank credit card sales					
(40% of cash and bank credit card sales × 97%)		162,960	203,700	285,180	651,840
Collections of accounts receivable:					
From credit sales the month before this month:					
Within cash discount period					
(Prior month's credit sales × 80% × 60% × 98%)		63,504	84,672	105,840	254,016
After the cash discount period					
(Prior month's credit sales × 80% × 40%)		43,200	57,600	72,000	172,800
From credit sales two months before this month					
(75% of 20% of credit sales two months prior)		18,000	20,250	27,000	65,250
Total cash receipts, net of bank service charge (3%) and discount (2%)		**$539,664**	**$681,222**	**$931,020**	**$2,151,906**

KERRY WINDOW SYSTEMS INC.
Cash Receipts Budget—Operating Activities
For the Quarter Ended June 30, 2022

60 percent cash and 40 percent credit card. The bank charges a 3 percent service fee to process credit card sales. In the cash receipts budget, estimated collections of bank credit card sales are reflected *net* of this service fee.

In terms of credit sales, KWS e-mails invoices to its customers on the first of each month. Credit terms are 2/10, n/eom. This means that customers who pay within 10 days receive a 2 percent discount; otherwise, the account is due on or before the end of the month (eom). *(Discounts for early payment of credit sales are recorded on the income statement as deductions from gross sales to arrive at net sales.)* These customers can access their accounts anytime on KWS's website to find out the status of their accounts. Eighty percent of these customers pay within the month; of these, 60 percent pay within the discount period. Seventy-five percent of the remaining balances at the end of the month pay within the following month. The remaining accounts are likely bad debts. (As indicated previously, the company uses the allowance method to account for bad debts expense. *Bad debts expense is included on the income statement as a noncash component of variable selling expenses.)* Most payments are made via electronic transfer of funds. Gross sales revenue was $400,000 in February and $450,000 in March of 2022.

Given the preceding information and the gross sales revenues reported in Exhibit 10.3, the accountant for KWS can now prepare the cash receipts budget for operating activities for the quarter ended June 30 (see Exhibit 10.11). Information from the last line of this budget is then incorporated into the cash budget for the quarter.

Cash Budget

Having adequate cash on hand at all times is crucial for an organization's survival and growth. This applies to for-profit enterprises, government entities, and NFP organizations (schools, hospitals, etc.). A **cash budget** depicts the cash effects of all budgeted activities. By preparing a cash budget, management can take steps to ensure having sufficient cash on hand to carry out planned activities, allow sufficient time to arrange for additional financing that may be needed during the budget period (and thus avoid high costs of

cash budget
A schedule depicting the effects on cash of all budgeted activities.

emergency borrowing), and plan for investments of excess cash on hand to earn the highest possible return.

The cash budget pulls data from almost all parts of the master budget. Preparing a cash budget requires a careful review of all budgets to identify all revenues, expenses, and other transactions that affect cash. A cash budget generally includes three major sections: (1) net cash flows from *operating activities,* (2) net cash flows from *investing activities,* and (3) net cash flows from *financing activities.* In short, the cash budget (and related statement of cash flows) provides the user with information regarding the cash-management ability of the company.

Although not represented in the present example, it is possible to secure a cash discount on payment of accounts payable within a discount period. (This opportunity mirrors the allowance of a cash discount on collection of accounts receivable within a discount period, as reflected in Exhibit 10.11.) From a cash-management perspective, it is important to consider taking advantage of such early-payment discounts. The opportunity cost of not doing this can be approximated as follows:

[Discount % ÷ (1 − Discount %)] × (365 ÷ Number of extra days allowed if discount is not taken)

For example, if purchase terms are 2/10, net 30, then the opportunity cost of *not* taking the cash discount is approximately 37.24 percent [(2% ÷ 98%) × (365 ÷ 20)].

You may be surprised at the opportunity cost associated with failure to take advantage of early-payment discounts, as illustrated by the above example. To motivate managers to take advantage of such discounts, the appropriate accounting practice would be to record purchases at their net-of-discount amount and then to record as "interest expense" or "purchase discounts lost" any cash discounts not taken advantage of.

Cash flows from operating activities reflect cash flows from the company's transactions and events related to its main operating activities. Cash flows from investing activities provide information regarding the net cash effect of acquisitions and divestitures of investments and long-term assets. Cash flows from financing activities provide information regarding the net effect of issuances of, payments toward, and retirements of borrowings (debt) and equity.

Exhibit 10.12 shows the cash budget of KWS for the quarter ended June 30, 2022. In addition to reviewing the information illustrated in Exhibits 10.3 through 10.11 to identify items that involve either cash inflow or cash outflow, management must gather additional information about the firm's operating characteristics and policies to complete the cash budget. The following are relevant operating characteristics and policies of KWS that affect the availability of cash or the requirement to expend cash during the budget period:

1. The firm expects to have $75,000 cash on hand on April 1 and has a requirement of maintaining a minimum cash balance of $50,000 each month.
2. KWS purchases direct materials with terms of n/30. The firm pays 60 percent of its purchases in the month of purchase and the remainder in the following month.
3. All expenses and wages are paid as incurred.
4. The firm purchased $155,000 of direct materials in March.
5. Equipment purchased in January for $200,000 will be delivered at the end of May, terms COD (cash on delivery). Depreciation deductions will commence in June.
6. KWS has a revolving 30-day account at 1 percent per month with the First National Bank for all temporary financing needs. The account must be drawn in increments of $50,000 with repayment occurring no sooner than 30 days after a draw. All borrowings take place at the beginning of the month while repayments (and interest payments) occur at the end of the month.

Budgeted Income Statement

The budgeted (pro forma) income statement describes the expected net income for an upcoming period. In the event that the budgeted income for the period falls short of the prespecified goal, management can investigate, during the budget-negotiation process, actions to improve operating results.

EXHIBIT 10.12   Cash Budget

	April	May	June	Quarter
KERRY WINDOW SYSTEMS INC. Cash Budget For the Quarter Ended June 30, 2022				
Cash balance, beginning of period (a)	$ 75,000	$ 84,781	$ 90,416	$ 75,000
Cash flows from operations:				
Operating cash inflows (cash receipts from cash sales, credit card sales, and collections of accounts receivable, Exhibit 10.11)	$539,664	$681,222	$ 931,020	$2,151,906
Operating cash outflows:				
Purchases of direct materials:				
From current month purchases (60% of current month's purchases, Exhibit 10.6)	$101,283	$129,825	$ 170,586	$ 401,694
From purchases made last month (40% of last month's purchases, Exhibit 10.6)	62,000*	67,522	86,550	216,072
Total cash payments for direct materials purchases	$163,283	$197,347	$ 257,136	$ 617,766
Direct labor (Exhibit 10.7, line 11)	144,000	179,200	233,600	556,800
Factory overhead (Exhibit 10.8, last line)	83,600	100,540	126,720	310,860
Selling and administrative expenses (Exhibit 10.10, last line)	139,000	147,000	163,000	449,000
Total operating cash outflows	$529,883	$624,087	$ 780,456	$1,934,426
Net cash flow from operations (b)	$ 9,781	$ 57,135	$ 150,564	$ 217,480
Investing activities:				
Equipment purchase	$ -0-	($200,000)	$ -0-	($ 200,000)
Net effect of investing activities (c)	$ -0-	($200,000)	$ -0-	($ 200,000)
Financing activities:**				
Bank borrowing beginning of month		$150,000		$ 150,000
Payments (i.e., cash outflows):				
Repayment of principal (@ end of month)			(150,000)	(150,000)
Interest (paid end of month; 1% per month)	-0-	(1,500)	(1,500)	(3,000)
Net effect of financing activities (d)	$ -0-	$148,500	$ (151,500)	$ (3,000)
Cash balance, end of period (a + b − c + d)	$ 84,781	$100,416	$ 100,480	$ 100,480

*March purchases = $155,000 (assumed).

**Note that the cash budget is not the same as the statement of cash flows prepared for external users, so we include interest expense as part of the financing activities.

Once the budgeted income statement has been approved, it can be used as the benchmark against which the performance of the period is evaluated. Exhibits 10.3, 10.9, and 10.10 provide the information needed to prepare the budgeted income statement for the period (Exhibit 10.13).

Budgeted Balance Sheet

The last step in a budget-preparation cycle usually is to prepare the budgeted (pro forma) balance sheet. The starting point in preparing a budgeted balance sheet is the expected financial position at the beginning of the budget period. Exhibit 10.14 presents the expected balance sheet as of March 31, the beginning of the current three-month budget period.

EXHIBIT 10.13
Budgeted Income Statement

KERRY WINDOW SYSTEMS INC.
Budgeted Income Statement
For the Quarter Ended June 30, 2022

	April	May	June	Quarter
Gross sales revenue (Exhibit 10.3)	$600,000	$750,000	$1,050,000	$2,400,000
Less: Cash discounts for early payment of credit sales (last month's credit sales × 80% × 60% × 2%)	1,296	1,728	2,160	5,184
Bank service charge (3% of bank credit card sales)*	5,040	6,300	8,820	20,160
Net sales	$593,664	$741,972	$1,039,020	$2,374,656
Less: Cost of goods sold (Exhibit 10.9)	371,750	465,450	653,818	1,491,018
Gross profit	$221,914	$276,522	$ 385,202	$ 100,638
Selling and administrative expenses (Exhibit 10.10)	175,000	185,250	205,750	566,000
Net operating income	$ 46,914	$ 91,272	$ 179,452	$ 317,638
Less: Interest expense (Exhibit 10.12)	0	1,500	1,500	3,000
Income before income taxes	$ 46,914	$ 89,772	$ 177,952	$ 314,638
Less: Income taxes (@30%)	14,074	26,932	53,386	94,391**
Net income	**$ 32,840**	**$ 62,840**	**$ 124,566**	**$ 220,247****

*These items can also be reflected as a component of "Selling, General, and Administrative Expense" (Exhibit 10.10).
**$1 difference between the sum of the rows and the totals is due to rounding.

The budgeted balance sheet incorporates the effects of all operations and cash flows during the budget period. Exhibit 10.15 shows the budgeted balance sheet for Kerry as of the end of June. For example, the amount of cash in Exhibit 10.15, $89,480, is taken from the ending cash balance of the cash budget for the period (Exhibit 10.12). The ending balance of direct materials, $28,080, is from Exhibit 10.5. The gross amount for Buildings and Equipment, $969,750, is the sum of the beginning balance in the Building and Equipment account reported in Exhibit 10.14, $769,750, and the purchase of new equipment during the budget period, $200,000, as shown in the cash budget for May and, again, for the quarter (Exhibit 10.12).

Uncertainty and the Budgeting Process

LO 10-5
Deal with uncertainty in the budgeting process.

The preceding section provides an overview of the master budgeting process, which culminates in a set of pro forma (i.e., budgeted) financial statements. As you can imagine, the validity of these statements is jointly affected by the validity of the underlying budgeting model and by the accuracy of the forecasted data going into the component budgets. Such data, because they are forecasts, are subject to various levels of uncertainty. Spreadsheet software (such as Excel) can be used to deal with uncertainty associated with the budget-preparation process. This software can be used to perform *what-if analysis, sensitivity analysis,* and *scenario analysis.* Each of these techniques is a way for managers to better understand and therefore deal with uncertainty and the budgeting process.

What-If Analysis

The intent of what-if analysis is to examine how a change in one or more budgetary items affects another variable or budget of interest. For example, management of Kerry Window Systems Inc. might use Excel to address the following questions:

- What would be the resulting impact on cash flow, or operating income, if management were able to increase product selling price by 8 percent while holding other factors constant?
- What would be the net effect on operating profit if KWS were to engage in a one-year product-promotion campaign that would cost $75,000 and increase sales by 20 percent?

EXHIBIT 10.14
Beginning-of-Budget-Period Balance Sheet

KERRY WINDOW SYSTEMS INC. Balance Sheet March 31, 2022			
Assets			
Current assets:			
Cash (Exhibit 10.12)		$ 75,000	
Net accounts receivable*		146,250	
Direct materials inventory (Exhibit 10.5)		16,800	
Finished goods inventory (Exhibit 10.9)		90,000	
Total current assets			$328,050
Property, plant, and equipment:			
Land		$ 40,000	
Buildings and equipment, gross	$769,750		
Less: Accumulated depreciation	168,000	601,750	
Total property, plant, and equipment			641,750
Total assets			$ 969,800
Liabilities and Stockholders' Equity			
Current liabilities:			
Accounts payable (Exhibit 10.12)		$ 62,000	
Income taxes payable		0	
Total liabilities			$ 62,000
Stockholders' equity:			
Common stock (given)		$303,300	
Retained earnings (given)		604,500	
Total stockholders' equity			907,800
Total liabilities and stockholders' equity			$ 969,800

*Net accounts receivable, March 31, 2022:

Gross accounts receivable:		
From credit sales made in February (20% a)	$ 24,000	
From credit sales made in March (100% of March's credit sales)	135,000	
Gross accounts receivable, end of March		$ 159,000
Less: Allowance for doubtful accounts:		
For February's credit sales (5%)	$ 6,000	
For March's credit sales (5%)	6,750	12,750
Net accounts receivable, March 31, 2022		$ 146,250

a That is, a total of 20% of each month's credit sales will be collected or written off in the second month following the month of sale.

- Assume KWS can invest in a new manufacturing technology. If direct labor costs, as a result of this investment, were to decrease by 8 percent, what would be the net impact on the company's short-term operating income?
- What would be the impact on operating income of a 7 percent increase in raw material costs accompanied by a commensurate percentage increase in selling price per unit?
- What would be the cash flow impact of investing in a program to better assess the financial wherewithal of potential customers if this investment reduced estimated bad debts expense by 50 percent?

An example of conducting a what-if analysis for KWS is presented in Exhibit 10.16.[4] In this simple example, the analysis responds to the following question: What would be the impact on the production schedule for each month of the quarter if the targeted ending inventory level were decreased from 30 percent to 20 percent of the following month's projected sales? As can be seen, budgeted production levels for KWS are relatively insensitive to changes in the targeted level of ending inventory. A similar analysis could be performed in terms of other budgeted items of interest—for example, the effect of the proposed change of targeted ending finished goods inventory on budgeted operating income or on budgeted cash flow from operations.

[4] An Excel spreadsheet containing all of the budgets and the pro forma financial statements from this chapter is available from your instructor. Note to instructor: This file is available by visiting *Connect*.

EXHIBIT 10.15
Budgeted Balance Sheet,
June 30, 2022

KERRY WINDOW SYSTEMS INC. Budgeted Balance Sheet June 30, 2022			
Assets			
Current assets:			
Cash (Exhibit 10.12)		$ 89,480	
Net accounts receivable[a]		333,000	
Direct materials inventory (Exhibit 10.5, line 11)		28,080	
Finished goods inventory (Exhibit 10.9)		224,852	
Total current assets			$ 675,412
Property, plant, and equipment:			
Land (Exhibit 10.14)		$ 40,000	
Buildings and equipment, gross	$969,750		
Less: Accumulated depreciation[b]	349,000	620,750	
Total property, plant, and equipment			660,750
Total assets			**$1,336,162**
Liabilities and Stockholders' Equity			
Current liabilities:			
Accounts payable[c]		$113,724	
Income tax payable (Exhibit 10.13)		94,391	
Total liabilities			$ 208,115
Stockholders' equity:			
Common stock (Exhibit 10.14)		$303,300	
Retained earnings[d]		824,747	
Total stockholders' equity			1,128,047
Total liabilities and stockholders' equity			**$1,336,162**

[a]Ending balance, accounts receivable, net of allowance for bad debts:

Gross accounts receivable:		
From credit sales made in May (20%)	$ 45,000	
From credit sales made in June (100%)	315,000	$360,000
Less: Allowance for doubtful accounts:		
From May's sales (5%)	$ 11,250	
From June's sales (5%)	15,750	27,000
Net accounts receivable, June 30, 2022		$333,000

[b]Accumulated depreciation, beginning of quarter (Exhibit 10.14) — $168,000

Plus: Depreciation expense for the quarter ending June 30, 2022:		
Factory (Exhibit 10.8)	$ 100,000	
Selling (Exhibit 10.10)	60,000	
Administrative (Exhibit 10.10)	21,000	181,000
Accumulated depreciation, June 30, 2022		$349,000

[c]Ending balance, accounts payable:

Direct materials purchases in June (Exhibit 10.6)	$ 284,310
Payments made in month of purchase (June), 60%	170,586
Accounts payable balance, June 30, 2022	$ 113,724

[d]Ending balance, retained earnings:

Beginning-of-quarter balance (Exhibit 10.14)	$ 604,500
Plus: Net income for quarter (Exhibit 10.13)	220,247
Retained earnings balance, June 30, 2022	$ 824,747

Sensitivity Analysis

As you might imagine, the pro forma financial statements that are produced as part of the master budgeting process assume a given operating strategy and scenario (state of the economy, level of product demand, achieved selling prices, etc.). Software, such as Excel, can be used to provide information about the sensitivity of the pro forma financial statements

REAL-WORLD FOCUS   Budgeting and Sensitivity Analysis—The Need for Incorporating Contingencies into the Planning Process

AT KRAFT HEINZ, ICONIC BRANDS ARE NOT IMMUNE FROM CHANGING LIFESTYLES

Kraft Heinz Co. owns such iconic brands as Oscar Mayer lunch meats, Miracle Whip, and Jell-O, but even names with high customer recognition and the feeling of nostalgia these brands may instill are no guarantee of strong customer demand. The company's revenue in 2018 was below the combined revenue of the two separate companies in 2014, before their merger. In 2019, the company wrote down the value of the iconic brands by nearly $17 billion. Higher-than-expected competition from store and other low-cost brands is part of the problem. Another factor that hurt the outlook for these brands is that a growing shift in consumer preferences away from processed foods has hurt the outlook for those brands.

INCREASED DEMAND DURING THE HOLIDAYS IS NO GUARANTEE OF GOOD RESULTS

A Mastercard survey found that, for the period from November 1 through Christmas Eve, online sales rose nearly 19%, a rate more than 10 times the 1.2% growth for in-store sales for the same period. Target's fourth-quarter results, which include that time period, were expected to fall short of the 3% to 4% predicted growth. Having a shorter period between Thanksgiving and Christmas and fewer electronic devices on the market are two of the possible reasons cited for the poorer-than-expected results.

Then there are the "black swan" events that are not foreseen. The COVID-19 pandemic has upended many operations and supply chains throughout the world. These disruptions will significantly affect the budgeting process. At the same time, the information value of the budgeting process is even more important for strategic and operational decision making. Particularly important budgets include the cash flow budget and many of the operating budgets.

The above examples indicate that potential effects of contingencies and eventualities can, and should, be incorporated formally into the planning/budgeting process. Dedicated software like SAP exists to aid in this type of analysis, but what-if and scenario analysis can also be done within Excel using 'What-if Analysis' tools and functions such as Solver and Scenario Manager. The use of such software will not prevent the various business pressures that firms experience, but it can help these firms develop appropriate contingency plans.

Sources: Annie Gasparro, "Kraft Heinz CEO, Pushing for Growth, Separates Winners from Losers; Miguel Patricio's Aim Is Fewer, Bolder Bets to Boost Sales: 'We Are Building a Strategy for the Future,'" *The Wall Street Journal (Online)*, January 26, 2020; Sarah Nassauer, "Target's Holiday Sales Disappoint—Results Spur Questions About Its Turnaround Efforts, Consumer Spending," *The Wall Street Journal*, Eastern ed., January 16, 2020, p. B1; J. C. Collins, "How to Use Scenario Manager," *Journal of Accountancy* 226, no. 5 (2018), pp. 70–71; David A. J. Axson "Strategic Implications of COVID-19 and Its Aftermath," Financial Management, June 2020 https://www.fm-magazine.com/issues/2020/jun/strategic-implications-of-coronavirus-and-its-aftermath.html, accessed June 27, 2020.

EXHIBIT 10.16
Results of What-If Analysis

	Decision Variable: Targeted Ending Inventory, Finished Goods			
		Budgeted Production (units) (Exhibit 10.4)		
	Target as % of Projected Sales	April	May	June
Original assumption	30%	22,500	28,000	36,500
Revised assumption	20%	20,000	27,000	36,000
Percentage change	(33%)	(11.1%)	(3.6%)	(1.4%)

to various assumptions made in preparing the component budgets. In fact, we can think of sensitivity analysis as a tool (or method) that budget planners use to determine the extent to which a change in the forecasted value of one or more budgetary inputs affects individual budgets and the set of pro forma financial statements produced as part of the master budgeting process.

An example of sensitivity analysis for KWS is provided in Exhibit 10.17. Management of the company is unsure about both the level of sales demand and product selling price. In addition to a best-guess estimate (Exhibit 10.3) used to prepare the master budget, management elicits from the marketing manager both high-end (optimistic) and low-end (pessimistic) estimates for both sales volume (in units) and selling price per unit. High-end and low-end estimated selling prices per unit were $35 and $25, respectively, while high-end and low-end estimates of sales volume were 22,500 and 17,500 units, respectively. Exhibit 10.17 provides estimated net operating income for a single month, April, under nine

EXHIBIT 10.17
Results of Sensitivity Analysis:
April 2022

Selling Price per Unit	Sales Volume (units)	Budgeted Net Operating Income	% Change from Master Budget Amount
$25.00	17,500	$ (67,877)	(244.6)%
25.00	20,000	(50,746)	(208.2)
25.00	22,500	(33,249)	(170.9)
30.00	17,500	17,575	37.5
30.00	**20,000**	**46,914**	**N/A**
30.00	22,500	76,619	163.3
35.00	17,500	103,028	219.6
35.00	20,000	144,574	308.2
35.00	22,500	186,487	397.5

different scenarios—that is, combinations of selling price and sales volume.[5] Note that in this analysis all other budgetary inputs (e.g., total fixed costs and variable cost per unit) are held constant.

One of the primary advantages of conducting sensitivity analysis is the ability to isolate risks associated with particular components of operations and to develop contingency plans for dealing with these risks. To the extent that the output variable of interest (e.g., operating income) is sensitive to changes in input factors (e.g., sales volume), management needs to know this. The ability to isolate these important factors is the primary planning benefit of performing sensitivity analysis as part of the master budgeting process.

In the present case (Exhibit 10.17), we see significant sensitivity of budgeted net operating income as a function of both sales volume and selling price. In fact, if the realized selling price can be set no higher than $25 per unit, our analysis shows that it is virtually impossible with the current cost structure for KWS to earn a profit. This situation would prompt managers to develop contingency plans to deal with this less-than-favorable situation.

Scenario Analysis

Both analyses described earlier assumed that certain inputs to the budget-planning model (e.g., selling price per unit) could be changed independently of other inputs (e.g., sales volume). Therefore, to the extent that the variables in our planning model are interrelated (e.g., a change in selling price leads to a change in sales demand), the preceding methods are deficient. In addition, the number of possible combinations of variables—even in a simplified real-life situation—can be exceedingly large, which makes the preceding approach unwieldy.

To address both of the preceding limitations, we might create and examine a small number of realistic scenarios (i.e., combinations of planning-model inputs). For each scenario, we could recalculate a budgetary figure of interest, such as operating income or operating cash flow.

At a minimum, we might prepare for management a set of budgets based on a "best-case scenario," a "worst-case scenario," and a "most-likely scenario." The best-case scenario would reflect the most optimistic (but realistic) values for selling price, sales volume, and so on, while the worst-case scenario would reflect just the opposite—that is, the most pessimistic (but realistic) combination of inputs in our budgeting model.

The range of outcomes for the scenarios we create gives us an idea of how bad or good things might be; the range of possible outcomes (e.g., budgeted operating income) provides a rough measure of risk. Assuming the numbers in Exhibit 10.17 reflect realistic scenarios, we see a most optimistic outcome of $186,487, a most pessimistic outcome of –$67,877, and a most likely outcome of $46,914.

Two concluding points regarding scenario analysis seem appropriate: (1) It is possible to enhance the analysis by assigning subjective probabilities to each of the various scenarios (in turn, we could calculate an expected value of operating income) and (2) the process of identifying realistic scenarios is complicated in practice and, therefore, suggests the need for a cross-functional team.

---

[5] Note, however, that these results are not generated from the actual underlying model depicted in the chapter. That is, the data were generated for illustrative purposes only.

Budgeting in Service Companies

LO 10-6

Identify unique characteristics of budgeting for service companies.

Service companies have different operating characteristics, operating environments, and considerations than those of manufacturing and merchandising firms. This section examines special considerations in budgeting for service companies.

Budgeting in Service Industries

Similar to budgeting for manufacturing or merchandising firms, budgeting for service firms consists of an integrated set of plans for an upcoming period. The difference is in the absence of production or merchandise purchases budgets and their ancillary budgets. A service organization achieves its budgeted goals and fulfills its mission through providing services. Therefore, an important focal point in its budgeting is personnel planning. A service firm must ensure that it has personnel with the appropriate skills to perform the services required for the budgeted service revenue.

As an example, AccuTax Inc. provides tax services to small firms and individuals. It expects to have the following revenues from preparing tax returns for the year ended December 31, 2022:

Tax returns for business firms		$1,000,000
Individual tax returns:		
Simple returns	$1,640,000	
Complex returns	1,200,000	2,840,000
Total revenues		$3,840,000

The firm has 2 partners, 8 senior consultants, and 20 consultants. On average, a partner works 50 hours a week and is paid $250,000 a year. Both senior consultants and consultants are expected to work 40 hours a week and are paid, respectively, $90,000 and $60,000 a year. The annual compensation for supporting staff is $40,000 per full-time equivalent. The number of supporting staff varies with the size of the firm. In general, one supporting staff person is needed for every 2 partners, one for every 4 senior consultants, and one for every 10 consultants. After allowing for vacation, sickness, and continuing education days, the weeks per year available to work with clients are 40 weeks for each partner, 45 weeks for each senior consultant, and 48 weeks for each consultant. All partners and senior consultants are full-time professional staff members. The firm estimates the following required proportions of professional staff times for each hour spent to complete each of the three different classifications of tax returns:

	Business Return	Simple Individual	Complex Individual
Partner	40%	—	10%
Senior consultant	60%	10%	40%
Consultant	—	90%	50%

General and administrative expenses are estimated as $150,000 per year, plus 10 percent of the total payroll. The firm charges $250 per hour for business returns, $100 per hour for individual returns with complicated tax matters, and $50 per hour for simple individual tax returns. The budgeted revenues and the total hours for each of the returns for the coming year are as follows:

	Budgeted Revenue		Hourly Charge Rate		Required Hours
Business returns	$1,000,000	÷	$250	=	4,000
Individual returns:					
Simple returns	1,640,000	÷	50	=	32,800
Complex returns	1,200,000	÷	100	=	12,000
Total	$3,840,000				48,800

Kraft Heinz Co. was formed by the merger of Kraft Foods Group and H. J. Heinz in July 2015. One of the stated goals of the merger was profitability improvement, which would come from increased manufacturing efficiency, cutting jobs, and shrinking budgets.

Kraft Heinz is actually run by 3G Capital Partners LP, a Brazilian private-equity firm. This firm has a reputation for mandating that the companies it acquires adopt zero-base budgeting. It is a method that requires departments to justify every cost at the start of each year, as opposed to just starting with the current budget as the basis for the next budget. Companies like Philip Morris International Inc. and Walgreens Boots Alliance Inc. have also adopted zero-based budgeting. While the concept has merit, there can be problems.

Three years after the merger, Kraft marked down its brand portfolio by $15 billion and the departing CEO felt that the focus on cost cutting failed to achieve the desired results. Many attribute a large part of the problem to the use of zero-based budgeting.

The global pandemic brought more attention to the value of zero-based budgeting. GM, Guess? Inc., and Signet Jewelers Ltd are three companies that not used zero-based budgeting as part of their regular financial planning before 2020. After the coronavirus outbreak their budgeting process shifted to a clean-sheet (zero-based) approach to building models store by store to estimate the number of associates needed to provide the level of service for expected demand.

Sources: Annie Gasparro, "Business News: Kraft Heinz Gets Boost from Cost-Cut Efforts," *The Wall Street Journal*, May 5, 2016, p. B8; John D. Stoll, "Business News—on Business: What's on Kraft's Menu Beyond Cuts?," *The Wall Street Journal*, Eastern ed., April 24, 2019, p. B6; Kristen Broughton, "Companies Turn to Zero-Based Budgeting to Cut Costs During the Pandemic," Wall Street Journal online edition, June 17, 2020, https://www.wsj.com/articles/companies-turn-to-zero-based-budgeting-to-cut-costs-during-the-pandemic-11592431029, accessed June 26, 2020.

The following table shows the professional staff requirements for the budgeted revenue:

	Total Hours	Partner	Senior Consultant	Consultant
Business returns	4,000	1,600	2,400	—
Complex individual returns	12,000	1,200	4,800	6,000
Simple individual returns	32,800	—	3,280	29,520
Total hours	48,800	2,800	10,480	35,520
Hours per week (given)		÷ 50	÷ 40	÷ 40
Equivalent number of work weeks		56	262	888
Weeks per year per professional staff (given)		÷ 40	÷ 45	÷ 48
Number of professional staff members needed		1.4	5.8	18.5

The budget shows that AccuTax has sufficient professional staff to support the expected activity. Assuming AccuTax plans no change in personnel and maintains the same staff level, its budgeted operating income will be $808,000, as shown in Exhibit 10.18.

Alternative Budgeting Approaches

LO 10-7

Describe alternative approaches to budgeting (viz., zero-base, activity-based, time-driven activity-based, and kaizen budgeting).

Over the years, alternative approaches have been proposed to facilitate budget preparation and improve operations. When used properly, these approaches—zero-base, activity-based, time-driven activity-based, and kaizen budgeting—improve budget effectiveness.

Zero-Base Budgeting

zero-base budgeting (ZBB)
A budgeting process that requires managers to prepare budgets each period from a base of zero.

Zero-base budgeting (ZBB) requires managers to prepare budgets each period from a baseline of zero. A typical budgeting process is incremental in nature in the sense that it starts with the current budget. The process assumes that most, if not all, current activities and functions will continue into the budget period. Thus, the primary focus in a typical budgeting process is on changes to the current operating budget.

In contrast, ZBB allows no activities or functions to be included in the budget unless managers can justify their needs. ZBB requires budgeting teams to perform in-depth reviews of all budget items. Such a budgeting process encourages managers to be aware of activities or functions that have outlived their usefulness or have been a waste of resources.

REAL-WORLD FOCUS   Budgeting in the Not-for-Profit World

Ducks Unlimited (DU), the world's largest private not-for-profit waterfowl and wetlands conservation organization, has had its financial ups and downs. The organization, which manages wetland and grassland habitats for North American waterfowl, found its mission was in jeopardy when it ran a financial deficit in 2009 and lacked financing reserves. In 2016, the picture was quite different. That year, DU had revenues in excess of $220 million and nearly $64 million in unrestricted net assets. Planning and budgeting were a big part of the turnaround. A new CEO joined DU in 2009 and, in coordination with the board of directors, a strategic plan was developed. As part of the process, a surplus budget strategy was adopted in order to ensure the organization could fulfill its mission. A business planning committee helped determine quantifiable objectives and a financial model. The plan was the connection point between the strategic plan and the annual operating budgets.

To be successful, management cannot simply prepare a budget and then forget about it. The budget should be continuously monitored throughout the year. The reason is to detect issues affecting funding or expenses in plenty of time for management to make informed decisions. By enabling well-informed, responsive management, a good budget and effective budgeting practices make for an efficient, effective, and successful not-for-profit organization.

Sources: Maria L. Murphy, "Using Surplus Budgeting to Advance and Sustain Your Mission," *Journal of Accountancy* 223, no. 2 (2017), pp. 40–43; *Budget Checkup: Critical Components to the Nonprofit Budget Review Process* (whitepaper published by Abila, Inc, 2017, available at https://www.abila.com/resource-library/whitepaper/budget-checkup-critical-components-to-the-nonprofit-budget-review-process/?utm_source=AICPA&utm_medium=banner).

EXHIBIT 10.18
Budgeted Operating Income with No Change in Staffing

ACCUTAX INC. Budgeted Operating Income For the Year Ended December 31, 2022		
Revenue		$3,840,000
Payroll expenses:		
Partners	2 × $250,000 = $ 500,000	
Senior consultants	8 × $90,000 = 720,000	
Consultants	20 × $60,000 = 1,200,000	
Supporting staff	5* × $40,000 = 200,000	2,620,000
General and administrative expenses	$150,000 + (10% × $2,620,000) =	412,000
Operating income		$ 808,000

*5 = (2 ÷ 2) + (8 ÷ 4) + (20 ÷ 10) = 1 + 2 + 2

The amount of work and time needed to apply a true ZBB to all aspects of operations of an organization can be monumental. An organization may find it practically impossible to review and examine all of its activities from the zero-base budget level every year. As an alternative, the organization can schedule ZBB periodically or perform ZBB for different divisions each year. For example, the highway department of a state government could adopt a rotating five-year ZBB process. All divisions of the department would be subject to in-depth review of their activities every fifth year, not every year as true ZBB requires, with the process applied to different divisions each year.

Activity-Based Budgeting

activity-based budgeting (ABB)
A budgeting process that is based on activities and associated activity costs to support production and sales; an extension of the traditional form of activity-based costing (ABC).

Activity-based budgeting (ABB) is an extension of the traditional form of activity-based costing (ABC) discussed in Chapter 5. ABB starts with the budgeted output and segregates costs required for the budgeted output into homogeneous activity cost pools such as unit, batch, product-sustaining, customer-sustaining, and facility-sustaining activity pools. Traditional budgeting and ABB are conceptually very different. Proponents of ABB maintain that use of this approach can lead to more accurate budgets pertaining to support activities, including factory (manufacturing) overhead.

For the majority of organizations, budgeting revolves around the chart-of-accounts structure. As a consequence, costs are budgeted on a departmental basis using descriptive accounts (salaries, depreciation, marketing, etc.). However, budgets expressed in these terms tell us little about the drivers of success for the organization. ABB attempts to fill this information

EXHIBIT 10.19 Factory Overhead Budget Using Activity-Based Budgeting

<table>
<tr><td colspan="6" align="center">KERRY WINDOW SYSTEMS INC.
Factory Overhead Budget (Activity-Based Budgeting)
For the Quarter Ended June 30, 2022</td></tr>
<tr><th></th><th></th><th>April</th><th>May</th><th>June</th><th>Quarter</th></tr>
<tr><td>A: Data</td><td></td><td></td><td></td><td></td><td></td></tr>
<tr><td>Units of output (assumed)</td><td></td><td>22,500</td><td>30,000</td><td>37,500</td><td>90,000</td></tr>
<tr><td>Direct labor hours:</td><td></td><td></td><td></td><td></td><td></td></tr>
<tr><td>Semiskilled (@ 0.5 hr./unit)</td><td></td><td>11,250</td><td>15,000</td><td>18,750</td><td>45,000</td></tr>
<tr><td>Skilled (@ 0.2 hr./unit)</td><td></td><td>4,500</td><td>6,000</td><td>7,500</td><td>18,000</td></tr>
<tr><td>Machine hours (@ 0.3 hr./unit)</td><td></td><td>6,750</td><td>9,000</td><td>11,250</td><td>27,000</td></tr>
<tr><td>Number of batches (@ 2,500/batch)</td><td></td><td>9</td><td>12</td><td>15</td><td>36</td></tr>
<tr><td>Number of products</td><td></td><td>1</td><td>2</td><td>3</td><td>6</td></tr>
<tr><td>B: Activity-Based Budget (ABB)</td><td>Activity</td><td></td><td></td><td></td><td></td></tr>
<tr><td>Overhead cost pools:</td><td>Cost Rate*</td><td></td><td></td><td></td><td></td></tr>
<tr><td>Semiskilled-hour-related</td><td>0.60</td><td>$ 6,750</td><td>$ 9,000</td><td>$ 11,250</td><td>$ 27,000</td></tr>
<tr><td>Skilled-hour-related</td><td>0.40</td><td>1,800</td><td>2,400</td><td>3,000</td><td>7,200</td></tr>
<tr><td>Machine-hour-related</td><td>3.20</td><td>21,600</td><td>28,800</td><td>36,000</td><td>86,400</td></tr>
<tr><td>Batch-related</td><td>2,000</td><td>18,000</td><td>24,000</td><td>30,000</td><td>72,000</td></tr>
<tr><td>Product-related</td><td>15,000</td><td>15,000</td><td>30,000</td><td>45,000</td><td>90,000</td></tr>
<tr><td>Facility-level</td><td>50,000</td><td>50,000</td><td>50,000</td><td>50,000</td><td>150,000</td></tr>
<tr><td>Total budgeted factory overhead</td><td></td><td>$113,150</td><td>$144,200</td><td>$175,250</td><td>$ 432,600**</td></tr>
</table>

*These data are assumed but in general are calculated for each cost pool as budgeted resource spending for an upcoming period divided by the practical capacity of resources (labor, utilities, equipment, etc.) supplied.

**The total budgeted overhead for KWS under ABB for the quarter ($432,600) differs from the total overhead under traditional costing ($410,860—see Exhibit 10.8) due to a combination of reasons (slightly different assumptions as to total units produced, different assumptions about product mix, different assumptions as to the underlying drivers of overhead costs, and some rounding).

void by focusing on the activities and associated resources needed to satisfy the projected level of customer demand.

ABB begins by budgeting activity requirements based on estimated product (or service) demand for the upcoming budget period. It then budgets the cost of resources needed to perform the set of budgeted activities needed to meet this demand. In so doing, a better match of the supply of and the demand for resources is effected. For example, management can budget intelligently for additional resources in specific areas or can plan to redeploy resources from one area of the organization to another. These insights would be difficult, if not impossible, to achieve in a traditional budgeting environment.

Of particular interest to most organizations today is the budgeting for labor (head count). How does the organization cut costs or manage its human capital when everyone appears fully employed? Which employees are involved in value-added activities, and which employees are performing non-value-added activities? What opportunities are there for redeploying people to activities within the organization that are value-added and strategically aligned? The application of ABB allows the organization to address these critical issues.

Exhibit 10.19 illustrates an ABB for the factory overhead budget for the quarter ended June 30 for Kerry Window Systems Inc. To better illustrate the difference between an ABB and a traditional budget for manufacturing overhead, we make some new assumptions. Specifically, we assume that in each of May and June, the company introduces a new product. In addition, we assume a constant batch size (2,500 units) and total output that is slightly different from the output level assumed earlier. These revised assumptions are reflected in Part A of Exhibit 10.19.

The result of an ABC analysis by KWS suggests that factory overhead cost varies with hours of semiskilled labor ($0.60 per hour), hours of skilled labor ($0.40 per hour), machine hours ($3.20 per hour), number of batches ($2,000 per batch), and number of products ($15,000 each). In addition, there is a $50,000 facility-level cost per month. These assumed amounts are reflected in Part B of Exhibit 10.19.

The firm has a standard batch size of 2,500 units and expects to operate 6,650, 9,000, and 11,250 machine hours, respectively, in April, May, and June. KWS plans to introduce one additional product in May and another new product in June.

EXHIBIT 10.20 Traditional vs. Activity-Based Budgeting

	Traditional Budgeting	Activity-Based Budgeting (ABB)
Budgeting unit	Expressed as the cost of functional areas or spending categories	Expressed as the cost of activities and cost drivers
Focus on orientation	Input resources	High-value-added activities
	Historical	Continuous improvement and capacity management
Roles of suppliers and customers	Does not formally consider suppliers and customers in budgeting	Coordinates with suppliers and considers the needs of customers
Control objective	Maximize managers' performance	Synchronize activities with level of demand
Budget base	Descriptive accounts in departmental budgets	Value-added versus non-value-added activities

Exhibit 10.20 contrasts traditional budgeting and ABB. As noted therein, firms with traditional costing systems usually prepare budgets for departmental units such as cutting, assembling, and finishing using volume-based drivers, as KWS did for the budget shown in Exhibit 10.8. Note that for KWS, the traditional budget for factory overhead for April was $113,600 compared with $119,230 under ABB. Aggregations of resource costs into functional units obscures relationships between resource consumption and output and complicates decisions regarding resource planning. As a result, traditional cost systems emphasize allocations of indirect costs to products via a broadly averaged and simplified volume-based measure, such as labor hours, machine hours, units of materials used, or output units. Such allocations generally do not represent resource demands (or resource consumption) of the organization's outputs and customers. Of course, some resources come in discontinuous amounts. For example, it is not possible to hire one-third of a person. Thus, the last step in ABB is for managers to decide whether to round up (and incur some idle-capacity costs) or to round down (which may adversely affect customer-service levels).

ABB facilitates continuous improvement. The process of preparing a budget under ABB highlights opportunities for cost reduction and elimination of wasteful activities. ABB facilitates the identification of high-value-added activities and the reduction or elimination of low-value-added activities. In contrast, history often is the underlying guidance in a traditional budget.

Time-Driven Activity-Based Budgeting

As discussed in Chapter 5, time-driven activity-based costing (TDABC) is an alternative to traditional ABC.[6] To build a TDABC system, management needs to provide only two estimates for each department or business process: (1) the total cost and amount of resources supplied for a period and (2) the amount of resource capacity, measured in time [i.e., consumed by each of the organization's cost objects (products, services, and customers)].

In stage one of the two-stage TDABC process, cost rates are calculated. For example, for an activity defined as *packaging activity,* we would divide the cost of resources supplied for this activity (labor, systems, etc.) by the amount of resources supplied, measured in *time* (e.g., minutes). In stage two, costs are then allocated to cost objects by multiplying estimated cost rates (e.g., $2 per minute) by the time requirements of the cost object (e.g., 4.0 minutes to package a standard, nonhazardous product that is shipped by air). Resource demands, and therefore allocated costs, of more complicated packaging activities can be captured through the use of time equations.

time-driven activity-based budgeting (TDABB)
A method of budget preparation used in conjunction with a time-driven activity-based cost (TDABC) system.

Time-driven activity-based budgeting (TDABB) is a method of budget preparation used in conjunction with a TDABC system. As with activity-based budgeting (ABB), TDABB works backward from forecasted sales volume (and mix) to calculate in a straightforward way resource spending needed to support production and sales plans. That is, the organization will have to estimate resource requirements in each process and department if the production and sales forecasts for the coming period are to be realized. To generate these estimates, time equations (discussed in Chapter 5) for each major activity or process can be used to extend the

[6] R. S. Kaplan and S. R. Anderson, *Time-Driven Activity-Based Costing: A Simpler and More Powerful Path to Higher Profits* (Boston: Harvard Business School Press, 2007).

basic approach described above. All of this detail can be supplied by the organization's enterprise resource planning (ERP) system. In sum, TDABC models can be used to streamline, and therefore significantly reduce the cost of, activity-based budgeting (ABB) processes. The resulting system allows managers to more accurately plan for the level of capacity needed to accomplish short-term profit goals.

Resource Capacity Planning

In both ABC and TDABC systems, we calculate cost-driver rates (e.g., the cost to ship an item, or the cost to process a customer order). As we argued in Chapter 5, these rates are best defined by dividing budgeted resource costs by the **practical capacity** of resources supplied for each activity or process. The use of this level of capacity allows us to estimate the cost of idle capacity at the end of each period for each activity or process. This estimate is defined as the difference between the total cost of resources *supplied* and the cost of resources *used* (or planned to be used) during the period, where the latter is defined as the product of the activity-cost rate (based on practical capacity) and the actual activity units used (or planned to be used) during the period.

A question arises as to what the appropriate treatment of idle capacity costs should be. Such costs should not be assigned to customers served or products produced during the period. To do so would overestimate the resource demands of these cost objects. Rather, these costs should be assigned to the level (product line, department, or a given manager) within the organization where the decision to acquire the capacity was made. For example, if the excess capacity was acquired to meet the anticipated demands of a given customer or market segment, then the cost of idle capacity, as a lump-sum amount, should be assigned to that segment.

The primary benefit of reporting the cost of idle capacity for each activity or resource is that this information can be used to manage the demand for and supply of capacity (e.g., personnel) within the organization. For example, if excess capacity is identified during the budgeting process, then management can take steps to reduce spending in these areas or to find alternative uses for this available capacity. This insight in large part distinguishes both ABB and TDABC budgeting from traditional budgeting practices.

Kaizen (Continuous-Improvement) Budgeting

Kaizen budgeting is a budgeting approach that incorporates continuous-improvement expectations in the budget. A kaizen budgeting approach adjusts required resource demands based on targeted efficiency and productivity gains. As such, it can be used as a complement to both traditional and activity-based budgeting systems.

A kaizen budget decrease is not the same as the budget cuts we often see firms or governments make when facing a budget crunch because of diminishing profits, decreasing sales, or declining tax revenues. A budget cut often is a reluctant passive response to a mandate that is accomplished by reducing productive activities or services. In contrast, kaizen budgeting promotes active engagement in reforming or altering practices. A decrease in cost in a kaizen budget is a result of performing the same activity more efficiently and with higher quality; it is not a result of arbitrary elimination of activities or components.

Kaizen budgeting is not limited to internal improvements. When considering the total value chain, firms could expect and demand continuous improvements from their suppliers and explicitly incorporate these effects on budgeted production cost and manufacturing schedules.

Behavioral Issues in Budgeting

A budget can be successful only if those responsible for its implementation make it happen. To encourage a successful budgeting process, management must consider a number of behavioral issues, as discussed next.

Budgetary Slack

Budgetary slack, or padding the budget, is the practice of managers knowingly including a higher amount of expenditures (or lower amount of revenue) in the budget than they actually believe will occur. When the actual cost (or revenue) amounts are realized and compared to "budgeted" figures, an appearance of successful effort is indicated.

practical capacity
Theoretical capacity reduced by normal output losses due to personal time, normal maintenance, and so on; the measure of capacity often recommended for estimating cost-driver rates under ABC and TDABC systems.

kaizen budgeting
A budgeting approach that incorporates continuous improvement expectations in the budget.

LO 10-8
Discuss various behavioral considerations in budgeting.

budgetary slack
The difference between budgeted performance and expected performance; a "cushion" managers intentionally build into budgets to help ensure success in meeting the budget.

In the article "Companies Get Budgets All Wrong," K. A. Merchant stated, "the annual budgeting process leads to bad decision-making . . . (and) needs a total overhaul." For example, he notes that traditional budgeting practices are thought to distract managers from doing their jobs and from taking appropriate risks. In response, Merchant offers a blueprint consisting of five prescriptions: (1) Adopt dynamic (rather than static) planning—when relevant factors (e.g., interest rates, oil prices, or completion) change, business plans should adapt immediately; (2) to encourage risk-taking, allow additional budgetary requests, but hold managers accountable for funding such unexpected (but important) needs; (3) decouple managerial performance evaluation (and incentive compensation) from the planning/budgeting process; rather, consider using relative-performance standards (as discussed in this textbook); (4) complement financial-performance indicators with nonfinancial-performance indicators (e.g., attaining significant new customers; successes in research and development; or improvements in production, customer satisfaction, or employee morale); and (5) make managerial bonuses incremental—align bonuses in direct relation to measured performance—with no upper or lower bounds.

Required

Provide at least two potential positive outcomes that could come from the proposed changes.

(Refer to Comments on Cost Management in Action at the end of the chapter.)

Managers often justify such practices as insurance against uncertain future events. After all, no one knows exactly how the future will unfold. Budgetary slack, however, wastes resources and could lead employees to make half-hearted efforts to meet or exceed the budget.

Goal Congruence

goal congruence
The consistency among the goals of the firm, its subunits, and its employees. It is achieved when the manager acts independently in such a way as to simultaneously achieve personal objectives and those of top management.

Goal congruence is a term that refers to the degree of consistency among the goals of the firm, its subunits, and its employees. In general, a firm's goals should be as consistent as possible with the goals of its employees. A budget devoid of considerations for goal congruence is not likely to achieve the most desirable results. A budget that aligns the firm's goals with those of its employees has a much better chance of realizing successful operations and attaining desirable results. As discussed below, there are at least three major factors that affect the level of goal congruence achieved: (1) the extent to which employees participate in the budgeting process, (2) the level of difficulty embedded in the budget, and (3) whether and how compensation is linked to budgeted performance.

Authoritative or Participative Budgeting?

Budgeting processes can be either top-down or bottom-up. In a top-down budgeting process, top management prepares budgets for the entire organization, including those for lower-level operations. This process often is referred to as *authoritative budgeting*. A *participative budgeting* process, on the other hand, is a bottom-up approach that involves the people affected by the budget, including lower-level employees, in the budget-preparation process.

Proponents argue that authoritative budgeting provides better decision-making control than does participative budgeting. Top management sets the overall goals for the budget period and prepares a budget for operating personnel to attain the goals. An authoritative budget, however, often lacks the commitment ("buy-in") of lower-level managers and employees responsible for implementing it.

A participative budget can be a good communication device. The process of preparing a budget often gives top management a better grasp of the problems their employees face and provides the employees a better understanding of the dilemmas that top management deals with. A participative budget also is more likely to gain employee commitment to fulfill budgetary goals. Unless properly controlled, however, a participative budget can lead to easy budget targets or targets not in compliance with the organization's overall strategy.

An effective budgeting process often combines both top-down and bottom-up budgeting approaches. Subunits prepare their initial budgets based on the budget guidelines issued by the firm's budget committee. Senior managers review and make suggestions to the proposed budget before sending it back to the divisions for revisions. The final budget usually is reached after several rounds of negotiations. For this reason, this is generally referred to as a *negotiated budgeting* process.

EXHIBIT 10.21
Budget Difficulty and Effort

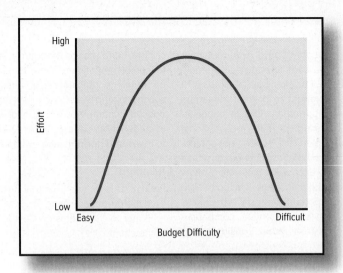

Difficulty Level of the Budget Target

An easy budget target may fail to encourage employees to give their best efforts. A budget target that is very difficult to achieve can, however, discourage managers from even trying to attain it. Exhibit 10.21 depicts research findings on the relationship between the level of employee effort and the level of difficulty of budget targets. Ideally, budget targets should be challenging yet attainable. But what is a challenging yet attainable budget target?

Research by Merchant and Manzoni suggests that a "highly achievable target," that is, one achievable by most managers 80 to 90 percent of the time, serves quite well in the vast majority of organizations, especially when accompanied by extra rewards for performances exceeding the target.[7] According to Merchant (1990), the advantages of using such a target include:

1. Increasing managers' commitment to achieving the budget target.
2. Maintaining managers' confidence in the budget.
3. Decreasing the cost of organizational control.
4. Reducing the risk that managers will engage in harmful "earnings management" practices or violate corporate ethical standards.
5. Allowing effective and efficient managers greater operating flexibility.
6. Improving the predictability of earnings or operating results.
7. Enhancing the usefulness of a budget as a planning and coordinating tool.

Linkage of Compensation and Budgeted Performance

Traditionally, budgets have played a role in determining employee and executive compensation. The traditional model is that such compensation would be at least partially a function of the difference between actual performance (sales, operating profit, net income, etc.) and budgeted performance for a given budget period, usually a year. This type of compensation plan is sometimes referred to as a **fixed-performance contract** because actual performance is compared to a fixed (budgeted) target.

While this traditional model may work well in some situations, we know that its usage can have dysfunctional consequences. That is, significant incentive (and ethical) issues arise when compensation is linked to a fixed-performance target. For example, such a reward system provides incentives for managers to submit biased information in their budgets.

fixed-performance contract
An incentive compensation plan whereby compensation (reward) is a function of actual performance compared to a fixed (budgeted) target.

[7] K. A. Merchant, "How Challenging Should Profit Budget Targets Be?," *Management Accounting,* November 1990, pp. 46–48; K. A. Merchant, *Rewarding Results: Motivating Profit Center Managers* (Cambridge, MA: Harvard Business School Press, 1989); and K. A. Merchant and J. Manzoni, "The Achievability of Budget Targets in Profit Centers: A Field Study," *The Accounting Review,* July 1989, pp. 539–558.

REAL-WORLD FOCUS   Contemporary Refinements to Traditional Budgeting Practices

Recent economic volatility (COVID-19 and the related economic recession) has motivated a growing number of companies to fundamentally rethink their budgeting and planning processes. To some CFOs, this means increasing the frequency of budget revisions and forecasts—so-called rolling forecasts. To others it means simplification: tracking a small set of high-level strategic performance indicators rather than thousands of line items (as is the case with a traditional master budget). To still others, it means routinely conducting scenario analysis (as described previously in this chapter)—what some have referred to as "perpetual planning." And, in order to make the budgeting process more meaningful, a growing number of companies are working to more actively engage lower-level managers and employees in the budgeting process—a combination of top-down and bottom-up efforts. Other companies (such as the publisher Houghton Mifflin Harcourt) are incorporating more macroeconomic factors into the sales-forecasting

component of budgeting. Changes in the nature and form of budgets is also causing CFOs to reconsider employee compensation systems. Rather than tying incentive compensation to performance relative to a static budget, companies are experimenting with systems where compensation is a function of performance compared to peer companies. The informed management accountant needs to be continually updated on new developments and contemporary refinements to traditional budgeting practices.

Sources: Kathleen Hoffelder, "Special Report: Forecasting Comes of Age," *CFO.com,* January 29, 2013 (available at ww2.cfo.com/budgeting/2013/01/special-report-forecasting-comes-of-age/); Russ Banham, "New Strategies around Strategy," *CFO.com,* August 29, 2013 (available at ww2.cfo.com/budgeting/2013/08/new-strategies-around-strategy/). "Covid-19 and Cash Flow Management," Crispin Dastoli, *Strategic Finance,* June 2017. https://sfmagazine.com/post-entry/june-2020-covid-19-and-cash-flow-management/.

gaming the performance measure

Non-value-adding actions taken by managers to improve indicated performance.

Budgetary slack, discussed earlier, is one example. In addition, the use of fixed targets reinforced by incentives motivates some managers to **game the performance measure**—that is, to take actions that make the performance indicator look better but do not increase the value of the firm. Finally, some would argue that the use of fixed budget targets unfairly rewards managers when actual performance is affected by factors, such as macroeconomic conditions, that are beyond the control or influence of the manager. In short, critics of the conventional fixed-performance model linked to compensation contend that this process is fundamentally flawed. At least two alternatives have been proposed as a way to deal with this problem: the use of linear compensation plans and the use of rolling forecasts combined with relative-performance indicators.

Use of Linear Compensation Plans[8]

Essentially, this option would sever the relationship between budgets and managerial compensation. In its place, incentive compensation would be based on a linear compensation plan. This strategy has two characteristics: (1) Managerial reward is independent of budgeted targets and (2) managerial reward is a linear function of actual performance—the greater the performance, the greater the managerial reward (both monetary and nonmonetary). In other words, this incentive system rewards people for what they actually *do,* not for what they do relative to what they *say* they can do. However, from a practical standpoint this strategy may be difficult to implement because of the use of budgeted targets in determining managerial rewards.

Use of Rolling Forecasts and Relative-Performance Contracts[9]

The displeasure with respect to current budgeting practices is perhaps best epitomized by a group referred to as the Beyond Budgeting Roundtable (BBRT; see **www.bbrt.org**). Instead of fixed-performance contracts, the BBRT recommends the use of *relative-performance (improvement) contracts* and *rolling financial forecasts.*

---

[8] This section draws on the following source: Michael C. Jensen, "Corporate Budgeting Is Broken—Let's Fix It," *Harvard Business Review,* November 2001, pp. 94–101.

[9] This discussion draws on the following source: Jeremy Hope and Robin Fraser, Beyond Budgeting: How Managers Can Break Free from the Annual Performance Trap (Boston: Harvard Business School Press, 2003).

relative-performance (or relative-improvement) contracts
Contracts that reward managers for performance based on a comparison of actual results with specified benchmarks, not budgeted (fixed) targets; contrast with *fixed-performance contracts.*

Relative-performance (or relative-improvement) contracts essentially reward managers for how their business units perform relative to some appropriate benchmark performance, not a fixed budget target. For example, an operating unit or division might be evaluated on the basis of its return on investment (ROI) for a period relative to the market or to best-in-class performance. Some organizations benchmark actual performance to the top quartile of their peer group. This change in incentive, at least conceptually, avoids much of the dysfunctional consequences associated with traditional budgeting systems. Units and managers are motivated to achieve to their highest level because their compensation/reward is tied to how they performed relative to a prespecified (external or internal) benchmark. In essence, this represents radical decentralization and significant reliance on self-regulation. Employees and operating managers in this model are vested with significant decision-making authority and are asked to use their own best judgment to achieve superior results, without being constrained by the plan embodied in a budget.

rolling financial forecast
A constant planning horizon with the use of regularly updated forecasts.

In addition to the use of relative-performance contracts, the BBRT model calls for the use of **rolling financial forecasts** rather than the annual master budget (described earlier in this chapter). These forecasts are updated regularly, for example, every quarter, to provide a constant planning horizon (e.g., five quarters into the future). Of particular note is the fact that these forecasts are separated from performance evaluation and control. They are prepared for a small set of key performance indicators (e.g., cash flow, sales, and number of customer orders) and serve as a high-level view of future performance. Their use is designed to allow employees to adapt to changing environments (including competitive threats) and to achieve the level of radical decentralization envisioned by the BBRT.

Summary

An organization's budget is a quantitative plan that identifies the resources required and commitments to fulfill the organization's goals for the budget period. Budgeting allows management to plan ahead, communicate the plan and performance expectations to all divisions and employees, and, when properly implemented, motivate employees. A budget can also serve as a basis for performance evaluation.

Strategy helps a firm to be more focused in its operations and to take advantage of its strengths and opportunities. A firm executes its strategy through long-range plans and master budgets. An annual master budget is an extension of the organization's long-range plan to fulfill organizational goals and objectives.

The master budget for a manufacturer includes sales, production, direct materials, direct labor, factory overhead, selling, and administration expense budgets, as well as a cash budget and budgeted financial statements.

A service firm prepares a budget following set procedures just as a manufacturing or merchandising firm does. A major difference between budgets for service firms and those for manufacturing or merchandising firms is the absence of a production budget or merchandise purchases budget for service firms. The budgeting procedures and all other budget items are essentially the same for both service and manufacturing or merchandising firms.

Budgets, by definition, are forward-looking and include estimates for key inputs such as sales volume, sales mix, total fixed (capacity-related) costs, variable cost per unit, and selling price per unit. What-if analysis can be performed to determine the effects of alternative scenarios (states of nature) and alternative plans. Sensitivity analysis allows us to determine the extent to which resulting budgets are affected by changes in the input factors. Together, these analyses allow the budget analyst to deal with uncertainty that is inherent in the budgeting process.

Refinements or alternatives to traditional budgeting practices include zero-base budgeting (ZBB), activity-based budgeting (ABB), time-driven activity-based budgeting (TDABB), and kaizen budgeting. By requiring budgets that start from a zero base each period, ZBB attempts to achieve a more realistic allocation of resources within the organization. ABB and TDABB are both extensions to modern cost-allocation systems, as discussed in Chapter 5. Kaizen budgeting incorporates continuous improvements into budgets that are produced.

In some sectors there is growing dissatisfaction, indeed frustration, with traditional budgeting practices, such as those described in this chapter. Critics contend that incentive compensation/employee reward should not be a function of the difference between budgeted and actual performance, a widespread approach in practice. In place of the annual fixed-performance contract, these critics suggest either that a linear compensation plan based on actual results be used or that budgets be replaced altogether with rolling forecasts and relative-performance contracts.

Key Terms

activity-based budgeting (ABB), *389*
budget, *366*
budgetary slack, *392*
budgeting, *366*
capital budgeting, *367*
cash budget, *379*
direct materials purchases budget, *373*
direct materials usage budget, *373*

financial budgets, *368*
fixed-performance contract, *394*
gaming the performance measure, *395*
goal congruence, *393*
kaizen budgeting, *392*
long-range plan, *367*
manufacturing cells, *375*
master budget, *368*
merchandise purchases budget, *376*

operating budgets, *368*
practical capacity, *392*
production budget, *372*
relative-performance (or relative-improvement) contracts, *396*
rolling financial forecast, *396*
sales budget, *370*
strategic budget expenditures, *367*
time-driven activity-based budgeting (TDABB), *391*
zero-base budgeting (ZBB), *388*

Comments on Cost Management in Action

Changing Traditional Budgeting Practice

Here are some possible positive outcomes:

1. Management of the organization is likely to become more adaptive and innovative, thereby making the organization better positioned to respond to new opportunities and threats because of the new focus on risk-taking and quick response to changed economic factors facing the company.

2. There is likely to be a decrease in the negative behavioral consequences of traditional budgetary practices that arise because the reward systems in many organizations are tied to the master budget. These negative consequences include managers building slack into the budget and setting artificially low performance targets in the budget.

3. The use of incremental bonuses (in place of a bonus for achieving a specific target) could provide the right incentive for managers to work hard, even after they have achieved the master budget target.

4. The use of nonfinancial as well as financial-performance indicators could lead managers to consider not only financial results, but also the important strategic factors that are nonfinancial in nature (new customers, customer service, quality control, etc.).

Of course, you are likely to come up with some additional points.

Source: K. A. Merchant, "Companies Get Budgets All Wrong," *The Wall Street Journal,* July 22, 2013, p. R5.

1. Master Budget

Hansell Company's management wants to prepare budgets for one of its products, Duraflex, for July 2022. The firm sells the product for $80 per unit and has the following expected sales (in units) for these months in 2022:

April	May	June	July	August	September
5,000	5,400	5,500	6,000	7,000	8,000

The production process requires 4 pounds of Dura-1000 and 2 pounds of Flexplas. The firm's policy is to maintain an ending inventory each month equal to 10% of the following month's budgeted sales, but in no case less than 500 units. All materials inventories are to be maintained at 5% of the production needs for the next month, but not to exceed 1,000 pounds. The firm expects all inventories at the end of June to be within the guidelines. The purchases department expects the materials to cost $1.25 per pound and $5.00 per pound for Dura-1000 and Flexplas, respectively.

The production process requires direct labor at two skill levels. The rate for labor at the K102 level is $50 per hour and $20 per hour for the K175 level. The K102 level can process one batch of Duraflex per hour; each batch consists of 100 units. The manufacturing of Duraflex also requires one-tenth of an hour of K175 workers' time for each unit manufactured.

Required   On the basis of the preceding data and projections, prepare the following budgets:

1. Sales budget for July (in dollars).
2. Production budget for July (in units).
3. Production budget for August (in units).
4. Direct materials purchases budget for July (in pounds).
5. Direct materials purchases budget for July (in dollars).
6. Direct manufacturing labor budget for July (in dollars).

2. Cash Budget and Budgeted Income Statement

Hansell Company expects its trial balance on June 30 to be as follows:

HANSELL COMPANY
Budgeted Trial Balance
June 30, 2022

	Debit	Credit
Cash	$ 40,000	
Accounts receivable	80,000	
Allowance for bad debts		$ 3,500
Inventory	25,000	
Property, plant, and equipment	650,000	
Accumulated depreciation		320,000
Accounts payable		95,000
Wages and salaries payable		24,000
Note payable		200,000
Stockholders' equity		152,500
Total	$795,000	$795,000

Typically, cash sales for Hansell represent 20% of sales while credit sales represent 80%. Credit sales terms by the company are 2/10, n/30. Hansell bills customers on the first day of the month following the month of sale. Experience has shown that 60% of the company's billings will be collected within the discount period, 25% by the end of the month after sales, and 10% by the end of the second month after the sale; 5% will ultimately be uncollectible. The company writes off uncollectible accounts after 12 months.

The purchase terms for materials are 2/15, n/60. Hansell makes all payments within the discount period. Experience has shown that 80% of the purchases are paid in the month of the purchase and the remainder are paid in the month immediately following. In June 2022, the firm budgeted purchases of $25,000 for Dura-1000 and $22,000 for Flexplas.

Variable manufacturing overhead is budgeted at $1,200 per batch (of 100 units) plus $80 per direct labor hour. In addition to variable overhead, the firm has a monthly fixed factory overhead of $50,000, of which $20,000 is depreciation expense. The firm pays all manufacturing labor and factory overhead when incurred.

Total budgeted marketing, distribution, customer service, and administrative costs for 2022 are $2,400,000. Of this amount, $1,200,000 is considered fixed and includes depreciation expense of $120,000. The remainder varies with sales. The budgeted total sales for 2022 are $4 million. All marketing and administrative costs are paid in the month incurred.

Management desires to maintain an end-of-month minimum cash balance of $40,000. The firm has an agreement with a local bank to borrow its short-term needs in multiples of $1,000 up to $100,000 at an annual interest rate of 12%. Borrowings are assumed to occur at the end of the month. Bank borrowing at July 1 is $0.

Required Using the information presented above:

1. Prepare the cash budget for July 2022.
2. Prepare the budgeted income statement for July 2022. (Assume that the company uses a LIFO cost-flow assumption.)

The Student Resources section of Connect includes video tutorials for the Self-Study Problems.

Questions

10-1 Describe at least three benefits that an organization can expect to realize from budgeting. **(CMA Adapted)**

10-2 Differentiate among master, operating, and financial budgets.

10-3 Many accountants believe that the most important benefit of the master budgeting process is the end result: a set of pro forma financial statements. What is the rationale for this view?

10-4 Some critics of budgeting believe that budgets are effective tools for planning but not for control purposes. What is the essence of this argument?

10-5 Why is the sales budget considered the cornerstone of the organization's master budget?

10-6 In addition to the sales budget, what information does a firm need to complete its materials purchases budget?

10-7 List the major components of a cash budget.

10-8 What is zero-base budgeting (ZBB)?

10-9 Define the term *budgetary slack*. Why is it common to find slack in budgets?

10-10 How does the use of a time-driven activity-based costing (TDABC) system facilitate the preparation of budgets for an organization?

10-11 What is the essence of a fixed-performance contract, and what dysfunctional consequences can occur through the use of this type of incentive system?

10-12 Define what is meant by the terms *what-if analysis* and *scenario analysis*.

10-13 Define the terms *relative-performance (relative-improvement) contract* and *rolling financial forecast*. What role for these is envisioned by critics of the traditional budgeting process?

Brief Exercises

[LO 10-4] 10-14 Kraft Bakeries introduced in 2022 a new line of frozen apple pie. For 2022, sales by quarter were as follows: 11,000 units, 16,000 units, 15,000 units, and 20,000 units. Because of aggressive marketing and promotion, the company expects that sales for each quarter of 2023 will be 25 percent higher than the respective quarter in 2022. The selling price per unit in 2023 is expected to be $4. What are the expected sales, in units and dollars, for the second quarter of 2023? For the third quarter of 2023?

[LO 10-4] 10-15 Resco, a local retail establishment, expects to make inventory purchases as follows for the first quarter of the year: January, $5,500; February, $6,500; and March, $8,000. Prior experience shows that 25 percent of a given month's purchases are paid in the month of purchase, with the balance paid in the following month. No purchase discounts apply. What is the total expected cash disbursement for February? For March?

[LO 10-4] 10-16 Ajax Manufacturing produces a single product, which takes 8.0 pounds of direct material per unit produced. The company's policy is to maintain an end-of-quarter inventory of materials equal to 25 percent of the following quarter's material requirements for production. Assume it is currently the end of the first quarter of the new year, and that at the end of the prior 4th quarter, there were 50,000 pounds of material on hand. How many units of product were planned for production in the first quarter? Under the assumption that production will increase by 10 percent in the second quarter, what are the direct material requirements (in pounds) for planned production in the second quarter?

[LO 10-4] 10-17 Grey Manufacturing Company expects sales to total 13,000 units in the first quarter, 12,000 units in the second quarter, and 15,000 units in the third quarter of the current fiscal year. Company policy is to have on hand at the end of each quarter an amount of inventory equal to 10 percent of the following quarter's sales. Given this information, how many units should be scheduled for production in the second quarter?

[LO 10-6, 10-7]   10-18 Easy Clean operates a chain of dry cleaners. It is experimenting with the use of a continuous-improvement (i.e., kaizen) budget for operating expenses. Currently, a typical location has operating expenses of $10,000 per month. Plans are in place to achieve labor and utility savings. The associated operational changes are estimated to reduce monthly operating expenses by a factor of 0.99 beginning in January. What are the estimated operating expenses for January? For June? For December?

[LO 10-4]   10-19 Campbell's Wholesale Company is preparing monthly cash budgets for the fourth quarter of the year. Monthly sales revenue in this quarter is estimated as follows: October, $30,000; November, $24,000; and December, $20,000. All sales are made on open credit with 70 percent collected in the month of sale and 30 percent collected in the following month. What is the estimated total cash collected in November? December?

[LO 10-4]   10-20 Royal Cigar Company is preparing a budget for cash collections. Its sales for November and December are estimated as $90,000 and $100,000, respectively. Past practice indicates that sales in any given month are collected as follows: month of sale, 75 percent; month following the month of sale, 20 percent; uncollectible accounts, 5 percent. The company allows a 2 percent discount for cash collections in the month of sale. What is the net cash estimated to be collected in December?

[LO 10-4]   10-21 The George Company has a policy of maintaining an end-of-month cash balance of at least $30,000. In months where a shortfall is expected, the company can draw in $1,000 increments on a line of credit it has with a local bank, at an interest rate of 12 percent per annum. All borrowings are assumed for budgeting purposes to occur at the beginning of the month, while all loan repayments (in $1,000 increments of principal) are assumed to occur at the end of the month. Interest is paid at the end of each month. For April, an end-of-month cash balance (prior to any financing and interest expense) of $18,000 is budgeted; for May, an excess of cash collected over cash payments (prior to any interest payments and loan repayments) of $22,000 is anticipated. What is the interest payment estimated for April (there is no bank loan outstanding at the end of March)? What is the total financing effect (cash interest plus loan transaction) for May?

[LO 10-4]   10-22 If the December 1 balance in the Direct Materials Inventory account was $37,000, the December 31 balance was $39,500, and $150,000 of direct materials were issued to production during December, what was the amount of direct materials purchased during the month?

[LO 10-4]   10-23 A company is formulating its marketing expense budget for the last quarter of the year. Sales in units for the third quarter amounted to 4,000; sales volume for the fourth quarter is expected to increase by 10 percent. Variable marketing expense per unit sold amounts to approximately $0.05, paid in cash in the month of sale. Fixed marketing expense per month amounts to $10,000 of salaries, $5,000 of depreciation (delivery trucks), and $2,000 of insurance (paid monthly). What is the total budgeted marketing *expense* for the fourth quarter of the year? What is the estimated *cash payment* for marketing expense for the fourth quarter?

Exercises

[LO 10-2, 10-4]   10-24 **Purchase Discounts**   It is typically beneficial for companies to take advantage of early-payment discounts allowed on purchases made on credit. To see why this is the case, determine the effective rate of interest associated with *not* taking advantage of the early-payment discount for each of the following situations. Assume in each case that payment is made on the 30th day of the billing cycle.

Required

1. What is the opportunity cost of not taking advantage of the discount associated with purchases made under the following terms: 2/10, n/30? (Show calculations.)

2. What is the opportunity cost of not taking advantage of the discount associated with purchases made under the following terms: 1/10, n/30? (Show calculations.)

3. To motivate managers to take early-payment discounts, what is the appropriate accounting treatment for purchase discounts?

[LO 10-4]   10-25 **Production and Materials Purchases Budgets**   White Corporation's budget calls for the following sales for next year:

| Quarter 1 | 90,000 units | Quarter 3 | 68,000 units |
| Quarter 2 | 76,000 units | Quarter 4 | 96,000 units |

Each unit of the product requires 3 pounds of direct materials. The company's policy is to begin each quarter with an inventory of product equal to 5 percent of that quarter's estimated sales requirements and an inventory of direct materials equal to 20 percent of that quarter's estimated direct materials requirements for production.

Required   Determine the production and materials purchases budgets for the second quarter.

[LO 10-4]   10-26   **Budgeted Cash Receipts and Cash Disbursements**   Timpco, a retailer, makes both cash and credit sales (i.e., sales on open account). Information regarding budgeted sales for the last quarter of the year is as follows:

	October	November	December
Cash sales	$100,000	$120,000	$ 80,000
Credit sales	100,000	150,000	90,000
Total	$200,000	$270,000	$170,000

Past experience shows that 5 percent of credit sales are uncollectible. Of the credit sales that are collectible, 60 percent are collected in the month of sale; the remaining 40 percent are collected in the month following the month of sale. Customers are granted a 1.5 percent discount for payment within 10 days of billing. Approximately 75 percent of collectible credit sales take advantage of the cash discount.

Inventory purchases each month are 100 percent of the *cost* of the following month's projected sales. (The gross profit rate for Timpco is approximately 30 percent.) All merchandise purchases are made on credit, with 25 percent paid in the month of purchase and the remainder paid in the following month. No cash discounts for early payment are available.

Required
1. Calculate the budgeted total cash receipts for November and December.
2. Calculate budgeted cash disbursements for November and December (budgeted total sales for January of the coming year equal $200,000).

[LO 10-4]   10-27   **Cash Disbursements Budget**   Bond Company budgets the following purchases of direct materials for the first quarter of the year:

	January	February	March
Budgeted purchases	$150,000	$120,000	$90,000

All purchases of direct materials are made on credit. On average, the company pays for 80 percent of its purchases in the month of acquisition and the remainder in the following month. Purchases take place fairly evenly throughout the month.

Required
1. For the months of February and March, what are the budgeted cash payments for purchases of direct materials under the assumption that there is no (cash) discount for early payment?
2. For the months of February and March, what are the budgeted cash payments for purchases of direct materials under the assumption that the purchase terms are 2/15, net 30? The company's policy is to take advantage of all cash discounts for early payment.
3. Provide an economic argument as to why it may be good (economic) policy to take advantage of early payment discounts, as in requirement 2.

[LO 10-4]   10-28   **Cash Budget—Financing Effects**   You are a relatively recent hire to Hartz & Co., a local manufacturer of plumbing supply products. You have been asked to prepare a condensed statement of cash flows for the months of November and December of the current year for presentation to the company's management.

Assume the cash balance at November 1 will be $75,000. It is the company's policy to maintain a minimum cash balance of $50,000 at the end of each month. Cash receipts (from cash sales and collection of accounts receivable) are projected to be $525,000 for November and $450,000 for December. Cash disbursements (sales commissions, advertising, delivery expense, wages, utilities, etc.) prior to financing activity are scheduled to be $450,500 in November and $550,000 in December.

Short-term borrowing, when needed, is done at the beginning of the month in increments of $1,000. The annual interest rate on any such loans is estimated to be 12 percent. Interest on any outstanding short-term loans is paid in cash at the end of the month. Repayments of principal (if any) are assumed to occur at the end of the month. As of November 1, the company has a $50,000 long-term loan from the local bank. This loan, including interest (at 12 percent per year) for the month of November, is payable at the end of November.

Required   Use the preceding information to prepare the cash budget for November and December. (*Hint:* The December 31 cash balance should be $50,480.)

[LO 10-4]   10-29 **Cash Budget**   Marsha Inc. has the following budgeted data for the coming year:

Cash balance, beginning	$15,000
Collections from customers	145,000
Direct materials purchases	25,000
Expenses:	
Operating expenses	50,000
Payroll	75,000
Income taxes	6,000
Other:	
Machinery purchases	30,000

Operating expenses include $20,000 depreciation for buildings and equipment. All purchases of materials are paid for in the period of purchase. The company requires a minimum cash balance of $25,000.

Required   Compute the amount the company needs to finance or the excess cash available for Marsha to invest.

[LO 10-4]   10-30 **Budgeted Cash Receipts: Cash Discounts Allowed on Receivables**   Yeopay Plumbing Supply accepts bank credit cards and offers established plumbers charge accounts with terms of 1/eom, n/45. Yeopay's experience is that 25 percent of its sales are for cash and bank credit cards. The remaining 75 percent are on credit. Of the cash sales, 40 percent pay cash and the remaining 60 percent pay with bank credit cards. Yeopay receives payments from the bank on credit card sales at the end of the day. However, Yeopay has to pay 3 percent for these services. An aging schedule for accounts receivable shows the following pattern on credit sales:

20% pay in the month of sale.
50% pay in the first month following the month of sale.
15% pay in the second month following the month of sale.
12% pay in the third month following the month of sale.
3% are never collected.

All accounts not paid by the end of the second month following the month of sale are considered overdue and are subject to a 2 percent monthly late charge. Yeopay has prepared the following sales forecasts:

June	$60,000
July	80,000
August	90,000
September	96,000
October	88,000

Required
1. Use Excel to prepare a schedule of cash receipts for September and October.
   a. At the top of a new spreadsheet, create an "Original Data" section with four subheads: Sales Data, Sales Breakdown and Terms, Breakdown of Cash/Bank Credit Card Sales, and Collection of Credit Sales.
   b. Enter all pertinent data listed above.
   c. Create a new section to calculate cash receipts for September with rows for Cash Sales, Bank Credit Card Sales, Collections of Accounts Receivable (4 rows), and Total Cash Receipts. Next, prepare columns for Total Sales, Percentage of Sales for cash/bank credit card sales versus credit sales (Sales %), Payment Percentage for the proportions collected (i.e., percentage collected to allow for cash discounts or late charges [Payment %]), and Cash Receipts.
   d. Program your spreadsheet to perform all necessary calculations for determining cash receipts for September. Do not type in any amounts. All the amounts you enter into this new section should derive from data from the Original Data section using a formula.
   e. Verify the accuracy of your spreadsheet by calculating the total cash receipts in September: $86,082.
   f. Create a new section titled October. Program your spreadsheet to perform all necessary calculations for determinations of cash receipts for October, and verify the accuracy of your spreadsheet by showing that the amount of total cash receipts for October is $88,141.
2. What is the appropriate accounting treatment for the bank service fees and the cash discounts allowed on collection of receivables?

[LO 10-4]   10-31 **Cash Receipts and Payments**   Information pertaining to Noskey Corporation's sales revenue follows:

	November 2021 (actual)	December 2021 (budgeted)	January 2022 (budgeted)
Cash sales	$ 80,000	$100,000	$ 60,000
Credit sales	240,000	360,000	180,000
Total sales	$320,000	$460,000	$240,000

Management estimates 5 percent of credit sales to be uncollectible. Of collectible credit sales, 60 percent is collected in the month of sale and the remainder in the month following the month of sale. Purchases of inventory each month include 70 percent of the next month's projected total sales (stated at cost) plus 30 percent of projected sales for the current month (stated at cost). All inventory purchases are on account; 25 percent is paid in the month of purchase, and the remainder is paid in the month following the month of purchase. Purchase costs are approximately 60 percent of the selling price.

Required   Determine for Noskey:
1. Budgeted cash collections in December 2021 from November 2021 credit sales.
2. Budgeted total cash receipts in January 2022.
3. Budgeted total cash payments in December 2021 for inventory purchases.

(CPA Adapted)

[LO 10-4]   10-32 **Retailer Budget**   D. Tomlinson Retail seeks your assistance in developing cash and other budget information for May, June, and July. The store expects to have the following balances at the end of April:

Cash	$100,500
Accounts receivable	437,000
Inventories	309,400
Accounts payable	133,055

The firm follows these guidelines in preparing its budgets:

- **Sales.** All sales are on credit with terms of 3/10, n/30. Tomlinson bills customers on the last day of each month. The firm books receivables at gross amounts and collects 60 percent of the billings within the discount period, 25 percent by the end of the month, and 9 percent by the end of the second month. The firm's experience suggests that 6 percent is likely to be uncollectible and is written off at the end of the third month.

- **Purchases and expenses.** All purchases and expenses are on open account. The firm pays its payables over a 2-month period with 54 percent paid in the month of purchase. Each month's units of ending inventory should equal 130 percent of the next month's cost of sales. The cost of each unit of inventory is $20. Selling, general, and administrative (SG&A) expenses, of which $2,000 is depreciation, equal 15 percent of the current month's sales.

Actual and projected sales follow:

Month	Dollars	Units	Month	Dollars	Units
March	$354,000	11,800	June	$342,000	11,400
April	363,000	12,100	July	360,000	12,000
May	357,000	11,900	August	366,000	12,200

Required
1. Prepare schedules showing budgeted merchandise purchases for May and June.
2. Prepare a schedule showing budgeted cash disbursements during June.
3. Prepare a schedule showing budgeted cash collections during May.
4. Determine gross and net balances of accounts receivable on May 31.

(CMA Adapted)

[LO 10-4, 10-5]   10-33   **Accounts Receivable Collections and Sensitivity Analysis**   Papst Company is preparing its cash budget for the month of May. The following information is available concerning its accounts receivable (based on sales made to customers on open account):

Actual credit sales for March	$130,000
Actual credit sales for April	$160,000
Estimated credit sales for May	$210,000
Estimated collections in the month of sale	25%
Estimated collections in the first month after the month of sale	60%
Estimated collections in the second month after the month of sale	10%
Estimated provision for bad debts (made in the month of sale)	5%

The firm writes off all uncollectible accounts at the end of the second month after the month of sale.

Required   Create an Excel spreadsheet and determine for Papst Company for the month of May:
1. The estimated cash receipts from accounts receivable collections.
2. The gross amount of accounts receivable at the end of the month (after appropriate write-off of uncollectible accounts).
3. The net amount of accounts receivable at the end of the month.
4. Recalculate requirements 1 and 2 under the assumption that estimated collections in the month of sale equal 60 percent and in the first month following the month of sale equal 25 percent.
5. What are the benefits and likely costs of moving to the situation described in requirement 4?

[LO 10-2, 10-4, 10-5]   10-34   **Budgeting for Marketing Expenses; Strategy**   You have been recruited by a former classmate, Susanna Wu, to join the finance team of a company that she founded recently. The company produces a unique product line of hypoallergenic cosmetics and relies for its success on an aggressive marketing program. The company is in a start-up phase and therefore has no significant history of expenses and revenues upon which to rely for budgeting and planning purposes. Given the restriction on available funds (most of the available capital has been used for new-product development and to recruit a management team), the control of costs, including marketing costs, is thought by the management team to be essential for the short-term viability of the company.

You have held a number of intensive discussions with Susanna and John Thompson, director of marketing for the firm. They have asked you to prepare an estimated budget for marketing expenses for a month of operations.

You are provided with the following data, which represent average actual monthly costs over the past three months:

Cost	Amount
Sales commissions	$120,000
Sales staff salaries	40,000
Telephone and mailing	38,000
Rental—office building	25,000
Gas (utilities)	12,000
Delivery charges	70,000
Depreciation—office furniture	8,000
Marketing consultants	25,000

Your discussions with John and Susanna indicate the following assumptions and anticipated changes regarding monthly marketing expenses for the coming year:

- Sales volume, because of aggressive marketing, should increase by 10 percent.
- To meet competitive pressures, sales prices are expected to decrease by 5 percent.
- Sales commissions are based on a percentage of sales revenue.
- Sales staff salaries, because of a new hire, will increase by 10 percent, regardless of sales volume.
- Because of recent industrywide factors, rates for telephone and mailing costs, as well as delivery charges, are expected to increase by 6 percent. However, both of these categories of costs are variable with sales volume.
- Rent on the office building is based on a two-year lease, with 18 months remaining on the original lease.
- Gas utility costs are largely independent of changes in sales volume. However, because of industrywide disruptions in supply, these costs are expected to increase by 15 percent, regardless of changes in sales volume.

- Depreciation on the office furniture used by members of the sales staff should increase because of new equipment that will be acquired. The planned cost for this equipment is $30,000, which will be depreciated using the straight-line (SL) method, with no salvage value, over a five-year useful life.
- Because of competitive pressure, the company plans to increase the cost of marketing consultants by $5,000 per month.

Required

1. Use the preceding information to develop an Excel spreadsheet that can be used to generate a monthly budget for marketing expenses. (Use the built-in function "SLN" to calculate monthly depreciation charges for the new equipment to be purchased.) What is the percentage change, by line item and in total, for items in your budget?

2. The management team is worried about the short-term financial position of the new company. Given the strain on available cash, the president has expressed a desire to keep marketing expenses over the next few months to a maximum of $350,000. Discussions with the marketing department indicate that telephone and mailing costs are the only category, in the short run, that can reasonably bear the planned-for reduction in marketing costs. The budget you have prepared includes an assumed 6 percent increase in telephone and mailing costs. What must this percentage change (positive or negative) be in order to achieve targeted monthly marketing costs? (*Hint:* Use the Goal Seek function in Excel, which is found under Data, then What-If Analysis.)

3. Comment on the use of the budget in this situation for cost-control purposes.

[LO 10-5] 10-35 **What-If Analysis** As the management accountant for the Tyson Company you have been asked to construct a financial planning model for collection of accounts receivable and then to perform a what-if analysis in terms of the assumption regarding estimated uncollectible accounts. You are provided with the following information:

Collection Pattern for Credit Sales: 65 percent of the company's credit sales are collected in the month of sale and 30 percent in the month following the month of sale; 5 percent are uncollectible.
Credit Sales: January 2022, $100,000; February 2022, $120,000; March 2022, $110,000.

Required

1. Generate a spreadsheet model regarding estimated bad debts expense under the following assumptions regarding the rate of uncollectible accounts: 1 percent, 3 percent, 5 percent (base case), and 8 percent. Prepare an estimate of bad debts expense for each of three months, January through March, and for the quarter as a whole.

2. What is the value to Tyson Company of creating a model and then performing the what-if analysis?

[LO 10-5] 10-36 **Profit Planning and Sensitivity Analysis** You are currently trying to decide between two cost structures for your business: one that has a greater proportion of short-term fixed costs and another that is more heavily weighted to variable costs. Estimated revenue and cost data for each alternative are as follows:

	Cost Structure	
	Alternative 1	Alternative 2
Selling price per unit	$ 100	$ 100
Variable cost per unit	85	80
Short-term fixed costs per year	40,000	45,000

Required

1. What sales volume, in units, is needed for the total costs in each cost-structure alternative to be the same?

2. Suppose your profit goal for the coming year is 5 percent of sales (i.e., operating profit ÷ sales = 5%). What sales level in units is needed under each alternative to achieve this goal?

3. Suppose again that your profit goal for the coming year is 5 percent of sales. What sales volume in dollars is needed under each alternative to achieve this goal?

[LO 10-5] 10-37 **Scenario Analysis** As part of the process of preparing the master budget for the coming year, you've been asked to perform What-If analyses, in the form of scenarios, on the original planning assumptions regarding product A produced by your company. The following are the baseline planning data for the coming year for this product:

Sales volume (annual, in units)	2,500
Selling price per unit	$ 1,500
Variable cost per unit	$ 1,000
Fixed costs (per year)	$200,000

Required

1. Based on the baseline planning data, what is the budgeted operating income for product A for the coming year?

2. Determine the estimated operating income under each of the following scenarios (for each scenario you should report both the new budgeted operating income and the percentage change in operating income from the baseline budgeted result):

   a. Selling price per unit is 10 percent higher than planned, while fixed costs per year are also 10 percent higher than planned.

   b. Variable cost per unit is 5 percent higher than planned, while fixed costs are lower by this same percentage.

   c. Selling price per unit is 10 percent higher than planned, while volume is decreased by 8 percent.

[LO 10-6]   **10-38 Cash Budgeting: Not-for-Profit (NFP) Contex**   *(contributed by Helen M. Savage)* Tri-County Social Service Agency is a not-for-profit organization in the Midwest. Use the following information to complete the cash budget for the year ending December 31:

- The Board of Trustees requires that Tri-County maintain a minimum cash balance of $8,000.
- If cash is short, the agency may borrow from an endowment fund the amount required to maintain the $8,000 minimum.
- It is anticipated that the year will begin with an $11,000 cash balance.
- Contract revenue is received evenly during the year.
- Mental health income is expected to grow by $5,000 in the second and third quarters; no change is expected in the fourth quarter.

Required

1. Within the context of a not-for-profit organization, what is an *endowment fund*?
2. Complete the cash budget for each quarter and the year as a whole, using the template that follows.
3. Determine the amount that the agency will owe the endowment fund at year-end.
4. Does the borrowing indicate a problem? What options would the agency have to increase revenues?
5. Do you think that a requirement to pay interest on the borrowings would have a positive impact on the agency's activities? Why or why not?

TRI-COUNTY SOCIAL SERVICE AGENCY
Quarterly and Annual Cash Budget (in thousands)

	Quarters				
	I	II	III	IV	Year
Cash balance, beginning	$ 11	?	?	?	$ 11
Receipts:					
Grants	80	$ 70	?	?	300
Contracts	?	?	?	?	80
Mental health income	20	?	?	?	105
Charitable donations	250	?	$200	$400	?
Total cash available	?	$473	$333	?	?
Less disbursements:					
Salaries and benefits	?	$342	?	?	$1,365
Office expenses	$ 70	?	$ 71	$ 50	256
Equipment purchases and maintenance	2	4	6	?	17
Specific assistance	20	15	18	?	73
Total disbursements	?	?	?	?	?
Excess (deficit) of cash available over disbursements	$(46)	?	?	$112	?
Financing:					
Borrowings from endowment fund	?	?	$112	?	?
Repayments	?	$(39)	?	?	?
Total financing effects	?	?	?	?	?
Cash balance, ending	?	?	?	?	?

[LO 10-1, 10-6] 10-39 **Budgeting: Not-for-Profit (NFP) Context** *(contributed by Helen M. Savage)* Catholic Charities Regional Agency serves several contiguous counties in Ohio. The finance committee of its board of directors monitors financial activity for the agency. This oversight includes decisions regarding the investment of excess funds and the management of endowment funds. These decisions are relevant to the annual budget preparation because the investment accounts serve as a source of needed funds and/or a use of excess funds.

As a Catholic Charities agency, the regional organization must adhere to guidelines adopted by the U.S. Conference of Catholic Bishops. Visit the council's website at **www.usccb.org/about/ financial-reporting/socially-responsible-investment-guidelines.cfm** to review its *Socially Responsible Investment Guidelines,* which discuss basic principles for investments and the stated investment policy of the organization.

Required
1. What is the meaning of the word *stewardship*? Should the religious or philosophical position of an organization affect decisions that are made as part of the budgeting process?
2. How should a board of directors for this organization apply these principles in making investment decisions tied to the annual budget?
3. Would you, as a board member, ignore such principles to increase investment gains? Why or why not?
4. If the agency's monies are managed by an investment firm, should the board request information about the stocks included in individual investment funds to verify compliance with the stated investment policy of the organization?

[LO 10-6] 10-40 **Budgeting for a Service Firm** Refer to the AccuTax Inc. example in the chapter. One of the partners is planning to retire at the end of the year. May Higgins, the sole remaining partner, plans to add a manager at an annual salary of $90,000. She expects the manager to work, on average, 45 hours a week for 45 weeks per year. She plans to change the required staff time for each hour spent to complete a tax return to the following:

	Business Return	Complex Individual Return	Simple Individual Return
Partner	0.3 hour	0.05 hour	—
Manager	0.2 hour	0.15 hour	—
Senior consultant	0.5 hour	0.40 hour	0.2 hour
Consultant	—	0.40 hour	0.8 hour

The manager is salaried and earns no overtime pay. Senior consultants are salaried but receive time and a half for any overtime worked. The firm plans to keep all the senior consultants and adjust the number of consultants as needed including employing part-time consultants, who also are paid on an hourly basis. Higgins has also decided to have five supporting staff at $40,000 each. All other operating data remain unchanged. The manager will share 10 percent of any profit over $500,000 before bonus.

Required
1. What are the budgeted total costs for overtime hours worked by senior consultants?
2. How many full-time consultants should be budgeted?
3. Determine the manager's total compensation and total pretax operating income for the firm, assuming that the revenues from preparing tax returns remain unchanged.

[LO 10-6, 10-7] 10-41 **Activity-Based Budgeting (ABB)** OFC Company of Kansas City prints business forms and other specialty paper products, such as writing paper, envelopes, note cards, and greeting cards. Its Business Services division offers inventory management services and desktop delivery on request. The division uses an activity-based costing (ABC) system. The budgeted usage of each activity cost driver and cost-driver rates for January 2022 for the Business Services division are:

Activity	Cost Driver	Budgeted Activity	Cost-Driver Rate
Storage	Cartons in inventory	400,000	$0.4925/carton/month
Requisition handling	Requisitions	30,000	12.50
Pick packing	Lines	800,000	1.50
Data entry	Lines	800,000	0.80
	Requisitions	30,000	1.20
Desktop delivery	Per delivery	12,000	30.00

For the month, the division expects to make 11,700 deliveries to deliver 1,170,000 cartons to customers.

Required

1. What is the total budgeted cost for each activity and for the Business Services division in January 2022?

2. Assume, in contrast to requirement 1, that activity-related information was not available. Rather, the only information available is that the budgeted fixed costs for the month are $1,000,000, and the budgeted variable cost per carton is estimated as $1.30. What is the budgeted total cost for the month using this single volume-based approach? Compare and comment on the difference in your answers to requirements 1 and 2.

3. Dories Supply Chain Management Company offers to install an electronic order-processing system that transmits customer requisitions via the Internet to the Business Services division for immediate pick, packing, and delivery. No requisition handling and data entry will be needed once the system is fully functional. How much savings can the Business Services division expect from switching to the new system before considering the payment to Dories? What would be necessary in order for the company to be able to realize these estimated cost savings? Can you estimate the amount of savings if the firm uses a single cost rate (based on the number of cartons delivered) to determine the budgeted cost for the division?

[LO 10-6, 10-7]   10-42   **Activity-Based Budgeting (ABB) with Continuous Improvement**   OFC Company (Exercise 10-41) has decided to implement a kaizen (continuous-improvement) program to enhance operational efficiency. After a careful study, management and employees agree that the firm will be able to reduce cost rates for batch-level activities by 2 percent and unit-level activities (other than Storage) by 1 percent per month during the first year of the program starting February 2022. The firm has decided to delay the implementation of the program for customer-sustaining and facility-level activities until 2023. The firm expects the amount of cost-driver usage in each of the next two months to be the same as those in January. (Use 4 decimal points for all cost rates.)

Required

1. Identify unit-level and batch-level activities.

2. What are the total budgeted costs for each activity and for the division as a whole in February and March?

3. Identify three factors that are likely to be critical for a successful kaizen (i.e., continuous-improvement) program.

4. What are primary criticisms regarding kaizen (i.e., continuous-improvement) budgeting?

[LO 10-7]   10-43   **Time-Driven Activity-Based Budgeting (TDABB)**   The company for which you work recently implemented time-driven activity-based costing (TDABC) in conjunction with its enterprise resource planning (ERP) system. Management is pleased with the revised product and customer cost information that the TDABC system produces. It is now wondering how this system can be used for budgeting purposes. You have been asked to provide an example of using time-driven activity-based budgeting, given the following information:

1. There are two resources (departments): indirect labor and computer support.

2. There are two primary activities that these resources support: handling production runs and product-level support.

3. Indirect labor support is consumed as follows:

    a. To handle production runs: 10 hours/run.

    b. To support products: 500 hours/product.

4. Computer support is consumed as follows:

    a. To handle production runs: 0.4 hour/run.

    b. To support products: 50 hours/product.

5. Resource practical capacity levels:

    a. Indirect labor: 20,000 hours per quarter.

    b. Computer support: 500 hours per quarter.

6. Cost of supplying resources:

    a. Indirect labor: $1,000,000 per quarter.

    b. Computer support: $500,000 per quarter.

Required

1. Calculate the budgeted resource cost per hour (at practical capacity) for each of the two resources, indirect labor support and computer support.

2. Determine the budgeted cost-driver rates for each of the two activities, handle production runs and support products.

3. Suppose that the total cost of resources supplied for the quarter just ended was exactly as budgeted (i.e., $1,500,000) but that only 18,000 indirect labor hours were used along with 450 computer hours.

Calculate, for each resource, the cost of idle capacity. How should this cost be handled for internal reporting purposes?

4. After implementing a total quality management (TQM) program, the company was able to implement process-efficiency changes, the end result of which was a 10 percent reduction in the indirect labor time associated with the activity handling production runs. Recalculate the indirect labor cost component of the cost to handle a production run. Also, recalculate the cost of idle capacity for indirect labor assuming the original facts but with the 10 percent efficiency gain. Assume that in the original case facts, 16,000 of the 18,000 hours relate to the activity handling production runs (while the remaining 2,000 hours relate to the activity product-level support).

[LO 10-8]   10-44   **Rolling Financial Forecasts**   You are given the following budgeted and actual data for the Grey Company for each of the months January through June of the current year.

In December of the prior year, sales were forecasted as follows: January, 100 units; February, 95 units; March, 100 units; April, 110 units; May, 120 units; June, 125 units. In January of the current year, sales for the months February through June were reforecasted as follows: February, 90 units; March, 100 units; April, 105 units; May, 110 units; June, 120 units. In February of the current year, sales for the months March through June were reforecasted as follows: March, 95 units; April, 105 units; May, 105 units; June, 120 units. In March of the current year, sales for the months April through June were reforecasted as follows: April, 105 units; May, 100 units; June, 110 units. In April of the current year, sales for the months May and June were reforecasted as follows: May, 90 units; June, 105 units. In May of the current year, sales for June were reforecasted as 105 units.

Actual sales for the six-month period, January through June, were as follows: January, 98 units; February, 95 units; March, 92 units; April, 108 units; May, 98 units; June, 100 units.

Required

1. Prepare a schedule of forecasted sales, on a rolling basis, for the months January through June, inclusive. (*Hint:* There will be only one forecasted number for January—this is the forecast done in December. For February, there will be two forecasts: one done in December and a second done in January. For June, there will be six forecasts, one done in each of the preceding six months.)

2. For each of the months March through June, determine the three-month forecast error rate, defined as 1 minus the absolute percentage error. For example, the forecast error rate for March's sales is found by dividing the absolute value of the forecast error for this month by the actual sales volume for the month. The forecast error for any month (e.g., March) is defined as the difference between the actual sales volume for the month and the sales volume for that month forecasted three months earlier (e.g., December). (Round error percentages to 2 decimal points; for example, 23.423% = 23.42%.) Also, indicate for each month whether the actual sales volume was above or below the forecasted volume generated three months earlier.

[LO 10-2, 10-7]   10-45   **Resource Capacity Planning/ABC**   Two years ago, in conjunction with revitalization efforts regarding the downtown area of Metro City, you and your partner purchased a local eatery. Though moribund at the time, you were able (through your hard work and dedicated efforts) to resurrect the establishment. In fact, the last few months appear to have been quite successful from a financial standpoint.

However, your establishment now faces a new competitor—an eatery located only several blocks away from yours. You and your partner are now evaluating strategic options as to how to deal with this new competition. Your facility is capable of serving 200 meals a day. (Because your clientele consists almost exclusively of college-age students, the basic menu is the same for lunch and dinner. Currently, your business does not serve breakfast.)

You and your partner have finally taken time to study the financial records carefully. Your investigation yields the following information:

1. The primary variable cost is food (i.e., the total food cost varies in response to changes in the number of meals served).

2. Fixed operating expenses (salaries, depreciation, etc.) average approximately $1,100 per day.

3. The average number of meals served per day over the past three months was 175.

In response to the above information, and in an attempt to fully recover your costs, you and your partner are contemplating a price increase.

Required

1. Compute the fixed cost per meal using the current capacity used and the fixed cost per meal using capacity available.

2. Given the competitive situation, what is the likely result of the decision to raise prices? Explain.

3. Suggest and defend an alternative approach for allocating budgeted fixed operating costs to each meal.

[LO 10-7]

10-46 Kaizen Budget/Activity-Based Budgeting (ABB) Refer to text Exhibit 10.19 (the ABB for KWS). As the management accountant for KWS, you have been asked to evaluate the possibility of implementing a continuous-improvement (i.e., kaizen) budgeting system. Assume that budgeted cost-driver usage data in part A of Exhibit 10.19 will continue over the foreseeable future.

Required

1. Recalculate the budgeted factory overhead costs for June under the assumption that, starting in May, each budgeted activity cost rate decreases by 0.5 percent relative to the preceding month.

2. In general, what are the anticipated benefits of using a kaizen approach to budgeting?

3. What do you envision as the principal concerns or limitations regarding the use of kaizen budgeting?

4. Provide some examples of how, in the KWS example, the company would be able to realize the budgeted cost savings referenced above in requirement 1.

[LO 10-7, 10-8]

10-47 Budgetary Slack and Zero-Base Budgeting (ZBB) Bob Bingham is the controller of Atlantis Laboratories, a manufacturer and distributor of generic prescription pharmaceuticals. He is currently preparing the annual budget and reviewing the current business plan. The firm's business unit managers prepare and assemble the detailed operating budgets with technical assistance from the corporate accounting staff. The business unit managers then present the final budgets to the corporate executive committee for approval. The corporate accounting staff reviews the budgets for adherence to corporate accounting policies but not for reasonableness of the line items within the budgets.

Bob is aware that the upcoming year for Atlantis could be a difficult one because of a major patent expiration and the loss of a licensing agreement for another product line. He also knows that during the budgeting process, slack is created in varying degrees throughout the organization. Bob believes that this slack has a negative effect on the firm's overall business objectives and should be eliminated where possible.

Required

1. Define the term *budgetary slack.*

2. Explain the advantages and disadvantages of budgetary slack from the point of view of (a) the business unit manager who must achieve the budget and (b) corporate management.

3. Bob Bingham is considering implementing zero-base budgeting (ZBB) in Atlantis Laboratories.

   a. Define *zero-base budgeting.*

   b. Describe how zero-base budgeting could be advantageous to Atlantis Laboratories in controlling budgetary slack.

   c. Discuss the disadvantages Atlantis Laboratories might encounter in using ZBB.

(CMA Adapted)

[LO 10-8]

10-48 Budgetary Pressure and Ethics Midwest Industries produces and distributes industrial chemicals in its Belco Division, which is located in Michigan's upper peninsula. Belco's earnings increased sharply in 2022, and bonuses were paid to the management staff for the first time in three years. Bonuses are based in part on the amount by which reported income exceeds budgeted income.

Maria Gonzales, vice president of finance, was pleased with reported earnings for 2022 and therefore thought that pressure to "show" financial results would subside. However, Tom Lin, Belco's division manager, told Gonzales that he "saw no reason why bonuses for 2023 should not be double those of 2022." As a result, Gonzales felt pressure to increase reported income to exceed budgeted income by an even greater amount, a situation that would ensure increased bonuses.

Gonzales met with Bill Wilson of P&R Inc., a primary vendor of Belco's manufacturing supplies and equipment. Gonzales and Wilson have been close business contacts for many years. Gonzales asked Wilson to identify all of Belco's purchases of perishable supplies as "equipment" on sales invoices issued by P&R. The reason Gonzales gave for her request was that Belco's division manager had imposed stringent budget constraints on operating expenses, but not on capital expenditures. Gonzales planned to capitalize (rather than expense) the cost of perishable supplies and then include them in the equipment account on the balance sheet. In this way, Gonzales could defer the recognition of expenses to a later year. This procedure would increase reported earnings, which in turn would lead to higher bonuses (in the short run). Wilson agreed to do as Gonzales had asked.

While analyzing the second quarter financial statements, Gary Wood, Belco's director of cost accounting, noticed a large decrease in supplies expense from a year ago. Wood reviewed the Supplies Expense account and noticed that only equipment, not supplies, had been purchased from P&R, a major source for such supplies. Wood, who reports to Gonzales, immediately brought this to the attention of Gonzales.

Gonzales told Wood of Lin's high expectations and of the arrangement made with Wilson (from P&R). Wood told Gonzales that her action was an improper accounting treatment for the supplies purchased from P&R. Wood requested that he be allowed to correct the accounts and urged that the arrangement with P&R be discontinued. Gonzales refused the request and told Wood not to become involved in the arrangement with P&R.

After clarifying the situation in a confidential discussion with an objective and qualified peer within Belco, Wood arranged to meet with Lin, Belco's division manager. At that meeting, Wood disclosed the arrangement Gonzales had made with P&R.

Required
1. Explain why the use of alternative accounting methods to manipulate reported earnings is unethical, if not illegal.
2. Is Gary Wood, Belco's director of cost accounting, correct in saying that the supplies purchased from P&R Inc. were accounted for improperly? Explain.
3. Assuming that the agreement of Gonzales with P&R was in violation of the IMA's *Statement of Ethical Professional Practice* (www.imanet.org/career-resources/ethics-center), discuss whether Wood's actions were appropriate or inappropriate.

(CMA Adapted)

Problems

[LO 10-4] 10-49 **Budgeting for a Merchandising Firm**   Goldberg Company is a retail sporting goods store that uses an accrual accounting system. Facts regarding its operations follow:
- Sales are budgeted at $250,000 for December and $225,000 for January, terms 1/eom, n/60.
- Collections are expected to be 50 percent in the month of sale and 48 percent in the month following the sale. Two percent of sales are expected to be uncollectible and recorded in an allowance account at the end of the month of sale. Bad debts expense is included as part of operating expenses.
- Gross margin is 30 percent of gross sales.
- All accounts receivable are from credit sales. Bad debts are written off against the allowance account at the end of the month following the month of sale.
- Goldberg desires to have 80 percent of the merchandise for the following month's sales on hand at the end of each month. Payment for merchandise is made in the month following the month of purchase.
- Other monthly operating expenses to be paid in cash total $25,000.
- Annual depreciation is $216,000, one-twelfth of which is reflected as part of monthly operating expenses.

Goldberg Company's statement of financial position at the close of business on November 30 follows:

GOLDBERG COMPANY
Statement of Financial Position
November 30, 2022

Assets	
Cash	$ 30,000
Accounts receivable (net of $4,000 allowance for doubtful accounts)	76,000
Inventory	132,000
Property, plant, and equipment (net of $680,000 accumulated depreciation)	870,000
Total assets	$1,108,000

Liabilities and Stockholders' Equity	
Accounts payable	$ 100,000
Common stock	800,000
Retained earnings	146,000
Total liabilities and equity	$1,108,000

Required
1. What is the total of budgeted cash collections for December?
2. How much is the book value of Accounts Receivable at the end of December?
3. How much is the income (loss) before income taxes for December?
4. What is the projected balance in Inventory on December 31, 2022?
5. What are budgeted purchases of inventory for December?
6. What is the projected balance in Accounts Payable on December 31, 2022?

(CMA Adapted)

[LO 10-4] 10-50 **Comprehensive Profit Plan** Spring Manufacturing Company makes two components identified as C12 and D57. Selected budgetary data for 2022 follow:

	Finished Components	
	C12	D57
Requirements for each finished component:		
RM 1	10 pounds	8 pounds
RM 2	0	4 pounds
RM 3	2 pounds	1 pound
Direct labor	2 hours	3 hours
Product information:		
Sales price	$ 150	$ 220
Sales (units)	12,000	9,000
Estimated beginning inventory (units)	400	150
Desired ending inventory (units)	300	200

	Direct Materials Information		
	RM1	RM2	RM3
Cost per pound	$ 2.00	$ 2.50	$ 0.50
Estimated beginning inventory in pounds	3,000	1,500	1,000
Desired ending inventory in pounds	4,000	1,000	1,500

The firm expects the average wage rate to be $25 per hour in 2022. Spring Manufacturing uses direct labor hours to apply overhead. Each year the firm determines the overhead application rate for the year based on budgeted direct labor hours for the year. The firm maintains negligible Work-in-Process Inventory and expects the cost per unit for both beginning and ending inventories of finished products to be identical.

	Factory Overhead Information
Indirect materials—variable	$ 10,000
Miscellaneous supplies and tools—variable	5,000
Indirect labor—variable	40,000
Supervision—fixed	120,000
Payroll taxes and fringe benefits—variable	250,000
Maintenance costs—fixed	20,000
Maintenance costs—variable	10,080
Depreciation—fixed	71,330
Heat, light, and power—fixed	43,420
Heat, light, and power—variable	11,000
Total	$580,830

	Selling and Administrative Expense Information
Advertising	$ 60,000
Sales salaries	200,000
Travel and entertainment	60,000
Depreciation—warehouse	5,000
Office salaries	60,000
Executive salaries	250,000
Supplies	4,000
Depreciation—office	6,000
Total	$ 645,000

The effective income tax rate for the company is 40 percent.

Required Prepare an Excel spreadsheet that contains the following schedules or statements for 2022:
1. Sales budget.
2. Production budget.
3. Direct materials purchases budget (units and dollars).

4. Direct labor budget.

5. Factory overhead budget.

6. Cost of goods sold and ending finished goods inventory budgets.

7. Selling and administrative expense budget, broken down into two components: Selling Expenses and Administrative Expenses

8. Budgeted income statement, the last item of which is labeled After-Tax Operating Income.

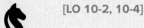

[LO 10-2, 10-4]   10-51 **Comprehensive Profit Plan**   (Use information in Problem 10-50 for Spring Manufacturing Company.) C12 is a mature product. The sales manager believes that the price of C12 can be raised to $160 per unit with no effect on sales quantity. D57 is a new product introduced last year. Management believes D57 has great potential and is considering lowering the price to $180 to expand market size and gain market share. The lowering of D57's price is likely to double the total units of D57 sold.

Required

1. Amend the eight budgets from Problem 10-50 to incorporate the changes outlined above.

2. What effect do these combined changes have on budgeted After-Tax Operating Income?

3. Would you recommend that the firm execute the proposed strategy? Explain.

[LO 10-2, 10-4, 10-7]   10-52 **Comprehensive Profit Plan (Kaizen Budgeting)**   (Use information in Problem 10-50 for Spring Manufacturing Company.) Spring Manufacturing Company has had a continuous-improvement (kaizen) program for the last two years. According to the kaizen program, the firm is expected to manufacture C12 and D57 with the following specifications:

Cost Element	C12	D57
Raw material 1	9 lbs.	7 lbs.
Raw material 2	-0-	3.6 lbs.
Raw material 3	1.8 lbs.	0.8 lb.
Direct labor	1.5 hrs.	2 hrs.

The company specifies that the variable factory overhead is to decrease by 10 percent while the fixed factory overhead is to decrease by 5 percent, except for depreciation expenses. The company does not expect the price of the raw materials to change. However, the hourly wage rate is likely to be $30.

Required

1. Prepare the following schedules or statements for 2022 assuming the firm can attain the expected operating level as prescribed by the kaizen program:

   • Sales budget
   • Production budget
   • Direct materials purchases budget (in units and in dollars)
   • Direct labor budget
   • Factory overhead budget
   • Cost of goods sold and ending inventory budgets
   • Selling and administrative expense budget
   • Income statement, the last line of which is labeled After-Tax Operating Income

2. What are the benefits of Spring Manufacturing Company adopting a continuous-improvement (kaizen) program? What are the primary limitations?

[LO 10-4, 10-5]   10-53 **Cash Flow Analysis, Rolling Sales Forecasts, and Sensitivity Analysis**   CompUSA Inc. sells computer hardware. It also markets related software and software-support services. The company prepares annual forecasts for sales, which are given below.

In a typical month, total sales are broken down as follows: cash sales, 30%; VISA® credit card sales, 65%; and 5% open account (the company's own charge accounts). For budgeting purposes, assume that cash sales plus bank credit card sales are received in the month of sale; bank credit card sales are subject to a 3% processing fee, which is deducted daily at the time of deposit into CompUSA's cash account with the bank. Cash receipts from collection of accounts receivable typically occur as follows: 20% in the month of sale, 50% in the month following the month of sale, and 27% in the second month following the month of sale. The remaining receivables generally turn out to be uncollectible.

CompUSA's month-end inventory requirements for computer hardware units are 30% of the following month's estimated sales. A one-month lead time is required for delivery from the hardware distributor. Thus, orders for computer hardware units are generally placed by CompUSA on the 25th of each month to ensure availability in the store on the first day of the month needed. These units are purchased on credit, under the following terms: n/45, *measured from the time the units are delivered to CompUSA*. Assume that CompUSA takes the maximum amount of time to pay its invoices. On average, the purchase price for hardware units runs 60% of selling price.

CompUSA Inc.
Forecasted Sales (units and dollars)
January–December 2022

	Number of Units	Hardware Sales	Software/ Support Sales	Total Revenue
January	120	$360,000	$140,000	$500,000
February	130	390,000	160,000	550,000
March	90	270,000	130,000	400,000
April	100	300,000	125,000	425,000
May	110	330,000	150,000	480,000
June	120	360,000	140,000	500,000
July				
August				
September				
October				
November				
December				
Totals	670	$2,010,000	$845,000	$2,855,000

Required

1. Calculate estimated cash receipts for April 2022 (show details).
2. The company is looking at the number of hardware units to order on January 25.
   a. Determine the estimated number of units to be ordered.
   b. Calculate the dollar cost (per unit and total) for these units.
3. Cash planning in this line of business is critical to success. Management feels that the assumption of selling price per unit ($3,000) is firm—at least for the foreseeable future. Also, it is comfortable with the 30% rate for end-of-month inventories. It is not so sure, however, about (a) the Cost of Goods Sold (COGS) rate (because of the state of flux in the supplier market) and (b) the level of predicted sales in March 2022. Discussions with marketing and purchasing suggest that three outcomes are possible for each of these two variables, as follows:

Outcome	March Sales	COGS%
Optimistic	100 units	55%
Expected	90 units	60
Pessimistic	80 units	65

The preceding outcomes are assumed to be independent, which means that there are nine possible combinations (3 × 3). You are asked to conduct a sensitivity analysis to determine the range of possible cash outflows for April 10, under different combinations of the above. Assume, for simplicity, that sales volume for April is fixed. Complete the following table:

Scenario	March Sales (units)	COGS %	Cash Payment April 10
1	100	55%	$ _____
2	100	60	_____
3	100	65	_____
4	90	55	_____
5	90	60	_____
6	90	65	_____
7	80	55	_____
8	80	60	_____
9	80	65	_____
	Maximum = ?		
	Minimum = ?		
	Range = ?		

4. As part of the annual budget process, CompUSA prepares a cash budget by month for the entire year. Explain why a company such as CompUSA would prepare monthly cash flow budgets for the entire year. Explain the role of *sensitivity analysis* in the monthly planning process.

5. Management is thinking about adopting rolling forecasts that would cover five quarters (15 months). As a starting point, use the Forecast Sheet function in Excel to create the forecast for hardware sales for the first three months of 2023. Create a 95% confidence interval and comment on the results.

(CMA Adapted)

[LO 10-5] **10-54 Profit Planning and What-If Analysis** As a newly hired management accountant, you have been asked to prepare a profit plan for the company for which you work. As part of this task, you've been asked to do some what-if analyses. Following is the budgeted information regarding the coming year:

Selling price per unit	$ 100.00
Variable cost per unit	70.00
Fixed costs (per year)	1,200,000

Required

1. What is the breakeven volume, in units and dollars, for the coming year?

2. Assume that the goal of the company is to earn a pretax (operating) profit of $300,000 for the coming year. How many units would the company have to sell to achieve this goal?

3. Assume that of the $70 variable cost per unit, the labor-cost component is $25. Current negotiations with the employees of the company indicate some uncertainty regarding the labor cost component of the variable cost figure presented above. What is the effect on the breakeven point in units if selling price and fixed costs are as planned, but the labor cost for the coming year is 4% higher than anticipated? What if labor costs are 6% higher than anticipated? What if labor costs turn out to be 8% higher than anticipated? (Show calculations.)

4. Assume now that management is convinced that labor costs will be 5% higher than originally planned when the budget for the year was put together. What selling price per unit must the company charge to maintain the budgeted ratio of contribution margin to sales? Round your answer to 2 decimal places. (*Hint:* Use the Goal Seek function in Excel to answer this question.)

5. Explain the role of what-if analysis in the budgeting process.

 [LO 10-5, 10-6] **10-55 Budgeting Customer Retention and Insurance-Policy Renewal; Sensitivity Analysis** National Insurance Company underwrites property insurance for homeowners. You have been charged with the responsibility of developing a portion of the monthly budget for the coming 12-month period for the company.

You have collected the following driver volumes, consumption rates, unit resource costs, and other data needed to prepare your 12-month budget for those active policyholders whose policies run from January to December:

Number of active policyholders beginning of month 1	100,000
Average monthly premium per policy	$100.00
Monthly midterm cancellation rate	0.50%
Policy renewal rate	85.00%

Required

1. Prepare, in good form, a monthly budget for customer retention and insurance premium revenue for the period January through December. Columns in your budget should represent months, while the rows in your budget should consist of the following: number of active policyholders at the beginning of the month, midterm cancellation rate (%), number of active policyholders at the end of the month, average number of active policyholders during the month, average monthly premium per policy, and total premiums earned per month from active policyholders. How many policies are projected to be renewed at the end of the year?

2. Within the context of budgeting, what do we mean by the term *what-if analysis*?

3. Recreate the original 12-month budget you prepared in requirement 1 to reflect what will happen if the policy-renewal rate falls to 80% and the monthly midterm cancellation rate increases to 0.75%.

4. What other information or data would be included in the full budget prepared each month for the company?

 [LO 10-6] **10-56 Budgeting Insurance Policy Volume and Monthly Revenues** National Auto Insurance Company underwrites automobile coverage for the consumer market. As part of the annual planning process, National Auto requires monthly estimates for the number of policies in force and the amount of premium revenue associated with this volume of business. You have been asked to prepare these estimates for the coming six-month period. Past experience indicates that the number of policies outstanding during a given month is influenced both by macro factors (e.g., market size [total number of households] and market growth rate) and company-specific factors (e.g., market share, cancellation rate experience).

At the beginning of January for the new budget year, the number of households is estimated as 100 million; further, past experience indicates that this will increase by approximately 0.05% per month. Your own research indicates that approximately 80% of households have one or more cars. On average, each household owns 2.2 cars. Because of legal requirements, the average percentage of cars insured is high—your best estimate is that this number is 85% and growing by 0.1% per month. Current market share of National Auto in the consumer market is 14,940,000, which is approximately 10%. Over the past 24 months, the rate of increase in market share for National Auto has been 0.005% per month. Because of aggressive levels of customer service, National Auto has been able to keep its monthly cancellation rate below average, to approximately 0.125%. Average monthly premium paid per auto insured for the coming year is assumed to be $100.

Required

1. For each of the months January–June in the coming year, prepare a budget broken down in three parts:

   a. Market size and volume.

   b. Volume for National Auto Insurance (number of policies outstanding).

   c. Premium revenues generated.

   For part (a), you should have seven rows of data as follows: total number of households (i.e., market size), percentage of households owning one or more cars, number of cars owned per household, percentage of car owners with insurance, total number of insured cars (marketwide), market share of National Auto, and number of autos insured by National Auto, end of the month. For part (b), your budget should have four rows as follows: number of cars insured, beginning of the month; cancellations during the month; number of insured autos, end of the month; and average number of insured autos during the month. For part (c), your budget should have the following three rows: average number of cars insured during the month, average insurance premium per car per month, and total monthly premium revenue.

2. What additional real-life refinements do you envision for the budgets you prepared in requirement 1? What additional budgets would you anticipate preparing for the company if you were in charge of the budget-preparation process?

3. The budgets you prepared in requirement 1 can be referred to as *driver-based budgets*. List some of the pros and cons of such budgets, relative to traditional budgeting practices.

[LO 10-6] 10-57 **Budgets for a Service Firm**   Triple-F Health Club (Family, Fitness, and Fun) is a not-for-profit, family-oriented health club. The club's board of directors is developing plans to acquire more equipment and expand club facilities. The board plans to purchase about $25,000 of new equipment each year and wants to establish a fund to purchase the adjoining property in four or five years. The adjoining property has a market value of about $300,000.

The club manager, Jane Crowe, is concerned that the board has unrealistic goals in light of the club's recent financial performance. She has sought the help of a club member with an accounting background to assist her in preparing a report to the board supporting her concerns.

The member reviewed the club's records, including this cash-basis income statement:

TRIPLE-F HEALTH CLUB

Income Statement (Cash Basis)

For Years Ended October 31

	2023	2022
Cash revenues:		
Annual membership fees	$355,000	$300,000
Lesson and class fees	234,000	180,000
Miscellaneous	2,000	1,500
Total cash revenues	$591,000	$481,500
Cash expenses:		
Manager's salary and benefits	$36,000	$36,000
Regular employees' wages and benefits	190,000	190,000
Lesson and class employees' wages and benefits	195,000	150,000
Towels and supplies	16,000	15,500
Utilities (heat and light)	22,000	15,000
Mortgage interest	35,100	37,800
Miscellaneous	2,000	1,500
Total cash expenditures	$ 496.1	$ 445.8
Increase in cash	$ 94,900	$ 35,700

- Other financial information as of October 31, 2023:
  - Cash in checking account, $7,000.
  - Petty cash, $300.
  - Outstanding mortgage balance, $360,000.
  - Accounts payable arising from invoices for supplies and utilities that are unpaid as of October 31, 2023, and due in November 2023, $2,500.
- No other unpaid bills existed on October 31, 2023.
- The club purchased $25,000 worth of exercise equipment during the current fiscal year. Cash of $10,000 was paid on delivery, with the balance due on October 1. This amount had not been paid as of October 31, 2023. An additional $25,000 (cash) of equipment purchases is planned for the coming year.
- The club began operations in 2022 in rental quarters. In October 2022, it purchased its current property (land and building) for $600,000, paying $120,000 down and agreeing to pay $30,000 plus 9% interest annually on the unpaid loan balance each November 1, starting November 1, 2023.
- Membership rose 3% in 2023. The club has experienced approximately this same annual growth rate since it opened, and this rate is expected to continue in the future.
- Membership fees increased by 15% in 2023. The board has tentative plans to increase these fees by 10% in 2024.
- Lesson and class fees have not been increased for three years. The board policy is to encourage classes and lessons by keeping the fees low. The members have taken advantage of this policy, and the number of classes and lessons has increased significantly each year. The club expects the percentage growth experienced in 2023 to be repeated in 2024.
- Miscellaneous revenues are expected to grow at the same rate as in 2023.
- Operating expenses expected to increase:
  - Hourly wage rates and the manager's salary: 15%.
  - Towels and supplies, utilities, and miscellaneous expenses: 25%.

Required

1. Prepare a cash budget for 2024 for the Triple-F Health Club.
2. Identify any operating problems that this budget discloses for the Triple-F Health Club. Explain your answer.
3. Is Jane Crowe's concern that the board's goals are unrealistic justified? Explain your answer.

(CMA Adapted)

[LO 10-2, 10-4, 10-5, 10-6]

10-58 **Budgeting and Sustainability** Neat-and-Clean handles both commercial laundry and individual customer dry cleaning. The company's dry cleaning process involves emitting a pollutant into the air. In addition, the commercial laundry service produces sediments and other elements that must receive special treatment before disposal. David Duncan, Neat-and-Clean's owner, is concerned about the cost of dealing with increasingly stringent laws and environmental regulations. Recent legislation in the state requires Neat-and-Clean to reduce the amount of its air pollution emissions.

Variable processing costs per 5-pound batch of laundry for Neat-and-Clean are estimated as follows (on average):

Service	Selling Price	Materials (per pound of laundry)	Labor (per 5-lb. batch)	Electricity (per 5-lb. batch)	Budgeted Batches per Year*
Commercial	$25.00	$1.00/lb.	$4.00	$1.50	7,500
Individual	20.00	0.50/lb.	4.00	$1.00	3,000

*Business is relatively smooth throughout the year.

The materials that are currently being used for dry-cleaning purposes have an unfortunate effect: excessive emissions that can be considered toxic in nature. The company can switch to a more environmentally friendly cleaning compound, which is currently selling at a price equal to $2.25 per pound of laundry. (For simplicity, assume that this cost applies to both commercial and individual laundry.) The owner is hesitant to switch over to the new cleaning compound because of the increase in processing cost per load of laundry. At the same time, he is acutely aware that in a neighboring town, a competitor business was subjected to a $60,000 fine by the relevant state authority. As such, Duncan is concerned that if he doesn't switch to the new compound, his business may be subject to a similar fine.

Required

1. Based solely on the data provided above, does it make financial sense for Duncan to switch to the more environmentally friendly cleaning compound? (Assume for this question that other costs are unaffected by this decision. Also, assume a one-year planning horizon.)

2. Independent of your answer to requirement 1, assume that Duncan "wants to do the right thing," for both his employees and the environment. As such, he chooses to switch to the new cleaning compound. The seller of this compound has suggested that, consistent with continuous-improvement (kaizen) budgeting, it may be possible to reduce both labor costs and electricity costs by 1% per month, starting with month 1 in a 12-month planning horizon. How close to being indifferent between incurring the fine and incurring the increased processing costs would Neat-and-Clean be after one year? (Show calculations.)

3. Use Goal Seek in Excel to answer each of the following questions, independently:

   a. What is the monthly cost-reduction rate (%) that would equate the net increase in year 1 processing costs with the amount of the anticipated fine ($60,000)?

   b. What is the cost per pound for the new compound that would equate the anticipated fine ($60,000) with year 1 processing costs, assuming no kaizen budgeting plan (i.e., no reduction in the labor and electricity processing costs over time)? What conclusion can you draw based on this analysis?

4. What options (i.e., operational changes) secure the cost savings referenced in requirement 2?

5. What other considerations (strategic and operational) might affect the ultimate decision by David Duncan?

[LO 10-8] 10-59 **Ethics in Budgeting/Budgetary Slack** Norton Company, a manufacturer of infant furniture and carriages, is in the initial stages of preparing the annual budget for the coming year. Scott Ford recently joined Norton's accounting staff and is interested in learning as much as possible about the company's budgeting process. During a recent lunch with Marge Atkins, sales manager, and Pete Granger, production manager, Scott initiated the following conversation:

Scott: Because I'm new around here and am going to be involved with the preparation of the annual budget, I'd be interested to learn how the two of you estimate sales and production numbers.

Marge: We start out very methodically by looking at recent history, discussing what we know about current accounts, potential customers, and the general state of consumer spending. Then, we add that usual dose of intuition to come up with the best forecast we can.

Pete: I usually take the sales projections as the basis for my projections. Of course, we have to make an estimate of what this year's closing inventories will be, and that sometimes is difficult.

Scott: Why does that present a problem? There must have been an estimate of closing inventories in the budget for the current year.

Pete: Those numbers aren't always reliable because Marge makes some adjustments to the sales numbers before passing them on to me.

Scott: What kind of adjustments?

Marge: Well, we don't want to fall short of our sales projections, so we generally give ourselves a little breathing room by lowering the initial sales projection anywhere from 5 to 10%.

Pete: So you can see why this year's budget is not a very reliable starting point. We always have to adjust the projected production rates as the year progresses, and, of course, this changes the ending inventory estimates. By the way, we make similar adjustments to expenses by adding at least 10% to the estimates; I think everyone around here does the same thing.

Required

1. Marge Atkins and Pete Granger have described the use of *budgetary slack.*

   a. Explain why Marge and Pete might behave in this manner, and describe the benefits they expect to realize from the use of budgetary slack.

   b. Explain how the use of budgetary slack can adversely affect Marge and Pete personally, and the organization as a whole.

2. As a management accountant, Scott Ford believes that the behavior described by Marge and Pete may be unethical and that he may have an obligation not to support this behavior. By citing the specific standards from the IMA's *Statement of Ethical Professional Practice* (**www.imanet.org/career-resources/ethics-center**, explain why the use of budgetary slack may be unethical.

(CMA Adapted)

[LO 10-2, 10-8]   10-60   **Criticisms of Traditional Budgeting/Incentive Issues**   As noted in the chapter, some individuals allege that the practice of tying managerial rewards to budgeted performance has dysfunctional consequences, including (but not limited to) gaming behavior. Search the Internet and pertinent literature (e.g., Michael C. Jensen, "Corporate Budgeting Is Broken—Let's Fix It," *Harvard Business Review,* November 2001, pp. 94–101) to further explore the issue of negative incentive effects associated with traditional budgeting practices. What alternatives are suggested to correct these negative consequences?

Solutions to Self-Study Problems

1. Master Budget

HANSELL COMPANY
a.   Sales Budget for July 2022

Budgeted sales in units	6,000
Budgeted selling price per unit	×$ 80
Budgeted sales	$480,000

HANSELL COMPANY
b.   Production Budget (in units) for July 2022

Budgeted sales for July 2022	6,000
Plus: Desired ending inventory (July 31)	
(The higher of 500 or 7,000 × 0.1)	+ 700
Total units needed for July 2022	6,700
Less: Beginning inventory (July 1)	
(The higher of 500 or 6,000 × 0.1)	− 600
	6,100

HANSELL COMPANY
c.   Production Budget (in units) for August 2022

Desired ending inventory (the higher of 500 and 8,000 × 0.1)	800
Budgeted sales	+ 7,000
Total units needed	7,800
Beginning inventory (August 1)	− 700
Units to manufacture in August	7,100

HANSELL COMPANY
d.   Direct Materials Purchases Budget (in pounds) for July 2022

	Direct Materials	
	Dura-1000 (4 lb. each)	Flexplas (2 lb. each)
Total direct materials needed for budgeted production (6,100 units of Duraflex)	24,400	12,200
Add: Desired direct materials ending inventory (lower of 1,000 or 5% of August production needs)	+ 1,000	+ 710
Total direct materials requirements	25,400	12,910
Less: Direct materials beginning inventory (lower of 1,000 or 5% of July's needs)	− 1,000	− 610
Direct materials to be purchased (in lbs.)	24,400	12,300

HANSELL COMPANY
e.   **Direct Materials Purchases Budget (in dollars) for July 2022**

	Budgeted Purchases (lbs.)	Expected Purchase Price per lb.	Total
Dura-1000	24,400	$1.25	$30,500
Flexplas	12,300	5.00	61,500
Budgeted purchases			$92,000

HANSELL COMPANY
f.   **Direct Manufacturing Labor Budget for July 2022**

Direct Labor Class	Direct Labor Hours per Batch	Number of Batches	Total Hours	Rate per Hour	Total
K102	1	61*	61	$50	$ 3,050
K175	10	61*	610	20	12,200
Total			671		$15,250

*No. of units ÷ 100 units/batch = 6,100/100 = 61 batches.

2. Cash Budget and Budgeted Income Statement

HANSELL COMPANY
Cash Budget for July 2022

Cash balance, beginning (given)		$40,000
Cash flow from operations:		
July cash sales	$480,000 × 20% = $ 96,000	
Collections of receivables from credit sales in June:		
Within the discount period	(5,500 × $80) × 80% × 60% × 98% = $206,976	
After the discount period	(5,500 × $80) × 80% × 25% = 88,000	
Collections of receivables from credit sales in May	(5,400 × $80) × 80% × 10% = 34,560	425,536
Cash disbursements:		
Materials purchases:		
June purchases	($25,000 + $22,000) × 20% × 98% = $ 9,212	
July purchases	$92,000 × 80% × 98% = 72,128	81,340
Direct manufacturing labor		15,250
Variable factory overhead	($1,200 × 61) + ($80 × 671) =	126,880
Fixed factory overhead	$50,000 − $20,000 =	30,000
Variable marketing, customer services, and administrative expenses	[($2,400,000 − $1,200,000) ÷ $4,000,000] × $480,000 =	144,000
Fixed marketing, customer services, and administrative expenses	($1,200,000 − $120,000) ÷ 12 =	90,000
Total cash flow from operations		$(61,934)
Investing activities:		
Purchases of investments and other long-term assets	$ 0	
Sales of investments and other long-term assets	$ 0	0
Financing activities:		
Repayment of existing debt, end of month	$ 0	
Interest payments, end of month	0	
New borrowing, end of month	$ 62,000	$ 62,000
Cash balance, July 31, 2022		$ 40,066

HANSELL COMPANY
Budgeted Income Statement for July 2022

Sales			$480,000
Cost of goods sold, LIFO basis*	$46.50 × 6,000 =		279,000
Gross margin			$201,000
Selling and administrative expenses:			
Variable (see cash budget, above)		$144,000	
Fixed	$1,200,000 ÷ 12 =	100,000	244,000
Operating income (loss) before tax			$ (43,000)
Direct materials:			
Dura-1000	4 lbs. × $1.25/lb. =	$ 40.00	
Flexplas	2 lbs. × $5.00/lb. =	10.00	$ 15.00
Direct labor:			
K102 labor	0.01 hour (i.e., 1 hr./100 units) × $50/hr. =	$ 0.50	
K175 labor	0.1 hour (given) × $20/hr. =	2.00	2.50
Factory overhead:			
Batch-related	(61 batches × $1,200/batch)/6,100 units =	$12.00	
Direct-labor hour-related	($80/direct labor hour ×		
	671 hours)/6,100 units =	8.80	
Fixed	($50,000/6,100 units) =	8.20	29.00
Cost per unit, July			$ 46.50

*Actual manufacturing cost per unit, July.

Please visit Connect to access a narrated, animated tutorial for solving this problem.

CHAPTER ELEVEN

Decision Making with a Strategic Emphasis

After studying this chapter, you should be able to . . .

LO 11-1 Define the decision-making process and identify the types of cost information relevant for decision making.

LO 11-2 Use relevant cost analysis and strategic analysis to make special-order decisions.

LO 11-3 Use relevant cost analysis and strategic analysis in the make-vs.-buy and lease-vs.-buy decisions.

LO 11-4 Use relevant cost analysis and strategic analysis in the decision to sell before or after additional processing.

LO 11-5 Use relevant cost analysis and strategic analysis in the decision to keep or drop products or services.

LO 11-6 Use relevant cost analysis and strategic analysis to evaluate service offerings of not-for-profit organizations.

LO 11-7 Use relevant cost analysis and strategic analysis to perform a constrained optimization (i.e., short-term product-mix) analysis.

LO 11-8 Discuss behavioral, implementation, ethical, and legal issues in decision making.

LO 11-9 Set up and solve in Excel a simple product-mix problem (appendix).

Alexey Boldin/Shutterstock

Apple Inc. produces a diverse, and expanding, set of technology-based products, including iPhones, computers (MacBook, MacBook Air, etc.), iPads, the Apple Watch, and a complement of software offerings (iOS, iWork, iLife, etc.). In the past, Apple has purchased many product components (e.g., semiconductors) from external suppliers such as Imagination Technologies Group, Synaptics Inc., and Cirrus Logic Inc. Recently, however, Apple has decided to make many of these components internally. (See Alex Webb and Ian King, "The Life of an Apple Supplier Is Getting Even Tougher," *Bloomberg,* April 19, 2017, **www.bloomberg.com/news/articles/2017-04-19/the-life-of-an-apple-supplier-is-getting-even-tougher.**)

How does Apple evaluate whether it is better to make or to buy the high-tech components in its products? A full analysis would consider the relevant costs of each of these two decision alternatives. In Apple's case, it would compare supplier costs to internal costs, the majority of which relate to increased research and development (R&D) spending and investment in more sophisticated manufacturing systems to accommodate an expanded product line. Apple would also likely consider the decreased leverage it has over supplier prices because of consolidation in the industry. (Greater competition in the supplier industry would give Apple greater leverage in terms of prices it secures for product components.) Ultimately, however, the company would also have to consider strategic factors associated with its make-vs.-buy decisions. For example, one important issue is the economic nationalism appearing in many countries, which has caused companies to consider reducing the outsourcing of production. In late 2016, Apple indicated it would look into the possibility of bringing some manufacturing back to the United States. Apple now does virtually none of its manufacturing in the U.S. but, instead, relies on production in Asia. Apple would also likely evaluate whether domestic or in-house production would make it easier for Apple to link software and hardware components. On the other hand, producing products in-house exposes Apple to what we might call *innovation risk* (smaller, focused suppliers may be more innovative in terms of producing specialty components). Accounting can play a major role in helping to inform managerial decisions, such as the Apple-related make-vs.-buy decision illustrated here.

This chapter provides a general framework for effective managerial decision making. The framework has two key elements: relevant cost analysis and strategic analysis. In this chapter, we will apply the decision-making framework to a variety of common decisions facing management. These examples are important because they illustrate in concrete terms how accounting can add organizational value.

The Five Steps of the Decision-Making Process

LO 11-1

Define the decision-making process and identify the types of cost information relevant for decision making.

In deciding among alternatives for a given situation, managers employ the five-step process outlined in Exhibit 11.1. The first step is to consider the organization's business environment and competitive strategy. This helps the decision maker focus on the right question. Strategic thinking is important to avoid decisions that might be best only in the short term. For example, a plant manager might incorrectly view the choice as being between whether to make or buy a part for a manufactured product when the correct decision might be to determine whether the product should be redesigned so the part is no longer needed.

The manager's second step is to specify the criteria—both quantitative and qualitative—by which the decision is to be made and to identify the alternative actions. Most often, the manager's principal objective is an easily quantified, short-term, achievable goal, such as to reduce cost, improve profit, reduce error rates, improve customer satisfaction, or maximize return on investment. In short, a manager most often is forced to think of multiple objectives, both the quantifiable, short-term goals and the more strategic, difficult-to-quantify goals.

In the third step, a manager performs an analysis in which decision-relevant information is developed and analyzed, using relevant cost analysis and strategic analysis. This step involves three sequential activities. The manager (1) identifies and collects relevant information about the decision, (2) makes predictions about the relevant information, and (3) considers the strategic issues involved in the decision.

Fourth, based on the relevant cost analysis and strategic analysis, the manager selects the best decision alternative and implements it. In the fifth and final step, the manager evaluates

EXHIBIT 11.1 **Five Steps in the Decision-Making Process**

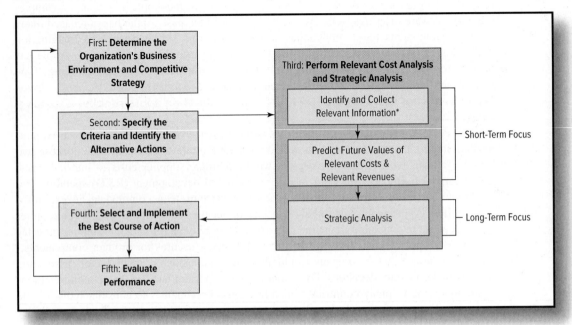

*Relevant information includes both quantitative (including financial) information as well as qualitative information.

the performance of the implemented decision as a basis for feedback to a possible recon-
sideration of this decision as it relates to future decisions. The decision process is thus a
feedback-based system in which the manager continually evaluates the results of prior analyses and decisions to discover any opportunities for improvement in decision making.

Relevant Cost Analysis

Relevant Cost Information

relevant cost
A future cost that differs between
and among decision alternatives;
an avoidable cost.

Relevant costs are future costs that differ between and among decision alternatives. A cost
that has been incurred in the past or is already committed for the future is not relevant; it is a
sunk cost because it will be the same whichever option is chosen. Similarly, costs that have
not been incurred but that would be the same whichever option is chosen are not relevant. In
effect, for a cost to be relevant, it must be a *cost that will be incurred in the future and will
differ between and among the decision maker's options.*

sunk costs
Costs that have been incurred
in the past or committed for
the future and are therefore
irrelevant for decision-making
purposes.

For example, consider the decision to purchase a new automobile to replace an existing
automobile. The purchase price of the new auto is relevant, while the price paid previously for the existing auto is irrelevant—you can't change that. Similarly, the cost of your
auto club membership, which will not change whichever car you choose, is irrelevant. This
would be true also for licenses and fees that would be the same regardless of the car you
select. Suppose further that you have narrowed your choice to two vehicles, and the dealer
for one is located some distance away, while the other dealer is nearby. The costs of travel
to the different dealers are irrelevant; they are "sunk" at the time the decision is made to
travel to both dealers. Various costs associated with the automobile purchase decision are
summarized in Exhibit 11.2.

A relevant cost can be either variable or fixed. Generally, variable costs are relevant
for decision making because they differ for each decision alternative and have not been
committed. In contrast, fixed costs often are irrelevant because typically they do not differ
between or across the decision alternatives. As indicated by the discussion below, the key
determinant is whether a given cost is both future and differential in terms of the decision
alternative(s).

EXHIBIT 11.2
Relevant and Irrelevant Costs: The Automobile Purchase Decision

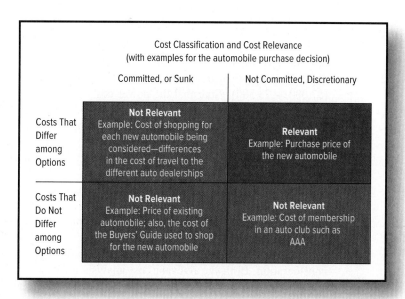

Occasionally, some variable costs are not relevant. For example, assume that a manager is considering whether to replace or repair an old machine. If the electrical power requirements of the new and old machines are the same, the variable cost of power is not relevant. On the other hand, fixed costs can be relevant. For example, if the new machine requires significant modifications to the plant building, the modification costs (which are fixed costs) are relevant because these costs have not yet been committed and they are associated with only one of the two decision alternatives.

To illustrate, assume a machine was purchased for $4,200 a year ago. This machine is to be depreciated over two years at $2,100 per year, and it has no trade-in or disposal value either currently or one year from now. At the end of the first year, the machine has a net book value of $2,100 ($4,200 − $2,100), but the machine needs to be repaired or replaced. Assume that the purchase price of a new machine is $7,000 and that this new machine is expected to last for one year with little or no expected trade-in or disposal value at the end of the year. The repair of the old machine would cost $3,500 and would be sufficient for another year of productive use. The power for either machine is expected to cost $2.50 per hour. The new machine is semiautomated, requiring a less-skilled operator and resulting in a reduction of average labor costs from $10.00 to $9.50 per hour for the new machine. If the firm is expected to operate at a 2,000-hour level of output for the next year, the total variable costs for power will be $2,000 × $2.50 = $5,000 for either machine, and labor costs will be $19,000 ($9.50 × 2,000) and $20,000 ($10 × 2,000) for the new and old machines, respectively.

Data for Machine-Replacement Example

Old machine:

Level of output	2,000 hours per year
Current net book value (NBV)	$2,100
Useful life (if repaired)	1 year
Disposal value (both current and one year from now)	$0
Operating cost (labor)	$10 per hour
Repair cost	$3,500

New machine:

Level of output	2,000 hours per year
Purchase price	$7,000
Useful life	1 year
Disposal value (one year from now)	$0
Operating cost (labor)	$9.50 per hour

The summary of relevant costs for this decision (see Exhibit 11.3) shows a $2,500 advantage for repairing the old machine. The projected $1,000 decrease in labor costs for the new machine is less than the projected $3,500 difference of replacement cost over repair cost ($7,000 − $3,500). Note that the power costs and the depreciation on the old machine are omitted because they are not relevant; they do not differ between the decision alternatives: repair vs. replace. As indicated by the last column of information in Exhibit 11.3, this type of report is sometimes referred to as a *differential cost analysis*. Finally, note that the ultimate decision will also be affected by relevant nonfinancial information, including qualitative factors (e.g., reliability and quality considerations).

To show that the analysis based on total costs provides the same answer, Exhibit 11.4 shows the analysis for total costs associated with each decision alternative. Under this approach, we include all costs whether relevant or not. Thus, the Total Costs columns in Exhibit 11.4 include both power costs and the depreciation expense associated with the old machine, neither of which are relevant costs to the equipment-replacement decision under consideration. Both the relevant cost analysis reflected in Exhibit 11.3 and the total cost analysis in Exhibit 11.4 lead to the same decision. Which approach is used is largely a matter of personal preference.

Batch-Level Cost Drivers

The preceding analysis includes the fixed cost associated with the purchase or repair of the machine but does not include the fixed cost of labor for machine setup. (Recall that under conventional accounting systems, set-up labor would likely be included as part of overhead cost and applied to products based on a volume-based cost-driver, such as number of units produced). Setup cost is, however, a batch-level cost that varies with the number of batches

EXHIBIT 11.3
Relevant Cost Analysis: Equipment-Replacement Decision

	Relevant Costs		Difference
	Repair	Replace	Replace Minus Repair
Variable costs:			
Labor (2,000 × $10, $9.50)	$20,000	$19,000	$(1,000)
Fixed costs:			
Old machine repair cost	3,500		(3,500)
Cost of new machine		7,000	7,000
Total costs	$23,500	$26,000	$ 2,500

The decision regarding whether a homeowner should install solar power, from a purely financial standpoint, is how quickly the proposed system will pay for itself. The short answer to this question is that it depends on where the homeowner lives. Specific factors that affect the financial viability of an investment in solar power include the following: available purchase subsidies (principally, tax credits at the federal, state, and local levels and rebates from states and public utilities), homeowner location (i.e., how much "sun power" is available), local utility rates (i.e., cost per kilowatt-hour of electricity), installation details (optimum is south-facing roof, tilted at 30 degrees), and projected power consumption (i.e.,

kilowatt-hours per year). In addition, to take full advantage of federal tax credits, the homeowner's tax bill in the year of purchase must be bigger than the credit. The source cited below contains a five-city comparison (Brooklyn, NY; Denver, CO; Los Angeles, CA; Minneapolis, MN; and Portland, OR) of payback period for a hypothetical system and assumed values of the factors cited in this section. An online calculator is available at **www.solar-estimate.org/?page=solar-estimate-notes**, **www.solarenergy.org/solar-calculator.**

Source: Yuliya Chernova, "The Economics of Installing Solar: Figuring Out Whether You Save Money Depends on a Lot of Factors—Especially Where You Live," *The Wall Street Journal,* September 17, 2012, p. R6.

EXHIBIT 11.4
Total Cost Analysis: Equipment-Replacement Decision

	Total Costs		Difference
	Repair	**Replace**	**Replace Minus Repair**
Variable costs:			
Labor	$20,000	$19,000	$(1,000)
Power	5,000	5,000	0
Fixed costs:			
Old machine:			
Depreciation	2,100	2,100	0
Repair cost	3,500		(3,500)
Cost of new machine		7,000	7,000
Total costs	$30,600	$33,100	$ 2,500

and not the units or hours of output on the machine. Suppose that there will be 120 setups done during the year, irrespective of whether the machine is replaced or repaired. This sounds irrelevant because the number of setups remains the same. But suppose further that because the automated machine is easier to set up, it takes only one hour to set up the new machine, while the old machine takes four hours to set up. Also, assume that the automated machine requires less-skilled setup labor so that the $9.50-per-hour labor rate applies and the firm uses only the needed setup labor; there is no unused capacity in setup labor. The machine-replacement analysis should also include the differential setup time and cost as follows:

Setup Costs for New Machine	Setup Costs for Old Machine
$9.50 per hour for labor	$10 per hour for labor
× 120 setups per year	× 120 setups per year
× 1 hour per setup	× 4 hours per setup
= $1,140 per year	= $4,800 per year

The new machine saves $3,660 ($4,800 − $1,140) in setup labor as well as $1,000 in direct labor. The total labor savings is, therefore, $4,660 ($3,660 + $1,000). This more than offsets the excess of the cost of the new machine over the cost of repair, $3,500 ($7,000 − $3,500), for a $1,160 ($4,660 − $3,500) net financial benefit of replacing the machine. See the revised analysis in Exhibit 11.5.

EXHIBIT 11.5
Relevant Cost Analysis:
Equipment-Replacement
Decision (including
consideration of setup costs)

	Relevant Costs		Difference
	Repair	Replace	Replace Minus Repair
Variable costs:			
Machine run-time labor	$20,000	$19,000	$(1,000)
Batch-level costs:			
Setup labor cost	4,800	1,140	(3,660)
Fixed costs:			
Old machine repair cost	3,500		(3,500)
Cost of new machine		7,000	7,000
Total costs	$28,300	$27,140	$(1,160)

Depreciation Expense: Relevant or Not?

Depreciation expense is an allocation of a cost already incurred. That is, it represents an allocation of a past cost over the life of the asset purchased. As such, it is not relevant for decision making. There is an exception to this rule: when tax effects are considered in decision making. In this context, depreciation has a positive value in that, as an expense, it reduces taxable income and, therefore, tax expense. If taxes are considered, depreciation has a role to the extent that it reduces tax liability. The decision maker often must consider the impact of local, state, federal, and (sometimes) international tax differences on the decision situation.

> "Intelligent people make decisions based on opportunity costs."
>
> *Charlie Munger, investor, businessperson, and philanthropist*

Other Relevant Information

opportunity cost
The benefit lost when choosing one option precludes receiving the benefits from an alternative option.

Managers should include in their decision process information such as the capacity usage of the plant. Capacity usage information is a critical signal of the potential relevance of **opportunity costs**—that is, the benefit lost when one chosen option precludes the benefits from an alternative option. When the plant is operating at full capacity, opportunity costs are an important consideration because the decision to produce a special order or add a new product line can cause the reduction, delay, or loss of sales of products and services currently offered. By definition, opportunity costs are always relevant and therefore should be included in the decision-making process.

Another important factor is the *time value of money,* which is relevant when deciding among alternatives with cash flows over an extended period of time (e.g., two or more years). These decisions are best handled by the methods described in Chapter 12.

Qualitative factors, such as differences in quality, functionality, timeliness of delivery, reliability in shipping, and service after the sale, can also strongly influence a manager's final decision and should be considered in addition to the analysis of relevant costs. This demonstrates the point that relevant information for decision making includes both financial and nonfinancial information and, as discussed below, strategic considerations as well.

Strategic Analysis

> "The task of management is not to apply a formula but to decide issues on a case-by-case basis. No fixed, inflexible rule can ever be substituted for the exercise of sound business judgment in the decision-making process."
>
> *Alfred P. Sloan, early president and CEO of General Motors*

Alfred Sloan had an important role in developing many of the financial management tools we use today, including relevant cost analysis and strategic analysis. Sloan knew that an inflexible

EXHIBIT 11.6
Relevant Cost Analysis vs. Strategic Cost Analysis

Relevant Cost Analysis	Strategic Cost Analysis
Short-term focus	Long-term focus
Not necessarily linked to strategy	Linked to the firm's strategy
Product-cost focus	Customer focus
Focused on individual product or decision situation	Integrative; considers all customer-related factors

"run the numbers" approach would not necessarily lead to good decisions. Instead, he used a consideration of the business and competitive context of the decision, together with the use of relevant costs, which we call *strategic cost analysis.* A consideration of the business and competitive context of the decision, together with an understanding of the firm's strategy and the relevant costs, ensures that each decision will help advance the firm's strategy, performance, and success.

To illustrate, a strategic decision to design the manufacturing process for high efficiency to produce large batches of product reduces overall production costs. At the same time, this decision might reduce the firm's flexibility to manufacture a variety of products and thus could increase the cost to produce small, specialized orders. The decision regarding cost efficiency cannot be separated from the determination of marketing strategy—that is, deciding what types and sizes of orders can be accepted.

As another example, the decision to buy rather than to make a part for the firm's product might make sense on the basis of a relevant cost analysis but be a poor strategic move if the firm's competitive position depends on product reliability that can be maintained only by manufacturing the part in-house. A good indication of a manager's failure to take a strategic approach is that the analysis will have a product-cost focus, while a strategic cost analysis also addresses broad and difficult-to-measure strategic issues. The strategic analysis directly focuses on adding value to the customer, going beyond only cost issues. (See Exhibit 11.6.)

We now consider the application of the relevant cost analysis and strategic cost analysis decision framework to the following decisions that managers often deal with: (1) the special-order decision, (2) make-vs.-buy (or lease-vs.-purchase) decisions, (3) the decision to sell before or after additional processing, (4) the decision of whether to keep or drop a product (or service) line, and (5) the determination of an optimum short-term product (or service) mix (also referred to as "constrained optimization analysis").

Special-Order Decisions

Relevant Cost Analysis

LO 11-2

Use relevant cost analysis and strategic analysis to make special-order decisions.

A special-order decision occurs when a firm has a one-time opportunity to sell a specified quantity of its product or service. The order frequently comes directly from the customer rather than through normal sales or distribution channels. Special-order decisions are infrequent and commonly represent a small part of a firm's overall business.

To make the special-order decision, managers begin with a relevant cost analysis for the special sales order. To illustrate, consider the special-order situation facing Tommy T-Shirt Inc. (TTS). TTS is a small manufacturer of specialty clothing, primarily T-shirts and sweatshirts with imprinted slogans and brand names. TTS has been offered a contract by the business honor society Alpha Beta Gamma (ABG) for 1,000 T-shirts printed with artwork publicizing a fund-raising event. ABG offers to pay $6.50 for each shirt. TTS normally charges $9.00 for shirts of this type and for this size order.

TTS's budgeted manufacturing costs for the current year are given in Exhibit 11.7. The budget is based on expected production of 200,000 T-shirts from an available capacity of 250,000. The 200,000 units are expected to be produced in 200 batches of 1,000 units each. The three groups of cost elements are as follows:

1. *Unit-level costs* vary with each shirt printed and include the cost of the shirt ($3.25 each), ink ($0.95 each), and labor ($0.85 each), for a total of $5.05 per unit.

EXHIBIT 11.7
Budget for TTS's
Manufacturing Costs:
Expected Output of 200,000
Units in 200 Batches

Cost Element	Variable Cost per Unit	Batch-Level Costs Per Batch	Batch-Level Costs Fixed Costs	Facility-Level Costs (all fixed)
Shirt	$3.25			
Ink	0.95			
Labor	0.85			
Subtotal	$5.05			
Setup		$130	$29,000	
Inspection		30	9,000	
Materials handling		40	7,000	
Subtotal		$200	$45,000	
Machine-related				$315,000
Other				90,000
Total	$5.05	$200	$45,000	$405,000

2. *Batch-level costs* vary, in part, with the number of batches produced. Batch-level costs include machine setup, inspection, and materials handling. These costs are partly variable (change with the number of batches) and partly fixed. For example, setup costs are $130 per setup ($26,000 for 200 setups) plus $29,000 fixed costs that do not change with the number of setups (e.g., setup tools or software). Setup costs for 200 batches total $55,000 ($26,000 + $29,000). Similarly, inspection costs are $30 per batch plus $9,000 fixed costs—$15,000 total [($30 × 200) + $9,000]. Materials handling costs are $40 per batch plus $7,000 fixed costs—$15,000 total [($40 × 200) + $7,000].

3. *Facility-level costs* are fixed (in the short run) and do not vary either with the number of units or the number of batches produced. These costs include depreciation and insurance on machinery ($315,000) and other fixed costs ($90,000), for a total of $405,000. Total fixed cost is the sum of fixed batch-level costs ($45,000) and fixed facility-level costs ($405,000), or $450,000.

The total cost-estimation equation for TTS for the year is:

$$\text{Total cost} = \$5.05 \text{ per unit} + \$200 \text{ per batch} + \$450,000$$

The question before TTS is whether it should accept or reject the order from ABG. This order requires the same unprinted T-shirt, ink, and labor time as other shirts, for a total of $5.05 per unit. In addition, the order from ABG will require $200 ($130 + $30 + $40) of incremental batch-level costs ($200 per batch ÷ 1,000 units per batch = $0.20 per unit). Thus, as reflected in Exhibit 11.8, the relevant cost of the special order is $5.25 per unit.

EXHIBIT 11.8
Relevant Cost Analysis of the
Special-Order Decision
Facing TTS

	Relevant Unit Costs	Relevant Cost for One Batch of 1,000 Units
Unit-level (i.e., variable) costs:		
Shirt	$3.25	$3,250
Ink	0.95	950
Labor	0.85	850
Total unit-level costs	$5.05	$5,050
Batch-level costs (that vary with the number of batches):		
Setup		130
Inspection		30
Materials handling		40
Total	$0.20	$ 200
Total relevant costs	$5.25	$5,250

To examine the short-term financial impact of accepting the order from ABG, we compare the relevant cost of $5.25 per unit to the offering price of $6.50 per unit. By accepting the order, TTS's operating income would increase by $1,250 (i.e., 1,000 units × $1.25 per unit). Thus, from a short-term financial perspective, it would be advantageous for the company to accept a selling price ($6.50 per unit) that is lower than its normal selling price ($9.00 per unit) for the special order. This conclusion assumes that the accountant has identified all relevant costs. For example, in this case, there may be an additional cost to design and/or apply the special logo requested by ABG, which would raise the per-unit relevant cost above $5.25.

Strategic Analysis

The preceding relevant cost analysis developed for TTS provides useful information regarding the short-term financial effect of the special sales order. At this point, it seems as if TTS should accept the special order because the order has a positive effect on operating income. But, before a decision is made, additional factors must be considered. At a minimum, TTS also should consider the strategic factors of capacity utilization and short-term versus long-term pricing.

Is TTS Operating at Full Capacity?

TTS currently has 50,000 units of excess capacity, more than enough to process the ABG order. But what if TTS were operating at or near full capacity: Would accepting the order cause the loss of other, possibly more profitable, sales? If so, TTS must consider the opportunity cost arising from the lost sales. Assume that TTS is operating at 250,000 units and 250 batches of activity and that accepting the ABG order would cause the loss of sales of other T-shirts that have a contribution margin per unit of $3.75 ($9.00 − $5.25). The opportunity cost is, therefore, $3.75 per shirt, and the proper short-term financial analysis is as follows:

Contribution from ABG order	$ 1,250
Less: Opportunity cost—lost sales (1,000 units × $3.75)	(3,750)
Net contribution (loss) for the order	$(2,500)

Exhibit 11.9 shows the short-term profit effect of accepting the ABG order: At full capacity, the order would (due to lost sales) reduce operating income by $2,500.

Note, too, that we can define the relevant cost of the special order as the sum of out-of-pocket costs ($5,250) plus the opportunity cost of lost business ($3,750), or a total of $9,000. Revenue from the special order is $6,500. Thus, by accepting the order, short-term operating income decreases by $2,500.

EXHIBIT 11.9
Special-Order Decision for TTS under Full Capacity

	With ABG Order	Without ABG Order
Sales:		
250,000 units at $9.00 per unit		$2,250,000
249,000 units at $9.00 per unit; 1,000 units at $6.50 per unit	$2,247,500	
Variable costs, at $5.25 per unit	1,312,500	1,312,500
Contribution margin	$ 935,000	$ 937,500
Fixed costs	450,000	450,000
Operating income	$ 485,000	$ 487,500
Net effect on short-term operating income		$ (2,500)

Excessive Relevant Cost Pricing

The relevant cost decision rule for special orders discussed earlier must be used with caution. Done on a regular basis, relevant cost pricing can erode normal pricing policies and lead to a loss in long-term profitability for firms such as TTS. The failure of some large companies in the airline, auto, and steel industries has been attributed in part to their excessive relevant cost pricing because a strategy of continually focusing on the short term can deny a company a successful long term. Special-order pricing decisions should not become the centerpiece of a firm's strategy.

Other Important Strategic Factors

In addition to capacity utilization and long-term pricing issues, TTS should consider qualitative factors, such as ABG's credit history, any potential complexities in the design that might cause production problems, and other issues such as whether the sale might lead to additional sales of other TTS products. TTS, before accepting the order, might also evaluate the likely impact of the sale on the ability of the company to maintain its pricing structure with existing customers. Finally, TTS should determine whether packaging, delivery, and selling costs (e.g., sales commissions) will differ for regular versus special sales orders.

Value Stream Accounting and the Special-Order Decision

value stream
A group of related products; useful for preparing profitability reports as part of lean accounting; all the activities required to create customer value for a family of products or services.

When using lean accounting (see Chapter 17 for more information on this topic), the management accountant puts families of products together in what is called a **value stream,** which consists of all the activities required to create customer value for that family of products or services. An example of a product family for a consumer electronics firm would be its group of DVD players, while another family of products would be its digital televisions. An example for a service firm, a bank, would be value streams for installment loans, mortgage loans, and commercial loans. When using lean accounting, special orders are evaluated within the context of the value stream in which they are located, so the analysis of costs includes relevant costs throughout the value stream and the strategic analysis is for the entire family of products in the value stream.

Make-vs.-Buy and Lease-vs.-Buy Decisions

Relevant Cost Analysis

LO 11-3

Use relevant cost analysis and strategic analysis in the make-vs.-buy and lease-vs.-buy decisions.

Make-vs.-Buy Decision

Generally, a firm's products are manufactured according to specifications set forth in what is called the *bill of materials,* which is a detailed list of the components of the manufactured product. (A bill of materials for the manufacture of furniture is illustrated in Chapter 4.) As illustrated by the discussion regarding Apple at the start of this chapter, an increasingly common decision for manufacturers is to choose which of the components of its product to manufacture in the firm's plant and which to purchase from outside suppliers. We refer to this as the make-vs.-buy decision.

The relevant cost information for the make-vs.-buy decision is developed in a manner similar to that of the special-order decision. The relevant cost of making the component consists of all avoidable costs (i.e., the costs that would be saved if the part were purchased). These costs are compared with the external purchase price for the part or component to determine the short-term financial consequence of making versus buying the part.

For example, consider Blue Tone Manufacturing, maker of clarinets and other reed-based musical instruments. Suppose that Blue Tone is currently manufacturing the mouthpiece for its clarinet but has the option to buy this piece from a supplier. The mouthpiece is plastic, while the remainder of the clarinet is made from wood. The following cost information assumes that fixed overhead costs will not change whether Blue Tone chooses to make or buy the mouthpiece (i.e., these costs are considered unavoidable):

Cost to buy the mouthpiece, per unit		$24.00
Cost to manufacture, per unit:		
Direct materials	$16.00	
Direct labor	4.50	
Variable overhead	1.00	
Total variable costs	$21.50	
Fixed overhead	6.00	
Total costs	$27.50	
Total relevant costs, per unit		$21.50
Per-unit savings from continuing to make		$ 2.50

In this example, while the total manufacturing cost is $27.50 per unit, the relevant per-unit cost to make the piece is $21.50. The fixed overhead cost ($6.00 on a per-unit basis) is not relevant to this decision as long as we assume that, in total, this cost is unavoidable (i.e., in the short run, this cost will not change in total regardless of the decision to make or buy).

The next step is for Blue Tone to complete a strategic analysis that considers, for example, the quality of the part, the reliability of the supplier, and the potential alternative uses of Blue Tone's plant capacity. With the combined cost and strategic analysis, Blue Tone is prepared to make the decision.

Lease-vs.-Purchase (Buy) Decision

A similar situation arises when a firm must choose between leasing or purchasing (i.e., buying) a piece of equipment. Such decisions are becoming ever-more frequent as the cost and terms of leasing arrangements continue to become more favorable.

To illustrate the lease-vs.-buy decision, we use the example of Quick Copy Inc., a firm that provides printing and duplicating services and other related business services. Quick Copy uses one large copy machine to complete most big jobs. It leases the machine from the manufacturer on an annual basis that includes general servicing. The annual lease includes both a fixed fee of $40,000 and a per-copy charge of $0.02.

The copier manufacturer has suggested that Quick Copy upgrade to the latest model copier that is not available for lease but would be available for purchase at a cost of $160,000. Quick Copy would use the purchased copier for one year, after which it could sell it back to the manufacturer for one-fourth the purchase price ($40,000). In addition, the new machine has a required annual service contract of $20,000, which includes all repair, service, and replacement of ink cartridges. Quick Copy's options for the coming year are to renew the lease for the current copier or to purchase the new copier. The relevant information is outlined in Exhibit 11.10. The lease-vs.-buy decision will not (by assumption) affect the cost of paper, electrical power, and employee wages, so these costs are irrelevant and are excluded from the analysis. For simplicity, we also ignore potential tax effects of the decision and the time value of money.

The initial step in the analysis is to determine which machine produces the lower total cost. Because there are short-term fixed costs associated with each decision alternative, the answer depends on the expected annual number of copies. Using cost-volume-profit analysis (Chapter 9) and Exhibit 11.11, Quick Copy's manager determines the indifference point, the

EXHIBIT 11.10
Quick Copy Lease-vs.-Buy Information

	Lease Option	Purchase (Buy) Option
Annual lease	$40,000	N/A
Charge per copy	$0.02	N/A
Purchase cost	N/A	$160,000
Annual service contract	N/A	$20,000
Value at end of period	N/A	$40,000
Expected number of copies a year	6,000,000	6,000,000

EXHIBIT 11.11
The Lease-vs.-Buy Example

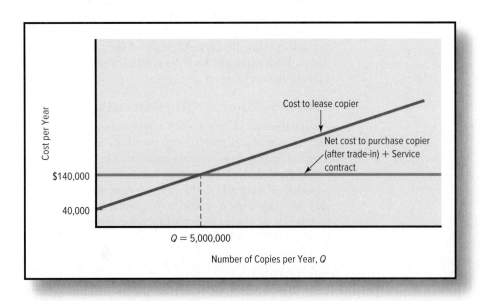

There are two sides to the buy parts of the make-or-buy decision, the customer and the supplier. Apple Inc. is widely recognized as a design company that outsources the actual production of its products. The company has chosen to buy instead of make. What about the suppliers that sit on the other side of this arrangement? AMS AG, an Austrian-based manufacturer, is just one of those many companies. In November 2018 it became the fourth key supplier to Apple to reduce its revenue forecast within a week. What was behind this trend? Apple was on a bit of a losing streak with respect to demand for its products. So, while Apple may be able to benefit from the

flexibility that comes with contracting out production by saving costs during a downturn, companies like AMS do not have that luxury. While AMS receives more than 20 percent of its revenue from Apple, Qorvo Inc. and Japan Display get 36 percent and 55 percent, respectively, from Apple. Perhaps these and other suppliers need to rethink their strategy of being a main supplier to the Cupertino, California–based company.

Source: Mark Gurman, "Apple's Outlook Dims as Suppliers Worldwide Sound the Alarm," Bloomberg.com, November 15, 2018, **www.bloomberg.com/news/articles/2018-11-14/ams-is-latest-apple-supplier-to-cut-sales-estimates-within-days**, accessed February 5, 2020.

number of copies per year at which the total annual cost of each decision alternative is the same. The calculations are as follows, where Q is the number of copies per year:

$$\text{Annual lease cost} = \text{Annual purchase cost}$$
$$\text{Annual fee} + \text{Per copy charge} = \text{Net purchase cost} + \text{Service contract}$$
$$\$40{,}000 + (\$0.02 \times Q) = (\$160{,}000 - \$40{,}000) + \$20{,}000$$
$$Q = \$100{,}000 \text{ per year} \div \$0.02 \text{ per copy}$$
$$= 5{,}000{,}000 \text{ copies per year}$$

As indicated in Chapter 9 (Exhibit 9.5), the Goal Seek routine in Excel also can be used to solve problems such as this.

The indifference point, 5,000,000 copies, is lower than the expected annual machine usage of 6,000,000 copies. This indicates that Quick Copy will have lower annual costs by purchasing the new machine. In fact, we show that costs will be lower by $20,000 per year:

$$\text{Cost of lease} - \text{Cost of purchase}$$
$$= [\$40{,}000 + (\$0.02 \times 6{,}000{,}000)] - (\$160{,}000 - \$40{,}000 + \$20{,}000)$$
$$= \$160{,}000 - \$140{,}000$$
$$= \$20{,}000 \text{ in favor of the purchase option}$$

In addition to the relevant cost analysis, Quick Copy should consider strategic factors such as the quality of the copy, the reliability of the machine (machine downtime costs could be significant), the benefits and features of the service contract, and any other factors associated with the use of the machine that might properly influence the decision.

Strategic Analysis

Make-vs.-buy and lease-vs.-purchase decisions often raise strategic issues. For example, a firm using value-chain analysis could find that certain of its activities in the value chain can be more profitably performed by other firms. The practice of choosing to have an outside firm provide a basic service function is called *outsourcing.* Many firms recently have considered outsourcing manufacturing and data processing, janitorial, or security services to improve profitability, as illustrated by the chapter opener (Apple) and the Real-World Focus examples in the chapter. In his book *The World Is Flat: A Brief History of the Twenty-First Century,* Thomas Friedman explains the breadth of outsourcing practices in the world today.[1] Even such simple activities as taking hamburger orders at the drive-thru of a fast-food restaurant are being outsourced around the world.

Because of the important strategic implications of make-vs.-buy and lease-vs.-purchase decisions, these decisions are often made on a two- to five-year basis, using projections of expected relevant costs and taking into account both income taxes and the time value of money (Chapter 12) where appropriate.

Decisions to Sell before or after Additional Processing

Relevant Cost Analysis

LO 11-4

Use relevant cost analysis and strategic analysis in the decision to sell before or after additional processing.

joint production process
A process that yields multiple outputs from a common resource input.

split-off point
The point in a joint production process where products with individual identities emerge.

joint production costs
Costs incurred prior to the split-off point; common (i.e., indirect) costs.

separable processing costs
In a joint production process, costs incurred after the split-off point that are traceable to individual products.

Another common decision concerns the option to sell a product or service before an intermediate processing step or to add further processing and then to sell the product or service for a higher price. The additional processing might add features or functionality to a product or add flexibility or quality to a service. For example, a travel agent preparing a group tour faces many decisions related to optional features to be offered on the tour, such as sidetrips, sleeping quarters, and entertainment. A manufacturer of consumer electronics faces a number of decisions regarding the nature and extent of features to offer in its products.

Yet another dimension of determining appropriate product features arises in what is called a **joint production process.** As discussed in Chapter 7, a joint production process is one in which multiple outputs arise from a common resource input. From this common resource (e.g., barrel of crude oil), multiple outputs are obtained. At a certain point in the process, products with individual identities emerge (e.g., diesel fuel, gasoline, aviation fuel). This point is referred to as the **split-off point.** Prior to this point, **joint production costs** are incurred; these, by definition, are not traceable to individual products. After the split-off point, **separable** (i.e., traceable) **processing costs** are incurred. Management typically has some discretion in either selling products at an intermediate stage (e.g., at the split-off point) or incurring additional processing costs and then selling the products.

As indicated in Chapter 7, for financial reporting purposes, it is important to allocate joint production costs to the various outputs. Full-cost data (including allocated joint product costs) are needed to prepare balance sheets and income statements. However, these allocated costs are generally irrelevant for short-term decision-making purposes. For example, when the decision is whether to sell a product at the split-off point or to process it further and then sell it, the only costs and revenues relevant to the decision are those that are incremental to the decision. By the time the product has reached the split-off point, the joint costs are considered sunk and, therefore, irrelevant to the decision. The only exception is that the joint costs would be relevant if the decision were whether to produce the set of joint products at all.

The analysis of features also is important for manufacturers in determining what to do with defective products. Generally, such products can either be sold in the defective state to outlet stores and discount chains or be repaired for sale in the usual manner. Therefore, the decision is whether the product should be sold with or without additional processing. Relevant cost analysis is again the appropriate model to follow in analyzing these situations.

To continue with the TTS example, assume that a piece of equipment used to print its T-shirts has malfunctioned and that 400 shirts are not of acceptable quality because some colors are missing or faded. TTS can either sell the defective shirts to outlet stores at a greatly reduced price ($4.50) or run them through the printing machine again. (The normal selling price per shirt is $9.00.) A second run will produce a salable shirt in most cases. The costs to run them through the printer a second time are for ink and labor, totaling $1.80 per shirt, plus the (assumed) setup, inspection, and materials handling costs for a batch of product. Thus, if TTS chooses to rework and then sell the shirts, the incremental contribution margin would be $2,680; if, on the other hand, it chooses to sell the shirts "as is" to a discounter, the incremental contribution margin would be only $1,800. In short, there is an $880 advantage ($2,680 vs. $1,800) to reprinting the shirts. See Exhibit 11.12.

[1] Thomas L. Friedman, *The World Is Flat: A Brief History of the Twenty-First Century* (New York: Farrar, Straus and Giroux, 2005). See also Thomas L. Friedman, *Hot, Flat, and Crowded* (New York: Farrar, Straus and Giroux, 2008).

In a broad sense, sustainability accounting relates to social and environmental performance of organizations. As indicated in the current chapter (and elsewhere in the text), management accountants—as part of their responsibility to help organizations implement their strategies successfully—are becoming increasingly involved in sustainability reporting and in defining a strategic role for sustainability accounting as part of an overall strategic management system. First, consider the linkage between sustainability accounting and the contents of the current chapter.

Second, describe what might be viewed as a traditional model of, or approach to, sustainability reporting. What are the broad characteristics of such a model? Where might you obtain information to guide the interpretation of sustainability performance for your organization? Finally, how might sustainability accounting be broadened in scope to have a more strategic (rather than traditional) performance-reporting role?

(Refer to Comments on Cost Management in Action at the end of the chapter.)

EXHIBIT 11.12
Relevant Cost Analysis of Reprinting 400 Defective T-Shirts

	Reprint	Sell to Discount Store
Revenue (400 @ $9.00, $4.50)	$3,600	$1,800
Relevant costs (assumed)		
Ink ($0.95 per unit)	380	
Labor ($0.85 per unit)	340	
Setup (per batch)	130	
Inspection (per batch)	30	
Materials handling (per batch)	40	
Total relevant costs	$ 920	
Incremental contribution margin	$2,680	$1,800
Net advantage to reprint	**$2,680 − $1,800 = $880**	

Alternatively, we could say that in terms of the decision to reprint the shirts, the revenue is $3,600 while the total cost is $2,720 (i.e., out-of-pocket costs of $920 [see Exhibit 11.12] plus opportunity costs of $1,800). Further, we could arrive at the same $880 net benefit of reprocessing the shirts by comparing the incremental revenue from further processing, $1,800 ($3,600 − $1,800), to the incremental cost of further processing, $920. Keep in mind that in terms of the decision to sell the shirts "as is" or to process them further and then sell them, the original manufacturing cost for the shirts is irrelevant—this cost is sunk and therefore the same regardless of the decision option chosen.

Strategic Analysis

Strategic concerns arise when considering selling to discount stores. Will this affect the sale of T-shirts in retail stores? Will the cost of packing, delivery, and sales commissions differ for these two types of sales? Will the lesser quality of these T-shirts affect the company's competitive position in the long run?

Another consideration is whether there is a discernible difference between the regular product and the reworked version. This is important because customers are essentially paying full price for a reworked product.

Further, while the decision at hand seems (on the surface) to be straightforward, perhaps the decision alternatives can be expanded. For example, could the company donate the shirts to a charitable organization, thereby securing favorable press (for being a socially conscious company)?

Finally, the decision to process the shirts further based on a relevant (short-term) cost analysis—such as presented here—can end up creating an infrastructure that would, in the absence of costly expansions and cost commitments, be difficult or impossible to support over the long term.

TS management must carefully consider these strategic issues in addition to the information provided by its relevant cost analysis.

Product- (or Service-) Line Profitability Analysis: Keep or Drop a Product (or Service) Line

Relevant Cost Analysis

LO 11-5

Use relevant cost analysis and strategic analysis in the decision to keep or drop products or services.

An important aspect of management is the regular review of product- (and service-) line profitability. This review should address issues such as:

- Which products (or services) are most profitable?
- Are the products (or services) priced properly?
- Which products (or services) should be promoted and advertised most aggressively?
- Which product (or service) managers should be rewarded?

This review has both a short-term and a long-term (strategic) focus. The short-term focus is addressed through relevant cost analysis. To illustrate, we use Windbreakers Inc., a manufacturer of sport clothing. Windbreakers manufactures three jackets: Calm, Windy, and Gale. Management has requested an analysis of Gale due to its low sales and low indicated profitability (see Exhibit 11.13).

The analysis of Gale should begin with the important observation that the $3.60 allocated fixed cost per unit is irrelevant for the analysis of the short-term profitability of the three products. Under this assumption, the $171,000 total fixed costs are unavoidable in the short run. As such, they are irrelevant for this analysis. That is, no changes in product mix, including the deletion of Gale, will affect total fixed costs in the coming year. The fact that the fixed costs are irrelevant is illustrated by comparing the contribution income statements in Exhibit 11.14, which assumes that Gale is dropped, and Exhibit 11.15, which assumes that Gale is kept. The only changes caused by dropping Gale are the loss of its revenues and the elimination of variable costs. Thus, in this situation, the only relevant costs for the short-term analysis are the variable costs associated with each product line. The total fixed costs are assumed unavoidable and therefore not relevant to the assessment of the short-term profitability of each product line. Further, the results presented in Exhibit 11.14 assume that there is no effect on the sales or costs of the other two products. Thus, dropping Gale causes a reduction in total contribution margin of $4 per unit times 3,750 units of Gale sold, or $15,000, and a corresponding reduction in operating profit ($15,000 = $144,000 − $129,000).

EXHIBIT 11.13
Sales, Cost, and Indicated Profitability Data for Windbreakers Inc.

	Calm	Windy	Gale	Total
Units sold last year	25,000	18,750	3,750	47,500
Revenue	$750,000	$600,000	$150,000	
Selling price per unit	$ 30.00	$ 32.00	$ 40.00	
Relevant costs:				
Variable cost per unit	24.00	24.00	36.00	
Contribution margin per unit	$ 6.00	$ 8.00	$ 4.00	
Nonrelevant (i.e., allocated) fixed costs	3.60	3.60	3.60	$171,000
Operating profit per unit	$ 2.40	$ 4.40	$ 0.40	

EXHIBIT 11.14
Contribution Income Statement Profitability Analysis: Gale Dropped (all fixed costs assumed unavoidable)

	Calm	Windy	Total
Sales	$750,000	$600,000	$1,350,000
Relevant costs:			
Variable cost ($24 per unit)	600,000	450,000	1,050,000
Contribution margin	$150,000	$150,000	$ 300,000
Nonrelevant costs:			
Fixed costs (unavoidable)			171,000
Operating profit without Gale			$ 129,000

EXHIBIT 11.15
Contribution Income Statement Profitability Analysis: Gale Retained

	Calm	Windy	Gale	Total
Sales	$750,000	$600,000	$150,000	$1,500,000
Relevant costs:				
Variable cost ($24, $24, $36 per unit)	600,000	450,000	135,000	1,185,000
Contribution margin	$150,000	$150,000	$ 15,000	$ 315,000
Nonrelevant costs:				
Fixed costs (unavoidable)				171,000
Operating profit with Gale				$ 144,000

Alternatively, we could show the $15,000 reduction in operating profit as the net effect of a cost savings (avoidable costs) of $135,000 and an opportunity cost (lost sales) of $150,000, as shown below:

Benefit: Saved variable costs of Gale	$135,000	$(36 × 3,750)
Cost: Opportunity cost—revenues from lost sales of Gale	(150,000)	$(40 × 3,750)
Decrease in operating profit from decision to drop Gale	$ (15,000)	$ (4 × 3,750)

Assume now that $60,000 of the $171,000 fixed costs are advertising costs to be spent directly on each of the three products: $25,000 for Calm, $15,000 for Windy, and $20,000 for Gale. That is, each of these is an avoidable cost. The remainder of the fixed costs, $111,000 ($171,000 − $60,000), are common fixed costs—that is, they are not traceable to any of the three products and are therefore allocated to each product as before. Because advertising costs are directly traceable to the individual products, and assuming that the advertising plans for Gale can be canceled without additional cost, the $20,000 of advertising costs for Gale are avoidable and therefore relevant to the decision to drop Gale.

Exhibit 11.16A shows that the total contribution margin for Gale is now a negative $5,000, providing a potential $5,000 increase in operating profit by dropping Gale because of the expected $20,000 savings in avoidable advertising costs. Exhibit 11.16B shows the results if Gale is dropped. Alternatively, management may choose to forgo the advertising for Gale and assess whether sales will fall with the loss of advertising; Gale could be profitable without advertising. We can interpret the contribution figures for Calm and Windy in the same way. The reduction in operating profit in choosing to drop Calm or Windy would be $125,000 and $135,000, respectively.

Strategic Analysis

In addition to the relevant cost analysis, the decision to keep or drop a product line should include relevant strategic factors, such as the potential effect of the loss of one product line on the sales of another. For example, some florists price cards, vases, and other related items at or below cost to better serve and attract customers to the most profitable product, the flower arrangements.

EXHIBIT 11.16A
Contribution Income Statement Profitability Analysis: Including Traceable (i.e., avoidable) Advertising Costs

	Calm	Windy	Gale	Total
Sales	$750,000	$600,000	$150,000	$1,500,000
Relevant costs				
Variable cost ($24, $24, $36 per unit)	600,000	450,000	135,000	1,185,000
Contribution margin	$150,000	$150,000	$ 15,000	$ 315,000
Other relevant costs (traceable)				
Advertising	25,000	15,000	20,000	60,000
Contribution after all relevant costs	$125,000	$135,000	$ (5,000)	$ 255,000
Nonrelevant costs (not traceable)				
Fixed cost (unavoidable portion)				$ 111,000
Operating profit				$ 144,000

EXHIBIT 11.16B
Contribution Income Statement Profitability Analysis: Gale Dropped; Avoidable Costs Removed

	Calm	Windy	Total
Sales	$750,000	$600,000	$1,350,000
Relevant costs			
Variable cost ($24, $24)	600,000	450,000	1,050,000
Contribution margin	$150,000	$150,000	$ 300,000
Other relevant costs (traceable)			
Advertising	25,000	15,000	40,000
Contribution after all relevant costs	$125,000	$135,000	$ 260,000
Nonrelevant costs (not traceable)			
Fixed cost (unavoidable portion)			$ 111,000
Operating profit			$ 149,000

Other important strategic factors include the potential effect on overall employee morale and organizational effectiveness if a product line is dropped. Moreover, managers should consider the sales growth potential of each product. Will the decision to drop a product place the firm in a strong competitive position sometime in the future? A particularly important consideration is the extent of available production capacity. If production capacity and production resources (such as labor and machine time) are limited, management should consider the relative profitability of the products and the extent to which they require different amounts of these production resources.

Profitability Analysis: Service Offerings of Not-for-Profit Organizations

Relevant Cost Analysis

LO 11-6

Use relevant cost analysis and strategic analysis to evaluate service offerings of not-for-profit organizations.

Triangle Women's Center (TWC) uses relevant cost analysis to determine the desirability of new services. TWC provides several services to the communities in and around a large southeastern city. It has not offered child care services but has received a large number of requests to do so in recent years. Now TWC is planning to add this service. The relevant cost analysis follows. TWC expects to hire a director ($65,000) and two part-time assistants ($30,000 each) for the child care service. TWC estimates variable costs per child at $60 per month. No other costs are relevant because none of the other operating costs of TWC are expected to change. TWC expects to receive funding of $100,000 from the United Way plus $30,000 from the city council. The analysis for the child care service's first year of operation is shown in Exhibit 11.17, which assumes that 20 children, the maximum number, will use the service.

The TWC analysis shows that the child care service will have a deficit of approximately $9,400 in the first year. Now TWC can decide whether it can make up the deficit from current funds or by raising additional funds. Relevant cost analysis provides TWC a useful method to determine the resource needs for the new program.

EXHIBIT 11.17
Triangle Women's Center
Analysis of Child Care Services

Relevant annual costs:	
Salary of director	$ 65,000
Salary for two part-time assistants	60,000
Variable costs for 20 children at $60 each per month	14,400
Total relevant costs	$139,400
Total funding:	
United Way	$100,000
City council	30,000
	$130,000
Expected deficit in the first year	**$ 9,400**

Strategic Analysis

Several important strategic considerations likely bear upon the current decision. It is stated that TWC does not have experience in offering child care services. Can TWC realistically expect to be able to recruit appropriate personnel who could develop and successfully implement a plan for the new service? Are there liability issues that need to be addressed (i.e., to what extent would the new service line expose TWC to increased risk)? Are there other, more productive, uses for the space (and perhaps other resources) that would be devoted to the child care service? Would the new service divert attention away from the service TWC currently provides? How confident is TWC that funding, on a continuing basis, would be available through United Way and through the local legislature? Is there a realistic backup plan should a funding shortfall occur? These are among the strategic issues that should accompany the short-term financial analysis conducted by TWC.

Constrained Optimization Analysis: Short-Term Product-Mix Decisions

LO 11-7

Use relevant cost analysis and strategic analysis to perform a constrained optimization (i.e., short-term product-mix) analysis.

The preceding relevant cost analyses were simplified by using a single product (or service offering) and assuming sufficient resources to meet all demands. The analysis changes significantly with two or more products and limited resources. The revised analysis is considered in this section. We continue the example of Windbreakers Inc., except that, to simplify the analysis, we assume that the Calm product is manufactured in a separate plant under contract with a major customer. Thus, the following analysis focuses only on the Windy and Gale products, which are manufactured in a single facility.

A key element of the relevant cost analysis is to determine the most profitable sales mix for Windy and Gale. If there are no production constraints, the answer is clear: Because the contribution margin per unit for each product is positive and total fixed costs are assumed joint or common with respect to the two products, we manufacture what is needed to meet demand for both Windy and Gale. However, when demand exceeds production capacity, management must make some trade-offs about the quantity of each product to manufacture, and, therefore, what amount of demand will be unmet. The answer requires considering the production possibilities given by the production constraints. Consider two important cases: (1) one production constraint and (2) two or more production constraints. In each of these cases, it may be necessary to incorporate demand constraints as well.

Case 1: One Production Constraint

Assume that the production of Windy and Gale requires an automated sewing machine to stitch the jackets and that this production activity is a limited resource: Sales demand for the two products exceeds the capacity of the plant's three automated sewing machines. Each machine can be run up to 20 hours per day five days per week, or 400 hours per month, which is its maximum capacity allowing for maintenance. This gives 1,200 (3 machines × 400 hours per machine) available hours for sewing each month. Assume further that the machine requires three minutes to assemble a Windy and two minutes to assemble a Gale.

Because only 1,200 hours of machine time are available per month and the Gale jacket requires less machine time, more Gale jackets can be made in a month than Windy jackets. The maximum number of Windy jackets is 24,000 per month (1,200 hours × 20 jackets per hour). Similarly, if sewing machine time were devoted entirely to Gale jackets, then 36,000 jackets per month could be produced (1,200 hours × 30 jackets per hour). This information is summarized in Exhibit 11.18.

A continuous trade-off possibility exists for the extreme situations: zero output of Windy and 36,000 units of Gale, or 24,000 units of Windy and zero units of Gale. These production and sales-mix possibilities can be shown graphically; all sales-mix possibilities are represented by the line in Exhibit 11.19. The line in Exhibit 11.19 (called an "iso-production" line) can be determined as follows:

$$\text{Slope} = -36,000 \div 24,000 = -3/2$$
$$\text{Intercept} = 36,000$$

The line in Exhibit 11.19 is thus given by

$$\text{Units of Gale} = 36,000 - (3/2 \times \text{Units of Windy})$$

To illustrate, if monthly production of Windy is 12,000 units, then the number of units of Gale that can be produced is 18,000, as follows:

$$\text{Units of Gale} = 36,000 - (3/2 \times 12,000) = 18,000$$

EXHIBIT 11.18

Windbreakers Data for the Windy and Gale Plant: One Production Constraint—The Sewing Machine

	Windy	Gale
Given:		
Contribution margin per jacket	$8	$4
Sewing time per jacket (minutes)	3 min.	2 min.
Then:		
Number of jackets per hour:	20	30
(60 min ÷ 3 min = 20; 60 min ÷ 2 min = 30)		
Contribution margin per hour:	$160	$120
(20 jackets per hour × $8 per jacket;		
30 jackets per hour × $4 per jacket)		
Also:		
The maximum production for each product,		
given the 1,200-hour constraint:		
For Windy: 1,200 hours × 20 jackets per hour	24,000	
For Gale: 1,200 hours × 30 jackets per hour		36,000

EXHIBIT 11.19

Windbreakers Production and Sales Possibilities: One Production Constraint—The Sewing Machine

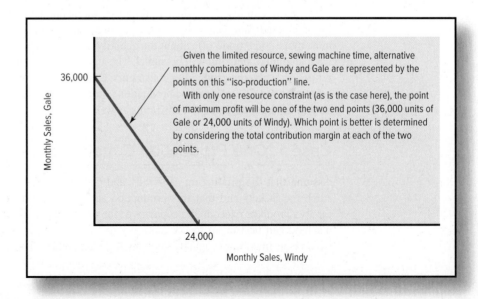

Given the limited resource, sewing machine time, alternative monthly combinations of Windy and Gale are represented by the points on this "iso-production" line.

With only one resource constraint (as is the case here), the point of maximum profit will be one of the two end points (36,000 units of Gale or 24,000 units of Windy). Which point is better is determined by considering the total contribution margin at each of the two points.

Now that we know the production possibilities, we can determine the best product mix. Note from Exhibit 11.18 that Windy has the higher contribution margin per machine hour, $160 (i.e., 20 jackets per hour × $8 per jacket). Because 1,200 machine hours are available per month, the maximum total contribution margin from the production possibilities is to produce only Windy and achieve a total contribution of 1,200 × $160 = $192,000 (or $8 per unit × 24,000 units = $192,000) per month. If Windbreakers chooses to produce and sell only Gale, the total contribution margin would be only $144,000 per month (1,200 hours × $120 per hour), a $48,000 reduction over the contribution margin from selling only Windy. *Thus, when there is only one production constraint and excess demand, it is generally best to focus production and sales on the product with the highest contribution per unit of scarce resource—in the present case, contribution margin per machine hour.*

Case 2: Two or More Production Constraints

When there are two or more production constraints, the choice of sales mix involves a more complex analysis, and in contrast to the case of one production constraint (in which the optimum solution will include only a single product, assuming sufficient demand for this product—see Exhibit 11.19), the solution can include both products when two constraints are involved. To continue with the Windbreakers case, assume that in addition to the use of sewing machine time, a second production activity is required. The second activity inspects and packages the completed product. This operation is done by 40 workers, each of whom can complete the operation for the Windy jacket in 15 minutes and for the Gale jacket in 5 minutes (because of differences in material quality, less inspection time is required for the Gale jacket). This means that 4 (60 min./15 min.) Windy jackets or 12 Gale (60 min./5 min.) jackets can be inspected and packaged in an hour. Because of the limited size of the facility, no more than 40 workers can be employed effectively in the inspection and packaging process. These employees work a 40-hour week, which means 35 hours of actually performing the operation, given time for breaks, training, and other tasks. Thus, 5,600 hours (40 workers × 35 hours/week × 4 weeks/month) are available per month for the inspection and packaging activity.

The maximum output per month for the Windy jacket, in terms of inspection and packaging activity, is 22,400 (5,600 hours × 4 jackets per hour). Similarly, the maximum output for the Gale jacket is 67,200 (5,600 hours × 12 jackets per hour). All of this information is summarized in Exhibit 11.20.

The production possibilities for two constraints are illustrated in Exhibit 11.21. In addition to the production possibilities for machine time, we show the production possibilities for the inspection and packaging activity. The darker shaded area indicates the range of possible outputs (the "feasible area") for both Gale and Windy. Note that it is not possible to produce more than 22,400 units of Windy because all 40 workers inspecting and packaging full-time would not be able to handle more than that number, even though sufficient sewing machine time is available for producing 24,000 units. That is, production of more than 22,400 units of

EXHIBIT 11.20
Windbreakers Data for the Windy and Gale Plant: The Second Constraint—Inspection and Packaging Activity

	Windy	Gale
Given:		
Contribution margin per jacket	$8	$4
Inspection and packaging time per jacket	15 min.	5 min.
Then:		
Number of jackets per hour	4	12
Contribution margin per labor hour	$32	$48
(4 jackets per hour × $8 per jacket;		
12 jackets per hour × $4 per jacket)		
Also:		
The maximum monthly production for each product,		
given the 5,600-hour constraint:		
For Windy: 5,600 hours/month × 4 jackets per hour	22,400	
For Gale: 5,600 hours/month × 12 jackets per hour		67,200

EXHIBIT 11.21
Windbreakers Production and Sales Possibilities (Feasible Area): Two Production Constraints—Sewing Machine and Inspection/Packaging Activity

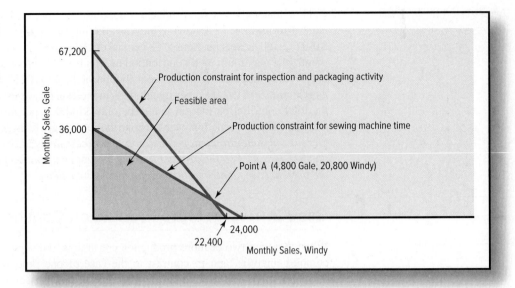

Windy is outside of the feasible area. Similarly, although Windbreakers could pack and ship 67,200 units of Gale by having all 40 individuals work full-time on this jacket, the firm could manufacture only 36,000 units of Gale because of limited capacity on the sewing machines.

We can determine the best production mix by examining all of the possible production possibilities in the darker shaded area, from 36,000 on the Gale axis to point A where the constraints intersect, and then to the point 22,400 on the Windy axis. The sales mix with the highest contribution must be one of these three points: 36,000 units of Gale, point A (20,800 units of Windy and 4,800 units of Gale), or 22,400 units of Windy. The optimal solution, called the *corner point analysis,* is obtained by finding the total contribution margin at each point and then choosing the point with the highest total contribution margin. The solution achieved in this manner is for production at point A: 20,800 units of Windy and 4,800 units of Gale.[2] A summary analysis of the three production possibilities is presented in the following table:

Corner Point	Windy	Gale	Total Contribution Margin
1	0	0	$ 0
2	0	36,000	144,000
3	22,400	0	179,200
4	**20,800**	**4,800**	**$185,600**

One way to see why point A represents an optimum short-term product mix is to impose on Exhibit 11.21 an iso-profit line, whose negative slope is equal to the ratio of the unit contribution margin of Gale to the unit contribution margin of Windy (i.e., −2.0). Extend this line to the right, from the origin until it just touches a point in the feasible region. This particular iso-profit line determines the optimum profit given the stated constraints and product contribution margins. Once again, you will see that the optimum short-term product mix is indicated by point A in Exhibit 11.21.

---

[2] Point A (20,800 units of Windy [W] and 4,800 units of Gale [G]) is obtained by solving the following two equations simultaneously:

$$15W + 5G = 336,000 \text{ minutes of inspection time (i.e., 40 workers} \times 35 \text{ hours per worker per week}$$
$$\times \text{ 4 weeks per month} \times 60 \text{ minutes per hour)}$$
$$3W + 2G = 72,000 \text{ minutes of sewing time (i.e., 3 machines} \times 400 \text{ hours per machine per month}$$
$$\times \text{ 60 minutes per hour)}$$

Linear programming, a mathematical method, permits the solution of much larger problems involving many products and both production and demand constraints. A linear program technique to solve the Windy and Gale case is shown in the appendix to this chapter. This technique uses the Solver function of Microsoft Excel.

Behavioral and Implementation Issues

Consideration of Strategic Objectives

LO 11-8

Discuss behavioral, implementation, ethical, and legal issues in decision making.

A well-known problem in business today is the tendency of managers to focus on short-term goals and neglect long-term strategic goals because their compensation is based on short-term accounting measures such as net income. Many critics of relevant cost analysis have raised this issue. As noted throughout the chapter, it is critical that the relevant cost analysis for decision making be supplemented by a careful consideration of the firm's long-term, strategic goals. Without strategic considerations, management could improperly use relevant cost analysis to achieve a short-term benefit and potentially suffer a significant long-term loss. For example, on the basis of a favorable relevant cost analysis, a firm might choose to accept a special order without properly considering that the special order could have a significant negative impact on the firm's image in the marketplace and perhaps a negative effect on sales of the firm's other products. The important message for managers is to keep the strategic objectives in the forefront in any decision situation.

Predatory Pricing Practices

predatory pricing

Exists when a company has set prices below average variable cost and plans to raise prices later to recover the losses from the lower prices.

The Robinson–Patman Act, administered by the U.S. Federal Trade Commission, addresses pricing that could substantially damage competition in an industry. This is called **predatory pricing.** In a 1993 decision, *Brooke Group Ltd. v. Brown & Williamson Tobacco Corp.* (B&W), the U.S. Supreme Court defined predatory pricing as a situation in which a company has set prices below average variable cost and plans to raise prices later to recover the losses from lower prices. This law is relevant for short-term *and* long-term pricing because it could require a firm to justify significant price cuts.

A variation on the issue of predatory pricing is the ability of countries to levy fines against global firms for "dumping" their products at anticompetitive prices. In the U.S., antidumping laws were enacted more than 90 years ago to protect against predatory pricing by global firms exporting to the United States. The laws state that the import price cannot be lower than the cost of production or the price in the home market.

Replacement of Variable Costs with Fixed Costs

Another potential problem associated with relevant cost analysis is that managers who are evaluated on their ability to reduce controllable variable costs will have the incentive to replace variable costs with fixed costs. This happens if mid-level and lower-level managers realize that because top managers rely on relevant cost analysis, upper management might overlook fixed costs. Lower-level managers might choose to upgrade or increase fixed assets in order to reduce variable costs, although this might increase fixed costs significantly. For example, a new machine might replace direct labor. The overall costs increase because of the cost of the new machine, although variable costs under the manager's control decrease and the contribution margin increases. Management's proper goal is to maximize contribution margin and to minimize fixed operating costs at the same time. Managers should use relevant cost analysis as a tool to maximize contribution but must also develop methods to manage fixed costs.

Proper Identification of Relevant Factors

Yet another potential problem associated with relevant cost analysis is that managers can fail to properly identify relevant costs. In particular, untrained managers commonly include irrelevant, sunk costs in decision making. Similarly, many managers fail to see that allocated fixed costs are irrelevant. When fixed costs are shown as fixed cost per unit, many managers tend to improperly view them as relevant. It is easier for these managers to see the fixed cost as irrelevant when the amount is given in a single sum; it is more difficult to see unit fixed costs as irrelevant.

REAL-WORLD FOCUS   How to Avoid Decision-Making/Judgment Biases

Fay and Montague note that decision makers often rely on "mental shortcuts" (or, in technical terms, decision heuristics). They argue further that an unintended consequence of using heuristics is *judgment bias,* which can take any of the following forms:

1. *Availability bias:* overreliance on information that is most readily accessible.
2. *Anchoring bias:* excessive influence on an initial amount or data point.
3. *Overconfidence:* overestimating one's ability or competence (to make accurate decisions, meet a deadline, etc.).

4. *Confirmation bias:* seeking information that helps confirm preconceived notions or beliefs; lack of professional skepticism.
5. *Rush-to-resolve:* failure to gather sufficient information (e.g., as a result of budgetary or time constraints).

The authors relate the decision-making biases to specific accounting and auditing contexts and offer (as an example) a strategy for dealing with *confirmation bias.*

Source: Rebecca Fay and Norma R. Montague, "I'm Not Biased, Am I?," *Journal of Accountancy,* February 2015, pp. 26–31 (available at www.journalofaccountancy.com/issues/2015/feb/auditing-judgment-bias.html).

These are illustrations of the pervasive biases present in many managers' decision making. Effective use of relevant cost analysis requires careful identification of relevant costs (i.e., future costs that differ between and among decision alternatives), as well as the correct recognition of sunk costs and unavoidable fixed costs, which are not relevant for short-term decision making.

Summary

Relevant costs for decision making are defined as future costs that differ between and among decision alternatives. Relevant costs can also be defined as the sum of out-of-pocket costs plus opportunity costs. Alternatively, relevant costs are called "avoidable costs"—that is, costs that can be avoided by choosing one decision alternative over another. The principle of relevant cost analysis can be applied in a number of specific decisions involving manufacturing, service, and not-for-profit organizations. Relevant cost analysis was illustrated in this chapter within the context of the following decisions: whether to accept or reject a special sales order, sourcing decisions (i.e., make-vs.-buy decisions), lease-vs.-purchase decisions, whether to sell or further process a product, and whether to keep or drop certain products.

When two or more products or services are involved, another type of decision must be made: to determine the correct short-term product (or service) mix. With one production constraint, the answer is to produce and sell as much as possible of the product that has the highest contribution margin per unit of the scarce (or constrained) resource, such as machine time. With two or more constrained activities, the analysis uses graphical and quantitative methods (such as linear programming—see the appendix) to determine the optimum short-term product (or service) mix.

Strategic analysis complements relevant cost analysis by having the decision maker consider the qualitative and strategic issues involved in the situation.

A number of key behavioral, implementation, and legal issues must be considered in using relevant cost analysis. Too strong a focus on relevant costs can cause the manager to overlook important opportunity costs and strategic considerations. Other issues include the tendency to replace variable costs with fixed costs when relevant cost analysis is used in performance evaluation and the pervasive tendency to view fixed costs as somehow controllable and relevant when in fact they are sunk costs.

linear programming
A mathematical technique that can be used to solve constrained optimization problems, such as the optimum short-term product (or service) mix.

Appendix

LO 11-9

Set up and solve in Excel a simple product-mix problem.

Linear Programming and the Product-Mix Decision

Linear programming is a mathematical technique that can be used to solve constrained optimization problems, such as the Windbreakers case illustrated in the chapter. Linear programming is particularly useful when the product-mix decision involves multiple constraints and three or more products—situations where graphical solutions to the problem become

Solver

An analytical tool available on the Data tab in Excel that can be used to solve linear programming (i.e., constrained-optimization) problems.

unwieldy or impossible. In this appendix, we illustrate the use of the **Solver** routine in Excel as one way to build and solve a linear programming model. Solver will appear as an option on Excel's Data tab.

The first step in using Solver is to enter the data for the problem into an Excel spreadsheet, in the form shown in Exhibit 11A.1.

Column A: These show the product names.

Column B: These are the "decision cells"; initially, you can simply enter a zero in cells B5 and B6.

Columns C, D, and E: These contain data inputs.

Columns F, G, and H: These contain formulas based on the data in columns C, D, and E; for example, cell F5 = B5 × C5; cell G5 = B5 × D5; cell F7 = SUM(F5:F6); cell G7 = SUM(G5:G6); and cell H7 = SUM(H5:H6). The target cell (i.e., the cell to be optimized) is F7.

The second step in using Solver is to enter the Solver parameters as shown in the dialog box in Exhibit 11A.2. The dialog box appears by selecting Solver from the Data tab. Note that the target cell is total contribution margin, located in cell F7. The "By Changing Variable Cells" section includes those cells representing unit sales of Windy (cell B5) and Gale (cell B6). The constraints for sewing time and inspection/packaging time are then entered in the "Subject to the Constraints" section as shown. Next, select the Simplex LP as the "Solving Method." Finally, select Solve in the dialog box, at which point a dialog box labeled "Solver Results" appears. Highlight the supplemental reports (Answer Report, Sensitivity Report, and Limits Report) you want (if any), and then click "OK." The LP solution now appears, as shown in Exhibit 11A.3.

Notice that cells B5 and B6 in Exhibit 11A.3 now show the optimum product mix for Windy and Gale (in units), and the cells in columns F, G, and H show the total contribution margin ($185,600) and total use of each of the two constraints. Note that the optimum contribution margin (cell F7) is precisely the same as the amount yielded by the "corner-point" analysis we conducted in conjunction with Exhibit 11.21.

Exhibit 11A.4 shows the "Answer Report" for the final solution. In addition to information contained in Exhibit 11A.3, the Answer Report includes information regarding each of the constraints (see rows 27 (sewing time constraint) and 28 (inspection/packaging time constraint). We see that all of the time available in both departments has been fully utilized in the optimum production plan. As a result, each constraint is "binding," with no "slack." In this situation, it may pay to relax each constraint.

Exhibit 11A.5 shows the "Sensitivity Report" for the final solution, which contains information regarding both the variable cells and the constraints. In terms of the variable cells, the following information is provided: final values (i.e., the optimum solution—here, number of unit sales for Windy and for Gale—see cells D9 and D10), objective coefficients (here, the contribution margin per unit for each of the two products—see cells F9 and F10), and the allowable increase and allowable decrease (i.e., the optimum solution holds as long as the objective function coefficients—the unit contribution margins reflected in cells F9 and F10—are within the ranges specified in cells G9:H9 and G10:H10, for Windy and Gale, respectively).

EXHIBIT 11A.1
Enter Data for the Windy and Gale Example

Source: Microsoft Excel

EXHIBIT 11A.2
Enter Solver Parameters for the Windy and Gale Example

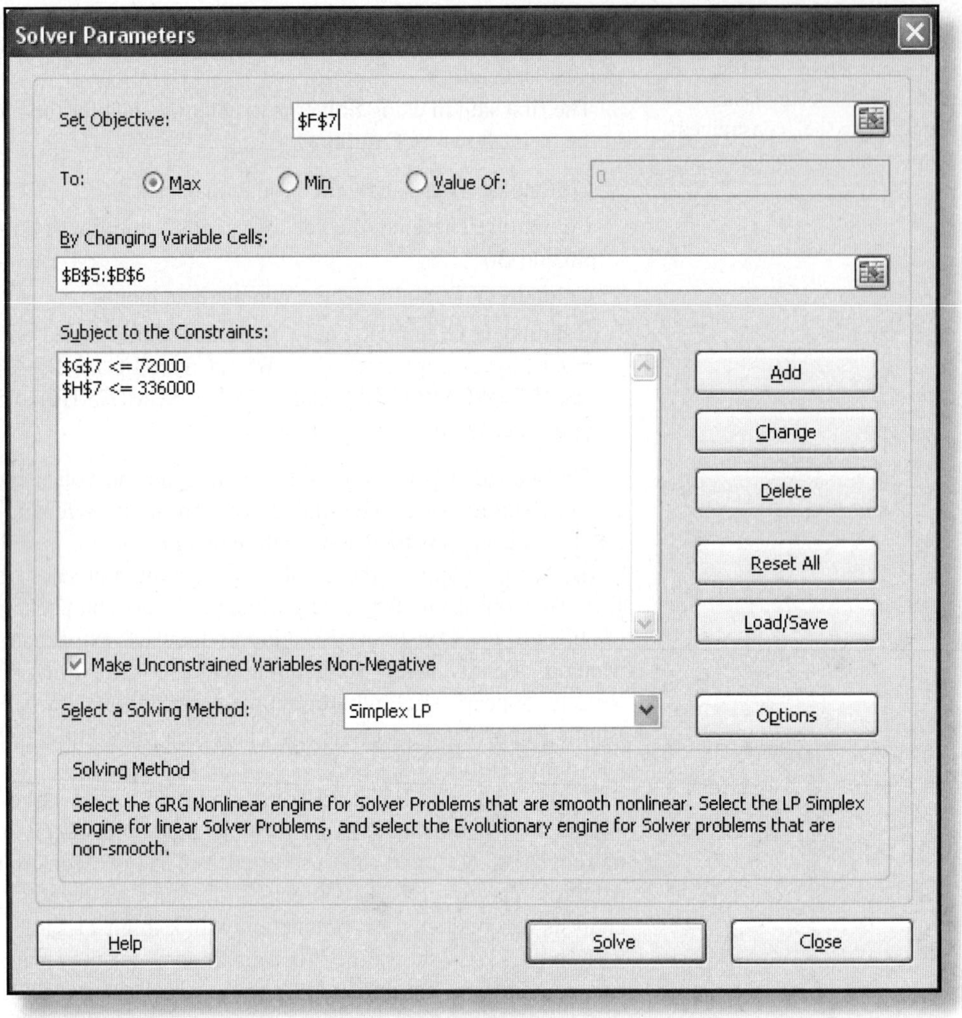

Solver Parameters

Set Objective: $F$7

To: ● Max   ○ Min   ○ Value Of: 0

By Changing Variable Cells:

$B$5:$B$6

Subject to the Constraints:

$G$7 <= 72000
$H$7 <= 336000

Add
Change
Delete
Reset All
Load/Save

☑ Make Unconstrained Variables Non-Negative

Select a Solving Method: Simplex LP   Options

Solving Method

Select the GRG Nonlinear engine for Solver Problems that are smooth nonlinear. Select the LP Simplex engine for linear Solver Problems, and select the Evolutionary engine for Solver problems that are non-smooth.

Help   Solve   Close

Source: Microsoft Excel

EXHIBIT 11A.3
Solver Solution for the Windy and Gale Example

	A	B	C	D	E	F	G	H
1	Windy and Gale Example							
2				Per-Unit Resource Consumption			Capacity Usage	
3		Sales	CM	Sewing	Inspection/	Total	Sewing	Inspect/Pack
4	Product	(units)	per Unit	Department	Packaging	CM	Time	Time
5	Windy	20,800	$8	3	15	$166,400	62,400	312,000
6	Gale	4,800	$4	2	5	$19,200	9,600	24,000
7						$185,600	72,000	336,000

Source: Microsoft Excel

In terms of the constraints, the following information is provided in Exhibit 11A.5: the final value of each constraint (i.e., the amount of the constraint used in the optimum solution—see cells D15 and D16, for sewing time and inspection/packaging time, respectively), the "shadow price" for each constraint (i.e., the amount we would be willing to pay for each additional unit of the constrained resource in question; see cells E15 and E16 for sewing time and inspection/packaging time, respectively), and the allowable increase and decrease for each constraint (i.e., the range of values over which the indicated shadow prices hold—see cells G15:H15 for sewing time, and cells G16:H16 for inspection/packaging time).

Finally, Exhibit 11A.6 contains the "Limits Report" for the Windy and Gale example. In addition to the optimum solution amount (cell D8 = $185,600), this exhibit also repeats

Chapter 11 Decision Making with a Strategic Emphasis 449

EXHIBIT 11A.4
Answer Report for the Windy and Gale Example

Objective Cell (Max)

Cell	Name	Original Value	Final Value
$F$7	CM	$0	$185,600

Variable Cells

Cell	Name	Original Value	Final Value	Integer
$B$5	Windy (units)	0	20,800	Contin
$B$6	Gale (units)	0	4,800	Contin

Constraints

Cell	Name	Cell Value	Formula	Status	Slack
$G$7	Sewing Time	72,000	$G$7<=72000	Binding	0
$H$7	Inspect/Pack Time	336,000	$H$7<=336000	Binding	0

Source: Microsoft Excel

EXHIBIT 11A.5
Sensitivity Report for the Windy and Gale Example

Microsoft Excel 16.0 Sensitivity Report

Variable Cells

Cell	Name	Final Value	Reduced Cost	Objective Coefficient	Allowable Increase	Allowable Decrease
$B$5	Windy (units)	20,800	0	$8.00	4.0000	2.0000
$B$6	Gale (units)	4,800	0	$4.00	1.3333	1.3333

Constraints

Cell	Name	Final Value	Shadow Price	Constraint R.H. Side	Allowable Increase	Allowable Decrease
$G$7	Sewing Time	72,000	1.3333	72,000	62,400	4,800
$H$7	Inspect/Pack Time	336,000	0.2667	336,000	24,000	156,000

Source: Microsoft Excel

EXHIBIT 11A.6
Limits Report for the Windy and Gale Example

Microsoft Excel 16.0 Limits Report

Objective

Cell	Name	Value
$F$7	CM	$185,600

	Variable		Lower	Objective	Upper	Objective
Cell	Name	Value	Limit	Result	Limit	Result
$B$5	Windy (units)	20,800	0	19,200	20,800	185,600
$B$6	Gale (units)	4,800	0	166,400	4,800	185,600

Source: Microsoft Excel

the optimum product mix (cells D13 and D14, for Windy and Gale, respectively). What's new, however, is the information presented in cells F13:J14. Cells G13:G14 and J13:J14 show the value of the objective function (total contribution margin) with each product in and out of the solution. For example, if only Gale is produced, then the total contribution margin drops from the optimum amount (cell D8) to $166,400 (cell G14), a reduction of $19,200 (i.e., 4,800 units × $4/unit).

Key Terms

joint production costs, *436*
joint production process, *436*
linear programming, *446*
opportunity cost, *428*

predatory pricing, *445*
relevant cost, *424*
separable processing costs, *436*
Solver, *447*

split-off point, *436*
sunk costs, *424*
value stream, *432*

Comments on Cost Management in Action

Defining a Strategic Role for Sustainability Accounting and Reporting

The primary theme of the present chapter is twofold: (1) Effective managerial decision making requires relevant financial and nonfinancial (including qualitative and strategic) information and (2) an appropriate and primary role of an organization's management accounting system is to collect and provide relevant information that informs decision making and that helps organizations implement their strategies successfully.

Perspectives can differ, but a "traditional" approach to sustainability accounting/reporting might be characterized as one that focuses on risk management, reporting (to both internal and external stakeholders), and operational efficiency (e.g., cost savings associated with implementing energy-saving production and delivery techniques). (See Bekefi and Epstein, 2016.) The references below can be consulted for corporate scorecards and sustainability reporting frameworks.

Bekefi and Epstein (2016) argue that, however well-intended, traditional approaches to sustainability practice and reporting may hinder break-through innovations in business models. In short, the authors argue (see page 33 of Bekefi and Epstein) that such practices may prevent organizations from doing things that keep them in business and that change the way business is done. The authors propose a more strategic role for sustainability—as the primary driver of innovation in an organization. They offer a framework for implementing this more strategic and value-creating role of sustainability. Corporate examples of break-through sustainability practices and performance include Nike, Levi Strauss, IKEA, Grovelabs, Tesla, and General Electric. Management accountants, as key information providers of both financial and key nonfinancial performance measures, can play a leadership role implementing both traditional and strategic frameworks regarding sustainability practices and results.

Sources: C. C. Verschoor, "Global Surveys Measure Non-financial Reporting," *Strategic Finance,* October 2016, pp. 16, 18; T. Bekefi and M. J. Epstein, "21st Century Sustainability," *Strategic Finance,* November 2016, pp. 29–37; https://www.spglobal.com/esg/csa/indices/; www.environmentalleader.com; sustainability.com/our-work/reports/the-2016-sustainability-leaders; https://home.kpmg/content/dam/kpmg/pdf/2015/12/KPMG-survey-of-CR-reporting-2015.pdf; www.aicpa.org/InterestAreas/BusinessIndustryAndGovernment/Resources/Sustainability/Pages/Sustainability%20Reporting.aspx; www.globalreporting.org/information/sustainability-reporting/Pages/default.aspx.

Self-Study Problem
(For answers, please see Solutions.)

1. Special-Order Pricing

HighValu Inc. manufactures a moderately priced set of lawn furniture (a table and four chairs) that it sells for $225. The company currently manufactures and sells 6,000 sets per year. The manufacturing costs include $85 for direct materials and $45 for direct labor per set. The overhead charge per set is $35, which consists entirely of fixed costs.

HighValu is considering a special purchase offer from a large retail firm, which has offered to buy 600 sets per year for three years at a price of $150 per set. HighValu has the available plant capacity to produce the order and expects no other orders or profitable alternative uses of the plant capacity.

Required
1. What is the total relevant cost per unit to produce the units requested by the retail firm?
2. What is the estimated net effect on annual operating income if HighValu accepts the special sales order?
3. Discuss relevant nonfinancial considerations related to this decision

2. The Make-vs.-Buy Decision

Assume that HighValu Inc., as described in Self-Study Problem 1, currently purchases the chair cushions for its lawn set from an outside vendor for $15 per set. HighValu's chief operations officer wants an analysis of the comparative costs of manufacturing these cushions to determine whether bringing the manufacturing in-house would save the company money. Additional information shows that if HighValu were to manufacture the cushions, the direct materials cost would be $6 and the direct labor cost would be $4 per set. In addition, to produce the cushions, HighValu would have to purchase cutting and sewing equipment, which would add $10,000 to annual fixed costs.

Required

1. What is the total relevant cost per year to purchase the chair cushions from the outside supplier?
2. What is the total relevant cost per year to produce the chair cushions internally?
3. What is the estimated net annual effect on operating income of producing the cushions internally rather than purchasing the cushions from an external supplier?
4. What strategic factors bear on the decision facing HighValu?

3. Constrained Optimization Analysis: The Short-Term Product-Mix Decision

Consider again the Windbreakers firm described in the text. Suppose that Windbreakers determines that dropping the Gale product line will release production capacity so that it can manufacture additional units of Windy. Assume that, as described in the text, the two production constraints are the automated sewing machine and the inspection and packaging operation. The automated sewing machine can make 20 Windys or 30 Gales per hour. As before, the inspection and packaging operation requires 15 minutes for a Windy (4 per hour) and 5 minutes for a Gale (12 per hour). Currently, 3,750 Gales and 18,750 Windys are being manufactured and sold. (Disregard whether this current solution is optimal.) Sales projections, determined on the basis of recent marketing analysis, show that sales of Windy could be increased to 30,000 units if additional capacity were available.

Required

1. If Windbreakers deletes Gale entirely, how many units of Windy can it manufacture solely because of the capacity released by discontinuing the production of Gale?
2. What is the dollar effect on operating income if Windbreakers drops the production and sale of Gale and uses the resulting released capacity—and only this released capacity—for Windy?
3. What other factors should Windbreakers consider in its decision to drop Gale and use the released capacity to produce additional units of Windy?

The Student Resources section of Connect includes video tutorials for the Self-Study Problems.

Questions

11-1 What are relevant costs? Provide several examples for the decision to repair or replace a piece of equipment.

11-2 List at least four different decisions for which the relevant cost analysis model can be used effectively.

11-3 What is the relevant cost when determining whether to sell a product before or after additional processing?

11-4 List four to six strategic factors that are often important in the make-vs.-buy decision.

11-5 How do short-term evaluations affect a manager's incentives and performance?

11-6 List four or five important limitations of relevant cost analysis.

11-7 How do strategic factors affect the proper use of relevant cost analysis?

11-8 List some of the behavioral, implementation, and legal problems to be anticipated in the use of relevant cost analysis.

11-9 How does the presence of one production constraint affect the relevant cost analysis model? Two or more production constraints?

11-10 What is the relationship, if any, between the relevant cost analysis method and cost-volume-profit analysis (discussed in Chapter 9)?

Brief Exercises

[LO 11-1]

11-11 Williams Auto has a machine that installs tires. The machine is now in need of repair. The machine originally cost $10,000 and the repair will cost $1,000, but the machine will then last two years. The labor cost of operating the machine is $0.50 per tire. Instead of repairing the old machine, Williams could buy a new machine at a cost of $5,000 that would also last two years; the labor cost would then be reduced to $0.25 per tire. Should Williams repair or replace the machine if it expects to install 10,000 tires in the next two years?

[LO 11-1]   11-12   Jackson Inc. disposes of other companies' toxic waste. Currently, Jackson loads the waste by hand into a truck, which requires labor of $20 per load. Jackson is considering a machine that would reduce the amount of time needed to load the waste. The machine would cost $200,000 but would reduce labor cost to $5 per load. Assume that Jackson averages 10,000 loads per year. How many years (rounded to 2 decimal places) would it take for Jackson to recover the cost of the new machine?

[LO 11-1]   11-13   Durant Co. manufactures glass bottles for dairy products. The contribution margin is $0.10 per bottle. Durant just received notification that one of its orders for 100,000 bottles contained misprinted labels, and thus it had to recall and reprint the bottle labels. If it will cost $0.05 per bottle to reprint the labels and $1,000 to reship the bottles, what will the net contribution margin be after the recall?

[LO 11-1]   11-14   Sweet Dream Hotel has labor costs that are mostly fixed, including registration desk, maintenance, and general repairs and cleaning. The housekeeping staff is hired in sufficient numbers to clean the rooms that need cleaning so that housekeeping is a variable cost for the number of occupied rooms. Which of these costs is relevant for determining the price of a room?

[LO 11-2]   11-15   Lance's Diner has a hot-lunch special each weekday and Sunday afternoon. The cost of food and other variable costs for each meal served is $3.50; weekly fixed costs (e.g., building depreciation and equipment rental costs) are $6,000, regardless of how many days the diner is open per week. Lance has an average of 500 customers per day. What is the lowest price *in total* (not per meal) that Lance should charge for a special group of 200 that wants to come on Saturday for a family reunion? What should be the lowest price *per meal* that Lance should charge for the hot-lunch special served on weekdays and Sunday afternoons?

[LO 11-2]   11-16   ElecPlus Batteries has two different products, AAA and AA batteries. The AA batteries have a contribution margin of $1 per package, and the AAA batteries have a contribution margin of $2 per package. ElecPlus has a capacity for 1 million batteries per month, and both batteries require the same amount of processing time. If a special order for 10,000 AAA batteries exceeds the monthly capacity, should ElecPlus accept the special order?

[LO 11-2]   11-17   Adams Furniture receives a special order for 10 sofas for a special price of $3,000. The direct materials and direct labor for each sofa are $100. In addition, supervision and other fixed overhead costs average $150 per sofa. Should Adams accept the special order? Why or why not? Would it make a difference to your answer if Adams is at full capacity and its current line of sofas sells for $500 each?

[LO 11-2]   11-18   Wings Diner has a box lunch that it sells on football game days at the local university. Each box lunch sells for $6, which includes $2.50 variable costs and $2.50 fixed costs, plus a $1 markup. In the short run, what is the minimum price Wings Diner should charge (i.e., what is the price below which the diner would not normally sell a meal)?

[LO 11-3]   11-19   The external purchase price is $35 for a part that can be manufactured internally for $33 per unit; the $33 manufacturing cost includes $5 per-unit allocated fixed overhead cost. What is the per-unit savings to make rather than to buy?

[LO 11-5]   11-20   Jamison Health Care is trying to decide if it should eliminate its orthopedic care division. Last year, the orthopedic division had a total contribution margin of $100,000 and allocated overhead costs of $200,000, of which $90,000 could be eliminated if the division were dropped. Based solely on the above financial information, should Jamison keep the division?

Exercises

[LO 11-1, 11-3]   11-21   **Solar Panels: Lease vs. Buy**   Consumers (including businesses and local governments) interested in using solar power generally have an option to purchase or lease the solar panels. To adequately address the questions below, you will have to first do some research on the Internet. Please remember to document the website (or other source) from which you obtain information related to this exercise.

Required
1. In general, what are the relevant costs associated with the lease decision and the purchase decision in regard to the acquisition of solar panels?
2. What are the primary nonfinancial considerations associated with both the decision to use solar energy and the choice to lease versus purchase? Address this question from the standpoint of individual consumers, businesses, and society at large (i.e., the environment).

[LO 11-2]   11-22 **Special Order; Opportunity Cost**   Grant Industries, a manufacturer of electronic parts, has recently received an invitation to bid on a special order for 20,000 units of one of its most popular products. Grant currently manufactures 40,000 units of this product in its Loveland, Ohio, plant. The plant is operating at 50 percent capacity. There will be no marketing costs on the special order. The sales manager of Grant wants to set the bid at $9 per unit because she is sure that Grant will get the business at that price. Others on the executive committee of the firm object, saying that Grant would lose money on the special order at that price.

Units	40,000	60,000
Manufacturing costs:		
Direct materials	$ 80,000	$120,000
Direct labor	120,000	180,000
Factory overhead	240,000	300,000
Total manufacturing costs	$440,000	$600,000
Unit cost	$ 11.00	$ 10.00

Required
1. Why does the unit cost decline from $11 to $10 when production level rises from 40,000 to 60,000 units?
2. What would be the impact on short-term operating income if the order is accepted at the price recommended by the sales manager? What do you think the minimum (short-term) bid price should be?
3. List some additional factors Grant should consider in deciding how much to bid on this special order.
4. What would the total opportunity cost be if by accepting the special order the company lost sales of 5,000 units to its regular customers? Assume the preceding facts plus a normal selling price of $20 per unit.

[LO 11-2]   11-23 **Special Order; Opportunity Cost**   Alton Inc. is working at full production capacity producing 20,000 units of a unique product. Manufacturing costs per unit for the product are as follows:

Direct materials	$ 9
Direct labor	8
Manufacturing overhead	10
Total manufacturing cost per unit	$27

The per-unit manufacturing overhead cost is based on a $4 variable cost per unit and $120,000 fixed costs. The nonmanufacturing costs, all variable, are $8 per unit, and the sales price is $45 per unit.

Sports Headquarters Company (SHC) has asked Alton to produce 5,000 units of a modification of the new product. This modification would require the same manufacturing processes. However, because of the nature of the proposed sale, the estimated nonmanufacturing costs per unit are only $4 (not $8). Alton would sell the modified product to SHC for $35 per unit.

Required   Set up an Excel spreadsheet to answer the following questions:
1. What is the impact on short-term operating profit of accepting the special sales order from SHC?
2. Suppose that Alton Inc. had been working at less than full capacity to produce 16,000 units of the product when SHC made the offer. What is the minimum price per unit that Alton should accept for the modified product under these conditions? (Round answer to 2 decimal places.) Explain.
3. To prove (or provide support for your answer to Requirement 2), use Goal Seek in Excel to determine the minimum price (per unit) that Alton should accept for the special sales order.

[LO 11-2]   11-24 **Special Order; Relevant Costs; Opportunity Cost**   Sharman Athletic Gear Inc. (SAG) is considering a special order for 15,000 baseball caps with the logo of East Texas University (ETU) to be purchased by the ETU alumni association. The ETU alumni association is planning to use the caps as gifts and to sell some of the caps at alumni events in celebration of the university's recent national championship by its baseball team. Sharman's full manufacturing cost per hat is $3.50, which includes $1.50 fixed overhead cost related to plant capacity and equipment. ETU has made a firm offer of $35,000 for the hats, and Sharman, considering the price to be far below production costs, decides to decline the offer.

Required
1. What is the impact of this decision on short-term operating profit, rounded to the nearest whole dollar?
2. How might this example be used to illustrate the notion of opportunity cost?

[LO 11-2]   11-25 **Special Order**   Earth Baby Inc. (EBI) recently celebrated its 10th anniversary. The company produces organic baby products for health-conscious parents. These products include food, clothing, and toys. Earth Baby recently introduced a new line of premium organic baby foods. Extensive research and scientific testing indicate that babies raised on the new line of foods will have substantial health benefits. EBI is able to sell its products at prices higher than those charged by its competitors because of its excellent reputation for superior products. EBI distributes its products through high-end grocery stores, pharmacies, and specialty retail baby stores.

Joan Alvarez, the founder and CEO of EBI, recently received a proposal from an old business school classmate, Robert Bradley, the vice president of Great Deal Inc. (GDI), a large discount retailer. Mr. Bradley proposes a joint venture between his company and EBI, citing the growing demand for organic products and the superior distribution channels of his organization. Under this venture, EBI would make some minor modifications to the manufacturing process of some of its best-selling baby foods, and the foods would then be packaged and sold by GDI. Under the agreement, EBI would receive $3.10 per jar of baby food and would provide GDI a limited right to advertise the product as manufactured for Great Deal by EBI. Joan Alvarez set up a meeting with Fred Stanley, Earth Baby's CFO, to discuss the profitability of the venture. Mr. Stanley made some initial calculations and determined that the direct materials, direct labor, and other variable costs needed for the GDI order would be about $2 per unit as compared to the full cost of $3 (direct materials, direct labor, and manufacturing overhead) for the equivalent EBI product.

Required   Should Earth Baby Inc. accept the proposed venture from GDI? Why or why not? Include in your answer strategic considerations.

[LO 11-3]   11-26 **Make versus Buy; Continuation of Exercise 9-22 (Chapter 9)**   Vista Company manufactures electronic equipment. In 2021, it purchased from an outside supplier the special switches used in each of its products. The supplier charged Vista $2 per switch. As an alternative, Vista's CEO considered purchasing either machine A or machine B so the company could manufacture its own switches. The CEO decided at the beginning of 2022 to purchase machine A, based on the following data:

	Machine A	Machine B
Annual fixed cost (depreciation)	$135,000	$204,000
Variable cost per switch	0.65	0.30

Required
1. Assume that machine A has not yet been purchased. What is the annual volume (rounded up to nearest whole number) that would make the company indifferent between the two decision alternatives (i.e., purchasing and then using machine A to make the switches versus purchasing the switches from the outside vendor)?
2. Assume that machine A has already been purchased. Is it preferable to use machine A to make the switches or to purchase the switches from the external supplier?
3. Assume that machine A has already been purchased. At what annual volume level (rounded to the nearest whole number) should Vista consider replacing machine A with machine B?
4. Use the Goal Seek function in Excel to confirm the volume-indifference level you calculated in requirement 3.

[LO 11-5]   11-27 **Product-Line Profitability Analysis**   Barbour Corporation, located in Buffalo, New York, is a retailer of high-tech products and is known for its excellent quality and innovation. Recently, the firm conducted a relevant cost analysis of one of its product lines that has only two products, T-1 and T-2. The sales for T-2 are decreasing and the purchase costs are increasing. The firm might drop T-2 and sell only T-1.

Barbour allocates fixed costs to products on the basis of sales revenue. When the president of Barbour saw the income statements (see below), he agreed that T-2 should be dropped. If T-2 is dropped, sales of T-1 are expected to increase by 10 percent next year, but the firm's cost structure will remain the same.

	T-1	T-2
Sales	$200,000	$260,000
Variable costs:		
Cost of goods sold	70,000	130,000
Selling & administrative	20,000	50,000
Contribution margin	$110,000	$ 80,000
Fixed expenses:		
Fixed corporate costs	58,700	76,300
Fixed selling and administrative	14,300	18,700
Total fixed expenses	$ 73,000	$ 95,000
Operating income	$ 37,000	$ (15,000)

Required

1. Find the expected change in annual operating income by dropping T-2 and selling only T-1. (Round answer to nearest whole dollar.)

2. By what percentage would sales from T-1 have to increase in order to make up the financial loss from dropping T-2? (Round your answer to 2 decimal places. For example, 56.568% = 56.57%.)

3. What is the required percentage increase in sales (rounded to 2 decimal places) from T-1 to compensate for lost margin from T-2, if total fixed costs can be reduced by $45,000?

4. What strategic factors should be considered in deciding whether to drop or to keep T-2?

[LO 11-4, 11-7] **11-28 Sell-or-Process-Further Decision; Product Mix** Cantel Company produces cleaning compounds for both commercial and household customers. Some of these products are produced as part of a joint manufacturing process. For example, GR37, a coarse cleaning powder meant for commercial sale, costs $1.60 a pound to make and sells for $2.00 per pound. A portion of the annual production of GR37 is retained for further processing in a separate department where it is combined with several other ingredients to form SilPol, which is sold as a silver polish, at $4.00 per unit. The additional processing requires ¼ pound of GR37 per unit; additional processing costs amount to $2.50 per unit of SilPol produced. Variable selling costs for SilPol average $0.30 per unit. If production of SilPol were discontinued, $5,600 of costs in the processing department would be avoided. Cantel has, at this point, unlimited demand for, but limited capacity to produce, product GR37.

Required

1. Calculate the minimum number of units of SilPol that would have to be sold in order to justify further processing of GR37. Round your answer to nearest whole number.

2. Assume that the cost data reported for GR37 are obtained at a level of output equal to 5,000 pounds, which is the maximum that the company can produce at this time. What is the expected operating income (to the nearest whole dollar) under each of the following scenarios: (a) all available capacity is used to produce GR37, but no SilPol; (b) 4,000 units of SilPol are produced, with the balance of capacity devoted to the production and sale of GR37; (c) 8,000 units of SilPol are produced, with the balance of capacity devoted to the production and sale of GR37; and (d) 10,000 units of SilPol are produced, with the balance of capacity devoted to the production and sale of GR37.

(CMA Adapted)

[LO 11-7] **11-29 Constrained Optimization Analysis: Product-Mix Decision** Sandalwood Company produces various lines of high-end carpeting in its Asheville, North Carolina, plant. This question pertains to two different grades of carpet in its Symphony line: commercial and residential. The former sells for $16 per square yard, while the latter sells for $25 per square yard (wholesale). Variable costs are $10 per square yard and $15 per square yard for the commercial and residential grade products, respectively. On average, it takes 12 labor hours to produce 100 square yards of commercial carpeting, and 18 labor hours for each 100 square yards of residential carpeting. Currently, the company is producing 28,000 square yards per week of commercial carpet and 6,000 square yards per week of residential carpet. Total labor-hour consumption at the plant is currently 4,440 hours per week. Fixed manufacturing costs ($17,300 per week) are allocated to products on the basis of labor hours. At the current volume and mix, this amounts to $0.4657 and $0.7013 for each square yard of commercial versus residential carpet produced, respectively. The company is currently evaluating its sales mix and the possibility of expanding its labor force.

Required

1. At the current output level and mix, what is the gross profit (gross margin) for each of the two products, in total and per square yard? Round total amounts to nearest whole number; round per-yard amounts to 2 decimal places.

2. What is the contribution margin for each of the two products, in total and per square yard? Round total amounts to nearest whole number; round per-yard amounts for contribution margin to 2 decimal places.

3. Assume that the company has recently conducted a marketing study, which revealed total estimated weekly demand of 30,000 and 8,000 square yards of commercial and residential carpeting, respectively. Assume, too, that the company is able to expand its labor force to 4,600 hours per week. (a) What is the contribution margin per labor hour (to 2 decimal places) for each product? (b) Given your answer to (a) above, and the labor-hour and product demand constraints, what is the optimum product mix, on a weekly basis? That is, how many square yards of each product should be produced each week? (Round answers to nearest whole number.) (c) Generate a graphical solution to this problem, similar to the solution presented in Exhibit 11.21.

4. What conceptual lesson (take-away) is associated with requirements 1–3 above?

5. What is the primary role of the management accountant in terms of addressing the short-term product- (or service-) mix problem?

[LO 11-1, 11-2, 11-3, 11-4, 11-7]   11-30 **Relevant Cost Exercises**   Each of the following situations is independent:

a. **Make or Buy**   Terry Inc. manufactures machine parts for aircraft engines. CEO Bucky Walters is considering an offer from a subcontractor to provide 2,000 units of product OP89 for $120,000. If Terry does not purchase these parts from the subcontractor, it must continue to produce them in-house with these costs:

	Cost per Unit
Direct materials	$28
Direct labor	18
Variable overhead	16
Allocated fixed overhead	4

Required

1. What is the relevant cost (per unit, rounded to 2 decimal places) to make the product internally?

2. What is the estimated increase or decrease in short-term operating profit of producing the product internally versus purchasing the product from a supplier? (Round your answer to nearest whole dollar.)

3. What strategic considerations likely bear on this make-vs.-buy decision?

b. **Disposal of Assets**   A company has an inventory of 2,000 different parts for a line of cars that has been discontinued. The net book value (NBV) of this inventory is $50,000. Either the parts can be re-machined at a total additional cost of $25,000 and then sold for $30,000, or the parts can be sold as-is for $2,500.

Required   What should the company do? Include both financial and strategic considerations.

c. **Asset Replacement**   An uninsured boat costing $90,000 was wrecked the first day it was used. It can be either sold as-is for $9,000 cash and replaced with a similar boat costing $92,000 or rebuilt for $75,000 and be brand new as far as operating characteristics and looks are concerned.

Required   What should be done? Include a consideration of both financial and strategic factors.

d. **Profit from Processing Further**   Deaton Corporation manufactures products A, B, and C from a joint process. Joint costs are allocated on the basis of relative sales value of the products at the split-off point. Additional information for Deaton Corporation follows:

	A	B	C	Total
Units produced	12,000	8,000	4,000	24,000
Joint costs	$144,000	$ 60,000	$36,000	$240,000
Sales value before additional processing	240,000	100,000	60,000	400,000
Additional costs for further processing	28,000	20,000	12,000	60,000
Sales value if processed further	280,000	120,000	70,000	470,000

Required

1. Define the following terms: joint production process, joint production costs, separable processing costs, and split-off point.
2. What is the impact on short-term operating income of processing each of the three products (A, B, and C) beyond the split-off point? Round each answer to nearest whole dollar.
3. Why do accountants allocate joint/common costs to individual products in a joint manufacturing process?

e. **Make-vs.-Buy (Sourcing Decision)**   Eggers Company needs 20,000 units of a part to use in producing one of its products. If Eggers buys the part from McMillan Company for $90 instead of making it, Eggers will not use the released facilities in another manufacturing activity. Forty percent of the fixed overhead will continue irrespective of CEO Donald Mickey's decision. The cost data are as follows:

Cost to make the part:	
Direct materials	$35
Direct labor	16
Variable overhead	24
Fixed overhead	20
	$95

Required

1. Determine which alternative is more attractive to Eggers, and by what amount.
2. What strategic factors might bear upon the ultimate decision?

f. **Short-Term Product-Mix Decision**   DVD Production Company produces two basic types of video games, Flash and Clash. Pertinent data for DVD Production Company follow:

	Flash	Clash
Sales price	$250	$140
Costs		
Direct materials	50	25
Direct labor (@ $25/hr.)	100	50
Variable factory overhead*	50	25
Fixed factory overhead*	20	10
Marketing costs (all fixed)	10	10
Total costs	$230	$120
Operating profit	$ 20	$ 20

*Based on direct labor hours: 4 direct labor hours (DLHs) per unit of Flash and 2 DLHs per unit of Clash.

The DVD game craze is at its height so that either Flash or Clash alone can be sold to keep the plant operating at full capacity. However, labor capacity in the plant is insufficient to meet the combined demand for both games. Flash and Clash are processed through the same production departments.

Required

1. What are the meaning and importance of the statement that "Flash and Clash are processed through the same production departments"?
2. Which of the two products should be produced? Briefly explain your answer.

g. **Special-Order Pricing**   Barry's Bar-B-Que is a popular lunch time spot. Barry is conscientious about the quality of his meals, and he has a regular crowd of 600 patrons for his $5 lunch. His variable cost for each meal is about $2, and he figures his fixed costs, on a daily basis, are about $1,200. From time to time, bus-tour groups with 50 patrons stop by. He has welcomed them because he has capacity to seat 700 diners in the average lunch period, and his cooking and wait staff can easily handle the additional load. The tour operator generally pays for the entire group on a single check to save the wait staff and cashier the additional time. Due to competitive conditions in the tour business, the operator is now asking Barry to lower the price to $3.50 per meal for each of the 50 bus-tour members.

Required

1. What is the incremental profit (loss) per bus-tour meal? Should Barry accept the bus-tour offer?
2. At least once per month, the tour company is in a position to guarantee 200 patrons (or four bus loads) in a single day. On those days, the tour company is asking for an even lower price of $3.00 per meal. What is the incremental profit (loss) for each meal? Is the offer financially attractive?

Problems

[LO 11-1]   11-31 **Budgeting and Sustainability**   If Problem 10-58 (Budgeting and Sustainability) has not already been assigned, it can be assigned here.

Note: For requirements 1 and 2, round answers to nearest whole number. For requirements 3a and 3b, round answer to 2 decimal places.

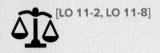

[LO 11-2, LO 11-8]   11-32 **Special Order**   Award Plus Co. manufactures medals for winners of athletic events and other contests. Its manufacturing plant has the capacity to produce 10,000 medals each month; current monthly production is 7,500 medals. The company normally charges $225 per medal. Variable costs and fixed costs for the current activity level of 75 percent follow:

	Current Product Costs
Variable costs	
Manufacturing	
Labor	$ 375,000
Material	300,000
Marketing	187,500
Total variable costs	$ 862,500
Fixed costs	
Manufacturing	$ 275,000
Marketing	225,000
Total fixed costs	$ 500,000
Total costs	$1,362,500

Award Plus has just received a special one-time order for 2,500 medals at $115 per medal. For this particular order, no variable marketing costs will be incurred. Cathy Senna, a management accountant with Award Plus, has been assigned the task of analyzing this order and recommending whether the company should accept or reject it. After examining the costs, Senna suggested to her supervisor, Gerard LePenn, who is the controller, that they request competitive bids from vendors for the raw materials because the current quote seems high. LePenn insisted that the prices are in line with those of other vendors and told her that she was not to discuss her observations with anyone else. Senna later discovered that LePenn is a brother-in-law of the owner of the current raw materials supply vendor.

Required

1. Calculate both the old (i.e., prior to the special order) average cost per unit and the revised average cost per unit, including the effect of the special sales order. (Round both answers to 2 decimal places.) Are either of these two figures relevant for evaluating whether to accept or reject the special order? Explain.

2. What is the short-term effect on operating profit (to the nearest whole dollar) if Award Plus Co. accepts the special sales order? (Round answer to nearest whole number.)

3. What is the breakeven selling price per unit for the special sales order, rounded to 2 decimal places?

4. Discuss at least three other considerations that Cathy Senna should include in her analysis of the special sales order.

5. Explain how Cathy Senna should try to resolve the ethical conflict arising out of the controller's insistence that the company avoid competitive bidding.

(**CMA Adapted**)

[LO 11-2, LO 11-8]   11-33 **Special Order**   Green Grow Inc. (GGI) manufactures lawn fertilizer. Because of the product's very high quality, GGI often receives special orders from agricultural research groups. For each type of fertilizer sold, each bag is carefully filled to have the precise mix of components advertised for that type of fertilizer. GGI's operating capacity is 22,000 one-hundred-pound bags per month, and it currently is selling 20,000 bags manufactured in 20 batches of 1,000 bags each. The firm just received a request for a special order of 5,000 one-hundred-pound bags of fertilizer for $130,000 from APAC, a research organization. The production costs would be the same, but there would be no variable selling costs. Delivery and other packaging and distribution services would cause a one-time $2,500 cost for GGI. The special order would be processed in two batches of 2,500 bags each. (No incremental batch-level costs are anticipated. Most of the batch-level costs in this case are short-term fixed costs, such as salaries and depreciation.) The following information is provided about GGI's current operations:

Sales and production cost data for 20,000 bags, per bag:	
Sales price	$40
Variable manufacturing costs	17
Variable selling costs	3
Fixed manufacturing costs	12
Fixed marketing costs	4

No marketing costs would be associated with the special order. Because the order would be used in research and consistency is critical, APAC requires that GGI fill the entire order of 5,000 bags.

Required

1. What is the total relevant cost of filling this special sales order, rounded to nearest whole dollar?

2. What would be the change in operating income (to nearest whole dollar) if the special order is accepted?

3. What is the breakeven selling price per unit for the special sales order (i.e., what is the selling price that would result in a zero effect on operating income)? Round answer to 2 decimal places.

4. Prepare comparative income statements, using the contribution format, for both the current situation and assuming the special order is accepted at the breakeven price determined in requirement 3.

5. Suppose that after GGI accepts the special order, it finds that unexpected production delays will not allow it to supply all 5,000 units from its own plants and meet the promised delivery date. It can provide the same materials by purchasing them in bulk from a competing firm. The materials would then be packaged in GGI bags to complete the order. GGI knows the competitor's materials are very good quality, but it cannot be sure that the quality meets its own exacting standards. There is not enough time to carefully test the competitor's product to determine its quality. What should GGI do? Specifically, discuss ethical and strategic issues associated with the decision.

[LO 11-2] 11-34 **Special Order; ABC Costing (Continuation of Problem 11-33)**   Assume the same information as for Problem 11-33, except that the $12.00 fixed manufacturing overhead cost per unit consists of facility-level costs ($9.00/unit at the 20,000-unit output level), with the remainder being setup-related (i.e., batch-level) costs. Assume that the setup-related costs increase in total with the number of batches produced and that the facility-level fixed costs do not vary in total, with either the number of units produced or the number of batches produced during a period.

Required

1. What is the total fixed manufacturing overhead cost for the period? Break down (that is, decompose) this total cost into its component parts (i.e., batch-related overhead costs and facility-related fixed overhead costs). Round all answers to nearest whole dollar.

2. Calculate the relevant unit and total costs of the special order, including the new information about batch-related costs. Assume, as before, the one-time delivery cost of $2,500. Round the total cost to the nearest whole dollar; round the per-unit relevant cost to 2 decimal places.

3. If accepted, how would the special order affect GGI's short-term operating income?

[LO 11-2] 11-35 **Special Order; Strategy; International**   Williams Company, located in southern Wisconsin, manufactures a variety of industrial valves and pipe fittings that are sold to customers in nearby states. Currently, the company is operating at about 70 percent capacity and is earning a satisfactory return on investment.

Glasgow Industries Ltd. of Scotland has approached management with an offer to buy 120,000 units of a pressure valve. Glasgow Industries manufactures a valve that is almost identical to Williams's pressure valve; however, a fire in Glasgow Industries's valve plant has shut down its manufacturing operations. Glasgow needs the 120,000 valves over the next four months to meet commitments to its regular customers; the company is prepared to pay $21 each for the valves.

Williams's product cost for the pressure valve, based on current attainable standards, follows:

Direct materials	$ 6
Direct labor (0.5 hour per valve)	8
Manufacturing overhead (1/3 variable)	9
Total manufacturing cost	$23

Additional costs incurred in connection with sales of the pressure valve are sales commissions of 5 percent and freight expense of $1 per unit. However, the company does not pay sales commissions on special orders that come directly to management. Freight expense will be paid by Glasgow.

In determining selling prices, Williams adds a 40 percent markup to product cost. This provides a $32 suggested selling price for the pressure valve, rounded to the nearest whole dollar. The marketing department, however, has set the current selling price at $30 to maintain market share.

Production management believes that it can handle the Glasgow Industries order without disrupting its scheduled production. The order would, however, require additional fixed factory overhead of $12,000 per month in the form of supervision and clerical costs.

If management accepts the order, Williams will manufacture and ship 30,000 pressure valves to Glasgow Industries each month for the next four months. Shipments will be made in weekly consignments, FOB shipping point.

Required

1. Determine how many additional direct labor hours (DLHs) will be required each month to fill the Glasgow order. Round your answer to the nearest whole number.

2. Prepare an analysis showing the impact on operating income of accepting the Glasgow order.

3. Calculate the minimum unit price that Williams's management could accept for the Glasgow order without reducing operating income. Round answer to 2 decimal places.

4. To prove your answer to requirement 3, use the Goal Seek function in Excel to calculate the minimum unit selling price (to 2 decimal places) for the special sales order.

5. Suppose now that if the Glasgow order were accepted, sales of 5,000 units per month to regular customers would be precluded (at a selling price of $30 per unit). All other facts are as given in this problem. What is the revised breakeven selling price per unit for the Glasgow special sales order? Round answer to 2 decimal places.

6. Identify the strategic factors that Williams should consider before accepting the Glasgow order.

7. Identify the factors related to international business that Williams should consider before accepting the Glasgow order.

(CMA Adapted)

[LO 11-3]   11-36 **Make vs. Buy; Strategy**   Martens Inc. manufactures a variety of electronic products. It specializes in commercial and residential products with moderate-to-large electric motors such as pumps and fans. Martens is now looking closely at its production of attic fans, which included 10,000 units in the prior year (see the table below). These costs included $100,000 of allocated fixed manufacturing overhead. Martens has capacity to manufacture 15,000 attic fans per year.

Martens believes demand in the coming year will be 20,000 attic fans. The company has looked into the possibility of purchasing the attic fans from another manufacturer to help it meet this demand. Harris Products, a steady supplier of quality products, would be able to provide up to 9,000 attic fans per year at a price of $46.00 per fan delivered to Martens's facility.

The following is based on the production of 10,000 units in the prior year:

Selling price per unit		$72.00
Costs per unit:		
Electric motor	$ 6.00	
Other parts	8.00	
Direct labor ($15/hour)	15.00	
Manufacturing overhead	15.00	
Selling and administrative cost	20.00	64.00
Profit per unit		$ 8.00

For each attic fan that Martens sells, regardless of whether the fan was purchased from Harris or was manufactured by Martens, there is an additional selling and administrative cost of $20.00 which includes (at a sales level of 10,000 units) fixed costs of $6.00 per unit.

Required

1. What is the (short-term) relevant manufacturing cost per fan for Martens? (Round your answer to 2 decimal places.)

2. Given the projected demand of 20,000 units, how many units should the company manufacture, and how many units (if any) should it purchase from Harris Products? Assume that the variable selling and administrative expense will be incurred for all sales. Explain your reasoning. Under this optimum plan, what is the total contribution margin?

3. Independent of requirement 2, assume that Beth Johnson, Martens's product manager, has suggested that the company could make better use of its fan department capacity by manufacturing marine pumps instead of fans. Johnson believes that Martens could expect to use the production capacity to produce and sell 25,000 pumps annually at a price of $60.00 per pump. Johnson's estimate of the costs to manufacture the pumps is presented below. If Johnson's suggestion is not accepted, Martens would sell 20,000 attic fans instead. Information on the sales price and costs for the marine pumps follows (assume that total fixed selling/administrative costs and total fixed overhead costs are the same, regardless of whether fans or pumps are produced):

Selling price per pump		$60.00
Cost per unit:		
Electric motor	$ 5.50	
Other parts	7.00	
Direct labor ($15/hour)	7.50	
Manufacturing overhead	9.00	
Selling and administrative cost	20.00	49.00
Profit per pump		$11.00

What would the total contribution margin be (to nearest whole dollar) from manufacturing and selling the marine pumps? Given this information, should Martens manufacture pumps or attic fans (based solely on short-term financial considerations)?

4. What are some of the strategic factors related to Martens's decisions in requirements 2 and 3?

[LO 11-3, LO 11-8]   11-37   **Make vs. Buy; Strategy; Ethics**   The Midwest Division of the Paibec Corporation manufactures subassemblies used in Paibec's final products. Lynn Hardt of Midwest's profit planning department has been assigned the task of determining whether Midwest should continue to manufacture a subassembly component, MTR-2000, or purchase it from Marley Company, an outside supplier. Marley has submitted a bid to manufacture and supply the 30,000 units of MTR-2000 that Paibec will need for 2022 at a per-unit price of $20.00. Marley has assured Paibec that the units will be delivered according to Paibec's production specifications and needs. The contract price of $20.00 is applicable only in 2022, but Marley is interested in entering into a long-term arrangement beyond 2022.

Lynn has submitted the following information regarding Midwest's cost to manufacture 25,000 units of MTR-2000 in 2021:

Direct materials	$168,750
Direct labor	100,000
Factory space rental	150,000
Equipment leasing costs	45,000
Other manufacturing costs	250,000
Total manufacturing costs	$713,750

Lynn has collected the following information related to manufacturing MTR-2000:

- Equipment leasing costs represent special equipment used to manufacture MTR-2000. Midwest can terminate this lease by paying the equivalent of one month's lease payment for each of the two years left on its lease agreement.

- Forty percent of the other manufacturing overhead is considered variable. Variable overhead changes with the number of units produced, and this rate per unit is not expected to change in 2022. The fixed manufacturing overhead costs are not expected to change (in total) whether Midwest manufactures or purchases MTR-2000. Midwest can use equipment other than the leased equipment in its other manufacturing operations.

- Direct materials cost used in the production of MTR-2000 is expected to increase 7 percent in 2022.

- Midwest's direct labor contract calls for a 4 percent wage increase in 2022.

- The facilities used to manufacture MTR-2000 are rented under a month-to-month rental agreement. Midwest would have no need for this space if it does not manufacture MTR-2000. Thus, Midwest can withdraw from the rental agreement without any penalty.

John Porter, Midwest's divisional manager, stopped by Lynn's office to voice his opinion regarding the outsourcing of MTR-2000. He commented, "I am really concerned about outsourcing MTR-2000. I have a son-in-law and a nephew, not to mention a member of our bowling team, who work on MTR-2000. They could lose their jobs if we buy that component from Marley. I really would appreciate anything you can do to make sure the cost analysis shows that we should continue making MTR-2000. Corporate is not aware of materials cost increases and maybe you can leave out some of those fixed costs. I just think we should continue making MTR-2000."

Required

1. Prepare a relevant cost analysis that shows whether the Midwest Division should make MTR-2000 or purchase it from Marley Company for 2022. Specifically, (a) what is the relevant cost per unit to make and the relevant cost per unit to buy externally? (Round both answers to 2 decimal places.) (b) What is the total difference in relevant costs between the two alternatives, assuming a volume of 30,000 units? (Round answer to nearest whole number.)

2. Identify and briefly discuss the strategic factors that Midwest should consider in this decision.

3. By referring to the specific ethical standards for management accountants outlined in Chapter 1, assess the ethical issues in John Porter's request of Lynn Hardt. (See **www.imanet.org/career-resources/ethics-center.**)

(CMA Adapted)

[LO 11-3, 11-6, LO 11-8]

11-38 Outsourcing Call Centers; Strategy; Ethics; Present-Value Analysis (Chapter 12)   Merchants' Bank (MB) is a large regional bank operating in 634 locations in the southeastern United States. Until 2014, the bank operated a call center for customer inquiries out of a single location in Atlanta, Georgia. MB understood the importance of the call center for overall customer satisfaction and made sure that the center was managed effectively. However, in early 2013, it became clear that the cost of running the center was increasing very rapidly, along with the firm's growth, and that some issues were arising about the quality of the service. To improve the quality and dramatically reduce the cost of the service, MB moved its call center to Bangalore, India, to be run by an experienced outsourcing firm, Naftel, which offers similar services to other banks like MB.

The Naftel contract was for five years, and in late 2017 it was time to consider whether to renew the contract, change to another call center service provider (in India or elsewhere), or bring the call center back to Atlanta.

Some important factors to consider in the decision:

- At the time of the decision in late 2017, assume that the value of the dollar was increasing relative to most other currencies.

- Recent worldwide events in the financial marketplace were starting to affect the banking business, and the outlook for growth for MB at the time had not been as rosy as it had been for the last few years. Top management and economic advisors for the bank had basically no idea what to forecast for the coming five years.

- At the time of the decision, the employment rate in Atlanta had been falling to the point where there was a good supply of talented employees who could have been recruited into the call center if the center were relocated back to Atlanta.

- The bank had just completed a new headquarters building in Atlanta and had a good bit of space in the building that MB had yet to lease. The outlook for the Atlanta economy was such that MB did not expect to lease much of this space for at least three years. If the call center were returned to Atlanta, it would occupy a space that could be rented for $100,000 per year, assuming there was a company that wanted to lease the space.

- If renewed, the Naftel contract would cost $4,200,000 per year for each of the next five years.

- The cost of salaries to staff the call center in Atlanta was expected to be $2,300,000 per year, the equipment would be leased for $850,000 per year, telecommunication services were expected to cost $500,000 per year, administrative costs for the call center were expected to be $600,000 per year, and the call center's share of corporate overhead was expected to be $400,000 per year.

Required

1. What is the five-year raw (i.e., undiscounted) total cost for the Naftel option? What is the five-year raw (i.e., undiscounted) cost of the Atlanta option? Round both answers to nearest whole dollar.

2. What is the discounted present-value cost of the Naftel option? What is the discounted present-value cost of the Atlanta option? (*Note:* For present-value [PV] calculations, assume a discount rate of 6 percent; use the formula at the bottom of Table 1, Appendix C, in Chapter 12 and in Excel to generate PV factors.)

3. What are the global and/or strategic issues related to the decision?

4. What ethical issues, if any, should have been considered in the decision?

[LO 11-5] 11-39 **Project Analysis; Sales Promotions** Hillside Furniture Company makes outdoor furniture from recycled products, including plastics and wood by-products. Its three furniture products are gliders, chairs with footstools, and tables. The products appeal primarily to cost-conscious consumers and those who value the recycling of materials. The company wholesales its products to retailers and various mass merchandisers. Because of the seasonal nature of the products, most orders are manufactured during the winter months for delivery in the early spring. Michael Cain, founder and owner, is dismayed that sales for two of the products are tracking below budget. The accompanying chart shows pertinent year-to-date data regarding the company's products.

Certain that the shortfall was caused by a lack of effort by the sales force, Michael has suggested to Lisa Boyle, the sales manager, that the company announce two contests to correct this situation before it deteriorates. The first contest is a trip to Hawaii awarded to the top salesperson if incremental glider sales are attained to close the budget shortfall. The second contest is a golf weekend, complete with a new set of golf clubs, awarded to the top salesperson if incremental sales of chairs with footstools are attained to close the budget shortfall. The Hawaiian vacation would cost $16,500 and the golf trip would cost $12,500.

	Glider		Chair with Footstool		Table	
	Actual	**Budget**	**Actual**	**Budget**	**Actual**	**Budget**
Number of units	2,600	4,000	6,900	8,000	3,500	3,300
Average sales price	$80.00	$85.00	$61.00	$65.00	$24.00	$25.00
Variable costs:						
Direct labor:						
Hours of labor	2.50	2.25	3.25	3.00	0.60	0.50
Cost per hour	$11.00	$10.00	$ 9.50	$ 9.25	$ 9.00	$ 9.00
Direct material	$16.00	$15.00	$11.00	$10.00	$ 6.00	$ 5.00
Sales commission	$15.00	$15.00	$10.00	$10.00	$ 5.00	$ 5.50

Required

1. What is the estimated financial impact of the first contest, net of the cost of the prize? What is the estimated financial impact of the second contest, net of the cost of the prize?

2. Supplement your analysis by determining the total contribution margin for the glider product and the chair-with-footstool product, under each of the following two scenarios: (a) actual sales volume at actual selling prices, actual costs, and actual resource usage and (b) actual sales volume at actual selling prices, budgeted resource usage, and budgeted costs. (Round all answers to nearest whole dollar.) What is the primary insight based on this supplemental analysis?

3. Explain the strategic issues guiding your choice about these contests.

(CMA Adapted)

[LO 11-5, 11-7] 11-40 **Profitability Analysis; Pro Forma Income Statement** RayLok Incorporated has invented a secret process to improve light intensity and, as a result, manufactures a variety of products related to this process. Each product is independent of the others and is treated as a separate profit/loss division. Product (division) managers have a great deal of freedom to manage their divisions as they think best. Failure to produce target divisional income is dealt with severely; however, rewards for exceeding one's profit objective are, as one division manager described them, lavish.

The DimLok Division sells an add-on automotive accessory that automatically dims a vehicle's headlights by sensing a certain intensity of light coming from a specific direction. DimLok has had a new manager in each of the three previous years because each manager failed to reach RayLok's target profit level. Donna Barnes has just been promoted to manager and is studying ways to meet the current target profit for DimLok.

DimLok's two profit targets for the coming year are $800,000 (20 percent return on the investment in the annual fixed costs of the division) and $20 (pretax) profit for each DimLok unit sold. Other constraints on the division's operations are as follows:

- Production cannot exceed sales because RayLok's corporate advertising program stresses completely new product models each year, although the models might have only cosmetic changes.

- DimLok's selling price cannot vary above the current selling price of $200 per unit but may vary as much as 10 percent below $200.

- A division manager can elect to expand fixed production or selling facilities; however, the target profit objective related to fixed costs is increased by 20 percent of the cost of any such expansion. Furthermore, a manager cannot expand fixed facilities by more than 30 percent of existing fixed cost levels without approval from the board of directors.

Donna is now examining data gathered by her staff to determine whether DimLok can achieve its target profits of $800,000 and $20 per unit. A summary of these reports shows the following:

- Last year's sales were 30,000 units at $200 per unit.

- DimLok's current manufacturing facility capacity is 40,000 units per year, but can be increased to 80,000 units per year with an increase of $1,000,000 in annual fixed costs.

- Present variable costs amount to $80 per unit, but DimLok's vendors are willing to offer direct materials discounts amounting to $20 per unit, beginning with unit number 60,001.

- Sales can be increased up to 100,000 units per year by committing large blocks of product to institutional buyers at a discounted unit price of $180. However, this discount applies only to sales in excess of 40,000 units per year.

Donna believes that these projections are reliable and is now trying to determine what DimLok must do to meet the profit objectives assigned by RayLok's board of directors.

Required
1. Determine the dollar amount of DimLok's present annual fixed costs per year.
2. Determine the number of units (rounded to the nearest whole number) that DimLok must sell to achieve both profit objectives. Be sure to consider all constraints in determining your answer.
3. Without regard to your answer in requirement 2, assume that Donna decides to sell 40,000 units at $200 per unit and 24,000 units at $180 per unit. (a) Prepare a budgeted income statement (contribution format) for DimLok showing budgeted operating income (to nearest whole dollar). (b) Would this projected operating income meet the stated profit objectives?
4. Provide a succinct description of DimLok's competitive strategy.
5. Identify critical success factors associated with the strategy that DimLok is pursuing.

(CMA Adapted)

[LO 11-7]   11-41 **Product-Profitability Analysis; Scarce Resources**   Creighton Corporation produces a variety of consumer electronic products. Unit selling prices and costs for three models of one of its product lines are as follows:

	No Frills	Standard Options	Super
Selling price	$40.00	$70.00	$86.00
Direct materials	10.00	14.00	16.00
Direct labor (@ $20/hour)	10.00	20.00	30.00
Variable overhead	3.00	6.00	9.00
Fixed overhead	3.00	6.00	6.00

Variable overhead is charged to products on the basis of direct labor dollars; fixed overhead is allocated to products on the basis of machine hours.

Required
1. What is fundamentally different about the fixed versus variable overhead assigned to products? (Answer the question within the context of the relevance of this difference to the determination of short-term product mix.)
2. Calculate for each product both the gross profit per unit and the contribution margin per unit. (Round answers to 2 decimal places, e.g., $15.459 = $15.46.) Are either of these profitability measures useful for planning the optimum short-term product mix? Explain.
3. If the company has excess machine capacity but a limited amount of labor time, how should the optimum short-term product mix be determined? That is, which product is most desirable (profitable)? Which of the three is least desirable (profitable)?
4. Assume now that machine hours, not direct labor hours, is the limiting resource. How, if at all, would this affect the product-mix decision? That is, which of the three products is the most desirable (profitable)? Which of the three is least desirable (profitable)?
5. How can the optimum product mix be determined when there are only two products and one or more constraints?
6. How can the optimum product mix be determined when there are more than two products and one or more constraints?
7. What is the primary role of the management accountant in terms of planning the optimum short-term product mix?

[LO 11-7] 11-42 **Sustainability** If not assigned previously, Problem 9-50 and 9-51 (CVP Analysis; Sustainability; Uncertainty; Decision Tables) can be assigned here.

[LO 11-9] 11-43 **Two Production Constraints; Corner Point Analysis; Linear Programming (Appendix)** Let us revisit the Windbreakers Inc. situation from the chapter. Information from Exhibit 11.16B is reproduced below and shows the results after Gale was dropped and the avoidable marketing expenses were also removed.

	Calm	Windy	Total
Sale in units	25,000	18,750	
Sales ($30 and $32 per unit)	$750,000	$600,000	$1,350,000
Variable cost ($24 per unit)	600,000	450,000	1,050,000
Contribution margin	$150,000	$150,000	$ 300,000
Traceable Advertising	25,000	15,000	40,000
Contribution after all relevant costs	$125,000	$135,000	$ 260,000
Fixed cost (unavoidable)			$ 111,000
Operating profit			$ 149,000

We will now assume that the production of the remaining products, Calm and Windy, requires an automated sewing machine to stitch the jackets and that this production activity is a limited resource: Sales demand for the two products exceeds the capacity of the plant's three automated sewing machines. Each machine can be run up to 20 hours per day five days per week, or 400 hours per month, which is its maximum capacity allowing for maintenance. This gives 1,200 (3 machines × 400 hours per machine) available hours for sewing each month. Assume further that the machine requires four minutes to assemble a Calm and three minutes to assemble a Windy.

A second activity inspects and packages the completed product, and this operation is done by 40 workers. Because of the limited size of the facility, no more than 40 workers can be employed effectively in the inspection and packaging process. These employees work a 40-hour week, which means 35 hours of actually performing the operation, given time for breaks, training, and other tasks. Thus, 5,600 hours (40 workers × 35 hours/week × 4 weeks/month) are available per month for the inspection and packaging activity. While the workers can complete the activity for the Calm jacket in 6 minutes, due to its heavier weight and the insulation, it takes the workers 15 minutes to complete the operation for the Windy jacket.

Required

1. Determine the contribution margin per hour, the maximum production per month, and the maximum contribution per month for each product if the sewing machines were the only constraining resource. From a strictly financial perspective, which product would you recommend Windbreakers produce?

2. Determine the contribution margin per hour, the maximum production per month, and the maximum contribution per month for each product if the inspection and packing activity were the only constraining resource. From a strictly financial perspective, which product would you recommend Windbreakers produce?

3. Recognizing there are two constraining resources, management decides to do a further analysis. Graph the maximum production results from requirements 1 and 2 and do a corner point analysis. For this requirement, ignore the avoidable fixed costs.

4. Redo requirement 3 using the Solver tool. Note that the online appendix for this chapter discusses the use of Solver.

[LO 11-3, 11-5, 11-8] 11-44 **Make vs. Buy; Strategy** GianAuto Corporation manufactures parts and components for manufacturers and suppliers of parts for automobiles, vans, and trucks. Sales have increased each year based, in part, on the company's excellent record of customer service and reliability. The industry as a whole has also grown as auto manufacturers continue to outsource more of their production, especially to cost-efficient manufacturers such as GianAuto. To take advantage of lower wage rates and favorable business environments around the world, GianAuto has located its plants in six different countries.

Among the various GianAuto plants is the Denver Cover Plant, one of GianAuto's earliest plants. The Denver Cover Plant prepares and sews coverings made primarily of leather and upholstery fabric and ships them to other GianAuto plants, where they are used to cover seats, headrests, door panels, and other GianAuto products.

Ted Vosilo is the plant manager for the Denver Cover Plant, which was the first GianAuto plant in the region. As other area plants were opened, Ted was given the responsibility for managing them in recognition of his management ability. He functions as a regional manager, although the budget for him and his staff is charged to the Denver Cover Plant.

Ted has just received a report indicating that GianAuto could purchase the entire annual output of Denver Cover from suppliers in other countries for $50 million. He was astonished at the low outside price because the budget for Denver Cover Plant's operating costs for the coming year was set at $82 million. He believes that GianAuto will have to close operations at Denver Cover to realize the $32 million in annual cost savings.

Denver Cover's budget for operating costs for the coming year follows:

DENVER COVER PLANT
Budget for Operating Costs
for the Year Ending December 31, 2022
(000s omitted)

Direct materials		$32,000
Labor		
Direct	$23,000	
Supervision	3,000	
Indirect plant	4,000	30,000
Other overhead		
Depreciation—equipment	$ 5,000	
Depreciation—building	3,000	
Pension expense	4,000	
Plant manager and staff	2,000	
Corporate allocation	6,000	20,000
Total budgeted costs		$82,000

Additional facts regarding the plant's operations are as follows:

- Due to Denver Cover's commitment to use high-quality fabrics in all its products, the purchasing department placed blanket purchase orders with major suppliers to ensure the receipt of sufficient materials for the coming year. If these orders are canceled as a result of the plant closing, termination charges would amount to 15 percent of the cost of direct materials.

- Approximately 400 plant employees will lose their jobs if the plant is closed. This includes all direct laborers and supervisors as well as the plumbers, electricians, and other skilled workers classified as indirect plant workers. Some would be able to find new jobs, but many would have difficulty doing so. All employees would have difficulty matching Denver Cover's base pay of $14.40 per hour, the highest in the area. A clause in Denver Cover's contract with the union could help some employees; the company must provide employment assistance to its former employees for 12 months after a plant closing. The estimated cost to administer this service is $1 million for the year.

- Some employees would probably elect early retirement because GianAuto has an excellent plan. In fact, $3 million of the 2022 pension expense would continue even if Denver Cover were closed.

- Ted and his staff would not be affected by closing Denver Cover. They would still be responsible for managing three other area plants.

- Denver Cover considers equipment depreciation to be a variable cost and therefore uses the units-of-production method to depreciate its equipment. The company uses the straight-line method to depreciate its building.

Required

1. Explain GianAuto's competitive strategy and how this strategy should be considered with regard to the Denver Cover Plant decision. Identify the key strategic factors that should be considered in the decision.

2. GianAuto Corporation wants you to prepare an analysis of whether to close the Denver Cover Plant. Specifically, what is the estimated year 1 cost savings associated with closing the plant (i.e., purchasing from an external supplier)? State your answer in thousands (000s), with the final answer rounded to the nearest thousand.

3. Supplement the financial analysis in requirement 2 with a consideration of global competition and GianAuto's competitive strategy.

(CMA Adapted)

[LO 11-4, 11-7, 11-8]   11-45 **Sell-or-Process-Further Decision**   Humbolt Electric manufactures electronic subcomponents that can be sold at the end of Process 1 or processed further, in Process 2, and then sold. Currently, the entire output of Process 1 can be sold at a price of $2 per unit. The output of Process 2 has in the past sold for $5.50 per unit; however, the selling price of this output has recently dropped to $5.10 (on average).

On the basis of an analysis of the preceding cost and selling price information, as well as an analysis of market trend data, the VP of marketing has suggested that output from Process 2 should be curtailed whenever the price of its output falls below $4.50 per unit. The VP of manufacturing has indicated that the total available capacity is interchangeable between the two processes. (That is, fixed manufacturing costs are largely independent of decisions regarding short-term product mix.) He recommends that, based on current prices, all sales should be from Process 2 output. His analysis follows:

	Output of Process 1	Output of Process 2
Selling price per unit	$2.00	$5.10
Unit costs:		
Direct materials (DM)	1.00	1.50
Direct labor (DL)	0.20	0.40
Manufacturing overhead	0.60	1.20
Transferred-in variable costs from		
Process 1 (DM + DL)	N/A	1.20
Operating profit	$0.20	$0.80

Direct materials (DM) and direct labor (DL) are variable costs. All manufacturing overhead costs are fixed and are allocated to units produced based on hours of capacity used.

Total hours of capacity available are 600,000. The products are produced in batches of 60 units. Each batch of output from Process 1 requires 1 hour of processing; each batch of output from Process 2 requires 2 *additional* hours of processing.

Required

1. Develop a schematic diagram of the two-stage production process. Include in your diagram relevant revenue (selling price per unit) as well as relevant costs (per unit of output).

2. Assume that the per-unit selling price for output from Process 2 for the coming year is expected to be $5.10. (a) What is the contribution margin per hour for output from Process 1 (rounded to 2 decimal places)? (b) What is the contribution margin per hour for output from Process 2 (rounded to 2 decimal places)? (c) What is the implication of this information if the goal of the company is to maximize short-term operating income?

3. What is the lowest acceptable selling price per unit (to 2 decimal places) for the output from Process 2 to make this output (in total) as profitable (in total) as the output from Process 1?

4. Suppose that 50 percent of the manufacturing overhead costs are variable. (a) What is the revised contribution margin per hour (rounded to 2 decimal places) for output from Process 1? (b) What is the revised contribution margin per hour (to 2 decimal places) for output from Process 2? (c) Does your answer to requirement 2 change, based on these revised calculations?

5. *Sensitivity analysis:* (a) Calculate the contribution margin per processing hour (to 2 decimal places) for both Process 1 output and Process 2 output under each of the following assumptions regarding the percentage of variable overhead costs: 0 percent, 25 percent, 50 percent, and 100 percent. Perform these calculations for Process 2 output for both a selling price of $5.10 per unit and a selling price of $5.50 per unit. (b) What general conclusion can you draw on the basis of this sensitivity analysis?

[LO 11-5]   11-46 **Profitability Analysis: Dropping a Product Line**   High Point Furniture Company (HPF) manufactures high-quality furniture for sale directly to exclusive hotels, interior designers, and select retail outlets throughout the world. HPF's products include upholstered furniture, dining tables, bedroom furniture, and a variety of other products, including end tables. Through attention to quality and design innovation, and by careful attention to changing consumer tastes, HPF has become one of the most successful furniture manufacturers worldwide. Hal Blin, the chief operating officer of HPF, is reviewing the most recent sales and profits report for the three best-selling end tables in HPF's product line—the Parker, Virginian, and Weldon end tables. Hal is concerned about the relatively poor performance of the Weldon line. He discusses the prospects for the line with HPF's marketing and sales vice president, Joan Hunt. Joan notes that there has been no significant trend up or down in any of the end table lines, though the direction of consumer tastes would probably favor the Virginian and Parker lines. Hal and Joan agree that this may be the time for further analysis to determine whether the Weldon line should be discontinued. Data for the most recent period for each product line and in total follow:

HPF Sales and Profits Report: End Tables

	Parker		Virginian		Weldon		
	Per Unit	Total	Per Unit	Total	Per Unit	Total	Total
Sales units		150,000		335,000		165,000	
Sales dollars	$459.00	$ 68,850,000	$365.00	$122,275,000	$248.00	$ 40,920,000	$232,045,000
Factory Costs							
Direct labor	$125.00	$ 18,750,000	$118.00	$ 39,530,000	$62.00	$ 10,230,000	$ 68,510,000
Direct materials	88.50	13,275,000	66.00	22,110,000	78.00	12,870,000	48,255,000
Power	23.50	3,525,000	15.60	5,226,000	13.80	2,277,000	11,028,000
Repairs	12.25	1,837,500	12.25	4,103,750	12.25	2,021,250	7,962,500
Factory equipment	33.50	5,025,000	33.50	11,222,500	33.50	5,527,500	21,775,000
Other	14.00	2,100,000	12.50	4,187,500	13.25	2,186,250	8,473,750
Total factory cost	$296.75	$ 44,512,500	$ 257.85	$ 86,379,750	$212.80	$ 35,112,000	$166,004,250
Selling and Administrative Expenses							
Selling expense	$ 45.00	$ 6,750,000	$ 36.00	$ 12,060,000	$ 25.00	$ 4,125,000	$ 22,935,000
Office expense	16.80	2,520,000	16.80	5,628,000	16.80	2,772,000	10,920,000
Administrative expense	27.50	4,125,000	27.50	9,212,500	27.50	4,537,500	17,875,000
Other	6.50	975,000	6.50	2,177,500	6.50	1,072,500	4,225,000
Total cost	392.55	58,882,500	344.65	115,457,750	288.60	47,619,000	221,959,250
Operating profit (loss)	$ 66.45	$ 9,967,500	$ 20.35	$ 6,817,250	$ (40.60)	$ (6,699,000)	$ 10,085,750

Note: Selling expense consists of fixed salaries for the sales staff, advertising, and the cost of marketing/sales management. The remaining selling and administrative expenses are also considered fixed. Power is for equipment used in manufacturing and varies with the number of units produced. The remaining three factory costs (that is, repairs, factory equipment, and other) are all considered fixed costs.

Required

1. Using Excel, develop an analysis that can help Hal decide about the future of the Weldon line. Specifically: (a) Calculate the contribution margin currently generated by each product line (round per-unit amounts to 2 decimal places). (b) What would be the short-term effect on operating profit by dropping the Weldon line? (c) Should this line be dropped? Why or why not?

2. Using the spreadsheet you developed in requirement 1, determine whether your answer would change if sales of Weldon are expected to fall by 80 percent.

3. Using the spreadsheet you developed in conjunction with requirement 1, determine the change in short-term operating income that would occur if the Weldon line were discontinued and the resources devoted to Weldon were used to increase sales by 10 percent in each of the other two lines.

4. Again using the spreadsheet you developed in conjunction with requirement 1 and the Goal Seek routine in Excel, determine the sales increase (in units, rounded to the nearest whole number) in the Parker line that would be necessary to attain the overall short-term operating income that exists before the Weldon line is discontinued. (For an illustration of Goal Seek, see Exhibit 9.5 in Chapter 9.)

5. Given your answers to requirements 1 through 4, consider the overall competitive environment facing HPF and make recommendations regarding the firm's strategic position and direction at this time.

[LO 11-5]   11-47 **Profitability Analysis**   "I'm not looking forward to breaking the news," groaned Charlie Wettle, the controller of Meyer Paint Company. He and Don Smith, state liaison for the firm, were returning from a meeting with representatives of the Virginia General Services Administration (GSA), the agency that administers bidding on state contracts. Charlie and Don had expected to get the specifications to bid on the traffic paint contract, soon to be renewed. Instead of picking up the bid sheets and renewing old friendships at the GSA, however, they were stunned to learn that Meyer's paint samples had performed poorly on the road test and the firm was not eligible to bid on the contract.

Meyer's two main product lines are traffic paint, used for painting yellow and white lines on highways, and commercial paints, sold through local retail outlets. The paint-production process is fairly simple. Raw materials are kept in the storage area that occupies approximately half of the plant space. Large tanks that resemble silos are used to store the latex that is the main ingredient in its paint. These tanks are located on the loading dock just outside the plant so that when a shipment of latex arrives, it can be pumped directly from the tank truck into these storage tanks. Latex is extremely sensitive to cold. It cannot be stored outside or even shipped in the winter without heated trucks, which are very expensive for a small firm such as Meyer.

Currently, Meyer has the traffic paint contracts for the states of Pennsylvania, North Carolina, Delaware, and Virginia. Of last year's total production of 380,000 gallons, 90 percent was traffic paint. Of this amount, 88,000 gallons were for the Virginia contract. Each state has unique specifications for color, thickness, texture, drying time, and other characteristics of the paint. For example, paint sold to Pennsylvania must withstand heavy use of salt on roads during the winter. Paint for North Carolina highways must tolerate extended periods of intense heat during summer months.

Due to the high cost of shipping paint, most paint producers can be competitive on price only in locations fairly close to their production facilities. Accordingly, Meyer has enjoyed an advantage in bidding on contracts in the eastern states close to Virginia. However, one of its biggest competitors, Heron Paint Company of Houston, Texas, is building a new plant in North Carolina. With lower costs due to its efficient new facility and its proximity, Heron will become a major competitive threat.

Meyer's commercial paint line includes interior and exterior house paints in a wide range of colors formulated to approximate authentic colonial colors. Because of the historical association, the line has been well received in Virginia. Most of these paints are sold through paint and hardware stores as the stores' second or third line of paint. The large national firms such as Benjamin Moore or Sherwin-Williams provide extensive services to paint retailers such as computerized color matching equipment. Partly because it lacks the resources to provide such amenities and partly because it has always considered the commercial paint a sideline, Meyer has never tried to market the commercial line aggressively. Meyer sells 38,000 gallons of commercial paint per year.

Charlie is worried about the future of the company. The firm's strategic goal is to provide a quality product at the lowest possible cost and in a timely fashion. After absorbing the shock of losing the Virginia contract, Charlie wondered whether the firm should consider increasing production of commercial paints to lessen the company's dependence on traffic paint contracts. Carl Bunch, who manages the day-to-day operation of the firm, believes the company can double its sales of commercial paint if it undertakes a promotional campaign estimated to cost $120,000. The average price of traffic paint sold last year was $20 per gallon. For commercial paint, the average price was $24.

Charlie assembled the following data to evaluate the financial performance of the two lines of paint. The primary raw material used in paint production is latex. The list price for latex is $32 per pound; 450 pounds of latex are needed to produce 1,000 gallons of traffic paint. Commercial paint requires 325 pounds of latex per 1,000 gallons of paint. In addition to the cost of the latex, other variable costs are as shown below:

	Traffic	Commercial
Raw materials cost per gallon of paint:		
Camelcarb (limestone)	$0.76	$1.08
Silica	0.74	1.04
Pigment	0.24	0.76
Other ingredients	0.12	0.06
Direct labor cost per gallon	0.92	1.70
Freight cost per gallon	1.56	0.86

Last year, fixed overhead costs attributable to the traffic paint totaled $170,000, including an estimated $50,000 of costs directly associated with the Virginia contract; the $50,000 can be eliminated in approximately two years. Fixed overhead costs attributable to the commercial paint are $26,000. Other fixed manufacturing overhead costs total $220,000. Charlie estimates that $80,000 of this amount is inventory-handling costs that will be avoided due to the loss of the Virginia contract. Both the remaining fixed manufacturing overhead ($140,000) and the general and administrative costs of $280,000 are allocated equally to all gallons of paint produced.

Required

1. Consider the following independent scenarios:

   Scenario A Current production, including the Virginia contract: (a) What is the contribution margin per unit (to 2 decimal places) for each of the two product lines? (b) What is the total margin for the company (rounded to nearest whole number)?

   Scenario B Without either the Virginia contract or the promotion to expand sales of commercial paint: What is the total contribution margin for the company, after considering the savings on inventory-handling costs?

   Scenario C Without the Virginia contract, but with the promotion to expand sales of the commercial paint: What is the total contribution margin for the company, after considering the savings on inventory-handling costs and the cost of the special promotion?

2. Based solely on the financial analysis performed in requirement 1, state whether scenario B or C should be chosen by Meyer.

3. What are the primary strategic considerations associated with the decision addressed in requirement 2?

4. *Sensitivity analysis:* Suppose that the sales of commercial paint are projected to increase by only 30 percent rather than 100 percent (an increase to 49,400 rather than 76,000 gallons). Recalculate the estimated total contribution margin associated with scenario B and scenario C. Which of the two scenarios has the higher projected total contribution margin (to the nearest whole dollar)?

[LO 11-9]   11-48 **Constrained Optimization Analysis; Linear Programming (Appendix)** Home Service Company offers monthly service plans to provide prepared meals that are delivered to customers' homes and need only be heated in a microwave or conventional oven. Home Service offers two monthly plans—premier cuisine and haute cuisine. The premier cuisine plan provides frozen meals that are delivered twice each month; the premier plan generates a contribution of $150 for each monthly service plan sold. The haute cuisine plan provides freshly prepared meals delivered on a daily basis and generates a contribution of $100 for each monthly plan sold. Home Service's strong reputation enables it to sell all meals that it can prepare.

Each meal goes through food preparation and cooking steps in the company's kitchens. After these steps, the premier cuisine meals are flash frozen. The time requirements per monthly meal plan and hours available per month follow:

	Preparation	Cooking	Freezing
Hours required:			
Premier cuisine	3	2	1
Haute cuisine	1	3	0
Hours available	80	120	45

For planning purposes, Home Service uses linear programming to determine the most profitable number of premier and haute cuisine meals to produce.

Required

1. Using the Solver function of Microsoft Excel, determine the most profitable product mix for Home Service given the existing constraints and contribution margins.

2. Generate and interpret the information contained in the "Sensitivity Report" associated with the solution in requirement 1.

3. Using the Solver function of Microsoft Excel, determine the most profitable product mix for Home Service given the existing contribution margins and all constraints except the preparation time constraint.

(CMA Adapted)

Solutions to Self-Study Problems

1. Special-Order Pricing

1. The key to this exercise is to recognize that the variable manufacturing costs of $130 ($85 for direct materials and $45 for direct labor) are the relevant ones, and that the fixed overhead costs, because they will not change, are not relevant to the decision.

2. The estimated net effect on annual operating income if HighValu accepts the special sales order is $12,000, as follows:

   600 units × ($150 − [$85 + $45])/unit

   600 units × $20/unit = $12,000 increase/year

3. HighValu also should consider strategic factors. For example, will the three-year contract be desirable? Perhaps the market conditions will change so that HighValu will have more profitable uses of the capacity in the coming years. Will the special order enhance or diminish the firm's competitive position?

2. The Make-vs.-Buy Decision

1. The total relevant cost per year to buy the cushions from an external supplier = $15/set of lawn furniture × 6,000 sets/year = $90,000 per year.

2. The total relevant cost per year to make the cushions internally = incremental costs per year = incremental variable costs per year + incremental fixed costs per year = [($6 + $4)/set × 6,000 sets] + $10,000 = $60,000 + $10,000 = $70,000.

3. The estimated net annual effect on operating income = relevant cost to buy the cushions externally − relevant cost to produce the cushions internally = $90,000/year − $70,000/year = $20,000/year. That is, operating income will be $20,000 higher per year if the cushions are made internally rather than being purchased from an external supplier.

4. HighValu also should consider relevant strategic factors, such as the quality and reliability of in-house production of the sets relative to supplier quality and reliability. Are there other, more attractive uses of the available capacity? Is there sufficient labor available (to produce internally)? Are there any more profitable uses of the capacity that will be devoted to the production of the cushions?

3. Constrained Optimization Analysis: The Short-Term Product-Mix Decision

1. To determine the number of Windys that can be manufactured if the 3,750 units of Gale are no longer produced, we consider the capacity released for each of the two constraints.

    For the automated sewing machine: The machine produces 20 Windys per hour or 30 Gales per hour, so that the number of Windys that could be produced from the released capacity of Gale is

    $$3,750 \times 20/30 = 2,500 \text{ Windys}$$

    For the inspection and packaging operation: The operation requires 15 minutes for Windy (4 per hour) and 5 minutes for Gale (12 per hour), so the number of Windys that could be inspected and packed in the released time is

    $$3,750 \times 4/12 = 1,250 \text{ Windys}$$

    In this case, the inspection and packaging activity is the effective constraint. As such, if Gale is deleted, the firm can produce 1,250 Windys with the resulting released capacity.

2. If 3,750 units of Gale are replaced with 1,250 units of Windy, the proper relevant cost analysis should consider the contribution margin of each product:

	Windy	Gale
Unit contribution margin	$ 8	$ 4
Units sold (giving up 3,750 units of Gale gives 1,250 of Windy, per requirement 1)	1,250	3,750
Total contribution margin	$10,000	$15,000

    Thus, the deletion of Gale and replacement with Windy would reduce the total contribution margin by $5,000 ($15,000 − $10,000).

3. The analysis in (2) above indicates that the company should continue making both Gale and Windy. Other factors to consider follow:

    a. At existing sales levels of 18,750 of Windy and 3,750 of Gale, Windbreakers is *not* operating at full capacity—in terms of both sewing time and inspection/packaging time. As shown in the appendix, with existing capacity, the optimum solution would be to produce 20,800 units of Windy and 4,800 units of Gale. The contribution margin earned on additional sales (beyond 18,750 units and 3,750 units for Windy and Gale, respectively), as well as the $5,000 amount calculated above in (2), suggests that eliminating Gale would be a very poor strategy. Note that this insight is facilitated by performing and interpreting the output of a "constrained optimization analysis" (as done in the appendix).

    b. Management should consider the effect of the loss of Gale on the firm's image and therefore the potential long-term effects on the sales of Windy.

    c. Management should also consider the long-term sales potential for Gale. Will its sales likely exceed the current 3,750 level in future years?

    d. If the company embraces a strategy of being a full-line supplier, it makes little sense to eliminate the Gale line.

Please visit Connect to access a narrated, animated tutorial for solving this problem.

CHAPTER TWELVE

Strategy and the Analysis of Capital Investments

After studying this chapter, you should be able to . . .

LO 12-1 Understand the strategic role of capital investment analysis.

LO 12-2 Describe how accountants can add value to the capital budgeting process.

LO 12-3 Provide a general model for determining relevant cash flows associated with capital investment projects.

LO 12-4 Apply discounted cash flow decision models for capital budgeting purposes.

LO 12-5 Deal with uncertainty in the capital budgeting process.

LO 12-6 Discuss and apply other capital budgeting decision models.

LO 12-7 Identify behavioral issues associated with the capital budgeting process.

LO 12-8 Understand and use alternative presentation formats for the asset replacement decision (Appendix A).

LO 12-9 Identify selected advanced considerations in making capital investment decisions (Appendix B).

David Becker/Getty Images

"Long-range planning does not deal with future decisions, but with the future of present decisions."

Peter S. Drucker

Strategic capital expenditures are a big deal at Intel Corporation. The technology company benefits from large investments by customers such as Google, Amazon, and Microsoft, which together spent about $50 billion in just the first nine months of 2019. Most of that investment was for expansion of networks that rely on Intel products such as server processors and other components. Meanwhile, Intel is making large capital investments of its own. The company announced it would spend $17 billion to update its chip-manufacturing process in 2020. That amount represents about 23% of Intel's projected revenue for the year.[1]

Expenditures of this magnitude are obviously risky. The benefits are expected to arise over a number of years, and customers' spending behavior is highly unpredictable. Yet Intel needs to make such investments, now and in the future, in order to avoid losing ground to competitors such as AMD, Qualcomm, and Samsung. With so much at stake, the need for informed forecasts and rigorous decision-making tools couldn't be higher.

These investment decisions are guided by the accounting methods and tools explained in this chapter. Intel and other companies use capital budgeting methods and strategic analysis to determine the proper type and scope of proposed investment projects. In this chapter, you will learn how to identify potentially successful projects and assess their expected profitability.

Strategy and the Analysis of Capital Expenditures

The Nature of Capital Expenditures

LO 12-1

Understand the strategic role of capital investment analysis.

capital investment

A project that involves a large up-front expenditure of funds and expected future benefits over a number of years.

Intel's chip manufacturing update is an example of a **capital investment**—an investment in a project that involves a large expenditure of funds and expected future benefits over a number of years. Examples of capital investments include the purchase of new manufacturing equipment, the implementation of a new manufacturing technology, the installation of a computer-based record-keeping system, the offering of new services by a government department, and the expansion of a business into new territories.

There are two principal types of investment projects: independent projects and dependent projects. An independent project is one whose cash flows are not affected by the cash flows of other projects. If two projects, A and B, are independent, either of the two projects could be accepted, one of the two projects could be accepted, or neither of the two projects could be accepted. By contrast, dependent projects are those whose cash flows are affected by the cash flows associated with other projects. Mutually exclusive projects represent an extreme form of project dependence: the acceptance of one investment alternative precludes the acceptance of one or more other alternatives. If two projects, A and B, are mutually exclusive, they are competing projects: accepting one means declining the other. For example, Amazon might be considering the choice between two alternative systems for moving and picking items in its distribution centers: The acceptance of one alternative necessarily eliminates the other. The issue of project selection for mutually exclusive projects is dealt with separately in Appendix B of this chapter.

Recent Developments in Capital Investment: Economic Protectionism and COVID-19

One of the consequences of economic protectionism is that heavy tariffs and strong oversight of foreign investment can create distrust between countries. As a result, investments in one country by companies headquartered in another country are likely to be impacted. A recent article in *The New York Times* indicates that foreign direct investment in the U.S. by Chinese organizations has been reduced by nearly 90 percent (from a high of $46.5 billion in 2016 to about $5.4 billion in 2018) as a result of a trade war between the two countries.[2]

---

[1] Dan Gallagher, "Intel Cushions Its Capital Pain," *The Wall Street Journal,* January 24, 2020.

[2] Alan Rappeport, "Chinese Money in the U.S. Dries Up as Trade War Drags On," *The New York Times,* July 21, 2019.

REAL-WORLD FOCUS
COVID-19, Electric Vehicles, and Capital Investments in the Auto Industry

When the COVID-19 (coronavirus) pandemic arose in early 2020, manufacturing shutdowns caused automakers to issue additional long-term debt as a way to raise cash. But this new debt added financial strain to balance sheets that were already highly leveraged. The reason? Massive recent investments by car companies and their suppliers in new technologies, primarily for electric vehicles. As these vehicles become more popular and emission standards become more strict, car companies are investing heavily to keep up. The result is a heavier debt load, and a longer time horizon for car companies to show positive

returns on invested capital. This example demonstrates the serious risks associated with long-term capital investment projects. Large, economy-slowing events (such as health pandemics like COVID-19) are often difficult to predict but can have lasting influence on investment outcomes. Factoring the possibilities and the consequences of these risks into capital investment decision-making is a critical way for management accountants to add value in their organizations.

Source: Stephen Wilmot, "The Car Industry's $1.1 Trillion Debt Problem," *The Wall Street Journal,* June 17, 2020.

You can see from this example that macroeconomic and political trends can have a huge influence on the "when, where, and how much" decisions companies make as part of their capital investment strategies.

The COVID-19 pandemic (first arising in early 2020) and the subsequent economic turmoil will also have broad implications for companies' capital investment decisions and their outcomes. The virus has caused operational shutdowns, reduced sales and earnings, and greater uncertainty about the future. As a result, many organizations will need to rethink how they invest their capital and when they can reasonably expect to see positive returns on those investments (if at all). See the nearby Real-World Focus item ("COVID-19, Electric Vehicles, and Capital Investments in the Auto Industry") for an example.

Strategic Analysis

capital budgeting
A process of identifying, evaluating, selecting, and controlling an organization's capital investments (i.e., its long-term projects and programs).

Capital investment decisions should support the underlying strategy of the organization. As noted in Chapter 1, firms can secure competitive advantage by pursuing either a low-cost (i.e., cost leadership) strategy or a product-differentiation strategy. In the case of the former, we would expect the use of large, highly automated manufacturing facilities, designed to capture economies of scale, and production efficiencies associated with the use of advanced manufacturing technologies (e.g., computer-integrated manufacturing, or CIM). In the case of the latter, the organization would likely devote a greater share of its capital investment budget to research, development, and product-promotion activities.

Given the strategic nature of capital investment decisions, organizations generally use a formal process to plan and control such expenditures. The process of identifying, evaluating, selecting, and controlling capital investments is called **capital budgeting.**

The Role of Accounting in the Capital Budgeting Process

LO 12-2
Describe how accountants can add value to the capital budgeting process.

You might wonder why capital budgeting is covered in an accounting textbook. Isn't this a finance topic? These are legitimate questions, particularly because the theory behind modern capital budgeting decision models comes from the field of finance. Thus, if accounting adds value to the capital budgeting process, it must come from somewhere other than model development. Within the context of capital budgeting, accounting plays a facilitative role, helping decision makers successfully implement decision models developed in finance. As noted below, accounting makes four specific contributions to the capital budgeting process: linkage to an organization's *master budget* (planning), linkage to *strategy* (planning) and to the organization's *balanced scorecard* (control), generation of *relevant data for investment analysis* purposes (decision making), and conducting of *post audits* (control) of capital investment projects.

Linkage to the Master Budget

An organization's **capital budget** for a given period consists of a listing of approved investment projects as well as anticipated cash outflows associated with these projects. As indicated in Chapter 10, the capital budget is part of the overall planning system known as the master budget.

Linkage to Strategy and the Balanced Scorecard

In Chapter 2, we introduced the notion of the balanced scorecard (BSC) as a critical element of an organization's strategic control system. Recall that a **strategic control system** refers to the processes an organization uses to monitor the progress of the organization in terms of accomplishing its strategic goals. The BSC can be an effective tool to communicate to employees and managers the mission and strategy of the organization. Fundamentally, a BSC represents a series of linked (i.e., cause-and-effect) relationships across four broad performance perspectives: learning and growth, customer, business processes, and financial. Included in these four dimensions is a mixture of financial and nonfinancial, internal and external, and lead versus lagged performance indicators.

It is management's responsibility, working with individuals throughout the organization (including accountants), to develop the list of relevant performance metrics. Presumably, the BSC will include some of the performance indicators—both financial and nonfinancial—used to evaluate capital investment proposals. Accounting's special role in this process is to collect and periodically summarize the performance metrics—both financial and nonfinancial—included within the organization's BSC.

Kaplan and Norton (2008)[3] describe a five-stage management system that can be used to develop strategy, translate the strategy into operational actions, and monitor and improve the effectiveness of both. Stage 2 of this process includes the development of a strategy map and associated balanced scorecard (BSC) and the identification of a set of strategic initiatives (investments) needed to achieve the organization's strategic objectives. The authors define strategic initiatives as "discretionary projects or programs, of finite duration, designed to close a performance gap" (p. 68). Such programs would complement capital expenditures designed to support current operations and would include, for example, a customer loyalty program or the implementation of a training program for Six Sigma. Strategic expenditures can also be made to support the organization's environmental performance and/or sustainability goals.

The evaluation of capital investment projects in terms of their relationship to strategy in general, and to the BSC in particular, is an interesting problem. How do organizations evaluate proposed projects in a comprehensive manner—that is, how do they include both financial and nonfinancial/qualitative considerations and ensure that such investments support the underlying strategy of the organization? The answer to this question may lie in the use of what

are called **multicriteria decision models**, which include more than a single decision criterion (such as after-tax rate of return or projected future cash flows). One of the more popular multicriteria decision models is the analytic hierarchy process (AHP).

The **analytic hierarchy process (AHP)** is a multicriteria decision technique that can combine qualitative and quantitative factors in the overall evaluation of decision alternatives; as such, the AHP can be used for capital budgeting purposes.[4] The AHP organizes a problem into smaller and smaller parts and then calls for the use of simple pairwise comparisons to develop a hierarchy of decision-maker preferences. This hierarchy is then manipulated analytically to produce a final matrix representing the overall priorities of the decision alternatives relative to one another. One can then make a logical decision based on the pairwise comparisons made between the decision alternatives (e.g., choice of competing capital budgeting projects) and the various criteria used for decision-making purposes (such as quality, cash flows, impact on brand image, and payback period). The AHP allows managers to consider

---

[3] Robert S. Kaplan and David P. Norton, "Mastering the Management System," *Harvard Business Review,* January 2008, pp. 63–77.

[4] A five-step procedure for implementing the AHP in a capital budgeting context is given in T. F. Monahan, M. J. Liberatore, and D. E. Stout, "Decision Support for Capital Budgeting: A Model for Classroom Presentation," *Journal of Accounting Education* 8 (1990), pp. 225–239; and in D. E. Stout, M. J. Liberatore, and T. F. Monahan, "Decision Support Software for Capital Budgeting," *Management Accounting,* July 1991, pp. 50–53.

REAL-WORLD FOCUS   Capital Expenditure Analysis by Oil-Exploration Companies

The sub-salt layer on the Brazilian continental shelf is estimated to contain a significant amount of deepwater oil reserves—as much as 50 billion barrels of recoverable oil according to some estimates. If true, this would position Brazil as a top-five crude oil producer in the world, behind Saudi Arabia, Russia, the U.S., and Iraq. Capital investment in this area of the world by companies such as ExxonMobil Corporation (Exxon) is complicated by two factors: (1) The oil reserves in question are owned/controlled by the Brazilian state-oil firm Petroleo Brasileiro SA (Petrobras) and (2) the oil in these fields is difficult to get at—it lies several miles below sea level and is covered by a thick layer of salt. In short, capital investments in these—and

similar—ultra-deep oil fields are both risky and expensive. To manage this risk, Exxon has partnered with Petrobras to develop oil and gas projects both inside and outside of Brazil. Risk associated with factors such as political shifts, worldwide demand and price changes in crude oil, and foreign exchange risk could be addressed through scenario analysis and by incorporating real options in the discounted cash flow (DCF) analysis of proposed capital investments by oil exploration companies. These topics are covered later in the chapter.

Source: E. Scheyder, "Exxon, Petrobras Form Alliance to Develop Oil, Gas Projects," *Reuters*, December 14, 2017; B. Olson and P. Kiernan, "Exxon Weighs Expansion in Brazil," *The Wall Street Journal*, April 5, 2017, p. B3.

both tangible and intangible factors when constructing the decision hierarchy, allowing managers to link capital budgeting decisions to strategy in a formal manner.[5]

Generation of Relevant Financial Data for Decision-Making Purposes

In Chapter 11, we defined relevant financial information for decision making as "future costs or revenues that differ between decision alternatives." We made the point that accountants assume primary responsibility for providing managers with such information. These points apply to capital budgeting as well: Management accountants supply decision makers with relevant *after-tax* cash flow data for analyzing the desirability of proposed capital investment projects and then participate actively in the decision-making process regarding these investment proposals.

Part of the relevant financial data pertaining to capital budgeting decisions consists of the income tax consequences of proposed capital expenditures. As we point out later in this chapter, tax savings due to depreciation deductions are important in the analysis of proposed capital expenditures.[6]

In late 2017, the U.S. Congress passed, and president Donald Trump signed into law, H.R.1, An Act to provide for reconciliation pursuant to titles II and V of the concurrent resolution on the budget for fiscal year 2018, otherwise known as the Tax Cuts and Jobs Act of 2017 (Public Law No. 115-97; www.congress.gov/bill/115th-congress/house-bill/1). The new law contains numerous and substantive changes to U.S. income tax law, as applied both to businesses and to individuals. Management accountants can add value by ensuring that all relevant tax-related factors and effects are included as part of the information set provided to managers for capital budgeting purposes.

Conducting Post Audits

post audit
An in-depth review of a completed capital investment project for the purpose of comparing its realized costs and benefits (both financial and nonfinancial) with the preinvestment estimates of these items.

Accountants can also add value in the final stage of the capital budgeting process. Various terms have been used to describe this stage, including post audit, post-completion audit, project reappraisal, post appraisal, and project review. We prefer the term **post audit** and define this as an in-depth review of a completed capital investment project for the purpose of comparing its realized costs and benefits (both financial and nonfinancial) with preinvestment estimates.

The following real-life example is offered as an overview of the strategic dimensions of the capital budgeting process. The rest of this chapter covers the technical and then behavioral factors associated with this process.

[5] A discussion of using the AHP to link capital budgeting decisions to strategy is provided in M. J. Liberatore, T. F. Monahan, and D. E. Stout, "A Framework for Integrating Capital Budgeting Analysis with Strategy,"*The Engineering Economist* 38, no. 1 (Fall 1992), pp. 31–43.

[6] Current rules for determining depreciation deductions are contained in IRS Publication 946, available at **www.irs.gov/publications/p946/**.

The Five Steps of Strategic Decision Making: Cost-Benefit Analysis of a Proposed Hospital Bar-Code Technology Investment[7]

1. **Determine the strategic issues surrounding the problem.** Errors in dispensing medications represent a significant and strategically important problem for hospital pharmacies. Costs of such errors, both out-of-pocket and opportunity (e.g., reputation effects), can be considerable. Thus, most hospitals attempt to control these quality-related costs. Recent advances in technology, including the use of a bar-code system, can be used by hospitals to manage the risks and costs of such errors.

2. **Identify the alternative actions.** In this situation, there are two broad decision alternatives. Hospital administrators can invest in employee training and the updating of existing monitoring systems associated with the control of pharmacy dispensing errors, or they can invest in and implement a new bar-code system that is designed to virtually eliminate human errors. Because this technology is relatively new, it is very expensive. Thus, one alternative is to delay the investment for a year, at which time the price of the technology will likely be significantly lower.

3. **Obtain information and conduct analyses of the alternatives.** The hospital would have to estimate the required investment outlay for the new dispensing system, both today and approximately one year from now. It would also have to estimate ongoing operating costs associated with the new monitoring system. These costs would be compared to the anticipated benefits of the system, both financial and nonfinancial. Financial benefits, in this example, are costs avoided by eliminating adverse effects from dispensing errors. Thus, both the number of event reductions and the dollar savings per event would have to be estimated. Other, more difficult, benefits are qualitative or strategic in nature and would complement the cost-benefit analysis described above.

4. **Based on strategy and analysis, choose and implement the desired alternative.** The proposed investment would be evaluated using anticipated future after-tax cash outflows and inflows (cost savings), discounted to a present value basis. This analysis of financial results would be supplemented by a strategic analysis of the proposed investment, conducted either informally or by using a multicriteria decision model such as the analytic hierarchy process (AHP). Finally, the cash flow analysis could be supplemented by including the effect of the option to delay the investment, which is one example of a *real option.* Given the uncertainties associated with the projected costs and benefits of this proposed investment, management would likely conduct a sensitivity analysis using, for example, a Monte Carlo simulation procedure.

5. **Provide an ongoing evaluation of the effectiveness of implementation in step 4.** Assuming the investment in the new technology is made, the hospital administrators could conduct a post audit of the decision to see how close the actual results were to the projected costs and benefits.

Identification of Relevant Cash Flow Data for Capital Investment Analysis

LO 12-3

Provide a general model for determining relevant cash flows associated with capital investment projects.

Data for evaluating the financial consequences associated with capital investment proposals differ from data used to prepare an organization's financial statements. The former relies on forecasted *cash flow* data, while the latter relies on the use of *accrual accounting* amounts.

Why Focus on Cash Flows and the Timing of These Cash Flows?

Accrual-based accounting income is determined under the matching principle. As such, there is no attempt to track cash flows into and out of an organization. However, in capital budgeting, the focus is on (after-tax) cash flows and the timing of these cash flows. This is true for two reasons. Conceptually, the financial markets value companies according to their ability to

---

[7] This example is drawn from the following: S. M. Maviglia, J. Y. Yoo, C. Franz, E. Featherstone, W. Churchill, D. W. Bates, T. K. Gandhi, and E. G. Poon, "Cost-Benefit Analysis of a Hospital Pharmacy Bar Code Solution," *Archives of Internal Medicine* 167, no. 8 (April 23, 2007), pp. 788–794. The five steps discussed in this section constitute a higher-level aggregation of the eight key principles of project appraisal presented in *Project Appraisal Using Discounted Cash Flow* (New York: IFAC, June 2008).

generate free cash flow. (Alternatively, companies are valued differently depending on their dividend-paying ability, which in turn is a function of their ability to generate free cash flow.) In addition, from a market perspective, the timing of cash flows generated by a company matters: A cash return to shareholders in the future does not have the same value (economic worth or buying power) as a dollar received today. In short, money has a time value.

Thus, managers strive to use capital budgeting decision models that (1) focus on cash flow amounts and (2) take into consideration the time value of money. The use of such decision models has the potential for increasing the value or economic worth of the firm.

Cash Flows—A Framework for Analysis[8]

A capital investment, such as the purchase of a new machine, usually starts with a large cash outflow, followed by future benefits in the form of reductions in cash expenditures, increases in cash inflows, or both. Additional funds could also be needed to support the investment over its useful life. The following structure can be used to accumulate relevant financial information associated with a simplified capital investment project, for example, whether to invest in a new piece of machinery:

1. *Project initiation*—Cash flows at this point include:

    a. Cash outflows, including installation costs, to acquire the investment and to begin operations (e.g., employee-training costs, machine-testing costs).

    b. Cash commitments for increases in **net working capital** (defined here as current assets other than cash, less current liabilities).

    c. Cash inflow associated with investment tax credits, if any. (For simplicity, we assume throughout this chapter that all tax-related cash flows occur in the same year as the related transaction.)

2. *Project operation*—Cash flows during the operating stage of a capital investment include:

    a. After-tax cash outflows for operating expenditures and, in some cases, additional capital investment(s) after the initial outlay.

    b. Commitments for additional net working capital needed to support operations.

    c. After-tax inflows of cash (or reductions in cash operating expenses) generated by the investment.

3. *Project disposal*—Cash flows at project disposal include:

    a. Cash inflows or outflows, net of tax, related to the investment's disposal. (For simplicity, we assume that any such cash flow effects are realized fully in the year of asset disposal.)

    b. Cash inflows from the recovery of net working capital.

Item 3b requires elaboration. The proposed project initially requires an increase in net working capital (see item 1b). When the project is terminated, this initial investment in net working capital is recovered (i.e., converted back into cash).

Sample Data Set: Mendoza Company— Equipment-Purchase Decision

To illustrate the calculation of relevant cash flows, we use the following example. The Mendoza Company manufactures high-pressure pipes for deep-sea oil drilling. The company is considering purchasing a new drilling machine at a base cost of $465,000, which will improve the efficiency of its drilling operations and therefore provide increased cash operating income. The controller expects the company to be in the 34% federal income tax bracket and to be subject to a combined state and local income tax rate of 6%.

Installation costs associated with the new machine are expected to be $5,000, and associated testing and adjusting expenses are estimated at $10,000. After its expected useful life of four years, the company expects to sell the machine for $100,000. In conjunction with this sale, the company expects to incur machine-removal and site-clearing expenses that total $95,000, all of

net working capital
For purposes of capital budgeting, current assets other than cash (CA − Cash) less current liabilities (CL).

---

[8] The framework presented here relates to a simplified investment. In a later section, we expand the framework to include an equipment replacement decision, alternative formats of which are presented in the templates included in Appendix A.

which are assumed to be deductible for tax purposes. Mendoza elects to use a double-declining-balance depreciation approach (following the Modified Accelerated Cost Recovery System (MACRS), which will be described later), with a zero salvage value, for tax purposes. After disposing of the investment, the company feels it can reassign all but 10 employees to other divisions without incurring significant expenses. However, at the end of year 4, the company expects to spend $150,000 for relocation, retraining, and work adjustment for these 10 employees. This expense is expected to be fully deductible for income tax purposes.

The company expects the new machine to generate $1 million of cash revenue from sales in each of the next four years. This level of sales activity is expected to require cash operating expenses, such as labor, materials, energy, and selling and administrative expenses, of $733,333 (pretax) per year. Mendoza expects additional cash costs of $50,000 (pretax) in the first year of operating the new machine, including expenditures for employee training, work adjustments, and learning effects.

Mendoza estimates that at the time the new machine is put in operation (time 0), its inventory and accounts receivable will increase $200,000 beyond the expected increase in current liabilities. That is, the amount of net working capital—current assets other than cash, minus current liabilities—is expected to increase because of the sales volume associated with the new machine. The company expects to fully recover (i.e., convert back to cash) the $200,000 amount at the end of the four-year life of the machine.

The purchase of the new machine is not expected to increase any corporate-level support costs. However, the investment will increase the cost-allocation base of the division that is acquiring the machine. As such, the new investment will increase the corporate-level support costs that are allocated to the division. The cost allocation rate used for performance-assessment purposes is $0.025 per dollar of sales. As noted earlier, the new machine is expected to generate cash sales of $1 million annually. Thus, total divisional expenses will increase by $25,000 per year in each of the four years of the new machine's life.

The preceding set of facts is summarized in Exhibit 12.1. It is through the proper gathering (and, ultimately, proper analysis and use) of such data that the accounting function can add value to the organization.

EXHIBIT 12.1
Data for Mendoza Company Capital Investment Decision

MENDOZA COMPANY Capital Budgeting Data Machine Purchase Decision	
New Machine	
Purchase price of machine, time 0	$465,000
Machine installation cost	$5,000
Testing and adjustments of new machine prior to new machine's use	$10,000
Expected life of new machine	4 years
Depreciation method (ignore salvage value for tax purposes)	3-year MACRS
Estimated sales (disposal) value of equipment at end of four years	$100,000
Salvage value assumed for tax-depreciation purposes	$0
Estimated costs related to sale of asset at end of four years (e.g., sales commission)	$95,000
Other Data	
Expected increase in *net* working capital, time 0	$200,000
Expected reduction in *net* working capital, end of year 4	$200,000
Annual cash sales associated with the new machine	$1,000,000
Annual operating cash expenses	$733,333
Pretax operating cash flow per year	$266,667
Combined income tax rate	40%
Corporate headquarters' allocation percentage	$0.025 per dollar of sales*
Additional pretax cash outlays, year 1 (employee training, etc.)	$50,000**
Employee pretax relocation expenses, end of year 4	$150,000**

*Note: The total corporate headquarters' expense is unaffected by whether or not the new machine is purchased. That is, the purchase of the new machine will not entail an increase in total operating expenses at the corporate level.
**Assume that these are fully deductible for tax purposes in the year incurred.

Determining After-Tax Cash Flows for Capital Investment Analysis

As noted earlier, cash flows for capital investment analysis must be stated on an *after-tax* basis. A summary analysis is presented in Exhibit 12.2. For simplicity in the cash flow calculations presented next, assume that the combined income tax rate is 40%.

Project Initiation

Asset Acquisition   As shown in Exhibit 12.2, the net cost of the machine at acquisition (i.e., at time 0) is $480,000 ($465,000 + $5,000 + $10,000). This is the depreciable (cost) basis of the asset.

Investment in Net Working Capital   In addition to the cost of the new asset, Mendoza feels that, in the year of asset acquisition (i.e., at time 0) it must commit net working capital (current assets other than cash, less current liabilities) to support the investment. Specifically, the company estimates that beyond a projected increase in current liabilities, its inventories and accounts receivable will increase by $200,000 per year during the life of the project. This excess of *additional* current assets (other than cash) over *additional* current liabilities is treated as an *additional* investment outlay at time 0. Note that at the end of year 4 the company expects to fully recover (i.e., convert back into cash) the $200,000 time 0 commitment of net working capital.

Project Operation

After-Tax Cash Operating Receipts   The new machine expects to generate $1 million of cash revenue per year. Such an amount, everything else held constant, will increase the annual income tax liability of the company. That is, the annual after-tax amount for this taxable cash receipt is found by subtracting from the gross cash inflow of $1,000,000 the associated $400,000 increase in income tax liability ($1,000,000 × 0.40). Thus, the

EXHIBIT 12.2 After-Tax Cash Flow Data

MENDOZA COMPANY After-Tax Cash Flow Data Machine Purchase Decision (000S)					
	Years				
	0	**1**	**2**	**3**	**4**
Project Inititation					
New cost of new machine	$(480.00)				
Commitment of net working capital	(200.00)				
Net initial cash outflow, after tax	$(680.00)				
Project Operation					
Cash revenues		$1,000.00	$1,000.00	$1,000.00	$1,000.00
Operating expenses:					
Cash items		(783.33)	(733.33)	(733.33)	(733.33)
Depreciation		(160.00)	(213.36)	(71.09)	(35.57)
Total operating expenses		(943.33)	(946.69)	(804.42)	(768.90)
Pretax operating income		56.67	53.31	195.58	231.10
Income taxes on operating income		(22.67)	(21.32)	(78.23)	(92.44)
After-tax operating income		34.00	31.99	117.35	138.66
Plus: Noncash expenses (depreciation—see above)		160.00	213.36	71.09	35.57
After-tax cash operating income		$194.00	$245.35	$188.44	$ 174.23
Project Disposal					
Net working capital released (i.e., recovered)					$ 200.00
After-tax proceeds from sale of machine					3.00
After-tax employee relocation expenses					(90.00)
Net cash flow, after tax, at project disposal					$ 113.00
Net (after-tax) cash flows	**($680)**	**$194**	**$245**	**$188**	**$287**

after-tax cash receipt each year is only $600,000. In summary, this transaction has two cash effects: a cash *inflow* and a cash *outflow* represented by the increased income tax liability. This leads to the following formula that can be used to determine the after-tax effect of taxable cash receipts:

$$\text{After-tax cash receipt} = \text{Taxable cash receipt} \times (1 - \text{Tax rate})$$

After-Tax Cash Operating Expenses   As shown in Exhibit 12.1, the increased revenue is expected to require $733,333 of cash operating expenses for each of years 2–4, and $783,333 for year 1 ($50,000 one-time employee-training costs). Consider, for sake of discussion, the $733,333 amount. Assuming that these expenses are fully deductible for income tax purposes, this annual transaction has two cash effects: a cash *outlay* of $733,333 and a reduction of income taxes in the amount of $293,333 ($733,333 × 0.40). Thus, the net effect of the expense is $440,000 (i.e., $733,333 × 0.60). In effect, the net cost to the company, per year, is only $440,000 after taking into consideration the tax savings realized because of the deductibility of the expense. The after-tax cash outlay in year 1 would be $470,000 (i.e., $783,333 × 0.60).

This leads to the following formula that can be used to determine the after-tax effect of cash operating expenses:

$$\text{After-tax cash expense} = \text{Pretax cash expense} \times (1 - \text{Tax rate})$$

After-Tax Cash Operating Income   Of course, the analyst can combine cash operating revenues (or cost savings) and cash operating expenses to produce the annual *cash operating income* associated with the proposed investment. In the case of the Mendoza Company, the expected pretax cash operating income would be $216,667 ($1,000,000 − $783,333) in year 1 and $266,667 ($1,000,000 − $733,333) thereafter. On an after-tax basis, this pretax cash operating income would yield $130,000 in year 1 and $160,000 in years 2–4.

The following formula can be used to estimate each year's after-tax cash operating income:

$$\text{After-tax cash operating income} = \text{Pretax cash operating income} \times (1 - \text{Tax rate})$$

Noncash Revenues   A word of caution is needed here. Noncash revenues that have tax effects also affect cash flows because of their effect on the tax liability of the company for the year. Because income tax liability (at least in the United States) is determined on an accrual-accounting basis, a noncash revenue, such as a credit sale planned to be collected in the following year, does not increase cash available to the firm this year, but does increase the company's taxable income for the current year. In turn, this transaction increases the cash outflows (taxes) for the current year. Thus, a noncash revenue for the current year *decreases,* rather than increases, cash available to the firm. The amount of the decrease is the increase in taxes resulting from the noncash revenue.

Note, however, that for the Mendoza Company the only information we have is for *cash* revenues and *cash* operating expenses associated with the proposed investment. As such, non-cash revenues are not an issue in this example.

Noncash Expenses   An increase in noncash expenses (e.g., depreciation, amortization costs) decreases taxable income and associated income taxes for the current period. Thus, a noncash expense increases, rather than decreases, cash flow. The deductibility of the noncash expense for income tax purposes reduces the tax liability that otherwise would exist.

Depreciation Calculations for Income Tax Purposes (MACRS)   Depreciation for income tax purposes in the United States is determined using the Modified Accelerated Cost Recovery System (MACRS). MACRS assigns all depreciable assets to one of eight classes, referred to as *recovery periods.* Exhibit 12.3 describes these classes and their depreciation methods and provides examples of assets in each class.

Exhibit 12.4 shows the depreciation rates each year for depreciable assets other than residential or nonresidential real estate. These percentages reflect the use of an accelerated depreciation method—150% or 200% of the straight-line (SL) depreciation rate, depending on

EXHIBIT 12.3 **Asset Classes (Recovery Periods) under MACRS**

Class	Depreciation Method	Example
3-year property	200% declining balance	Light tools and handling equipment
5-year property	200% declining balance	Computers and peripheral equipment, office machinery, automobiles, light trucks
7-year property	200% declining balance	Office furniture, appliances, carpet, and furniture in residential rental property and any asset that does not have an assigned class
10-year property	200% declining balance	Manufacturing assets for food products, petroleum refining, tobacco
15-year property	150% declining balance	Road and shrubbery, telephone distribution plant
20-year property	150% declining balance	Multipurpose farm structures
27.5-year property	Straight line	Residential rental property
31.5-year property	Straight line	Nonresidential real property, office building, warehouse

the property class. With the exception of residential and nonresidential real estate properties (see the last two classes of assets in Exhibit 12.3), a half-year convention is used to determine the depreciation expense for the first and last years of the asset's recovery period.

To illustrate, the first-year depreciation of a five-year property is 20% of the asset's cost—regardless of when the asset was placed into service during the year. The depreciation deduction for the second year for this asset would be 32% of the asset's cost. This amount is determined using the double-declining-balance (DDB) approach. That is, the SL rate for an asset with a five-year recovery period would be 20% per year. In year 1 (under the half-year convention), 20% of the asset's cost would be written off, leaving 80% to be deducted over the remaining four years. For year 2, the depreciation deduction (32%) is equal to 40% of this 80%. To ensure that 100% of an asset's cost is written off over the specified recovery period, the depreciation method under MACRS ultimately reverts to the SL method. For example, the switch-over for five-year property occurs in year 4.

Taxpayers in the United States can choose to use the optional SL method instead of the percentages specified in the MACRS tables.[9] Except for the midyear, or in some cases midquarter, convention that affects the amount of depreciation charges for the first and last years of an asset's life, the optional SL method provides for a constant depreciation deduction per year. For example, for a three-year property subject to the midyear convention, the relevant depreciation rates would be 16.67% for year 1; 33.33% for years 2 and 3; and 16.67% for year 4. Note that under MACRS, the salvage value is ignored for depreciation calculations, including when the SL method is chosen.

For the Mendoza example, we made the assumption that the company chose the double-declining-balance method under MACRS and that the new machine qualifies as a three-year asset. With the midyear convention, this means that depreciation expense is recognized in all four years of the asset's life. As shown in Exhibit 12.2, the annual depreciation deductions for Mendoza Company are calculated using the depreciation rates provided in Exhibit 12.4. Given a 40% combined tax rate, these deductions provide income tax savings in each year.

Earlier we referenced the Tax Cuts and Jobs Act of 2017 in the U.S. Portions of the new law affect depreciation deductions, particularly under IRS Code Sections 168 (alternative depreciation system for residential and nonresidential property and the determination of bonus depreciation) and 179 (immediate expensing of capital expenditures). Details in these provisions (some of which have significant cash flow effects) should always be considered as part of any analysis of an actual capital investment proposal.

Project Disposal

Investment Disposal At the project disposal stage, there are potential cash flow effects that should be included in any capital investment analysis.

In some situations, there are end-of-project after-tax cash expenses that need to be considered. These costs include asset-removal costs, restoration costs (i.e., costs needed to bring the

[9] The use of the optional SL method may be attractive to start-up firms (because they generally are unprofitable during the early stages of the business) and to firms experiencing financial difficulty. For such situations, the firm in question may want to defer rather than accelerate its depreciation deductions.

EXHIBIT 12.4
MACRS Depreciation Rates

Year	3-year	5-year	7-year	10-year	15-year	20-year
1	33.33	20.00	14.29	10.00	5.00	3.75
2	44.45	32.00	24.49	18.00	9.50	7.22
3	14.81	19.20	17.49	14.40	8.55	6.68
4	7.41	11.52*	12.49	11.52	7.70	6.18
5		11.52	8.93*	9.22	6.93	5.71
6		5.76	8.92	7.37	6.23	5.28
7			8.92	6.55*	5.90*	4.89
8			4.47	6.55	5.90	4.52
9				6.56	5.91	4.46*
10				6.55	5.90	4.46
11				3.28	etc.	etc.

*First year of switching to the straight-line method.

Source: www.irs.gov/publications/p946/.

asset, such as land, back to an original state), and any employee-related costs (e.g., severance pay, relocation costs, and retraining costs).

In addition, at the end of the project's life, the investment asset could possibly be sold—an event that could trigger a taxable gain or loss. Any cash received from the disposal of the asset at the end of its life must be adjusted by the tax effect of the transaction. Refer to Exhibit 12.5 for a summary of the procedures used for determining the after-tax cash flow effect of an asset disposal.

In the case of the Mendoza Company (Exhibit 12.2), the after-tax cash inflow from the sale of the four-year-old asset is projected to be $3,000; that is, $5,000 net proceeds minus $2,000 income tax paid on the gain. In this example, and throughout the rest of this chapter, we assume that gains or losses on the disposal of depreciable assets are taxed at the same rate as ordinary income.

Recovery of Investment in Net Working Capital   Recall that Mendoza Company committed $200,000 of net working capital at the onset of the investment, which, at the end of year 4, is no longer needed. Thus, at the end of year 4, we include a $200,000 (nontaxable) cash inflow for the conversion of this net working capital back into cash.

Additional Measurement Issues

Following are four additional measurement issues that need to be considered by accountants as they gather relevant information for the analysis of capital expenditure proposals.

Inflation   For simplicity, we have assumed that the annual cash revenues and cash expenses associated with the proposed project, including the recovery of net working capital at the end of the project's life, are constant in amount; that is, they are not affected by inflation. In an actual capital budgeting analysis, however, the accountant would incorporate inflation adjustments for future cash flows. Typically, the discount rate that is used in capital budgeting models is an inflation-adjusted rate. Thus, to achieve consistency in the discounting process, the cash flows that are being discounted should incorporate the anticipated effects of inflation.

EXHIBIT 12.5
After-Tax Proceeds from an Asset Disposal

Net Effect of Asset Disposal on After-Tax Cash Flow, End of Year 4
Terminology
Net book value (NBV) = Original cost − Accumulated depreciation
Net proceeds = Selling (disposal) price of asset − Disposal costs (selling commissions, etc.)
Gain on disposal: If net proceeds > NBV
Loss on disposal: If net proceeds < NBV
Net after-tax cash flow:
For *gain* situation: Net cash effect = Net proceeds − (Gain on disposal × Tax rate)
For *loss* situation: Net cash effect = Net proceeds + (Loss on disposal × Tax rate)

Note: Assume, for simplicity, that any tax effects are realized in full in the year of asset disposal.

Opportunity Costs—Include These in Cash Flow Analysis As noted in Chapter 11, opportunity costs are always relevant for decision making, including the analysis of proposed capital expenditures. Consider, for example, the decision to expand manufacturing facilities to meet projected demand for a firm's product(s). Suppose that the land on which the facilities would be built could otherwise be sold for $250,000. While an out-of-pocket cost would not be involved, there is nonetheless an economic cost of using the land for the new manufacturing facilities. In this example, the opportunity cost would be equal to the after-tax amount that the firm could get by selling the land; as such, this amount should be included as a relevant cash flow for capital budgeting purposes.

Sunk Costs—Ignore These In Chapter 11, it was noted that these costs, because they are historical (i.e., sunk), are irrelevant for decision-making purposes. Consider the example earlier. The original purchase price of the land is irrelevant to the facilities-expansion decision—it is a sunk cost. Because such costs will be the same regardless of whether or not the firm invests in the new facilities, these costs should be ignored for capital budgeting purposes.

Allocated Overhead Costs—Be Careful of These As discussed elsewhere in the text, there are various circumstances in which accountants must allocate common, or shared, costs of the organization. The requirement of generating full product cost information for financial statement purposes is one such use. However, there are certain circumstances in which the allocation of these kinds of costs should be avoided.

The basic rule here is to ask whether overhead costs (administrative and/or manufacturing) will increase if a given project is accepted, or whether these costs will be largely unaffected in total. In the former case, the *incremental* overhead should be included (as an after-tax cash outflow) for capital budgeting purposes. In the latter case, regardless of the amount allocated to the project for accounting purposes, these costs should not be charged against the project for decision-making purposes.

In the Mendoza Company example (Exhibit 12.1), corporate headquarters' expenses are not likely to change in total if the company invests in the new machine. Thus, even though an allocation of such expenses may be appropriate for some other reason (such as full product costing), no portion of these expenses should be charged against the project for capital budgeting purposes.

Recap—After-Tax Cash Flow Information for the Mendoza Company Investment Proposal

After-tax cash flow information for the Mendoza Company investment proposal is summarized in Exhibit 12.2. Data in this exhibit have been divided according to the three primary stages of the proposed project: (1) project initiation, (2) project operation, and (3) project disposal.

How can managers use this information to assess the financial consequences of the proposed investment? We turn now to a discussion of various capital budgeting decision models that can be used to answer this question.

Discounted Cash Flow Capital Budgeting Decision Models

LO 12-4

Apply discounted cash flow decision models for capital budgeting purposes.

Types of Capital Budgeting Decision Models

Models for evaluating capital investment proposals fall into one of two categories: discounted cash flow (DCF) models and non-DCF models.[10] The former category includes the net present value (NPV) model, the internal rate of return (IRR) model, and the profitability index (PI) model. The latter category includes the payback model and the accounting (book) rate of return (ARR) model.

---

[10] The mechanics of discounting are covered elsewhere in the curriculum (e.g., finance or management accounting courses) and as such will not be covered here. A useful reference is V. Martinez, "Time Value of Money Made Simple: A Graphic Teaching Method," *Journal of Financial Education* 39, no. 1/2 (Spring/Summer 2013), pp. 96–113. This article presents a visual aid for structuring a variety of time-value-of-money problems, including future value of a lump sum, present value of a lump sum, future value of an annuity, present value of an annuity, and present value of a perpetuity. As such, the article may be helpful in responding to some of the end-of-chapter assignments in this chapter.

REAL-WORLD FOCUS   Discount Rates and Pension Funding

The discount rate matters! American state and local pensions make contributions to fund their obligations to public workers based on assumed rates of return, or discount rates. You can think of the discount rate in this context as the hypothetical interest rate that a pension would expect on a bond today to fund future obligations; the lower the rate, the greater the pension liability in present value terms. Yet, as the *Wall Street Journal* article cited in this section indicates, many pension systems are funding their obligations using discount rates that are probably overly optimistic, creating large funding gaps. For example, if the California Public Employees' Retirement System (known as Calpers) reduced its assumed discount rate (currently 6.1%) to a more realistic 5.1%, its funding gap (the difference between its long-term obligations and the cash available to pay those obligations) would increase by around $30 billion. The increased contributions needed to fill that gap would bankrupt many of the cities served by Calpers.

Source: S. Jakab, "Heard on the Street: America's Public Pensions Are Stuck in the Clouds,"*The Wall Street Journal*, July 26, 2019.

discounted cash flow (DCF) models
Capital budgeting decision models that incorporate the present value of future after-tax cash flows.

discount rate
A generic term that refers to the rate used for converting estimated future cash flows to a present-value basis.

average-risk projects
Projects that approximate the risk of the firm's existing assets and operations; the WACC (weighted-average cost of capital) is used in DCF (discounted cash flow) models to evaluate average-risk investment projects.

hurdle rate
The minimum acceptable rate of return on an investment for capital budgeting purposes, also referred to as the *required rate of return;* for average-risk projects, the hurdle rate is defined as the weighted-average cost of capital (WACC).

weighted-average cost of capital (WACC)
An average of a firm's (after-tax) cost of debt and equity capital in which each source of funds is proportionately weighted.

capital structure
The mix of debt and equity capital by which a company is financed.

Given the prominence of DCF models in practice today, particularly for large companies, we discuss these models next, using data from the Mendoza Company. We discuss the non-DCF models (payback and accounting rate of return) in a separate section of the chapter. Appendix B includes a discussion of some advanced capital budgeting topics.

DCF Models: Specifying the Discount Rate

The **discounted cash flow (DCF) models** evaluate capital investment projects by converting anticipated future after-tax cash flows to a present-value basis. That is, in evaluating capital investments, DCF models explicitly take into consideration the time value of money. This process is conceptually appealing because it is consistent with the process that investors use in assigning value to securities issued by individual firms.

Unfortunately, the terminology regarding the discounting process can be confusing. In this text, when we speak of the rate used to convert future cash flows to a present-value basis, we use the term **discount rate.** For capital budgeting purposes, the discount rate can be approximated as the firm's weighted-average cost of capital (WACC). However, the use of a firm's WACC as the discount rate for capital budgeting purposes is only appropriate (as explained later) for **average-risk projects.** In the situation where a project under consideration exhibits higher or lower risk than average, an adjustment to the firm's WACC is needed (upward for higher-risk projects, downward for lower-risk projects).[11] Some refer to a project-specific discount rate as the **hurdle rate.** They consider this the minimum acceptable rate of return.

Unless otherwise noted, for purposes of discussion, assume that the appropriate discount rate used for capital budgeting purposes is the firm's WACC.

Estimating the WACC[12]

A company obtains funds (capital) from both equity and debt sources. The cost to the firm for each source of funds is the return demanded by lenders and investors who buy the firm's securities. A firm's **weighted-average cost of capital (WACC)** therefore, is a calculation of the firm's cost of capital in which each source of funds is proportionately weighted. You could think of the WACC as the expected rate of return that investors would demand on a portfolio consisting of all of the firm's securities. The weights in determining the WACC are based on the firm's **capital structure**—that is, its mix of debt and equity capital, expressed in market-value terms.

---

[11] In the study by J. Graham and C. Harvey, "How Do CFOs Make Capital Budgeting and Capital Structure Decisions?," *Journal of Applied Corporate Finance* 15, no. 1 (Spring 2002), pp. 8–23, 60% of respondents said they used a single company-wide rate for investment analysis purposes; 51% said they used a "risk-matched" rate for a given project (thereby suggesting that some companies use *both* approaches).

[12] An interactive spreadsheet model for estimating WACC is provided in S. G. Berry, C. E. Betterton, and I. Karagiannidis, "Understanding Weighted-Average Cost of Capital: A Pedagogical Application,"*Journal of Financial Education* 40, no. 1/2 (Spring/Summer 2014), pp. 115–136. The model allows students to explore alternative mixes of debt and equity in terms of estimating a company's WACC.

REAL-WORLD FOCUS   Deductibility of Interest Payments for U.S. Income Tax Purposes

A key provision of the Tax Cuts and Jobs Act of 2017 in the U.S. affects the deductibility of interest payments and therefore the calculation of an entity's weighted-average cost of capital (WACC). After 2021, the deductibility of interest payments will be limited to 30 percent of EBIT (earnings before interest and taxes). The effect of this change will serve to increase the after-tax cost of debt financing for most businesses (public utilities, for example, are exempt from these changes)—particularly those companies with large amounts of depreciation and/or amortization expense. The new limit on the deductibility

of interest is also likely to affect smaller businesses (on average, interest expense for large companies is a small portion of profits) and companies in industries (such as health care providers and pharmaceutical companies) that tend to use greater amounts of debt financing. For entities subject to U.S. tax law, this change will have to be factored into the estimation of an entity's WACC.

Source: Justin Lahart, "The One Tax Change That Really Bites Businesses," *The Wall Street Journal*, December 20, 2017, p. B1.

After-Tax Cost of Debt

Because interest payments are tax deductible, we must calculate the cost of debt on an after-tax basis. Because market values are used to determine the weight attached to each type of security (including debt instruments), we need to estimate the current yield of the debt instruments in a company's capital structure. That is, we need to use the effective, not nominal, interest rate of the debt.[13] Thus, we define the after-tax cost of debt, K_d, as follows:

$$K_d = \text{Effective interest rate} \times (1 - t)$$

where

t = marginal income tax rate

Note: For an important change regarding the deductibility of interest expense for U.S. tax purposes, see the related Real-World Focus box.

Cost of Common Equity

capital asset pricing model (CAPM)
Model that depicts the risk-return relationship for equity securities and that can be used to estimate the required rate of return on equity for a given company; a rate equal to the risk-free rate of return plus a risk premium measured as the product of β and the market-risk premium.

beta coefficient (β)
A measure of the sensitivity of a given stock's return to fluctuations in the overall market; the average beta of all stocks is 1.0; a beta coefficient greater than 1 implies greater sensitivity to market fluctuations, while a beta less than 1 implies lower sensitivity of return to fluctuations in the overall market.

The cost of common stock (and retained earnings) is defined as the rate of return demanded by investors; that is, it is the risk-adjusted return needed to attract investors to purchase the common stock of a company. For companies whose shares of stock are listed on an exchange, the **capital asset pricing model (CAPM)** can be used to estimate this rate of return, K_e, as follows:

$$K_e = r_f + \beta(r_m - r_f)$$

where

r_f = risk-free rate

r_m = the percentage return (dividends + capital gains) on a market portfolio of securities

β = the firm's **beta coefficient** (an index of how the rate of return of a particular security moves as the rate of return of the market moves)

An intuitive explanation of the CAPM is that the expected rate of return on a given stock is a function of two factors: the current risk-free rate of return (e.g., the yield on U.S. Treasury bills) and a market risk premium equal in amount to the second component on the right-hand side of the preceding equation. Alternatively, you can view the former term as compensation for the time value of money and the second term as a premium that investors demand. This second term is a function of the sensitivity of a given stock's return to

[13] For example, the *effective interest rate* on a 10-year, 8.0%, $100,000 bond with semiannual interest payments that was sold for $88,448 is 9.84%, not 8.0%. (Note: This amount can be found using the Yield function in Excel.) If the issuing firm faces a marginal income tax rate of 40%, the after-tax cost of this security is 5.91% (i.e., 9.84% × 0.60).

market risk premium
The spread between the expected rate of return on a market portfolio of securities and the risk-free rate of return; represented as $(r_m - r_f)$, where r_m = return on a market portfolio of securities and r_f = risk-free rate of return.

the fluctuations in the overall market (i.e., its β coefficient) and the **market risk premium** (defined as the spread between the expected rate of return on a market portfolio of securities, r_m, and the risk-free rate of return, r_f). In sum, under the CAPM the expected rate of return on a stock is equal to the risk-free rate plus the specific stock's beta coefficient times the market risk premium.

Cost of Preferred Stock

The cost of preferred stock, K_p, is conceptually equal to the current yield that holders (i.e., investors) of the stock demand. This is also referred to as the *dividend yield* on the share of preferred stock. That is,

$$K_p = \text{Current dividend on preferred stock} \div \text{Current market price per share}$$

Determining Weights

Market, not book (accounting), values are needed conceptually to determine the weights associated with each source of funds in determining the WACC. As an example, consider a company in the 40% marginal income tax bracket. This company has a $100,000 long-term bank loan outstanding with a 12% interest rate; $500,000 face value of 8.396%, 20-year bonds, currently selling at 90% of face value (interest on the bonds is paid semiannually; the bonds mature in 10 years); $200,000 of 15%, $20 preferred stock with a current market value of $300,000; and 10,000 shares of $1 par value common stock that the firm sold originally for $5 per share. The common stock has a current market price of $75 per share. Assume that application of the CAPM (as described above) yields an estimated rate of return (yield) of approximately 20%. Given this information, the company's WACC is approximately 13.4%, as shown in Exhibit 12.6.

Software that calculates a company's WACC and that generates estimates of underlying common stock value for the company is available (e.g., www.valuepro.net). Also, from http://people.stern.nyu.edu/adamodar/New_Home_Page/datafile/wacc.htm and https://dpcostofcapital.com/ (subscription basis), you can obtain estimated cost of capital (both cost of equity and WACC) information from a sample of U.S. industries, income tax rate and beta information for individual U.S. stocks, and international industry data of interest to U.S. investors.

Net Present Value Decision Model
Estimating a Project's NPV

net present value (NPV)
The difference between the present value of future cash inflows and the present value of future cash outflows of an investment project.

The estimated **net present value (NPV)** of an investment is the difference between the present value of the project's estimated cash inflows and the present value of the project's estimated cash outflows (where outflows are characterized as positive numbers). If outflows are expressed as negative numbers, then we can define the estimated NPV of a project as the sum of the present value of cash inflows and the present value of the cash outflows of

EXHIBIT 12.6 Estimation of Weighted-Average Cost of Capital (WACC) (Hypothetical Example)

Source of Funds	(1) Book Value	(2) Pretax Effective Rate of Return	(3) After-Tax Rate or Expected Return	(4) Total Current Market Value	(5) Weight (Based on Market Values)	(6) = (3) × (5) Components for WACC Calculation
Bank loan	$100,000	12%	7.20%	$ 100,000	6.250%	0.4500%
Bonds	500,000	10*	6.00	450,000	28.125	1.6875
Preferred stock	200,000	15	10.00**	300,000	18.750	1.8750
Common stock	50,000		20.00	750,000	46.875	9.3750
Total	**$850,000**			**$1,600,000**	**100.000%**	**13.3875%**

Notes:

*The estimated effective interest rate (yield to maturity) on the bonds, 10%, was found using the YIELD function in Excel.

**Number of preferred shares outstanding = $200,000 ÷ $20 par value per share = 10,000 shares. Current market price per share = $300,000 ÷ 10,000 shares outstanding = $30.00. Preferred stock dividend per share = 15% × $20 par value per share = $3.00. Therefore, the current dividend yield on preferred stock = $3.00 ÷ $30.00 = 10%

present value (PV)
Future cash flows expressed
in terms of current purchasing
power; also referred to as
time-adjusted value or current
equivalent value.

an investment. The **present value (PV)** of a future cash flow is its current equivalent dollar value, using an appropriate discount rate—such as the firm's WACC. The decision rule is to accept a proposed investment if the projected NPV of the project is positive; that is, accept a project if the PV of cash inflows is greater than the PV of cash outflows. If a project has a positive expected NPV, then the project is expected to add to shareholder value.

Estimating NPV with Uniform Net Cash Inflows

Some capital expenditure projects are characterized by an investment outlay in year 0 followed by an annuity—that is, a uniform stream of estimated future cash inflows. Such a project's NPV can be determined in either of two ways. We illustrate these methods by using assumed data for Bradley Inc. Bradley is considering investing in a four-year project that requires an outlay at time 0 of $555,000 and expected after-tax inflows of $200,000 per year. Bradley's WACC is assumed to be 10%.

Method 1: Annuity Table

To convert the future stream of cash inflows back to its present value, you could obtain (from Appendix C, Table 2) the appropriate annuity factor for 10%, four years: 3.170. (This annuity factor can be generated directly using the formula in the note that appears at the bottom of Appendix C, Table 2.) Note that this factor (3.170) is simply the sum of the four present-value factors presented in Appendix C, Table 1, under the 10% column.

Thus, the PV of the future annuity is $634,000 ($200,000 × 3.170), and the expected NPV of this project is $634,000 − $555,000 = $79,000. This implies that the investment is expected to provide the company with an economic return greater than 10% (WACC). Alternatively, you can say that this investment is expected to earn a 10% return on the invested funds plus an additional $79,000 (in current dollars).

Method 2: Excel Formula

You can use a built-in function in Excel to estimate a project's NPV, as indicated in the screenshot presented next. The formula is as follows:

$$= NPV(rate, values)$$

In this formula, *rate* refers to the discount rate (usually the WACC) to be used for the analysis; *values* is an array or a reference to cells that contain a series of outflows (negative values) and/or inflows (positive values) occurring at regular periods.

Note that the difference of $26.91 ($79,000 − $78,973.09) in NPV amounts that you observe is due to rounding (to 3 decimal points) that took place when Table 2 was constructed. Note, too, that if the amount in cell C1 were entered as a negative number, then the formula in cell B9 would be slightly different—the last item would be +C1, not −C1.

	A	B	C	D
1	Initial Investment		$555,000	
2	After-tax Cash Inflows:			
3	Year 1	$200,000		
4	Year 2	$200,000		
5	Year 3	$200,000		
6	Year 4	$200,000		
7	Discount Rate		10.00%	
8			Formula in Cell B9	
9	NPV =	$78,973.09	=NPV(C7,B3:B6)-C1	

Source: Microsoft Excel

Estimating NPV with Uneven Cash Inflows

To illustrate the calculation of NPV when the anticipated future cash flows are uneven, return to the cash flow data for the Mendoza Company presented in Exhibit 12.2. The net investment outlay at time zero is $680,000. The after-tax cash inflows (rounded) from the proposed investment are $194,000 (year 1), $245,000 (year 2), $188,000 (year 3), and $287,000 (year 4).

With this information, and an assumed (after-tax) discount rate of 10%, we calculate the esti-mated NPV of this proposed investment as $36,115, as follows:[14]

	A	B	C	D
1	Initial Investment		($680,000)	
2	After-tax Cash Inflows:			
3	Year 1	$194,000		
4	Year 2	$245,000		
5	Year 3	$188,000		
6	Year 4	$287,000		
7	WACC		10.00%	
8			Formula in Cell B9	
9	NPV =	$36,115	=NPV(C7,B3:B6)+C1	

Source: Microsoft Excel

The formula in cell B9 assumes that the initial cash outlay (cell C1) is entered as a negative number. As such, C1 is added in the formula to the present value of cash inflows (=NPV(C7,B3:B6)+C1).

Internal Rate of Return Decision Model

internal rate of return (IRR)
An estimate of the true (i.e., economic) rate of return on a proposed investment.

The **internal rate of return (IRR)** represents an estimate of the true (i.e., economic) rate of return on a proposed investment. Mathematically, the IRR is defined as the rate of return that produces an NPV of zero.[15] The decision rule using the IRR model is simple: Accept an investment if its projected IRR exceeds the firm's discount rate (WACC). If a project's IRR is greater than the company's WACC, it means that the project has a positive NPV.

Estimating a Project's IRR: Uniform Cash Inflows

If the project consists of an initial investment outlay followed by a stream of constant cash inflows, the project's IRR is defined as the discount rate that satisfies the following equation:

Initial investment outlay = PV of future cash inflows at a specified discount rate
= Annual after-tax cash inflow × Annuity discount factor associated with the life of the project

Using $A_{r,n}$ to denote the last term in the above equation, the equation can be restated as follows:

$A_{r,n}$ = Initial investment outlay ÷ Annual after-tax cash inflow from the investment

where

$A_{r,n}$ = annuity factor that makes the PV of the stream of future after-tax cash inflows equal to the initial investment outlay

n = life of the project (e.g., in years)

r = discount rate

As an example, for a four-year project that has an initial investment outlay of $555,000 and annual after-tax cash inflows of $200,000, the estimated IRR is determined as follows:

$$\$555,000 = \$200,000 \times A_{r,4}$$
$$A_{r,4} = \$555,000 \div \$200,000 = 2.775$$

[14] Alternatively, we could use the PV factors in Appendix C, Table 1, to determine the PV of the stream of after-tax cash inflows. From this, we would subtract the required investment outlay, $680,000, to arrive at the project's estimated NPV. It is also possible to use an array formula to calculate the NPV of a project. To do this, refer to the Excel screenshot above. First, define variable names (go to Formulas, then Define Names). For example, define cell C7 as "WACC," cells A4 through A8 as "Year," and cells B4 through B8 as "CF." Then, enter into an open cell (e.g., B10) the following formula to calculate the estimated NPV of this project: =SUM(CF/(1 + WACC)^Year) + C1. Finally, rather than hitting "Enter," you now (to enter the array formula) hit Control + Shift + Enter. Cell B10 should now display the correct amount, $36,115 (rounded).

[15] The IRR can also be interpreted as a constant rate of return on the declining balance of an investment. As such, and similar to a typical mortgage, each receipt (or payment in a mortgage context) consists of a partial return on investment and a partial return of the original investment (capital). See S. P. Rich and J. T. Rose, "Re-Examining an Old Question: Does the IRR Method Implicitly Assume a Reinvestment Rate?," *Journal of Financial Education* 40, no. 1/2 (Spring/Summer 2014), pp. 152–166.

An annuity factor of 2.775 in Appendix C, Table 2, for a project with a four-year useful life corresponds to a discount rate, r, of between 15% and 20%. Because this rate exceeds the firm's WACC (10.0%), the project should be accepted.[16]

Estimating a Project's IRR: Uneven Cash Inflows

When the projected future cash inflows are not even, the project's IRR can be estimated using a trial-and-error approach. That is, a discount rate, say 10%, is chosen to begin the process. Using this discount rate, you would compute the project's NPV. If the resulting NPV at this discount rate is positive, the discount rate you chose is too low (and vice versa). Thus, a higher discount rate is chosen and the project's NPV at this new rate is determined. The process stops when the resulting NPV is close to zero: The discount rate at this point represents the project's estimated IRR. The interpolation process explained in footnote 16 can be used to generate a more accurate estimate of a project's IRR.

Alternatively, we could use the IRR function in Excel to estimate the project's IRR:

$$= \text{IRR}(\text{values},[\text{guess}])$$

Because Excel uses iteration to compute the IRR, it starts with a guess that you can provide. The guess is optional, and if none is provided, Excel uses 10% as a default.

Using the cash flow data for Mendoza Company (Exhibit 12.2), Excel computes the following:

	A	B	C	D
1	After-tax Cash Flows:			
2	Year	CF		
3	0	($680,000)		
4	1	194,000		
5	2	245,000		
6	3	188,000		
7	4	287,000		
8			Cell Formulas	
9	IRR =	12.31%	=IRR(B3:B7,0.09)	
10	NPV =	$0.00	=B3+NPV(B9,B4:B7)	
11				
12	Note: in the IRR formula, 0.09 is a "guess,"			
13	which is needed to start the algorithm used by			
14	Excel to estimate a project's IRR.			

Source: Microsoft Excel

Note that we confirm that the project's estimated IRR is 12.31%. At this discount rate, the estimated NPV of the project is zero. Given a WACC of 10% for the Mendoza Company, this project should therefore be accepted. Managers generally find the IRR decision rule intuitively appealing: *accept projects that provide a rate of return* (e.g., 12.31%) *that exceeds the company's WACC* (e.g., 10%).

Of course, you can also use the built-in function in Excel to estimate a project's IRR when the future cash inflows are equal (rather than using the trial-and-error procedure described earlier).

[16] To generate a more accurate estimate of this project's IRR, we can use the following interpolation procedure:

	Interest rate, r		Annuity factor, Ar_4	
At lower rate	15.00%	15.00%	2.855	2.855
Target rate	?	?		2.775
At higher rate	20.00%		2.589	—
Difference	5.00%	—	0.266	0.080

The difference in annuity factors between the interest rates on either side of the target annuity factor (2.775) is 0.266. This suggests that an increase of 5% in interest rates, from 15% to 20%, increases the annuity factor by 0.266. Thus, to get to 2.775 we need to increase the interest rate proportionately to the decrease in the annuity factor. That is, the annuity factor must be reduced by 30.08% (0.080/0.266). Thus, the needed increase in interest rate to decrease the annuity factor by 0.266 is 30.08% of 5%, or 1.50%. The project's estimated IRR is therefore 16.50% [i.e., 15% + (30.08% × 5.00%)]. Note that this linear interpolation process produces an *estimate* of the true IRR. The true IRR, found using the built-in Excel function, is 16.42%. See if you can reproduce this result and verify that at this discount rate the NPV of the project is zero.

The Modified Internal Rate of Return

Survey evidence suggests that the IRR is widely used in practice, in large part because of its intuitive appeal to managers. Students in accounting should be aware of a particular controversy regarding the use of IRR for evaluating capital budgeting projects: the reinvestment rate assumption.

Critics argue that the IRR metric ignores the reinvestment potential of intermediate positive cash flows from a project. These same critics maintain that the IRR inherently assumes that such cash flows are reinvested at the IRR rate and that in most cases this rate is unrealistically high. Thus, they claim, conventional IRR calculations build in reinvestment assumptions that make bad projects look better and good ones look great. This can result in major capital budgeting distortions.

These critics suggest that a more conservative assumption regarding the reinvestment rate of return on interim cash flows be used. In most cases, this rate is better approximated by the organization's discount rate (WACC). To do this, the **modified internal rate of return (MIRR)** can be used to assess capital budgeting projects. As the name implies, MIRR is a modification of the conventional IRR measure. The MIRR assumes all positive cash flows are reinvested at a particular rate of return (usually at the WACC) for the remaining duration of the project.

A built-in function in Excel, MIRR, provides an estimate of a project's modified internal rate of return, as follows:[17]

modified internal rate of return (MIRR)
The internal rate of return (IRR) of a capital investment adjusted to account for an assumed rate of return associated with interim project cash inflows.

MIRR(values, finance_rate, reinvest_rate)

In this formula, *finance_rate* is the discount rate (i.e., WACC) used for DCF analysis of capital budgeting projects and *reinvest_rate* is the estimated reinvestment rate (i.e., the rate of return on the periodic cash flows provided by the project—generally, this will also be the WACC).

Based on the after-tax cash flow data for the Mendoza Company presented in Exhibit 12.2, we find an estimated MIRR of 11.43%, as follows:

	A	B	C	D
1	WACC	10.00%		
2	After-tax Cash Flows:			
3	Year	CF		
4	0	($680,000)		
5	1	194,000		
6	2	245,000		
7	3	188,000		
8	4	287,000		
9			Cell Formula	
10	MIRR=	11.43%	=MIRR(B4:B8,B1,B1)	

Source: Microsoft Excel

Three points are worth making regarding the reinvestment rate controversy. One, the MIRR suffers from some of the same drawbacks as the more conventional IRR metric. Relying on either can lead to an incorrect choice between mutually exclusive investments; we deal with this issue in Appendix B. Two, a search of the internet under "MIRR" suggests heated debate as to whether or not the conventional IRR metric has an inherent reinvestment rate assumption. Some of these arguments are arcane and embedded in mathematical theory. Students of accounting should, therefore, simply be aware that there are different points of view regarding this issue. Three, as noted next, in most cases (e.g., other than when capital needs to be rationed), a safe bet would be to use NPV as the financial performance metric associated with proposed investments.

---

[17] See https://support.microsoft.com/en-us/article/MIRR-function-b020f038-7492-4fb4-93c1-35c345b53524; and J. Carlton Collins, "Microsoft Excel: 3 Ways to Calculate Internal Rate of Return in Excel," *Journal of Accountancy,* February 2017, http://www.journalofaccountancy.com/issues/2017/feb/calculate-internal-rate-of-return-in-excel.html.

Comparison of NPV and IRR Methods: Which to Use?

If the decision is limited to accepting or rejecting a given investment project, the NPV model and the IRR model will lead to the same conclusion. There are, however, several situations that complicate capital budgeting decisions in the real world. Appendix B to this chapter deals with three of these issues: (1) the problem of multiple IRRs, (2) choosing between mutually exclusive projects, and (3) capital budgeting under the situation of capital rationing. Given such real-world complications, modern financial theory generally argues for the use of the NPV decision model, except in the case of capital rationing. In this case, a company's capital budget should be allocated to projects on the basis of *relative profitability,* that is, on the basis of NPV per dollar invested.

Uncertainty and the Capital Budgeting Process

Capital budgeting decision models rely on estimates of key input variables, such as the discount rate, life of a proposed project, after-tax cash flows, and alternative future states of nature (e.g., good economy vs. bad economy, high price of energy vs. low price of energy). By definition, these estimates and states of nature are subject to uncertainty; the longer the time horizon for the investment, the greater is the uncertainty regarding these estimates. Management accountants, as part of the decision-making team, need to understand approaches that can be used to address this uncertainty. Here we consider two broad approaches to the problem: (1) conducting sensitivity analysis as part of the capital budgeting process and (2) incorporating real options into the analysis of proposed investments.

Sensitivity Analysis

sensitivity analysis
The name for a variety of methods that examine how an amount changes if factors involved in predicting that amount change.

Decision makers want to know how sensitive their capital budgeting decisions (e.g., whether to accept or reject a proposed investment) are to estimates of the decision inputs (e.g., discount rate). In more formal terms, this assessment process is referred to as **sensitivity analysis.** In the sections that follow, we provide an overview of three types of sensitivity analysis: what-if analysis, scenario analysis, and Monte Carlo simulation.

What-If Analysis

What-if questions attempt to determine the impact on project profitability of changes in the value of a single input variable. For example, we might be interested in knowing the impact on NPV if the after-tax cash flows for a project are only 90% of their projected amount. Separately, what if a given project has a three-year rather than four-year life? The more general question to be asked is: Which variables in the decision model have the greatest potential to alter the expected profitability (and hence desirability) of an investment? Once this is known, management may want to refine its estimate of the variable(s) that has (have) the greatest impact on project profitability.

Following is an Excel screenshot of a basic what-if analysis for a project with an investment outlay of $18 and a three-year life. The table in the screenshot shows the independent impact of changes in the discount rate and changes in the amount of annual after-tax cash flows on the estimated NPV of the investment.[18]

	A	B	C	D
1	NPV as a Function of Changes in After-tax Cash			
2	Flows and Discount Rate (Initial Cash Outflow = $18;			
3	Project Life = 3 years)			
4				
5		Annual After-tax Cash Flows		
6	Discount Rate	$7.00	$8.00	$9.00
7	0.10	($0.59)	$1.89	$4.38
8	0.11	($0.89)	$1.55	$3.99
9	0.12	($1.19)	$1.21	$3.62

Source: Microsoft Excel

[18] Excel provides a structured way to conduct and report one-variable and two-variable sensitivity analyses, using "Data Tables." In Excel, go to Data, then What-If Analysis, then Data Table. The following online tutorial can be consulted: https://support.office.com/en-us/article/Calculate-multiple-results-by-using-a-data-table-e95e2487-6ca6-4413-ad12-77542a5ea50b?CorrelationId=76a788fa-1fb5-46ad-8cda-9dcc54b14852&ui=en-US&rs=en-US&ad=US&ocmsassetID=HP010342214.

REAL-WORLD FOCUS   Scenario Planning at Royal Dutch Shell

In the mid-1960s, Royal Dutch Shell started experimenting with what it called "scenario planning"—that is, a new way of looking into the future to anticipate changes in critical factors such as oil prices, worldwide inflation, political instabilities, and the emergence of alternative energy sources. Today, over 50 years later, it is still using this method for long-range planning. The company asserts that this approach is designed principally to break the habit of assuming that the future for a company will look much like the past. Research suggests that the use of scenario planning adds value principally through an enhanced

capacity to perceive, interpret, and respond to change, as well as promote organizational learning. In short, advocates of scenario planning believe that this exercise provides a safe place for discussing and acknowledging uncertainty. As noted in the text, the same principle can be used in conjunction with the analysis of proposed capital investments.

Source: A. Wilkinson and R. Kupers, "Living in the Futures: How Scenario Planning Changed Corporate Strategy," *Harvard Business Review,* May 2013, pp. 119–127.

breakeven after-tax cash flow
The minimum annual after-tax cash inflows needed for an investment project to be acceptable (in a present value sense).

In addition, the decision maker might be interested in determining the breakeven point associated with a given variable. In the preceding example, managers might feel fairly certain that the appropriate discount rate (WACC) is 11%. A reasonable question to ask is: What is the **breakeven after-tax cash flow**—that is, the minimum annual after-tax cash inflows needed for an investment project to be acceptable? In other words, what is the annual after-tax cash inflow amount that would result in a zero NPV? The Goal Seek function in Excel can be used to answer this question.[19]

Assume a model that calculates the NPV of a three-year project with an initial investment of $18, annual after-tax cash inflows of $7 per year, and a discount rate of 11%. The NPV function of Excel for this example shows a projected NPV of ($0.89), as indicated below:

	A	B	C	D	E	F
1	Original investment outlay		$ 18.00			
2	Annual after-tax cash flow		$ 7.00			
3	Discount rate		11%			
4	NPV		($0.89)	(=NPV(C3,C2,C2,C2,)-C1)		

Source: Microsoft Excel

To find the breakeven after-tax cash flow, access the Goal Seek function using the What-If Analysis button under the Data tab, and do the following:

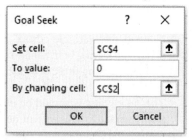

Source: Microsoft Excel

After clicking OK in the dialog box above, the following solution should appear:

	A	B	C	D	E	F
1	Original investment outlay		$ 18.00			
2	Annual after-tax cash flow		$ 7.37			
3	Discount rate		11%			
4	NPV		$0.00	(=NPV(C3,C2,C2,C2,)-C1)		

Source: Microsoft Excel

Thus, a project that costs $18 and that has an after-tax cash flow of $7.37 for each of three years will, at a discount rate of 11%, result in an NPV of $0. (See the end-of-chapter Self-Study Problem for another application of the Goal Seek option in Excel.)

[19] To find a quick tutorial on how to use the Goal Seek function in Excel, visit the Office Help and Training site at **https://support.office.com.**

Access and Read the Following Items: S. Mark Young, James J. Gong, and Wim A. Van der Stede, "Using Real Options to Make Decisions in the Motion Picture Industry," *Strategic Finance,* May 2012, pp. 53–59 (available at http://sfmagazine.com/wp-content/uploads/sfarchive/2012/05/Using-Real-Options-to-Make-Decisions-in-the-Motion-Picture-Industry.pdf); Tom Copeland and Peter Tufano, "A Real-World Way to Manage Real Options," *Harvard Business Review,* March 2004 (https://hbr.org/2004/03/a-real-world-way-to-manage-real-options); Wim Van der Stede, "Hollywood Studios Appear to Plan Sequels before They Produce the Original Movie" (2015) (http://eprints.lse.ac.uk/63736/1/blogs.lse.ac.uk-Hollywood%20studios%20appear%20to%20plan%20sequels%20before%20they%20produce%20the%20original%20movie.pdf); and Institute of Management Accountants (IMA), *Certified Management Accountant* (CMA) *Learning Outcome Statements* (revised September 2, 2016), p. 26 (www.imanet.org/cma-certification/taking-the-exam).

Required

Provide an overview of how real options analysis can help decision makers deal with uncertainty in the analysis of capital investment projects. How, specifically, can real options analysis be used to evaluate investment decisions in the film (motion picture) industry? What aspects of the topic of real options are covered on the current CMA (Certified Management Accountant) exam?

(Refer to Comments on Cost Management in Action at the end of the chapter.)

A word of caution regarding what-if analyses is in order. The basic approach looks at the *independent effects* of individual variables. In reality, variables included in the NPV model may be related to one another. That is, a change in one variable (e.g., variable costs) might be related to a change in another variable (e.g., fixed costs). The effect of such interrelationships cannot be captured by the use of what-if analyses, which look only at the effects of changing one variable at a time. In short, there are technical limits as to how far you can take this type of sensitivity analysis.

Scenario Analysis

scenario analysis
Simultaneous effect on a decision variable of interest of changing the values of a set of input factors; a special form of sensitivity analysis that is appropriate when the variables in a decision model are interrelated.

Decision makers may be interested in how their proposed investment would look under different combinations of variables, called *scenarios.* Scenario analysis is a form of sensitivity analysis that does just this: It examines the profitability of a project (e.g., its expected NPV) under a variety of plausible scenarios.[20]

Typically, decision makers specify the expected outcomes of an investment project as the base case. The associated NPV assumes a specific scenario (e.g., the market price of oil, whether the U.S. economy is in recession or expansion, the state of labor relations with a key supplier, and so forth). Then, separate NPV analyses can be conducted for each of several additional scenarios. It is common to label such scenarios with descriptive terms such as *disaster scenario* (i.e., worst-case scenario values for variables such as sales price, sales demand, and variable costs), *disappointing* (reflecting less-than-favorable values), and *optimistic* (reflecting better-than-expected values).

In generating these scenarios, it is not uncommon for accountants to work with other managers (like marketing managers and/or the vice president of strategic planning, for example). These individuals should be most knowledgeable about possible macroeconomic and uncontrollable factors that determine various scenarios. In short, scenario analysis allows managers to examine the effects of different scenarios represented as the joint effect of a set of related variables captured in the NPV model. These scenarios are best developed through the use of cross-functional teams within the organization.

Monte Carlo Simulation[21]

As noted above, risk analysis of capital budgeting projects using traditional spreadsheets is inherently limited. For example, scenario analysis yields only a single output value (e.g., expected NPV) for a set of inputs. Scenario analysis does not have the ability to measure an outcome's probability of occurrence, which is a key measure of risk within a modeled relationship.

[20] To find a quick tutorial on how to conduct scenario analysis in Excel, visit the Office Help and Training site at https://support.office.com.

[21] This discussion draws on the following source: D. F. Togo, "Risk Analysis for Accounting Models: A Spreadsheet Simulation Approach," *Journal of Accounting Education* 22, no. 2 (2004), pp. 153–163.

Thus, risk analysis can be enhanced if managers are able to generate probabilities associated with alternative values of the outcome variable (e.g., NPV, IRR) in a capital budgeting decision model. Spreadsheet add-ons, such as Oracle Crystal Ball,[22] are able to generate such probability distributions. Oracle Crystal Ball specifies more than 30 possible probability distributions (normal, uniform, binomial, triangular, etc.) that can be used to describe each input variable (such as project life or discount rate). The end result is that this process transforms what was previously a deterministic model (e.g., NPV or IRR) into a probabilistic model that can be analyzed through **Monte Carlo simulation (MCS)**. Monte Carlo simulation is an extension to scenario analysis in which a computer provides a distribution of possible outcomes based on repeated sampling from a distribution associated with one or more input variables in a decision model.

A capital budgeting simulation computes the value of an outcome variable of interest (e.g., a project's expected NPV) many times over. Each time it simulates the project's NPV, it draws a combination of input values (sales price per unit, variable cost per unit, sales volume, etc.) based on a prespecified probability distribution of each of these variables. Based on these inputs, an associated NPV is generated. In essence, the simulation allows the decision maker to substitute a probability distribution for the mean value of each input variable in a decision model. When the simulation is complete (e.g., after 10,000 iterations), a probability distribution of NPVs for a given investment proposal is generated. Associated output from the simulation includes the mean, maximum result, minimum result, standard deviation, skewness, and percentile probabilities. The latter are particularly important as they allow statements such as, "Given the probability distributions of the variables in our capital budgeting model, this investment proposal has a 48% probability of having a negative NPV and a 35% probability of having an NPV of at least $25,000."

Real Options[23]

The use of DCF models, such as NPV, is recommended as the preferred method of evaluating capital budgeting proposals. However, these models have an inherent assumption that may be unrealistic: They assume passive behavior on the part of management once an investment decision has been made. Alternatively, we can describe the traditional analysis as "take it or leave it." But in reality, some investment projects are dynamic in nature. They may contain one or more options for dealing with risk and uncertainty as new information (e.g., market conditions) is revealed over time. Management might expand a project in the future if things go well, or it might scale back or abandon a project altogether if things are not going well. These opportunities are collectively referred to as **real options** (or options on **real assets**). In this context, real assets represent investments in both tangible property (e.g., a new manufacturing facility) and intangible property (e.g., a new information system). Traditional capital budgeting decision models, such as DCF models, do not explicitly incorporate options on real assets that may be embedded in a proposed investment.

Real options are analogous to financial options—puts and calls. The latter gives the holder of the option the right, but not obligation, to purchase stock at a fixed price, called the *strike price* or *exercise price,* up to the expiration date of the option; the former gives the holder of the option the right, but not obligation, to sell stock for a fixed price on or before the exercise date of the option. These financial options have value and, in fact, are traded between investors on an organized exchange. Financial options have value precisely because they allow investors to capitalize on new information about a company that unfolds over time. Similarly, options on real assets have value because they allow decision makers to react to favorable or

Monte Carlo simulation (MCS)
An extension to scenario analysis in which a computer provides a distribution of possible outcomes—for example, project NPVs—based on repeated sampling from a distribution associated with one or more input variables in a decision model.

real options
Flexibilities and/or growth opportunities embedded in capital investment projects; can be contrasted with financial options, which are traded on an organized exchange.

real assets
Investments in both tangible property (e.g., a manufacturing facility) and intangible property (e.g., a new information system).

[22] Crystal Ball is available from Oracle (www.oracle.com/crystalball/). An academic version of this software is available for student/faculty use. For an extended example of using Crystal Ball to perform Monte Carlo simulation within a capital budgeting context, consult N. Dhiensiri and N. Balsara, "An Introductory Application of Monte Carlo Simulation in Capital Budgeting Analysis,"*Journal of Financial Education* 40, no. 1/2 (Spring/Summer 2014), pp. 94–114. The following can be consulted for developing limited Monte Carlo simulations within Excel: T. E. McKee and Linda J. B. McKee, "Using Excel to Perform Monte Carlo Simulations,"*Strategic Finance,* December 2014, pp. 47–51.

[23] The material in this section is drawn from the following two sources: D. E. Stout, Y. A. Xie, and H. Qi, "Improving Capital Budgeting Decisions with Real Options," *Management Accounting Quarterly* 9, no. 4 (Summer 2008), pp. 1–10; and D. E. Stout, H. Qi, Y. A. Xie, and S. Liu, "Incorporating Real Options into the Capital Budgeting Process: A Primer for Accounting Educators," *Journal of Accounting Education* 26 (2008), pp. 213–230.

unfavorable information by dynamically adjusting the capital budgeting decision. Unfortunately, conventional capital budgeting decision models, such as DCF, do not incorporate into the valuation process the value of real options. Not explicitly including the value of embedded options effectively assigns any such options a value of zero.

There are four common types of real options: (1) the option to *expand* an investment (i.e., to make follow-on investments if the immediate investment project succeeds), (2) the option to *abandon* a project on the basis of new information revealed over time, (3) the option to wait and learn before investing (i.e., the option to *delay* an investment—some refer to this as an investment-timing option), or (4) the option to *scale back* the magnitude of a project (e.g., by varying output or its production methods). Items 1 and 3 are analogous to call options; items 2 and 4 are analogous to put options. We discuss the topic of real options in this section of the chapter because their inclusion in the capital budgeting process provides an additional opportunity for dealing formally with risk and uncertainty. As we demonstrate with the following example, real options may change a project's expected cash flows and risk, and for this reason they should be formally considered in the analysis of capital investment projects.

Incorporating Real Options Into the Capital Budgeting Process

There are, in general, two approaches to incorporating real options into the analysis of long-term investment projects: the use of *scenario analysis combined with decision trees* and the use of an *options-pricing model* (such as the Black-Scholes model[24]). The following discussion illustrates the former approach. The latter approach is illustrated in selected finance texts.

For purposes of illustration, assume that XYZ Company is considering investing in the production of a new technology (e.g., a handheld communications device), the target market for which is young college graduates. The estimated investment cost for this project is $100 million. Demand for the product, and therefore the project's risk, is a function of the demand for wireless internet connections. The CFO of XYZ, working with marketing, estimates a 25% chance that such demand will be high, a 50% probability that demand will be medium, and a 25% probability that demand will be low. After-tax cash flows under each of these market scenarios are estimated as follows: $70 million, $50 million, and $5 million. For projects of this nature, a 15% discount rate (the firm's estimated weighted-average cost of capital) is assumed.

Assume that XYZ can make the investment today (time period 0), or it can delay the decision for one year. The advantage of the delay option is that over the coming year, additional information regarding consumer demand for this project will be revealed. For simplicity, assume the same investment outlay cost ($100 million) and the same projected after-tax cash flows. The difference, however, is that if XYZ delays its investment by a year, the cash inflows will also be delayed (and therefore worth less in a present-value sense). Finally, assume (and this is a strong assumption) that if the project is delayed one year, the true level of consumer demand will be revealed with certainty (or near certainty). You can see that this investment-timing option is similar to a call option on a stock. In essence, management of XYZ needs to decide whether to defer the investment one year. If the company does delay the investment, then one year from now XYZ can exercise its option to invest in the project. Note, however, that it will choose to do this only if the expected NPV at time 0 is positive. In this sense, the inclusion of real options complements a traditional DCF analysis of a proposed investment, as discussed earlier in this chapter.

Traditional (DCF) Analysis

Details regarding the proposed investment are provided in the *decision tree* depicted in Panel A of Exhibit 12.7. As used here, the decision tree depicts three different scenarios (states of nature) associated with the proposed investment (today) of $100 million: high level of demand for the product, medium level of demand, and low level of demand. Each level of

---

[24] The Black-Scholes Option Pricing Model (OPM) is used to estimate the value of a call option (i.e., an option that the holder of the option has to buy shares at a specified price—called the strike price or exercise price—up to the expiration date of the option). The Black-Scholes OPM specifies the value of a call option as a function of the current market price of the underlying stock, the option's time to expiration, the risk-free rate of interest, the estimated variance in the returns for the stock, and the strike (exercise) price of the option.

Flexcell International Corporation, a Swiss company producing lightweight solar panels for a wide variety of applications, recently complemented a traditional DCF analysis with a real options analysis in conjunction with making an investment decision regarding the location of a new factory complex. Specifically, the company included in its evaluation of three different sites the value of flexibility (i.e., an investment-timing option) regarding this decision. Based on this approach, the company determined that manufacturing from its home base was more cost effective than going abroad.

More recent work addresses the following strategic issue: How does the company balance the competitive pressure to commit to new investments against the flexibility of keeping investment options open? That is, the value of a company's capital investments

is a joint function of the evolution of industry demand and prices and the additional investments it and its competitors make. One solution to this dilemma is to blend together real options analysis and game theory (into "option games"). Ferreira et al. (2009) report the application of this method to decisions made by a real, but disguised, mining company that recently faced the decision whether to add new capacity in the face of demand and competitive uncertainties. The indicated choice (invest now) differed from that revealed by a conventional DCF analysis.

Sources: Nelson Ferreira, Jayanti Kar, and Lenos Trigeorgis, "Option Games: The Key to Competing in Capital-Intensive Industries," *Harvard Business Review,* March 2009, pp. 101–107; Suzanne de Treville and Lenos Trigeorgis, "It May Be Cheaper to Manufacture at Home," *Harvard Business Review,* October 2010, pp. 84–87.

demand (state of nature) in our example is shown as a separate branch of the decision tree (see rows 7, 8, and 9 in Panel A, and rows 20, 21, and 22 in Panel B).

The demand levels and their associated probabilities (e.g., cells C7:C9 in Panel A) allow us to calculate the expected NPV of the proposed investment. This expected value is defined as the weighted average of the three possible states of nature (product demand levels), with the weights represented by the given demand probabilities.

Given an after-tax discount rate of 15%, the expected NPV of this investment is *negative* $0.109 million (cell H10 in Exhibit 12.7). Based on this conventional analysis, the project should not be undertaken: The project's expected rate of return is less than the weighted-average cost of capital (15%); as such, this project, based on a conventional DCF analysis, would not add to shareholder value.

Investment Analysis with Investment-Timing Option

As shown earlier, the expected NPV of the proposed investment is slightly negative. However, that analysis of the project failed to incorporate the value of the timing (or delay) option associated with the project. In reality, XYZ company has the option to delay its investment in the project for one year. This situation is analogous to having a call option on a stock. In this case, the company has the ability to "purchase" the investment next year, for the indicated price, based on the revealed level of consumer demand for the proposed product.

The essence of the approach is to estimate, as before, the NPV (at $t = 0$) of the proposed investment. What is different, however, is that the planning horizon must now be extended

EXHIBIT 12.7

Decision Trees: Real Options Analysis (Investment-Timing Option)

Source: Microsoft Excel

	A	B	C	D	E	F	G	H	I	J	K
1	Panel A: Expected NPV--Invest in Project Today (time 0); amounts in $ millions										
2											
3	Discount rate (WACC) =	15.00%									
4											
5	Cash Outflow	Market Demand			End-of-Period Cash Inflows		NPV of	Weighted			
6	@ time 0	(Scenario)	Probability	1	2	3	Scenario	NPV			
7		High	0.25	$70	$70	$70	$59.826	$14.956			
8	$100	Medium	0.50	$50	$50	$50	$14.161	$7.081			
9		Low	0.25	$5	$5	$5	($88.584)	($22.146)			
10			1.00				Expected NPV =	($0.109)			
11											
12	Panel B: Expected NPV--Delay Investment by One Year, Only if NPV is Increased; amounts in $ millions										
13											
14	Discount rate (WACC) =	15.00%									
15	Risk-free rate =	5.00%									
16	Cash outflow in one year =	$100									
17											
18		Market Demand			End-of-Period Cash Inflows			PV of Cash	PV of Cash	Weighted	
19		(Scenario)	Probability	1	2	3	4	Outflows*	Inflows†	NPV @ time 0‡	
20		High	0.25	($100)	$70	$70	$70	($95.238)	$138.979	$10.935	
21		Medium	0.50	($100)	$50	$50	$50	($95.238)	$99.271	$2.016	
22		Low	0.25	$0	$0	$0	$0	$0.000	$0.000	$0.000	
23			1.00						Expected NPV =	$12.951	
24	* discounted at risk-free rate of interest										
25	† discounted at WACC (weighted-average cost of capital); formula for cell I20: =PV(B14,1,(PV(B14,3,E20)))										
26	‡ formula for cell J20: =(I20+H20)*C20										
27											
28											

to four periods. Also, ***in the determination of the weighted-average NPV of the project, we include only those individual scenarios that have a positive NPV.*** For example, if the NPV of any scenario at $t = 1$ is negative, then this scenario is not included in the computation of the weighted-average return on the project. This is precisely because at $t = 1$, the company is assumed to possess revealed information regarding the level of consumer demand. If, for example, it is revealed at $t = 1$ that demand is going to be low, then XYZ would not be forced to exercise its option to purchase the investment. On the other hand, if at $t = 1$ the revealed level of consumer demand is high, then most likely the NPV of this scenario, at $t = 1$, would be positive. As such, this scenario would be included in the computation of the expected value of the proposed investment. Note, however, that in order to be able to compare our NPV analysis with the conventional approach (Panel A of Exhibit 12.7), we must bring all future cash flows (both inflows and outflows) back to time period 0. Because we assume that the investment outlay cost of $1 million is known with certainty (or near certainty), it would be appropriate to use the risk-free rate of return to discount this amount to present value at $t = 0$. For the current example, we assume that the risk-free rate of return is 5%. All of the information pertaining to the investment-timing option analysis is presented in Panel B of Exhibit 12.7.

We see from Panel B that at $t = 1$, XYZ Company would invest in the project *only if* the revealed level of demand was either high or medium. If the company invests (at $t = 1$) in the project, then it will spend $100 million and will expect to receive either $70 million or $50 million in cash inflows for each of three years. If consumer demand turns out to be low, then no investment is made at $t = 1$. Thus, given the probabilities for the three specified levels of demand, we can proceed to calculate the weighted present value of each scenario (see cells J20:J22 in Exhibit 12.7) and finally the weighted-average NPV of the project. As shown in cell J23, this value is $12.951 million, an amount considerably higher than indicated in the conventional NPV analysis presented in Panel A of Exhibit 12.7. In short, the project's expected NPV is considerably higher after considering the existence of the investment-timing option. As indicated earlier in the chapter, the decision maker normally would, as part of the evaluation, conduct a sensitivity analysis on the inputs to the decision model. This issue is pursued in Problem 12-53.

Finally, we note that the same approach as discussed earlier, and demonstrated in Exhibit 12.7, can be used to deal with other types of real options, for example, the option to abandon a project. Problem 12-54 provides an example of an abandonment option embedded in a proposed investment. The approach, however, is basically the same as that illustrated earlier. A decision tree can be used to represent various scenarios or states of nature (e.g., levels of consumer demand). The NPV of the proposed project can first be determined using the conventional approach and then again after incorporating the effect of the real option. The decision, from a purely financial standpoint, is a function of the NPVs of the decision alternatives. Just remember that these NPVs, for comparability purposes, are calculated at time 0.

Determinants of the Value of Real Options

As members of the decision-making team that evaluates capital budgeting proposals, accountants should have some knowledge of the drivers or determinants of value for real options. In effect, the same factors that affect the value of financial options also affect the inherent value of real options. In this regard, we offer the following three comments:

1. *All other things being equal,* the value of a real option is higher if the value of the underlying asset is high relative to the exercise price of the option (for XYZ, an estimate of the value of the asset is $99.891 million [because, as shown in Exhibit 12.7, the estimated NPV of the project, if made at time 0, is negative $0.109 million], while the exercise price of the project at time 0 is $100 million).
2. The farther away the expiration date is, the higher the value of an option is. (The one-year expiration period in the case of XYZ is probably considered long.)
3. Perhaps most important, the value of an option increases as the risk of the project increases. (In the case of XYZ, the value of the delay option increases as the volatility of project returns increases. In essence, when project returns are considered risky, there is greater value in delaying the decision until consumer demand levels are revealed, or at least better revealed. The delay option available to XYZ therefore provides value to the company in terms of dealing with project risk.)

Other Capital Budgeting Decision Models

non-DCF models
Capital budgeting decision models that are not based on an analysis of the present value of future cash flows.

payback period
The length of time (in years, months, etc.) required for the cumulative after-tax cash inflows from an investment to recover the initial investment outlay.

The preceding sections argue for the theoretical superiority of discounted cash flow (DCF) models for the analysis of capital investments. Survey evidence, in fact, indicates that a majority of firms use DCF models for this purpose. However, we also observe the use of complementary decision tools for capital investment analysis, which we refer to here as **non-DCF models**. Given the complexity of capital budgeting decisions in practice, it is not surprising that firms use a variety of decision models and analytical tools. As such, the management accountant must be aware of these alternative models, focusing on how they work, what they tell us, and what their limitations are. In this section we discuss the payback period model (as well as a variant of this model, called the discounted payback period model) and the accounting (book) rate of return of model.

Payback Period

The **payback period** of an investment is the length of time required for the cumulative after-tax cash inflows from an investment to recover the initial investment outlay. At that point, the investor has recovered the amount of money invested in the project.

Determining the Payback Period with Uniform Annual Cash Inflows

For an investment that provides uniform future after-tax cash inflows, the payback period (in years) can be determined as follows:

Payback period = Total initial capital investment ÷ Annual after-tax cash inflows

For example, assume an initial capital investment outlay (time 0) of $1,110,000. This project is projected to have a four-year life. Each year, the investment is expected to provide an after-tax cash inflow of $387,000. Based on this information, the project has a payback period of 2.87 years (i.e., $1,110,000 ÷ $387,000).

Determining the Payback Period with Uneven Cash Inflows

Refer back to Exhibit 12.2, which contains cash flow information regarding the machine purchase decision facing the Mendoza Company. With uneven cash inflows, as is the case here, the payback period is defined as the number of years it takes for the *cumulative* after-tax cash inflows to equal the initial investment outlay ($680,000). The necessary analysis is presented in Exhibit 12.8.

The amount needed in year 4 to reach the payback period is $53,000; under the assumption that the after-tax cash inflows in year 4 occur evenly throughout the year, the payback period is 3 + ($53,000 ÷ $174,000) years = 3.30 years. If we assume, as is the case when we calculate a project's NPV or IRR, that the cash inflows occur at year-end, then the payback period for this project would be four years.

Evaluation of the Payback Period Model

Advantages   The principal advantage of the payback period model is that once cash flow data have been collected, the payback period is easy to compute and comprehend. Business people, particularly owners of small businesses, seem to have an intuitive understanding of payback periods.

EXHIBIT 12.8
Payback Period Calculation for the Mendoza Company Example

(1)	(2)	(3)
Year	After-Tax Cash Flows (Exhibit 12.2)	Cumulative After-Tax Net Cash Flows
0	$(680,000)	$(680,000)
1	194,000	(486,000)
2	245,000	(241,000)
3	188,000	(53,000)
4	174,000*	121,000

*For purposes of determining the payback period, we have (temporarily) ignored the cash inflows expected to occur at the end of year 4. The cash inflows reflected in Exhibit 12.8 are the operating cash inflows, which in the present analysis are assumed to occur evenly throughout the year.

We note, too, that the payback period addresses the issue of liquidity. Projects with shorter payback periods provide increased flexibility in the sense that they provide funds for other investment opportunities. The value of such flexibility is thought to be particularly important for evaluating large-scale investments and investments in industries characterized by high growth and/or change.

The length of the payback period can serve as a rough measure of the risk associated with a proposed investment. The longer the payback period, the more risky the project is. The underlying logic is that the farther out into the future the payback period is, the more uncertainty about future cash flows there is. For example, the longer it takes to recover the original investment, the more likely it is that the underlying product or service will become obsolete or attract competition, making it more difficult to earn cash flows as projected. Thus, all other things equal, managers prefer projects with shorter payback periods.

Limitations   The use of payback period information for investment decision making is subject to four primary limitations:

1. *The model fails to consider returns over the entire life of the investment.* That is, the payback model considers cash inflows from the initiation of the project until its payback period but ignores cash flows after the payback period. Notice that in the Mendoza example, the calculation ignores the significant cash inflows scheduled to occur at the end of year 4.
2. *If unadjusted, the payback period ignores the time value of money.* It considers only the length of time required to recover the investment, regardless of differences in the timing or pattern of cash flows. For example, as long as the payback period for each of two projects is the same, the model considers them equally desirable. This is the case even if one project generates most of its cash inflows in the early years of its payback period while the other project generates most of its cash inflows in the latter years of its payback period.
3. *The decision criterion for accepting/rejecting a project is not well defined; that is, it is subjective.* This contrasts with the two DCF decision models we discussed earlier and their more objective decision rules. For the NPV model, the rule is: accept a project if its NPV is greater than 0; for the IRR model, the rule is: accept a project if its IRR is greater than the WACC (or another specified hurdle rate).
4. *Use of the model may encourage excessive investment in short-term projects, at the expense of investments critical to long-term success.* Some investments needed to secure competitive advantage—such as an investment in computer-integrated manufacturing (CIM)—can take many years to recover the original investment. A company that fails to make such strategic investments may not be competitive in the long run.

Present Value (or Discounted) Payback Period

To avoid the second criticism listed in the prior section, some companies use the present value of future cash inflows to determine the investment's payback period. Because discounted cash flows are used, the resulting payback period is referred to as the **present value (or discounted) payback period.** As with the NPV model, the present value of future after-tax cash inflows from an investment is estimated using the firm's WACC (or another specified hurdle rate).

As shown in Exhibit 12.9, the present value payback period for the machine investment by the Mendoza Company, if we consider only recurring after-tax cash inflows, is greater than the life of the project (four years). If we consider the additional after-tax cash inflow

present value (or discounted) payback period
The length of time required for the cumulative *present value* of after-tax cash inflows to recover the initial investment outlay.

EXHIBIT 12.9
Present Value Payback Period for the Mendoza Company Investment Proposal

Year	After-Tax Cash Flow	Discount Factor @ 10%	PV of After-Tax Cash Flow	Cumulative PV of After-Tax Cash Flows
0	$(680,000)	1.000	$(680,000)	$(680,000)
1	194,000	0.909	176,346	(503,654)
2	245,000	0.826	202,370	(301,284)
3	188,000	0.751	141,188	(160,096)
4	174,000	0.683	118,842	(41,254)

Note: Similar to Exhibit 12.8, we consider in Exhibit 12.9 only the operating after-tax cash inflows in each year.

of $113,000 (see Exhibit 12.2), then the present value payback period on this proposed investment is approximately four years, which is the life of the project. As noted earlier, the unadjusted (i.e., nondiscounted) payback period is approximately 3.30 years.

Because it considers the time value of money, the present value payback model is considered superior to the unadjusted payback period model. Because it relies on the use of discounted cash inflows, this version of the payback model has an important implication: *If the discounted payback period is less than the life of the project, then the project must have a positive NPV.* This result holds because the cash inflows that accrue up to the discounted payback period are, by definition, just sufficient (in a present-value sense) to cover the initial investment outlay; any cash inflows that come after the payback point will ensure a positive NPV for the project.

However, the discounted payback model suffers the same weaknesses of the unadjusted model in other respects: (1) use of the model for capital budgeting decisions can motivate excessive investment in short-term projects, (2) the model ignores investment returns beyond the (discounted) payback period, and (3) the decision criterion under this model is not set objectively—that is, the cut-off period for determining project acceptance is set subjectively (i.e., by management policy). The second limitation is particularly important because it may lead managers to incorrectly reject some positive NPV investment opportunities.

Finally, one technical note is in order. The Mendoza example is simplified in the sense that it reflects a single cash outflow (time period 0) followed by a series of future cash inflows. It is possible, however, that a project requires a series of cash outflows, beyond time period 0. To calculate the payback period in this case, you should first sum these cash outflows (or discounted cash flows) against which you would compare cumulative cash inflows (either unadjusted or discounted) to estimate the payback (or discounted payback) period for a proposed investment.

Accounting (Book) Rate of Return

accounting (book) rate of return (ARR)
A rate of return on a project measured as the ratio of some measure of accounting profit associated with the project to some measure of investment in the project.

The **accounting (book) rate of return (ARR)** on a project is equal to the ratio of some measure of accounting profit to some measure of investment in the project. One specification of the ARR is:

$$\text{ARR} = \text{Average annual net operating income} \div \text{Average investment}$$

Be aware, however, that there are differences in practice regarding how both the numerator and the denominator for the ARR are defined. That is, there is more than a single way to calculate the ARR of an investment.

One way to define the denominator of the ARR is to take a simple average of the book value of the net investment at the beginning of the project's life and the sum of the after-tax disposal value of the asset (if any) at the end of the project's life and the amount of net working capital recovered at the end of the project's life. A second, more rigorous approach is to compute the average book value of the net investment in each year, and take the average of those averages as the denominator of the ARR equation.

As an example of the first approach, refer back to Exhibit 12.2 for financial information regarding the machine purchase decision for the Mendoza Company. In this case, the average book value of the proposed investment can be calculated as follows:

Net initial investment = $680,000

End-of-project amounts recovered (Exhibit 12.2) = $203,000 (i.e., $3,000 + $200,000)

Average investment over life of project = ($680,000 + $203,000) ÷ 2 = $441,500

The proposed investment for the Mendoza Company is expected to earn an average annual after-tax operating income of $58,000, as follows (see Exhibit 12.2):

Year	After-Tax Operating Income
1	$ 34,000
2	31,990
3	117,350
4	48,660 ($138,660 − $90,000)
Average	$ 58,000

Thus, when the denominator of the calculation is defined as the *average investment* (as calculated above), the proposed project's ARR is 13.14% ($58,000 ÷ $441,500). This result means that, on average, the proposed project returns approximately 13 cents of after-tax operating profit per year for each dollar associated with the average investment in the project.

Some companies define the denominator of the ARR as the net original investment rather than the average. If the ARR is calculated based on this measure ($680,000), the calculated ARR for the proposed project would be 8.53%.

Evaluation of the Accounting (Book) Rate of Return Model

Advantages To a large extent, the ARR model uses the same kind of data routinely generated for financial reporting purposes. For this reason, the ratio is called the *accounting rate of return*. Some would argue that relative to DCF-based outputs, ARR numbers are easier for managers to understand. Further, as indicated in Chapter 19, accounting rate of return measures are used by many companies to evaluate the financial performance of operating divisions and managers. Thus, the use of ARR for capital budgeting purposes would be consistent with the way subsequent financial performance is typically measured and reported. This can be helpful when a company needs to be concerned about how performance appears to external stakeholders (for example, if there are plans to access the capital markets in the near future).

The ARR has an additional advantage over the payback period model in that it looks at financial returns (e.g., changes in after-tax operating income) over the entire life of a project. That is, the ARR gives managers an idea of how future accounting income numbers will be affected if the project is accepted.

Limitations As with the payback period model, the ARR decision model ignores the time value of money. Another limitation pertains to the use of accounting numbers in the numerator and denominator. While such numbers are useful for financial reporting purposes, financial theory tells us that cash flow information is preferable for making capital budgeting decisions. In essence, the use of DCF decision models aligns internal decision making with the process that, in theory, investors use in valuing stocks in the financial marketplace.

As indicated earlier, there are multiple ways to define both the numerator and the denominator in the ARR calculation. For example, one possibility is to define the denominator simply as the net cost of the asset acquired ($480,000 in the case of the Mendoza Company). While simplifying the calculation (i.e., average investment would now be defined as ($480,000 + $0) ÷ 2 = $240,000), this approach ignores the fact that the proposed project required a commitment of net working capital during the life of the project. The treatment of after-tax proceeds from the sale of the asset at the end of the project and, for asset replacement decisions, the after-tax proceeds from the sale of an existing asset provides additional areas of differences in practice. In short, there is no universally accepted practice as to how the components of ARR are measured. At a minimum, this leads to comparability problems across companies and potentially within divisions of the same company.

Finally, as with the case of the payback model, there is no objectively defined decision criterion for making project acceptance decisions. What is an acceptable ARR? Any response is determined subjectively, usually using rules of thumb that may or may not be ideal.

Behavioral Issues in Capital Budgeting

LO 12-7

Identify behavioral issues associated with the capital budgeting process.

To this point, we have dealt mainly with technical issues associated with the capital budgeting process. It is worth noting that the success of this process is also affected by a number of behavioral considerations, as discussed below.

Common Behavioral Problems: Cost Escalation, Incrementalism, and Uncertainty Intolerance

Escalating commitment is common in the capital budgeting process; in an attempt to recoup past losses, a decision maker may consider past costs or losses as relevant in making capital budgeting decisions. For example, elimination or reduction of losses from past investments may, erroneously, be included as savings associated with a proposed investment. As indicated in Chapter 11, such amounts do not meet the test of information relevancy and, as such, should not be included in formal decision models, such as those used for analyzing capital investment projects. Research suggests that escalating commitments are more likely to occur when current managers are the ones responsible for the negative results of past actions.[25]

Another common behavioral problem, incrementalism, refers to situations in which needed capital investments may not be pursued because of the amount of time and work required to secure their approval. Projects that cost less than those that must be approved as a capital investment are undertaken instead. As a result, managers may choose to invest in multiple small additions that require no approval from above, rather than investing in a major capital project such as computer-integrated manufacturing (CIM) or a flexible manufacturing system (FMS) that would vastly improve the firm's competitive position. Failure to make necessary capital investments can reduce the firm's competitiveness, erode its market share, and jeopardize its long-term profitability and survival.

Intolerance of uncertainty may lead managers to require short payback periods for capital investments. Once a project pays for itself, the amount of risk is substantially reduced. This makes projects with short payback periods the preferred choice for some decision makers. However, many capital investments of strategic importance do not have short payback periods. These projects may require a lengthy time to install, test, adjust, train personnel, and gain market acceptance; examples include investments in new manufacturing technologies, new product development, and expansion into new territories. Requiring short payback periods makes the acceptance of such projects unlikely, even if they would be beneficial in the long term.

Goal Congruence Issues

Perhaps the greatest behavioral challenge in capital budgeting is the need to align DCF decision models (such as NPV) with models used to evaluate subsequent financial performance. Typically, accrual-based measures of profitability, such as return on investment (ROI—see Chapter 19), are used to evaluate the financial performance of managers and organizational subunits. As the following example shows, managers may not be motivated to make decisions that are in the best interest of the organization in situations where NPV is used for decision making, but accrual accounting numbers are used for performance evaluation purposes.

Assume an investment of $12,000 today that is expected to generate, for each of three years, an increase in cash contribution margin (CM) of $5,000. Further, assume no income taxes, a three-year depreciation period for the investment, zero salvage value, and the use of straight-line depreciation. Finally, assume that the financial performance of the manager and subunit is evaluated each year using return on investment (ROI), defined as operating income divided by beginning-of-year (BOY) book value of the asset. Given these assumptions, the following rates of return would be anticipated:

Item	Year 1	Year 2	Year 3
Cash CM	$ 5,000	$ 5,000	$ 5,000
Less: Depreciation	4,000	4,000	4,000
Operating income	$ 1,000	$ 1,000	$ 1,000
NBV of asset (BOY)	$12,000	$ 8,000	$ 4,000
ROI	8.33%	12.50%	25.00%

Assuming a discount rate of 11.0%, this project has a projected NPV of $218.57 (details omitted) and therefore should be accepted.

The issue, however, is whether a rational decision maker/manager would be motivated to accept the investment given the projected ROIs over the coming three years. If compensation is

[25] G. Whyte, "Escalating Commitment to a Course of Action: A Reinterpretation," *Academy of Management Review,* 1986, pp. 311–321.

tied to reported ROI, there may be a disincentive to invest, in spite of the fact that accepting the project would be consistent with adding shareholder value. This disincentive would be stronger:

- If the individual were likely to be transferred out of the division (job advancement, retirement, etc.).
- If the project life is long (i.e., the cash flow benefits are not realized until later in the project's life).
- If the discount rate is high.
- If the disposal of any existing assets would result in a reported loss (which would, in turn, reduce reported ROI in year 1).
- If accelerated depreciation methods are used for accounting purposes.

Addressing the Goal Congruence Problem

The preceding example illustrates a pervasive problem in control system design: Conflicts can arise when DCF-based models are used for decision-making purposes and accrual-based accounting income numbers are used subsequently for evaluating the financial performance of managers and organizational subunits. Top management cannot expect goal congruence under these conditions, which are, unfortunately, fairly common in practice.

What can organizations do, then, to better align the goals of decision makers with the goals of the overall organization? To a large extent, this issue is one of the unsolved problems in control system design. An extended discussion of these issues is presented in Chapter 19. Within the context of capital budgeting, however, three possible solutions are offered.

Economic Value Added (EVA®)

economic value added (EVA®)
A measure of financial performance designed to approximate an entity's *economic profit;* calculated most often as net operating profit after taxes (adjusted for accounting "distortions") less an imputed charge based on the level of invested capital.

As will be discussed more fully in Chapter 19, **economic value added (EVA®)** is a financial performance indicator that includes a charge for use of invested capital. That is, *economic profitability* is not indicated until the organization generates sufficient cash flow to cover *all* expenses, including an imputed charge for capital invested in the business. As such, both NPV and EVA assume that shareholder value is created only when projects recover their capital costs. Thus, the use of EVA for evaluation of financial performance is one way to avoid the behavioral conflict noted earlier.

Separating Incentive Compensation from Budgeted Performance

In Chapter 10, we discussed some of the negative incentive effects of traditional budgeting systems, including those where an annual fixed performance contract is used to determine compensation.[26] Budgeted performance, against which actual performance (income earned, ROI, etc.) is compared, is reflected in the master budgeting process and the set of pro forma financial statements produced as a result of that process. Among other things, linking managerial rewards to a comparison between budgeted and actual performance penalizes managers for factors that emerge during the year that are beyond their control (general price level changes, changes in the price of energy, etc.). It simultaneously rewards such managers for market (or industry-wide) positive results. Further, linking compensation to budgeted performance encourages dysfunctional, perhaps even unethical, behaviors as managers game the performance indicator in order to achieve budget targets.

As we discussed in Chapter 10, some feel that relative performance indicators are superior to the fixed performance model described earlier. In such cases, actual financial performance for a subunit or manager is compared to the contemporaneous performance of a comparable manager or subunit for the purpose of determining incentive rewards and/or compensation. This approach can provide strong incentives while protecting managers from common uncertainty and uncontrollability, resulting in greater goal congruence.

Post Audit

Another way to achieve goal congruence in the capital budgeting process is to forgo the use of accrual-based accounting income numbers in performance evaluation altogether. Rather,

---

[26] See Michael C. Jensen, "Corporate Budgeting Is Broken—Let's Fix It," *Harvard Business Review,* November 2001, pp. 94–101.

top management might focus on a post-decision comparison between forecasted and realized amounts for a given investment project. As indicated earlier in this chapter, such a comparison is referred to as a *post audit.* The principal benefit of post audits is the collection, for performance evaluation purposes, of the same cash inflow and outflow information used for investment decision-making purposes (e.g., NPV). In turn, this should eliminate (or at least reduce) disincentives associated with the use of different models for decision making and assessment of subsequent financial performance.

Summary

Capital budgeting decisions represent long-term commitments of substantial amounts of resources. As indicated in Chapter 10, the capital budget is a key component of an organization's overall planning system. Accountants can add value to the capital budgeting process of an organization by linking the capital budget with the master budget, by connecting capital budgeting decisions with organizational strategy, by gathering relevant financial and nonfinancial information, and by designing post-audit mechanisms to monitor the capital budgeting process. The determination of what financial information is relevant follows the same procedure outlined in Chapter 11: To be relevant for decision making, a given cost or revenue item must be incremental to the decision—that is, only future costs and revenues that *differ* between (or among) decision alternatives are relevant for capital expenditure analysis.

In general, managers can optimize an organization's capital budget by using the net present value (NPV) decision model, which compares the present value of after-tax cash inflows to the present value of after-tax cash outflows. Typically, the discount rate used in DCF models is the organization's weighted-average cost of capital (WACC). Another DCF model is the internal rate of return (IRR), which computes the discount rate at which the NPV of a project would equal zero. Non-DCF models include the payback period and the accounting rate of return (ARR). Each model has advantages and disadvantages.

Cash outflows from investments can occur at three points: (1) *project initiation*—to acquire the investment and begin operations, to provide needed net working capital for the project, and to dispose of any replaced or discarded assets; (2) *project operation*—to cover operating expenditures, any additional investments, and additional net working capital; and (3) *project disposal*—to dispose of the investment, to restore facilities, and to provide training or relocation benefits for personnel whose positions have been terminated. An investment generates net cash inflows during its existence through increases in revenues or decreases in expenses, through recovery of its investment in net working capital, and from the disposal of assets. For a profit-seeking organization, all such cash flows should be stated on an after-tax basis.

Exhibit 12.10 summarizes the definitions, computation procedures, advantages, and weaknesses of the various capital budgeting decision models covered in the chapter. Some advanced considerations in using DCF models for the analysis of capital investments are presented in the appendices to this chapter.

The determination of a project's NPV requires the use of forecasts and assumptions. Sensitivity analysis can be used to determine how sensitive the capital budgeting decision is with respect to these assumptions. The chapter presents three examples of sensitivity analysis: what-if analysis, scenario analysis, and Monte Carlo simulation analysis. An alternative approach to dealing with risk and uncertainty in capital budgeting is to incorporate the existence of real options that may exist in a project into the analysis.

Finally, managers need to understand that the capital budgeting process is affected by a number of important behavioral considerations. Foremost among these considerations is the conflict that arises from using DCF models for investment decision making but accrual accounting numbers (such as ROI) for evaluation of financial performance, and also from incentive conflicts associated with the use of fixed performance contracts. The use of EVA® for performance appraisal, the use of relative performance indicators for compensation and reward, and the use of post audits may help reduce this conflict and achieve greater goal congruence between decision makers and the organization as a whole.

EXHIBIT 12.10   Capital Investment Decision Models

Model	Definition	Computation Procedure	Advantages	Disadvantages
Payback period	Number of years to recover the initial investment	*Uniform cash flow:* Investment *divided by* net cash flow *Uneven cash flow:* Number of years for the cumulative cash inflow to equal the initial investment	1. Simple to use and understand 2. Focuses on liquidity 3. Rough measure of risk	1. Ignores timing and time value of money 2. Ignores cash flows beyond payback period 3. Decision rules are subjective
Accounting (book) rate of return (ARR)	Ratio of some measure of profit to some measure of investment	Average net income *divided by* investment book value	1. Data are readily available 2. Consistent with other financial measures 3. Readily interpretable by managers	1. Ignores timing and time value of money 2. Uses accounting numbers, not after-tax cash flows
Net present value (NPV)	Difference between present value (PV) of cash inflows and PV of cash outflows	PV of after-tax cash inflows − PV of after-tax cash outflows	1. Considers the time value of money 2. Focuses on after-tax cash flows 3. Consistent with goal of maximizing shareholder value	1. Can possibly lead to suboptimal capital budgeting under condition of capital rationing
Internal rate of return (IRR)	Discount rate that makes the PV of cash inflows equal to the PV of cash outflows	For uniform cash inflows—solving for *i* in the following equation: PV annuity factor for *i* × Annual after-tax cash inflow = Initial investment	1. Considers time value of money 2. Focuses on after-tax cash flows 3. Ratios are intuitively appealing to managers	1. Inherent assumption regarding reinvestment rate could be unrealistic 2. Complex to compute if done manually 3. May not lead to optimum capital budget
Modified internal rate of return (MIRR)	Discount rate that makes the PV of cash inflows equal to the PV of cash outflows, under the assumption that interim cash inflows are reinvested at a specified rate	Rate at which PV costs = PV terminal value, where the left-hand term is the PV of outlays, discounted at the WACC, and the numerator of the right-hand term is the compounded future value of the interim cash inflows, reinvested at the WACC, and the denominator is $(1 + MIRR)^n$, where n = number of periods	1. Considers the time value of money 2. Focuses on after-tax cash flows 3. Ratios are intuitively appealing to managers 4. Avoids overly optimistic rates of return associated with the use of IRR	1. Complex to compute if done manually 2. May not lead to optimum capital budget 3. Discrepancy as to whether there is a reinvestment rate assumption inherent in the IRR calculation
Profitability index (PI) (see Appendix B)	Ratio of PV of cash inflows (or NPV) to initial investment	PV of after-tax cash inflows (or NPV) *divided by* initial investment	1. Considers time value of money 2. Focuses on after-tax cash flows 3. Useful under conditions of capital rationing	1. When capital budget is not limited, use could lead to suboptimal capital budget

Appendix A

LO 12-8

Understand and use alternative presentation formats for the asset replacement decision.

Structuring an Asset Replacement Decision Problem— Spreadsheet Templates

Most of the chapter focused on straightforward capital investment decisions. In this appendix, we consider a more complicated decision: whether to keep or replace an existing asset (such as a piece of machinery). In this case, as we stressed in Chapter 11, relevant cost and revenue data consist of future amounts that differ between the decision alternatives. Thus, to properly structure an asset replacement problem, we must identify all costs and revenues that are differential to the decision. These items are then subjected to a discounted cash flow analysis using either the NPV method or the IRR method, as discussed earlier.

At the time of the initial investment (time period 0), we must calculate the after-tax proceeds (if any) from the sale of the existing asset. Exhibit 12.5 provides guidelines to accomplish this. During the life of the investment, we need to calculate *incremental* (or *differential*) after-tax operating cash flows associated with the new asset versus the existing asset. We also need to include the differential tax benefit each year associated with depreciation expenses calculated on the basis of the old versus new asset. Finally, at the termination of the life of the project, we need to calculate two amounts: (1) differential after-tax cash proceeds from the sale/disposal of the old versus the new asset and (2) differential recovery of net working capital associated with the old versus the new asset. In short, we embrace the same perspective as used in Chapter 11: We focus on differential revenues and differential costs. In Chapter 12, we employ the same guideline; however, for this analysis, the relevant costs and revenues are subjected to a discounting process to express all amounts on a present-value basis.

To illustrate these points, let's recast the Mendoza example (Exhibit 12.2) to reflect a machine replacement decision. Assume the company is currently using a machine that it purchased six years ago for $320,000. The accumulated depreciation on this machine at the replacement date (time period 0) is $192,000. (For tax purposes, assume that the machine is being depreciated using the straight-line method over 10 years, with zero salvage value assumed.) A used equipment broker, who charges a commission of 10% of the selling price, has secured a buyer for the old machine. The buyer is willing to pay $80,000 for the machine; however, Mendoza would have to pay all asset removal costs, estimated to be $2,000 (pretax).

The net cash proceeds from the sale (i.e., gross selling price minus sales-related costs, such as sales commissions) would be $70,000 (i.e., $80,000 − $8,000 − $2,000). Given a net book value (NBV) of $128,000 (i.e., $320,000 − $192,000), Mendoza would realize a tax-deductible loss of $58,000 on the sale of the old machine. At a combined tax rate of 40%, this loss would result in a tax savings of $23,200. As indicated in Exhibit 12.5, the net cash effect of this entire transaction would be $93,200 (net cash proceeds of $70,000, plus tax savings due to the deductibility of the loss on the sale, $23,200).

Further, assume that if the current machine is not sold, it is expected to generate cash revenues of $400,000 and cash operating expenses of $320,000 per year in each of the next four years. At the time the existing machine was put into service (six years ago), Mendoza committed additional working capital of $50,000, which is expected to be fully recovered four years from now, at the end of the asset's life. At that point, the net-of-sales-commission estimated sales value of the existing machine is expected to be $1,500 (pretax).

The net cost of the new machine as well as the working capital commitment is the same as the amounts reflected in Exhibit 12.2. However, we now assume that if the new machine is purchased, total cash revenues are expected to be $1,400,000 per year, while operating cash expenses are expected to be $1,000,000 per year. (The amounts in the original example were $1,000,000 and $783,333, respectively.) To simplify the analysis, we also now assume that Mendoza would choose to depreciate the new machine using the straight-line (SL) method over four years without the midyear convention. Thus, depreciation expense each year would be $120,000 ($480,000 ÷ 4), resulting in an annual depreciation tax shield of $48,000 ($120,000 × 0.40). All other information regarding the new machine is as assumed earlier.

Relevant information for evaluating this machine replacement decision for Mendoza is presented in Exhibit 12A.1. These data are used in the three templates included in this appendix.[27] Panel A (shown in Exhibit 12A.2) contains the first of two alternative templates that can be used in conjunction with what we call the *differential approach* to a decision analysis. The 10% discount factors shown in cells L33:L36 were calculated using the following formula: factor $= 1/(1 + 0.10)^i$, where i represents year (1, 2, 3, 4). (Note: All numbers in cells I34 through I40 were determined using actual discount factors from cells L33 through L37, not the rounded values shown in column H.) Panel B (shown in Exhibit 12A.3) contains an alternative format for the differential approach to structuring a decision analysis. Note that the PV factors in line 67 are copied from cells L33:L36. Note also that the estimated NPV of the project (cell F71) is exactly the same as the amount contained in Panel A (cell I45). Both presentation formats indicate an NPV of $148,536 in favor of replacing the existing machine. An advantage of the format reflected in Panel B is that it facilitates the calculation of the investment's IRR, in this case, 20.5%.

Finally, Panel C (Exhibit 12A.4) provides an alternative presentation format, one that reveals the opportunity costs associated with purchasing the new machine separately. This format is, in fact, consistent with the decision models discussed in Chapter 11. Once again, we find (cell I102) that the NPV of the decision to replace the existing machine is $148,536.

EXHIBIT 12A.1

Spreadsheet Data for Mendoza Company Asset Replacement Decision

Source: Microsoft Excel

	A	B	C	D	E	F	G	H
1	**Input Data**							
2	Discount rate (WACC) =				10.00%			
3	Combined income tax rate =				40.00%			
4	**New Machine:**							
5	Net cost of new equipment, year 0 =				$480,000	($465,000 + $5,000 + $10,000)		
6	Useful life of new asset (in years) =				4			
7	Estimated salvage value, Yr. 4 =				-			
8	One-time employee training costs, Yr. 1 =				50,000			
9	Working capital required, Yr. 1 =				200,000			
10	Recovery of working capital, Yr. 4 =				200,000			
11	After-tax proceeds, sale of machine (Yr. 4) =				3,000	($100,000 – $95,000 – $2,000)		
12	After-tax employee relocation costs (Yr. 4) =				90,000	($150,000 × (1 - 0.40))		
13	Cash revenues, per year =				1,400,000			
14	Cash operating costs, per year =				1,000,000			
15	Recurring after-tax operating cash flows, years 1–4:				240,000	(($1,400,000 – $1,000,000) × (1 – 0.40))		
16	Annual depreciation charges (SL basis)				120,000	($480,000 – $0) ÷ 4 years		
17	Annual depreciation tax shield (SL basis)				48,000	($120,000 × 0.40)		
18	**Existing Machine:**							
19	After-tax proceeds, sale of old machine (Yr. 0) =				93,200	($70,000 + $23,300)		
20	Existing NBV of machine =				128,000	($320,000 - $192,000)		
21	Return of working capital, Year 4				50,000			
22	Net (pretax) proceeds, sale of old machine (Yr. 4)				1,500	(given/assumed)		
23	After-tax proceeds, sale of old machine (Yr. 4) =				900	($1,500 × (1 - 0.40))		
24	Cash revenues, per year =				400,000	(given)		
25	Cash operating costs, per year =				320,000	(given)		
26	Recurring after-tax operating cash flows, years 1–4				48,000	($400,000 - $320,000) × (1 – 0.40)		
27	Annual depreciation charge (SL basis) =				32,000	($128,000 ÷ 4 years)		
28	Annual depreciation tax shield (SL basis) =				12,800	($32,000 × 0.40)		

Note: For the asset-replacement example, the assumption regarding expected cash revenues per year ($1,400,000—see cell E13) and cash operating costs per year ($1,000,000—see cell E14) were changed from the amounts assumed for the Mendoza asset-purchase decision covered in the body of the chapter (and reflected in Exhibit 12.2).

[27] For guidance in developing a more general Excel template for asset-replacement decisions, see R. J. Balik, "Excel Best Practices," *Managerial Finance* 35, no. 5 (2009), pp. 410–426. For a general discussion of structuring the equipment-replacement capital budgeting decision, see Su-Jane Chen and Timothy R. Mayes, "A Note on Capital Budgeting: Treating a Replacement Project as Two Mutually Exclusive Projects," *Journal of Financial Education* 38 (Spring/Summer 2012), pp. 46–55.

EXHIBIT 12A.2
Differential Approach 1 (Panel A)

Source: Microsoft Excel

		Amount	Year(s)	PV Factor [@ WACC]	PV of Cash Flows			
30	**Panel A: DCF Analysis--Differential Approach #1**							
31		Amount	Year(s)	PV Factor [@ WACC]	PV of Cash Flows			
32	**Differential After-tax Cash Inflows:**						**Discount Factors, 10%**	
33	PV of differential after-tax operating cash flows:						Year 1 =	0.9090909
34	Recurring operating cash flows after taxes	$192,000	1-4	3.1698654	$608,614		Year 2 =	0.8264463
35	One-time employee training costs, after taxes	$30,000	1	0.9090909	($27,273)		Year 3 =	0.7513148
36	Differential depreciation tax shield =	$35,200	1-4	3.1698654	$111,579		Year 4 =	0.6830135
37	PV of differential terminal values:						Annuity =	3.1698654
38	Differential working capital recovered =	$150,000	4	0.6830135	$102,452			
39	Differential after-tax proceeds, sale of machines =	$2,100	4	0.6830135	$1,434			
40	After-tax employee relocation expenses =	$90,000	4	0.6830135	($61,471)			
41	**Net Investment:**							
42	Net cost of new equipment, Yr. 0 =	($480,000)	0	1.0000000	($480,000)			
43	After-tax salvage value, old machine (Yr. 0) =	93,200	0	1.0000000	$93,200			
44	Increase in working capital, Yr. 0 =	($200,000)	0	1.0000000	($200,000)			
45		($586,800)		NPV =	$148,536			

EXHIBIT 12A.3
Differential Approach 2 (Panel B)

Source: Microsoft Excel

		0	1	2	3	4
47	**Panel B: DCF Analysis--Differential Approach #2**					
48				Year		
49		0	1	2	3	4
50	**I. Net Cash Flow at Time Investment Is Made**					
51	Net cost of new machine, Yr. 0	$480,000				
52	After-tax salvage value of existing machine, Yr. 0	$93,200				
53	Increase in net working capital required, Yr. 0	$200,000				
54	Total	$586,800				
55	**II. Differential After-tax Operating Cash Flows Over Life of the Asset:**					
56	One-time employee-training costs, after tax		$30,000			
57	Incremental net operating cash flows, after tax		$192,000	$192,000	$192,000	$192,000
58	Incremental depreciation tax shield		$35,200	$35,200	$35,200	$35,200
59	Totals		$197,200	$227,200	$227,200	$227,200
60	**III. Differential Terminal After-tax Cash Flows:**					
61	Differential working capital released ($200,000 – $50,000)					$150,000
62	Differential after-tax salvage value of assets ($3,000 – $900)					$2,100
63	Differential employee relocation costs, after tax ($150,000 x 0.60)					$90,000
64	Total					$62,100
65	**IV. Differential Net Cash Flow (After-tax) per Year**	($586,800)	$197,200	$227,200	$227,200	$289,300
66	**V. NPV Determination:**					
67	PV Factors	1.0000000	0.9090909	0.8264463	0.7513148	0.6830135
68						
69	PV of After-tax Cash Flows =	$735,336				
70	Net Investment Outlay =	($586,800)				
71	NPV =	$148,536				
72	**VI. IRR Estimation:**					
73	IRR =	20.5%				

EXHIBIT 12A.4
Opportunity Cost Approach (Panel C)

Source: Microsoft Excel

				Existing Machine	New Machine			
75	**Panel C: Analysis of Equipment-Replacement Decision--Opportunity Cost Approach**							
76				Existing Machine	New Machine			
77	Annual cash revenues (pretax)			$400,000	$1,400,000			
78	Less: Annual cash operating costs, pretax			$320,000	$1,000,000			
79	Less: Depreciation expense, SL basis			$32,000	$120,000			
80	Annual pretax cash operating income			$48,000	$280,000			
81	Less: Income taxes			$19,200	$112,000			
82	After-tax income			$28,800	$168,000			
83	Plus: Depreciation expense			$32,000	$120,000			
84	After-tax cash operating income per year			$60,800	$288,000			
86	**Decision Alternatives**			Amount	Year(s)	PV Factor [@ WACC]	PV of Cash Flows	
87	**Purchase New Machine:**							
88	Net incremental investment, after-tax			$480,000	0	1.0000000	($480,000)	
89	Required investment in working capital, Yr. 0			$200,000	0	1.0000000	($200,000)	
90	Net-of-tax salvage value, sale of old machine (Yr. 0) a			$93,200	0	1.0000000	$93,200	
91	Annual after-tax cash income (total)			$288,000	1-4	3.1698654	$912,921	
92	One-time operating cash outflow, after-tax, Yr. 1			$30,000	1	0.9090909	($27,273)	
93	Ater-tax proceeds from sale of the asset, Yr. 4			$3,000	4	0.6830135	$2,049	
94	After-tax employee relocation expenses, Yr. 4			$90,000	4	0.6830135	($61,471)	
95	End-of-investment recovery of working capital, Yr. 4			$200,000	4	0.6830135	$136,603	
96	Net present value of this decision alternative						$376,029	
97	**Less: Opporunity Costs:**							
98	After-tax cash operating income, per year			$60,800	1-4	3.1698654	$192,728	
99	After-tax salvage value of existing equipment, 4 years hence			$900	4	0.6830135	$615	
100	Recovery of working capital, end of year 4			$50,000	4	0.6830135	$34,151	
101							$227,493	
102	**Difference in NPV, Purchase New Machine vs. Keep Existing Machine**						$148,536	

Appendix B

DCF Models: Some Advanced Considerations

In the main part of the chapter, we have considered the rather simple situation where the firm is evaluating independent projects, each on a yes/no basis. In such situations, the NPV method and the IRR method normally lead to the same decision as to whether a proposed project should be accepted or rejected. However, there are some pitfalls associated with the use of IRR for capital budgeting purposes. We deal briefly with these pitfalls below. In addition, we look briefly at the capital budgeting decision when the firm faces a capital (funds) constraint. Except for the capital rationing situation, the primary conclusion of this appendix is that managers should be guided by project NPVs in making capital budgeting decisions.

THE POTENTIAL FOR MULTIPLE IRRs

normal cash flows
This involves one or more cash outflows followed by one or more cash inflows (or vice versa).

non-normal cash flows
This involves a series of alternating cash flows, with a minimum of two sign changes (positive to negative, then negative to positive).

In a normal investment project, there will be a large cash outflow at time 0 for the project, followed by a series of positive after-tax cash inflows during the life of the project. In this case, we say that the project has **normal cash flows** (i.e., one or more cash outflows followed by one or more cash inflows (or vice versa). In this case, there is only one sign change in the pattern of cash flows, and as such, there will be only a single IRR associated with the proposed investment.

Some projects, however, have **non-normal cash flows**, which we define as a series of alternating cash flows, with a minimum of two sign changes (positive to negative followed by negative to positive, or vice versa). For example, new machinery might require a major overhaul (cash outflow) sometime during the life of the asset. A strip-mining company might incur end-of-project reclamation costs (e.g., to restore to its original state the land that was mined). In both cases, there are two sign changes in the pattern of cash flows. In each of these two cases, there can be *up* to two IRRs associated with the project—one IRR for each sign change. If there are five sign changes, then there can be *up* to five IRRs. Thus, the basic rule to accept a project if its IRR is greater than the firm's weighted-average cost of capital breaks down. The solution to this problem is to base the decision on the NPV of the proposed investment: *If the NPV is greater than 0, accept the project.*[28]

Alternatively, the analyst may calculate a project's MIRR (rather than IRR). Each project has a single MIRR, regardless of the nature of its cash flows. Thus, we would accept a project if its MIRR were greater than the firm's WACC.

COMPARISON OF NPV AND IRR METHODS: MUTUALLY EXCLUSIVE PROJECTS

All of the examples in the body of the chapter involve take-it-or-leave-it decisions. That is, each investment project is considered independently of other investments. The basic decision, therefore, is whether to accept or reject the individual project being considered. However, in the real world almost all capital budgeting decisions involve a choice in which the selection of one alternative precludes the selection of one or more other alternatives. For example, your university may be considering whether to build a three-story or a four-story parking garage on campus—the university can invest in one but not both alternatives. The new garage could involve the use of electronic surveillance equipment or the use of security guards. As noted at the start of the chapter, these alternatives are said to be *mutually exclusive projects* in the sense that acceptance of one alternative precludes the acceptance of one or more other (competing) alternatives.

In analyzing mutually exclusive projects on a DCF basis, should the analyst use NPV or IRR? Although there are situations where NPV and IRR both give the same result regarding which of two (or more) competing investments should be chosen, there are also situations

---

[28] For an intuitive interpretation of multiple IRRs, see David Johnstone, "What Does an IRR (or Two) Mean?," *Journal of Economic Education,* Winter 2008, pp. 78–87.

where the two methods provide different signals to managers. For discussion purposes, consider the following two examples of mutually exclusive projects:

1. Each of two projects has roughly the same initial investment outlay but different useful lives; the project with the longer life also has more distant returns and a higher NPV but a lower IRR compared to the project with the shorter life.
2. Each of two projects has the same useful life but a different initial outlay.

In choosing between mutually exclusive projects, modern financial theory specifies that the decision maker should choose the project with the higher NPV. In the case of the first example, it can be shown that the IRR method mistakenly favors the project with the quicker payback and higher IRR in spite of the fact that the alternative project has a higher NPV. In the case of the second example, it can be shown that the IRR decision rule can mistakenly favor smaller projects with high rates of return but lower NPVs. The arguments are developed more fully in a corporate finance textbook.

In general, the point here is that high economic rates of return (project IRRs) are not an end in and of themselves. The shareholders of a company benefit to the extent that managers choose projects that increase share value, and this increase is accomplished by choosing among investment alternatives on the basis of projected NPVs.

CAPITAL RATIONING (CAPITAL CONSTRAINT)

We stated earlier that, in general, decision makers should use the NPV criterion for capital budgeting purposes. This rule states that all projects with a positive NPV should be accepted. This rule, however, assumes that the organization has access to capital markets to raise, if need be, additional capital (presumably at its WACC). For many large companies, this assumption would seem to be reasonable. But many small companies, and some larger companies as well, have either self-imposed or externally imposed constraints on their ability to raise capital. This situation is referred to as **capital rationing**; in the context of a capital constraint, the overall goal of management is to allocate in an optimal manner the investment funds (capital) it has available.

In fact, the situation here is similar to the constrained optimization problem we considered in Chapter 11 when we addressed the issue of determining the optimal short-run product mix. Under capital rationing, the appropriate decision rule is: Allocate capital to investment projects on the basis of the NPV per dollar of the investment capital associated with each project. This relative measure of profitability is referred to as the **profitability index (PI)** and is calculated as follows:

$$PI = NPV \div \text{Initial investment (I)}$$

Under the situation of capital rationing, managers should allocate available capital (investment funds) to projects that provide the greatest NPV per dollar of investment. Consider the following two independent projects and an after-tax discount rate of 10% for the firm attempting to set an optimum capital budget for the period:

capital rationing
The case where investment capital for a given accounting period is limited—hence the need for these funds to be "rationed."

profitability index (PI)
A rate-of-return measure, defined as the ratio of the NPV of a project to the original investment outlay for the project; useful for project-selection purposes when capital funds are limited and therefore need to be rationed.

	After-Tax Cash Flows (Undiscounted)					
Project	Period 0	Period 1	Period 2	Period 3	NPV	PI = NPV ÷ I
1	$(36.00)	$20.00	$20.00	$15.00	$9.98	0.28
2	(50.00)	25.00	25.00	25.00	12.17	0.24

If there is no capital rationing, the firm would accept both projects because the NPV of each project, at 10%, is positive. Under capital rationing, Project 1 would be preferred over Project 2 because it has the higher ratio of NPV to investment (0.28) than Project 2 (0.24). In a sense, the underlying logic is one of getting the most bang for the buck. Remember, though, that the use of PI for ranking investment projects is appropriate only under conditions of capital rationing.

Appendix C

Present Value Tables

TABLE 1   **Present Value of $1**

Periods	4%	5%	6%	7%	8%	9%	10%	11%	12%	13%	14%	15%	20%	25%	30%
1	0.962	0.952	0.943	0.935	0.926	0.917	0.909	0.901	0.893	0.885	0.877	0.870	0.833	0.800	0.769
2	0.925	0.907	0.890	0.873	0.857	0.842	0.826	0.812	0.797	0.783	0.769	0.756	0.694	0.640	0.592
3	0.889	0.864	0.840	0.816	0.794	0.772	0.751	0.731	0.712	0.693	0.675	0.658	0.579	0.512	0.455
4	0.855	0.823	0.792	0.763	0.735	0.708	0.683	0.659	0.636	0.613	0.592	0.572	0.482	0.410	0.350
5	0.822	0.784	0.747	0.713	0.681	0.650	0.621	0.593	0.567	0.543	0.519	0.497	0.402	0.328	0.269
6	0.790	0.746	0.705	0.666	0.630	0.596	0.564	0.535	0.507	0.480	0.456	0.432	0.335	0.262	0.207
7	0.760	0.711	0.665	0.623	0.583	0.547	0.513	0.482	0.452	0.425	0.400	0.376	0.279	0.210	0.159
8	0.731	0.677	0.627	0.582	0.540	0.502	0.467	0.434	0.404	0.376	0.351	0.327	0.233	0.168	0.123
9	0.703	0.645	0.592	0.544	0.500	0.460	0.424	0.391	0.361	0.333	0.308	0.284	0.194	0.134	0.094
10	0.676	0.614	0.558	0.508	0.463	0.422	0.386	0.352	0.322	0.295	0.270	0.247	0.162	0.107	0.073
11	0.650	0.585	0.527	0.475	0.429	0.388	0.350	0.317	0.287	0.261	0.237	0.215	0.135	0.086	0.056
12	0.625	0.557	0.497	0.444	0.397	0.356	0.319	0.286	0.257	0.231	0.208	0.187	0.112	0.069	0.043
13	0.601	0.530	0.469	0.415	0.368	0.326	0.290	0.258	0.229	0.204	0.182	0.163	0.093	0.055	0.033
14	0.577	0.505	0.442	0.388	0.340	0.299	0.263	0.232	0.205	0.181	0.160	0.141	0.078	0.044	0.025
15	0.555	0.481	0.417	0.362	0.315	0.275	0.239	0.209	0.183	0.160	0.140	0.123	0.065	0.035	0.020
16	0.534	0.458	0.394	0.339	0.292	0.252	0.218	0.188	0.163	0.141	0.123	0.107	0.054	0.028	0.015
17	0.513	0.436	0.371	0.317	0.270	0.231	0.198	0.170	0.146	0.125	0.108	0.093	0.045	0.023	0.012
18	0.494	0.416	0.350	0.296	0.250	0.212	0.180	0.153	0.130	0.111	0.095	0.081	0.038	0.018	0.009
19	0.475	0.396	0.331	0.277	0.232	0.194	0.164	0.138	0.116	0.098	0.083	0.070	0.031	0.014	0.007
20	0.456	0.377	0.312	0.258	0.215	0.178	0.149	0.124	0.104	0.087	0.073	0.061	0.026	0.012	0.005
22	0.422	0.342	0.278	0.226	0.184	0.150	0.123	0.101	0.083	0.068	0.056	0.046	0.018	0.007	0.003
24	0.390	0.310	0.247	0.197	0.158	0.126	0.102	0.082	0.066	0.053	0.043	0.035	0.013	0.005	0.002
25	0.375	0.295	0.233	0.184	0.146	0.116	0.092	0.074	0.059	0.047	0.038	0.030	0.010	0.004	0.001
30	0.308	0.231	0.174	0.131	0.099	0.075	0.057	0.044	0.033	0.026	0.020	0.015	0.004	0.001	0.000
35	0.253	0.181	0.130	0.094	0.068	0.049	0.036	0.026	0.019	0.014	0.010	0.008	0.002	0.000	0.000
40	0.208	0.142	0.097	0.067	0.046	0.032	0.022	0.015	0.011	0.008	0.005	0.004	0.001	0.000	0.000

Note: The present value (PV) factor for N periods and rate r per period $= 1 \div (1 + r)^N$. For example, the PV factor for 10%, 5 years $= 1 \div (1 + 0.10)^5 = 0.621$ (rounded).

TABLE 2 Present Value of Annuity of $1

Periods	4%	5%	6%	7%	8%	9%	10%	11%	12%	13%	14%	15%	20%	25%	30%
1	0.962	0.952	0.943	0.935	0.926	0.917	0.909	0.901	0.893	0.885	0.877	0.870	0.833	0.800	0.769
2	1.886	1.859	1.833	1.808	1.783	1.759	1.736	1.713	1.690	1.668	1.647	1.626	1.528	1.440	1.361
3	2.775	2.723	2.673	2.624	2.577	2.531	2.487	2.444	2.402	2.361	2.322	2.283	2.106	1.952	1.816
4	3.630	3.546	3.465	3.387	3.312	3.240	3.170	3.102	3.037	2.974	2.914	2.855	2.589	2.362	2.166
5	4.452	4.329	4.212	4.100	3.993	3.890	3.791	3.696	3.605	3.517	3.433	3.352	2.991	2.689	2.436
6	5.242	5.076	4.917	4.767	4.623	4.486	4.355	4.231	4.111	3.998	3.889	3.784	3.326	2.951	2.643
7	6.002	5.786	5.582	5.389	5.206	5.033	4.868	4.712	4.564	4.423	4.288	4.160	3.605	3.161	2.802
8	6.733	6.463	6.210	5.971	5.747	5.535	5.335	5.146	4.968	4.799	4.639	4.487	3.837	3.329	2.925
9	7.435	7.108	6.802	6.515	6.247	5.995	5.759	5.537	5.328	5.132	4.946	4.772	4.031	3.463	3.019
10	8.111	7.722	7.360	7.024	6.710	6.418	6.145	5.889	5.650	5.426	5.216	5.019	4.192	3.571	3.092
11	8.760	8.306	7.887	7.499	7.139	6.805	6.495	6.207	5.938	5.687	5.453	5.234	4.327	3.656	3.147
12	9.385	8.863	8.384	7.943	7.536	7.161	6.814	6.492	6.194	5.918	5.660	5.421	4.439	3.725	3.190
13	9.986	9.394	8.853	8.358	7.904	7.487	7.103	6.750	6.424	6.122	5.842	5.583	4.533	3.780	3.223
14	10.563	9.899	9.295	8.745	8.244	7.786	7.367	6.982	6.628	6.302	6.002	5.724	4.611	3.824	3.249
15	11.118	10.380	9.712	9.108	8.559	8.061	7.606	7.191	6.811	6.462	6.142	5.847	4.675	3.859	3.268
16	11.652	10.838	10.106	9.447	8.851	8.313	7.824	7.379	6.974	6.604	6.265	5.954	4.730	3.887	3.283
17	12.166	11.274	10.477	9.763	9.122	8.544	8.022	7.549	7.120	6.729	6.373	6.047	4.775	3.910	3.295
18	12.659	11.690	10.828	10.059	9.372	8.756	8.201	7.702	7.250	6.840	6.467	6.128	4.812	3.928	3.304
19	13.134	12.085	11.158	10.336	9.604	8.950	8.365	7.839	7.366	6.938	6.550	6.198	4.843	3.942	3.311
20	13.590	12.462	11.470	10.594	9.818	9.129	8.514	7.963	7.469	7.025	6.623	6.259	4.870	3.954	3.316
22	14.451	13.163	12.042	11.061	10.201	9.442	8.772	8.176	7.645	7.170	6.743	6.359	4.909	3.970	3.323
24	15.247	13.799	12.550	11.469	10.529	9.707	8.985	8.348	7.784	7.283	6.835	6.434	4.937	3.981	3.327
25	15.622	14.094	12.783	11.654	10.675	9.823	9.077	8.422	7.843	7.330	6.873	6.464	4.948	3.985	3.329
30	17.292	15.372	13.765	12.409	11.258	10.274	9.427	8.694	8.055	7.496	7.003	6.566	4.979	3.995	3.332
35	18.665	16.374	14.498	12.948	11.655	10.567	9.644	8.855	8.176	7.586	7.070	6.617	4.992	3.998	3.333
40	19.793	17.159	15.046	13.332	11.925	10.757	9.779	8.951	8.244	7.634	7.105	6.642	4.997	3.999	3.333

Note: The present value (PV) annuity factor for N periods and a rate of r per period $= [1 - (1 + r)^{-N}] \div r$. For example, for $N = 5$ and $r = 0.10$, the PV annuity factor = 3.791 (rounded).

Key Terms

Comments on Cost Management in Action

Real Options Analysis in the Motion Picture (Film) Industry

As noted in the chapter (and the suggested readings), traditional discounted cash flow (DCF) models for making capital investment decisions use a *static analysis.* That is, these models assume that decision makers invest in *discrete* projects, rather than projects that adapt or unfold over time, based on newly revealed information (e.g., information related to the realized level of consumer acceptance or demand). A DCF model such as NPV provides a single go/no-go decision, based on the discounted value of estimated after-tax future cash flows.

Critics argue, however, that the estimated NPV of a proposed investment does not reflect investment options that may be embodied in the investment—for example, the option to delay a project, the option at a future point to expand a project, or the option to abandon a project. In other words, projects are dynamic in nature—investments in many kinds of projects (including those in the motion picture industry) unfold over time. These same critics argue that the use of *real options* analysis is a structured/formal way to incorporate uncertainty into the analysis of capital investment projects. Conceptually, real options have value similar to the value associated with financial options (viz., put options and call options).

In the motion picture industry, you are likely aware that large sums of money are committed to film projects. Young et al. (2012) provide a lucid account of how real options analysis can be applied to the evaluation of such projects. The authors specifically consider two real options that may be embodied in a given motion picture: a *growth option* (i.e., the ability to produce a motion picture sequel, on the basis of the commercial success of the original movie) and an *abandonment option* (i.e., the level of advertising expenditures committed to a film, as determined by tracking data and box-office receipts).

Section E of Part Two of the CMA (Certified Management Accountant) exam contains the following two learning objectives related to the topic of real options in the capital budgeting process: (1) explain how the value of a capital investment is increased if consideration is given to the possibility of adding on, speeding up, slowing down, or discontinuing early and (2) demonstrate an understanding of real options and identify examples of the different types of real options (calculations not required).[29]

Sources: S. Mark Young, James J. Gong, and Wim A. Van der Stede, "Using Real Options to Make Decisions in the Motion Picture Industry," *Strategic Finance,* May 2012, pp. 53–59 (available at http://sfmagazine.com/wp-content/uploads/sfarchive/2012/05/Using-Real-Options-to-Make-Decisions-in-the-Motion-Picture-Industry.pdf). Also see Tom Copeland and Peter Tufano, "A Real-World Way to Manage Real Options," *Harvard Business Review,* March 2004, https://hbr.org/2004/03/a-real-world-way-to-manage-real-options, and Wim A. Van der Stede, "Hollywood Studios Appear to Plan Sequels before They Produce the Original Movie" (2015), http://eprints.lse.ac.uk/63736/1/blogs.lse.ac.uk-Hollywood%20studios%20appear%20to%20plan%20sequels%20before%20they%20produce%20the%20original%20movie.pdf.

Self-Study Problem
(For answers, please see Solution.)

Capital Budgeting for Expanding Productive Capacity

Ray Summers Company operates at full capacity of 10,000 units per year. The company, however, is still unable to fully meet the demand for its product, estimated at 15,000 units annually. This level of demand is expected to continue for at least another four years.

---

[29] Institute of Management Accountants (IMA), *Certified Management Accountant* (CMA) *Learning Outcome Statements* (revised September 2, 2016), p. 26, available at www.imanet.org/cma-certification/taking-the-exam.

To meet the demand, the firm is considering the purchase of new equipment for $580,000. This equipment has an estimated useful life of four years; estimated sales (disposal) value of this asset at the end of four years is $50,000 (pretax). The engineering division estimates that installing, testing, and training for the use of the equipment will cost $12,000. These costs are to be capitalized as part of the cost of the new equipment.

An adjacent vacant warehouse can be leased for the duration of the project for $10,000 per year, which cost would be included as part of fixed manufacturing overhead. The warehouse needs $58,000 of renovations to make it suitable for manufacturing. The renovation cost is to be capitalized as part of the cost of the new equipment. The lease terms call for restoring the warehouse to its original condition at the end of the lease. The restoration is estimated to cost $20,000, a cost that is expected to be fully deductible for tax purposes. Current pretax operating profit per unit is as follows:

			Per Unit
Sales price			$200
Variable costs:			
Manufacturing	$60		
Marketing	20	$80	
Fixed costs:			
Manufacturing	$25		
Marketing and administrative	15	40	120
Operating profit before tax			$ 80

The new equipment would have no effect on the variable costs per unit. All current fixed costs are expected to continue with the same total amount. The per-unit fixed cost includes depreciation expenses of $5 for manufacturing and $4 for marketing and administration.

Additional fixed manufacturing costs of $140,000 (excluding depreciation on the new equipment) will be incurred each year if the equipment is purchased. The company must also hire an additional marketing manager to serve new customers. The annual cost for the new marketing manager, support staff, and office expense is estimated at approximately $100,000. The company expects to be in the 40% tax bracket for each of the next 4 years. The company requires a minimum after-tax rate of return of 12% on investments and for tax purposes uses straight-line depreciation with a $50,000 salvage value assumed.

Required

1. What is the required net initial investment outlay (year 0)? Round your answer to nearest whole dollar.

2. (a) What is the projected increase in after-tax operating profit for each of the first three years if the new equipment is purchased? (Assume for each year that sales equals production.) (b) What is the projected year 4 increase in after-tax operating profit if the new equipment is purchased? Round all answers to the nearest whole dollar.

3. (a) If the new equipment is purchased, what is the projected increase in after-tax cash inflow for each of the first three years of the asset's life? (b) What is the projected year 4 increase in after-tax cash inflow if the new equipment is purchased? Round all answers to nearest whole dollar.

4. Compute the (unadjusted) payback period of the proposed investment under the assumption that cash inflows occur evenly throughout the year. Round your answer to 2 decimal places (e.g., 4.207 years = 4.21 years).

5. Compute the accounting (book) rate of return (ARR) of the proposed investment, based on the average book value of the investment. Round your answer to 2 decimal places.

6. Compute the estimated net present value (NPV) of the proposed investment under the assumption that all cash inflows occur at year-end. Round your answer to the nearest whole dollar.

7. Compute the discounted payback period of the proposed investment under the assumption that cash inflows at the end of each year. (Note: It is sufficient for this answer to state adjacent years under which the discounted payback period falls. For example, an acceptable answer might be: "The discounted payback period is between seven and eight years.")

8. Compute the internal rate of return (IRR) of the proposed investment (to 1 decimal place) under the assumption that all cash inflows occur at year-end.

9. Use the MIRR function in Excel to estimate the modified internal rate of return (MIRR) for the proposed investment. Round your answer to 1 decimal place (e.g., 21.57% = 21.6%).

10. Assume now that the company expects the variable manufacturing cost per unit to increase once the new equipment is in place. What is the most that the *per-unit* variable manufacturing cost can increase and still allow the company to earn the minimum rate of return on this investment? (*Hint:* Use the Goal Seek option in Excel.) Round your answer to 2 decimal places (e.g., $23.441 = $23.44).

The Student Resources section of Connect includes video tutorials for the Self-Study Problems.

Questions

12-1   What are the distinguishing characteristics of capital budgeting decisions?

12-2   In what ways can accountants add value to the capital budgeting process?

12-3   What is the analytic hierarchy process (AHP), and how can it be used in making capital budgeting decisions?

12-4   In capital budgeting analysis, what is meant by the *income tax effect*? Give three examples of the tax effect pertaining to the acquisition of new factory (manufacturing) equipment.

12-5   What are the limitations of the payback period method for making capital budgeting decisions (e.g., whether to accept or reject a proposed investment)? Does the present value payback period overcome these limitations?

12-6   Does the accounting (book) rate of return (ARR) method provide a valid (or meaningful) measure of the return on investment? How about the investment's internal rate of return (IRR)?

12-7   What should be the decision criterion when using the NPV method to evaluate capital investments? Does the IRR method use the same criterion?

12-8   List at least three important behavioral issues related to the capital budgeting process.

12-9   "The net present value (NPV) method weighs early receipts of cash much more heavily than more distant receipts of cash." Do you agree? Why?

12-10 "Depreciation expenses have no effect on cash flows and, therefore, are not relevant in capital expenditure analysis." Do you agree? Why or why not?

12-11 Should the firm accept the independent projects described below? Why or why not? (a) The firm's cost of capital is 10% and the estimated internal rate of return (IRR) of the project is 11%. (b) A capital project requires a $150,000 initial investment. The firm's cost of capital is 10% (after-tax), and the present value of the expected after-tax cash inflows from the project is $148,000.

12-12 Provide a short explanation of the modified internal rate of return (MIRR) financial performance metric. How does MIRR differ from IRR? (In addition to the discussion in the text, see, for example, www.journalofaccountancy.com/issues/2017/feb/calculate-internal-rate-of-return-in-excel.html.)

12-13 (Appendix B): What decision criterion should be used to choose investment projects for a firm with unlimited funds available at a weighted-average cost of 10% (after tax)? Can the firm use the same decision criterion if it has only a limited amount of available funds, say $100 million? Explain.

12-14 (Appendix B): When analyzing a proposed capital investment, what conditions or factors may lead the results to differ between the net present value (NPV) and internal rate of return (IRR) decision models?

12-15 (Appendix B): How does the size of the initial investment affect the indicated internal rate of return (IRR) and net present value (NPV) of a proposed investment?

Brief Exercises

[LO 12-3] 12-16 For a firm facing a marginal income tax rate of 34%, what is the after-tax cash flow effect of (a) a $1,000 increase in contribution margin during the year and (b) a $500 increase in cash operating expenses?

[LO 12-3] 12-17 Use the appropriate function in Excel (= SLN) to calculate the annual straight-line (SL) depreciation charge for an asset that has a $10,000 acquisition cost, an estimated salvage value of $500, and a useful life of four years.

[LO 12-3] 12-18 Calculate the net after-tax cash flow effect of the following information: sales, $260; expenses other than depreciation, $140; depreciation expense, $50; marginal income tax rate, 35%. (*Hint:* You can use either a direct or an indirect approach to arrive at the answer.) Round your answer to 2 decimal places.

[LO 12-3] 12-19 Refer to Exhibit 12.4 in the text. What is the depreciation expense deduction in each of four years for a $10,000 asset classified under MACRS as three-year property?

[LO 12-3] 12-20 A company purchases an asset that costs $10,000. This asset qualifies as three-year property under MACRS. The company uses an after-tax discount rate of 12% and faces a 40% income tax rate. (a) Use the appropriate present value factors found in Appendix C, Table 1, to determine the present value of the depreciation deductions for this firm over the specified four-year period. (b) Use the built-in NPV function in Excel to verify your answer.

[LO 12-3] 12-21 Given an asset with a net book value (NBV) of $25,000, what are the after-tax proceeds for a firm in the 34% tax bracket if this asset is sold for $35,000 cash? What are the after-tax proceeds for this same firm if the asset is sold for $15,000 cash?

[LO 12-4] 12-22 What is the present value of $1,000 to be received two years from now, if the discount rate is (a) 10%, (b) 14%, and (c) 20%? Do the calculations first using the present value factors given in Appendix C, Table 1, then using the formula that appears at the bottom of Appendix C, Table 1 to generate present value factors.

[LO 12-4] 12-23 What is the present value of a stream of five end-of-year annual cash receipts of $500 given a discount rate of 14%? (a) Use the appropriate table in the text (i.e., Appendix C, Table 2) and (b) the appropriate function in Excel (= PV) to answer this question.

[LO 12-4] 12-24 Given the following attributes of an investment project with a five-year life and an after-tax discount rate of 12%, calculate both the IRR and MIRR of the project using the built-in functions in Excel: investment outlay, time 0, $5,000; after-tax cash inflows, year 1, $800; year 2, $900; year 3, $1,500; year 4, $1,800; and year 5, $3,200. What accounts for the difference in these two measures?

[LO 12-4] 12-25 MicroTech Corporation is subject to a 35% income tax rate. Given the following information about the firm's capital structure, calculate the corporation's weighted-average cost of capital (WACC), rounded to 1 decimal place:

Source of Funds	Market Value	After-Tax Rate or Expected Return
Long-term debt	$40 million	7.0%
Preferred stock	20 million	9.0
Common stock	60 million	12.0

[LO 12-5] 12-26 Create an Excel spreadsheet for Brief Exercise 12-20 and demonstrate that the PV of the depreciation deductions, when the income tax rate is 40%, is $3,218 (rounded to the nearest dollar). Given an after-tax discount rate of 12%, what tax rate (rounded to 2 decimal places, e.g., 38.712% = 38.71%) would be needed in order for the PV of the depreciation deductions to equal $4,000? Use the Goal Seek function of Excel.

[LO 12-6] 12-27 Given the following attributes of an investment project with a five-year life: investment outlay, year 0, $5,000; after-tax cash inflows, year 1, $800; year 2, $900; year 3, $1,500; year 4, $1,800; and year 5, $3,200. (a) Use the built-in NPV function of Excel to estimate the NPV of this project. Round your answer to the nearest whole dollar. Assume an after-tax discount rate of 12.0%. (b) Estimate the payback period, in years, for this project under the assumption that cash inflows occur evenly throughout the year. Round your answer to one (1) decimal place.

Exercises

[LO 12-3] 12-28 **Identifying Relevant Cash Flows; Asset Purchase Decision**   This exercise parallels the machine purchase decision for the Mendoza Company discussed in the body of the chapter. Assume that Mendoza is exploring whether to enter a complementary line of business. The existing business line generates annual cash revenues of approximately $5,000,000 and cash expenses of $3,600,000, one-third of which are labor costs. The current level of investment in this existing division is $12,000,000. (Sales and costs of this division are not affected by the investment decision regarding the complementary line.)

Mendoza estimates that incremental (noncash) net working capital of $30,000 will be needed to support the new business line. No additional facility-level costs would be needed to support the new line—there is currently sufficient excess capacity. However, the new line would require additional cash expenses (overhead costs) of $400,000 per year. Raw materials costs associated with the new line are expected to be $1,200,000 per year, while the total labor cost is expected to double.

The CFO of the company estimates that new machinery costing $2,500,000 would need to be purchased. This machinery has a seven-year useful life and an estimated salvage (terminal) value of $400,000. For tax purposes, assume that the Mendoza Company would use the straight-line method (with estimated salvage value considered in the calculation).

Assume, further, that the weighted-average cost of capital (WACC) for Mendoza is 14% (after-tax) and that the combined (federal and state) income tax rate is 40%. Finally, assume that the new business line is expected to generate annual cash revenue of $3,600,000.

Required   Determine relevant cash flows (after-tax) at each of the following three points: (1) project initiation, (2) project operation, and (3) project disposal (termination). For purposes of this last calculation, you can assume that the asset is sold at the end of its useful life for the salvage value used to establish the annual straight-line depreciation deductions; further, you can assume that at the end of the project's life Mendoza will fully recover its initial investment in net working capital. Also, separately identify any irrelevant cost and revenue data associated with this decision.

[LO 12-3]   **12-29 Value of Accelerated Depreciation: Sum-of-Years'-Digits (SYD) and Double-Declining-Balance (DDB) Methods**   Freedom Corporation acquired a fixed asset for $100,000. Its estimated life at time of purchase was four years, with no estimated salvage value. Assume a discount rate of 8% and an income tax rate of 40%.

Required
1. What is the incremental present value (rounded to the nearest whole dollar) of the tax benefits resulting from calculating depreciation using the sum-of-the-years'-digits (SYD) method rather than the straight-line (SLN) method on this asset? Use the SYD and SLN functions in Excel to calculate depreciation charges.
2. What is the incremental present value (rounded to the nearest whole dollar) of the tax benefits resulting from calculating depreciation using the double-declining-balance (DDB) method rather than the straight-line (SLN) method on this asset? Use the SLN and DDB functions in Excel to calculate depreciation charges.
3. What is the incremental present value (rounded to the nearest whole dollar) of the tax benefits resulting from using MACRS rather than straight-line (SLN) depreciation? The asset qualifies as a three-year asset. Use the half-year convention. (Refer to Exhibit 12.4 for MACRS depreciation rates.)

(CPA Adapted)

[LO 12-4, 12-5]   **12-30 Cash Receipts Frequency and Present Value Consequences**   Assume that you are about to sell property (a vacant parcel of real estate) you own but otherwise have no use for. The net-of-sales-commission selling price for the property is $500,000. You are willing to finance this transaction over a 20-year period and have told the buyer that you expect a 12% pretax return on the transaction. The buyer has asked you for a payment schedule under several alternatives.

Required
1. What will be your total cash receipts, to earn a 12% return, if payments are received from the purchaser:
   a. At the end of each week?
   b. At the end of each month?
   c. At the end of each quarter?
   d. At the end of each year?
2. What general conclusion can you draw based on the calculations in requirement 1?

[LO 12-4]   **12-31 Weighted-Average Cost of Capital (WACC)**   Below is information regarding the capital structure of Micro Advantage Inc. On the basis of this information you are asked to respond to the following three questions:

Required
1. Micro Advantage issued a $5,000,000 par value, 20-year bond a year ago at 98 (i.e., 98% of par value) with a stated rate of 9%. Today, the bond is selling at 110 (i.e., 110% of par value). If the firm's tax bracket is 30%, what is the current after-tax cost of this debt, rounded to 2 decimal places?
2. Micro Advantage has $5,000,000 preferred stock outstanding that it sold for $24 per share. The preferred stock has a per share par value of $25 and pays a $3 dividend per year. The current market price is $30 per share. The firm's tax bracket is 30%. What is the after-tax cost of the preferred stock, rounded to 2 decimal places?
3. In addition to the bonds and preferred stock described in requirements 1 and 2, Micro Advantage has 50,000 shares of common stock outstanding that has a par value of $10 per share and a current market price of $170 per share. The expected after-tax market return on the firm's common equity is 20%. What is Micro Advantage's weighted-average cost of capital (WACC), rounded to 2 decimal places?

[LO 12-4]   **12-32 After-Tax Net Present Value and IRR (Non-MACRS Rules—Straight-Line vs. Double-Declining-Balance Depreciation Methods)**   eEgg is considering the purchase of a new distributed network computer system to help handle its warehouse inventories. The system costs $60,000 to purchase and install and $30,000 to operate each year. The system is estimated to be useful for four years. Management expects the new system to reduce the cost of managing inventories by $62,000 per year. The firm's cost of capital (discount rate) is 10%.

Required
1. What is the net present value (NPV) of the proposed investment under each of the following independent situations? Use the NPV built-in function in Excel; round answers to the nearest whole dollar.
   a. The firm is not yet profitable and therefore pays no income taxes.
   b. The firm is in the 30% income tax bracket and uses straight-line (SLN) depreciation with no salvage value. Assume MACRS rules do *not* apply; calculate depreciation expense using the SLN function in Excel.

c. The firm is in the 30% income tax bracket and uses double-declining-balance (DDB) depreciation with no salvage value. Given a four-year life, the DDB depreciation rate is 50% (i.e., $2 \times 25\%$). In year 4, record depreciation expense as the net book value (NBV) of the asset at the start of the year.

2. What is the internal rate of return (IRR) of the proposed investment for situations in requirement 1, parts (a) through (c)? Use the built-in IRR function in Excel and round answers to 1 decimal place (e.g., $23.348\% = 23.3\%$).

[LO 12-4] 12-33 **Using Arrays in Excel; NPV Analysis**   Please refer to footnote 14 and the data referenced in the footnote.

Required

1. Follow the directions given in footnote 14 to calculate the NPV of the referenced investment project. (*Hint:* If necessary, consult the following: https://support.office.com/en-us/Search/results?query =array+formulas&src=as.)

2. Repeat the procedure using a discount rate (WACC) of 10% and the following cash flows, time 0 through time 10: ($1,000), $100, $200, $300, $400, $500, $600, $700, $800, $900, $1,000. (*Hints:* The NPV should be $1,903.59; remember to use the Name Manager (Ctrl+F3) under the Formulas tab in Excel.)

[LO 12-3, 12-4] 12-34 **Determining Relevant Cash Flows; Basic Capital Budgeting**   Rockyford Company must replace some machinery that has zero book value and a current market value of $1,800. One possibility is to invest in new machinery costing $40,000. This new machinery would produce estimated annual pre-tax cash operating savings of $12,500. Assume the new machine will have a useful life of four years and depreciation of $10,000 each year for book and tax purposes. It will have no salvage value at the end of four years. The investment in this new machinery would require an additional $3,000 invest-ment of net working capital. (Assume that when the old machine was purchased, the incremental net working capital required at the time was $0.)

If Rockyford accepts this investment proposal, the disposal of the old machinery and the invest-ment in the new one will occur on December 31 of this year. The cash flows from the investment are expected to occur over a four-year period.

Assume that Rockyford is subject to a 40% income tax rate for all ordinary income and capital gains and has a 10% weighted-average after-tax cost of capital. All operating and tax cash flows are assumed to occur at year-end.

Required

1. What is the after-tax cash flow arising from disposing of the old machinery?

2. What is the present value of the after-tax cash flows for the next four years attributable to the cash oper-ating savings? Use the appropriate annuity factor from Appendix C, Table 2 for this calculation.

3. What is the present value of the tax-shield effect of depreciation expense for year 1? Use the appropriate present value factor from Appendix C, Table 1 for this calculation.

4. Which one of the following is the proper treatment for the additional $3,000 of net working capital required in the current year?

   a. It should be ignored in capital budgeting because it is not a capital investment.

   b. It is a sunk cost that needs no consideration in capital budgeting.

   c. It should be treated as part of the initial investment when determining the net present value.

   d. It should be spread over the machinery's four-year life as a cash outflow in each of the years.

   e. It should be included as part of the cost of the new machine and depreciated.

(**CMA Adapted**)

[LO 12-3, 12-4] 12-35 **Cash Flow Analysis; NPV; Spreadsheet Analysis; Double-Declining-Balance (DDB) Deprecia-tion Using the VDB Function in Excel**   Lou Lewis, the president of Lewisville Company, has asked you to give him an analysis of the best use of a warehouse the company owns. *Note:* The company has a 40% effective tax rate.

   a. Lewisville Company is currently leasing the warehouse to another company for $5,000 per month on a year-to-year basis. (*Hint:* Use the PV function in Excel to calculate, on an after-tax basis, the PV of this stream of *monthly* rental receipts.)

   b. The warehouse's estimated sales value is $200,000. A commercial Realtor believes that the price is likely to remain unchanged in the near future. The building originally cost $60,000 and is being depreciated at $1,500 annually. Its current net book value (NBV) is $7,500.

   c. Lewisville Company is seriously considering converting the warehouse into a factory outlet for furniture. The remodeling will cost $100,000 and will be modest because the major attraction will be rock-bottom prices. The remodeling cost will be depreciated over the next five years using the double-declining-balance method. (*Note:* Use the VDB function in Excel to calculate depreciation charges. The advantage of using the VDB, rather than the DDB, function is that there is a (default) option in the former that provides an automatic switch to the straight-line method when it is advantageous to do so.)

d. The inventory and receivables (net of current liabilities) needed to open and sustain the factory outlet would be $600,000. This total is fully recoverable whenever operations terminate.

e. Lou is fairly certain that the warehouse will be condemned in 10 years to make room for a new highway. The firm most likely would receive $200,000 from the condemnation.

f. Estimated annual operating data, exclusive of depreciation, are as follows:

Sales (cash)	$900,000
Operating expenses	$500,000

g. Nonrecurring sales promotion costs at the beginning of year 1 (i.e., at time 0) are expected to be $100,000. (These costs are fully deductible for tax purposes.)

h. Nonrecurring termination costs at the end of year 5 are $50,000. (These costs are fully deductible for tax purposes.)

The after-tax discount rate for capital budgeting purposes is 14%. (To calculate the present value factor for each year, $i, i = 1, 5$, use the following formula: PV factor$_i = (1 \div 1.14^i)$. The company is in the 40% tax bracket (federal and state combined).

Required

1. Show how you would handle the individual items (a through h above) in determining whether the company should continue to lease the space or convert it to a factory outlet. Use the company's analysis form, which is set up as follows:

			Cash Flows in Year					
Item	Description	Present Value	0	1	2	3	4	5
a.								
b.								
.								
.								
.								
h.								

Identify any items that are irrelevant for decision making.

2. After analyzing all relevant data, compute the estimated net present value (NPV) of the proposed investment. Use the appropriate built-in functions in Excel (PV and NPV) for all present value calculations. Indicate which course of action, based only on these data, should be taken.

 [LO 12-4, 12-5]   **12-36 Future and Present Values (including Annuity Due); Spreadsheet Application**

It is said that the Indian who sold Manhattan for $24 was a sharp salesman. If he had put his $24 away at 6% compounded semiannually, it would now be worth more than $9 billion, and he could buy most of the now-improved land back! Assume that this seller invested on January 1, 1701, the $24 he received.[30]

Required

1. Use Excel to determine the balance (in billions) of the investment as of December 31, 2021, assuming a 6% interest rate compounded *semiannually*. (*Hints:* Use the FV function in Excel. Also, you can use the NPER function in Excel to determine the number of years between the end year and the start year. Remember that there are two semiannual periods in every year.)

2. Carry out the same calculation using an 8% annual interest rate, compounded semiannually.

3. What would be the balances for requirements 1 and 2 if interest is compounded quarterly?

4. Assume that the account consisting of this investment had a balance of $9.5 billion as of December 31, 2021. How much would the total amount be on December 31, 2027, if the annual interest rate is 8%, compounded semiannually?

5. In 2000, a star major-league baseball player signed a 10-year, $252 million contract with the Texas Rangers. Assume that equal payments would have been made each year to this individual and that the

[30] See the following websites for more information: http://blog.nmai.si.edu/main/2011/08/americas-first-urban-myth.html and http://mentalfloss.com/article/12657/wasmanhattan-really-bought-24.

owners' cost of capital (discount rate) was 12% at the time the contract was signed. What is the present value cost of the contract to the owners as of January 1, 2000, the date the contract was signed, in each of the following independent situations?

a. The player received the first payment on December 31, 2000.

b. The player received the first payment on January 1, 2000, the date the contract was signed. (This situation is referred to as an annuity due rather than an ordinary annuity. See **www.accountingtools.com/ articles/what-is-an-annuity-due.html.** In the PV formula in Excel, this situation is handled by setting "type" to 1.)

c. Assuming the owner is in the 45% income tax bracket, recalculate your answer for requirement a.

[LO 12-4, 12-5] 12-37 **NPV; Sensitivity Analysis** Griffey & Son operates a plant in Cincinnati and is considering opening a new facility in Seattle. The initial outlay will be $3,500,000 and should produce after-tax net cash inflows of $600,000 per year for 15 years. Due to the effects of the ocean air in Seattle, however, the plant's useful life may be only 12 years. The cost of capital (discount rate) is 14%.

Required

1. Based on an NPV analysis, should the project be accepted if a 15-year useful life is assumed? What if a 12-year useful life is used? Use appropriate present value annuity factors from Appendix C, Table 2, and round final answers to the nearest whole dollar.

2. How many years (to 1 decimal place) will be needed for the Seattle facility to earn at least a 14% return? (*Hint:* Use the =NPER function in Excel or the formula for the present value annuity factor given at the bottom of Appendix C, Table 2 to answer this question.)

 [LO 12-4, 12-5] 12-38 **Uneven Cash Flows; NPV; Sensitivity Analysis** MaxiCare Corporation, a not-for-profit organization, specializes in health care for senior citizens. Management is considering whether to expand operations by opening a new chain of care centers in the inner city of large metropolitan areas. For a new facility, initial cash outlays for lease, renovations, net working capital, training, and other costs are expected to be about $15 million. The corporation expects the cash inflows of each new facility in its first year of operation to equal the initial investment outlay for the facility. Net cash inflows are expected to increase to $1 million in each of years 2 and 3; $2.5 million in year 4; and $3 million in each of years 5 through 10. The lease agreement for the facility will expire at the end of year 10, and MaxiCare expects the cost to close a facility will pretty much exhaust all cash proceeds from the disposal. Cost of capital for MaxiCare is estimated as 12%. Assume that all cash flows occur at year-end.

Required

1. Compute (using the built-in NPV function in Excel) the net present value (NPV) for the proposed investment. Round your answer to nearest whole dollar.

2. Compute (using the built-in IRR function in Excel) the internal rate of return (IRR) for the proposed investment. Round your answer to 2 decimal places (e.g., 14.347% = 14.35%).

3. What is the breakeven selling price for this investment, that is, the price that would yield an NPV of $0? (Use the Goal Seek function in Excel to determine the breakeven selling price. See the instructions in the Uncertainty and the Capital Budgeting Process section of this chapter.)

[LO 12-4, 12-5] 12-39 **Risk and NPV; Sensitivity Analysis** J. Morgan of SparkPlug Inc. has been approached to take over a production facility from B.R. Machine Company. The acquisition will cost $1,500,000, and the after-tax net cash inflows are expected to be $275,000 per year for 12 years.

SparkPlug currently uses 12% as its after-tax cost of capital. Tom Morgan, production manager, is very much in favor of the investment. He argues that the total after-tax net cash inflow is more than the cost of the investment, even if the demand for the product is somewhat uncertain. "The project will pay for itself even if the demand is only half the projected level." Cindy Morgan (corporate controller) believes that the cost of capital should be 15% because of the declining demand for SparkPlug products.

Required

1. What is the estimated NPV of the project if the after-tax cost of capital (discount rate) is 12%? Use the built-in NPV function in Excel; round your answer to the nearest whole dollar.

2. What is the estimated NPV of the project if the after-tax cost of capital (discount rate) is 15%? Use the built-in NPV function in Excel; round your answer to the nearest whole dollar.

3. Use the built-in function in Excel to estimate the project's IRR, rounded to 1 decimal place.

4. Use the Goal Seek function in Excel to calculate the maximum amount (rounded to the nearest whole dollar) that can be invested up front in order to generate an economic rate of return (i.e., IRR) equal to the 15% rate of return specified by management as appropriate for the proposed investment. (See the Goal Seek instructions in the Uncertainty and the Capital Budgeting Process section of this chapter.)

5. Is adjusting the discount rate or the desired rate of return an effective way to deal with risk or uncertainty?

[LO 12-4, 12-6]   12-40   **Basic Capital Budgeting Techniques**   Answer each independent question (a) through (e).

a. Project A costs $5,000 and will generate annual after-tax net cash inflows of $1,800 for five years. What is the payback period (in years, rounded to 2 decimal places) for this investment under the assumption that the cash inflows occur evenly throughout the year?

b. Project B costs $5,000 and will generate after-tax cash inflows of $500 in year 1, $1,200 in year 2, $2,000 in year 3, $2,500 in year 4, and $2,000 in year 5. What is the payback period (in years, rounded to 2 decimal places) for this investment assuming that the cash inflows occur evenly throughout the year?

c. Project C costs $5,000 and will generate net cash inflows of $2,500 before taxes each year for five years. The firm uses straight-line depreciation with no salvage value and is subject to a 25% tax rate. What is the payback period (in years, and rounded to 2 decimal places) under the assumption that all cash inflows occur evenly throughout the year?

d. Project D costs $5,000 and will generate sales of $4,000 each year for five years. The cash expenditures will be $1,500 per year. The firm uses straight-line depreciation with an estimated salvage value of $500 and has a tax rate of 25%.

   a. What is the accounting (book) rate of return based on the original investment, rounded to 2 decimal places?

   b. What is the book rate of return based on the average book value, rounded to 2 decimal places?

e. What is the NPV for each of the projects A through D? Assume that the firm requires a minimum after-tax return of 8% on all investments. Use the built-in NPV function for all calculations; round all answers to nearest whole dollar.

[LO 12-3, LO 12-4, 12-6]   12-41   **Capital Budgeting with Multiple Measures and Taxes (MACRS-Based Depreciation)**   Steadman Company is considering an investment in a new machine for an independent five-year project. The machine's cost is $500,000 with no salvage value at the end of five years. Net cash inflows from the project are expected to be $140,000 annually. Steadman would depreciate the machine using the MACRS schedule, and the machine qualifies as a five-year asset. Steadman uses a discount rate of 8%, and its tax rate is 30%.

Required

1. Determine the after-tax net income and after-tax cash flows from the investment. Refer to Exhibit 12.4 for the five-year MACRS deprecation schedule.

2. Determine the NPV of the project. Round to the nearest dollar.

3. Determine the IRR of the project. Round your answer to two decimal places.

4. Determine the payback period of the project, assuming that cash flows occur evenly in each year.

5. Determine the book (accounting) rate of return using both (a) the initial investment as the denominator and (b) the average book value of the investment as the denominator.

[LO 12-4, 12-5, 12-6]   12-42   **Straightforward Capital Budgeting with Taxes (Non-MACRS-Based Depreciation); Sensitivity Analysis**   Dorothy & George Company is planning to acquire a new machine at a total cost of $30,600. The machine's estimated life is six years and its estimated salvage value is $600. The company estimates that annual cash savings from using this machine will be $8,000. The company's after-tax cost of capital is 8%, and its income tax rate is 40%. The company uses straight-line depreciation (non-MACRS-based).

Required

1. What is this investment's net after-tax annual cash inflow, rounded to nearest whole dollar?

2. Assume that the net after-tax annual cash inflow of this investment is $5,000. What is the payback period in years, rounded to 2 decimal places (e.g., 4.418 years = 4.42 years)?

3. Assume that the net after-tax annual cash inflow of this investment is $5,000. What is the net present value (NPV) of this investment? Use the built-in NPV function; round your final answer to the nearest whole dollar.

4. What are the minimum net after-tax annual cost savings that make the proposed investment acceptable (i.e., the dollar cost savings that would yield an NPV of $0)? The present value factor for 8%, six years (Appendix C, Table 1) is 0.630; the present value annuity factor for 8%, six years (Appendix C, Table 2) is 4.623. Round final answer to the nearest whole dollar.

(CPA Adapted)

[LO 12-4, 12-5, 12-6] 12-43 **Capital Budgeting with Taxes (Non-MACRS Depreciation); Sensitivity Analysis** Gravina Company is planning to spend $6,000 for a machine that it will depreciate on a straight-line basis over 10 years with no salvage value. The machine will generate additional cash revenues of $1,200 a year. Gravina will incur no additional costs except for depreciation. Its income tax rate is 35%. The present value annuity factor for 15%, 10 years (from Appendix C, Table 2) is 5.019.

Required

1. What is the payback period of the proposed investment (in years, and rounded to 1 decimal place) under the assumption that the cash inflows occur evenly throughout the year?
2. What is the accounting (book) rate of return (ARR) based on the initial investment outlay? Round your answer to 1 decimal place (e.g., 13.571% = 13.6%).
3. What is the maximum amount that Gravina Company should invest if it desires to earn an internal rate of return (IRR) of 15%? Round your answer to the nearest whole dollar.
4. What is the minimum annual (pretax) cash revenue required for the project to earn an IRR of 15%? Round answer to the nearest whole dollar. (Use the PV annuity factor from Appendix C, Table 2 to answer this question.)
5. Prepare a single schedule to show the NPVs associated with a 10-year life under annual after-tax cash flows of $500, $1,000, and $2,000, *and* discount rates of 10%, 15%, and 20%.

(CPA Adapted)

[LO 12-3, 12-8] 12-44 **Identifying Relevant Cash Flows; Asset Replacement Decision**   Assume that it is January 1, 2022, and that the Mendoza Company is considering the replacement of a machine that has been used for the past three years in a special project for the company. This project is expected to continue for an additional five years (i.e., until the end of 2026). Mendoza will either keep the existing machine for another five years (eight years total) or replace the existing machine now with a new model that has a five-year estimated life. Pertinent facts regarding this decision are as follows:

	Keep Existing Machine	Purchase New Machine
Purchase price of machine (including transportation, setup charges, etc.)	$150,000	$190,000
Useful life (determined at time of acquisition)	8 years	5 years
Estimated salvage value, end of 2026*	$20,000	$25,000
Expected cash operating costs, per year:		
Variable (per unit produced/sold)	$0.25	$0.19
Fixed costs (total)	$25,000	$24,000
Estimated salvage (terminal) values:		
January 1, 2022	$68,000	
December 31, 2026	$12,000	$22,000
Net working capital committed at time of acquisition of existing machine (all fully recovered at end of project, December 31, 2026)	$30,000	
Incremental net working capital required if new machine is purchased on January 1, 2022 (all fully recovered at end of project, December 31, 2026)		$10,000
Expected annual volume of output/sales (in units), over the period 2022–2026	500,000	500,000

*These amounts are used for depreciation calculations.

Assume further that Mendoza is subject to a 40% income tax, for both ordinary income and gains/losses associated with disposal of machinery, and that all cash flows occur at the end of the year, except for the initial investment. Assume that straight-line depreciation is used for tax purposes and that any tax associated with the disposal of machinery occurs at the same time as the related transaction.

Required

1. Determine the relevant cash flows (after-tax) at the time of purchase of the new machine (i.e., time 0: January 1, 2022).
2. Determine the relevant (after-tax) cash inflow each year of project operation (i.e., at the end of each of years 1 through 5).
3. Determine the relevant (after-tax) cash inflow at the end of the project's life (i.e., at the project's disposal time, December 31, 2026).
4. Identify any irrelevant cost and revenue data associated with this asset replacement decision.
5. Determine the undiscounted net cash flow (after tax) for the new machine and determine whether, on this basis, the old machine should be replaced.

(CMA Adapted)

[LO 12-3, 12-4, 12-8] 12-45 **Asset-Replacement Decision; NPV Analysis** Assume a situation in which a company has an existing asset, A, that has a current net book value (original cost less accumulated depreciation to date) of $300,000. This asset has a useful life of three additional years. Its estimated disposal (sales) value both today and at the end of three years is estimated to be zero. Asset B, which would replace A, could be purchased today for $600,000. If purchased, B would generate annual (cash) operating cost savings (pretax) of $280,000 for each year of its three-year useful life. In determining depreciation deductions for tax purposes, assume the straight-line method and zero salvage value for both assets. The company is subject to a combined (federal, state, and local) income tax rate of 40%, for both operating income and gains/losses related to the sale of assets. Other than the initial outlay for asset B, assume that all cash flows (and related tax payments) occur at the end of the year. Assume a weighted-average cost of capital of 10%.

Required

1. Determine the relevant (i.e., *differential*) cash flows (after-tax) at each of the following three points related to this asset replacement decision: (1) project initiation (i.e., time 0), (2) project operation (i.e., end of years 1, 2, and 3), and (3) project disposal/termination (i.e., end of year 3).
2. What is the estimated net present value of the decision to replace asset A (the existing asset) with asset B? Use the built-in NPV function in Excel and round your final answer to the nearest whole dollar.
3. What is the weighted-average cost of capital (WACC) that would make the company indifferent between keeping or replacing asset A? Use the Goal Seek option in Excel to answer this question; round your answer to 2 decimal places (e.g., 13.418% = 13.42%.)

[LO 12-3, 12-4, 12-8] 12-46 **Machine Replacement with Tax Considerations; Spreadsheet Application; Double-Declining-Balance (DDB) Depreciation** A computer chip manufacturer spent $2,500,000 to develop a special-purpose molding machine. The machine has been used for one year and is expected to be obsolete after an additional three years. The company uses straight-line (SLN) depreciation for this machine.

At the beginning of the second year, a machine salesperson offers a new, vastly more efficient machine. This machine will cost $2,000,000, reduce annual cash manufacturing costs from $1,800,000 to $1,000,000, and have zero disposal value at the end of three years. Management has decided to use the double-declining-balance (DDB) depreciation method for tax purposes for this machine if purchased. (*Note:* Make sure to switch to SLN depreciation in year 3 to ensure that the entire cost of the asset is written off. You may find it useful to use the VDB function in Excel to calculate depreciation charges.)

The old machine's salvage value is $300,000 now and is expected to be $50,000 three years from now; however, no salvage value is provided in calculating straight-line (SLN) depreciation on the old machine for tax purposes. The firm's income tax rate is 45%. The firm desires to earn a minimum after-tax rate of return of 8%.

Required

1. What is the present value (rounded to the nearest whole dollar) of tax savings associated with depreciating the existing machine (using the straight-line method)?
2. What is the present value (rounded to the nearest whole dollar) of tax savings associated with depreciating the new machine using the double-declining-balance method? Use the VDB built-in function in Excel to calculate depreciation deductions.
3. What is the present value of net after-tax cost associated with the existing machine? Round your answer to the nearest whole dollar. (*Hint:* There will be three items to consider.)
4. What is the present value (rounded to the nearest whole dollar) of the net after-tax cost of using the replacement (new) machine?
5. What is the estimated net present value (NPV) of the decision to replace the existing machine with the new machine. Round your final answer to the nearest whole dollar.

(*Note:* Use the PV and NPV functions in Excel to calculate all present value amounts.)

[LO 12-3, LO 12-4, 12-8]

12-47 **Equipment Replacement Decision; MACRS Depreciation** VacuTech manufactures sophisticated instruments for testing microcircuits. Each instrument sells for $3,500; variable manufacturing cost per unit (all cash) equals $2,450. An essential component of the company's manufacturing process is a sealed vacuum chamber where the interior approaches a pure vacuum. The technology of the vacuum pumps that the firm uses to prepare its chamber for sealing has been changing rapidly. On June 1, 2018, VacuTech bought the latest in electronic high-speed vacuum pumps that can evacuate a chamber for sealing in only six hours. The company paid $400,000 for the pump. Recently, the pump's manufacturer approached VacuTech with a new pump that would reduce the evacuation time to two hours.

VacuTech's management is considering the purchase of this new pump and has asked Doreen Harris, the company controller, to evaluate the financial impact of replacing the existing pump with the new model. Doreen has gathered the following information prior to preparing her analysis:

- The new pump could be installed and placed in service on January 1, 2022. The pump's cost is $608,000; installing, testing, and debugging the machine will cost $12,000 (which should be capitalized). The pump would be assigned to the three-year class for depreciation under the Modified Accelerated Cost Recovery System (MACRS) and is expected to have an $80,000 salvage value when it is sold at the end of four years. Depreciation on the equipment would be recognized starting in 2022, and MACRS rates (rounded) would be as follows:

Year 1	33%
Year 2	45
Year 3	15
Year 4	7

- The current pump is being depreciated under MACRS and will be fully depreciated by the time the new pump is placed in service. If the firm purchases the new pump, it will sell the current pump for a net price of $50,000.
- At the current rate of production, the new pump's greater efficiency will result in annual pretax cash savings of $125,000.
- VacuTech is able to sell all testing instruments that it can produce. Because of the new pump's increased speed, output is expected to increase by 30 units in 2022, 50 units in both 2023 and 2024, and 70 units in 2025. Cash-based manufacturing costs for all additional units would be reduced by $150 per unit (in addition to the $125,000 savings noted above).
- VacuTech is subject to a 40% income tax rate. For evaluating capital investment proposals, management assumes that annual cash flows occur at the end of the year and uses a 15% after-tax discount rate.

Required

1. Determine whether VacuTech should purchase the new pump by calculating the net present value (NPV) at January 1, 2022, of the estimated after-tax cash flows that would result from its acquisition. (Use the built-in NPV function in Excel to estimate the NPV of the proposed investment.) Round final answer to the nearest whole dollar.

2. Describe the factors, other than the net present value, that VacuTech should consider before making the pump replacement decision.

(CMA Adapted)

[LO 12-4, 12-9]

12-48 **Comparing Mutually Exclusive Projects; Uneven Cash Flows; Strategy** Gunnell Inc. is considering two mutually exclusive 10-year investments. The initial cash outlays and expected net after-tax cash flows are shown below.

	Project 1	Project 2
Initial	$ (2,500,000)	$ (1,800,000)
Year 1	200,000	400,000
Year 2	200,000	375,000
Year 3	235,000	350,000
Year 4	280,000	350,000
Year 5	325,000	325,000
Year 6	450,000	200,000
Year 7	500,000	185,000
Year 8	600,000	170,000
Year 9	700,000	160,000
Year 10	900,000	130,000

Required

1. Calculate the NPV and IRR of each project. Assume Gunnell Inc. uses a discount rate of 8%. Round your NPV answer to the nearest dollar and your IRR answer to two decimal points.

2. Which project would you recommend to Gunnell management? Are there strategic or risk factors that might lead you to recommend the project with the lower NPV? Explain with specific evidence.

Problems

[LO 12-4, 12-6]   **12-49   Basic Capital Budgeting Techniques; No Taxes, Uniform Net Cash Inflows; Spreadsheets**   Bob Jensen Inc. purchased a $650,000 machine to manufacture specialty taps for electrical equipment. Jensen expects to sell all it can manufacture in the next 10 years. To encourage capital investments, the government has exempted taxes on profits from new investments. This legislation is to be in effect for the foreseeable future. The machine is expected to have a 10-year useful life with no salvage value. Jensen uses straight-line depreciation. The net cash inflow is expected to be $150,000 each year for 10 years. Jensen uses a 12% discount rate in evaluating capital investments. Assume, for simplicity, that MACRS depreciation rules do not apply.

Required   Using Excel (including built-in functions for NPV, IRR, and MIRR), compute the following for the above-referenced investment:

1. The payback period, under the assumption that cash inflows occur evenly throughout the year. Round your answer to 1 decimal place (e.g., 4.581 years = 4.6 years).

2. The accounting (book) rate of return based on (a) initial investment and (b) average investment. Round both answers to 1 decimal place (e.g., 23.418% = 23.4%).

3. The net present value (NPV) of the proposed investment under the assumption that cash inflows occur at year-end. Round your answer to nearest whole dollar.

4. The present value payback period, in years, of the proposed investment under the assumption that cash inflows occur evenly throughout the year. (*Note:* Because of this assumption, the present value calculations will be approximate, not exact.) To calculate present value amounts, use the appropriate factors from Appendix C, Table 1. Round your answer to 1 decimal place. For example, 3.481 years = 3.5 years.

5. The internal rate of return (IRR), rounded to 1 decimal place (e.g., 13.612% = 13.6%).

6. The modified internal rate of return (MIRR), rounded to 1 decimal place. (In conjunction with this requirement, you might want to consult either of the following two references: https://support.office.com/en-us/Search/results?query=mirr+function&src=as and/or www.journalofaccountancy.com/issues/2017/feb/calculate-internal-rate-of-return-in-excel.html.)

[LO 12-4, 12-6]   **12-50   Basic Capital Budgeting Techniques; Uneven Net Cash Inflows with Taxes; Spreadsheet Application**   Use the same information for this problem as you did for Problem 12-49, except that the discount rate is 10% (not 12%), the investment is subject to taxes, and the projected pretax operating cash inflows are as follows:

Year	Pretax Cash Inflow	Year	Pretax Cash Inflow
1	$ 65,000	6	$300,000
2	80,000	7	270,000
3	120,000	8	240,000
4	200,000	9	120,000
5	240,000	10	80,000

Jensen has been paying 25% for combined federal, state, and local income taxes, a rate that is not expected to change during the period of this investment. The firm uses straight-line depreciation. Assume, for simplicity, that MACRS depreciation rules do not apply.

Required   Using Excel, compute the following for the proposed investment:

1. The payback period (in years), under the assumption that the cash inflows occur evenly throughout the year. Round your answer to 1 decimal place.

2. The accounting (book) rate of return based on (a) initial investment and (b) average investment. Round both answers to 1 decimal place (e.g., 13.417% = 13.4%).

3. The net present value (NPV), rounded to the nearest whole dollar.

4. The present value payback period of the proposed investment under the assumption that the cash inflows occur evenly throughout the year. (*Note:* Use the formula at the bottom of Appendix C, Table 1 to calculate present value factors.)

5. The internal rate of return (IRR), rounded to 1 decimal place (e.g., 5.491% = 5.5%).

6. The modified internal rate of return (MIRR), rounded to 1 decimal place. (In conjunction with this requirement, you might want to consult either of the following two references: https://support.office.com/en-us/Search/results?query=mirr+function&src=as and/or www.journalofaccountancy.com/issues/2017/feb/calculate-internal-rate-of-return-in-excel.html.)

[LO 12-4, 12-6] **12-51 Basic Capital Budgeting Techniques; Uneven Net Cash Inflows; Taxes; MACRS Depreciation**
Use the data in Problem 12-50 for Bob Jensen Inc. and MACRS. The asset qualifies as a five-year property.

Required Compute the following for the proposed investment:

1. Its payback period (in years) under the assumption that the cash inflows occur evenly throughout the year. Round your answer to 1 decimal place (e.g., 4.341 years = 4.3 years).

2. Its accounting (book) rate of return based on (a) the initial investment and (b) an average investment (calculated here as a simple average of the 10 average annual book values; for each year, the average book value is the sum of the beginning-of-year and end-of-year book values, divided by two; note: the average book value for each of the last four years is $0). Round both answers to 1 decimal place (e.g., 13.417% = 13.4%).

3. Its estimated net present value (NPV). Use the built-in NPV function in Excel; round your answer to the nearest whole dollar.

4. Its internal rate of return (IRR). Use the built-in IRR function in Excel; round your answer to 1 decimal place (e.g., 5.491% = 5.5%).

5. Its modified internal rate of return (MIRR), rounded to 1 decimal place. (In conjunction with this question, you might want to consult either of the following two references: https://support.office.com/en-us/Search/results?query=mirr+function&src=as and/or www.journalofaccountancy.com/issues/2017/feb/calculate-internal-rate-of-return-in-excel.html.)

[LO 12-4, 12-5] **12-52 Real Options—Basic Concepts** This problem pertains to the XYZ Company example in the body of the chapter and the associated discussion of real options.

Required

1. Define the term *real option.* Provide an example of each of the four common types of real options.

2. Define the terms *put option* and *call option.* Which of the four common types of real options are similar to put options? Which are similar to call options?

3. Based on the stated probabilities for the individual states of nature (i.e., level of consumer demand):
   a. What is the expected value each year (1, 2, 3) for the after-tax cash inflows associated with the proposed investment, without considering the investment delay option? As in Exhibit 12.7, express data in millions of dollars ($ millions). Round answers to 2 decimal places.
   b. What is the estimated NPV of the proposed investment, without considering the investment delay option? Do *not* express data in millions of dollars ($ millions) (i.e., use raw numbers). Round your answer to the nearest dollar.

4. We see from Panel B of Exhibit 12.7 that XYZ should invest in the project only if the revealed level of consumer demand was high or medium. Show calculations as to why no investment should be made if the revealed level of demand (in period 1) was low.

5. In Panel B of Exhibit 12.7, show for each of the three scenarios (levels of market demand) the calculation for the present value (at $t = 0$) of cash outflows (cells H20:H22) (at the risk-free rate), the present value of cash inflows (cells I20:I22) (at the indicated discount rate), and the weighted net present value amounts @ time 0 (cells J20:J22).

6. What is the interpretation of the expected NPV of the project (i.e., a positive $12.951 million)?

[LO 12-4, 12-5] **12-53 Real Options and Sensitivity Analysis** Refer to the XYZ Company example in the chapter and the results in Panels A and B of Exhibit 12.7. On the basis of this information, management of the company has decided to delay the implementation of the project for one year. Those managers are now interested in knowing how sensitive this decision is with respect to the assumptions they've made regarding the basic analysis. Therefore, they have asked you to prepare some supplementary analyses regarding Panel B of Exhibit 12.7.

Required

1. Holding everything else constant, what is the expected NPV of the decision if the probabilities for the three scenarios are as follows: high (20%), medium (50%), and low (30%)? (Express amounts in millions of dollars; round expected NPV result to 3 decimal places.)

2. Holding everything else constant, what is the expected NPV of the decision if the probabilities for the three scenarios are as follows: high (30%), medium (40%), and low (30%)? (Express amounts in millions of dollars; round expected NPV result to 3 decimal places.)

3. Prepare a 5 × 3 table containing the estimated NPV of the decision to delay for each combination of the following: risk-free rate of interest (4%, 5%, 6%) and weighted-average cost of capital (13%, 14%, 15%, 16%, and 17%). For example, one cell in your table would be the estimated NPV of the project if the risk-free rate of interest is 4% and the weighted-average cost of capital is 13%. (Express data inputs in millions of dollars; round expected NPV results in your 5 × 3 table to 2 decimal places.) What does your analysis suggest?

[LO 12-4, 12-5]   **12-54 Real Options—the Option to Abandon a Project**   You and several of your classmates have just graduated from college and are evaluating various investment opportunities, including a startup company that would produce high-quality jackets embroidered with a college logo. If demand for this customized product is high, you expect to sell approximately 100,000 units per year, at a price per unit of $80. On the other hand, because of stiff competition in the field, a pessimistic estimate is that demand for your new product would be only 40,000 units per year at a selling price of $70. Anticipated variable costs per jacket amount to $40. Capacity-related (i.e., short-term fixed) costs other than the cost of manufacturing equipment are thought to be negligible. Manufacturing equipment (with a 10-year life, a cost of $12 million, and a zero salvage value) would have to be purchased as part of this project. Assume that, for income tax purposes, your company will use straight-line depreciation over the life of the proposed investment. Your anticipated income tax bracket for this endeavor is $33\frac{1}{3}$%. You are unsure of what discount rate to use for capital budgeting purposes, but you believe the appropriate rate is somewhere between 10% and 14% on an after-tax basis.

Required
1. What is the anticipated after-tax cash flow for this investment for each of the two possible states of nature/scenarios? Round both answers to the nearest whole dollar.

2. Under the assumption that the two scenarios (level of product demand) are equally likely, what is the expected NPV of the proposed investment, rounded to the nearest whole dollar? Assume a discount rate of 12%. Based on the amount you estimated, should you invest in the project?

3. How sensitive is your decision to the assumption regarding the discount rate? To answer this question, prepare an estimated NPV for the proposed project using discount rates, in 1% increments, from 10% to 14%. (Round all answers to the nearest whole dollar.) Is the decision to accept or reject the investment sensitive to the discount rate used in the calculation of NPV?

4. Suppose your company could abandon the project and dispose of the manufacturing equipment for $10.4 million if demand for your product turns out to be weak. You and your colleagues would make this decision at the end of the first year of operations. What is the expected NPV of the proposed project, with the abandonment option? (Use a discount rate of 12%; round your final answer to nearest whole dollar.) Comment on the value of the abandonment option in this example.

[LO 12-1, 12-4, 12-8]   **12-55 Equipment Replacement and Strategic Considerations**   The management of Devine Instrument Company is considering the purchase of a new drilling machine, model RoboDril 1010K. According to the specifications and testing results, RoboDril will substantially increase productivity over AccuDril X10, the machine Devine is currently using.

The AccuDril was acquired eight years ago for $120,000 and is being depreciated using the straight-line method over a 10-year expected life and an estimated salvage value of $20,000. The engineering department expects the AccuDril to keep going for another three years after a major overhaul at the end of its expected useful life. The estimated cost for the overhaul is $100,000. The overhauled machine will be depreciated using straight-line depreciation with no salvage value. The overhaul will improve the machine's operating efficiency approximately 20% for each of years 3, 4, and 5. No other operating conditions will be affected by the overhaul.

RoboDril 1010K is selling for $250,000. Installing, testing, rearranging, and training will cost another $30,000. The manufacturer is willing to take the AccuDril as a trade-in for $40,000. The RoboDril will be depreciated using the straight-line method with no salvage value. New technology most likely will make RoboDril obsolete to the firm in five years.

Variable operating cost for either machine is the same: $10 per machine hour (cash-based). Other pertinent data follow:

	AccuDril X10	RoboDril 1010K
Units of output (per year)	10,000	10,000
Machine hours	8,000	4,000
Selling price per unit	$100	$100
Variable manufacturing cost—cash-based (not including machine hours)	$40	$40
Other annual expenses (tooling and supervising)	$95,000	$55,000
Disposal value—today	$25,000	
Disposal value—in 5 years	$0	$50,000

Devine Instrument Company's weighted-average cost of capital (WACC) is 12%, and it is in the 40% tax bracket. Use the PV factors (Appendix C, Table 1) for calculating the NPV of each decision alternative.

Required

1. Determine for each of years 0 though 5 (inclusive) the after-tax cash flows for items that differ between the two alternatives. Express all cash flow amounts in thousands (000s); round individual amounts to 1 decimal place.

2. Compute the payback period (in years) for purchasing RoboDril 1010K rather than having AccuDril X10 overhauled in two years. Assume for this calculation only that all cash flows (other than those related to the net acquisition cost of the replacement asset)—including tax effects—occur evenly throughout the year. Round your answer to 1 decimal place (e.g., 2.812 years = 2.8 years).

3. Using results generated in requirement 1, what is the present value of each decision alternative, keep vs. replace? State all cash flows in thousands (000s); round each of your two answers to 1 decimal place. (Use the built-in NPV function in Excel to calculate present values.)

4. What other factors, including strategic issues, should the firm consider before making a final decision?

[LO 12-5, 12-8] 12-56 **Sensitivity Analysis; Spreadsheets** Use the information in Problem 12-55 to answer the following questions (for calculations below, do NOT round data to 000s—use raw data).

Required

1. What would the maximum machine annual operating cost of the overhauled AccuDril need to be (before tax) in order for the replacement decision to be an incorrect financial decision? (Use the appropriate PV factors and/or PV annuity factor from Appendix C to answer this question.) Round final answer to the nearest whole dollar.

2. Use the Goal Seek function in Excel to determine what the maximum amount of annual after-tax operating costs for the new machine must be in order to change the decision. (*Hint:* Set up a spreadsheet to calculate the PV of after-tax cash flows for each alternative. Use the built-in functions in Excel, NPV and/or PV, to determine the present values of these cash flows.) State final answer to nearest whole dollar.

3. New technologies make it possible to overhaul this machine now for $80,000. Both the overhaul cost and the undepreciated cost (book value) of the existing asset are to be depreciated over two years. The overhaul will improve the machine's productivity by 20% and reduce the cost of a major overhaul two years from now to $30,000. All overhaul costs will be depreciated using the straight-line method. With either overhaul, the machine will have no salvage value. Either overhaul can be scheduled during regular maintenance and will not affect production. Despite the old saying, "If it ain't broke, don't fix it," should you overhaul it now or wait for two years to do the overhaul as planned originally, assuming that no funds are currently available to purchase RoboDril 1010K? (Use the built-in functions PV and/or NPV for your present value calculations. Round your answer (NPV) to the nearest whole dollar.)

4. Performing the overhaul now also improves product quality. Management believes that the quality improvement is rather subtle and very difficult to quantify. Should the firm overhaul now?

[LO 12-1, 12-4, 12-5, 12-6] 12-57 **Comparison of Capital Budgeting Techniques; Sensitivity Analysis; Strategy** Rob Roy Corporation has been using its present facilities at its annual full capacity of 10,000 units for the last three years. Still, the company is unable to keep pace with continuing demand for the product that is estimated to be 25,000 units annually. This demand level is expected to continue for at least another four years. To expand manufacturing capacity and take advantage of the demand, Rob Roy must acquire equipment costing $1,000,000. The equipment will double the current production quantity. This equipment has a useful life of 10 years and can be sold for $200,000 at the end of year 4 or $30,000 at the end of year 10. Analysis of current operating data provides the following information:

			Per Unit
Sales price			$200
Variable costs:			
Manufacturing	$97		
Marketing	10	$107	
Fixed costs:			
Manufacturing	$45		
Other	25	70	177
Pretax operating income			$ 23

The fixed costs include depreciation expense of the current equipment. The new equipment will not change variable costs, but the firm will incur additional fixed manufacturing costs (excluding depreciation on the new machine) of $250,000 annually. The firm needs to spend an additional $200,000 in fixed marketing costs per year for additional sales. Rob Roy is in the 35% tax bracket. Management has set a minimum rate of return of 14% after-tax for all capital investments. Assume, for simplicity, that MACRS depreciation rules do *not* apply.

Required

1. Assume that the equipment will be depreciated over a four-year period using the straight-line method. What effects will the new equipment have on after-tax operating income in each of the four years?

2. What effect will the new equipment have on after-tax cash inflows in each of the four years?

3. Compute the proposed investment's payback period (in years) under the assumption that after-tax cash inflows occur evenly throughout the year. Round your answer to 2 decimal places (e.g., 14.816% = 14.82%).

4. Compute the accounting (book) rate of return (ARR) based on the average investment. Round your answer to 2 decimal places.

5. Compute the net present value (NPV) of the proposed investment. (Use the built-in function in Excel (NPV). Round your answer to nearest whole dollar.)

6. Compute the internal rate of return (IRR) of the proposed investment using the built-in IRR function in Excel. Round your answer to 2 decimal places.

7. Compute the modified internal rate of return (MIRR) of the proposed investment using the built-in MIRR function in Excel. Round your answer to 2 decimal places. (In responding to this requirement, you might find the following resource to be helpful: **www.journalofaccountancy.com/issues/2017/feb/calculate-internal-rate-of-return-in-excel.html.**)

8. Management has decided to invest in the new equipment but is unsure of the reliability of some of the estimates and as such has asked some "what-if" questions. Treat each of the following two cases independently.

   a. By how much can the unit variable cost for units produced by the new equipment increase and still justify the purchase of the equipment (i.e., have the investment generate an after-tax IRR of exactly 14%, its cost of capital)? Round your answer to 2 decimal places. (*Hint:* The present value annuity factor from Appendix C, Table 2 for four years, 14% is 2.914.)

   b. The company is anticipating an increase in competition. Management believes that, in response, it will have to reduce the selling price of the product. By how much can the firm decrease the per-unit selling price (for all units sold) and still be able to justify the purchase of the new equipment? Round your answer to 2 decimal places. What percentage decrease in selling price (rounded to 2 decimal places) does this represent?

9. What strategic considerations and other factors might bear on this investment decision? How can such considerations be dealt with formally in the planning and decision-making process?

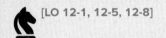

[LO 12-1, 12-5, 12-8] 12-58 **Sensitivity Analysis; Equipment-Replacement Decision**   The Mendoza Company discussed in the chapter is now considering replacing a piece of equipment that the company uses to monitor the integrity of metal pipes used for deep-sea drilling purposes. The company's pretax WACC (discount rate) is estimated as 10%. The following data are pertinent to the question you've been asked to analyze:

	Existing Asset	Replacement
Annual (pretax) variable operating expenses	$200,000	(?)
Current purchase price	N/A	$500,000
Current salvage value of existing asset	$ 40,000	N/A
Current book value of existing asset	$ 60,000	N/A
Expected useful life (years)	6	6
Expected salvage value, end of year 6	$ 10,000	$100,000

Required

1. What is the maximum amount of annual variable operating expenses, pretax, that would make this an attractive investment from a present-value standpoint? In answering this question, use the appropriate PV factor(s) from Appendix C, Table 1 and the appropriate PV annuity factor from Appendix C, Table 2. Round your answer to the nearest whole dollar.

2. Assume now that the company expects, over the coming six years, to be subject to a combined income tax rate of 35%, including any gain/loss realized on the sale of the existing equipment. Assume that the current net book value of the existing asset is $60,000 and that the after-tax WACC (discount rate) for

Mendoza is 8.0%. Finally, assume that the company will use straight-line depreciation, with no salvage value, for income tax purposes. In this situation, what is the maximum amount of variable operating costs (on both a pretax and an after-tax basis) that can be incurred in order to make the proposed purchase attractive in a present-value sense? In answering this question, use the appropriate PV annuity factor from Appendix C, Table 2. Round both answers to the nearest whole dollar.

3. What strategic considerations might affect the decision whether to invest in this new equipment?

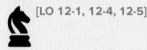

[LO 12-1, 12-4, 12-5]   12-59   **Present Value Analysis; Sensitivity Analysis; Spreadsheet Application**   Because of increased consumer demand for fuel-efficient, alternative-energy automobiles, Global Auto Company is considering investing in a new hybrid crossover vehicle. Development costs each year for a two-year period for this new vehicle are estimated as $750 million. Tooling and other setup costs in year 2 are estimated at $1 billion. Actual production and sales are estimated to begin in year 3. It is anticipated that the plant being envisioned could produce vehicles for six years. Each vehicle sold is estimated to provide $3,500 of net cash flow (pretax). The estimated salvage value of the manufacturing plant after six years of operation is thought to be $250 million. Assume that all cash flows take place at year-end and that the pretax WACC (discount rate) for Global Auto is 15%. Income tax effects can be ignored in this problem.

Required

1. What minimum volume of car sales (per year, in the six-year life of the plant) is needed to make this proposed investment acceptable using NPV as the decision criterion? Round your answer to the nearest whole number. (*Note:* For calculating present values of after-tax cash flows, use the following formula rather than the PV factors presented in Table 1 in Appendix C: $PV_i = 1 \div (1 + r)^i$, where r = discount rate (WACC) and i (year) = 1–8. Also, use the Goal Seek function in Excel to answer this question.)

2. How does your answer in requirement 1 change if the company's pretax WACC is 16%? 14%? (In each case, round your answer to the nearest whole number.) Do you think the estimated NPV of this project is sensitive to the estimate of the company's discount rate? Explain.

3. What strategic considerations, including those related to risk management, would likely bear on this decision?

[LO 12-1, 12-4, 12-5]   12-60   **MACRS Depreciation and Capital Budgeting Analysis; Spreadsheet Application; Sensitivity Analysis**   You and your spouse have recently inherited money from a distant relative and are considering a number of investment opportunities, one of which would involve residential real estate. Specifically, you have an opportunity to purchase an apartment complex with 25 rental units. The total price for these units, including sales commission expense, is estimated as $500,000. You estimate that to make each unit suitable for renting, average remodeling costs of $20,000 per unit would be needed. Fifteen of the units have a single bedroom and rent for $500 per month; the remaining units contain two bedrooms and rent for $650 per month. A friend of yours who is in the business suggests that ordinary maintenance and repair costs be budgeted, annually, at 16% of rental revenue. Both the purchase price of the units and the remodeling costs qualify as 27.5-year MACRS property.

In terms of calculating depreciation expense for tax purposes, you can assume that MACRS-based deductions for the first 27 years will be the same; in year 28, one-half year of depreciation will be deducted. The present value of MACRS-based depreciation deductions can be found by multiplying the following three items: depreciable cost of the asset, tax rate (t), and PV depreciation factor (which you must calculate—-see below for calculated amounts).

If the remodeling is undertaken and annual maintenance is done as scheduled, the investment should last at least 30 years. The estimated net salvage value of the investment 30 years from now is $0.

Assume, initially, an opportunity cost of capital of 10% for purposes of evaluating this investment proposal. You and your spouse feel that your combined income tax rate for the foreseeable future would be approximately 40%.

Required

1. What is the estimated NPV of this proposed investment, rounded to the nearest whole dollar? (*Hints:* As noted above, at a discount rate of 10%, the present value of MACRS-based depreciation deductions for 27.5-year property is equal to the product of the tax rate [t], the initial investment outlay, and 0.33588. For other present value calculations, use the appropriate present value annuity factor for 10%, 30 years found in Appendix C, Table 2 [that is, 9.427].)

2. What would the estimated NPV (rounded to the nearest whole dollar) be if the discount rate were 8% rather than 10%? (*Hint:* The present value of MACRS-based depreciation deductions for the property in question equals the product of the tax rate [t], the depreciable cost of the asset, and 0.39851.) The present value annuity factor for 8%, 30 years (Appendix C, Table 2) is 11.258.

3. What would the estimated NPV (rounded to the nearest whole dollar) be if the discount rate were 12% rather than 10%? (*Hint:* The present value of MACRS-based depreciation deductions for the property in question equals the product of the tax rate [*t*], the depreciable cost of the asset, and 0.28828.) The present value annuity factor for 12%, 30 years (Appendix C, Table 2) is 8.055.

4. What additional factors might you have to consider before investing in this apartment complex?

[LO 12-4, 12-5]   12-61   **Environmental Cost Management**   Myers Manufacturing Inc. wants to build a booth for painting the boxes it makes for small transformers used to power neon signs. The company can choose either a solvent-based or a powder-based paint process. The following table summarizes the costs and investment required by each approach:

	Solvent-Paint Process	Powder-Paint Process
Initial investment	$400,000	$1,200,000
Unit paint cost	$0.19	$0.20
Estimated life in years	10	10
Annual units	2,000,000	2,000,000

The firm will incur additional environmental costs with the solvent-paint process but not with the powder-paint process. The firm estimates annual environmental costs for the solvent-paint process as follows:

	Units	Unit Cost
Monthly pit cleaning	12	$ 1,000
Hazardous waste disposal	183	3,000
Superfund fee	18,690	0.17
Worker training	2	1,500
Insurance	1	10,000
Amortization of air-emission permit	0.2	1,000
Air-emission fee	44.6	25
Recordkeeping	0.25	45,000
Wastewater treatment	1	50,000

The firm estimates its after-tax cost of capital to be 12%. Either system is a 10-year property under MACRS (see text Exhibit 12.4). The firm pays a total of 40% in income taxes.

Required

1. What is the total cost, in present value terms, of the solvent-paint process? Use the built-in NPV function in Excel, and round final answer to nearest whole dollar.

2. What is the total cost, in present value terms, of the powder-paint process? Use the built-in NPV function in Excel, and round final answer to nearest whole dollar.

3. What is the most the firm should be willing to pay for the powder-based process? Round your answer to the nearest whole number.

(Adapted from German Böer, Margaret Curtin, and Louis Hoyt, "Environmental Cost Management," *Management Accounting,* September 1998, pp. 28–38.)

[LO 12-9]   12-62   **The Potential for Multiple IRRs**   A proposed investment has the following projected after-tax cash flows over its three-year life:

Initial outlay (time 0) = ($1,000)

End of year 1 = $2,000

End of year 2 = $2,000

End of year 3 = ($3,700)

Required

1. In a capital budgeting context, explain the difference between a normal and a non-normal cash flow pattern. What is the importance of this distinction for estimating the internal rate of return (IRR) of a proposed investment?

2. For the proposed investment project just described, how many IRRs will there be? Why?

3. Use Excel to prepare a graph of the net present value (NPV) profile of the proposed investment described herein. On the *X*-axis, show discount rates from 0% to 120%, in increments of 5%. On the *Y*-axis, show the estimated NPV of the project for each of the specified discount rates. (Use the built-in NPV function in Excel to estimate the NPVs.) Based on a visual examination of the graph, what are the two estimated IRRs for the proposed investment?

4. Use the built-in IRR function in Excel to estimate each of the two IRRs for the proposed investment. You will have to do this twice, once for each solution. In using the IRR function, choose a "guess" (initial estimate) percentage close to the X-intercepts depicted in the graph prepared in requirement 3. (If you omit the initial estimate, the default value used by Excel is 10%.) Round your answers to 2 decimal places.

5. What are the primary implications of the preceding analyses, in terms of the capital budgeting process?

[LO 12-9] 12-63 **Comparison of NPV and IRR: The Case of Mutually Exclusive Projects** Estimated cash-flow data for each of two projects, A and B, and the discount rate, *r*, to be used for the analysis of capital investment projects are given below:

Year	Project A	Project B
0	($10,000)	($10,000)
1	$7,000	$2,000
2	$3,000	$3,000
3	$2,000	$4,000
4	$2,000	$6,000

Discount rate, $r = 10.0\%$.

Required

1. In a capital budgeting context, explain the difference between independent and mutually exclusive investments. Give an example of each type of investment project. What is the primary implication of this distinction for the analysis of capital investment projects?

2. Use the built-in functions in Excel to calculate the IRR and the NPV for each investment project. Which of these projects—if either—should be accepted if they are considered independent projects? Round IRRs to 2 decimal places and NPVs to the nearest whole dollar.

3. An NPV profile for a project is a plot of the project's NPV as a function of the discount rate, *r*, used to determine NPV. Use Excel to prepare a single chart (graph) containing the NPV profile for the two projects, A and B. To generate the plot, use the following values for *r*: 0%, 4%, 8%, 12%, 16%, and 20%. Interpret each of the following points on your chart: the Y-intercepts; the point at which the two NPV profiles cross each other (defined as the crossover rate); and the X-intercepts.

4. Of what interpretive value is the chart (graph) you prepared in requirement 3? (*Hint:* Link the discussion to the situation where projects A and B are mutually exclusive rather than independent. If you could choose only one of these two projects, which would you choose, if either?)

5. What is the primary implication (i.e., take-away) from the preceding analyses, in terms of the capital budgeting process?

[LO 12-4, 12-5] 12-64 **NPV Analysis; Sensitivity Analysis; Data Tables in Excel** This assignment is designed to introduce you to the preparation of both a one-variable and a two-variable Data Table in Excel. Such tables are useful for conducting and reporting the results of a series of what-if analyses. Assume that a hypothetical five-year investment would require a net investment outlay of $350,000 and would have annual (after-tax) cash inflows of $100,000. Assume, too, that the company considering this investment uses a 10% discount rate (weighted-average cost of capital) for present-value calculations.

Required

1. Consult the specified online help file (Microsoft website) regarding the preparation of Data Tables. (See footnote 18.)

2. Prepare a one-variable Data Table where you depict the NPV of the proposed investment at each of the following discount rates: 8% to 12%, in increments of 0.5%. Round your answers to nearest whole dollar.

3. Prepare a two-variable Data Table where, in addition to the 10 discount rates assumed in requirement 2, you want to consider three possible levels of after-tax cash inflows per year: $90,000, $100,000, and $110,000. (Thus, your table will include 10 × 3 = 30 cells.) Round your answers to nearest whole dollar.

Solution to Self-Study Problem

Capital Budgeting for Expanding Productive Capacity

1. Net initial investment outlay, time 0:

Purchase price of the new equipment	$580,000
Installation, testing, and training	12,000
Capitalized renovation costs for the leased warehouse	58,000
Net initial investment outlay, time 0	$650,000

2. Effect of the acquisition on total after-tax operating profit, years 1 through 4:

Incremental sales (15,000 − 10,000)	$200 × 5,000		$1,000,000
Cost of goods sold:			
Variable manufacturing costs	$ 60 × 5,000	$300,000	
Additional fixed manufacturing overhead($140,000 + $10,000)		150,000	
Depreciation on new equipment (SL basis) ($650,000 − $50,000) ÷ 4 years*		150,000	600,000
Gross margin			$ 400,000
Marketing and administrative expenses:			
Variable marketing expenses	$ 20 × 5,000	$100,000	
Additional fixed marketing expenses		100,000	200,000
Incremental operating profit before tax			$ 200,000
Less: Income taxes (@40%)			80,000
Incremental after-tax operating profit, each of years 1 through 3			$ 120,000
The company can expect its after-tax operating profit in year 4 to increase by $108,000, as follows:			
Net operating income before restoration expenses (see above)			$ 120,000
Less: After-tax restoration expenses:			
Restoration expenses		$ 20,000	
Less: Income tax savings on restoration expenses (@40%)		8,000	12,000
Incremental after-tax operating profit, year 4			$ 108,000

*Unlike the example in the body of the chapter, we are assuming here that for tax purposes, the depreciable cost of the asset is equal to cost less estimated salvage value, an assumption that may or may not comport with current tax law.

3. The incremental after-tax cash inflow is anticipated to be $270,000 for each of the first three years and $308,000 in year 4, as follows:

	Years 1–3	Year 4
Incremental after-tax operating profit (see part 2)	$120,000	$108,000
Add: Noncash expenses included in determination of after-tax operating profit: depreciation expense	150,000	150,000
Add: After-tax cash inflow from disposal of equipment	-0-	50,000*
Incremental after-tax cash inflows	$270,000	$308,000

*Sales (salvage) value equals net book value (NBV) of the asset. Therefore, there is no tax-related gain or loss on the transaction.

4. The (unadjusted) payback period for this investment (under the assumption that cash inflows occur evenly throughout the year) is approximately 2.41 years, as follows:

$$\text{Payback period} = \text{Initial investment} \div \text{Annual cash inflow after-tax}$$
$$= \$650,000 \div \$270,000 = 2.41 \text{ years (rounded), or 2 years and 5 months}$$

5. The accounting (book) rate of return (ARR), based on average investment, is approximately 33.43%, as follows:

$$\text{Average net operating income} = [(\$120,000 \times 3) + \$108,000] \div 4 \text{ years} = \$117,000 \text{ per year}$$
$$\text{Average investment} = (\text{Book value beginning of year 1} + \text{Book value at end of year 4}) \div 2$$
$$= (\$650,000 + \$50,000) \div 2 = \$350,000$$
$$\text{Accounting rate of return (ARR)} = \$117,000 \div \$350,000 = 33.43\%$$

6. The net present value (NPV) of the proposed investment, at a 12% discount rate, is $194,428 (rounded to nearest whole dollar), as follows (under the assumption that cash inflows occur at year-end):

PV of after-tax cash inflows, years 1 through 3, at 12%:	
$270,000 × 2.402 =	$648,540
PV of after-tax cash inflow, year 4: $308,000 × 0.636 =	195,888
Total PV of after-tax cash inflows	$844,428
Net initial investment outlay (i.e., year 0)	650,000
NPV	$194,428

Alternative Solutions: Using an Excel Spreadsheet

Two Excel-based solutions are possible, as reflected in the screenshot below:

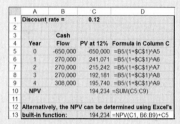

	A	B	C	D
1	Discount rate =		0.12	
2				
3		Cash		
4	Year	Flow	PV at 12%	Formula in Column C
5	0	-650,000	-650,000	=B5/(1+$C$1)^A5
6	1	270,000	241,071	=B5/(1+$C$1)^A6
7	2	270,000	215,242	=B5/(1+$C$1)^A7
8	3	270,000	192,181	=B5/(1+$C$1)^A8
9	4	308,000	195,740	=B5/(1+$C$1)^A9
10	NPV		194,234	=SUM(C5:C9)
11				
12	Alternatively, the NPV can be determined using Excel's			
13	built-in function:		194,234	=NPV(C1, B6:B9)+C5

Source: Microsoft Excel

The first of the above-two solutions uses the formula presented at the bottom of Table 1 in Appendix C to calculate present value (PV) factors, which are then used to calculate PV amounts (cells C5:C9) of the after-tax cash flows reflected in cells B5:B9.

The second of the above-two solutions uses the NPV function in Excel (see formula in cell C13).

Note that the above-two Excel-generated solutions are exact, while the method based on the present value tables is an approximation because the present value factors in the tables are rounded to 3 decimal places.

7. Under the assumption that cash inflows occur at the end of each year, the discounted payback period for the proposed project is slightly more than three years, as follows:

	A	B	C	D	E
1					Cumulative
2		After-tax	Discount	PV of After-	PV of After-
3		Cash	Factor	tax Cash	tax Cash
4	Year	Inflow	@ 12.0%	Flow	Flows
5	0	($650,000)	1.000	($650,000)	($650,000)
6	1	$270,000	0.893	$241,110	($408,890)
7	2	$270,000	0.797	$215,190	($193,700)
8	3	$270,000	0.712	$192,240	($1,460)
9	4	$308,000	0.636	$195,888	$194,428

Source: Microsoft Excel

8. Under the assumption that cash inflows occur at year-end, the estimated internal rate of return (IRR) for this investment (rounded to 1 decimal place) is 25.3%, which can be determined using either a trial-and-error approach or using a built-in function for Excel, as follows:

Trial-and-error: We can surmise from our solution to requirement 6 earlier that the IRR must be significantly greater than the discount rate, 12%. Thus, we might choose IRR candidates of 25% and 30% in our attempt to find a rate that produces an NPV of 0.

	@25%	@30%
PV of after-tax cash inflows (details omitted)	$653,320	$598,120
Less: Initial investment outlay	650,000	650,000
NPV at indicated discount rate	$ 3,320	$(51,880)

Thus, the IRR of this project lies between 25% and 30%. By interpolation we have

$$\text{IRR} = 25\% + [\$3{,}320 \div (\$3{,}320 + \$51{,}880)] \times 5\%$$
$$= 25\% + (\$3{,}320 \div \$55{,}200) \times 5\% = 25\% + (0.06 \times 5\%) = 25.3\%$$

Excel-based formula approach:

	A	B	C	D
1		After-Tax		
2	Year	Cash Flows		
3	0	($650,000)		
4	1	$270,000		
5	2	$270,000		
6	3	$270,000		
7	4	$308,000		
8			Formula	
9	IRR =	25.3%	=IRR(B3:B7,0.12)	

Source: Microsoft Excel

(*Note:* In the IRR function, the 0.12 represents an initial guess; if omitted, Excel uses 10% as the starting point in its algorithm to estimate the IRR of an investment project.)

9. The MIRR of the proposed investment is (rounded to 1 decimal place) 19.6%, as follows:

	A	B	C	D
2	Year	Cash Flows		
3	0	($650,000)		
4	1	$270,000		
5	2	$270,000		
6	3	$270,000		
7	4	$308,000		
8	WACC =	12.00%		
9			Formula	
10	MIRR =	19.6%	=MIRR(B3:B7,B8,B8)	

Source: Microsoft Excel

10. Prior to presenting the solution based on Goal Seek, it may be instructive to work through the following manual solution. The most that variable costs can increase (to 2 decimal places) and still have the project return the minimum rate of return (12%), *holding everything else constant,* is $21.34 per unit, as follows:

   The current projected NPV of the project is $194,428; thus, the PV of future after-tax cash inflows can drop by a maximum of $194,428 (if they fell by this amount, then the IRR on the project would be exactly 12%). The amount by which the annual pretax cash flows could decrease is $106,700, as follows:

Maximum annual decrease in annual *after-tax* cash = $194,428 ÷ 3.037 = $ 64,020
inflows (through increased variable costs, using
annuity factor @ 12%)
Given a 40% marginal income tax rate, the above amount = $64,020 ÷ (1 − 0.40) = $106,700
represents 60% (i.e., 1 − 40%) of the pretax amount;
thus, the maximum amount that pretax income can fall

   Therefore, the variable cost per unit can increase by $106,700 ÷ 5,000 units = $21.34 per unit. If everything else remains constant and the variable cost per unit increases by $21.34, the proposed project will yield a 12.0% return.

   We now use the Goal Seek function in Excel to confirm the above manually determined result. The following two-step process is used to determine the maximum change in variable costs that could be realized such that the investment would yield an IRR of 12%:

Step 1: Set Up the Current Situation

	A	B	C	D	E
1	Incremental sales per year (in units) =		5,000		
2	Selling price per unit =		$200.00		
3	Variable costs per unit =		$80.00		
4	Cash fixed costs per year =		$250,000		
5	Marginal income tax rate =		0.4		
6	Annual depreciation deduction (SL) =		$150,000		
7	Current level of after-tax operating cash flows per year =		$270,000		
8					
9	Current NPV of investment proposal =		$194,428	(given, Part 6)	
10	PV annuity factor, 12%, 4 years =		3.037	(Appendix C, Table 2)	
11					
12	Thus, decrease in annual *after-tax* cash inflows can be		$64,020	=C9/C10	
13	New level of annual *after-tax* cash inflows can decrease to		$205,980	=C7-C12	
14					
15	Incremental annual *pretax* cash income =		$350,000	─C1*(C2 C3) C4	
16	Minus: Income taxes on above (@40%) =		$140,000	=C5*C15	
17	Plus: Depreciation tax savings =		$60,000	=C5*C6	
18	After-tax, annual increase in operating cash flows =		$270,000	=C15-C16+C17	

Source: Microsoft Excel

This initial spreadsheet reflects the current investment proposal and the allowable decrease in annual after-tax cash inflows (cell C12) that can occur, given the goal of generating an IRR of 12.0% on the project.

Step 2: Use the Goal Seek Function of Excel

Next, go to the Goal Seek option under Data, What-If Analysis, then Goal Seek. Given the preceding spreadsheet, complete the Goal Seek dialog box as follows:

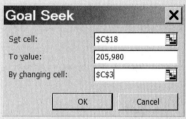

Source: Microsoft Excel

The preceding entries tell Excel to vary cell C3 (variable costs per unit) until the amount of annual increase in operating cash flows, after-tax (cell C18), has been reduced to $205,980 ($270,000 − $64,020). After clicking "OK," your spreadsheet should change to:

	A	B	C	D	E
1	Incremental sales per year (in units) =		5,000		
2	Selling price per unit =		$200.00		
3	Variable costs per unit =		$101.34		
4	Cash fixed costs per year =		$250,000		
5	Marginal income tax rate =		0.4		
6	Annual depreciation deduction (SL) =		$150,000		
7	Current level of after-tax operating cash flows per year =		$270,000		
8					
9	Current NPV of investment proposal =		$194,428	(given, Part 6)	
10	PV annuity factor, 12%, 4 years =		3.037	(Appendix C, Table 2)	
11					
12	Thus, decrease in annual *after-tax* cash inflows can be		$64,020	=C9/C10	
13	New level of annual *after-tax* cash inflows can decrease to		$205,980	=C7-C12	
14					
15	Incremental annual *pretax* cash income =		$243,300	=C1*(C2-C3)-C4	
16	Minus: Income taxes on above (@40%) =		$97,320	=C5*C15	
17	Plus: Depreciation tax savings =		$60,000	=C5*C6	
18	After-tax, annual increase in operating cash flows =		$205,980	=C15-C16+C17	

Source: Microsoft Excel

Thus, variable costs per unit can increase to $101.34 (or $21.34 over the initial assumption of $80.00 per unit); if everything else other than variable cost per unit is held constant, the IRR of the project will be 12%.

Please visit Connect to access a narrated, animated tutorial for solving this problem.

Cost Planning for the Product Life Cycle: Target Costing, Theory of Constraints, and Strategic Pricing

After studying this chapter, you should be able to . . .

LO 13-1   Explain how to use target costing to facilitate strategic management.

LO 13-2   Apply the theory of constraints to strategic management.

LO 13-3   Describe how life-cycle costing facilitates strategic management.

LO 13-4   Outline the objectives and techniques of strategic pricing.

Having some of the world's best-selling cars, including the Camry, the Corolla, and the Prius, Toyota is among the world's most successful automakers. This distinction can be attributed, in part, to Toyota's success in consistently producing high-quality cars with attractive features and competitive prices. Target costing, a method Toyota pioneered in the 1960s, is one

Shutterstock/Zoran Karapancev

method used to provide high-quality and desirable features at a competitive price. As we will see in this chapter, the method is a design approach in which cost management plays a large part. Using target costing, a company designs a product to achieve a desired profit while satisfying the customer's expectations for quality and product features. The balancing of costs, features, and quality takes place throughout the design, manufacturing, sale, and service of the car but has the strongest influence in the design phase. When design alternatives are being examined and selected, Toyota, like most any manufacturer, has the maximum flexibility for choosing options that affect manufacturing and all other product costs such as customer service and warranty work.

Once the design is complete, manufacturing begins. The cost consequences of the choice of features and manufacturing methods are set until the next model change, meaning cost-effective design is critical. Target costing places a strong focus on using the design process to improve the product and reduce its cost. For example, in the redesign of the Camry, Toyota made the running lamps part of the headlamp assembly and made the grille part of the bumper, which saves time and materials in manufacturing and produces a more crash-resistant bumper—a win/win for Toyota and the car buyer. The focus on costs, however, should not blind management to continuing to provide the functionality and quality demanded by customers. Toyota saw that firsthand with the recall of millions of cars due to problems with airbags.

Target costing is only the first of four costing methods covered in this chapter. Each of the methods is used for cost planning during the product (or service) life cycle. For example, target costing is used at an early phase in the product's life cycle to help create a product designed to achieve a desired profit. The other methods, which are used at different phases in the life cycle, are the theory of constraints, life-cycle costing, and strategic pricing. While managers once focused only on manufacturing costs, they now look at costs both before manufacturing (upstream) and after manufacturing (downstream) to obtain a comprehensive analysis of product cost and profitability over a product's cost life cycle.

cost life cycle

The sequence of activities within the firm that begins with research and development, followed by design, manufacturing, marketing/ distribution, and customer service.

The **cost life cycle** is the sequence of activities within the organization that begins with research and development, followed by design, manufacturing (or providing the service), marketing and distribution, and customer service. It is the life cycle of the product or service from the viewpoint of costs incurred. The cost life cycle is illustrated in Exhibit 13.1.[1]

Of the four methods used for cost planning, target costing, the theory of constraints, and life-cycle costing are based on the product or service's cost life cycle. For example, target costing considers the role of product design (an upstream activity) in reducing costs in the manufacturing and downstream phases of the life cycle. Then, the theory of constraints can be used in the manufacturing phase to reduce manufacturing costs and to speed up delivery downstream. Next, life-cycle costing provides a comprehensive evaluation of the profitability of the different products, including costs throughout the product life cycle. The fourth method used for cost planning, strategic pricing, uses both cost life cycle and sales life cycle concepts in pricing decisions.

EXHIBIT 13.1
The Cost Life Cycle of a Product or Service

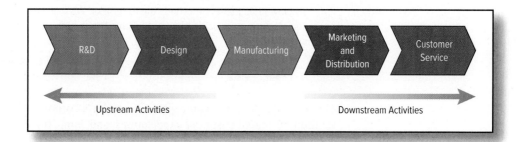

[1] The *cost life cycle* also is called a *value chain* by many writers to emphasize that each activity must add value for the ultimate consumer (Michael Porter, *Competitive Advantage* [New York: Free Press, 1985]). Note that this concept of the value chain differs from that introduced in Chapter 2. Chapter 2 describes the industry-level value chain; the cost life-cycle concept in this chapter describes the firm-level value chain. We use the broader concept of the industry-level value chain in Chapter 2 to facilitate the strategic focus in that chapter. For a discussion of the two types of value chains, see "Value Chain Analysis for Assessing Competitive Advantage," *Statement on Management Accounting,* Institute of Management Accountants, 1999.

EXHIBIT 13.2
The Sales Life Cycle of a
Product or Service

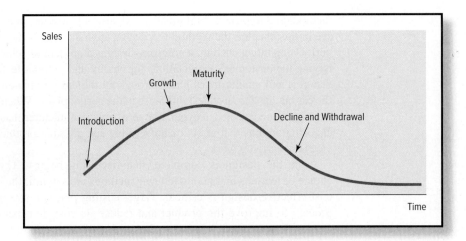

sales life cycle
The sequence of phases in a product's or service's life in the market—from the introduction of the product or service to the market; to growth in sales; and finally to maturity, decline, and withdrawal from the market.

The **sales life cycle** is the sequence of phases in the product's or service's life in the market from the introduction of the product or service to the market; to growth in sales; and finally to maturity, decline, and withdrawal from the market. Sales are at first small, but then grow until they peak in the maturity phase, and then decline, as illustrated in Exhibit 13.2.

These four methods are commonly used by manufacturing firms, where new product development, manufacturing speed, and efficiency are important. Because a product with physical characteristics is involved, applications in manufacturing firms are more intuitive and easily understood. However, each method can also be used in service organizations. For example, a local government could use the theory of constraints to speed the process of billing and collection for water services and reduce the related processing costs.

Target Costing

To start this section, consider the words of Henry Ford.

LO 13-1

Explain how to use target costing to facilitate strategic management.

"Our policy is to reduce the price, extend the operations, and improve the article. You will notice that the reduction of price comes first. We have never considered costs as fixed. Therefore we first reduce the price to the point where we believe more sales result. Then we go ahead and try to make the prices. We do not bother about the costs. The new price forces the costs down. The more usual way is to take the costs and then determine the price, and although that method may be scientific in the narrow sense, it is not scientific in the broad sense, because what earthly use is it to know the cost if it tells you that you cannot manufacture at a price at which the article can be sold? But more to the point is the fact that although one may calculate what a cost is, and of course all of our costs are carefully calculated, no one knows what a cost ought to be. One of the ways of discovering . . . is to name a price so low as to force everybody in the place to the highest point of efficiency. The low price makes everybody dig for profits. We make more discoveries concerning manufacturing and selling under this forced method than by any method of leisurely investigation."

Henry Ford, My Life and My Work*, 1923*

Henry Ford's thinking would fit well in today's corporate boardrooms, where global competition, increased customer expectations, and competitive pricing in many industries have forced companies to look for ways to reduce costs year after year while producing products or services with increased levels of quality and functionality (different types of product features).

What Ford is describing is a technique called *target costing,* in which the firm determines the allowable (i.e., target) cost for the product or service, given a competitive market price, so the firm can earn a desired profit. The formula is

$$\text{Target cost} = \text{Competitive price} - \text{Desired profit}$$

The target cost is just that, a target, and the firm has two options for managing costs to reach the target level:

1. By integrating new manufacturing technology, using advanced cost management techniques such as activity-based costing, and seeking higher productivity.
2. By redesigning the product or service.

These options are not mutually exclusive, so firms may choose to employ both options in their target costing efforts to achieve increased productivity and a low-cost design.

Auto manufacturers, software developers, and other consumer product manufacturers must also have a design process that anticipates the number and types of features to include in periodic updates of a product. Target costing, based on analysis of functionality/cost trade-offs, is an appropriate management tool for these firms. With its positioning in the early upstream phases of the cost life cycle, target costing can clearly help a firm reduce total costs (see Exhibit 13.3).

Toyota, Honda, Boeing, Intel, and many other firms worldwide use target costing. These companies have global supply chains, which adds an additional level of complexity to target costing. One obvious complexity comes from the currency fluctuations that occur in global markets, which can affect the costs of resources. However, there are also the risks that are associated with a growing trend toward economic nationalism that threaten cross-border relationships. Companies must carefully consider their strategies for future ties with foreign suppliers to mitigate the risks to the plan to achieve target costs.

Many firms find it difficult to compete successfully on cost leadership or differentiation alone; they must compete on both price and functionality. Target costing uses the following five-step process to manage the trade-offs between functionality and cost:

1. Determine the market price.
2. Determine the desired profit.
3. Calculate the target cost at market price less desired profit.
4. Use value engineering to identify ways to reduce product cost.
5. Use kaizen and operational control to further reduce costs.

The first three steps require little additional explanation. In step 2, the determination of desired profit can be done in a variety of ways. A common approach is to set a desired per-unit profit, meaning that if the product's price falls and target costs fall by the same dollar amount, then profits will remain the same after the price change, assuming the firm meets the new price and sales in units do not change. Another approach is to set the desired profit as a percentage of sales dollars. The section on pricing at the end of this chapter gives some additional examples of pricing methods. The following sections explain the fourth and fifth steps: the use of value engineering and kaizen and operational control.

Value Engineering

"Innovation is not about saying yes to everything. It's about saying NO to all but the most crucial features."

Steve Jobs

EXHIBIT 13.3
Target Costing in the Cost Life Cycle

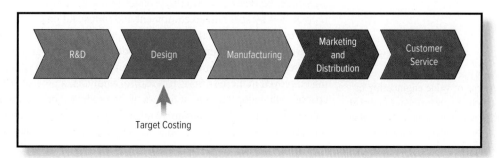

In competitive industries such as computers, consumer electronics, and autos, manufacturers continuously look for ways to reduce cost and increase value throughout the value chain. Because of intense pricing pressures and increased customer expectations, target costing methods can help identify and analyze the options for competitive advantage. Going abroad is the solution for many firms but for different reasons. We look at the practices in two industries: automobile manufacturing and consumer electronics and computer products.

AUTOMOBILE MANUFACTURING

In the global marketplace for automobile production, one company stands out as the world's biggest contract car manufacturer, Magna

International. What advantage is gained by companies ranging from Ford and Honda to BMW and Jaguar Land Rover by outsourcing production to Magna? If, and how, are these advantages threatened by the current trend to economic nationalism?

CONSUMER ELECTRONICS AND COMPUTER PRODUCTS

Computer and electronics companies such as Apple and Hewlett-Packard have outsourced manufacturing to plants operated by contract manufacturers, such as Foxconn in China. Why is this an advantage to these companies?

(Refer to Comments on Cost Management in Action at the end of the chapter.)

REAL-WORLD FOCUS   Product Designed to Meet a Price Target

The low prices at IKEA are legendary, and the prices often decline over time. The low prices, however, do not mean lower quality. How can quality be high and prices low? Target costing is the answer. Once the decision is made as to what to sell, a price is selected and then IKEA's designers work with suppliers to make sure the product can be profitable at that price. Many elements go in to keeping costs down, including

the materials used, bulk production to get economies of scale and supplier discounts, and even its well known flat-packing of merchandise.

Source: Jessica Taylor, "Here Are IKEA's Secrets to Keeping Its Prices So Low," *Business Insider,* October 12, 2018, www.businessinsider.com/why-ikea-is-so-cheap-2018-10; Oliver Roeder, "The Weird Economics of IKEA," *FiveThirtyEight,* October 21, 2016, https://fivethirtyeight.com/features/the-weird-economics-of-ikea/.

The philosophy behind the words of Steve Jobs is one of providing customers with what they value, and not wasting resources by including all the features and functions that might be possible. Value engineering is one of the tools available to assist management in these efforts.

value engineering
Used in target costing to reduce product cost by analyzing the trade-offs between different types of product functionality and total product cost.

Value engineering is used in target costing to reduce product cost by analyzing the trade-offs between different types of product functionality (different types of product functions or features) and total product cost. An important first step in value engineering is performing a consumer analysis during the design stage to identify critical consumer preferences that define the desired functionality for the new product.

The type of value engineering used depends on the product's functionality. For one group of products—including automobiles, computer software, and many consumer electronics products (such as cameras and audio and video equipment)—functionality can be added or deleted relatively easily. These products have frequent new models or updates, and customer preferences may change frequently. The manufacturer in effect chooses the particular bundle of features to include with each new model of the product. For automobiles, this can mean new performance and safety features; for computer software, it might mean the ability to perform certain new tasks or analyses.

In contrast, for a product in which customer preferences are relatively stable, the functionality must be designed into the product rather than added on. Products in this group are best represented by specialized equipment and industrial products such as construction equipment, heavy trucks, and specialized medical equipment.

functional analysis
A type of value engineering in which the performance and cost of each major function or feature of the product is examined.

Target costing is more useful for products in the first group (autos, consumer products, etc.) because the firm has some discretion about a larger number of features. A type of value engineering employed in these firms is **functional analysis**, a process of examining the performance and cost of each major function or feature of the product. The objective of the analysis is to determine a desired balance of functionality and cost. An overall desired level of performance achievement for each function is obtained while keeping the cost of all functions below the target cost.

REAL-WORLD FOCUS Cost Savings through Recycling

Fuel economy is sought by many automobile consumers, but how can this feature be provided cost-effectively by manufacturers? In designing its 2015 F-150, Ford Motor Company's management decided to make the vehicle lighter by using aluminum body panels. The new material added about $1,000 to the cost of each vehicle, but the production process also generated a significant amount of scrap aluminum. Ford implemented

processes to collect, separate, and shred the aluminum waste, making the scrap worth nearly 90% of the price of the original raw material cost. Recycling the scrap material allowed Ford to recapture nearly $300 per vehicle, thereby reducing the cost of providing better fuel efficiency.

Source: Mike Ramsey and John Miller, "How Recycling Shaves Ford's Material Costs," *The Wall Street Journal*, December 17, 2014, p. B8.

Benchmarking (discussed in Chapter 1) is often used at this step to determine which features give the firm a competitive advantage. In a release of new software, for example, each desired feature of the updated version is reviewed against the cost and time required for its development. The objective is an overall bundle of features for the software that achieves the desired balance of meeting customer preferences while keeping costs below targeted levels. In another example, auto manufacturers must decide which performance and safety features to add to the new model. This decision is based on consumer analysis and a functional analysis of the feature's contribution to consumer preferences compared to its cost. For instance, improved safety air bags could be added, but target cost constraints could delay an improved sound system until a later model year. As noted in the Real-World Focus design changes to meet customer demands may lead to opportunities to offset the costs of meeting those needs.

design analysis
A form of value engineering in which the design team prepares several possible designs of the product, each having similar features with different levels of both performance and cost.

Design analysis is a form of value engineering for products in the second group, industrial and specialized products. The design team prepares several possible designs of the product, each having similar features with different levels of both performance and cost. Benchmarking and value-chain analysis help guide the design team in preparing designs that are both low cost and competitive. The design team works with cost management personnel to select the one design that best meets customer preferences while not exceeding the target cost.

A useful comparison of different target costing and cost-reduction strategies in well-known firms, based on a study done for Consortium of Advanced Management International (CAM-I), is illustrated in Exhibit 13.4. Note that the different market demands for functionality result in different cost-reduction approaches. Where customers' expectations for functionality are increasing, as for Boeing, there is more significant use of target costing. In contrast, at Caterpillar, the emphasis is on value engineering and productivity improvement. Note also that firms such as Daimler, which uses both internal and external sourcing for parts and components, use target costing at both the product level and the component level. The overall product-level target cost is achieved when targeted costs for all components are achieved.[2]

cost tables
Computer-based databases that include comprehensive information about the firm's cost drivers.

Other cost-reduction approaches include cost tables and group technology. **Cost tables** are computer-based databases that include comprehensive information about the firm's cost drivers. Cost drivers include, for example, the size of the product, the materials used in its manufacture, and the number of features. Firms that manufacture parts of different sizes from the same design (pipe fittings, tools, and so on) use cost tables to show the difference in cost for parts of different sizes and different types of materials.

group technology
A method of identifying similarities in the parts of products manufactured so the same part can be used in two or more products, thereby reducing costs.

Group technology is a method of identifying similarities in the parts of products manufactured so the same parts can be used in two or more products, thereby reducing costs. Large manufacturers of diverse product lines, such as in the automobile industry, use group technology in this way. A point of concern in the use of group technology is that it reduces manufacturing costs but might increase service and warranty costs if a failed part is used in many different models. The combination of group technology and total quality management can, however, result in lower manufacturing and service/warranty costs.

---

[2] Dan Swenson, Shahid Ansari, Jan Bell, and Il-Woon Kim, "Best Practices in Target Costing," *Management Accounting Quarterly* 4, no. 2 (Winter 2003), pp. 12–17.

EXHIBIT 13.4 **Target Costing Examples**

Firm/Industry	Cost-Reduction Approach	Strategy
Boeing/Aerospace	Target costing using value engineering; the concept of functionality for the price point	Prices are set by desired customers' expectations about functionality; focus on managing functionality versus customer willingness to pay
Daimler/Automotive	Value engineering by product and by each component of each product; then increase price or reduce functionality	Prices are set by desired customers' expectations about functionality; after functionality is set, target cost is used to find savings, especially from suppliers
Caterpillar/Heavy machinery	Design analysis to determine alternative designs; functional analysis to develop cost/functionality trade-offs	Primary focus is on cost control rather than redesign or functional analysis

concurrent engineering
An engineering method that integrates product design with manufacturing and marketing throughout the product's life cycle; also called *simultaneous engineering.*

Concurrent engineering, or *simultaneous engineering,* is an important development in the design of products that is replacing the traditional approach of product designers working in isolation on specialized components of the overall design project. In contrast, concurrent engineering relies on an integrated approach. The engineering/design process takes place throughout the cost life cycle using cross-functional teams. Information is solicited from and used at each phase of the value chain to improve the product design. For example, customer feedback in the service phase is used directly in product design. Manufacturers such as Toyota Motor Corp. and Moen Inc. are increasingly using product design in a very flexible manner by continuously incorporating product improvements. Some experts argue that this approach has saved firms as much as 20% of total product cost.

Being able to identify, estimate, and track the costs associated with providing each feature of the product, each function of the product, or each design option that is being considered is an important part of value engineering. Consequently, advanced costing methods, such as ABC, should probably play a role in the value engineering process. The activity analysis component of ABC cost systems is particularly useful for helping managers in product design, purchasing, manufacturing, and marketing gain a common understanding of the costs of different features and options.

Target Costing and Kaizen

The fifth step in target costing is to use continuous improvement (kaizen) and operational control to further reduce costs. Target costing incorporates kaizen at the manufacturing stage, where the effects of value engineering and improved design are already in place; the role for cost reduction at this phase is to develop new manufacturing methods (such as flexible manufacturing systems) and to use new management techniques such as operational control (Chapters 14, 15, and 16), total quality management (Chapter 17), and the theory of constraints (next section) to further reduce costs. Kaizen means *continuous* improvement—that is, the ongoing search for new ways to reduce costs in the manufacturing process of a product with a given design and functionality. Toyota, for example, uses kaizen to reduce manufacturing costs on its hybrid vehicles so that it can bring down the premium it must now charge for these vehicles.

Exhibit 13.5 shows the relationship between target costing and kaizen. Price is assumed to be stable or decreasing over time for firms for which target costing is appropriate because of intense competition on price, product quality, and product functionality. These firms respond to the competitive pressure by periodically redesigning their products using target costing to simultaneously reduce price and improve value. Consider the two points labeled first and second target cost in Exhibit 13.5. The time period between product redesigns is approximately the product's sales life cycle. In the time between product redesigns, the firm uses kaizen to reduce product cost in the manufacturing process by streamlining the supply chain and improving both manufacturing methods and productivity programs. Thus, target costing and kaizen are complementary methods used to continually reduce cost and improve value.

An Illustration: Target Costing in Health Product Manufacturing

Health Products International Inc. (HPI) is conducting a target costing analysis of a major product, a hearing aid. The HPI-2 is a reliable second-generation hearing aid that has 30% of the worldwide market. HPI-2 sells for $750 and costs $650 to produce, generating a profit of

EXHIBIT 13.5
Price, Cost, Kaizen, and Target Costing

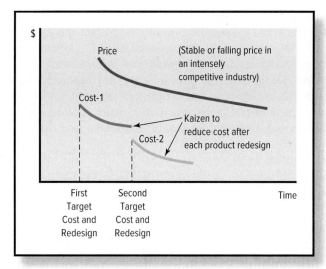

$100 per unit. A competitor has recently introduced a third-generation product that incorporates a computer chip, thereby significantly improving performance. The competitor's price is $1,200. Customer analysis has revealed that cost-conscious consumers will still buy the HPI-2, but HPI can maintain market share only if the price is lowered to $600. The target profit for HPI-2, however, remains at $100, so redesigning the product and/or the manufacturing process is required.

With a price of $600 and a target profit of $100, the target cost for HPI-2 is $500. Management must find a way to reduce costs by $150 ($650 − $500), and because the product has no add-on features, design analysis is the preferred approach. The following table summarizes the three alternatives being considered:

Alternative A	Projected Impact
Reduce R&D expenditures	($ 30)
Replace microphone with one of nearly equal sensitivity	($ 30)
Replace power switch with a cheaper and almost as reliable version	($ 30)
Replace current inspection procedure with an integrated quality review	
process at each assembly station	($ 40)
Total impact	($ 150)

Alternative B	Projected Impact
Replace the amplifier with one having slightly less power but not	
enough difference to be noticed by most users	($ 30)
Replace microphone with one of nearly equal sensitivity	($ 30)
Replace power switch with a cheaper and almost as reliable version	($ 30)
Replace current inspection procedure with an integrated quality review	
process at each assembly station	($ 20)
Total impact	($ 150)

Alternative C	Projected Impact
Increase R&D expenditures to develop a third-generation computer	
chip–based hearing aid	($ 40)
Replace the amplifier with one having slightly less power but not	
enough difference to be noticed by most users	($ 50)
Replace microphone with one of nearly equal sensitivity	($ 30)
Replace power switch with a cheaper and almost as reliable version	($ 30)
Replace current inspection procedure with an integrated quality review	
process at each assembly station	($ 40)
Renegotiate contract with supplier of plastic casings	($ 20)
Replace plastic earpiece material with a lower-quality material that will	
still meet user's expectations of a 6- to 10-year useful life	($ 20)
Total impact	($ 150)

Manufacturing and marketing managers agree that the design changes proposed in all the options would not significantly alter the market appeal of the current product. After a review of its alternatives, HPI chooses alternative C, primarily because it includes an increase in research and development expenditures that will start to position the firm to compete in the market for the new type of hearing aid. Key managers also determine that this alternative is strategically important because the new technology, while only a fraction of the market now, could be dominant in the next 10 to 15 years as prices come down on the new units and users become more aware of the benefits of the computer chip.

An Illustration Using Quality Function Deployment

quality function deployment (QFD)
The integration of value engineering, marketing analysis, and target costing to assist in determining which components of the product should be targeted for redesign.

Quality function deployment (QFD) is the integration of value engineering, marketing analysis, and target costing to assist in determining which components of the product should be targeted for redesign or cost reduction. QFD helps designers and managers break down the total product target cost into the components that make up the product. There are four steps in QFD, and we will use the example of a table saw product to explain those steps:

1. Determine the customer's purchasing criteria for this product and how these criteria are ranked. For the saw, the customer criteria could be safety, performance, and economy.
2. Identify the components of the product and the manufacturing cost of each component. For simplicity, assume the components of the table saw are the motor, the saw, and the frame.
3. Determine how each component contributes to customer satisfaction. How much does the motor contribute to the customer's desired safety, performance, and economy? What about the contribution of the saw or the frame? Recognize that in actual practice, there are likely to be more components and more criteria.
4. The final step is to determine the importance index of each component, by combining the information in steps 1 and 3 and then comparing this to the cost information in step 2.

To illustrate, suppose customers were asked to use a scale of 1 to 100 to rate the importance of each criterion. It is the relative rather than the absolute importance that is significant. Calculate the relative importance by dividing the score for each criterion by the total points awarded. The customer ranking and relative importance results appear in the following table:

First: Customer Criteria and Ranking

	Importance	Relative Importance	
Safety	95	46.34%	= 95 ÷ 205
Performance	60	29.27	= 60 ÷ 205
Economy	50	24.39	= 50 ÷ 205
Total	205	100.00%	

Second, identify the components and both the absolute and relative costs (the "cost index") of each:

Second: Product Components and Cost

	Cost	Cost Index	
Motor	$40	53.3%	= 40 ÷ 75
Saw	20	26.7	= 20 ÷ 75
Frame	15	20.0	= 15 ÷ 75
Total	$75	100.0%	

Third, determine the contribution of each component to satisfying customer criteria. This step usually requires a cross-functional team that may include marketing, operations, and cost management analysts. In this example, the desired criterion of safety is achieved primarily by the frame (60%) and then by the saw (30%) and motor (10%):

Third: Determine How Components Contribute to Customer Satisfaction

	Customer Criteria		
Components	Safety	Performance	Economy
Motor	10%	10%	60%
Saw	30	50	10
Frame	60	40	30
	100%	100%	100%

Fourth, determine the importance index for each component, which reflects the value of the component to the customer. To compute the importance index, multiply the relative importance of each criterion by each component's percentage contribution and then sum those amounts. For example, the 22.195% index for the motor is determined as follows:

$$(46.34\% \times 10\%) + (29.27\% \times 10\%) + (24.39\% \times 60\%) = 22.195\%$$

Fourth: Determine Importance Index for Each Component

	Customer Criteria			Importance Index
	Safety	Performance	Economy	
Relative importance of each criterion (step 1)	46.34%	29.27%	24.39%	
The % contribution of each component to each customer criterion (from step 3):				
Motor	10%	10%	60%	22.195%
Saw	30	50	10	30.976
Frame	60	40	30	46.829
	100%	100%	100%	100.000%

The importance index can now be compared to the cost information in step 2 to identify components where cost reductions are needed and components where additional design features might be appropriate. Dividing the importance index by the cost index yields a value index. If a value index is greater than 1, it means the relative importance of the component is greater than the relative spending on the component. Conversely, a value index of less than 1 means the relative spending is higher than the relative importance.

Components	Importance Index	Cost Index	Value Index
Motor	22.195%	53.33%	0.42
Saw	30.976	26.67	1.16
Frame	46.829	20.00	2.34
	100.000%	100.00%	

The preceding comparison shows that far too much is being spent on the motor relative to its value to the customer. In contrast, not enough is being spent on the frame, relative to customer criteria.

This information is a guide to both the redesign of the product and the determination of the target cost for each component.

REAL-WORLD FOCUS   Design for the Market

Thomas Sedran was hired as strategy chief at Volkswagen in 2016, and he quickly moved to help change the culture that contributed to the emissions scandal the company had faced. One change was to the Product Strategy Committee, the group that oversaw product development. Where once that group often added product features sought by the engineers, managers in charge of a car model must now show that any new option will generate enough profit to justify the cost of the feature.

Similarly, in an effort to compete against top appliance manufacturer Whirlpool, Electrolux revamped the way it developed and updated its lineup. In an effort to get new products to market as much as 30% faster, the company moved away from a production-development process run mainly by accountants and engineers. Electrolux's new process makes use of an "innovation triangle" that includes design, research and development, and marketing. There are also customer focus groups involved, and

any proposal that receives less than a 70% approval rating is not ready for production. As one example of the process, researchers watched people use a vacuum cleaner. It was discovered that many dust particles start to fly around when the vacuum is emptied. One idea was to compact the dust into a disk to eliminate the dust particles. Then a decision had to be made regarding how to compress the particles. One option was a manual piston and the other was a motorized compactor. The manual piston won out because the motorized version was more expensive and would require batteries. However, before a final decision was made, additional customer focus groups were involved, with the 70% approval rule applied at every step.

Source: Christoph Rauwald and Chris Reiter, "Reinventing These Wheels," *Bloomberg Businessweek,* December 19, 2016, pp. 19–20; Carol Matlack, "Electrolux's Holy Trinity," *Bloomberg Businessweek,* November 4, 2013, pp. 55–56.

Benefits of Target Costing

Target costing can be beneficial because it

- Orients the organization toward the customer, as design is focused on customer values.
- Reduces costs, through more effective and efficient design.
- Helps the firm achieve desired profitability on new or redesigned products.
- Can decrease the total time required for product development, through improved coordination of design, manufacturing, and marketing functions.
- Can increase communication and cooperation among departments.
- Can improve overall product quality, as the design is carefully developed and manufacturing issues are considered explicitly in the design phase.

Target costing also involves costs due to the:

- Need to develop detailed cost data.
- Time demands associated with cooperation and coordination throughout the organization.

The Theory of Constraints

LO 13-2

Apply the theory of constraints to strategic management.

"Remember that time is money."

Benjamin Franklin

Benjamin Franklin must be right. Most strategic initiatives undertaken by firms today focus on improving the speed of their operations throughout the cost life cycle because speed can provide a competitive edge. Customers expect quick response to inquiries and fast delivery of the product. Shorter sales life cycles in many industries mean that manufacturers are working to reduce product development and delivery time. One of the most successful business models of recent years, used by Amazon.com, was built on speed.

In this part of the chapter, we present one of the key methods used to improve speed, the theory of constraints (TOC). Before looking closely at TOC, consider the issue of how speed is measured and improved throughout the cost life cycle, as illustrated in Exhibit 13.6. The

cycle time
The amount of time between receipt of a customer order and shipment of the order.

manufacturing cycle time
The time from the start of production to the shipment of the order.

manufacturing cycle efficiency (MCE)
The ratio of processing time to manufacturing cycle time.

measures are defined in different ways by different firms, depending on the nature of the firm's operations. For example, **cycle time** (or *lead time*) is commonly defined as follows:

$$\text{Cycle time} = \text{Amount of time between the receipt of a customer order and the shipment of the order}$$

Similarly, **manufacturing cycle time** is defined as the time from the start of production to the shipment of the order. Recognize that some firms may define *start time* as the time a production batch is scheduled, the time the raw materials are ordered, or the time that production on the order is started. Similarly, the *finish time* of the cycle can be defined as the time that production is completed or the time the order is ready for shipping.

Another useful measure is **manufacturing cycle efficiency (MCE)**:

$$\text{MCE} = \frac{\text{Processing time}}{\text{Manufacturing cycle time}}$$

For example, if the processing time is 2 days and the manufacturing cycle time is 10 days, then the MCE ratio is $2 \div 10$, or 20%.

MCE separates manufacturing cycle time into the time required for each of the various activities: processing (value-added work on the product), inspection, materials handling, waiting, and so on. Most firms would like to see their MCE close to 1, which reflects less time wasted on moving, waiting, inspecting, and other non-value-added activities.[3]

The theory of constraints (TOC) was developed to help managers reduce cycle times and operating costs.[4] Prior to TOC, managers often devoted efforts to improve efficiency and speed *throughout* the manufacturing process instead of focusing attention on just those activities that were constraints (i.e., bottlenecks) in the process. **Constraints** are activities or policies that slow a product's total cycle time or limit throughput. Goldratt and Cox use as an example a troop of Boy Scouts on a hike. The goal is to have every scout complete the hike, so the slowest hiker is the constraint and sets the overall pace for the troop. Manufacturers have learned that increased efficiency and speed with activities that are not constraints could be

constraints
Those activities or policies that slow the product's total manufacturing cycle time or limit throughput.

EXHIBIT 13.6 Measures of Speed and How to Improve Speed at Each Step of the Cost Life Cycle

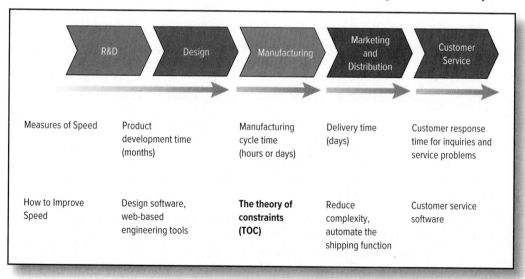

---

[3] While 100% is a theoretical maximum for MCE, many firms find their MCE ratios somewhat smaller because of delays and wasted time in the manufacturing process. For example, statistics from the auto industry show that some firms have cycle times of over 30 days and product assembly times of 1 to 2 days—an MCE of approximately 5%. Also, note that the terms used here are *manufacturing* measurements and that similar measures are used by firms to examine the firm's progress in *filling customer orders*. For example, customer lead time (or customer cycle time) is usually defined as the time from the receipt of an order to the delivery of the product.

[4] E. Goldratt and J. Cox, *The Goal* (New York: Free Press, 1986); E. Goldratt, *The Theory of Constraints* (New York: North River Press, 1990). See also Thomas Corbett, *Throughput Accounting* (New York: North River Press, 1998).

dysfunctional. Using resources to increase the efficiency of nonconstraints is likely to result in the buildup of work-in-process for activities prior to the constraint (just as the faster scouts would be "bunched up" behind the slowest scout) and to divert attention and resources from the actual slowdown in cycle time. TOC focuses attention on improving speed at the constraints, which causes a favorable decrease in the overall cycle time and inventory. TOC can be compared to just-in-time manufacturing (JIT) in that both are aimed at reducing cycle time and reducing inventory levels. JIT accomplishes this by methods that coordinate manufacturing processes so that materials are available just in time for the process, thereby increasing processing speed and reducing or eliminating inventory.

The Use of the Theory of Constraints in Health Product Manufacturing

To illustrate the five steps of TOC, return to the example involving Health Products International Inc. (HPI). Suppose that HPI adopts alternative C from the list of three possible alternatives presented earlier in this chapter. Further assume HPI is currently manufacturing both the second-generation (HPI-2) and a new third-generation (HPI-3) hearing aid. The prices for the HPI-2 and HPI-3 are competitive at $600 and $1,200, respectively, and are not expected to change. However, increasing cycle times have led to a backlog of orders for both products. Orders average 3,000 units for the HPI-2 and 1,800 units for the HPI-3, and new customers are told they may have to wait three or more weeks for their orders. Management is concerned about the need to improve speed in the manufacturing process and is planning to use TOC. Here are the steps HPI would take to use TOC.

Steps in the Theory of Constraints Analysis

TOC analysis has five steps:

1. Identify the constraint.
2. Determine the most profitable product mix given the constraint.
3. Maximize the flow through the constraint.
4. Add capacity to the constraint.
5. Redesign the manufacturing process for flexibility and fast cycle time.

Step 1: Identify the Constraint

flow diagram
A flowchart of the work done that shows the sequence of processes and the amount of time required for each.

The management accountant works with manufacturing managers and engineers to identify the constraints in the manufacturing process by developing a **flow diagram** of the work done. The flow diagram shows the sequence of processes and the amount of time each requires. The five processes for HPI follow, and their flow diagram is shown in Exhibit 13.7.

Process 1. Assemble earpiece.
Process 2. Test and program computer chip (product HPI-3 only).
Process 3. Install other electronics.
Process 4. Perform final assembly and test.
Process 5. Pack and ship.

The raw materials cost for each unit is $300 for the HPI-2 and $750 for the HPI-3 ($450 for the computer chip and $300 for other electronics).

The constraint is identified by using the flow diagram to analyze the total time required for each process given the current level of demand. Exhibit 13.8 shows a summary of the data for this analysis, including the number of employees available for each process and the total time available per month for all employees (assuming a 40-hour work week in which 30 hours are available for work and 10 hours are used for breaks, training, etc.). HPI processes are very specialized, and employees are able to work only within their assigned process. Moreover, because of the specialized skills required, HPI has difficulty maintaining adequate staffing in all processes except process 5, pack and ship.

Step 1 in Exhibit 13.8 shows the total time required in each process given the current level of demand. Each of the five processes except process 4 has slack time. Therefore, the constraint occurs with process 4, perform final assembly and test. Because of inadequate time

EXHIBIT 13.7
Flow Diagram for HPI Inc.

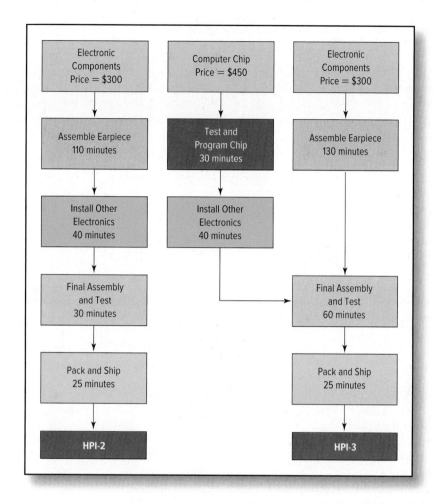

(900 hours too few) available in this process, HPI will not be able to meet the total demand for HPI-2 and HPI-3 and will delay some orders or perhaps not fill them at all. HPI must now determine which orders to fill and which not to fill. This takes us to the second step of TOC.

Step 2: Determine the Most Profitable Product Mix Given the Constraint

The most profitable product mix is the combination of products that maximizes total profits for the given demand across all products. Should we produce all 3,000 units of HPI-2 and whatever we can of HPI-3, or should we produce all 1,800 units of HPI-3 and whatever we can of HPI-2? Or some other mix? The step 2 analysis in Exhibit 13.8 provides the answer.[5]

throughput margin
A TOC measure of product profitability; it equals price less materials cost, including all purchased components and materials handling costs.

To determine the most profitable product mix, we first determine the most profitable product, given the constraint. TOC measures product profitability using the **throughput margin**, which is the product price less materials cost (which includes the costs of all materials used, purchased components, and materials-handling costs). All other manufacturing costs are excluded in determining profitability because they are assumed to be fixed and will not change regardless of which product mix is chosen.[6] Step 2, part 1, in Exhibit 13.8 shows that throughput margins for HPI-2 and HPI-3 are $300 and $450 per unit, respectively. Although HPI-3 has the higher margin, the profitability analysis is not complete without considering the time each product requires from the constrained process 4, final assembly and test. Because HPI-3 involves twice as much constraint time as HPI-2 (60 versus 30 minutes), HPI can produce twice as many HPI-2 models for each HPI-3 produced. In effect, the relevant measure of profitability

---

[5] Note that the analysis in step 2, part 1, and step 2, part 2, of Exhibit 13.8 is identical to that explained in Chapter 11 under the heading of "Constrained Optimization Analysis: Short-Term Product-Mix Decisions," for one production constraint. The determination of the optimal product mix is arrived at in the same manner. Step 2, part 2, can be solved using the Solver tool in Excel, as illustrated in Chapter 11.

[6] Note that TOC analysis assumes that factory labor is not a direct and variable cost but is a fixed cost. This assumption applies when labor is a small or an unchanging part of total cost.

EXHIBIT 13.8 Summary of Data for HPI Inc., TOC Analysis

	HPI-2	HPI-3
Demand (per month)	3,000	1,800
Price	$600	$1,200
Materials cost	$300	$750

Process	Minutes Required for Each Product per Unit		Number of Employees	Total Hours Available per Month
	HPI-2	HPI-3		
1: Assemble earpiece	110	130	80	9,600
2: Test and program computer chip	0	30	8	960
3: Install other electronics	40	40	30	3,600
4: Perform final assembly and test	30	60	20	2,400
5: Pack and ship	25	25	18	2,160

Step 1: Identify the Constraint (the process for which total hours required for the given demand exceeds available hours—process 4)

	Hours Required				
	HPI-2	HPI-3	Total Hours	Hours Available	Slack Hours
Process 1: Assemble earpiece (5,500 hrs. = 3,000 × 110 ÷ 60, etc.)	5,500	3,900	9,400	9,600	200
Process 2: Test and program chip	0	900	900	960	60
Process 3: Install other electronics	2,000	1,200	3,200	3,600	400
Process 4: Perform final assembly and test	1,500	1,800	3,300	2,400	(900)
Process 5: Pack and ship	1,250	750	2,000	2,160	160

Step 2, Part 1: Identify Most Profitable Product = HPI-2

	HPI-2	HPI-3
Price	$600.00	$1,200.00
Materials cost	300.00	750.00
Throughput margin	$300.00	$ 450.00
Constraint time (for process 4)	30	60
Throughput margin per minute	$ 10.00	$ 7.50

Step 2, Part 2: Determine the Most Profitable Product Mix

	HPI-2	HPI-3	Hours per Unit	Constraint Time (process 4)
Total monthly demand	3,000 units	1,800 units		
Constraint process time available				2,400 hours
Time required to meet demand for most profitable product	3,000 units		× 0.50 =	1,500 hours
Constraint process time remaining to meet remaining demand and quantity that can be produced in the remaining time available		900 units	× 1.00 =	900 hours
Unmet demand	-0-	900 units		

is throughput margin *per minute of time in final assembly and test*—that is, a throughput per minute of $10 for HPI-2 and $7.50 for HPI-3. This means each minute of final assembly and test used to produce HPI-2 earns $10, while each minute used to produce HPI-3 earns only $7.50. HPI-2 is the more profitable product when final assembly and test is the constraint.

The best product mix is determined in step 2, part 2, of Exhibit 13.8. Because it is the more profitable product, HPI produces all 3,000 units of demand for HPI-2 and then determines the remaining capacity in final assembly. Finally, HPI determines the number of units of HPI-3 it can produce with the remaining capacity on the constraint. Despite the demand for 1,800 units of HPI-3, only 900 can be produced with the available capacity. Thus, the optimal product mix is 3,000 units of HPI-2 and 900 units of HPI-3.

The assumption in our illustration of the TOC approach is that minimal or no inventory of HPI-3 is maintained so that it is not possible to fill the unmet demand for HPI-3 out of inventory. This assumption is in keeping with the TOC approach, which emphasizes the reduction of cost and speed of product flow by removing constraints and reducing inventory levels.

Step 3: Maximize the Flow through the Constraint

In this step, the management accountant looks for ways to speed the flow through the constraint by simplifying the process, improving the product design, reducing setup time, and reducing other delays due to unscheduled and non-value-added activities such as inspections or machine breakdowns, among others.

Takt time
The speed at which units must be manufactured to meet customer demand.

A commonly used method for identifying constraints and smoothing production flow is the use of **Takt time**. *Takt* is a German word meaning the conductor's baton, or rhythm. It is the ratio of the total time available to the expected customer demand in units. For example, suppose a manufacturing plant operates for eight hours per day, and that after allowing for break time, 400 minutes of manufacturing time are available per day. Also, because the average customer demand per day is 800 units, the Takt time is 30 seconds per unit:

$$\text{Takt time} = \frac{\text{Available manufacturing time}}{\text{Customer demand}}$$

$$\text{Takt time} = \frac{400 \text{ minutes}}{800 \text{ units}} = \frac{1}{2}\text{minute} \left(\text{or } 30 \text{ seconds}\right) \text{ per unit}$$

This means that each unit must be manufactured in an average of 30 seconds to meet customer demand. To illustrate how Takt time can be used to identify constraints, consider a product that has demand of 18,000 units per week, with total operating time available per week at 75 hours. The Takt time is:

$$\frac{\text{Available time}}{\text{Demand}} = \frac{75 \text{ hours} \times 60 \text{ minutes} \times 60 \text{ seconds}}{18,000 \text{ units}}$$

$$= \frac{270,000 \text{ seconds}}{18,000 \text{ units}}$$

$$= 15 \text{ seconds per unit}$$

The plant must produce a unit each 15 seconds to keep up with demand. Assuming the manufacturing process has three operations in sequence, each requiring 15 seconds of processing time, a product will be completed every 15 seconds. Now, assume that the first operation requires 10 seconds, the second operation requires 20 seconds, and the third requires 15 seconds. The processing line is now unbalanced; the first operation moves quickly and work-in-process will build up at the relatively slower second operation. Furthermore, the total demand of 18,000 units cannot be met because the second process requires more than the 15 seconds of Takt time. The second operation is a constraint. In fact, the plant will be able to meet a demand of only 13,500 units (13,500 = 270,000 seconds ÷ 20 seconds per unit) because of the relatively slow second operation. Only when the three operations are balanced at or near the Takt time of 15 seconds will the demand be met. The goal of implementing Takt time is to balance the processing of the operations so that the processing time of each operation is preferably a little below the overall Takt time. An operation that has a very low processing time relative to Takt time has too much capacity, making it more efficient to reduce capacity (and thus increase processing time) on that operation, as long as processing time remains below Takt time.

Disruptions come in many forms, and while some disruptions might be anticipated, others can be completely unexpected.

DISRUPTIONS OF THE MANUFACTURING PROCESS

In its fiscal year 2016 10-K filing, global medical technology company Anika Therapeutics noted "manufacturing processes involve inherent risks, and disruption could materially adversely affect our business, financial condition and results of operations." These disruptions are the drivers of reduced production volumes, which generate an opportunity cost. The opportunity cost comes in the form of the profit lost, which can be determined with throughput analysis.

Source: Ge Bai, Takehisa, Kajiwara, and Jianbo Liu, "The Cost of Manufacturing Disruptions," *Strategic Finance,* December 2015, pp. 41–45.

UNEXPECTED SOCIAL CRISIS

The unfortunate outbreak of the coronavirus in China in early 2020 disrupted the production of many of Apple's devices. Unlike one if its rivals, Samsung Electronics, Apple had not diversified its manufacturing base, and China was manufacturing most of Apple's iPads, iPhones, and Mac computers. Apple's leaders had recognized the reliance on China as a strength but may have underestimated the vulnerability of that strategy. The delay in manufacturing might not be able to be made up, and the impact of the virus could be greater than that of the trade tariffs that had been put in place in 2019.

Source: Tripp Mickle, "Apple Faces Risk in Its Reliance on Chinese Factories," *The Wall Street Journal,* February 6, 2020, p. A6.

Step 4: Add Capacity to the Constraint

As a longer-term measure to relieve the constraint and improve cycle time, management should consider adding capacity to the constraints by adding new or improved machines and/or additional labor.

Step 5: Redesign the Manufacturing Process for Flexibility and Fast Cycle Time

The most complete strategic response to the constraint is to redesign the manufacturing process, including the introduction of new manufacturing technology, the deletion of some hard-to-manufacture products, and the redesign of some products for greater ease of manufacturing. Simply removing one or more minor features on a given product might speed up the production process significantly. The use of value engineering as described earlier might help at this point.

The Five Steps of Strategic Decision Making for Speed and Efficiency in the Fashion Industry

Founded in 1856, London-based Burberry Group PLC has become one of the top 10 most valuable luxury brands in the world. The company has several hundred retail stores worldwide providing its famous trench coats and a variety of fashion clothing and accessories for women, men, and children. Burberry CEO Angela Ahrendts, upon taking the position in July 2006, noticed that the company was making "way too much stuff." There were too many product lines—for example, 20 different versions of men's and women's polo shirts. The complexity of the large number of products resulted in delay throughout the value chain—design, manufacturing, and distribution.[7] The five steps of strategic decision making for Burberry, the fashion retailer, follow.

1. **Determine the strategic issues surrounding the problem.** Burberry, as a fashion retailer, competes on the basis of design and fashion innovation, a differentiation strategy.
2. **Identify the alternative actions.** The company can continue to focus on product development, design, and innovation, with the expectation that the delays will not affect customer satisfaction or profitability. Alternatively, the company could review its product lines and look for efficiency throughout the value chain and expect to maintain the unique designs that have satisfied its customers in the past.

[7] The information is from Burberry's 2018 annual report and from Cecilie Rohwedder, "Burberry CEO Retrenches: Fewer Items, Faster Delivery," *The Wall Street Journal,* May 24, 2007, p. B1. Other high fashion designers including Valentino, Gucci, and Zara are also changing design and manufacturing processes for greater speed and flexibility; see Christina Passariello, "Logistics Are in Vogue with Designers," *The Wall Street Journal,* June 27, 2008, p. B1; Kerry Capell, "Zara Thrives by Breaking All the Rules," *BusinessWeek,* October 20, 2008, p. 66; Christina Binkley, "Tracking the Trousers Cycle," *The Wall Street Journal,* August 16, 2007, p. D1.

3. **Obtain information and conduct analyses of the alternatives.** Ahrendts directed the CFO to prepare a report showing what amount each product contributed to overall sales. The findings were that 20% of the products produced 80% of total sales. The enterprise system SAP was later introduced to help determine product profitability.

4. **Based on strategy and analysis, choose and implement the desired alternative.** Based on the CFO's information and her understanding that the firm's strategy required comprehensive, coherent product development, Ahrendts decided to reduce the number of Burberry's products by one-third and to switch from two large collections of fashion per year to five smaller collections. At the same time, she coordinated product development from London so that all Burberry lines provided ". . . one brand and one message." The changes allowed the company to design and produce its fashions much more quickly, to adjust much more rapidly to changes in customer expectations, and to reduce costs through more efficient processes.

5. **Provide an ongoing evaluation of the effectiveness of implementation in step 4.** The changes made the company more competitive, more profitable, and better able to meet customer expectations. However, because design and innovation are the hallmarks of the fashion industry and for Burberry, the company must maintain a priority on these facets of the business as well. To this point, the company had a brand relaunch in 2017 under the direction of a new chief creative officer.

Theory of Constraints Reports

When a firm focuses on improving cycle time, eliminating constraints, and improving speed of delivery, the performance evaluation measures also focus on these critical success factors. A common approach is to report throughput margin as well as selected operating data in a *theory of constraints (TOC) report.* TOC reports are useful for identifying the most profitable product and for monitoring success in achieving the critical success factors. An example of this report used by a manufacturer of automotive glass is shown in Exhibit 13.9. Note in the exhibit that window styles H and B are the most profitable because they have far higher throughput margins based on the binding constraint, hours of furnace time. The throughput margin per hour is $3,667 for style H and $2,371 for style B; in contrast, the throughput margin per hour for styles C and A is less than $1,000.

Activity-Based Costing and the Theory of Constraints

Firms using such cost management methods as target costing and the theory of constraints may also employ activity-based costing (ABC). Like TOC, ABC is used to assess the profitability of products. The difference is that TOC takes a short-term approach to profitability analysis by emphasizing only materials-related costs, while ABC costing develops a long-term analysis by including all product costs.

EXHIBIT 13.9
The TOC Report for an Automotive Glass Manufacturer

Source: R. J. Campbell, "Pricing Strategy in the Automotive Glass Industry," *Management Accounting,* July 1989, pp. 26–34.

	Style C	Style A	Style H	Style B
Window size	0.77	0.073	7.05	4.95
Sales volume	High	Moderate	High	Moderate
Units in unfilled orders	1,113	234	882	23
Average lead time (days)	16	23	8	11
Market price	$2.82	$6.68	$38.12	$24.46
Direct production costs				
Materials	0.68	0.64	5.75	4.02
Scrap allowance	0.06	0.05	0.42	0.34
Materials handling	0.12	0.12	1.88	1.61
Subtotal	0.86	0.81	8.05	5.97
Throughput margin	$1.96	$5.87	$30.07	$18.49
Furnace hours per unit	0.0062	0.0061	0.0082	0.0078
Throughput margin per hour	$ 316	$ 962	$3,667	$2,371

EXHIBIT 13.10
Comparison of the TOC and ABC Costing Methods

	TOC	ABC
Main objective	Short-term focus; throughput margin analysis based on materials and materials-related costs	Long-term focus; analysis of all product costs, including direct materials, direct labor, and overhead
Resource constraints and capacities	Included explicitly; a principal focus of TOC	Not included explicitly except as shown in time-driven ABC (see Chapter 5)
Cost drivers	No direct utilization of cost drivers	Develops an understanding of cost drivers at the unit, batch, product, and facility levels
Major use	Optimization of production flow and short-term product mix	Strategic pricing and profit planning

ABC, unlike TOC, does not explicitly include the resource constraints and capacities of production activities. Thus, ABC cannot be used to determine the best short-term product mix. ABC and TOC are thus *complementary* methods; ABC provides a comprehensive analysis of cost drivers and accurate unit costs as a basis for strategic decisions about long-term pricing and product mix. In contrast, TOC provides a useful method for improving the short-term profitability of the manufacturing plant through short-term product mix adjustments and through attention to production constraints. The differences between ABC and TOC are outlined in Exhibit 13.10.

Life-Cycle Costing

LO 13-3

Describe how life-cycle costing facilitates strategic management.

Typically, product or service costs are measured and reported for relatively short periods, such as a month or a year. Life-cycle costing provides a long-term perspective because it considers the entire cost life cycle of the product or service (see Exhibit 13.11). It therefore provides a more complete perspective of product or service costs and profitability. For example, a product that is designed quickly and carelessly, with little investment in design costs, could have significantly higher marketing and service costs later in the life cycle. Managers are interested in the total costs to the company, over the entire life cycle, not manufacturing costs only.

While cost management methods have tended to focus only on manufacturing costs, upstream and downstream costs can account for a significant portion of total life-cycle costs, especially in certain industries:

Industries with High Upstream Costs

Computer software
Specialized industrial and medical equipment
Pharmaceuticals

EXHIBIT 13.11
Life-Cycle Costing in the Cost Life Cycle

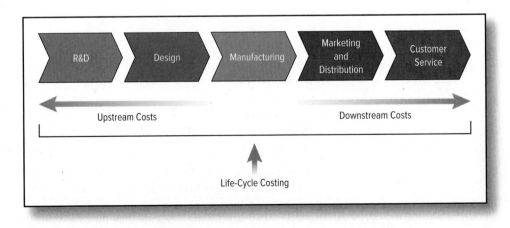

Industries with High Downstream Costs

Fashion apparel

Perfumes, cosmetics, and toiletries

The Importance of Design

As managers consider upstream and downstream costs, decision making at the design stage is critical. Target costing, as explained earlier in this chapter, shows that although the costs incurred at the design stage may account for only a very small percentage of the total costs over the entire product life cycle, design-stage decisions commit a firm to a given production, marketing, and service plan. Therefore, they lock in most of the remaining life-cycle costs.

This concept is illustrated in Exhibit 13.12, which shows the difference, in terms of time, between when costs are committed versus when those costs are actually incurred.

While Exhibit 13.12 shows the difference in timing between committing and incurring costs, Exhibit 13.13 provides an example of the effects of poor design and quality on life-cycle costs.

The critical success factors at the design stage include the following:

- **Reduced time to market.** In a competitive environment where the speed of product development and the speed of delivery are critical, efforts to reduce time to market have high priority.
- **Reduced expected service costs.** By careful, simple design and the use of modular, interchangeable components, the expected service costs can be greatly reduced.

EXHIBIT 13.12   Committed versus Incurred Costs

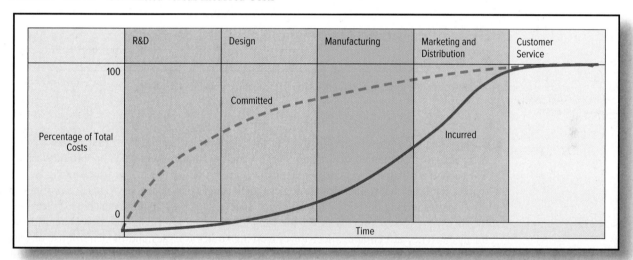

EXHIBIT 13.13
Value Chain Showing Upstream and Downstream Linkages for a Manufacturer

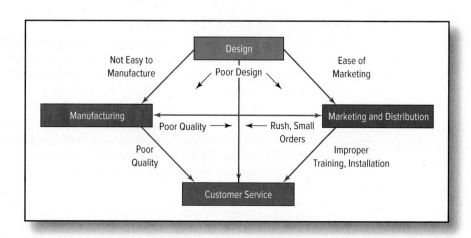

REAL-WORLD FOCUS   Social and Regulatory Pressures on Pricing

Companies are not free of outside pressures when setting prices. States around the U.S. are pushing pharmaceutical companies to justify price increases. A Nevada law goes so far as to require disclosures about production costs for specific drugs and the amounts spent on marketing of the product. Insurers are also putting downward pressure on the profit margins of retail drugstores by pitting pharmacy chains like Walgreens and CVS against each other in an effort to lock in lower costs.

Cost-conscious consumers can also make use of an app that helps patients find the best prices because, as the founder of Rx Savings Solutions said, "It is the same drug wherever you go, and people don't want to pay a premuim because it has Walgreens on the bottle or CVS on the bottle."

Sources: Robert Pear, "Companies Fighting Efforts by States to Rein in Drug Prices," The News & Observer, August 19, 2018, p.A4; "Trouble at the Corner Drugstore," Bloomberg Businessweek, April 22, 2019, p.18.

- **Reduced product environmental impact.** Product design should focus on sustainability; that is, efforts should be made to reduce or lower the product's carbon footprint (use of greenhouse gases) in manufacturing and in later use, to incorporate recycled materials, and so on.[8]

- **Improved ease of manufacture.** To reduce production costs and speed production, the design must be easy to manufacture.

- **Process planning and design.** The plan for the manufacturing process should be flexible, allowing for fast setups and product changeovers, using flexible manufacturing concepts, computer-integrated manufacturing, computer-assisted design, and concurrent engineering.

Strategic Pricing Using the Product Life Cycle

LO 13-4

Outline the objectives and techniques of strategic pricing.

"The single most important decision in evaluating a business is pricing power."

Warren Buffet

Management accountants are involved in three pricing situations: The first is the special-order decision (explained in Chapter 11) in which a nonrecurring sales opportunity arises. The second context is target costing (explained earlier in this chapter), in which a firm faces a market price and determines how to achieve the level of costs necessary to make a profit. The third type of pricing decision—not involving special orders or market-determined prices—is the focus in this section. These are the long-term, strategic pricing decisions facing many managers. They are complex decisions involving strategic issues and the careful use of cost information. To assist in these pricing decisions, the management accountant prepares cost information from the perspective of the cost life cycle and the sales life cycle and through the use of analytical pricing methods.

Pricing Using the Cost Life Cycle

Pricing based on costs is a common approach for manufacturing and service firms. Those companies that compete on cost leadership use cost information to improve operating efficiency to reduce costs and price. Prices are set by the most efficient producers: the ones that are best able to reduce costs. In contrast, firms that compete on differentiation have more discretion in setting prices. The differentiated firm's goal might be to increase profits by setting an initial high price for those willing to pay, followed by lower prices for the cost-conscious customers (called *skimming*). Alternatively, the firm's goal might be to increase market share by lowering the price (called *penetration*). A third approach would be to build longer-term customer relationships by utilizing "value pricing" in which pricing is based on meeting

---

[8] For information on the role of accountants regarding sustainability, see the IMA Statement on Management Accounting, *The Evolution of Accountability, Sustainability Reporting for Accountants* (2014).

specific customer needs. A firm's pricing policy is also influenced by patterns in the industry. For example, firms with seasonal demand (clothing, appliances, furniture, among others) usually offer discounts and promotions during the slow periods of the year. Other industries are sensitive to interest rates, stock market returns, other factors in the economy (automobiles and construction, among others), and new products or pricing policies of competitors. To deal with the complexity of the pricing decision, firms like GE Lighting, DHL, and Hewlett-Packard use web-based software systems to determine prices more quickly and accurately for different customers. The systems speed up the process of quoting prices and assist in determining the timing and location of discount programs. Thus, a number of seasonal, cyclical, economic, and other strategic factors influence the pricing policies of the firm, and cost information is only the starting point of the pricing decision. The cost information for pricing is commonly based on one of these four methods: (1) full manufacturing cost plus markup, (2) life-cycle cost plus markup, (3) full cost and desired gross margin percent, and (4) full cost plus desired return on assets.

Full Manufacturing Cost Plus Markup

In this method, a firm uses the total of variable and fixed manufacturing costs and applies a markup percentage to cover other operating costs plus profit. The markup percentage could be determined by industry practice, judgment, or a desired level of profit. Suppose that a firm has a markup rate of 40% and, using ABC costing, determines the full manufacturing cost is $150. The resulting price would be $210, calculated as $150 + (150 \times 40\%)$.

Life-Cycle Cost Plus Markup

The life-cycle approach to pricing uses the full life-cycle cost instead of manufacturing cost only. Suppose that in addition to manufacturing costs of $150 per unit, the example firm has selling and administrative costs of $25 per unit, for a total life-cycle cost of $175. The firm uses a markup rate of 25% based on life-cycle costs. The calculated price is now $218.75:

$$\text{Total life-cycle costs} \times \text{Markup} = \text{Price}$$
$$\$175 \times 125\% = \$218.75$$

The life-cycle approach has the advantage that all costs are included so that the markup percentage can be directly tied to a desired level of profit.

Full Cost and Desired Gross Margin Percentage

In this variation, the price is determined based upon achieving a desired gross margin percentage. To continue with the previous example, suppose that the desired gross margin is 30% of sales. Then, the price would be $214.29:

$$\text{Price} = \frac{\text{Full manufacturing cost}}{(1 - \text{Desired gross margin percentage})}$$
$$= \frac{\$150}{((1 - 0.3))} = \$214.29$$

This price would produce a gross margin of $214.29 - \$150 = \$64.29$, which is 30% of sales. Alternatively, a variation of this method could be used to achieve a desired percentage return on life-cycle costs. For example, if the desired percentage return on life-cycle costs is 15%, then the price would be $205.88:

$$\text{Price} = \frac{\text{Full life-cycle cost}}{(1 - \text{Desired life-cycle margin percentage})}$$
$$= \frac{\$175}{((1 - 0.15))} = \$205.88$$

Full Cost Plus Desired Return on Assets

Another pricing approach is to set the price to achieve a desired return on assets. Starting with the same information, now assume that the firm has an average of $3.5 million in assets committed to the production of the product and desires a 10% before-tax return on assets.

REAL-WORLD FOCUS   Setting Prices for Profitability

Setting prices can be tricky for any organization. While some companies compete on price, others compete on the basis of performance and adjust the price accordingly. The key is to identify value opportunities. One manufacturer of rubber stoppers was able to charge a premium for a product that was very similar to, but not exactly the same as, a low-priced stopper. The company was able to charge a premium because of the tighter tolerances and greater quality control needed by the customer because of the high-value application of the stopper.

Sometimes the value of differentiation is found by accident. Headset.com erroneously posted its products at cost rather than retail and found only a marginal increase in sales before the error was caught and corrected. It found that customer service, not price, was driving sales. Following that event, the company raised prices 8% and found virtually no change in sales volume, so revenue went up by about 8%.

In some cases, it is transparency that helps customers feel good about the prices they pay. The leather goods company Oliver Cabell provides a cost breakdown of all of its products on its website. One item, for example, had the following cost information for a pair of shoes priced at $188: Leather: $8.04, Lining: $3.12, Outsoles: $6.60, In-soles: $1.80, Cutting/Manufacturing/Quality Control: $29.88, Packaging: $3.96, Transit: $12.43, Duties: $5.36, Shipping: $11.50. In addition, the company provides information on the sources of the materials and where the work is done. The information for these same shoes included the fact that the laces were made of Italian cotton and that the shoes were hand stitched in Marche, Italy. This information appeals to certain customers and helps them feel better about the price.

Sources: Frank Cespedes, Elliot Ross, and Benson Shapiro, "Raise Your Prices," *The Wall Street Journal,* May 24, 2010, p. R8; Eilene Zimmerman, "Real-Life Lessons in the Delicate Art of Setting Prices," *The Wall Street Journal,* April 21, 2011, p. B4.

Sales are expected to be 10,000 units. Using a life-cycle cost approach (a full manufacturing cost approach could be used in a similar manner), the markup percentage would be 20%.

$$\text{Markup rate} = \frac{\text{Desired before-tax profit}}{\text{Life-cycle cost of expected sales}}$$
$$= \frac{\$3,500,000 \times 10\%}{10,000 \times \$175} = 20\%$$

And the price would then be $210:

$$\text{Price} = \text{Life-cycle cost} \times 120\% = \$175 \times 120\% = \$210$$

Each of these illustrations assumes that all sales are for the price determined. The desired price could be adjusted to reflect expected discounts or losses due to spoilage or theft.

Strategic Pricing for Phases of the Sales Life Cycle

Strategic pricing depends on the position of the product or service in the sales life cycle. As the sales life cycle becomes shorter (only months in some industries such as consumer electronics), the analysis of the sales life cycle becomes increasingly important. In contrast to the cost life cycle just described, the sales life cycle refers to the phase of the product's or service's sales in the market, from introduction of the product or service to decline and withdrawal from the market. (Exhibit 13.2 illustrates the phases of the sales life cycle.)

Phase 1: Introduction. The first phase involves little competition, and sales rise slowly as customers become aware of the new product or service. Costs are relatively high because of high R&D expenditures and capital costs for setting up production facilities and marketing efforts. Prices are relatively high because of product differentiation and the high costs at this phase. Product variety is limited.

Phase 2: Growth. Sales begin to increase rapidly, as does product variety. The product continues to enjoy the benefits of differentiation. Competition increases, and prices begin to fall.

Phase 3: Maturity. Sales continue to increase but at a decreasing rate. The number of competitors and product variety both decline. Prices fall further, and differentiation is no longer important. Competition is based on cost given competitive quality and functionality.

Phase 4: Decline. Sales and prices decline, as do the number of competitors. Control of costs and an effective distribution network are key to continued survival.

REAL-WORLD FOCUS   AI and Big Data Come to Pricing

It used to cost $16.95 for an adult to enter the Indianapolis Zoo, but now the price can be somewhere between $8 and $30, depending on the day and time the person wishes to enter. The zoo uses data on advance sales and from history to price the tickets dynamically. Since introducing this approach to pricing, the zoo's revenues are up 12%, and the zoo is not alone in adopting these practices.

One day in 2017, the price of a gallon of gas at a Shell-branded gas station rose 3½ cents over the course of the afternoon. The station manager was using artificial intelligence algorithms to set the price. This practice moves beyond

dynamic pricing by crunching historical and real-time data to predict reactions to price changes under different scenarios. The station manager can set a goal, such as boosting sales revenue, and the algorithms do the rest. The manager said, "It's about making margin on people who don't care and giving away margin to people who do care."

Sources: Sam Schechner, "To Set Prices, Stores Turn to Algorithms—Potential Consumer Downside: Software Can Cause Firms to Charge More," *The Wall Street Journal*, May 9, 2017, p. A1; Jack Nicas, "The Price You Pay Depends on Your Timing," *The Wall Street Journal*, December 14, 2015, p. B1.

In the first phase, the focus of management is on design, differentiation, and marketing. The focus shifts to new product development and pricing strategy as competition develops in the second phase. In the third and fourth phases, management's attention turns to cost control, quality, and service as the market continues to become more competitive. Thus, the firm's strategy for the product or service changes over the sales life cycle from differentiation in the early phases to cost leadership in the final phases.

Similarly, the strategic pricing approach changes over the product or service life cycle. In the first phase, pricing is set relatively high to recover development costs and to take advantage of product differentiation and the new demand for the product. In the second phase, pricing is likely to stay relatively high as the firm attempts to build profitability in the growing market. In the latter phases, pricing becomes more competitive, and target costing and life-cycle costing methods are used as the firm becomes more of a price taker than a price setter and makes efforts to reduce upstream and downstream costs.

Strategic Pricing: Analytical and Peak Pricing Methods

Increasingly, retailers, manufacturers, and even service providers use a strategic approach to pricing in which they determine prices by what the customer is willing to bear, often using analytical methods based upon extensive data analysis of customers' buying behaviors. Consider, for example, the variability in the prices charged to fly between two destinations, the higher price for electricity in the middle of the day, the difference in the cost of a hotel room on a weekend versus a weekday, or the cost of peak versus off-peak minutes for a cell phone plan. Another example is the use of a "fighter brand," a low-priced version of the well-known product. The fighter brand is especially common in a recessionary environment, as consumers of high-end products look for less expensive substitutes.[9]

Summary

The strategic cost management concepts introduced in the preceding chapters are extended here. First, we discuss four cost management methods used to analyze the product's or service's life cycle: target costing, the theory of constraints, life-cycle costing, and strategic pricing. Target costing is a tool for analyzing the cost structure to help management identify the proper design features and manufacturing methods to allow the firm to meet a competitive price.

Target costing has five steps:

1. Determine market price.
2. Determine desired profit.
3. Calculate target cost.
4. Use value engineering to identify ways to reduce costs.
5. Use kaizen and operational control to further reduce costs.

[9] Thomas H. Davenport and Jeanne G. Harris, *Competing on Analytics* (Boston: Harvard Business School Press, 2007); Josh Hyatt, "And in This Corner, the Fighter Brand," *CFO.com*, December 1, 2008; Rebecca Smith, "Electricity: The New Math," *The Wall Street Journal*, July 19, 2010, p. A6; Scott McCartney, "You Paid What for That Flight?," *The Wall Street Journal*, August 26, 2010, p. D1.

The theory of constraints (TOC) is a tool that assists managers in identifying bottlenecks (constraints) and scheduling production to maximize throughput and profits. TOC analysis has five steps:

1. Identify the constraint.
2. Determine the most efficient product mix given the constraint.
3. Maximize the flow through the constraint.
4. Add capacity to the constraint.
5. Redesign the manufacturing process for flexibility and fast throughput.

Life-cycle costing assists managers in minimizing total costs over the product's or service's entire life cycle. Life-cycle costing brings a focus to the upstream (before production) activities (research and development, engineering) and downstream (after production) activities (marketing, distribution, service), as well as the manufacturing and operations that cost systems traditionally focus on. Especially important is a careful consideration of the effects of design choices on downstream costs.

Strategic pricing helps management determine the price of the product or service based on its life-cycle costs or its position in the different phases of its sales life cycle.

Key Terms

concurrent engineering, *544*
constraints, *549*
cost life cycle, *539*
cost tables, *543*
cycle time, *549*
design analysis, *543*

flow diagram, *550*
functional analysis, *542*
group technology, *543*
manufacturing cycle efficiency (MCE), *549*
manufacturing cycle time, *549*

quality function deployment (QFD), *546*
sales life cycle, *540*
Takt time, *553*
throughput margin, *551*
value engineering, *542*

Comments on Cost Management in Action

Why Go Abroad?

In competitive industries such as computers, consumer electronics, and auto, manufacturers continuously look for ways to reduce cost and increase value throughout the value chain. These industries have chosen to locate extensive manufacturing operations and/or partners in Latin America and China to reduce costs and to benefit from innovative manufacturing methods and facilities. Wage costs are lower and, using target costing and value engineering, manufacturing processes are built around modular manufacturing methods that reduce the number of parts in the product, speeding the manufacturing process and reducing costs.

Automobile Manufacturing   The cost of designing and developing a new car could run into the billions of dollars. Once designed, the automobiles may have thousands of components, obtained from hundreds of suppliers. The Canadian company Magna International can help manufacturers minimize these costs by mass-producing components. For example, Magna manufactures nearly 10 million cameras per year for the cars of competing manufacturers. Each car company benefits from the lower cost of production, and it can focus on design and placement of the cameras rather than the expertise to produce them. Also, as companies such as Uber and Apple consider whether to build and sell self-driving cars, they will need the expertise of a company like Magna to develop the hardware, allowing the companies themselves to focus their resources on the essential software.

The trend to economic nationalism, along with other anti-globalization and anti-immigration efforts, threatens these cross-border relationships. Companies such as Magna and Ford must carefully consider their strategies for future ties such as this, to preserve their business success in coming years.

Consumer Electronics and Computer Products   Why is outsourcing manufacturing to foreign plants an advantage to Apple and Hewlett-Packard? The contract manufacturers' manufacturing experience and technology give them a cost advantage. Foxconn and the other contract manufacturers also can focus on the manufacturing process rather than the entire product value chain. Moreover, they gain economies of scale by manufacturing similar products for different clients. The use of contract manufacturing is an important part of the strategy to achieve target costs while maintaining product leadership in design and customer service. These arrangements are not, however, without risks in terms of both supply and reputation.

Sources: Alex Webb, Gerrit DeVynck, and Elisabeth Behrmann, "The Foxconn of the Auto Industry," *Bloomberg Businessweek,* September 2016, p. 32; Justin Scheck, "Dell Plans to Sell Factories in Effort to Cut Costs," *The Wall Street Journal,* September 5, 2008, p. 1; Jason Dean and Ting-I Tsai, "Suicides Spark Inquiries; Apple, H-P to Examine Asian Supplier after String of Deaths at Factory," *The Wall Street Journal* (Online), May 26, 2010; Aries Poon, Loretta Chao, and Yukari Iwatani Kane, "Factory Blast Roils Tech Supply Chain; China's Hon Hai Closes Product Polishing Workshops," *The Wall Street Journal* (Online), May 24, 2011.

Best Brand Lighting Inc.

Best Brand Lighting Inc. (BBL) manufactures lighting fixtures. The two major markets for BBL products are major retailers (including Home Depot, Walmart, and Kmart) and specialty lighting stores. The former sell primarily to homeowners, and the latter primarily to electrical contractors.

Although its standard sizes and models typically are sold to the large retailers, BBL sells its products with more specialized features and sizes only to the specialty stores. Thus, the design and manufacturing costs of the products going to the specialty stores are slightly higher. The products in both markets have similar sales life cycles of about 2 years.

Because of the difference in consumers, BBL has a larger marketing cost for the products sold to the large retailers—advertising in major media to attract homeowners. In contrast, the marketing for the specialty shops consists mainly of catalogs and advertisements in trade publications, resulting in a lower overall marketing cost. The sales policies also differ somewhat for the two markets. Sales to specialty stores are priced higher but include significant discounts and attractive return policies. In contrast, sales to the major retailers have restrictive return policies and offer little, if any, discount.

BBL management is interested in an in-depth analysis of the profitability of its two markets. As a first step, it has asked for the average costs and other data for all BBL products:

	Major Retailers	Specialty Stores
Design costs	$ 0.80	$ 1.10
Manufacturing costs	5.20	5.90
Marketing costs	0.95	0.10
Returns	0.05	0.95
Discounts	0.10	0.95
Average price	10.55	12.50
Total market ($000) in BBL's sales region	188,000	32,000
Current unit sales ($000)	9,200	8,000

Required   Using the methods discussed in this chapter, analyze BBL's two market segments. What questions would you want to ask management and which fact-finding studies would be appropriate to support this analysis?

The Student Resources section of Connect includes video tutorials for the Self-Study Problems.

13-1   What is target costing?

13-2   Explain the two methods for reducing total product costs to achieve a desired target cost. Which is more common in the consumer electronics industries? In the specialized equipment manufacturing industries?

13-3   What does the term *sales life cycle* mean? What are the phases of the sales life cycle? How does it differ from the cost life cycle?

13-4   Do pricing strategies change over the different phases of the sales life cycle? Explain how.

13-5   Do cost management practices change over the product's sales life cycle? Explain how.

13-6   What does the concept of value engineering mean? How is it used in target costing?

13-7   For what types of firms is target costing most appropriate and why?

13-8   What is life-cycle costing? Why is it used?

13-9   Name the five steps of the theory of constraints and explain the purpose of each. Which is the most important step and why?

13-10   What does the term *constraints* mean in the theory of constraints analysis?

13-11   What is the role of the flow diagram in the theory of constraints analysis?

13-12   What is the main difference between activity-based costing and the theory of constraints? When is it appropriate to use each one?

13-13   For what types of firms is the theory of constraints analysis most appropriate? Why?

13-14   How important is product design in life-cycle costing? Why?

13-15   For what types of firms is life-cycle costing most appropriate? Why?

13-16   Explain the difference in intended application between strategic pricing and life-cycle costing.

13-17   How is Takt time calculated, and what is it used for?

13-18   Distinguish pricing based on the cost life cycle and pricing based on the sales life cycle, and give an example method for each.

13-19   At what phase in the product sales life cycle will prices likely be the highest: introduction, growth, maturity, or decline?

Brief Exercises

[LO 13-1] 13-20 The market price for a product has been $50 per unit, but competitive pressures have reduced the market price to $45. The firm manufactures 10,000 of these products per year at a manufacturing cost of $38 per unit (including $22 fixed cost and $16 variable cost per unit). Other selling and administrative costs for the product are $8 per unit. What is the firm's target manufacturing cost for this product if the profit per unit is to remain unchanged?

[LO 13-4] 13-21 The firm in Brief Exercise 13-20 ignores competitive prices because it has a differentiated product. It uses full manufacturing cost–based pricing with a 40 percent markup. What is the firm's price?

[LO 13-4] 13-22 The firm in Brief Exercise 13-20 ignores competitive prices because it has a differentiated product. It uses life-cycle cost-based pricing with a 10 percent markup. What is the firm's price?

[LO 13-1] 13-23 Comdex Inc. manufactures parts for the telecom industry. One of its products that currently sells for $160 is now facing a new competitor that offers the same product for $140. The parts currently cost Comdex $130. Comdex believes it must reduce its price to $140 to remain competitive. What is the target cost of the product if Comdex desires a 25 percent profit on sales dollars?

[LO 13-2] 13-24 If a customer order is placed on May 1, the company expects to begin processing it on May 10, and the order is shipped on May 20, the manufacturing cycle time is then how many days long?

[LO 13-2] 13-25 If Toyota Motor Company receives an order on May 1, begins production on May 19, and ships the order on May 20 immediately following production, then what is the manufacturing cycle efficiency (MCE) ratio?

[LO 13-2] 13-26 If customer demand is 200,000 units per month, and available manufacturing capacity is 6,000 hours per week, what is the Takt time for this firm?

[LO 13-4] 13-27 Why do prices at theme parks in Orlando, Florida, remain high despite seasonal and economic cyclical ups and downs? What type of strategic pricing is used by these theme parks?

Exercises

[LO 13-1] 13-28 **Target Costing** MaxiDrive manufactures a wide variety of parts for recreational boating, including a gear and driveshaft part for high-powered outboard boat engines. Original equipment manufacturers such as Mercury and Honda purchase the components for use in large, powerful outboards. The part sells for $610, and sales volume averages 25,000 units per year. Recently, MaxiDrive's major competitor reduced the price of its equivalent unit to $550. The market is very competitive, and MaxiDrive realizes it must meet the new price or lose significant market share. Management has begun paying closer attention to costs and has reconfirmed the existing standard costs. The controller then assembled the following cost and usage data for the most recent year for MaxiDrive's production of 25,000 units:

	Budgeted Quantity	Budgeted Cost	Actual Quantity	Actual Cost
Direct materials		$ 6,500,000		$7,000,000
Direct labor		2,500,000		2,625,000
Indirect labor		2,500,000		2,400,000
Inspection (hours and cost)	920	300,000	1,000	350,000
Materials handling (number of purchases and cost)	3,500	500,000	3,450	485,000
Machine setups (number and cost)	1,400	750,000	1,500	725,000
Returns and rework (number of times and cost)	300	80,000	500	130,000
		$13,130,000		$13,715,000

Required
1. Calculate the target cost for maintaining current market share and profitability.
2. Can the target cost be achieved? How?

[LO 13-1] 13-29 **Target Costing** Bowman Specialists Inc. (BSI) manufactures specialized equipment for polishing optical lenses. There are two models—one (A–25) principally used for fine eyewear and the other (A–10) for lenses used in binoculars, cameras, and similar equipment.

The following table shows how the manufacturing cost of each unit is calculated, using activity-based costing, for these manufacturing cost pools.

Cost Pools	Allocation Base	Costing Rate
Materials handling	Number of parts	$2.25 per part
Manufacturing supervision	Hours of machine time	$23.50 per hour
Assembly	Number of parts	$2.55 per part
Machine setup	Each setup	$44.60 per setup
Inspection and testing	Logged hours	$35.00 per hour
Packaging	Logged hours	$15.00 per hour

BSI currently sells the A–10 model for $1,050 and the A–25 model for $725. Manufacturing costs and activity usage for the two products follow:

	A–10	A–25
Direct materials	$143.76	$66.44
Number of parts	121	92
Machine hours	6	4
Inspection time	1	0.6
Packing time	0.7	0.4
Setups	2	1

Required

1. Calculate the product cost and product margin for each product.

2. A new competitor has entered the market for lens-polishing equipment with a superior product at significantly lower prices, $825 for the A–10 model and $595 for the A–25 model. To try to compete, BSI has made some radical improvements in the design and manufacturing of its two products. The materials costs and activity usage rates have been decreased significantly, as follows:

	A–10	A–25
Direct materials	$78.65	$42.45
Number of parts	110	81
Machine hours	5	2
Inspection time	1	0.5
Packing time	0.7	0.2
Setups	1	1

Calculate the total product costs with the new activity usage data. Can BSI make a positive gross margin with the new costs, assuming that it must meet the price set by the new competitor?

3. Assume the information in requirement 2, but further assume that BSI management is not satisfied with the gross margin on the A–10 after the cost improvements. BSI wants a $50 gross margin on A–10. Suppose you are able to change the number of parts to reduce costs further to achieve the desired $50 margin. How much would the number of parts have to change to provide the desired gross margin? (*Hint:* Use the Excel Goal Seek function.)

4. What cost management method might be useful to BSI at this time, and why?

[LO 13-1]   13-30   **Target Costing in a Service Firm** Take-a-Break Travel Company offers spring break travel packages to college students. Two of its packages, a 7-day, 6-night trip to Cancun and a 5-day, 4-night trip to Jamaica, have the following characteristics:

Package Specifications	Cancun	Jamaica	Cost Data
Oceanfront room; number of nights	6	4	$55/night
Meals:			
Breakfasts	6	4	$10/ea
Lunches	7	5	$15/ea
Dinners	6	4	$25/ea
Scuba diving trips	3	2	$75/ea
Water skiing trips	4	2	$50/ea
Airfare (round trip from Miami)	1	1	$375 (Cancun), $550 (Jamaica)
Transportation to and from airport	1	1	$25 (Cancun), $40 (Jamaica)

The Cancun trip sells for $1,750, and the Jamaica trip sells for $1,500, and both packages allow two bags to be checked for free.

Required

1. What are the current profit margins on both trips?

2. Take-a-Break's management believes that it must drop the price of each trip by $100 in order to remain competitive in the market. Recalculate profit margins for both packages at these price levels.

3. Describe two ways that Take-a-Break Travel could cut its costs to get the profit margins back to their original levels.

[LO 13-1]   13-31   **Target Costing Using Quality Function Deployment (QFD)** Rick's is a popular restaurant for fine dining. The owner and chef, Rick Goetz, is pleased with his success and is now considering expanding his existing restaurant or perhaps opening a second restaurant. Before making his decision, Rick wants to find out more about his competitive position. There are three other restaurants that compete directly with him on food quality and price. Rick knows that his profitability depends on his ability to provide a satisfying meal at the market price. His first step was to gather some information about his customers, using an independent market research firm, which informed him that his customers were looking for taste, comfort (the ambiance, service, and overall presentation of the food), and enjoyment (the distinctiveness of the dining experience, a degree of excitement). He was surprised to find that comfort and enjoyment ranked highest:

First: Customer Criteria and Ranking

	Importance	Relative Importance
Taste	45	15.00%
Comfort	95	31.67
Enjoyment	160	53.33
Total	300	100.0%

Next, he worked with his key wait staff and chefs to try to identify the three main components, and related costs, of the service Rick's provides:

Second: Components and Cost

Components	Cost	Percentage of Total
Menu and food preparation	$ 8	30.77%
Wait staff	12	46.15
Food ingredients	6	23.08
Total	$26	100.00%

Having the customer criteria and components, Rick now again worked with his staff to assess how each component contributes to the desired customer criteria:

Third: Determine How Components Contribute to Customer Satisfaction

	Customer Criteria		
Components	Taste	Comfort	Enjoyment
Menu and food preparation	30%	20%	45%
Wait staff	30	60	35
Food ingredients	40	20	20
	100%	100%	100%

Required

1. Using the information Rick has developed, determine the importance index for each component (menu and food preparation, wait staff, and food ingredients).

2. Compare your findings in requirement 1 to the cost of the components. What conclusions can you draw from this comparison?

[LO 13-2]   13-32   **Manufacturing Cycle Efficiency** Waymouth Manufacturing operates a contract manufacturing plant located in Dublin, Ireland. The plant provides a variety of electronics products and components to consumer goods manufacturers around the world. Cycle time is a critical success factor for Waymouth, which has developed a number of measures of manufacturing speed. Waymouth has studied the matter and found that competitive contract manufacturers have manufacturing cycle efficiency (MCE) of about 40 percent. When last calculated, Waymouth's MCE was 35 percent.

Key measures from the recent month's production, averaged over all the jobs during that period, are as follows:

Activity	Average Time (hours)
New product development	30
Materials handling	2
Order setup	6
Machine maintenance	3
Order scheduling	1
Inspection of completed order	5
Pack and move to storage or ship	2
Manufacturing assembly	24
Order taking and checking	3
Receiving and stocking raw materials	6
Inspection of raw materials at start of production	2

Required   Determine the manufacturing cycle efficiency (MCE) for the recent month. What can you infer from the MCE you calculated?

[LO 13-2]   13-33   **Takt Time** Johnson Electronics manufactures a power supply used in a variety of electronics products, including printers, modems, and routers. The demand for the part is 8,400 units per week. The production of the power supply requires six different manufacturing operations, each in sequence and each having the following processing times. The net available time to work is 70 hours per week, using two shifts.

Operation	Processing Time (seconds)
Operation 1	25
Operation 2	22
Operation 3	30
Operation 4	24
Operation 5	34
Operation 6	28

Required
1. What is the Takt time, in seconds, for this product?
2. Is the processing line properly balanced for this product? Why or why not?
3. What is the strategic role of Takt time, and how is it implemented by the cost management analyst?

[LO 13-3]   13-34   **Life-Cycle Costing; Service Department** In the chapter, we illustrated the use of the life-cycle concept for both the cost and sales life cycles of a company's product lines. It can also be useful to extend the cost life cycle to the service department. In Chapter 7, we were interested in the allocation of service department costs to product lines. Here we are interested in managing the costs of a service department over its life cycle. The information technology department (IT) is a good example. The costs incurred in IT have the following phases:

1. Acquire IT assets, including computers, hubs, cables, and other assets.
2. Acquire software and deploy IT for the desired application and functionality.
3. Maintain management and operations of the IT assets.
4. Provide user support.
5. Retire the assets on a planned schedule and replace as needed.

Required   How can life-cycle costing help in the management of the IT department?

[LO 13-4]   13-35   **Pricing** Williams Inc. produces a single product, a part used in the manufacture of automobile transmissions. Known for its quality and performance, the part is sold to luxury auto manufacturers around the world. Because this is a quality product, Williams has some flexibility in pricing the part. The firm calculates the price using a variety of pricing methods and then chooses the final price based on that information and other strategic information. A summary of the key cost information follows. Williams expects to manufacture and sell 50,000 parts in the coming year. While the demand for Williams's part has been growing in the past 2 years, management is not only aware of the cyclical nature of the automobile industry, but also concerned about market share and profits during the industry's current downturn.

	Total Costs
Variable manufacturing	$ 4,680,000
Variable selling and administrative	855,650
Facility-level fixed overhead	2,345,875
Fixed selling and administrative	675,495
Batch-level fixed overhead	360,000
Total investment in product line	22,350,000
Expected sales (units)	50,000

Required (round prices to 4 decimal places)

1. Determine the price for the part using a markup of 45 percent of full manufacturing cost.
2. Determine the price for the part using a markup of 25 percent of full life-cycle cost.
3. Determine the price for the part using a desired gross margin percentage to sales of 40 percent.
4. Determine the price for the part using a desired life-cycle cost margin percentage to sales of 25%.
5. Determine the price for the part using a desired before-tax return on investment of 15 percent.
6. Determine the contribution margin and operating profit for each of the methods in requirements 1 through 5. Which price would you choose, and why?

[LO 13-4]   13-36   **Pricing Military Contracts** The Pentagon is constantly seeking ways to procure the most effective combat equipment and systems at the lowest possible cost. A key element in most procurement contracts is a fixed fee based on a percentage of the full cost for the contract plus a percentage fixed fee that is incentive-based. The latter is based on meeting contract deadlines and meeting or exceeding other contract performance measures. An actual Pentagon contract with Boeing involved a 10 percent fixed fee on cost incurred and another 5 percent as an incentive award.

Required Evaluate the compensation plan for this contract, with the fixed fee of 10 percent and the incentive fee of 5 percent. What do you think is the role of the incentive fee, and do you think it is too large or too small?

[LO 13-4]   13-37   **Life-Cycle Pricing** Matt Simpson owns and operates Quality Craft Rentals, which offers canoe rentals and shuttle service on the Nantahala River. Customers can rent canoes at one station, enter the river there, and exit at one of two designated locations to catch a shuttle that returns them to their vehicles at the station they entered. Following are the costs involved in providing this service each year:

	Fixed Costs	Variable Costs
Canoe maintenance	$ 2,300	$ 2.50
Licenses and permits	3,000	0
Vehicle leases	5,400	0
Station lease	6,920	0
Advertising	6,000	0.50
Operating costs	21,000	0.50

Quality Craft Rentals began business with a $25,000 expenditure for a fleet of 30 canoes. These are expected to last 10 more years, at which time a new fleet must be purchased. Rentals have been stable at about 6,400 per year.

Required Matt is happy with the steady rental average of 6,400 per year. For this number of rentals, what price should he charge per rental for the business to make an annual 20 percent before-tax return on assets using life-cycle costs?

Problems

[LO 13-1]

13-38   Target Costing in a Service Firm UR Safe Systems installs home security systems. Two of its systems, the ICU 100 and the ICU 900, have these characteristics:

Design Specifications	ICU 100	ICU 900	Cost Data
Video cameras	1	3	$150/ea
Video monitors	1	1	$75/ea
Motion detectors	5	8	$15/ea
Floodlights	3	7	$8/ea
Alarms	1	2	$15/ea
Wiring	700 ft.	1,100 ft.	$0.10/ft.
Installation	16 hr	26 hr	$20/hr

The ICU 100 sells for $810 installed, and the ICU 900 sells for $1,520 installed.

Required

1. What are the current gross profit margin percentages on both systems?

2. UR Safe's management believes that it must drop the price on the ICU 100 to $750 and on the ICU 900 to $1,390 to remain competitive in the market. Recalculate gross profit margin percentages for both products at these price levels and then compute the target cost needed for each product to maintain the current gross profit margin percentages.

3. Describe two ways that UR Safe could cut its costs to get the gross profit margins back to their original levels.

[LO 13-1]

13-39   Target Costing; Review of Chapter 11 Morrow Company is a large manufacturer of auto parts for automakers and parts distributors. Although Morrow has plants throughout the world, most are in North America. Morrow is known for the quality of its parts and for the reliability of its operations. Customers receive their orders in a timely manner, and there are no errors in the shipment or billing of these orders. For these reasons, Morrow has prospered in a business that is very competitive, with competitors such as Delphi, Visteon, and others.

Morrow just received an order for 100 auto parts from National Motors Corp., a major auto manufacturer. National proposed a $1,500 selling price per part. Morrow usually earns a 20 percent operating margin as a percent of sales. Morrow recently decided to use target costing in pricing its products. An examination of the production costs by the engineers and accountants showed that this part was assigned a standard full life-cycle cost of $1,425 per part (this includes $1,000 production, $200 marketing, and $225 general and administration costs per part). Morrow's Value Assessment Group (VAG) undertook a cost reduction program for this part. Two production areas that were investigated were the defective unit rate and the tooling costs. The $1,000 production costs included a normal defective cost of $85 per part. Group leaders suggested that production changes could reduce defective cost to $25 per part.

Forty-five tools were used to make the auto part. The group discovered that the number of tools could be reduced to 30 and that less expensive tools could be used on this part to meet National's product specifications. These changes saved an additional $105 of production cost per part. By studying other problem areas, the group found that general and administration costs could be reduced by $50 per unit through use of electronic data interchange with suppliers and just-in-time inventory management.

In addition, Morrow's sales manager told the group that National might be willing to pay a higher selling price because of Morrow's quality reputation and reliability. He believed National's proposed price was a starting point for negotiations. Of course, National had made the same offer to some of Morrow's competitors.

Required

1. What is Morrow's target cost per auto part? Explain.

2. As a result of the Value Engineering Group's efforts, determine Morrow's estimated cost for the auto part. Will Morrow meet the target cost for the part? Do you recommend that Morrow take National's offer? Explain your reasons.

(Adapted from a problem by Joseph San Miguel)

[LO 13-1]

13-40   Target Costing; Health Care VIP-MD is a health maintenance organization (HMO) located in North Carolina. Unlike the traditional fee-for-service model that determines the payment according to the actual services used or costs incurred, VIP-MD receives a fixed, prepaid amount from subscribers. The per member, per month rate (PMPM) is determined by estimating the health care cost per enrollee within a geographic location. The average health care coverage in North Carolina costs $368 per month, which is the same amount irrespective of the subscriber's age. Because individuals are demanding quality care at reasonable rates, VIP-MD must contain its costs to remain competitive. A major competitor, National Physicians, entered the North Carolina market early in the current year with a monthly premium of $325. VIP-MD wants to maintain its current market penetration and hopes to increase the number of its enrollees in the current year. The latest data on the number of enrollees and the associated costs follow:

Age	Enrollment in Current Year	Projected Enrollment Next Year	Average Monthly Cost in Current Year
1–4	45,688	48,977	$ 11,147,872
5–14	82,456	84,663	10,059,632
15–19	95,873	95,887	8,436,824
20–24	66,246	67,882	9,539,424
25–34	133,496	132,554	26,432,208
35–44	166,876	175,446	38,882,108
45–54	85,496	90,889	22,741,936
55–64	99,624	101,923	28,691,712
65–74	156,288	161,559	49,518,144
75–84	67,895	72,465	33,432,760
85 years and older	23,499	26,849	24,286,475
	1,023,437	1,059,094	$263,169,095

Required

1. Calculate the target cost required for VIP-MD to maintain its current market share and profit per enrollee in the current year.

2. Costs in the health care industry applicable to VIP-MD and National Physicians are expected to increase by 7 percent in the coming year. VIP-MD is planning for the year ahead and is expecting all providers, including VIP-MD and National Physicians, to increase their rates by $25 to $350. Calculate the new target cost assuming again that VIP-MD wants to maintain the same profit per enrollee as in the current year.

3. Identify the critical success factors for VIP-MD. How can the HMO maintain its market share?

[LO 13-1] 13-41 **Target Cost; Warehousing** Caldwell Supply, a wholesaler, has determined that its operations have three primary activities: purchasing, warehousing, and distributing. The firm reports the following operating data for the year just completed:

Activity	Cost Driver	Quantity of Cost Driver	Cost per Unit of Cost Driver
Purchasing	Number of purchase orders	1,000	$150 per order
Warehousing	Number of moves	8,000	30 per move
Distributing	Number of shipments	500	80 per shipment

Caldwell buys 100,000 units at an average unit cost of $10 and sells them at an average unit price of $20. The firm also has fixed operating costs of $250,000 for the year.

Caldwell's customers are demanding a 10 percent discount for the coming year. The company expects to sell the same amount if the demand for price reduction can be met. Caldwell's suppliers, however, are willing to give only a 2 percent discount.

Required Caldwell has estimated that it can reduce the number of purchase orders to 680 and can decrease the cost of each shipment by $3 with minor changes in its operations. Any further cost savings must come from reengineering the warehousing processes. What is the target cost for warehousing if the firm desires to earn the same amount of profit next year?

[LO 13-1] 13-42 **Target Costing; International** Harpers Ltd. is a UK manufacturer of casual shoes for men and women. It has sustained strong growth in the UK market in recent years due to its close attention to fashion trends. Harpers's shoes also have a good reputation for quality and comfort. To expand the business, Harpers is considering introducing its shoes to the U.S. market, where comparable shoes sell for an average of $90 wholesale, more than $16 above what Harpers charges in the UK (average price, £57, and average exchange rate of $1.30 per £). Management has engaged a marketing consultant to obtain information about what features U.S. consumers seek in shoes if they desire different features. Harpers also has obtained information on the approximate cost of adding these features:

Features Desired in the United States	Cost to Add (in U.S. $)	Importance Rating (5 is most important)
Colorfast material	$4.50	3
Lighter weight	6.75	5
Extra-soft insole	3.00	4
Longer-wearing sole	3.00	2

The current average manufacturing cost of Harpers's shoes is £43 (approximately $56 U.S.), which provides an average profit of £14 ($18 U.S.) per pair sold. Harpers would like to maintain this profit margin; however, the firm recognizes that the U.S. market requires different features and that shipping and advertising costs would increase approximately $10 U.S. per pair of shoes.

Required
1. What is the target manufacturing cost for shoes to be sold in the United States?
2. Which features, if any, should Harpers add for shoes to be sold in the United States?
3. Strategically evaluate Harpers's decision to begin selling shoes in the United States.

[LO 13-1]   13-43 **Target Costing; Quality Function Deployment (QFD)** Hilton Yacht manufactures a line of family cruiser/racing sailboats. The boats are well known for their quality, safety, and performance. Hilton hired Matthew Perry, a well-known sailboat designer and racer, to design a new sailboat, the M33. The M33 will have advanced materials in the hull and rigging to enhance the safety and performance of the boat and also to improve its overnight comfort. Safety and comfort are the two most important boat-buying criteria of Hilton's customers, rated at 34 percent and 33 percent respectively, on a 100-point scale. The other two criteria are performance (20 percent) and styling (13 percent). The overall length of the boat is about 33 feet; its two sleeping areas have room for five or six people. Hilton projects a sales price of approximately $200,000 and estimates the costs of manufacturing the M33 as shown in Table 1.

Table 1

Component	Projected Cost	Percentage of Total
Hull and keel	$39,000	30%
Standing rig	22,100	17
Sails	19,500	15
Electrical	19,500	15
Other	29,900	23
Total	$130,000	100%

A team of engineers and sales managers studied the projected cost and identified how each component of the planned boat contributed to satisfying customers' criteria. The results of this study, based on careful estimates, are shown in Table 2. For example, the estimates show that 30 percent of customers' desire for safety is satisfied by the construction of the hull and keel, another 30 percent by the standing rig, and so on.

Table 2

Component	Safety	Styling	Performance	Comfort
		Criteria		
Hull and keel	30%	40%	50%	30%
Standing rig	30	20	20	10
Sails	10	10	30	10
Electrical	20	10	—	—
Other	10	20	—	50
	100%	100%	100%	100%

Required

1. Using the information in Table 2 developed by the team of engineers and sales managers, together with the customer criteria, compute:

   a. The importance index for each component of the sailboat.

   b. The cost index of each component.

   c. The value index of each component.

2. Take your findings in requirement 1 and compare them against the projected cost figures in Table 1. What conclusions can you draw from this comparison?

[LO 13-1]   **13-44 Target Costing; Quality Function Deployment** Bridal Photography Inc. (BPI) specializes in preparing wedding pictures, including a large book of photos for the wedding couple. Each couple works directly with a single BPI photographer, who helps the couple plan the photos to be made on the wedding day, select the wedding photo book, and choose the photos it is to contain. The standard fee for each wedding is $6,000, which includes all of the firm's services, including the book of wedding photos. BPI is experiencing increased competition, especially based on price. BPI wants to protect its reputation and to continue to expand its business, and for this purpose, it has decided to use quality function deployment (QFD) to better understand the cost and value trade-offs in its business. As a first step, BPI defined the four key buying criteria that couples use in choosing and evaluating photographers: (1) fast service, (2) great photos at the wedding, (3) quality of the photo finishing (color, clarity, etc.), and (4) the quality of the photo book. A select sample of prior customers was asked to rate these criteria and, on a 300-point scale, they provided scores of 30, 120, 60, and 90, respectively.

The BPI accounting records showed the average weekly cost of $5,000 could be traced to four activities: (1) a planning meeting in which the couple and the photographer determined what types of photos were desired, set dates for the photography and proofs, etc.; (2) photography on the wedding day; (3) preparation of proofs from which the couple would select the photos to be used in the book; and (4) preparation of the final photos and the wedding photo book. The average costs of the four activities were $800, $2,400, $600, and $1,200, respectively.

As a final step, BPI managers, photographers, and staff worked together to determine an estimate of the contribution of each of the four activities to achieving the buying criteria. The results were as follows:

Activity/Criteria	Fast Service	Great Photos	Finishing Quality	Book Quality
Conduct planning meeting	30%	40%	—	35%
Take photos	5	60	—	15
Prepare proofs	35	—	50%	—
Prepare photo book	30	—	50	50
	100%	100%	100%	100%

Required

1. Using the information provided, compute:

   a. The importance index for each component of the product,

   b. The cost index of each component, and

   c. The value index of each component.

2. Indicate some business and competitive issues that should be taken into account when interpreting the values from requirement 1.

[LO 13-2]   **13-45 Theory of Constraints; Strategy** Colton Furniture Co. is a small but fast-growing manufacturer of living room furniture. Its two principal products are end tables and sofas. The flow diagram for the manufacturing at Colton follows. Colton's manufacturing involves five processes: cutting the lumber, cutting the fabric, sanding, staining, and assembly. One employee cuts fabric and two do the staining. These are relatively skilled workers who could be replaced only with some difficulty. Two workers cut the lumber, and two others perform the sanding operation. There is some skill to these operations, but these skills are less critical than those for staining and fabric cutting. Assembly requires the lowest skill level, and there is currently a total of 175 hours of working time per week provided by a single full-time employee plus some part-timers. The other employees work a 40-hour week, with 5 hours off for breaks, training, and personal time. Assume a 4-week month and that, by prior agreement, none of the employees can be switched from one task to another. The current demand for Colton's products and sales prices are as follows, although Colton expects demand to increase significantly in the coming months if it is able to successfully negotiate an order from a motel chain.

	End Tables	Sofas
Price	$250	$450
Current demand (units per month)	400	150

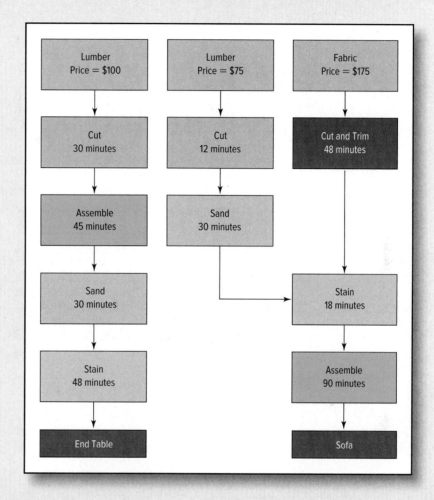

Required

1. Which of the activities is the constraint?

2. Using the constraint identified in requirement 1, calculate the throughput margin per hour for each product.

3. Given the results to requirements 1 and 2, how many of each product should be produced?

4. How would you apply steps 3 through 5 of the theory of constraints to Colton's manufacturing operations? What would you recommend for each step?

[LO 13-2]   13-46 **Theory of Constraints** Chemical Products Company (CPC) produces a variety of chemicals—primarily adhesives, lubricants, and polymers—for industrial use by manufacturers to produce plastics and other compounds. Don Leo, the production vice president, has been informed of a disturbing trend of increasing customer complaints regarding late deliveries from the Canton, Kentucky, plant. The Canton plant is one of the firm's newest and most modern plants and is dedicated to the manufacture of two products, Polymer 1 and Polymer 2. Don has downloaded some incomplete recent information about the Canton plant onto his laptop; he plans to analyze the information in the hour or so he has before his next meeting of the CPC executive committee. He is concerned that some comments will be made about the problems at Canton, and he wants to have an idea of how to respond. Because CPC views Polymer 1 and Polymer 2 as very promising in terms of both sales and profit potential, the news of these problems is likely to spark some comment. The data downloaded by Don are as follows:

Activity	Number of Hours Required for Each Product		Hours Available per Week
	Polymer 1	Polymer 2	
Filtering	2	4	320
Stripping	2	3	320
Reacting	3	5	320
Final filtering	2	1	160
Mixing	3	3	320
Other information Current sales			
demand (per week)	60	40	
Price	$145	$185	
Total material costs	$45	$60	

Don has sketched the following flow diagram for the Canton plant. He believes it is relatively accurate because of his frequent contact with the plant.

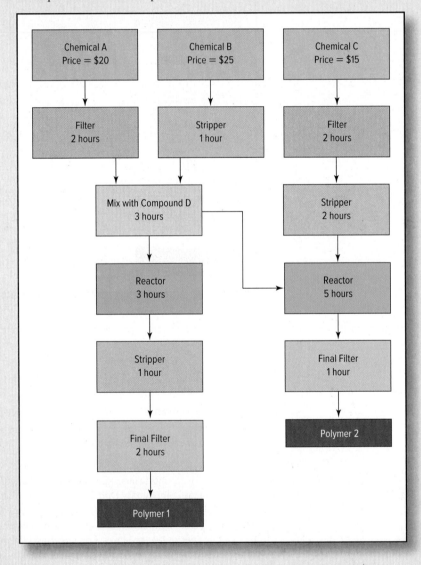

Required

1. Which of the activities is the constraint?

2. Using the constraint identified in requirement 1, calculate the throughput margin per hour for each product.

3. Given the results to requirements 1 and 2, how much of each product should be produced?

[LO 13-2]   13-47   **Theory of Constraints for a Restaurant**   Taylor's is a popular restaurant that offers customers a large dining room and comfortable bar area. Taylor Henry, the owner and manager of the restaurant, has seen the number of patrons increase steadily over the last two years and is considering whether and when she will have to expand its available capacity. The restaurant occupies a large home, and all the space in the building is now used for dining, the bar, and kitchen, but space is available on the property to expand the restaurant. The restaurant is open from 6 p.m. to 10 p.m. each night (except Monday) and, on average, has 24 customers enter the bar and 50 enter the dining room at the beginning of each of those hours. Taylor has noticed the trends over the last 2 years and expects that within about 4 years, the number of bar customers will increase by 50 percent and the dining customers will increase by 20 percent. Taylor is worried that the restaurant will be not be able to handle the increase and has asked you to study its capacity. In your study, you consider four areas of capacity: the parking lot (which has 80 spaces), the bar (54 seats), the dining room (100 seats), and the kitchen. The kitchen is well-staffed and can prepare any meal on the menu in an average of 12 minutes per meal. The kitchen, when fully staffed, is able to have up to 20 meals in preparation at a time, or 100 meals per hour (60 min/12 min × 20 meals). To assess the capacity of the restaurant, you obtain the additional information:

- Diners typically come to the restaurant by car, with an average of 3 persons per car, while bar patrons arrive with an average of 1.5 persons per car.
- Diners, on average, occupy a table for an hour, while bar customers usually stay for an average of 2 hours.
- Due to fire regulations, all bar customers must be seated.
- The bar customer typically orders one drink per hour at an average of $7 per drink; the dining room customer orders a meal with an average price of $22; the restaurant's cost per drink is $1, and the direct costs for meal preparation are $5.

Required   (*Note:* When calculating capacity usage, you must round numbers up to the nearest whole digit.)
1.   a.   Given the current number of customers per hour, what is the amount of excess capacity in the bar, dining room, parking lot, and kitchen?
      b.   Calculate the expected total throughput margin for the restaurant per hour, day, and month (assuming a 26-day month).
2.   a.   Given the expected increase in the number of customers, determine if there is a constraint for any of the four areas of capacity. What is the amount of needed capacity for each constraint?
      b.   If there is a constraint, reduce the demand on the constraint so that the restaurant is at full capacity (assume some customers would have to be turned away). Calculate the expected total throughput margin for the restaurant per hour, day, and month (assuming a 26-day month).
3.   Taylor has obtained construction estimates. To increase the capacity of the bar to 80 seats, the dining room to 120 seats, and the kitchen to 25 meals at the same time would cost $250,000, which Taylor could finance for $5,000 per month for the next 4 years. There would be no change to the parking lot. Given your analysis above, prepare a brief recommendation to Taylor regarding expanding the restaurant.

[LO 13-3]   13-48   **Life-Cycle Costing**   Kate Stephens, the COO of BioDerm, has asked her cost management team for a product-line profitability analysis for her firm's two products, Xderm and Yderm. The two skin care products require a large amount of research and development and advertising. After receiving the following statement from BioDerm's accountants, Kate concludes that Xderm is the more profitable product and that perhaps cost-cutting measures should be applied to Yderm:

	Xderm	Yderm	Total
Sales	$2,900,000	$2,000,000	$4,900,000
Cost of goods sold	(2,000,000)	(1,500,000)	(3,500,000)
Gross profit	$ 900,000	$ 500,000	$1,400,000
Research and development			(800,000)
Selling expenses			(100,000)
Profit before taxes			$ 500,000

Required
1.   Explain why Kate may be wrong in her assessment of the relative performance of the two products.
2.   Suppose that 75 percent of the R&D and selling expenses are traceable to Xderm. Using this assumption, compute the life-cycle income for each product and the return on sales for each product.

3. Consider your answers to requirements 1 and 2 with the following additional information: R&D and selling expenses are substantially higher for Xderm because it is a new product. Kate has strongly supported development of the new product, including the high selling and R&D expenses. She has assured senior managers that the Xderm investment will pay off in improved profits for the firm. What are the ethical issues, if any, facing Kate as she reports to top management on the profitability of the firm's two products?

[LO 13-3]   13-49 **Life-Cycle Costing; Health Care; Present Values** Forever Young Inc. has developed a drug that will diminish the effects of aging. Forever Young has spent $1,000,000 on research and development and $2,108,000 for clinical trials. Once the drug is approved by the FDA, which is imminent, it will have a 5-year sales life cycle. Laura Russell, Forever Young's chief financial officer, must determine the best alternative for the company among three options. The company can choose to manufacture, package, and distribute the drug; outsource only the manufacturing; or sell the drug's patent. Laura has compiled the following annual cost information for this drug if the company were to manufacture it:

Cost Category	Fixed Costs	Variable Cost per Unit
Manufacturing	$5,000,000	$70.00
Packaging	380,000	20.00
Distribution	1,125,000	6.50
Advertising	2,280,000	15.00

Management anticipates a high demand for the drug and has benchmarked $245 per unit as a reasonable price based on other drugs that promise similar results. Management expects sales volume of 3,000,000 units over 4 years and uses a discount rate of 10 percent.

If Forever Young chooses to outsource the manufacturing of the drug while continuing to package, distribute, and advertise it, the result would be a reduction of fixed manufacturing cost from $5,000,000 to $1,350,000 and an increase of variable manufacturing costs from $70 to $74 per unit. For the sale of the patent, Forever Young would receive $300,000,000 now and $25,000,000 at the end of every year for the next 4 years.

Required
1. Determine the life-cycle income for each option.
2. Which option would you recommend for Forever Young? Support your answer.

Solutions to Self-Study Problem

Best Brand Lighting Inc.

A thorough analysis will require a good deal more inquiry of management and fact finding than is available from the limited information provided earlier, but a few useful observations can be made.

1. Encourage BBL to consider increasing the effort put into design to reduce manufacturing costs and to reduce the relatively high rate of product returns in the specialty segment. The cost of design appears low relative to manufacturing and downstream costs, especially in the specialty segment. Inquire about which types of design approaches are being used. Urge BBL to adopt concurrent engineering-based methods, especially because of the relatively short sales life cycles in the industry. Kaizen procedures should also be adopted.

2. Consider additional analysis of pricing. Because of BBL's strong acceptance in the specialty segment and because the differentiation strategy is likely to be important in that segment, a price increase might yield higher profits with little or no loss in market share.

   Cost leadership appears to be the appropriate strategy in the major retail segment; inquire what methods the company is using to reduce overall product costs in this segment.

   Also, investigate further the rate of customer returns for each product. Is this due to design problems or problems in sales management?

3. Consider a further analysis of marketing expenses. Would an increase in marketing effort in the major retailer segment improve sales in this segment?

4. Consider the need to perform a detailed analysis by product category within each market segment. A detailed analysis might uncover important information about opportunities to reduce cost and add value within the products' value chain.

5. Because of the relatively short sales life cycles, consider whether target costing could be used effectively at BBL. How intense is the level of competition in the industry, and to what extent are trade-offs made between functionality and price in the development and introduction of each new product? If the level of competition is very intense, and if trade-offs between functionality and price are key strategic decisions, target costing should be a useful management tool.

6. Investigate the costing system. Is it activity-based? How accurate are the cost figures that it develops?

Please visit Connect to access a narrated, animated tutorial for solving this problem.

PART THREE

Operational-Level Control

The objective of the four chapters comprising Part Three is to present some key tools used to evaluate the performance of mid-level managers and operating personnel, what we refer to as *operational control*. By its nature, operational control focuses on short-term financial and relevant nonfinancial performance. The performance of high-level managers (i.e., *management control*) is examined in Part Four. The essence of control is a comparison of actual performance to budgeted or expected performance.

In Chapters 14 through 16, we cover methods based on the use of standard costs and flexible budgets. The flexible budget allows a comparison of expected financial performance to the actual performance for a given period. The use of flexible budgets and standard costs provides a number of ways to break down and explain what we call the master (or static) budget variance for the period—that is, the difference between actual operating profit and budgeted operating profit for the period. Because profit is a function of five factors (sales volume, selling price, variable cost per unit, sales mix, and total fixed costs), the master budget variance can be broken down into components associated with each of these five factors.

In Chapter 14, we begin by defining the master budget variance and then breaking down this total variance into a sales volume variance and a total flexible budget variance. We show how the latter variance can, for a manufacturing company, be broken down into a selling price variance and component variances related to two direct manufacturing costs (labor and materials). (As noted below, in Chapter 15 we look at the manufacturing overhead variance components of the total flexible budget variance for the period.) Chapter 14 also looks at relevant nonfinancial performance indicators that are useful complements to the variances calculated earlier in the chapter.

Chapter 15 focuses on the variances that arise from differences between budgeted and actual indirect manufacturing costs (i.e., manufacturing overhead). As with Chapter 14, we use flexible budgets and standard costs to further break down the total flexible budget variance for the period. Chapter 15 also deals with the issue of recording standard overhead costs and associated variances for a period, the application of overhead variance analysis in conjunction with ABC systems, and decision rules associated with the variance investigation decision. Chapter 15 also includes a discussion of resource capacity planning issues. The variance investigation decision under uncertainty is covered in a separate online supplement for Chapter 15.

Chapter 16 completes the master budget variance analysis by looking in more detail at the sales volume variance. Specifically, we show how the total sales volume variance can be broken down into components based on market size and market share, among others. Chapter 16 also looks at various measures of operating productivity.

Part Three closes with a study, in Chapter 17, of the management and control of quality, including topics of cost of quality (COQ), Six Sigma, lean manufacturing, and lean accounting. These topics are presented from the standpoint of how cost management systems can be refined to support strategic initiatives on the part of management.

CHAPTER FOURTEEN

Operational Performance Measurement:
Sales, Direct Cost Variances, and the Role of Nonfinancial Performance Measures

After studying this chapter, you should be able to . . .

LO 14-1 Explain control systems in general and operational control systems in particular.

LO 14-2 Define and interpret the master budget variance for a given period.

LO 14-3 Develop a general framework for subdividing the master budget variance into component variances.

LO 14-4 Develop standard costs for product costing, performance evaluation, and control.

LO 14-5 Record manufacturing cost flows and associated variances in a standard cost system.

LO 14-6 Discuss major operating functions and the need for nonfinancial performance indicators.

Newscast/Shutterstock

Founded in 1907 to provide private messenger and delivery services in the Seattle, Washington (USA), area, United Parcel Services (UPS) has become the world's largest package delivery company and one of the leading global providers of specialized transportation and logistics services. On average, UPS delivers nearly 22 million packages and documents per day, in more than 220 countries and territories. In 2019, the company generated revenue of more than $60 billion from its package operations alone and earned a higher profit than its competitors. In 2020, the company was 33rd on *Fortune Magazine*'s list of the world's most admired companies, and first in its industry (**http://fortune.com/worlds-most-admired-companies/2020/ups/**). How does UPS do it?

UPS has become known for its strict adherence to standards in all phases of its work. Every day, each delivery truck driver knows the exact number of packages and documents he or she will be delivering that day. A long-haul driver is expected to travel a certain distance within the time allowed. UPS customers can track packages on its website to find out the time that packages were or will be delivered; on a typical business day, UPS handles more than 100 million (online) tracking requests. Through use of strict work standards, the company has been able to deliver as promised and has become one of the best-run companies in the United States.

Standards are performance criteria and targets that most organizations can use to set performance expectations, evaluate and control operations, motivate employees, and encourage efforts toward their goals. Use of standards allows a manager to identify the cost of manufacturing and selling a product or providing a service, to find causes and attributes of cost overruns or inefficient operations, and to manage by exception. Manufacturing firms can use standards to specify the amount of materials and the number of hours to be used to manufacture their products. Retail stores have specific sales-related standards (e.g., sales density, or sales per square foot). Standards provide useful benchmarks to which actual results can be compared. As such, they represent a key element of operational control systems.

"Don't lower your expectations to meet your performance. Raise your level of performance to meet your expectations."

Ralph Marston, American writer

The Schmidt Machinery Company

Schmidt Machinery Company, the hypothetical firm for this chapter and the next, produces a line of all-weather furniture for use on patios and decks and in sunrooms. The company competes on the basis of a differentiation strategy. Because of increased competitive threats, however, the company must also keep an eye on and control of its operating costs. In short, the company would benefit from a strong and effective operational control system—one that focuses on major business processes and that includes both financial and nonfinancial performance indicators.

To illustrate basic concepts associated with building an operational control system, we focus on a single product produced by Schmidt: product XV-1, a lightweight but durable lounge chair. Because of its high quality and reputation for design innovation, Schmidt's products are sold largely by catalog and over the firm's website; a few high-end retailers also carry the brand. The company currently has few direct competitors in this country, but there are a growing number of competitors from Europe and Asia. At present, concerted efforts to control costs have helped Schmidt maintain its domestic sales and provided some opportunities for foreign sales, but management is concerned that foreign competitors will soon be able to reduce their prices and compete more effectively. Thus, the company is looking for ways to better manage its costs and improve manufacturing efficiency.

Conceptually, the underlying business of Schmidt can be broken down into four major processes: operating processes, customer management processes, innovation processes, and regulatory/social processes. Schmidt's goal is to design and implement a comprehensive management accounting and control system that will enable it to successfully meet competitive threats in a sustainable manner. As a start, the company has decided to focus on a control system associated with its operating processes—*operational control,* for short.

The topic of operational control systems, as part of a comprehensive management accounting and control system, is the subject of Part Three of the text (i.e., Chapters 14, 15, 16, and 17, inclusive). In this chapter, we introduce you to the notion of *financial control,* which begins at the end of a period (e.g., month or quarter) by comparing actual operating income to budgeted income. This difference, which we call a variance, can then be broken down into component variances related to costs, sales volume, sales price, and sales mix.

In this chapter, we focus on the determination of the sales volume variance and what is called the *total flexible budget variance.* The latter variance can be further broken down into a sales price variance and component variances associated with two direct manufacturing costs: labor and materials. In Chapter 15, we extend the analysis to include a breakdown and analysis of variances associated with indirect manufacturing costs (i.e., manufacturing overhead costs). In Chapter 16, we provide a further discussion of sales-related and productivity variances. Finally, in Chapter 17, we look at the issue of operational control from the standpoint of quality initiatives and how management accounting systems can be refined to support such initiatives.

In all four chapters, we make the point that to develop a comprehensive management accounting and control system, we need to supplement financial performance indicators with relevant nonfinancial measures of performance. Thus, as we will see, operational control systems (such as the one discussed for Schmidt Company) can be thought of as including both financial and nonfinancial performance metrics.

"In business, the idea of measuring what you are doing, picking the measurements that count, like customer satisfaction and performance . . . you thrive on that."

Bill Gates, quote from BrainyQuote.com

Management Accounting and Control Systems

control

The set of procedures, tools, and systems that organizations use to reach their goals.

management accounting and control system

An organization's core performance measurement system.

LO 14-1

Explain control systems in general and operational control systems in particular.

operational control

The monitoring of short-term operating performance; takes place when mid-level managers monitor the activities of operating-level managers and employees.

financial control

The comparison of actual and budgeted financial results.

variances

Differences between budgeted and actual amounts, for either financial or nonfinancial measures.

In business, we use the term **control** in a general sense to refer to the set of procedures, tools, and systems organizations use to ensure that progress is being made toward accomplishing the goals and objectives of the organization. In accounting, we refer to an organization's **management accounting and control system** as its core performance measurement system, one that includes both planning and evaluation (feedback) components.

Comprehensive management accounting and control systems can be subdivided for discussion purposes into management control systems and operational control systems. In this text, we use the term **operational control** to refer to the subset of an organization's overall management accounting and control system that focuses on *short-term operational performance.* That is, operational control focuses on the control of basic business processes (or activities) that are performed to produce and deliver the organization's outputs (goods or services) to customers.

There are fundamentally two performance dimensions covered by operational control systems: financial and nonfinancial. An effective operational control system will include performance indicators of both types.

Financial control is accomplished by comparing actual to budgeted financial amounts. Thus, budgets are useful in the financial control process because they provide the standard against which actual financial results can be compared. Differences between budgeted amounts and actual financial results are referred to as **variances.** In this text, we use the labels F and U to refer, respectively, to favorable and unfavorable variances. Favorable variances are those that increase short-term operating income, while unfavorable variances have the opposite effect.

The following example provides a broad overview of the tasks involved in developing an effective operational control system for Schmidt Machinery Company.

Developing an Operational Control System: The Five Steps of Strategic Decision Making for Schmidt Machinery

1. **Determine the strategic issues surrounding the problem.** Schmidt is a differentiated manufacturer, selling a high-priced product to those who value its quality, design, and functionality. With the growth of foreign competition and the possibility of price competition in the coming years, Schmidt is now looking for ways to maintain its profitability and quality by improving operational efficiency.

2. **Identify the alternative actions.** One approach, as explained in Chapter 13, would be to use target costing in the context of product redesign aimed at reducing the cost while maintaining the quality of the product that Schmidt produces. Another approach would be to implement an operational control system. Thus, the company is currently considering whether to implement such a system, either in conjunction with or in lieu of the target costing procedures discussed in Chapter 13.

3. **Obtain information and conduct analyses of the alternatives.** An operational control system, if fully implemented, will capture both financial and nonfinancial performance data. Financial data include budgeted results (sales volume, sales mix, selling prices, variable cost per unit, and total fixed costs). Budgeted costs on a per-unit basis are referred to as *standard costs*. To experiment with a new financial control system, Schmidt develops standard costs for the production of one of its products, XV-1 (see Exhibit 14.5 later in the chapter). Product design engineers have been asked to consider the possibility of redesigning XV-1 and to estimate the potential savings from the redesign.

4. **Based on strategy and analysis, choose and implement the desired alternative.** Management decides that a product redesign would be too risky at this point, jeopardizing the quality image of the company. So the firm chooses to proceed with the development and implementation of an operational control system.

5. **Provide an ongoing evaluation of the effectiveness of implementation in step 4.** As the competitive environment becomes clearer, management should revisit and reevaluate its approach to delivering the company's differentiated product profitably. In the future, therefore, the company will evaluate each of the following options: the management and control of quality (Chapter 17), productivity analysis (Chapter 16), and the theory of constraints (Chapter 13).

Short-Term Financial Control

LO 14-2

Define and interpret the master budget variance for a given period.

master budget variance
The difference between actual operating income and the master budget operating income for the period.

An important short-term financial goal for a company is to achieve the budgeted operating income for the period. At the end of a period, management wants to know whether the planned operating income was attained. The difference between the actual operating income and the master budget operating income (see Chapter 10) is called the **master budget variance** for the period.

Consider the analysis of operations for Schmidt Machinery Company presented in Exhibit 14.1. The bottom line of column (2) shows that the budgeted operating income for October 2022 is $200,000, while column (1) reports that the firm actually earned an operating income of $128,000 for the period. This difference is the master budget variance for the period, $72,000 unfavorable [column (3)].

Exhibit 14.1 also reports the difference between the master budget and the actual result for units sold, sales dollars, variable cost per unit, and total fixed costs. For example, we see from Exhibit 14.1 that actual units sold, 780 units, is 220 units less than the sales units in the master budget.

Exhibit 14.1 also reports that total variable costs in October were $99,050 less than budget; we refer to this difference as a favorable variance. This result may lead us to conclude that the primary reason for Schmidt's failure to be effective in earning its budgeted operating income is the shortfall in sales, not its failure to control variable costs. The shortfall is so large that even with a good control of expenses, as evidenced by the substantial favorable variance in total variable costs, the firm still failed to achieve its budgeted operating income for the month.

EXHIBIT 14.1
Comparison of Actual and
Budgeted Operating Income

	SCHMIDT MACHINERY COMPANY Analysis of Operating Income For October 2022					
	(1) **Actual Operating Income**		**(2)** **Master Budget**		**(3)** **Variances**	
Units	780		1,000		220U*	
Sales	$639,600	100%	$800,000	100%	$160,400U	
Variable costs	350,950	55	450,000	56	99,050F**	
Contribution margin	$288,650	45%	$350,000	44%	$ 61,350U	
Fixed costs	160,650***	25	150,000†	19	10,650U	
Operating income	$128,000	20%	$200,000	25%	**$ 72,000U**	

*U denotes an *unfavorable* effect on operating income.
**F denotes a *favorable* effect on operating income.
***Actual fixed factory overhead cost = $130,650; actual fixed selling and administrative costs = $30,000.
†Budgeted fixed factory overhead cost = $120,000; budgeted fixed selling and administrative costs = $30,000.

That conclusion is misleading. Direct comparisons between the actual operating results and the master budget amounts for total variable costs can be meaningless. In this instance, the variable costs in the master budget are for operations at a higher level than were actually attained. Variable costs for 780 units should be less than the variable costs for 1,000 units. Schmidt should not credit its management for having good control of variable costs based only on the fact that the variable costs incurred are below the master budgeted amount for the period.

The master budget variance ($72,000 unfavorable for Schmidt in October) reveals only whether the firm achieved the budgeted operating income for the period; it does not identify causes for the deviation or help the firm identify courses of action to reduce or eliminate similar deviations in the future. Schmidt needs to conduct additional analyses to learn the reason for missing the target. Flexible budgets and standard costs can be used to break down and explain the master budget variance for a period.

Flexible Budgets and Profit-Variance Analysis

The Flexible Budget

LO 14-3
Develop a general framework for subdividing the master budget variance into component variances.

The budget prepared prior to the beginning of a period, as discussed in Chapter 10, is a *master budget* for the period; it lays out expectations and provides blueprints of operations for the coming period. This budget is referred to as a *static budget* because it is developed for only a single output level.

The master budget is useful for initial planning and coordination of activities for a given period. Operating conditions, however, seldom turn out exactly the way they were expected or forecasted when the master budget was prepared. Whenever the output (e.g., sales volume) attained differs from the budgeted output, the organization needs to revise the master budget before assessing short-run financial performance. This revised budget is referred to as a *flexible budget.*

flexible budget
A budget that adjusts revenues and costs to reflect varying levels of output activity (i.e., different levels of volume and mix).

A **flexible budget** is a budget that adjusts revenues and expenses to the actual output level and sales mix achieved. Changes in output (e.g., units sold for a manufacturing firm, number of patient-days for a hospital, or number of students for a school district) change the firm's expected revenues and expenses. For financial control purposes, a firm prepares a flexible budget at the end of a period when the total work done or the actual output level for the period is known.

Flexible budgets are useful for assessing short-term financial performance. The data for Schmidt Machinery Company in Exhibit 14.1 show that the period's operating income is $72,000 less than the budgeted amount. On receiving the report, management would likely raise the following questions:

1. Why was operating income less than expected?
2. Why have costs gone from 75% of sales to 80% of sales? Can management do something to prevent the same thing from happening next period?

EXHIBIT 14.2   Master Budget Variances (Single-Product Example: Product XV-1)

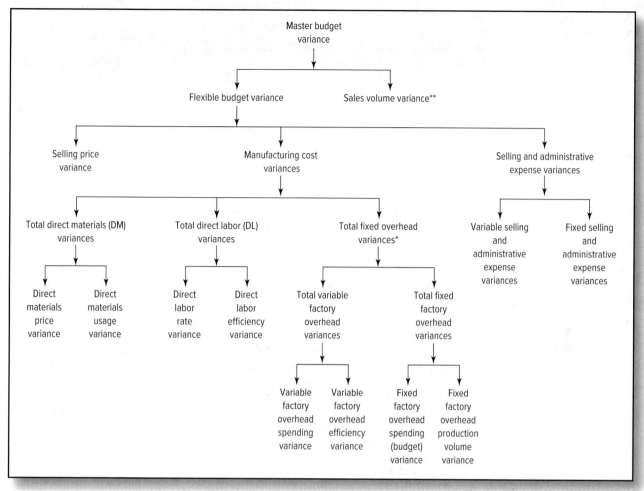

*The decomposition of this variance is covered in Chapter 15.

**As explained in the text, and as illustrated in Exhibit 14.4, the sales volume variance can be calculated and expressed in terms of each major component of the income statement (revenues, variable costs, contribution margin, and operating income).

3. Why were short-term fixed costs $10,650 more than expected?
4. Were the disappointing financial results attributable to changes in:

    a. Units sold?

    b. Sales price?

    c. Sales mix?

    d. Production costs?

    e. Selling and administrative costs?

Preparing a flexible budget allows management to adjust the original budget to the actual output level and sales mix achieved, thereby allowing management to answer the above questions. That is, the use of flexible budgets and standard costs (discussed later in this chapter) allows us to subdivide the master budget variance for the period into component variances related to each of the five factors that combine to determine short-run operating profit—namely, selling price, sales volume, sales mix, variable cost per unit, and total fixed costs. A framework for subdividing into these component variances is presented in Exhibit 14.2. This exhibit gives you an overall picture of the variance-decomposition process. All of the component variances that can be calculated, when summed, equal the master budget variance for the period. The ability to explain this overall variance is the essence of the traditional

EXHIBIT 14.3
Flexible and Master Budgets for Schmidt Machinery Company: October 2022

	(1) Flexible Budget		(2) Master Budget	
Units	780		1,000	
Sales ($800 per unit)	$624,000	100%	$800,000	100%
Variable costs ($450 per unit)	351,000	56	450,000	56
Contribution margin ($350 per unit)	$273,000	44%	$350,000	44%
Fixed costs	150,000	24	150,000*	19
Operating income	$123,000	20%	$200.000	25%

*Budgeted fixed factory overhead costs = $120,000; budgeted fixed selling and administrative costs = $30,000. See Exhibit 14.1.

financial control model. For simplicity, Exhibit 14.2 deals with a single-product situation. We cover the issue of sales mix in Chapter 16.

Flexible budgets differ from the master budget only in terms of the number of units embodied in the budget. Exhibit 14.3 illustrates the flexible budget for Schmidt for October 2022. As noted earlier, for simplicity in Chapter 14 we assume that Schmidt produces only a single product, XV-1. Schmidt developed this flexible budget in three steps:

Step 1. **Determine the output of the period.** Schmidt manufactured and sold 780 units of XV-1. The flexible budget, therefore, would be based on an output level of 780 units.

Step 2. **Use the selling price and the variable cost per unit data from the master budget to calculate the budgeted sales revenues and budgeted variable expenses, respectively, for the output of the period and to compute the flexible budget contribution margin.** The selling price per unit and variable cost per unit in the master budget are $800 and $450, respectively. Thus, at 780 units:

Flexible budget total sales = 780 units × $800 per unit	$624,000
Flexible budget total variable expenses = 780 units × $450 per unit	351,000
Flexible budget contribution margin = 780 units × $350 per unit*	$273,000

*$800 − $450 (total variable cost per unit consists of manufacturing costs of $400 plus $50 of selling and administrative costs).

Step 3. **Determine the budgeted amount of fixed costs and then compute the flexible budget operating income.** Schmidt Company has determined that the manufacturing and selling of 780 units is within the same operating range as the master budget operating level. Thus, the total fixed cost for the flexible budget is $150,000, and the flexible budget operating income is:

$$\$273,000 - \$150,000 = \$123,000$$

Note that the amount of fixed costs in a flexible budget may differ from the amount in the master budget if the actual operating level is substantially different from the operating level anticipated by the firm at the time it prepared the master budget.

In summary, total sales and total expenses for a flexible budget are calculated using these formulas:

$$\text{Total sales} = \text{Actual number of units sold} \times \text{Budgeted selling price per unit}$$
$$\text{Total variable expenses} = \text{Actual number of units sold} \times \text{Budgeted variable cost per unit}$$
$$\text{Total fixed expenses} = \text{Amount of fixed expenses in the master budget}$$

An organization can prepare a budget for different levels of output or activity. In this text we use the term *pro forma* when referring to budgets prepared for multiple output levels. We use the term *flexible budget* in a more limited sense—that is, the budget based on the actual activity level achieved during a period.

Sales Volume Variance and the Flexible Budget Variances

With the help of a flexible budget, we can now separate the $72,000U master budget variance (Exhibit 14.1) into two components: a *total flexible budget variance* ($5,000F) and a *sales volume variance* ($77,000U). (See Exhibit 14.4.) Each of these two variances can, in turn, be decomposed into finer components. The details for this decomposition are shown in Exhibit 14.4 and are discussed next.

EXHIBIT 14.4
Breakdown of the Master Budget Variance

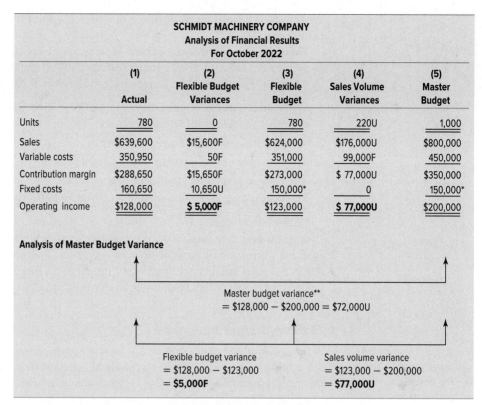

	(1) Actual	(2) Flexible Budget Variances	(3) Flexible Budget	(4) Sales Volume Variances	(5) Master Budget
Units	780	0	780	220U	1,000
Sales	$639,600	$15,600F	$624,000	$176,000U	$800,000
Variable costs	350,950	50F	351,000	99,000F	450,000
Contribution margin	$288,650	$15,650F	$273,000	$ 77,000U	$350,000
Fixed costs	160,650	10,650U	150,000*	0	150,000*
Operating income	$128,000	$ 5,000F	$123,000	$ 77,000U	$200,000

SCHMIDT MACHINERY COMPANY
Analysis of Financial Results
For October 2022

Analysis of Master Budget Variance

Master budget variance**
= $128,000 − $200,000 = $72,000U

Flexible budget variance
= $128,000 − $123,000
= **$5,000F**

Sales volume variance
= $123,000 − $200,000
= **$77,000U**

*Budgeted fixed factory overhead cost = $120,000; budgeted fixed selling and administrative expense = $30,000.
Note: U denotes an *unfavorable* effect on operating income; F denotes a *favorable* effect on operating income.

Sales Volume Variance

sales volume variance
For each income statement item, the difference between the flexible budget amount for that item and the amount for that item reflected in the master budget for the period.

The **sales volume variance** for the period is the difference between the flexible budget operating income and master budget operating income. As indicated in Exhibit 14.4, the sales volume variance for Schmidt for October 2022 ($77,000U) is the difference between $123,000 and $200,000. This variance is unfavorable because actual sales volume for the month was 220 units less than anticipated.

Note from Column (4) of Exhibit 14.4 that the sales volume variance can be expressed for each income statement item as the difference between the flexible budget amount for that item and the amount for that item reflected in the master budget for the period. Thus, we can express the sales volume variance in terms of units (220U), sales ($176,000U), variable costs ($99,000F), and contribution margin ($77,000U), as well as in terms of operating income ($77,000U).

Also note that the sales volume variance in terms of operating income is normally the same as the contribution margin sales volume variance. This is because, as noted earlier, fixed expenses in the master budget and in the flexible budget usually are the same. Thus, an alternative way to compute the sales volume variance is to multiply the master budget contribution margin per unit (here $350) by the difference between the actual units sold and the units in the master budget.

$$\text{Sales volume variance} = \left(\begin{array}{c} \text{Actual units} \\ \text{sold} \end{array} - \begin{array}{c} \text{Units budgeted} \\ \text{to be sold} \end{array} \right) \times \begin{array}{c} \text{Master budget contribution} \\ \text{margin per unit} \end{array}$$

$$= (780 - 1,000) \text{ units} \times \$350 \text{ per unit}$$

$$= \$77,000U$$

Note: Both in the above calculation and throughout the rest of the chapter, the "sign" (positive or negative) of the difference in parentheses should be ignored. As stated in the note to Exhibit 14.4, individual variances are labeled favorable (F) or unfavorable (U) based on their effect on short-term operating income. Those that increase short-term operating income are labeled favorable (F), while those that decrease short-term operating income are labeled unfavorable (U).

The sales volume variance expressed in terms of operating income shows that, holding everything else constant, a sales volume decrease of 220 units would decrease operating income by $77,000. The sales volume variance may be a result of one or more of the following:[1]

1. The market for the product has changed. The total demand for the product grew (or declined) at a rate higher than expected.
2. The firm lost market share to competitors.
3. The firm failed to set a proper goal for the period.
4. The firm set an inappropriate selling price for the product.
5. The marketing and promotion programs were not effective.

Each of these causes may be a result of one or more contributing factors. For example, a firm might have lost market share because of quality problems that led to customer dissatisfaction, shifts in customer preferences and tastes, ineffective advertising, reduction in the number of sales calls or salespeople, or products not available due to production problems, among others. The proper response to a sales volume variance depends on the identified cause of the variance.

Flexible Budget Variances

flexible budget variance
The difference between actual and flexible budget amounts on the income statement.

A **flexible budget variance** for each income statement item refers to the difference between the actual amount of that item and the flexible budget amount for that item. As indicated in column (2) of Exhibit 14.4, for any income statement item:

$$\text{Flexible budget variance} = \text{Actual results} - \text{Flexible budget results}$$

Thus, there is a flexible budget variance for sales, for variable costs, for fixed costs, and for operating income. The sum of these individual variances equals the total flexible budget variance for the period.

total flexible budget variance
The difference between the flexible budget operating income and the actual operating income for the period.

The **total flexible budget variance** for a period is also equal to the difference between the actual operating income and the flexible budget operating income for the period. In Exhibit 14.4, we see that the total flexible budget variance for October is $5,000 favorable, as follows:

$$\frac{\text{Total flexible budget}}{\text{variance}} = \frac{\text{Actual operating}}{\text{income earned}} - \frac{\text{Flexible budget}}{\text{operating income}}$$
$$= \$128{,}000 - \$123{,}000$$
$$= \$5{,}000\text{F}$$

As noted earlier (Exhibit 14.2), the total flexible budget variance for the period can be broken down into a selling price variance, a total variable cost flexible budget variance, and a total fixed cost flexible budget variance. As shown by the details that follow, the present $5,000 favorable total flexible budget variance consists of a $15,600 favorable selling price variance, a $50 favorable total variable cost variance, and a $10,650 unfavorable total fixed cost variance.

Selling Price Variance   As the name implies, the selling price variance reflects the effect on operating income of a difference between actual and budgeted selling prices. Thus, the

selling price variance
The difference between the total actual sales revenue for a period and the sales revenue in the flexible budget for the period.

selling price variance can be determined by taking the difference between actual sales revenues for a period and the sales revenue in the flexible budget for the period. The difference between these two amounts, if any, results from deviations of the actual selling price per unit from the budgeted selling price per unit:

$$\text{Actual sales revenue} = \text{Units sold} \times \textit{Actual} \text{ selling price per unit}$$
$$\text{Flexible budget sales revenue} = \text{Units sold} \times \textit{Budgeted} \text{ selling price per unit}$$

---

[1] For a multiproduct firm, the sales volume variance can be decomposed into a pure volume variance and a sales mix variance. This topic is covered in Chapter 16. Also, in Chapter 16 we discuss how to separate the total sales volume variance into market size and market share components.

In the preceding two equations, both sales revenue figures are for the actual number of units sold during the period. The difference between these two sales revenue amounts is due solely to the difference between actual and budgeted selling price per unit. For this reason, we refer to this difference as the selling price variance for the period.

$$\begin{aligned}\text{Selling price} \atop \text{variance} &= {\text{Actual sales} \atop \text{revenue}} - {\text{Flexible budget} \atop \text{sales revenue}}\\[2mm]
&= \left({\text{Units} \atop \text{sold}} \times {\text{Actual selling} \atop \text{price per unit}}\right) - \left({\text{Units} \atop \text{sold}} \times {\text{Budgeted selling} \atop \text{price per unit}}\right)\\[2mm]
&= \left({\text{Actual selling} \atop \text{price per unit}} - {\text{Budgeted selling} \atop \text{price per unit}}\right) \times {\text{Units} \atop \text{sold}}\end{aligned}$$

Exhibit 14.4 shows that in October 2022, Schmidt sold 780 units of XV-1 for $639,600, or $820 per unit. The budgeted selling price, however, was $800 per unit. Using the budgeted selling price of $800 per unit, the total sales revenue in the flexible budget for 780 units actually sold is $624,000. The difference, $15,600, is a result of the actual selling price per unit being $20 higher than the budgeted selling price per unit for each of the 780 units sold, as shown here:

$$\begin{aligned}\text{Selling price} \atop \text{variance} &= {\text{Actual} \atop \text{sales revenue}} - {\text{Flexible budget} \atop \text{sales revenue}}\\[2mm]
&= \$639,600 - \$624,000 = \$15,600\text{F}\\[2mm]
\text{Selling price} \atop \text{variance} &= \left({\text{Actual selling} \atop \text{price per unit}} - {\text{Budgeted selling} \atop \text{price per unit}}\right) \times {\text{Units} \atop \text{sold}}\\[2mm]
&= (\$820 - \$800)\text{ per unit} \times 780 \text{ units}\\[2mm]
&= \$15,600\text{F}\end{aligned}$$

total variable cost flexible budget variance
The difference between total variable cost incurred during a period and the total variable cost in the flexible budget for the period.

standard cost sheet
A document that lists the standard costs of manufacturing and selling one unit of a product.

Total Variable Cost Flexible Budget Variance   The **total variable cost flexible budget variance** is the difference between the total variable cost incurred during a period and the total variable cost in the flexible budget for the period. Thus, this variance reflects the deviation of the actual variable cost incurred during the period from the total standard variable cost for the output of the period.

Note in Exhibit 14.4 that Schmidt incurred $350,950 total variable costs in October 2022 to produce and sell 780 units of XV-1. Budgeted variable costs per unit for Schmidt for all variable cost items are referred to as *standard costs* and are reflected on the **standard cost sheet** illustrated in Exhibit 14.5. The standard variable manufacturing cost is $400 per unit (including $140 for direct materials, $200 for direct labor, and $60 for variable manufacturing overhead). For 780 units, the total standard variable manufacturing cost is therefore $312,000 ($400 per unit × 780 units). In addition, the standard variable selling and administrative cost is $50 per unit, or $39,000 in total ($50 per unit × 780 units). This brings the total budgeted variable cost for manufacturing and selling 780 units to $351,000 ($312,000 + $39,000). The difference between the actual variable costs incurred during the period ($350,950) and the total variable costs in the flexible budget for the units manufactured and sold during the period ($351,000) is the *total variable cost flexible budget variance,* which in the present case is $50 favorable (see Exhibit 14.4):

$$\begin{aligned}\text{Total variable cost} \atop \text{flexible budget variance} &= {\text{Total variable} \atop \text{cost incurred}} - {\text{Total flexible budget} \atop \text{variable cost}}\\[2mm]
&= \$350,950 - [(\$140 + \$200 + \$60 + \$50)\text{ per unit} \times 780 \text{ units}]\\[2mm]
&= \$350,950 - (\$450 \text{ per unit} \times 780 \text{ units})\\[2mm]
&= \$350,950 - \$351,000\\[2mm]
&= \$50\text{F}\end{aligned}$$

EXHIBIT 14.5
Standard Cost Sheet, Product XV-1

SCHMIDT MACHINERY COMPANY Standard Cost Sheet Product: XV-1				
Descriptions	**Quantity**	**Cost Rate**	**Subtotal**	**Total**
Direct materials:				
Aluminum	4 pounds	$25 per pound	$100	
PVC	1 pound	40 per pound	40	
Direct labor	5 hours	40 per hour	200	
Variable factory overhead	5 hours	12 per hour	60	
Total variable manufacturing cost				$400
Fixed factory overhead*	5 hours	24 per hour	120	120
Standard manufacturing cost per unit				$520
Standard variable selling and administrative cost per unit				$ 50

*Budgeted fixed factory overhead cost = $120,000.

Further Analysis of the Total Variable Cost Flexible Budget Variance   The total variable cost flexible budget variance is the sum of the flexible budget variances of all variable costs and expenses, including flexible budget variances for direct materials, direct labor, variable overhead, and variable selling and administrative expenses.

$$
\begin{array}{c}
\text{Total variable} \\
\text{cost} \\
\text{flexible budget} \\
\text{variance}
\end{array}
=
\begin{array}{c}
\text{Total direct} \\
\text{materials} \\
\text{flexible budget} \\
\text{variance}
\end{array}
+
\begin{array}{c}
\text{Total direct} \\
\text{labor} \\
\text{flexible budget} \\
\text{variance}
\end{array}
+
\begin{array}{c}
\text{Total variable} \\
\text{overhead} \\
\text{flexible budget} \\
\text{variance}
\end{array}
+
\begin{array}{c}
\text{Total variable selling} \\
\text{and administrative} \\
\text{expenses} \\
\text{flexible budget} \\
\text{variance}
\end{array}
$$

More detailed information regarding the total variable cost flexible budget variance is provided in Exhibit 14.6. The $50 favorable total variable cost flexible budget variance may not in and of itself be of concern to the management of Schmidt Machinery Company. However, this seemingly insignificant net variance could be the result of large but offsetting component variances. For this reason, we can decompose this net variance using a two-step process. Step 1 is to calculate a flexible budget variance for each variable cost, as shown in Exhibit 14.8. For example, the total direct labor cost variance for October was $8,580F. Step 2 is to use the following model to break down this variable cost variance into its price and quantity components.

General Model for the Analysis of Variable Cost Variances   Any purely variable cost is a function of two factors, price (P) and quantity (Q). Thus, any flexible budget variance for a given variable cost, such as direct materials or direct labor, can be decomposed into a *price* (or rate) *variance* and a *quantity* (or efficiency) *variance*. A general model for the analysis of variable cost flexible budget variances is provided in Exhibit 14.7.

The price variance for direct materials can be calculated either at the time materials are purchased or at the time materials are issued to production. If the former is the case, then AQ in Exhibit 14.7 means "actual quantity of materials *purchased*" and the resulting variance is referred to as a *materials purchase price variance*. Regardless of when the price variance for materials is calculated, the quantity variance for direct materials is calculated at the end of the period, once production (i.e., output for the period) is known. The term *AQ* in the materials quantity variance *always* refers to the actual quantity of materials consumed for a given period's output.

We now apply the general model to the analysis of variable cost flexible budget variances for the Schmidt Machinery Company, October 2022.

Direct Materials Variances   As indicated in Exhibit 14.7, the direct materials flexible budget variance for each direct material is the difference between the actual direct materials cost and the total standard direct materials cost for a period's output. This variance reflects efficiency (or inefficiency) in buying and using direct materials. Attaining efficiency in buying

EXHIBIT 14.6   Comparison of Actual Variable Costs and Flexible Budget Variable Costs: Product XV-1 (October 2022)

	SCHMIDT MACHINERY COMPANY October 2020		
Product XV-1			
Units Manufactured: 780			
Actual Results			
Direct materials:			
Aluminum	3,630 pounds at $26 per pound	$94,380	
PVC	720 pounds at $41 per pound	29,520	$123,900
Direct labor	3,510 hours at $42 per hour		147,420
Variable factory overhead			40,630
Total variable cost of goods manufactured			$311,950
Variable selling and administrative expenses			39,000
Total variable costs for the period			$350,950
Flexible Budget			
Budgeted variable cost of goods manufactured:			
Standard variable manufacturing cost per unit (from Exhibit 14.5)		$400	
Number of units manufactured		× 780	$312,000
Budgeted variable selling and administrative expenses (780 units × $50 per unit)			39,000
Total budgeted variable costs for 780 units			$351,000
Total variable cost flexible budget variance for the period			$ 50F

EXHIBIT 14.7
General Model for Analyzing Variable Cost Variances

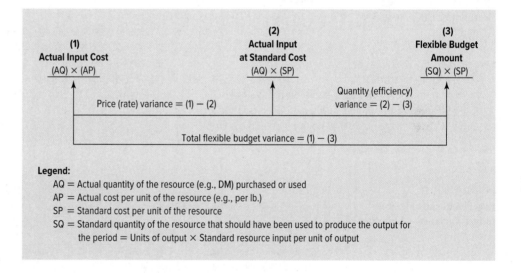

and using materials requires good controls over both the price paid for the materials and the quantity of the materials used in production. Because price and usage can move in opposite directions, we must analyze a total variance for each direct material by breaking the variance down into its price and quantity components.

Exhibits 14.8 and 14.9 illustrate an analysis of direct materials costs using the October 2022 operating data of the Schmidt Company. In this example, there are two direct materials: aluminum and PVC. We illustrate here the analysis of the flexible budget variance for aluminum. Exhibit 14.8 (top portion) shows that Schmidt used 3,630 pounds of aluminum at a total cost of $94,380 to manufacture 780 units of XV-1. The standard cost sheet reported in Exhibit 14.5 indicates that the standard cost for one unit of XV-1 is 4 pounds of aluminum at $25 per pound. For October, the total flexible budget cost for aluminum, given an output of 780 units, is therefore $78,000. (See the middle section of Exhibit 14.8.)

EXHIBIT 14.8   A Detailed Comparison of Actual Variable Costs and Flexible Budget Variable Costs: Product XV-1 (October 2022)

SCHMIDT MACHINERY COMPANY October 2022			
Product XV-1			
Units Manufactured: 780			
Actual Variable Costs Incurred			
Direct materials:			
Aluminum	3,630 pounds* at $26 per pound	$94,380	
PVC	720 pounds at $41 per pound	29,520	$123,900
Direct labor	3,510 hours at $42 per hour		147,420
Variable factory overhead			40,630
Total variable cost of goods manufactured			$311,950
Variable selling and administrative expenses			39,000
Total variable costs incurred			$350,950
Flexible Budget for Variable Costs			
Direct materials:			
Aluminum	780 units × 4 pounds per unit × $25 per pound =	$78,000	
PVC	780 units × 1 pound per unit × $40 per pound =	31,200	$109,200
Direct labor	780 units × 5 hours per unit × $40 per hour =		156,000
Variable factory overhead	780 units × 5 hours per unit × $12 per hour =		46,800
Total standard variable cost of goods manufactured			$312,000
Variable selling and administrative expenses			39,000
Total flexible budget variable costs			$351,000
Variable Cost Flexible Budget Variances			
Direct materials:			
Aluminum	$94,380 − $78,000 =	$16,380U	
PVC	29,520 − 31,200 =	1,680F	$14,700U
Direct labor	147,420 − 156,000 =		8,580F
Variable factory overhead	40,630 − 46,800 =		6,170F
Variable manufacturing cost flexible budget variance			$ 50F
Variable selling and administrative expense variance			0
Variable cost flexible budget variance (see Exhibit 14.6)			$ 50F

*Assume that pounds purchased = pounds used.

EXHIBIT 14.9
Direct Materials Flexible Budget Variance—Aluminum

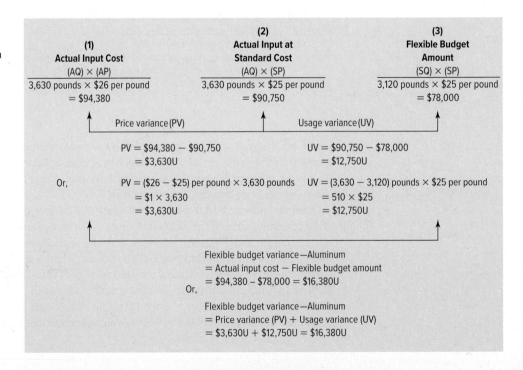

direct materials flexible budget variance
For each material, the difference between the total direct materials cost incurred and the flexible budget amount for this period's output.

Direct Materials Flexible Budget Variance   The **direct materials flexible budget variance** for each material is the difference between the total direct material cost incurred and the flexible budget amount for this period's output. Schmidt spent $94,380 for aluminum (Exhibit 14.8, top portion). Thus, the total flexible budget variance for aluminum for October is $16,380 unfavorable ($94,380 − $78,000). This same approach can be used to calculate the total flexible budget variance for PVC, $1,680F (Exhibit 14.8, bottom portion).

Further Analysis of the Direct Materials Flexible Budget Variance
Price Variance

direct materials price variance
For each direct material, the difference between the actual and standard costs per unit of the material multiplied by the actual quantity of direct materials used (or purchased) during the period.

The **direct materials price variance** for each material is the difference between the actual and the standard costs per unit of direct material multiplied by the quantity of the direct materials used (or purchased) during the period.[2] Exhibit 14.8 shows that in October, Schmidt Machinery Company paid $26 per pound for the 3,630 pounds of aluminum used in production. The standard cost sheet (Exhibit 14.5) specifies the standard price for aluminum is $25 per pound. Thus, the actual price paid is $1 per pound more than standard. For the 3,630 pounds used, the price variance is $3,630 unfavorable [column (1) − column (2), Exhibit 14.9]. Alternatively,

$$
\begin{aligned}
\text{Direct materials price variance} &= \left(\begin{array}{c} \text{Actual price paid} \\ \text{for one unit of} \\ \text{direct material} \end{array} - \begin{array}{c} \text{Standard price} \\ \text{for one unit of} \\ \text{direct material} \end{array} \right) \times \begin{array}{c} \text{Total number of units} \\ \text{of the direct material} \\ \text{used in production} \end{array} \\
&= (AP - SP) \times AQ \\
&= (\$26 - \$25) \text{ per pound} \times 3,630 \text{ pounds} \\
&= \$1 \text{ per pound} \times 3,630 \text{ pounds} \\
&= \$3,630 \text{ Unfavorable}
\end{aligned}
$$

Interpreting the Direct Materials Price Variance   A direct materials price variance can result from failure to take purchase discounts, unexpected changes in the price of materials, changes in freight costs, variation in grades of materials, or other causes. The purchasing department is often the office most likely to provide an explanation or have the responsibility for materials price variances.

Care must be taken in interpreting direct materials price variances. A favorable direct materials price variance could lead to excessively high manufacturing costs if the low-cost materials are of poor quality. Downstream costs such as scrap, rework, schedule disruptions, or field service costs could exceed the price savings from lower materials prices. A firm with a differentiation strategy is likely to fail if it pursues favorable price variances by purchasing low-quality materials. A firm that competes on low cost also is likely to be adversely affected if the quality of its products is below customer expectations or if poor-quality materials increase other manufacturing costs or downstream (i.e., post-production) costs.

materials usage ratio
The ratio of the quantity used to the quantity purchased.

In addition to price variances, many firms also compute usage ratios in evaluating the performance of purchasing departments. A **materials usage ratio** is the ratio of quantity used over quantity purchased. A low materials usage ratio suggests that the purchasing department purchased for reasons other than the operational needs of the period (for example, to secure favorable price variances). Such a move can actually be more costly because carrying and additional materials handling costs can often exceed the savings from low purchase prices. A firm with warehouses full of materials and supplies purchased in bulk at low prices could have a higher overall cost than a firm that buys in small quantities and maintains only a minimum amount of direct materials on hand, even if the firm paid higher purchase prices for these materials. Thus, the benefit of any favorable price variance should be evaluated along with the cost of carrying surplus inventory.

direct materials usage variance
For each material, the difference between the actual direct material units used during the period and the number of standard units that should have been used for the output of the period, multiplied by the standard cost per unit of the direct material.

Usage Variance

The **direct materials usage variance** refers to the efficiency with which each raw material was used during the period. For each raw material, this variance is calculated as the difference between the actual raw material units used during the period and the standard units that

---

[2] As we discuss later in this chapter, for control purposes it is preferable to calculate the materials price variance at the time materials are purchased. In this case, we use the more specific term *materials purchase price variance*. See Exhibit 14.11 and the related discussion.

should have been used for the output of the period, multiplied by the standard cost per unit of the direct material. This variance is also referred to as an *efficiency* or *quantity variance.*

In October 2022, Schmidt Machinery Company used 3,630 pounds of aluminum to manufacture 780 units of XV-1. According to the standard cost sheet (Exhibit 14.5), each unit of XV-1 requires 4 pounds of aluminum. The total standard quantity of aluminum for the 780 units manufactured during the period, therefore, is 3,120 pounds (780 units × 4 pounds per unit). This says that the 3,630 pounds of aluminum used in production is 510 pounds more than the total standard quantity for the 780 units of XV-1 manufactured during the period. At the standard price of $25 per pound, the usage variance this period for aluminum is $12,750 unfavorable [column (2) − column (3), Exhibit 14.9]. Alternatively,

$$\begin{array}{c}\text{Direct}\\\text{materials}\\\text{usage variance}\end{array} = \left(\begin{array}{c}\text{Total quantity}\\\text{of the direct}\\\text{material used}\end{array} - \begin{array}{c}\text{Total standard quantity of}\\\text{the direct material for}\\\text{the units manufactured}\end{array}\right) \times \begin{array}{c}\text{Standard cost per}\\\text{unit of the direct}\\\text{material}\end{array}$$

$$= (AQ - SQ) \times SP$$
$$= (3{,}630 - 3{,}120) \text{ pounds} \times \$25 \text{ per pound}$$
$$= 510 \text{ pounds} \times \$25 \text{ per pound}$$
$$= \$12{,}750 \text{ Unfavorable}$$

Interpreting the Direct Materials Usage Variance A significant direct materials usage variance suggests that operations consumed a significantly different amount of direct materials than the amount specified for the output of the period. This variance measures efficiency in using direct materials and can result from the efforts of production personnel, substitutions of materials or production factors, variation in the quality of direct materials, inadequate training or inexperienced employees, poor supervision, or other factors.

Direct Labor Variances

As indicated in Exhibit 14.7, a direct labor flexible budget variance is a result of the total direct labor cost of a period being different from the total standard direct labor cost for the output of the period. As with the direct materials flexible budget variance, a direct labor flexible budget variance also can be divided into two components: a rate (price) variance and an efficiency (quantity) variance. As shown in Exhibit 14.8, the total direct labor flexible budget variance for October 2022 is $8,580F. The procedure for further analysis of this variance is similar to the procedure discussed earlier for direct materials. Exhibit 14.10 shows calculations of

EXHIBIT 14.10
Direct Labor Flexible Budget Variance—Schmidt Machinery Company (October 2022)

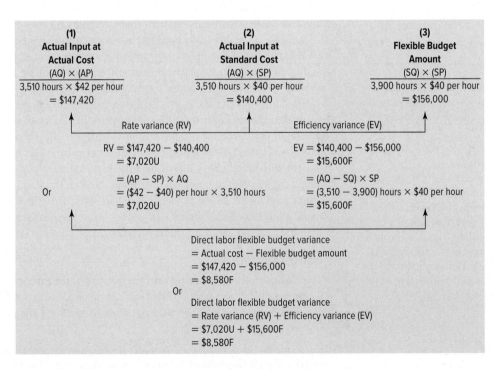

(1) Actual Input at Actual Cost (AQ) × (AP)	(2) Actual Input at Standard Cost (AQ) × (SP)	(3) Flexible Budget Amount (SQ) × (SP)
3,510 hours × $42 per hour = $147,420	3,510 hours × $40 per hour = $140,400	3,900 hours × $40 per hour = $156,000

Rate variance (RV)   Efficiency variance (EV)

RV = $147,420 − $140,400   EV = $140,400 − $156,000
    = $7,020U   = $15,600F

Or
    = (AP − SP) × AQ   = (AQ − SQ) × SP
    = ($42 − $40) per hour × 3,510 hours   = (3,510 − 3,900) hours × $40 per hour
    = $7,020U   = $15,600F

Direct labor flexible budget variance
= Actual cost − Flexible budget amount
= $147,420 − $156,000
= $8,580F

Or

Direct labor flexible budget variance
= Rate variance (RV) + Efficiency variance (EV)
= $7,020U + $15,600F
= $8,580F

the direct labor rate variance and the direct labor efficiency variance for Schmidt Machinery Company for October 2022.

direct labor rate variance
The difference between the actual and standard hourly wage rate multiplied by the actual direct labor hours worked during the period.

Direct Labor Rate Variance The **direct labor rate variance** is the difference between the actual and the standard wage rates multiplied by the actual direct labor hours worked during the period. As indicated in the top portion of Exhibit 14.8, Schmidt Machinery Company paid an average wage rate of $42 per hour for 3,510 direct labor hours in October. The standard cost sheet, however, calls for a wage rate of $40 per hour. Thus, the firm paid $2 per hour more than the standard hourly rate. With 3,510 total hours actually worked, the total direct labor rate variance is $7,020 unfavorable [Exhibit 14.10, column (1) – column (2)]. Alternatively,

$$\begin{matrix} \text{Direct labor} \\ \text{rate variance} \end{matrix} = \left(\begin{matrix} \text{Actual hourly} \\ \text{wage rate paid} \end{matrix} - \begin{matrix} \text{Standard hourly} \\ \text{wage rate} \end{matrix} \right) \times \begin{matrix} \text{Total direct labor} \\ \text{hours worked} \end{matrix}$$

$$= (AP - SP) \times AQ$$
$$= (\$42 - \$40) \text{ per direct labor hour} \times 3,510 \text{ direct labor hours}$$
$$= \$7,020 \text{ Unfavorable}$$

A direct labor rate variance reflects the effect on operating income when the actual hourly wage rate during the period deviates from the standard hourly wage rate. This could result from not using workers with the skill level specified in the standard cost sheet for the work performed or from using an out-of-date standard.

The personnel department usually is responsible for direct labor rate variances. Production, however, could be responsible for the variance if it chooses to use employees with a different skill level than that specified in the standard cost sheet.

direct labor efficiency variance
The difference between the actual direct labor hours worked and the standard direct labor hours allowed for the units manufactured, multiplied by the standard wage rate per hour.

Direct Labor Efficiency Variance A **direct labor efficiency variance** occurs when the total direct labor hours worked deviate from the total standard direct labor hours allowed for the actual output of the period. It is calculated by multiplying the difference between the actual and the standard allowed hours by the standard hourly wage rate, as follows:

$$\begin{matrix} \text{Direct labor} \\ \text{efficiency} \\ \text{variance} \end{matrix} = \left(\begin{matrix} \text{Total direct} \\ \text{labor hours} \\ \text{worked} \end{matrix} - \begin{matrix} \text{Total standard direct} \\ \text{labor hours allowed for} \\ \text{the output of the period} \end{matrix} \right) \times \begin{matrix} \text{Standard} \\ \text{direct labor} \\ \text{hourly rate} \end{matrix}$$

As indicated in the upper panel of Exhibit 14.8, Schmidt Machinery Company used 3,510 direct labor hours to manufacture 780 units of XV-1 in October 2022. The standard cost sheet (Exhibit 14.5) allows five direct labor hours for one unit of XV-1. The total standard hours allowed for 780 units of XV-1, therefore, is 3,900 hours (780 units × 5 hours per unit). Thus, Schmidt used 390 fewer direct labor hours than the standard hours allowed this period. At a standard wage rate of $40 per hour, the total direct labor efficiency (quantity) variance is $15,600 favorable [column (2) – column (3), Exhibit 14.10]. Alternatively,

$$\begin{matrix} \text{Direct labor} \\ \text{efficiency variance} \end{matrix} = \left(\begin{matrix} 3,510 \text{ actual} \\ \text{hours} \end{matrix} - \begin{matrix} 3,900 \text{ standard} \\ \text{hours allowed} \end{matrix} \right) \times \$40 \text{ per hour}$$

$$= (AQ - SQ) \times SP$$
$$= \$15,600 \text{ Favorable}$$

A direct labor efficiency variance reflects the effect on operating income of using a number of direct labor hours during the period that differs from the standard hours allowed during the period. This variance usually is the responsibility of the production department. Besides the employees' efficiency or inefficiency in carrying out their tasks, however, several other factors can lead to a direct labor efficiency variance, including:

- Employees or supervisors are new on the job or are inadequately trained.
- Employees' skill levels are different from those specified in the standard cost sheet.
- Batch sizes are different from the standard size.
- Materials are different from those specified.
- Machines or equipment are not in proper working condition.
- Supervision is inadequate.
- Scheduling is poor.

Timing of Variance Recognition   Identification of variances helps managers to be aware of deviations from expected performance. For maximum control, managers should recognize variances at the earliest feasible time.

As noted earlier, a direct materials price variance can be identified either at the time of purchase or at the time the materials are issued to production. The discussion to this point has assumed that the price variance for materials is calculated at the time materials are issued to production. By contrast, recognition of the price variance at the point of purchase allows the firm to take proper actions, preventing the continuation of an unfavorable variance or attaining the most benefit from favorable variances. As indicated in the top half of Exhibit 14.11, when the materials price variance is calculated at the point of purchase, actual quantity (AQ) in the variance calculation formula refers to the quantity of materials purchased. In this case, the materials price variance is referred to by the more descriptive term *materials purchase price variance.*

Recognizing materials price variances at the time of purchase lets the firm carry all units of the same material in the inventory account at one price—the standard cost of the material. Using one price for the same materials greatly simplifies accounting work. For example, such a firm needs to maintain materials subsidiary ledgers only in terms of quantity.

If a price variance is not recorded until the materials are issued to production, then AQ in the price variance formula refers to the quantity of materials *used* in production and the direct materials are carried on the books at their actual purchase prices.

EXHIBIT 14.11
Analyzing Direct Materials Variances When the Materials Purchase Price Variance Is Calculated at Point of Purchase

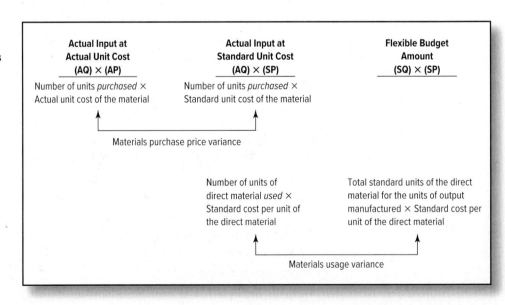

Regardless of when a direct materials price variance is recognized, the number of units of direct materials actually consumed in production is used to compute the direct materials usage variance, as shown in the lower portion of Exhibit 14.11.

Standard Costs

LO 14-4

Develop standard costs for product costing, performance evaluation, and control.

A **standard cost** is a carefully determined cost a firm or organization sets for an operation—the cost the firm or organization should incur for the operation under relatively efficient conditions. A standard cost usually is expressed on a per-unit-of-output basis. Standard costs are incorporated into budgets and as such can be used to monitor and control operations and evaluate performance.

Standard Costs vs. a Standard Cost System

standard cost
The cost a firm should incur for a process or activity.

A standard cost prescribes expected performance. A complete standard cost for a product or service includes carefully established standards for each cost element, including manufacturing, selling, and administrative expenses, as illustrated earlier in Exhibit 14.5. Although the discussions in this and the next chapter focus on standard cost systems for manufacturing operations, these concepts and procedures can be applied to service contexts as well.

standard cost system
An accounting system in which standard, not actual, costs flow through the formal accounting records.

It is useful to distinguish between standard costs and a **standard cost system**. The latter refers to an accounting system in which standard costs, and associated standard cost variances, are recorded in the formal accounting system. The flow of direct manufacturing costs in the accounting records is illustrated in the next section of this chapter.[3] Note, however, that standard costs can be used for control purposes outside of the formal accounting system. That is, at the end of the accounting period, accountants can compare actual and standard costs and analyze variances using the procedures discussed in the previous section of this chapter, regardless of whether standard costs are incorporated formally in the accounting system.

A standard cost system can be applied in either a job-order or a process costing context. Because of the repetitive nature of operations, it is generally simpler to establish standards in conjunction with a process costing system. Also, the use of standard costs in a process costing system greatly simplifies the determination of equivalent unit costs: The standard (predetermined) costs serve as the cost per equivalent unit for direct materials, direct labor, and manufacturing overhead.

Types of Standards

Firms have different expectations for the proper level at which to set their standards. Differences in expectations lead to two basic types of standards: ideal and currently attainable.

Ideal Standards

ideal standard
A standard that reflects perfect implementation and maximum efficiency in every aspect of the operation.

An **ideal standard** (sometimes called a theoretical standard) reflects maximum efficiency in every aspect of an operation. By definition, ideal standards are difficult, but not impossible, to achieve. They assume peak operating efficiency and the absence of any production disruptions. That is, ideal standards assume perfection across all operations. As such, the use of ideal standards can lead to undue stress on employees that, in turn, may lead to decreases in morale and ultimately decreases in productivity.

continuous-improvement standard
A standard that gets progressively tighter over time.

As an alternative to the use of ideal standards, some organizations employ what are referred to as **continuous-improvement standards**. Such standards, as a function of time (e.g., months), become progressively tighter (i.e., more difficult to achieve). The use of this approach is somewhat analogous to the Japanese use of kaizen costing.

Organizations that use ideal standards often modify performance evaluation and reward structures so that employees are not frustrated by frequent failures to attain the standards. Organizations can, for example, use progress toward an ideal standard rather than deviations from it as the primary benchmark in their performance evaluation and reward systems.

---

[3] Journal entries for recording standard indirect manufacturing costs (i.e., manufacturing overhead), as well as associated standard cost variances, are presented in Chapter 15.

This chapter discusses standard costing and the computation of cost variances as common (and useful) features of traditional short-term financial control systems. When executed properly, these tools can provide valuable information for managers to identify problems as well as opportunities that can help organizations operate more effectively and efficiently.

However, not all organizations are likely to benefit equally from the use of standard costing and variance analysis systems. In fact, some organizations may find them obsolete. To understand why, read the article at the following website (**https://sfmagazine.com/post-entry/june-2016-leaning-away-from-standard-costing/**). What is lean management? Why would companies adopting principles of lean management find that traditional standard costing systems are not in their best interest?

(Refer to **Comments on Cost Management in Action** at the end of the chapter.)

Currently Attainable Standards

currently attainable standard
A level of performance that workers with proper training and experience can attain most of the time without having to exert extraordinary effort.

A **currently attainable standard** (sometimes called a practical standard) sets the performance expectation at a level that a person with proper training and experience can attain most of the time without having to exert extraordinary effort. A currently attainable standard emphasizes normality and allows for some imperfections and inefficiencies.

Suppose that a firm sets the standard for the amount of plywood needed to produce 1,000 tabletops at 525 sheets of plywood, although two tabletops can be cut from one sheet. The additional 25 sheets allow for such things as less-than-ideal input quality, occasional maladjustment of the equipment used in production, worker fatigue, and varying experience and skill levels of the personnel involved in production. By using a standard that allows for normal fluctuations in relevant manufacturing factors, employees exerting reasonable effort usually can meet the standard.

Selection of Standards

Which standards—ideal or currently attainable—should a firm use? There is no single answer for all situations.

Firms struggling for survival in intensely competitive industries may choose to use ideal (or continuous improvement) standards to motivate employees to put forth their best efforts. Ideal standards are not effective, however, if frequent failures in meeting the standards discourage employees or lead them to ignore the standards.

Currently attainable standards, however, may have built into them some degree of inefficiency. Allowing some inefficiencies is strategically unwise if the firm operates in an intensely competitive environment. In the preceding example, a standard that allows 25 additional sheets of plywood for every 1,000 tabletops produced conveys to production that it has attained acceptable performance as long as it does not use more than 525 sheets for every 1,000 tabletops produced.

Standard-Setting Procedures

authoritative standard
A standard determined solely or primarily by management.

participative standard
A method of establishing standards whereby employees affected by the standards participate in the development of those standards.

A firm can use either an authoritative or a participative procedure when setting standards. An **authoritative standard** is determined solely or primarily by management. In contrast, a **participative standard** calls for the active participation of employees affected by the standard. A firm uses an authoritative process to ensure proper consideration of all operating factors, to incorporate management's desires or expectations, or to expedite the standard-setting process. Firms using an authoritative process in standard setting, however, should keep in mind that a standard is useless if ignored by employees.

Participative standards usually require more time and effort to create, yet they can have valuable behavioral effects. For example, employees are more likely to accept standards they helped to determine. Participation also reduces the chance that employees will view a standard as unreasonable and increases the likelihood that they will buy into or adopt it as their own.

Establishing Standard Costs

Establishing a standard cost often is a joint effort. Managers, product-design engineers, industrial engineers, management accountants, production supervisors, the purchasing department, the personnel department, and employees affected by the standard may all be involved.

Establishing the Standard Cost for Direct Materials

The first step in establishing a standard cost is to specify the quality of the direct materials. The quality of direct materials determines the quality of the product and affects many phases of the manufacturing process, including the quantity of direct materials needed or used in manufacturing, the prices of direct materials, processing time, and the extent and frequency of supervision needed to complete manufacturing. Once a firm determines the quality of the direct materials, management accountants work with the industrial engineering and production departments to set the standard for the quantity of direct materials needed to manufacture the product.

Quality, quantity, and (sometimes) the timing of purchases can all affect material cost standards. In a competitive environment, many companies emphasize long-term relationships with selected suppliers that are reliable in delivering quality materials on time. For a firm that emphasizes long-term benefits and the reliability of its supply chain, the price standard needs to be revised only when a change occurs in the underlying long-term factors that affect material prices.

Establishing the Standard Cost for Direct Labor

Direct labor costs vary with types of work, product complexity, employee skill level, the nature of the manufacturing process, and the type and condition of the equipment to be used. After considering these factors, industrial engineering, production, personnel, labor union representatives, and management accountants jointly determine the quantity standard for direct labor.

The personnel department determines the standard wage rate for the type and skill level of employees needed for the manufacturing process. The standard labor rate for direct labor includes not only the wage paid, but also the fringe benefits provided to employees and the required payroll taxes associated with wages and salaries. Fringe benefits include health and life insurance, pension plan contributions, and paid vacations. Payroll taxes include unemployment taxes and the employer's share of an employee's Social Security assessment.

A question normally arises as to how overtime premiums are treated, both for product costing and for subsequent variance analysis purposes. In many cases, **overtime premiums** are treated as part of factory overhead. This is true when production (or service) scheduling is random or when the overtime is caused by taking on more jobs than can be handled during a standard workweek. In this case, the overtime premium should be spread over production in general—that is, over all output for the period. In other cases, however, the overtime premium might be attributed to a specific job, client, or customer—for example, a rush order. In this case, the premium can be traced and, therefore, should be treated as part of direct labor cost. Such excess payments would typically appear as part of the direct labor rate variance for the period.

overtime premium
The *excess* wage rate per hour over the standard hourly wage rate.

Recording Standard Costs

When standard costs (including both price and quantity) have been established, they are documented on the standard cost sheet for each product. As described earlier and shown in Exhibit 14.5, the standard cost for one unit of XV-1 includes 4 pounds of aluminum at $25 per pound, 1 pound of PVC at $40 per pound, 5 hours of direct labor at $40 per hour, and factory overhead of $36 ($12 + $24) per direct labor hour. The standard cost sheet for product XV-1 also records the budgeted variable selling and administrative expense of $50 per unit.

Recording Cost Flows and Variances in a Standard Cost System

LO 14-5
Record manufacturing cost flows and associated variances in a standard cost system.

Standard cost systems use the same accounts for inventory and for recording manufacturing costs that actual or normal costing systems use. Thus, they have accounts such as Direct Materials Inventory, Accrued Payroll, Factory (Manufacturing) Overhead, Work-in-Process Inventory, Finished Goods Inventory, and Cost of Goods Sold. Manufacturing costs flow through inventory and manufacturing cost accounts in ways that are similar to cost flows in an actual or a normal cost system. Of course, standard cost systems have standard costs instead of actual or normalized costs flowing through the accounts.

Another difference is the use of variance accounts in standard cost systems. Firms that use a standard cost system have a separate ledger account for each variance. Favorable

EXHIBIT 14.12 **Standard Manufacturing Cost Flows (Direct Labor and Direct Materials)***

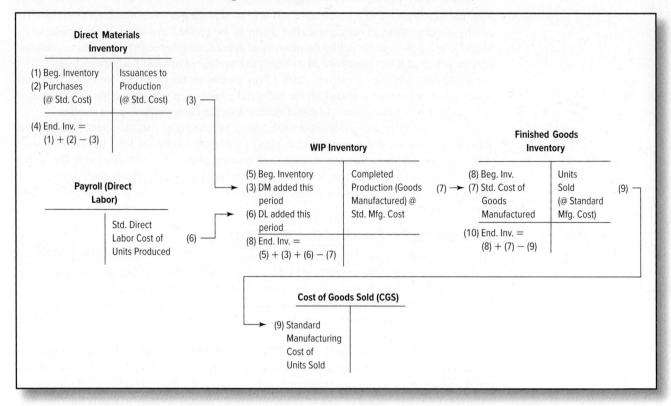

*The accounting for standard manufacturing overhead costs is covered in Chapter 15.

variances will have *credit* balances while unfavorable variances will have *debit* balances. The end-of-period disposition (closing) of these variance accounts is covered in Chapter 15. A diagrammatic representation of the cost-recording process for a standard cost system is given in Exhibit 14.12.

Direct Materials Cost

A firm that uses a standard cost system and that recognizes material price variances at the point of purchase records purchases of direct materials as follows:

	Account	Amount
Debit:	Direct Materials Inventory	Total standard cost of the purchased materials
	Direct Materials Purchase Price Variance *(if unfavorable)*	Amount of *unfavorable* variance
Credit:	Cash or Accounts Payable	Purchase cost of materials
	Direct Materials Purchase Price Variance *(if favorable)*	Amount of *favorable* variance

To illustrate, on October 7, Schmidt Machinery Company purchased 3,630 pounds of aluminum at $26 per pound, as shown in Exhibit 14.6 and Exhibit 14.8. The terms of purchase were 1/EOM, n/180. The standard cost sheet (Exhibit 14.5) lists the cost at $25 per pound. The firm records all cash discounts when earned.[4] The journal entry for the purchase is as follows:

---

[4] If, for example, payment were made before the end of October, the appropriate journal entry would be:

Dr. Account Payable 94,380.00

   Cr. Cash ($94,380 × 0.99) 93,436.20

   Cr. Purchase Discounts Taken 943.80

Date	Account	Amount
Oct. 7	Direct Materials Inventory (3,630 × $25)	90,750
	Direct Materials Purchase Price Variance—Aluminum (3,630 × $1)	3,630
	Accounts Payable (3,630 × $26)	
	Purchase of 3,630 pounds of aluminum at $26 per pound.	94,380
	Terms = 1/EOM, n/180; standard price is $25 per pound.	

The purchase price Schmidt agreed to pay is $3,630 higher than the total standard cost for 3,630 pounds of aluminum—an unfavorable direct materials purchase price variance. Schmidt records the unfavorable variance by *debiting* the variance account.

The journal entry at the end of the month to record the issuance of direct materials, after the output for the month could be determined, takes the following form:

	Account	Amount
Debit:	Work-in-Process Inventory	Total standard quantity of materials, at standard cost, for the output of the period
	Direct Materials Usage Variance *(if unfavorable)*	Amount of *unfavorable* variance
Credit:	Direct Materials Inventory	Total quantity of materials used, at standard cost
	Direct Materials Usage Variance *(if favorable)*	Amount of *favorable* variance

As shown in Exhibit 14.9, during October the production department used 3,630 pounds of aluminum for the production of 780 units of XV-1. Thus, the end-of-month journal entry is:

Date	Account	Amount
Oct. 31	Work-in-Process Inventory (780 × 4 = 3,120; 3,120 × $25)	78,000
	Direct Materials Usage Variance—Aluminum	12,750
	(3,630 − 3,120 = 510; 510 × $25)	
	Direct Materials Inventory (3,630 × $25)	90,750
	Issued 3,630 pounds of aluminum to production for the manufacture of 780 units of XV-1. Standard usage is 4 pounds per unit of XV-1.	

Direct Labor Cost

The cost of the manufactured units is increased by direct labor costs. To accomplish this, the Work-in-Process Inventory account is debited for the total standard direct labor cost for the units manufactured. An associated credit entry is made to the Accrued Payroll account for the total direct labor wages incurred for the period.

	Account	Amount
Debit:	Work-in-Process Inventory	Total number of standard hours, at the standard hourly wage rate, for the units manufactured
	Direct Labor Rate or Efficiency Variance *(if unfavorable)*	Amount of *unfavorable* variance
Credit:	Accrued Payroll	Actual wage expense
	Direct Labor Rate or Efficiency Variance *(if favorable)*	Amount of *favorable* variance

The difference between the amount debited (the amount that should have been incurred for the units manufactured) and the amount credited (the total amount of direct labor wages incurred) is the total direct labor flexible budget variance for the period; as shown in Exhibit 14.10, this total variance can be broken down into a labor rate variance and a labor efficiency (quantity) variance. Each of these two component variances is entered into its own account.

During October, Schmidt spent 3,510 direct labor hours for $147,420 to complete the production of 780 units of XV-1, or $42 per hour. The standard (Exhibit 14.5) calls for 5 direct labor hours per unit of XV-1 at $40 per hour. Thus, the end-of-month journal entry is:[5]

Date	Account	Amount	
Oct. 31	Work-in-Process Inventory (780 × 5 = 3,900; 3,900 × $40)	156,000	
	Direct Labor Rate Variance (3,510 × [$42 − $40 = $2])	7,020	
	Direct Labor Efficiency Variance ([3,900 − 3,510 = 390] × $40)		15,600
	Accrued Payroll (3,510 × $42)		147,420
	Used 3,510 direct labor hours to manufacture 780 units of XV-1.		
	Standard cost allows 5 hours per unit of XV-1 at $40 per hour.		

This single journal entry captures both the labor efficiency variance (favorable because Schmidt spent fewer direct labor hours [3,510] than indicated by the standard [3,900] to make 780 units) and the labor rate variance (unfavorable because Schmidt incurred a higher hourly labor rate [$42] than indicated by the standard [$40]).

Application of Standard Factory Overhead Costs

In addition to direct materials costs and direct labor costs, production for the period should be charged with standard factory overhead costs. According to Exhibit 14.5, the standard overhead cost per unit produced is $180 ($60 variable overhead plus $120 fixed overhead). The application of standard overhead costs for the period is accomplished as follows:

Date	Account	Amount	
Oct. 31	Work-in-Process Inventory (780 units × $180 per unit)	$140,400	
	Factory Overhead Applied		$140,400

Note: A full accounting of overhead costs and associated variances is covered in Chapter 15.

Completion of Production

Upon completion of production, the total standard cost of the units manufactured is transferred out of the Work-in-Process Inventory account and into the Finished Goods Inventory account. The standard cost sheet (Exhibit 14.5) specifies that the total standard manufacturing cost per unit of XV-1 is $520. The following journal entry, on October 31, records the completion of 780 units of XV-1 during October:

Date	Account	Amount	
Oct. 31	Finished Goods Inventory (780 units × $520 per unit)	405,600	
	Work-in-Process Inventory		405,600
	Completed 780 units of XV-1 at a standard manufacturing cost		
	per unit of $520.		

Exhibit 14.13 summarizes the cost flows through ledger accounts in a standard cost system. (The recording of manufacturing overhead costs, including overhead cost variances, is covered in Chapter 15.)

---

[5] When the liability is paid (extinguished), Schmidt would simultaneously debit the Accrued Payroll account and credit Cash for $147,420.

EXHIBIT 14.13 **Partial Cost Flows and General Ledger Entries in a Standard Cost System**

Direct Materials Inventory		Work-in-Process Inventory	
Beginning inventory at standard cost per unit xxx	Units issued to production × Standard cost per unit 90,750	Beginning inventory at standard cost xxx	Units completed × Standard manufacturing cost per unit 405,600
Units purchased × Standard cost per unit 90,750		Total standard quantity of direct materials for units manufactured × Standard cost per unit of direct materials 78,000	

Direct Materials Purchase Price Variance†			
Unfavorable variances 3,630	Favorable variances	Total standard direct labor hours for units manufactured × Standard wage rate per hour 156,000	

Direct Materials Usage Variance†			
Unfavorable variances 12,750	Favorable variances	Total units produced × Standard factory overhead cost per unit 140,400	

Finished Goods Inventory	
Beginning inventory at standard manufacturing cost xxx	Units sold × Standard manufacturing cost per unit xxx

Accrued Payroll	
	Direct labor hours worked × Actual hourly wage rate 147,420

Finished Goods Inventory continued:

Units completed × Standard manufacturing cost per unit 405,600	

Direct Labor Rate Variance†		Cost of Goods Sold	
Unfavorable variances 7,020	Favorable variances	Units sold × Standard manufacturing cost per unit xxx	

Direct Labor Efficiency Variance†		Accounts Payable	
Unfavorable variances	Favorable variances 15,600		Actual purchase cost of materials 94,380

†The end-of-period disposition (closing) of these accounts is covered in Chapter 15.

The Strategic Role of Nonfinancial Performance Indicators

LO 14-6

Discuss major operating functions and the need for nonfinancial performance indicators.

Thus far, this chapter has focused on the use of flexible budgets, standards, and various operating income variances to assess short-run financial performance. However, long-term organizational success will not likely be achieved if the accounting and control system focuses only on short-run financial performance indicators. This section explains some of the limitations of short-term financial performance indicators and introduces the use of nonfinancial performance indicators as part of a comprehensive management accounting and control system.

Limitations of Short-Term Financial Control

When used carefully, the financial-control model discussed thus far in the chapter can be helpful for organizations as they strive for competitive advantage. However, management

REAL-WORLD FOCUS   Cost Savings in the Cloud

Chief information officers (CIOs) are always on the lookout for ways to streamline operations and reduce costs. A number of companies are improving their sustainability efforts to accomplish this, particularly by reducing their carbon footprints. Brokerage firm TD Ameritrade Holding Corp. is consolidating its data centers from three to two, while payroll and human resources services company Automatic Data Processing Inc. has decommissioned 20 data center facilities in the past five years. Other companies (such as Atlassian Corp., a Sydney-based

company that develops online collaboration tools for businesses) are moving their data storage facilities to the cloud, using companies such as Amazon Web Services (AWS). Cloud computing services offer companies the opportunity to reduce costs by eliminating physical facilities. Specialty service providers such as AWS have their own sustainability commitments and can achieve efficiency-based cost reductions.

Source: Sara Castellanos, "Shift to Cloud, Renewable Energy Top CIOs' Sustainability Agendas," *The Wall Street Journal*, December 26, 2019.

accountants need to recognize the following major limitations of the use of standard costs and variance analysis for operational control purposes:

- Because of the short-term nature of the performance indicators, employees and decision makers may take actions that improve short-term financial performance at the expense of long-term performance. For example, favorable labor rate variances may be realized by employing substandard labor. However, the use of such labor may result in a deterioration of product or service quality, which could result in the erosion of market share and long-term profitability.

- Focusing on individual variances may result in optimizing local, but not global, performance. For example, the purchase of nonstandard raw materials may result in a favorable materials purchase price variance for the purchasing manager. However, those lower-quality materials may result in increased scrap and other quality-related costs, increased machine-hour consumption, and increased labor (i.e., processing) costs. The net effect of this chain of events could very well be an unfavorable flexible budget variance for the period.

- Operating personnel may not be able to interpret or act upon financial performance indicators, such as the cost variances discussed earlier in this chapter. That is, they may not find such information useful for improving operating performance.

- Financial performance indicators are basically backward-looking measures. They tell us something about operating performance in the past but do not necessarily tell us much about the drivers of future financial performance.

- The construction, application, updating, and use of a standard cost system may incur significant costs.

For all of the above reasons, we suggest that nonfinancial operating performance measures be used as a complement to the financial control information achieved through the use of standard costs, flexible budgets, and resulting variances. A fuller discussion of expanding the scope of the performance evaluation model, in the form of a balanced scorecard, is presented in Chapter 18. In the remainder of this chapter, we provide an overview of the role that nonfinancial performance indicators can play in terms of achieving operational control. As the name implies, nonfinancial performance indicators are measures expressed in terms other than dollars. These performance indicators focus on, or relate to, basic business processes, as described next.

Business Processes

At the beginning of this chapter, we noted that there are multiple business processes in which many, if not most, organizations engage. Common business processes include:

- *Operating processes* (i.e., the day-to-day activities that produce the outputs of the organization and that deliver them to customers).
- *Customer management processes* (i.e., activities that focus on creating customers and then expanding and deepening relationships with these customers).

As noted in the text, one strategy for improving operating processes is adopting a JIT philosophy. Ultimately, the adoption of JIT should be based on a comparison of costs and benefits. The following examples illustrate the primary benefits associated with JIT implementations:

- **Toyota:** With rigid adherence to quality standards, the company is able to maintain only minimal levels of inventories at each manufacturing stage. Parts enter the manufacturing process only as needed; as a result, inventory holding costs are reduced, while the company is able to respond more quickly to changing customer demands.
- **Dell:** Suppliers, not Dell, maintain most of the inventory of items needed in production; supplier arrangements specify short lead times for manufacturing components. In this way, Dell is able to maintain short production lead times and quicker customer response times.

- **Harley Davidson:** Under JIT, the company has committed to continuous process improvements and inventory reductions that, together, have allowed the company to dramatically reduce the amount of inventory holdings (and associated costs).
- **McDonald's:** On-demand order-filling (i.e., "demand pull") is possible because of a reduction in setup costs and standardization of the production process in this fast-food provider; in this environment, inventory holding costs (e.g., food spoilage) are decreased dramatically.

Source: David Kiger, "Analyzing Top Examples of Just-in-Time Inventory and Production Management" (https://davidkigerinfo.wordpress.com/2016/02/22/analyzing-top-examples-of-just-in-time-inventory-and-production-management/).

- *Innovation processes* (i.e., activities designed to produce new processes, services, and products).
- *Social/regulatory processes* (i.e., activities related to the organization's environmental and community responsibilities, as well as its legal responsibilities, at both local and national levels).

Organizations succeed by managing the set of activities associated with each of these four classes of business processes. Thus, an effective operational control system would establish specific objectives for each of the four business processes and then monitor performance by developing one or more key performance measures for each specified objective. For example, in the innovation processes category, management might specify the following two critical objectives: (1) manage the development cycle cost and (2) reduce new product development time. To monitor performance of the former, the organization might compare actual spending versus budgeted spending on each project at each development stage. To monitor performance in terms of the latter objective, management might measure the development manufacturing cycle time (elapsed time from initial concept to the time the product in question comes to market) and/or the number of projects delivered on time (i.e., according to plan). In the following section, we provide a more detailed discussion of the use of both financial and nonfinancial performance indicators for improving operating processes. The monitoring of customer management, innovation, and social/regulatory processes is covered in greater detail in Chapter 18.

Operating Processes

As noted above, operating processes include activities such as acquiring raw materials from suppliers, producing outputs (i.e., services or products), and delivering products or services to customers. Depending on the strategy the organization is pursuing, it would likely give differential weight to each of the following operating process objectives: time, cost, and quality. For each of these critical dimensions on which the organization could compete, the management accountant would help to identify a series of specific objectives and associated measures, similar to the example given earlier. In the remainder of this section, we provide an extended discussion of a particular operating strategy: the switch from a conventional manufacturing process to a just-in-time (JIT) process.

The goal of the discussion is to illustrate the expansion of a management accounting system for control of an operating process.

Just-in-Time Manufacturing

just-in-time (JIT) manufacturing
A process in which production at any stage of the process does not take place until an order is received.

A **just-in-time (JIT) manufacturing** process is one in which production at any stage of a process does not take place until an order, from an internal or external customer, is received. In this sense, the underlying system is sometimes referred to as demand pull. One implication of JIT manufacturing is the reduction, if not elimination, of inventory buffer stocks (which, many would argue, serve as a cushion for poor-quality outputs). When inventory stocks are kept to a minimum, quality at each stage of the production process is required. Obviously, the adoption of a JIT philosophy, with a focus on the elimination of waste and inefficiency, is a strategic choice made by management. What are the costs and benefits associated with a move to JIT? The management accountant can help answer this question.

Costs of Implementing JIT

In concept, a JIT system is straightforward: reduce inventories, eliminate waste, and produce only to order. In reality, however, the successful implementation of a JIT system, as an operating process, can require significant resources—to educate and train employees, to reconfigure the production layout (e.g., to a cellular approach), to modify/improve information systems, to coordinate activities with customers and suppliers, and to monitor operating performance in the new environment (i.e., to revise the organization's management accounting and control system). The organization's management accounting system can help by identifying and reporting to management the sources of delay, error, and waste in the system. While conventional systems monitor labor and materials usage, with large-batch production, the focus on a JIT system would be on measures such as defect rates, manufacturing cycle times, percentage of on-time deliveries, and machine up-times.

Benefits of Implementing JIT

A switch from a conventional to a JIT manufacturing system provides the following key benefits, all of which could be estimated by the organization's management accounting system:

- Reduction in out-of-pocket inventory carrying costs. Under JIT, the clerical process of recording and monitoring inventory levels (raw materials, work-in-process, and finished goods) is significantly reduced. This results in both labor savings as well as reduced information processing costs.
- Reduction in inventory-related opportunity (holding) costs. All assets that are held require that capital be tied up (i.e., not available for an alternative use). Reductions in inventory result in reductions in imputed costs associated with holding inventory.
- Possible increases in sales, market share, and profitability:

- ○ Increases in product/service quality can result in increased sales and market share for the organization, particularly if the organization is pursuing a differentiation strategy.
- ○ Reductions in cycle/processing time (i.e., faster customer response times) may also lead to increased sales and market share for the organization.
- Decreased production costs. Improvements in product/service quality are reflected in manufacturing costs. For example, under JIT, we would anticipate reductions in defect-related quality costs (e.g., a reduction in the cost of reworking defective outputs).
- Improved management of the supply chain and resulting cost savings. Through improvements in the way the organization transacts and pays for purchases, suppliers can realize and pass on to the organization cost savings. Supplier cost reductions can result from not having to invoice the organization, through automatic payments received from the purchaser, elimination of purchase orders altogether (if suppliers are able to directly access the organization's production schedule), etc. Changing the way the organization does business with suppliers is part of a larger concept "activity-based management," as discussed in Chapter 5.

The preceding discussion focuses on financial performance indicators associated with a strategic move to JIT manufacturing. Such indicators, in a mature management accounting system, should be supplemented with relevant nonfinancial operating performance indicators.

Exhibit 14.14 provides an example of a **customer response time (CRT)** model that the management accountant can use to monitor and report time-based performance in conjunction with the adoption of a JIT production system. This model would be particularly useful for an organization that competes on the basis of time. Notice that the total customer response time in this model can be broken down into three major elements: receipt time, manufacturing lead (cycle) time, and delivery time. Manufacturing cycle time (or manufacturing lead time) represents the total time from the start of production to the time the product is finished. As you see from Exhibit 14.14, manufacturing cycle time can be further broken down into manufacturing wait time and actual processing (manufacturing) time. Behind each of these times, we would envision one or more activities that are being performed. An activity analysis, similar to the analysis required in conjunction with the implementation of an ABC system (Chapter 5), can be performed to motivate improvements in these time-based measures. The main point, however, is that the CRT model is but one example of a nonfinancial performance indicator that could be used as part of an operational control system.

Manufacturing Cycle Efficiency (MCE)

An alternative (and complementary) measure of operating process efficiency in a manufacturing setting is called **manufacturing cycle efficiency (MCE)**. As noted in Chapter 13, MCE

customer response time (CRT)
A measure of operating performance defined as the elapsed time between the time the customer places an order and the time the customer receives the order.

manufacturing cycle efficiency (MCE)
A measure of operating performance in a manufacturing setting, defined as the ratio of processing time to total manufacturing time (or the ratio of value-added time to total time).

EXHIBIT 14.14
Model of Customer Response Time (CRT)

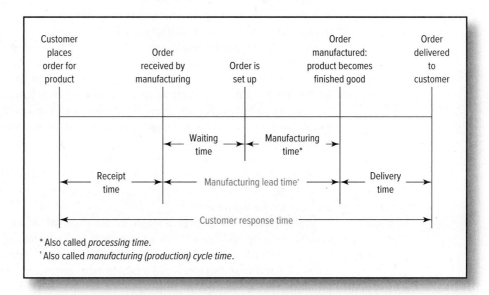

* Also called *processing time*.
† Also called *manufacturing (production) cycle time*.

is a method of assessing process efficiency, based on the relationship between *actual processing time* and *total production time*. In formula form, we can define MCE as:

MCE = Processing time ÷ Total manufacturing time

MCE = Processing time ÷ (Processing time + Moving time + Storage time + Inspection time)

Alternatively, we can view MCE as the ratio of value-added time to the sum of value-added time and non-value-added time. The notion of value-added and non-value-added is precisely the same as we saw in Chapter 5. The classifications are viewed from the standpoint of the customer; that is, an external, not internal, perspective is taken when classifying activities as value-added or non-value-added. Notice that increases in performance are reflected by increases in MCE. The optimum situation is when MCE equals 1.

Advantages of Nonfinancial Measures of Business Process Performance

Nonfinancial performance measures complement the financial measures discussed earlier in the chapter and in conjunction with the JIT example presented earlier. Both types of measures are useful in terms of building a comprehensive management accounting and control system. As well, both types of measures can be incorporated into an organization's strategic management system, such as its balanced scorecard (BSC). In short, the two groups of measures complement one another.

Relative to financial measures, nonfinancial performance measures have the following advantages:

- They are often easy to quantify and can be understood by operating personnel. This is a significant benefit when building an effective operational control system.
- They direct attention to basic business processes and hence focus on the precise problem areas that need attention.
- They are typically available on a real-time (or nearly real-time) basis—far earlier than financial performance indicators are typically available.
- They can often be viewed as drivers (or at least leading indicators) of future financial performance.

Summary

This chapter is the first of four that address the topic of operational control. We define operational control systems as a subset of an organization's overall (i.e., comprehensive) management accounting and control system. A modern operational control system consists of *both* financial and nonfinancial performance indicators. Financial control is achieved through the use of flexible budgets, standard costs, and associated variances for reporting and interpreting the short-term financial results of operations. A comprehensive operational control system will also include performance indicators associated with basic business processes (operating, customer, innovation, and regulatory/social).

For any given period (e.g., a month or a quarter), an organization will typically realize an actual amount of operating income that differs from the operating income reflected in its master (or static) budget. Any such difference is referred to as the *master budget variance* for the period. This total variance is a function of five factors: sales volume, selling price per unit, variable cost per unit, total fixed costs, and sales mix. Through the use of flexible budgets and standard costs, we are able to subdivide the master budget variance into amounts associated with each of these five factors. This variance decomposition process is the essence of the short-term financial control model discussed in the chapter. Exhibit 14.15 provides a summary of the variance decomposition process we conducted for the Schmidt Machinery Company for October 2022. Our goal in this regard was to explain the $72,000U master budget variance for the month.

In this chapter, we assume a single product/output and show how to calculate the sales volume variance and the total flexible budget variance for any given operating period. As can be seen in Exhibit 14.15, the total flexible budget variance can be subdivided into a series of fixed cost variances and variable cost variances. All variable cost variances can

EXHIBIT 14.15 Variance-Decomposition Summary: Schmidt Machinery Company Example (October 2022)

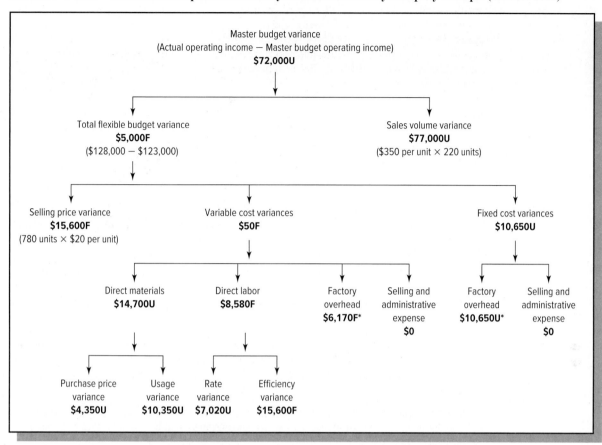

*Decomposition (breakdown) of these variances is covered in Chapter 15. In addition, Chapter 15 discusses the end-of-period disposition of standard cost variance amounts.

then be subdivided into a price (rate) component and a quantity (efficiency) component. In Chapter 15, we continue the variance-decomposition process by calculating and interpreting variances for indirect manufacturing costs. In Chapter 16, we take a further look at sales variances (e.g., by introducing sales mix into the analysis), and to complement the analysis, we look at various productivity measures.

When standard costs are incorporated into the formal accounting system, the organization is said to be using a standard cost system. The standard cost for each product is reflected on what is called a standard cost sheet. Except for the inclusion of standard cost variances (e.g., materials purchase price variance), the recording of manufacturing costs under a standard cost system parallels the process we discussed earlier in the text for job costing systems and process costing systems. (The issue of how standard cost variances are disposed of at the end of an accounting period is discussed in Chapter 15.)

In this chapter, we discuss major classes of business processes, including operating processes. Each business process consists of a number of activities. Thus, the control of operating processes focuses on managing these activities, a point we made earlier in the text (Chapter 5) in our discussion of ABC. This implies the use of nonfinancial operating performance indicators as a complement to the financial indicators discussed earlier in the chapter. We argue that an effective operational control system includes both financial and nonfinancial performance indicators. One example of an operating process is the production/manufacturing process. The chapter concludes with an extended discussion of one manufacturing strategy: just-in-time (JIT) production. As an example of how nonfinancial performance indicators of operating performance can be constructed to support the organization's strategy, we discuss the following two time-related metrics: customer response time (CRT) and manufacturing cycle efficiency (MCE).

Key Terms	authoritative standard, *596*	direct materials usage	operational control, *580*
	continuous-improvement	variance, *591*	overtime premium, *597*
	standard, *595*	financial control, *580*	participative standard, *596*
	control, *580*	flexible budget, *582*	sales volume variance, *585*
	currently attainable standard, *596*	flexible budget variance, *586*	selling price variance, *586*
	customer response time	ideal standard, *595*	standard cost, *595*
	(CRT), *605*	just-in-time (JIT)	standard cost sheet, *587*
	direct labor efficiency	manufacturing, *604*	standard cost system, *595*
	variance, *593*	management accounting and	total flexible budget
	direct labor rate variance, *593*	control system, *580*	variance, *586*
	direct materials flexible budget	manufacturing cycle efficiency	total variable cost flexible
	variance, *591*	(MCE), *605*	budget variance, *587*
	direct materials price	master budget variance, *581*	variances, *580*
	variance, *591*	materials usage ratio, *591*	

Comments on Cost Management in Action

Could Standard Costing and Variance Analysis Be a Bad Idea?

The article referred to in the chapter (found at https://sfmagazine.com/post-entry/june-2016-leaning-away-from-standard-costing/) indicates that for organizations that are embracing lean manufacturing, standard costing and variance analysis are obsolete. So what are lean manufacturing principles, and why are they inconsistent with standard costing?

Lean manufacturing techniques refer to organizational efforts to increase product flow and product quality, reduce inventory, reduce waste and inefficiency, improve decision making, and increase profitability. The ultimate goal is to achieve excellence with reduced levels of all necessary inputs: labor, materials, time, space, and energy. Standard cost systems may suffer from weaknesses that limit their usefulness for companies adopting lean manufacturing techniques. These include:

- *Inconsistent updating of standards.* Typically, companies establish standards of cost and usage at the beginning of the year, far too infrequently for variance information to be useful for lean companies that are constantly trying to improve the efficiency of operations and reduce costs.

- *Time-lagged data.* Lean manufacturing depends on real-time feedback to correct inefficiencies. The typical pattern of creating and investigating cost variance reports weeks after the data are available creates a time lag that conflicts with this objective.

- *Need for more granular feedback.* Standard cost systems tend to produce variance reports that aggregate data, hiding details that lean manufacturers need to optimize production efficiencies.

Companies that operate in dynamic and fast-changing industries, where response time and operating efficiencies are critical, are likely to find that standard costing systems may not provide the detailed and timely information they need to compete and excel. Lean manufacturing and the associated accounting principles are described in more detail in Chapter 17.

Sources: Andrew Bargerstock and Ye Shi, "Leaning Away from Standard Costing," *Strategic Finance,* June 2016, pp. 39–45. See also Institute of Management Accountants, "Accounting for the Lean Enterprise" (2014), www.imachina.org.cn/Uploads/File/2019/02/21/u5c6e74387624a.pdf.

Self-Study Problems

(For answers, please see Solutions.)

1. Sales Volume and Flexible Budget Variances/JIT Manufacturing

Solid Box Fabrications manufactures boxes for workstations. The firm's standard cost sheet prior to October of the current year and actual results for October are as follows:

	Budget Information		Actual Results October
	Standard Price and Variable Costs per Unit	Fixed Costs	
Units			9,500
Sales	$50.00		$ 551,000
Variable costs:			
Direct materials			
5 pounds at $2.40			
per pound	$12.00		48,000 lbs.* × $3 per pound = $ 144,000

	Budget Information			
	Standard Price and Variable Costs per Unit	Fixed Costs		Actual Results October
Direct labor				
0.5 hour at $14 per hour	7.00			4,800 hrs. × $16 per hour = 76,800
Manufacturing overhead	2.00			19,000
Selling and administrative	5.00			55,100
Total variable costs	$26.00			$ 294,900
Contribution margin	$24.00			$ 256,100
Fixed costs:				
Manufacturing (factory)				
overhead		$50,000		$ 55,000
Selling and administrative		20,000		24,000
Total fixed costs		$70,000		$ 79,000
Operating income				$ 177,100

*Assume that pounds purchased = pounds issued to production (i.e., a JIT inventory policy).

In preparing the master budget for October, the firm recognized that several items on the standard cost sheet were expected to change. For example, the selling price of the product was expected to increase by 8%. Suppliers have notified the firm that starting October 1, materials prices would be 5% higher. The labor contract prescribes a 10% increase, starting October 1, on wages and benefits. Fixed manufacturing costs were expected to increase $5,000 for insurance, property taxes, and salaries. Fixed selling and administrative costs were expected to increase as follows: $2,000 in managers' salaries and $2,000 for advertising during October. The unit sales for October were expected to be 10,000 units. Solid Box Fabrications uses a JIT approach in all of its operations, including materials acquisitions and product manufacturing.

Required

1. Prepare the master budget and pro forma budgets for 9,500 units and 11,000 units for October.
2. Calculate and label as favorable or unfavorable the master budget variance for October. Break this variance down into the sales volume variance and the total flexible budget variance for the period.
3. Compute and label as favorable or unfavorable each of the following variances for October: selling price variance, total variable cost flexible budget variance, and total fixed cost variance.
4. Break down the total direct materials flexible budget variance and the total direct labor flexible budget variance into their price (rate) and quantity (efficiency) components. Label each component variance as favorable or unfavorable.
5. Define what is meant by a just-in-time (JIT) manufacturing process. What are the primary benefits, both financial and nonfinancial, of a JIT system compared to a conventional manufacturing process?

2. Direct Materials Price and Usage Variances, Direct Labor Rate and Efficiency Variances, and Journal Entries

Chemical Inc. has set the following standards for direct materials and direct labor for each 20-pound bag of Weed-Be-Doom:

	Per Bag
Direct materials: 25 pounds XF–2000 @ $0.08 per pound	$2.00
Direct labor: 0.05 hour @ $32 per hour	1.60

The firm manufactured 100,000 bags of Weed-Be-Doom in December and used 2,700,000 pounds of XF–2000 and 5,200 direct labor hours. During the month, the firm purchased 3,000,000 pounds of XF–2000 at $0.075 per pound and incurred a total payroll of $182,000 for direct labor. The firm records purchases at standard cost and therefore recognizes the direct materials price variance at point of purchase.

Required

1. Compute the price and usage variances for direct materials and the rate and efficiency variances for direct labor.
2. Prepare journal entries to record the preceding events.

The Student Resources section of Connect includes video tutorials for the Self-Study Problems.

Questions

14-1 What is the difference among a master budget, pro forma budgets, and a flexible budget?

14-2 Explain how standard costs and flexible budgets can be used for short-term profit analysis—that is, for financial control purposes.

14-3 Explain what is meant by the term *management by exception* (see, for example, www.myaccount-ingcourse.com/accounting-dictionary/management-by-exception). What is the relationship between the process of standard cost variance analysis and management by exception?

14-4 Should the performance of a division be deemed less than satisfactory if all of its variances are "unfavorable"? Explain.

14-5 Explain the possible causes for direct materials *price* and direct materials *usage* (efficiency) variances. Who in the organization normally has influence over or responsibility for each of these variances?

14-6 Explain some of the possible causes of direct labor *rate* and direct labor *efficiency* variances. Who normally has responsibility for or influence over each of these variances?

14-7 Will overtime premiums affect direct labor variances? If so, which ones?

14-8 Which of the following should a firm use as the standard in assessing production efficiencies: standards based on ideal performance, standards based on attainable performance, or standards based on the average of recent historical performance? Explain.

14-9 Discuss behavioral concerns in establishing and implementing a standard cost system.

14-10 This chapter deals with control systems associated with business processes, such as operating processes. Provide a definition and some examples of operating processes. In what other processes would an organization engage in the normal course of business?

14-11 Describe how a just-in-time (JIT) manufacturing system is fundamentally different from a conventional manufacturing system. List two primary financial benefits associated with a shift to JIT manufacturing. What effect does the adoption of JIT have on the design of management accounting and control systems?

14-12 One of the purported benefits of moving to a JIT system is improvements in customer response time (CRT). Define the following terms: *total customer response time, manufacturing (production) cycle time, manufacturing cycle efficiency (MCE), value-added time,* and *non-value-added time.*

Brief Exercises

[LO 14-2] 14-13 The Baldwin Company, in its master budget for 2022, predicted total sales of $160,000, variable costs of $48,000, and fixed costs of $52,000 ($24,000 manufacturing and $28,000 nonmanufacturing). Actual sales revenue for 2022 turned out to be $180,000. Actual costs were as follows: variable, $54,000, and fixed, $50,000. (1) What was the total master budget variance for 2022? (Round your answer to the nearest whole dollar.) (2) Was this total variance favorable or unfavorable?

[LO 14-2, 14-3] 14-14 Edwards and Bell market a single line of home computers, dubbed the XL-98. The master budget for the coming year contained the following items: sales revenue, $400,000; variable costs, $250,000; fixed costs, $100,000. Actual results for the year were as follows: sales revenue, $350,000; variable costs, $225,000; fixed costs, $95,000. The flexible budget operating income for the year was $35,000. (1) What is the total master budget variance in operating profit for the period? (2) What portion of the total master budget variance is attributable to actual sales volume being different from planned sales volume? (3) What portion of the total variance is due to a combination of selling price and costs (variable cost per unit and total fixed costs) being different from budgeted amounts? (Round all answers to the nearest whole dollar.)

[LO 14-3] 14-15 The Ace Company sells a single product at a budgeted selling price per unit of $20. Budgeted fixed manufacturing costs for the coming period are $10,000, while budgeted fixed marketing expenses for the period are $24,000. Budgeted variable costs per unit include $2 of selling expenses (commission) and $4 of manufacturing costs. What is the budgeted operating income if the anticipated sales volume for the period is (1) 10,000 units and (2) 15,000 units? (Round answers to the nearest whole number.)

[LO 14-3] 14-16 Davidson Corp. produces a single product: fireproof safety deposit boxes for home use. The budget going into the current year anticipated a selling price of $55 per unit. Because of competitive pressures, the company had to cut selling prices by 10% during the year. Budgeted variable costs per unit are $32, and budgeted total fixed costs are $156,000 for the year. Anticipated sales volume for the year was 10,000 units. Actual sales volume was 5% less than budget. (1) What was the sales price variance for the year? (Round your answer to the nearest whole dollar.) (2) Label this variance favorable or unfavorable, as appropriate.

[LO 14-3]   14-17 Chapman Inc. sells a single product, Zud, which has a budgeted selling price of $24 per unit and a budgeted variable cost of $12 per unit. Budgeted fixed costs for the year amount to $45,000. Actual sales volume for the year (47,000 units) fell 3,000 units short of budgeted sales volume. Actual fixed costs were $46,000. With everything else held constant, what impact did the shortfall in volume have on profitability for the year? (Round your answer to the nearest whole number; indicate whether the effect was favorable or unfavorable in terms of its effect on operating income.)

[LO 14-3]   14-18 Refer to Exhibit 14.8 and the accompanying discussion in the text. Demonstrate that the materials usage variance for PVC during October 2022 was $2,400F.

[LO 14-3]   14-19 Refer to Exhibit 14.8 and the accompanying discussion in the text. Demonstrate that the purchase price variance for PVC during October 2022 was $720U.

[LO 14-3]   14-20 Refer to Exhibit 14.8 and the accompanying discussion in the text. Demonstrate that the flexible budget variance for PVC during October 2022 was $1,680F.

[LO 14-3]   14-21 Mom's Apple Pie Company uses a standard cost system. The standard direct labor time for each pie is 10 minutes. During the most recent month, the company produced and sold 6,000 pies. The standard direct labor rate is $8 per hour; the actual labor rate per hour for the month was $8.40. The company used a total of 980 labor hours. (a) What was the direct labor efficiency variance for the month? (Round your answer to 2 decimal places.) (b) Was this variance favorable or unfavorable?

[LO 14-3]   14-22 Refer to the data in Brief Exercise 14-21. (a) What was the direct labor rate variance for the month, rounded to 2 decimal places? (b) Was this variance favorable or unfavorable?

Exercises

[LO 14-1, 14-2, 14-3]   14-23 **Flexible Budgets; Master Budget Variance; Breakdown of the Master Budget Variance; Spreadsheet Application**   The following information is available for Brownstone Products Company for the month of July:

	Actual	Master Budget
Units	3,800	4,000
Sales revenue	$53,200	$60,000
Variable manufacturing costs	19,000	16,000
Fixed manufacturing costs	16,000	15,000
Variable selling and administrative expenses	7,700	8,000
Fixed selling and administrative expenses	10,000	9,000

Required

1. What was the master budget variance for July, rounded to the nearest whole dollar? Was this variance favorable or unfavorable?

2. Set up a spreadsheet to compute the July sales volume variance and the flexible budget variance for the month, both in terms of contribution margin and in terms of operating income. Round all dollar amounts to the nearest whole number.

3. Discuss implications of these variances on strategic cost management for Brownstone.

4. Configure your spreadsheet so that it will allow the firm to prepare pro-forma budgets for activities within its relevant range of operations. Use your spreadsheet to prepare a flexible budget for each of the following two output levels (round all dollar amounts in the flexible budgets to the nearest whole number):

   a. 3,750 units.
   b. 4,150 units.

(CMA Adapted)

[LO 14-2, 14-3]   14-24 **Master Budget Variance and Its Components**   As the new accountant for Cohen & Co., you have been asked to provide a succinct analysis of financial performance for the year just ended. You obtain the following information that pertains to the company's sole product:

	Actual	Master Budget
Units sold	40,000	45,000
Sales	$380,000	$450,000
Variable costs	210,000	270,000
Fixed costs	145,000	135,000

Required

1. What was the actual operating income for the period? Show calculations; round your answer to the nearest whole dollar.

2. What was the company's master budget operating income for the period? Show calculations, and round your answer to the nearest whole dollar.

3. (a) What was the total master budget variance, in terms of operating income, for the period (rounded to nearest whole dollar)? (b) Is this variance favorable or unfavorable? Why?

4. The total master budget variance for a period can be decomposed into a total flexible budget variance and a sales volume variance. (a) What was (to the nearest whole dollar) the total flexible budget variance for the period? (b) Was this variance favorable or unfavorable? (c) What was the sales volume variance (to the nearest whole dollar) for the period? (d) Was this variance favorable or unfavorable?

5. Define the meaning of the *total flexible budget variance* and the *sales volume variance*.

[LO 14-2, 14-3]   14-25 **Flexible Budgets and the Breakdown of the Master Budget Variance**   Assume that in October 2022 the Schmidt Machinery Company (Exhibit 14.1) manufactured and sold 950 units for $835 each. During this month, the company incurred $475,000 total variable costs and $180,000 total fixed costs. The master budget data for the month are as given in Exhibit 14.1.

Required   (Round all your answers to the nearest whole number):

1. Prepare a flexible budget for the production and sale of 950 units.

2. Compute for October 2022:

   a. The sales volume variance, in terms of operating income. Indicate whether this variance was favorable or unfavorable.

   b. The sales volume variance, in terms of contribution margin. Indicate whether this variance was favorable or unfavorable.

3. Compute for October 2022:

   a. The total flexible budget variance. Indicate whether this variance was favorable or unfavorable.

   b. The total variable cost flexible budget variance. Indicate whether this variance was favorable or unfavorable.

   c. The total fixed cost flexible budget variance. Indicate whether this variance was favorable or unfavorable.

   d. The selling price variance. Indicate whether this variance was favorable or unfavorable.

[LO 14-3]   14-26 **Direct Materials and Direct Labor Variances**   Assume that Schmidt Machinery Company had the standard costs reflected in Exhibit 14.5. In a given month, the company used 3,450 pounds of aluminum to manufacture 920 units. The company paid $28.50 per pound during the month to purchase aluminum. At the beginning of he month, the company had 50 pounds of aluminum on hand. At the end of the month, the company had only 30 pounds of aluminum in its warehouse. Schmidt used 4,200 direct labor hours during the month, at an average cost of $41.50 per hour.

Required   Compute the following variances for the month, all rounded to the nearest whole dollar:

1. The purchase price variance for aluminum. Indicate whether this variance is favorable or unfavorable.

2. The usage variance for aluminum. Indicate whether this variance is favorable or unfavorable.

3. The direct labor rate variance. Indicate whether this variance is favorable or unfavorable.

4. The direct labor efficiency variance. Indicate whether this variance is favorable or unfavorable.

[LO 14-3]   14-27 **Direct Materials Price and Usage Variances**   DES Company manufactures folding chairs. Direct materials include hard plastic for the seat and back and metal beams for the legs. The standard cost sheet for a single chair includes the following direct materials information:

Material	Quantity	Cost per Unit	Total Cost
Hard plastic	2 sheets	$2.65 per sheet	$ 5.30
Metal beams	4 beams	$1.20 per beam	4.80
			$10.10

Last month, DES purchased 41,500 sheets of hard plastic at a cost of $102,920. The company also purchased 82,700 metal beams at a cost of $107,510. DES produced 20,800 chairs. There was no beginning or ending inventory of plastic sheets or metal beams during the month.

Required

1. Compute the following for last month's operations at DES Company:
   a. The price variance for hard plastic. Indicate whether the variance is favorable or unfavorable.
   b. The price variance for metal beams. Indicate whether the variance is favorable or unfavorable.
   c. The *total* direct materials price variance. Indicate whether the variance is favorable or unfavorable.
   d. The usage variances for hard plastic and metal beams, and the *total* direct materials usage variance. Indicate whether each variance is favorable or unfavorable.

2. What are the advantages and disadvantages of computing *total* price and usage variances when there are multiple material inputs?

[LO 14-3]   14-28   **Standard Direct Labor Wage Rate and Direct Labor Efficiency Variance**   Information regarding Maxwell's direct labor cost for the month of January follows:

Direct labor hourly rate paid	$28.50
Total standard direct labor hours forunits produced this period	11,000
Direct labor hours actually worked	10,800
Direct labor rate variance	$16,000 favorable

Required   Compute the following:

1. Standard direct labor wage rate per hour, rounded to 2 decimal places, in January.
2. Direct labor efficiency variance for January; round your answer to the nearest whole dollar. Was this variance favorable or unfavorable?

[LO 14-3]   14-29   **Generating a Flexible Budget; Spreadsheet Application**   Crane Corporation's master budget for the year is shown below:

Sales (60,000 units)		$1,860,000
Cost of goods sold:		
Direct materials	$168,000	
Direct labor	450,000	
Overhead (variable overhead		
applied at 40% of direct labor cost)	240,000	858,000
Gross profit		$1,002,000
Selling expenses:		
Sales commissions (all variable)	$167,400	
Rent (all fixed)	40,000	
Insurance (all short-term fixed)	30,000	
General expenses:		
Salaries (all short-term fixed)	92,000	
Rent (all short-term fixed)	77,000	
Depreciation (all short-term fixed)	50,000	456,400
Operating income		$ 545,600

Required

1. During the year, the company manufactured and sold 55,000 units of product. Prepare an Excel spreadsheet that contains a flexible budget for this level of output. Round all budget figures to nearest whole dollar.

2. Now suppose that the actual level of output was 65,000 units. Rerun your spreadsheet to generate a flexible budget for this output level. Round all budget figures to the nearest whole dollar.

3. Of what relevance is the notion of the "relevant range" when preparing pro forma budgets or a flexible budget for control purposes?

[LO 14-3, 14-4]   14-30   **Behavioral Considerations and Continuous-Improvement Standards**   At a recent seminar you attended, the invited speaker was discussing some of the advantages and disadvantages of standard costs in terms of evaluating performance and motivating goal-congruent behavior on the part of employees. One criticism of standard costs in particular caught your attention: The use of conventional standard costs may not provide appropriate incentives for improvements needed to compete effectively with world-class organizations. The speaker then discussed so-called continuous-improvement standard costs. Such standards embody systematically lower costs over time. For example, on a monthly basis, it might be appropriate to budget a 1.0% reduction in per-unit direct labor cost.

Assume that the standard wage rate into the foreseeable future is $30.00 per hour. Assume, too, that the budgeted labor-hour standard for October of the current year is 1.50 hours and that this standard is reduced each month by 1.0%. During December of the current year the company produced 10,000 units of XL-10, using 14,800 direct labor hours. The actual wage rate per hour in December was $32.00.

Required

1. Prepare a table that contains the standard labor-hour requirement per unit and standard direct labor cost per unit for the four months, October through January. (*Note:* Carry the labor-hour requirement per unit to 5 decimal places and the standard labor costs per unit to 2 decimal places.)

2. Compute the direct labor efficiency variance for December. (Show calculations, and round your answer to the nearest whole dollar.) Was this variance favorable or unfavorable?

3. What behavioral considerations apply to the decision to use continuous-improvement standards?

[LO 14-3, 14-4]   14-31   **Flexible Budget Variances and Sales Volume Variances**   RTI Company's master budget calls for production and sale of 18,000 units for $81,000, variable costs of $30,600, and fixed costs of $20,000. During the most recent period, the company incurred $32,000 of variable costs to produce and sell 20,000 units for $85,000. During this same period, the company earned $25,000 of operating income.

Required

1. Determine the following for RTI Company (Round all answers to the nearest whole dollar):

    a. Flexible budget operating income.

    b. Flexible budget variance, in terms of contribution margin. Was this variance favorable or unfavorable?

    c. Flexible budget variance, in terms of operating income. Was this variance favorable or unfavorable?

    d. Sales volume variance, in terms of contribution margin. Was this variance favorable or unfavorable?

    e. Sales volume variance, in terms of operating income. Was this variance favorable or unfavorable?

2. Explain why the contribution margin sales volume variance and the operating income sales volume variance for the same period are likely to be identical.

3. Explain why the contribution margin flexible budget variance is likely to differ from the operating income flexible budget variance for the same period.

[LO 14-1, 14-4, 14-6]   14-32   **Applicability of Standard Cost Systems**   Portfolio management is a powerful concept in finance and marketing. The marketing application of the concept is to develop and manage a balanced portfolio of products. Market share and market growth can be used to classify products for portfolio purposes, and the product classifications often are extended to the organizational units that make the product. The market share/growth classifications can be depicted as follows:

	Market Share	
Market Growth Rate	High	Low
High	Rising star	?
Low	Cash cow	Dog

The question mark is the classification for products that show high growth rates but have small market shares, such as new products that are similar to their competitors. A rising star is a high-growth, high-market-share product that tends to mature into a cash cow. A cash cow is a slow-growing established product that can be milked for cash to help the question mark and introduce new products. The dog is a low-growth, low-market-share item that is a candidate for elimination or segmentation. Understanding where a product falls within this market share/growth structure is important when applying a standard cost system.

Required

1. Discuss the major advantages of using a standard cost accounting system.

2. Describe the types of information that are useful in setting standards and the conditions that must be present to support the use of standard costing.

3. Discuss the applicability or nonapplicability of using standard costing for a product classified as (a) a cash cow and (b) a question mark.

4. What are some primary criticisms of using standard cost systems in today's manufacturing environment?

(CMA Adapted)

[LO 14-4]   14-33 **Determining Standard Direct Materials Cost**   Agrichem manufactures Insect-Be-Gone. Each bag of the product contains 60 pounds of direct materials. Twenty-five percent of the materials evaporate during manufacturing. The budget allows the direct materials to be purchased at $2.50 per pound (gross cost) under terms of 2/10, n/30. The company's stated policy is to take all available cash discounts.

Required   Determine the standard direct materials cost for one bag of Insect-Be-Gone.

[LO 14-4]   14-34 **Ethical Considerations; the Role of the Management Accountant**   A number of ethical issues arise in the design of management control systems. For example, such issues might arise when an individual's performance relative to budget or standard cost affects the individual's compensation or reward. Assume you are the management accountant for a manufacturing firm. The reward system at your firm is such that the purchasing manager earns a financial reward when a significant favorable materials purchase price variance is realized. Suppose, too, that this manager has an opportunity to get an extremely low price on raw materials that the manager knows are of substandard quality. Finally, assume that the purchasing manager believes that any problems attributable to the low-grade materials are not likely to surface until the product from which these materials is made has been in use for a while by consumers.

Required

1. Access the IMA's Statement of Ethical Professional Practice (updated July 1, 2017, and available at https://www.imanet.org/career-resources/ethics-center). Put aside for the moment whether the purchasing manager's behavior is governed by the IMA ethical standards. Which, if any, of the these standards contained in the statement are at issue in this case, from the standpoint of the behavior of the purchasing manager?

2. Assume you are the management accountant at the manufacturing plant where the preceding scenario takes place. According to the IMA's Statement of Ethical Professional Practice, what are your obligations in this situation?

3. What other observations can you make regarding the role of the management accountant in the present scenario?

[LO 14-4]   14-35 **Standard Costs and Ethics**   Ohio Apple Orchards Inc. (OAO) produces an organic, super-premium apple juice that it markets to specialty food outlets. OAO purchases its apples from a select group of farmers located in the Midwest. Recently, a graduate of the local university, Susanna Wu, joined the staff of OAO. Among Susanna's first responsibilities was the charge to develop and implement a standard costing system for OAO. The company thought that the introduction of such an accounting system would be a helpful response to what it saw as competition from new and aggressive entrants to the organic foods market. Susanna discussed her task with the controller of the company, Mary Whitman, who indicated that unrefined apple juice would cost $1.50 per liter, the price she intended to pay her college pal, Bill O'Neal, who had, since graduation, been operating his own apple orchard at a loss. Because of favorable weather conditions during the most recent growing season, the price for comparable apple juice in the region dropped to $1.10 per liter. Mary felt that the $1.50 price, if maintained throughout the current year, would be sufficient to make Bill's operation profitable—at last.

Required   Is Mary's behavior regarding the cost information she provided to Susanna ethical? Support your answer by reference to the Institute of Management Accountant's Statement of Ethical Professional Practice (updated July 1, 2017, and available at https://www.imanet.org/career-resources/ethics-center). **(CMA Adapted)**

[LO 14-1, 14-4]   14-36 **Financial vs. Operational Control; Behavioral Considerations in the Standard-Setting Process**   You have been assigned to a strategic leadership committee that has been charged by the CEO with developing and implementing a comprehensive management accounting and control system. At the first planning session that you attended, the subject of financial-control systems arose, but there was some uncertainty regarding the nature of such systems and some of the behavioral considerations that might have to be made in the design process. You have been asked by the chair of the committee to prepare a short written document that could be used as the basis of discussion at the next meeting. Specifically, you have been asked to define and distinguish between operational control and financial control and how such systems relate to an organization's management accounting and control system; explain the theory behind the use of flexible budgets, standard costs, and variance analysis as elements of a financial-control system; and provide input regarding how standards/budgets for performance evaluation should be set (i.e., whether authoritative standards, participative standards, or perhaps a combination approach should be used in the standard-setting process).

Required   Compose your response as requested.

[LO 14-5]   14-37   **Journal Entries**   Use the data in Exhibit 14.5. On October 7, Schmidt Machinery Company purchased 720 pounds of PVC at $41.00 per pound. On October 9, Schmidt's production department used 720 pounds of PVC for the 780 units of XV-1 it manufactured.

Required   Make the necessary journal entries to record the purchase and usage of PVC during October. (Round all amounts to nearest whole dollar.)

[LO 14-3, 14-5]   14-38   **Journal Entries in a Standard Cost System**   Boron Chemical Company produces a synthetic resin that is used in the automotive industry. The company uses a standard cost system. For each gallon of output, the following direct manufacturing costs are anticipated:

Direct labor: 2 hours at $25.00 per hour	$50.00
Direct materials: 2 gallons at $10.00 per gallon	$20.00

During December of the current year, Boron produced a total of 2,500 gallons of output and incurred the following direct manufacturing costs:

Direct labor: 4,900 hours worked at an average wage rate of $19.50 per hour
Direct materials:
   Purchased: 6,000 gallons @ $10.45 per gallon
   Used in production: 5,100 gallons

Boron records price variances for materials at the time of purchase.

Required   Prepare journal entries for the following events and transactions. (Round all amounts to nearest whole dollar.)
1. Purchase, on credit, of direct materials.
2. Direct materials issued to production.
3. Direct labor cost of units completed this period.
4. Direct manufacturing cost (direct labor plus direct materials) of units completed and transferred to Finished Goods Inventory.
5. Sale (on credit), for $150.00 per gallon, of 2,000 gallons of output. (*Hint:* You will need two journal entries here.)

[LO 14-3, 14-5]   14-39   **Direct Materials Variances—Journal Entries**   Steinberg Company had the following direct materials costs for the manufacturing of product T in March:

Actual purchase price per pound of direct materials	$7.50
Standard direct materials allowed for units of product T produced	2,100 pounds
Decrease in direct materials inventory	100 pounds
Direct materials used in production	2,300 pounds
Standard price per pound of material	$7.25

Required
1. What was Steinberg's direct materials purchase price variance and its direct materials usage variance for March? Indicate whether each variance was favorable or unfavorable. (Round both answers to the nearest whole dollar.)
2. Prepare the appropriate journal entries for March.

[LO 14-1, 14-6]   14-40   **Financial vs. Nonfinancial Performance Indicators for Operational Control**   As indicated in the text, both financial and nonfinancial performance indicators play important roles in an organization's overall operational control system. Explain, concisely, the relative advantage of each type of performance indicator. That is, what role would each type of performance indicator play in helping to ensure that operations are in control? (*Hint:* Think about this issue both from the standpoint of managers and from the standpoint of operating personnel.)

[LO 14-1, 14-4, 14-6]   14-41   **Behavioral and Strategic Considerations**   Chen Inc. produces a line of soy-based products, including a premium soy milk that comes in different flavors. This company, founded by Alan Chen, has been doing business in the United States for the past 15 years. In the face of competition associated with recent entrants into this line of business, the controller of the company, Rosita Chang, implemented a standard cost system to better control costs of the soy milk product line.

Financial reports for tracking performance are issued monthly, and any unfavorable cost variances are investigated by management.

Recently, the production manager of the soy milk line complained to Chang that the standards were unrealistic; that they have a negative impact on motivation (because the system focuses only on unfavorable variances); and that because of global forces of supply and demand, they quickly become out of date. The production manager noted that his recent switch to a newly available homogenizing agent resulted in higher acquisition costs for direct materials but decreased labor hours to produce the soy milk. These two changes, when combined, had a negligible effect on manufacturing cost per unit. However, the monthly performance reports continued to show a favorable labor variance (despite evidence that the workers were slowing down or slacking off a bit) and an unfavorable materials variance.

Required

1. Describe several ways that a standard cost system could improve (i.e., strengthen) an overall management control system.

2. Give at least two reasons a standard cost system could have a negative impact on employee motivation.

3. Explain strategic issues regarding the decision to adopt a standard costing system, particularly in light of competitive forces confronting this company. (*Hint:* Think in terms of the costs and benefits associated with the use of standard costs as part of a comprehensive management accounting and control system.)

(CMA Adapted)

[LO 14-1, 14-6]   14-42 **Control of Operating Processes; Financial and Nonfinancial Performance Indicators**   This chapter deals with the design of effective control systems associated with business processes, including operating processes. As indicated in the text, a comprehensive management accounting and control system will have both financial indicators and nonfinancial performance indicators. Financial indicators can include (among other things) the operating income variances that can be calculated each period by using standard costs and flexible budgets. This question deals with the use of nonfinancial performance indicators as a complement to financial performance indicators that are useful for controlling operating processes.

Required

1. List and define the primary business processes in which organizations engage in their attempt to meet customer expectations.

2. Fundamentally, control systems (including management accounting and control systems) collect information regarding the extent to which specified objectives are being accomplished. Consider both the production process and the distribution process for a manufacturer. For each of these two operating processes provide a listing of possible objectives that the organization might pursue. For each listed objective, provide one or more relevant *financial* and one or more relevant *nonfinancial* performance indicators (performance metrics) that the organization's management accounting and control system might collect and report to management.

[LO 14-1, 14-6]   14-43 **JIT and Manufacturing Cycle Efficiency (MCE)**   Zodiac Sound Co. manufactures audio systems, both made-to-order and mass-produced systems, that are typically sold to large-scale manufacturers of electronics equipment. For competitive reasons, the company is trying to increase its manufacturing cycle efficiency (MCE) measure. As a strategy for improving its MCE performance, the company is considering a switch to JIT manufacturing. While the company managers have a fairly good feel for the costs of implementing JIT, they are unsure about the benefits of such a move, both in financial and nonfinancial terms. To help inform the ultimate decision regarding a move to a JIT system, you've been asked to provide some input. Fortunately, you've recently attended a continuing professional education (CPE) workshop on the costs and benefits of moving to JIT and therefore feel comfortable responding to management's request.

Required

1. Define the terms *value-added time, non-value-added time,* and *manufacturing cycle efficiency (MCE).* Conceptually, how are activities included in the first two categories determined? (That is, how does one know what activities are considered "value-added"?)

2. Define the terms *manufacturing cycle time* and *processing (manufacturing) time.* How can processing time be broken down further?

3. Given the estimated data below, calculate and interpret the MCE (to 2 decimal places, e.g., 0.38456 = 38.46%) for both the current manufacturing process and the proposed process after implementing JIT:

Activity	Current System	After JIT Implementation
Storage	60 minutes	20 minutes
Inspection	30 minutes	15 minutes
Moving	45 minutes	15 minutes
Processing	60 minutes	30 minutes

4. What is the percentage change (to 2 decimal places) in average MCE anticipated under JIT?
5. What additional nonfinancial performance indicators might management monitor in conjunction with the move to JIT?

Problems

[LO 14-2, 14-3]   14-44 **Master Budget, Flexible Budget, and Operating Income Variance Analysis; Spreadsheet Application**   Going into the period just ended, Ortiz & Co., manufacturer of a moderately priced espresso maker for retail sale, had planned to produce and sell 3,900 units at $100.00 per unit. Budgeted variable manufacturing costs per unit are $50.00. Ortiz pays its salespeople a 10.0% sales commission, which is the only variable nonmanufacturing cost for the company. Fixed costs are budgeted as follows: manufacturing, $50,000; marketing, $36,000.

Actual financial results for the period were disappointing. While sales volume was up (4,000 units sold), actual operating profit was only $20,000 for the period. Fixed manufacturing costs were as budgeted, but fixed marketing expenses exceeded budget by $4,000. Actual sales revenue for the period was $390,000, and actual variable costs (manufacturing and nonmanufacturing combined) were $70.00 per unit (the actual sales commission cost was 10.0% of sales revenue generated).

Required
1. Develop an Excel spreadsheet that is able to produce a profit-variance report similar to the one presented in Exhibit 14.4. Use your spreadsheet (and the data presented above) to complete the profit-variance report for the period. (Round all variances to the nearest whole dollar.) Make sure that you calculate each of the following variances:
   a. Total master budget variance.
   b. Total flexible budget variance.
   c. Flexible budget variance for total variable costs, plus the flexible budget variance for:
      (1) Variable manufacturing costs.
      (2) Variable nonmanufacturing costs.
   d. Flexible budget variance for total fixed costs, plus the flexible budget variance for:
      (1) Fixed manufacturing costs.
      (2) Fixed nonmanufacturing costs.
2. Provide an interpretation for each of the variances calculated in requirement 1.
3. Using the variances you calculated in requirement 1 and, in as much detail as the data allow, prepare a separate summary report similar to Exhibit 14.2.

[LO 14-3]   14-45 **Direct Materials Purchase Price Variance and Foreign Exchange Rates**   Jonas Materials Science (JMS) purchases its materials from several countries. As part of its cost-control program, JMS uses a standard cost system for all aspects of its operations, including purchases of direct materials. The company establishes standard costs for direct materials at the beginning of each fiscal year.

Pat Butch, the purchasing manager, is happy with the result of the year just ended. He believes that the purchase price variance for direct materials for the year will be favorable and is very confident that his department has at least met the standard prices. The preliminary report from the controller's office confirms his jubilation. Following is a portion of the preliminary report:

Total quantity purchased	40,000 kilograms
Average price per kilogram	$50.00
Standard price per kilogram	$60.00
Budgeted quantity per quarter	5,000 kilograms

In the fourth quarter, the purchasing department increased purchases from the budgeted normal volume of 5,000 to 25,000 kilograms to meet the increased demands, which was a result of the firm's unexpected success in a fiercely competitive bidding. The substantial increase in the volume to be purchased forced the purchasing department to search for alternative suppliers. After frantic searches, it found suppliers in several foreign countries that could meet the firm's needs and could provide materials with higher quality than that of JMS's regular supplier. The purchasing department was very reluctant to make the purchase because the negotiated price was $77.00 per kilogram, including shipping and import duty. However, this original reluctance disappeared upon learning that the actual cost of the purchases would be much lower than expected due to currency devaluations (the result of financial turmoil in several of the countries in the region).

Patricia Rice, the controller, does not share the purchasing department's euphoria. She is fully aware of the following quarterly purchases of direct materials:

	First Quarter	Second Quarter	Third Quarter	Fourth Quarter
Quantity	5,000	5,000	5,000	25,000
Purchase price (per kilogram)	$68.00	$69.00	$74.00	?

Required
1. Calculate the direct materials purchase price variance (to nearest whole dollar) for the fourth quarter and for the year. How much of each purchase price variance is attributable to changes in foreign currency exchange rates?
2. Evaluate the purchasing department's performance.

[LO 14-3] 14-46 **Joint Direct Materials Variance** Acme Manufacturing produces corrugated board containers that the nearby wine industry uses to package wine in bulk. Acme buys kraft paper by the ton, converts it to heavy-duty paperboard on its corrugator, and then cuts and glues it into folding boxes. The boxes are opened and filled with a plastic liner and then with the wine.

Many other corrugated board converters are in the area, and competition is strong. Acme is eager to keep its costs under control. The company has used a standard cost system for several years. Responsibility for variances has been established. For example, the purchasing agent is responsible for the direct materials price variance, and the general supervisor answers for the direct materials usage variance.

Recently, the industrial engineer and the company's management accountant participated in a workshop sponsored by the Institute of Management Accountants (IMA) at which there was some discussion of variance analysis. They noted that the workshop proposed that the responsibility for some variances was properly dual. The accountant and engineer reviewed Acme's system and were not sure how to adapt the new information to it.

Acme has the following standards for its direct materials:

Standard direct materials cost per gross of finished boxes = 5 tons of kraft paper at $10 per ton = $50.00

During May, the management accountant for the company assembled the following data:

Units of finished product: 5,000 gross of finished boxes
Actual cost of direct materials used during the month: $324,000 for 27,000 tons
Direct materials put into production (used): 27,000 tons
Acme began and finished the month of May with no inventory of direct materials

Required Determine the following for Acme (round all variances to the nearest whole dollar):
1. Direct materials price variance, calculated at point of production. Was this variance favorable or unfavorable?
2. Direct materials usage variance. Was this variance favorable or unfavorable?
3. "Pure" direct materials price variance [defined as SQ × (AP − SP)]. Was this variance favorable or unfavorable?
4. Direct materials joint price-quantity variance [defined as (AP − SP) × (AQ − SQ)]. Was this variance favorable or unfavorable? (*Hint:* You can determine the sign of the joint price-quantity variance by working backward from the total DM variance [= (AP × AQ) − (SP × SQ)], subtracting the "pure" price variance and the usage variance [both of which are calculated above].)

(CMA Adapted)

[LO 14-3, 14-4]   14-47   Standard Cost Sheet and Use of Variance Data   Tastyfreeze Company is a small producer of fruit-flavored frozen desserts. For many years, its products have had strong regional sales because of brand recognition; however, other companies have begun marketing similar products in the area, and price competition has become increasingly important. Dan O'Mara, the company's controller, is planning to implement a standard cost system for Tastyfreeze and has gathered considerable information from his coworkers about production and materials requirements for Tastyfreeze's products. Dan believes that the use of standard costs will allow the company to improve cost control, make better pricing decisions, and enhance strategic management.

Tastyfreeze's most popular product is raspberry sherbet. The sherbet is produced in 10-gallon batches, each of which requires 6 quarts of good raspberries and 10 gallons of other ingredients. The fresh raspberries are sorted by hand before they enter the production process. Because of imperfections in the raspberries and normal spoilage, 1 quart of berries is discarded for every 4 accepted. The standard direct labor time for sorting to obtain 1 quart of acceptable raspberries is 4 minutes. The acceptable raspberries are then blended with the other ingredients; blending requires 12 minutes of direct labor time per batch. After blending, the sherbet is packaged in quart containers. Dan has gathered the following price information:

- Tastyfreeze purchases raspberries for $5.00 per quart. All other ingredients cost $2.50 per gallon.
- Direct labor is paid at the rate of $16.00 per hour.
- The total packaging cost (labor and materials) for the sherbet is $0.75 per quart.

Required

1. Develop the standard cost for the direct cost components of a 10-gallon batch of raspberry sherbet. For each direct cost component, the standard cost should identify the following:
   a. Standard quantity.
   b. Standard rate (or price).
   c. Standard cost per 10-gallon batch, rounded to 2 decimal places (e.g., $13.431 = $13.43).
2. As part of the implementation of a standard cost system at Tastyfreeze, Dan plans to train those responsible for maintaining the standards to use variance analysis. He is particularly concerned with the causes of unfavorable variances.
   a. Discuss the possible causes of unfavorable direct materials price variances, identify the individuals who should be held responsible for them, and comment on the implications of these variances on strategic cost management.
   b. Discuss the possible causes of unfavorable direct labor efficiency variances, identify the individuals who should be held responsible for them, and comment on the implications of these variances on strategic cost management.

(CMA Adapted)

[LO 14-4]   14-48   Standard Cost Systems—Behavioral Considerations   Mark-Wright Inc. (MWI) is a specialty frozen food processor located in the midwestern states. Since its founding in 1982, MWI has enjoyed a loyal local clientele willing to pay premium prices for the high-quality frozen foods prepared from special recipes. In the last two years, MWI has experienced rapid sales growth in its operating region and has had many inquiries about supplying its products on a national basis. To meet this growth, MWI expanded its processing capabilities, which resulted in increased production and distribution costs. Furthermore, MWI has been encountering pricing pressure from competitors outside its normal marketing region.

Because MWI desires to continue its expansion, Jim Condon, CEO, has engaged a consulting firm to assist the company in determining its best course of action. The consulting firm concluded that, although premium pricing is sustainable in some areas, MWI must make some price concessions if sales growth is to be achieved. Also, to maintain profit margins, the company must reduce and control its costs. The consulting firm recommended using a standard cost system that would facilitate a flexible budgeting system to better accommodate the changes in demand that can be expected when serving an expanding market area.

Jim met with his management team and explained the consulting firm's recommendations. He then assigned the team the task of establishing standard costs. After discussing the situation with their respective staffs, the management team met to review the matter.

Jane Morgan, purchasing manager, noted that meeting expanded production would necessitate obtaining basic food supplies from sources other than MWI's traditional ones. This would entail increased raw materials and shipping costs and could result in supplies of lower quality. Consequently, the processing department would have to make up these increased costs if current cost levels are to be maintained or reduced.

Alan Chen, processing manager, countered that the need to accelerate processing cycles to increase production, coupled with the possibility of receiving lower-grade supplies, could result in a slip in quality and a higher product rejection rate. Under these circumstances, per-unit labor utilization cannot be maintained or reduced, and forecasting future unit labor content becomes very difficult.

Tina Lopez, production engineer, advised that failure to properly maintain and thoroughly clean the equipment at prescribed daily intervals could affect the quality and unique taste of the frozen food products. Jack Reid, vice president of sales, stated that if quality could not be maintained, MWI could not expect to increase sales to the levels projected.

When the management team reported these problems to Jim, he said that if agreement could not be reached on appropriate standards, he would arrange to have the consulting firm set the standards, and everyone would have to live with the results.

Required
1. With respect to a standard cost system, list:
   a. Its major advantages.
   b. Its major disadvantages.
2. Identify those who should participate in setting standards, and describe the benefits of their participation.
3. Explain the general features and characteristics associated with the introduction and operation of a standard cost system that make it an effective tool for cost control.
4. What could the consequences be if Jim Condon, CEO, has the outside consulting firm set MWI's standards?

(CMA Adapted)

[LO 14-3, 14-5]   14-49   **Standard Costs in Process Costing (Chapter 6); All Variances and Journal Entries**   Dash Company adopted a standard costing system several years ago. The standard costs for the prime costs (i.e., direct materials and direct labor) of its single product are:

Material	(8 kilograms × $5.00 per kilogram)	$ 40.00
Labor	(6 hours × $18.20 per hour)	109.20

All materials are added at the beginning of processing. The following data were taken from the company's records for November:

In-process beginning inventory	None
In-process ending inventory	800 units, 75% complete as to direct labor
Units completed	5,600 units
Budgeted output	6,000 units
Purchases of materials	50,000 kilograms
Total actual direct labor costs	$600,000
Actual direct labor hours	36,500 hours
Materials usage variance	$1,500 Unfavorable
Total materials variance	$750 Unfavorable

Required
1. Compute for November:
   a. The direct labor efficiency variance, rounded to the nearest whole dollar. Is this variance favorable or unfavorable?
   b. The direct labor rate variance, rounded to the nearest whole dollar. Is this variance favorable or unfavorable?
   c. The actual number of kilograms of material used in the production process during the month, rounded to the nearest whole number.
   d. The actual price paid per kilogram of material during the month, rounded to 3 decimal places (e.g., $3.4591 = $3.459); the company calculates the direct materials price variance at point of purchase.
   e. The amount of direct materials cost and direct labor cost transferred to the Finished Goods Inventory account, each rounded to the nearest whole dollar.
   f. The total amount of direct materials cost and direct labor cost in the Work-in-Process Inventory account at the end of the month, rounded to the nearest whole dollar.
2. Prepare journal entries to record all transactions, including the variances in requirement 1.

(CMA Adapted)

[LO 14-2, 14-3, 14-6]   14-50   **Flexible Budgets and Operating Income Variances** Phoenix Management helps rental property owners find renters and charges the owners one-half of the first month's rent for this service. For August 2022, Phoenix expects to find renters for 100 apartments with an average first month's rent of $700. Budgeted cost data per tenant application for 2022 follow:

- Professional labor: 1.5 hours at $20.00 per hour
- Credit checks: $50.00

Phoenix expects other costs, including the lease payment for the building, secretarial help, and utilities, to be $3,000 per month. On average, Phoenix is successful in placing one tenant for every three applicants.

Actual rental applications in August 2022 were 270. Phoenix paid $9,500 for 400 hours of professional labor. Credit checks went up to $55 per application. Other costs in August 2022 (lease, secretarial help, and utilities) were $3,600. The average first monthly rentals for August 2022 were $800 per apartment unit for 90 units.

Required

1. Prepare an operating income variance report similar to text Exhibit 14.4. (a) What is the master budget variance for August 2022? (b) What is the total flexible budget variance for the month? (c) What is the sales volume variance for the month? (Round all answers to the nearest whole dollar.)

2. Determine the professional labor rate and labor efficiency variances for August 2022, each rounded to the nearest whole dollar.

3. What nonfinancial factors should Phoenix consider in evaluating the effectiveness and efficiency of professional labor?

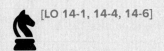

[LO 14-1, 14-4, 14-6]   14-51   **Standard Costing; Variance Analysis; Strategic Considerations**   In a *Wall Street Journal* article, the author notes that various retailers in the United States (e.g., Meijer, Gap, and Office Depot) are turning to consulting firms, such as Accenture, to develop engineered labor standards for cashiers and other retail workers. Monitoring labor-hour consumption (i.e., labor efficiency) under such standards involves timing from the first scan of an item in a customer's purchase to the production of a sales receipt for the customer. A commentator for Meijer states that the system now in use has enabled the company to more efficiently staff stores while concomitantly increasing customer service ratings. A representative from another client of Accenture states that the new system allows the retailer to determine how many workers to schedule at a given time, resulting in a labor-cost reduction of approximately 8%. Engineered standards were developed many years ago in a manufacturing environment, at places such as Westinghouse, by time and motion study experts. Unlike factory workers, however, most retail clerks deal directly with customers. This raises interesting questions as to whether and how the use of such monitoring (i.e., control) systems affects customer relations, including customer satisfaction. Uncertainties associated with nonstandard transactions or events are also thought to have negative motivational effects on employees whose performance is assessed using such engineered standards. (**Source:** Vanessa O'Connell, "Stores Count Seconds to Cut Labor Costs," *The Wall Street Journal,* November 13, 2008, pp. A1, A15. For additional information regarding "workforce-management systems," go to the website of Accenture Ltd. (**www.accenture.com/home.asp**) and search under "Operations Workforce Optimization.")

Required

1. The article refers to the terms *engineered labor standards* and *time and motion studies.* Define each of these two terms.

2. Define the terms *labor rate variance* and *labor efficiency variance.* Which of these two variances is the basis for monitoring a cashier's performance, as described in the above-referenced article?

3. What is it about the activities performed by cashiers that might complicate efforts to develop engineered labor standards for this context?

4. As described in the chapter, any control/monitoring system is likely to have behavioral consequences. In the present context, what employee morale problems and customer service problems might arise from using engineered standards for evaluating employees' time in completing tasks? What steps do you think a retailer, such as those described in the article, can take to monitor this situation?

5. How can information about cashier time-management be used strategically by a retailer? For example, how can such information be used to lower labor costs for retail stores? For which types of firms would such detailed information likely be of greater value?

[LO 14-1, 14-2, 14-3,
14-6]   14-52   **Master Budgets; Flexible Budgets; Operating Income Variance Analysis**   As part of its comprehensive planning and control system, Mopar Company uses a master budget and subsequent variance analysis. You are given the following information that pertains to the company's only product, XL-10, for the month of December.

Required

1. Using text Exhibit 14.4 as a guide, complete the missing parts of the following profit report for December. Round all entries to nearest whole number.

	Actual Results	Flexible-Budget Variances	Flexible Budget	Sales Volume Variances	Master Budget
Unit sales	100,000	____	____	____	90,000
Sales	$500,000	____	____	____	$450,000
Variable costs	$375,000	____	____	____	270,000
Contribution margin	$125,000	____	____	____	$180,000
Fixed costs	55,000	____	____	____	75,000
Operating income	$ 70,000	____	____	____	$105,000

2. Based on your completed profit report, determine the dollar amount, and label (F or U) each of the following variances for December:

   a. Total master budget variance.

   b. Total flexible budget variance.

   c. Sales volume variance, in terms of operating income.

   d. Sales volume variance, in terms of contribution margin.

   e. Selling price variance.

3. Explain what is meant by the labels "favorable" and "unfavorable" in terms of a profit-variance report of the type you just prepared for the Mopar Company.

4. What information is contained in the total flexible budget variance for the period? Include in your answer a short discussion of the component variances that can be calculated to explain the causes of the total flexible budget variance.

5. Some individuals have recently criticized the use of standard costs and flexible budgets to perform the kinds of variance analyses covered in this chapter. Provide an overview of the arguments for and against the use of standard costs and flexible budgets for operational control purposes.

[LO 14-1, 14-4, 14-6] 14-53 **Production Planning and Control Strategy** This is a story about manufacturing performance at one plant of a large company. It begins with Kristen Reynolds, a relatively new plant manager, coming to visit Bryan Simpkins, the plant's head of manufacturing. Kristen and Bryan work for ITR Incorporated, a manufacturer of lighting fixtures with plants located in six countries and worldwide sales. The plant that Kristen and Bryan manage is located in Canada near Hamilton, Ontario. It is the one plant in ITR's system that focuses on custom orders that require special materials, setup, and assembly. The other five plants supply ITR's high-volume, standardized products. Because of changes in the residential and commercial construction industries, the demand for custom orders at the Ontario plant has been increasing steadily. Unfortunately, the plant has not been filling these orders as quickly as Kristen would like. Many solid customers are waiting days or weeks longer for their orders than they did a year ago; moreover, some ITR salespeople have begun to be evasive when customers ask how soon their orders can be filled. Kristen does not know how this is affecting sales or customer goodwill.

Kristen: Hi, Bryan. It's good to see you. I hope all is well with you and the family.

Bryan: Going great—though I just learned that Jimmy will have to have braces on his teeth. I don't even want to think of how much that will cost.

Kristen: Hey, I've been through that too. No fun. (pause) Bryan, I haven't visited the plant operations in some time. Would you take me for a quick tour?

Bryan: Let's go.

Bryan and Kristen first visit an operation where a skilled worker is operating a machine that molds a metal frame on which multiple light fixtures will later be installed. They watch as the worker (his name badge says Ed) completes the last of a batch of 15 frames. Kristen asks how long this batch took him, and he says 82 minutes. "I know this exactly because I have productivity standards to meet, and I must record my time on all jobs. My standard is 6 minutes per item, so I beat my goal." Ed then examines each frame and finds that one has a bad twist and must be rejected; this takes about 10 minutes. He then pushes a button near the machine that calls another worker to remove the defective frame. Meanwhile, Ed loads the 14 good ones on a cart and moves them to the next manufacturing station. Bryan and Kristen note that many frames are already waiting at the next station.

The worker who was called to remove the defective frame tags it, writes up the potential cause(s) for the defect, and then moves the frame to the area of the plant designated for scrap and rework. Kristen and Bryan look at the defect report and note that it indicates two possibilities, which will be studied further by another worker assigned to the scrap and rework area. The two possibilities are poor-quality materials, as determined by apparent weaknesses in portions of the framing material, and poor work quality (Ed could have damaged the frame accidentally by banging it against one of the roof support beams located next to his work area). Kristen and Bryan note that Ed's workstation area is indeed pretty cramped.

They move to another workstation, which has no operator. By asking a worker at the adjacent station, they determine that the station is down because the machine needs repair. "Joe usually works that station, but he is helping out in the shipping department until his machine is repaired."

They move to another workstation that looks very busy. An order marked "urgent" is waiting at this station, while Dan, the operator, quickly finishes another order. Bryan asks Dan why he has not started the urgent order, and Dan explains that he cannot afford to stop the machine and set it up for another order. This would cost him some time that would lower his productivity on the current job. Dan explains that it is important that he get the items done in the current order quickly, within a standard level of productivity, or production supervisors will be coming to call. Dan says he sees the urgent sign and is working quickly to get to it. He says he might even delay lunch to start it.

To investigate some of the things they observed, Kristen and Bryan next visit the purchasing department. Here they find that the frame material Ed used was purchased from a relatively new vendor at an unbelievably low price. The purchasing department manager approved the purchase because other purchases in the month had gone over budget and this was a way to help meet the budget. The budget is a predetermined amount that the purchasing department is expected to spend each month. Plant policy requires an investigation of any large variances from the budget.

Next, Kristen and Bryan inquire about Joe's machine. A check at the job scheduler's desk shows that the workstation had been in use constantly for the last few weeks. Joe said that he noticed a funny noise but had not reported it because he had some jobs to finish and his productivity was measured by how quickly he finished them. His time between jobs is not measured, but doing jobs quickly is important. Bryan asks the job scheduler why Ed's work area is so crowded since there appears to be plenty of room elsewhere in the plant. The job scheduler says that he is not sure, but that it probably has to do with the fact that each production department is charged a certain amount of plant overhead based on the amount of square feet of space that department occupies. Thus, the department manager for whom Ed works is likely to have reduced the space as much as possible to reduce these overhead charges.

As the story ends, Bryan and Kristen are looking for an answer to how urgent orders are scheduled and moved through the plant.

Required   Consider the manufacturing processes observed in ITR's Ontario plant. What recommendations do you think Bryan and Kristen should make?

Solutions to Self-Study Problems

1. Sales Volume and Flexible Budget Variances/JIT manufacturing

1. Master and pro forma budgets:

	Master Budget	Pro Forma Budgets	
Units	10,000	9,500	11,000
Sales ($54 per unit)	$540,000	$513,000	$594,000
Variable costs:			
Direct materials ($12.60 per unit)	$126,000	$119,700	$138,600
Direct labor ($7.70 per unit)	77,000	73,150	84,700
Manufacturing overhead ($2.00 per unit)	20,000	19,000	22,000
Selling and administrative ($5.00 per unit)	50,000	47,500	55,000
Total variable costs ($27.30 per unit)	$273,000	$259,350	$300,300
Contribution margin ($26.70 per unit)	$267,000	$253,650	$293,700
Fixed costs:			
Manufacturing	$ 55,000	$ 55,000	$ 55,000
Selling and administrative	24,000	24,000	24,000
Total fixed costs	$ 79,000	$ 79,000	$ 79,000
Operating income	$188,000	$174,650	$214,700

2. Total master budget variance = Actual operating income − Master budget operating income

   = $177,100 − $188,000 = **$10,900U**

   Sales volume variance, in terms of operating income = Flexible budget operating income − Master budget operating income
   = $174,650 − $188,000 = **$13,350U**

   or

   = Standard contribution margin per unit × (Actual sales volume − Master budget sales volume)
   = ($54.00 − $27.30) per unit × (9,500 − 10,000) units = **$13,350U**

   Total flexible budget variance = Actual operating income − Flexible budget operating income

   = $177,100 − $174,650 = **$2,450F**

3. Selling price variance = Actual sales revenue − Flexible budget sales revenue

   = $551,000 − $513,000 = **$38,000F**

   or

   = AQ × (AP − SP) = 9,500 units × ($58.00 − $54.00) per unit = **$38,000F**

   Total variable cost flexible budget variance = Actual total variable costs − Flexible budget total variable costs

   = $294,900 − $259,350 = **$35,550U**

   or

   = AQ × (AP − SP) = 9,500 units × ($31.0421 − $27.30) per unit =**$35,550U**

   Total fixed cost flexible budget variance = Actual fixed costs − Flexible budget fixed costs

   = $79,000 − $79,000 = **$0**

   Check: Total flexible budget variance = Selling price variance + Total variable cost flexible budget
   variance + Total fixed cost flexible budget variance
   $2,450F = $38,000F + $35,550U + $0

4. Direct materials purchase price variance, direct materials usage variance, direct labor rate variance, and direct labor efficiency variance:

Direct Materials

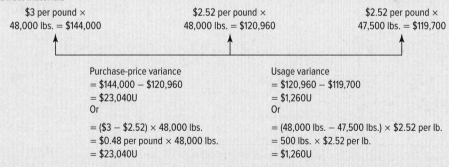

$3 per pound ×	$2.52 per pound ×	$2.52 per pound ×
48,000 lbs. = $144,000	48,000 lbs. = $120,960	47,500 lbs. = $119,700

Purchase-price variance
= $144,000 − $120,960
= $23,040U
Or

= ($3 − $2.52) × 48,000 lbs.
= $0.48 per pound × 48,000 lbs.
= $23,040U

Usage variance
= $120,960 − $119,700
= $1,260U
Or

= (48,000 lbs. − 47,500 lbs.) × $2.52 per lb.
= 500 lbs. × $2.52 per lb.
= $1,260U

Direct Labor

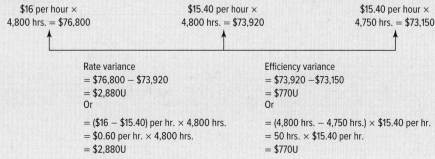

$16 per hour ×	$15.40 per hour ×	$15.40 per hour ×
4,800 hrs. = $76,800	4,800 hrs. = $73,920	4,750 hrs. = $73,150

Rate variance
= $76,800 − $73,920
= $2,880U
Or

= ($16 − $15.40) per hr. × 4,800 hrs.
= $0.60 per hr. × 4,800 hrs.
= $2,880U

Efficiency variance
= $73,920 −$73,150
= $770U
Or

= (4,800 hrs. − 4,750 hrs.) × $15.40 per hr.
= 50 hrs. × $15.40 per hr.
= $770U

5. A just-in-time (JIT) process is one in which products, components, and subassemblies are produced only when needed—that is, on a so-called demand-pull basis. Based originally on the Toyota production system, this philosophy requires a commitment to total quality (to ensure smooth flowing of the production line), elimination of waste and inefficiency, and a minimization of inventory holdings. In effect, the JIT philosophy reflects a new business model for the organization, as follows:

> Make only what you've sold, rather than stockpiling large quantities of goods that may remain in inventory for an extended period of time. Make use of raw materials as soon as they are delivered. Deliver to customers finished goods shortly after rolling off the assembly line.

Financial benefits from implementing a JIT manufacturing strategy include increased sales/market share (especially for companies embracing a differentiation strategy), reduction in inventory-holding costs (both out-of-pocket costs and opportunity costs), and decreased quality-related costs (e.g., internal failure costs and external failure costs—see Chapter 17). Nonfinancial benefits associated with JIT manufacturing systems include faster *manufacturing cycle times,* increased inventory turnover ratios (i.e., ratio of cost of goods sold to average inventory), improvements in defect rates, increased uptime for machinery and equipment, and improvements in on-time deliveries to customers. Of course, to obtain these benefits, the organization generally must make sizable investments in employee training, information systems, and a reconfigured plant layout (e.g., a move to *cellular manufacturing*).

2. Direct Materials Price and Usage Variances, Direct Labor Rate and Efficiency Variances, and Journal Entries

1. **Variance Calculations**

Direct Materials—XF–2000
Total standard quantity of direct materials for the product manufactured (SQ)
= 100,000 bags × 25 lbs. of XF–2000 per bag = 2,500,000 lbs.

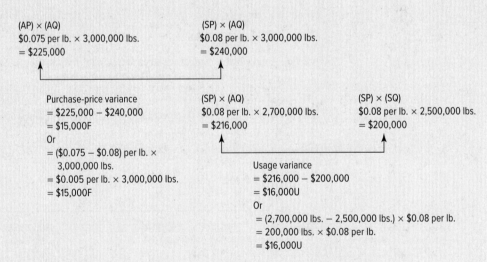

Direct Labor
Actual wage rate per direct labor hr. (AP)
= $182,000 ÷ 5,200 hrs. = $35 per hr.
Total standard direct labor hrs. for the product manufactured (SQ)
= 100,000 bags × 0.05 hr. per bag = 5,000 hrs.

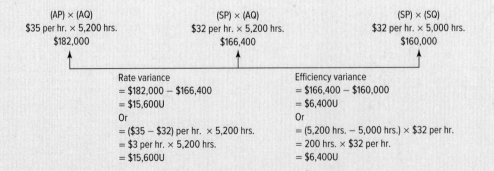

2. **Journal Entries**

Materials Inventory (3,000,000 × $0.08)	240,000	
Materials Purchase Price Variance (3,000,000 × $0.005)		15,000
Accounts Payable (3,000,000 × $0.075)		225,000
Purchased 3,000,000 pounds of XF–2000 at $0.075 per pound.		

Work-in-Process Inventory ($0.08 × 2,500,000)	200,000	
Materials Usage Variance (200,000 × $0.08)	16,000	
Materials Inventory (2,700,000 × $0.08)		216,000
Issued 2,700,000 pounds of XF–2000 for the production of 100,000 bags of Weed-Be-Doom.		

Work-in-Process Inventory (5,000 × $32)	160,000	
Labor Rate Variance (5,200 × $3)	15,600	
Labor Efficiency Variance (200 × $32)	6,400	
Accrued Payroll (5,200 × $35)		182,000
Direct labor wages for the manufacturing of 100,000 bags of Weed-Be-Doom for 5,200 hours at $35 per hour.		

Please visit Connect to access a narrated, animated tutorial for solving these problems.

CHAPTER FIFTEEN

Operational Performance Measurement: Indirect Cost Variances and Resource Capacity Management

After studying this chapter, you should be able to . . .

LO 15-1 Distinguish between the product costing and control purposes of standard costs for factory (manufacturing) overhead.

LO 15-2 Use flexible budgets to calculate and interpret standard cost variances for factory (manufacturing) overhead.

LO 15-3 Record overhead costs and associated standard cost variances.

LO 15-4 Dispose of standard cost variances at the end of a period.

LO 15-5 Apply standard costs in service organizations.

LO 15-6 Analyze overhead variances in a traditional (i.e., non-time-driven) activity-based costing system.

LO 15-7 Understand decision rules that can be used to guide the variance investigation decision.

Southwest Airlines has been consistently listed by *Fortune* magazine as one of the world's most admired companies, ranking as number 11 in 2020. The company is recognized for its HR practices, its focus on sustainability, the quality of its rewards program, its work–life balance policies, and, perhaps most of all, its low-cost strategy. To a large extent, Southwest's low costs are attributable to the fact that, since 1987, the airline has almost exclusively flown only a single model: the Boeing 737. Flying a single model saves the company on training and maintenance costs, and allows Southwest to pass those savings on to customers. The results have been impressive: In 2019 Southwest celebrated 46 consecutive years of profitability and reported record-setting profits of $2.5 billion.

However, in 2019 federal regulators around the world grounded the newest version of the Boeing 737 (called the 737 Max) after software flaws were found to have caused two significant crashes. No clear timeline for the plane's return to service has been established. Because it has relied almost exclusively on the 737, Southwest now faces two significant problems: Its operating costs may rise as it shifts to other models, and its ability to manage flight capacity is uncertain.[1]

---

[1] Darryl Campbell, "The 737 Built Southwest, and the 737 Max Could Be Its Undoing," *The Verge*, October 23, 2019, www.theverge.com/2019/10/23/20927213/boeing-737-max-southwest-planes-crash-budget-airlines-grounded-cost-maintenance.

Chris Parypa/Essentials/rypson/iStockphoto

Capacity-related costs (that is, costs related to the supply, but not actual use, of capacity) are a major cause of the profitability swings that are associated with the airline industry. Too much capacity leads to operational risk (e.g., failure to break even); too little capacity results in significant opportunity costs, particularly when the economy strengthens. Put differently, airline carriers want full flights, but not so full that they must turn away high-yielding business travelers or experience unpleasant consequences from "bumping" passengers. The issue of managing capacity-related resources is particularly important for airline carriers such as Southwest given the slim profit margins in the industry and the magnitude of capacity-related costs for individual airlines.

In this chapter, we continue the discussion from Chapter 14 for Schmidt Manufacturing by examining production volume and other indirect cost variances that the company could use to monitor short-term financial performance. (Recall that although Schmidt competes on the basis of differentiation, competitive pressures mean that cost control is increasingly important.) Specifically, we expand the discussion of standard costs, flexible budgets, and variance analysis concepts to the control of overhead (i.e., indirect manufacturing) costs for Schmidt Manufacturing. Part of the discussion is how information from the analysis of fixed overhead costs can be used to manage resource capacity (i.e., capacity-related costs). We then consider how overhead variances could be applied to service organizations and how overhead cost variances can be determined in a traditional ABC (activity-based costing) system (see Chapter 5). This chapter also deals with recording standard overhead costs, overhead cost variances, and the end-of-period disposition of standard cost variances. We conclude the chapter by discussing the variance investigation decision—that is, decision rules that management can use to guide the variance investigation decision. A separate online supplement (available through Connect) provides an extended discussion of the variance investigation decision under uncertainty.

Standard Overhead Costs: Planning vs. Control

LO 15-1

Distinguish between the product costing and control purposes of standard costs for factory (manufacturing) overhead.

As pointed out in Chapter 14, standard costs can be used alone for control purposes, or they can be incorporated formally into the accounting records for both product costing and control purposes. In Chapter 14, we used a flexible budget at the end of the period to calculate various revenue and cost variances, which helped explain why actual operating income for the period differed from operating income reflected in the master budget. For *cost control purposes,* we

EXHIBIT 15.1
Variable Factory Overhead: Product Costing vs. Control Purposes

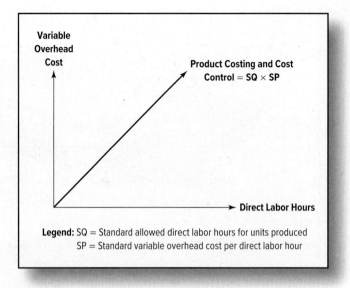

calculated a total flexible budget variance and then proceeded to explain this total variance by calculating a selling price variance, a set of fixed cost variances (for both manufacturing and nonmanufacturing costs), and a total flexible budget variance for direct manufacturing costs.[2] We then subdivided the variance for direct labor and direct materials into price and efficiency components. The breakdown of the flexible budget variance for factory overhead (i.e., indirect manufacturing costs) was left for this chapter. However, before looking at standard cost variances associated with factory overhead, we need to differentiate the product costing and cost control purposes of standard costs used for factory overhead.

For *variable* factory overhead, the underlying model for cost control and product costing purposes is the same, as illustrated in Exhibit 15.1. Recall from Chapter 14 that the Schmidt Machinery Company uses direct labor hours as the allocation base (or driver) for applying overhead costs. Other drivers, such as number of machine hours, could have been used by the company.

Exhibit 15.2 reproduces the manufacturing cost portion of the standard cost sheet for the Schmidt Machinery Company presented in Chapter 14 (Exhibit 14.5). As you can see, the standard variable overhead rate per unit is $60 (5 standard direct labor hours per unit × $12

EXHIBIT 15.2
Standard Manufacturing Cost Sheet (partial reproduction of Exhibit 14.5)

SCHMIDT MACHINERY COMPANY				
Standard Manufacturing Cost Sheet				
Product: XV-1				
Descriptions	**Quantity**	**Unit Cost**	**Subtotal**	**Total**
Direct materials:				
Aluminum	4 pounds	$25	$100	
PVC	1 pound	40	40	
Direct labor	5 hours	40	200	
Variable factory overhead	5 hours	12	60	
Total variable manufacturing cost				$400
Fixed factory overhead	5 hours	24	120	120*
Standard manufacturing cost per unit				$520

*As noted in Exhibit 14.1, budgeted fixed factory overhead cost is $120,000 per month. The master budget in Exhibit 14.1 is based on an output level of 1,000 units for the month. Thus, the $120-per-unit figure in Exhibit 15.2 is found by dividing budgeted fixed factory overhead cost ($120,000) by the planned level of output for the month, 1,000 units. Because the budgeted direct labor hours per unit equals 5, we can also say that the budgeted fixed factory overhead cost is $24 per standard direct labor hour, as indicated above in Exhibit 15.2.

[2] As you may recall, in order to explain the master (static) budget variance for the period, in Chapter 14 we also calculated a sales volume variance. Further analysis of this variance is covered in Chapter 16. Please refer back to Exhibit 14.15 for a summary of the variance decomposition process used by Schmidt each period to explain the master (static) budget variance for the period.

EXHIBIT 15.3
Fixed Factory Overhead Costs:
Product Costing vs. Control

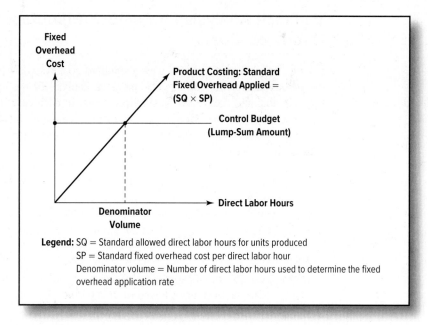

Legend: SQ = Standard allowed direct labor hours for units produced
SP = Standard fixed overhead cost per direct labor hour
Denominator volume = Number of direct labor hours used to determine the fixed overhead application rate

standard variable overhead cost per direct labor hour). It is this amount that is charged to production for the period (product costing purpose) and that is used in the flexible budget (cost control purpose) in Exhibit 14.8 (see the middle section). In short, the graph depicted in Exhibit 15.1 for variable overhead cost is similar in form to what we could have prepared in Chapter 14 for either direct materials cost or direct labor cost. This makes sense because all three (direct materials, direct labor, and variable overhead) are variable costs.

The situation for fixed costs, however, is different, as reflected in the graph presented as Exhibit 15.3. For cost control purposes, we see that budgeted (lump-sum) fixed overhead costs are used—see the horizontal line in Exhibit 15.3. At the end of the period, this budgeted amount is compared to the actual fixed overhead cost incurred. The resulting difference (if any) is called a *spending variance.* The spending variance for fixed overhead, along with the spending variance for nonmanufacturing fixed costs, is used to explain a portion of the total master budget variance for the period (see Exhibit 14.15).

For product costing purposes, however, we must "unitize" fixed factory overhead costs.[3] As indicated in Exhibit 15.3, for product costing purposes, we treat fixed factory overhead costs *as if* they were variable costs. In the Schmidt Machinery Company case, total fixed costs for October 2022 are budgeted at $150,000 [see Exhibit 14.1, column (2)]. In this chapter, we expand the discussion further and break these costs into $120,000 for fixed factory overhead and $30,000 for fixed selling and administrative expenses. Given a budgeted output level of 1,000 units per month (Exhibit 14.1), budgeted fixed factory overhead cost *for product costing purposes* can be expressed as $120 per unit (or, equivalently, 5 standard direct labor hours per unit × $24 per direct labor hour = $120 per unit).

"There is never a time in a company's history when cost control can be relegated to the back burner."

Felix Dennis, publisher, poet, and philanthropist

---

[3] This holds for what is called the *absorption* or *full-cost approach* to product costing, which is currently required for external reporting and for federal income tax purposes in the United States. An alternative product-costing approach called *variable costing* treats fixed production costs as period (i.e., non-inventoriable) costs. Variable costing is covered in Chapter 18. U.S. income tax rules regarding inventory valuation are contained in Internal Revenue Code (IRC) Section 263 ("Uniform Capitalization Rules"). Treasury Regulation § 1.263 requires that indirect (manufacturing) costs be "reasonably allocated" to outputs.

Variance Analysis for Factory (Manufacturing) Overhead Costs

Schmidt Machinery Company uses a standard cost system. Thus, at the end of each period, the accountant for the company prepares an analysis of the total standard cost variance for both variable and fixed factory overhead costs. In each case, the goal will be to explain the difference between the actual overhead cost incurred and the standard overhead cost charged to production (units produced) for the period. As shown later, these variances are recorded at the end of the period in separate variance accounts.

For product costing purposes, the total overhead cost variance for the period (also called the total under/overapplied overhead) is equal to the difference between actual overhead cost incurred and the standard overhead cost applied to production. For Schmidt, the total overhead standard cost variance for October 2022 is $30,880U, as follows (you can refer to Exhibits 14.1, 14.5 and 14.8 to find the numbers shown here):

Total overhead cost variance = Total actual overhead cost − Total applied overhead cost

= (Total variable overhead + Total fixed overhead) − (Total overhead application rate × Standard labor hours allowed for this period's production)

= ($40,630 + $130,650) − [$36 per hour × (780 units × 5 hours per units)]

= $171,280 − $140,400 = $30,880U (i.e., $30,880 *under*applied overhead)

As explained below, the total overhead cost variance for the period can be subdivided into a set of variable overhead cost variances and a set of fixed overhead cost variances.

Variable Overhead Cost Analysis

Exhibit 15.4 provides a graphical representation of the process used to decompose the **total variable overhead cost variance** for the period. As indicated in Exhibit 14.8 (bottom portion), this variance for the Schmidt Machinery Company in October 2022 is $6,170F, which is the difference between actual variable overhead cost incurred ($40,630) and the standard variable overhead cost charged to production during October [$46,800 = (780 units × 5 standard direct labor hours per unit) × $12 standard variable overhead cost per direct labor hour]. Note that these figures are obtained from Exhibit 14.8. Note, too, that this total variance, from a product costing standpoint, could be called *total over/underapplied variable overhead cost* for the period, a point consistent with Exhibit 15.1. Because the actual variable factory overhead

EXHIBIT 15.4
Schmidt Machinery Company Variance Analysis: Variable Factory Overhead Cost

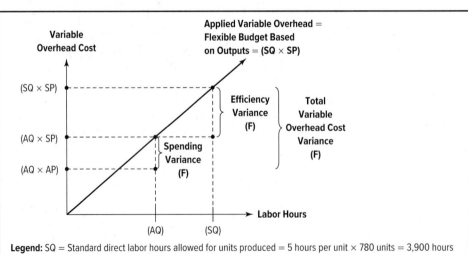

Legend: SQ = Standard direct labor hours allowed for units produced = 5 hours per unit × 780 units = 3,900 hours
SP = Standard variable overhead cost per direct labor hour = $12 (see Exhibit 15.2)
AQ = Actual direct labor hours worked = 3,510 hours (Exhibit 14.6)
AP = Actual variable overhead cost per direct labor hour worked = $40,630 ÷ 3,510 = $11.5755 (rounded)
Total variable overhead variance = Spending variance + Efficiency variance
F = A favorable effect on operating income

cost was less than the variable factory overhead cost applied to production, we call the $6,170 difference *over* applied variable overhead.

Cost Control: Breakdown of the Total Variable Overhead Cost Variance

We see from Exhibit 15.4 that the total variable factory overhead cost variance for a period ($6,170F in our example) can be broken down into a **variable overhead spending variance** and a **variable overhead efficiency variance,** as follows:

variable overhead spending variance
The difference between actual variable overhead cost incurred and the flexible budget for variable overhead based on *inputs* for the period (e.g., actual direct labor hours worked).

$$\frac{\text{Variable overhead}}{\text{spending variance}} = \frac{\textit{Actual} \text{ variable overhead}}{\text{incurred}} - \frac{\textit{Flexible budget} \text{ for variable}}{\text{overhead based on } \textit{inputs}}$$
$$\text{for the period}$$
$$= (AQ \times AP) - (AQ \times SP)$$
$$= AQ \times (AP - SP)$$

variable overhead efficiency variance
The difference between the flexible budget for variable overhead based on *inputs* (e.g., actual labor hours worked) and the flexible budget for variable overhead based on *outputs* (i.e., standard allowed labor hours for units produced).

From Exhibit 14.8 (top portion), we see that Schmidt used 3,510 direct labor hours in October 2022 to produce 780 units; total variable overhead cost incurred for the month was $40,630. Based on a standard variable overhead cost per direct labor hour of $12 and an actual variable overhead rate of $11.5755 per direct labor hour ($40,630 ÷ 3,510 direct labor hours), the variable overhead spending variance for the month is $1,490F, as follows:

$$= \$40,630 - (3,510 \text{ direct labor hours} \times \$12 \text{ per direct labor hour})$$
$$= \$40,630 - \$42,120 = \$1,490F$$

Or

$$= 3,510 \text{ direct labor hours} \times (\$11.5755 - \$12) \text{ per direct labor hour} = \$1,490F \text{ (rounded)}$$

Next, we calculate the variable overhead efficiency variance, as follows:

$$\frac{\text{Variable overhead}}{\text{efficiency variance}} = \frac{\textit{Flexible budget} \text{ for variable}}{\text{overhead based on } \textit{inputs}} - \frac{\textit{Flexible budget} \text{ for variable}}{\text{overhead based on } \textit{outputs}}$$
$$= (AQ \times SP) - (SQ \times SP)$$
$$= SP \times (AQ - SQ)$$

As implied by the graph in Exhibit 15.1, the amount of standard overhead cost applied to production (product costing purpose) and the flexible budget based on output (cost control purpose) for variable overhead are always equal. Thus, the second term on the right-hand side of the above equation could have been expressed as "standard variable overhead costs applied to production."

The standard for direct labor is 5 hours per unit. Thus, the variable overhead efficiency variance for October 2022 is:

$$= \$42,120 - [(780 \text{ units} \times 5 \text{ direct labor hours per unit}) \times \$12.00 \text{ per direct labor hour}]$$
$$= \$42,120 - \$46,800 = \$4,680F$$

Or

$$= \$12.00 \text{ per direct labor hour} \times (3,510 - 3,900) \text{ direct labor hours} = \$4,680F$$

In sum, the above procedures have been used to break down the total variable overhead standard cost variance for October ($6,170F) into a variable overhead *spending variance* ($1,490F) and a variable overhead *efficiency variance* ($4,680F).

Interpretation and Implications of Variable Overhead Variances

In traditional accounting systems, such as the system used by Schmidt Machinery Company, only a single activity variable (e.g., direct labor hours or machine hours) is used to assign manufacturing overhead costs to outputs. Further, as illustrated above, traditional systems use this single activity variable for cost control purposes. That is, the flexible budget for such companies is based on a single, usually volume-related, activity variable. This simple approach requires careful interpretation of the resulting standard cost variances for variable overhead. While the formulas for these variances may look the same as those covered in Chapter 14 for direct labor and direct materials costs, the meaning and interpretation of these variances are not the same. In short, the imperfect relationship between variable factory overhead costs and the chosen activity variable (e.g., direct labor hours) that a company uses to allocate these costs to outputs requires careful interpretation of variable overhead variances.

Variable Overhead Spending Variance

The variable overhead spending variance results from a difference between the actual spending for variable overhead items *per unit of the activity variable* and the standard variable overhead cost per unit of the activity variable. In the Schmidt Machinery Company example for October 2022, the budgeted spending for variable overhead cost per direct labor hour is $12. The actual variable overhead cost per direct labor hour is approximately $11.5755 ($40,630 ÷ 3,510 hours). Thus, spending for variable overhead items per direct labor hour worked is less than standard; for this reason, the resulting variable overhead spending variance for the period ($1,490) is labeled *favorable.* The key to understanding this is to remember that the variable overhead application rate refers to the standard variable overhead cost per unit of the activity variable used for product costing purposes and for constructing the flexible budget for cost control purposes.

If the variable overhead spending variance is considered material or significant, a follow-up analysis of individual variable overhead items is indicated. Essentially, managers of the Schmidt Machinery Company will want to know *why* spending for variable overhead items per labor hour was different from expectations. To answer this question, a follow-up analysis of each variable overhead cost component would be required.

Variable Overhead Efficiency Variance

Simply put, the variable overhead efficiency variance reflects efficiency or inefficiency in the use of the activity variable used to apply variable overhead costs to products. In the case of Schmidt Machinery Company, this variable is direct labor hours. Thus, to the extent that the incurrence of variable overhead cost for Schmidt is related to the number of direct labor hours worked and the company uses a nonstandard number of labor hours, it will incur both a direct labor efficiency variance (Chapter 14) and a variable overhead efficiency variance (Chapter 15). For October 2022, Schmidt used 3,510 direct labor hours to produce 780 units of output. The standard direct labor hours allowed for this level of output was 3,900 hours (780 units × 5 direct labor hours per unit). Thus, the company worked 390 fewer direct labor hours than standard for the period. *If* variable overhead is incurred at the rate of $12 per direct labor hour worked, then this 390-hour savings would translate to a savings of $4,680 in variable overhead costs.

Because this variance is related to efficiency or inefficiency in the use of whatever driver is used to apply variable overhead for product costing purposes, it reinforces the need to choose the proper activity variable for allocating variable overhead costs (ideally, a variable that is highly correlated with those costs). Also, whoever is responsible for controlling the use of this activity variable would be responsible for controlling the variable overhead efficiency variance. In the case of the Schmidt Machinery Company, this would most likely be the production supervisor.

Fixed Overhead Cost Analysis

total fixed overhead variance
The difference between actual fixed overhead costs for the period and the standard fixed overhead costs applied to production based on a standard fixed overhead application rate; also called *over- or underapplied fixed overhead* for the period; this variance can be broken down into a fixed overhead spending variance and a fixed overhead production volume variance.

Exhibit 15.5 provides a graphical representation of the process used to decompose the **total fixed overhead variance** for the Schmidt Machinery Company for October 2022. For product costing purposes, the total variance is $37,050U, which is the difference between actual fixed overhead costs incurred ($130,650, see Exhibit 14.1) and the standard fixed overhead costs charged to production during October ($93,600 = 780 units × 5 standard direct labor hours per unit × $24 standard fixed overhead rate per direct labor hour—see Exhibit 15.2). Note, too, that this total variance, from a product costing standpoint, could be called *total over- or underapplied fixed overhead cost* for the period. When the actual fixed overhead costs are greater than the fixed overhead costs assigned to production, as they were for Schmidt for the month of October, we label the figure *under* applied fixed overhead.

Measuring and managing capacity utilization for companies and industries with significant levels of fixed costs (what we referred to as "operating leverage" in Chapter 9) is an important strategic issue. For example, in response to growing consumer demand, many U.S. automakers have expanded capacity by building new plants and/or expanding existing plants. If demand turns out to be strong, these companies will benefit from having the expanded capacity to meet that demand. However, when demand is weak, the excess fixed costs associated with expanded or new facilities provide a significant drag on profits. Auto companies are most profitable when operating near 100% of capacity; when operating at approximately 80% of capacity, losses begin to mount rapidly. In such cases (as occurred around the time of the 2008–2009 market collapse in the United States), price wars among the manufacturers may ensue—a situation that facilitated Chrysler's and General Motors's slide into bankruptcy in 2009.

Generally, then, high operating leverage and high fixed costs are great when demand is high but costly when demand falls. When future demand is uncertain, a highly leveraged strategy is very risky. Domestic manufacturers, such as Chrysler and General Motors, may find this to be the case if the recent trend toward economic nationalism continues and these companies can no longer import parts and subassemblies (because the automakers are not making them, the imported parts are variable costs to them). Then to bring manufacturing jobs back home, the automakers will have to trade variable costs (purchase of parts) for investments in manufacturing capacity and related fixed costs; that is, even higher operating leverage.

Required

Consider what you think would be the right strategy for an automaker regarding operating leverage during a time of economic nationalism—that is, how do you manage the balance of fixed and variable costs in a time of uncertainty about demand for automobiles?

(Refer to Comments on Cost Management in Action at the end of the chapter.)

EXHIBIT 15.5
Schmidt Machinery Company Variance Analysis: Fixed Factory Overhead Cost

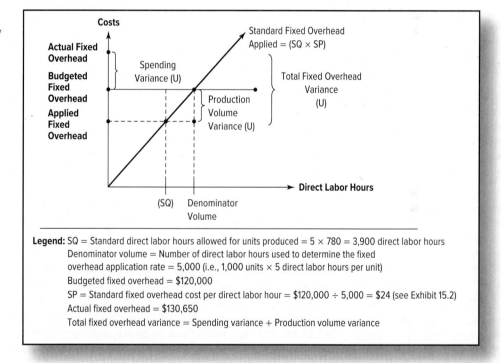

Legend: SQ = Standard direct labor hours allowed for units produced = 5 × 780 = 3,900 direct labor hours
Denominator volume = Number of direct labor hours used to determine the fixed overhead application rate = 5,000 (i.e., 1,000 units × 5 direct labor hours per unit)
Budgeted fixed overhead = $120,000
SP = Standard fixed overhead cost per direct labor hour = $120,000 ÷ 5,000 = $24 (see Exhibit 15.2)
Actual fixed overhead = $130,650
Total fixed overhead variance = Spending variance + Production volume variance

The Production (Denominator) Volume Variance

As noted earlier in footnote 3, for U.S. federal income tax and U.S. GAAP purposes, companies must report inventories on a full (also called absorption) cost basis. This means that in addition to absorbing variable manufacturing costs, each unit produced must also absorb a share of fixed factory overhead costs. In turn, this requires that fixed overhead costs be "unitized" for product costing purposes (see Chapter 18 for a comprehensive treatment of full costing versus variable costing). The following four-step process can be used for this purpose.

Step 1: Determine budgeted total fixed factory overhead. Fixed factory (manufacturing) overhead costs, by definition, do not vary in the short run in response to changes in output or activity. As such, these costs are often referred to as *capacity-related* manufacturing support costs. Thus, once an organization has determined its capacity for an upcoming period (e.g., one year), it constructs a budget for capacity-related costs. In the case of Schmidt Machinery Company, the capacity-related manufacturing (i.e., fixed factory overhead) costs are estimated at $120,000 per month.

Step 2: Choose an appropriate activity measure for applying fixed factory overhead. For product costing purposes, capacity-related manufacturing costs are assigned to outputs based on one or more activity measures (machine hours, labor hours, etc.). Usually, this is the same activity measure used to apply variable overhead costs to outputs. The Schmidt Machinery Company uses direct labor hours as the activity measure for assigning fixed overhead costs to production (output).

Step 3: Choose a denominator activity level. In order to unitize fixed overhead costs for product costing purposes, we must choose some level of output (activity) over which the budgeted fixed factory overhead costs for the period (in this case, $120,000 per month) can be spread. The Schmidt Machinery Company uses 5,000 direct labor hours per month (i.e., 1,000 units × 5 direct labor hours per unit) for this purpose. The general term used to describe the level of output (activity) used to establish the standard **fixed overhead application rate** (here, $24 per direct labor hour) is **denominator activity level** or **denominator volume**. Several alternatives exist for defining the denominator activity level: two "supply-based" alternatives and two "demand-based" alternatives.

Supply-Based Definitions of Capacity The denominator activity level can be defined in terms of output capacity supplied. In this regard it is useful to think in terms of two alternatives: **theoretical capacity** (the maximum level of activity or output based on available capacity) or **practical capacity** (theoretical capacity reduced by normal employee breaks, machine downtime for maintenance, and other "expected" loss of output). As a rough rule of thumb, you might think of practical capacity as somewhere in the neighborhood of 85% to 90% of theoretical capacity. Thus, the notion of practical capacity is not rigidly defined.

Demand-Based Definitions of Capacity It is also possible to define capacity in terms of the demand for the organization's output. For example, we could use **budgeted capacity utilization** (the expected level of activity or output for the upcoming period, usually a year) or **normal capacity** (the average level of demand for the company's product projected over an intermediate-level number of years into the future, say, three to five years).

Given these choices, which activity level should be chosen when determining the fixed overhead application rate? The answer is partly subjective. This is due largely to the fact that the resulting product-cost information can be used for different purposes, ranging from product pricing decisions, to performance evaluation purposes, to tax and external reporting requirements in accounting. In terms of the latter, generally accepted accounting principles (GAAP) [FASB ASC 330-10-30: Inventory—Overall—Initial Measurement (previously, *SFAS No. 151:* Inventory Costs—An Amendment of ARB No. 43)] require that allocation of fixed production overhead cost to products be based on the *normal capacity* of the production facilities. According to **FASB ASC 330-10-30,** normal capacity is the production expected to be achieved over a number of periods or seasons under normal circumstances, taking into account the loss of capacity resulting from planned maintenance. According to this financial reporting standard, some variation in production levels from period to period is expected and establishes a range of normal capacity. As noted in footnote 3, current U.S. income tax requirements specify only that methods used to allocate indirect costs to inventory should result in reasonable allocations across outputs. Additional guidance for U.S. income tax purposes regarding the use of alternative denominator volume levels for determining income under the full costing approach is given in Treasury Regulation § 1.471-11: Inventories of Manufacturers.

Note that different definitions of the denominator volume will result in different fixed overhead application rates, different amounts of fixed overhead costs charged to production, and therefore different amounts for the production volume variance. Depending on how variances

fixed overhead application rate
A term used for product-costing purposes; the rate at which fixed overhead cost is charged to production per unit of activity (or output).

denominator activity level
The output (activity) level used to establish the predetermined fixed overhead application rate; generally defined as *practical capacity;* also called the *denominator volume.*

denominator volume
The output (activity) level used to calculate the predetermined fixed overhead application rate; generally defined as *practical capacity;* also called the *denominator activity level.*

theoretical capacity
A measure of capacity (output or activity) that assumes 100% efficiency; maximum possible output (or activity).

practical capacity
Theoretical capacity reduced by normal output losses due to personal time, normal maintenance, and so on; the measure of capacity often recommended for estimating cost-driver rates under ABC and TDABC systems.

budgeted capacity utilization
The planned (forecasted) output for the coming period, usually a year.

normal capacity
The expected average demand per year over an intermediate term—for example, the upcoming three to five years.

FASB ASC 330-10-30
GAAP financial reporting guidance regarding the determination of overhead allocation rates and the treatment of abnormal idle-capacity variances.

are disposed of at the end of the year, the financial statements can be affected by the choice of denominator activity level.[4]

Our position is that for internal reporting purposes, *practical capacity* should be used as the denominator level for setting the fixed overhead allocation rate. We maintain this position for several reasons. First, though not necessarily controlling, the use of practical capacity (as noted above) is consistent with current federal income tax requirements in the United States. Second, relative to budgeted output, the use of practical capacity provides more uniform data over time, which facilitates decision making on the part of management. (That is, managers do not have to continually reevaluate decisions based on changing product cost data over time.) Third, the use of practical capacity in the denominator is logically consistent with the numerator in the fixed overhead rate calculation. That is, the numerator represents the costs of the capacity supplied and the denominator represents, in practical terms, the amount of capacity supplied.[5] Fourth, and perhaps most important, the use of practical capacity means that current customers and current production will not be burdened with the cost of unused (i.e., idle) capacity, which would be the case if budgeted output were used and budgeted output is less than practical capacity. From a pricing standpoint, this can help managers avoid the so-called death-spiral effect. This refers to a situation where an organization uses cost-based pricing and includes in "cost" both the cost of capacity used and the cost of unused (idle) capacity. These larger costs result in decreased demand, which in turn leads to higher fixed costs per unit, and so forth. Finally, the resulting production volume variance data (discussed below) can be interpreted, loosely, as the *cost of unused (i.e., cost of idle) capacity* and therefore can be used for **resource capacity planning** purposes. This information can facilitate decisions by management as to the appropriate *supply* of capacity-related resources (and associated costs).

resource capacity planning
Procedures used to ensure adequate but not excessive supply of capacity-related resources.

Step 4: Calculate the predetermined fixed overhead application rate. The last step in the process is to divide budgeted fixed factory overhead cost for the period by the denominator activity level. For Schmidt, this calculation results in a rate of $24 per direct labor hour, as reported in Exhibit 15.2. Thus, for product costing purposes each unit produced is assigned $120 of fixed factory overhead (i.e., $24 per direct labor hour × 5 direct labor hours).

In summary, for product costing purposes, a company must choose an activity level over which it spreads budgeted fixed (i.e., capacity-related) manufacturing costs for a given period. If the company actually operates at the level assumed when the application rate was determined, it will have assigned to production an amount exactly equal to the budgeted fixed overhead cost for the period. If, on the other hand, the company operates at any level of activity other than the denominator activity level, then it will have applied to production an amount greater or lesser than budgeted fixed overhead. It is this over- or underapplied budgeted fixed overhead that we call the **fixed overhead production volume variance** for the period. For brevity, we will refer to this variance more simply as the production volume variance. Keep in mind, however, that in practice some refer to this as the denominator volume variance. Because of this, we will use these terms interchangeably.

fixed overhead production volume variance
The difference between budgeted (lump-sum) fixed overhead cost for the period and the standard fixed overhead cost applied to production (using the predetermined fixed overhead allocation rate); also called the *production volume variance* or the *denominator volume variance.*

Refer back to Exhibit 15.5. The line emanating from the origin represents the standard fixed overhead cost applied to production. The slope of this line is equal to the fixed overhead application rate, which in the case of Schmidt Machinery Company is $24 per direct labor hour (or $120 per unit). You will note that the only situation where the total fixed overhead applied exactly equals budgeted fixed overhead is when the output (activity) for the period is 5,000 standard allowed hours (or, equivalently, 1,000 units produced). The production volume variance is therefore defined as the difference between budgeted fixed factory overhead

[4] As explained later in this chapter, there are different ways of disposing of standard cost variances at the end of the year. One of these methods is to restate cost of goods sold (COGS) and ending inventory amounts to actual costs by recalculating, at year-end, the actual fixed overhead cost per unit of output. Another approach is to allocate (prorate) variances to the ending inventory and COGS accounts. Under either of these approaches, the denominator activity level chosen at the beginning of the year for product costing purposes during the year will have little or no effect on the financial statements for the year. The choice of denominator volume will, however, affect financial statements when standard cost variances are written off in their entirety to COGS. In short, in some cases, the choice of denominator volume will affect an organization's financial statements for the year.

[5] Practical capacity can change over time due to changes in manufacturing layout, improvements in worker efficiencies, and so on.

(lump-sum) cost and the standard fixed overhead cost applied to production. For October, this variance for the Schmidt Machinery Company is $26,400U, as follows:

$$\text{Production volume variance} = \text{Budgeted fixed factory overhead cost} - \text{Standard fixed overhead cost assigned to production}$$

$$= \$120,000 - [(780 \text{ units produced} \times 5 \text{ direct labor hours per unit}) \times \$24 \text{ per direct labor hour}]$$

$$= \$120,000 - \$93,600 = \$26,400U$$

Or

$$= SP \times (\text{Denominator activity hours} - SQ)$$
$$= \$24 \text{ per direct labor hour} \times [5,000 \text{ direct labor hours} - (780 \text{ units} \times 5 \text{ direct labor hours per unit})]$$
$$= \$24 \text{ per direct labor hour} \times (5,000 - 3,900)$$
$$\text{direct labor hours} = \$26,400U^{6}$$

Fixed Overhead Spending (Budget) Variance

fixed overhead spending (budget) variance
The difference between budgeted and actual fixed factory overhead costs for a period.

Refer to Exhibit 15.5. We see that the **fixed overhead spending (budget) variance** is defined as the difference between budgeted and actual fixed factory overhead cost for the period. For Schmidt Machinery Company, the fixed overhead spending (budget) variance for October was $10,650U, as follows:

$$\text{Fixed overhead spending variance} = \text{Actual fixed overhead} - \text{Budgeted fixed overhead}$$
$$= \$130,650 - \$120,000$$
$$= \$10,650U$$

Note that this is the amount reported in the variance decomposition summary contained in Exhibit 14.15 and the four-variance analysis reflected in Panel 1 of Exhibit 15.7.

Interpretation of Fixed Overhead Variances
Production (Denominator) Volume Variance

The production (denominator) volume variance is an artifact of unitizing fixed overhead costs for product costing purposes. As indicated in Exhibit 15.5, in and of itself this variance has no meaning for cost control purposes. However, as we indicated earlier in this chapter, if practical capacity is used to establish the fixed overhead application rate, then the production volume variance can be viewed as a rough measure of capacity utilization. This is because the variance reflects differences between available capacity and actual capacity usage. In short, the reporting of production volume variances over time provides decision makers with information that can be used to manage *spending* on capacity-related resources. For example, consistently reported underapplied fixed overhead (i.e., unfavorable production volume variances) may signal the need to reduce spending on capacity-related costs or motivate action to better utilize the capacity that does exist.

death spiral effect
Continual raising of selling prices in an attempt to recover fixed costs, in spite of successive decreases in demand; generally described as one of the dangers of cost-plus pricing.

As noted above, if the fixed overhead allocation rate were based on expected (budgeted) output, then the cost of unused capacity would be hidden—that is, charged to the units actually produced during the period. To the extent that selling prices are based on indicated costs and budgeted output is less than practical capacity, the use of budgeted output could lead to successively increasing units costs (and, therefore, selling prices) over time, a situation referred to as the **death spiral effect.** In this case, fixed overhead costs get allocated over successively lower output quantities.

When practical capacity is used to calculate the fixed overhead application rate, the cost of unused capacity becomes visible to management through the amount and direction of the production volume variance. To avoid misinterpretations, yet communicate information regarding capacity usage, some companies prefer to report the fixed overhead production volume variance in physical terms only.

---

[6] Given the way costs are applied to outputs under a standard cost system, the fixed overhead production volume variance can also be calculated as Standard fixed overhead rate per unit × (Denominator volume, in units − Actual units produced). In the above example, we would have $120 per unit × (1,000 units − 780 units) = $26,400 underapplied (or $26,400 unfavorable). This approach to calculating the fixed overhead production volume variance would, in fact, be the approach used by a company that produces a single product.

Finally, we note the importance of not placing too much emphasis on individual variances because of the interrelatedness of these performance indicators. For example, a production department in a manufacturing facility can generate a favorable fixed overhead production volume variance by overproducing for the period—that is, producing more units than needed to meet sales demand. Such practice, of course, runs counter to the JIT philosophy. In this case, a financial performance indicator (production volume variance) might be accompanied by one or more nonfinancial performance indicators (e.g., inventory turnover or spoilage/obsolescence rates).

Fixed Overhead Spending (Budget) Variance

Fixed overhead spending variances typically arise when the budget procedure for the organization fails to anticipate or incorporate changes in spending for fixed overhead costs. For example, a budget that inadvertently neglects scheduled raises for factory managers, changes in property taxes on factory buildings and equipment, or purchases of new equipment creates unfavorable spending variances for fixed manufacturing overhead.

Unfavorable fixed overhead spending variances can also result from excessive spending due to improper or inadequate cost controls. Events such as emergency repairs, impromptu replacement of equipment, or the addition of production supervisors for an unscheduled second shift all would result in unfavorable fixed overhead spending variances for the period.

Alternative Analyses of Overhead Variances

In the earlier discussion, we separated the total variable overhead variance and the total fixed overhead variance each into two components. Such an analysis is referred to as a *four-variance analysis of factory overhead.* A general model for performing a four-variance analysis, which combines Exhibits 15.4 and 15.5, is presented in Exhibit 15.6. Exhibit 15.7 (panel 1) provides a four-variance analysis of the total overhead variance for Schmidt Machinery Company for October 2022. Not all companies, however, want or need to analyze factory overhead costs in this level of detail. Furthermore, a company's chart of accounts may not separate total overhead into its fixed and variable components. In the following sections, we discuss alternative, less-detailed ways to analyze overhead variances.

EXHIBIT 15.6
General Model: Four-Variance Analysis of Total Factory Overhead Cost Variance

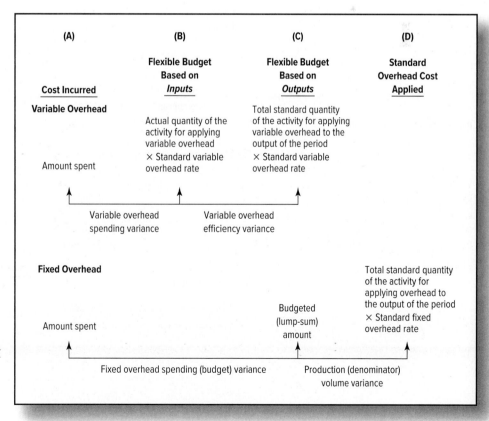

EXHIBIT 15.7   Schmidt Machinery Company, Factory Overhead Variance Analyses, October 2022

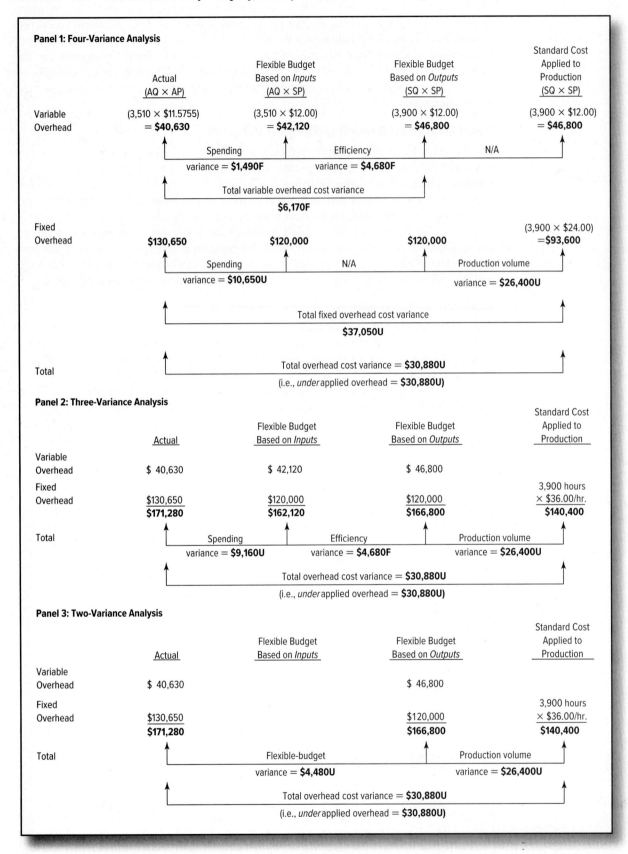

Three-Variance Analysis of the Total Overhead Variance

total overhead spending variance
The difference between actual factory overhead cost incurred during a period and the flexible budget for overhead based on inputs (i.e., based on actual direct labor hours worked during the period).

As shown in panel 2 of Exhibit 15.7, the three-variance analysis of factory overhead separates the total overhead variance into three components: **total overhead spending variance,** variable overhead efficiency variance, and fixed overhead production volume variance. That is, in a three-variance analysis, the variable overhead spending variance and the fixed overhead spending variance are combined into a single overhead variance. Thus, Schmidt's total overhead variance for the period, $30,880U, can be subdivided into a total spending variance, $9,160U ($10,650 unfavorable fixed overhead spending variance + $1,490 favorable variable overhead spending variance); a favorable variable overhead efficiency variance, $4,680; plus an unfavorable production volume variance of $26,400.

Two-Variance Analysis of the Total Overhead Variance

total flexible budget variance for overhead
The difference between the total actual overhead cost for a period and the flexible budget for total overhead based on *output*.

Companies that do not separate fixed from variable overhead costs for product costing purposes perform what is called a two-variance analysis of the total overhead variance. That is, the total overhead variance for the period is broken down into a **total flexible budget variance for overhead** and a production volume variance (which pertains only to the product costing purpose of standard costing, as described earlier). A two-variance breakdown of the total factory overhead variance is represented in the bottom portion of Exhibit 15.7 (panel 3).

For the Schmidt Machinery Company, the total factory overhead cost variance in October, as before, is $30,880U. This variance is broken down as follows:

Total flexible-budget variance for factory overhead

= Total actual factory overhead cost − Flexible budget for total factory overhead based on output (i.e., based on allowed labor hours for units produced)

= (Actual fixed overhead + Actual variable overhead) − [Budgeted fixed overhead + (Standard allowed direct labor hours × Standard variable overhead rate per direct labor hour)]

= ($130,650 + $40,630) − [$120,000 + ($12.00 per direct labor hour × 3,900 direct labor hours)]

= $171,280 − $166,800 = $4,480U

Note that $4,480 is the net amount of the two overhead flexible budget variances contained in Exhibit 14.15: a total *variable* overhead cost variance of $6,170F plus a total *fixed* overhead cost variance of $10,650U.

The second variance in a two-variance breakdown of the total overhead cost variance ($30,880U) is the production volume variance, as follows:

$$\text{Production volume (denominator) variance} = \text{Flexible budget for overhead based on } output - \text{Applied factory overhead}$$

= $166,800 − (3,900 direct labor hours × $36.00 per direct labor hour)

= $26,400U

Note that the production volume variance is exactly the same as the amount calculated under the four-variance and the three-variance breakdowns.

Summary of Overhead Variances

Exhibit 15.7 provides a summary of the various approaches to the analysis of overhead variances. In each case, the total variance to be explained for the Schmidt Machinery Company for October 2022 is $30,880U. The fixed overhead production volume variance ($26,400U) relates to the product costing use of standard costs. That is, this variance will occur only if a company uses a standard cost *system* and defines product cost as full manufacturing cost. The other variances can be calculated regardless of whether the firm uses a standard cost system.

Before leaving this discussion, it is important to point out some alternative terminology for the variances referred to earlier. When standard costs are incorporated formally into the accounting records (i.e., when a standard cost system is used), we have already indicated that the total overhead variance for the period can also be referred to as *total over- or underapplied overhead.* Also, note that the production volume variance is also referred to as the *capacity variance,* the *idle capacity variance,* the *denominator-level variance,*

REAL-WORLD FOCUS   The Key to Cutting Costs? Employees

Flexible budgets and variances are used by management to know what questions need to be asked to reduce costs and improve efficiency. Employees can be a vital part of the question-asking process because of their knowledge and operational experience. Bob Knowling, COO of Ameritech, learned the importance of employee support when he rolled out new performance metrics to motivate employees to cut unneeded overhead costs. However, one employee asked, "Why should I support this?," suspecting that lower-level employees would be among the first to lose their jobs if the company were able to improve efficiency. After Knowling was able to address the issue by announcing there would be no layoffs in the offices that improved on the new metrics, operating costs dropped rapidly as employees brought ideas and ingenuity to the effort. Employee support was key in using variance information and budgets to improve efficiency and lower costs.

Source: B. Fotsch and J. Case, "The Missing Link: Why Lean So Often Fails," *Forbes*, February 19, 2019.

the *output-level overhead variance,* or, simply, the *denominator variance.* The spending variance for variable overhead is sometimes referred to as a *price variance* or a *budget variance.* The total flexible budget variance for overhead (and, by extension, the total flexible budget variance for fixed overhead and the total flexible budget variance for variable overhead) is sometimes referred to as a *controllable variance.* This latter term is more descriptive of the use of standard costs and related variances for cost control purposes. For this reason, the production volume variance is sometimes referred to as the *uncontrollable overhead variance.* The important point is that, unfortunately, this is an area where the terminology is not standard.

Supplementing Financial Results with Nonfinancial Performance Indicators

As is the case for the material presented in Chapter 14, the cost variances covered in this chapter are directed at short-term financial control. These variances are calculated through the use of standard cost information and the use of flexible budgets. The overall intent of these variances is to tell management whether the organization is meeting its short-term financial goals. In the case of for-profit entities, financial control looks at the drivers of short-term profit—for example, the organization's ability to control costs for a given level of sales. Students of accounting should keep in mind, however, that financial control should be viewed as part of a larger and more comprehensive management accounting and control system.

The cost variances we cover here and in Chapter 14 are inherently limited because they relate only to short-term financial performance. As such, they are subject to the same criticisms as any other short-term performance measure. That is, the amount of variance can, at least to some extent, be manipulated in the short run. For example, production volume variances can be decreased by increasing production (thereby absorbing more fixed overhead costs into inventory). Spending variances for fixed overhead items can be affected by managerial choice: cutting discretionary spending on short-term fixed overhead will lead to favorable (short-run) spending variances for fixed overhead costs.

We know, too, that financial measures (such as the cost variances discussed in this chapter and in Chapter 14) don't tell us what is wrong with a process or operation. They can tell us that perhaps something was wrong (because the financial results are not as expected), but we generally need to rely on an accompanying analysis of nonfinancial performance indicators to determine why operations are not proceeding as planned. For example, we might monitor quality; customer-response time; the ability to meet production schedules; employee motivation; employee safety; and the organization's commitment to ethical, social, and environmental commitments. In short, if a subunit of an organization is evaluated solely on the basis of its short-term financial performance (e.g., cost control), employees of that unit may ignore the unmeasured attributes of performance, such as output quality and manufacturing cycle time. It is precisely for this reason that the notion of a balanced scorecard (BSC) as a strategic management system is of value. We introduced the BSC in Chapter 2 and will discuss it in greater detail in Chapter 18.

Finally, there is a question about the appropriate role of financial performance data for operating personnel. Certainly, managers of operating units require periodic financial performance results. At the operational level, however, employees are probably better served with nonfinancial performance data, presumably on as close to a real-time basis as possible. These nonfinancial measures are likely predictors (i.e., leading indicators) of financial performance. In addition, they are expressed in terms that operating personnel can understand. Examples would include actual machine hours consumed per unit produced, actual energy consumption (e.g., kilowatt-hours) per machine hour, amount of indirect materials consumed per unit (or batch) of output, percentage of first-pass yields, defect rates, and so on.

Recording Standard Overhead Costs

Journal Entries and Variances for Overhead Costs

LO 15-3

Record overhead costs and associated standard cost variances.

As noted earlier and in Chapter 14, a standard cost *system* incorporates standard product costs in the formal accounting records [Direct Materials Inventory, Work-in-Process (WIP) Inventory, Finished Goods Inventory, and Cost of Goods Sold (COGS)]. As in the case of direct materials and direct labor, the standard overhead cost of the output of the period is charged to production, while actual overhead costs are recorded separately, in descriptive accounts such as Utilities Payable, Accumulated Depreciation, and Salaries Payable.

Assume that for October 2022, Schmidt Machinery Company incurred the following variable overhead costs: utilities, $30,000, and indirect materials, $10,630. These actual overhead costs would be recorded as incurred, in entries such as the following:

Factory Overhead	40,630	
Utilities Payable		30,000
Indirect Materials Inventory		10,630

At the end of the month (process costing system) or at the completion of one or more jobs (job-order costing system), the WIP Inventory account must be charged for the standard variable overhead cost of the 780 units produced. The standard variable overhead rate is $12 per direct labor hour and the standard number of direct labor hours per unit is 5. Thus, for October 2022 the appropriate journal entry would be:

WIP Inventory [(780 units × 5 hrs. per unit) × $12.00 per hr.]	46,800	
Factory Overhead		46,800

From the preceding two journal entries, we can see that the balance in the Factory Overhead account ($40,630 dr. + $46,800 cr. = $6,170F) is the total variable overhead cost variance for the period (see Exhibit 15.7, panel 1).

Assume now, for simplicity, that the actual fixed factory overhead cost for October 2022 consisted of only two items: $100,000 supervisory salaries plus $30,650 of depreciation charges. The journal entry to record actual fixed factory overhead costs for the month would be:

Factory Overhead	130,650	
Accumulated Depreciation		30,650
Salaries Payable		100,000

Recall that the standard fixed factory overhead rate is $24 per standard direct labor hour allowed or, equivalently, $120 per unit produced (because there are 5 standard direct labor hours per unit produced). The journal entry to charge production with standard fixed factory overhead cost would be:

WIP Inventory [(780 units × 5 hrs. per unit) × $24 per hr.]	93,600	
Factory Overhead		93,600

Similar to entries we made in Chapter 14 for direct materials and direct labor, we would then use the following journal entry to transfer the standard overhead cost of completed production from WIP Inventory to Finished Goods Inventory:

Finished Goods Inventory ($180 per unit × 780 units)	140,400	
WIP Inventory		140,400

After these entries are posted to the ledger, the Factory Overhead account contains the net overhead balance for the period, $30,880 debit (i.e., net unfavorable variance). The component variances calculated using one of the approaches described earlier could be calculated at this point and used to close out the $30,880 balance in the Factory Overhead account.

Assume that Schmidt Machinery Company uses the four-variance approach for overhead analysis. The appropriate journal entry to simultaneously close out the balance in the Factory Overhead account ($30,880 debit) and record the four standard overhead cost variances for October 2022 (see Panel 1, Exhibit 15.7) would be as follows:

Production Volume Variance	26,400	
Fixed Overhead Spending Variance	10,650	
Factory Overhead		30,880
Variable Overhead Spending Variance		1,490
Variable Overhead Efficiency Variance		4,680

End-of-Period Disposition of Variances

LO 15-4

Dispose of standard cost variances at the end of a period.

Variance Disposition

For interim purposes (e.g., preparation of monthly or quarterly financial statements), the standard cost variances calculated in this chapter and in Chapter 14 are typically not disposed of. That is, the variance accounts are carried forward on the balance sheet under the assumption that, over the course of the year, favorable and unfavorable interim variances will offset one another. If interim financial statements are prepared, the cost variances can be shown in a temporary (i.e., holding) account on the balance sheet awaiting ultimate disposition at the end of the year.

At the end of the year, the appropriate treatment for standard cost variances depends on the size (materiality) of the net variance. Assume, for example, that variance data for Schmidt Machinery from Chapters 14 and 15 relate to the fiscal year, not just the month of October. These cost variances are as follows:

Variance	Source	Amount
DM Purchase Price Variance	Exhibit 14.15	$ 4,350U
DM Usage Variance	Exhibit 14.15	10,350U
DL Rate Variance	Exhibit 14.15	7,020U
DL Efficiency Variance	Exhibit 14.15	15,600F
Variable Overhead Spending Variance	Exhibit 15.7, panel 1	1,490F
Variable Overhead Efficiency Variance	Exhibit 15.7, panel 1	4,680F
Fixed Overhead Spending Variance	Exhibit 15.7, panel 1	10,650U
Production Volume Variance	Exhibit 15.7, panel 1	26,400U
Net standard manufacturing cost variance for the year		$37,000U

Net Variance Considered Immaterial

If the net manufacturing cost variance of $37,000U is not considered to be material, then an appropriate treatment at year-end would be to close all variances to Cost of Goods Sold. If the net variance is favorable, then it is closed out by crediting (i.e., reducing) Cost of Goods Sold. If, as in the present case, the net standard cost variance is unfavorable, the Cost of Goods Sold

REAL-WORLD FOCUS Expensing the Cost of Idle Capacity

As indicated in the text, for U.S. financial reporting purposes, FASB ASC 330-10-30 (paragraphs 1–8) provides guidance both for estimating "normal capacity" (which is the required denominator for the fixed overhead rate calculation) and for dealing with abnormal amounts of idle capacity expense, which must be written off to the income statement (and, therefore, not included as part of inventory cost). Abnormally low production could be caused, for example, by significantly reduced product demand, labor and material shortages, and unplanned facility or equipment downtime. In March 2020, the spread of COVID-19 (known as the coronavirus) grounded more than 2,000 aircraft

around the world. This unplanned event represents an example of how idle capacity expenses can become an issue for companies. The rules surrounding this issue also reinforce the importance of distinguishing between cost data for internal (i.e., managerial) purposes and cost data for external (financial reporting) purposes. Accountants should always be aware of the need to consider costs differently depending on the purpose of the calculation.

Source: A. Sider, B. Katz, and D. Cameron, "Global Fear of Flying Spawns Crisis for Airlines," *The Wall Street Journal,* March 9, 2020.

account is debited (i.e., increased) by the amount of the net variance. The following journal entry closes out the net unfavorable variance of $37,000 to Cost of Goods Sold:

Cost of Goods Sold	37,000	
Direct Labor Efficiency Variance	15,600	
Variable Overhead Spending Variance	1,490	
Variable Overhead Efficiency Variance	4,680	
Direct Materials Purchase Price Variance		4,350
Direct Materials Usage Variance		10,350
Direct Labor Rate Variance		7,020
Fixed Overhead Spending Variance		10,650
Production Volume Variance		26,400

Under the assumption that the results for October represent annual results for the Schmidt Machinery Company, its condensed income statement for 2022 is reflected in Exhibit 15.8. As noted earlier, this treatment of the net variance for the period is appropriate when the amount involved is considered immaterial.

Net Variance Considered Material in Amount

If the net manufacturing cost variance is considered material in amount, the net variance should be allocated to the inventory and Cost of Goods Sold (COGS) accounts. This allocation should

EXHIBIT 15.8
Annual Income Statement with Write-off of the Net Manufacturing Cost Variance

SCHMIDT MACHINERY COMPANY		
Income Statement		
For 2022		
Sales (Exhibit 14.4), at standard selling price	$624,000	
Add: Selling price variance (Exhibit 14.4)	15,600F	
Net sales, at actual selling price		$639,600
Cost of goods sold (at standard: 780 units × $520 per unit) (Exhibit 15.2)	$405,600	
Add: Net manufacturing cost variance	37,000U*	
Total cost of goods sold		442,600
Gross margin		$197,000
Selling and administrative expenses ($39,000 variable + $30,000 fixed)**		69,000
Operating income (before disposition of sales volume variance—see Chapter 16)		$128,000

*$50F net variable cost variance (Exhibit 14.8) + $37,050U net fixed cost variance (Exhibit 15.7, panel 1).

**Note that, in this example, the actual variable selling and administrative expenses per unit equaled the standard cost ($50 per unit) and the actual fixed selling and administrative expenses for the period equaled the budgeted amount, $30,000. That is, there were no cost variances for selling and administrative expenses. See Exhibits 14.8 and 14.15 (variable selling and administrative cost variance = $0) and Exhibit 14.15 (fixed selling and administrative cost variance = $0).

REAL-WORLD FOCUS   Technology Is Key to Nonprofit Success

Since 2007, nonprofit jobs have grown four times faster than for-profit jobs in the U.S., currently employing about 1 in 10 in the private workforce. This growth brings heightened interest in how nonprofits manage the money they receive. A common metric for that interest is a nonprofit's *overhead ratio,* or the percentage of its budget that is committed to operating expenses rather than going directly to the nonprofit's primary cause. Staying at or below a target overhead ratio (a common benchmark is 10%) is essential for the continued support of donors, who want to see the maximum amount of their contributions dedicated to the organization's core mission.

While striving to cut costs so as to be more efficient, many nonprofits are simultaneously making larger investments in technology for the same purpose. Although technology investments may cause unfavorable variances in the short run, the increased efficiencies made possible (through better use of data, team management, and work scaling) can reduce operating expenses and allow more of the contributed funds to be used for core organizational purposes. Managers of these nonprofits are willing to increase spending to drive down expenses in the near future, hoping to give more to their cause in the end.

Source: M. Duva, "Technology Improves Nonprofit Sector Growth," *Forbes,* November 5, 2019.

be based on the relative amount of this period's standard cost in the end-of-period balance of each affected account. This means that the direct materials price variance from Chapter 14 will be apportioned to five accounts—Direct Materials Inventory, Materials Usage Variance, WIP Inventory, Finished Goods Inventory, and COGS—based on the amount of this period's standard direct materials cost in each account at the end of the period. The direct materials usage variance would be allocated only to WIP Inventory, Finished Goods Inventory, and COGS. This is because the direct materials usage variance occurs *after* direct materials are issued to production.

Note that, as a practical matter, some companies allocate the price variance only to the ending inventory and COGS accounts.

Any direct labor variances and variable overhead variances would be allocated to WIP Inventory, Finished Goods Inventory, and COGS on the basis of this period's standard direct labor and standard variable overhead costs, respectively, in these accounts at year-end. The fixed overhead spending variance should be allocated to four accounts: WIP Inventory, Finished Goods Inventory, COGS, and the Production Volume Variance. The production volume variance, if allocated, would then be apportioned among WIP Inventory, Finished Goods Inventory, and COGS.

Some companies take a simpler approach to the variance allocation decision. For example, they may use the total end-of-period account balances, rather than this period's standard cost, in each end-of-period account to allocate the net manufacturing cost variance. Other companies, in particular those that have minimal ending inventories, choose to write off the net variance against COGS, regardless of its size, because most of the variance would be allocated to COGS anyway. Under this approach, the error of not allocating a portion of the variance to inventories, as well as COGS, is minimal.

Note, however, that some accountants argue that any variance that results from inefficiencies that could have—in the judgment of management—been avoided, regardless of amount, should be written off against COGS rather than carried forward on the balance sheet, as is the case with the proration method discussed below. Not to do this implies that asset values reflected on the balance sheet (i.e., inventories) necessarily contain the cost of inefficiencies, a situation that some accountants would dismiss as improper.

Finally, note that FASB ASC 330-10-30 requires that for U.S. external reporting purposes, any abnormal amount of "idle capacity cost" (which we have called the fixed overhead production volume variance) must be written off on the current period's income statement. One implication of this reporting requirement is that the amount of fixed overhead allocated to each unit of production is not increased as a consequence of abnormally low production or an idle plant.

The Effects of Denominator Level Choice on Full Costing Income

earnings management
The manipulation of reported income.

Before leaving this section, we discuss one additional topic, principally because it deals with the issue of **earnings management** through the selection of the denominator level used to establish the fixed overhead application rate. We noted earlier in this chapter that alternative denominator volume levels lead to different (fixed) overhead application rates, which in turn lead to different product costs and, ultimately, to different levels of the fixed overhead production volume variance. The accounting disposition of the production volume variance essentially provides management with an opportunity to smooth, or manage, income as determined under full costing.

Under full (i.e., absorption) costing, a portion of fixed manufacturing overhead costs are either absorbed into or released from inventory, depending on the relationship between production volume and sales volume during the period. For example, for a given level of sales, the production of extra units shifts fixed overhead costs to the balance sheet (inventory) so that reported profit increases with increases in production. The opposite is true if inventory is decreasing. For a given level of sales, decreases in production require not only this period's fixed overhead to be released as an expense on the income statement; they also imply the release of some previously capitalized fixed overhead costs (from inventory). Thus, for a given level of sales, full costing income decreases as production decreases.

Note, however, a key point: The amount of fixed overhead costs absorbed or released is affected by the denominator level chosen for the predetermined overhead rate. Thus, the effect of a change in inventory can be intensified or reduced based on how the fixed overhead production volume variance is disposed of at the end of the period. Specifically, this ability to affect reported income is confined to the situation where the production volume variance is written off entirely to cost of goods sold (COGS), as follows:

- If inventory is *increasing,* choosing a *lower* denominator volume level will *enhance* the increase in full costing income due to the deferral of fixed overhead in inventory.
- If inventory is *decreasing,* choosing a *higher* denominator level will *moderate* the decrease in full costing income due to the release of fixed overhead into COGS.

Thus, it is through the interaction of how the fixed overhead rate is set and how the resulting production volume variance is accounted for that provides management an opportunity to manage earnings under full costing. The above points suggest that managers can increase short-run operating income by (1) choosing larger denominator levels if they expect inventory to decrease or (2) choosing smaller denominator levels if they expect inventory to increase. Note, however, that if the fixed overhead production volume variance is prorated based on the units creating the variance, then the denominator-level choice has no effect on full costing income. This is because prorating this variance effectively changes the budgeted overhead application rate to the actual overhead application rate.

Standard Costs in Service Organizations

LO 15-5

Apply standard costs in service organizations.

As noted in Chapter 14, a standard cost system facilitates planning (i.e., budget preparation) and short-term financial control (through standard cost variance analysis) that helps managers make decisions about product pricing and resource management. These benefits, however, are not limited to manufacturing companies. Service organizations can also benefit from the use of standard cost systems.

Most costs in a service organization are short-term fixed costs (i.e., they are capacity-related costs). The bulk of labor costs are for professional personnel who usually are paid a monthly salary. Variations from one period to the next for salaried personnel should be small or nonexistent. Other overhead costs for these organizations often consist of expenses related to facilities and equipment and are, therefore, also fixed in the short run. Other service-sector companies have minimal labor costs relative to capacity-related costs. Examples include the airline industry, the shipping industry, and much of the telecommunications industry. The predominance of capacity-related costs for such companies increases the importance of monitoring fixed cost spending variances and idle capacity variances.

It is also important to remember that service organizations use varied measures of output. As shown in Exhibit 15.9, hospitals measure output using patient days, colleges and universities measure output using credit hour production, and so on. These are certainly relevant measures, but they are usually imperfect indicators of service organization output. The amount and type of work performed by a service organization to complete an output unit often

EXHIBIT 15.9
Output Measures for Selected Service Organizations

Organization	Output Measure
Airline	Revenue-producing passenger miles
Hospital	Patient days
Hotel	Occupancy rate or number of guests
Accounting, legal, and consulting firms	Professional staff hours
Colleges and universities	Credit hours
Primary and secondary schools	Number of students

vary from one client to the next or from one patient day to another. For example, the amounts and types of work performed for two patients with identical heart diseases during their 10-day stays can be vastly different, although the number of patient days and the treated illnesses are the same. Not all patient days are equal.

Differences in the resources that are consumed to produce a unit of output reduce the information about the efficiency and cost of service organization operations that a traditional standard cost system can provide. Service organizations are therefore more likely to benefit from designing their standard costing systems to better reflect how resource consumption drives costs. As discussed in Chapter 5 and in the following section of this chapter, activity-based costing (ABC) can provide a more accurate mapping of resources to costs than simple volume-based costing systems, and can be particularly valuable for service organizations.

Overhead Cost Variances in Traditional ABC Systems

LO 15-6

Analyze overhead variances in a traditional (i.e., non-time-driven) activity-based costing system.

The business environment has evolved over the last few decades, and many new management techniques have been developed during this period to emphasize continuous improvement, total quality management, and managing activities rather than cost. These emphases have changed product costing, strategic and operational decisions, and cost determination methods, as discussed in the preceding chapters. They also influence the ways in which many firms use standard cost systems as management tools, including the preparation of flexible budgets, the selection of performance evaluation criteria, and the implications of reported variances.

ABC-Based Flexible Budgets for Control

Because a number of different activities influence factory overhead costs, the accountant needs to carefully select the activity measure, or measures, that will be used to construct the flexible budget for control purposes. The Schmidt Machinery Company, as illustrated thus far in the chapter, uses a single, volume-based activity measure (direct labor hours) for allocating overhead costs to outputs and for determining standard cost variances for control purposes.

As described in Chapter 5, more modern cost systems, such as activity-based costing (ABC), apply overhead costs to outputs on the basis of the activities performed for each product. That is, ABC attempts to assign costs to products on the basis of the resource consumption of each output. To accomplish this, ABC systems use a broader set of activity measures, both volume-related and non-volume-related, in the cost allocation process.

Costs can be classified using a hierarchical framework that reflects the level at which an activity takes place.[7] The framework classifies manufacturing support costs as unit-level, batch-level, product-level, or facility-level costs. Unit-level costs are those that increase or decrease as more units are produced; thus, unit-level measures relate to output volume and include machine hours, direct labor hours, units of output, and units of raw materials. Batch-level costs are those that increase or decrease as batches are produced or ordered (i.e., regardless of whether many or few units are produced or ordered in a batch). Batch-level activity measures include the number of production setups, the number of times materials and parts are moved during the manufacturing process, and the number of receipts of materials. Product-level costs are those that increase or decrease with the number of products (rather

---

[7] R. Cooper, "Cost Classification in Unit-Based and Activity-Based Manufacturing Cost Systems," *Journal of Cost Management for the Manufacturing Industry,* Fall 1990, pp. 4–14. The use of these cost classifications results in what can be considered "traditional" ABC systems.

than units or batches) that are produced. Product-level activity measures typically relate to engineering support activities and can include things such as the number of products, the number of processes, the number of engineering change orders (ECOs), and the number of schedule changes. At the top of the cost hierarchy are facility-level costs, which are related to the capacity or ability to produce, rather than the variety of outputs, the number of batches produced, or the volume of output.

Exhibit 15.10 illustrates a traditional flexible budget prepared for a company that applies factory overhead cost to outputs on the basis of standard direct labor hours, similar in nature to the example discussed thus far in this chapter. The master budget in this exhibit is based on a planned output of 3,000 units for the period (1,500 standard direct labor hours). The flexible budget is based on the actual output of the period, 2,000 units (or, equivalently, 1,000 standard direct labor hours). The company in this example spent 1,200 direct labor hours to manufacture the 2,000 units. Exhibit 15.11 shows a typical financial report for manufacturing costs incurred during the period.

In contrast, Exhibit 15.12 illustrates a flexible budget for the period prepared under traditional (i.e., non-time-driven) ABC. This representation specifies that manufacturing costs are assigned to outputs on the basis of multiple activity measures (or drivers). In the present example, three different volume-related drivers are used (units produced, direct labor hours, and machine hours) as well as one non-volume-related driver (number of production setups). Note that there is a single facility-level cost, insurance, that essentially has no well-defined driver. Because this cost is not related to volume of output, number of batches, or number of products, it is allocated to products using a systematic, but essentially arbitrary, method, such as square feet in the factory devoted to the production of each product.

Compared to the simpler control budget presented in Exhibit 15.10, the ABC-based flexible budget presented in Exhibit 15.12 provides a more accurate representation of the manufacturing costs that should have been incurred for the production of 2,000 units. A financial performance report for the period, based on the ABC flexible budget, is presented in Exhibit 15.13.

EXHIBIT 15.10   **Master Budget and Traditional Flexible Budget for Control**

Cost Item	Variable	Fixed	Flexible Budget for 2,000 Units (1,000 standard direct labor hours)	Master Budget for 3,000 Units (1,500 standard direct labor hours)
Direct materials	$20 per unit		$ 40,000	$ 60,000
Direct labor	$30 per direct labor hour		30,000	45,000
Indirect materials	$2 per direct labor hour		2,000	3,000
Repair and maintenance	$5 per direct labor hour		5,000	7,500
Receiving		$ 5,000	5,000	5,000
Insurance		30,000	30,000	30,000
Setup		75,000	75,000	75,000
Total			$187,000	$225,500

EXHIBIT 15.11
Traditional Financial Performance Report

	Actual Cost	Flexible Budget Based on Output	Flexible-Budget Variance
Direct materials	$ 50,000	$ 40,000	$10,000U
Direct labor	36,000	30,000	6,000U
Indirect materials	3,000	2,000	1,000U
Repair and maintenance	6,500	5,000	1,500U
Receiving	3,000	5,000	2,000F
Insurance	30,000	30,000	—
Setup	50,000	75,000	25,000F
Total	$178,500	$187,000	$ 8,500F

The total manufacturing cost flexible budget variance for the period, based on the approach illustrated earlier in the chapter, is $8,500 favorable (Exhibit 15.11). In contrast, the ABC approach yields a $17,000 unfavorable variance for the same period (Exhibit 15.13). Exhibit 15.14 compares these short-run financial performance reports.

Exhibit 15.14 demonstrates that cost variances identified using a traditional approach (single activity for applying factory overhead) can be misleading. Substantial differences are

EXHIBIT 15.12   Representation of Manufacturing Costs under a Traditional ABC System

Data	Activity Measure	Cost Function Variable	Fixed	Flexible (Control) Budget	Master Budget
Operating Data					
Output	Number of units			2,000 units	3,000 units
Standard direct labor hours				1,000 hours	1,500 hours
Standard machine hours				300,000 hours	450,000 hours
Number of setups				2 setups	3 setups
Cost Data					
Direct materials	Number of units	$20 per unit	—	$ 40,000	$ 60,000
Direct labor	Direct labor hours	$30 per hour, 0.5 hour per unit	—	30,000	45,000
Indirect materials	Direct labor hours	$2 per direct labor hour	—	2,000	3,000
Repair and maintenance	Machine hours	$0.01 per machine hour	$ 3,000	6,000	7,500
Receiving	Number of setups	$1,500 per setup	500	3,500	5,000
Setup	Number of setups	$25,000 per setup	—	50,000	75,000
Insurance	Facility-level		$30,000	30,000	30,000
Total				$161,500	$225,500

EXHIBIT 15.13   Financial Performance Report Using a Traditional (i.e., Non-Time-Driven) ABC Model

	Cost Incurred		Flexible (Control) Budget	Flexible Budget Variance
Direct materials	$ 50,000	$ 40,000	(2,000 units × $20 per unit)	$10,000U
Direct labor	36,000	30,000	(2,000 units × 0.5 labor hour per unit × $30 per labor hour)	6,000U
Indirect materials	3,000	2,000	(1,000 labor hours × $2 per labor hour)	1,000U
Repair and maintenance	6,500	6,000	[(300,000 machine hours × $0.01 per machine hour) + $3,000]	500U
Receiving	3,000	3,500	[(2 setups × $1,500 per setup) + $500]	500F
Insurance	30,000	30,000	($30,000 per period)	—
Setup	50,000	50,000	(2 setups × $25,000 per setup)	—
Total	$178,500	$ 161,500		$17,000U

EXHIBIT 15.14
Financial Performance Reports: Comparison of Traditional Costing and ABC

	Variance		
	Traditional	Activity-Based	Difference
Direct materials	$10,000U	$10,000U	—
Direct labor	6,000U	6,000U	—
Indirect materials	1,000U	1,000U	—
Repair and maintenance	1,500U	500U	$ 1,000
Receiving	2,000F	500F	1,500
Insurance	—	—	—
Setup	25,000F	—	25,000
Total	$ 8,500F	$17,000U	$25,500

found in variances for repair and maintenance, receiving, and setups. The traditional costing approach in our example considers repair and maintenance as a cost that varies with direct labor hours. In contrast, the ABC approach identifies repair and maintenance as a mixed cost with the variable portion of the cost varying with machine hours. As a result, the cost variance for repair and maintenance decreases from $1,500 unfavorable to $500 unfavorable. The traditional costing approach considers both receiving and setups as fixed costs, while the ABC approach classifies receiving as having both a fixed and a (batch-related) variable component, and setup costs as variable in response to number of setups (a batch-level activity). As illustrated in Exhibit 15.14, the difference in the net variance between these two approaches is $25,500.

Flexible Budget Analysis under Traditional ABC When There Is a Standard Batch Size for Production Activity

When production occurs in a standard (i.e., predetermined) batch size, the accountant can modify the preceding traditional ABC analysis to provide more detailed information regarding the cause of any observed overhead cost variances. In the sections below, we discuss these procedures within the context of production-related setup costs.

Fixed Setup Costs in a Traditional ABC System

The short-term fixed cost component of setup costs is controlled using the same procedures discussed previously in this chapter. That is, the difference between actual fixed setup costs and budgeted fixed setup costs is called a *spending* (or *flexible budget*) *variance.* And the difference between the fixed setup costs allocated to production and budgeted fixed setup costs is called a *production volume variance.* The only complicating factor in terms of calculating the latter is the possible need to convert actual units produced to standard number of batches. This is necessary only when setup-related support costs are allocated on the basis of *setup hours* (not number of setups). We make this conversion by dividing actual output by the standard (i.e., budgeted or planned) batch size.

Variable Setup Costs in a Traditional ABC System

If output is produced in a standard batch size, we must first convert (as we did above for fixed setup-related costs) the actual output of the period to number of standard batches allowed. We then convert this to the standard allowed setup hours. This latter figure, when multiplied by the standard variable setup cost per setup hour gives us the flexible budget for variable setup overhead costs. As we did earlier in the chapter, we then define the total flexible budget variance for variable setup overhead cost as the difference between actual variable setup costs and the flexible budget for variable setup overhead costs. Finally, this total flexible budget variance is decomposed into a *spending variance* and an *efficiency variance* using the procedures discussed earlier.

Interpretation of Setup-Related Standard Cost Variances

Management accountants can add value to their organization by accompanying cost-variance data with plausible explanations for these variances. This holds true regardless of whether the organization is using a traditional cost system or a traditional ABC system.

Fixed spending variances for setup activities are likely to be relatively small but could arise if new setup equipment is leased or if the leasing charge actually incurred on setup equipment is different from the planned amount. They might also occur if salaries paid to supervisors or engineers allocated to setup activity are different from those planned. The production volume variance for fixed setup costs can be viewed roughly as a measure of capacity utilization. One limitation of this interpretation, however, is the fact that it does not consider the income effect of reduced output. That is, lower-than-anticipated output volume could have been sold at a higher-than-budgeted selling price, thereby resulting in a net increase to short-term operating profit.

The *variable setup spending variance* exists because the actual variable cost per setup hour is different from the budgeted cost per setup hour. The interpretation of this variance follows the interpretation discussed earlier in this chapter. That is, this variance is partly due to the fact that the actual quantity of individual resources (e.g., energy) per setup hour is different than planned and/or the prices paid for these items are different from planned amounts. The *variable setup efficiency variance* is due to the actual number of setup hours, for the actual output of the period, being different from the standard setup hours allowed. This variance could be due to batch size being different from the planned size and/or a different number of setup hours per batch compared with standard.

Extension of ABC Analysis: GPK and RCA

Grenzplankostenrechnung (GPK) and **resource consumption accounting (RCA)** are two other sophisticated cost management systems that are being proposed as alternatives to ABC systems. Both GPK and RCA can be used to allocate indirect (i.e., support) costs across the value chain. Both of these systems rely on a significant number of cost centers and cost-allocation pools—far more than are typically found in an ABC system. As such, both GPK and RCA are usually paired with an **enterprise resource planning (ERP)** system that tracks and maintains detailed information regarding resources and activities associated with business processes.

GPK is a German cost management system that attempts to establish a strong relationship between resources consumed and the appropriate cost driver. Notably, GPK distinguishes between flexible and short-term fixed (capacity-related) resources. In contrast, ABC systems typically embrace a long-term or strategic time horizon. Thus, GPK is proposed as a tool for managing short-run financial performance. RCA, on the other hand, can loosely be thought of as a combination of ABC and GPK. Therefore, it is a mix of activity-based and direct assignment based on resource consumption. Proponents of RCA maintain that RCA provides increased product-cost accuracy because it only includes the cost of resources used.

Implementation results for GPK and RCA to date suggest that these systems are more effective in large organizations that have highly routine and repetitive operations. Such a context would seem conducive to the construction of the many resource cost pools characteristic of GPK and RCA. It will be interesting to see whether these systems for short-term planning and cost control will gain acceptance in the United States. As indicated in Chapter 5, some U.S. companies have been reluctant to implement a traditional ABC system because of the perceived complexity. GPK and RCA systems would seem to be even more complex. Thus, additional experimentation in the United States is needed before we are able to draw a conclusion regarding the role of these systems. It may be the case that there is room for both ABC systems and more detailed systems such as GPK and RCA. The former may be used for short-term financial control, while the latter may yield relevant information for strategic decision making.

Investigation of Variances

Identifying and reporting cost variances are the first steps in reducing variances and improving financial performance. Not all variances call for investigation and corrective action, however. In general, the proper response to a variance depends on the causes and the controllability of the variance.

Causes and Controllability

The causes and the controllability of variances fall into two categories: random and systematic. **Random variances** are beyond the control of operators, either technically or financially. Many standards are point estimates of long-term average performance. Small variances in either direction occur in operations, and firms usually cannot benefit from investigating or responding to them. For example, prices of goods or services acquired in open markets fluctuate with, among other factors, supply and demand at the time of acquisition and the amount of time allowed to acquire the goods or services. These variances are essentially random and require no management action.

Systematic variances, by contrast, are persistent and are likely to recur until corrected. They usually are controllable by management or can be eliminated or reduced through actions of management. Systematic variances that are material in amount require prompt corrective action. Among causes for systematic variances are errors in prediction, modeling,

---

Grenzplankostenrechnung (GPK)
Detailed German cost accounting system, roughly translated as *flexible standard costing* or *Flexible Analytic Cost Planning and Accounting;* an extension of ABC.

resource consumption accounting (RCA)
A comprehensive and fully integrated management accounting approach that provides management with decision support information based on an operational view of the organization.

enterprise resource planning (ERP)
The process by which a company manages and integrates key business processes (e.g., planning, purchasing, inventory, sales, marketing, finance, and human resources).

LO 15-7
Understand decision rules that can be used to guide the variance investigation decision.

random variances
Variances beyond the control of management, either technically or financially.

systematic variances
Variances that, until corrected, are likely to recur; also called *nonrandom variances.*

EXHIBIT 15.15 **Variance Causes and Corrective Actions**

Controllability	Cause	Corrective Action	Example
Uncontrollable (random)	Random error	None	Overtime wages paid to make up time lost by employees ill with the flu Materials lost in a fire
Controllable (systematic)	Prediction error	Modify standard-setting processes	Materials prices increase faster than expected
	Modeling error	Revise model or modeling process	Failure to consider learning-curve effect in estimating product costs Not allowing for normal materials lost
	Measurement error	Adjust accounting procedure	Bonus attributed to the period paid, not in the period earned Costs assigned to wrong jobs
	Implementation error	Take proper actions to correct the causes	Failure to provide proper training for the task

measurement, and implementation. Each of these factors has its own implications regarding the need for further investigation or proper managerial action to correct the variance. Exhibit 15.15 classifies variances according to controllability, causes, and corrective action.

prediction error
A deviation from a standard because of an inaccurate estimation of the amounts for variables used in the standard-setting process.

Prediction errors result from inaccurate estimation of the variable amounts included in the standard-setting process. For example, management expected a 5% price increase for a direct material when the price increased 10%, or it expected to have adequate $25 per hour workers available when a shortage forced the firm to hire workers at $35 per hour.

modeling error
A deviation from the standard because of the failure to include all relevant variables or because of the inclusion of wrong or irrelevant variables in the standard-setting process.

Modeling errors result from failing to include all relevant variables or from including wrong or irrelevant variables in the standard-setting process. For example, a modeling error occurs when a firm uses the production rate of experienced workers as a standard, although most of its workers are new hires with little or no experience. The unfavorable direct labor efficiency variance that the firm experiences is a result of a modeling error, not of inefficient operations. The standard of making 100 gallons of output from every 100 gallons of input material is a modeling error when the manufacturing process has a 5% normal evaporation rate. Corrective actions for both prediction and modeling errors require the firm to change its standard and the standard-setting process.

measurement errors
Incorrect numbers resulting from improper or inaccurate accounting systems or procedures.

Measurement errors are incorrect numbers resulting from improper or inaccurate accounting systems or procedures. Including bonuses for extraordinary productivity as a cost of the period in which the bonuses are paid rather than the period in which they are earned is a measurement error. Charging overhead incurred for setups based on direct labor hours rather than the number of setups is a measurement error. Corrective actions for measurement errors include redesigning the firm's accounting system or procedures.

implementation error
A deviation from standard due to operator errors.

Implementation errors are deviations from the standard due to operator errors. Unfavorable materials usage variances from using materials of lesser quality than those specified by the standard are implementation errors. The direct labor rate or efficiency variance in an operation that assigned workers with a different skill level than the one called for in the standard is an implementation error. Setting a cutting machine to cut tubes in lengths of 2 feet 9.7 inches, instead of 2 feet 10 inches as required, is an implementation error.

Some implementation errors are temporary and disappear in subsequent periods in the normal course of operations. Other implementation errors could be persistent and reappear until the firm takes proper corrective action. An incorrectly set cutting machine continues to manufacture products with wrong lengths until the problem is corrected. Use of wrong or excessive materials in production, on the other hand, might occur in one or only a few production runs.

Role of Control Charts

Managers and employees can use control charts to identify random versus systematic variances. A control chart plots measures of an activity or event over time; this widely used tool helps managers identify out-of-control variances. A control chart has a horizontal axis, a vertical axis, a horizontal line at the level of the desirable characteristic, and one or two additional horizontal lines for the allowable range of variation. The horizontal axis represents time intervals, batch numbers, or production runs. The vertical line denotes scales for the characteristic of interest, such as the amount of the cost variance. Upper and lower limits indicate the allowable range of the variance. Variances within these limits are deemed random and no further action is needed unless a pattern emerges.

It is management's responsibility to set upper and lower control limits in control charts, ideally based on a statistical analysis of past data. When the control limits are established using a statistical procedure, the chart is called a **statistical control chart.** See Chapter 17 for a fuller discussion of the use of control charts.

statistical control charts
Charts that set control limits using a statistical procedure.

Summary

Establishing standard overhead application rates requires the selection of appropriate activity measures. These rates can be determined using relatively simple procedures (e.g., a single, volume-related activity measure, such as number of direct labor hours) or more sophisticated procedures, such as ABC. The resulting standard cost data can be used both for product costing purposes and, through their inclusion in flexible budgets, for control purposes.

For control purposes, actual factory overhead costs (both variable and fixed) are compared to flexible budget costs. The total variable overhead cost variance (also referred to as the total variable overhead flexible budget variance or the total over- or underapplied variable overhead cost) is calculated as the difference between actual variable overhead cost for the period and the flexible budget for variable overhead based on *outputs* (i.e., based on allowed activity for the number of units manufactured during the period). Variable overhead spending and efficiency variances are components of the total variable overhead cost variance.

The total fixed overhead cost variance (also called the total over- or underapplied fixed overhead cost) is calculated as the difference between the actual and the applied fixed overhead for the period. This variance can be decomposed into a fixed overhead spending variance and a production volume variance. The former variance is defined as the difference between the actual fixed factory overhead costs and the budgeted (lump-sum) fixed overhead costs for the period. The fixed overhead production volume variance exists only because of the product costing need to assign a share of fixed factory overhead costs to each unit produced. To do this, the accountant develops a fixed overhead allocation rate, which is defined as budgeted fixed factory overhead cost divided by an assumed level of activity, called the denominator volume. If the denominator volume is defined as practical capacity, then the production volume variance can be thought of as a rough measure of capacity utilization.

If a company uses a standard cost system, it records inventory and Cost of Goods Sold (COGS) amounts at standard cost. In such a system, variances from standard cost are recorded in separate accounts. At the end of the year, the company can dispose of standard cost variances by charging them to COGS. Alternatively, the company can prorate the variances among the COGS, ending Work-in-Process Inventory, and ending Finished Goods Inventory accounts. Generally accepted accounting principles in the United States provide guidance for disposing of fixed overhead production volume variances for external reporting purposes.

Changes in manufacturing environments in recent years have motivated changes in cost systems. Increasingly, companies are using systems with multiple activity measures, both volume-based and non-volume-based. Flexible budgets based on ABC systems provide more accurate data for cost control purposes. The use of practical capacity for establishing ABC rates yields relevant information regarding the existence and cost of unused capacity. This information can be used over time for resource capacity planning. For operational control purposes, financial results such as cost variances should be accompanied by relevant nonfinancial performance indicators.

Whether to investigate a particular variance is a function of the identified cause of the variance. Causes of variances can be random or systematic. The former generally require no follow-up, while the latter require some type of intervention by managers. Statistical control charts can be used to isolate random versus nonrandom variances.

Variance Investigation under Uncertainty Supplement (online)

A special online supplement that deals with the variance investigation decision under uncertainty is available in Connect. *This supplement provides advanced coverage of the variance investigation decision and is subdivided into three major parts:* **payoff tables** *[i.e., the cost of alternative management actions (investigate vs. do not investigate the cause of an observed variance) under alternative states of nature (variance is random vs. systematic)],* **indifference probability** *(i.e., the probability regarding states of nature that would make management indifferent between investigating vs. not investigating the cause of an observed variance), and* **the expected value of perfect information** *(EVPI) (i.e., the maximum amount a rational decision maker would be willing to pay for "perfect information" regarding whether the underlying process is in control or out of control). A separate Self-Study Problem and three end-of-chapter assignments covering the variance investigation decision under uncertainty are also available in* Connect.

Key Terms

budgeted capacity utilization, *636*
death spiral effect, *638*
denominator activity level, *636*
denominator volume, *636*
earnings management, *646*
enterprise resource planning (ERP), *652*
FASB ASC 330-10-30, *636*
fixed overhead application rate, *636*
fixed overhead production volume variance, *637*
fixed overhead spending (budget) variance, *638*

Grenzplankostenrechnung (GPK), *652*
implementation error, *653*
measurement errors, *653*
modeling error, *653*
normal capacity, *636*
practical capacity, *636*
prediction error, *653*
random variances, *652*
resource capacity planning, *637*
resource consumption accounting (RCA), *652*
statistical control charts, *654*
systematic variances, *652*

theoretical capacity, *636*
total fixed overhead variance, *634*
total flexible budget variance for overhead, *641*
total overhead spending variance, *641*
total variable overhead cost variance, *632*
variable overhead efficiency variance, *633*
variable overhead spending variance, *633*

Comments on Cost Management in Action

Strategic Importance of Capacity Utilization: The U.S. Auto Industry

An automaker should first recognize that, from the manufacturing side, the effect of economic nationalism is likely to push the company to a higher level of operating leverage (i.e., the relative amount of fixed costs in the company's cost structure). This is because the reduction in imports of foreign-made parts and subassemblies into the United States, which is now a variable cost, would be transformed into a fixed cost as the company ramps up production capacity in the United States to manufacture those parts. Given uncertainty about demand for auto sales, it is likely that the company had previously determined a desired level of operating leverage to balance fixed and variable costs in the longer term. Because the effect of economic nationalism is to move the company to a higher level of operating leverage, the prudent thing would be for the company to take steps to readjust leverage to the desired lower level by, in some fashion, converting other fixed costs to variable costs. This could be done, for example, by domestically sourcing parts that were previously purchased from abroad—that is, developing new domestic suppliers. The result would be that a previously variable cost would remain a variable cost; the company would not invest in plant and equipment to secure the desired parts, thus avoiding additional fixed costs and higher operating leverage.

Other options for reducing fixed costs could also be considered. For example, the automaker might look for ways to outsource (to a domestic supplier) a portion of current in-house manufacturing costs. Note that any attempt to outsource manufacturing to a domestic supplier will surely reduce the automaker's employment while increasing employment at its domestic suppliers. This movement in employment is likely to be challenged by the automaker's current workforce and perhaps also by those who support economic nationalism.

The topics of cost structure, operating leverage, and cost/profit planning are covered comprehensively in Chapter 9.

Sources: J. Eckstein, "How Ford Makes Money," *Investopedia,* October 6, 2019 (available at **www.investopedia.com/articles/markets/082115/how-ford-makes-money.asp**); Neil E. Boudette, "Auto Makers Dare to Boost Capacity: North American Factories Will Build One Million More Cars a Year," *The Wall Street Journal,* January 14, 2014 (available at **http://online.wsj.com/news/articles/SB10001424052702304549504579318952857858762**).

Self-Study Problem

(For answer, please see Solution.)

Analysis of the Total Overhead Cost Variance

Simpson Manufacturing has the following standard cost sheet for one of its products:

		Total
Direct materials	5 pounds at $2 per pound	$ 10
Direct labor	2 hours at $25 per hour	50
Variable factory overhead	2 hours at $5 per hour	10
Fixed factory overhead	2 hours at $20 per hour	40
Cost per unit		$110

The company uses a standard cost system and applies factory overhead cost based on direct labor hours and determines the factory overhead rate based on a practical capacity of 400 units of the product. Simpson has the following actual operating results for the year just completed:

Units manufactured	360	
Direct materials purchased and used	1,800 pounds	$19,800
Direct labor incurred	750 hours	20,250
Variable factory overhead incurred		4,800
Fixed factory overhead incurred		15,800

Before closing the periodic accounts, the (standard cost) entries in selected accounts follow:

Account	Debit (total)	Credit (total)
Work-in-Process Inventory	$153,000	$134,640
Finished Goods Inventory	134,640	111,690
Cost of Goods Sold	111,690	

Required

1. Determine for the period the following items:
   a. Flexible budget for variable factory overhead cost based on output for the period.
   b. Total variable overhead cost applied to production during the period.
   c. Total budgeted fixed factory overhead cost.
   d. Total fixed factory overhead cost applied to production during the period.
2. Compute the following factory overhead cost variances using a four-variance analysis:
   a. Total variable overhead cost variance.
   b. Variable overhead spending variance.
   c. Variable overhead efficiency variance.
   d. Total underapplied or overapplied variable overhead.
   e. Fixed overhead spending variance.
   f. Fixed overhead production volume variance.
   g. Total fixed overhead cost variance.
   h. Total underapplied or overapplied fixed overhead.
3. Compute the following factory overhead cost variances using three-variance analysis:
   a. Overhead spending variance.
   b. Overhead efficiency variance.
   c. Fixed overhead production volume variance.
4. Compute the total overhead flexible budget variance and the fixed overhead production volume variance using a two-variance analysis.
5. Using a single overhead account (e.g., Factory Overhead), make proper journal entries for:
   a. Incurrence of factory overhead costs.
   b. Application of factory overhead costs to production.
   c. Identification of overhead variances assuming that the firm uses the four-variance analysis identified in requirement 2.

    d. Close all factory overhead cost items and their variances of the period if:

        (1) The firm closes all variances to the Cost of Goods Sold account.

        (2) The firm prorates variances to the inventory accounts and the Cost of Goods Sold account.

The Student Resources section of Connect includes video tutorials for the Self-Study Problems.

Questions

15-1 "As long as the total actual factory overhead cost is not significantly different from the total standard applied factory overhead cost for the period, there is no need to conduct further analyses of the factory overhead variance." Do you agree? Why or why not?

15-2 What is the difference between the applied variable overhead cost and the total variable overhead cost in the flexible budget? What is the difference between the applied factory overhead cost and the total flexible budget cost for fixed overhead?

15-3 List causes that could lead to a variable overhead spending variance.

15-4 List causes that could lead to a variable overhead efficiency variance.

15-5 List causes that could lead to a fixed overhead spending variance.

15-6 List causes that could lead to a fixed overhead production volume variance.

15-7 Would the choice of denominator level affect the amount of the fixed factory overhead budget variance? Fixed overhead production volume variance? Explain.

15-8 What are the justifications for using practical capacity as the denominator volume when calculating the fixed overhead application rate?

15-9 Why do some firms choose to use a two-variance analysis instead of a three-variance or a four-variance analysis of the total overhead cost variance for the period?

15-10 Explain two available treatments for disposing of overhead cost variances at the end of a period.

15-11 What provisions of U.S. GAAP (viz., FASB ASC 330-10-30, previously *SFAS No. 151*—available at **www.fasb.org**) pertain to the issue of end-of-period disposition of overhead cost variances? Be specific.

15-12 What factors should be considered in determining whether to investigate a variance?

15-13 "The direction of a variance (favorable or unfavorable) is irrelevant in decisions regarding whether or not to investigate the variance." Do you agree? Why or why not?

Brief Exercises

[LO 15-2]   **15-14** Sipple Furniture's master budget for the year includes $360,000 for fixed supervisory salaries. Practical capacity, which is used to set the fixed overhead allocation rate, is 500 units per month. Supervisory salaries are expected to be incurred uniformly throughout the year. During August, the company produced 250 units, incurred production supervisory salaries of $29,000, and reported underapplied fixed overhead of $14,000 for supervisory salaries. What is Sipple Furniture's supervisory salaries spending (budget) variance (rounded to the nearest whole dollar) for August? Is this variance favorable (F) or unfavorable (U)?

[LO 15-2]   **15-15** Baxter Corporation's master budget calls for the production of 5,000 units per month and $144,000 indirect labor costs for the year. Baxter considers indirect labor as a component of variable factory overhead cost. During April, the company produced 4,500 units and incurred indirect labor costs of $10,100. What amount (rounded to the nearest whole dollar) would be reported in April as a flexible budget variance for indirect labor? Is this variance favorable (F) or unfavorable (U)?

[LO 15-2]   **15-16** Patel and Sons Inc. uses a standard cost system to apply factory overhead costs to units produced. Practical capacity for the plant is defined as 50,000 machine hours per year, which represents 25,000 units of output. Annual budgeted fixed factory overhead costs are $250,000 and the budgeted variable factory overhead cost rate is $4 per unit. Factory overhead costs are applied on the basis of standard machine hours allowed for units produced. Budgeted and actual output for the year was 20,000 units, which took 41,000 machine hours. Actual fixed factory overhead costs for the year amounted to $245,000, while the actual variable overhead cost per unit was $3.90. What was (a) the fixed overhead spending (budget) variance for the year and (b) the production volume variance for the year? Round each answer to the nearest whole dollar, and indicate whether each variance was favorable (F) or unfavorable (U).

[LO 15-2]   **15-17** Refer to the data in Brief Exercise 15-16. Given this information, what was (a) the variable overhead spending variance for the year and (b) the variable overhead efficiency variance for the year? Round answers to the nearest whole dollar; indicate whether each variance was favorable (F) or unfavorable (U).

[LO 15-3]   15-18   Refer to the data in Brief Exercise 15-16. Provide the correct summary journal entries for actual and applied factory overhead costs (both variable and fixed) for the year. Assume that the company uses a single account, Factory Overhead, to record both actual and applied factory overhead. Also, assume that the only variable overhead cost was electricity and that actual fixed overhead consisted of depreciation of $150,000 and supervisory salaries of $95,000. Finally, assume that both electricity expense and the supervisory salaries expense have been incurred but not yet paid (i.e., both are current liabilities).

[LO 15-4]   15-19   Refer to your answers to Brief Exercises 15-16 and 15-17 and the journal entries made in conjunction with Brief Exercise 15-18. Given this information, provide the appropriate journal entries (a) to record the overhead cost variances for the period (thereby closing out the balance in the Factory Overhead account) and (b) to close the variance accounts to the Cost of Goods Sold (COGS) account at the end of the period.

[LO 15-4]   15-20   As an extension of Brief Exercise 15-19, assume that at the end of the year, management of Patel and Sons decides that the overhead cost variances should be allocated to WIP Inventory, Finished Goods Inventory, and Cost of Goods Sold (COGS) using the following percentages: 10%, 20%, and 70%, respectively. Provide the proper journal entry to close out the manufacturing overhead variances for the year.

[LO 15-2]   15-21   Refer to the information in Brief Exercise 15-16. Calculate and label the following factory overhead variances for the year: (a) total overhead cost variance, (b) total flexible budget variance, and (c) production volume variance. Round each answer to the nearest whole dollar, and indicate whether each variance is favorable (F) or unfavorable (U).

[LO 15-3]   15-22   Refer to the variances you calculated in conjunction with Brief Exercise 15-21 and to the information in Brief Exercises 15-16 and 15-18. Prepare the appropriate journal entries to record (a) actual factory overhead costs for the year, (b) the applied factory overhead costs for the year (both variable and fixed), and (c) the total flexible budget variance and the production volume variance for the period (as calculated above in Brief Exercise 15-21).

[LO 15-4]   15-23   Refer to the journal entries made in Brief Exercise 15-22. Provide an appropriate end-of-year closing entry for each of the following two independent situations: (a) the net factory overhead cost variance is closed entirely to Cost of Goods Sold (COGS) and (b) the net factory overhead variance is allocated among WIP Inventory, Finished Goods Inventory, and COGS using the following percentages: 10%, 20%, and 70%, respectively.

Exercises

[LO 15-1]   15-24   **Flexible Overhead Budgets for Control**   Johnny Lee Inc. produces a line of small gasoline-powered engines that can be used in a variety of residential machines, ranging from different types of lawnmowers, to snowblowers, to garden tools (such as tillers and weed-whackers). The basic product line consists of three different models, each meant to fill the needs of a different market. Assume you are the cost accountant for this company and that you have been asked by the owner of the company to construct a flexible budget for factory overhead costs, which seem to be growing faster than revenues. Currently, the company uses machine hours (MHs) as the basis for assigning both variable and fixed factory overhead costs to products.

Within the relevant range of output, you determine that the following fixed factory overhead costs per month should occur: engineering support, $15,000; insurance on the manufacturing facility, $5,000; property taxes on the manufacturing facility, $12,000; depreciation on manufacturing equipment, $13,800; and indirect labor costs of supervisory salaries, $14,800; setup labor, $2,400; and materials handling, $2,500. Variable factory overhead costs are budgeted at $21.00 per machine hour, as follows: electricity, $8.00; indirect materials for Material A of $1.00 and for Material B of $4.00; indirect labor—maintenance, $6.00; and production-related supplies, $2.00.

Required

1.   Prepare a flexible budget for Johnny Lee for each of the following monthly levels of machine hours: (a) 4,000, (b) 5,000, and (c) 6,000. (*Hint:* Provide in your response a separate line for each of the factory overhead costs for the company.)

2.   Generate an equation to represent, within the relevant range, the factory overhead costs per month for Johnny Lee (state the variable overhead cost rate to 2 decimal places). Use this equation to estimate monthly total overhead cost for machine hours of 3,000 to 6,000, in increments of 500.

3.   Use the Chart function in Excel to generate a graphical representation of the monthly factory overhead cost function for Johnny Lee over the range of 3,000–6,000 machine hours per month.

[LO 15-1, 15-2] 15-25 **Graphical Analysis—Variable Overhead Cost Variances** You are in charge of making a presentation to operating managers regarding the meaning of the total factory overhead variance that appears each month on their performance reports. The controller suggested that a graphical presentation might be an effective way to communicate the essential points to your audience. As such, she provided you with this partially completed graph. This graph represents a situation where (1) machine hours are used to apply variable overhead costs to products and (2) there is both an unfavorable variable overhead spending variance and an unfavorable variable overhead efficiency variance for the period in question. The controller also indicated that she would like you to use the following notation for some of the items to be included in your chart: actual number of machine hours worked during the period = AQ; standard number of machine hours allowed for the output of the period = SQ; actual variable overhead cost per machine hour worked during the period = AP; and standard variable overhead cost per machine hour = SP.

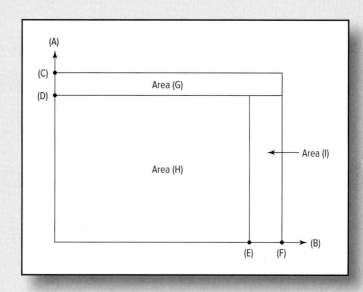

Required Based on the preceding assumptions and information, properly label or describe (as appropriate) the following components of the above graph:
1. Label (A)
2. Label (B)
3. Point (C)
4. Point (D)
5. Point (E)
6. Point (F)
7. Area (G)
8. Area (H)
9. Area (I)
10. Sum of areas (G), (H), and (I)

[LO 15-1, 15-2] 15-26 **Graphical Analysis—Fixed Overhead Cost Variances** (Continuation of Exercise 15-25) The controller is satisfied with the graphical representation you prepared in conjunction with Exercise 15-25. She thinks this graphical representation of variable overhead variances will be well received by operating managers of the company. As such, she asks you to prepare an accompanying graph for fixed overhead variances. She indicates that you should assume the following in constructing your graph: (1) fixed factory overhead is applied to production on the basis of standard machine hours allowed for the output of the period (the standard total factory overhead cost per machine hour is $10.00, while the standard variable factory overhead cost per machine hour is $6.00); (2) during the example case, there was a favorable production volume variance and an unfavorable spending (budget) variance for fixed overhead. Based on these assumptions, the controller has asked you to properly label or interpret (as appropriate) the components (A) through (L) in the graph.

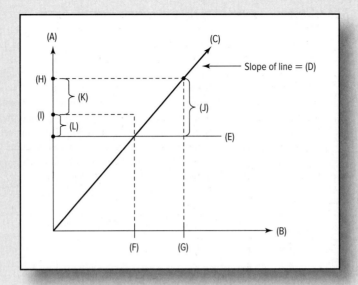

Required
1. Label (A)
2. Label (B)
3. Line (C)
4. Slope (D)
5. Amount (E)
6. Amount (F)
7. Amount (G)
8. Amount (H)
9. Amount (I)
10. Vertical distance (J)
11. Vertical distance (K)
12. Vertical distance (L)

[LO 15-1, 15-2]   15-27   **Fixed Overhead Rate; Denominator Level; Two-Variance Breakdown of Total Factory Overhead Cost Variance**   Overhead information for Cran-Mar Company for October follows:

Total factory overhead cost incurred	$30,000
Budgeted fixed factory overhead cost	$ 7,125
Total standard overhead rate per machine hour (MH)	$ 4.90
Standard variable factory overhead rate per MH	$ 3.00
Standard MHs allowed for the units manufactured	3,600

Required
1. What is the standard fixed factory overhead rate per machine hour (MH)?
2. What is the denominator activity level that was used to establish the fixed factory overhead application rate? (Round your answer to the nearest whole number.)
3. Two-way analysis (breakdown) of the total factory overhead cost variance: Using panel 3 in Exhibit 15.7 as a guide, calculate the following factory overhead cost variances for October. [*Note:* Round answers to the nearest whole dollar, and indicate whether each variance is favorable (F) or unfavorable (U).]
   a. Total flexible budget variance.
   b. Production volume variance.
   c. Total overhead cost variance.
4. Confirm your answer to requirement 3b above by using the model at the bottom of Exhibit 15.6 to calculate the production volume variance. Round your answer to the nearest whole dollar and indicate whether the variance is favorable (F) or unfavorable (U).

[LO 15-1, 15-2]   15-28   **Flexible Budget and Variances for Depreciation**   Clark Company's master budget includes $360,000 for equipment depreciation. The master budget was prepared for an annual volume of 120,000 chargeable hours. This volume is expected to occur uniformly throughout the year. During September, Clark performed 9,000 chargeable hours and recorded $28,000 of depreciation.

Required

1. Determine the flexible budget amount (to nearest whole dollar) for equipment depreciation in September.

2. Compute the spending variance for the depreciation on equipment, rounded to nearest whole dollar. Was the variance favorable (F) or unfavorable (U)?

3. Calculate the fixed overhead production volume variance for depreciation expense in September, rounded to nearest whole dollar. Was this variance favorable (F) or unfavorable (U)? What is the interpretation of this variance?

4. List possible reasons for the observed spending variance.

[LO 15-2, 15-3]   15-29   **Variable Factory Overhead Variances; Journal Entries**   The Platter Valley factory of Bybee Industries manufactures field boots. The cost of each boot includes direct materials, direct labor, and manufacturing (factory) overhead. The firm traces all direct costs to products, and it assigns overhead cost to products based on direct labor hours.

    The company budgeted $15,000 variable factory overhead cost and 2,500 direct labor hours to manufacture 5,000 pairs of boots in March.

    The factory used 2,700 direct labor hours in March to manufacture 4,800 pairs of boots and spent $15,600 on variable overhead during the month.

Required

1. Compute the factory overhead flexible budget variance, the factory overhead spending variance, and the efficiency variance for variable factory overhead for March. Round each variance to the nearest whole dollar, and state whether each variance is favorable (F) or unfavorable (U).

2. Provide the appropriate journal entry to record the variable overhead spending variance and a second entry to record the variable overhead efficiency variance for March. Assume that the company uses a single account, Factory Overhead, to record overhead costs.

3. Comment on the factory's operation in March with regard to variable factory overhead cost.

[LO 15-2, 15-3]   15-30   **Fixed Factory Overhead Cost Variances; Journal Entries**   (Continuation of Exercise 15-29) For March, the Platter Valley factory of Bybee Industries budgeted $90,000 for fixed factory overhead cost. Its practical capacity is 2,500 direct labor hours per month (to manufacture 5,000 pairs of boots). The factory used 2,700 direct labor hours in March to manufacture 4,800 pairs of boots. The actual fixed overhead cost incurred for the month was $92,000.

Required

1. Compute the fixed overhead spending (budget) variance and the production volume variance for March. Round each variance to the nearest whole number, and indicate whether each variance is favorable (F) or unfavorable (U).

2. Compute the fixed overhead flexible budget variance for March, rounded to the nearest whole number. Is this variance favorable (F) or unfavorable (U)?

3. Provide the appropriate journal entry to record the fixed overhead spending variance and the appropriate journal entry to record the production volume variance for March. Assume that the company uses a single account, Factory Overhead, to record overhead costs.

4. Comment on the factory's results in March with regard to fixed overhead costs.

[LO 15-2, 15-3]   15-31   **Three-Variance vs. Four-Variance Analysis of the Total Factory Overhead Cost Variance** (Continuation of Exercises 15-29 and 15-30) The Platter Valley factory of Bybee Industries currently uses a four-variance analysis of the total factory overhead cost variance but is thinking of changing to a three-variance analysis.

Required

1. Use the data given in Exercises 15-29 and 15-30 to compute the total overhead spending variance, the (variable overhead) efficiency variance, and the production volume variance for March. Round all answers to the nearest whole number, and indicate whether each variance is favorable (F) or unfavorable (U).

2. Prepare the appropriate journal entries at the end of March to record each of the following: (a) the total overhead spending variance, (b) the variable overhead efficiency variance, and (c) the production volume variance. Assume that all overhead costs are recorded in a single account called "Factory Overhead."

3. Describe the primary difference between information contained in a three-way versus a four-way analysis of the total factory overhead variance.

[LO 15-2]   15-32   **Two-Variance vs. Four-Variance Breakdown of the Total Factory Overhead Cost Variance**   (Continuation of Exercises 15-29 and 15-30) The Platter Valley factory of Bybee Industries uses a two-variance analysis of the total factory overhead variance.

Required

1. Use the data given in Exercises 15-29 and 15-30 to compute the total flexible budget variance for overhead and the production volume variance for March. What was the total factory overhead cost variance for March? Round all variances to the nearest whole dollar, and indicate whether each variance is favorable (F) or unfavorable (U).

2. Use your answers for requirement 1 of Exercises 15-29 through 15-31 to show the three components of the total flexible budget variance for overhead (i.e., the variable overhead spending variance, the variable overhead efficiency variance, and the fixed overhead spending variance); in addition, show the production volume variance for March. Indicate whether each variance is favorable (F) or unfavorable (U).

3. What information is contained in each of the variances in a two-variance breakdown of the total overhead variance?

[LO 15-1, 15-2]   15-33   **Factory Overhead Analysis—Two, Three, and Four Variances**   Walkenhorst Company's machining department prepared its 2022 budget based on the following data:

Practical capacity	40,000 units
Standard machine hours per unit	2
Standard variable factory overhead	$3.00 per machine hour
Budgeted fixed factory overhead	$360,000

The department uses machine hours to apply factory overhead to production. In 2022, the department used 85,000 machine hours and incurred $625,000 in total manufacturing overhead cost to manufacture 42,000 units. Actual fixed overhead cost for the year was $375,000.

Required   Determine for the year:

1. The fixed, variable, and total factory overhead application rates (per machine hour). Round all answers to 2 decimal places. For example, $3.451 = $3.45.

2. The total flexible budget, to the nearest whole dollar, for factory overhead cost based on output achieved in 2022.

3. The production volume variance, to the nearest whole dollar. State whether this variance was favorable (F) or unfavorable (U).

4. The total overhead spending variance, to the nearest whole dollar. State whether this variance was favorable (F) or unfavorable (U).

5. The overhead efficiency variance, to the nearest whole dollar. State whether this variance was favorable (F) or unfavorable (U).

6. The variable overhead spending variance and the fixed overhead spending variance, each to the nearest whole dollar. State whether each variance is favorable (F) or unfavorable (U).

[LO 15-2, 15-3, 15-4]   15-34   **Journal Entries for Factory Overhead Costs and Standard Cost Variances**   Refer to the information for Johnny Lee Inc. in Exercise 15-24. Assume that in a given month (December) the standard allowed machine hours for output produced was 5,500. Also, assume that the denominator activity level for setting the predetermined overhead application rate is 6,550 machine hours per month.

Actual fixed overhead costs for the month of December were as follows: engineering support, $15,500 (salaries); factory insurance, $5,500; property taxes, $12,000; equipment depreciation, $13,800; supervisory salaries, $14,800; setup labor, $2,200; materials-handling labor, $2,400. The actual variable overhead cost per machine hour worked in December was equal to the standard cost except for the following two items: electricity, $8.50 per machine hour; and manufacturing supplies, $2.10 per machine hour. All salary and wage amounts have not yet been paid. The company used 5,600 machine hours in December.

The company uses a single overhead account, Factory Overhead, and performs a two-way analysis of the total factory overhead cost variance each month.

Required

1. Calculate (a) the total factory overhead cost variance, (b) the total flexible budget variance, and (c) the production volume variance for the month. Round each factory overhead cost variance to the nearest whole number and state whether each variance was favorable (F) or unfavorable (U).

2. Provide the summary journal entry to record (separately) each of the following: (a) actual variable overhead costs, (b) actual fixed overhead costs, (c) standard variable overhead cost applied to production, and (d) standard fixed overhead cost applied to production. *Note:* Accrued payroll costs are recorded in Salaries and Wages Payable, while transactions regarding indirect materials and manufacturing supplies are recorded in the Indirect Materials Inventory account.

3. Provide a single journal entry to record the two factory overhead cost variances for the month.

4. Assume that the variances calculated above represent net overhead cost variances for the year. Provide the required journal entry to close these two variances to the Cost of Goods Sold (COGS) account.

[LO 15-6] 15-35 **Traditional ABC Costing** Alden Company uses a three-variance analysis for factory overhead variances. Practical capacity is defined as 32 setups and 32,000 machine hours to manufacture 6,400 units for the year. Selected data for 2022 follow:

Budgeted fixed factory overhead:		
Setup cost	$64,000	
Other	200,000	$264,000
Total factory overhead cost incurred		$480,000
Variable factory overhead rate:		
Per setup		$600
Per machine hour		$5.00
Total standard machine hours allowed for the units manufactured		30,000 hours
Machine hours actually worked		35,000 hours
Actual total number of setups		28
Actual number of units produced during the year		6,000
Standard number of setups for units produced during the year		30

Required

1. Compute (a) the total overhead spending variance, (b) the overhead efficiency variance, and (c) the total overhead flexible budget variance for 2022. Label each variance as favorable (F) or unfavorable (U); round all variances to the nearest whole dollar.

2. Assume that the company includes all setup costs as variable factory overhead. The budgeted total fixed overhead, therefore, is $200,000, and the standard variable overhead rate per setup is $2,600. What are (a) the total overhead spending variance, (b) the overhead efficiency variance, and (c) the total overhead flexible budget variance for the year? Label each variance as favorable (F) or unfavorable (U); round all variances to nearest whole dollar.

3. Assume that the company uses only machine hours as the activity measure to apply both variable and fixed overhead, and that it includes all setup costs as variable factory overhead. What are (a) the total overhead spending variance, (b) the overhead efficiency variance, and (c) the total overhead flexible budget variance for the year? [*Note:* Round the standard variable overhead application rate per machine hour to 2 decimal places; round variance calculations to nearest whole dollar; indicate whether each variance is favorable (F) or unfavorable (U).]

4. What is the primary conceptual lesson derived from the preceding calculations?

[LO 15-6] 15-36 **ABC and Practical Capacity; Spreadsheet Application** The XYZ Manufacturing Company produces two products, S-101 and C-110. You have obtained the following information regarding the annual manufacturing support (i.e., factory overhead) costs associated with the manufacturing process used to produce these two products:

Cost Pools	Budgeted Costs	Activity Measure (Cost Driver)	Practical Capacity	Budgeted Activities for the Coming Year	
				S-101	C-110
Setup activity	$250,000	Setup hours	5,000	2,500	2,350
Packing and shipping	50,000	Number of shipments	2,000	1,200	775
Inspection	30,000	Number of batches	1,000	250	700
Machining	750,000	Units produced	150,000	100,000	40,000
Purchase ordering	40,000	Number of orders	300	50	110
Total	$1,120,000				

Required

1. Prepare an Excel spreadsheet that provides activity-based costing (ABC) cost allocation rates based on budgeted activity units as the denominator activity level for the coming year. (a) What is the budgeted manufacturing support (i.e., factory overhead) cost per unit for S-101? (b) What is the budgeted manufacturing support cost per unit for C-110? (Display each answer to 4 decimal places.)

2. Using your spreadsheet, recalculate the ABC cost allocation rates, this time based on practical capacity as the denominator activity level. (a) What is the budgeted manufacturing support cost per unit for S-101? (b) What is the budgeted manufacturing support cost per unit for C-110? (Display each answer to 4 decimal places.)

3. Compute, for each cost pool, the difference (rounded to nearest whole dollar) between the budgeted cost for the year and the total cost allocated to production. Label each of these differences (variances) as *underapplied* or *overapplied*.

4. How do you interpret the variances (differences) identified in requirement 3?

[LO 15-7] **15-37 The Variance Investigation Decision** As noted in the text, identifying and reporting standard cost variances (such as those covered in Chapters 14 and 15) is the first step in one strategy for controlling costs and improving short-term financial performance.

Required What guidelines can you suggest for determining which cost variances are investigated for their underlying cause(s)? Include in your answer the notion of costs vs. benefits and a discussion of random vs. systematic variances.

Problems

[LO 15-2] **15-38 Capacity Levels and Fixed Overhead Rates** At its Sutter City plant, Yuba Machine Company manufactures nut shellers, which it sells to nut processors throughout the world. Since its inception, the family-owned business has used actual factory overhead costs in costing factory output. On December 1, 2022, Yuba began using a predetermined factory overhead application rate to determine manufacturing costs on a more timely basis. The following information is from the 2022–2023 budget for the Sutter City plant:

Plant maximum (theoretical) capacity	100,000 DLHs
Variable factory overhead costs	$3.00 per DLH
Fixed factory overhead costs:	
Salaries	$80,000
Depreciation and amortization	50,000
Other expenses	30,000
Total fixed factory overhead	$160,000

Based on these data, the predetermined factory overhead application rate was established at $4.60 per direct labor hour (DLH).

A variance report for the Sutter City plant for the six months ended May 31, 2023, follows. The plant incurred 40,000 DLHs, which represents one-half of the company's *practical capacity* level.

	Variance Report		
	Actual Costs	**Applied***	**Variance†**
Total variable factory overhead	$120,220	$120,000	$ (220)
Fixed factory overhead:			
Salaries	$ 39,000	$ 32,000	$ (7,000)
Depreciation and amortization	25,000	20,000	(5,000)
Other expenses	15,300	12,000	(3,300)
Total fixed factory overhead	$ 79,300	$ 64,000	$(15,300)

*Based on 40,000 direct labor hours (DLHs).
†Favorable (Unfavorable).

Yuba's controller, Sid Thorpe, knows from the inventory records that one-quarter of this period's applied fixed overhead costs remain in the Work-in-Process Inventory and Finished Goods Inventory accounts. Based on this information, he has included $48,000 of fixed overhead (i.e., three-quarters of the period's applied fixed overhead) as part of the cost of goods sold in the following interim income statement:

YUBA MACHINE COMPANY
Interim Income Statement
For Six Months Ended May 31, 2023

Sales	$625,000
Cost of goods sold	380,000
Gross profit	$245,000
Selling expense	44,000
Depreciation expense	58,000
Administrative expense	53,000
Operating income	$ 90,000

Required

1. Define the term *maximum (theoretical) capacity,* and explain why it might not be a satisfactory basis for determining the fixed factory overhead application rate. What other capacity levels can be used to set the fixed factory overhead allocation rate? Provide a short definition of each of these alternative capacity levels.

2. Prepare a revised variance report for Yuba Machine Company using *practical capacity* as the basis for determining the fixed factory overhead application rate. Round each applied overhead cost and each overhead cost variance to the nearest whole dollar. Indicate whether each of the five overhead cost variances in the revised variance report is favorable (F) or unfavorable (U).

3. What would Yuba's reported (a) cost of goods sold (COGS) and (b) operating income be for the 6 months ending May 31, 2023, if the fixed factory overhead rate is based on practical capacity rather than on maximum capacity? Round each answer to the nearest whole dollar.

4. What capacity level should companies use to determine the factory overhead application rate? Why?

(CMA Adapted)

[LO 15-2, 15-4]   15-39   **Ethics and Overhead Variance**   New Millennium Technologies uses a standard cost system. It budgeted 50,000 machine hours to manufacture 100,000 units in 2022. The budgeted total fixed factory overhead was $9,000,000. The company manufactured and sold 80,000 units in 2022 and would report a loss of $9,600,000 after charging the production volume variance to Cost of Goods Sold (COGS) of the period.

Bob Evans, VP–Finance, believes that the denominator activity level of 50,000 machine hours is too low. The maximum capacity of the firm is between 5,000,000 and 6,000,000 machine hours. Bob considers a denominator level at half the low-end capacity to be reasonable. Furthermore, he believes that the unfavorable production volume variance should be capitalized (rather than written off against the current period's earnings) because the demand for the firm's products has been increasing rapidly. A conservative projection of the firm's sales places the total sales at a level that will require at least 5 million machine hours in less than 5 years. Bob was able to show a substantial improvement in operating income after revising the cost data. He used the revised operating results in briefing financial analysts.

Required

1. Consider the two changes being considered: (a) What is the estimated operating income (loss) if both changes are implemented? (b) What portion of the change identified in part (a) is attributable to the elimination of the unfavorable production volume variance? (c) What portion of the change identified in part (a) is attributable to the decrease in fixed overhead cost applied to production?

2. Is it ethical for Bob to make the changes? (Consult www.imanet.org/career-resources/ethics-center for the IMA's Statement of Ethical Professional Practice, revised July 1, 2017.)

3. Do the provisions of GAAP regarding inventory costing (viz., FASB ASC 330-10-30, previously *SFAS No. 151*—available at www.fasb.org) bear upon the current issue? If so, how?

4. How does the choice of the denominator volume level in setting fixed overhead application rates provide managers with an opportunity to manage earnings?

[LO 15-2, 15-4]   15-40   **Income Statement Effects of Alternative Denominator Activity Levels; Spreadsheet Application**
At a recent board meeting of the Grayson Manufacturing Company, several individuals in attendance expressed concern that they could not understand how the choice of an activity level for determining overhead application rates for the company could affect reported operating profits. The controller, Susanna Wu, told members of the board that, in fact, companies have some latitude in

how overhead application rates are set. For example, she told members of the board that companies can spread budgeted fixed overhead for the period over budgeted (forecasted) activity, normal capacity, practical capacity, or even theoretical (maximum) capacity. All of this didn't resonate well with members of the board, who basically saw the discussion as just another example of how accounting can be used to manage income (i.e., "cook the books"). The chair of the finance committee of the board asked Susanna to generate a concise report that would illustrate, in concrete terms, the issues involved. In turn, you have been asked to prepare this report, which will be distributed to attendees at the next meeting of the finance committee. These committee members are adept at using spreadsheets and therefore have requested that your report be distributed to them electronically.

Based on your subsequent discussions with the controller, you have come up with the following information that is pertinent to your task:

a. Basis for applying factory overhead costs to units produced = Standard machine hours.

b. Budgeted fixed overhead (total) = $350,000 per year.

c. Standard number of machine hours per unit produced = 2.0.

d. Sales data: Units sold = 11,500; unit selling price = $100.

e. Standard variable manufacturing cost per unit produced = $60.25.

f. Beginning inventory of finished goods = 0 units.

g. Budgeted operating costs: Variable = $4.95 per unit sold; fixed = $65,000 per year.

h. Actual number of units produced during the year = 12,250.

i. Capacity levels (in machine hours): Theoretical capacity = 30,000 hours; practical capacity = 27,000 hours; normal capacity = 25,000 hours; budgeted (forecasted) usage = 24,000 hours.

Required

1. Develop an Excel spreadsheet to calculate the amount of the fixed overhead production volume variance (rounded to the nearest whole dollar) under each of the following denominator activity levels that can be used to set the fixed overhead allocation rate: (a) theoretical capacity, (b) practical capacity, (c) normal capacity, and (d) budgeted capacity usage. Indicate in each case whether the variance is favorable (F) or unfavorable (U).

2. Determine the end-of-year balance in the Finished Goods Inventory account (at standard manufacturing cost) under each of the following denominator activity levels for establishing the fixed overhead allocation rate: (a) theoretical capacity, (b) practical capacity, (c) normal capacity, and (d) budgeted capacity usage. Round each answer to nearest whole number.

3. Assume that the practice of the company at the end of the year is to close any standard cost variances to cost of goods sold (COGS). What is the amount of operating profit that would be reported for each of the following choices for defining the denominator activity level for purposes of calculating the fixed overhead allocation rate: (a) theoretical capacity, (b) practical capacity, (c) normal capacity, and (d) budgeted capacity usage? Round each answer to nearest whole dollar.

4. What conclusions can be drawn based on the preceding analyses you conducted? That is, what is the bottom-line information you would like to convey to members of the finance committee?

5. How do the provisions of GAAP regarding inventory costing (viz., FASB ASC 330-10-30, previously *SFAS No. 151*) affect the decision as to how the fixed overhead production volume variance (also known as the idle capacity variance) is handled at the end of a period?

[LO 15-2, 15-4] 15-41 **Managing Earnings; Denominator Capacity Level; Ethics** Any given cost information system is a function of a number of design choices. For product costing purposes, one such design choice relates to how overhead, particularly fixed manufacturing overhead, application rates are determined. As controller for your company, you have been asked to prepare a written presentation for an upcoming meeting of the board of directors of your company. In preparing this assignment, assume that board members are reasonably knowledgeable about financial reporting issues, but not necessarily about the intricacies of cost accounting. Your memo should address the three issues listed below.

Required

1. Explain how manufacturing overhead rates are constructed in conventional cost accounting systems and in activity-based costing systems. Speak separately about fixed versus variable overhead application rates. What key choices must be made in establishing these rates? In answering this question, you might want to discuss differences (if any) between current IRS (income tax) requirements, internal reporting needs, and financial reporting requirements (e.g., FASB ASC 330-10-30, previously *SFAS No. 151*— available at www.fasb.org).

2. Your company uses a standard cost system. As such, at the end of each period, it must "clean up" the accounts by disposing of any standard cost variances that might have occurred during the period. Explain how the variances for fixed manufacturing overhead are disposed of at the end of the period. In your answer, pay particular attention to the following two financial reporting issues: (a) the requirements of FASB ASC 330-10-30 and (b) how, under absorption costing, reported earnings can be "managed" by choice of the denominator volume used to establish the fixed overhead application rate.

3. Access the Institute of Management Accountant's Statement of Ethical Professional Practice, revised July 1, 2017 (www.imanet.org/career-resources/ethics-center). Explain whether any of the stated standards relate to the issue of setting fixed overhead application rates and how any resulting production volume variances are disposed of at the end of the period for financial reporting purposes? Be specific.

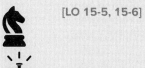

[LO 15-5, 15-6]   15-42   **Strategy, Resource Capacity Planning, and Time-Driven ABC (TDABC)**   Obtain and read the following article: Robert S. Kaplan and David P. Norton, "Mastering the Management System," *Harvard Business Review,* January 2008, pp. 63–77 (available at ftp://public. dhe.ibm.com/software/data/sw-library/cognos/pdfs/whitepapers/wp_mastering_the_ management_system.pdf). The authors of this article propose a five-stage management system designed to balance strategy and operations—that is, short-term operational concerns with long-term (strategic) priorities. [*Note:* The following additional source, available for download from the Harvard Business Publishing website, may also be helpful: Robert S. Kaplan, "Resource Capacity Planning in the Strategy Execution System," *Balanced Scorecard Report,* Reprint No. B0809A (2008).]

Required   After reading the above-referenced article(s), respond to the following questions:

1. Provide an overview of the five-step cycle that comprises the (strategic) management system proposed by the authors of this article.

2. Stage 3 of the proposed (strategic) management system focuses on "Plan Operations," a significant component of which deals with planning resource capacity. Describe the process of resource capacity planning within the context of the five-stage (strategic) management cycle proposed by the authors. In particular, discuss the strategic importance of managing the linkage of Stage 3 to both Stage 2 and Stage 4 of the proposed management cycle.

3. The authors indicate that their preferred tool for resource capacity planning is time-driven activity-based costing (TDABC). Provide a brief overview of TDABC, including how this implementation differs from traditional ABC models. (*Hint:* In addition to the article, refer to Chapter 5 of the text.)

4. Refer to the Towerton Financial example presented in the article. How did this organization use TDABC results to determine the level of resource capacity (people and computing) needed to implement its strategy?

[LO 15-4, 15-5]   15-43   **Strategic Control of Capacity-Related Manufacturing Costs**   Obtain from your library (or instructor or course pack, as appropriate) a copy of the following article: K. Snead, D. Stott, and A. Garcia, "The Causes of Misapplied Capacity Related Manufacturing Costs and Corresponding Reporting Implications: A Conceptual Perspective," *Journal of Accounting Education* 28 (2010), pp. 85–102 (available at www.sciencedirect.com/science/article/pii/S0748575111000170).

Required   After reading the above-referenced article, answer the following questions:

1. In general, how does this article relate to the material covered in this chapter?

2. What do the authors of this article mean when they refer to misapplied fixed (i.e., capacity-related) manufacturing overhead costs?

3. Into what components do the authors feel the production volume variance should be decomposed? How are each of the component variances calculated and interpreted?

4. What is the connection between the variance decomposition model proposed by the authors and the strategic control of capacity-related manufacturing costs?

5. What do the authors of this article indicate are the financial-reporting consequences of their proposed framework?

[LO 15-4]   15-44   **Proration of Variances; Chapters 14 and 15**   Butrico Manufacturing Corporation uses a standard cost system, records materials price variances when direct materials are purchased, and prorates all variances at year-end. Variances associated with direct materials are prorated based on the balances of direct materials in the appropriate accounts, and variances associated with direct labor and manufacturing overhead are prorated to Finished Goods Inventory and to Cost of Goods Sold (COGS) on the basis of the relative direct labor cost in these accounts at year-end.

The following information is for the year ended December 31:

The company had no beginning inventories and no ending Work-in-Process (WIP) Inventory. It applies manufacturing overhead at 80% of standard direct labor cost.

Finished Goods Inventory at 12/31:	
Direct materials	$ 87,000
Direct labor	130,500
Applied manufacturing overhead	104,400
Direct Materials Inventory at 12/31	65,000
Cost of Goods Sold for the year ended 12/31:	
Direct materials	$348,000
Direct labor	739,500
Applied manufacturing overhead	591,600
Direct Materials Price Variance (unfavorable)	10,000
Direct Materials Usage Variance (favorable)	15,000
Direct Labor Rate Variance (unfavorable)	20,000
Direct Labor Efficiency Variance (favorable)	5,000
Actual manufacturing overhead incurred	690,000

Required

1. Compute (to nearest whole dollar) the amount of Direct Materials Price Variance to be prorated to Finished Goods Inventory at December 31.

2. Compute (to nearest whole dollar) the total amount of *direct materials cost* in the Finished Goods Inventory at December 31, after all materials variances have been prorated. (*Hint:* The correct amount is $85,732.)

3. Compute (to nearest whole dollar) the total amount of *direct labor cost* in the Finished Goods Inventory at December 31, after all variances have been prorated. (*Hint:* The correct amount is $132,750.)

4. Compute (to nearest whole dollar) the total Cost of Goods Sold (COGS) for the year ended December 31, after all variances have been prorated. (*Hint:* The correct amount is $1,681,678.)

5. How, if at all, would the provisions of GAAP regarding inventory costing (i.e., FASB ASC 330-10-30, previously *SFAS No. 151*—available at www.fasb.org) bear upon the end-of-period variance disposition question?

6. Under absorption (i.e., full) costing, explain how reported earnings can be managed by the method used to dispose of (fixed) overhead cost variances at the end of the period.

(CMA Adapted)

[LO 15-1, 15-2, 15-3, 15-4]

15-45 **Four-Variance Analysis; Journal Entries**   Edney Company employs a standard cost system for product costing. The per-unit standard cost of its product is:

Raw materials	$14.50
Direct labor (2 direct labor hours × $8.00 per hour)	16.00
Manufacturing overhead (2 direct labor hours × $11.00 per hour)	22.00
Total standard cost per unit	$52.50

The manufacturing overhead rate is based on a normal capacity level of 600,000 direct labor hours. (Normal capacity is defined as the level of capacity needed to satisfy average customer demand over a period of two to four years. Operationally, this level of capacity would take into consideration sales trends and both seasonal and cyclical factors affecting demand.) The firm has the following annual manufacturing overhead budget:

Variable	$3,600,000
Fixed	3,000,000
	$6,600,000

Edney incurred $433,350 in direct labor cost for 53,500 direct labor hours to manufacture 26,000 units in November. Other costs incurred in November include $260,000 for fixed manufacturing overhead and $315,000 for variable manufacturing overhead.

Required

1. Determine each of the following for November. [*Note:* Round each overhead variance to nearest whole dollar, and indicate whether each variance is favorable (F) or unfavorable (U).]

    a. The variable overhead spending variance.

    b. The variable overhead efficiency variance.

    c. The fixed overhead spending (budget) variance.

    d. The fixed overhead production volume variance.

    e. The total amount of under- or overapplied manufacturing overhead (i.e., the total manufacturing overhead cost variance for the period).

2. Provide the following four journal entries: (a) to record actual variable overhead costs, (b) to record actual fixed overhead costs, (c) to record standard overhead costs applied to production, and (d) to record all four overhead cost variances. The company uses a single account, Factory Overhead, to record all overhead costs. Assume that the actual variable manufacturing overhead consists of utilities payable of $165,000, indirect materials of $100,000 (all materials, direct and indirect, are recorded in a single account, Materials Inventory), and $50,000 depreciation on factory equipment (determined under the units-of-production method). Assume that the fixed manufacturing overhead consists of accrued (i.e, unpaid) salaries of $60,000 and factory depreciation of $200,000. All unpaid salaries should be recorded in a single account, Accrued Payroll.

3. Give the appropriate journal entry to close all manufacturing overhead variances to the cost of goods sold (COGS) account. (Assume the cost variances you calculated above are for the year, not the month.)

4. How, if at all, would the provisions of GAAP regarding inventory costing (viz., FASB ASC 330-10-30, previously *SFAS No. 151*— available at www.fasb.org) bear upon the end-of-period variance disposition question?

5. Explain how reported earnings under absorption costing can be managed by the method used to dispose of (fixed) overhead cost variances at the end of the period.

(CMA Adapted)

[LO 15-2, 15-5] 15-46 **Control of Overhead Costs; Strategy** See the following: K. P. Coyne, S. T. Coyne, and E. J. Coyne Jr., "When You've Got to Cut Costs Now: A Practical Guide to Reducing Overhead by 10%, 20%, or (wince) 30%," *Harvard Business Review,* May 2010, pp. 74–82 (available at http://my.gartner.com/html/itexecutives/downloads/ExecPicks_ITCost_CutCosts_0610.pdf).

Required After reading the above-referenced article, answer the following questions:

1. In general, how does this article relate to the material covered in this chapter?

2. The authors of the article state that "administrative cost-reduction opportunities follow similar patterns everywhere." What two major conclusions do the authors offer, based on their accumulated experience in implementing successful cost-cutting programs?

3. The authors of this article also state that cost-reduction goals typically require "ten or more actions." For each of the three classifications of cost-reduction goals discussed in the article, provide examples of specific actions that managers can pursue in an attempt to meet the stated cost-reduction goal.

4. Provide a concise summary of the authors' recommended approach for determining the "right level of overhead."

[LO 15-5, 15-6] 15-47 **ABC Data; Resource Capacity Planning; Nonfinancial Performance Indicators** Zenon Computer competes at the retail level on the basis of customer service. It has invested significant resources in its customer service department. Recently, the company has installed a traditional activity-based costing (ABC) system to provide better cost information for pricing, decision making, and customer profitability analysis. Most of the costs of running the customer service department are considered committed (i.e., short-term fixed) costs (principally, personnel and equipment costs). The budgeted cost for the upcoming period is $800,000. Activity analysis, recently conducted when the ABC system was implemented, revealed the following information:

Activities	Percentage of Employee Time	Estimated (Budgeted) Cost Driver Quantity
Handling customer orders	75%	8,000 customer orders
Processing customer complaints	10	400 customer complaints
Conducting customer credit checks	15	500 credit checks

Required

1. Based on the preceding information, calculate (to 2 decimal places) the activity cost driver (ABC) rates for each of the three activities performed by the customer service department. Assume that during the period, actual cost driver activity levels are exactly as planned. Under this situation, what is the total cost allocated to each of the three activities? For each activity, what is the cost of unused (that is, idle) capacity, rounded to the nearest whole dollar?

2. Suppose that during the upcoming period, activities (i.e., cost-driver quantities) are exactly as budgeted. Suppose, too, that the practical capacity level for each of these activities is 10,000 customer orders, 500 customer complaints, and 500 credit checks. Using cost-driver rates based on the practical capacity level for each activity: (a) What is the cost assigned to each of the three activities, rounded to the nearest whole dollar? (b) What is the unused capacity for each activity (rounded to the nearest whole number)? (c) What is the cost of unused capacity for each activity, rounded to the nearest whole dollar?

3. What actions might the management of Zenon Computer take in response to the analysis conducted in response to requirement 2?

4. What nonfinancial performance indicators do you recommend Zenon Computer monitor in terms of its customer service department? In general, how are these indicators chosen? (That is, how do you justify the items you are recommending?)

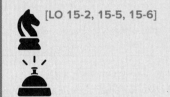

[LO 15-2, 15-5, 15-6]

15-48 **Managing Resource Capacity through Traditional Activity-Based Costing (ABC)** This assignment involves the use of a traditional (i.e., non-time-driven) ABC system to address the problem of measuring and managing the cost of capacity. As controller for Zen Company, you've been asked to provide input regarding the appropriate level of resource capacity needed to support the strategic initiatives of the company, as identified in the company's strategic planning system (e.g., its balanced scorecard system and associated strategy maps—see Chapter 18).

Because of the company's focus on exceptional customer service, you've decided to run a pilot test by focusing on a single activity: *handling customer orders*. During the most recent year, total resource costs of this activity were $600,000. You've determined that, during the year, 8,000 customer orders were handled by the company. Observations of the process and your own interviews with knowledgeable personnel indicate that the current level of resource spending in this area provides the capacity to efficiently process approximately 10,000 customer orders. (That is, the practical capacity of resources supplied is 10,000 customer orders.) An analysis of past accounting data and the application of the cost-estimation techniques covered in Chapter 8 suggest that resource spending for this activity in the coming year will be approximately $720,000. The company expects to handle 9,000 customer orders during the coming year; practical capacity remains at 10,000 customer orders. Your basic task is to determine how the use of ABC data can facilitate decisions regarding the appropriate level of spending to support the handling of customer orders.

Required

1. Distinguish between short-term variable costs and short-term fixed (i.e., capacity-related) costs. For many organizations today, including the Zen Company, which type of costs characterize support costs, such as the cost of handling customer orders?

2. ABC fundamentally deals with the issue of assigning costs to activities and then activity-based costs to outputs such as products, services, or customers. From the start, however, you are a bit bewildered: Which data at your disposal should be used to calculate the cost of handling a customer order? Include in your answer a discussion of choice of the capacity level (denominator volume) used to generate ABC costs, an explanation of the term *practical capacity,* and a short discussion of what is referred to as the *death spiral effect.*

3. How can the use of ABC data assist managers in managing spending on resource capacity? [*Hint:* Calculate each of the following for the support activity "handling customer orders": (a) support cost rate (to 2 decimal places), per order handled; (b) the cost of unused capacity for order-handling activity (rounded to nearest whole dollar); and (c) percentage capacity utilization for order-handling activity (rounded to 2 decimal places, e.g., 87.872% = 87.87%).] Why is the management of resource capacity costs of strategic importance to companies such as Zen?

4. Assume that Zen, in an effort to improve the process of handling customer orders, implements a total quality management (TQM) or similar initiative, the effect of which is to increase the number of orders that can be handled efficiently. As a result, the practical capacity of the process increases to approximately 12,000 orders per year. Assume a total cost, as before, of $720,000 and that, as before, the company in the coming year expects to process 9,000 customer orders. After the TQM implementation: (a) What is the support cost rate, to 2 decimal places, for handling a customer order? (b) What is the estimated cost of unused capacity after TQM implementation (rounded to nearest whole dollar)? (c) What is the capacity utilization rate (percentage) after TQM implementation, rounded to 2 decimal places? (d) What is the primary lesson based on a comparison of results from requirements 3 and 4?

5. What strategies are available to managers for reducing or eliminating unused capacity?

6. What recommendation would you make to management regarding how the cost of unused (i.e., idle) capacity should be assigned?

[LO 15-5] 15-49 **Two-Variance Analysis: Service Company Example** Acme Financial issues letters of credit to importers for overseas purchases. The company charges a nonrefundable application fee of $4,000 and, on approval, an additional service fee of 2.0% of the amount of credit requested.

    The company's budget for the year just completed included fixed expenses for office salaries and wages of $600,000, leasing office space and equipment of $60,000, and utilities and other operating expenses of $10,000. In addition, the budget also included variable expenses for supplies and other variable overhead costs of $1,000,000. The company estimated these variable overhead costs to be $2,000 for each letter of credit approved and issued. The company approves, on average, 75% of the applications it receives.

    During the year, the company received 600 requests and approved 70% of them. The total variable overhead was 10.0% higher than the standard amount applied; the total fixed expenses were 5.0% lower than the amount budgeted.

    In addition to these expenses, the company paid a $270,000 insurance premium for the letters of credit issued. The insurance premium is 1.0% of the amount of credits issued in U.S. dollars. The actual amount of credit issued often differs from the amount requested due to fluctuations in exchange rates and variations in the amount shipped versus the amount ordered by importers. The strength of the dollar during the year decreased the insurance premium by 10.0%.

Required

1. Calculate (or determine) the following budgeted overhead costs for the year: (a) the variable overhead application rate (per letter of credit issued), (b) the insurance cost percentage (to 1 decimal place), and (c) the fixed overhead application rate (per letter of credit issued).

2. Prepare an analysis of the overhead cost variances for the year just completed and in so doing answer the following questions: (a) What is the total overhead flexible budget variance for the period, rounded to the nearest whole dollar? (b) What is the overhead volume variance for the period, rounded to the nearest whole dollar? (c) What is the total overhead cost variance for the year, rounded to the nearest whole dollar? Indicate whether each of the above variances is favorable (F) or unfavorable (U).

[LO 15-2, 15-6] 15-50 **ABC vs. Traditional Approaches to Control of Batch-Related Overhead Costs** The Bangor Manufacturing Company makes mechanical toy robots that are typically produced in batches of 250 units. Prior to the current year, the company's accountants used a standard cost system with a simplified method of assigning manufacturing support (i.e., overhead) costs to products: All such costs were allocated to outputs based on the standard machine hours allowed for output produced. You have recently joined the accounting team and are developing a proposal that the company adopt an ABC system for both product costing and control purposes. To illustrate the benefit of such a system in terms of the latter, you decide to put together an analysis of batch-related overhead costs. You chose these costs because a previous investigation indicated that there is both a variable component to these costs (materials plus power) plus a fixed component (depreciation and salaries). Last year's budget indicated that the variable overhead cost per setup hour was $20.00 and that the fixed overhead production setup costs per year were $20,000. Output was budgeted at 10,000 units for the year. Typically, a batch takes 4 hours of setup time. For cost control purposes, assume that the flexible budget is based on the budgeted number of setup hours for the output of the period.

    You have also collected data regarding actual results for the past year. Specifically, the company produced (and sold) 9,000 toy robots, which were produced in an average batch size of 200 units. The actual setup hours per batch last year turned out to be 4.25 hours, and the actual variable overhead cost per setup hour was $19.00. Actual fixed setup-related overhead costs were $21,000 last year.

    Your discussion with the company controller indicates that under the previous accounting system, all setup-related overhead costs were allocated to production based on machine hours. The standard machine hours allowed per unit produced was 1.50 hours. The denominator activity level assumed for applying fixed manufacturing support costs to units produced was 15,000 machine hours.

Required

1. Under the ABC approach, what were (a) the spending variance and (b) the production volume variance last year for the *fixed setup-related overhead costs* described above? Round answers to nearest whole dollar (e.g., $998.891 = $999), and indicate whether each variance is favorable (F) or unfavorable (U). How would you explain these results to management?

2. Under the ABC approach, what were (a) the spending variance and (b) the efficiency variance last year for the *variable setup-related overhead costs* described above? Round answers to 2 decimal places (e.g., $188.784 = $188.78), and indicate whether each variance is favorable (F) or unfavorable (U). How would you explain these results to management?

3. Write a brief statement outlining the projected costs and benefits of using an ABC approach for the day-to-day control of the overhead costs referred to above as compared to the use of a more traditional cost system.

4. The Bangor Manufacturing Company is currently experiencing severe cost-based pressure from foreign competitors. As such, top management of the company is interested in improving the existing financial-control system in the organization. What other recommendation might you have for management in this regard? That is, what do you recommend to accompany the type of financial analysis referred to above?

[LO 15-2]   **15-51   Standard Cost Variance Analysis and Interpretations**   Glavine & Co. produces a single product, each unit of which requires three direct labor hours (DLHs). Practical capacity (for setting the factory overhead application rate) is 30,000 DLHs, on an annual basis. The information below pertains to the most recent year:

Standard direct labor hours (DLHs) per unit produced	3.00
Practical capacity, in DLHs (per year)	30,000
Variable Overhead Efficiency Variance	$5,000 unfavorable (U)
Actual production for the year	9,500 units
Budgeted fixed manufacturing overhead	$600,000
Standard direct labor wage rate	$ 20.00 per DLH
Total overhead cost variance for the year	$50,000 favorable (F)
Direct Labor Efficiency Variance	$10,000 unfavorable (U)

Required

1. What was the actual number of direct labor hours (DLHs) worked during the year? (Round answer to nearest whole number.) [*Hint:* Recall from Chapter 14 that the DL Efficiency Variance = SP × (SQ − AQ), where SP = standard labor rate per hour, SQ = standard # of DLHs for output produced, and AQ = actual number of DLHs worked.]

2. What was the standard variable overhead rate per DLH during the year? (Round answer to 2 decimal places, e.g., $13.231 = $13.23.) [*Hint:* Recall that the Variable Overhead Efficiency Variance = SP × (SQ − AQ), where [assuming variable overhead is applied on the basis of DLHs] SP = standard variable overhead cost per DLH, SQ = standard # of DLHs for output produced, and AQ = actual # of DLHs worked during the period.]

3. What was the total overhead application rate per direct labor hour (DLH) during the year? (Round answer to 2 decimal places, e.g., $15.679 = $15.68.)

4. What was the total actual overhead cost incurred during the year, rounded to the nearest whole dollar?

5. What was the Production Volume Variance (to the nearest whole dollar) for the year? Was this variance favorable (F) or unfavorable (U)?

6. What was the total Overhead Spending Variance (to the nearest whole dollar) for the year? Was this variance favorable (F) or unfavorable (U)?

7. Provide a short interpretive statement regarding the financial performance of the company for the current year.

8. What recommendations can you offer to the company in terms of achieving increases in operational control?

[LO 15-2, 15-3, 15-4]   **15-52   Summary Problem—Four-Variance Breakdown of the Total Overhead Variance; Journal Entries**   ACME manufacturing is a low-cost producer of a single, commodity product: RGL-01. Standard overhead cost information for one unit of this product is presented below:

Standard number of machine hours per unit produced	0.5
Standard variable overhead rate per machine hour	$30.00
Budgeted fixed overhead (for the year)	$300,000
Practical capacity, in units (annual basis)	10,000
Budgeted output for the coming year, in units	8,000
Normal capacity, in units (per year)	9,000
Actual production for the year (in units)	9,200
Actual overhead costs incurred during the year:	
Fixed overhead	$288,000
Variable overhead	$142,600
Actual number of machine hours per unit for work done this period	0.49

Required

1. Calculate the fixed overhead application rate per machine hour (rounded to 2 decimal places) using (a) budgeted output, (b) normal capacity, and (c) practical capacity.

2. What is the total overhead application rate per machine hour (rounded to 2 decimal places) for each of the three choices identified in requirement 1?

3. What is the total overhead variance for the year when the overhead application rate per machine hour is determined under each of the following options: (a) budgeted output, (b) normal capacity, and (c) practical capacity? [Round answers to nearest whole number, and indicate whether each variance is favorable (F) or unfavorable (U).]

4. What is causing the results you observe in requirement 3?

5. What is the Overhead Efficiency Variance (= Variable Overhead Efficiency Variance) for the year when the overhead application rate per machine hour is determined under each of the following options: (a) budgeted output, (b) normal capacity, and (c) practical capacity? [Round answers to nearest whole number, and indicate whether each variance is favorable (F) or unfavorable (U).]

6. Provide an interpretation of the results reported in requirement 5.

7. What is the total Overhead Spending Variance for the year under each of the following assumptions regarding the denominator activity level used to set the overhead application rate for the year: (a) budgeted output, (b) normal capacity, and (c) practical capacity? Round answers to nearest whole dollar, and state whether each variance is favorable (F) or unfavorable (U).

8. Break down the Total Overhead Spending Variance (as determined in requirement 7) into (a) a Fixed Overhead Spending Variance and (b) a Variable Overhead Spending Variance. Round answers to nearest whole dollar, and state whether each variance is favorable (F) or unfavorable (U).

9. Provide an interpretation of the results reported in requirements 7 and 8.

10. Calculate the Production Volume Variance when the overhead application rate per machine hour is determined under each of the following options: (a) budgeted output, (b) normal capacity, and (c) practical capacity. Round answers to nearest whole dollar, and state whether each variance is favorable (F) or unfavorable (U).

11. Provide an interpretation of the results reported in requirement 10.

12. Summary analysis: Prepare a four-variance analysis of the total overhead variance for the period under each of the following options for determining the fixed overhead application rate: (a) budgeted output, (b) normal capacity, and (c) practical capacity.

13. Provide summary journal entries at the end of the year to (a) record all four overhead cost variances (calculated above, in requirement 12) and (b) close the variances to Cost of Goods Sold (COGS). Assume that variances were determined using "practical capacity" as the denominator volume level for establishing the fixed overhead application rate and the total overhead application rate. Also assume that the company uses a single account, Factory Overhead, to record overhead costs.

Solution to Self-Study Problem

Analysis of the Total Overhead Cost Variance

1. a.	Units manufactured during the period	360
	Standard direct labor hours allowed per unit produced	× 2
	Total standard direct labor hours allowed for the units manufactured	720
	Standard variable factory overhead rate per direct labor hour (given)	× $5.00
	Flexible budget for variable factory overhead for the units produced	$3,600
b.	The total variable factory overhead cost applied to production (same as the flexible budget for variable overhead based on output)	$3,600
c.	Practical capacity (units)	400
	Standard direct labor hours per unit	× 2
	Total standard direct labor hours at practical capacity	800
	Standard fixed factory overhead rate per direct labor hour (given)	× $20
	Total budgeted fixed factory overhead for the period	$16,000
d.	Total standard direct labor hours for the units manufactured (from 1a)	720
	Standard fixed factory overhead rate per direct labor hour (given)	× $20
	Total fixed factory overhead applied	$14,400

2. a, b, and c.

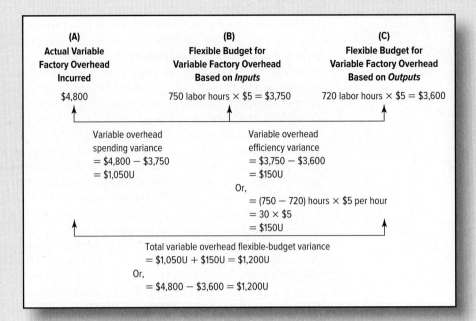

d. Total underapplied variable factory overhead = Total variable overhead flexible budget variance = $1,200

e, f, and g.

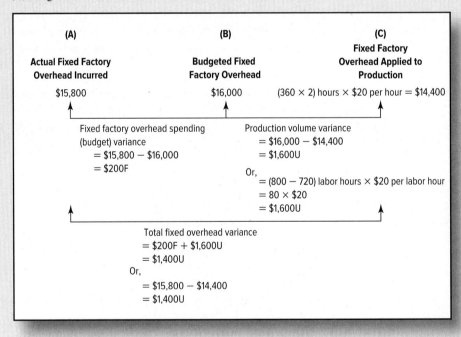

h. Total underapplied fixed factory overhead = Total fixed overhead variance = $1,400U

3. a. $\text{Overhead spending variance} = \text{Variable factory overhead spending variance} + \text{Fixed factory overhead spending variance}$
    = $1,050U + $200F
    = $850U

    b. $\text{Overhead efficiency variance} = \text{Variable factory overhead efficiency variance} = \$150U$

    c. Fixed overhead production volume variance = $1,600U

4. $$\text{Total overhead} \atop \text{flexible-budget variance} = \text{Overhead} \atop \text{spending variance} + \text{Overhead} \atop \text{efficiency variance}$$
$$= \$850U + \$150U$$
$$= \$1,000U$$

Fixed overhead production volume variance is $1,600U, the amount identified in both four-variance and three-variance analyses.

5. a.	Factory Overhead	20,600	
	Cash, Prepaid Accounts, Accumulated Depreciation, and/or Sundry Payable Accounts		20,600
b.	Work-in-Process Inventory	18,000	
	Factory Overhead		18,000
c.	Variable Factory Overhead Spending Variance	1,050	
	Variable Factory Overhead Efficiency Variance	150	
	Fixed Overhead Production Volume Variance	1,600	
	Factory Overhead		2,600
	Fixed Factory Overhead Spending Variance		200
d.(1)	Cost of Goods Sold	2,600	
	Fixed Factory Overhead Spending Variance	200	
	Variable Factory Overhead Spending Variance		1,050
	Variable Factory Overhead Efficiency Variance		150
	Fixed Overhead Production Volume Variance		1,600

d.(2) Ending balances at standard cost:

Work-in-Process Inventory ($153,000 − $134,640)	$18,360
Finished Goods Inventory ($134,640 − $111,690)	22,950
Cost of Goods Sold (COGS)	111,690
Total	$153,000

Account	Standard Cost	Percentage of Total	Proration of Net Variance	Adjusted Cost
Work-in-Process Inventory	$18,360	12%	$2,600 × 0.12 = $ 312	$ 18,672
Finished Goods Inventory	22,950	15	2,600 × 0.15 = 390	23,340
Cost of Goods Sold	111,690	73	2,600 × 0.73 = 1,898	113,588
Total	$153,000	100%	$2,600	$155,600

Cost of Goods Sold	1,898	
Work-in-Process Inventory	312	
Finished Goods Inventory	390	
Fixed Factory Overhead Spending Variance	200	
Variable Factory Overhead Spending Variance		1,050
Variable Factory Overhead Efficiency Variance		150
Fixed Overhead Production Volume Variance		1,600

Please visit Connect to access a narrated, animated tutorial for solving the Self-Study problem for this chapter.

CHAPTER SIXTEEN

Operational Performance Measurement:
Further Analysis of Productivity and Sales

After studying this chapter, you should be able to . . .

LO 16-1   Explain the strategic role of the flexible budget in analyzing productivity and sales.

LO 16-2   Calculate and interpret the measures for total productivity, partial operational productivity, and partial financial productivity.

LO 16-3   Use the flexible budget to calculate and interpret the sales quantity, sales mix, market size, and market share variances.

LO 16-4   Use the flexible budget to analyze sales performance over time.

"Stressing output is the key to improving productivity, while looking to increase activity can result in just the opposite."

Paul Gauguin, artist

The quote from this nineteenth-century artist seems to be telling us that more activity is not the same as more productivity. Measuring and managing productivity can be tricky and difficult at times, and productivity improvement does not have much benefit if there is no demand for the resulting outputs. This chapter covers the measures of performance for both productivity (employee output per labor hour or other measure of input) and sales growth. Productivity and sales growth can both be measured on many dimensions, and a comprehensive analysis of these many dimensions is often the key to tracking performance and attaining strategic goals. Productivity and sales growth have been much in the news, and the news is not good. In December 2019, the U.S. Bureau of Labor Statistics reported nonfarm business sector labor

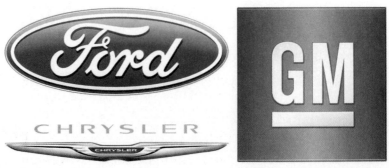

Rvlsoft/Shutterstock

productivity decreased 0.2 percent in the third quarter of 2019. The report stated that, while output increased 2.3 percent, hours worked increased 2.5 percent. The results do not compare well to an average annual increase of 2.2 percent since World War II. This drop is not an outlier because there were several consecutive quarters of productivity decline in 2016.[1]

As an example of the relevance of productivity and sales growth measures, the period 2008–2011 was a challenge for the auto industry worldwide; sales fell by 30 percent or more at many auto companies. The recession's effect on unemployment, the increase in gasoline prices, the March 2011 earthquake and tsunami in Japan, and the 2011 flooding in Thailand had a dramatic effect on the industry worldwide. This period also saw both GM and Chrysler go through bankruptcy and move from unprofitable to profitable companies. Dramatic reductions in output and labor costs led the way. In fact, by late 2011, labor and benefits costs per hour at the "Detroit Big Three" averaged $55, which was very close to that of Japanese rivals. What a change! In 2007, for example, GM paid $1,400 more in labor costs per vehicle than Toyota. After its bankruptcy reorganization, GM's labor costs had come down significantly. In just three years, the Detroit automakers came close to parity in productivity with other worldwide automakers. However, the competition is not standing still, as can be seen by Volkswagen's goal to increase productivity by 30 percent by 2025. Recent improvements in profitability have also led union negotiators to ask for wage increases. GM, for example, may be faced with paying its Canadian workers the auto industry's second highest rates in the world.[2]

The measurement of productivity and sales growth turns out to be an extension of the operational performance measures introduced in Chapters 14 and 15—standard costing and the flexible budget, nonfinancial operational performance measures, and resource-capacity planning. This chapter extends Chapters 14 and 15 through coverage of an extension of the flexible budget—productivity measures and additional sales variance measures. Other methods for improving efficiency and financial control are covered elsewhere in the text (see Chapter 1 for a summary), including target costing, benchmarking, business process improvement, and total quality management.

The Strategic Role of the Flexible Budget in Analyzing Productivity and Sales

LO 16-1

Explain the strategic role of the flexible budget in analyzing productivity and sales.

The strategic role of sales analysis is to better understand the reasons behind an increase (or decrease) in total sales dollars relative to the budgeted amount or an increase (decrease) over the prior year. The key question for a competitive analysis is how the change in sales has affected the firm's profitability and growth in desired market areas. Is the firm meeting strategic sales goals? Are sales changing in profitable or unprofitable product lines? To begin to answer these questions, the total amount of change in sales is decomposed into many components, each of which holds some answers about these strategic questions. For example, the total dollar change in sales over (or under) the budget can be explained in terms of changes in selling prices and changes in the volume of units sold. A change in prices or volume will affect total sales. The decomposition of total sales into these two variances, the selling price and sales volume variances, is illustrated using the flexible budget in Chapter 14. Chapter 16 now takes one of these two variances, the sales volume variance, and further decomposes it into elements that explain the effect of changes in product mix (the proportion of total sales for each of the products), the size of the markets for the firm's products, and the firm's share in these markets. This extended analysis allows managers to see how changes in product mix, market size, and market share affect profits. The decomposition of the sales variances uses the flexible budget in two ways:

[1] Jeffrey Sparshot, "U.S. News: U.S. Productivity, Past and Present," *The Wall Street Journal,* May 5, 2017, p. A2; Ben Leubsdorf, "Productivity Fall Imperils Growth," *The Wall Street Journal,* August 10, 2016, p. A1.

[2] Data from the Center for Automotive Research, a nonprofit research group, as cited on **Cars.com**, October 14, 2011. See also Bill Vlasic, "With New Labor Contracts, Detroit Protects Turnaround," *The Wall Street Journal,* October 28, 2011, pp. B1–2; "A Jump in Labor Costs," *Bloomberg Businessweek,* August 29, 2011, p. 16; "How America Started Selling Cars Again," *Time,* December 19, 2011, pp. 31–41; Nagesh Gautham Nagesh and Paul Vieira, "Detroit Opens Canada Talks—Auto Workers Union Pushes to Save Jobs as More Investment Moves into Mexico," *The Wall Street Journal,* August 11, 2016, p. B3; "Increased Productivity at the Heart of Volkswagen," **www.volkswagenag.com/en/news/stories/2019/02/productivity-and-efficiency-at-volkswagen-production.html**, accessed January 30, 2020.

(1) analyzing differences between actual sales and the master budget sales (the approach illustrated in Chapter 14) and (2) analyzing changes in sales over the prior year.

The strategic role of productivity analysis is to assist management in identifying the drivers of productivity and to implement methods that improve productivity and profitability. The news is mixed with regard to productivity. While it may be true that productivity in most countries has been increasing in recent years, the increases may not match historical trends. In the United States, data from the Bureau of Labor Statistics show that productivity in the 1950s and 1960s grew an average of about 2.6 percent annually. In recent years, it has been as low as 0.6 percent. However, productivity has differed substantially across industries, depending on the industry's ability to control waste and labor costs and to develop product and manufacturing process innovations. For example, some of the industries that have been slow to innovate relative to other industries include home construction, printing, and food manufacturing.

The key determinants of productivity for most organizations are:

1. Control of waste.
2. Product and manufacturing process innovation.
3. Fluctuations in demand or resource usage due to changes in the business cycle or for other reasons.

First, the control of waste is achieved through efforts in work flow management and quality control. A good example is the Toyota Production System (TPS), which has helped Toyota be recognized as one of the most productive automakers in the world. The main elements of TPS are (1) a long-term focus on relationships with suppliers and coordination with these suppliers; (2) an emphasis on balanced, continuous flow manufacturing with stable production levels; (3) continuous improvement in product design and manufacturing processes with the objective of eliminating waste; and (4) flexible manufacturing systems (FMSs) in which different vehicles are produced on the same assembly line and employees are trained for a variety of tasks. The focus on waste and balanced production flows is also called *lean manufacturing*.

Product and process innovation is the second key determinant of competitiveness in productivity, often achieved through the implementation of information technology. Third, it is important to understand that productivity in a firm or industry is greatly influenced by the business cycle. Higher productivity is usually seen when a firm is coming out of a low point in the business cycle, as the firm stretches existing resources to meet demand, and then productivity growth slows as resources are added. So it is always important to analyze productivity within the larger context of the competitive environment and business cycle in which the firm operates. While many of the examples to follow are in the manufacturing context, the topic of productivity applies as well in service companies where labor costs are a high proportion of total costs. Examples of productivity analysis in the service industries are included in the end-of-chapter problems.

Analyzing Productivity

LO 16-2

Calculate and interpret the measures for total productivity, partial operational productivity, and partial financial productivity.

"The single best measure of a country's average standard of living is productivity: the value of output of goods and services a country produces per worker. The more workers produce, the more income they receive, and the more they can consume. Higher productivity results in higher standards of living."

Martin Neil Baily and Matthew J. Slaughter,
former members of the U.S. president's
Council of Economic Advisers

productivity
The ratio of output to input.

Looking at the quote above, one might argue that productivity is key to the success of a country, a company, and an individual worker. **Productivity** is measured as the ratio of output to input.

$$\text{Productivity} = \frac{\text{Output}}{\text{Input}}$$

As noted in the introduction to the chapter, the most common way to improve total productivity is to reduce the workforce. This approach was used widely during the 2008–2010 recession, during which approximately 9 million jobs were lost in the United States. In more recent times, the use of tariffs, trade wars, and moves toward economic nationalism have also impacted demand. Here are some examples of how companies have lowered their costs and improved their operational productivity.

WORKING LEANER

In 2016 falling demand caused Caterpillar to lay off workers. As demand picked up, not everyone was rehired. In one plant in North Carolina, the company was able to produce more loaders with 30 percent fewer people. One way to do this was through the use of flexible contracts for nearly one-third of the 550 factory employees. Another action was to redesign new equipment to reduce the number of parts by over 20 percent.

Sources: Rajesh Kumar Singh, "Caterpillar Leans on Old Playbook to Cope with Trump Tariffs," Reuters.com, September 21, 2018, www.reuters.com/article/us-caterpillar-cuts/caterpillar-leans-on-old-playbook-to-cope-with-trump-tariffs-idUSKCN1M10DH; Rajesh Kumar Singh, "Caterpillar Lays off 120 Workers as Trade War Hits Sales," Reuters.com, November 4, 2019, www.reuters.com/article/caterpillar-layoffs/update-3-caterpillar-lays-off-120-workers-as-trade-war-hits-sales-idUSL2N27K15W, accessed February 3, 2020.

REDUCING MATERIALS CONTENT (IMPROVING MATERIALS PRODUCTIVITY)

The fashion industry reduces costs by reducing the workforce, as in many other industries. But companies that produce large quantities of men's pants have found that costs can also be reduced significantly by making small changes in the garment—removing the watch pocket, eliminating cuffs and pleats, using less expensive buttons, working with coarser fabric, and cutting the fabric more carefully. These reductions require careful market analysis because the changes cannot be changes that are easily perceived by the customer, such as pockets that are so shallow that loose change falls out.

Source: Chris Burritt, "Why 'Less Is More' Rules Fashion," *Bloomberg Businessweek,* May 30, 2011, pp. 18–19.

RETURNING MANUFACTURING JOBS TO THE UNITED STATES FROM CHINA

As productivity has improved in the United States in recent years, it has slowed in China due to wage increases there. Projections of labor productivity show the productivity gap between the United States and China closing over the next five years. In response, Caterpillar, Ford, General Electric, and NCR (maker of ATMs) plan to return some work positions from China back to the United States.

Sources: Peter Coy, "A Renaissance in U.S. Manufacturing," *Bloomberg Businessweek,* May 9, 2011, pp. 11–13; James R. Hagerty, "Once Made in China: Jobs Trickle Back to U.S. Plants," *The Wall Street Journal,* May 22, 2012, p. 1; Louis Uchitelle, "The U.S. Gains Factory Jobs, but Workers Give Ground on Wages," *The New York Times,* December 30, 2011, p. B1.

AUTOMATION

Airbus has a backlog of orders for nearly 6,000 of their A320 jets, making improving the efficiency of the production process a priority. They built a new production facility that took a modular approach to producing the jets, an approach not normally seen in aircraft production. Within the new facility, the company can use 20 percent fewer people to produce the same number of planes. More productivity improvement through automation is planned, but one consulting firm estimates it may be up to 10 years before the production process is more than 65 percent automated.

Source: Dimitra Kessenides and David Rocks, "A Ballet of Airbus Jets," *Bloomberg Businessweek,* April 22, 2019, pp. 43–45.

STRATEGY SUPERSEDES COST CUTTING

However, sometimes strategy outweighs the focus on productivity improvement. General Electric built a new locomotive factory in a tiny impoverished village in India as part of a survival strategy in an environment of rising national protectionism. The company incurred the high costs of building in this inhospitable location because of the growing need to have local roots in a nation to win business.

Source: Ted Mann and Brian Spegele, "Why GE Builds More Factories Overseas—Rising Protectionism Led Conglomerate to a Flood-Challenged Locomotive Plant in India," *The Wall Street Journal,* June 30, 2017, p. A1.

A firm that spends five days to manufacture 100 units has a productivity of 20 units per day. A social service worker who processes 75 cases over a four-week period has a productivity of 18.75 cases per week. A firm that uses 24.5 pounds of material for each unit manufactured is more productive than a firm that uses 25 pounds of the same materials to manufacture one unit of the same product. To improve productivity, firms need to know the productivity levels of their operations.

A measure of productivity can be either an operational or a financial productivity measure. **Operational productivity** is the ratio of output units to input units. Both the numerator and the denominator are physical measures. **Financial productivity** is also a ratio of output to input, except that either the numerator or the denominator is a dollar amount, or both are in dollar amounts. For example, the number of tables made from a sheet of plywood involves operational productivity; the number of tables per dollar cost of plywood reflects financial productivity.

operational productivity
The ratio of output units to the number of units of an input factor.

financial productivity
The ratio of output to the dollar amount of one or more input factors.

partial productivity
A productivity measure that focuses only on the relationship between one of the inputs and the output attained.

total productivity
A productivity measure that includes all input resources in computing the ratio of the output attained to the input resources consumed.

A productivity measure may include all production factors or focus on a single factor or part of the production factors that the firm uses in manufacturing. A productivity measure that focuses on the relationship between one of the input factors and the output attained is a **partial productivity** measure. The following are examples of partial productivity:

- Direct materials productivity (output per unit of direct material used).
- Workforce productivity (output per labor hour or output per person employed).
- Process productivity (output per machine hour or output per kilowatt-hour).

A productivity measure that includes all input resources used in production is a **total productivity** measure. The number of tables manufactured per dollar of manufacturing costs is a total productivity measure because the denominator, manufacturing costs, includes all manufacturing costs incurred to make the tables. Exhibit 16.1 provides examples of productivity measures.

Exhibit 16.2 presents selected production data of Erie Precision Tool Company's drill bit manufacturing for 2021 and 2022. The manufacturing costs include total fixed factory overhead and other operating expenses of $300,000 per year and variable manufacturing costs consisting of metal alloy (direct materials) and direct labor.

The firm earned $1,100,000 operating income in 2022, a 17 percent increase over the $940,000 earned in 2021. Without examining the operating data in detail, management would probably be happy with the improvement. The increase in operating income, however, compares unfavorably to the improvement in total sales. The total sales in 2022 are 120 percent of the total sales in 2021. With the fixed factory overhead and other fixed operating expenses remaining unchanged at $300,000 each year, the increase in operating income should have been more than the 20 percent increase in total sales. The lower increase in operating income is a result of a higher-than-proportional increase in the firm's variable costs for direct materials and direct labor. The total variable costs increased 32 percent [($1,000,000 − $760,000) ÷ $760,000], while the total sales increased only 20 percent.

Several factors could have contributed to the increase in direct materials and direct labor costs, including increases in the number of units manufactured and sold, changes in the amounts and/or the proportions of the inputs used in production, and increases in the unit cost

EXHIBIT 16.1   Examples of Productivity Measures

	Partial Productivity		Total Productivity	
	Operational	**Financial**	**Total Units of Output**	**Sales Value of Output**
Numerator (output)	Units of output	Units of output	Units of output	Sales value of output
Denominator (input)	Units of input	Dollar value of input	Dollar value of input	Dollar value of input
Productivity measure (output/input)	Units of output per unit of input	Units of output per dollar value of input	Units of output per dollar value of input	Dollar value of output per dollar value of input

EXHIBIT 16.2
Operating Data of Erie Precision Tool Company

ERIE PRECISION TOOL COMPANY Operating Data		
	2022	**20121**
Units manufactured and sold	4,800	4,000
Sales ($500 per unit)	$2,400,000	$2,000,000
Direct materials (25,000 lbs. at $24/lb. in 2021 and 32,000 lbs. at $25/lb. in 2022)	800,000	600,000
Direct labor (4,000 hrs. at $40 per hr. in 2021 and 4,000 hrs. at $50/hr. in 2022)	200,000	160,000
Fixed factory overhead and other fixed operating expenses	300,000	300,000
Operating income	$1,100,000	$ 940,000

REAL-WORLD FOCUS   Productivity vs. Profitability: An Either/Or Situation?

As companies started emerging from the recession in June 2009, productivity rose rapidly. During the recession, companies had learned to be lean and efficient, requiring workers to do more with less. However, productivity nearly stalled, averaging less than a 1 percent increase per year for several years. As noted by Phillips and Coy, "Workers were actually less efficient in the first quarter of 2014." Why the decline? One primary reason is that companies were not investing in their workers. Growth in capital spending was low and workers were not getting the new equipment, software, and other infrastructure items they needed to be more productive. In fact, the Bureau of Economic Analysis states that the average age of equipment in the United States is now 7.4 years, the highest in 20 years. Also, over the past 5 years, the average output per worker hour has grown at an annual rate of just 1.3 percent, well below the 2.3 percent average over the 20 years prior to the recession. Lower productivity makes companies less efficient,

which depresses wages. Companies have cash—the cash on corporate balance sheets increased nearly 70 percent in the 4 years after the recession. However, companies are choosing to spend their cash on dividends and stock buybacks rather than investing in capital. Dividends do not reduce income, and stock buybacks increase earnings per share because fewer shares are outstanding. Therefore, Wall Street has been rewarding those companies that do not invest in productivity. According to Morgan Stanley, "Companies that haven't spent on new equipment have outperformed those that have spent for most of the recovery." Perhaps a change in investor sentiment will start to reward companies that invest in productivity.

Sources: Matthew Phillips and Peter Coy, "Choosing Profits over Productivity," *Bloomberg Businessweek,* May 10, 2014, pp. 12–13; Justin Lahart, "America Inc.'s Cure for Higher Wage Costs: Start Spending," *The Wall Street Journal,* July 21, 2014, p. C6.

of resources. The firm should identify factors that caused the changes so that management can decrease manufacturing costs and increase operating income.

Productivity measurements discussed in this chapter examine the effect of a firm's productivity on its operating income. Increased productivity decreases costs and increases operating income. Changes in the productivity of different resources, however, do not always occur in the same direction or at an equal rate. A firm's productivity of direct materials usage can improve while its direct labor productivity might deteriorate. For instance, a furniture manufacturer increased materials productivity by reducing waste due to improper cutting of lumber. However, to reduce improper cutting of lumber, workers spent more labor hours to cut the boards carefully. The labor hour productivity decreased. Management needs to know the changes in productivity of individual production resources, which partial productivity measures provide.

Partial Productivity

A partial productivity measure depicts the relationship between output and one of the required input resources used in producing the output:

$$\text{Partial productivity} = \frac{\text{Number of units manufactured}}{\text{Number of units or cost of a single input resource}}$$

For example, the partial productivity of the direct materials for the Erie Precision Tool Company in 2021 is 0.16 unit of output per pound of material, as computed here:

$$\text{Partial productivity of direct materials in 2021} = \frac{4,000}{25,000} = 0.16 \text{ unit/pound}$$

Partial Operational Productivity

Firms often use benchmarks in assessing productivity. Benchmarks often used include past productivity measures of the firm, the productivity of another firm in the same industry, the industry standard or average, or benchmarks established by top management as the goal for the firm to attain. Sources of benchmarking information include industry and national associations focused on productivity and quality, such as the APICS (www.apics.org), the American Productivity & Quality Center (http://www.apqc.org), and the American Society for Quality (http://www.asq.org). In this example, we use Erie Precision Tool Company's productivity level in 2021 as the benchmark to assess productivity in 2022.

EXHIBIT 16.3
Partial Productivity of Erie Precision Tool Company

ERIE PRECISION TOOL COMPANY		
Partial Productivity—Direct Materials and Direct Labor		
	Partial Operational Productivity	
	2022	**2021**
Direct materials	4,800 ÷ 32,000 = 0.15	4,000 ÷ 25,000 = 0.16
Direct labor	4,800 ÷ 4,000 = 1.20	4,000 ÷ 4,000 = 1.00
	Partial Financial Productivity	
	2022	**2021**
Direct materials	4,800 ÷ $800,000 = 0.006	4,000 ÷ $600,000 = 0.0067
Direct labor	4,800 ÷ $200,000 = 0.024	4,000 ÷ $160,000 = 0.025

A comparison of partial productivity from 2021 to 2022 shows that the partial productivity of direct materials decreased. The firm manufactured 0.16 unit in 2021 but only 0.15 unit in 2022 from 1 pound of direct materials, a 6.25 percent decrease in productivity. (See Exhibit 16.3 for calculations.) Partial productivity of direct labor, however, improved in 2022. The firm manufactured one unit for each direct labor hour in 2021 and 1.2 units per hour in 2022, a 20 percent increase in productivity.

Changes in productivity also can be examined by computing the amount of input resources that the firm would have used in 2022 had it maintained the 2021 partial productivity, as shown in Exhibit 16.4. In this case, the 4,800 units manufactured and sold in 2022 would have required only 30,000 pounds of direct materials (4,800 ÷ 0.16). The decreased partial productivity required the use of an additional 2,000 pounds in 2022 (32,000 − 30,000). Similarly, the firm would have used 4,800 direct labor hours in 2022 had it had the same direct labor partial productivity in 2022 as in 2021. The firm saved the cost for 800 hours of direct labor (4,800 − 4,000) when its partial productivity in 2022 for direct labor increased from 1.0 to 1.2.

Partial Financial Productivity

The bottom panel of Exhibit 16.3 reports the partial financial productivity of direct materials and direct labor. The partial financial productivity indicates the number of units of output manufactured for each dollar the firm spent on the input resource. The partial financial productivity for direct materials is determined by dividing the output (4,800 units in 2022 and 4,000 units in 2021 by the cost of the resource for the year (cost of direct materials: $800,000 in 2022 and $600,000 in 2021). The partial financial productivity for direct materials is 0.0060 in 2022 and 0.0067 in 2021, a decrease in productivity from 2021 to 2022 of 10 percent [(0.0067 − 0.006) ÷ 0.0067].

The direct labor partial financial productivity is 0.025 for 2021 and 0.024 for 2022, a decrease of 4 percent [(0.025 − 0.024) ÷ 0.025]. This result is in conflict with the direct labor partial operational productivity reported earlier (20 percent improvement). These results suggest that although employee productivity per hour increased, the cost increase due to higher hourly wages more than offset the gain in productivity per hour.

EXHIBIT 16.4
Changes in Operational Partial Productivity of Erie Precision Tool Company

ERIE PRECISION TOOL COMPANY					
Effects of Changes in Operational Partial Productivity of Direct Materials and Direct Labor					
Input Resource	(1) 2022 Output	(2) 2021 Partial Operational Productivity	(3) = (1) ÷ (2) 2022 Output at 2021 Productivity	(4) Input Used in 2022	(5) = (3) − (4) Savings (Loss) in Units of Input
Direct materials	4,800	0.16	30,000	32,000	(2,000)
Direct labor	4,800	1.00	4,800	4,000	800

Factors that may contribute to the difference in manufacturing costs between two operations are differences in output level, input cost, or productivity. Panel 1 of Exhibit 16.5 shows how the flexible budget can be used for determining the effects of each of these factors. Point A is the actual operating results of 2021. The amounts for all three factors at point A are the actual 2022 figures: units of output, productivity, and input cost. Point B is the cost to manufacture the 2022 output at the 2021 productivity level and 2022 input cost. The only difference

EXHIBIT 16.5 **Partitioning Partial Financial Productivity Using the Flexible Budget**

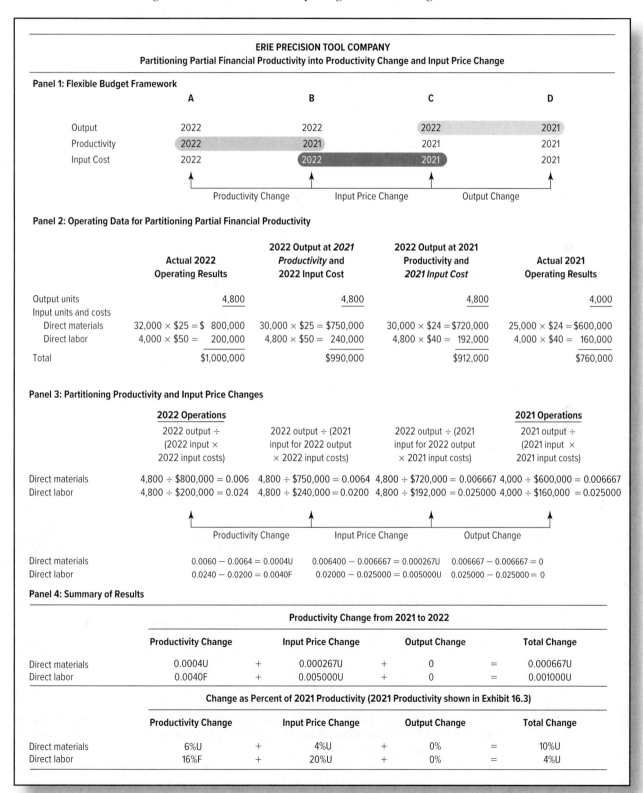

between points A and B is in productivity. Thus, any difference between points A and B is attributable to changes in productivity between 2022 and 2021.

Point C is the cost to manufacture the 2022 output at the 2021 productivity level and 2021 input cost. The only difference between points B and C is in the unit cost of the input resource in each of the years. Point B uses the 2022 cost per unit for the input resource while point C uses the 2021 cost per unit for the input resource. The difference between the amounts in points B and C, if any, results from the difference in unit cost of the input resource.

Point D is the cost to manufacture the 2021 output at 2021 productivity and 2021 unit cost of the input resource. Any difference in the costs between points C and D is because of different output levels between these two points. The output is then divided by the total cost of the required resource to manufacture the output. Because the total cost of the required resource in each of the years is determined using the same productivity level (2021 productivity) and the same unit cost of the input resource (2021 cost per unit of the input resource), the total cost of the required resource in each of the years is in proportion to their respective output levels. As a result, the ratios of output to input (costs) at points C and D are always identical, and the change in productivity for output change from 2021 to 2022 is always equal to zero. The column for point D is included for completeness to show the total change from the actual results of 2021 compared to the actual results of 2022; the change in productivity from 2021 to 2022 is the result of two changes only: the change in input prices and the change in materials or labor productivity.

The analysis shows that of the 10 percent decrease in partial financial productivity of direct materials (from 0.0067 to 0.006, Exhibit 16.3), 6 percent ($0.0004 \div 0.0067$, bottom of panel 4, Exhibit 16.5) is attributable to productivity change. The remaining 4 percent (bottom of panel 4, Exhibit 16.5) reflects the price change in the cost per pound of direct materials ($24 in 2021 to $25 in 2022).

The 2022 partial financial productivity of direct labor is 4 percent lower than that of 2021 (from 0.025 in 2021 to 0.024 in 2022, Exhibit 16.3). The lower partial financial productivity of direct labor in 2022 is not due to decreased productivity of direct labor in 2022, however. The partial productivity of direct labor increased by 16 percent (bottom of panel 4, Exhibit 16.5). The $10 increase in wages ($40 per hour in 2021 and $50 per hour in 2022) more than offsets the gain in labor productivity. As a result, total direct labor cost increased and the partial financial productivity decreased by 4 percent.

Partial Productivity: Operational vs. Financial

Both the numerator and the denominator of a partial operational productivity measure are physical units. Using physical measures makes partial operational measures easy for operational personnel to understand and use in operations. The fact that an operational productivity measure is unaffected by price changes or other factors also makes it easier to benchmark.

Partial financial productivity has the advantage of considering the effects of both cost and quantity of an input resource on productivity. At the management level, the effect of cost, not merely the physical quantity, is the main concern. In addition, partial financial productivity can be used in operations that use more than one production factor. Partial operational productivity, on the other hand, measures only one input resource at a time.

Limitations of Partial Productivity Analysis

A partial productivity measure has several limitations. First, it measures only the relationship between an input resource and the output; it ignores any effect that changes in other manufacturing factors have on productivity. For example, an improved partial productivity measure could be obtained by decreasing the productivity of one or more other input resources. For example, Erie Precision Tool Company can improve its partial productivity of direct labor by speeding up labor usage, though waste of direct materials might increase. Or it can boost direct materials partial productivity through reduction in direct materials waste by using more labor hours to cut each piece of material carefully. Management accountants call this the cross-substitution of factors of input.

A second limitation is that partial productivity ignores any effect that changes in other production factors have on productivity. For example, increases in materials quality are likely to raise the partial productivity of direct materials as well as direct labor. Erie Precision Tool Company might have workers with more experience or higher skill in 2022 than in 2021. As a result, the partial productivity of labor would increase in 2022 because the average hourly wage rate for workers with more experience or higher skill is higher. Is it worthwhile for the firm to make the trade-off? Unfortunately, an analysis of operational partial productivity cannot provide an answer.

Third, the analysis and interpretation of partial productivity should include effects that changes in the firm's operating characteristics have on the productivity of the input resource. For example, installation of high-efficiency equipment can also improve direct labor partial operational productivity.

Fourth, an improved partial productivity does not necessarily mean that the firm or division operates efficiently. For example, as computed in Exhibit 16.5, an improvement may simply mean productivity is better than last year.

Partial Productivity, the Flexible Budget, and Standard Costs (Review of Chapter 14)

It is common for productivity analysis as illustrated earlier to use the year-to-year analytical framework. The analysis could also be based upon a budget or standard, and then the analysis would be very much like the application of the flexible budget in Chapter 14. For example, in Exhibit 16.5, panel 2, the differences in total costs for each of the points A, B, C, and D represent differences in costs very much like the variances calculated in Chapter 14. The difference is that in Chapter 14, we compared actual performance to the master budget using the flexible budget to distinguish volume and flexible budget variances. Note that one can compute the volume variance in dollars in Exhibit 16.5, panel 2, as $152,000 ($912,000 − $760,000), which is the increased cost for producing 800 more units at standard productivity and price. Now, look back and review the calculation of the sales volume variance in Exhibit 14.4. The sales volume variance for variable costs of $99,000 in column 4 of Exhibit 14.4 is calculated in the same way as the volume variance in Exhibit 16.5, panel 2; the only difference is that the benchmark in Exhibit 14.4 is the master budget, and the benchmark in Exhibit 16.5 is the prior year's results. Similarly, the flexible budget variances for direct labor and direct materials in Chapter 14 are computed in a way similar to the computation of the input price and productivity variances in Exhibit 16.5, panel 2.

In effect, the use of the flexible budget in Chapters 14 and 16 is quite similar, but there are different objectives. The flexible budget in Chapter 14 was used to identify the volume and flexible budget variances for direct materials and direct labor *for changes in volume relative to the master budget.* In contrast, the flexible budget is used in Exhibit 16.5 to identify changes in input prices and productivity *from year to year* (rather than in comparison to the master budget). The variances in Chapter 14 calculate the effect of differences in usage or price for a given level of good output, at a standard level of input. Chapter 14 works with the direct materials or direct labor standard of a certain number of direct materials units or direct labor hours *per unit of output,* while productivity analysis looks at the inverse: the number of units of output *per unit of direct materials or direct labor input.*

Both standard cost analysis (Chapter 14) and productivity analysis (Chapter 16) are widely used and have different objectives. Standard cost analysis focuses on meeting standards of direct materials and direct labor usage, while productivity analysis analyzes changes in productivity over time.

Total Productivity

Total productivity is the ratio of output to the total cost of all input resources used to produce the output.

$$\text{Total productivity} = \frac{\text{Units or sales value of output}}{\text{Total cost of all input resources}}$$

Total productivity is a financial productivity measure. The numerator can be either the number of units or the sales value of the output attained. The denominator is the total dollar amount of all resources used in the production of the output.

The first panel of Exhibit 16.6 shows the computation of Erie Precision Tool Company's total productivity of manufacturing costs for 2021 and 2022. The computation of total

REAL-WORLD FOCUS   Maximizing the Use of Available Capacity

Productivity looks at the relationship between outputs and inputs. Increasing productivity means getting more output from the currently available capacity (inputs). That capacity could be measured in terms of space utilization, but it could also be measured in terms of time available.

USE OF SPACE IN RETAIL

There is a glut of department store retail space, and companies like Sears Holding, Macy's, and J.C. Penney are closing stores in order to improve the level of sales per square foot. One consulting firm estimated that J.C. Penney would have to close nearly 31 percent of it stores to return to the productivity levels of 2006, but this prediction was made before J.C. Penney filed for bankruptcy due to the impact of Covid-19 in early 2020. At the same time, the firm predicted Nordstrom would have to close nearly one-quarter of its stores.

MONITORING TIME AT AMAZON

In the case of Amazon, the capacity is the time a worker has available during a shift in a fulfillment center. In 2019 it was reported that Amazon not only tracks the productivity of its employees, but also fires those who underperform. The termination decision may come with little human intervention. A law firm that represents Amazon said, "Amazon's system tracks the rates of each individual associate's productivity and automatically generates any warnings or terminations regarding quality or productivity without input from supervisors."

Source: Greg Ip, "For Lower-Paid Workers, the Robot Overlords Have Arrived; Software and Algorithms Are Used to Screen, Hire, Assign and Now Terminate Workers," *The Wall Street Journal (Online),* May 1, 2019, www.wsj.com/articles/for-lower-paid-workers-the-robot-overlords-have-arrived-11556719323, accessed February 3, 2020.

productivity involves three steps. First, determine the output of each period: 4,000 units in 2021 and 4,800 units in 2022. Second, calculate the total costs incurred to produce the output: $1,300,000 in 2022 and $1,060,000 in 2021 (Exhibit 16.5, panel 2). Third, compute the total productivity by dividing the amount of output by the total cost of variable input resources: 0.003692 in 2022 and 0.003774 in 2021.

The total productivity indicates that for every thousand dollars of costs incurred in 2022, the firm manufactured 3,692 units of output. The total productivity in 2021 is 0.003774, indicating that the firm manufactured 3,774 units for every thousand dollars of costs.

The total productivity of the resources required to manufacture the output is often used in assessing production operations. Achieving higher productivity by making more units is an important first step for a successful firm.

Limitations of Total Productivity

Total productivity measures the combined productivity of all operating factors. As such, use of a total productivity measure in performance evaluations decreases the possibility of manipulating some of the manufacturing factors to improve the productivity measure of other manufacturing factors.

However, total productivity is a financial productivity measure. Personnel at the operational level may have difficulty linking financial productivity measures to their day-to-day operations. Furthermore, deterioration in total productivity can result from an increase in

EXHIBIT 16.6
Total Productivity for Erie Precision Tool Company

ERIE PRECISION TOOL COMPANY		
Total Productivity		
Panel 1: Total Productivity in Units	**2022**	**2021**
(a) Total units manufactured	4,800	4,000
(b) Total costs incurred	$1,300,000	$1,060,000
(c) Total productivity: (a) ÷ (b)	0.003692	0.003774
(d) Productivity decrease: 0.003692 − 0.003774 = (0.000081), or −2.15% (0.000081 ÷ 0.003774)		
Panel 2: Total Productivity in Sales Dollars		
(a) Total sales	$2,400,000	$2,000,000
(b) Total variable manufacturing costs incurred	$1,300,000	$1,060,000
(c) Total productivity: (a) ÷ (b)	1.846154	1.886762
(d) Productivity decrease: 1.846154 − 1.886792 = (0.040639) or −2.15% (0.040639 ÷ 1.886792)		

Sometimes it takes real savvy to understand what the productivity numbers really mean. For example, when a company outsources some of its processes, the output per hour of effort might not change, but the output per company employee will go up because contract workers are not employees. However, the cost per hour for a contract worker could be higher than the hourly employee who was replaced. The reverse can also happen. Before Mike McNamara became the CIO at Target Corp., about 70 percent of the IT jobs were outsourced. That number was closer to 30 percent in early 2017. There may have been a cost savings, but output per employee goes down.

Productivity measures provided by government and trade organizations are subject to bias and errors. The measures are constantly updated and revised as the underlying wage cost and output data are updated. Economists advise it may take several months of updates to get reliable figures for productivity in any given prior period. Moreover, economists have argued that the manner in which productivity is calculated can be misleading. For example, the different ways of counting imported parts (used in assembling finished products here in the United States) in the determination of manufacturing output can bias the productivity numbers.

Required

As a management accountant and consultant who advises companies on operational efficiency and strategy, how would you explain the importance of these productivity measurement issues to your clients?

(Refer to Comments on Cost Management in Action at the end of the chapter.)

the cost of resources or a decrease in the productivity of some of the input resources, both of which may be beyond the control of the manager. Ambiguity in the relationship between the controllability of operations and a performance measure based on total productivity could defeat the purpose of having a productivity measurement.

In addition, productivity measures can ignore the effects of changes in demand for the product, changes in selling prices of the goods or services, and changes in special purchasing or selling arrangements on productivity. For example, a special arrangement to sell products at a discount price decreases the productivity in dollars of output per input unit. Alternatively, a special purchase of materials increases financial productivity. Neither of these actions can be attributed to a loss or gain in productivity.

Analyzing Sales: Comparison with the Master Budget

In comparing the master budget to actual results for sales, this section uses the flexible budget to help answer strategic questions about sales performance. Are sales increasing at the expected rate? Are sales as profitable as expected? How much success has the firm had at increasing its share of the market in its industry? What factors have contributed to the increase or decrease in sales growth and profitability? These questions can be answered by further analyzing the sales variances first introduced in Chapter 14. For a quick review, look at Exhibit 14.4 and note that the comparison of actual sales with budgeted sales, using the flexible budget, identifies the two variances to explain the difference between actual and budgeted sales dollars. These two variances are the sales volume variance (measured in sales dollars rather than contribution) and the selling price variance. The sales volume variance is due to a change in units sold times budgeted selling price. In Exhibit 14.4, budgeted unit sales were 1,000 units, budgeted price was $800, the actual sales in units were 780 units, and total actual sales dollars were $639,600. The actual price received was $639,600 ÷ 780, or $820, a $20 improvement over the budgeted price. The sales volume variance, in terms of sales dollars, of $176,000 unfavorable is computed in Exhibit 14.4 as follows:

$$\text{Sales volume variance} = \text{Budgeted sales price} \times \text{Change in sales volume}$$
$$\$176,000U = \$800 \times (1,000 - 780) = \$800,000 - \$624,000$$

We use the U after the variance to indicate it is unfavorable because unit sales were below budget. The selling price variance, in terms of sales dollars, is completed in a similar fashion. Note that it is favorable because of the $20 increase in price.

$$\text{Selling price variance} = \text{Actual sales units} \times \text{Change in price}$$
$$\$15,600F = 780 \times (\$820 - \$800) = \$639,600 - \$624,000$$

The favorable selling price variance reflects the positive effect on profits of an increase in selling price over the budget. For simplicity, this example has assumed a single product, so the sales price and sales volume variances are easy to interpret. The more common case is there are two or more products. The selling price variance could then be computed for each product in a manner similar to that shown earlier. Management would also investigate whether a change in the price of one product might be associated with or caused by a change in the price of another product. A more complete coverage of pricing issues is provided in Chapter 13.

When there are multiple products, the sales volume variance could also be computed for each product in a manner similar to that shown earlier. Also, the volume variance can be partitioned into two further parts, one that relates to the mix, or proportion, of products in total sales and the other to the total quantity of sales. The further analysis allows managers to see how changes in product mix and total quantity affect profits. While the selling price variance is measured in sales dollars (as we have shown earlier), when the volume variance is partitioned into the quantity and mix variances, these three variances are commonly measured in terms of *contribution margin,* as we will see next.

LO 16-3

Use the flexible budget to calculate and interpret the sales quantity, sales mix, market size, and market share variances.

Sales Volume Variance Partitioned into Sales Quantity and Sales Mix Variances

Sales Quantity Variance

One contributing factor to the sales volume variances of firms with multiple products is the difference between the budgeted and the actual sales units—the sales quantity variance. The **sales quantity variance** focuses on deviations between the number of units sold and the number of units budgeted to be sold and measures the effect of these deviations on contribution and income. A product's sales quantity variance is the product of three elements:

1. The difference in *total units of all products* between the actual units sold and the units budgeted to be sold.
2. The budgeted sales mix ratio of the product. The sales mix for a product is its sales in units as a percentage of total sales in units.
3. The budgeted contribution margin per unit of the product.

The sales quantity variance focuses on the difference between the total actual units sold and the budgeted sales in units. Therefore, we also use the budgeted amounts for the other two elements, sales mix and contribution margin per unit, to compute the sales quantity variance.

sales quantity variance
The product of three elements: (1) the difference between the budgeted and actual total sales quantity, (2) the budgeted sales mix of the product, and (3) the budgeted contribution margin per unit of the product. It measures the effect of the change in the number of units sold from the number of units budgeted to be sold.

$$\begin{array}{c}\text{Sales}\\\text{quantity}\\\text{variance of}\\\text{a product}\end{array} = \begin{pmatrix}\text{Total units}\\\text{of all}\\\text{products}\\\text{sold}\end{pmatrix} - \begin{pmatrix}\text{Budgeted}\\\text{total units}\\\text{of all}\\\text{products}\end{pmatrix} \times \begin{array}{c}\text{Budgeted}\\\text{sales mix}\\\text{of the}\\\text{product}\end{array} \times \begin{array}{c}\text{Budgeted}\\\text{contribution}\\\text{margin per unit}\\\text{of the product}\end{array}$$

Notice that the calculation of the sales quantity variance for a product uses the budgeted sales mix and the budgeted contribution margin per unit of the product. However, the difference in quantity is the difference between the total number of units sold and the total number of units budgeted to be sold for all of the firm's products.

Sales Mix Variance

The second component of the volume variance is the sales mix variance. **Sales mix** is the relative proportion of a product's sales to total sales. A product's **sales mix variance** refers to the effect that a change in the relative proportion of the product from the budgeted proportion has on the total contribution margin of the period. It is calculated by multiplying the difference between budgeted and actual sales mix by the actual number of total units sold and the budgeted contribution margin per unit:

sales mix
The relative proportion in which a company's products (or services) are sold.

sales mix variance
The product of the difference between the actual and budgeted sales mix multiplied by the actual total number of units of all products sold and by the budgeted contribution margin per unit of the product.

$$\begin{array}{c}\text{Sales mix}\\\text{variance of}\\\text{a product}\end{array} = \begin{pmatrix}\text{Actual sales}\\\text{mix of the}\\\text{product}\end{pmatrix} - \begin{pmatrix}\text{Budgeted sales}\\\text{mix of the}\\\text{product}\end{pmatrix} \times \begin{array}{c}\text{Total}\\\text{units}\\\text{sold}\end{array} \times \begin{array}{c}\text{Budgeted contribution}\\\text{margin per unit of}\\\text{the product}\end{array}$$

Illustration of the Calculation of the Sales Quantity and Sales Mix Variances

The calculations for the sales quantity and sales mix variances can be illustrated using information from the Schmidt Machinery Company (used in Chapter 14). Assume that, as in Chapter 14, we have product XV-1 but that, in addition, we now have product FB-33. These are the only two products sold by Schmidt Machinery. In contrast to the results for the month of October 2022 used in Chapter 14, we are now considering budgeted and actual results for the month of December 2022; the budgeted information is shown in Exhibit 16.7 and the actual information is shown in Exhibit 16.8. Note in comparing Exhibits 16.7 and 16.8 that there are no differences in prices, variable costs, or fixed costs; the only differences are in units sold. This allows us to focus strictly on the sales quantity and sales mix variances for these two products. To begin the analysis, we calculate the budgeted and actual sales mix, as follows:

Product	Units Sold	Actual Sales Mix	Budgeted Sales Mix	Budgeted Sales
XV-1	1,600	32% = 1,600 ÷ 5,000	25% = 1,000 ÷ 4,000	$1,000
FB-33	3,400	68 = 3,400 ÷ 5,000	75 = 3,000 ÷ 4,000	3,000
Total	5,000	100%	100%	$4,000

The calculations of the sales mix and quantity variances for each product for December 2022 are illustrated in Exhibit 16.9, using the flexible budget. Panel 1 of Exhibit 16.9 shows the flexible budget framework that is used to calculate the variances. Note that the master

EXHIBIT 16.7
Master Budget for Schmidt Machinery

SCHMIDT MACHINERY COMPANY
Master Budget
For the Month Ended December 31, 2022

	XV-1		FB-33		Both Products
	Total	Per Unit	Total	Per Unit	Total
Units	1,000		3,000		4,000
Sales	$800,000	$800	$1,800,000	$600	$2,600,000
Variable costs	450,000	450	960,000	320	1,410,000
Contribution margin	$350,000	$350	$ 840,000	$280	$1,190,000
Fixed costs	150,000		450,000		600,000
Operating income	$200,000		$ 390,000		$ 590,000

EXHIBIT 16.8
Income Statements for Two Products

SCHMIDT MACHINERY COMPANY
Income Statement
For the Month Ended December 31, 2022

	XV-1		FB-33		Both Products
	Total	Per Unit	Total	Per Unit	Total
Units	1,600		3,400		5,000
Sales	$1,280,000	$800	$2,040,000	$600	$3,320,000
Variable costs	720,000	450	1,088,000	320	1,808,000
Contribution margin	$560,000	$350	$ 952,000	$280	$1,512,000
Fixed costs	150,000		450,000		600,000
Operating income	$410,000		$ 502,000		$ 912,000

EXHIBIT 16.9   Sales Mix and Quantity Variances

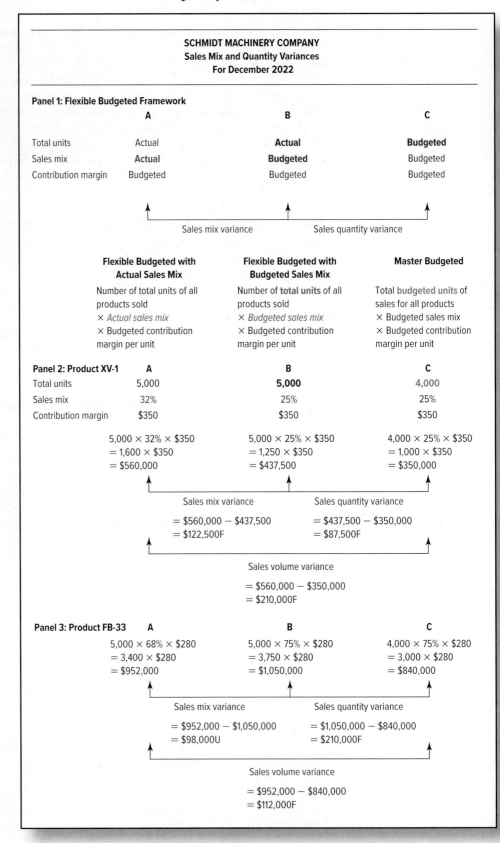

SCHMIDT MACHINERY COMPANY
Sales Mix and Quantity Variances
For December 2022

Panel 1: Flexible Budgeted Framework

	A	B	C
Total units	Actual	**Actual**	**Budgeted**
Sales mix	**Actual**	**Budgeted**	Budgeted
Contribution margin	Budgeted	Budgeted	Budgeted

Sales mix variance   Sales quantity variance

Flexible Budgeted with Actual Sales Mix	Flexible Budgeted with Budgeted Sales Mix	Master Budgeted
Number of total units of all products sold	Number of **total units** of all products sold	Total **budgeted units** of sales for all products
× *Actual sales mix*	× *Budgeted sales mix*	× Budgeted sales mix
× Budgeted contribution margin per unit	× Budgeted contribution margin per unit	× Budgeted contribution margin per unit

Panel 2: Product XV-1

	A	B	C
Total units	5,000	**5,000**	4,000
Sales mix	32%	25%	25%
Contribution margin	$350	$350	$350

5,000 × 32% × $350   5,000 × 25% × $350   4,000 × 25% × $350
= 1,600 × $350   = 1,250 × $350   = 1,000 × $350
= $560,000   = $437,500   = $350,000

Sales mix variance   Sales quantity variance
= $560,000 − $437,500   = $437,500 − $350,000
= $122,500F   = $87,500F

Sales volume variance
= $560,000 − $350,000
= $210,000F

Panel 3: Product FB-33

A	B	C
5,000 × 68% × $280	5,000 × 75% × $280	4,000 × 75% × $280
= 3,400 × $280	= 3,750 × $280	= 3,000 × $280
= $952,000	= $1,050,000	= $840,000

Sales mix variance   Sales quantity variance
= $952,000 − $1,050,000   = $1,050,000 − $840,000
= $98,000U   = $210,000F

Sales volume variance
= $952,000 − $840,000
= $112,000F

(*Continued*)

EXHIBIT 16.9 *(Continued)*

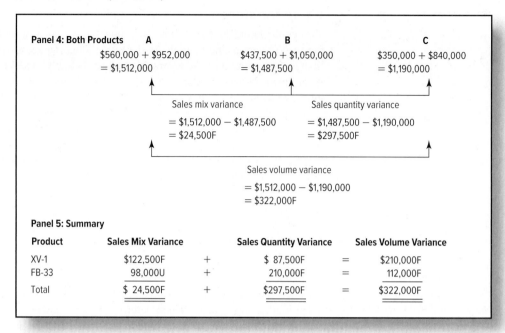

Panel 4: Both Products

	A	B	C
	$560,000 + $952,000	$437,500 + $1,050,000	$350,000 + $840,000
	= $1,512,000	= $1,487,500	= $1,190,000

Sales mix variance
= $1,512,000 − $1,487,500
= $24,500F

Sales quantity variance
= $1,487,500 − $1,190,000
= $297,500F

Sales volume variance
= $1,512,000 − $1,190,000
= $322,000F

Panel 5: Summary

Product	Sales Mix Variance		Sales Quantity Variance		Sales Volume Variance
XV-1	$122,500F	+	$ 87,500F	=	$210,000F
FB-33	98,000U	+	210,000F	=	112,000F
Total	$ 24,500F	+	$297,500F	=	$322,000F

budget is in column C, while column A has the actual sales mix and column B has the budgeted sales mix. The difference between columns B and C is the budgeted (column C) and actual (column B) total units sold. Panel 2 of Exhibit 16.9 shows the calculation of the mix and quantity variances for product XV-1, while panel 3 shows the calculations for product FB-33. Panel 4 shows the total for both products, and panel 5 shows the summary of the results for each product and in total. Note that the sales quantity variance plus the sales mix variance for each product equals the sales volume variance for that product. Also, the sales volume variance calculated here can be reconciled to the volume variance as determined directly from the comparison of actual and budgeted results in Exhibits 16.8 and 16.7, respectively. Because actual sales price equals budget sales price in this example, the selling price variance equals zero, and because the volume variance plus the selling price variance is the total sales variance, the entire difference between the actual and budgeted contribution margin is the sales volume variance ($1,512,000 – $1,190,000 = $322,000). See panel 4 of Exhibit 16.9.

The analysis has partitioned the sales volume variance into meaningful components. For example, with the information in Exhibits 16.8 and 16.9, managers would note that the change in sales mix in favor of a higher proportion of sales of XV-1 (an increase to 32 percent of total sales versus a budget of 25 percent) has a net positive effect on contribution and profit because XV-1 has a higher unit contribution ($350 per unit) than FB-33 ($280 per unit). The favorable quantity variance reflects that total sales units were greater than the number indicated in the master budget (for XV-1, an increase of 600 units = 1,600 – 1,000; for FB-33, an increase of 400 units = 3,400 – 3,000).

Note that the sale mix, sales quantity, and sales volume variances can be calculated on the basis of contribution margin (as we have done above) or on the basis of total sales in units or sales dollars. For example, if we were to use sales dollars to complete the analysis in Exhibit 16.9, then the sales mix variance for XV-1 would have been:

$$(1,600 - 1,250) \times \$800 = \$280,000$$

rather than as is currently calculated, based on contribution margin:

$$(1,600 - 1,250) \times \$350 = \$122,500$$

Both methods are used in practice, but the contribution margin method is more commonly used.

Sales Quantity Variance Partitioned into Market Size and Market Share Variances

Two contributing factors of the sales quantity variance are changes in the market size and the firm's share of the market. As the total global market for its products increases, a firm is likely to sell more units. Conversely, the firm is likely to sell fewer units when the market for its products decreases. Also, when a firm's share of the market increases, the firm sells more units and sales fall when market share decreases.

At the time Schmidt prepared the budget for December 2022, the firm expected that the total combined global market for both its products, XV-1 and FB-33, would be 40,000 units per month and that Schmidt would have 10 percent of the total global market. The master budget data for December is shown in Exhibit 16.7. Exhibit 16.8 shows the actual operations of the month. Exhibit 16.9 shows that the firm had a favorable total sales quantity variance of $297,500, an amount that can be attributed to both a change in market size and a change in market share.

Market Size Variance

market size variance
A measure of the effect of changes in the total market size on the firm's total contribution margin.

Market size is the total units for the industry. The **market size variance** measures the effect of changes in market size on a firm's total contribution margin. In computing the market size variance, the focus is on the change in market size: the difference between the actual and budgeted market size (units). When determining the market size variance of a firm, we assume that the firm maintains the budgeted market share and the budgeted average contribution margin per unit. The equation for computing a market size variance follows:

$$\begin{matrix} \text{Market} \\ \text{size} \\ \text{variance} \end{matrix} = \left(\begin{matrix} \text{Actual} \\ \text{market size} \\ \text{in units} \end{matrix} - \begin{matrix} \text{Budgeted} \\ \text{market size} \\ \text{in units} \end{matrix} \right) \times \begin{matrix} \text{Budgeted} \\ \text{market} \\ \text{share} \end{matrix} \times \begin{matrix} \text{Weighted-average} \\ \text{budgeted contribution} \\ \text{margin per unit} \end{matrix}$$

The first term on the right side of the equation is the focus of the variance: the difference in market size (in units) between the actual and the budgeted market size. The second term is the budgeted market share. The product of the first two terms is the effect of the change in market size on unit sales if the firm maintains the budgeted market share. To estimate the effect on contribution of the change in sales units, we multiply the number of units by the contribution margin per unit, the last term in the equation. Notice that the contribution margin per unit is the weighted-average budgeted contribution margin per unit of all of the firm's products in the same market, not the contribution margin per unit of an individual product. The weighted-average budgeted contribution margin per unit for a firm is determined by dividing the total units of the firm into the total contribution margin of the firm. Some managers refer to this contribution margin as the *composite contribution margin per unit*. Schmidt Machinery Company budgeted to sell 4,000 units of XV-1 and FB-33 to earn a total contribution margin of $1,190,000, as shown in Exhibit 16.7. Thus, the weighted-average budgeted contribution per unit is $297.50 ($1,190,000 ÷ 4,000 units).

The firm budgeted to sell 4,000 units and expected the total market to be 40,000 units. The budgeted market share is 10 percent of the total market. The total market for December 2022 turned out to be 31,250 units; the total market size decreased. Panel 1 of Exhibit 16.10 shows the calculation of Schmidt's market size variance, which is $260,312.50 unfavorable.

The actual market size of the industry (31,250 units) is a decrease of 8,750 units from the budgeted market size of 40,000 units. If the firm maintained its budgeted market share of 10%, the 8,750 units decrease in market size would have decreased Schmidt's total sales by 875 units. With a weighted-average contribution margin of $297.50 per unit, the decrease in units (875) would have decreased Schmidt's total contribution margin and operating income by $260,312.50.

Market Share Variance

Market share is a firm's proportion of a particular market. The market share of a firm is a function of its core competencies and competitive environment and reflects the firm's competitive

EXHIBIT 16.10
Market Size and Market Share Variances

SCHMIDT MACHINERY COMPANY
Market Size and Share Variances
For December 2022

Panel 1: Market Size Variance
= **Difference in market size × Budgeted market share × Weighted-average budgeted contribution margin per unit**
= (31,250 − 40,000) × 10% × $297.50 = $260,312.50U

Panel 2: Market Share Variance
= **Difference in market share × Actual market size × Weighted-average budgeted contribution margin per unit**
= (16% − 10%) × 31,250 × $297.50 = $557,812.50F

Panel 3: Reconciliation

Market size variance	$260,312.50U
Market share variance	557,812.50F
Sales quantity variance	$297,500.00F

market share variance
A comparison of the firm's actual market share to its budgeted market share and measurement of the effect of changes in the firm's market share on its total contribution margin and operating income.

position. A successful firm maintains or increases its market share. A firm experiencing continuous erosion in its market share is likely to experience financial difficulties.

The **market share variance** compares a firm's actual market share to its budgeted market share and measures the effect of the difference in market share on the firm's total contribution margin and operating income. Three items are involved in determining the market share variance: the difference between the firm's actual and budgeted market share, the total actual market size, and the weighted-average budgeted contribution margin per unit. Notice that the computation uses the *actual,* not budgeted, total market size and the *budgeted,* not actual, weighted-average contribution margin per unit. The product of these three factors—the difference in market share, total actual market size, and weighted-average budgeted contribution margin per unit—is the market share variance. The equation is:

$$\begin{array}{l} \text{Market} \\ \text{share} \\ \text{variance} \end{array} = \left(\begin{array}{c} \text{Actual} \\ \text{market} \\ \text{share} \end{array} - \begin{array}{c} \text{Budgeted} \\ \text{market} \\ \text{share} \end{array}\right) \times \begin{array}{c} \text{Total actual} \\ \text{market size} \\ \text{(in units)} \end{array} \times \begin{array}{c} \text{Weighted-average} \\ \text{budgeted contribution} \\ \text{margin per unit} \end{array}$$

Panel 2 of Exhibit 16.10 shows the calculation of the market share variance for Schmidt Machinery Company's December 2022 operations.

Although the total market for the industry decreased to 31,250, Schmidt's total units sold are higher than the budgeted sales for the period. Its market share increased from the budgeted 10 percent to 16 percent (5,000 units ÷ 31,250 units = 16%). With the actual total market size being 31,250 units, the increase in the market share increased Schmidt's total sales by 1,875 units. At a budgeted weighted-average contribution margin of $297.50 per unit, the increase of 1,875 units increased its total contribution margin and operating income by $557,812.50.

Together, the market size variance and market share variance equal the sales quantity variance of the period. Panel 3 of Exhibit 16.10 confirms this result. For December 2022, the total of these two variances is $297,500 favorable, which equals the sales quantity variance reported in Exhibit 16.9.

Exhibit 16.11 shows the calculation of the market size and market share variances for December 2022 using a flexible budget framework. The results are the same as in Exhibit 16.10. Remember that market share and market size variances explain the firm's sales quantity variance. The total variance in Exhibit 16.11, the difference between columns A and C, is the total sales quantity variance for both products. Column A of Exhibit 16.11 shows the budgeted total contribution margin that the firm would have earned from the actual number of units sold. Starting from the industry's total market size, the total number of units sold by the firm is the product of the industry's total actual market size and the firm's actual market share:

$$31,250 \text{ units} \times 16\% = 5,000 \text{ units}$$

EXHIBIT 16.11   Analyzing Market Size and Market Share Variances Using Columnar Form

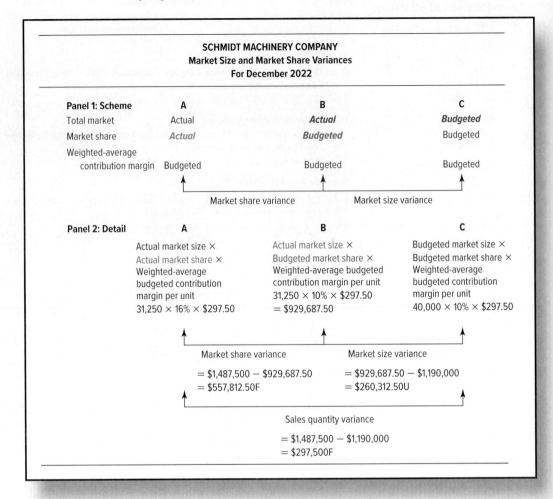

The weighted-average budgeted contribution margin per unit is $297.50. Therefore, the total budgeted contribution margin from 5,000 actual sales units is $1,487,500, as shown in column A of panel 2.

Column B is the budgeted total contribution margin the firm would have earned, given the actual market size, had it maintained the budgeted market share. With the actual market size of 31,250, the firm would have sold 3,125 total units if it had maintained its budgeted market share of 10 percent. At the weighted-average budgeted contribution margin of $297.50 per unit, the total contribution margin would be $929,687.50. The only difference between column A and column B is in market share. The $557,812.50 difference ($1,487,500 − $929,687.50) between these two columns, therefore, is a market share variance. This variance is favorable because the actual market share is 16 percent, as opposed to the budgeted 10 percent.

Column C is the master budget. The budgeted total units of sales in the master budget is the product of the budgeted market size and the budgeted market share:

$$40,000 \times 10\% = 4,000 \text{ units}$$

At the weighted-average budgeted contribution margin of $297.50 per unit, the total budgeted contribution margin in the master budget is:

$$4,000 \text{ units} \times \$297.50 \text{ per unit} = \$1,190,000$$

The only difference between column B and column C is in the total market size: actual market size in column B and budgeted market size in column C. The difference, therefore, is

EXHIBIT 16.12 Components of Sales Variances

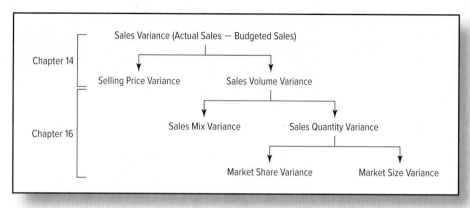

a market size variance, which is $260,312.50. The variance is unfavorable because the actual market size (31,250) is smaller than the budgeted market size (40,000) anticipated at the time the firm prepared the master budget for December 2022. The various components of sales performance are summarized in Exhibit 16.12.

Note that the market share and market size variances can be calculated on the basis of contribution margin (as we have done above) or on the basis of total sales in units or sales dollars. All three methods are used in practice, but the contribution margin method is most common and therefore is the one we use in this chapter.

The Five Steps of Strategic Decision Making for Schmidt Machinery

Schmidt Machinery is a well-established firm that produces very-high-quality, all-weather furniture that is used on patios and decks and in sunrooms. Product XV-1 is a lightweight but durable lounge chair, and FB-33 is a lightweight and durable table. Because of its very high quality and reputation for design innovation, Schmidt's products are sold largely by catalog and over the firm's website; a few high-end retailers also carry the brand. The firm has few direct competitors in the United States, but there are a growing number of competitors from Europe and Asia. Also, the decline of the dollar against other currencies in prior years helped Schmidt maintain its domestic sales and have some opportunities for foreign sales. However, the global economic recession and a recent rise in the dollar have reduced sales worldwide. While Schmidt's sales have increased, the company is concerned that the recession will deepen and that sales of its products will eventually be affected. Schmidt is facing questions such as which production lines to scale back and which products to increase or decrease should that happen. Schmidt knows that the XV-1 product has a larger percentage of its sales overseas than FB-33, but Schmidt is not sure which of its two products should be supported at this difficult time.

1. **Determine the strategic issues surrounding the problem.** Schmidt is a differentiated manufacturer, selling a high-priced product to those who value its quality, design, and functionality. With the growth of foreign competition and the increased price competition, Schmidt is now looking for ways to maintain its profitability by determining an effective marketing strategy for its two products.

2. **Identify the alternative actions.** The question facing Schmidt is whether to scale back production and marketing of one or both of its products.

3. **Obtain information and conduct analyses of the alternatives.** Schmidt calculates the sales quantity and market share and market size variances as illustrated in Exhibit 16.9 and 16.11. Schmidt also conducts further economic analysis, which shows that in the coming years, the dollar will likely rise against other currencies and that the worldwide recession will continue to show lower levels of consumer spending.

4. **Based on strategy and analysis, choose and implement the desired alternative.** Based on an analysis of the quantity, market share, and market size variances for both products (which show an unfavorable market size variance but a favorable market share variance and a favorable quantity variance), and given the negative news about the dollar and the global recession, Schmidt decides to make contingency plans for the possible reduction in the production and sales of the FB-33 product. One reason is the lower unit contribution of the FB-33 product. The second reason is that while the global recession will affect sales worldwide and XV-1 has a greater share of worldwide sales, Schmidt expects that the recession will have the greatest negative impact on sales in the United States and thus a relatively greater impact on FB-33.

5. **Provide an ongoing evaluation of the effectiveness of implementation in step 4.** As the global economic environment becomes more predictable, including potential changes in the value of the dollar, management should continue to review its planning for the two products. Also, management should consider obtaining additional information about the market size for each product (e.g., by country or region) so that the company can further partition the market share and market size variances for each product.

Analyzing Sales: Comparison with Prior Period Results

LO 16-4

Use the flexible budget to analyze sales performance over time.

A common application of sales performance analysis is to partition the difference between the current period's profit and the prior period's profit. The analytical framework, based on the flexible budget, is the same as for the analysis of the master budget. For example, suppose that Schmidt Machinery has another month of operations to consider, the month of January 2023. We use the actual data for December, as used in the prior section, and analyze the change in sales performance from December to January. The relevant information is shown in Exhibit 16.13. We assume that fixed costs do not change, and because unit variable costs have not changed, the only changes to analyze in this example are changes in units sold and prices for the two products.

Notice that the December 2022 data are the same as shown in Exhibit 16.8. As shown in Exhibit 16.14, our first step is to calculate the income statements for January and December.

Analysis of Selling Price and Volume Variances

The next step is to decompose the total difference in contribution margin (or difference in operating income) of \$4,950 (\$1,512,000 − \$1,507,050; or also \$912,000 − \$907,050) by calculating the selling price and volume variances for January, as shown in Exhibit 16.15.

The selling price variance is a net unfavorable variance of \$28,050, composed of a favorable selling price variance for XV-1 of \$7,650 and an unfavorable selling price variance for FB-33 of \$35,700. The selling price variance for XV-1 is due to the price increase of \$5: \$7,650 = 5,100 × 0.3 × \$5. The selling price variance for FB-33 is due to the price decline of \$10: \$35,700 = 5,100 × 0.7 × \$10.

EXHIBIT 16.13
Schmidt Machinery Company Actual Data

	January 2023	December 2022
Sales units	5,100	5,000
Sales mix for each product		
XV-1	30%	32%
FB-33	70%	68%
Price		
XV-1	\$805	\$800
FB-33	590	600
Variable cost per unit		
XV-1	450	450
FB-33	320	320
Contribution margin per unit		
XV-1	355	350
FB-33	270	280

EXHIBIT 16.14
Comparative Income Statements for Schmidt Machinery Company

	January 2023	December 2022
Sales XV-1	$1,231,650	$1,280,000
Sales FB-33	2,106,300	2,040,000
Total sales	3,337,950	3,320,000
Variable costs	1,830,900	1,808,000
Contribution margin	1,507,050	1,512,000
Fixed costs	600,000	600,000
Operating income	$ 907,050	$ 912,000

EXHIBIT 16.15 **Selling Price and Volume Variances for January 2022 vs. December 2022**

	January 2023	Sales Price Variance	Flexible Budget	Sales Volume Variance	December 2022
Sales					
XV-1	$1,231,650	$7,650	$1,224,000	$(56,000)	$1,280,000
FB-33	2,106,300	(35,700)	2,142,000	102,000	2,040,000
Total sales	3,337,950	(28,050)	3,366,000	46,000	3,320,000
Variable costs					
XV-1	688,500	–	688,500	(31,500)	720,000
FB-33	1,142,400	–	1,142,400	54,400	1,088,000
Total variable costs	1,830,900		1,830,900	22,900	1,808,000
Contribution margin					
XV-1	543,150	7,650	535,500	(24,500)	560,000
FB-33	963,900	(35,700)	999,600	47,600	952,000
Total contribution margin	1,507,050	$(28,050)	$1,535,100	$ 23,100	1,512,000
Fixed costs	600,000	0	600,000	0	600,000
Operating income	$ 907,050	($28,050)	$ 935,100	$ 23,100	$ 912,000

As noted in Chapter 14, the sales volume variance can be expressed, for each income statement item, as the difference between the flexible budget amount for that item and the amount for that item reflected in the master budget for the period. Thus, we can express the sales volume variance in terms of sales ($46,000F), variable costs ($22,900UF), and contribution margin ($23,100F), as well as in terms of operating income ($23,100F). Looking at the sales volume variance for revenue, we see a net favorable variance of $46,000. The volume for XV-1 fell by 70 units [(0.32 × 5,000) – (0.3 × 5,100)], at a price of $800 each, or $56,000 unfavorable. In contrast, the sales of FB-33 increased by 170 units [(0.7 × 5,100) – (0.68 × 5,000)], at a price of $600 each, or $102,000. For the variable costs, the costs of XV-1 were lower than expected, which is a favorable variance. The variable costs of FB-33 were higher by $47,600, which is an unfavorable variance. The net effect is an unfavorable variable cost variance of $22,900. The contribution margin is the net of the sales and variable cost variances and is $23,100 favorable.

The flexible budget column in the center of Exhibit 16.15 is determined from January sales in units (based on the January sales mix), December prices, and December unit variable costs. For example, the flexible budget for sales of the two products is:

$$\text{XV-1: } \$1,224,000 = 5,100 \text{ units} \times 30\% \text{ mix} \times \$800$$
$$\text{FB-33: } \$2,142,000 = 5,100 \text{ units} \times 70\% \text{ mix} \times \$600$$

The flexible budget for variable costs for the two products is determined in a similar way:

$$\text{XV-1:   } \$688,500 = 5,100 \text{ units} \times 30\% \text{ mix} \times \$450$$
$$\text{FB-33: } \$1,142,400 = 5,100 \text{ units} \times 70\% \text{ mix} \times \$320$$

In this case, because January unit variable costs are the same as December unit variable costs, the flexible budget for variable costs is the same as the total actual variable cost for January.

Overall, the analysis of sales data for January shows that the relatively small selling price changes are associated with offsetting changes in sales volume and selling price variances. Total sales increased by $17,950 ($46,000 – $28,050; or equivalently, $3,337,950 – $3,320,000), which is the net effect of the selling price and sales volume variances for both products. Looking at the details, the price for product XV-1 increased and there was a significant favorable selling price variance but a much larger unfavorable sales volume variance. The case for product FB-33 is somewhat different. The price decrease caused a significant unfavorable selling price variance but a much larger favorable sales volume variance. However, variable costs increased by $22,900 ($1,830,900 – $1,808,000) due to the increase in sales volume; that is, the increase in sales of 100 units caused an increase in total variable cost (170 units increase for FB-33 at $320 each, less 70 units reduction in sales volume for XV-1 at $450 each). The net effect is a relatively small reduction in total contribution and operating income of $4,950 ($912,000 – $907,050).

Analysis of Mix and Quantity Variances

The earlier analysis can be enhanced by computing the mix and quantity variances for each product, as illustrated in Exhibit 16.16.

The mix variances are determined as follows:

Change in mix × Units sold in January 2023 × December 2022 unit contribution

$$\text{XV-1:} \quad (0.30 - 0.32) \times 5,100 \times \$350 = \$35,700 \text{ unfavorable}$$
$$\text{FB-33:} \quad (0.70 - 0.68) \times 5,100 \times \$280 = 28,560 \text{ favorable}$$

The quantity variances are determined as follows:

Change in total units sold × December 2022 sales mix × December 2022 contribution margin

$$\text{XV-1:} \quad (5,100 - 5,000) \times 0.32 \times \$350 = \$11,200 \text{ favorable}$$
$$\text{FB-33:} \quad (5,100 - 5,000) \times 0.68 \times \$280 = \$19,040 \text{ favorable}$$

Note that the total of the mix and quantity variances equals the volume variance for each product, as expected. In effect, the analysis of the change in operating income from December 2022 to January 2023 is very similar to the analysis for a comparison with the master budget, and the interpretation of the variances is also similar. In the period-to-period analysis, the interpretation focuses on changes from the prior period, instead of on variances between performance and the master budget.

EXHIBIT 16.16
Sales Mix and Quantity Variances by Product Line

	Sales Mix Variance	Sales Quantity Variance	Volume Variance
XV-1	$(35,700)U	$11,200F	$(24,500)U
FB-33	28,560F	19,040F	47,600F
Contribution margin	$ (7,140)U	$30,240F	$ 23,100F

Analysis of Variable Cost Variances

The preceding approach can also be extended to analyze the changes in unit variable costs. This would involve calculating price and usage variances for direct materials and direct labor, much like the procedures used in Chapter 14. Again, the flexible budget based on actual output and prior year actual unit variable costs would provide the desired framework. For example, if the unit variable cost in January for product XV-1 was $460 rather than $450, as shown in Exhibit 16.13, and assuming that the unit variable cost for XV-1 was $450 in December, then we can calculate a variable cost variance as follows for January:

$$\text{Variable cost flexible budget variance} = (\$460 - \$450) \times 5,100 \times 0.3 = \$15,300U$$

The variable cost flexible budget variance could also then be partitioned into the six variances for usage and price of direct materials and direct labor, and usage of and spending for the components of variable overhead. The partitioning would be done in the same manner as explained and illustrated in Chapters 14 and 15.

Summary

Productivity is the ratio of output to input. Improvements in productivity enable firms to do more with fewer resources. A productivity measure is often compared to the performance of a prior period, another firm, the industry standard, or a benchmark in assessing a firm's productivity.

Partial productivity is the ratio of output level attained to the amount of an input resource used in the operation. Total productivity, on the other hand, measures the relationship between the output achieved and the total input costs and is usually a financial productivity measure. In either case, the higher the ratio, the better. Partial operational productivity refers to the required physical amount of an input resource to produce one unit of output. The partial financial productivity of an input resource is the number of units or the value of output manufactured for each dollar spent on the input resource. A partial financial productivity measure can be separated into changes in productivity, input price, and output. The productivity change is the difference between the actual amount used and the expected amount of input resources to manufacture the output. The input price change accounts for the effects of the difference between the budgeted (or benchmark) and the actual prices for the input resource on the operating income of the period.

Measures of productivity are applicable to all organizations, including service firms and not-for-profit organizations. However, imprecise measures for output, or lack of definite relationships between output and input resources, may limit the usefulness of productivity measures for some service or not-for-profit organizations.

Increasing global competition and rapid changes in technologies require management to be constantly alert to changes in resource productivity. Management must be aware of levels and changes in its productive factors, such as materials, labor, energy, and processes.

To effectively evaluate sales performance, management must be fully informed of the effects of changes in selling prices, sales volumes, sales mixes, market sizes, and market shares on the firm's sales. The sales volume variance reflects the difference in contribution margin or operating income between a flexible budget and the master budget. The sales volume variance for a single product firm can be determined by multiplying the budgeted contribution margin per unit of the product by the difference between the number of units sold and the budgeted units to be sold. The sales volume variance of firms with multiple products can be separated into sales mix and sales quantity variances. The sales mix variance is the product of three components: (1) the difference between the actual sales mix (defined as the ratio of the units of the product to the total units of all products) and the budgeted sales mix, (2) the total number of units of all products sold during the period, and (3) the product's budgeted contribution margin.

A product's sales quantity variance has three elements: (1) the difference between the firm's total actual units sold and budgeted sales units, (2) the product's budgeted sales mix, and (3) the budgeted contribution margin. The product of these three elements is the product's sales quantity variance. A sales quantity variance assesses the difference between the units sold and budgeted unit sales and measures the effect of this difference on total contribution margin and operating income.

A sales quantity variance can be separated further into market size and market share variances. A market size variance assesses the effect of changes in the industry's total market size on the firm's total contribution margin and operating income. A market size variance is the product of three factors: (1) the difference between the actual and the budgeted total market size (in number of units), (2) the firm's budgeted market share, and (3) the weighted-average budgeted contribution margin per unit. The market size variance is favorable if the actual total market size is larger than the market size expected when the master budget was prepared. A market share variance measures the effect of changes in the firm's market share on its operating income. A market share variance is the product of three elements: (1) the actual total number of units in the market (actual market size), (2) the difference between the firm's actual and budgeted market share, and (3) the weighted-average budgeted contribution margin per unit.

Sales performance can be analyzed from either of two benchmarks, the master budget or the prior period. The period-to-period analysis also uses the flexible budget, and the same variances are calculated, with similar interpretations.

Key Terms	financial productivity, *679*	partial productivity, *680*	sales quantity variance, *688*
	market share variance, *693*	productivity, *678*	total productivity, *680*
	market size variance, *692*	sales mix, *688*	
	operational productivity, *679*	sales mix variance, *688*	

Comments on Cost Management in Action

Productivity: Not So Easy to Measure

The example from Target Corp. is not limited to retailers. In a 2015 earnings conference call, executives of a bank were asked why revenue per employee was lower than that of its competitors. It could just be a function of outsourcing work. Other examples include Pfizer using contract workers to perform clinical trials, and Google's parent company, Alphabet, employing about 70,000 temps, vendors, and contract workers to perform duties ranging from reviewing legal documents to test-driving the self-driving cars.

The measurement issues that economists advise about are important issues. Managers rely on the productivity statistics to guide them, along with other considerations, in determining when and where to add capacity to their operations. New investment is likely to be drawn to areas with higher productivity. Productivity statistics are also used as benchmarks to help managers assess the performance of their own operations. Timely and reliable productivity data are valuable also for strategic decisions—such as when to add new products and when to add or cut the workforce.

Sources: Lauren Weber, "The End of Employees—U.S. Companies Shift Work Once Considered Core to Contractors, Pruning Costs and Job Security," *The Wall Street Journal,* February 3, 2017, p. A1; Ben Leubsdorf, "Productivity Fall Imperils Growth," *The Wall Street Journal,* August 10, 2016, p. A1; Justin Lahart, "Portion of Recent Gains Could Be an Illusion," *The Wall Street Journal,* May 6, 2010, p. A16; Alexander Kowalski and Ilan Kolet, "Productivity Is Not the Savior You Think It Is," *Bloomberg Businessweek,* October 24, 2011, pp. 13–14.

Self-Study Problems

(For answers, please see Solutions.)

1. Productivity Variances

Carlson Automotive Company manufactures fuel-injection systems. It manufactured and sold 60,000 units in 20X1 and 64,000 units in 20X2 at $25 per unit. In 20X1, the firm used 75,000 pounds of alloy TPX–45 at $7.20 per pound and used 10,000 direct labor hours at an hourly wage rate of $30. In 20X2, the firm used 89,600 pounds of alloy TPX–45 at $6.80 per pound and used 10,847 direct labor hours at an hourly wage rate of $32. The total amount of all other expenses remains the same at $450,000 each year. Jerry Olson, CEO, was disappointed that although the total sales increased in 20X2, operating income declined from $210,000 in 20X1 to $193,616 in 20X2.

Required   Analyze the following:
1. Partial operational productivity of direct material and direct labor for both 20X1 and 20X2.
2. Partial financial productivity of direct material and direct labor for both 20X1 and 20X2.
3. Detailed partition of partial financial productivity.
4. Total productivity for 20X1 and 20X2 as measured in both units and sales dollars.

2. Sales Variances

Springwater Brewery has two main products: premium and regular ale. Its operating results and master budget for 20XX (000s omitted) follow:

	Operating Results of 20XX			Master Budget for 20XX		
	Premium	Regular	Total	Premium	Regular	Total
Barrels	180	540	720	240	360	600
Sales	$28,800	$62,100	$90,900	$ 36,000	$43,200	$79,200
Variable expenses	16,200	40,500	56,700	21,600	27,000	48,600
Contribution margin	$12,600	$21,600	$34,200	$ 14,400	$16,200	$30,600
Fixed expenses	10,000	5,000	15,000	10,000	5,000	15,000
Operating income	$ 2,600	$16,600	$19,200	$ 4,400	$11,200	$15,600

Pam Kuder, CEO, expected the total industry sales to be 1,500,000 barrels during the period. After the year, Mark Goldfeder, the controller, reported that the total sales for the industry were 1,600,000 barrels.

Required Calculate the following:
1. Selling price variances for the period for each product and for the firm.
2. Sales volume variances for the period for each product and for the firm.
3. Sales quantity variances for each product and the firm.
4. Sales mix variances for the period for each product and for the firm.
5. The sum of the sales quantity variance and sales mix variance. Also, verify that this total equals the sales volume variance.
6. Market size variance for the period.
7. Market share variance for the period.
8. The sum of the market size variance and market share variance. Also, verify that this total equals the sales quantity variance.

The Student Resources section of Connect includes video tutorials for the Self-Study Problems.

Questions

16-1 What is productivity? What does it measure?

16-2 Discuss why improving productivity is important for a firm that competes on a cost leadership strategy.

16-3 List benchmarks or criteria often used in assessing productivity, and discuss their advantages and disadvantages.

16-4 What is operational productivity? Financial productivity?

16-5 What is partial productivity? Total productivity?

16-6 "A financial productivity measure contains more information than an operational productivity measure does." Do you agree, and why or why not?

16-7 "A total productivity measure encompasses all partial productivity measures." Do you agree, and why or why not?

16-8 "Partial productivity measures should be calculated only for high-value-added activities." Do you agree, and why or why not?

16-9 Why do manufacturing personnel prefer operational productivity measures to financial productivity measures?

16-10 "A productivity measure such as machine-hour productivity is more important in a JIT environment than in a non-JIT environment." Do you agree, and why or why not?

16-11 Which of the following statements is true?
a. The lower the partial productivity ratio, the greater the productivity.
b. Productivity improves when partial productivity increases.
c. Prices of inputs are incorporated in the partial operational productivity ratio.
d. The partial productivity ratio measures the number of outputs produced per multiple inputs.

16-12 List important measures in assessing marketing effectiveness.

16-13   What are the types of sales variances?

16-14   Distinguish between a selling price variance and a sales volume variance.

16-15   What is the difference between a sales quantity variance and a sales volume variance?

16-16   "As long as a firm sells more units than the units specified in the master budget, it will not have an unfavorable sales volume variance." Do you agree? Why or why not?

16-17   What are the relationships among a selling price variance, a sales mix variance, a sales quantity variance, and a sales volume variance?

16-18   Distinguish between a market size variance and a market share variance.

16-19   "A favorable sales quantity variance indicates that the marketing manager has done a good job." Do you agree? Can you give an example in which a market size variance or market share variance is opposite to that of the sales quantity variance?

16-20   What are the relationships between a market size variance, a market share variance, a sales quantity variance, and a sales volume variance?

16-21   "An improvement in earnings growth can be achieved at the expense of market share (i.e., an unfavorable market share variance)." Do you agree, and why or why not?

Brief Exercises

[LO 16-2]   16-22   Darwin Inc. provided the following information:

Budgeted production	10,000 units
Actual production	9,500 units
Budgeted input	9,750 gallons
Actual input	8,950 gallons

What is the partial operational productivity ratio?

Use the following information for Brief Exercises 16-23, 16-24, and 16-25. CompuWorld sells two products, R66 and R100, and calculates sales variances using the contribution margin. Pertinent data for the current year follow:

	Budgeted		Actual	
	R66	**R100**	**R66**	**R100**
Selling price	$ 50	$160	$ 55	$ 155
Variable cost per unit	40	90	43	95
Contribution margin	$ 10	$ 70	$ 12	$ 60
Fixed cost per unit	6	30	5	25
Operating income	$ 4	$ 40	$ 7	$ 35
Sales in units	1,200	400	1,000	1,000

[LO 16-3]   16-23   What is the R100 sales mix variance?

[LO 16-3]   16-24   What is the total sales volume variance?

[LO 16-3]   16-25   What is the R66 sales quantity variance?

Use the following information for Brief Exercises 16-26, 16-27, and 16-28. C. W. McCall sells a goldplated souvenir mug; McCall expects to sell 1,600 units for $45 each to earn a $25 contribution margin per unit. Janice McCall, president, expects the year's total market to be 32,000 units. For the year just completed, the local college won the national hockey championship, and as a result, the total actual market was 100,000 units. C. W. McCall sold 3,000 units and calculates sales variances using contribution margin.

[LO 16-3]   16-26   What is the firm's market size variance?

[LO 16-3]   16-27   What is the firm's sales volume variance?

[LO 16-3]   16-28   What is the firm's market share variance?

Exercises

[LO 16-1]

Note regarding rounding errors: Many of the exercises and problems in this chapter require a series of calculations. Rounding errors can accumulate and affect totals unless each calculation is carried to a recommended four or more digits after the decimal point. If you are using a calculator, make sure all your calculations are done to 4 or more digits after the decimal. To avoid rounding errors entirely, use a spreadsheet package like Excel to set up and solve these problems.

[LO 16-1]

16-29 **Productivity and Strategy; Manufacturing**   To maintain profit growth, several manufacturing companies have responded to the recession by cutting jobs. After the 2008–2010 recession, for example, Harley-Davidson reduced its workforce by 1,400 in one year and 1,600 more in the next year. As sales declined, the company reduced labor capacity at many plants. The same is true at General Electric, Texas Instruments, Coca-Cola, and many other companies that have reduced capacity at certain plants, closed selected plants entirely, or dropped product lines. In many of these companies, the profits are held as cash, and the companies are holding off on making any new investments until economic conditions improve. Some analysts say the companies are just shrinking their operations to match the decline in expected future demand; the companies are profitable but smaller.

Required
1. Do the actions by these companies support their long-term strategies?
2. How do the productivity gains at these companies affect profits in the short-term and long-term?

16-30 **Productivity; Sustainability**   Telematics is a system of sensors installed on cars and trucks that provides current information on the status and operation of many of the vehicle's parts. It can be used to show the location of the vehicle, the oil level, the condition of the brake pads, whether all lights are working, and whether a seatbelt is buckled, among many other potential measures. United Parcel Service (UPS) uses telematics on nearly one-half of its 55,000-vehicle U.S. truck fleet.

Required
1. Describe what you think is UPS's strategy. Does telematics support UPS's strategy, and if so, how?
2. How can telematics be used to improve productivity and sustainability at UPS?

[LO 16-2]

16-31 **Productivity and Quality Improvement in Retail**   Most manufacturers have long adopted quality improvement techniques to reduce or eliminate errors, defects, and waste and speed the flow of product to the consumer. Many retailers are now following the lead. For example, Best Buy was able to save approximately $20 million through a quality improvement program that streamlined the installation of appliances. Target has also adopted quality improvement as a means of reducing waste and cost in its retail operations.

Required   How does quality improvement as described above differ from productivity?

[LO 16-2]

16-32 **Partial Financial Productivity**   ABC Corporation makes small parts from steel alloy sheets. Management has the flexibility to substitute direct materials for direct manufacturing labor and vice versa. If workers cut the steel carefully, more parts can be manufactured from a metal sheet, but this requires additional direct manufacturing labor hours. Alternatively, ABC can use fewer labor hours if it is willing to tolerate more waste of direct materials. ABC decided to improve materials productivity this year, and the following provides information for the current and prior year:

	Prior Year	Current Year
Output units	400,000	490,000
Direct manufacturing labor hours	10,000	13,500
Wages per hour	$26	$24
Direct materials used	160 tons	180 tons
Direct materials cost per ton	$3,375	$3,250

Required
1. Compute the partial financial productivity for both direct materials and direct labor for each of the 2 years.
2. Calculate ABC's combined direct labor and direct material productivity in units per dollar in each of the 2 years.
3. Evaluate management's decision to substitute one production factor for another.

[LO 16-2]

16-33 **Partial Operational and Financial Productivity**   Software Solution (SOS) helps subscribers solve software problems. All transactions are made over the telephone. For the year 2021,

10 engineers, most of whom are recent graduates, handled 100,000 calls. The average yearly salary for software engineers was $45,000. Starting in 2022, the firm retained and hired only software engineers with at least 2 years of experience. SOS raised the engineers' salary to $60,000 per year. In 2022, eight engineers handled 108,000 calls.

Required
1. Calculate the partial operational productivity ratio for both years.
2. Calculate the partial financial productivity ratio for both years.
3. Did the firm make the right decision to hire only software engineers with at least 2 years' experience?
4. List other factors that should be considered in making the decision.

[LO 16-1, 16-2]   16-34   **Productivity: Which Way to Lean?**   Lean manufacturing is what a lot of manufacturing firms are after these days. This requires a renewed focus on productivity and profitability, particularly for firms that compete using a cost leadership strategy and are facing increased global low-cost competition. Adopting the right accounting approach to facilitate improvements in productivity is critical for these companies. Companies like Whirlpool, Pratt-Whitney (a unit of United Technologies), General Electric, and many other manufacturers are adopting the methods of lean manufacturing.

Required
1. How can productivity measures described in this chapter help a company to achieve lean manufacturing?
2. The founding principles of lean manufacturing are based in part on the Toyota Production System. What is the Toyota Production System, and list its four main elements.

[LO 16-1, 16-2]   16-35   **Cost Control, Quality, and Productivity**   Each summer, the Harbour Report (www.oliverwyman.com/index.html) rates the productivity of the major automakers, including the "Detroit Big Three," Toyota, Honda, and many other brands. The report is closely watched as a barometer of the future profitability of the firms. However, some have argued that the productivity reports are insufficient. For example, a company can temporarily raise its productivity by laying off or "buying out" employees. Also, some would argue that the focus on productivity fails to draw attention to other key strategic factors such as quality, design, and customer service. For example, the J.D. Power organization (www.jdpower.com/autos) rates the initial quality of many new cars.

Required   What do you think are the priorities for the auto companies: quality, productivity, customer service, design, or some other key strategic success factor? Briefly explain your answer.

[LO 16-2]   16-36   **Productivity and the Economy**   The U.S. Bureau of Labor Statistics (https://data.bls.gov/timeseries/PRS85006092) provides quarterly data for labor productivity in business, nonfarm business, and manufacturing industries. The Bureau of Labor Statistics also breaks down these data into industry segments. The data for the annual percentage change in labor productivity for the category of nonfarm business productivity from right before the Great Recession up until recent times is as follows:

Year	Percentage Change in Labor Productivity
2007	1.6%
2008	0.8
2009	3.6
2010	3.4
2011	0.0
2012	0.9
2013	0.5
2014	0.9
2015	1.3
2016	0.3
2017	1.3
2018	1.3

Required   Economists argue that the changes in productivity are influenced by changes in the economy—for example, the economic downturn of 2000–2001 as well as the recession that started in 2008. Others argue that productivity is most affected by advances in and adoption of information technology, investments in research and development, and capital investment in new plant and equipment (i.e., more highly automated and efficient manufacturing facilities). The preceding data show that productivity did decline in 2008 but was on the rise in the period 2009–2010 and improved again in 2012 but actually declined in 2016.

Based on the preceding information and the data from the Census Bureau, what productivity change would you forecast for 2019 and the following couple of years?

[LO 16-2] 16-37 **Alternative Measures of Productivity** A common measure of productivity, as explained in this chapter and as used by many business and trade organizations, including the U.S. Bureau of Labor Statistics, is the ratio of output to input, where input is typically measured in units of materials, labor hours, or related measures. An alternative is to use the ratio of capacity available to capacity utilized. For example, the amount of capacity in the U.S. manufacturing industries has almost doubled over the past two decades. However, the rate of capacity utilization (output/capacity available) has fallen slightly over this period of time, with a steep drop in 2009 followed by slow increases in 2010 and 2011. Some would say that this measure gives a better picture of productivity than the one we have used in the chapter.

Required Compare the measure of productivity based on capacity utilization with the measure used in the chapter. Which measure do you think is more useful for assessing the state of the manufacturing sector of the economy? Explain briefly.

[LO 16-2] 16-38 **Productivity Measures for Service Businesses** Our examples in the chapter have focused on manufacturing, where the output is units of product and the inputs are manufacturing activities or costs. The concept of productivity can be applied in a variety of settings, wherever there are inputs and outputs. For example, consider LandscapeCity, a landscape design company that specializes in small landscape projects for people living in cities. Amanda Caldwell, the assistant manager, is in the process of trying to determine if productivity has been improving since she was hired 6 months ago. Because it is a design firm, labor is the only significant expense, but Amanda is unsure if the number of projects or the dollar of sales volume should be used when computing productivity. She has collected these data for sales and labor expenses for the past 6 months:

Month	Labor Expense	Number of Projects	Sales Dollars
1	$16,470	34	$20,090
2	19,200	40	21,900
3	19,392	50	28,780
4	13,194	13	18,560
5	13,926	18	21,680
6	20,592	50	21,520

Required
1. Calculate the productivity for each month and the change in productivity from month to month using number of projects as the measure of output.
2. Calculate the productivity for each month and the change in productivity from month to month using sales dollars as the measure of output.
3. Which of these measures of productivity is Amanda likely to prefer, and why?

[LO 16-3] 16-39 **Sales Volume, Sales Quantity, and Sales Mix Variances** The Greensboro Performing Arts Center (GPAC) has a total capacity of 7,500 seats: 2,000 center seats, 2,500 side seats, and 3,000 balcony seats. The budgeted and actual tickets sold for a Broadway musical show are as follows:

		Percentage Occupied	
	Ticket Price	Budgeted Seats	Actual Seats
Center	$70	90%	95%
Side	60	80	85
Balcony	50	85	75

The actual ticket prices were the same as those budgeted. Once a show has been booked, the total cost does not vary with the total attendance.

Required Compute the following for the show (Round the variances to the nearest whole dollar):
1. The budgeted and actual sales mix percentages for different types of seats.
2. The budgeted average contribution margin per seat. Assume the ticket price is also the contribution margin.
3. The total sales quantity variance and the total sales mix variance.
4. The total sales volume variance.

[LO 16-4]   16-40   **Sales Variances; Quarter to Quarter**   Hathaway Products Inc. produces an innovative lighting system used in restaurants and high-end retail stores to provide a pleasing, warm atmosphere. Hathaway produces two versions of the product, called Starlight and Moonlight. Sales management at Hathaway wants to complete a sales performance analysis and has collected the following information for the first quarter (Qtr. 1) and the second quarter (Qtr. 2) of the current fiscal year:

	Qtr. 2	Qtr. 1
Sales units	12,000	10,000
Sales mix for each product		
Starlight	20%	25%
Moonlight	80%	75%
Price		
Starlight	$35.00	$35.00
Moonlight	$85.00	$90.00
Variable cost per unit		
Starlight	$22.00	$22.00
Moonlight	$48.00	$48.00
Fixed cost	$150,000	$150,000

Required

1. Prepare a flexible-budget contribution income statement for Qtr. 2, showing the Qtr. 2 results, the Qtr. 1 results, and the flexible budget. Use Exhibit 16.15 as a guide.

2. Calculate the sales volume variance for each product based on both sales dollars and contribution margin.

3. Determine the sales mix variance and the sales quantity variance for each product, based on contribution margin.

Problems

[LO 16-2]   16-41   **Partial Operational Productivity**   Ashley Technology Inc. manufactures a scrambling device for cellular telephones. The device's main component is a delicate part, CT140. CT140 is easily damaged and requires careful handling. Once damaged, it must be discarded. The firm hires only skilled laborers to manufacture and install CT140; however, some are still damaged. Robotic instruments process all other parts. Ashley's operating data for 2 years are as follows:

Note regarding rounding errors: Many of the exercises and problems in this chapter require a series of calculations. Rounding errors can accumulate and affect totals unless each calculation is carried to a recommended four or more digits after the decimal point. If you are using a calculator, make sure all your calculations are done to 4 or more digits after the decimal. To avoid rounding errors entirely, use a spreadsheet package like Excel to set up and solve these problems.

	2022	2021
Units manufactured	750,000	1,000,000
Number of CT140 used	900,000	1,050,000
Number of direct labor hours spent	150,000	200,000
Cost of CT140 per unit	$156	$135
Direct labor wage rate per hour	$56	$62

Required

1. Compute the partial operational productivity for both direct materials and direct labor for each of the 2 years.

2. On the basis of the partial operational productivity that you computed, what conclusions can you draw about the firm's productivity in 2022 relative to 2021?

[LO 16-2]   16-42   **Partial Financial Productivity**   Use the data for Ashley Technology Inc. in Problem 16-41 to complete the following requirements:

Required

1. Compute the partial financial productivity ratios for direct materials and direct labor for each of the 2 years.

2. On the basis of the partial financial productivity ratios you computed, what conclusions can you draw about the firm's productivity in 2022 relative to 2021?

3. Separate the changes in the partial financial productivity ratios from 2021 to 2022 into productivity changes, input price changes, and output changes.

4. Does the detailed information provided by separating the change of the partial financial productivity ratio offer any additional insight into the relative productivity for either 2021 or 2022?

[LO 16-2]   16-43 **Total Productivity**   Use the data for Ashley Technology Inc. in Problem 16-41 to complete the following requirements. Also assume that fixed manufacturing costs are $50 million in both 2021 and 2022.

Required

1. Compute the total productivity ratios for 2021 and 2022.

2. On the basis of the total productivity that you computed, what conclusions can you draw about the firm's productivity in 2022 relative to 2021?

[LO 16-2]   16-44 **Partial Operational and Financial Productivity**   In the fourth quarter of last year, Colditz Company embarked on a major effort to improve productivity. It redesigned products, reengineered manufacturing processes, and offered productivity improvement courses. The effort was completed in the last quarter of the current year. The controller's office has gathered the following year-end data to assess the results of this effort:

	Current Year	Prior Year
Units manufactured and sold	20,000	16,000
Selling price of the product	$40	$40
Direct materials used (pounds)	14,000	13,000
Cost per pound of materials	$10	$8
Direct labor hours	5,250	6,000
Hourly wage rate	$25	$20
Power (kWh)	2,000	1,000
Cost of power per kWh	$2	$2

Required

1. Prepare a summary contribution income statement for each of the 2 years, and calculate the change in operating income.

2. Compute the partial operational productivity ratios for each production factor in each year.

3. Compute the partial financial productivity ratios for each production factor in each year.

4. On the basis of the partial operational and financial productivity ratios computed in requirements 2 and 3, what conclusions can you make about the firm's productivity last year relative to the current year?

5. Separate the changes in the partial financial productivity ratios from the prior year to the current year into productivity changes, input price changes, and output changes.

6. Consider the changes calculated in requirement 5. Does this detailed information offer any additional insight into the relative productivity of Colditz for the prior year and the current year?

[LO 16-2]   16-45 **Partial Operational and Financial Productivity; Total Productivity**   Katrina Design has decided to experiment with two alternative manufacturing approaches, identified as MF and LI, for producing men's fashions. The firm expects the total demand to be 20,000 suits. Management estimates the required input resources using the different manufacturing approaches are:

	Direct Materials (yards)	Direct Labor (hours)
MF	240,000	100,000
LI	180,000	120,000

The cost of direct materials is $10 per yard; the cost of direct labor is $26 per hour.

Required

1. Compute the partial operational productivity ratios for each of the production approaches. Which approach would you select based on the partial operational productivity ratios?

2. Calculate the partial financial productivity ratios for each of the production approaches. Which approach would you select based on the partial financial productivity ratios?

3. Compute the total productivity ratios for each of the production approaches. Which approach would you select based on the total productivity ratios?

[LO 16-2]   16-46 **Direct Labor Rate and Efficiency Variances; Productivity Measures; Review of Chapter 14**
Textron Manufacturing Inc. assembles industrial testing instruments in two departments, assembly and testing. Operating data for the current and prior years follow:

	Current Year	Prior Year
Assembly department		
Actual direct labor hours per instrument	20	25
Actual wage rate per hour	$36	$30
Standard direct labor hours per instrument	21	24
Standard wage rate per hour	$35	$28
Testing department		
Actual direct labor hours per instrument	10	12
Actual wage rate per hour	$24	$20
Standard direct labor hours per instrument	11	14
Standard wage rate per hour	$25	$21

The firm assembled and tested 20,000 instruments in both years.

Required
1. Calculate the direct labor rate and efficiency variances for both departments in both years.
2. Calculate the direct labor partial operational productivity ratio for both departments in both years.
3. Calculate the partial financial productivity ratio for both departments in both years.
4. Compare your answers for requirements 2 and 3. Comment on the results.
5. How do productivity measures differ from variance analysis, in terms of the types of perspectives they offer for the firm's strategic decision making?

[LO 16-2]   16-47 **Productivity and Market Share in the Auto Industry; Internet Exercise**   The following data were obtained from the 2018 financial statements for two U.S. automakers (in millions of dollars):

	Ford	GM
Sales	148,294	$151,092
Cost of goods sold	136,269	138,082

Required
1. Calculate and interpret total productivity in dollars for the two automakers.
2. Go to the internet for these companies and look under investor information to find the 2016 financial statements for each company. Review the sections on management's discussion and analysis and the related financial statements and disclosures and find the market size and market share information provided by these firms.

Ford: https://shareholder.ford.com/investors/financials-and-filings/default.aspx
GM: http://www.gm.com/investors/index.html

[LO 16-2]   16-48 **Productivity and Ethics**   Janice Interiors installs custom interiors for luxury mobile homes. In its most recent negotiation with the union, the firm proposed to share productivity gains in direct labor equally with the union. In return, the union agreed not to demand wage increases. Most union members, however, are skeptical about management's honesty in calculating productivity measures. Nevertheless, union members voted to try the program. Kim Tomas, the management accountant responsible for determining productivity measures, collected these data at the end of the current year:

	Current Year	Prior Year
Number of installations	560	500
Direct labor hours	115,000	99,000

Steve Janice, the CEO, is very eager to demonstrate the firm's good intentions by showing the labor union a positive result. He suggests to Kim that some of the direct labor hours are actually indirect. For example, some of the labor hours are indirect because these hours cannot be allocated to specific types of work.

Required

1. Compute the partial labor productivity for each year.

2. Recompute the partial productivity for the current year assuming 8,000 hours are reclassified as indirect.

3. Would it be ethical for Kim to modify her calculations?

[LO 16-2]

16-49 **Partial Operational and Financial Productivity; Medical Practice** Family Medical Care (FMC) is a family medical practice with 6 physicians, a nursing staff of 8 to 10 nurses, and an administrative staff that varies from 4 to 7 personnel. Rajat Patel, the chief physician at FMC, is interested in studying the efficiency of the practice as a basis to set some benchmarks for further improvement, for rewarding his staff, and for comparing the efficiency of the FMC practice to other family medical practices. He is able to get comparable data for other practices from industry sources. So that the data are consistent with the industry sources, Patel has asked Marin & Associates, his accounting firm, to develop a set of productivity measures that would satisfy this requirement. Upon investigation, Joseph Marin finds that the measures to be used are the partial financial and operational productivity measures as defined in the chapter. The following information is for the last 2 years for the FMC practice:

	Current Year	Prior Year
Patient visits	33,000	28,600
Nursing hours used	20,300	19,400
Administrative hours used	13,425	13,425
Cost of nursing support per hour	$39.00	$38.00
Cost of administration per hour	$25.56	$24.00
Industry average financial productivity		
Nursing	0.035	0.034
Administrative	1.120	1.140

Required

1. Compute the partial financial productivity ratios for nursing and administrative support for the current and prior years.

2. Separate the change in the partial financial productivity ratio from the prior year to the current year into productivity changes, input price changes, and output changes.

3. Write a brief memo from Joseph Marin to Rajat Patel interpreting the findings above.

[LO 16-3]

16-50 **Sales Variances; Flexible-Budget Variance; Review of Chapter 14** Robinson Company has two products, A and B. Robinson's budget for August follows:

	Master Budget	
	Product A	Product B
Sales	$240,000	$300,000
Variable cost	140,000	180,000
Contribution margin	$100,000	$120,000
Fixed cost	80,000	40,000
Operating income	$ 20,000	$ 80,000
Selling price	$ 120	$ 50

On September 1, these operating results for August were reported:

	Operating Results	
	Product A	Product B
Sales	$180,400	$341,120
Variable cost	106,600	216,480
Contribution margin	$ 73,800	$124,640
Fixed cost	80,000	40,000
Operating income	$ (6,200)	$ 84,640
Units sold	1,640	6,560

Required
1. For each product, determine the following variances measured in dollars of contribution margin:
   a. Flexible budget variance.
   b. Sales volume variance.
   c. Sales quantity variance.
   d. Sales mix variance.
2. Explain the amount of the flexible budget variance using the amounts of the selling price and variable cost variances.

[LO 16-1, 16-3]   **16-51 Sales Variances; Flexible-Budget Variance; Review of Chapter 14**   Jay Banning, CEO and a major stockholder of Banning Inc., was unhappy with its operating results for the past year. The company manufactures two environmentally friendly, industrial-caliber cleaning machines used primarily in automobile repair shops, gas stations, and auto dealerships. The master budget and operating results for the year (000s omitted except for the selling price per unit) follow:

	Actual		Budget	
	T10	**S40**	**T10**	**S40**
Sales	$126,000	$58,500	$100,000	$40,000
Variable cost	61,200	34,500	50,000	25,000
Contribution	$ 64,800	$24,000	$ 50,000	$15,000
Fixed cost	10,000	10,000	10,000	10,000
Operating income	$ 54,800	$14,000	$ 40,000	$ 5,000
Units sold	1,200	1,500		
Unit selling price			$100	$40

Required
1. Compute the contribution margin flexible budget variance, contribution margin sales volume variance, contribution margin sales quantity variance, and contribution margin sales mix variance for each product and for the firm.
2. Write a memo to Jay Banning about the implications of the variances that you just computed on the firm's strategy, planning, and operational control.

[LO 16-3]   **16-52 Sales Volume, Sales Quantity, and Sales Mix Variances**   Margot's Ice Cream operates several stores in a major metropolitan city and its suburbs. Its budget and operating data for the current year follow:

	Budgeted Data			Actual Operating Results		
Flavor	**Gallons**	**Selling Price per Gallon**	**Variable Costs per Gallon**	**Gallons**	**Selling Price per Gallon**	**Variable Costs per Gallon**
Vanilla	240,000	$1.25	$0.55	180,000	$1.10	$0.45
Chocolate	300,000	1.50	0.60	270,000	1.35	0.50
Strawberry	200,000	1.80	0.70	330,000	2.00	0.75
Anchovy	60,000	2.50	1.00	180,000	3.00	1.20

Required
1. Compute these variances for the individual flavors and total quantity sold:
   a. Sales volume.
   b. Sales mix.
   c. Sales quantity.
2. Assess sales in the current year based on your analyses.

[LO 16-3]   **16-53 Market Size and Share Variances**   TransPacific Airlines (TPA) budgeted 80 million passenger miles, or 5 percent of the total market for the year just completed, at a contribution margin of 40 cents per mile. The budgeted average price was 52 cents per passenger mile.

The operating data for the year show that TPA flew 69.12 million passenger miles with an average price of 48 cents per passenger mile. The terrorist activity in the early part of the year in several countries in the region decreased the total miles flown by all airlines for the year by 10 percent. There is no flexible budget variance for all costs.

Required

1. In an effort to understand the operating results, you are asked to compute the following:
   a. Selling price variance.
   b. Sales volume variance.
   c. Market size variance.
   d. Market share variance.

2. Explain the risks posed by the global economic environment for TPA, and suggest strategies for mitigating those risks.

[LO 16-3]   16-54   **Market Size and Market Share Variances for Small Business**   Diane's Designs is a small business run out of its owner's house. For the past 6 months, the company has been selling two products, a welcome sign and a birdhouse. The owner has been concerned about the company's marketing effectiveness. The master budget and actual results for March of this year follow:

	Master Budget		
	Welcome Sign	**Birdhouse**	**Total**
Units	50	25	75
Sales	$1,000	$250	$1,250
Variable costs	890	120	1,010
Contribution margin	$ 110	$130	$ 240
Fixed costs	75	75	150
Operating income	$ 35	$ 55	$ 90

	Actual Results		
	Welcome Sign	**Birdhouse**	**Total**
Units	45	35	80
Sales	$675	$420	$1,095
Variable costs	580	270	850
Contribution margin	$ 95	$150	$ 245
Fixed costs	75	75	150
Operating income	$ 20	$ 75	$ 95

The total market for welcome signs for each of the last 6 months was 500 budgeted and 500 actual. Diane expected the total market for birdhouses to be 200 units per month; the actual volume for the entire market, however, turned out to be only 175 units per month.

Required

1. Compute Diane's actual market share for welcome signs and birdhouses.
2. What is the market share contribution margin variance?
3. What is the market size contribution margin variance?
4. Explain possible reasons for these variances.

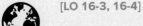

[LO 16-3, 16-4]   16-55   **Market Size, Market Share, Price, Mix, and Volume Variances; Foreign Currency Fluctuations**   Tall Pines Brewery (TPB) makes two specialty beers in its microbrewery: Golden Ale and Dark Ale. Both beers sell for the same price per case in the U.S. market and in the export market. The latter market is primarily European countries. Both beers also have the same variable production costs, though the export product has slightly higher variable costs due to shipping and other distribution costs associated with the export beers. The price, cost, and market information for the two beers are shown below:

	Budgeted	Actual	Budgeted Wt Avg CM
Sales units (cases)			
Domestic	22,000	22,350	
Export	12,000	14,500	
Total	34,000	36,850	
Price per case			
Domestic	$88	$87	
Export	90	92	
Variable cost per case			
Domestic	$62	$62	
Export	68	68	
Contribution margin per case			
Domestic	$26	$25	
Export	22	24	
Total contribution margin			
Domestic	$572,000	$558,750	
Export	264,000	348,000	
Total contribution margin	$836,000		$24.5882

	Industry Budget	Industry Actual
Sales units (cases)		
Domestic	901,500	924,550
Export	635,400	645,750

The budget was prepared with the expectation that the currency exchange rate would be $1.07 per euro. The actual average exchange rate for the period reflected the falling dollar, at $1.23 per euro.

Required

1. What is the market share variance?
2. What is the market size variance?
3. What are the selling price variance and sales volume variance?
4. What are the sales mix variance and sales quantity variance?
5. Explain possible reasons for these variances, including a consideration of the effect of the change in the currency exchange rate for the dollar and the euro.

[LO 16-4]   16-56   **Comparative Income Statements and Sales Performance Variances; Current to Prior Year**   Clippers Inc. (CI) manufactures two types of garden clippers. A light-duty model, called the "half-inch," is intended for clipping branches and stems up to one-half-inch thick. The "one-inch" model is designed for heavier stems and branches. To boost sales, CI decided at the beginning of the current year to reduce the price of the half-inch model to better position its price relative to some key competitors. On the other hand, CI felt that the one-inch model was technically superior to competitors' models and decided that a small price increase was appropriate. The data for the current and prior years are as follows:

	Current Year	Prior Year
Sales units	7,200	6,500
Sales mix for each product		
Half-inch model	50%	30%
One-inch model	50%	70%
Price		
Half-inch model	$12.00	$14.00
One-inch model	$36.00	$32.00
Variable cost per unit		
Half-inch model	$6.00	$6.00
One-inch model	$8.00	$8.00
Fixed cost	$35,000	$35,000

Required

1. Prepare a comparative contribution income statement for CI for the current year that shows the sales volume and selling price variances for each product. (*Hint:* Use Exhibit 16.15 as an example.)
2. Determine the sales mix variance and the sales quantity variance for each product, based on contribution margin.
3. Did the price change have the expected results? Why or why not?

[LO 16-4]   16-57 **Comparative Income Statements and Sales Performance Variances; Current to Prior Year**   Green Grow Inc. manufactures riding lawn mowers that it sells to the large discount stores such as Walmart, Lowe's, and Home Depot. The mowers are marketed as a "value" product, with good quality at a very good price. The company's two products are the Quality mower, which last year sold for $1,200 (the discounters retailed it for $1,500), and the Heavy Duty model, which Green Grow sold for $1,600 (and was retailed for $2,200). At the end of last year, the company had come under increased price competition from other manufacturers. The company management believes it must reduce its price in the current year on both products to keep its current market share with sales of 3,500 units. The unit variable costs for the Quality and Heavy Duty products are $800 and $950, respectively. Management does not believe it can reduce these variable costs for the coming year but will begin to study ways to do so for future years. In the meantime, the company management believes it can maintain its total market share by increasing its advertising expenses by $150,000 and cutting the price on both models by 10 percent. Fixed costs, including advertising, were $550,000 last year and are not expected to change, with the exception of the increase in advertising. Last year, the sales mix was 40 percent for Quality and 60 percent for Heavy Duty. In the current year, the sales mix is 50 percent for Quality and 50 percent for Heavy Duty.

Required

1. Prepare a comparative contribution income statement for Green Grow Inc. for the current year that shows the volume and selling price variances for each product based on contribution margin. (*Hint:* Use Exhibit 16.15 as an example.)
2. Determine the sales mix variance and the sales quantity variance for each product, based on contribution margin.
3. Did the price change and increase in advertising have the expected results? Why or why not?
4. What methods should Green Grow adopt to become more competitive in the current and coming years?

[LO 16-4]   16-58 **Sales and Variable Cost Variances; Current to Prior Year; Review of Chapter 14**   RJM Enterprises is a manufacturer of consumer electronics products. The industry is very competitive, and RJM has seen its profits fall in recent years, including an operating loss of $18,585 last year. RJM was able to turn that around this year by aggressively cutting costs. The summarized financial results for RJM are shown below:

	Current Year	Prior Year
Gross sales:	$934,920	$1,273,545
Less variable costs		
Direct materials	550,368	746,200
Direct labor	329,280	511,875
Total contribution margin	$ 55,272	$ 15,470
Fixed costs	33,509	34,055
Operating income	$ 21,763	$ (18,585)

Jim Green, the management accountant at RJM, is analyzing the company's performance for this year in order to explain to management the specific aspects that drove the company to success. Some of the information Jim obtained follows:

	Current Year	Prior Year
Sales units	39,200	45,500
Price	$23.85	$27.99
Direct materials cost per unit of material	$7.80	$8.20
Direct materials required per unit	1.80	2.00
Direct labor required per unit	0.60	0.75
Wage rate ($/hour)	$14.00	$15.00

Assume that RJM, for efficiency and to reduce cost, maintains little or no direct materials or work-in-process inventory.

Required

1. Determine the selling price variance for the current year based on sales dollars. Determine the sales volume variance based on contribution margin.
2. Determine the following variable cost variances:
   a. The usage and price variances for direct materials.
   b. The efficiency and rate variances for direct labor.
3. Interpret your findings in requirements 1 and 2.

Solutions to Self-Study Problems

1. Productivity Variances

1. Operational partial productivity

		20X1				20X2		
	Output		Input Resource Used	Partial Productivity	Output		Input Resource Used	Partial Productivity
Direct material	60,000	÷	75,000	= 0.8	64,000	÷	89,600	= 0.7143
Direct labor	60,000	÷	10,000	= 6.0	64,000	÷	10,847	= 5.9002

2. Financial partial productivity

		20X1				20X2		
	Units of Output		Cost of Input Resource Used	Partial Productivity	Units of Output		Cost of Input Resource Used	Partial Productivity
Direct material	60,000	÷	$540,000	= 0.1111	64,000	÷	$609,280	= 0.1050
Direct labor	60,000	÷	$300,000	= 0.2000	64,000	÷	$347,104	= 0.1844

3. Partition of financial partial productivity

	(A) 20X2 Output with 20X2 Productivity at 20X2 Input Costs	(B) 20X2 Output with 20X1 Productivity at 20X1 Input Costs	(C) 20X2 Output with 20X1 Productivity at 20X1 Input Costs	(D) 20X1 Output with 20X1 Productivity at 20X1 Input Costs
Direct materials	64,000 ÷ $609,280 = 0.1050	64,000 ÷ $544,000 = 0.1176	64,000 ÷ $576,000 = 0.1111	60,000 ÷ $540,000 = 0.1111
Direct labor	64,000 ÷ $347,104 = 0.1844	64,000 ÷ $341,333 = 0.1875	64,000 ÷ $320,000 = 0.2000	60,000 ÷ $300,000 = 0.2000

	Productivity change	Input price change	Output change
Direct materials	0.1050 − 0.1176 = 0.0126U	0.1176 − 0.1111 = 0.0065F	0.1111 − 0.1111 = 0
Direct labor	0.1844 − 0.1875 = 0.0031U	0.1875 − 0.2000 = 0.0125U	0.2000 − 0.2000 = 0

Summary of Results:

	Productivity Change	Input Price Change	Total Change	Change as Percent of 20X1 Productivity* Productivity Change	Input Price Change	Total Change
Direct material	0.0126U	0.0065F	0.0061U	11.34%U	5.85%F	5.49%U
Direct labor	0.0031U	0.0125U	0.0156U	1.55%U	6.25%U	7.8%U

*20X1 productivity: Direct materials   60,000 units ÷ (75,000 pounds × $7.20 per pound) = 0.111111
                     Direct labor   60,000 units ÷ (10,000 hours × $30 per hour) = 0.2

Change as percent of 20X1 productivity:

	Productivity Change	Input Price Change	Total Change
Direct material	0.0126 ÷ 0.111111 = 11.34%	0.0065 ÷ 0.111111 = 5.85%	0.0061 ÷ 0.111111 = 5.49%
Direct labor	0.0031 ÷ 0.2 = 1.55%	0.0125 ÷ 0.2 = 6.25%	0.0156 ÷ 0.2 = 7.8%

4. Total productivity

Total Productivity in Units	20X1	20X2
(a) Total units manufactured	60,000	64,000
(b) Total manufacturing costs incurred	$1,290,000	$1,406,384
(c) Total productivity (a) ÷ (b)	0.0465	0.0455
(d) Decrease in productivity		0.0465 − 0.0455 = 0.0010

Total Productivity in Sales Dollars	20X1	20X2
(a) Total sales	$1,500,000	$1,600,000
(b) Total manufacturing costs incurred	$1,290,000	$1,406,384
(c) Total productivity (a) ÷ (b)	1.1628	1.1377
(d) Decrease in productivity		1.1628 − 1.1377 = 0.0251

2. Sales Variances

1. Selling price variances (in 000s)

Flexible Budget Sales:

	Total Sales		Units		Budgeted Selling Price per Unit		Total Units Sold in 20XX		Flexible Budget Sales
	Master Budget for 20XX								
Premium	$36,000	÷	240	=	$150	×	180	=	$27,000
Regular	43,200	÷	360	=	120	×	540	=	64,800

Selling Price Variances:

	Premium			Regular		
	Actual	Flexible Budget	Selling Price Variance	Actual	Flexible Budget	Selling Price Variance
Barrels	180	180		540	540	
Sales	$28,800	$27,000	$1,800F	$62,100	$64,800	$2,700U
Total Selling price variance				$900U		

2. Sales volume variances (in 000s) for the period for each product and for the firm.

Flexible Budget Variable Expenses:

	Total Variable Expenses		Number of Units		Budgeted Variable Expenses per Unit		Total Units Sold in 20XX		Flexible Budget Variable Expenses
	Master Budget for 20XX								
Premium	$21,600	÷	240	=	$90	×	180	=	$16,200
Regular	27,000	÷	360	=	75	×	540	=	40,500

Sales Volume Variances:

	Premium			Regular		
	Flexible Budget	Master Budget	Sales Volume Variance	Flexible Budget	Master Budget	Sales Volume Variance
Barrels	180	240	60U	540	360	180F
Sales	$27,000	$36,000	$9,000U	$64,800	$43,200	$21,600F
Variable expenses	16,200	21,600	5,400F	40,500	27,000	13,500U
Contribution margin	$10,800	$14,400	$3,600U	$24,300	$16,200	$ 8,100F
Fixed expenses	10,000	10,000	—	5,000	5,000	—
Operating income	$ 800	$ 4,400	$3,600U	$19,300	$11,200	$ 8,100F
Total sales volume variance				$4,500F		

3. Sales quantity variances for the firm and for each product. (See the solution for requirement 4.)
4. Sales mix variances for the period for each product and for the firm (000s omitted).

Sales Mixes:

	Budgeted		Actual	
	Total Sales in Units	**Sales Mix**	**Total Sales in Units**	**Sales Mix**
Premium	240	0.40	180	0.25
Regular	360	0.60	540	0.75
Total	600	1.00	720	1.00

Budgeted contribution margin per unit =
Budgeted selling price per unit (item 1 above) − Budgeted variable
cost per unit (item 2 above)

Premium = \$150 − \$90 = \$60
Regular = \$120 − \$75 = \$45

Sales mix and sales quantity variances:

Flexible Budget		Master Budget
Total units of all products sold × **Actual sales mix** × Budgeted contribution margin per unit	*Total units of all products sold* × **Budgeted sales mix** × Budgeted contribution margin per unit	***Total budgeted units of all products to be sold*** × Budgeted sales mix × Budgeted contribution margin per unit

Premium

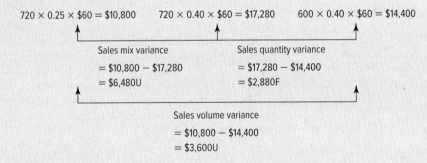

Regular

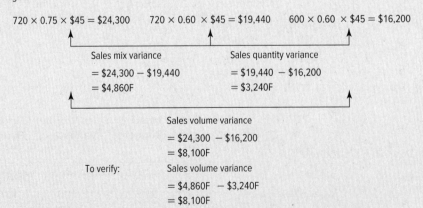

Total (both premium and regular)

Sales mix variance = \$6,480U + \$4,860F = \$1,620U
Sales quantity variance = \$2,880F + \$3,240F = \$6,120F

5. Verification

Sales mix variance + Sales quantity variance = Sales volume variance

Premium	$6,480U	+	$2,880F	=	$3,600U
Regular	4,860F	+	3,240F	=	8,100F
Total	$1,620U	+	$6,120F	=	$4,500F

6. Market size variance. (See the solution for requirement 7.)
7. Market share variance (000s omitted).

Weighted-Average Budgeted Contribution Margin per Unit

Master budget total contribution margin	$30,600
Master budget total sales units	÷ 600
Total	$ 51

Market Shares:

Budgeted: Total sales in units 600 ÷ Total sales of the industry 1,500 = 0.40
Actual: Total sales in units 720 ÷ Total sales of the industry 1,600 = 0.45

Market Share and Size Variances:

Actual total market size × **Actual market share** × Average budgeted contribution margin per unit	**Actual total market size × Budgeted market share** × Average budgeted contribution margin per unit	**Budgeted total market size** × Budgeted market share × Average budgeted contribution margin per unit

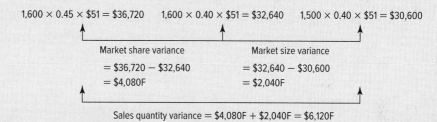

8. The sum of the market size variance and market share variance follows. It verifies that this total equals the sales quantity variance.

Total market size variance + Total market share variance = Total sales quantity variance
$2,040F + $4,080F = $6,120F

Please visit Connect to access a narrated, animated tutorial for solving these problems.

CHAPTER SEVENTEEN

The Management and Control of Quality

After studying this chapter, you should be able to . . .

LO 17-1 Discuss the strategic importance of quality.

LO 17-2 Define accounting's role in the management and control of quality.

LO 17-3 Develop a comprehensive framework for the management and control of quality.

LO 17-4 Understand alternative approaches for setting performance expectations (Six Sigma, goalpost vs. absolute specifications, and Taguchi quality loss functions).

LO 17-5 Prepare and interpret relevant financial information to support quality-related initiatives.

LO 17-6 Discuss the use of nonfinancial performance data to support quality-related initiatives.

LO 17-7 Describe and understand tools that can be used to detect and correct quality problems.

LO 17-8 Describe lean manufacturing and changes in management accounting systems needed to support a change to "lean."

Panchenko Vladimir/Shutterstock

"Quality is everyone's responsibility."

W. Edwards Deming, engineer, statistician, and business consultant

The competitive landscape of the business world has changed dramatically. Today, high quality of products and services is a nonnegotiable standard. Global competition gives consumers many choices, and consumers today are much more cost- and value-conscious. Most organizations, to varying degrees, have responded with quality-related management programs, with names such as total quality management (TQM), Six Sigma, Lean Six Sigma, and lean management (or lean manufacturing). Organizations that fail to embrace such initiatives may find themselves at a competitive disadvantage.

Consider, for example, the health care industry. Probably no other industry (at least in the U.S.) has been the focus of more intense discussion in the recent past—in terms both of the quality of delivery and of cost management and operating efficiency. Management of patient care quality and health care finances is complicated by the following factors (see **www.isixsigma. com/industries/healthcare/six-sigma-powerful-strategy-healthcare-providers/**):

- *Changing demographics in the U.S.* Over the next 10 to 15 years, a significant number of baby boomers will retire and add significant demands to the health care system.
- *Financial constraints.* There is a practical limit to how much the U.S. as a nation can afford to spend on health care.
- *Staffing shortages.* Particularly in terms of nurses, there are severe staffing shortfalls (see **www.healthcarefinancenews.com/news/nearly-half-nurses-consider-changing-careers-nationwide-shortage-looms-rnnetwork-study-says**).
- *Increased litigation.* The risk of personal injury judgments places additional demands on an already burdened financial model for health care.

All of the above factors are related—directly or indirectly—to heath care quality. The following examples, or "success stories," illustrate how management accountants can add value by developing and implementing systems that help control costs and manage health care quality:

- Morton Plant Hospital in Clearwater, Florida, recently used a variety of tools discussed in this chapter (e.g., lean, Six Sigma, and cost of quality) to improve patient satisfaction (an external nonfinancial measure of quality), reduce emergency department length of service, and significantly reduce cost of quality (COQ) spending (see **http://asq.org/healthcaresixsigma/**).
- Mountain States Health Alliance, with facilities in northeastern Tennessee and southwestern Virginia, recently adopted lean management practices not only to cut costs (e.g., savings related to reductions in inventory and medical supplies), but also to improve quality (as measured by both patient and employee satisfaction and by the average appointment time per patient) (see **www.beckershospitalreview.com/hospital-management-administration/lean-management-for-cutting-costs-and-a-happier-hospital.html**).
- Akron Children's Hospital recently employed quality tools (lean and Six Sigma) and control charts generated by a statistical software program (Minitab) to reduce patient waiting times, reduce insurance eligibility denials, improve operating efficiency (e.g., reduced need for overtime costs and reductions in prescription fill times by the Outpatient Pharmacy unit), and improve overall patient care (see **www.minitab.com/en-us/Case-Studies/Akron-Childrens-Hospital/**).

In each of the above cases, the organization initiated programs to improve quality (defined here as patient care and satisfaction), control costs, reduce waste, increase speed of delivery, or refine operational processes. Given the challenges facing the health care sector in the United States, these managerial initiatives are strategically important for patients, health care providers, and the public at large.

This discussion raises the following question: How can cost management systems be configured to support strategic initiatives related to *quality,* similar to the health care examples listed above? Chapter 17 is devoted to this question. In the next section, we discuss the strategic importance of quality in greater detail. This is followed by a discussion of accounting's role in the management and control of quality. Next, we derive a comprehensive framework (Exhibit 17.3) that can be used to manage and control quality. The remainder of the chapter discusses the elements of the framework depicted in Exhibit 17.3. Throughout this chapter, our task is to demonstrate how accounting can add organizational value by providing managers with information that supports quality-related initiatives in the organization.

The Strategic Importance of Quality

LO. 17-1

Discuss the strategic importance of quality.

Many firms have engaged in major efforts to improve the quality of their products and services. In this text, we refer to such efforts collectively as **total quality management (TQM)**—that is, the unyielding and continuous effort by everyone in the organization to understand, meet, and exceed the expectations of customers. In fact, continuous improvement has become a way of life for many firms and organizations, as evidenced by the quality standards and awards discussed next.

total quality management (TQM)

Total quality management (TQM) is a method by which management develops policies and practices to ensure that the firm's products and services exceed customers' expectations.

Baldrige Quality Award

In 1987, the U.S. Congress established the Malcolm Baldrige National Quality Award to enhance the competitiveness of U.S. businesses by promoting quality awareness; recognizing quality and performance achievements; and publicizing successful performance strategies of U.S. organizations in the areas of manufacturing, service, small business, and—added in 1999—education and health care. Seven broad categories make up the award criteria: leadership, strategic planning, customer and market focus, measurement/analysis/knowledge management, workforce, operations, and results. The award is managed by the National Institute of Standards and Technology (NIST), within the U.S. Department of Commerce.

The 2019 Baldrige Award recipients include organizations in health care, education, local government, and the first-ever public pension fund to receive the award (see **www.nist.gov/news-events/news/2019/11/six-health-care-nonprofit-and-education-organizations-win-baldrige-awards**):

- Adventist Health White Memorial, Los Angeles, CA (health care).
- Center for Organ Recovery & Education, Pittsburgh, PA (health care).
- City of Germantown, Germantown, TN (nonprofit)
- Howard Community College, Columbia, MD (education)
- Illinois Municipal Retirement Fund, Oak Brook, IL (nonprofit)
- Mary Greeley Medical Center, Ames, IA (health care)

An organization can be nominated for the award in one of six business sectors: education, health care, manufacturing, nonprofit, service, or small business. As of 2019, 129 awards have been made. The competition to win the award is evidence of the importance U.S. organizations place on being recognized for the quality of their operations.

ISO 9000

A set of guidelines for quality management and quality standards developed by the International Organization for Standardization (ISO), located in Geneva, Switzerland.

ISO 14000

A set of quality standards that address various aspects of environmental performance, including life-cycle analysis, communication, and auditing of environmental performance.

ISO 9000 and ISO 14000

In 1947, a specialized agency (the International Organization for Standardization, **www.iso.org**) was formed to standardize quality management practices. The current set of quality-management standards developed by the ISO is referred to as the **ISO 9000** standards. These standards provide guidance and tools for companies and organizations that want to ensure their products and services consistently meet customers' requirements and that quality is consistently improved.

ISO 14000 is a set of standards that relate to environmental management—that is, what an organization does to minimize harmful effects to the environment. As with ISO 9000, ISO 14000 is concerned with quality management—specifically, processes in place that ensure the ability of an organization to identify and control its environmental impact and constantly improve its environmental performance.

Quality and Profitability: Conceptual Linkage

Whether a company competes through a strategy of cost leadership or product differentiation, quality issues permeate every aspect of operations. A company choosing to compete through low prices is not necessarily choosing to produce low-quality products. Its low-priced products must still meet customer expectations. Similarly, a differentiation strategy will not be successful, or at least will not be as successful as it could be, if the company fails to build quality into its products and services. Thus, a key question for top management is how best to control quality, quality-related costs, and investments in quality-related initiatives.

Exhibit 17.1 shows one possible model of how and why a manufacturing firm with improved quality can achieve competitive advantage and enjoy improved financial performance [e.g., higher profitability and/or a higher rate of return on investment (ROI)]. Improved quality decreases product returns. Lower sales returns decrease warranty costs and repair expenses. Improved quality typically lowers inventory levels for raw materials, components, and finished products because the firm has more reliable manufacturing processes and schedules. Improved product quality also lowers manufacturing costs as, for example, the firm reduces or eliminates rework costs and increases productivity. Customers are likely to perceive quality products as having higher values, which may allow the firm to charge higher prices and enjoy a larger market share. Higher prices and greater market shares increase revenues and profits. Improved quality also decreases manufacturing cycle time. Faster cycle times increase delivery speed; prompt delivery produces satisfied customers, creates new demand, and increases market shares. Higher revenues and lower costs boost net income and increase the firm's ROI.

Accounting's Role in the Management and Control of Quality

LO 17-2

Define accounting's role in the management and control of quality.

Quality programs such as TQM are management initiatives rather than accounting initiatives. Thus, an appropriate question is how accounting can add value to, or support, quality-related initiatives of management. An inspection of Exhibit 17.1 suggests that accountants can add value to the process by providing managers with relevant and timely information (both financial and nonfinancial) that helps managers make better quality-related decisions.

EXHIBIT 17.1
Conceptual Relationship between Improved Quality and Financial Performance

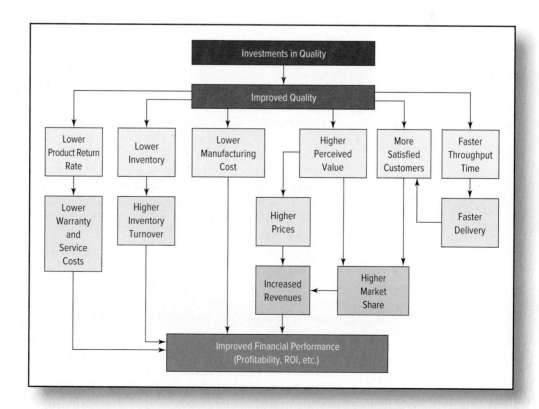

The following example provides an overview of the five-step process that was used to develop internal accounting procedures for measuring and managing quality in the pharmaceutical industry.

The Five Steps of Strategic Decision Making: Improving Quality in Pharmaceutical and Medical Product Companies[1]

Many world-class manufacturers, including producers of semiconductors and goods for the aerospace and electronics industries, have implemented effective systems for measuring and managing product quality. However, the situation in the pharmaceutical and medical products sectors is different. Historically, quality control was superseded in importance by a focus on product innovation and compelling marketing initiatives.

1. **Determine the strategic issues surrounding the problem.** Lack of effective systems for monitoring and controlling quality in the pharmaceutical and medical products industry ("pharma" for short) is becoming costly for these firms. Over the period 2001–2007, the industry incurred more than $700 million in fines and, it is estimated, suffered billions more in lost revenues. Thus, for some firms in this industry, adopting world-class manufacturing processes can create a competitive advantage—both by reducing regulatory risk and by reducing production costs. One such process (discussed later in the chapter) is the movement to lean manufacturing coupled with Six Sigma quality-performance expectations.

2. **Identify the alternative actions.** At one level, corporate management may feel that strict regulation in the industry obviates the need for investing in a new quality-management system. At another level, however, executives may feel that a new system is needed to secure competitive advantage and reduce regulatory risk. In terms of a new system, choices need to be made about (a) what data should be collected (e.g., qualitative vs. quantitative, including financial data regarding product quality), (b) to whom such data should be reported, (c) how often the data should be reported, and (d) how targeted performance in terms of quality (e.g., Six Sigma) should be specified. Finally, a decision needs to be made about the methods that should be used to isolate and correct quality-related problems.

3. **Obtain information and conduct analyses of the alternatives.** Corporate management would have to estimate the required investment outlay for the new monitoring and control system, as well as ongoing operating costs associated with the system. Benefits of the new quality- and compliance-management system would have to be quantified and reported over time. These costs would be compared to anticipated benefits of the new system, both financial and nonfinancial in nature (e.g., improved relationship with regulators). Financial benefits would include opportunity costs as well as out-of-pocket costs, as discussed in Chapters 11 and 12.

4. **Based on strategy and analysis, choose and implement the desired alternative.** The company in question can choose to implement a comprehensive system for managing and controlling quality. This system might consist of a cost of quality (COQ) reporting framework that would report, on a time-series basis using activity-based costing (ABC) data, both out-of-pocket and opportunity cost information. Such data could be benchmarked against best-in-class performers (either within or external to the company). Nonfinancial performance indicators would be derived from an explicit statement of strategy and would be analyzed statistically to justify their continued use. If lean production methods are adopted, then the company must consider whether and how to change its internal reporting system to support this change in production philosophy.

5. **Provide an ongoing evaluation of the effectiveness of implementation in step 4.** Assuming the investment in the new system is made, management could institute a post-audit review of the decision, to see how close the actual results were to the projected costs and benefits of the new system. (The topic of conducting post audits in conjunction with capital budgeting decisions was introduced in Chapter 12.)

---

[1] Background information for this example is taken from Anil G. D'souza, David J. Keeling, and Richard D. Phillips, "Improving Quality in 'Pharm' Manufacturing," *The McKinsey Quarterly,* September 2007, pp. 1–7.

Comprehensive Framework for Managing and Controlling Quality

LO 17-3

Develop a comprehensive framework for the management and control of quality.

quality

Defined as customer satisfaction with the total experience of a product or service. An overall measure of quality is the difference between customer expectations and actual performance of the product or service.

design quality

The extent to which actual product design matches customer expectations (for attributes, services, functionality, etc.).

performance quality

The extent to which the actual performance of the product matches (or is consistent with) design specifications of the product.

The Meaning of Quality

For purposes of discussion, we define the term **quality** to mean the total level of customer satisfaction with the organization's product or service. Defined in this manner, we can decompose quality into two broad components: *features* and *performance.* Features refer to the extent to which product/service design is consistent with customer expectations (in terms of product/service characteristics, attributes, or functionality)—in short, **design quality.** Outputs that fail to meet such expectations result in quality-of-design failure costs. Conceptually, you can think of design failure as the difference between the actual features of the product (or service) and the features that the customer wants. Such failures (or gaps) represent one component of total quality cost.

The other broad component of quality, **performance quality,** is defined as the difference between the design specifications of the product and the actual performance of the product. Thus, a personal computer whose electronic mouse consistently malfunctions or whose operating system constantly locks up suffers what are called performance-quality failures.

These two broad categories of quality (and related costs) are depicted in Exhibit 17.2. The issue of how to build quality of design into products was covered in Chapter 13 (target costing). In this chapter, we focus on the left-hand side of Exhibit 17.2: performance quality and related costs. Exhibit 17.1 provides broad guidance for the development of a comprehensive framework (or system) for the management and control of quality. One possible framework is presented in Exhibit 17.3. This exhibit serves as the focal point for the discussion in the rest of the chapter. The discussion should reinforce the principle that cost management systems are dynamic in nature and need to evolve over time to meet the changing information needs of top management.

Knowledge of Business Processes

Because the framework presented in Exhibit 17.3 is comprehensive, it presumes knowledge of key business processes. Thus, the development and implementation of a comprehensive framework for managing and controlling quality is best thought of as a cross-functional effort, with input from individuals across the firm's entire value chain. Because of their record-keeping and reporting responsibilities, management accountants can be viewed as the key point of contact across various subunits and managers within the organization. Thus, the development of such a comprehensive system requires the management accountant to have broad business knowledge, including knowledge of fundamental business processes.

Role of the Customer

In the past, most quality control reporting systems had a decidedly inward focus. That is, measures and techniques were developed and used based on what the *organization* felt were appropriate to the situation. More recently, however, organizations have begun to realize a fundamental flaw in system design: failure to embrace an outward (i.e., *customer-based*) viewpoint. Thus, in the comprehensive model shown in Exhibit 17.3, we depict customer expectations as the cornerstone of the entire framework. In this sense, then, the model can be

EXHIBIT 17.2
Dimensions of Quality

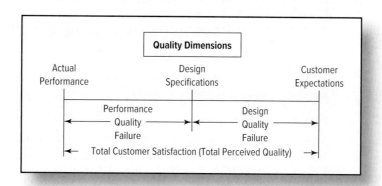

REAL-WORLD FOCUS   How Costly Is Poor Quality?

As noted earlier, some organizations have a quality orientation and embrace managerial initiatives such as TQM to support this competitive strategy. For each of the following examples, consider how costly poor quality can be and how management accounting and control systems (including both financial and nonfinancial performance indicators) could be used to help manage and control quality:

- In 2019, Japanese air bag manufacturer Takata Corp. was forced to issue another recall of over 4.4 million inflaters used in over 1.4 million cars. This came after Takata already agreed to a $70 million fine related to the widespread sale of rupture-prone air bags in 2015. In both instances, the inflater was found to explode after a buildup of moisture and send shrapnel into the vehicle. Billions of dollars have been set aside by auto makers such as Toyota, Honda, and Audi to cover air bag–related settlements and replacement costs.

- In 2020, Boeing was subjected to fines of over $25 million by the FAA for a software glitch that made a warning light inoperable in more than 80% of its airplanes. The glitch was

found in 2017 by the company, but Boeing chose not to fix the problem or inform U.S. regulators. The same glitch was cited as a factor in the crash of a Lion Air jet in 2018. That crash, and the subsequent grounding of the 737 Max world-wide, will cost the company an estimated $18.6 billion.

- In 2019, Fisher-Price paid $27 million to recall and warn of the dangers of its inclined sleeper, the Rock 'n Play. The company released the angle-inclined sleeper in 2009 with the promise of better sleep for babies than a flat-lying crib or bassinet. However, the company never sought the advice of pediatricians or performed clinical research. The Rock 'n Play sleeper has been involved in over 30 deaths after infants turned over while unrestrained. Lawsuits against the company are expected to cost millions more in the future.

Sources: B. Foldy, "New Problems with Takata Air Bags Prompt Recall of 1.4 Million Cars," *The Wall Street Journal,* December 4, 2019; A. Levin, "A Malfunctioning 737 Max Warning Light Could Cost Boeing Millions in New FAA Fines," *Fortune,* February 21, 2020; T. Frankel, "Fisher-Price Invented a Popular Baby Sleeper without Medical Safety Tests and Kept Selling It, Even as Babies Died," *The Washington Post,* May 30, 2019.

EXHIBIT 17.3

Comprehensive Framework for Managing and Controlling Quality

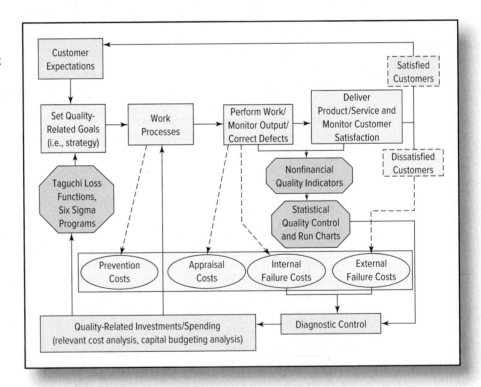

viewed as customer-based. The model also captures (as "external failure costs") various costs associated with dissatisfied customers.

Financial Component

You will notice that the reporting of quality *cost* information is a key element of the compre-hensive framework shown in Exhibit 17.3. In fact, we depict cost information in four separate categories (prevention, appraisal, internal failure, and external failure) to give prominence to the different types of quality costs that organizations incur. This financial approach to the management and control of quality, known as *cost of quality (COQ)*, is dealt with in greater detail later in the chapter.

Nonfinancial Performance Indicators

As illustrated in Exhibit 17.3, the financial performance indicators of our comprehensive reporting framework are complemented by both internal and external nonfinancial performance indicators. As we explain later in the chapter, nonfinancial performance indicators can be leading indicators (i.e., predictors) of future financial performance. As such, any comprehensive framework for managing and controlling quality should have a combination of both financial and nonfinancial performance indicators.

Feedback Loops

You will notice that Exhibit 17.3 contains a number of feedback loops designed to inform future decisions and to support an organization's overall goal of continuous improvement. Thus, for example, the entire model continually helps the organization better understand "customer expectations" and, in turn, set appropriate quality goals for the organization.

Relevant Cost Analysis of Quality-Related Spending and Investments

As indicated in Exhibit 17.3, management accountants can provide financial information that can be used by managers to evaluate quality-related spending and investment decisions. Thus, the framework presented in Exhibit 17.3 draws directly from the material covered in Chapters 11 (relevant cost analysis) and 12 (capital budgeting analysis) of the text.

Link to Operations Management and Statistics

The framework presented in Exhibit 17.3 provides a good example of cross-disciplinary inputs to a management process. As noted above, accounting has primary reporting responsibility for relevant financial and nonfinancial performance measures. The question then is how managers, after receiving such information, identify and analyze quality-related problems. For this, the fields of operations management and statistics have developed techniques such as control charts, Pareto diagrams, and cause-and-effect diagrams. As part of the decision-making team, management accountants should have at least cursory knowledge of these techniques, all of which are discussed later in the chapter.

Breadth of the System

In the past, for many organizations (particularly manufacturers), quality was assumed to be the responsibility of production (i.e., the manufacturing process). However, as indicated by the discussion at the beginning of this chapter (and implied by the model presented in Exhibit 17.3), many organizations today are emphasizing a broader responsibility for quality—one that stretches across all elements of the value chain. Any comprehensive framework developed to support a TQM strategy should therefore have a broad reporting perspective. You will note that the performance measures associated with Exhibit 17.3 cut across the entire value chain.

In the remaining sections of this chapter, we discuss in greater detail the elements of the conceptual framework illustrated in Exhibit 17.3.

Alternative Approaches to Setting Quality-Related Expectations

LO 17-4

Understand alternative approaches for setting performance expectations (Six Sigma, goalpost vs. absolute specifications, and Taguchi quality loss functions).

As seen from Exhibit 17.3, the actual quality goals embraced by the organization are affected principally by customer demands—that is, the level of quality (including product functionality) customers are willing to pay for. In this section we first discuss the Six Sigma approach to setting quality-related performance standards. This is followed by a discussion of an alternative approach: the use of "goalpost" versus absolute conformance standards. We conclude with a discussion of Taguchi quality loss functions, which can be used in conjunction with absolute performance standards.

Setting Quality Expectations: A Six Sigma Approach

In statistics, the Greek letter *sigma* stands for standard deviation (i.e., a measure of dispersion of a set of observations around the mean value of these observations). We can use a standard normal curve (i.e., one for a distribution with a mean of zero and a standard deviation of 1) to represent probabilities. For example, the area to the right of +3 standard deviations (i.e., 3 sigma) is very small: approximately 1.4%. In turn, these probabilities can be converted to number of defects per million. A 3-sigma performance level, then, would be approximately 1,400 defects per million. A 4-sigma performance level would translate to approximately 32 defects per million, while a 6-sigma performance level would translate to only 0.001 defect per million. (In practice, be aware that adjustments to these figures are made to capture process drift or shift.) In short, sigma can be used to set (or express) quality expectations: the higher the sigma level, the higher the quality expectation. As noted next, however, the term Six Sigma can also be used to refer to a process-improvement philosophy.

Six Sigma[2], as a management philosophy or goal, has been embraced by many organizations as the guiding principle that drives improvements in products, services, and processes (e.g., product development, logistics, sales, marketing, and distribution). **Six Sigma** can be defined as a business process improvement approach that seeks to find and eliminate causes of defects and errors, reduce manufacturing cycle times and costs, improve productivity, better meet customer expectations, and achieve higher asset utilization and return on investment in both manufacturing and service operations.[3]

The following are actual examples of improvements realized by adopting a Six Sigma philosophy:[4]

- Reduction of scrap in a ball-bearing manufacturing plant and capacity assembly plant.
- Identification and reduction of unnecessary spare parts inventory for a paper cup plant.
- Reduction of defects and product variation in a textile finishing plant.
- Reduction of lead times for product development and scale-up in a pharmaceutical company.
- Reduction of wait time for loan approval notification (from the bank).

Six Sigma is based on a simple problem-solving methodology, **DMAIC**—**D**efine, **M**easure, **A**nalyze, **I**mprove, and **C**ontrol. Typically, the application of Six Sigma uses cross-functional teams, more or less on a consulting project basis. In the design stage of the project, the Six Sigma team *defines* the problem and specifies the deliverables of the project. In the *measure* stage, the team collects relevant process performance data. In the *analyze* stage, the team tries to uncover root causes of an underlying quality problem. This is followed by the *improve* stage, in which proposed solutions to the underlying problem(s) are generated and then implemented. Finally, in the *control* stage of the project, appropriate controls are put in place to ensure that the identified problem does not recur. Motorola Inc. pioneered the concept of Six Sigma as a structured approach for assessing and improving both product and service quality. Today, this approach has gained notoriety and credibility because of its adoption by firms such as Honeywell and General Electric.

As noted previously, the term *Six Sigma* actually comes from statistics: In a normal distribution, the area outside of +/− six standard deviations from the mean is very, very small. From a control standpoint, we can express this area in terms of relative number of defects. The move from, say, a 3-sigma to a 6-sigma quality level (where "sigma" refers to process standard deviations, and therefore the area under a normal curve) is dramatic. For example, a change from 3 to 4 sigma represents a 10-fold improvement in quality; a change from 4 to 5 sigma, a 30-fold improvement; and a change from 5 to 6 sigma, a 70-fold improvement. For this reason, Six Sigma is not likely the goal for all processes and operations. The appropriate

Six Sigma
An overall strategy to accelerate improvements and achieve unprecedented performance levels by focusing on characteristics that are critical to customers and identifying and eliminating causes of errors or defects in processes.

[2] Six Sigma is a federally registered trademark and service mark of Motorola Inc., now Motorola Solutions Inc.
[3] J. R. Evans and W. M. Lindsay, *An Introduction to Six Sigma and Process Improvement* (Mason, OH: South-Western, 2005), p. 3.
[4] F. Rudisill and D. Clary, "The Management Accountant's Role in Six Sigma," *Strategic Finance,* November 2004, pp. 35–39.

quality expectation is a function of the strategic importance of the process and the anticipated costs of taking the process to an increasingly higher level of quality.

Implementation Tips: Six Sigma[5]

Following are steps management can take to ensure the success of Six Sigma projects:

- First and foremost, *provide necessary leadership and resources.* As with many other strategic initiatives, the CEO and top management team must exhibit strong support for the Six Sigma program. Such support can come in the form of employee training and making sure that there is appropriate buy-in for the concept on the part of key managers in the organization.

- *Implement a reward system.* Bonus and incentive schemes for the organization might have to be amended to accommodate rewards associated with reaching Six Sigma goals.

- *Provide ongoing training.* Because Six Sigma is a *process* (think of the DMAIC approach as a repeated cycle), employee training should be ongoing, reinforcing the strategic importance of the process and the need for continuous improvement.

- *Judiciously select early projects.* As noted above, Six Sigma principles can be applied to processes throughout the entire value chain of the organization. It is recommended, however, that top management start with easy, nonpolitical, and noncontroversial projects that support the strategic goals of the organization. Given success with these projects, Six Sigma can then be rolled out to more complicated and difficult projects.

- *Break up difficult projects.* Top management should try to parse complicated projects into smaller, short-term segments, each with its own milestone. This allows individuals to experience success along the way and to be recognized for their efforts to help the organization succeed.

- *Avoid employee layoffs.* From a motivational standpoint, it is crucial that improvements based on Six Sigma should not jeopardize the jobs of those who helped accomplish the goal. Judicious job reassignment is one strategy for dealing with this situation; layoffs should be viewed as a last resort.

Setting Quality Expectations: Goalpost vs. Absolute Conformance Standards

tolerance
An acceptable range of a quality characteristic, such as thickness (measured, e.g., in centimeters).

An alternative approach to defining quality expectations, or product **tolerances,** is to choose between goalpost and absolute conformance standards. One advantage of the latter is that it is consistent with the use of Taguchi quality loss functions for control purposes, a subject dealt with later in this section of the chapter.

Goalpost Conformance

goalpost conformance
Refers to a quality specification expressed as a specified range around a targeted performance level.

Goalpost conformance refers to a quality specification expressed as a specified range around the targeted performance level. The target is the ideal or desirable outcome of the operation. The range around the target is referred to as the *quality tolerance.*

For example, the target for a production process to manufacture 0.5-inch sheet metal is 0.5-inch thickness for all sheet metal manufactured. Recognizing that meeting the target every time in manufacturing is difficult (and costly), a firm often specifies a tolerance range. A firm that specifies a tolerance of ± 0.05 inch meets the stated quality standard when the thickness of its products is between 0.55 inch and 0.45 inch.

absolute quality conformance (robust quality approach)
Conformance that aims for all products or services to meet the quality target value *exactly,* with no variation.

This approach assumes that the customer would accept any value within the tolerance range. As such, the approach assumes that quality-related costs do not depend on the actual value of the quality characteristic, as long as this value falls within a specified range. Exhibit 17.4 depicts the goalpost conformance specifications for the sheet metal example.

Absolute Quality Conformance

robust quality approach
See *absolute quality conformance.*

Absolute quality conformance, or the **robust quality approach,** aims for all products or services to meet the quality target value *exactly,* with no variation. Continuing with the

---

[5] This discussion is adapted from P. C. Brewer and J. E. Eighme, "Using Six Sigma to Improve the Finance Function: Here Are Some Tips for Success," *Strategic Finance,* May 2005, pp. 27–33.

EXHIBIT 17.4
Goalpost Conformance

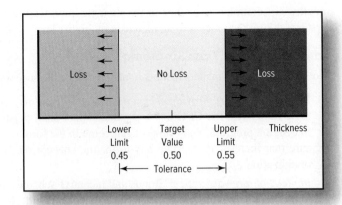

EXHIBIT 17.5
**Absolute Conformance
(Robust Quality Approach):
Quality Cost (Loss) as a
Function of Deviations from
the Targeted Quality Value**

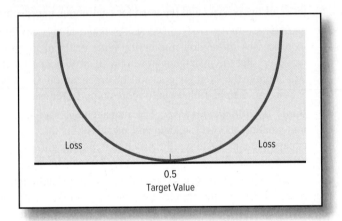

previous example, an absolute conformance standard requires all sheet metal to have a thickness of 0.5 inch, not 0.5 inch $\pm$ 0.05 inch or even 0.5 inch $\pm$ 0.0005 inch. Exhibit 17.5 depicts the robust quality approach. This approach assumes that the smaller the departure from the target value, the better the quality.

Variations from the target value are assumed to have negative economic consequences. As indicated in Exhibit 17.5, the "cost" (or loss) of deviating from the target value is assumed to be nonlinear. Thus, robustness in quality comes with meeting the exact target consistently. Any deviation from the target is viewed as a quality failure and weakens the overall quality of the product or service. You will notice that the slope of the function depicted in Exhibit 17.5 increases as the observed quality characteristic, *x,* deviates from the targeted value. Put another way, the amount of the quality cost/loss is increasing at an increasing rate as we depart from the targeted value of the quality characteristic.

Goalpost or Absolute Conformance?

Goalpost conformance assumes that a firm incurs no quality or failure cost or loss if all quality measures fall within the specified limits. That is, the firm suffers quality costs or losses only when the measure is outside these limits. No such quality tolerance exists in absolute conformance, which views quality costs or losses as a continuously increasing function starting from the target value. Quality costs, hidden or out-of-pocket, occur whenever the quality measure deviates from its target value.

Which of these two approaches, goalpost or absolute conformance, is better? Perhaps we can find an answer in the experience Sony had in two of its plants that manufacture color televisions.[6]

The two Sony plants manufacture the same television sets and follow the same specification for color density. The two plants, however, have adopted different types of quality conformance. The San Diego plant uses goalpost conformance, and the Tokyo plant adopts

[6] J. R. Evans and W. M. Lindsay, *The Management and Control of Quality,* 6th ed. (Mason, OH: South-Western, 2005).

EXHIBIT 17.6
Color Density of Sony TV Sets Manufactured in the San Diego Plant and a Japanese Plant

Source: J. R. Evans and W. M. Lindsay, *The Management and Control of Quality*, 6th ed. (Mason, OH: South-Western, 2005), p. 113.

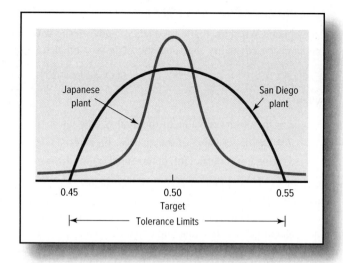

absolute conformance. On examining the operating data over the same period, Sony found that all the units produced at the San Diego plant fell within the specifications (zero defects), but some of those manufactured at the Japanese plant did not. The quality of the Japanese units, however, was more uniform around the target value, while the quality of the San Diego units was uniformly distributed between the lower and upper limits of the specification, the goalpost, as depicted in Exhibit 17.6.

The average quality cost (loss) per unit of the San Diego plant, however, was $0.89 higher than that of the Japanese plant. One reason for the higher quality cost for units produced at the San Diego plant was the need for more frequent field service. Customers are more likely to complain when the density is farther away from the target value. Although the plant in Tokyo had a higher rejection rate, it experienced lower warranty and repair costs for its products. For firms desiring to attain long-term profitability and customer satisfaction, absolute conformance may be the better approach.

Taguchi Quality Loss Function (QLF)

Genichi Taguchi and Yuin Wu proposed the absolute quality conformance approach as an *offline* quality control.[7] Taguchi and Wu hypothesize that any variation from the exact specifications entails a cost or loss to the firm. This cost or loss can be depicted by a quadratic function, similar to the one shown in Exhibit 17.5.

Taguchi quality loss function (QLF)

Depicts, in the form of a quadratic function, the relationship between quality costs and level of deviation from the target quality level or specification.

The **Taguchi quality loss function (QLF)** depicts the cost function associated with deviations from the target quality level or specification. The loss grows larger as the variation increases (a quadratic function); that is, the total loss increases as the magnitude of a quality characteristic of the product or service moves farther away from the target value. In a quadratic function, the loss quadruples when the deviation from the target value doubles. For instance, if the loss is $4 when the deviation is 0.1 from the target value, the loss will be $16 when the deviation doubles, or is 0.2 from the target value.

In Chapter 11, we noted that relevant costs for decision making include both out-of-pocket costs and opportunity costs. This same model can be applied to the present context. Here, the total cost of deviations from the quality target includes *direct (out-of-pocket) costs* in manufacturing as well as *hidden quality costs* (i.e., opportunity costs). Direct costs are costs such as rework, warranty repair or replacement, additional production costs, and loss on disposal. The hidden quality losses include customer dissatisfaction, loss of future business, loss of market share, and the imputed cost associated with holding additional inventory. Management accountants can add value to the organization by helping to estimate these various costs.

---

[7] Genichi Taguchi and Yuin Wu, *Introduction to Off-Line Quality Control* (Central Japan Quality Control Association, 1985). See also Evans and Lindsay, *The Management and Control of Quality*, pp. 594–597; T. L. Albright and H. P. Roth, "The Measurement of Quality Costs: An Alternative Paradigm," *Accounting Horizons*, June 1992, pp. 15–27.

Quality Loss Function (QLF)

Taguchi and Wu show that for a quality characteristic with the target value T, the loss from having an observed quality characteristic x can be estimated by the following quadratic function:

$$L(x) = k(x - T)^2$$

where

$x =$ the observed value of the quality characteristic

$T =$ the target value of the quality characteristic (e.g., 0.50 inch)

$k =$ the cost coefficient, determined by the firm's costs of failure

Note that k is a constant estimated for the quality characteristic based on the total production and hidden (i.e., opportunity) costs to the firm due to deviation of the quality characteristic from the target value. You might recall that a graphical representation of any quadratic equation (including the Taguchi quality loss function depicted above) is called a *parabola*, an example of which is provided in Exhibit 17.5. Finally, we note that the cost coefficient, k, determines the steepness or flatness of the parabola: the greater the value of k, the steeper the slope of the parabola.

The value of k in a particular Taguchi QLF can be estimated as follows:

$$k = \text{Total quality cost} \div (\text{Tolerance allowed})^2$$

where tolerance allowed = product specification (i.e., allowable deviation from the targeted value).

For example, assume that a company has determined that no customer will accept sheet metal deviating more than 0.05 inch from the target value in thickness; we therefore define *tolerance allowed* as 0.05 inch. Further, assume that the target thickness (T) is 0.5 inch and that the estimated cost to the firm is $5,000 for each rejection by a customer (i.e., for each unit where the thickness exceeds 0.55 inch or is less than 0.45 inch). The $5,000 estimated cost to the firm includes repair or replacement, processing, service costs, and other costs due to customer dissatisfaction. Then, based on the above formula we have:

$$k = \$5,000 \div 0.05^2$$
$$k = \$5,000 \div 0.0025 = \$2,000,000$$

Once we have an estimate for the cost coefficient, k, we can then use the QLF to estimate quality costs for different values of x. For example, if the actual thickness of a unit is 0.47 (that is, $x = 0.47$), then the estimated quality cost (or loss) for this unit, $L(0.47)$, is

$$L(0.47) = \$2,000,000 \times (0.47 - 0.50)^2$$
$$= \$2,000,000 \times 0.009 = \$1,800$$

If, however, the thickness is 0.46, then the estimated total loss from the deviation increases to $3,200, as follows:

$$L(0.46) = \$2,000,000 \times (0.46 - 0.50)^2$$
$$= \$2,000,000 \times 0.0016 = \$3,200$$

Note from an inspection of Exhibit 17.5 and the above two calculations that (1) the only time the quality cost function is zero is when the observed quality characteristic, x, is equal to the targeted value, T, and (2) there is a cost of deviating from the targeted value, and the cost of this deviation increases quadratically as the quality characteristic, x, moves farther away from the target value, T.

Total Loss and Average Loss

Each of the losses calculated above, $L(x)$, represents the estimated loss from having one unit of output with the observed quality characteristic, x. The total loss for all the units manufactured during a period is the sum of the losses from all units whose observed value of the quality characteristic deviated from the target value.

Alternatively, the total loss due to variations in the quality characteristic can be determined by multiplying the average loss per unit by the total number of units manufactured. The average loss per unit is the expected loss due to variations in the quality characteristic. Exhibit 17.7

EXHIBIT 17.7
Total Estimated Quality Losses Using a Taguchi Quality Loss Function (QLF)

(1)	**(2)**	**(3)**	**(4) = (2) × (3)**	**(5)**	**(6) = (2) × (5)**
x	*L(x)*	Plant A		Plant B	
Measured Thickness	Quality Cost (or Loss)	Probability	Weighted Loss	Probability	Weighted Loss
0.43	$9,800	0.00	$ 0	0.02	$196
0.46	3,200	0.20	640	0.03	96
0.48	800	0.20	160	0.15	120
0.50	0	0.20	0	0.60	0
0.52	800	0.20	160	0.15	120
0.54	3,200	0.20	640	0.03	96
0.57	9,800	0.00	0	0.02	196
Expected loss		1.00	$1,600	1.00	$824

shows the calculations of the expected total losses in two plants identified as A and B. These two plants have different probability distributions of deviations from the target value, as noted in columns (3) and (5).

The output from plant A spreads evenly over the range from 0.46 to 0.54, with no unit falling outside the tolerance limits. In contrast, the output from plant B concentrates near the specified target value (0.50), but not all units lie within the tolerance limits.

The expected, or average, loss per unit can be determined using the variance and the square of the mean deviation from the target value, as follows:[8]

$$E(L(x)) = k(\sigma^2 + D^2)$$

where

$E(L(x))$ = expected (average) loss per unit, based on quality characteristic, x

σ^2 = variance of the quality characteristic around the mean value of the quality characteristic[9]

D = the deviation of the mean value of the quality characteristic from the target value, $T = \bar{x} - T$

Note that the variance is 0.0008 for plant A[10] and 0.000412 for plant B, and that the value of D is 0 for both plants.[11] Thus,

$$(\text{Plant A: } E(L(x)) = \$2,000,000 \times (0.000800 + 0) = \$1,600$$
$$(\text{Plant B: } E(L(x)) = \$2,000,000 \times (0.000412 + 0) = \$824$$

[8] Albright and Roth, "The Measurement of Quality Costs," p. 23.
[9] Variance, σ^2, is computed as follows:

$$\sigma^2 = \Sigma(x - \bar{x})^2 f(x)$$

where,

x = quality characteristic, e.g., measured thickness, as in Exhibit 17.7

$\bar{x}$ = mean value of quality characteristic, $\bar{x} = \Sigma x f(x)$

$f(x)$ = probability of observing quality characteristic, x; each value of $f(x)$ lies between 0 and 1, and all values of $f(x)$ sum to 1

[10] For plant A,

$$\bar{x} = \text{column(1)} \times \text{column(3)} = \Sigma x f(x) = (0.46 \times 0.20) + (0.48 \times 0.20) + (0.50 \times 0.20) + (0.52 \times 0.20)$$
$$+ (0.54 \times 0.20) = 0.50$$

and, $\sigma^2 = [(0.46 - 0.50)^2 \times 0.20] + [(0.48 - 0.50)^2 \times 0.20] + [(0.50 - 0.50)^2 \times 0.20] + [(0.52 - 0.50)^2 \times 0.20]$
$$+ [(0.54 - 0.50)^2 \times 0.20]$$
$$= 0.0008$$

[11] The mean value of the quality characteristic is 0.50 for plant A, as calculated in footnote 10. The target value of the quality characteristic is also 0.50. Therefore, for plant A, $D = 0.50 - 0.50 = 0$. Verify that the value of D is also zero for plant B by carrying out the same procedure. Note that many times in actual practice, D is a positive number rather than zero (as is the case here). In such cases, the QLF is extremely helpful in assessing the cost of processes that may be "in control" yet not precisely centered on the target engineering specifications. Put another way, the QLF helps managers understand the relative costs of having an improperly centered process or one with too wide a variability. The reader is encouraged to evaluate the above QLFs for different assumed values of D.

Notice the similarity in the quality characteristic between plant A and that observed in the Sony plant at San Diego (as depicted in Exhibit 17.6)—all units are within and spread evenly over the specified tolerance limits. The quality characteristic of plant B is similar to that observed in the Sony plant in Japan—not all units lie within the tolerance limits, but most units cluster around the target value. Some units, however, fall outside the tolerance limits. Plant B, like the Sony plant in Japan, incurs a smaller average cost per unit. Even though all units of plant A fall within the tolerance limits while some units of plant B are outside the limits, plant B has a lower expected loss than that of plant A.

Finally, while the mathematics presented above are without dispute, there are at least two caveats that should be kept in mind as we consider the use of the QLF in practice. First, the QLF function may be sensitive to the value of the estimated cost coefficient, k. Some would contend that managers tend to underestimate the value of k because they fail to include a realistic estimate of the cost of customer dissatisfaction and other external failure costs. Second, and related to point number one above, some would maintain that there should be two quality loss functions—one for situations where output is within specifications and a separate one for situations where the quality characteristic, x, falls outside specifications. In other words, the conventional (i.e., single equation) approach may seriously underestimate the costs associated with output beyond acceptable limits. These observations lead some managers—those who embrace TQM, for example—to conclude that the goal should be zero defects (i.e., no output outside of specifications).

Using the Taguchi Quality Loss Function (QLF) for Tolerance Determination

The Taguchi QLF can also be used to set tolerances for an operation. Assume a situation in which a firm can repair any rejected units that exceed the specified tolerance level. Even though such repairs cost money, repairs that correct defects save downstream quality costs such as field repairs, warranty costs, and loss of customer satisfaction. By contrasting the estimated repair cost with the quality cost of not detecting and repairing defects, the firm can determine an acceptable tolerance level for its outputs. Rewriting the equation for estimating the value of k:

$$\text{Total quality cost} = k \times (\text{Tolerance})^2$$

Let's return to our sheet metal example. Assume that the cost to the firm in question is estimated as $300 if the firm repairs the product before shipping. Assume, too, that the firm repairs all units that exceed the tolerance level for thickness. Then, this firm can determine the tolerance as follows:

$$\$300 = \$2,000,000 \times (\text{Tolerance})^2$$

Solving the equation,

$$\text{Tolerance} = 0.0122 \text{ (rounded)}$$

Alternatively, the tolerance can be determined as shown below.

$$\text{Tolerance} = T_0 \sqrt{C_1 \div C_2}$$

where

T_0 = current (or customer) tolerance

C_2 = manufacturer's quality cost when the product fails to meet customer's specification

C_1 = manufacturer's cost to rework or scrap the unit before shipping

In the example above, the firm expects the external failure cost, C_2, to be $5,000; the cost to the firm is estimated to be $300 if the firm repairs, reworks, or scraps the defective unit before shipping (C_1); and the customer's tolerance is assumed to be 0.05. Given these assumptions, the firm would then set the tolerance at 0.0122, as follows:

$$\text{Tolerance} = 0.05 \sqrt{\$300 \div \$5,000}$$
$$= 0.05 \times 0.24495$$
$$= 0.0122 \text{ (rounded)}$$

Financial Measures and Cost of Quality

There are two major ways management accountants can provide relevant financial information as part of a comprehensive framework for managing and controlling quality: relevant cost (and revenue) data for decision-making purposes and cost of quality (COQ) performance reports.

Relevant Cost Analysis for Decision Making

Quality-related spending (investment) affects the target level of quality and ultimately work processes and outputs—as depicted in Exhibit 17.3. In terms of spending on quality-related initiatives, we can employ the same decision framework that we presented in Chapter 11. That is, financial information relevant to quality-related decisions consists of future costs (and revenues) that differ between decision alternatives. In terms of relevant costs, we can also use the term *avoidable costs* because, by definition, these are future costs that can be avoided by choosing one decision alternative over another. As discussed in Chapter 12, long-term investments in quality are evaluated using relevant cost (and revenue) information and discounted cash flow (DCF) decision models, such as net present value (NPV).

Activity and process decisions are prime examples of quality-related investments. For example, some manufacturers are moving from process layouts (batch processing) to cellular manufacturing. Other firms are embracing a just-in-time (JIT) production philosophy. Obviously, there can be significant outlay costs associated with a plant layout change or a change in manufacturing philosophy.

At the same time, improvements in quality provide an opportunity for increasing revenues and for significant cost savings. The management accountant can provide decision makers with accurate estimates of costs and benefits associated with quality-related spending, such as a move to JIT. Benefits could include the contribution margin associated with increased sales (because of decreased manufacturing cycle times associated with JIT production or the use of cellular manufacturing). Benefits could also include reduced spending on rework/scrap costs, lower financing costs associated with inventory reductions, reduced inventory obsolescence costs, reduced spending on inventory-recording costs, and reduced inventory-handling and storage-activity costs. Note that, as in Chapter 11, relevant costs include both opportunity costs and out-of-pocket costs.

Cost of Quality (COQ) Reporting

Quality costs for many companies are essentially buried in the company's financial statements. For example, in the case of a manufacturer, some costs appear in manufacturing (factory) overhead accounts (e.g., product testing, materials inspection, normal spoilage costs), while other quality costs are included as part of general and administrative expenses. Still others are reflected in decreased sales revenues due to abandonment by existing customers and failure to attract new customers. When warranted, traditional cost accounting systems—both job and process—separately report the cost of abnormal spoilage.

However, as indicated in Exhibit 17.3, quality costs are associated with activities across the value chain—from the design of work processes, to production of outputs (goods and services), to delivery of outputs to customers. Thus, quality costs also include costs associated with support functions such as product design, purchasing, public relations, and customer services.

The traditional general ledger is an effective instrument for what it is designed to do: post and summarize transactions into specific account balances. But the expense data in this format (e.g., salaries, supplies, depreciation) are structurally deficient for decision support, including measuring the total **cost of quality (COQ)** for the organization. They disclose what was spent but not why, for what, or for whom. Expense data must be transformed into the costs of the activities within processes that traverse the departmental cost centers reported in a general ledger system—and ultimately transformed into the cost of products, services, and customers.

Thus, an expansive view would define COQ as the cost of activities associated with the prevention, identification, repair, and rectification of poor quality, as well as opportunity costs from lost production and lost sales as a result of poor quality. For performance evaluation purposes, we might subdivide total COQ into the following four categories: prevention costs, appraisal costs, internal failure costs, and external failure costs. These terms are defined below. Exhibit 17.8 provides examples of the components of COQ. Consistent with the discussion in Chapter 11, we include both out-of-pocket as well as opportunity costs in the analysis of COQ.

cost of quality (COQ)
A comprehensive reporting framework for classification of quality-related costs.

EXHIBIT 17.8
Examples of Quality Costs, by Category

Prevention Costs	Appraisal Costs
Training:	Raw materials inspection**
Instructor fees	Work-in-process inspection
Testing equipment	Finished goods inspection
Tuition for external training	Packaging inspection
Wages and salaries for time spent on training and education	Test equipment:
Planning and execution of a quality program:	Depreciation
Salaries	Salaries and wages paid to equipment operators
Cost of meetings/quality circles	Maintenance
Supplier evaluations	Software
Investments:	**External Failure Costs**
Product redesign (for continuous product improvement)	Sales returns and allowances (i.e., discounts allowed because of defects)
Process improvement	Warranty cost/field service
Equipment maintenance	Customer support
Internal Failure Costs	Contribution margin of canceled sales orders*
Scrap disposal (net cost)	Contribution margin of lost sales orders*
Rework (materials, labor, overhead)	Product recalls
Loss due to downgrades*	Customer complaint resolution
Reinspection costs	Product liability lawsuits/claims
Spoilage	
Machine repair costs	
Loss due to work interruptions*	

*Opportunity cost.
**Some organizations may classify this as a prevention cost.

Prevention Costs

prevention costs
Costs incurred to keep quality defects from occurring.

Prevention costs are incurred to keep quality defects from occurring. Prevention costs include the following:

- **Quality training costs.** Costs incurred to conduct internal training programs and for employees to participate in external programs to ensure proper manufacturing, delivering, and servicing of products and services and to improve quality. These costs include salaries and wages for time spent in training, instruction costs, clerical staff expenses and miscellaneous supplies, and costs expended to prepare handbooks and instructional manuals.
- **Equipment maintenance costs.** Costs to install, calibrate, maintain, repair, and inspect production equipment.
- **Supplier assurance costs.** Costs incurred to ensure that materials, components, and services received meet the firm's quality standards. These include costs of selection, evaluation, and training of suppliers to conform with the requirements of total quality management (TQM).
- **Information system costs.** Costs expended for developing data requirements and measuring, auditing, and reporting quality data.
- **Product redesign and process improvement.** Costs incurred to evaluate and improve product designs and operating processes to simplify manufacturing processes or to reduce or eliminate quality problems.
- **Quality circles.** Costs incurred to establish and operate quality circles to identify quality problems and to offer solutions to improve the quality of products and services.

quality circle
A small group of employees from the same work area that meets regularly to identify and solve work-related problems and to implement and monitor solutions to these problems.

Appraisal Costs

appraisal (detection) costs
Costs associated with detecting output that doesn't conform to quality standards.

Appraisal (detection) costs are costs devoted to determining conformity of outputs to specifications. These costs are incurred during the production process (including inspection of incoming materials and parts) and prior to delivery to customers. Through the measurement, analysis, and monitoring of manufacturing processes and the inspection of products and services prior to delivery, firms identify defective items and ensure that all units meet or exceed customer requirements. Appraisal costs include (among other items) the following costs:

- **Test and inspection costs.** Costs incurred to test and inspect incoming materials, work in process, and finished goods, and the cost incurred to inspect machinery; also, costs associated with field testing of products at the site of the customer.
- **Test equipment and instruments.** Expenditures incurred to acquire, operate, or maintain facilities, software, machinery, and instruments for testing or appraising the quality of products, services, or processes.

Note that some companies may choose to classify inspection costs associated with incoming materials and parts as prevention (not appraisal) costs. The logic is that if materials and parts are inspected upon receipt, then inferior inputs to the manufacturing process would never (or should never) occur. As such, the costs associated with this activity are viewed as prevention costs. Note, too, that if nonconforming materials and parts are returned to the vendor (or credit is given by the vendor), then inspection costs are truly prevention costs.

On the other hand, if the purchaser has to incur the cost of inferior materials and parts, then one could argue that the inspection cost is a product cost and therefore properly classified as an appraisal cost. Some companies choose to define appraisal costs more loosely to include ANY inspection—pre-production, post-production, or during the actual manufacturing process itself. Doing so simplifies the classification challenges.

The above discussion illustrates two important points: (1) accounting practice is not always uniform—special conditions or situations may result in slightly different applications of what you are learning—and (2) it is precisely because of the example discussed above (are inspection costs associated with incoming materials and parts appraisal costs or prevention costs?) that many COQ advocates do not dwell so much on the four categories of COQ as they do on the two broader categories, viz., prevention plus appraisal costs versus failure costs (see the discussion of conformance costs vs. noncomformance costs below). Put another way, it is probably more important that a firm classifies a given quality-related cost consistently over time than whether, for example, that cost is classified by the organization as a prevention cost or as an appraisal cost.

Internal Failure Costs

Internal failure costs are quality-related costs associated with defective processes or defective products detected before delivery to customers. These costs include (but are not limited to) the following examples:

- **Costs of corrective action.** Costs of time spent to find the cause of failure and to correct the problem.
- **Rework and (net) scrap costs.** Materials, labor, and overhead costs for items that are scrapped or that need to be reworked.
- **Process costs.** Costs expended to redesign the product or processes; unplanned machine downtime for adjustment; and lost production (an opportunity cost) due to process interruption for repair or rework.
- **Expediting costs.** Costs incurred to expedite manufacturing operations due to time spent for repair or rework.
- **Reinspection and retest costs.** Salaries, wages, and expenses incurred during reinspection or retesting of reworked or repaired items.
- **Lost contribution due to increased demand on constrained resources—an opportunity cost.** Constrained resources spent on defective units increase manufacturing cycle time and reduce total output. Contribution margin lost from units not produced because of the unavailability of the constrained resources reduces the operating income of the firm.

External Failure Costs

External failure costs are costs associated with defective/poor-quality outputs detected after being delivered to the customer. External failure costs include (among other items) the following costs:

- **Repair or replacement costs.** Repair or replacement of returned products.
- **Costs to handle customer complaints and returns.** Salaries and administrative overhead of the customer service department; allowances or discounts granted for poor quality; and freight charges for returned products.
- **Product recall and product liability costs.** Administrative costs to handle product recalls, repairs, or replacements; legal costs; settlements resulting from legal actions.
- **Lost sales and customer ill-will due to defective outputs.** Lost contribution margin on canceled orders, lost sales, and decreased market share. These are opportunity costs.
- **Costs to restore reputation.** Costs of marketing activities to minimize damages from a tarnished reputation and to restore the firm's image and reputation.

Conformance Costs and Nonconformance Costs

Conceptually, the total cost of quality (COQ) can be categorized into conformance costs and nonconformance costs. Prevention and appraisal costs are **costs of conformance** because they are incurred to ensure that products or services meet customer expectations. Internal failure costs and external failure costs are **costs of nonconformance.** They are costs incurred because of poor-quality products or services and include opportunity costs. The total COQ is the sum of conformance and nonconformance costs.

Prevention costs are usually the least expensive and the easiest among the four costs of quality for management to control. Internal and external failure costs are among the most expensive costs of quality, especially external failure costs. In a typical scenario, the cost of prevention may be $0.10 per unit, the cost of testing and replacing poor quality parts or components during production may be $5, the cost of reworking or reassembling may be $50, and the cost of field repair and other external costs may be $5,000 or higher.

Better prevention of poor quality reduces all other costs of quality. With fewer problems in quality, less appraisal is needed because products are made right the first time. Fewer defective units also reduce internal and external failure costs as repairs, rework, and recalls decrease. By spending more on prevention and appraisal, companies spend less on internal or external failure costs. The savings alone can be substantial. Meanwhile, the firm enjoys higher perceived values of its products, increased sales and market share, and improved earnings and return on investment, as depicted earlier in Exhibit 17.1.

COQ Reports

The purpose of reporting quality costs is to make management aware of the magnitude of these costs, to motivate continuous improvement in COQ, and to provide a baseline against which the impact of quality-improvement investments can be measured.

Report Format

A COQ report is useful only if its recipients understand, accept, and can use the content of the report to improve operations. Each organization should select and design a reporting system that (1) can be integrated into its information system and (2) promotes the quality initiatives specified by top management. To facilitate assessment of the magnitude of quality costs and their impact, the organization should express its COQ component costs relative to some baseline amount, such as net sales (or total operating costs) for the period.

A cost of quality matrix, as illustrated in Exhibit 17.9, is a convenient and useful tool in reporting total quality costs for an organization. With columns identifying functions or departments across the value chain and rows delineating COQ categories, a cost of quality matrix enables each department, function, process, or product line to identify and recognize the effects of its actions on the total cost of quality and to pinpoint areas of improvement.

Illustration of a COQ Report

Exhibit 17.10 illustrates a COQ report.[12] Bally Company is a small, midwestern manufacturing company with annual sales of around $9 million. The company operates in a highly competitive environment and has been experiencing increasing pressures from new and existing competitors to raise quality and lower cost. The report shows that, in year 0, the external

EXHIBIT 17.9   Cost of Quality (COQ) Matrix

	Design Engineering	Purchasing	Production	Finance	Accounting	Other	Totals	Percent of Sales
Prevention costs:								
Quality planning								
Training								
Other								
Appraisal costs:								
Test and inspect								
Instruments								
Other								
Internal failure costs:								
Scrap								
Rework								
Other								
External failure costs:								
Returns								
Recalls								
Other								
Totals								

Source: J. R. Evans and W. M. Lindsay, *Managing for Quality and Performance Excellence,* 8th ed. (Mason, OH: South-Western, 2011), p. 391.

[12] Adapted from "Managing Quality Improvements," *Statement of Management Accounting No. 4-R* (Montvale, NJ: Institute of Management Accountants, 1993).

EXHIBIT 17.10   Cost of Quality (COQ) Report for Bally Company

	Year 2	Percent of Sales	Year 0	Percent of Sales	Percent Change in Cost
Prevention Costs					
Training	$ 90,000		$ 20,000		350%
Quality planning	86,000		20,000		330
Other quality improvement	60,000		40,000		50
Supplier evaluation	40,000		30,000		33
Total	$ 276,000	3.07%	$ 110,000	1.38%	151
Appraisal Costs					
Testing	$ 120,000		$ 100,000		20
Quality performance measurement	100,000		80,000		25
Supplier monitoring	60,000		10,000		500
Customer surveys	30,000		10,000		200
Total	$ 310,000	3.44%	$ 200,000	2.50%	55
Internal Failure Costs					
Rework and reject	$ 55,000		$ 150,000		(63)
Reinspection and testing	35,000		30,000		16
Equipment failure	30,000		50,000		(40)
Downtime	20,000		50,000		(60)
Total	$ 140,000	1.56%	$ 280,000	3.50%	(50)
External Failure Costs					
Product liability insurance	$ 70,000		$ 250,000		(72)
Warranty repairs	100,000		120,000		(17)
Customer losses (estimated)	600,000		1,400,000		(57)
Total	$ 770,000	8.55%	$1,770,000	22.12%	(56)
Total Quality Costs	$1,496,000	**16.62%**	$2,360,000	**29.50%**	(37)
Total sales	$9,000,000	100.00%	$8,000,000	100.00%	

failure costs for items such as warranty claims, customer dissatisfaction, and loss of market share accounted for 75% of the total COQ ($1,770,000 ÷ $2,360,000, or 22.12% ÷ 29.5%).

To be more competitive and to increase market share, Bally began a company-wide three-year TQM process. The firm started with substantial increases in prevention and appraisal expenditures. The investment started to pay off in year 2. Internal failure, external failure, and total quality costs have all decreased. COQ reports over time (i.e., time-series reports) can help document these improvements.

Exhibit 17.10 compares the current year's quality costs to those of a base year. Alternative bases for comparisons can be the budgeted amounts, flexible budget costs, or long-range goals.

To better communicate results, the accountant can transform time series (i.e., multiperiod) data, such as the data presented in Exhibit 17.10, into one or more histograms. Based on before-and-after histograms (or "pie charts") and/or stacked bar charts, managers are more able to see improvement in overall COQ spending—and the mix of COQ spending—that has occurred over time. The visual representation of the histograms also enables managers to better evaluate trade-offs, such as increased spending in prevention and appraisal with the expectation of reductions in total failure costs. This process of feedback and evaluation makes COQ more than just an accounting framework—it becomes a financial investment justification tool.

Cost of Quality (COQ) and Activity-Based Costing

An ABC system is ideally suited to the preparation of COQ reports. An ABC system identifies cost with activities and thus increases the visibility of costs of quality. Costs of activities that are the result of poor quality become clear to the organization. Traditional costing systems, in contrast, focus the cost reporting on organizational functions such as production, sales, and administration. An organization with a good ABC system in place needs only to identify costs and activities relating to COQ and classify these costs according to the COQ categories that the firm chooses to use.

Nonfinancial Quality Indicators

LO 17-6

Discuss the use of nonfinancial performance data to support quality-related initiatives.

As seen from the preceding discussion, relevant financial data are needed to guide investment decision making and to plan and control quality-related costs. However, as indicated in Exhibit 17.3, *nonfinancial* performance data also play an important role in a comprehensive framework for managing and controlling quality. It is useful for discussion purposes to divide nonfinancial performance indicators into internal and external subgroups.

Internal Nonfinancial Quality Metrics

Organizations strive to specify internal dimensions of quality on which they must focus in order to meet customer expectations. The following are examples of internal nonfinancial quality measures:

- Process yield (i.e., good output/total output).
- Productivity (i.e., ratio of acceptable outputs—goods or services—to resource inputs).
- Percentage of first-pass yields (i.e., percentage of initial output meeting quality standards).
- Number of defective parts produced [e.g., parts per million (ppm)].
- Machine downtime.
- Trend in dollar amount of inventory held.
- Safety record (e.g., number of accidents per month, number of days since last accident).
- Throughput (i.e., outputs—goods or services—produced and delivered to customers).
- Production (manufacturing) lead time (i.e., difference between when an order is received by manufacturing and when that order is completed).
- Cycle-time efficiency (i.e., ratio of time spent on value-added activities to the sum of time spent on value-added and non-value-added activities).
- New product (or service) development time.

Note that many of the preceding metrics relate to process efficiency. Improving quality should improve many, if not most, of these measures. In practice, responsibility for implementing process changes designed to improve these measures is assigned to cross-functional teams. Also, some type of benchmark, either internal or external, is generally used as the standard against which actual performance is compared.

Finally, note that the preceding metrics are not necessarily confined to the manufacturing sector; some apply to the service sector as well. For example, consider a patient's visit to a health care professional. What proportion of time spent by the patient would be considered "value-added"? If a visit to a local dentist, on average, requires patients to spend 10 minutes on administrative tasks (e.g., completing forms), 20 minutes of wait time in the lobby, and 30 minutes of time spent undergoing dental-related work, the cycle time efficiency for this setting would be 0.50 (i.e., 30 minutes ÷ 60 minutes). In this example, average *office-visit cycle time* is 60 minutes; of this amount, only 50% would be considered value-added time by that patient. Catherine Booth Hospital (South Africa) reports significant improvements in two measures of quality—patient cycle time and waiting time—after it recently implemented quality-focused principles, tools, and techniques. Its focus was to use these tools to identify and eliminate non-value-added patient time.

"A satisfied customer is the best business strategy of all."

Michael LeBoeuf, American businessperson

REAL-WORLD FOCUS Airline Quality Ratings and Competitive Benchmarking

What nonfinancial performance data are available to passengers of U.S. domestic airlines? How can these airlines benchmark their operating performance in terms of critical success factors? Since 1991 such data have been provided on an annual basis in what is called the *Airline Quality Rating* (AQR) report (available at https://airlinequalityrating.com/). For each domestic carrier, the AQR contains monthly performance data in 15 areas and four major categories, based on data obtained from the U.S. Department of Transportation's monthly *Air Travel Consumer Report* (www.dot.gov/airconsumer). The *Airline Quality Rating 2019* report reflects monthly AQR scores for calendar-year 2018. The AQR for an airline is based on a weighted average of performance measures in four major areas that are deemed important to customers, as follows:

$$AQR = \frac{(+8.63 \times OT) + (-8.03 \times DB) + (-7.92 \times MB) + (-7.17 \times CC)}{(8.63 + 8.03 + 7.92 + 7.17)}$$

where

OT = on-time arrival

DB = denied boarding

MB = mishandled baggage

CC = customer complaints (12 separate items: fares, refunds, etc.)

The creators of the model state that the AQR provides both consumers and industry watchers with a means of looking at comparative quality for each airline on a timely basis using objective, performance-based data.

AQRs for the top 3 and bottom 3 domestic airlines for 2018 and 2017, as well as composite (industry-average) data (all airlines combined), are as follows:

	2018 AQR		2017 AQR	
Airline	**Score**	**Rank**	**Score**	**Rank**
Delta	−0.36	1	−0.44	2
JetBlue	−0.48	2	−0.58	3
Southwest	−0.62	3	−0.73	5
Spirit	−1.00	7	−1.66	12
American	−1.10	8	−1.03	9
Frontier	−1.53	9	−1.23	11
Industry Average	−0.66		−0.79	

A separate ranking of 9 major U.S. airlines (McCartney, 2020), based on a composite of seven operational performance indicators [on-time arrivals, extreme delays (over 45 minutes), two-hour tarmac delays, canceled flights, bumped passengers, mishandled bags, and passenger complaints], shows Delta Air Lines, Alaska Airlines, and Southwest Airlines holding the top three spots. The bottom 3 airlines in the 2019 rankings are Frontier, United, and American Airlines.

Sources: B. D. Bowen and D. E. Headly, *Airline Quality Rating 2019*, April 2019 (available at https://commons.erau.edu/cgi/viewcontent.cgi?article=1029&context=aqrr); S. McCarthy, "The Best and Worst U.S. Airlines of 2019," *The Wall Street Journal*, January 15, 2020 (available at www.wsj.com/articles/the-best-and-worst-u-s-airlines-of-2019-11579097301).

External (Customer Satisfaction) Quality Metrics

A comprehensive framework for managing and controlling quality will also include a set of external quality measures. These metrics are customer-based, as shown by the following examples:

- Number of defective units shipped to customers as a percentage of total units shipped.
- Number of customer complaints.

customer loyalty
An indication of customer satisfaction, measured (for example) by repeat purchases or customer retention rates or by percentage growth in business with existing customers.

- **Customer loyalty** (measured, e.g., by repeat purchases or customer retention rates or by percentage growth in business with existing customers).
- Percentage of products that experience early or excessive failure.
- Market share.
- Delivery delays (e.g., difference between scheduled delivery date and date requested by the customer).
- On-time delivery rate (e.g., percentage of shipments made on or before the scheduled delivery date).
- Market research information on customer preferences and satisfaction with specific product features (e.g., see the customer version of the "Loyalty Acid Test" at www.loyaltyrules.com/loyaltyrules/acid_test_customer.html for a sample customer-satisfaction survey).
- Customer-response time (CRT), or the total lapse of time between when a customer places an order and when the customer actually receives the completed goods. This total time can

Rankings of colleges and universities are a function of a number of financial and nonfinancial indicators. There are various sources that a prospective student can consult before making the college-selection decision. One of the recent entries to the field is the *Wall Street Journal (WSJ)/Times Higher Education (THE)* ranking of U.S. colleges (see **www.wsj.com/news/collection/college-rankings-2020-5987b790?mod=article_inline** for the 2020 rankings of more than 1,000 U.S. colleges and universities).

Required

How is the discussion of college/university rankings related to the material covered in the present chapter?

Source: M. Korn and D. Belkin, "The Top-Ranked College Is . . . ," *The Wall Street Journal,* September 4, 2019, p. R1.

(Refer to Comments on Cost Management in Action at the end of the chapter.)

be broken down into three components: receipt time, manufacturing lead time, and delivery time. (See Exhibit 14.14.)

net promoter score (NPS)
A measure of customer satisfaction, defined as the difference between the percentage of customers classified as "promoters" and those classified as "detractors" (those not recommending the business plus those who are neutral).

- **Net promoter score** [i.e., willingness of customers to recommend your business, defined as the difference between the percentage of "promoters" (those strongly recommending the company) and "detractors" (those who would not recommend your company plus those that are neutral)]. The net promoter score (NPS) is recommended as a nonfinancial, customer-related performance metric based on research that indicates that a customer's willingness to recommend a company is correlated positively with the future growth and profitability of the company. Academic research shows that only truly loyal customers are classified as "promoters" of the company's business. "Detractors," on the other hand, are customers who can harm the company's brand value and reputation.[13]

The preceding list is meant to be illustrative, not exhaustive. In practice, the actual metrics used should be based on an organization's strategy. As with internal quality measures, external metrics require some benchmark (standard) against which actual performance can be compared.

Role of Nonfinancial Performance Measures

Internal and external nonfinancial measures of quality are important components of the framework presented in Exhibit 17.3 for a number of reasons:

- They are, for the most part, readily available (for example, compared to activity-based cost information, most nonfinancial quality-performance data are much less costly to obtain).

- Such information is relevant to operations and sales personnel (production employees, salespersons, etc.)—that is, these individuals understand these metrics and therefore can use them as a guide for improving operations and downstream activities such as sales.

- Because many of these measures relate to physical processes, they focus attention on precise problem areas that need attention.

- Such information is more timely than financial measures of quality—in the extreme, these measures of quality can be reported on a real-time basis (i.e., instantaneously as operations occur). Thus, nonfinancial quality indicators provide immediate short-run feedback on whether quality-improvement efforts are, in fact, succeeding in improving quality.

- Nonfinancial performance measures can be useful predictors (i.e., leading indicators) of future financial performance.

---

[13] F. Reichheld, "The One Number You Need to Grow," *Harvard Business Review,* December 2003, pp. 46–54; F. Reichheld, *The Ultimate Question: Driving Good Profits and True Growth* (Boston: Harvard Business Press, 2008). To calculate the net promoter score, the organization analyzes responses to the following question: "How likely is it that you would recommend our company/firm to a friend or colleague?" Respondents use a 10-point scale, from 1 = "extremely unlikely" to 10 = "extremely likely." "Promoters" are defined as individuals responding with either a 9 or a 10. "Detractors" are defined as those answering 1 through 6, inclusive. (Those who provide a response of 7 or 8 are ignored, under the assumption that these responses provide no information regarding customer loyalty.) The number of respondents in each of the two groups is then converted to a percentage (i.e., percentage of "promoters" and percentage of "detractors"). The net promoter score is the difference in these two percentages.

Detecting and Correcting Poor Quality

"Don't find fault, find a remedy."

Henry Ford, American industrialist

LO 17-7

Describe and understand tools that can be used to detect and correct quality problems.

As indicated in Exhibit 17.3, a comprehensive framework for managing and controlling quality relies on the use of a number of techniques for detecting poor quality and then taking appropriate corrective action if need be. These techniques come principally from the field of statistics, and secondarily from the field of operations management and industrial engineering. In general, you can think of these techniques as embracing a single, overall goal: improving underlying business processes. As indicated in Chapter 2, assessing the performance of business processes (operating, innovation, customer management, and social/environmental/regulatory) is one key element of an organization's balanced scorecard (BSC).

Detecting Poor Quality

Once an appropriate set of financial and nonfinancial performance indicators has been specified, management needs to determine how to analyze the data to look for potential indications of poor quality. The overall goal is to determine when an underlying process is not in control and, therefore, is in need of correction. We define a process to be in control when variation in process data points (or observations) is random. A nonrandom observation suggests a systematic change in the process, and therefore may indicate an out-of-control process. One way to isolate random and nonrandom observations, and therefore to identify a potentially out-of-control process, is through the use of control charts.

control chart

A graph that depicts successive observations of an operation (or cost) taken at constant intervals over a specified time.

A **control chart** plots successive observations of a quality characteristic (or cost), taken at constant intervals, to help determine whether a process is in control.

A typical control chart has a horizontal axis representing units, time intervals, batch numbers, or production runs, and a vertical axis denoting a financial or nonfinancial performance measure. The vertical measure has a specified range of variations, which are referred to as *upper* and *lower limits,* respectively. As such, control charts are appropriate for use with goalpost performance standards. Note, however, that the goalpost standards described earlier were external to the manufacturing process; that is, they were customer-imposed specifications. In the present discussion, we use the term *control limits* in a statistical sense. That is, we assume that the control limits are based on the mean and standard deviation of the observed quality characteristic (or cost) under a given manufacturing process. Exhibit 17.11 contains example control charts for manufacturing 1/8-inch drill bits in three workstations.

EXHIBIT 17.11
Control Charts for 1/8-Inch Drill Bit

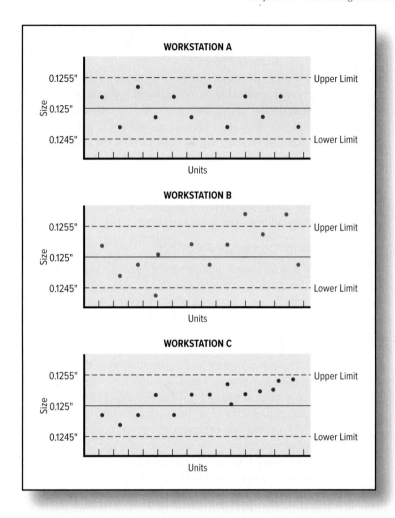

Assume that a firm has determined that all drill bits must be within 0.0005 inch of the specified diameter. All units from workstation A are within the specified range ($\pm$ 0.0005 inch), and the variation appears to be random; therefore, no further investigation is necessary. Three units from workstation B are outside the specified range—an indication that the process in workstation B may be out of control. Management may want to investigate the cause of the aberration to prevent further quality failures. Although all units manufactured by workstation C are within the acceptable range, the control chart reveals that the size observations are drifting upward. (Used in this manner, the control chart is often referred to as a **run chart.** A run chart shows the trend of observations over time.) Management may want to launch an investigation because the trend suggests that in the near future the operation may produce drill bits outside the control limits.

run chart
A chart that shows trends in observations of a quality characteristic (or cost) over time.

As noted earlier, when the central line and the limits in a control chart are determined through a statistical process, the control chart is referred to as a *statistical quality control (SQC) chart* or *statistical process control (SPC) chart.* The control charts presented in Exhibit 17.11 are SQC (or SPC) charts if the line in the center, 0.125 inch, is determined by calculating the arithmetic mean (μ read *mu*) of the observations and the limits, 0.1255 inch and 0.1245 inch, are determined based on the standard deviation (σ read *sigma*) of the observations. For example, the standard deviation of the drill bits is, say, 0.00025 inch, and the firm has determined that variations within 2 standard deviations of the mean are acceptable. Thus, the limits are $\mu \pm 2\sigma$ or 0.125 inch $\pm$ 2 $\times$ 0.00025 inch, which are 0.1255 inch and 0.1245 inch for upper and lower limits, respectively.

The purpose of a (statistical) control chart like the example in Exhibit 17.11 is to help distinguish between random and nonrandom variations. A process (or operation, or cost) is considered to be in *statistical control* if no sample observation is outside the established limits. Variations that fall within the established limits are deemed *random* variations so that no further investigation is needed. Observations outside the limits may signal quality failures or an out-of-control process.

However, for observations within the established limits to be considered random, the observations should show no apparent patterns or runs, with an approximately equal number of observations above and below the centerline and most points nearing the center line. A process may be out of (statistical) control if the observations show trends, cycles, clusters, or sudden shifts hugging the centerline or the control limits. Consider, for example, the situation depicted for workstation C in Exhibit 17.11: Even though all observations are within the specified control limits, the trend (or "drift") may be evidence that the process may not be in statistical control. Posting control charts in a common area facilitates early detection of quality problems, promotes awareness of workers on the quality status of their products or services, and encourages active participation in efforts to manage and control quality.

Taking Corrective Action

Once control charts indicate that a process may be out of control, what techniques are available for diagnostic purposes—that is, to guide corrective action? Histograms, Pareto charts (diagrams), and cause-and-effect diagrams are useful tools for diagnosing causes of quality problems and therefore possible solutions to these problems.

Histograms

histogram
A graphical representation of the frequency of attributes or events in a given set of data.

A **histogram** is a graphical representation of the frequency of attributes or events in a given set of data. Patterns or variations that are often difficult to see in a set of numbers become more apparent in a histogram. Exhibit 17.12 contains a histogram of factors that contribute to the quality problems identified by a company that makes chocolate mousse.

The company has experienced uneven quality in one of its products and has identified six contributing factors to the problem: substandard chocolate, improper liqueur mixture, uneven egg size, uneven blending speed, variant blending time, and improper refrigeration after production. Over a recent period, the company identified 210 batches as having poor quality (i.e., production outside of established specifications). The histogram in Exhibit 17.12 suggests that variations in egg size may be the largest contributor to the quality problem, followed by uneven speed in blending ingredients.

EXHIBIT 17.12
Histogram of Quality Problems: Contributing Factors

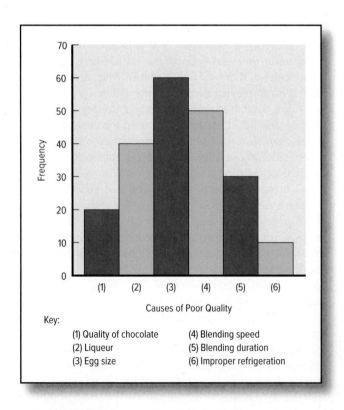

Key:
(1) Quality of chocolate
(2) Liqueur
(3) Egg size
(4) Blending speed
(5) Blending duration
(6) Improper refrigeration

EXHIBIT 17.15
Cause-and-Effect Diagram for the Chocolate Mousse Quality Problem

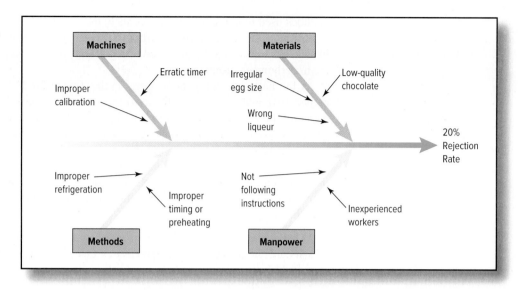

Lean Manufacturing and Accounting for "Lean"

Lean Manufacturing

LO 17-8

Describe lean manufacturing and changes in management accounting systems needed to support a change to "lean."

The practice of total quality management (TQM), when combined with a strategic focus on productivity (Chapter 16) and an emphasis on increasing the speed of product flow and reducing inventory levels and customer lead times (the theory of constraints, Chapter 13), has led a number of companies to adopt what is called *lean manufacturing*. The goal of lean manufacturing ("lean," for short) is to increase product flow and product quality, reduce inventory, reduce waste and inefficiency, improve decision making, and increase profitability. In short, the ultimate goal of lean is the ability to do "more" with "less"—less human effort, less raw material, less developmental time, less space, and less energy.

In 1988, to "promote awareness of Lean manufacturing concepts," and to honor Japanese industrial engineer Shigeo Shingo, the *Shingo Prize* was instituted. Originally, the prize focused solely on North American manufacturers. More recently, the scope of the award has broadened to a focus on operational excellence (including, but going beyond, lean principles). Today, the award is based on the extent to which the *Shingo Guiding Principles* of the *Shingo Model*™ are embraced by employees throughout an organization to drive continuous improvement and enterprise excellence. The award is made through the Shingo Institute, which is part of the Jon M. Huntsman School of Business at Utah State University (USA). As the following list of recent recipients illustrates, the Shingo Prize is no longer confined to North American manufacturers:

- 2019: Merit Medical System, Inc., Tijuana, Mexico (medical device manufacturer)
- 2018: AbbVie Ballytivnan, Sligo, Ireland (biopharmaceutical research and manufacturing company)
- 2017: Ball Beverage Packaging Europe, Naro Forminsk, Russia (manufacturer of aluminum beverage can ends).

Organizations adopting lean usually also adopt lean accounting, a new approach to costing and performance measurement that helps the organization show the financial benefits of the lean manufacturing initiative. Chapter 13 explains how lean manufacturing is related to productivity goals and measures. In Chapter 11, we show how lean accounting can play a role in the application of cost-volume-profit (CVP) analysis and short-term decision making, respectively. And in Chapter 18, we provide a short discussion of the role that lean accounting plays in performance measurement. The objective of the discussion of lean in this chapter is to outline the strategic role of lean manufacturing and lean accounting and to illustrate the methods used to implement them. As such, the material in this section can be considered an extension of the topics covered earlier in this chapter. The more general lesson here for the management accountant is the need to reexamine and redesign cost management systems as the underlying environment changes.

At the heart of lean manufacturing is the Toyota Production System (TPS), which has helped Toyota become one of the most productive automakers in the world.[15] The main elements of TPS are (1) a long-term focus on supplier relationships and coordination; (2) an emphasis on balanced, continuous-flow manufacturing with stable production levels; (3) continuous improvement in product design and manufacturing processes, with the objective of eliminating waste; and (4) flexible manufacturing systems in which different vehicles are produced on the same assembly line and employees are trained for a variety of tasks. Lean manufacturing is an approach to operations that has similar goals. The five principles of lean manufacturing follow:[16]

1. **Value.** Lean starts with what is of worth to the customer; rather than focus on internal standards of performance, lean measures success in terms of what the customer considers valuable.

2. **Value stream.** The value stream consists of all the activities required to create customer value for a family, or group, of related products or services. Lean organizations do not focus on the cost of individual products but on the costs and profitability of each specified value stream. As such, the cost accounting system is greatly simplified, which gives rise to the notion of "lean accounting."

3. **Pull and flow.** A lean production process is scheduled to satisfy customer orders as these orders arrive at the company; this is the concept of *pull* production. The emphasis is on reducing lead time—the time it takes to process a customer's order. The company does not produce to meet a production forecast or budget; this is called the push approach. The push approach can result in excess inventory, especially when the inventory does not satisfy changed customer needs.

4. **Empowerment.** The lean manufacturing system has measures of performance, both financial and nonfinancial, that help employees achieve the organization's lean goals. In the lean system, these measures are collected in what is called a *box score,* which is similar to the balanced scorecard. The lean approach produces these measures frequently (daily or weekly) so that operating and management personnel have real-time information on their progress toward meeting goals.

5. **Perfection.** The lean approach emphasizes Six Sigma, continuous improvement, and elimination of non-value-added processes.

In Chapter 13 we introduced the term *kaizen* to represent the process of continuous improvement. In the context of lean, kaizen can be applied to the process of eliminating waste in all areas of the value stream. Waste can be found in at least the following seven areas: transportation/conveyance (of information, parts, or materials), waiting/delay (idle facilities, people, and systems), overproduction (i.e., "push" vs. "pull" philosophy), defective outputs (not meeting customer quality expectations—both internal and external customers), inventory build-up, unnecessary movement/motion (equipment, people, materials, etc.), and extra processing/ overprocessing (i.e., any processing that does not add value to the product/service being produced). Identification of areas of waste across the entire value chain of activities is facilitated by preparing what is referred to as a *value-stream map*—that is, a graphical representation of the flow of materials and information as a product (or service output) makes its way through to the customer (internal or external).

In terms of the health care example used at the beginning of this chapter, we might identify the following sources of waste: *transportation* (excessive movement of patients, e.g., for

---

[15] Taiichi Ohno, *Toyota Production System: Beyond Large Scale Production,* (Productivity Inc., 1988).

[16] Institute of Management Accountants (IMA), *Statements on Management Accounting,* "Accounting for the Lean Enterprise: Major Changes to the Accounting Paradigm" and "Lean Enterprise Fundamentals" (**www.imanet.org/ publications_statements.asp**).

testing/treatment, or excessive movement of test samples and specimens collected for analysis), *waiting* (physicians waiting for lab-test results, health care teams waiting for specialists, etc.), *overproduction* (excessive testing, perhaps due to liability concerns), *inventories* (excessive supplies of medicines and supplies, lab results completed and awaiting distribution, physician dictation awaiting transcription, etc.), *movement* (excessive time spent trying to locate missing charts, medicines, patient charts, etc.), *defects* (patient misdiagnoses, blood/specimen redraws, incorrect procedure performed and/or medicine administered, etc.), and *excess processing* (medical retests, non-value-added paperwork, etc.).

The key concepts of lean manufacturing as compared to traditional production systems are summarized in Exhibit 17.16. While the discussion to this point has centered on the manufacturing sector, we note that the concept of lean applies to all types of organizations and all processes that create customer value.

Accounting for Lean

Accounting for lean (lean accounting, for short) uses value streams to measure the financial benefits of a firm's progress in implementing lean manufacturing. Lean accounting places the firm's products and services into value streams, which are groups of related products or services. For example, a company manufacturing consumer electronics might have two groups of products (and therefore two value streams)—digital cameras and video cameras—with several models in each group. Accounting for value streams significantly reduces the need for cost allocations (because the products are aggregated into value streams), which can help the firm to better understand the profitability of its process improvements and product groups.

A second motivation for value-stream accounting arises from the fact that organizations implementing lean may see the operating improvements rather quickly, but traditional financial statements will not show these improvements for some time. The organization's commitment to lean manufacturing may take several months or years to complete, so failure to see improvements in the financial statements for a long period could undermine the commitment and success of the effort.

There are three reasons improvements in financial results typically appear later than the operating improvements from implementing lean manufacturing:

1. Customers will benefit from improved manufacturing flexibility by ordering in smaller, more diverse quantities. In the short term, this means that total sales (and overall financial results) may fall. In the longer term, the increased value added to the customers will increase sales and the overall volume of customer demand should increase.

2. Improvements in productivity will create excess capacity; as equipment and facilities are used more efficiently, some will become idle. The result is no improvement in short-term financial results. When the excess capacity is reduced over time, or redeployed, the financial results will show the improvement from cost savings.

3. Because full cost accounting methods include all manufacturing costs as part of product cost, fixed manufacturing costs are included in the balance sheet as part of inventory until the product is sold. The decrease in inventory that results from lean means that using full-cost accounting, the fixed costs incurred in prior periods (when inventory was increasing) flow through the income statement when inventory is decreasing.

EXHIBIT 17.16
Lean vs. Traditional Manufacturing Processes

	Traditional Production	Lean Manufacturing
Key focus points	Reduce cost; reduce idle time	Meet customer demand with short lead time; reduce overproduction and inventory levels
Manufacturing scheduling	Goal is to meet forecasted demand (push); production is in batches	Goal is to meet a customer order received (pull); production is driven by the receipt of customer orders
Batch production	Reduce *number* of setups to reduce setup costs	Reduce setup *time* to maximize manufacturing flexibility and to reduce inventory; maximize the ability to meet diverse customer needs; the principle of one-piece flow

Value-stream income statements can be adapted to separate the effects of each of the above items from operating income. An example of a value-stream income statement that addresses the third item above (i.e., the effect of inventory reduction) is shown in Exhibit 17.17. Rimmer Company has two value streams: digital cameras and video cameras. Assume that operating and other value-stream costs directly traceable to each of the two value streams total $830,800. Costs that cannot be traced to a value stream ($209,000 in total) are assigned only to the total company. Note also that the recent implementation of lean has resulted in a decline in inventory and that the prior-period fixed manufacturing costs flowing through the current income statement are shown separately: $10,000 for the digital cameras stream and $20,000 for the video cameras stream. The temporary total effect on income, $30,000, is set apart; lean managers would argue that, taking a long-term view, total operating income should be interpreted as $85,200 ($55,200 + $30,000).

The Strategic Role of Lean Accounting

Lean manufacturing and lean accounting can play a key role in an organization's success. Lean is particularly appropriate for firms in dynamic and competitive environments, where there are product complexity and changing customer expectations. These are the types of firms that Robin Cooper describes in his study of lean enterprises—firms like Toyota, Nissan, and Sony.[17] These companies have long embraced the principles of lean, just-in-time (JIT), and continuous improvement. A commodity-based firm (agribusiness, building products, etc.) with a few homogeneous products and integrated manufacturing processes would probably focus on efficiency and many of the lean manufacturing principles but have little need for the value-stream income statement. Similarly, firms such as Coach and Tiffany that succeed on the basis of a strong differentiated

EXHIBIT 17.17
Sample Value-Stream Income Statement

	RIMMER COMPANY Value-Stream Income Statement					
	Digital Cameras		**Video Cameras**		**Total**	
Sales		$585,000		$540,000	$1,125,000	
Operating costs:						
Materials	$ 25,200		$ 12,800			
Labor	168,000		88,000			
Equipment-related costs	92,400		48,400			
Occupancy costs	11,200		4,800			
Total operating costs		296,800		154,000	450,800	
Less: Other value-stream costs						
Manufacturing	120,000		240,000			
Selling and administration	10,000	130,000	10,000	250,000	380,000	
Value-stream profit before inventory change		$158,200		$136,000	$ 294,200	
Less: Cost of decrease in inventory		(10,000)		(20,000)	(30,000)	
Value-stream profit		$148,200		$116,000	$ 264,200	
Less: Nontraceable costs						
Manufacturing					$ 155,000	
Selling and administration					54,000	
Total nontraceable fixed costs					$ 209,000	
Operating income					$ 55,200	

[17] Robin Cooper describes a type of competition that differs from cost leadership and differentiation, as described by Michael Porter and explained in Chapter 1 of this text. Cooper studied firms that compete on both cost and product leadership, in very competitive environments. See Robin Cooper, *When Lean Enterprises Collide: Competing through Confrontation* (Cambridge, MA: Harvard Business School Press, 1995).

EXHIBIT 17.18 Summary Comparison: Traditional (Full Cost) Accounting vs. Lean Accounting

	Full Cost Accounting	Lean Accounting
Key focus points	Causality; linking resources, cost drivers, and cost objects	Process flow and throughput; speed up product throughput
	Obtain accurate product costs	Facilitate the five principles of lean manufacturing Support just-in-time (JIT) and theory-of-constraints (TOC) efforts; reduce inventory and customer lead time
Strategy implementation	Full cost based; can be used to support long-term decisions	Short-term focus on reducing lead times, inventory levels, and value-stream income; value-stream goals can be linked to company strategy Focus on day-to-day decisions
Cost allocation	Trace direct costs and use cost drivers for indirect costs	The goal is to avoid cost allocation; the use of the value stream, by aggregating products into product families, means that many costs can be traced directly to the value stream so that allocation is not needed
Nonfinancial performance measures	Can be a supplement, as in a balanced scorecard	Included in the box score report that includes operational, capacity usage, and financial measures
Product cost detail and product-mix analysis	Individual product; product mix at the detail level	Aggregation of products; product cost at the value-stream level; analysis of average product cost within value stream
Reflects the financial benefits of lean manufacturing?	Only in the long term	Directly shows the financial benefits of lean efforts, through value-stream accounting and through the recognition of the cost of decreasing inventory levels
Product costs for pricing	Product costs may or may not play a role in pricing	Assumes that the firm is a price-taker; costs are not used in pricing
Reporting interval	Often monthly	Frequent; often weekly or daily

brand would likely focus on performance measures that advance their brands, rather than emphasizing the principles of lean. Exhibit 17.18 provides a summary of the strategic role that can be played by the lean approach relative to full cost accounting.

Summary

In today's globally competitive environment, with short product life cycles and rapidly changing technologies and consumer tastes, organizations can sustain long-term survival and profitability only by manufacturing quality products and rendering quality services.

A quality product or service meets or exceeds customer expectations at a price customers are willing to pay. To achieve quality products or services, many firms adopt *total quality management,* which requires continuous efforts by everyone in an organization to understand, meet, and exceed the expectations of both internal and external customers.

How can accounting add value to the organization by supporting quality-related initiatives of management? We propose, in Exhibit 17.3, a comprehensive framework that can be used to manage and control quality for a business. The framework implies an iterative or continuous process that begins and ends with the goal of meeting customer expectations. One primary role for accounting in this process is to provide relevant financial information, which informs the decision-making process. We identify two such examples: relevant cost (and revenue) data for evaluating spending and investments in quality and the preparation of cost of quality (COQ) reports. Such financial information regarding quality is supplemented with internal and external nonfinancial measures of quality. Run charts and control charts can be used to assess process and activity stability (i.e., to determine whether a process or activity is producing predictably). Such information is foundational to making process and activity changes, if needed. Histograms, Pareto diagrams, and cause-and-effect diagrams can be used for diagnostic purposes—that is, to identify the source of quality problems in order to motivate and guide corrective action once quality problems are identified.

Management accountants—with training and expertise in analyzing, measuring, and reporting information—can help design and implement the type of comprehensive control system depicted in Exhibit 17.3.

Recently, some companies have embraced lean manufacturing initiatives. In response, the management accounting and control systems for these organizations may have to be revised to better reflect and support such initiatives. The use of value-stream income statements was illustrated in the chapter as one possible revision. The primary conceptual lesson is the organic nature of cost management systems. Such systems need to change in response to changes in business strategy—a lesson that has been a primary theme throughout this text.

Key Terms

absolute quality conformance, *727*	external failure costs, *736*	quality, *723*
appraisal (detection) costs, *735*	goalpost conformance, *727*	quality circle, *735*
cause-and-effect diagram, *745*	histogram, *744*	robust quality approach, *727*
control chart, *742*	internal failure costs, *736*	run chart, *743*
cost of quality (COQ), *734*	ISO 9000, *720*	Six Sigma, *726*
costs of conformance, *736*	ISO 14000, *720*	Taguchi quality loss function
costs of nonconformance, *736*	net promoter score (NPS), *741*	(QLF), *729*
customer loyalty, *740*	Pareto diagram, *745*	tolerance, *727*
design quality, *723*	performance quality, *723*	total quality management
	prevention costs, *735*	(TQM), *720*

Comments on Cost Management in Action

Rankings of U.S. Colleges and Universities

The WSJ/THE rankings of institutional quality are based on "how well a college will prepare students for life after graduation," as predicted by a total score on 15 separate items across the following four performance categories (category weights shown in parentheses): the institution's academic resources (30%); student outcomes, including a measure of graduate salaries (40%); student engagement (20%); and the academic environment, i.e., the diversity of the institution's students and staff (10%). (For a fuller explanation of the scoring scheme used to create institutional rankings, go to **www.timeshighereducation. com/USmethodology2020?mod=article_inline#survey-answer**). Performance data are obtained from the U.S. government [the Integrated Postsecondary Education Data System (IPEDS), the College Scorecard, and the Bureau of Economic Analysis (BEA)], the *THE* US Student Survey, the *THE* Academic Survey, and the Elsevier bibliometric dataset. Survey data for the 2020 rankings were obtained from approximately 100,000 students attending U.S. colleges and universities. The results include a tool that allows individuals to create customized institutional rankings based on category weights different from those specified above.

At least two general observations are suggested on the basis of the present example. (1) Overall quality rankings of U.S. institutions of higher education are a function of both financial and nonfinancial performance indicators—similar to the argument raised earlier regarding the comprehensive framework for the management and control of quality, presented as Exhibit 17.3. Financial measures include factors such as the "earning power" of graduates (measured as the difference between predicted and actual mean salaries earned by graduates of each institution), debt burdens students attending the institution may take on, and academic spending per student. Nonfinancial measures of quality include factors such as student-faculty ratios, research output, student perceptions regarding the helpfulness of the institution in securing internship opportunities, student perceptions regarding inspiration (i.e., an environment in which students are inspired and motivated), breadth of academic options available to students, and extent to which students at the institution feel engaged with their professors and their education. (2) Management accountants can add value by applying cost management concepts—concepts learned by studying the material in this textbook—to novel questions and issues, such as quality rankings of colleges and universities.

Thus, students should be challenged to think about how the frameworks presented in Exhibits 17.1 through 17.3 in the chapter could apply to nonmanufacturing contexts, such as the service industry (including higher education). Managers of service organizations (including colleges and universities) might use these frameworks for managing and monitoring institutional quality as measured, for example, by the Wall Street Journal/Times Higher Education rankings model referenced in this Cost Management in Action example.

Self-Study
Problems
(For answers, please see
Solutions.)

1. Relevant Cost Analysis: Quality-Improvement Program

An automobile manufacturer plans to spend $1 billion to improve the quality of a new model. The manufacturer expects the quality-improvement program to eliminate the need for recall and reduce the costs for other warranty repairs. The firm's experience had been, on average, 1.5 recalls for each new model at a cost of $300 per vehicle per recall. The average cost per recall, if one is needed, is expected to increase by 10% for the new model. Costs for other warranty repairs are expected to decrease from $200 to $80 per unit sold. Sales of the new model were expected to be 500,000 units without the quality-improvement program. The company believes that the well-publicized quality-improvement program will increase total sales to 650,000 units. If there is a profit of $5,000 per unit on any incremental sales attributable to the quality-improvement program, is the $1 billion expenditure justified?

2. Taguchi Quality Loss Function (QLF)

Marlon Audio Company manufactures video tapes. The desired speed of its model SF2000 is 2 inches per second. Any deviation from this value distorts pitch and tempo, resulting in poor sound quality. The company sets the quality specification to 2 ± 0.25 inch per second because an average customer is likely to complain and return the tape if the speed is off by more than 0.25 inch per second. The cost per return is $36.00. The repair cost before the tape is shipped, however, is only $3.00 per tape.

Required
1. Compute $L(x)$ if x is 2.12 inches per second.
2. Estimate the tolerance for the firm to minimize its quality-related cost (loss).

3. Cost of Quality (COQ) Report

Precision Electric Instruments manufacturers fans for mini and microcomputers. As a first step to focus on quality improvements, the firm has compiled the following operating data for 2022 (in thousands):

Line inspection	$ 55
Training	120
Returns	100
Warranty repairs	68
Preventive equipment maintenance	20
Recalls	157
Design engineering	67
Scrap (net of salvage value)	30
Downtime	40
Product-testing equipment	88
Product liability insurance	20
Supplier evaluation	15
Rework	35
Inspection and testing of incoming materials	25
Litigation costs to defend allegation of defective products	240

Required Prepare a cost of quality (COQ) report and classify the costs as prevention, appraisal, internal failure, and external failure. Express each category subtotal as a percentage of total COQ.

The Student Resources section of Connect includes video tutorials for the Self-Study Problems.

Questions

17-1 Provide a brief explanation of the conceptual relationship between improvements in quality and improvements in financial performance.

17-2 Define *quality*. For management accounting and control purposes, define the two primary components of quality.

17-3 In what respect are traditional accounting systems deficient for the goal of managing and controlling quality?

17-4 Describe the major elements of a comprehensive framework for managing and controlling quality, such as the framework presented in text Exhibit 17.3.

17-5 What is meant by Six Sigma? What five steps are usually associated with Six Sigma applications?

17-6 There are two basic approaches to setting quality standards (expectations). Discuss the difference between *goalpost conformance* and *absolute quality conformance*.

17-7 Taguchi argues that being within specification limits is not enough to be competitive in today's global economy. Explain his argument.

17-8 What functions does a cost of quality (COQ) report play in a quality improvement program?

17-9 Of the four categories in a typical COQ report, which category of quality cost is the most damaging to the organization? Why is this the case?

17-10 From a design standpoint, what are some desirable characteristics of a COQ reporting system? That is, if you were to design such a system from scratch, what would be the key attributes of the system?

17-11 Name and briefly describe three methods that companies can use to either identify or correct quality problems.

Brief Exercises

[LO 17-4] 17-12 Assume that a plasma TV company is working at a 3-sigma level of quality in terms of each of 100 component parts in each TV it manufactures. Because of the high price associated with these TV sets, the company defines a product defect as any unit with one or more defective components. (That is, a good-quality output is defined as a TV set with zero defective parts.) On average, what is the probability (rounded to 3 decimal places, e.g., $0.3331 = 0.333$) of producing a unit with zero defects? [*Note:* You will need to use the NORMDIST function in Excel to find the two-tailed z-value corresponding to the specified sigma level. This probability value is the probability associated with a single good-quality component part, under a 3-sigma performance level. Use the following formula: =(NORM. DIST(Sigma value,0,1,TRUE)*2)-1, where "sigma value" is the quality level assumed. For this exercise, you should replace "sigma value" with "3" because we are looking at a 3-sigma level of quality. To calculate the probability of producing a defect-free unit with n components (e.g., $n = 100$), you will need to raise the calculated probability value associated with a single component to the n-th power (e.g., if the probability for a good-quality single component is 0.90, then the probability that a given unit with 100 components would be error-free is 0.90^100 (i.e., 0.90 raised to the 100th power).]

[LO 17-4] 17-13 Solidtronic Inc., an original equipment manufacturer (OEM), has a product specification of 75 ± 5 (i.e., T [the target value] = 75). The cost for warranty services (when the quality characteristic, x, is either 70 or 80) is estimated as $500 per unit. What is the value of k, the cost coefficient (rounded to the nearest whole number), in the Taguchi quality loss function (QLF) for this situation?

[LO 17-4] 17-14 Refer to the information in Brief Exercise 17-13. Calculate the estimated total quality loss (cost) when the measured quality characteristic, x (e.g., circumference, measured in inches), is 78. Round your answer to the nearest whole number.

[LO 17-4] 17-15 Refer to the information in Brief Exercise 17-13. What is the expected average loss (cost) per unit, $E(L(x))$, based on a Taguchi quality loss function (QLF), if the manufacturing process is centered on the target specification with a standard deviation (σ) of 2.0? Round your answer to the nearest whole number.

[LO 17-5] 17-16 Listed below are selected items from the cost of quality (COQ) report for Watson Products for last month:

Category	Amount
Rework	$ 725
Equipment maintenance	1,154
Product testing	786
Field-service costs	560
Spoilage	459
Product liability insurance	780
Product repair	695

What is Watson's total prevention and appraisal cost for the month?

[LO 17-5] 17-17 In 2023, a manufacturing company instituted a total quality management (TQM) program producing the comparative report shown below:

Summary COQ Report (in thousands)			
	2022	2023	% Change
Prevention costs	$ 200	$ 300	+50
Appraisal costs	210	315	+50
Internal failure costs	190	114	−40
External failure costs	1,200	621	−48
Total COQ	$1,800	$1,350	−25

On the basis of this report, which one of the following statements is *most likely* correct?

a. An increase in conformance costs resulted in a higher-quality product and, therefore, a decrease in nonconformance costs.

b. An increase in inspection costs was solely responsible for the decrease in quality costs.

c. Quality costs such as scrap and rework decreased by 48%.

d. Quality costs such as returns and repairs under warranty decreased by 40%.

e. Nonconformance costs increased by 50% and conformance costs decreased by approximately 47%.

[LO 17-6] 17-18 A customer's order is delivered (received by the customer) on December 1, 2022. This order was placed with the company on September 1, 2022, and received by the manufacturing department on September 15, 2022. Actual production on the order began on October 15, 2022, and was completed November 15, 2022. Based on this information, calculate the following for this order: (a) total customer-response time (CRT), (b) order receipt time, (c) manufacturing lead (cycle) time, (d) manufacturing wait time, (e) manufacturing (processing) time, and (f) delivery time. (*Hint:* Refer to Exhibit 14.14 and the accompanying discussion.) Use the DAYS function in Excel to generate all answers.

[LO 17-6] 17-19 A customer places an order on January 1. Ten days later, that order is received by the manufacturing department. Fifteen days later, the order is put into production. Processing (manufacturing) time is 20 days for this order. The completed order is then shipped 10 days later. For this order, what was the total customer-response time (CRT), in days? (*Hint:* Refer to Exhibit 14.14 and accompanying discussion.)

[LO 17-6] 17-20 On average, the manufacturing (processing) time spent per order is approximately 4 days. In addition, a typical order spends 4 days moving from process to process, 3 days in storage, and 2 days in inspection. For an average order, what is the manufacturing cycle efficiency (%), rounded to 1 decimal place (e.g., 32.463% = 32.5%)? (*Hint:* Refer to Exhibit 14.14 and accompanying discussion.)

[LO 17-6] 17-21 For a typical order, assume the following times (in hours): storage time (in between processes), 5.0; inspection time, 1.0; move time (from process to process), 2.0; and manufacturing (processing) time, 8.0. Given this information, what is the manufacturing cycle efficiency (%), rounded to 1 decimal place (e.g., 45.156% = 45.2%)? (*Hint:* Refer to Exhibit 14.14 and accompanying discussion.)

[LO 17-1] 17-22 Which of the following would *not* typically be associated with improved quality of a manufacturer's output?

a. Reduced manufacturing cost

b. Higher levels of inventory holdings

c. Faster throughput times

d. Higher selling prices and increased revenues

[LO 17-1] 17-23 Which of the following would *not* be a desirable outcome from an organization's investments in quality?

a. An increase in the sales return rate

b. A decrease in warranty and service-related costs

c. Higher product/service selling prices

d. Reduced manufacturing cost

[LO 17-2] 17-24 "Total perceived quality" (i.e., total customer satisfaction with a product or service) can be defined as the difference between

a. "design specifications" and "customer expectations."

b. "customer expectations" and "performance quality."

c. "performance quality" and "quality design."

d. "actual performance" (of the product or service) and "customer expectations."

[LO 17-4] 17-25 Which of the following is a distinguishing characteristic of using *goalpost conformance* for setting quality expectations?

a. The use of Six Sigma performance standards

b. The use of the DMAIC (define, measure, analyze, improve, and control) problem-solving method

c. The use of Taguchi quality loss functions for control purposes

d. The use of quality expectations expressed as a specified range around a targeted quality-performance level

[LO 17-4] 17-26 Which of the following is a distinguishing characteristic of using absolute quality conformance for setting quality expectations?

a. The ability to incorporate Taguchi quality loss functions

b. The use of the DMAIC (define, measure, analyze, improve, and control) problem-solving method

c. The ability to set performance standards as a range (or tolerance) around a targeted quality-performance level

d. The ability to express the quality expectation in terms of Six Sigma performance expectations

[LO 17-4]   17-27   A Taguchi quality loss function (QLF)

a. is used to define the tolerance range in the goalpost quality approach to setting quality standards.

b. predicts decreasing quality-related costs as deviations from targeted quality increases.

c. would show a doubling of costs when the deviation from standard is quadrupled.

d. depicts the relationship between quality costs and the level of deviation from targeted quality using a quadratic cost function.

[LO 17-5]   17-28   Which of the following statements regarding cost of quality (COQ) reporting is correct?

a. Total COQ consists of conformance costs plus nonconformance costs.

b. Total COQ consists of conformance costs plus appraisal costs.

c. A typical COQ report includes out-of-pocket costs, but not opportunity costs.

d. The focus of reporting is the production segment of the internal value chain.

[LO 17-5]   17-29   Which of the following costs is *not* properly characterized as a *prevention cost* under a COQ reporting system?

a. Quality training costs

b. Supplier assurance costs

c. Testing and inspection costs

d. Equipment maintenance costs

[LO 17-5]   17-30   Which of the following costs is *not* properly characterized as an *external failure cost* under a COQ reporting system?

a. Sales returns and allowances

b. Lost contribution due to increased demand on constrained resources

c. Lost sales and customer ill-will due to defective products

d. Repair or replacement costs

[LO 17-5]   17-31   Which of the following costs is *not* a desirable characteristic of a COQ reporting system?

a. Exclusion of opportunity costs in the COQ report

b. Comparison of quality costs to some baseline amount for the period

c. Use of activity-based cost data to estimate quality-related costs

d. Use of time-series data

[LO 17-6]   17-32   Total customer-response time (CRT) can be defined as which of the following? (*Hint:* Refer to text Exhibit 14.14 and the accompanying discussion.)

a. The difference between when a customer's order is set up and when the order is finished

b. The elapsed time between when a customer places an order for a product and when that order is delivered to the customer

c. Manufacturing lead (cycle) time for the order

d. The time between when an order is received by manufacturing and when that order is completed

[LO 17-6]   17-33   Which of the following is *not* a characteristic of nonfinancial performance quality indicators?

a. They relate to physical processes and therefore focus attention on precise problem areas in need of attention.

b. They can provide immediate feedback on whether quality-improvement efforts have succeeded in improving quality.

c. They are typically less expensive to obtain compared to cost of quality (COQ) data.

d. They are predicted by a set of relevant financial indicators.

[LO 17-7]   17-34   Part of the process of managing and controlling quality consists of detecting poor quality and then taking appropriate corrective action. Which of the following is *not* a mechanism that management would typically use to *detect* poor quality outputs?

a. Histogram (of frequency of causes of poor-quality outputs)

b. Run chart (trend in quality measures over time)

c. Statistical control chart (SQC) (statistical process control mechanism)

d. Control chart (plot of observations of an operation, or cost, taken at constant intervals over time)

[LO 17-7] 17-35 A cause-and-effect (i.e, "fish-bone" or "Ishikawa") diagram is most helpful for which of the following?

    a. Estimating nonlinear cost functions

    b. Diagnostic purposes (i.e., guiding corrective action once poor-quality outputs have been determined)

    c. Detecting poor-quality outputs

    d. Developing cost of quality (COQ) reports

[LO 17-8] 17-36 Which of the following is a primary motivation for using a value-stream income statement?

    a. To measure the financial benefits of a firm's progress in implementing lean manufacturing

    b. To identify the existence of poor-quality outputs or processes

    c. To guide corrective action once quality-related failures have been detected

    d. To sort out "root causes" of a quality problem after that problem has been identified

Exercises

[LO 17-1] 17-37 **Ethics** Keystone Electronics Corporation (KEC) is an 8-year-old company that has developed a process to produce highly reliable electronic components at a cost well below the established competition. In seeking to expand its overall components business, KEC decided to enter the digital scanning business because there was a niche for lower-priced scanning machines in a vigorously growing marketplace. The market KEC pursued consisted of small regional businesses not yet approached by the larger vendors. KEC sells its scanning machines with a 1-year warranty and has established a maintenance force to handle machine breakdowns.

    As KEC customers learned of the benefits of digital scanning equipment, some increased their usage significantly. After 6 months, large-volume users began experiencing breakdowns, and the field technicians' portable test equipment was not sophisticated enough to detect hairline breaks in the electronic circuitry caused by the heavier-than-expected usage. Consequently, field technicians were required to replace the damaged components and return the defective ones to the company for further testing.

    This situation caused an increase in maintenance costs, which added to the cost of the product. Unfortunately, there was no way to determine how many of the businesses would become heavy users and be subject to breakdowns. Some of the heavier-volume users began switching to the more expensive scanning machines available from the larger competitors. Although new sales orders masked the loss of heavier-volume customers, the increased maintenance costs had an unfavorable impact on earnings. In a report prepared for the quarterly meeting of the board of directors, Mary Stein, KEC's assistant controller, summarized this situation and its anticipated effect on earnings.

    Jim March, vice president of manufacturing, is concerned that the report does not provide any solutions to the problem. He asked Maria Sanchez, the controller, to have the matter deferred so that his engineering staff could work on the problem. He believes that the electronic components can be redesigned. This redesigned model, while more costly, could be an appropriate solution for the heavier-volume users, who should not expect a low-cost model to serve their anticipated needs. March expects that the board may decide to discontinue the product line if no immediate solution is available, and the company could miss a potentially profitable opportunity. March further believes that the tone of the report places his organization in an unfavorable light.

    The controller called Stein into her office and asked her to suppress the part of the formal report related to the component failures. Sanchez asked Stein to just cover it orally at the meeting, noting that "engineering is working with marketing on the situation to reach a satisfactory solution." Stein feels strongly that the board will be misinformed about a potentially serious impact on earnings if she follows the advice of Sanchez.

Required

1. Refer to the IMA's Statement of Ethical Professional Practice (www.imanet.org/career-resources/ethics-center). Explain why the request from Maria Sanchez to Mary Stein is unethical. Cite both actions and nonactions on the part of Sanchez that result in an unethical situation.

2. Identify steps that Mary Stein should follow to resolve the situation.

(CMA Adapted)

[LO 17-4] 17-38 **Taguchi Quality Loss Function (QLF) Analysis; Spreadsheet Application** North Platt Machinery Company manufactures a shaft that must fit inside a sleeve. The firm has just received an order of 50,000 units from Southernstar Exploration Company for $80 per unit. North Platt can manufacture the shaft at $50 per unit. Southernstar desires the diameter of the shaft to be 1.275 cm.

The diameter of the shaft must not be less than 1.25 cm in order to fit properly inside the sleeve. To be able to insert the shaft into a sleeve without the use of force, the diameter cannot be larger than 1.30 cm. A defective shaft is discarded and a replacement has to be shipped via express freight to locations around the world. North Platt estimates that the average cost of handling and shipping a replacement shaft will be approximately $70. Shown below are the diameters from a sample of 80 shafts manufactured during a trial run:

Diameter	Number of Units	Diameter	Number of Units	Diameter	Number of Units
1.232	1	1.273	6	1.292	2
1.240	2	1.274	7	1.293	1
1.250	3	1.275	18	1.294	4
1.258	2	1.276	8	1.298	2
1.262	2	1.277	5	1.300	2
1.270	3	1.280	2	1.304	1
1.272	6	1.288	2	1.320	1

Required   Set up an Excel spreadsheet that uses a Taguchi quality loss function to determine:

1. The expected loss (total quality cost) *per unit*, $E[L(x)]$, from this process. Round final answer to 2 decimal places.

2. The diameter tolerance (in cm, and rounded to 4 decimal places) that should be set for the manufacture of the shaft.

3. Specifications: (a) what is the upper specification (limit) of the tolerance range and (b) what is the lower specification (limit) of the tolerance range that should be set for this process? Round each answer to 3 decimal places. (*Hint:* The target value, *T*, will be the midpoint in the tolerance range.)

[LO 17-4]   **17-39**   **Six Sigma Interpretation; Spreadsheet Application**   (1) To what (one-tailed) probabilities does each of the following sigma levels correspond, based on a standard normal curve: 3 sigma, 4 sigma, 5 sigma, and 6 sigma? (*Hint:* Use the NORM.DIST function in Excel. Note that this function returns the standard normal cumulative distribution function—that is, you will generate a one-tail probability associated with each listed sigma value. The distribution has a mean of 0 (zero) and a standard deviation of 1.) Round one-tailed probabilities (percentages) to 7 decimal places (e.g., 2.1845423%). **Check Figures:** For 3 sigma, the one-tailed probability equals 0.2699796%; for 6 sigma, the one-tailed probability level is 0.0000002%. (2) To what level of defects per million does each of the one-tailed probabilities correspond? (Round answers to 3 decimal points.) (3) What is the point of these calculations? (*Hint:* In responding, it might be helpful to consult the following source: **www.qualitydigest.com/may01/html/sixsigma.html.**)

[LO 17-4]   **17-40**   **Management Accounting's Role in Six Sigma**   This chapter contains an overview of the Six Sigma process that many organizations are using today to improve the quality of their services and products. One could get the impression from the discussion that this topic is more properly a management or an operations management issue. Respond to this position by speculating as to the appropriate role of the management accountant in the Six Sigma process. (*Hint:* Use as the basis of structuring your response the DMAIC implementation approach that is commonly associated with Six Sigma.)

[LO 17-1, 17-4]   **17-41**   **Applying Six Sigma Principles to the Accounting Function**   In an article by P. C. Brewer and F. A. Kennedy ("Putting Accountants on a 'Lean Diet,'" *Strategic Finance,* February 2013, pp. 27–34, accessible at **http://sfmagazine.com/wp-content/uploads/sfarchive/2013/02/Putting-Accountants-on-a-Lean-Diet.pdf**), the authors provide a framework (or "road map") that management accountants can use to apply lean principles to the accounting function. After reading this article, discuss the broad steps that were used to implement lean and improve the efficiency of the accounting function at Candler Industrial Products (CIP), a fictional name for an actual manufacturing company located in Reading, Pennsylvania (USA). Figure 3 in the article ("Lean Transformation: Putting It All Together") can be used to organize your response.

Note: The interested reader can consult P. C. Brewer and J. E. Eighme, "Using Six Sigma to Improve the Finance Function," *Strategic Finance,* May 2005, pp. 27–33, for an alternative case study of applying Six Sigma (and the DMAIC [**D**esign, **M**easure, **A**nalyze, **I**mprove, and **C**ontrol] process) to improve the accounting function.

[LO 17-4]   **17-42**   **Taguchi Quality Loss Function (QLF) Analysis**   Flextronchip, an OEM manufacturer, has a fifth-generation chip for cell phones, with chip specification of 0.2 ± 0.0002 mm for the distance between two adjacent pins. The loss due to a defective chip has been estimated as $20.

Required

1. Compute (to the nearest whole dollar) the value of k, the cost coefficient in the Taguchi quality loss function (QLF), $L(x) = k(x - T)^2$.

2. Assume that the quality control manager takes a sample of 100 chips from the production process. The results are as follows:

Measurement	Frequency
0.1996	2
0.1997	5
0.1998	12
0.1999	11
0.2000	45
0.2001	10
0.2002	8
0.2003	5
0.2004	2

    a. Use the appropriate Taguchi quality loss function, $L(x)$, to calculate the estimated quality loss (to 2 decimal places) for each of the observed measurements.

    b. Calculate the expected (i.e., average) loss per unit (to 2 decimal places) for the production process as a whole.

3. Using the data from requirement 2 above:

    a. Determine the square of the deviation of the mean of the actual x-values from the targeted value, T. (*Note:* In the text, this requested amount is denoted D^2.) Round your answer to 12 decimal places.

    b. Determine, using the formula given in footnote 9, the variance (σ^2) of the observed values of the quality characteristic, x, around the mean value of x, denoted x-bar. Round your answer to 12 decimal places.

    c. Using the formula provided by Albright and Roth (1992) and the results from requirements 3a and 3b above, calculate $E(L(x))$, that is, the expected (average) per-unit loss of the process (rounded to 2 decimal places). *Source:* T. L. Albright and H. P. Roth, "The Measurement of Quality Costs: An Alternative Paradigm," *Accounting Horizons*, June 1992), pp. 15–27. (See Exhibit 17.7 and footnote 9.)

[LO 17-4]   **17-43**   **Using a Taguchi Quality Loss Function (QLF) to Determine Tolerance**   The desired distance for Flextronchip customers is 0.2 mm between two adjacent pins. Any deviation from this value causes interference. The process of handling complaints costs the firm at approximately $40.00 per chip. The engineers of the firm expect the average customer will be likely to complain when the distance is off target by at least 0.0001 mm. At the factory, the adjustment can be made at a cost of $1.60, which includes the labor to make the adjustment and additional testing.

Required

1. What is the value of k, the cost coefficient, in the Taguchi QLF based on the above data?

2. Based on a Taguchi QLF, what should the tolerance be (to 5 decimal places) before an adjustment is made at the factory?

3. Based on your answer to requirement 2 above, what are the specification limits (upper and lower, to five decimal places) for the production of the product in question?

[LO 17-4]   **17-44**   **Taguchi Quality Loss Function (QLF) Analysis**   Duramold specializes in manufacturing molded plastic panels to be fitted on car doors. The blueprint specification for the thickness of a high-demand model calls for 0.1875 ± 0.0025 inch. It costs $120 to manufacture and $150 to scrap a part that does not meet these specifications. The thickness measure for the unit just completed is 0.1893 inch.

Required

1. Use the Taguchi QLF, $L(x)$, to determine:

    a. The value of the cost coefficient, k (rounded to the nearest whole dollar)

    b. The estimated loss (total quality cost) for the unit just completed, that is, the dollar amount for $L(x)$ where $x = 0.1893$. Round your answer to 2 decimal places.

2. Assume that Duramold can eliminate the uneven thickness by adding a production worker, at the critical production point, for $6.00 per unit. Under this assumption:

    a. At what tolerance (to 4 decimal places) should the panels be manufactured? (*Hint:* For this calculation, the total quality cost, $L(x)$, is equal to the above-referenced $6.00 per unit figure.)

    b. What should be the production specification for these panels? That is, what is the upper specification limit (to 4 decimal places) and what is the lower specification limit (to 4 decimal places) for the quality characteristic?

[LO 17-1, 17-5]   17-45 **Graphical Depiction: Is There an Optimal Level of Spending on Quality, or Is Quality "Free"?**   Some proponents of TQM assert that quality is free—that is, that quality is a never-ending quest and that improving product/service quality will reduce a firm's total spending on quality. Others believe that after a point, there are diminishing returns to additional expenditures on quality. Provide a graphical representation of each of these arguments. [*Hint:* Let the vertical axis of your graph represent $ (e.g., revenues or costs), and let the horizontal axis represent the level of quality—the higher the value on the *X*-axis, the greater the indicated quality level.] Supplement your graphs with appropriate explanations/interpretations.

[LO 17-5]   17-46 **COQ Histogram; Spreadsheet Application**   Genova Company classifies its costs of quality into four categories. The costs of quality (COQ) as a percentage of cost of goods sold for the last three years are as follows:

	2022	2023	2024
Prevention costs	1.00%	4.00%	2.00%
Appraisal costs	3.00	2.50	1.50
Internal failure costs	27.00	23.00	14.00
External failure costs	31.00	18.00	12.00

Required
1. Use a spreadsheet to prepare a histogram that shows the COQ trends as a percentage of cost of goods sold.
2. Comment on the trends in COQ over the 3-year period from 2022 to 2024.
3. Based on the observed trends, what total COQ can the company expect in 2025? Explain.

[LO 17-5]   17-47 **Quality Cost Classification**

Required   Classify each of the following costs into one of the four quality cost (i.e., COQ) categories:
1. Materials, labor, and overhead costs of scrapped units.
2. Engineering time spent to determine the causes of failures to meet product specification.
3. Wages and salaries for the time spent by workers to gather quality measurements.
4. Information systems costs expended to develop data requirements.
5. Clerical staff expenses to coordinate training programs.
6. Salaries for members of problem-solving teams.
7. Payment to settle a product-liability lawsuit.

[LO 17-1, 17-5]   17-48 **Cost of Quality (COQ) Reporting for Environmental Performance**   This chapter includes an overview of a COQ reporting system. Such a system has, in fact, been applied in practice by a number of companies. This exercise pertains to the application of a COQ reporting framework to environmental management.

Required
1. What motivation is there to implement an accounting and control system for environmental performance?
2. Construct a sample environmental cost of quality report using the four categories that comprise a traditional COQ report (i.e., prevention costs, appraisal/detection costs, internal failure costs, and external failure costs).
3. Do you think firms would be motivated to provide to shareholders information contained in the environmental COQ report you propose in requirement 2? Why or why not?

[LO 17-5]   17-49 **Cost of Quality (COQ) Report: Environmental Management**   You are given the following environmental quality-related costs:

Employee training	$100,000
Product design	140,000
Supplier certification	40,000
Process inspection	320,000
Depreciation—pollution-control equipment	400,000
Maintain pollution-control equipment	200,000
Clean up polluted lake	500,000
Restore land after use	700,000
Property damage claim	600,000

Required

1. Prepare a COQ report of environmental management for the year. Determine subtotals for each of the four reporting categories, and express each subtotal as a percentage of total operating expenses ($10,000,000) for the year. (*Hint:* Classify the pollution-control costs as internal failure costs, under the assumption that the process pollutes and that the pollution-control equipment used by the company controls the release of pollutants into the environment.)

2. Based on the report you prepare, what conclusions can you draw regarding the company's environmental quality performance for the year?

3. Can you offer management suggestions for the design of an effective COQ reporting system for the environmental program? (That is, what would make for a good reporting system?)

[LO 17-5]   17-50 **Cost of Quality Improvement—Relevant Cost Analysis**   PIM Industries Inc. manufactures electronics components. Each unit costs $30 before the final test. The final test rejects, on average, 5% of the 50,000 units manufactured per year. The average rejection rate of the industry is 3%. A consultant has determined that poor lighting is the most likely cause of this high rejection rate. It would cost $100,000 to install adequate lighting in the assembly department, which would be useful for 5 years. With adequate lighting (which will cost an additional $5,000 of operating costs per year), the firm expects to reduce its rejection rate to no higher than the industry average.

Required

1. Should the firm install the lighting? That is, what would be the projected five-year impact on operating profit? (Show calculations.)

2. What other considerations might affect this decision?

3. What is the primary role of the management accountant in this decision context?

[LO 17-1, 17-5]   17-51 **Relevant Cost Analysis—Conversion to JIT; Spreadsheet Application**   As part of its commitment to quality, the J. J. Borden manufacturing company is proposing to introduce just-in-time (JIT) production methods. Managers of the company have an intuitive feel regarding the financial benefits associated with a change to JIT, but they would like to have some data to inform their decision making in this regard. You are provided with the following data:

Item	Existing Situation	After Adopting JIT
Manufacturing Costs as Percentage of Sales:		
Product-level support	12%	5%
Variable manufacturing overhead	28	10
Direct materials	30	20
Direct manufacturing labor	22	15
Other Financial Data:		
Sales revenue	$1,350,000	$1,650,000
Inventory of WIP	180,000	30,000
Other Data:		
Manufacturing cycle time	60 days	30 days
Inventory financing costs (per annum)	10%	10%

Required

1. As the management accountant for the company, construct an Excel spreadsheet that can be used to estimate the financial benefits associated with the adoption of JIT. Specifically, what is the estimated change in annual operating income (to the nearest whole dollar) attributable to the JIT implementation?

2. Provide some explanations as to how or why sales would be expected to increase after a JIT implementation.

3. In the above example, a reduction of both direct and indirect (i.e., support) costs is predicted. Explain how or why a reduction in each of these two classes of cost might occur in conjunction with a JIT implementation.

[LO 17-5]   17-52 **Relevant Cost Analysis: Decision Making**   Pack-and-Go, a new competitor to FedEx and UPS, does intra-city package deliveries in seven major metropolitan areas. The performance of Pack-and-Go is measured by management as (1) delivery time (relative to budgeted delivery time), (2) on-time delivery rates (defined as agreed-upon delivery date/time plus or minus a specified cushion), and (3) percentage of lost or damaged deliveries. In response to competitive pressures, Pack-and-Go is evaluating an investment in new technology that would improve customer service and delivery quality, particularly in terms of items 2 and 3 above. The annual cost of the new technology, for each of the seven metropolitan areas serviced by Pack-and-Go, is expected to be $80,000. You have gathered the following information regarding delivery performance both under existing operations and after implementing the new technology:

	Decision Alternative	
Item	Current System	After Implementing New Technology
On-time delivery rate	80%	95%
Variable cost per package lost or damaged	$ 30	$ 30
Allocated fixed cost per package lost or damaged	$ 10	$ 10
Annual no. of packages lost or damaged	300	100

Based on a recent marketing study commissioned by Pack-and-Go, the company estimates that each percentage point increase in the on-time performance rate would lead to an annual revenue increase of $10,000. The average contribution margin ratio for packages delivered by Pack-and-Go is estimated as 40%.

Required
1. From a financial perspective, should Pack-and-Go invest in the new technology? That is, what would be the estimated net change in annual operating profit (to the nearest whole dollar) if the company makes the proposed investment?
2. Based on the data collected by Pack-and-Go, the company is fairly confident about the reduction in costs associated with lost or damaged packages. However, because of uncertainties in terms of pricing in the markets in which Pack-and-Go operates, it is less sure about the predicted increase in revenues associated with the implementation of the new technology. What is the breakeven increase in annual revenue (to the nearest whole dollar) that would justify the investment in the new technology?
3. What other factors are likely relevant to the present investment decision facing Pack-and-Go?

[LO 17-5]   17-53 **Cost of Quality (COQ) Reporting** CVI Inc. had November sales totaling $4,200,000 and incurred the following quality-related costs:

Spoiled work-in-process inventory disposal	$28,000
Downtime, due to quality problems	24,000
Field test of new computer	74,000
Support of a customer complaint department	26,000
Product liability insurance	18,000
Quality training	12,000
Reinspection	13,000
Rework (labor and overhead)	8,000
New vendor verification and facilities inspection	25,000
Technical support provided to vendors	4,000
Equipment inspection	20,000
Test and inspection of purchased parts	32,000
Warranty repairs	22,000

Required
1. Prepare a COQ report for November, with appropriate classifications. For each of the four major categories in your report, present total category cost as a percentage of total COQ for the period and as a percentage of sales. (Round all percentages to 2 decimal places.)
2. Offer some observations regarding the data presented in your report, in terms of the process of managing and controlling quality costs.
3. What are the primary limitations of COQ reports (similar to the one you prepared)?

[LO 17-5]   17-54 **Relevant Cost Analysis—Quality Improvements** Destin Company produces water control valves, made of brass, that it sells primarily to builders for use in commercial real estate construction. These valves must meet rigid specifications (i.e., the quality tolerance is small). Valves that, upon inspection, get rejected are returned to the Casting Department; that is, they are returned to stage 1 of the four-stage manufacturing process. Rejected items are melted and then recast. As such, no new materials in Casting are required to rework these items. However, new materials must be added in the Finishing Department for all reworked valves. As the cost accountant for the company, you have prepared the following cost data regarding the production of a typical valve:

Cost	Casting	Finishing	Inspection	Packing	Total
Direct materials	$200	$ 12	$-0-	$ 8	$220
Direct labor	110	120	20	20	270
Variable manufacturing overhead	100	150	20	20	290
Allocated fixed overhead	70	80	40	10	200
	$480	$362	$80	$58	$980

The company, spurred by intense price pressures from foreign manufacturers, recently initiated a number of quality programs. As a result, the rejection rate for valves has decreased from 5.0% to 3.5% of annual output (equal in total to 15,000 units). The reduction in reject rates has enabled the company to reduce its inventory holdings from $400,000 to $250,000. Destin estimates that the annual financing cost associated with inventory holdings is 12%.

Required
1. What are the estimated manufacturing cost savings per year (to the nearest whole dollar) associated with the reduction in rework costs?
2. What are the annual financing cost savings (to the nearest whole dollar) associated with the reduction in inventory holdings?
3. Provide a dollar estimate of the total annual cost savings (to nearest whole dollar) associated with the recently enacted quality improvements.

[LO 17-1, 17-6] 17-55 **Nonfinancial (Operational) Control Measures: Environmental Performance** Assume that the company for which you are working is interested in implementing a comprehensive monitoring and control system regarding environmental performance. The company is convinced that improved performance in this area will lead to reduced costs, an improved corporate image, greater market share, and, ultimately, greater financial returns. To supplement a number of financial performance indicators in the area of environmental quality, the company is interested in developing a set of nonfinancial performance indicators, which (it is hoped) will motivate better environmental quality. In this regard, the company has embraced five strategic objectives: minimize hazardous materials, minimize raw/virgin materials usage, minimize energy requirements, minimize release of residues into the environment, and maximize opportunities to recycle.

Required For each of the five strategic objectives referenced above, provide at least two relevant nonfinancial performance indicators that could lead to improved environmental performance.

[LO 17-1, 17-6] 17-56 **Nonfinancial Quality Indicators** ABC Mfg. is evaluating the desirability of implementing process improvements and is seeking your help in determining whether it should proceed with the proposed improvements. One area of focus is how the improvements will affect processing time (manufacturing cycle time efficiency). Estimated activities and associated times for these activities both under the current process and after process improvements are as follows:

Process Activity	Current Process	After Process Improvements
Wait time	4 hours	1 hour
Inspection	40 minutes	5 minutes
Moving	80 minutes	20 minutes
Processing (manufacturing)	2 hours	75 minutes

Required (*Note:* In responding to the following questions, it may be helpful to refer back to text Exhibit 14.14 and the accompanying discussion.)
1. Determine the manufacturing (production) lead time (in minutes) for each of the two decision alternatives.
2. Determine the manufacturing cycle efficiency (MCE) for each decision alternative. (Round decimal answers to 2 places, e.g., 0.3143 = 0.31.)
3. Calculate (to 2 decimal places each) the following: (a) the percentage improvement in MCE, new vs. old, and (b) the ratio of the new manufacturing lead time to the old manufacturing lead time, in decimal form (e.g., 0.4275 = 0.43).

4. Based on only the figures calculated in requirements 1, 2, and 3, should the company implement the proposed process improvements? Why or why not?

5. Why would process improvements, such as those referenced above, likely lead to improved financial results?

[LO 17-6] 17-57 **Nonfinancial Quality Measures: Net Promoter Score (NPS)** Cope Farm Equipment has recently conducted market research regarding a number of issues, including customer loyalty and customer satisfaction. In regard to the latter, Cope obtained the following responses to the question, "How likely is it that you would recommend Cope to a friend or relative?" The response scale for this question ranged from 1 ("Extremely Unlikely") to 10 ("Extremely Likely").

Score	No.
10	962
9	1,898
8	1,880
7	340
6	822
5	740
4	536
3	95
2	63
1	164
Total	7,500

Required
1. What is meant by the term *net promoter score (NPS)*?
2. What is the potential value of the NPS to the management and control of quality?
3. Given the above results, what is the NPS for Cope? (Round your answer to the nearest whole percentage, e.g., 18.819% = 19%).
4. How is the NPS for an organization interpreted?

[LO 17-6] 17-58 **Manufacturing Cycle Efficiency (MCE)** Grey Company is evaluating two manufacturing process layout options, each of which has the following characteristics for producing a batch of output:

	Minutes per Batch	
	Alternative 1	**Alternative 2**
Setup time	50	20
Movement time (from start to finish)	20	28
Waiting time	6	32
Inspection time	10	14
Processing time	80	60

Required (*Note:* In responding to the following questions, it may be helpful to refer back to Exhibit 14.14 and the accompanying discussion.)
1. Determine the manufacturing lead time (in minutes) per batch for each decision alternative.
2. Determine the manufacturing cycle efficiency (MCE) for each layout (i.e., for each of the two decision alternatives). (Round decimal answers to 2 places, e.g., 0.3143 = 0.31.)
3. Which of the two systems do you recommend? Why? [*Hint:* Calculate the processing time per batch for each decision alternative and (to the nearest whole percentage) the percentage difference for alternative 2 vs. alternative 1.]

[LO 17-3, 17-7] 17-59 **Pareto Diagram (Chart)** The following causes of absenteeism for a fellow student are for the year just completed:

Cause of Absenteeism	Occurrences
Personal illness	12
Child's illness	26
Car broke down	8
Personal emergency	32
Overslept	9
Unexpected visitor	11

Required   Construct a Pareto diagram (chart). In conjunction with the framework presented in Exhibit 17.3, what is the primary role of these diagrams?

[LO 17-7]   17-60   **Control Chart; Spreadsheet Application**   Refer to the background information in Exercise 17-54 for the Destin Company. Based on customer requirements for on-time delivery, management has determined that the target performance level for manufacturing cycle time is 14.0 minutes with a tolerance of ±2 minutes. To monitor the company's ability to meet these specifications, management of the company has recently introduced the use of run charts and control charts. Over the most recent 12-day period, you have obtained the following average manufacturing cycle time data regarding the valve-production process:

Day	Average Manufacturing Cycle Time (minutes)
1	12.5
2	18.0
3	15.0
4	10.0
5	15.5
6	12.8
7	23.5
8	16.5
9	17.5
10	11.0
11	14.5
12	16.0

Note: For ease of illustration, Exercise 17-60 uses only 12 data points; in practice, an application of control charts would likely involve the use of many more data points.

Required

1. Use Excel to prepare a run chart from the daily, sequential observations given above.

2. Provide a short discussion of how run charts can be used in the overall process of measuring and managing quality.

3. What is the mean (to 2 decimal places) and what is the standard deviation (to 2 decimal places) of the 12 manufacturing cycle-time observations?

4. What preliminary conclusion can you draw about the process, based on the results in requirement 3 above relative to the product specifications? What suggestion(s) might you have regarding the present data-collection effort?

5. What is the difference between product specifications and control limits (in a statistical control chart)?

[LO 17-7]   17-61   **Using a Run Chart to Examine Process Stability; Spreadsheet Application**   All processes illustrate some variation (in quality, conformance to specification, etc.). One hallmark of a quality process is stability. As noted in the text, both control charts and run charts (as well as histograms) can be used to examine process stability. In this exercise, you are provided with some information regarding loan processing times at a bank (for an individual loan officer) over a 20-day period. In sequential order, these data are as follows: 90, 73, 62, 88, 47, 68, 87, 68, 50, 69, 26, 78, 80, 30, 32, 73, 60, 50, 36, and 89.

Required

1. Use Excel to plot the above data, in time series fashion. What is the median processing time (to 2 decimal places)? What is the mean (average) processing time (to 2 decimal places)?

2. What is meant by the term *process stability*?

3. What techniques might you use to support a conclusion as to whether this process is stable?

[LO 17-8]   17-62   **Benefits and Challenges of Lean**   Much discussion at your organization recently has centered on the notion of lean. In preparation for an upcoming meeting of senior managers across business functions, you have been asked to prepare an explanatory memo. Your memo should address, at a minimum, the following issues: (1) the definition of *lean,* (2) the strategic value of adopting lean principles for your organization, (3) the anticipated costs and benefits of moving to lean, (4) implications of the move for cost-system design, and (5) suggested sources for additional information regarding these issues.

Required   Prepare a memo for management that addresses the five issues noted above. In responding to this assignment, you should read the following Statement of Management Accounting: *Accounting for the Lean*

Enterprise: Major Changes to the Accounting Paradigm (Montvale, NJ: Institute of Management Accountants, 2014, accessible at www.imanet.org/-/media/f56cba3786e148f486a61df52b0c03ee.ashx ?as=1&mh=200&mw=200).

[LO 17-8]   17-63   **Implementation of Lean Accounting**   Watlow Electric Manufacturing Company introduced lean principles in 2005 and reported a successful implementation in 2008. Watlow began with the implementation of lean principles and then adopted value-stream management (VSM) using the value-stream income statement. As expected, the use of VSM achieved better decision making (previously, the firm had treated direct labor as a purely variable cost that varied with volume; after VSM, it was clear that the behavior of labor costs was far more complex), reduced inventory, reduced manufacturing cycle times, and improved communication and coordination among employees. It was this latter result—better communication—that surprised Watlow management as employees began to work as teams that focused on the key success factors for the firm. The steps taken by Watlow to implement lean included:

- Identify the main value streams of the company (Watlow selected value streams consisting of 25–150 employees each; more than 90% of the company's employees were assigned to a value stream).
- Determine the key measures for achieving the company's strategic goals (these included measures of quality, safety, on-time delivery, and cost).
- Adapt the accounting system to VSM (this included changes in the accounting for direct materials, direct labor, and overhead).

Required   Given the implementation of lean as described above, what do you see as the challenges ahead for Watlow? What features of lean accounting have yet to be implemented? (*Hint:* Among other items, the following articles may be accessed and used as the basis of in-class discussion: Jan P. Bosnahan, "Unleash the Power of Lean Accounting," *Journal of Accountancy,* July 2008, pp. 60–66; Brian Maskell and Bruce Baggaley, "Lean Accounting; What's It All About?," accessible at www.ame.org/sites/default/files/target_articles/06-22-1-Lean_Accounting.pdf)

[LO 17-8]   17-64   **Value-Stream Income Statement**   Marshall Company is a large manufacturer of office furniture. The company has recently adopted lean accounting and has identified two value streams—office chairs and office tables. Total sales in the most recent period for the two streams are $245 and $310 million, respectively.

In the most recent accounting period, Marshall had the following operating costs, which were traced to the two value streams as follows (in thousands):

	Chairs	Tables
Operating costs:		
Materials	$ 16,500	$14,500
Labor	123,000	96,500
Equipment-related costs	44,500	62,800
Occupancy costs	11,350	12,600

In addition to the traceable operating costs, the company had manufacturing costs of $116.750 million, and selling and administrative costs of $25 million that could not be traced to either value stream. Due to the implementation of lean methods, the firm has been able to reduce inventory in both value streams significantly. Marshall has calculated the fixed cost of prior-period inventory that is included in the current income statement to be $5.5 million for the office chair stream and $22.5 million for the office table stream.

Required   Prepare, in good form (i.e., using Exhibit 17.17 as a guide), the value-stream income statement for Marshall Company.

Problems

[LO 17-2, 17-4]   17-65   **Managing the Employee–Customer Encounter in a Sales and Service Setting: Six Sigma vs. "Human Sigma"; Strategy**   Obtain a copy of the following article: John H. Fleming, Curt Coffman, and James K. Harter, "Manage Your Human Sigma," *Harvard Business Review,* July–August 2005, pp. 107–114 (available at https://hbr.org/2005/07/manage-your-human-sigma). The authors of this article state (p. 114): "Ask any CEO to list his or her most pressing business challenges, and you will no doubt hear concerns about customer and employee retention, authentic and sustainable growth, eroding margins, and cost efficiencies. . . . We are confident that measuring and managing two simple factors—employee and customer engagement—can lead to breakthrough improvements in all aspects of your business."

Required   After reading the above-referenced article, answer the following questions:

1. What is the general issue addressed by the authors of this article? That is, what managerial problem are they discussing?

2. How, conceptually, is the Human Sigma approach developed by the authors of this article similar to or distinct from Six Sigma? What is the connection between this discussion and the role of the management accountant (i.e., why is the topic relevant to management accounting)?

3. How do the authors propose to measure the effectiveness of the employee–customer encounter? What evidence do they offer regarding the predictive value of the performance metric they are proposing?

4. Developing appropriate performance metrics is one component of effective performance management system design. The other key component is developing ways to deploy (implement) such metrics successfully. According to the authors, what strategies can an organization use to improve the quality of employee–customer interactions, as measured by the performance metric referenced in requirement 3?

[LO 17-1, 17-2, 17-5, 17-6]

17-66   **Benefits of Switching to JIT**   You have recently been hired as the management accountant for Delta Technologies Inc. The company produces a broad line of subassemblies that are used in the production of flat-screen TVs and other electronic equipment. Competitive pressures, principally from abroad, have caused the company to reexamine its competitive strategy and associated management accounting and control systems. More to the point, the company feels a pressing need to adopt JIT manufacturing, to improve the quality of its outputs (in response to ever-increasing demands by consumers of electronic products), and to better manage its cost structure.

A year ago, Delta acquired, via a 5-year lease, new manufacturing equipment, the annual cost of which is $500,000. To support the move to JIT, however, Delta would have to acquire new, computer-controlled manufacturing equipment, the leasing cost of which is estimated at $1 million per year for 4 years. If the company were to break its existing lease, it would incur a one-time penalty of $275,000.

The replacement equipment is expected to provide significant decreases in variable manufacturing cost per unit, from $50 to $35. This reduction is attributed to faster setup times with the new machine, faster processing speed, a reduction in direct material waste, and a reduction in direct labor expenses (because of increased automation). In addition, improvements in manufacturing cycle time and improvements in product quality are expected to increase annual sales (in units) by approximately 25% (based on a current volume of 40,000 units).

Additional financial information regarding each decision alternative (existing equipment versus replacement equipment) is as follows:

Item	Pre-JIT	Post-JIT
Selling cost per unit	$ 5.00	$ 5.00
Average per-unit cost of Direct Materials Inventory	15.00	12.00
Average per-unit cost of WIP Inventory	25.00	20.00
Average per-unit cost of Finished Goods Inventory	40.00	30.00
Selling price per unit	70.00	70.00

The increased automation, including computer-based manufacturing controls, associated with the replacement equipment will greatly reduce the need for inventory holdings. The annual inventory holding cost, based on the company's (after-tax) weighted-average cost of capital, is 10%. Based on engineering estimates provided to Delta by the lessor company, all inventory holdings (direct materials, WIP, and finished goods) can safely be cut in half from current levels. Currently, Delta holds, on average, 4 months of raw materials inventory, 3 months of WIP inventory, and 2 months of finished goods inventory—all of which are based on production requirements.

Required

1. Essentially, how is a JIT manufacturing system different from a conventional system?

2. What is an appropriate role for management accounting regarding a company's adoption of a JIT manufacturing system?

3. Based on the information presented above, determine the annual financial benefit (including reduction in inventory carrying costs) associated with the proposed move by the company to JIT. (Round your final answer to the nearest whole dollar.)

4. What is the projected first-year net financial effect of investing in the new equipment in conjunction with a move to JIT? Based on an analysis of financial considerations alone, should the company make the switch to JIT? Why or why not?

5. What additional considerations (both qualitative and quantitative) might bear on the decision at hand?

[LO 17-1, 17-2, 17-6]   17-67   **Assessing the Use and Role of Nonfinancial Performance Indicators**   This question pertains to the use of nonfinancial performance indicators as part of a comprehensive management accounting and control system. You are asked to think critically about the value and challenges of using such data for performance evaluation purposes. The following source should be accessed and read prior to answering the questions that appear below: Christopher D. Ittner and David F. Larcker, "Coming Up Short on Non-financial Performance Measurement," *Harvard Business Review,* November 2003, pp. 88–95.

Required

1. What are the primary benefits of incorporating nonfinancial performance indicators as part of a comprehensive management accounting and control system?

2. Why do Ittner and Larcker believe that many companies fail to realize the kinds of benefits listed in requirement 1?

3. In 2008, the Institute of Management Accountants (IMA) revised its definition of *management accounting* (see **www.imanet.org/-/media/6c984e4d7c854c2fb40b96bfbe991884.ashx?as=1&mh=200&mw=20**). After accessing this statement, comment on an appropriate role of the management accountant with regard to the development and use of nonfinancial performance indicators.

[LO 17-2, 17-5, 17-6]   17-68   **Relevant Costs and Quality Improvement**   Lightening Bulk Company is a moving company specializing in transporting large items worldwide. The firm has an 85% on-time delivery rate. Thirteen percent of the items are misplaced and the remaining 2% are lost in shipping. On average, the firm incurs an additional $65 per item to track down and deliver misplaced items. Lost items cost the firm about $300 per item. Last year, the firm shipped 6,000 items with an average freight bill of $200 per item shipped.

The firm's manager is considering investing in a new scheduling and tracking system costing $125,000 per year. The new system is expected to reduce misplaced items to 1% and lost items to 0.5%. Furthermore, the firm expects total sales to increase by 10% with the improved service. The average contribution margin ratio on any increased sales volume, after cost savings associated with a reduction in misplaced and lost items, is expected to be 37.5%.

Required

1. Based on a relevant cost analysis, should the firm install the new tracking system? That is, what is the estimated change in pretax cash flow under the proposed system? Show calculations and round answer to the nearest whole dollar.

2. What other factors does the firm's manager need to consider in making the decision?

3. Upon further investigation, the manager discovered that 80% of the misplaced or lost items either originated in or were delivered to the same country. What is the maximum amount (to the nearest whole dollar) the firm should spend to reduce the cost of problems in that country by 90%?

[LO 17-1, 17-2, 17-5, 17-6]   17-69   **Relevant Costs and Quality Improvement; Chapter 12**   Each year, Worrix Corporation manufactures and sells 3,000 premium-quality multimedia projectors at $12,000 per unit. At the current production level, the firm's manufacturing costs include variable costs of $2,500 per unit and annual fixed costs of $6,000,000. Selling, administrative, and other expenses (not including 15% sales commissions) are $10,000,000 per year.

The new model, introduced a year ago, has experienced a flickering problem. On average, the firm reworks 40% of the completed units and still has to repair under warranty 15% of the units shipped. The additional work required for rework and repair caused the firm to add additional capacity with annual fixed costs of $1,800,000. The variable costs per unit are $2,000 for rework and $2,500, including transportation cost, for repair.

The chief engineer, Patti Mehandra, has proposed a modified manufacturing process that will almost entirely eliminate the flickering problem. The new process will require $12,000,000 for new equipment (including installation cost) and $3,000,000 for training. The firm currently inspects all units before shipment. Patti believes that current appraisal costs of $600,000 per year and $50 per unit can be eliminated within 1 year after the installation of the new process. Furthermore, if the new investment is made, warranty repair cost per unit is estimated to be only $1,000, for no more than 5% of the units shipped.

Worrix believes that none of the fixed costs of rework or repair can be saved and that a new model will be introduced in 3 years. This new technology would most likely render obsolete the equipment the company purchased a year ago.

The accountant estimates that warranty repairs now cause the firm to lose 20% of its potential business.

Required

1. What is the total required initial investment cost (cash outlay) associated with the new manufacturing process?

2. What is the total expected change (i.e., increase or decrease) in cost of quality over the next 3 years from using the new manufacturing process being proposed?

3. Based solely on financial considerations, should Worrix invest in the new process? Specifically: (a) What is the cumulative (i.e., 3-year) estimated change in pretax cash flow assuming the new system is implemented? (b) What is the estimated payback period for the proposed investment (see Chapter 12)? (c) What is the estimated pretax internal rate of return (IRR) (to 2 decimal places) for the proposed investment? (Use the built-in IRR function in Excel to answer this question.)

4. What additional factors should be considered before making the final decision?

5. A member of the company's board of directors is very concerned about the substantial amount of additional funds needed for the new process. Because the current model will be replaced in about 3 years, the board member suggests that the firm should take no action and the problem will go away in 3 years. Do you agree? Why or why not?

[LO 17-5, 17-6] 17-70 **Cost of Quality (COQ) Analysis; Nonfinancial Performance Measures** (*Note:* This problem can be solved as a spreadsheet application and should be set up on a spreadsheet if Problem 17-71 is also assigned.) Acme Materials Company manufactures and sells synthetic coatings that can withstand high temperatures. Its primary customers are aviation manufacturers and maintenance companies. The following table contains financial information pertaining to COQ in 2022 and 2023 (in thousands of dollars):

	2022	2023
Sales	$16,000	$20,000
Materials inspection	300	60
In-process (production) inspection	160	125
Finished product inspection	250	70
Preventive equipment maintenance	20	60
Scrap (net)	500	300
Warranty repairs	700	450
Product design engineering	150	270
Vendor certification	10	60
Direct costs of returned goods	275	80
Training of factory workers	40	140
Product testing—equipment maintenance	60	60
Product testing labor	210	90
Field repairs	70	40
Rework before shipment	240	200
Product-liability settlement	360	60
Emergency repair and maintenance	200	75

Required

1. Classify the cost items in the table into COQ categories.

2. Calculate the ratio of each COQ category to revenues in each of the 2 years. (Round all answers to 2 decimal places.)

3. Comment on the results. In conjunction with answering this question, calculate and refer to the following results:

   a. Percentage change (to 2 decimal places) in total COQ as a percentage of sales, from 2022 to 2023.

   b. Total COQ in 2023 expressed as a percentage (to 2 decimal places) of 2022 sales dollars.

   c. Percentage change in total prevention costs (to 2 decimal places), 2022 to 2023.

   d. Percentage change in total appraisal costs (to 2 decimal places), 2022 to 2023.

   e. Percentage change in total internal failure costs (to 2 decimal places), 2022 to 2023.

   f. Percentage change in total external failure costs (to 2 decimal places), 2022 to 2023.

4. In addition to the financial measures listed in the table, what nonfinancial measures might Acme monitor in its effort to achieve overall improvements in quality?

5. Are financial or nonfinancial quality measures likely of more use to (a) managers or (b) operating personnel? Why?

[LO 17-5]   17-71 **Cost of Quality (COQ) Analysis; Spreadsheet Application**   Use the data in Problem 17-70 to respond to the requirements that follow.

Required

1. If you haven't done so already (in conjunction with Problem 17-70), prepare in Excel a COQ report for 2022 and 2023. Show subtotals each year for each of the four COQ categories. As well, show category costs each year as a percentage of revenue for the year. Finally, show each year total COQ as a percentage of revenue for the year. and set up a spreadsheet for this information. Round all percentages to 2 decimal places.

2. Move to another area of your spreadsheet and title the area "Cost of Quality—Trend Analysis." Show, for both 2022 and 2023, COQ spending (both category-level and in total) as a percentage of sales for the year. Show all percentages to 2 decimal places.

3. Create a bar chart to compare the percentages of each of the COQ categories and the total COQ for 2023 vs. 2022.

4. Do a sensitivity analysis by making the following (joint) changes to the 2023 amounts:
   - Increase the total sales by 5%.
   - Increase total prevention cost by 6%.
   - Decrease total internal failure cost by 60%.
   - Decrease total external failure cost by 50%.

   For each of the four COQ categories, what is the revised (i.e, 2023) category cost as a percentage of sales, rounded to 2 decimal places?

[LO 17-6]   17-72 **Net Promoter Score (NPS)**   Upon graduation, you and a friend established a computer-consultancy business. Your business has generally been successful, but you and your colleague wish to expand the business significantly over the next 3 years. You have always assumed that the service your firm rendered to clients was of sterling quality. However, up to this point you have not attempted to measure customer satisfaction. Recently, you prepared and sent to your clients a customer-satisfaction survey that, among other items, asked the following question: "How likely is it that you would recommend our services to a friend or business associate?" Customers responded to this question using a 10-point scale, with 10 = "Extremely Likely," 5 = "Neutral/Uncertain," and 1 = "Extremely Unlikely." You received 290 responses to this question, which were as follows:

Score	No. of Responses
1	6
2	8
3	9
4	21
5	23
6	30
7	16
8	72
9	70
10	35

Required

1. What is meant by the term *net promoter score*?

2. Given the above data (customer responses), calculate the NPS for your consulting firm. (Round your answer to 1 decimal place, e.g., 10.817% = 10.8%.)

3. Of what strategic importance are nonfinancial customer performance measures in general and the NPS in particular?

[LO 17-5, 17-7]   17-73 **Cost of Quality (COQ) Reporting; Spreadsheet Application**   Carrie Lee, the president of Lee Enterprises, was concerned about the results of her company's new quality control efforts. "Maybe the emphasis we've placed on upgrading our quality control system will pay off in the long run, but it doesn't seem to be helping us much right now. I thought improved quality would give a real boost to sales, but sales have remained flat at about $10,000,000 for the last 2 years."

Lee Enterprises has seen its market share decline in recent years because of increased foreign competition. An intensive effort to strengthen the quality control system was initiated a year ago (on January 1, 2023) in the hope that better quality would strengthen the company's competitive position and reduce warranty and servicing costs. The following costs (in thousands) relate to quality and quality control over the last 2 years:

	2022	**2023**
Warranty repairs	$420	$140
Rework labor	140	200
Supplies used in testing	4	6
Depreciation of testing equipment	22	34
Warranty replacements	60	18
Field servicing	180	120
Inspection	76	120
Systems development	64	106
Disposal of defective products	54	76
Net cost of scrap	86	124
Product recalls	340	82
Product testing	98	160
Statistical process control (SPC)	—	74
Quality engineering	56	80

Required

1. Prepare a spreadsheet that produces a COQ report for both 2022 and 2023. For each individual cost, for each of the four category totals, and for total COQ spending, calculate (to 2 decimal places, e.g., 42.884% = 42.88%) the percentage change from 2022 to 2023.

2. Use your spreadsheet to prepare a histogram showing total COQ spending and spending by COQ category. (*Note:* Your histogram should include results for both 2022 and 2023.)

3. Prepare a written evaluation to accompany the reports you have prepared in requirements 1 and 2. This evaluation should discuss the distribution of quality costs in the company, changes in this distribution that you detect have taken place over the last year, and any other information you believe would be useful to management.

4. A member of the management team believes that employees will be more conscientious in their work if they are held responsible for mistakes. He suggests that workers should do rework on their own time and that they also should pay for disposal of defective units and the cost of scrap. The proposal estimates that the firm can save another $400,000 in quality costs and the employees are less likely to make as many errors. Should the firm implement the proposal? Why or why not?

(CMA Adapted)

[LO 17-7] 17-74 **Constructing and Interpreting a Control Chart** As indicated in the text, various tools from operations management and statistics are used to help support Six Sigma goals and process improvements in a lean environment. One such tool is a control chart—a key element used to assess statistical process control (SPC). You are given the following error rates for a loan-processing activity at a bank: 2.8, 2.4, 2.4, 4.2, 1.8, 2.8, 3.8, 3.4, 3.2, 3.2, 2.2, 1.6, 1.4, 1.4, 2.4, 1.8, 2.6, 2.0, 2.4, 2.4, 2.2, 2.8, and 2.4.

Note: For illustrative purposes, we have intentionally chosen to use a reduced sample of observations. In actual settings, we would likely use a minimum of 30 observations (data points) in creating control charts (*x*-bar charts, *R*-charts, and *p*-charts, for example).

Required

1. Define the term *control chart*. What is the difference between a control chart and a run chart? What do these charts have in common?

2. Use the data on error rates to construct a control chart for the loan-processing operation. Although there are various ways to construct the chart (see any text on operations management or quality control for details), define the upper control limit (UCL) of your chart as the mean plus 2 standard deviations; define the lower control limit (LCL) of your chart as the mean less 2 standard deviations. (In each case, use the sample mean and sample standard deviation for the data set at hand. Round all calculations to 2 decimal places.)

3. Provide an interpretation of the control limits you established in requirement 2.

4. Using a control chart, what techniques can be used to judge whether a process is in *statistical* control?

5. Control charts were developed many years ago for application in the manufacturing sector. However, these charts can be used in other contexts as well. What quality measure might you collect, for use in a control chart, for each of the following nonmanufacturing settings: hospital, insurance company, hotel, and local police department?

[LO 17-8] 17-75 **Applying Lean Principles to Knowledge Work** Can lean principles be applied to so-called knowledge work? This issue is addressed in the following article: D. R. Staats and D. M. Upton, "Lean Knowledge Work," *Harvard Business Review,* October 2011, pp. 101–110 (available at **https://hbr.org/2011/10/lean-knowledge-work**). After accessing and reading this article, respond to the following set of questions.

Required

1. Define what is meant by the term *lean* (or *lean management*). To date, what types of organizations have successfully applied lean? Why have these contexts proven fruitful for the application of lean? What is the role of lean (or lean management) in terms of helping an organization implement its strategy successfully?

2. According to the authors, what is meant by the term *knowledge work*? Why is it more difficult/challenging to apply lean principles to this work context?

3. Based on their own research, what do the authors claim to be the primary benefits of applying lean principles to knowledge work?

4. Based on their experience with more than 1,800 projects, the authors developed six principles that they say could be used to guide the implementation of lean in regard to knowledge work (such as software and IT-development projects). Provide an overview of each of these principles.

5. Of what relevance is the above discussion to the work of the management accountant?

[LO 17-3, 17-5, 17-6]   17-76   **Decision Analysis—Cost of Quality (COQ) Trade-offs**   Drago Company produces a line of brass-based products, one of which is a flow control valve (for regulating the flow of water). The production of this valve requires the use of specialized equipment by highly trained employees. Recently, the company has been experiencing a variety of quality-related problems, which strategically puts this product at competitive risk.

To address these problems, management is considering two decision alternatives. Alternative 1 would be to redesign the production layout process to secure both an increase in product quality and a decrease in manufacturing cycle time. Alternative 2 would be to lease (on a year-to-year basis) state-of-the-art inspection/testing equipment, which would allow the company to better and more accurately identify poor-quality output before that output leaves the plant.

Because of limitations on available capital to support additional investments (i.e., the capital spending budget for the year has already been constructed and is committed to other projects) and the possible need in the near future to redesign the flow-control valve, the company feels that it cannot pursue both of the above-referenced alternatives; it must choose one or the other.

The management accounting team for the company has gathered the following information that bears on the decision now facing management:

Decision Alternative 1: One-time engineering (process) redesign costs	$160,000
Decision Alternative 2: Annual leasing cost for inspection/testing equipment	$100,000

The following fully allocated (i.e., variable plus fixed) costs are budgeted for quality-related activities for the coming year:

Cost to rework defective products	$100 per hour
Transportation costs (for obtaining repair parts)	$150 per delivery
Customer-support costs	$50 per hour
Repair costs in the field (i.e., warranty costs)	$120 per hour

Estimates of the variable cost component of each of the above activity costs are as follows:

	Estimated Variable Cost Component (%)
Cost to rework defective products	30
Transportation costs (for obtaining repair parts)	60
Customer-support costs	50
Repair costs in the field (i.e., warranty costs)	40

Estimated savings of quality-related activities under each decision alternative is:

	Savings Under	
	Decision Alternative 1	Decision Alternative 2
Rework hours (for defective products) avoided	3,000	2,000
Saved deliveries (associated with avoided repairs)	75	50
Reduction in customer-support hours	300	200
Reduction in field-service (warranty) hours	2,800	2,600

The average contribution margin ratio for the product in question, over the past 3 years, and based only on direct labor and direct materials costs (i.e., quality-related savings are captured in their entirety above), has been 30%. Incremental sales (resulting from producing a better product) under each of the two decision alternatives are estimated as follows:

Decision Alternative 1 =	$800,000
Decision Alternative 2 =	$600,000

Required

1. What is the incremental cost (cash outlay) for each of the two decision alternatives? (*Hint:* No calculations are needed here.)

2. What is the estimated year 1 financial benefit associated with each decision alternative? Round both answers to the nearest whole dollar.

3. What is the estimated year 1 net difference between the decision alternatives? That is, based on a 1-year financial analysis, which of the two decision alternatives is preferable (and by how much)? (*Hint:* Remember to factor in both costs and benefits, that is, both cash outflows and cash inflows.)

4. Comment on the results obtained in requirements 1, 2, and 3, particularly in terms of the COQ reporting model and any other pertinent concepts from Chapter 17.

5. What strategic considerations (including both financial and nonfinancial) bear upon the decision facing Drago?

[LO 17-4, 17-7]   17-77 **Goalpost Conformance, Histograms, Run Charts, and Statistical Quality Control Charts**   Assume that Allied Manufacturing Co. produces sheet metal, with a target thickness of 0.750 inch. Below are the observed thicknesses of output each day over the past 30 working days. Because the company has only recently begun operations and is eager to compete effectively in the market for specialty rolled-steel products, it is interested in developing and implementing an effective quality-control system. As the management accountant for Allied, you have been invited to participate in the design of this system.

Day	Output Thickness (inch)
1	0.734
2	0.754
3	0.755
4	0.727
5	0.722
6	0.708
7	0.734
8	0.749
9	0.728
10	0.731
11	0.744
12	0.761
13	0.731
14	0.776
15	0.693
16	0.754
17	0.786
18	0.833
19	0.761
20	0.795
21	0.766
22	0.771
23	0.781
24	0.749
25	0.755
26	0.789
27	0.812
28	0.766
29	0.801
30	0.821

Required

1. Prepare a histogram using the 30 observations presented above. (*Hints:* In conjunction with the Histogram option under Charts, choose Axis Options, Bins, No. of bins = 12, and choose to show Numbers on the horizontal axis to 2 decimal places; resize the resulting chart to increase its clarity.) Show the sample mean and sample standard deviation for the 30 observations. (Round answers to 3 decimal places.)

2. What information is conveyed in the histogram you prepared, and what information (of interest to the present discussion) is not conveyed by the histogram? In general, what cautions might you offer (or what questions might you ask) when attempting to interpret information from a histogram, similar to the one you prepared in requirement 1?

3. The time interval between each of the 30 observations above is equal. Therefore, the sample number (1, 2, 3, etc.) can be used to as a surrogate for "time." Use Excel to prepare a "run chart" [i.e., a line graph in which observations are plotted over time; the vertical axis is the observed quality characteristic (thickness), while the horizontal axis represents the time scale]. (*Hints:* Prepare an *XY* scatter chart, with Smooth Lines and Markers. For the vertical axis, use 0.65 for the minimum bound and 0.85 for the maximum bound, under Format Axis, Axis Options.) What can you conclude from a visual examination of the chart you prepared? What is the mean value of the first 16 observations (to 3 decimal places), and what is the mean value of the last 14 observations (to 3 decimal places)?

4. Statistical control chart: Assume that, after collecting additional data over time, the company concludes that the process is in control, with a mean thickness of rolled steel (in inches) of 0.750 and a standard deviation of 0.025 inch. Given these characteristics, what are the upper control limit and the lower control limit for the process of producing rolled steel by Allied, assuming a 95% confidence level? (Round answers to 3 decimal places. For example, 0.7846 = 0.785.)

5. Assume that the data presented above represent a new sample of observations, collected after the construction of the statistical control limits set in requirement 4 above. Use conditional IF statements in Excel to scan the set of 30 observations to isolate any observations outside the statistical control limits determined in requirement 4. What conclusion(s) can you draw based on this analysis?

6. Suggest follow-up activities that might be pursued as a result of the findings from requirements 1 through 5.

[LO 17-3, 17-5]   17-78 **Multiperiod COQ Reporting**   This problem is an extension to the Bally Company COQ reporting example, reflected in Exhibit 17.10. At year 0, the management team for the company was presented with its first COQ report for the company. Top management was justifiably concerned both about the total spending on quality (COQ) and the breakdown of spending into the four categories reflected in the COQ report it received. Bally formed a new team to recommend possible responses to the observed competitive threat the company was experiencing. As the top management accountant for the company, you were invited to join the team. Over the coming 4 years, the team saw the implementation of several quality-related initiatives. Assume that financial results for year 4 (including those related to COQ) have just been made available. Your task, for an upcoming management meeting, is to prepare for discussion a financial analysis of COQ spending over the past 5 years (i.e., years 0 through 4, inclusive). The key question to be addressed at the meeting is whether the company has been successful in managing and controlling quality costs. As a first step in responding to this question, you have assembled the COQ spending data presented below:

	COQ Spending Category				
Year	Prevention	Appraisal	Internal Failure	External Failure	Sales
0	$125,000	$200,000	$280,000	$1,770,000	$ 8,000,000
1	150,000	250,000	200,000	1,250,000	8,500,000
2	276,000	310,000	240,000	770,000	9,000,000
3	380,000	250,000	150,000	500,000	9,000,000
4	575,000	150,000	150,000	550,000	10,000,000

Required

1. For each of the 5 years (0 through 4, inclusive), compute COQ spending, in total and by category, as a percentage of sales. Round answers to 1 decimal place (e.g., 34.0144% = 34.0%).

2. What preliminary conclusions can be drawn based on the results generated in requirement 1?

3. Prepare a multiyear bar chart of total COQ spending as a percentage of sales over the 5-year period.

4. What conclusion can be drawn based on the chart prepared in response to requirement 3?

5. Prepare a 5-period bar graph showing for each year COQ spending (as a percentage of sales) by category (prevention, appraisal, internal failure, and external failure). Also, prepare two pie charts showing for each of the four COQ categories relative COQ spending (prevention cost as a percentage of total COQ spending, etc.), for both year 0 and year 4.

6. What conclusions can be drawn based on the graphs prepared in requirement 5? [*Hints:* As part of your answer, you might want to break down, for each of the 5 years, total COQ as a percentage of sales into the following two components: conformance costs as a percentage of sales and nonconformance costs as a percentage of sales. It would also be appropriate to generate a stacked bar chart, which shows (for each of the 5 years) conformance cost as a percentage of total COQ and nonconformance cost as a percentage of total COQ.]

7. Assume (perhaps unrealistically) that all quality-related costs are variable, in response to changes in sales. Use the results in year 0 to calculate a variable cost rate for total COQ spending. Given actual sales in year 4, what is the projected total quality cost for year 4, using the calculated variable cost rate from year 0? (Round final answer to nearest whole dollar.)

8. What is the estimated year 4 increase in operating income because of the quality-related initiatives embraced by the company since year 0? (Round answer to nearest whole dollar.) Comment on the accuracy of (and therefore your degree of confidence in) the dollar estimate you generate.

9. As indicated in the discussion accompanying Exhibit 17.10, Bally is experiencing a competitive threat from both new and existing competitors. Provide a short discussion of the role of quality and of COQ in helping Bally respond to the competitive threats it is now facing.

Solutions to Self-Study Problems

1. Relevant Cost Analysis: Quality-Improvement Program

Cost of the quality-improvement program		$1,000,000,000
Savings from eliminating recalls	$300 × 110% × 1.5 × 500,000 = $247,500,000	
Decrease in cost of repairs	($200 − $80) × 500,000 = 60,000,000	
Profit from increased sales	(650,000 − 500,000) × $5,000 = 750,000,000	1,057,500,000
Increase in profit from the quality-improvement program		$ 57,500,000

Yes, the increase in profit from the additional sales and the decrease in the projected cost of warranty repairs and recalls exceed the $1 billion cost of the improvement program.

2. Taguchi Quality Loss Function (QLF)

1. $36 = k(0.25)^2$
   $k = \$576$
   $L(2.12) = \$576 \times (2.12 - 2.0)^2 = \$8.2944$

2. $\$3 = \$576 \times (\text{Tolerance})^2$
   $\text{Tolerance} = 0.0722$

   Therefore, the specification should be set at 2 inches $\pm$ 0.0722 inch.

3. Cost of Quality (COQ) Report

PRECISION ELECTRIC INSTRUMENTS
Cost of Quality (COQ) Report
For the Year 2020
(data in thousands)

		Percent of Total
Prevention costs:		
Training	$ 120	
Design engineering	67	
Preventive equipment maintenance	20	
Supplier evaluation	15	
Total prevention costs	$ 222	20.6
Appraisal costs:		
Line inspection	$ 55	
Product-testing equipment	88	
Inspection and testing of incoming materials*	25	
Total appraisal costs	$ 168	15.5
Internal failure costs:		
Scrap (net)	$ 30	
Downtime	40	
Rework	35	
Total internal failure costs	$ 105	9.7
External failure costs:		
Returns	$ 100	
Warranty repairs	68	
Recalls	157	
Product liability insurance	20	
Litigation costs	240	
Total external failure costs	$ 585	54.2
Total cost of quality (COQ)	$1,080	100.0

*Some may classify this cost as a prevention cost, under the assumption that such testing would (or should) prevent inferior materials from being used, thereby *preventing* failure costs. If inferior materials can be returned to the vendor (or credit received for such materials), then the inspection cost is more clearly a prevention cost. If, on the other hand, the manufacturer would have to "eat" the cost of any inferior materials detected during the inspection process, then one could argue that the inspection cost is part of appraisal. Still others would choose to define appraisal more broadly, to include ANY inspection-related costs. What is more important is that however a given firm chooses to classify such costs (appraisal or prevention), consistency of classification over time is maintained.

Please visit Connect to access a narrated, animated tutorial for solving these problems.

PART FOUR

Management-Level Control

A common element of Parts Three and Four is the focus on control (performance evaluation)—that is, the methods, procedures, and systems used to monitor performance to ensure the organization is implementing its strategy. As part of a comprehensive management accounting and control system, we discuss incentives and rewards for individuals and managers to work most effectively in implementing the organization's strategy. Part Three focuses on the level of operations (*operational control*), while Part Four focuses on the higher level—that is, *management control*.

The objective of the three chapters in Part Four is to present a variety of tools that top managers (such as CFOs) use to evaluate mid-level managers and the organization as a whole. Mid-level managers include plant managers, product-line managers, heads of research and development (R&D) departments, and regional sales managers. They all have significant responsibility in helping the organization achieve its strategic goals.

In Chapters 18 and 19, we introduce the concept of responsibility accounting and a performance evaluation framework that consists of the following organizational subunits: cost centers, revenue centers, profit centers, and investment centers. Tied to the concept of controllability, different mechanisms are used to evaluate the short-term financial performance of each of these subunits of the organization. The coverage in Part Four of the text has a strong strategic focus because mid-level managers have a significant responsibility for achieving strategic goals, and it is critical that the performance evaluation be aligned with these strategic goals. The strategic focus is emphasized in our presentation of *comprehensive* management control systems that, like the balanced scorecard, include both financial and nonfinancial measures.

The comparison of variable costing with full costing (Chapter 18) is included as part of the coverage of assessing profit centers. We cover this topic in Part Four because of its importance in performance evaluation; variable costing is also extensively covered in Part Two, while full costing is covered in Part One.

Chapter 19 covers investment center evaluation, including the key topics of return on investment, residual income, and EVA®. Transfer pricing, also covered in Chapter 19, is an important topic for the assessment of both profit centers and investment centers. When buying and selling exist between units within the organization, the determination of the transfer price will affect the performance evaluation of both the buying unit and the selling unit. Therefore, we cover the topic of transfer pricing both as an *incentive issue* (having the right incentive for the unit managers to choose to trade inside or outside the firm in a manner that achieves the firm's strategic and financial goals) and as a *motivation issue* (the choice of a transfer price should result in a fair measure of performance for both units).

Management compensation, covered in Chapter 20, discusses the link from performance to rewards and the motivation that is needed for managers to achieve strategic goals. Going one step further, the performance of the firm as a whole can be evaluated (i.e., evaluate top managers, collectively). Chapter 20 provides different ways to develop this assessment.

CHAPTER EIGHTEEN

Strategic Performance Measurement:
Cost Centers, Profit Centers, and the Balanced Scorecard

After studying this chapter, you should be able to . . .

LO 18-1　Identify the objectives of management control.

LO 18-2　Identify the types of management control systems and understand factors that affect the design of management control systems.

LO 18-3　Explain the objectives and applications of strategic performance measurement for cost centers, revenue centers, and profit centers.

LO 18-4　Explain the role of variable costing and full costing in evaluating profit centers.

LO 18-5　Explain the role of the balanced scorecard in strategic performance measurement.

Sundry Photography/Shutterstock

> "It is not enough to do your best: you must know what to do, then do your best."
>
> *W. Edwards Deming*

Deming, the influential business consultant and innovator, understood the importance of performance measurement in strategy implementation. He also understood the importance of aligning managers' incentives with the organization's strategic goals. When incentives are aligned, managers are evaluated and rewarded for achieving the critical success factors that contribute to the organization's success. Many of the most successful companies use this approach, often with the help of the balanced scorecard (BSC), a key tool for aligning performance and strategic goals. The BSC has helped many organizations achieve strategic goals, including Northwestern Mutual (life insurance), Cisco Systems, 7-Eleven Stores, Saatchi & Saatchi (advertising agency), Teach for America, the Boston Lyric Opera, and Duke Children's Hospital.[1] The BSC helped United Parcel Service (UPS) significantly increase its revenues. As Kaplan and Norton note:

> The Balanced Scorecard made the difference. Each organization executed strategies using the same physical and human resources that had previously produced failing performance. The strategies were executed with the same products, the same facilities, the same employees, and the same customers. The difference was a new senior management team using the Balanced Scorecard to focus all organizational resources on a new strategy. The scorecard allowed these successful organizations to build a new kind of management system—one designed to manage strategy.

The BSC is particularly important in difficult economic times when traditional profit-based measures can be distorted and difficult to compare against established benchmarks such as prior-year earnings, industry earnings, and competitors' earnings. Moreover, the manager's objective during difficult times is to look for actions taken currently that are expected to lead to profit growth in the future. This means a refocus on nonfinancial measures that define the organization's competitive advantage—the critical success factors. Additionally, in difficult economic times, a company may need to change strategic direction—to move from a focus on product development and innovation to cost control or to make another type of strategic change. Firms with a strong ability to reduce costs and meet customer expectations will be more successful. The BSC can help firms position themselves to meet customer needs and continue to grow.

This chapter covers tools and measures for evaluating management performance. These tools include topics introduced in previous chapters, such as the balanced scorecard, the contribution income statement, cost allocation, the flexible budget, and outsourcing. These topics are covered here in the context of the important role they play in management performance evaluation. For example, an understanding of the difference between the contribution income statement and the full cost income statement is important in an effective analysis of performance. We begin with an explanation of the broad concepts underlying performance measurement and control.

performance measurement
A process that identifies and gathers information about the work performed and the results achieved by an individual, activity, process, or organizational unit as compared to preestablished criteria.

Performance Measurement and Control

LO 18-1

Identify the objectives of management control.

Performance measurement is the process by which managers at all levels gain information about the performance of tasks within the firm and judge that performance against expectations established in budgets, plans, and goals.

---

[1] Robert S. Kaplan and David P. Norton, *The Strategy-Focused Organization: How Balanced Scorecard Companies Thrive in the New Business Environment* (Boston: Harvard Business School Press, 2001); Robert S. Kaplan and David P. Norton, *Strategy Maps* (Boston: Harvard Business School Press, 2004). See The Palladium Group's website (**www.thepalladiumgroup.com**) for more examples of how organizations in diverse industries and numerous countries around the world are successfully using the balanced scorecard.

Performance is evaluated at many different levels in the firm: top management, middle management, and the operating level of individual production and sales employees. In operations, the performance of individual production supervisors at the *operating level* is evaluated by plant managers, whose performance, in turn, is evaluated by executives at the *management level*. Similarly, individual salespersons are evaluated by sales managers, who are evaluated, in turn, by upper-level sales management.

Management control refers to the evaluation of the performance of mid-level managers by upper-level managers. **Operational control** refers to the evaluation of operating-level employees by mid-level managers. Part Three of the text, which includes Chapters 14 through 17, covers operational-level control. Operational control is explained more fully in the introduction to Chapter 14. Part Four, which begins with this chapter and includes Chapters 19 and 20, covers management control. Because upper-level managers are more directly responsible for implementing the organization's strategy, we call control at this level *strategic performance measurement.* In contrast, control at the operating level is called *operational performance measurement.*

management control
The system used by upper-level managers to evaluate the performance of mid-level managers.

operational control
The monitoring of short-term operating performance; takes place when mid-level managers monitor the activities of operating-level managers and employees.

Operational Control vs. Management Control

In contrast to operational control, which focuses on detailed short-term performance measures, management control focuses on higher-level managers and long-term, strategic issues. Operational control has a management-by-exception approach; that is, it identifies units or individuals whose performance (which is often measured with both financial and nonfinancial metrics) does not comply with expectations so that problems can be promptly corrected. In contrast, management control is more consistent with a management-by-objectives approach, in which long-term objectives such as growth and profitability are determined and performance is periodically measured against these goals.

Management control also has a broader and more strategic objective: to evaluate a unit's overall profitability as well as the performance of its manager, to decide whether the unit should be retained or closed, and to motivate the manager to achieve top management's goals. Because of this broader focus, various objectives for management control generally have multiple measures of performance rather than a single financial or operating measure, as is sometimes true in operational control. Exhibit 18.1 presents a simplified organization chart that illustrates where management control and operational control are implemented.

Objectives of Management Control

In a management-by-objectives approach, top management assigns a set of responsibilities to each mid-level manager. The nature of these responsibilities and, therefore, the precise nature

EXHIBIT 18.1
Organization Chart:
Operational and Management
Control

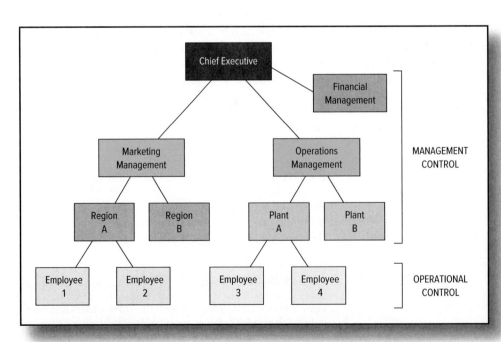

of top management's objectives depend on the functional area involved (operations, marketing, etc.) and on the scope of authority of the mid-level manager (the extent of the resources under the manager's control).

These areas of responsibility are often called *strategic business units*. The concept of a strategic business unit is particularly useful for diversified firms that need performance measures to manage the different business units. General Electric Company (GE) is widely cited as a pioneer in the concept.

A **strategic business unit (SBU)** consists of a well-defined set of controllable operating activities over which a manager is responsible. Generally, SBU managers have autonomy for making decisions and for managing the SBU's human and physical resources. In practice, a variety of terms are used for the SBU: business unit, center, division, or simply unit. For consistency throughout this text, we will use the concept of *SBU* when referring to strategic performance measurement in a general sense, and the term *center* when referring to the four types of SBUs covered in this chapter and the following chapter: cost centers, profit centers, revenue centers, and investment centers. Each of these centers is a type of SBU.

The objectives of management control are to:

1. *Motivate* managers to exert a high level of effort to achieve the goals set by top management.
2. Provide the right *incentives* for managers to make decisions consistent with the goals set by top management—that is, to align managers' efforts with desired strategic goals. The alignment of managers' goals with those of top management is also referred to as *goal congruence.*
3. *Determine fair rewards* to be earned by managers for their effort and skill and the effectiveness of their decision making.

A concise summary of top management's objectives is to provide fair compensation to the SBU manager for working hard and making the right decisions, all within the context of autonomous action by the manager. A common mechanism for achieving these objectives is to develop an **employment contract** between the manager and top management that covers each of these points. Assuming that managers act in autonomous self-interest, the contract is designed to provide incentives for them to act independently while achieving top management's objectives and earning the desired compensation. The contract specifies the desired behaviors and the compensation to be awarded for achieving specific outcomes using these behaviors. Contracts can be explicit and written; as such, they are legal and enforceable by the courts. Other contracts are unwritten and/or implied. For clarity and effectiveness, organizations often use explicit written contracts.

Employment Contracts

An economic model called the **principal–agent model** provides a framework that contains the key elements contracts must have to achieve the desired objectives. The model describes three important aspects of management performance that affect the contracting relationship: controllability, risk aversion, and information asymmetry.

Controllability

Each manager operates in an environment that is influenced by factors beyond the manager's control—operating factors such as unexpected and unpreventable machine breakdowns and external factors such as fluctuations in market prices and demand. The potential for uncontrollable events means that there will always be some uncertainty about the effects of the manager's actions on contracted outcomes, independent of the efforts and abilities the manager brings to the job.

Risk Aversion

The presence of uncontrollability in the manager's environment means that it is important to also consider the manager's tolerance for risk. A manager's risk preferences are important in management and control because they can have unexpected and undesirable effects on the manager's behavior. Risk preferences describe the way individuals view decision options; based on these preferences, certain outcomes and uncertain outcomes are given different weights. The risk associated with uncertain outcomes may be undesirable (or desirable) to

---

strategic business unit (SBU)
A well-defined set of controllable operating activities over which an SBU manager is responsible.

employment contract
An agreement between the manager and top management, designed to provide incentives for the manager to act autonomously to achieve top management's objectives.

principal–agent model
A conceptual model that contains the key elements that contracts must have to achieve the desired objectives.

the decision maker, irrespective of the value of the outcome itself. It is necessary to separate the value of the outcome from the positive or negative weight associated with the risk due to uncertainty. For example, it is common for managers to be averse to risk and thus to prefer a certain $50 over a 50-50 chance of winning $100. A risk-neutral manager would see these options as equivalent. One who prefers risk would prefer to have the chance at winning the $100, but this type of risk-seeking behavior is less common among managers.

Risk has implications for performance evaluation measures, so a manager's risk preferences should be taken into account when choosing among alternatives. For example, a risk-averse manager is most likely to be motivated by supervision and rewards that reduce risk. Moreover, risk preferences can interfere with proper decision making. For example, a risk-averse manager may choose not to take a risky action that top management would take (e.g., to install a costly new machine that would probably reduce operating costs) because of the personal consequences of a potentially unfavorable outcome. For proper motivation and decision making, management control systems should be designed to reduce the negative effects of risk preferences.

Information Asymmetry

Management contracts are often characterized by *information asymmetry:* The manager generally possesses information that top management does not have, and the efforts and decisions made by the manager are often not observable by top management. Because of the manager's independent and unobservable actions, top management is able to observe only the outcomes of those actions, not the efforts that led to those outcomes. The principal–agent model assumes that the manager, in addition to being risk-averse, is also effort-averse.

These three features of the job environment complicate the contracting relationship. Ideally, with no uncontrollability or information asymmetry, the manager and top management would base their contract on the amount of effort the manager is to supply. The desired effort would be assured because it could be observed. However, the presence of these complications means that the contract between the manager and top management must be designed to provide effective incentives to motivate the manager. Three general principles can help structure contracts:

1. The principal–agent model assumes that managers will pursue their own self-interest before the interests of anyone else. Therefore, the contract should be designed so that the manager (the *agent*) is rewarded for achieving the same outcome goals that top management (the *principal*) desires. For example, top managers seeking to maximize firm profit may create incentives (such as bonus compensation) for managers to maximize the profit of their units. If top management seeks to maximize free cash flow, then the contract should tie rewards to that measure. This is called the principle of *alignment.*

2. The contract's ability to motivate the manager is limited when the contract includes performance measures or other factors that the manager can't control. Therefore, top management should strive to exclude known uncontrollable factors from the contract.

3. Top management is assumed to be more risk-seeking than the manager is (because of its ability to diversify risk over the entire organization). Therefore, it is often in the best interests of both parties to introduce some risk-sharing features into the contract. This is why many contracts include both fixed-pay and pay-for-performance components that increase compensation as certain performance measures improve. The fixed-pay aspect provides protection for the manager against the risk of factors that could reduce performance despite the manager's efforts, and the pay-for-performance component provides motivation for the manager to work hard.

In the principal–agent model illustrated in Exhibit 18.2, top management supplies compensation to the manager, who operates in an environment of uncertainty (uncontrollability). The manager supplies effort and decision-making skills and is influenced by a degree of risk aversion. The effect of the effort and decision-making skills on the factors in the environment produces the outcomes. The outcomes are multifaceted, including financial and nonfinancial results: earnings, customer satisfaction, operating efficiency, and so on. The accountant prepares a performance report consisting of financial and nonfinancial measures of the outcomes of the manager's decisions and efforts; the performance report goes to top management, who

EXHIBIT 18.2
The Principal–Agent Model

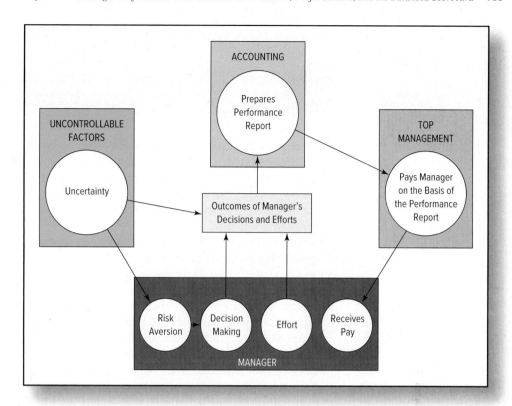

uses it to determine the manager's pay. In this way, the principal–agent model shows the relationships among the key factors that affect the manager's performance and compensation.[2]

Design of Management Control Systems for Motivation and Evaluation

LO 18-2

Identify the types of management control systems and understand factors that affect the design of management control systems.

Developing a management control system involves clearly identifying the *who, what,* and *when* for the evaluation of performance. We start with the *who*—that is, who is interested in evaluating the organization's performance? The four recipients of performance reports are (1) the firm's owners, directors, or shareholders; (2) its creditors; (3) the community or governmental units affected by its operations; and (4) its employees. Each has a different view about what performance is desired.

The second aspect of management control is *what* is being evaluated. Commonly, the evaluation is of the individual manager to assess the effectiveness and efficiency of the manager's performance. Alternatively, the focus of the evaluation might be the SBU under the manager's control for the purpose of determining whether to expand or to divest the SBU. Rather than focusing on the individual manager, the evaluation might be focused on a team of managers. A manager's performance can be compared either with that of other managers or with the manager's own previous performance. Comparison to other managers is common, but comparison to the manager's previous performance is preferable when comparison to others is inappropriate or uninformative.

The third aspect of management control is *when* the performance evaluation is conducted. There are two considerations. First, the evaluation can be done on the basis of either the *resources provided* to the manager or the *outputs* of the manager's efforts. The first approach uses the master budget (Chapter 10), while the second uses the flexible budget (Chapter 14). The focus is on inputs when measuring the outputs of the manager's efforts is difficult or when the nature and extent of the manager's control over the outputs are not clear. Then the

---

[2] The principal–agent model illustrates the concept of what is called *moral hazard*—the risk that the manager might take advantage of the information asymmetry to claim and receive rewards that are not earned under the employment contract.

EXHIBIT 18.3
Sales Life Cycle of
Management Control

Stage of Product's Sales Life Cycle	Appropriate Performance Evaluation Measures
Early	Revenue, market penetration
Growth	Profitability, asset management
Mature	Profitability, strategy

manager's evaluation is performed *ex ante*—that is, before the manager's efforts and decisions have been made. In effect, the manager negotiates with top management for the amount of resources needed. This approach is common in service and not-for-profit organizations, for which outputs are often difficult to measure. In contrast, in manufacturing, where the inputs and outputs are often relatively easy to measure, the *ex post* approach based on actual outputs is more commonly used.

An option for many companies using the ex post approach is to tie performance evaluation to the product life cycle. The life cycle of a product or service is the time from its introduction to its removal from the market. In the early stages of a product's sales life cycle, management focuses primarily on nonfinancial factors such as market penetration and success in developing certain customers. The appropriate performance measures at this time include revenue according to customer class and area, the number of back orders, the number of new customers, and customer satisfaction. As the product achieves market acceptance, profitability and asset management become more important, and the performance measures change. Finally, when the product is in its mature phase—when the nature of the competition is established and the future of the market is clear—the focus on profitability continues with the addition of interest in strategic issues, such as customer satisfaction, information regarding product modifications, and potential new markets. Top management must choose the types of performance measures that are appropriate for the sales life-cycle stage of the product or service, as illustrated in Exhibit 18.3.

The systems for management control are of two types, formal and informal. Formal systems are developed with explicit management guidance, while informal systems arise from the unmanaged, and sometimes unintended, behavior of managers and employees. Informal systems reflect the managers' and employees' reactions and feelings that result from the positive and negative aspects of the work environment. An example is the positive feelings of security and acceptance held by an employee in a company that has a successful product and offers generous employee benefits.

Informal Control Systems

Informal systems are used in firms at both the individual and the team levels. At the individual level, performance is influenced by the individual drives and aspirations employees bring to the workplace; these are separate from any incentives and guidance provided by management. Such individual motivators explain performance differences among employees.

When informal systems exist at the work group or team level, shared team norms, such as a positive attitude to help the firm achieve quality goals or to improve sales, influence the performance of team members. At a broader level, organization-level norms can influence the behavior of teams and of individual employees. For example, some firms have an organizational strategy of commitment to customer service (e.g., IBM and Nordstrom); others have a culture devoted to quality (Toyota, FedEx) or innovation (3M, Apple). Management accountants must consider these informal systems to properly develop controls that have the desired impact on employees' performance.

Formal Control Systems

The most important formal management control systems at the individual employee level are (1) hiring policies, (2) promotion policies, (3) leadership development, and (4) strategic performance measurement systems. In each system, management sets expectations for desired employee performance. Hiring and promotion policies are critical in all companies and supplement strategic performance measurement systems. Leadership development includes training courses, readings and other media, meetings, policies, and procedures that help managers become more effective. Strategic performance measurement systems are the most common method for evaluating managers.

EXHIBIT 18.4
Systems for Management Control

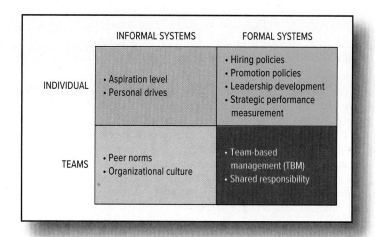

Less is known about formal systems for management control at the team level, although the increased emphasis on teamwork in recent years has led to the development of team-based management (TBM) programs and resources, particularly in organizations focusing on customer relationship management and quality management. The four management control systems are summarized in Exhibit 18.4.

Strategic Performance Measurement

Strategic performance measurement is a system used by top management to evaluate SBU managers. It is used when responsibility can be effectively delegated to SBU managers and adequate measures for evaluating the performance of the managers exist. Before designing strategic performance measurement systems, top managers determine when delegation of responsibility (called *decentralization*) is desirable.

Decentralization

Decentralization is a decision-making approach in which top management chooses to delegate a significant amount of decision authority and responsibility to SBU managers. In contrast, a centralized firm reserves many decision rights at the top management level. For example, in a centralized multistore retail firm, all pricing, purchasing, and advertising decisions are made at the top management level, typically by top-level marketing and operations executives. In contrast, a decentralized retail firm allows local store managers to decide which products to purchase and the type and amount of advertising to use.

The strategic benefit of the centralized approach is that top management retains control over key business functions. With involvement in most decisions, the expertise of top management can be effectively utilized, and the activities of different units within the firm can be effectively coordinated. For many firms, however, a decentralized approach is preferable. The main reason is that top management cannot effectively manage the operations at a detailed level; it lacks the necessary expertise and local knowledge. Decisions at lower levels in the firm must often be made quickly using the information at hand to make the firm more responsive to customers. For example, the retail store manager must often make quick changes in inventory, pricing, and advertising to respond to local competition and changing customer buying habits and tastes.

Although the main reason for decentralization is the use of local or specialized knowledge by SBU managers, other important incentives exist. First, many managers would say that decentralized strategic performance measurement is more motivating because it provides them the opportunity to demonstrate their skill and their desire to achieve as well as to receive recognition and compensation for doing so. Second, because of the direct responsibility assumed by SBU managers, the decentralized approach provides a type of training for future top-level managers. Finally, most managers would agree that the decentralized approach is a better basis for performance evaluation. It is perceived to be more objective and to provide more opportunity for the advancement of hard-working, effective managers.

LO 18-3

Explain the objectives and applications of strategic performance measurement for cost centers, revenue centers, and profit centers.

strategic performance measurement
A system used by top management for the evaluation of SBU managers.

decentralization
A decision-making approach in which top management delegates a significant amount of decision authority and responsibility to subunit (SBU) managers.

REAL-WORLD FOCUS   Wells Fargo and the Dangers of Decentralization

There are numerous potential benefits to a decentralized organizational structure, but there are some real dangers as well. In 2016 Wells Fargo, one of the largest banks in the U.S., reported that 5,300 employees had been fired for aggressive sales tactics, including the creation of more than 2 million accounts using fictitious or unauthorized customer information. An investigation revealed that these tactics went unnoticed or unaddressed for years, in large part due to the bank's highly decentralized structure. The broad delegation

of decision-making authority to department heads allowed them to impose enormous pressure on employees to meet sales goals and to withhold information about the problems that such pressure was creating. This scandal highlights the need for proper controls and oversight in situations where department heads and other mid-level managers are given far-reaching discretion to manage their units.

Source: Emily Glazer, "Wells Fargo Slams Former Bosses' High-Pressure Tactics," *The Wall Street Journal* (Online), April 10, 2017.

EXHIBIT 18.5
Advantages and Disadvantages of Decentralization

Advantages of Decentralization	Disadvantages of Decentralization
• Uses local knowledge • Allows for timely and effective response to customers • Trains managers • Motivates managers • Offers objective method of performance evaluation	• Can hinder coordination among SBUs • Can cause potential conflict among SBUs

As shown in Exhibit 18.5, decentralization has a downside as well. It can hinder coordination within the firm. The increased focus on competition also could cause increased conflict among managers, which can lead to counterproductive actions and reduced overall performance.

Types of Strategic Business Units

The four types of SBUs are cost centers, revenue centers, profit centers, and investment centers.

Cost centers are a firm's production or support SBUs that are evaluated on the basis of cost. Examples include a plant's assembly department, data processing department, and shipping and receiving department. When the focus is on the selling function, centers are called **revenue centers** and are defined either by product line or by geographic area. When an SBU both generates revenues and incurs the major portion of the cost for producing those revenues, it is a **profit center**. Profit center managers are responsible for both revenues and costs and therefore seek to achieve a desired operating profit. The use of profit centers is an improvement over cost and revenue centers in many firms because they align the manager's goals more directly with top management's profit goals.

The choice of a profit, cost, or revenue center depends on the nature of the production and selling environment in the firm. Products that have little need for coordination between the manufacturing and selling functions are good candidates for cost centers. These include many commodity products such as food and paper products. For such products, the production manager rarely needs to adjust the functionality of the product or the production schedule to suit a particular customer. For this reason, production managers should focus on reducing costs while sales managers focus on sales; this is what cost and revenue centers accomplish.

In contrast, sometimes close coordination is needed between the production and selling functions. For example, high-fashion and consumer products require close coordination so that consumer information coming into the selling function promptly reaches the design and manufacturing functions. Cost and revenue centers could fail to provide the incentive for coordination; in this case, production managers would be focusing on cost control and not responding to the ever-changing customer demand information coming from the selling

cost center
A firm's production or support unit that is evaluated on the basis of cost.

revenue center
A business unit with responsibility for sales, defined either by product line or by geographic area, that focuses on the selling function.

profit center
A business unit whose manager is responsible for revenues and expenses, but not the level of invested capital, in the unit.

REAL-WORLD FOCUS   IT Services—From Cost Centers to Revenue Centers

In most firms, the information technology (IT) function has traditionally been defined as a cost center, charged with managing the costs of providing IT services throughout the firm. In recent years, however, many firm owners and top managers have come to see the IT function as a key driver of firm revenue and are evaluating IT managers using revenue-based measures. In a 2017 survey by executive consulting and recruiting firm Korn/Ferry International, 84% of chief information officers (CIOs) agreed with the statement that their departments are viewed as revenue generators rather than cost centers, with 46% strongly agreeing and only 5% disagreeing. This shift in expectations will require CIOs to change the way they manage their units. Instead of focusing exclusively on the costs of providing IT services, they will need to understand how new IT initiatives can help drive revenue and which IT measures can depict (and motivate) improved revenue-generating performance.

Sources: CIO *Journal,* "CIO Stats: More CIOs Expected to Drive Revenue," *The Wall Street Journal* (Online), May 23, 2017; *CIO Journal,* "Top CIOs Hash Out Tech's Business Value," *The Wall Street Journal* (Online), May 22, 2017.

function. A preferred option is to define a profit center for both the revenue and production managers so that they coordinate their efforts to achieve the highest overall profit for the firm.

When a firm has many different profit centers because it has many different product lines, comparing their performance could be difficult because they vary greatly in size and in the nature of their products and services. A preferred approach is to use **investment centers**, which include assets employed by the SBUs as well as profits in the performance evaluation. Investment centers are covered in Chapter 19.

investment center
A business unit that includes in its financial-performance metric the level of assets (capital) employed by the unit as well as profit generated by that unit.

The Balanced Scorecard

Each of the four types of centers described earlier focuses on a critical financial measure of performance. Rather than focus on financial performance only, most firms use multiple measures of performance to evaluate centers, often in the form of a balanced scorecard. The balanced scorecard provides a more comprehensive performance evaluation, one that can be more effective in meeting the objectives of motivation, fairness, and proper incentives for the alignment of managers' efforts with strategic goals.

Cost Centers

Cost SBUs include manufacturing plants or direct manufacturing departments such as assembly or finishing and manufacturing support departments (also called service departments) such as materials handling, maintenance, or engineering. Direct manufacturing and manufacturing support (service) departments are often evaluated as cost centers because these managers have significant direct control over costs but little control over revenues or decision making for investment in facilities.

Strategic Issues Related to Implementing Cost Centers

Three strategic issues arise when implementing cost centers: (1) cost shifting, (2) excessive focus on short-term objectives, and (3) the miscommunication between managers and top management arising from budgetary slack.

Cost Shifting

Cost shifting occurs when a department replaces its controllable costs with noncontrollable costs. For example, the manager of a production cost center that is evaluated on controllable costs has the incentive to replace variable costs with fixed costs. The reason for this is that the manager generally is not held responsible for increases in noncontrollable fixed costs. The net effect might be higher overall costs for the firm, although controllable costs in the manager's department might decrease; fixed costs go up while variable costs go down. The effective use of cost centers requires top management to anticipate and prevent cost shifting by requiring an analysis and justification of equipment upgrades and any changes in work patterns that affect other departments.

Excessive Short-Term Focus

A second strategic issue is the broad concern that many performance measurement systems focus excessively on annual cost figures; this motivates managers to attend only to short-term costs and to neglect long-term strategic issues. This concern is an important reason why cost centers should use nonfinancial strategic information as well as financial information about costs.

Role of Budgetary Slack

A third strategic issue in implementing cost-based SBUs involves recognizing the negative and positive roles of budgetary slack. Budgetary slack is the difference between budgeted and expected performance. The majority of SBUs have some amount of slack, evidenced by a budgeted cost target that is somewhat easier to attain than is reasonably expected. Managers often plan for a certain amount of slack in their performance budgets to allow for unexpected unfavorable events. However, a significant amount of slack might result from SBU managers' attempts to simply make their performance goals easier to achieve.

The positive view of slack is that it effectively addresses the decision-making and fairness objectives of performance evaluation. By limiting managers' exposure to environmental uncertainty, it reduces their relative risk aversion. The resulting evaluation therefore satisfies fairness objectives, and the reduced risk helps managers make decisions that are more congruent with the goals of top management.

Implementing Cost Centers in Departments
Production and Support Departments

There are two methods for implementing cost centers for production and support departments: the discretionary-cost method and the engineered-cost method. These two methods have different underlying cost behaviors and different focuses: inputs and outputs, respectively. When costs are predominantly fixed, an input-oriented planning focus is appropriate because fixed costs are not controllable in the short term. The planning approach is taken so that top management can effectively budget for expected costs in each discretionary-cost center; the focus is on beginning-of-period planning for expected costs rather than end-of-period evaluation of the amount of costs expended. In contrast, if costs are primarily variable and therefore controllable, an output-oriented approach, based on end-of-period evaluation of controllable costs, is appropriate. The input-oriented approach is called the **discretionary-cost method** because costs are considered to be largely uncontrollable and discretion is applied at the planning stage. The output-oriented approach is called the **engineered-cost method** because costs are variable and, therefore, "engineered," or controllable.

Another factor in choosing between the discretionary- and engineered-cost methods is the complexity of the work environment. Cost centers that have relatively poorly defined outputs (e.g., research and development) or have less well-defined goals are therefore more likely to be evaluated as discretionary-cost centers. Cost centers in which operations are well-defined and output goals are more clearly determined will take an engineered-cost approach. See Exhibit 18.6.

Thus, cost behavior in a production department is important in choosing the cost method. As explained in Chapter 5, the behavior of an activity measure depends on the level of analysis: the facility, the product, the batch of production, or the unit of production. Similarly, when defining a cost center, we must know on which level of analysis it operates. For example, costs in the engineering department are driven primarily by product-level activity measures: the number of new products or product changes. Also, costs in the inspection department are caused primarily by batch-level activity measures: the number of production runs or setups.

discretionary-cost method
Used when costs are considered largely uncontrollable; an input-oriented approach that applies discretion at the planning stage.

engineered-cost method
An output-oriented method that considers costs to be variable and, therefore, controllable.

EXHIBIT 18.6
Cost Centers for Production and Support Departments

Discretionary-Cost Approach	Engineered-Cost Approach
Costs are mainly fixed and uncontrollable	Costs are mainly variable and controllable
Firms use an input-oriented planning focus	Firms use an output-oriented evaluation focus
Outputs are poorly defined	Outputs are well-defined
The focus is on planning	The focus is on evaluation

Relatively few cost drivers exist at the facility level because most of its costs are fixed and do not fluctuate with short-run changes in production level, production mix, or product. Therefore, most departments at this level are evaluated as discretionary-cost centers.

For cost departments at the unit, batch, and product levels, managers commonly implement the engineered-cost method based on the appropriate cost driver for that production activity. For example, for the engineering department, where the cost driver activity is at the product level, the engineered-cost method uses the number of engineering changes to new and existing products as the cost driver and evaluates the performance of the engineering department on its costs for each engineering change completed. Similarly, for the inspection department, where the cost driver activity is at the batch level (inspection is done for each batch), the appropriate cost center method is again the engineered-cost method, in which management reviews the cost incurred for the number of batches inspected.

Some production departments are more difficult to classify as batch, product, or facility level. For example, the maintenance department can be viewed as a facility-level activity because much of the demand for maintenance is for plant and equipment that is not influenced by production levels (units or batches). However, because the wear on equipment is greater at a higher level of production or for a larger number of batches, batch and unit cost drivers also can be appropriate. The choice of method depends in part on management's objectives. If management wants to motivate a reduction in maintenance use (because of rising maintenance costs or overall budget constraints), the engineered-cost method is appropriate because it rewards cost reduction. In contrast, if management is concerned about the low overall serviceability of plant and equipment (due perhaps to a prior lack of maintenance), the discretionary-cost method provides the proper incentive because it does not affect the manager's performance evaluation for the current use of maintenance, and thereby motivates the proper additional expenditures on maintenance.

Another option for management control of the engineering or maintenance departments is to treat each as a profit center and to charge internal departments a price for their services. The effects of using a profit center method are added emphasis on cost control and an incentive for the center to provide quality service and perhaps seek markets outside the firm.

Administrative Support Departments

Administrative support departments such as human resources, research and development, information technology services, and printing and duplicating are also commonly evaluated as cost centers. They seldom have a source of revenue, but the department managers control most of the costs, so the cost center method is appropriate. The choice of a discretionary-cost or engineered-cost method for these departments depends on the cost behavior in the department and on management's objectives, as explained earlier. The proper choice of method might change over time. For example, when cost reduction is a key objective, the human resources department might be treated as an engineered-cost center for a time. Later it might be changed to a discretionary-cost SBU to motivate managers to focus on long-term goals such as the design of new employee bonus systems.

Cost behavior in administrative support departments is often a step cost, as illustrated in Exhibit 18.7. As clerical and/or service support personnel are added, labor costs increase in a step-cost pattern. Suppose that one clerk is required to process 100 new employee applications per month and that each clerk is paid $3,000 per month. If the firm processes 250 applications per month, it needs three clerks at a total cost of $9,000 per month. If the discretionary-cost method is used, the supervisor of personnel management is likely to have negotiated for three clerks *at the beginning of the year,* and therefore the budget is $9,000 and there is no meaningful *ex post* evaluation. The discretionary-cost method is represented by the horizontal line in Exhibit 18.7.

Recognizing that processing each application in effect costs $30 ($3,000 ÷ 100), management might choose to use an engineered-cost method that evaluates the personnel department manager by comparing the budget of $7,500 (250 applications × $30 per application) to the actual expenditure of $9,000. Because slack or overcapacity can exist due to the nature of the step cost, an unfavorable cost variance is likely; only when the operation is exactly at one of the full-capacity points (100, 200, 300, etc.) will there be no variance. Therefore, the interpretation of the cost variances must include both the productivity of labor and the underutilization of labor due to excess capacity.

EXHIBIT 18.7
Step-Cost Administrative
Support Costs: Discretionary-
Cost versus Engineered-Cost

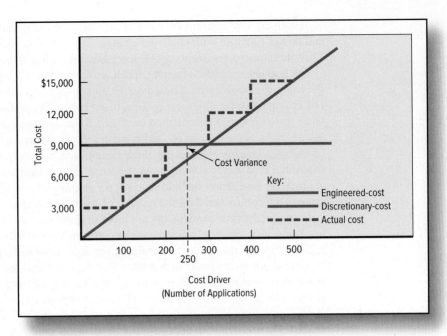

Outsourcing or Consolidating Cost Centers

Outsourcing is the term used to describe a firm's decision to have a service or product sup-plied by an outside firm instead of an internal support department. Many firms have found that the use of an outside source is an effective way to obtain reliable products or services at a reasonable cost without the risk of obsolescence and other potential management problems. It can also enable a firm to gain access to new technologies. The cost of outsourcing is that the firm loses control over a potentially strategic resource and must rely on the outside firm's competence and reliability. For this reason, firms analyze this decision thoroughly, select the vendors carefully, and develop precisely worded contracts. Outsourcing is increasingly used by many firms for their manufacturing, customer service, engineering, and other services.

Another option often used by companies is to consolidate decentralized cost centers into one or a few centralized cost centers. The goals are to reduce overall costs and to increase the overall quality of the services provided. Accounting and human resource service departments are often consolidated for these reasons.

Cost Allocation

When a cost center is centralized, an important issue is how to allocate the jointly incurred costs of service departments—such as IT, engineering, human resources, or maintenance—to the departments using the services. The various cost allocation methods are explained in Chapter 7. The choice of method affects the amount of cost allocated to each cost center and therefore is critical in effective cost center evaluation. For example, if the cost of maintenance is allocated based on the square feet of space in each production department, the departments with more space have higher allocated costs. The incentives of such an allocation method are not clear because the production departments likely cannot control the amount of space they occupy. Alternatively, if maintenance costs are allocated on the basis of the number of main-tenance jobs requested, the production departments can control their allocated maintenance costs by controlling usage.

The criteria for choosing the cost allocation method, as explained in Chapter 7, are the same as the objectives of management control: to (1) motivate managers to exert a high level of effort, (2) provide an incentive for managers to make decisions consistent with top management's goals, and (3) provide a basis for a fair evaluation of managers' performance. For example, when management wants to encourage production departments to reduce the amount of maintenance, allocation based on usage provides the desired incentive. In contrast,

REAL-WORLD FOCUS   Outsourcing, Toys, and Median Pay Levels

Though they compete in the same industry and report similar amounts of revenue, toy makers Hasbro Inc. and Mattel Inc. have very different manufacturing strategies. Hasbro outsources almost all of its toy production to outside contractors (primarily in China and other Far East countries) as a way to reduce costs. In contrast, while Mattel also produces most of its toys in Asia, the company owns and operates its own factories and employs its own workers. The company argues that this arrangement helps management respond more quickly to changes in market trends.

The difference in these strategic approaches to outsourcing was highlighted when U.S. public companies were first required to disclose median employee pay levels in 2018. Mattel's median pay was $6,300 per year, while Hasbro's was $74,000. The explanation? Mattel employs 35,280 people, most of them production employees working outside the U.S. Hasbro, however, directly employs only 5,400 people, most of them in the U.S. What a difference production strategy makes!

Sources: Theo Francis, "Why Mattel and Hasbro Workers Are a World Apart on Pay," *The Wall Street Journal* (Online), April 13, 2018; Paul Ziobro, "Mattel Closes Factories as It Revamps Supply Chain," *The Wall Street Journal* (Online), February 9, 2020.

---

if management wants the departments to increase the use of maintenance to improve the serviceability of the equipment, the most effective incentive might be not to allocate the maintenance cost or perhaps to subsidize it in some way.

A useful approach to achieving the three criteria just explained is to use dual allocation. **Dual allocation** is a cost allocation method that separates fixed and variable costs. Variable costs are directly traced to user departments, and fixed costs are allocated on some logical basis. For example, the variable costs of maintenance, such as supplies, labor, and parts, can be traced to each maintenance job and charged directly to the user department. This approach is both fair and positively motivating. The fixed costs of the maintenance department (training, manuals, equipment, etc.) that cannot be traced to specific maintenance jobs should be allocated to the user departments using a basis that fairly reflects each department's use of the service. For example, those departments for which maintenance jobs require more expensive equipment might be allocated a higher proportion of the maintenance department's fixed costs.

To improve dual allocation, indirect costs could be traced to cost centers using activity-based costing (Chapter 5). This approach tends to produce the most accurate cost assignment and therefore would be the most motivating and fairest to SBU managers.

dual allocation
A cost allocation method that separates fixed and variable costs and traces variable service department costs to the user departments; fixed costs are allocated based on either equal shares among departments or a predetermined budgeted proportion.

Revenue Centers

Management commonly uses revenue drivers in evaluating the performance of revenue centers. **Revenue drivers** in manufacturing firms are the factors that affect sales volume, such as price changes, promotions, discounts, customer service, changes in product features, delivery dates, and other value-added factors. In service firms, the revenue drivers focus on many of the same factors, with a special emphasis on the quality of the service—is it courteous, helpful, and timely?

The marketing and sales departments can be viewed as both revenue and cost centers. The revenue center responsibility stems from the fact that these departments manage the revenue-generating process. These managers must therefore report revenues—typically by product line and often also by sales area and salesperson. Top management uses the revenue reports to assess performance in achieving desired sales goals. Often this analysis is performed at a detailed level to determine the separate effects of changes in price, quantity, and sales mix on overall sales dollars.[3]

revenue drivers
The factors that affect sales volume, such as price changes, promotions, discounts, customer service, changes in product features, delivery dates, and other value-added factors.

---

[3] Sales variances are explained in Chapter 16. Also, some marketing managers have a relatively broad view of the responsibility of the marketing function, which includes responsibility for sales and cost of sales. This is suggested, for example, by the Institute of Marketing's definition: "Marketing is the management process for identifying, anticipating, and satisfying customer requirements profitably."

Many firms evaluate employee performance using subjective measures in addition to objective measures such as cost, revenue, or SBU profit. Subjective performance evaluation offers a variety of benefits in strategic performance measurement systems. Many performance dimensions are difficult to assess with objective measures; examples include leadership, attitude, professionalism, and customer service. Subjective measures give managers the ability to evaluate (and therefore motivate) performance on these dimensions, which improves the alignment of the employment contract. In addition, unanticipated and/or uncontrollable events and other factors may distort the effort signal created by objective measures (e.g., hotel profit may suffer due to extreme weather conditions out

of the manager's control, despite a high level of effort). Subjectivity allows managers to incorporate this kind of information into the evaluation, which reduces the risk the employee faces and improves effort incentives.

Required

Can you think of some potential disadvantages of subjective performance evaluation? Remember that subjectivity involves flawed human beings evaluating other flawed human beings. How could these disadvantages be addressed?

(Refer to Comments on Cost Management in Action at the end of the chapter.)

The marketing and sales departments also can be cost centers. In the pharmaceuticals, cosmetics, software, games and toys, and specialized electrical equipment industries, the cost of advertising and promotion is a significant portion of the total cost of producing and selling the product. The marketing and sales departments incur two types of costs: order-getting and order-filling costs. **Order-getting costs** are expenditures to advertise and promote the product. They include samples, demonstrations, advertising and promotion, travel and entertainment expenses, commissions, and marketing research. Because showing how these costs have directly affected sales is often difficult, managers frequently evaluate order-getting costs using a discretionary-cost center approach and focus on planning these expenditures rather than evaluating their effectiveness. In contrast, other firms have developed extensive analyses of order-getting costs to identify the most effective activities for improving sales. Such efforts might consist of statistical analysis of general economic data and the firm's sales and operating data, as well as operational analysis of sales ratios (e.g., sales per salesperson, sales per number of follow-ups on inquiries, and returns and allowances per product and salesperson).

A second category of marketing costs is **order-filling costs**, which include freight, warehousing, packing and shipping, and collections. These costs usually have a more direct relationship to sales volume, and as a result, they can often be effectively managed using an engineered-cost center approach. The engineered-cost approach could be implemented by using customer cost analysis tools as explained in Chapter 5 and Chapter 8 or by developing appropriate operating ratios—average shipping cost per item, average freight cost per sales dollar, and so on.

order-getting costs
Expenditures to advertise and promote the product.

order-filling costs
Expenditures for freight, warehousing, packing and shipping, and collections.

Profit Centers

Profit centers are defined where SBU managers have authority to make decisions that affect both revenues and costs. The profit center manager's goal is to earn profits. A key advantage of the profit center is that it brings the manager's incentives into congruence with those of top management: to improve the firm's profitability. Moreover, the profit center should also motivate individual managers because by earning profits, the managers are contributing directly to the firm's financial success. For these reasons, the profit center meets the management control objectives of motivation and decision making.

Strategic Role of Profit Centers

Three strategic issues cause firms to choose profit centers rather than cost or revenue centers. First, profit centers provide incentive for the desired coordination among the marketing, production, and support functions. The handling of rush orders is a good example. A cost center would view a rush order unfavorably because of the potential added cost associated with the disruption of the production process, but a revenue center would view it favorably. If they are in separate cost and revenue centers, the production manager has little incentive to meet with the marketing manager to coordinate the rush order. In contrast, if the production unit is part

EXHIBIT 18.8
Cost Leadership, Differentiation, and SBUs

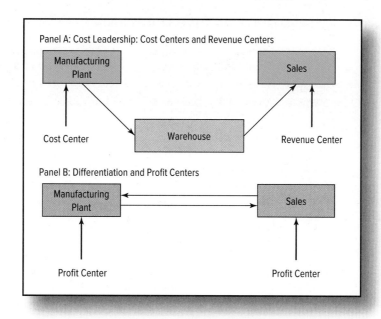

of a profit center, its manager accepts the order if it improves the center's profit, a decision that is consistent with the goals of both the production unit and top management.

This idea is illustrated in Exhibit 18.8. Panel A of Exhibit 18.8 shows a cost leadership firm in which a commodity is manufactured to certain standard quality and functionality specifications. These standards are common in the industry and firms compete primarily on price. In this case, the manufacturing plant's role is to provide product for sale at the lowest cost; this can be visualized as filling the warehouse, as shown in the exhibit. The warehouse might be small if the firm's supply chain management system is effective. The function of the sales organization is to sell product from the warehouse. In effect, the sales and manufacturing units are logically separate and can be evaluated simply: the plant as a cost center and the sales organization as a revenue center. These performance measures align very well with the objectives of the plant and the sales function in this case.

In contrast, see Panel B of Exhibit 18.8, which reflects a firm that competes on differentiation. The arrows shown going in both directions between the plant and the sales function indicate that this product requires extensive coordination between manufacturing and sales. An example is fashion apparel. The design and manufacturing of the apparel must be closely coordinated with sales because styles may change frequently, and the new style preferences must be communicated from sales to the plant in a closely coordinated way. Structuring both the plant and the sales organization as profit centers provides the right incentive in this case because both the plant and sales management are required to attend to both customer preferences and manufacturing costs. An alternative approach is to assign responsibility to the product lines (responsible for both manufacturing and sales) and evaluate each product line as a profit center rather than separate the manufacturing and sales functions.

A second reason that firms use profit centers rather than cost centers is to motivate managers to consider their product or service as marketable to outside customers. Production departments that provide products and services primarily for other internal departments might find that they can market their products or services profitably outside the firm or that the firm can purchase the product or service at a lower price outside the firm.

The third reason for choosing profit centers is to motivate managers to develop new ways to make profit from their products and services. For example, an increasing number of companies find that service contracts (for home entertainment equipment, business equipment, appliances, and so on) provide a significant source of profit in addition to the sale of the product. In the software industry, revenues from providing service and upgrades can be as important as the software's original sales price. Coordination among marketing, production, and design is critical for the success of these efforts, and because many of these contracts are for three years or more, the expected future costs of the service must be carefully analyzed.

EXHIBIT 18.9   **Machine Tools Inc. Contribution Income Statement (000s omitted)**

	Company as a Whole	Company Breakdown into Profit Centers		Breakdown of Division B to Product-Level Profit Centers			
		Division A	Division B	Not Traceable	Product 1	Product 2	Product 3
Net revenues	$2,000	$600	$1,400		$400	$700	$300
Variable costs	900	200	700		100	350	250
Contribution margin	$1,100	$400	$ 700		$300	$350	$ 50
Controllable fixed costs	250	100	150	$ 25	25	100	0
Controllable margin	$ 850	$300	$ 550	(25)	$275	$250	$ 50
Noncontrollable fixed costs	400	120	280	20	10	130	120
Contribution by profit center (CPC)	$ 450	$180	$ 270	$(45)	$265	$120	$ (70)
Nontraceable costs	200						
Operating income	$ 250						

In a profit center, managers have the incentive to develop creative new products and services because the profit center evaluation rewards the incremental profits.

The Contribution Income Statement

contribution income statement
In a contribution income statement, variable costs are subtracted from sales to get total contribution margin, from which fixed costs are subtracted, to yield the amount of operating profit for the period.

A common form of profit center evaluation is the **contribution income statement**, which is based on the contribution margin developed for each profit center and for each relevant group of profit centers. The contribution income statement is illustrated in Exhibit 18.9 for Machine Tools Inc. (MTI). MTI has two operating divisions, A and B, each of which is considered a profit center. The level of detail at which the contribution income statement is developed varies depending on management's needs. For a firm with a limited number of products, the level of detail in Exhibit 18.9 is common. For a firm with several products, a more extensive contribution income statement would be required to provide sufficient detail for management analysis.

contribution by profit center (CPC)
Measures profit after all traceable costs and is therefore a performance measure that is controllable by the profit center manager.

This contribution income statement is an extension of the income statement illustrated in Exhibits 11.14, 11.15, and 11.16 of Chapter 11. Chapter 11 introduces the idea of traceable fixed costs—that is, fixed costs that can be traced directly to a product line or production unit. Exhibit 18.9 shows both contribution margin and contribution margin less traceable fixed costs, which is known as **contribution by profit center (CPC)**. The concept of CPC is important because it measures profit after *all* traceable costs and is therefore controllable by the profit center manager. CPC is a more complete and fair measure of performance than either contribution margin or operating income.

controllable fixed costs
Fixed costs that the profit center manager can influence in approximately a year or less.

This chapter expands the contribution income statement by distinguishing controllable and noncontrollable fixed costs. **Controllable fixed costs** are fixed costs that the SBU manager can influence in approximately a year or less. That is, the manager typically budgets these costs in the annual budget; some of them involve contractual relationships for a year or less. Examples include advertising; sales promotion; certain engineering, data processing, and research projects; and management consulting. In contrast, **noncontrollable fixed costs** are those that are not controllable within a year's time; usually they include facilities-related costs such as depreciation, taxes, and insurance.

noncontrollable fixed costs
Costs that are not controllable within a year's time, usually including facilities-related costs such as depreciation, taxes, and insurance.

As illustrated in Exhibit 18.9, the firm develops a useful measure of the SBU manager's short-term performance by subtracting controllable fixed costs from the contribution margin to determine the **controllable margin**. In contrast, to measure the manager's performance in managing both short- and long-term performance, the CPC measure is most appropriate because it includes both short-term and long-term fixed costs.

controllable margin
A margin determined by subtracting short-term controllable fixed costs from the contribution margin.

One complication in completing the contribution income statement is that some costs that are not traceable at a detailed level are traceable at a higher level of aggregation. The nontraceable costs column in the income statement represents costs traceable to division B but not traceable to any of the product lines. For example, the $25,000 controllable fixed costs might consist of the cost of advertising that was arranged at the division level to benefit all three products, so it is not traceable to any one product.

In addition to providing useful measures of the manager's performance in managing costs, the contribution income statement can be used to determine whether a profit center should be dropped or retained, much like the contribution margin analysis in Exhibit 11.16. The analysis is now enhanced because of our ability to distinguish controllable and noncontrollable fixed costs. For example, using the analysis in Exhibit 18.9, MTI can determine that if it drops product 3, the short-term effect will be to reduce profit by $50,000, the amount of the controllable margin. All costs involved in the determination of the controllable margin are avoidable within a period of one year. Taking the longer-term view, suppose that MTI could ultimately save an additional $120,000 of noncontrollable fixed costs by dropping product 3. Then, in the long term, MTI can save a net of $70,000 by dropping product 3, the amount of the CPC for product 3. The preceding analysis has assumed that the sales of the products are independent—that a change in sales of one product will not affect the level of sales of another product. Sales interdependencies between products must also be included in the analysis when they occur.

The Contribution Income Statement and Value Streams

In applications of lean accounting, products and services are grouped into families called *value streams*. The value-stream income statement shows the contribution of each of the organization's value streams in much the same way as the contribution income statement illustrated in Exhibit 18.9; each value stream is a profit center. Moreover, a unique feature of the value-stream income statement is that it shows separately the increase or decrease in profit due to a change in inventory; in effect, the value-stream income statement adjusts the full costing income statement to contribution-based variable costing. The ability to see the inventory effect as a separate item on the income statement provides significant additional information for managers. This is one of the key contributions of value streams in lean accounting.[4]

Variable Costing vs. Full Costing for Evaluating Profit Centers

LO 18-4

Explain the role of variable costing and full costing in evaluating profit centers.

The use of the contribution income statement is connected with what is called **variable costing** because it separates variable and fixed costs. Only variable costs are included in determining the cost of sales and the contribution margin. All fixed costs are treated as period costs and are expensed in the period they are incurred. In contrast, **full costing** (also called absorption costing) is a system that includes fixed production costs in product cost and cost of sales. Full costing is the conventional costing system because it is required by financial reporting standards (generally accepted accounting principles) and by the Internal Revenue Service in the U.S. for determining taxable income. A key reason full costing is preferred for financial reporting is that it satisfies the matching principle; that is, in determining cost of goods sold, it matches the revenues of the period with the full manufacturing cost of the product. The details of full costing systems are explained in Chapters 3, 4, 5, 6, and 7.

The advantage of variable costing is that it meets the three objectives of management control systems by showing separately those costs that can be traced to, and controlled by, each profit center. In this section, we see an additional reason for using variable costing. Although operating income determined using full costing is affected by changes in inventory levels, operating income using variable costing is not. Exhibits 18.10A and 18.10B show how using full costing affects operating income.

variable costing

A costing system in which only variable production costs are included in the calculation of cost of sales. Under variable costing, fixed production costs are not included in inventory cost but are expensed in the period they are incurred.

full costing

A costing system in which all production costs (both fixed and variable) are included in the calculation of cost of sales. Full costing (also called absorption costing) is required by GAAP.

---

[4] Refer to Chapter 17 for a discussion of value-stream income statements as a key feature of lean accounting.

EXHIBIT 18.10A
Comparison of Full and
Variable Costing—Period 1

Panel 1 Data Summary	Period 1	Period 2	
Units			
Beginning inventory	0	40	
Price	$100	$100	
Sold	60	140	
Produced	100	100	
Unit variable costs			
Manufacturing	$30	$30	
Selling and administrative costs	$5	$5	
Fixed costs			Per unit
Manufacturing	$4,000	$4,000	$40
Selling and administrative costs	$1,200	$1,200	

Panel 2

Period 1 Income Statement	Full Costing		Variable Costing	
Sales (60 × $100)		$6,000		$ 6,000
Less: Cost of goods sold				
Beginning inventory	$ 0		$ 0	
+ Cost of goods produced	7,000		3,000	
	(= 100 × $70)		(= 100 × $30)	
= Cost of goods available for sale	7,000		3,000	
− Ending inventory ($1,600 difference)	2,800		1,200	
	(= 40 × $70)		(= 40 × $30)	
= Cost of goods sold		4,200		1,800
Less: Variable selling and administrative costs		N/A		300
Gross margin		**$1,800**		
Contribution margin				**$ 3,900**
Less: Fixed manufacturing costs		N/A	$4,000	
Less: Selling and administrative costs				
Variable	$ 300		N/A	
Fixed	1,200		$1,200	
Total other costs		1,500		5,200
Operating income ($1,600 difference)		**$ 300**		**$(1,300)**

Recap

Difference in ending inventory = $2,800 − $1,200 = $1,600 (or 40 units × $40/unit = $1,600)
Difference in income = $300 − $(1,300) = $1,600

Difference in
ending inventory =
$2,800 − $1,200 = $1,600

Difference in
operating income =
$300 − $(1,300) = $1,600

N/A = not applicable.

Panel 1 in Exhibit 18.10A shows the data used in the illustration, including units produced and sold and costs for two periods. Panel 2 shows both the full and variable costing income statements for the first of two periods. Two periods are used to show the differences for both possible cases, increasing or decreasing inventory. In the first period, inventory increases; in the second period, it decreases. Exhibit 18.10B shows the comparison of the two income statements for period 2.

In period 1, inventory increases by 40 units because production of 100 units exceeds sales of 60 units. Inventory decreases by the same amount in period 2. Using full costing, the unit product cost is $30 variable plus $40 fixed, or $70 per unit in both periods. The $70 unit cost is used to calculate the cost of goods sold on the income statements in periods 1 and 2 for full costing. The selling and administrative costs ($5 variable and $1,200 fixed) are deducted after gross margin to determine the income of $300 in period 1 and $2,300 in period 2.

The variable costing income statement uses only variable costs to determine product cost. The cost of sales and inventory figures are determined using variable manufacturing costs of

EXHIBIT 18.10B

Comparison of Full and Variable Costing—Period 2

Difference in beginning inventory = $2,800 − $1,200 = $1,600

Period 2 Income Statement		Full Costing	Variable Costing
Sales (140 × $100)		$14,000	$14,000
Less: Cost of goods sold			
Beginning inventory ($1,600 difference)	$2,800		$ 1,200
+ Cost of goods produced (for 100 units, same as period 1)	7,000		3,000
= Cost of goods available for sale	9,800		4,200
− Ending inventory	0		0
= Cost of goods sold		9,800	4,200
Less: Variable selling and administrative		N/A	700
Gross margin		**$ 4,200**	
Contribution margin			**$ 9,100**
Less: Fixed manufacturing costs	N/A		$ 4,000
Less: Selling and administrative costs			
Variable	$ 700		N/A
Fixed	1,200		$ 1,200
Total other costs		1,900	5,200
Operating income ($1,600 difference)		$ 2,300	$ 3,900
Recap			
Difference in beginning inventory = $2,800 − $1,200 = $1,600			
Difference in operating income = $3,900 − $2,300 = $1,600			

Difference in operating income = $2,300 − $3,900 = $1,600

N/A = not applicable.

$30 per unit. To calculate the total contribution margin, the variable selling and administrative costs of $5 per unit sold are deducted along with the $30 variable manufacturing costs per unit. The result is a total contribution margin of $3,900 in period 1 and $9,100 in period 2. In variable costing, all fixed costs (both manufacturing fixed costs of $4,000, and selling and administration fixed costs of $1,200) are deducted from the contribution margin, to get a $1,300 loss in period 1 and $3,900 income in period 2.

The difference in operating income in period 1 for full and variable costing is $1,600 ($300 income compared to a $1,300 loss), which is exactly the amount of fixed cost included in the increase in inventory under full costing ($1,600 = increase of 40 units × $40 per unit fixed cost). Note that the amount of ending inventory in period 1 differs by $1,600 ($2,800 for full costing versus $1,200 for variable costing). This amount is also the difference in operating income for variable and full costing for both periods 1 and 2, when period 2 inventory decreases by 40 units. Note the shaded areas in Exhibit 18.10 (A and B), which show the difference of $1,600 in operating income for each period is due to the difference in the value of inventory (ending inventory for period 1 and beginning inventory for period 2 because the two periods combined start and end with no inventory). Therefore, a useful guide is that *full costing income exceeds variable costing income (by the amount of fixed cost in the inventory change) when inventory (in units) increases, and variable costing income exceeds full costing income when inventory (in units) decreases.* Given this guide, the following rule can be used to calculate the operating income difference between the two costing approaches:

Difference in income = Change in inventory × Fixed manufacturing cost per unit

The critical point is that variable costing is not affected by changes in inventory because all fixed costs (both manufacturing and nonmanufacturing) are deducted from income in the period in which they occur; fixed manufacturing costs are not included in inventory so inventory changes do not affect operating income. For this reason, variable costing operating income can be considered a more reliable measure and is preferable for use in strategic performance measurement. When full costing is used (as required for financial reporting), operating income may be inflated by overproduction of inventory, which effectively shifts current-period fixed costs onto the next period's income statement (when those overproduced items are actually sold). Thus, the management accountant must use special caution in interpreting the amount of full costing operating income and attempt to determine what portion, if any, might be due to inventory changes. This is especially important if operating income is used as a basis for performance evaluation as it is in profit centers (because the profit center manager has an incentive to overproduce, which may boost short-term operating profit, and even stock price, but can harm the firm's long-term profitability and cash flows). A survey of senior financial executives showed that a majority (76%) use full costing for both financial reporting and internal purposes such as performance evaluation and decision making; the remaining 24% use variable costing for internal purposes.

Strategic Performance Measurement and the Balanced Scorecard

LO 18-5

Explain the role of the balanced scorecard in strategic performance measurement.

> "The sacred obligation of senior leadership: Vision: What will it be? Goals: What four or five things must we do to get there? Alignment: Translate the work of each person into an alignment with the goals."
>
> *Soichiro Honda, founder of Honda Motor Company*

Cost, revenue, and profit centers are widely used methods to facilitate strategic performance measurement. A common characteristic of these SBUs in practice is that they use little or no nonfinancial information. However, a complete strategic performance evaluation necessarily attends to all critical success factors of the business, including nonfinancial factors. A useful approach for a complete strategic performance evaluation is to include both financial and nonfinancial measures for the SBU using the balanced scorecard. The balanced scorecard measures the SBU's performance in four key areas (called perspectives): (1) financial performance, (2) customer satisfaction, (3) internal processes, and (4) learning and innovation. Cost, revenue, and profit centers tend to focus on the financial dimension. The main concept of the balanced scorecard is that no single measure can properly evaluate the SBU's progress to strategic success. Rather, multiple measures typically grouped in the four key perspectives provide a more comprehensive evaluation of the SBU's performance. Moreover, by attending directly to the firm's critical success factors, the balanced scorecard effectively aligns the performance measurement/evaluation process with the firm's strategy.

Implementing the Balanced Scorecard and the Strategy Map for Performance Evaluation

There are several important considerations for effectively implementing the balanced scorecard (BSC) and strategy map for performance evaluation (you can refer to Chapter 2 for more information about understanding and building BSCs and strategy maps):

- The BSC and strategy map are more likely to be used in an evaluation of performance over time rather than for performance of an SBU relative to other SBUs. The reason is that the scorecard measures for one unit may not be appropriate for another SBU, and therefore, it is difficult to compare them.
- Many studies have shown that the BSC is widely used for strategic planning, and also for performance evaluation, but less often in management compensation. To effectively tie performance to strategic objectives, the BSC should also be used in determining management compensation.
- Successful implementation of a BSC requires validation of the links among measures that are assumed to improve performance throughout the scorecard. Without validation, the company cannot be sure that attention to the measures will produce the desired results. Validation involves using a statistical model to test the effects of the measures on performance.

In an article about strategy evaluation, Emett and Tayler discuss research suggesting that managers may be subject to a self-selection bias when evaluating strategies that they have selected themselves. These managers can use cherry-picked data to draw conclusions that masquerade as data-driven decisions. The authors recommend the use of the balanced scorecard to constrain the bias that may exist in these evaluations. Why might this be effective? The belief is that having managers select the strategy as well as the scorecard measures will cause management biases to work against themselves—that is, the selection of good scorecard measures will, by their very nature, provide a more unbiased evaluation of strategic initiatives. This comes from the fact that managers have to think about the balanced scorecard as a causal chain. The authors

present Domino's Pizza as an example. In 2009, executives at Domino's implemented a strategy to include higher-quality ingredients in their pizzas while rebranding the company as a low-cost, high-quality restaurant. The company then tracked customer loyalty to gauge the success of the initiative. Within two years, Domino's was ranked in the top 100 for customer loyalty, the only pizza chain to make the list. While customer loyalty is nice, it does not necessarily mean additional profits, but as it turns out, Domino's saw improvements not only in its customer loyalty scores, but also in its sales and profitability scores. It was obvious, therefore, that the initiative was a measurable success.

Source: Scott Emett and William Tayler, "Is Your Strategy Evaluation Biased?," *Strategic Finance,* November 2013, pp. 27–34.

- Managers must be informed about the strategic linkages in the scorecard. One study has shown that those evaluating the performance of a business relied more on the strategically linked measures than other measures when they were provided information on the strategically relevant measures. In contrast, the nonstrategically linked measures were most commonly used when the strategic linkage information was not provided.[5]
- Many large firms have installed extensive computer systems called *enterprise resource planning (ERP)* systems. They provide an information system base that stores the detailed information for the balanced scorecard. Firms without an ERP system might have difficulty developing and maintaining the data needed for the scorecard.
- In contrast to financial data that are subject to financial audit and control systems, much of the nonfinancial information used in the scorecard is not subject to control or audit. Thus, the reliability and accuracy of some of the nonfinancial data could be questionable.
- Performance reviews of managers tend to occur at regular intervals—usually every quarter or every year—which fits well with the typical firm's quarterly and annual preparation of financial statements. In contrast, nonfinancial information is often prepared on a weekly or daily basis for effective use in operations and decision making. This variance in preparation cycles can complicate the nature and timing of reviews.
- Typically, all financial data used by cost or profit SBUs are developed internally, using well-developed information systems. In contrast, some of the most valuable nonfinancial information, such as customer surveys, are developed outside the firm, which creates additional issues regarding the timeliness and reliability of this nonfinancial information.

Implementing Strategy Using the Balanced Scorecard

While many organizations thrive using the BSC, others do not. Research conducted on BSC companies has found that many implementations fail for the following reasons:

- Not linking nonfinancial measures to strategy.
- Linking performance measures to desired outcomes without validating the supporting assumptions.
- Setting the wrong performance targets.
- Measuring results incorrectly.

[5] Rajiv D. Banker, Hsihui Chang, and Mina J. Pizzini, "The Balanced Scorecard: Judgmental Effects of Performance Measures Linked to Strategy," *The Accounting Review,* January 2004, pp. 1–23.

To address the need for more effective implementation of nonfinancial measures, researchers suggest the following six steps:[6]

1. **Develop a predictive model.** Think carefully about the predicted links between measures of performance and desired outcomes.
2. **Gather data.** Maximize the available inputs by pulling from all the different information systems employed by the firm.
3. **Turn the data into information.** Use regression analysis and other statistical methods to test the validity of the model developed in step 1.
4. **Continually refine the model.** Monitor internal and external events and rebuild the model on a timely basis, as needed.
5. **Base actions on findings.** Have the confidence in the model to follow where it leads.
6. **Assess outcomes.** Continuously assess the effectiveness of the model and the actions taken in step 5 to produce the desired outcomes. Does the model work?

Management Control in Service Firms and Not-for-Profit Organizations

Management control in service firms and not-for-profit organizations is commonly implemented in the form of a cost center or a profit center. Similar to manufacturing and retail firms, these organizations choose a cost center when the manager's critical mission is to control costs; a profit center is preferred when the department manager must manage both costs and revenues or, alternatively (in a not-for-profit organization), manage revenues without exceeding budgeted costs.

The most common type of SBU in service firms and not-for-profit organizations is the cost center. For example, the performance of a bank's consumer loan department often is monitored as a cost center, as illustrated in Exhibit 18.11. Note that the structure of the performance report is much like that of the profit center analysis in Exhibit 18.9. The difference is that the focus in Exhibit 18.11 is on costs, which are separated into variable costs such as labor and supplies, controllable fixed costs such as supervision salaries, and noncontrollable fixed costs such as data processing and facilities management. In addition, Exhibit 18.11 includes information regarding certain operating measures critical to the department's success: the number of new accounts, the number of closed accounts, the number of transactions processed, and

EXHIBIT 18.11
Performance Report for the Consumer Loan Department

Variable costs	
Direct labor	$23,446
Supplies	3,836
Controllable fixed costs	
Supervision salaries	15,339
Advertising	6,500
Fees and services	4,226
Other	766
Noncontrollable fixed costs	
Facilities	650
Data processing	2,200
Other	899
Total costs	$57,862
Operating performance	
Number of accounts at end of month	1,334
Number of new accounts	54
Number of closed accounts	22
Number of transactions processed	1,994
Number of inquiries processed	334

[6] Christopher D. Ittner and David F. Larcker, "Coming Up Short on Nonfinancial Performance Measurement," *Harvard Business Review* 81, no. 11 (November 2003), pp. 88–95.

the number of inquiries handled. This information is used to evaluate the department's performance over time and perhaps to compare its performance to that of related departments such as the mortgage loan department. Note that the report does not include the cost of funds provided for the loans because it is assumed that the department manager cannot control either the supply or the cost of those funds.

Summary

One of the principal purposes of management control systems is to facilitate strategic performance measurement. The goal of top management in using strategic performance measurement is to motivate managers to provide a high level of effort, to guide them to make decisions that are congruent with the goals of top management, and to provide a basis for determining fair compensation.

A large number of management control systems are used in practice, including both formal and informal systems and individual or team-based systems. The chapter focuses on one type of formal control system at the individual level: the strategic performance measurement system.

Strategic performance measurement systems are implemented in four different forms, depending on the nature of the SBU manager's responsibilities: revenue center, cost center, profit center, and investment center. Revenue, cost, and profit centers are covered in this chapter, and investment centers are covered in Chapter 19.

The four types of SBUs are employed in manufacturing firms as well as service firms and not-for-profit and governmental organizations. Typical cost centers in manufacturing firms are production and production-support departments. Cost centers often are evaluated as either engineered-cost centers or discretionary-cost centers. Discretionary-cost centers focus on planning desired cost levels; engineered-cost centers focus on evaluation of achieved cost levels.

The marketing and sales departments may be evaluated as revenue centers or cost centers. As revenue centers, these departments focus on sales growth; as cost centers, they focus on managing order-getting and order-filling costs.

The profit center is used when the manager is responsible for both costs and revenues and when coordination between the marketing and production areas is needed—for example, in handling special or rush orders. Evaluation on profit provides incentive for the departments to work together. Profit centers are also used to set a desirable competitive tone. All departments have the profit incentive to compete with other providers of the product or service, inside or outside the firm.

The contribution income statement is an effective method for evaluating profit centers because it identifies each profit center's controllable costs. It has the benefit of not being affected by changes in finished goods inventory. In contrast, income as determined by the conventional income statement based on full costing is affected by inventory changes.

A key issue in the effective use of strategic performance measurement systems is the integration of strategic considerations into the evaluation. This requires an identification of the firm's critical success factors and the appropriate measurement and reporting of these factors, commonly in the form of a balanced scorecard. In many cases, a substantial portion of these factors is nonfinancial, including operating and economic data from sources external to the firm.

Key Terms

contribution by profit center (CPC), *794*
contribution income statement, *794*
controllable fixed costs, *794*
controllable margin, *794*
cost center, *786*
decentralization, *785*
discretionary-cost method, *788*
dual allocation, *791*

employment contract, *781*
engineered-cost method, *788*
full costing, *795*
investment center, *787*
management control, *780*
noncontrollable fixed costs, *794*
operational control, *780*
order-filling costs, *792*
order-getting costs, *792*
performance measurement, *779*

principal–agent model, *781*
profit center, *786*
revenue center, *786*
revenue drivers, *791*
strategic business unit (SBU), *781*
strategic performance measurement, *785*
variable costing, *795*

<table>
<tr><td>

Comments on Cost Management in Action

</td><td>

Subjective Performance Evaluation

Subjectivity offers managers the ability to evaluate their subordinates on *all* dimensions of job performance. This is a powerful benefit in many job settings, where objective measures are either too broad (i.e., they capture many factors other than just the employee's efforts) or too narrow (i.e., they provide information on only a small and specific part of the employee's total duties). Subjectivity can also reduce the risk employees feel about their contracts because factors outside of their control can be accounted for and filtered out so that performance measures provide a more informative signal about their actual efforts.

However, there can be a number of disadvantages and pitfalls when using subjectivity in performance evaluation. These include:

1. **Data gathering costs.** It is time-consuming and often difficult to observe and record employee performance on the subjective dimensions. Failure to gather the necessary information can lead to uninformative and distorted subjective evaluations.

2. **Bias.** Because subjective evaluations rely on judgments, perceptions, and opinions, they can be biased due to the social effects and cognitive limitations associated with human information processing and decision making. Some forms of bias include:

   a. *Centrality.* Managers often group subjective evaluations closely together because of the psychological cost (i.e., discomfort) of distinguishing among subordinates.

   b. *Leniency.* Managers often shift the distribution of subjective evaluations upward because they are uncomfortable giving low ratings. Together, centrality and leniency result in evaluation distributions that are narrow and shifted toward the top of the range; for example, most evaluations on a rating scale from 1 to 5 tend to fall in the range of 3 to 5.

   c. *Favoritism.* Managers may use subjectivity as a way to reward favored employees in ways that do not reflect actual performance. In addition to uninformative ratings, favoritism also gives rise to "influence activities" in which employees seek higher evaluations by engaging in behaviors that please the manager but do not add value to the firm.

   d. *Spillover.* Many contracts include both objective and subjective performance measures. Research shows that when managers know the objective performance measures of an employee, their subjective evaluations are biased to be consistent with those objective measures, even when they capture different and unrelated dimensions of performance.

Firms can try to minimize these negative effects through training and oversight. Some firms use "forced rankings," in which evaluators must place a certain percentage of their employees into each rating category (e.g., 1, 2, or 3) as a way to eliminate the tendencies toward centrality and leniency. GE was the first to begin this practice on a wide scale, but it comes with its own dangers. For example, employees who know that they are effectively competing with their colleagues for spaces in rating categories are less likely to help each other succeed, and may even sabotage their colleagues' efforts.

Sources: A. Frederiksen, F. Lange, and B. Kriechel, "Subjective Performance Evaluations and Employee Careers," *Journal of Economic Behavior & Organization,* February 2017, pp. 408–429; J. Bol and S. Smith, "Spillover Effects in Subjective Performance Evaluation: Bias and the Asymmetric Influence of Controllability," *The Accounting Review,* July 2011, pp. 1213–1230; P. Cappelli and A. Travis, "The Performance Management Revolution," *Harvard Business Review,* October 2016, pp. 58–67.

</td></tr>
<tr><td>

Self-Study Problem
(For answers, please see Solution.)

</td><td>

Discretionary-Cost and Engineered-Cost Methods

C. B. (Chuck) Davis is the manager of the claims processing department for Liberty Life Insurance Co. He has 12 clerks working for him to process approximately 900 claims per month. Each clerk earns a monthly salary of $2,400, including benefits. The number of claims varies somewhat, and in recent years, it has been as low as 810 and as high as 1,020 per month. Chuck has argued with Liberty officials that his 12 clerks are not enough to handle 1,000 or more claims; he knows from a recent study of his department that it takes a well-trained clerk an average of 121 minutes to process a claim (processing time also varies widely, from as little as a few minutes to as much as several hours, depending on the claim's complexity). While Liberty management agrees that 12 clerks are not sufficient for a month with 1,000 claims, it notes that most months require that only 800 claims be processed. Management concludes, therefore, that 12 clerks are about right. Assume that each clerk works an 8-hour day except for 40 minutes of break time and that each month has an average of 22 working days. In the most recent month, January, the department processed 915 claims.

Required

1. What type of SBU does Liberty management appear to use for the claims processing department?

2. Assuming that Liberty uses the discretionary-cost method to implement cost centers, what is the budgeted cost in the claims department for January?

</td></tr>
</table>

3. Assuming that Liberty uses the engineered-cost method to implement cost centers, what is the budgeted cost in the claims department for January?

4. If you were Chuck Davis, what would you use as a more effective argument to top management in requesting additional clerks?

The Student Resources section of Connect includes video tutorials for the Self-Study Problems.

Questions

18-1 What are the differences among performance evaluation, management control, and operational control?

18-2 What is strategic performance measurement, and why is it important for effective management?

18-3 Does an effective performance evaluation focus on individual or team performance?

18-4 Explain the difference between informal and formal control systems. What type of control system is strategic performance measurement?

18-5 Name two types of organizational design and explain how they differ.

18-6 What are four types of SBUs, and what are the goals of each?

18-7 Because full costing is accepted for financial reporting purposes and variable costing is not, why should we be concerned about the difference between them? What is the difference, and why is it important?

18-8 What are some important behavioral and implementation issues in strategic performance measurement? How does the management accountant deal with these issues?

18-9 What is the role of cost allocation in strategic performance measurement?

18-10 Can strategic performance measurement be used for service firms and not-for-profit organizations? How?

18-11 In what situations is a cost center most appropriate? A profit center? A revenue center?

18-12 How do centralized and decentralized firms differ? What are the advantages of each?

18-13 Can the marketing department be both a revenue center and a cost center? Explain.

18-14 Which type of cost center has a planning focus, and which type has an evaluation focus?

18-15 What is the role of risk preference in performance evaluation?

18-16 Explain the difference between the engineered-cost and discretionary-cost approaches to evaluating support departments.

Brief Exercises

[LO 18-3] 18-17 An internationally known food processing company has acquired a mineral mining company. The decision to acquire the mining company is considered strategic based on the anticipated growing demand for the minerals used to create the packages for the company's products. The mining operation continues to be run by its local management group, which makes all its own investment decisions, independent of the management of the food processing company.

The mining company described above is most likely what type of strategic business unit (SBU)?

a. Cost center

b. Revenue center

c. Profit center

d. Investment center

[LO 18-3] 18-18 Colleen Stevens is the North Carolina senior account manager for a national medical equipment manufacturer. Colleen has overall responsibility for the Southeast sales division. The division employs approximately eight sales representatives. Colleen's representatives sell equipment, but equipment maintenance is provided by the maintenance division, which is coordinated through the national headquarters.

Colleen is most likely in charge of which type of strategic business unit (SBU)?

a. Cost center

b. Revenue center

c. Profit center

d. Investment center

[LO 18-4] 18-19 Pepper's Automotive produces auto parts for various automotive retailers. Pepper's is evaluating the exhaust system division of the company and has come up with the following data for the year: net revenues are $1,000,000, variable costs are $300,000, and fixed costs are $400,000. Of the fixed costs, controllable fixed costs are $100,000 and noncontrollable fixed costs are $300,000.

Required
1. What is the controllable margin?
2. What is the total contribution by profit center (CPC)?

[LO 18-4]   18-20   Pepper's Automotive (see Brief Exercise 18-19) has further analyzed the exhaust system division into three products: exhaust pipes, intake valves, and intake pipes. The income statement is available below.

	Exhaust Pipes	Intake Valves	Intake Pipes
Net revenues	$500,000	$300,000	$200,000
Variable costs	50,000	150,000	100,000
Contribution margin	450,000	150,000	100,000
Controllable fixed costs	50,000	50,000	0
Controllable margin	400,000	100,000	100,000
Noncontrollable fixed costs	100,000	150,000	50,000
Contribution by profit center	$300,000	$ (50,000)	$ 50,000

Required
1. What would be the change in profit *in the short run* if the company dropped intake valves from its product line?
2. What would be the change in profit *in the long run* if the company dropped intake valves from its product line?

[LO 18-4]   18-21   Calabria Healthcare supplies prescription drugs to pharmacies. As the management accountant, you are required to analyze the financial statements for this quarter. You already have analyzed the company's two divisions, Name Brand and Generic, and your supervisor wants an analysis of the comparable profitability of the SBUs. The contribution margins are $500,000 and $200,000, respectively; the controllable fixed costs are $200,000 and $50,000; and the noncontrollable fixed costs are $50,000 and $100,000. Assume there are no nontraceable fixed costs.

Required
1. What is the total contribution by profit center (CPC) for the Name Brand division?
2. What is the total CPC for the Generic division?

[LO 18-4]   18-22   Phelps Glass Inc. has reported the following financial data: net revenues of $10 million, variable costs of $5 million, controllable fixed costs of $2 million, noncontrollable fixed costs of $1 million, and nontraceable costs of $500,000.

Required
1. What is the controllable margin?
2. What is the contribution by profit center (CPC)?
3. What is operating income?

[LO 18-4]   18-23   Manuel Inc. produces textiles in many different forms. After recording lower-than-anticipated profits last year, Manuel has decided to shut down one of its divisions that is not performing well. The accounting manager has compiled the following data on the two divisions being considered for closing and has asked you to evaluate the short-term and long-term effects on profits of closing each division.

	Winter Outerwear	High-End Suits
Net revenues	$1,000,000	$5,000,000
Variable costs	500,000	2,000,000
Contribution margin	500,000	3,000,000
Controllable fixed costs	0	2,000,000
Controllable margin	500,000	1,000,000
Noncontrollable fixed costs	750,000	1,500,000
Contribution by profit center	$ (250,000)	$ (500,000)

Which division should be closed if Manuel is most concerned with increasing long-run profits?

a. Winter Outerwear

b. High-End Suits

c. Closing either division would have the same impact on long-term profits.

[LO 18-4]   18-24   Meargia Plastics is evaluating its plastic bottles division. The accounting manager has come up with the following data for the year: contribution margin of $500,000, controllable fixed costs of $200,000, and noncontrollable fixed costs of $50,000.

Required

1. What is the controllable margin?

2. What is the total contribution by profit center (CPC)?

Exercises

[LO 18-1]   18-25   **Risk Aversion and Decision Making; Strategy**   John Smith is the production manager of Elmo's Glue Company. Because of limited capacity, the company can produce only one of two possible products. The two products are:

a. A space-age bonding formula that has a 15% probability of making a profit of $1,000,000 for the company and an 85% chance of generating $200,000 in profit.

b. A reformulated household glue that has a 100% chance of making a profit of $310,000.

John gets a bonus of 20% of the profit from his department. John has the responsibility to choose between the two products. Assume John is more risk-averse than the top management of Elmo's Glue Company.

Required

1. Compute the expected profit of the space-age bonding formula.

2. Which product is John most likely to choose? Is that the product Elmo's would prefer? Why or why not?

3. How could Elmo's change its reward system to increase the likelihood that John will make decisions that are consistent with top management's wishes?

[LO 18-1]   18-26   **Risk Aversion; Strategy**   John Holt is the production supervisor for ITEXX, a manufacturer of plastic parts with customers in the automobile and consumer products industries. On a Tuesday morning, one of ITEXX's sales managers asks John to reschedule his manufacturing jobs for the rest of the week to accommodate a special order from a new customer. The catch is that getting the customer requires fast turnaround on the order and means not only delaying the current production schedule, but also running the production equipment all three shifts for the remainder of the week. This will make it impossible to complete the regularly scheduled maintenance on the equipment that John has planned for midweek. The sales manager is keen on getting the new customer, which could mean an important increase in overall sales and output at the plant. However, John is worried not only about the delay of the current jobs, but the chance that the delay in maintenance will cause one of the machines to fail, which would back up the orders in the plant for at least a week, meaning a substantial delay for the new order as well as those currently scheduled.

Required   Explain how you think John should resolve this problem. What would be a good policy for handling issues like this in the future?

[LO 18-1]   18-27   **Research and Development: Risk Aversion and Performance Measurement; Strategy**   When the economic outlook becomes uncertain, some managers look to cut costs in research and development to provide a short-term boost to profits. The problem with this strategy is that it reduces the opportunities for new products and product improvements in the coming years, which are necessary for the long-term competitiveness of the firm. As Intel chair Craig Barrett says, "You cut off your future if you do not invest."

Required

1. What role does risk aversion play in determining the amount to invest in research and development on an ongoing basis? How might a firm manage risk aversion so as to continue the desired level of spending on research and development?

2. What type of strategic business unit would you choose to evaluate the performance of the research and development department? Explain your choice briefly.

[LO 18-2]   18-28   **Leadership Development**   Training courses and other forms of professional development are commonly used by organizations to improve managers' effectiveness in leading teams, providing the desired motivation to their employees, and leading their SBUs to success. Often these training efforts are designed to develop effective leadership behaviors. For example, a study conducted within Google identified the following eight behaviors of effective managers:

- Be a good coach.
- Empower your team and do not micromanage.
- Express interest in team members' success and personal well-being.
- Be productive and results-oriented.
- Be a good communicator and listen to your team.
- Help your employees with career development.
- Have a clear strategy for the team.
- Develop and maintain key technical skills needed by all team members.

Required For each of the eight desired behaviors, develop one or two examples of that behavior. For example, providing constructive feedback is a behavior that a good coach would employ.

[LO 18-3] **18-29 Departmental Cost Allocation in Profit Centers** Elvis Wilbur owns two restaurants, the Beef Barn and the Fish Bowl. Each restaurant is treated as a profit center for performance evaluation. Although the restaurants have separate kitchens, they share a central baking facility. The principal costs of the baking area include depreciation and maintenance on the equipment, materials, supplies, and labor.

Required
1. Elvis allocates the monthly costs of the baking facility to the two restaurants based on the number of tables served in each restaurant during the month. In April the costs were $24,000, of which $12,000 is fixed cost. The Beef Barn and the Fish Bowl each served 3,000 tables.
   a. How much of the joint cost should be allocated to the Beef Barn?
   b. How much of the joint cost should be allocated to the Fish Bowl?
2. In May, total fixed and unit variable costs remained the same, but the Beef Barn served 2,000 tables and the Fish Bowl served 3,000.
   a. How much should be allocated to the Beef Barn?
   b. How much should be allocated to the Fish Bowl?
3. Assume Elvis decides to use a dual allocation approach in which variable costs are traced directly to the user (based on tables served) and fixed costs are allocated evenly (because, on average, the two restaurants have equal activity levels). Assume the same table service outcomes as in requirement 2.
   a. How much should be allocated to the Beef Barn?
   b. How much should be allocated to the Fish Bowl?
4. Why would the managers of the Beef Barn and the Fish Bowl be upset about the cost allocations in requirement 2? Explain why the allocation method in requirement 3 is fairer and more motivating.

[LO 18-3] **18-30 Allocation of Marketing and Administrative Costs; Profit Centers** Chilton Day School allocates marketing and administrative costs to its three schools on the basis of each school's annual tuition revenue (as a percentage of the total). Last year the allocations (000s omitted) were as follows:

	Preschool	Middle School	High School	Total
Tuition revenue	$1,500	$1,800	$2,200	$5,500
Marketing and administration	275	325	400	1,000

In the current year, the middle and high schools experienced no change in revenues, but the preschool's tuition revenue increased to $1.9 million. Marketing and administrative costs rose to $1,250,000.

Required
1. Using revenue as an allocation base, how much current year cost will be allocated (rounded to the nearest dollar) to the:
   a. Preschool?
   b. Middle School?
   c. High School?
2. What are the shortcomings of this allocation method?

[LO 18-3]   18-31 **Allocation of Administrative Costs; Ethics**   Wical Rental Management Services manages four apartment buildings, each with a different owner. Wical's CEO has observed that the apartment buildings with more expensive rental rates tend to require more of her time and also the time of her staff. The four apartment buildings incur a total annual operating expense of $7,345,733, and these operating expenses are traced directly to the apartment buildings for the purpose of determining the profit earned by the building owners. The annual management fee that Wical earns is based on a percentage of total annual operating expenses and is negotiated each year. For the current year, the fee rate is 6%, and Wical has the following information for current-year average rental rates and occupancy rates:

Apartment Complex	Number of Units	Average Occupancy	Average Rent
Cape Point	100	88.0%	$1,895
Whispering Woods	250	77.0	1,295
Hanging Rock	200	72.0	995
College Manor	350	82.0	895
Total	900		

For the current year, Wical must choose between the number of units in each complex, the average occupancy, or the total annual rental revenue in each complex to allocate the management fee.

Required
1. How much of the management fee would be charged to Cape Point under each of the three allocation bases? (Round your final answers to the nearest dollar)
    a. Number of units
    b. Average occupancy
    c. Total annual rental revenue
2. Explain which allocation base you would choose and why. What ethical issues, if any, are involved in the choice of allocation base?

[LO 18-3]   18-32 **Responsibility for Inefficiency; Ethics**   General Hospital leases its diagnostic equipment from Normed Leasing, which is also responsible for maintaining the equipment. Recently, the hospital's MRI machine needed repair and physicians were required to order expensive nonemergency laboratory tests for their patients to diagnose conditions that could have been diagnosed more easily (and less expensively) using the MRI machine. Rather than bill its patients for the entire cost of these tests, the hospital billed the patients for the cost of an MRI and billed the difference to Normed. Normed disputes the charge, claiming that the physicians should have postponed diagnosis of the patients' conditions until the MRI machine could be repaired.

Required   What issues should be addressed to determine how the charge should be handled properly? How can this situation be prevented? If appropriate, include ethical issues in your response.

[LO 18-3]   18-33 **Assigning Responsibility**   Kristen Langdon, the sales manager at a large bicycle manufacturer, has secured an order from a major department store that is due to ship on November 1. She is eager to please the department store in the hope of getting more future business. She asks Bryan Collins, the company's purchasing agent, to procure all necessary parts in time for production to begin on October 10. Bryan orders from reputable suppliers, and most of the parts arrive by October 7. George Watkins, the production manager, begins production as scheduled on October 10, although the gears that Bryan ordered were delayed because of quality control problems at the manufacturer. Bryan assures George that the gear shipment will arrive before October 16, when those parts are scheduled to be attached to the bicycles. The shipment finally arrives on October 18 after production has been delayed for 2 days.

Required   Which department should bear the responsibility for the 2 days' downtime? How can similar problems be avoided in the future?

[LO 18-3]   18-34 **Outsourcing; Choice of Strategic Business Unit (SBU)**   The management of office printing, duplicating, filing, and overall document storage is one of the most significant overhead costs in many companies, especially companies with large and complex product lines and/or a diverse customer base, such as the large consumer products company, Procter & Gamble (P&G). Increasingly, companies like P&G are outsourcing their overall document management activity to service providers such as Xerox, Hewlett-Packard (HP), or Canon. Xerox and HP provide the equipment, materials, and labor for the activity in what is often called "managed print services" (MPS). MPS has reduced P&G's costs significantly and also provides P&G an opportunity to better focus its efforts on strategic marketing and operational matters.

Required

1. What type of SBU was probably used by P&G to manage print services prior to outsourcing? What type of responsibility accounting is probably being used by P&G now, after outsourcing? Explain briefly.

2. How would the decision to outsource print services affect the sustainability objectives of a firm such as Procter & Gamble?

[LO 18-3]   **18-35   Outsourcing; Strategy**   Some years ago, Walmart's Sam's Club outsourced 10,000 jobs (about 9% of its workforce) to independent marketing firms. The marketing firms provide in-store product demonstrations. Most of the 10,000 jobs were part-time jobs. Industry analysts suggested the change was a smart move because it allowed Sam's Club to focus on other key strategic issues and to eliminate a significant portion of the high costs associated with training, hiring, and managing a part-time workforce.

Required

1. What type of strategy do you think Sam's Club follows, cost leadership or differentiation, and why?

2. Do you think Sam's Club's decision to outsource the product demonstration activity is consistent with the firm's strategy? Explain briefly.

[LO 18-3]   **18-36   Cost Allocation; Sharing Cab Fare**   Suppose there are three passengers sharing a single cab ride and that passenger A's usual fare to his destination would be $12, passenger B's usual fare to her destination would be $18, and passenger C's fare would be $30. Because they are sharing the cab, and assuming no surcharge, the total cab fare is $30, rather than the $60 they would have had to pay in total individually. So there is a $30 saving to sharing the cab.

Required

1. Assume the passengers decide to split the $30 savings based on the relative proportion of how much each passenger would have paid individually if they had not shared the cab. How much will each passenger pay?

2. Assume, instead, that the passengers decide to split the cab fare so that each passenger saves the same absolute amount of money. How much will each passenger pay?

3. Explain how you would split the total cost of the cab fare and why. Are there other ways that could be sensible and/or fair?

[LO 18-3, 18-5]   **18-37   Intangibles; Validating the Balanced Scorecard**   Intangibles such as customer relationships can account for a massive amount of the total assets of firms in the United States, though such assets are not recorded on firms' balance sheets under current U.S. accounting standards. The importance of nonfinancial measures is one of the motivations for the increased use of the balanced scorecard, which includes a perspective on customer relationships. However, according to research, data on intangibles such as customer satisfaction can improve forecasts of earnings only when the data are analyzed in conjunction with financial statistics and tied to corporate strategy. This result is based on a wide range of customer relationship data (e.g., customer satisfaction, employee turnover, the speed of loan processing, and the average number of products and services purchased) from 115 retail banks and represents potentially useful guidance for managers wanting to know how to use nonfinancial measures effectively.

Required   Comment on the implications of the research for the use of the balanced scorecard relative to profit centers. We have noted in the text that it is important to validate the balanced scorecard. What does it mean to validate the scorecard in the context of the retail bank example above?

[LO 18-3]   **18-38   Managing the Research and Development Department**   Effective use of research and development (R&D) is an important part of any firm's competitive strategy. Some firms take an "incrementalist" approach to R&D, continually striving to add value to their products and services. Other firms take a quite different approach by looking only for "breakthrough" results from R&D. The breakthrough results are those that fundamentally change the nature of the products, the services, and the competition in the industry. An example of a breakthrough result is General Electric's digital X-ray technology, first sold in 1996, which uses digital imaging to replace the conventional film-based technology. Other examples include Apple's iPhone and Toyota's hybrid vehicles.

Many firms employ both strategies: One R&D department uses the incrementalist approach that focuses on continually improving existing products, and another R&D department uses the breakthrough approach that develops fundamental changes. The incrementalist R&D projects help to keep the current product lines competitive while the breakthrough projects hold the promise of a successful future.

Required   Describe what type of SBU you would recommend for each of the two types of R&D departments and explain why.

[LO 18-3]   18-39   **Financial Reporting and SBU Performance**   Samentech Inc. operates in the highly competitive agribusiness industry. Recently, rising fuel costs have added a significant financial burden to day-to-day operations, and top management has become increasingly concerned about the financial performance of several of its business units. Business unit performance and the performance of the unit managers is evaluated using the financial information in the "Segment Reporting" section of Samentech's annual report. Samentech uses this approach to evaluation because it knows that the information is audited and therefore accurate.

Some key executives have noticed that many business unit leaders seem unwilling to cooperate and coordinate with other business units; difficulties have arisen, for example, in convincing unit managers to share certain services when the result would be to reduce total costs to the company. A recent example is the failure of the unit managers to agree to share the services of an insurance firm that offered lower rates if all units used the same insurance policy; some unit managers wanted to maintain individual insurance coverage for their units so that they had maximum flexibility in choosing the terms of the coverage.

Moreover, the financial performance of many units and for Samentech overall has been behind industry averages, and the firm's stock price has been declining as well. These issues were largely ignored in recent years because there were "more important issues" at hand. But the pace of decline in stock price has alarmed Frank Ramirez, the CFO of Samentech Inc., who believes that the lackluster performance of many of the business units may be due to inadequacies in the company's performance measurement system.

Required   Mr. Ramirez asks you to help him prepare a report for top management in which you:
1. Explain why Samentech should or should not use information from the company's annual financial report to evaluate leaders of business units.
2. Provide a proposed new evaluation plan for business unit leaders.
3. Explain the long-term benefits Samentech could gain if it adopts a more effective evaluation strategy for its business unit leaders.

[LO 18-3]   18-40   **Financial Incentives and Auto Repair/Inspections Companies**   Some states in the United States are encountering increased pressure from citizen groups and other organizations to increase efforts to reduce carbon emissions. One of the key producers of carbon emissions is the automobile, so some states have become more strict in implementing auto inspection procedures that include compliance with emissions standards. The goal is to reduce emissions overall in the vehicles operating in the state. Some environmental groups that support the emissions tests have suggested that the financial incentive for those inspecting vehicles is to be strict with the testing because any failed tests would require some repair that could then be performed by the inspector. However, research shows the unexpected—the Environmental Protection Agency (EPA) estimates that approximately 50% of inspections for which the vehicle fails to comply with state-level emission standards are allowed to pass the inspection without the repair needed for compliance. In most states, vehicle inspections are performed by auto mechanics, auto dealers, and other companies that repair autos.

Required   Develop a brief explanation of the finding that many inspections are not in compliance with state standards. What incentives are necessary to improve the rate of compliance? Are there ethical issues you identified in developing your answer? Are there sustainability issues you identified in developing your answer?

[LO 18-3]   18-41   **Allocation of Central Costs; Profit Centers**   Woodland Hotels Inc. operates four resorts in the heavily wooded areas of northern California. The resorts are named after the predominant trees at the resort: Pine Valley, Oak Glen, Mimosa, and Birch Glen. Woodland allocates its central office costs to each of the four resorts according to the annual revenue the resort generates. For the current year, the central office costs (000s omitted) were as follows:

Front office personnel (desk, clerks, etc.)	$ 8,000
Administrative and executive salaries	4,000
Interest on resort purchase	3,000
Advertising	600
Housekeeping	2,000
Depreciation on reservations computer	80
Room maintenance	800
Carpet-cleaning contract	50
Contract to repaint rooms	400
Total	$18,930

	Pine Valley	Oak Glen	Mimosa	Birch Glen	Total
Revenue (000s)	$ 5,350	$ 7,995	$8,857	$ 6,550	$ 28,752
Square feet	55,475	76,599	41,774	83,664	257,512
Rooms	86	122	66	174	448
Assets (000s)	$92,345	$136,745	$72,355	$57,499	$358,944

Required (Round calculations to the nearest dollar)

1. Based on annual revenue, what amount of the central office costs are allocated to each resort? What are the shortcomings of this allocation method?

2. Suppose that the current methods were replaced with a system of four separate cost pools with costs collected in the four pools allocated on the basis of revenues, assets invested in each resort, square footage, and number of rooms, respectively. Which costs should be collected in each of the four pools?

3. Using the cost pool system in requirement 2, how much of the central office costs would be allocated to each resort? Is this system preferable to the single-allocation base system used in requirement 1? Why or why not?

[LO 18-4] **18-42 Product Cost under Full vs. Variable Costing** Kate's Kale Chips produces a healthy snack made primarily of kale. Each bag of the product sells for $5. The company computes the manufacturing overhead rate on a quarterly basis based upon the planned number of units to be produced that quarter. The following data are from the projections of Kate's Kale Chips for the upcoming quarter:

	Projections
Sales	20,000 bags
Production	22,000 bags
Variable manufacturing cost per bag	$2.00
Sales and distribution costs per bag	$0.15
Total fixed manufacturing overhead	$33,000
Fixed administrative overhead	$18,000

Required (Round calculations to the nearest dollar)

1. Compute the projected product cost per bag produced under full costing.
2. Compute the projected product cost per bag under variable costing.

[LO 18-4] **18-43 Full Costing and Variable Costing; Operating Income** Start Me Up, Inc., manufactures a caffeinated energy drink that sells for $4 each. The results for its first year of operations appear in the table below:

Number of drinks produced	52,000
Number of drinks sold	50,000
Direct materials per drink	$0.55
Direct labor per drink	$0.25
Variable manufacturing overhead per drink	$0.15
Total fixed manufacturing overhead	$39,000
Total fixed selling and administrative costs	$50,000

Required
1. Compute the operating income for the first year under full costing.
2. Compute the operating income for the first year under variable costing.

[LO 18-3, 18-4]   18-44 **Profit Centers: Comparison of Variable and Full Costing** Yale Company manufactures hair brushes that sell at wholesale for $3 per unit. The company had no beginning inventory in the prior year. These data summarize the current and prior year operations:

	Prior Year	Current Year
Sales (000s)	1,800 units	2,200 units
Production (000s)	2,000 units	2,000 units
Production cost		
Factory—variable (per unit)	$0.60	$0.60
—fixed (000s)	$1,000	$1,000
Marketing—variable (per unit)	$.40	$.40
Administrative—fixed (000s)	$500	$500

Required (Round calculations to the nearest dollar)
1. Prepare an income statement for each year based on full costing.
2. Prepare an income statement for each year based on variable costing.
3. Prepare a reconciliation and explanation of the difference each year in the operating income resulting from using the full costing method and variable costing method.

[LO 18-3, 18-4]   18-45 **Full vs. Variable Costing** Security Technology Inc. (STI) is a manufacturer of an electronic control system used in the manufacture of certain special-duty auto transmissions used primarily for police and military applications. The part sells for $55 per unit and STI had sales of 24,000 units in the current year, 2021. STI had no inventory on hand at the beginning of 2021 and is projecting sales of 26,000 units in 2022. STI is planning the same production level for 2022 as in 2021, 25,000 units. The variable manufacturing costs for STI are $16, and the variable selling costs are only $.50 per unit. The fixed manufacturing costs are $200,000 per year, and the fixed selling costs are $500 per year.

Required (Round calculations to the nearest dollar)
1. Prepare an income statement for each year using full costing.
2. Prepare an income statement for each year using variable costing.
3. Prepare a reconciliation and explanation of the difference each year in the operating income resulting from the full and variable costing methods.

[LO 18-3, 18-4]   18-46 **Profit Centers: Comparison of Variable and Full Costing (Underapplied Overhead)** Mark Hancock Inc. manufactures a specialized surgical instrument called the HAN-20. The firm has grown rapidly in recent years because of the product's low price and high quality. However, sales have declined this year primarily due to increased competition and a decrease in the surgical procedures for which the HAN-20 is used. The firm is concerned about the decline in sales and has hired a consultant to analyze the firm's profitability. The consultant was provided the following information:

	2021	2022
Sales (units)	3,200	2,800
Production	3,800	2,300
Budgeted production and sales	4,000	3,400
Beginning inventory	800	1,400
Data per unit (all variable)		
Price	$ 2,095	$ 1,995
Direct materials and labor	1,200	1,200
Selling costs	125	125
Fixed costs		
Manufacturing overhead	$700,000	$595,000
Selling and administrative	120,000	120,000

Top management at Hancock explained to the consultant that a difficult business environment for the firm in 2021 and 2022 had caused the firm to reduce its price and production levels and reduce its fixed manufacturing costs in response to the decline in sales. Even with the price reduction, there was a decline in sales in both years. This led to an increase in inventory in 2021, which the firm was able to reduce in 2022 by further reducing the level of production. In both years, Hancock's actual production was less than the budgeted level so that the overhead rate for fixed overhead, calculated from budgeted production levels, was too low, and a production volume variance was calculated to adjust cost of goods sold for the underapplied fixed overhead (the calculation of the production volume variance is explained fully in Chapter 15 and reviewed briefly below).

The production volume variance for 2021 was determined from the fixed overhead rate of $175 per unit ($700,000 ÷ 4,000 budgeted units). Because the actual production level was 200 units short of the budgeted level in 2021 (4,000 − 3,800), the amount of the production volume variance in 2021 was 200 × $175 = $35,000. The production volume variance is underapplied because the actual production level is less than budgeted, and the production volume variance is therefore added back to cost of goods sold to determine the amount of cost of goods sold in the full costing income statement. The full costing income statement for 2021 is shown below:

Sales		$6,704,000
Cost of goods sold:		
Beginning inventory	$1,100,000	
Cost of goods produced	5,225,000	
Cost of goods available for sale	$6,325,000	
Less ending inventory	1,925,000	
Cost of goods sold:		$4,400,000
Plus unfavorable production volume variance		35,000
Adjusted cost of goods sold		$4,435,000
Gross margin		$2,269,000
Less selling and administrative costs		
Variable	$ 400,000	
Fixed	120,000	520,000
Operating income		$1,749,000

Required (Round calculations to the nearest dollar)

1. Using the full costing method, prepare the income statement for 2022.

2. Compute operating income for each period under variable costing, and explain the difference in operating income from that obtained in requirement 1.

3. Write a brief memo to the firm to explain the difference in operating income between variable costing and full costing.

[LO 18-5] 18-47 **Strategy; Balanced Scorecard: Health Care** Consumers, employers, and governments at all levels are very concerned about the rising costs of health care. As a result, health care systems nationwide are experiencing an ongoing demand to improve the efficiency of their operations. The health care industry faces significant challenges due to changing patient needs, reduced reimbursement, and the fierce competitive environment. The industry is experiencing consolidations through systemwide mergers and acquisitions as a way to reduce operating costs. Patients and payors are demanding a one-stop shopping approach. While improving operations is necessary, the quality of the health care delivered must not be jeopardized.

The Medical University of Greenbelt is feeling the impact of the increasing penetration of its market by managed care companies. As a result, management has been asked to develop a strategic plan to ensure that its funding sources will continue to meet the demands of its patients. Because it is an academic medical center, the Medical University of Greenbelt's mission encompasses three components: clinical care, education, and research. Management must consider these competing objectives in the proposed plan.

Required

1. How could the balanced scorecard and strategy map help ensure the success of the Medical University of Greenbelt?

  a. By communicating the university's strategy to managers throughout the company.

b. By articulating the connection from nonfinancial performance (i.e., critical success factors) to financial performance.

c. By helping to develop incentives that are aligned with strategy and value creation.

d. All of the above.

2. Determine three or four critical success factors for each of the four areas within the balanced scorecard.

Note: This information is adapted from Problem 2-46.

[LO 18-5]   18-48 **Strategy; Balanced Scorecard** Fowler's Farm is a 1,000-acre dairy and tobacco farm located in southern Virginia. Jack Fowler, the owner, has been farming since 1982. He initially purchased 235 acres and has made the following purchases since then: 300 acres in 1985, 150 acres in 1988, dairy equipment and buildings worth $350,000 in 1988, and 315 acres in 1998. The cost of farmland has inflated over the years so that, although Jack has a total investment of $1,850,000, the land's current market value is $2,650,000. The current net book value of his buildings and equipment is $300,000, with an estimated replacement cost of $1,250,000. Current price pressures on farm commodities have affected Fowler's Farm as well as others across the country. Jack has watched as many of his neighbors either have quit farming or have been consolidated into larger, more profitable farms.

Fowler's Farm consists of three different operating segments: dairy farming, tobacco, and corn and other crops intended for livestock feed. The dairy farm consists of 198 milk-producing cows that are grazed on 250 acres of farmland. The crop farm consists of the remaining acreage that covers several types of terrain and has several types of soil. Some of the land is high and hilly, some of it is low and claylike, and the rest is humus-rich soil. Jack determines the fertilizer mix for the type of soil and type of crop to be planted by rules of thumb based on his experience.

The farm equipment used consists of automated milking equipment; six tractors; two tandem-axle grain bed trucks; and numerous discs, plows, wagons, and assorted tractor and hand tools. The farm has three equipment storage barns, an equipment maintenance shed, and a 90,000-bushel grain elevator/drier. The equipment and buildings have an estimated market value of $1,500,000.

Jack employs five full-time farmhands, a mechanic, and a bookkeeper and has contracted part-time accounting/tax assistance with a local CPA. All employees are salaried; the farmhands and the bookkeeper make $25,000 a year, and the mechanic makes $32,000 annually. The CPA contract costs $15,000 a year.

In the most recent year, the farm produced 256,000 gallons of raw milk, 23,000 bushels of tobacco, and 75,300 bushels of corn. Jack sells the tobacco by contract and auction at the end of the harvest. The revenue this year was $1,345,000, providing Jack a net income after taxes of $233,500.

Jack's daughter Kelly has just returned from college. She knows that the farm is a good business but believes that the use of proper operating procedures and cost management systems could increase profitability and improve efficiency, allowing her father to have more leisure time. She also knows that her father has always run the farm from his experience and rules of thumb and is wary of scientific concepts and management principles. For example, he has little understanding of the accounting procedures of the farm; has not participated in the process; and has adopted few, if any, methods to maintain control over inventories and equipment. He has trusted his employees to maintain the farm appropriately without using any accounting or operating procedures over inventories or equipment, preventive maintenance schedules, or scientific application of crop rotation or livestock management.

Required   Prepare a balanced scorecard for Fowler's Farm.

Note: This information is adapted from Problem 2-47.

[LO 18-5]   18-49 **Strategy; Balanced Scorecard** Tartan Corporation has been manufacturing high-quality home lighting systems for more than 90 years. The company's first products in the 1920s—the Classic line—were high-quality floor lamps and table lamps made of the highest-quality materials with features that other manufacturers did not attempt: multiple switches, adjustable heights, and stained glass. In the 1950s and 1960s, the company introduced a number of new products that were in demand at the time, including track lighting and lava lamps, which became the company's Modern line. In keeping with its brand image, Tartan ensured that these new products also met the highest standards of quality in the industry. A new customer style emerged in the 1960s and 1970s, which resulted in another new line of products, Contemporary. It was followed in more recent years by two new product lines, Margaret Stewart and Western. Jess Jones, the company's chief financial officer, had become concerned about the performance of some of the product lines in recent years. Although total sales were growing at an acceptable rate, approximately 10% per year, the sales mix was changing significantly, as shown in the following product line sales report. Jess was particularly concerned about the Classic line because of its sharp drop in sales and its high costs. Because of the high level of craftsmanship required for the Classic line, it always had higher-than-average costs for labor and materials. Furthermore, attracting and retaining the highly skilled workers necessary for this product line was becoming more and more difficult. The workers in the Classic line in 2022 were likely to be older and very loyal employees who were paid well because of their skill and seniority. These workers displayed the highest level of workmanship in the company and, some would argue, in the entire industry. Few newer employees seemed eager to learn the skills required in this product line.

Product Line Sales Report

	Classic	Contemporary	Margaret Stewart	Modern	Western
2019	20%	33%	5%	40%	2%
2020	16	35	11	34	4
2021	14	33	14	33	6
2022	9	31	18	31	11

Moreover, manufacturing capacity was experiencing an increasing strain. The sharper-than-expected increase in sales for the Western styles had created a backlog of orders for them, and plant managers had been scrambling to find the plant capacity to meet the demand. Some plant supervisors suggested shutting down the Classic line to make capacity for the Western line. Some managers of the Margaret Stewart line argued the same thing. However, eliminating the Classic line would make obsolete about $233,000 worth of raw materials inventory that is used only in the manufacture of Classic line products.

Tom Richter, the firm's sales manager, acknowledged that sales of the Classic line were more and more difficult to find and that demand for the new styles was increasing. He also noted that the sales of these products reflected significant regional differences. The Western line was popular in the South and the West, and the Contemporary, Modern, and Stewart styles were popular nationally. The Classic line tended to have strong support only in the northeast states. In some sales districts in these states, Classic sales represented a relatively high proportion of total sales.

Kelly Arnold, the firm's CEO, is aware of these concerns and has decided to set up a task force to consider the firm's options and strategy in regard to these problems.

Required   Prepare a balanced scorecard for Tartan Corporation.
Note: This information is adapted from Problem 2-51.

Problems

[LO 18-3, 18-4, 18-5]   18-50   **Profit Center Limitations** Kenneth Merchant and Tatiana Sandino summarize clearly some of the potential limitations of profit center evaluation in the article "Four Options for Measuring Value Creation," *Journal of Accountancy,* August 2009, pp. 34–37 (available here: www.journalofaccountancy.com/issues/2009/aug/20091518.html). While profit centers are commonly used, these limitations are well known. Here are two of the most prominent:

a. Profit is a measure of past performance and not a measure of past or future value creation; that is, profit does not directly measure the improvement or decline in the market value of the company. The value of a public or privately held company can be measured in a variety of ways (see Chapter 20).

b. Profit as determined by U.S.-based generally accepted accounting principles (GAAP) is conservatively biased; for example, GAAP tends to use valuations based on purchase cost rather than current market values.

Merchant and Sandino propose four approaches to improving the profit center approach for strategic performance measurement:

a. Use market measures, such as stock price among others.

b. Use non-GAAP alternative measures of profit that reduce the conservative bias. Some of these measures, such as EVA®, are explained in Chapter 19.

c. Use a measure of profit that extends beyond the usual quarterly or annual statements; instead, look for long-term profit performance over 3 to 6 years or more.

d. Use a combination of measures. The balanced scorecard is one example of this approach.

Required

1. Do you agree with Merchant and Sandino's assessment of the limitations of profit center measurement? Explain briefly.

2. Do you think the authors' proposals for improvement are practical and potentially effective?

[LO 18-3] 18-51 **Contribution Income Statement; Spreadsheet Application** Fashionisto Inc. is an upscale clothing store in New York City and London. Each store has two main departments, Men's Apparel and Women's Apparel. Marie Phelps, Fashionisto's CFO, wants to use strategic performance measurement to better understand the company's financial results. She has decided to use the profit center method to measure performance and has gathered the following information about the two stores and the two departments of the New York City store:

Total net sales	$3,500,000
Fixed costs	
Partly traceable and controllable	250,000
Partly traceable but noncontrollable	220,000
Nontraceable costs	70,000
Total net sales (percent)	
London store	40%
New York store	60
New York—Men's Apparel	40
New York—Women's Apparel	60
Cost of goods sold—variable (percent of sales)	
London store	52%
New York—Men's Apparel	45
New York—Women's Apparel	60
Variable operating costs (percent of sales)	
London store	36%
New York—Men's Apparel	22
New York—Women's Apparel	32
Fixed controllable costs—partly traceable (percent of total)	
London store	40%
New York total	40
Men's Apparel	45
Women's Apparel	40
Could not be traced to Men's or Women's Apparel	15
Could not be traced to London or New York	20
Fixed noncontrollable costs—partly traceable (percent of total)	
London store	50%
New York total	40
Men's Apparel	35
Women's Apparel	15
Could not be traced to Men's or Women's Apparel	50
Could not be traced to London or New York	10

Required

1. Using this information, prepare a contribution income statement for Fashionisto showing contribution margin, controllable margin, and contribution by profit center (CPC) for both the London and New York stores and for both departments of the New York store (Exhibit 18.9 provides a useful template for this requirement).

2. What are the global issues that are an important part of the profit center evaluation for Fashionisto Inc.?

[LO 18-3, 18-5] 18-52 **Validating the Balanced Scorecard; Spreadsheet Application** Whitehouse Gardens Inc. is a chain of home supply and gardening product stores. Last year, Whitehouse adopted the balanced scorecard (BSC) for evaluation of store and store manager performance. The BSC has helped Whitehouse to identify the critical success factors for sales and profitability. In particular, it has helped Whitehouse better understand its competitive environment and the drivers of success in that environment. On the advice of its chief financial officer, Whitehouse's board has requested that the company president conduct a study to validate the BSC. The objective of the study is to make sure that the scorecard measures being used are, in fact, the key measures associated with success. The following data have been obtained for the most recent quarter's results for each of the company's 30 stores, listed in order of when the store was opened (the most recent is store 30). There are five district managers, each of whom is responsible for six of the stores. In this study, a store manager's success is measured by increase in sales of each store for the current quarter over the same quarter last year. The data below include the percentage change in sales and four of the measures included in the customer perspective of the company's BSC. The scorecard measures include:

a. A survey of customers: this measure is taken from a survey form that is handed to customers on a random basis as they leave the store. The customers rate the store's performance on a scale of 0 to 100, where 100 is the highest score.

b. Manager review: each district manager evaluates each store once a quarter, also using a scale from 0 to 100, where 100 is the highest score.

c. Average wait time: the district managers have a staff that on a random basis measures the wait time in the checkout line for customers in each store. The figures shown here are the average wait times, in seconds, for the samples taken in the most recent quarter.

d. Average number of store employees who have had one or more of the company's in-house training courses in the past quarter, as a proportion of total employees at the store.

Store Number	Sales	Survey	Manager Review	Average Wait Time	Employee Training
1	−17.1%	65	33	95	56
2	−14.3	54	54	92	30
3	1.0	72	86	81	45
4	−10.8	50	94	89	60
5	−5.5	53	40	85	75
6	0.0	57	86	81	52
7	7.5	61	80	75	48
8	15.5	67	74	69	90
9	20.6	70	70	80	90
10	31.5	79	61	71	65
11	35.0	81	88	68	30
12	12.5	64	76	80	18
13	−2.6	54	38	83	33
14	3.5	59	27	78	48
15	20.6	71	70	65	63
16	7.8	62	80	75	78
17	14.5	66	43	69	93
18	20.0	71	70	65	55
19	29.4	77	63	58	39
20	39.4	84	55	50	67
21	45.7	88	49	59	34
22	59.4	84	87	49	78
23	63.8	89	56	45	48
24	35.6	81	58	62	36
25	5.2	60	82	77	51
26	11.8	64	77	72	66
27	30.7	77	62	57	81
28	7.8	77	73	68	96
29	15.1	73	67	62	57
30	24.8	77	62	57	36

Required

1. Construct a correlation matrix in Excel to analyze the validity of the four scorecard measures in the customer perspective of the BSC (if necessary, see the Excel tutorial associated with Chapter 6 in Connect for instructions on how to create a correlation matrix). Which BSC measure has the strongest correlation with sales?

   a. Survey

   b. Manager review

   c. Average wait time

   d. Employee training

2. Use regression in Excel to analyze the relationship between customer survey scores and sales at Whitehouse (if necessary, see the Excel tutorial associated with Chapter 8 in Connect for instructions on how to conduct regression analysis). What is the coefficient on the *Survey* variable in the regression equation (rounded to 2 decimal places)?

3. What observations or suggestions can you make from your correlation and regression analyses?

4. Briefly compare the benefits of the balanced scorecard relative to the profit center approach to strategic performance measurement.

[LO 18-3]   18-53   **Contribution Income Statement for Profit Centers; Strategy, International** Stratford Corporation is a diversified company whose products are marketed both domestically and internationally. Its major product lines are pharmaceutical products, sports equipment, and household appliances. At a recent meeting, Stratford's board of directors had a lengthy discussion on ways to improve overall corporate profitability without new acquisitions. New acquisitions are problematic because the company already has a lot of debt. The board members decided they needed additional financial information about individual corporate operations to target areas for improvement. Dave Murphy, Stratford's controller, has been asked to provide additional data to assist the board in its investigation. Stratford is not a public company and, therefore, has not prepared complete income statements by product line. Dave has regularly prepared an income statement by product line through contribution margin. However, he now believes that income statements prepared through operating income along both product lines and geographic areas would provide the directors with more insight into corporate operations. Dave has the following data available:

| | Product Lines | | | |
	Pharmaceutical	Sports	Appliances	Total
Production/sales in units	160,000	180,000	160,000	500,000
Average selling price per unit	$8.00	$20.00	$15.00	
Average variable manufacturing cost per unit	4.00	9.50	8.25	
Average variable selling expense per unit	2.00	2.50	2.25	
Fixed factory overhead excluding depreciation				$ 500,000
Depreciation of plant and equipment				400,000
Administrative and selling expense				1,160,000

Dave had several discussions with the division managers from each product line and compiled this information:

- The division managers concluded that Dave should allocate fixed factory overhead on the basis of the ratio of the total variable costs per product line or per geographic area to total overall variable costs.

- Each division manager agreed that a reasonable basis for the allocation of depreciation on plant and equipment would be the ratio of units produced per product line or per geographic area to the total number of units produced.

- There was little agreement on the allocation of administrative and selling expenses, so Dave decided to allocate only those expenses that were directly traceable to the SBU—that is, manufacturing staff salaries to product lines and sales staff salaries to geographic areas. He used these data for this allocation:

Manufacturing Staff		Sales Staff	
Pharmaceutical	$120,000	United States	$ 60,000
Sports	140,000	Canada	100,000
Appliances	80,000	Europe	250,000

The division managers provided reliable sales percentages for their product lines by geographic area:

| | Percentage of Unit Sales | | |
	United States	Canada	Europe
Pharmaceutical	40%	10%	50%
Sports	40	40	20
Appliances	20	20	60

Dave prepared this product-line income statement:

STRATFORD CORPORATION
Statement of Income by Product Lines
For the Fiscal Year Ended April 30

| | Product Lines | | | | |
	Pharmaceutical	Sports	Appliances	Unallocated	Total
Sales in units	160,000	180,000	160,000		500,000
Sales	$1,280,000	$3,600,000	$2,400,000	—	$7,280,000
Variable manufacturing and selling costs	960,000	2,160,000	1,680,000	—	4,800,000
Contribution margin	$ 320,000	$1,440,000	$ 720,000	—	$2,480,000
Fixed costs					
Fixed factory overhead excluding depreciation	$ 100,000	$ 225,000	$ 175,000	—	$ 500,000
Depreciation of plant and equipment	128,000	144,000	128,000	—	400,000
Administrative and selling expense	120,000	140,000	80,000	$ 820,000	1,160,000
Total fixed costs	$ 348,000	$ 509,000	$ 383,000	$ 820,000	$2,060,000
Operating income (loss)	$ (28,000)	$ 931,000	$ 337,000	$(820,000)	$ 420,000

Required (Round answers to the nearest dollar)   Prepare a contribution income statement for Stratford Corporation based on the company's geographic areas of sales.

1. Which geographic region has the highest contribution margin?
2. What is the total amount of unallocated fixed costs?
3. Which geographic region has the highest operating income?
4. As a result of the information disclosed by both income statements (by product line and by geographic area), recommend areas on which Stratford Corporation should focus its attention to improve corporate profitability.
5. What changes would you make to Stratford's strategic performance measurement system? Include the role, if any, of the firm's international business operations in your response.

(CMA Adapted)

[LO 18-3]   18-54 **Centralization vs. Decentralization: Banking** RNB is a bank holding company for a statewide group of retail consumer-oriented banks. RNB was formed in the early 1960s by investors who believed in a high level of consumer services. The number of banks owned by the holding company expanded rapidly. These banks gained visibility because of their experimentation with innovations such as free-standing 24-hour automated teller machines, automated funds transfer systems, and other advances in banking services.

RNB's earnings performance has been better than that of most other banks in the state. The founders organized RNB and continue to operate it on a highly decentralized basis. As the number of banks owned has increased, RNB's executive management has delegated more responsibility and authority to individual bank presidents, who are considered to be representatives of executive management. Although certain aspects of each bank's operations are standardized (such as procedures for account and loan applications and salary rates), bank presidents have significant autonomy in determining how each bank will operate.

The decentralization has led each bank to develop individual marketing campaigns. Several of them have introduced unique "packaged" accounts that include a combination of banking services; however, they sometimes fail to notify the other banks in the group as well as the executive office of these campaigns. One result has been interbank competition for customers where the market overlaps. The corporate marketing officer had also recently begun a statewide advertising campaign that conflicted with some of the individual banks' advertising. Consequently, customers and tellers have occasionally experienced both confusion and frustration, particularly when the customers attempt to receive services at a bank other than their "home" bank.

RNB's executive management is concerned that earnings will decline for the first time in its history. The decline appears to be attributable to reduced customer satisfaction and higher operating costs. The competition among the banks in the state is keen. Bank location and consistent high-quality customer service are important. RNB's 18 banks are well located, and the three new bank acquisitions planned for next year are considered to be in prime locations. The increase in operating costs appears to be directly related to the individual banks' aggressive marketing efforts and new programs. Specifically, expenditures increased for advertising and for the special materials and added personnel related to the "packaged" accounts.

For the past 3 months, RNB's executive management has been meeting with the individual bank presidents to review RNB's recent performance and seek ways to improve it. One recommendation that appeals to executive management is to make the organization's structure more centralized. The specific proposal calls for reducing individual bank autonomy and creating a centralized individual bank management committee of all bank presidents to be chaired by a newly created position, vice president of bank operations. The individual banks' policies would be set by consensus of the committee to conform to overall RNB plans.

Required

1. Discuss the advantages of a decentralized organizational structure.

2. Identify disadvantages of a decentralized structure. Support each disadvantage with an example from RNB's situation.

3. Do you think the proposed more centralized structure is in the strategic best interests of RNB? Why or why not?

(CMA Adapted)

[LO 18-3, 18-5] 18-55 **Balanced Scorecard; Strategic Business Units; Ethics** Pittsburgh-Walsh Company Inc. (PWC) manufactures lighting fixtures and electronic timing devices. The lighting fixtures division assembles units for the upscale and mid-range markets. The trend in recent years as the economy has been expanding is for sales in the upscale market to increase while those in the mid-range market have been relatively flat. Over the years, PWC has tried to maintain strong positions in both markets, believing it is best to offer customers a broad range of products to protect the company against a sharp decline in either market. PWC has never been the first to introduce new products but watches its competitors closely and quickly follows their lead with comparable products. PWC is proud of its customer service functions, which have been able to maintain profitable relationships with several large customers over the years.

The electronic timing devices division manufactures instrument panels that allow electronic systems to be activated and deactivated at scheduled times for both efficiency and safety purposes. Both divisions operate in the same manufacturing facilities and share production equipment.

PWC's budget for the year ending December 31 follows; it was prepared on a business unit basis under the following guidelines:

- Variable expenses are directly assigned to the division that incurs them.
- Traceable fixed overhead expenses are directly assigned to the division that incurs them.
- Common fixed expenses are allocated to the divisions on the basis of units produced, which bears a close relationship to direct labor. Included in common fixed expenses are costs of the corporate staff, legal expenses, taxes, marketing staff, and advertising.
- The company plans to manufacture 8,000 upscale fixtures, 22,000 mid-range fixtures, and 20,000 electronic timing devices during the year.

PITTSBURGH-WALSH COMPANY INC.
Budget
For the Year Ending December 31
(amounts in thousands)

	Lighting Fixtures Upscale	Lighting Fixtures Mid-Range	Electronic Timing Devices	Totals
Sales	$1,440	$770	$800	$3,010
Variable expenses				
Cost of goods sold	720	439	320	1,479
Selling and administrative	170	60	60	290
Contribution margin	$ 550	$271	$420	$1,241
Fixed overhead	140	80	80	300
Divisional contribution	$ 410	$191	$340	$ 941
Common fixed expenses				
Fixed factory overhead	48	132	120	300
Selling and administrative	11	31	28	70
Operating Income	$ 351	$ 28	$192	$ 571

PWC established a bonus plan for division management that provides a bonus for the manager if the division exceeds the planned product line income by 10% or more.

Shortly before the year began, Jack Parkow, the CEO, suffered a heart attack and retired. After reviewing the current budget, Joe Kelly, the new CEO, decided to close the lighting fixtures mid-range product line by the end of the first quarter and use the available production capacity to grow the remaining two product lines. The marketing staff advised that electronic timing devices could grow by 40% with increased direct sales support. Increasing sales of the electronic timing devices and the upscale lighting fixtures product lines would require expanded advertising expenditures to increase consumer awareness of PWC as an electronics and upscale lighting fixtures company. Joe approved the increased sales support and advertising expenditures to achieve the revised plan. He advised the divisions that for bonus purposes, the original product-line income objectives must be met and that the lighting fixtures division could combine the income objectives for both product lines for bonus purposes.

Prior to the close of the fiscal year, the division controllers were given the following preliminary actual information to review and adjust as appropriate. These preliminary year-end data reflect the revised units of production amounting to 12,000 upscale fixtures, 4,000 mid-range fixtures, and 30,000 electronic timing devices.

PITTSBURGH-WALSH COMPANY INC.
Preliminary Actual Information
For the Year Ending December 31
(amounts in thousands)

	Lighting Fixtures Upscale	Lighting Fixtures Mid-Range	Electronic Timing Devices	Totals
Sales	$2,160	$140	$1,200	$3,500
Variable expenses				
Cost of goods sold	1,080	80	480	1,640
Selling and administrative	260	11	96	367
Contribution margin	$ 820	$ 49	$ 624	$ 1,493
Fixed overhead	140	14	80	234
Divisional contribution	$ 680	$ 35	$ 544	$1,259
Common fixed expenses				
Overhead	78	27	195	300
Selling and administrative	60	20	150	230
Operating Income (less)	$ 542	$(12)	$ 199	$ 729

Because of the better-than-expected performance in the current year, the controller of the lighting fixtures division, anticipating a similar bonus plan for the coming year, is contemplating (1) deferring some revenue into the next year on the pretext that the sales are not yet final and (2) accruing, in the current year, expenditures that will be applicable to the first quarter of the coming year. The corporation would meet its annual plan, and the division would exceed the 10% incremental bonus plateau in the current year despite the deferred revenues and accrued expenses contemplated.

Required

1. Did the new CEO make the correct decision? Why or why not?

2. Outline the benefits that an organization realizes from profit center reporting, and evaluate profit center reporting on a variable costing basis versus a full costing basis.

3. Why would the management of the electronic timing devices division be unhappy with the current reporting? Should the current performance measurement system be revised?

4. Explain why the adjustments contemplated by the controller of the lighting fixtures division may or may not be unethical by citing specific standards in the Institute of Management Accountants's Statement of Ethical Professional Practice (available here: www.imanet.org/-/media/b6fbeeb74d964e6c9fe-654c48456e61f.ashx).

5. Develop a balanced scorecard for PWC, providing three to five perspectives and four to six measures for each perspective. Make sure your measures are quantifiable.

[LO 18-3]   18-56   **Choice of Strategic Business Unit** Hamilton-Jones, a large consulting firm in Los Angeles, has experienced rapid growth over the last 5 years. To better serve its clients and to better manage its practice, the firm decided 2 years ago to organize into five strategic business units, each of which serves a significant base of clients: accounting systems, executive recruitment and compensation, client-server office information systems, manufacturing information systems, and real-estate consulting. Each SBU is served by a variety of administrative services within the firm, including payroll and accounting, printing and duplicating, report preparation, and secretarial support. Hamilton-Jones's management closely watches the trend in the total costs for each administrative support area on a month-to-month basis. Management has noted that the costs in the printing and duplicating area have risen 40% over the last 2 years, a rate that is twice that of any other support area.

Required Should Hamilton-Jones evaluate the five strategic business units as cost, revenue, or profit centers? Why? How should the administrative support areas be evaluated?

[LO 18-3] 18-57 **Choice of Strategic Business Unit** MetroBank is a fast-growing bank that serves the region around Jacksonville, Florida. The bank provides commercial and individual banking services, including investment and mortgage banking services. The firm's strategy is to continue to grow by acquiring smaller banks in the area to broaden the base and variety of services it can offer. The bank now has 87 strategic business units, which represent different areas of service in different locations. To support its growth, MetroBank has invested several million dollars in upgrading its information services function. The number of networked computers and of support personnel has more than doubled in the last 4 years and now accounts for 13% of total operating expenses. Two years ago, MetroBank decided to charge information services to the SBUs based on the head count (number of employees) in each SBU. Recently, some of the larger SBUs have complained that this method overcharges them and that some of the smaller SBUs are actually using a larger share of the total information services resources. MetroBank's controller has decided to investigate these complaints. His inquiry of the director of the information services department revealed that the larger departments generally use more services, but some small departments in fact kept him pretty busy. Based on this response, the controller is considering changing the charges for information services to the basis of actual service calls in each SBU rather than the head count.

Required Is the information services department at MetroBank a profit center or a cost center? Which type of unit should it be, and why? Also, evaluate the controller's decision regarding the basis for charging information services costs to the SBUs.

[LO 18-3] 18-58 **Profit Centers: Hospitals** Suburban General Hospital owns and operates several community hospitals in North Carolina. One of its hospitals, Cordona Community Hospital, is a not-for-profit institution that has not met its financial targets in the past several years because of decreasing volume. It has been losing market share largely because of the entrance of a new competitor, Jefferson Memorial Hospital. Jefferson has successfully promoted itself as the premier provider of quality care; its slogan is "Patients Come First." To compete with Jefferson, Cordona has developed a new department, guest services, to improve patient relations and overall customer service. Guest services personnel will be positioned throughout the hospital and at major entrances to help patients and their families get where they are going. Guest services will also be visible in the waiting rooms of high-volume areas such as cardiovascular services and women's services to help guide the patients throughout their visit. Cordona's management is wrestling with how to charge guest services to the various profit centers in the hospital.

Required What are some different ways to allocate the costs of guest services, and what would be the effect of each on the behavior of the managers of the different profit centers?

[LO 18-3, 18-5] 18-59 **Performance Measurement; Balanced Scorecard; Hospital** Braxton Hospital and Health Care Services (BHHS) in Braxton, Mississippi, is a part of the Pillford University Health System. BHHS is a 450-bed community teaching hospital with the following mission: "In six years, Braxton Hospital and Health Care Services, as an integral part of the Pillford Health System, will be the system patients choose, the system to which physicians and payers refer, and the employer of choice for health care personnel."

To transform this mission to reality, BHHS adopted the balanced scorecard for performance measurement and a plan to implement it by the end of the sixth year. In the first year of the scorecard, BHHS identified 12 scorecard perspectives and 56 critical success factors across these 12 perspectives. In the second year, BHHS refined the scorecard to include the following five perspectives (which included 35 nonquantitative critical success factors):

a. *Organizational health* (teamwork, leadership development, communications, facilities, etc.).

b. *Process improvement* (reducing delays, streamlining processes, maximizing the effective use of technology, etc.).

c. *Quality improvement* (patient satisfaction, improving patient outcomes, external recognition for patient care, etc.).

d. *Volume and market share growth* (expanded clinical services, etc.).

e. *Financial health* (financial returns, system efficiencies, etc.).

Required

1. Why did BHHS reduce the number of scorecard perspectives and critical success factors in the second year? The number of perspectives was further reduced to four in the third year; state which you think are the remaining four perspectives, and explain why.

2. For the five perspectives in the second-year plan, develop two to five measurable critical success factors that the hospital might use to measure performance toward the goals of each perspective.

3. Will the scorecard as described in the second-year be effective in helping BHHS achieve its mission?

4. Develop a strategy map for BHHS, incorporating each of the five perspectives of the second-year plan. Explain why you have developed the map in this way.

5. Would a profit center approach work for BHHS? Why or why not?

[LO 18-3]   18-60   **Value Streams and Profit Centers** Levine Company is a manufacturer of very inexpensive cell phones and television sets. The company uses recycled parts and a highly structured manufacturing process to keep costs low so that it can sell at very low prices. The company uses lean accounting procedures to help keep costs low and to examine financial performance. Levine uses value streams to study the profitability of its two main product groups, cell phones and TVs. Information about finished goods inventory, sales, production, and average sales price follows:

	Cell Phone Group	TV Group
Units		
Beginning inventory	2,000	7,000
Price	$ 90	$ 140
Sold	13,500	15,600
Budgeted and actual production	14,000	15,000

Levine's costs for the current quarter are as follows. Note that some of the company's manufacturing and selling costs are traceable directly to the two value streams, while other costs are not traceable. Levine considers all traceable fixed costs to be controllable by the manager of each group. Also, Levine's value stream shows operating income determined by the full costing method; the difference from the traditional full costing income statement is that the effect on income from a change in inventory is shown as a separate item on the value-stream income statement:

	Cell Phone Group	TV Group	Total
Unit variable costs			
Manufacturing	$ 50	$ 85	
Selling and administrative	5	5	
Traceable fixed costs			
Manufacturing	140,000	258,000	$398,000
Selling and administrative	100,000	100,000	200,000
Nontraceable fixed costs			
Manufacturing			130,000
Selling and administrative			85,000

Required   Consider Levine's two value streams as profit centers, and use the contribution income statement as a guide to develop a value-stream income statement for the company. (See Exhibit 18.9 for an example of a contribution income statement.) In your solution, replace the term *controllable margin* (in Exhibit 18.9) with *value-stream profit*. Be sure to include the inventory effect on profit as a separate line item in your value-stream income statement.

1. What is the effect of the inventory change (and in what direction) on the value stream profit of cell phones?

2. What is the value stream profit of TVs?

3. Interpret the information revealed by the value stream income statements.

4. What is the benefit of the use of value streams for evaluating profit centers relative to the use of the contribution income statement for individual product lines?

[LO 18-3]   18-61   **Contribution Income Statement for Profit Centers** Cardio World Inc. (CWI) is a sporting goods retailer that specializes in bicycles, running shoes, and related clothing. The firm has become successful by careful attention to trends in cycling, running, and changes in the technology and fashion of sport clothing. In recent years, however, the profit margins have begun to fall, and CWI has decided to employ a contribution income statement to further analyze the company's profitability. The company has two stores, one in Hartford, Connecticut, and the other in Boston, Massachusetts. The total sales for the two stores for the most recent year are $7,025,000 and $5,875,000 for the Hartford and Boston stores, respectively. Both stores are considered profit centers, and within each store are two profit centers: one for clothing and the other for cycle and running shoes (called "cycle & run" below). The breakdown of sales within the two stores is approximately 50% clothing and 50% cycle & run for Boston but is estimated to be 60%/40% for Hartford due to the greater interest in cycling in the Boston area. CWI is interested in finding the profit contribution of clothing and cycle & run at the Hartford store but not at the Boston store.

Cost of purchases for resale averages 60% of retail value at Boston; at Hartford, the cost is 70% for clothing and 50% for cycle & run. Variable operating costs at each store are similar: 30% of retail sales at Boston, and at Hartford, variable operating costs are 25% of retail sales for the clothing unit and 35% for the cycle & run unit. CWI estimates it has a total of $1,175,000 fixed cost, of which $325,000 cannot be traced to either store; of the remaining $850,000, $475,000 is traceable to the stores and controllable by store managers, and $375,000 can be traced to the stores but cannot be controlled in the short term by the store managers. These fixed costs are estimated to be traceable to the stores as follows:

Fixed Controllable Costs	Percent of Total Cost
Boston	45%
Hartford total	45
Clothing	50
Cycle & run	30
Could not be traced to clothing or cycling at Hartford	20
Could not be traced to Boston or Hartford	10

Fixed Noncontrollable Costs	Percent of Total Cost
Boston	40%
Hartford total	50
Clothing	55
Cycle & run	35
Could not be traced to clothing or cycling at Hartford	10
Could not be traced to Boston or Hartford	10

Required

1. Prepare a contribution income statement for CWI showing the contribution margin, controllable margin, and contribution by profit center for both the Boston and Hartford stores, and also for the clothing and cycle & run units of the Hartford store.

2. Interpret the contribution income statement you prepared in requirement 1. What recommendations do you have for the management of CWI?

[LO 18-3]   18-62 **Choice of Strategic Business Unit**

Required   For each of the following cases, determine whether the business unit should be evaluated as a cost center or a profit center and explain why. If you choose cost center, then explain which type of cost center—the discretionary-cost center or the engineered-cost center.

1. A trucking firm has experienced a rapid increase in fuel costs and has only been partly successful in passing along the increased costs to customers. In recent months, fuel prices have come back down, but the firm's management knows to expect a continued volatility in the cost of fuel. To secure the firm's profits when fuel costs are rising, the company has established an Office of Sustainability to develop and implement a strategy for reducing costs and reducing the firm's overall carbon footprint.

2. To more effectively compete in a dynamic market for consumer electronics, a manufacturer of consumer electronics products has established a new department for Innovation and Refinement that reports directly to the chief operating officer (COO). The role of the new department is to develop new products and to refine existing products that keep the firm on the leading edge of innovation in the industry. A key tool of the new department is to use business analytics—a type of statistical analysis that is used to analyze market trends, consumer data, and economics forecasts—to best identify the products that consumers want and the types of innovation most likely to be valued.

3. A recent economic downturn has convinced Marshall Clothing Stores Inc. to initiate risk management practices and to locate this activity in a new department that reports directly to the chief financial officer (CFO). The objectives of risk management are to identify significant new risks that could potentially affect the company in the coming 1 to 5 years and to develop plans for adapting to the risk. For example, the company is concerned about the rapidly increasing inventories in certain departments of its stores, due to an unexpected decrease in demand in these areas. The company faces losses on selling these items at a discount.

[LO 18-3, 18-5]   18-63 **Research Assignment; Sustainability** Read the following article by Marc J. Epstein, Adriana Rejc Buhovac, and Kristi Yuthas: "Implementing Sustainability: The Role of Leadership and Organizational Culture," *Strategic Finance*, April 2010, pp. 41–47. The article explains the use of management control systems in the context of a firm's sustainability objectives. The research for this article was funded by the Institute of Management Accounting (IMA).

Required

1. What is the difference between local and corporate decision making, and what is the significance of the difference for sustainability?

2. Study the Corporate Sustainability Model in Figure 1 within the article. Based on this study, do you think sustainability should be managed by means of a cost center, profit center, the balanced scorecard, or some other method? Why?

3. Identify two of the leading companies in the area of sustainability, and explain why you think each of these companies has chosen to take a leadership role in sustainability.

4. Review Exhibit 18.4. Do you think sustainability is best managed as part of an informal or a formal type of management control system? Briefly explain your answer.

5. Explain briefly the role of leadership in sustainability management.

6. Explain briefly the role of organization culture in sustainability management.

Solution to Self-Study Problem

Discretionary-Cost and Engineered-Cost Methods

1. Liberty management is apparently using a cost center for its claims department because it generates no revenues. Because management has chosen not to adjust the number of clerks for the changing number of claims each month, it appears to be using a discretionary-cost method to budget these costs. That is, management has determined it is more effective to provide a reasonable resource (12 clerks) for the claims processing area and has chosen not to be concerned directly with the clerks' efficiency, the slack during slow times, or the hectic pace at peak load times. Management's view is that the work averages out over time.

2. If Liberty uses the discretionary-cost method, the budget would be the same each month and would not depend on the level of claims to be processed. The budget would include the costs to provide the number of clerks that management judges to be adequate for the job (12 clerks × $2,400 = $28,800 per month).

3. If Liberty uses the engineered-cost method, each claim that is processed has a budgeted cost based on the average time used as determined by a work flow study. Assume that each clerk works an 8-hour day except for 40 minutes of break time; the number of claims a clerk can process each month (assuming 22 working days) is

$$\frac{[(8 \text{ hours} \times 60 \text{ minutes/hour}) - 40 \text{ minutes}]/\text{day} \times 22 \text{ days/month}}{121 \text{ minutes/claim}} = 80 \text{ claims per month}$$

The cost per claim is thus

$$\$2,400/\text{month} \div 80 \text{ claims/month} = \$30 \text{ per claim}$$

The engineered-cost budget for January is

$$915 \text{ claims} \times \$30 \text{ per claim} = \$27,450$$

The unfavorable variance for January using the engineered-cost method is $1,350 ($28,800 actual expenditure less $27,450 budgeted expenditure). This unfavorable variance is best interpreted as the cost of unused capacity for processing claims. Because the capacity for processing claims is 80 × 12 = 960 claims, the department has unused capacity of 45 claims (960 − 915 = 45 claims), or approximately one-half of one clerk.

4. Chuck could make the strategic argument that the claims processing department should be staffed for peak capacity rather than for average capacity to ensure promptness and accuracy during the busy months and to provide a better basis for employee morale, which is an important factor in performance during the low-volume months as well.

Please visit Connect to access a narrated, animated tutorial for solving this problem.

CHAPTER NINETEEN

Strategic Performance Measurement:
Investment Centers and Transfer Pricing

After studying this chapter, you should be able to . . .

LO 19-1　Explain the use and limitations of return on investment for evaluating the short-term financial performance of investment centers.

LO 19-2　Explain the use and limitations of residual income for evaluating the short-term financial performance of investment centers.

LO 19-3　Explain the use and limitations of economic value added for evaluating the short-term financial performance of investment centers.

LO 19-4　Explain the objectives of transfer pricing and describe the advantages and disadvantages of various transfer pricing alternatives.

LO 19-5　Understand important international issues that arise in transfer pricing.

Ezra Shaw/Getty Images

When the Golden State Warriors won the NBA Championship in 2017, it capped one of the most successful regular season and postseason performances in the history of professional basketball. The team won 67 of their 82 regular season games, and had an amazing 16-1 record in their playoff run to the championship. But was it a financial success for the team's owners? That season, the Warriors added Kevin Durant, one of the best players in the world, to a roster that already had a number of All-Star players (including Stephen Curry, Klay Thompson, and Draymond Green). As a result, the Warriors's payroll was high; the team started the 2016–2017 season with an active salary cap of $97,520,106, the 11th highest in the NBA.

It turns out that the investment paid off, at least on the measure of "amount spent per win." The Warriors ended up paying $1,455,524 per regular season win and $6,095,007 per postseason win. Both of those spend-per-win numbers are smaller than any of the teams with higher salary cap amounts; for example, the San Antonio Spurs had the second lowest spend-per-win during the regular season ($1,719,127), and the Cleveland Cavaliers had the second lowest spend-per-win during the postseason ($9,625,537).

The spend-per-win measure is helpful for teams to know how well their financial investments (i.e., player salaries) are doing at generating the outcomes they seek (i.e., wins). In other words, it is a form of *return on investment,* a performance measure that helps portray outcomes in the context of the investment that was made to generate those outcomes. In most cases, the outcome firms are interested in is profit; in this case, the outcome is wins. Whatever the outcome of interest, return on investment is among the most common measures by which the performance of investment centers, and entire firms (or teams), is evaluated.

As we have discussed, one of the challenges of decentralization is the need to implement an effective performance measurement system. In Chapter 18, we looked at how top management can evaluate the financial performance of lower-level units of the organization (e.g., cost centers and profit centers). This chapter covers issues related to the performance of investment centers—the highest subunit level of an organization. By definition, managers of these units exercise control over revenues, costs, and level of investment. Thus, the evaluation of financial performance of these units should logically incorporate a measure of invested capital (such as player salaries in the case of NBA teams). Such measures allow top management to compare the financial performance of different investment centers within the organization. As indicated in the vignette that follows, the task of evaluating the performance of investment units is complicated when these units exchange goods and services with one another. That is, in such situations a transfer price between units must be chosen to evaluate the financial performance of both the buying unit and the selling unit. Setting an appropriate transfer price is especially challenging in an international context.

Five Steps in the Evaluation of the Financial Performance of Investment Centers in an Organization

Global Electronics Inc. (a fictitious company) was started five years ago by a small group of entrepreneurial students. The company produces innovative electronics products that appeal to young, educated individuals. Global is pursuing a low-cost, high-volume strategy. In fact, from its inception, the company has grown rapidly and now does business in all 50 states in the United States as well as selected countries abroad. Its incentive to go abroad is to reduce cost and to facilitate growth in foreign sales. The company is decentralized and organized for performance evaluation purposes into a series of cost centers, profit centers, and investment centers. Recently, to take advantage of income tax opportunities, Global established several foreign subsidiaries that both produce and distribute the company's products. Initially, the company felt little need for a comprehensive performance evaluation system. However, with recent growth and development, the owners of the company are looking at alternative models for evaluating the performance of the various subunits of the organization. Business consultants with whom the owners met recently recommended the following five-step process for developing a performance measurement system for Global.

1. **Determine the strategic issues surrounding the problem.** Global Electronics Inc. has organized itself into a number of decentralized units, including investment centers where the managers have broad responsibility over operating decisions and level of investment in the unit. The owners of the company want to institute a performance measurement system that will allow them to effectively evaluate the performance of each investment center.

2. **Identify the alternative actions.** The first task is to choose one or more short-term financial performance indicators that incorporate the unit's level of investment. Possible indicators include return on investment (ROI), residual income (RI), and economic value added (EVA®).[1] Global must also choose the time period over which financial performance will be evaluated (i.e., one year versus a time-series basis). For interdivisional transfers of products and services, Global must choose an appropriate transfer pricing system from among the following alternatives: variable cost, full cost, market price, or negotiated price. Further, the company must determine whether transfer prices will be recorded at actual, budgeted, or standard cost.[2]

3. **Obtain information and analyze the alternatives.** The choice of a performance evaluation system for decentralized units, such as investment centers, has important behavioral consequences. For example, to a greater or lesser extent, each choice mentioned maintains or decreases managerial autonomy, increases or decreases managerial motivation, and results in varying degrees of goal congruency. Further, some system choices are simpler to implement and maintain. In terms of selecting the appropriate transfer pricing method, there are significant income tax considerations, particularly given the (now) international scope of the company's operations. To protect itself, the company is considering entering into an advance pricing agreement (APA) with the Internal Revenue Service (IRS) regarding its transfer pricing method to be used for both domestic and international purposes. Finally, the company is concurrently considering the introduction of a balanced scorecard (BSC) (see Chapter 18), so management needs to consider the selection of performance metrics in conjunction with the design of its BSC.

4. **Based on strategy and analysis, choose and implement the desired alternative.** After discussion of these issues with its consultants, the company chooses a mix of financial performance indicators and a specific transfer pricing system that the company hopes will balance implementation costs with behavioral benefits and income tax considerations. The high-level financial performance indicators should be linked strategically to the company's BSC. Overall, the proposed performance evaluation system for its investment centers will help Global implement its growth strategy and determine where growth is most profitable.

5. **Provide ongoing evaluation of the effectiveness of the step 4 implementation.** The financial performance of all strategic investment centers of the company is evaluated quarterly, in conjunction with both subunit and corporate scorecards. Further, the financial performance metrics are benchmarked to best-in-class performance of Global's competitors. Changes to the way financial performance is evaluated, as well as potential changes to the transfer pricing system used by the company, are discussed during quarterly meetings with company owners.

The rest of this chapter is divided into two parts. In Part One, we discuss alternatives for evaluating the short-term financial performance of investment centers. In Part Two, we discuss the issue of transfer pricing. In both cases, our approach is to discuss both the advantages and limitations of various alternatives. As you will see, evaluation of the short-term financial performance of investment centers is important but incomplete. Thus, a strategic analysis of the performance of an investment center must also include nonfinancial performance indicators, such as those included in an entity's balanced scorecard.

---

[1] EVA® is a registered trademark of Stern Stewart & Co. ROI, RI, and EVA® are covered later in this chapter.

[2] As noted in Chapter 14, standard costs are *normative*—they represent the costs that *should be* incurred under relatively efficient operating conditions.

Under the principle of controllability, it is appropriate for top management to evaluate the profitability of each investment center in relation to the amount of capital invested in the subunit. In this regard, top management can use one or a combination of the following metrics: return on investment (ROI), residual income (RI), or economic value added (EVA®). Each of these measures is discussed in this part of the chapter. In general, we evaluate each of these alternatives along the following dimensions:

- The extent to which the measure motivates a high level of effort on the part of investment center managers.
- The extent to which the use of the measure results in goal congruence (consistency between decisions made by managers and the goals of top management).
- The extent to which the measure rewards managers fairly for their effort and skill, and for the effectiveness of the decisions they make.

Please keep these criteria in mind as you study the rest of this chapter.

Return on Investment

LO 19-1

Explain the use and limitations of return on investment for evaluating the short-term financial performance of investment centers.

The most commonly used measure of short-term financial performance of an investment center is **return on investment (ROI)**, which is defined as a measure of profit divided by a measure of investment in the business unit. ROI is a percentage, and the larger the percentage, the better the ROI. The achieved level of ROI depends on several factors, including general economic conditions, and, in particular, the current economic conditions of the company's industry. For example, cyclical industries such as airlines and home construction have ROIs that vary significantly under differing economic conditions. In calculating ROI, profit for an investment center is typically defined as divisional operating income. The amount of investment is often defined as the assets of the business unit.

return on investment (ROI)
A measure of profit divided by a measure of investment in a business unit.

Return on Investment Equals Return on Sales Times Asset Turnover (ROI = ROS × AT)[3]

ROI is the product of two components, return on sales and asset turnover. Because sales and profits relate to a period of time, for consistency, the amount of assets used to calculate ROI is usually determined from the simple average of the amount of assets at the start of the period and at the end of the period:

$$\text{ROI} = \text{Return on sales} \times \text{Asset turnover}$$
$$\text{ROI} = \frac{\text{Profit}}{\text{Sales}} \times \frac{\text{Sales}}{\text{Average Assets}}$$

return on sales (ROS)
The amount of profit per sales dollar; measures the manager's ability to control expenses and increase revenues to improve profitability.

Return on sales (ROS), or profit per sales dollar, measures the manager's ability to control expenses and increase revenues to improve profitability. **Asset turnover (AT)**, the amount of sales dollars generated per dollar of investment, measures the manager's ability to increase sales from a given level of investment. Together, the two components of ROI tell a more complete story of the manager's short-term performance and therefore enhance top management's ability to evaluate and compare different units within the organization. For example, research has shown that firms with different operating strategies also tend to have a different mix of return on sales versus asset turnover. Firms with high operating leverage (see Chapter 9) tend to have low asset turnover and high return on sales; those with low operating leverage and commodity-like products tend to have the highest asset turnover and the lowest return on sales. See the nearby Real-World Focus item for an elaboration on these points. Note that for performance evaluation purposes, a business unit can be defined in various ways. As illustrated in the CompuCity example that follows, business units can be defined in terms of product lines, geographic regions, or even product lines within geographic regions.

asset turnover (AT)
The amount of sales dollars generated per dollar of investment; measures the manager's ability to increase sales from a given level of investment.

[3] ROI based on ROS and AT is often referred to as the *DuPont approach* because it was originated by Donaldson Brown, chief financial officer of DuPont Corporation in the early 1900s.

The accompanying figure shows the relationship between asset turnover (AT) and return on sales (ROS) for a return on investment (ROI) of 10%. Any point falling above the line would represent an ROI of greater than 10%; a point falling below this line would be an ROI of less than 10%. The curve shows that there are lots of different combinations of AT and ROS that will produce an ROI of 10%. Also, it is common that different industries will fall at different points of the figure. For example, restaurants typically have low ROS and higher AT, so they will appear to the upper left of the figure [e.g., in 2019, Darden Restaurants Inc. (DRI), which owns companies such as Olive Garden and Longhorn Steakhouse, had an ROS of 8.4% and AT of 1.5, for an ROI of 12.6%]. In contrast, technology companies typically have higher ROS and lower AT [e.g., Microsoft (MSFT) in 2019 had an ROS of 30.1% and AT of 0.42, for an ROI of 12.6%].

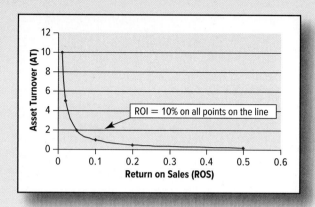

Illustration of Short-Term Financial Performance Evaluation Using ROI

Assume that CompuCity is a retailer with three product lines: computers, software, and computer help books. The company has stores in three regions: the Boston region, South Florida, and the Midwest. Each store sells computers, software, and books. CompuCity's profits for the Midwest region declined last year, due in part to increased price competition in the computer product line.

Top management uses ROI to study and investigate the financial performance of the Midwest region. Each of the three product lines (as well as each of the three geographic regions) is considered an investment center for performance evaluation purposes. CompuCity knows that the markups are highest in software and lowest for computers because of price competition. Investment in each product line consists of the inventory for sale, the value of the real estate, and improvements to the retail stores. Inventory is relatively low in the computer product line because merchandise is restocked quickly from the manufacturers. Inventory is also low in the book product line because about 40% of CompuCity's books are on consignment from publishers.

The current book value (recorded cost) of the real estate and store improvements is allocated to each of the three product lines in the Midwest region on the basis of square feet of floor space used. The software product line occupies the largest amount of floor space, followed by computers and books. Panel A of Exhibit 19.1 shows the operating income, sales, and investment information for the Midwest region of CompuCity in 2021 and 2022. Panel B shows the calculation of ROI, including ROS and asset turnover, for the Midwest region for both 2021 and 2022.

The data in Exhibit 19.1 indicate that the Midwest region's ROI has fallen (from 14.4% in 2021 to 13.5% in 2022) due mainly to a decline in overall ROS (from 6.1% in 2021 to 5.1% in 2022). Further analysis shows that the drop in ROS is due to the sharp decline in ROS for the computer product line (from 4% in 2021 to 2% in 2022). The computer product line's decline in ROS is likely the result of the increased price competition.

The analysis also shows that software is the most profitable product line for the Midwest region (based on an ROI of 20% in 2022); this is so primarily because of the relatively high ROS (highest at 10% because the markup on software products is relatively high). ROI for the software line also improved because of the decline in investment, due either to a reduction in inventory or a decrease in floor space for software (recall that investment is allocated to the three product lines on the basis of floor space).

EXHIBIT 19.1 Return on Investment, Return on Sales, and Asset Turnover for CompuCity (*Midwest Region*)

Panel A: Operating Income, Investment, and Sales

Product Line	Operating Income		Investment (Average Assets)		Sales	
	2021	2022	2021	2022	2021	2022
Computers	$ 8,000	$ 5,000	$ 50,000	$ 62,500	$200,000	$250,000
Software	15,000	16,000	100,000	80,000	150,000	160,000
Books	3,200	5,000	32,000	50,000	80,000	100,000
Total	$26,200	$26,000	$182,000	$192,500	$430,000	$510,000

Panel B: Return on Sales, Asset Turnover, and Return on Investment

Product Line	Return on Sales (ROS)		Asset Turnover (AT)		Return on Investment (ROI)	
	2021	2022	2021	2022	2021	2022
Computers	4% = 8,000 ÷ 200,000	2% = 5,000 ÷ 250,000	4.00 = 200,000 ÷ 50,000	4.00 = 250,000 ÷ 62,500	16% = 8,000 ÷ 50,000	8% = 5,000 ÷ 62,500
Software	10% = 15,000 ÷ 150,000	10% = 16,000 ÷ 160,000	1.50 = 150,000 ÷ 100,000	2.00 = 160,000 ÷ 80,000	15% = 15,000 ÷ 100,000	20% = 16,000 ÷ 80,000
Books	4% = 3,200 ÷ 80,000	5% = 5,000 ÷ 100,000	2.50 = 80,000 ÷ 32,000	2.00 = 100,000 ÷ 50,000	10% = 3,200 ÷ 32,000	10% = 5,000 ÷ 50,000
Total	6.09% = 26,200 ÷ 430,000	5.10% = 26,000 ÷ 510,000	2.36 = 430,000 ÷ 182,000	2.65 = 510,000 ÷ 192,500	14.40% = 26,200 ÷ 182,000	13.51% = 26,000 ÷ 192,500

Note: The values for investment in this exhibit represent the simple average of beginning-of-year and end-of-year values of product line assets.

The computer line saw a significant one-year decline in ROI (from 16% to 8%), driven by the aforementioned decline in ROS from 2021 to 2022. For the book product line, a 20% one-year decrease in asset turnover (AT) was offset by a 25% increase in return on sales (ROS), leaving ROI constant over the two-year period.

Strategic Analysis Using ROI

Use of ROI enables CompuCity to evaluate the short-term financial performance of each of the three product lines within the Midwest region. CompuCity can set performance goals for each product line in terms of both return on sales (ROS) and asset turnover (AT). Product line managers then have clear goals to increase sales and reduce costs, reduce inventory, and use floor space effectively. To be effective, the goals should recognize differences in the competitive factors among the product lines. For example, a lower ROS should be expected of the computer product line because of competitive pricing that affects that line.

Exhibit 19.1 data also reflect the way that competitive factors in the computer product line and business relationships regarding inventory in the computer and book product lines affect profitability. This provides a useful basis for an improved analysis for determining how the firm should position itself strategically. How should CompuCity's competitive approach be changed in view of recent and expected changes in the competitive environment? Perhaps the computer product line should be reduced and the software product line expanded. Which stores in the Midwest are successful, and why? A value-chain analysis might provide insight into strategic competitive advantages and opportunities. For example, CompuCity might find it more profitable to reduce or eliminate its computer product line and replace it with a potentially more profitable line, such as printers, smartphones, supplies, or computer accessories.

Return on Investment: Measurement Issues

If ROI is used to evaluate the relative financial performance of business units (such as product lines or regions, or product lines within regions), the following evaluation guidelines should be kept in mind:

1. Income and investment should be measured in the same way for each business unit, to the extent possible. For example, all units to be evaluated should use the same inventory cost flow assumption (e.g., FIFO or LIFO) and the same depreciation method.
2. The measurement method must be reasonable and fair for all business units. For example, the use of net book value (NBV) for assets can significantly bias ROI measures in favor of units with older assets.

To illustrate the effect of an accounting policy on divisional ROIs, assume that all business units of CompuCity expense all furniture and other items used to display products; these items cost $2,000 per year. Suppose the computer product line in the Midwest region decides to capitalize these expenses. What is the short-term effect on ROI if depreciation is $500 per year on these items? The increase in the NBV of assets for the computer product line in the Midwest region is $1,500, and the net effect on income for this product line is $1,500. Exhibit 19.2 compares the computer product line to the book product line for the Midwest region before the change (Panel A) and after the change (Panel B).

EXHIBIT 19.2

Effect on ROI of Capitalizing Certain Costs: CompuCity (*Midwest Region*)

Panel A: ROI Prior to Capitalizing Display Materials (same as Exhibit 19.1, 2022)		
	Computer Unit	**Book Unit**
Assets	$62,500	$50,000
Income	$5,000	$5,000
ROI	8%	10%

Panel B: Year-One Results—Book Unit Expenses Display Costs; Computer Unit Capitalizes Display Costs		
Assets	**$64,000** = $62,500 + $1,500	$50,000
Income	**$6,500** = $5,000 + $1,500	$5,000
ROI	**10.16%** = $6,500 ÷ $64,000	10%

The illustration shows that the decision to capitalize the display costs in the short run increased the computer product line's assets, income, and ROI. Although the book product line has the higher ROI when both units expense display costs, the computer product line's decision to capitalize these costs while the book product line does not has caused the computer product line to have the higher ROI (at least temporarily).

Which Assets to Include in the ROI Calculation

A key criterion for including an asset in the ROI calculation is the degree to which the business unit controls the asset. For example, if the unit's cash balance is controlled at the firmwide level, only a portion (or perhaps none) of the cash balance should be included in the investment amount for calculating ROI for that unit. Similarly, receivables and inventory should include only those that are controllable at the unit level. Long-lived assets are commonly included in investment if they are traceable to the business unit (for shared assets, see the next section).

For idle assets, the main issue again is controllability. If idle assets have an alternative use or are readily saleable, they should be included in the investment amount for ROI. Also, if top management wants to encourage the divestment of idle assets, including idle assets in the determination of ROI would motivate the desired action because divestment would simultaneously reduce investment and increase ROI. Alternatively, if top management sees a potential strategic advantage to holding the idle assets, excluding them from ROI would provide the most effective motivation because holding idle assets would not affect the ROI calculation.

Measuring Investment: Allocating Shared Assets

When shared facilities, such as a common maintenance facility, are involved, management must determine a fair allocation arrangement. As with joint cost allocation (Chapter 7), top management should trace the assets to the business units that used them and allocate—on a basis that is as close to actual usage as possible—the assets that cannot be traced. For example, the investment in a vehicle maintenance facility might be allocated on the basis of the number of vehicles in each unit or on the basis of the total value of those vehicles.

Alternatively, the required capacity—and therefore the investment in the joint facility—is sometimes large because the user units require high levels of service at periods of high demand. In this case, the assets should be allocated according to the *peak demand* by each individual business unit; units with higher peak-load requirements would be allocated a relatively larger portion of the total investment cost. For example, an information technology department might require a high level of computer capacity because certain units within the company require a large amount of service at certain times.

Measuring Investment: Current Values

historical cost

In conjunction with measuring ROI or RI (residual income) of an investment center, a measure of investment equal to the book value of current assets plus the net book value (NBV) of long-lived assets.

net book value (NBV)

The original (acquisition) cost of a depreciable asset less accumulated depreciation to date on that asset.

The amount of investment is typically the **historical cost** of divisional assets, which is defined as the book value of current assets plus the net book value (NBV) of long-lived assets. **Net book value (NBV)** for a depreciable asset is the difference between the original cost of the asset and accumulated depreciation on that asset. A problem arises when long-lived assets are a significant portion of the total investment base because most long-lived assets are stated at historical cost, and price changes since the purchase date can make historical cost figures irrelevant and misleading.

If the relatively small historical cost value is used to measure the level of investment for purposes of calculating ROI, then *ROI can be significantly overstated* relative to ROI determined on the basis of the current value of the assets. The consequence is that the use of historical cost ROI can mislead strategic decision makers as the inflated ROI figures can create an illusion of profitability. The illusion is removed when the assets are measured at their current value.

For example, a business unit that enjoys a relatively high ROI of 20% based on NBV of assets (e.g., income of $200,000 and NBV of assets of $1,000,000) would find that if replacement cost of the assets were four times book value (4 × $1,000,000 = $4,000,000), the ROI after replacement would become a relatively low 5% ($200,000 ÷ $4,000,000). Strategically, the firm should have identified the low profitability of this business unit in a timely manner, but use of historical cost ROI can delay this recognition. Thus, instead of measuring assets at

Deciding which business segments to keep and which to dispose of is a complex decision, with strategic implications for the parent entity. Unilever PLC recently needed to find a way to appease investors after rejecting a $143 billion takeover offer from Kraft Heinz Co. The company conducted a review of its diverse set of product lines (including Hellmann's mayonnaise, Ben & Jerry's ice cream, and Dove soap), using ROI to help identify underperforming divisions. The review resulted in an announcement that Unilever would sell its

145-year-old margarine and spreads business, including such well-known names as Country Crock and I Can't Believe It's Not Butter. The sale will allow Unilever to concentrate its efforts on faster-growing product lines such as personal-care and home products. About the strategic shift, Unilever CEO Paul Polman said, "We need to accelerate our plans to unlock further value, faster."

Source: D. Roland and S. Chaudhuri, "Unilever Looks to Shed Businesses In Revamp," *The Wall Street Journal* (Asia Edition), April 7, 2017, p. A1.

historical cost (for purposes of calculating ROI), an organization may choose some measure of current value of these assets. Presumably, the resulting ROIs better inform management about the true profitability of the organization's various business units. Note, however, that if current value data are not currently being reported (e.g., for financial accounting purposes), the organization will incur additional information-gathering costs.

In addition to its strategic value, the use of current value helps to reduce the unfairness of historical cost NBV when comparing among business units with *different aged assets.* Units with older assets under the NBV method may have significantly higher ROIs than business units with newer assets because of the effect of price changes and accumulated depreciation over the life of the assets. If the old and new assets are contributing equivalent service, the bias in favor of the unit with older assets is unfair to the manager of a unit with newer assets.

Measures of Current Value   The three methods for developing or estimating the current values of assets are (1) gross book value, (2) replacement cost, and (3) liquidation value. **Gross book value (GBV)** is historical cost without the reduction for accumulated depreciation. It is a rough estimate of the current value of the assets. GBV improves on NBV because it removes the bias due to differences in the age of assets and differences in depreciation methods used across different business units. However, it does not address potential price changes in the assets since the time of original purchase.

Replacement cost represents the estimated cost to replace the assets at the current level of service and functionality. In contrast, **liquidation value** is the estimated price that could be received from the sale of the assets of a business unit. In effect, replacement cost is a purchase price and liquidation value is a sales price. Generally, replacement cost is higher than liquidation value.

GBV is preferred by those who value the objectivity of a historical cost number; original purchase cost is reliable and verifiable. In contrast, replacement cost is preferred when ROI is used to evaluate the manager or the business unit as a continuing enterprise because the use of replacement cost is consistent with the idea that the assets will be replaced at the current cost and the business will continue. On the other hand, liquidation value is most useful when top management is using ROI to evaluate the business unit for potential disposal and the relevant current cost is the sales (i.e., liquidation) value of the assets of the business unit.

To illustrate, consider CompuCity's three marketing regions, each of which is considered a separate business unit for performance evaluation purposes. CompuCity has 15 stores in the Midwest, 18 in the Boston region, and 13 in South Florida. CompuCity owns and manages each store. Exhibit 19.3 shows the NBV, GBV, estimated replacement cost, and estimated liquidation value for 2022 for the stores in each region.

The stores in the Boston region, where CompuCity began, are among the oldest and are located in areas where real estate values have risen considerably. The newer stores (in the Midwest and Florida) are also experiencing significant appreciation in real estate values. ROI based on NBV shows the Boston region to be the most profitable. Additional analysis based on GBV, however, shows that when considering that stores in the Boston region are somewhat older, the ROI figures for all three regions are comparable, illustrating the potentially misleading information from ROI based on NBV.

gross book value (GBV)
An asset's historical (i.e., acquisition) cost without the reduction for accumulated depreciation.

replacement cost
The current cost to replace an asset at the current level of service and functionality of that asset.

liquidation value
The estimated price that could be received from the sale of the assets of a business unit.

EXHIBIT 19.3
Investment Data and ROI for
CompuCity's Three Marketing
Regions (000s omitted)

		Measure of Assets			
Region	Operating Income	Net Book Value	Gross Book Value	Replacement Cost	Liquidation Value
Financial data:					
Midwest	$26,000	$192,500	$250,500	$388,000	$ 332,000
Boston region	38,500	212,000	445,000	650,000	1,254,600
South Florida	16,850	133,000	155,450	225,500	195,000
Return on investment (ROI):					
Midwest		13.5%	10.4%	6.7%	7.8%
Boston region		18.2	8.7	5.9	3.1
South Florida		12.7	10.8	7.5	8.6

Note: The values for net book value and gross book value in Exhibit 19.3 represent the simple average of beginning-of-year and end-of-year values (beginning and ending values are not shown). Replacement cost and liquidation value are estimated as of the point when ROI is calculated.

Replacement cost is useful in evaluating managers' performance because it best measures the investment in the continuing business: The ROI figures show that all three regions are somewhat comparable, with South Florida slightly in the lead.

Liquidation value provides a somewhat different picture. The ROI based on liquidation value for the Boston region is very low relative to the other two regions. Because of the significant appreciation in real estate values of stores in the Boston region, the liquidation value for the Boston region is quite high. The replacement cost figure is lower than liquidation cost because of the assumption that if CompuCity replaces its stores in the Boston region, these stores would be located where the real estate values are lower. The analysis of liquidation-based ROIs is useful for showing CompuCity management that the real estate value of these stores could now exceed their value as CompuCity retail locations. Perhaps the company should sell these stores and relocate elsewhere in areas where values are near those suggested by the replacement cost figures.

Strategic Issues Regarding the Use of ROI

The use of ROI for performance evaluation purposes is well established in business practice. However, management accountants should be aware of some of the limitations or deficiencies of using ROI to evaluate the performance of investment centers. We address four such issues: applicability of ROI as a performance indicator in the knowledge-based economy; goal-congruence problems associated with the use of any short-term financial performance indicator, such as ROI; behavioral consequences associated with using different models for investment decision making (e.g., NPV) and subsequent performance evaluation (e.g., ROI); and incentive effects regarding new investment by the most profitable units of the organization.

Value Creation in the New Economy

As indicated in footnote 3, the ROI metric was developed in the U.S. for use by industrial-age companies (DuPont, General Motors, etc.). For such companies, the ROI performance indicator served its purpose well: It allowed top management to effectively allocate capital across business units (such as product lines or geographic territories). In short, companies in that era competed on how effectively they managed physical assets (plant, property, and equipment). It was entirely appropriate, therefore, to evaluate business units on the basis of the amount of profit generated by the use of those physical assets.

Today's business environment is drastically different. Value creation for many companies in what can be called the *knowledge-based economy* consists of managing intangible, as well as tangible, assets. Examples of such assets are the skill level of the organization's employees (i.e., human capital); distinctive processes, including supply chains; loyal customers; and innovative products and services. Thus, in today's competitive environment, a broader performance measurement and control system is required, such as the balanced scorecard (BSC), covered in Chapters 2 and 18.

Short-Term Focus of ROI

A somewhat related factor is that ROI (and, as we shall see, residual income) is a short-term measure of profitability and, as such, is subject to manipulation on the part of business unit managers. Because ROI is a ratio, managers (particularly those whose bonuses are tied to realized ROI figures) are motivated to do whatever it takes to increase the numerator of the calculation, decrease the denominator, or both. Some actions may be unethical or even illegal. Other actions (e.g., delaying needed repairs and maintenance or reducing spending on critical research and development activities or on productivity-improvement programs) can be myopic in nature. That is, they may provide a short-term boost to reported profits (i.e., to the numerator of the ROI metric) but be harmful to the long-term competitive position of the business.

On the denominator side, the use of ROI can provide further goal congruence problems: It can discourage managers of business units from making investments that would increase the value of the organization as a whole. There are two dimensions to this problem: (1) There can be a disconnect between the method used to make capital budgeting decisions (e.g., discounted cash flow [DCF] decision models, as discussed in Chapter 12) and the method used subsequently to evaluate managerial performance and (2) disincentive effects related to the short-term ROI associated with new investment opportunities may exist. We explore these issues in the following two sections. Both situations can motivate suboptimal decision making on the part of business unit managers.

Decision Model and Performance Model Inconsistency   As we argued in Chapter 12, long-term investment projects should be evaluated using a discounted cash flow (DCF) decision model, such as net present value (NPV). Such a model compares the present value of expected after-tax cash flows from a project to the present value of cash outflows (investment outlays) for the project. If the NPV is positive, the project in question should be accepted because the expectation is that the project will increase the value of the organization.

In practice, the business unit manager's financial performance may be judged using an accounting-based metric such as ROI. The use of two different metrics, one for making the investment decision (NPV) and the other for evaluating subsequent financial performance (ROI), creates an inherent and significant incentive problem: It may discourage managers from making investments that add value to the organization (i.e., NPV > 0) yet have unfavorable short-term effects on the business unit's ROI. One solution to this problem is to calculate depreciation, for ROI purposes, on a present value basis. (This issue is explored in Problem 19-37 at the end of this chapter.) The end result is that the use of present value depreciation aligns the decision-making model with the model used subsequently to evaluate the financial performance of the business unit.

As demonstrated in the following section, investment disincentive effects can exist even when ROI, rather than NPV, is used to evaluate long-term investment proposals.

ROI: Disincentive for New Investment by the Most Profitable Units   Business units evaluated on the basis of ROI have an important disincentive that conflicts with the goals of the firm: ROI encourages units to invest only in projects that earn *a higher rate of return than the unit's current ROI* so that the addition of the investment improves the unit's overall ROI. Thus, the most profitable business units (i.e., those with relatively high ROIs) have a corresponding disincentive to invest in any project that does not exceed their current ROI, even projects that, on a present value basis, are attractive to the organization as a whole.[4]

The disincentive for new investment hurts the firm strategically in two ways. First, it rejects investment projects that would be beneficial. Second, to take advantage of a unit's apparent management skill, ROI evaluation provides a disincentive for the best units to grow. In contrast, the units with the lowest ROI have an incentive to invest in new projects to improve their ROI. Management skills could, however, be lacking in the low-ROI units.

The disincentive can be illustrated if we assume that CompuCity's Boston region has an option to purchase, for $22,500, a telephone switch that can increase the capacity of its toll-free service number and reduce operating costs by $10,000 per year. The switch is expected

---

[4] As we noted in Chapter 12 and as noted above, an attractive project is one that has a positive estimated net present value (NPV).

EXHIBIT 19.4   ROI for Boston Region's Proposed Investment

	First Year	Second Year	Third Year
Depreciation expense (straight-line method)	$7,500 = \dfrac{\$22,500}{3}$	$7,500	$7,500
NBV at year-end	$15,000 = $22,500 − $7,500	$7,500 = $15,000 − $7,500	$0 = $15,000 − $7,500
Average NBV for the year	$18,750 = \dfrac{(\$22,500 + \$15,000)}{2}$	$11,250 = \dfrac{(\$15,000 + \$7,500)}{2}$	$3,750 = \dfrac{(\$7,500 + \$0)}{2}$
ROI	$13.33\% = \dfrac{\$10,000 - \$7,500}{\$18,750}$	$22.22\% = \dfrac{\$10,000 - \$7,500}{\$11,250}$	$66.67\% = \dfrac{\$10,000 - \$7,500}{\$3,750}$

to last for three years and have no salvage value. Exhibit 19.4 shows the determination of ROI for the purchase of the switch using the straight-line method of depreciation. The ROI for its purchase is expected to be 13.33% in the first year and 22.22% and 66.67% in the second and third years, respectively.[5]

Using NBV, the Boston region's ROI is currently 18.2% (Exhibit 19.3). Consequently, the manager of the Boston region might not purchase the switch because the first year's return of 13.3% on the proposed investment is less than the current ROI for the Boston region. Buying the switch would reduce Boston's ROI from 18.2% to 17.8% [($38,500 + $10,000 − $7,500) ÷ ($212,000 + $18,750)] in the first year. In later years, the ROI from the switch would substantially exceed Boston's current ROI, but the manager might not be able (or willing) to wait for that improvement if strong pressure for current ROI exists.

Moreover, from a firmwide perspective, because the rate of return on the switch in each year exceeds the firm's threshold rate of return of 12%, the Boston region should purchase it. Thus, a significant limitation of ROI is that it can cause business unit managers to decline some investments, in conflict with the firm's interests. This situation is an excellent example of a goal congruence problem: *The use of ROI to evaluate the short-term financial performance of business unit managers might not motivate decisions that increase the value of the business as a whole.* One way to address this limitation is to use an alternative measure of business unit profitability, called residual income.

Residual Income

LO 19-2

Explain the use and limitations of residual income for evaluating the short-term financial performance of investment centers.

In contrast to ROI, which is a percentage, **residual income (RI)** is a dollar amount equal to the income of a business unit less an imputed charge for the level of investment in the unit. The charge is determined by multiplying a desired minimum rate of return by the level of investment in the business unit.[6] Residual income can be interpreted as the income earned after the division has "paid" a charge for the funds invested in the business unit by top management.

The RI calculation for CompuCity is illustrated in Exhibit 19.5 using an assumed minimum rate of return of 12%. Note that because all three business units (regions) have an ROI higher than 12%, all also have a positive RI. Note, too, that in this case, each unit's ranking on ROI is the same as its ranking based on RI: The Boston region unit has the highest ROI and residual income. However, this will not always be the case.

residual income (RI)
A dollar amount equal to the income of a business unit less an imputed charge for the level of investment in the division.

The issues regarding the measurement of investment and income for RI are the same as those discussed earlier for ROI. However, RI does have the advantage of motivating a business unit to pursue an investment opportunity as long as the investment's expected return exceeds the minimum return set by the firm. For example, using RI, the Boston region would *accept* the opportunity to purchase the telephone switch described in Exhibit 19.4 because

[5] Using the discounted cash flow (DCF) methods explained in Chapter 12, the purchase of the switch has an internal rate of return (IRR) of approximately 16% ($22,500 ÷ $10,000 = 2.250; the PV annuity factor for 16% and three years is 2.246).

[6] Conceptually, the minimum desired rate of return is defined as an entity's weighted-average cost of capital (WACC). However, we are speaking here about the evaluation of an investment center, not firmwide performance. Thus, adjustments to the firm's WACC are likely appropriate when evaluating *subunit* performance.

REAL-WORLD FOCUS   Calculating the Human Capital Return on Investment

In a knowledge-based economy, people are the most important asset. Managing human capital is therefore a strategic concern for many organizations today. Numerous useful metrics have been developed to help companies assess the financial returns to their investments in human capital. One of these metrics is called the *human capital return on investment,* or HCROI. HCROI is calculated as the ratio of pretax profit, prior to employment costs, to employee investment (total compensation), as follows:

$$HCROI = \frac{Revenue - Nonwage\ costs}{Total\ compensation}$$

Because the metric is in ratio form, it is useful for making comparisons across commercial sectors, regions, and nations. This metric covers all of the following: revenue production, cost incurrence, employment level, and amount invested in employees. As such, it provides direction for improving an organization's return on human capital.

Source: Chartered Institute of Personnel and Development, "Human Capital Metrics and Analytics: Assessing the Evidence of the Value and Impact of People Data," Technical Report, May 2017.

EXHIBIT 19.5

Illustration of Residual Income Calculations for CompuCity Geographic Regions

	Financial Data (from Exhibit 19.3)	
	Operating Income	Net Book Value (NBV) of Assets
Regions:		
Midwest	$26,000	$192,500
Boston region	38,500	212,000
South Florida	16,850	133,000
Return on investment (ROI):		
Midwest	13.5%	
Boston region	18.2%	
South Florida	12.7%	
Residual income (RI):		
Midwest	$2,900 = $26,000 − (0.12 × $192,500)	
Boston region	**$13,060 = $38,500 − (0.12 × $212,000)**	
South Florida	$890 = $16,850 − (0.12 × $133,000)	

this investment would increase the unit's residual income. The RI in the first year after the investment in the switch would be:

$$\$13,310 = (\$38,500 + \$10,000 - \$7,500) - [0.12 \times (\$212,000 + \$18,750)]$$

This amounts to a $250 improvement over the unit's current RI ($13,060, from Exhibit 19.5).

An additional advantage of RI is that a firm can adjust the required rates of return for differences in risk. For example, business units with higher business risk can be evaluated at a higher minimum rate of return. The increased risk might be due to obsolete products, increased competition in the industry, or other economic factors affecting the business unit. In Exhibit 19.5, we used the same minimum rate of return (12%) when calculating the RI of each geographic region of CompuCity. However, we could have used different rates of return for each region, in order to capture risk differences across the three regions.

Another advantage is that it is possible to calculate a different investment charge for different types of assets. For example, a higher minimum rate of return could be used for long-lived assets that are more likely to be specialized in use and thus not so readily sellable.

Time Period of Analysis: Single vs. Multiperiod Perspective

Both ROI and RI are *short-term* indicators of financial performance. That is, they both generally reflect one-year performance. Because of this, some organizations choose to evaluate these performance indicators over multiple years. Trend analysis, perhaps combined with competitive benchmarking, would yield more informative indications of an investment center's financial performance. By including multiple years in the evaluation window, there may be less incentive to engage in short-term behaviors that are dysfunctional in terms of long-term

EXHIBIT 19.6   **The Effect of Business Unit Size and Minimum Desired Rate of Return on Residual Income (RI)**

	Business Unit A	Business Unit B
Investment	$10,000,000	$750,000
Operating income	$1,500,000	$112,500
Return on investment (ROI)	15% = $1,500,000 ÷ $10,000,000	15% = $112,500 ÷ $750,000
Residual income (RI), at a minimum desired return of 12%	$300,000 = $1,500,000 − (0.12 × $10,000,000)	$22,500 = $112,500 − (0.12 × $750,000)

profitability. Finally, in the discussion of ROI, we pointed out that the use of present value depreciation is one mechanism for achieving compatibility between the model used for long-term investment decision making and the model used subsequently to evaluate managerial performance. The use of multiyear residual income (RI) figures is thought to accomplish the same objective. Why? Because the NPV of residual incomes over the life of a project, if cash flows are exactly as predicted, will be exactly equal to the NPV of net after-tax cash flows. In short, the use of multiyear RI figures helps to achieve goal congruence.

Limitations of Residual Income

Although the residual income measure deals effectively with the disincentive problem of ROI, it has its own limitations. A key issue is that because RI is not a percentage, it is not useful for comparing units of significantly different sizes. RI favors larger units that would be expected to have larger residual incomes, even with relatively poor performance. Moreover, relatively small changes in the minimum rate of return can dramatically affect the RI for business units of different size, as illustrated in Exhibit 19.6. Although business units A and B both have the same ROI of 15%, the RI amount differs significantly: $300,000 for business unit A, but only $22,500 for business unit B. The difference would be greater for a smaller minimum return.

ROI and RI can complement each other in the evaluation of investment centers. The advantages and limitations of each measure are summarized in Exhibit 19.7.

Economic Value Added

economic value added (EVA®)
A measure of financial performance designed to approximate an entity's *economic profit;* calculated most often as net operating profit after taxes (adjusted for accounting "distortions") less an imputed charge based on the level of invested capital.

Economic value added (EVA®) is an estimate of a business's *economic profit* generated during a given period. In its simplest form, EVA® can be defined as profit less an imputed charge for the use of assets (capital) during the period. We might depict this measure of earnings as follows:

> Sales
> Less: Operating expenses (including taxes)
> Less: Financing expense (Cost of capital × Amount of invested capital)
> EVA®

As with RI and ROI, EVA® is a potentially useful metric for evaluating the financial performance of investment units because it explicitly incorporates the level of invested capital. That is, similar to residual income (RI), no measure of return on investment is indicated until there is a recovery of the cost of capital. Similar to RI, EVA® motivates managers to increase investment as long as such investments return at least $1 beyond the cost of capital. In this sense, the use of EVA® is thought to better align the interests of shareholders and managers of a company.

On the surface, RI and EVA® look confusingly similar. There is a major difference, however. RI is calculated entirely using reported (i.e., GAAP-based) accounting data. As such, RI suffers from all of the limitations associated with historical-based accounting statements. By contrast, EVA® attempts to approximate economic, rather than accounting, earnings and level of invested capital.

Thus, RI and EVA® are similar in form but strikingly different in terms of measurement. The overall objective of EVA® is to provide an estimate of the *value added* to (or destroyed by) each division of an organization (or the entire organization itself) during a given period. As such, EVA® is one approach to what we call *value-based management.*

EXHIBIT 19.7   **Advantages and Limitations of ROI and Residual Income (RI)**

	Advantages	Limitations
Return on investment (ROI)	• Easily understood by managers • Comparable to interest rates and rates of return on alternative investments • Widely used	• Disincentive for high-ROI units to invest in projects with ROI higher than the minimum rate of return but lower than the unit's current ROI • Can lead to goal congruence problems (e.g., suboptimal investment decision making)
Residual income (RI)	• Supports incentive to accept all projects with ROI above the minimum rate of return • Can use the minimum rate of return to adjust for differences in risk • Can use a different minimum rate of return for different types of assets	• Favors large units • Can be difficult to determine a minimum rate of return for organizational subunits
Both ROI and RI	• *Comprehensive financial measure;* includes key elements important to top management: revenues, costs, and level of investment • *Comparability;* expands top management's span of control by allowing comparison of business units	• Can mislead strategic decision making; not as comprehensive as the balanced scorecard, which includes customer satisfaction, business processes, and learning, as well as financial measures; the balanced scorecard is linked to strategy • Measurement issues; variations in the measurement of inventory and long-lived assets and in the treatment of nonrecurring items, income taxes, foreign exchange effects, and the use/cost of shared assets • Short-term focus; investments with long-term benefits might be neglected; captures financial performance for only a single year; may cause goal congruence problems within the organization • Failure to capture value-creating activities (i.e., managing an organization's intangible assets)

Estimating EVA®

The equation listed earlier for EVA® can be expanded as follows:

$$\text{EVA}^® = \text{NOPAT} - (k \times \text{Average invested capital})$$

where NOPAT = After-tax cash operating income, after depreciation (i.e., "the total pool of cash funds available to suppliers of capital")

= Revenues − Cash operating costs − Depreciation − Cash taxes on operating income

It is because of the deduction for depreciation that the earnings figure in the computation of EVA® is referred to as net operating profit after tax (i.e., NOPAT). In the above formulation, invested capital = economic capital = cash contributed by suppliers of funds to the business (or business unit).

Finally, note that in determining the imputed charge for invested capital, k represents the weighted-average cost of capital (WACC).[7]

An alternative specification of EVA® is:

$$\text{EVA}^® = (r - k) \times \text{Invested capital}$$

where

r = Rate of return on capital (what economists might call cash-on-cash *return*)

= NOPAT ÷ Invested capital

[7] See Chapter 12 for a discussion of the calculation of the weighted-average cost of capital (WACC) for a company as a whole. As indicated in footnote 6, adjustments to the firmwide WACC may be needed when estimating *divisional* discount rates.

REAL-WORLD FOCUS   Long-Term Strategy and Economic Profit

Economists and business leaders have argued for many years that companies are most successful when their strategic priorities and efforts are focused on long-term value creation rather than succumbing to pressure from investors and analysts to focus on short-term earnings and stock price movements. A recent study from researchers at McKinsey Global Institute and FCLT Global provides compelling evidence that, over a 15-year period, companies taking a long-term perspective outperformed companies with a more short-term focus. Long-term companies had higher average revenue and earnings growth, as well as higher growth in market capitalization. But the metric on which the difference was greatest was

"economic profit," another term for residual income (of which EVA® is a specific version). On average, long-term companies increased their economic profit by an amazing 63% more than short-term companies over the period of study. This research demonstrates the value of residual income for measuring companies' use of capital to generate profits, and the results provide clear evidence that companies pursuing a long-term strategic vision are more likely to create real value through superior investments.

Source: D. Barton, J. Manyika, and S. K. Williamson, "Finally, Evidence That Managing for the Long Term Pays Off," *Harvard Business Review* (Online), February 9, 2017.

and

$$k = \text{WACC}$$

The primary advantage of the preceding formulation is its associated interpretation:

If $r > k$ during a period, then shareholder value was increased during that period (i.e., EVA® was positive).

As seen from the above, in order to calculate EVA® for a period, we need to estimate both NOPAT and capital. Stewart, in the seminal work in the area, lists 164 possible adjustments to reported accounting data to estimate NOPAT and capital.[8] In the EVA® literature, adjustments to the capital figures reported in financial statements are referred to as *equity-equivalent (EE)* adjustments.

The actual number of adjustments in practice is typically much less than 164. Note that if no adjustments to reported accounting data are made, then the EVA® metric reduces to RI.

The following table lists some common adjustments that analysts can make when estimating EVA®.

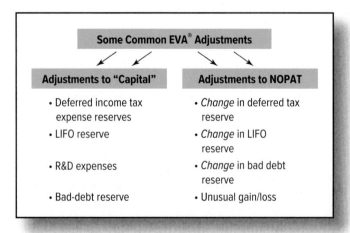

Alternative Approaches to Estimating EVA® NOPAT and EVA® Capital

Stewart provides two alternative ways for estimating an entity's EVA®: the *financing approach* and the *operating approach*. Which of the two methods you use is simply a matter of personal preference. If applied correctly, both yield the same estimate of EVA®.

[8] G. Bennett Stewart III, *The Quest for Value* (New York: Harper Collins, 1995).

Financing Approach

In the financing approach, NOPAT is estimated by building up to the rate of return on capital from the standard return on equity (ROE) calculation in three steps:

1. Eliminate financial leverage (i.e., the effect of debt financing).
2. Eliminate so-called financial distortions.
3. Eliminate so-called accounting distortions.

As a result of the first two adjustments above, NOPAT will represent the total returns available to *all* providers of capital to the company. The NOPAT return therefore represents the productivity of capital employed in the business, irrespective of how investments in that capital were financed.

To calculate EVA® capital using the financing approach, you would first determine the total of interest-bearing debt. To this figure, you would add the book value of common equity (par value of stock, capital in excess of par, and retained earnings), the book value of preferred stock, and noncontrolling interests (if any). Finally, it is necessary to adjust for equity equivalents, such as the balance sheet amount of deferred taxes and the LIFO reserve (if any). The resulting amount represents an estimate of EVA® capital.

Operating Approach

The operating approach to estimating NOPAT essentially consists of starting with (cash) sales and then subtracting depreciation and recurring cash economic expenses. Next, we deduct the amount of cash operating taxes, after which we are left with EVA® NOPAT. In estimating the amount of cash taxes paid, we adjust reported income tax expense by the change in the deferred tax account during the period. Note that interest expense, because it is a financing charge, is ignored in the determination of EVA® NOPAT. What this means, therefore, is that we must remove (i.e., add back to income tax expense) the assumed income tax benefit associated with the deductibility of interest expense. Finally, to estimate EVA® NOPAT we make a number of "EE" adjustments (e.g., the effect of a change in the LIFO reserve account). The resulting profit figure should be the same as the NOPAT figure calculated under the financing approach.

Under the operating approach, EVA® capital is estimated by looking at the left-hand side of the entity's balance sheet. We define EVA® capital as net working capital (NWC) plus net fixed assets (NFA), where NWC is defined as (adjusted) current assets less NIBCLS (non-interest-bearing current liabilities). A typical EE adjustment that would be made to reported balance sheet data is an adjustment for the LIFO reserve.

Problems 19-44 and 19-45 at the end of the chapter explore the issue of estimating EVA® using the operating approach and financing approach, respectively.[9]

Using Average Total Assets

For purposes of calculating ROI, RI, and EVA®, at what point in the accounting period are assets measured? In practice, accountants use the average of the beginning and ending balances of the year for total assets in these performance metrics. The reason is that because income is applicable to the entire year, then using a simple average of the amount of total assets for the year is consistent with the period covered by the income.

Part Two: Transfer Pricing

transfer pricing
The determination of an exchange price for a product or service when different business units within a firm exchange it; used to evaluate the financial performance of profit and investment centers.

Transfer pricing is the determination of an exchange price for a product or service when different business units within a firm exchange it. The products can be final products sold to outside customers or intermediate products provided to other internal units. Regardless of

[9] Additional guidance for estimating EVA® NOPAT and EVA® capital are provided in the following sources: G. Bennett Stewart III, *The Quest for Value* (New York: Harper Collins, 1995); D. S. Young and S. F. O'Byrne, *EVA® and Value-Based Management: A Practical Guide to Implementation* (New York: McGraw-Hill, 2001). A discussion of 11 concerns about EVA®, in three categories (computational issues, measurement issues, and effectiveness), can be found in H. Kent Baker, Prakash Deo, and Tarun Mukherjee, "EVA Revisited," *Journal of Financial Education,* Fall 2009, pp. 1–22. Also see G. Bennett Stewart III, *Best-Practice EVA* (John Wiley & Sons, 2013).

whether business units of an organization are considered profit centers (Chapter 18) or investment centers (Chapter 19), transfer prices are needed for performance evaluation purposes. For example, without transfer prices it would not be possible to implement the performance metrics discussed in Part One of this chapter (i.e., ROI, RI, and EVA®).

When Is Transfer Pricing Important?

Transfers of products and services between business units are most common in firms with a high degree of vertical integration. Such firms engage in a number of different value-creating activities in the value chain. Wood product, food product, and consumer product firms are examples. For instance, a computer manufacturer must determine transfer prices if it produces the chips, boards, and other components and assembles the computer itself. (See Exhibit 2.3 in Chapter 2.) A useful way to visualize the transfer pricing context is to create a graphic such as the one in Exhibit 19.8 that illustrates the business units involved in the transfer of products and services and identifies them as inside or outside the firm, nondomestic or domestic. Exhibit 19.8 shows the transfers for a hypothetical computer manufacturer, High Value Computer (HVC), that purchases a key component, the x-chip, from both internal and external suppliers and purchases other components from nondomestic sources. The internal unit that manufactures x-chips sells them both internally and externally. Where it is known, the transfer price is shown.

The management accountant's role is to help determine the proper transfer price for the internal sales of the x-chip. We begin by considering the objectives of transfer pricing.

Objectives of Transfer Pricing

There are three primary objectives for transfer prices:

1. To motivate a high level of effort on the part of business unit managers (i.e., the extent to which a particular transfer pricing method maintains autonomy of the business units).

2. To achieve goal congruence (i.e., consistency between decisions made by managers of business units and the goals of top management); for example, one important goal of transfer pricing is to minimize, within allowable limits, income tax consequences of internal transfers of goods and services.

3. To reward business unit managers fairly for their effort and skill and for the effectiveness of the decisions they make.

EXHIBIT 19.8

Transfer Pricing Context for High Value Computer (HVC) Example

Note: "Internal to the firm" refers to interdivisional transfers of goods and/or services. In the HVC example, internal units include both domestic and nondomestic units/divisions.

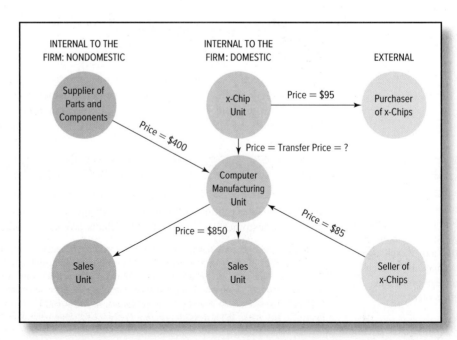

From a practical standpoint, specific transfer pricing alternatives can also be evaluated in terms of implementation/administrative costs. In the next section, we discuss several transfer pricing methods, including advantages and disadvantages of each.

Transfer Pricing Methods

The four available methods for determining the transfer price are variable cost, full cost, market price, and negotiated price.[10]

The **variable cost method** sets the transfer price equal to the seller's variable cost, with or without a markup. This method is desirable when the seller has excess capacity and the seller's variable cost is less than the external purchase price. The relatively low transfer price encourages buying internally, a situation that benefits the firm as a whole. To help ensure an internal transfer, and because of equity considerations, some companies add a markup to variable cost when determining the transfer price. One alternative in this regard is to add a lump-sum amount to variable costs. Also, variable costs can be defined as either actual or standard costs.

The **full cost method** sets the transfer price equal to the seller's variable cost plus an allocated share of the seller's fixed costs, with or without a markup for profit. Advantages of this approach are that it is well understood and that the information for determining the transfer price is readily available in the accounting records. A key disadvantage is that it includes fixed costs, which can cause improper decision making (Chapter 11). To improve on the full cost method, firms can use the activity-based costing (ABC) method described in Chapter 5.[11] Again, costs can be defined either as actual or as standard costs.

The **market price method** sets the transfer price as the current price of the product (or service) in the external market. Its key advantage is objectivity; it best satisfies the arm's-length criterion desired for both management and tax purposes. Further, using market prices generally (but not necessarily always) provides proper economic incentives. A key disadvantage is that the market price, especially for intermediate products, is often not available.

The **negotiated price method** involves a negotiation process and sometimes arbitration between divisions to determine the transfer price. This method is desirable when the divisions have a history of significant conflict and negotiation can result in an agreed-upon price. One could also argue that the use of negotiated transfer prices is consistent with the theory of decentralization. The primary limitation is that the method can reduce the desired autonomy of the divisions. Further, this method may be costly and time-consuming to implement.

Firms can also use two or more methods, called **dual pricing**. For example, when numerous conflicts exist between two divisions, standard full cost might be used as the buyer's transfer price, while the seller might use market price.[12]

The advantages and limitations of each of the four methods are summarized in Exhibit 19.9.

Choosing the Right Transfer Pricing Method: The Firmwide Perspective

One aspect of transfer pricing is whether the transfer price will lead to actions that benefit the organization as a whole. Looked at differently, we might ask whether the transfer price motivates an internal transfer when this benefits the firm, and whether it motivates an external

variable cost method
In transfer pricing, the transfer price equals the selling unit's variable cost, with or without a markup.

full cost method
A transfer price set equal to the variable cost of the selling unit, plus an allocated share of the selling unit's fixed costs, with or without a markup for profit.

market price method
A transfer price set as the current price of the product (or service) in the external market.

negotiated price method
The determination of a transfer price through a negotiation process and sometimes arbitration between units.

dual pricing
Involves the use of multiple prices for an internal transfer or cost allocation, one based on variable cost and one based on fixed cost.

[10] Administered transfer prices are also possible. In this situation, the transfer price is set either by management or by an arbiter. Such "imposed" prices are sometimes used when a specified internal transaction occurs frequently. While avoiding confrontations sometimes associated with a negotiated transfer price, we note that an imposed transfer price impinges on business unit autonomy and therefore the spirit of decentralization.

[11] For an explanation of the use of activity-based costing in transfer pricing, see Robert S. Kaplan, Dan Weiss, and Eyal Desheh, "Transfer Pricing with ABC," *Management Accounting*, May 1997, pp. 20–28; Gary J. Colbert and Barry H. Spicer, "Linking Activity-Based Costing and Transfer Pricing for Improved Decisions and Behavior," *Journal of Cost Management*, May–June 1998, pp. 20–26.

[12] For an illustration of dual allocation in transfer pricing, see David W. Young, "Two-Part Transfer Pricing Improves IDS Financial Control," *Healthcare Financial Management*, August 1998, pp. 56–65.

EXHIBIT 19.9   **Advantages and Limitations of Alternative Transfer Pricing Methods**

Method	Advantages	Limitations
Variable cost	• Provides proper motivation for the manager to make the correct *short-term decision,* in which the seller's fixed costs are not expected to change; when the seller's variable cost is less than the buyer's outside price, the variable cost transfer price will cause internal sourcing, the correct decision	• Inappropriate for long-term decision making in which fixed costs are relevant and prices must cover fixed as well as variable costs • Unfair to seller if seller is profit or investment center (i.e., no profit recognized on the transfer)
Full cost	• Easy to implement • Intuitive and easily understood • Preferred by tax authorities over variable cost • Appropriate for long-term decision making in which fixed costs are relevant and prices must cover fixed as well as variable costs	• Irrelevance of fixed costs in short-term decision making; fixed costs should be ignored in the buyer's choice of whether to buy inside or outside the firm • If used, should be standard rather than actual cost (allows buyer to know cost in advance and prevents seller from passing along inefficiencies)
Market price	• Helps to preserve division autonomy • Provides incentive for the seller to be competitive with outside suppliers • Has arm's-length standard desired by taxing authorities • Usually provides proper economic incentives	• Intermediate products often have no market price • Should be adjusted for any cost savings associated with an internal transfer, such as reduced selling costs
Negotiated price	• Can be the most practical approach when significant conflict exists • Is consistent with the theory of decentralization	• Need negotiation rule and/or arbitration procedure, which can reduce autonomy • Potential tax problems; might not be considered arm's length • Can be costly and time-consuming to implement • Resulting profitability measures (e.g., ROI or RI) are partly a function of the negotiating skills of the manager, rather than the operational performance of the division

sale when such a sale is warranted (from an organization-wide perspective). To guide such a decision, three questions must be addressed:

1. Is there an outside (i.e., an external) supplier?
2. Is the seller's variable cost (or, more generally, its incremental cost) less than the external market price?
3. Is the seller operating at full capacity?

Exhibit 19.10 shows the influence of each of these three factors on the choice of a transfer price and the decision to purchase inside or outside the firm.

First: Is there an external supplier? If not, there is no market price, and the best transfer price is based on cost or negotiated price. If there is an outside supplier, we must consider the relationship of the inside seller's variable cost (or, more generally, its incremental cost) to the market price of the external supplier by answering the second question.

Second: Is the seller's variable (or incremental) cost less than the external market price? If not, the seller's costs are likely far too high, and from the standpoint of the organization as a whole the buyer should buy externally. On the other hand, if the

EXHIBIT 19.10   Choosing the Right Transfer Price

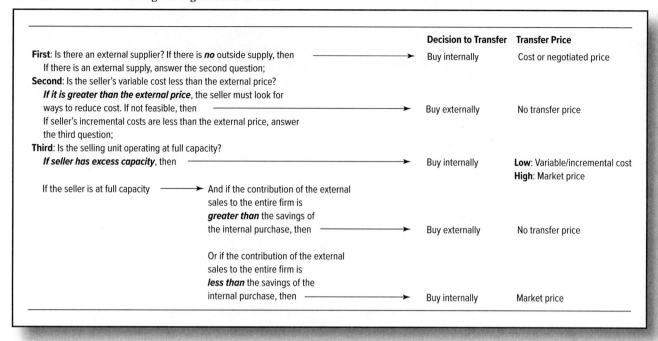

seller's incremental costs are less than the market price, we must consider the capacity of the seller (i.e., the third question).[13]

Third: Is the seller operating at full capacity? That is, will the order from the internal buyer cause the seller to deny other sales opportunities? If not, the selling division should provide the order to the internal buyer at a transfer price somewhere between variable cost and market price. In contrast, if the seller is at full capacity, we must determine and compare the cost savings of internal sales versus the selling division's opportunity cost of lost sales. If the cost savings to the internal buyer are higher than the cost of lost sales to the seller, then from the standpoint of the organization as a whole, the buyer should buy inside, and the proper transfer price should be the market price.

Determining the correct transfer price and correct transfer decision can be illustrated using the High Value Computer (HVC) case (Exhibit 19.8). HVC has the option to purchase the x-chip outside the firm for $85 or to manufacture it. Note that if the computer manufacturing division of HVC purchases the x-chip from the outside suppler, it must add a component to the x-chip at a variable cost of $5 to make the x-chip function as desired; this additional step is not necessary if the x-chip is purchased internally. Also, note that the x-chip production division can sell its chip outside for $95, but there is a variable selling cost of $2 per unit; there is no selling cost for internal transfer. The relevant information is presented in the top portion of Exhibit 19.11. The lower portion of Exhibit 19.11 shows the calculation of the relevant costs for each of the two options.

A comparison of options 1 and 2 in Exhibit 19.11 shows that the firm as a whole benefits (in the short run) under option 1 when the computer manufacturing division of HVC purchases the x-chip externally and the x-chip product division of HVC sells externally. The reason is that the computer manufacturing division's savings of $30 from internal transfer ($30 = $85 outside price plus $5 for additional variable cost to add a component to the x-chip less $60 variable cost of the internal x-chip production division) is less than the x-chip production division's opportunity cost of lost sales, $33 ($95 less $60 manufacturing cost less $2 selling cost). The opportunity cost of the x-chip production division is important because the division is assumed to be working at full capacity. The $450,000 difference between the

---

[13] We focus on variable costs in this second step because commonly the transfer pricing issue is addressed as a short-term decision in which fixed costs are not expected to differ, regardless of whether the internal transfer is made or not made. In this case, the analysis is very much like the make-or-buy decision problem covered in Chapter 11—the fixed costs of the seller generally are irrelevant because they will not change in the short run.

EXHIBIT 19.11
Transfer Pricing Example: The High Value Computer (HVC) Example

Key assumptions:
 The computer manufacturing division can buy the x-chip inside or outside the firm.
 The x-chip production division can sell inside or outside the firm.
 The x-chip production division is at full capacity (150,000 units).
 One x-chip is needed for each computer manufactured by HVC.
Other information:

Sales price of computer for HVC's computer manufacturing division	$850
Variable manufacturing cost of the computer manufacturing division (excluding x-chip) ($400 parts and $250 labor)	650
Variable x-chip manufacturing cost for HVC's x-chip production division	60
Price of x-chip from outside supplier, to HVC's computer manufacturing division	85
Variable cost to computer manufacturing division to add needed component to outside supplier's x-chip	5
Price of x-chip from HVC's x-chip production division to outside buyer	95
Variable selling cost to the x-chip production division for outside sales	2

Option 1: X-Chip Production Division Sells Outside

HVC manufactures 150,000 computers, using x-chips purchased for $85 from outside supplier; HVC's x-chip production division sells 150,000 units for $95 each to an outside buyer.

Contribution Income Statement*
(000s omitted)

	Computer Manufacturing Division	X-Chip Production Division	Total
Sales (price = $850, $95)	$127,500	$14,250	$141,750
Less: Variable costs			
x-chip ($85 + $5)	13,500		13,500
Other costs ($650, $60 + $2)	97,500	9,300	106,800
Contribution margin	$ 16,500	$ 4,950	$ 21,450

Option 2: X-Chip Production Division Sells Inside (to HVC's Computer Manufacturing Division)

HVC manufactures 150,000 computers, using x-chips purchased for $60 (variable cost) from the inside supplier.

	Computer Manufacturing Division	X-Chip Production Division	Total
Sales (price = $850, $60)	$127,500	$9,000	$136,500
Less: Variable costs			
x-chip ($60)	9,000		9,000
Other costs ($650, $60)	97,500	9,000	106,500
Contribution margin	$ 21,000	—	$ 21,000

*It is assumed that fixed costs will not differ for the two options; thus, these costs are excluded from the analysis.

two options is due to the net difference identified above ($33 − $30) × 150,000 = $450,000. In summary, we can answer the same three questions for HVC in the following way:

> **First: Is there an external supplier?** HVC has an outside supplier, so we must compare the internal seller's incremental costs (in this case, its variable costs) to the external seller's price.
>
> **Second: Is the seller's variable (or incremental) cost less than the external market price?** For HVC, it is, so we must consider the utilization of capacity in the inside selling division.
>
> **Third: Is the seller operating at full capacity?** For HVC, it is, so we must consider the contribution of the selling division's external sales relative to the savings from selling internally. Again, for HVC, the contribution of the selling division's external sales is $33 per unit, which is higher than the savings from selling internally ($30). Therefore, HVC's x-chip production division should choose outside sales and make no internal transfers.

Many companies are converting what used to be cost centers into profit centers or even investment centers. Examples include PepsiCo and MasterCard (converting the marketing function) as well as ExxonMobil Corp. and Aflac (converting the IT function). This shift can be challenging for division managers who used to focus exclusively on managing costs but who will now be evaluated on their ability to generate revenues and profits. This shift is likely to change how division managers think about transfer prices for the goods and services they provide to other internal divisions.

Required

How would a shift from cost center to profit center affect a manager's approach to transfer pricing? Can you think of how top management could help division managers succeed in their new roles?

(Refer to Comments on Cost Management in Action at the end of the chapter.)

By way of summary, we note that from the standpoint of HVC as a whole, setting an appropriate transfer price is important because it motivates divisional actions that may either increase or decrease the total operating profits of the firm. You can see this by looking at the total contribution margins associated with each of the two options listed in Exhibit 19.11. A transfer price that motivates option 1 increases total contribution margin (and therefore operating income). In short, setting the appropriate transfer price affects the "size of the pie." We turn next to a discussion of a general model that can be used to help guide the determination of the correct transfer price from the standpoint of the firm as a whole. Later, we consider a second situation where the "size of the pie" (i.e., the amount of firmwide profit) is affected by the transfer price chosen: transfers between domestic and nondomestic divisions, each of which may be subject to its own set of income tax rates, customs duties, and so on.

General Transfer Pricing Rule

The preceding discussion, captured in Exhibit 19.10, may seem overwhelming, but it can be summarized by the following general transfer pricing rule:

$$\text{Minimum transfer price} = \text{Incremental cost of the producing division}$$
$$+ \text{Opportunity cost to the organization (if any)}$$
$$\text{by making an internal transfer}$$

From the standpoint of the firm as a whole, this rule will generally ensure that the optimal decision (about whether to transfer internally or not) will be motivated. Refer once again to the data (and two options) presented in Exhibit 19.11. There is a pretax benefit to HVC as a whole if option 1 is chosen: HVC is better off, at least in the short run, if the computer manufacturing division purchases its chips externally and the x-chip production division sells its chips externally. As we'll see next, a transfer price based on this general rule will motivate this decision:

Variable manufacturing cost		$60
Opportunity cost of making an internal transfer:		
External sales price	$95	
Less: Incremental costs:		
Selling cost	2	
Variable manufacturing cost	60	
Foregone contribution—external sales		$33
Minimum transfer price		$93

Thus, the minimum transfer price should be set at $93 (i.e., $60 + $33). At this price, the computer manufacturing division at HVC would be motivated to purchase externally, at $90 per chip. By doing so, HVC as a whole would generate a total contribution margin of $21,450,000 (compared to $21,000,000, as determined under option 2).

Remember that the amount indicated by the general rule is a minimum amount that the selling division should accept. This same principle was introduced in Chapter 11: In deciding whether a business should accept a special order, the minimum specified price was the sum of out-of-pocket costs plus opportunity cost. (Recall the definition of opportunity cost: a benefit forgone by taking a particular course of action.) The same logic applies in the transfer pricing case. Here, opportunity cost is the contribution margin the organization gives up, if any, by transferring internally rather than selling to an external party.

Estimating opportunity costs may not be an easy task, or even possible in some situations. For example, unless the product in question is traded in a purely competitive market (e.g., commodity-type products), then selling price—and therefore opportunity cost—are partly a function of the amount of internal versus external sales by the producer. These interactions complicate efforts to determine an opportunity cost associated with internal transfers. As another example, the product in question may be in the form of an intermediate product for which no organized external market exists. In such cases, the organization would have to rely on the use of one of the other transfer pricing options.

International Issues in Transfer Pricing

LO 19-5

Understand important international issues that arise in transfer pricing.

arm's length standard
A transfer price set to reflect the price that unrelated parties acting independently would have set.

comparable price method
Establishes an arm's length transfer price by using the sales prices of similar products made by unrelated firms.

resale price method
A transfer pricing method based on cost plus an appropriate markup based on gross profits of unrelated firms selling similar products.

cost plus method
Within the context of transfer pricing, a method that determines the price based on the selling unit's cost plus a gross profit percentage determined by comparing the seller's sales to those of unrelated parties (or by comparing unrelated parties' sales to those of other unrelated parties).

Transfer pricing is perhaps the most important international tax issue faced by multinational corporations (MNCs). Most countries now accept the Organization for Economic Cooperation and Development's model treaty, which calls for transfer prices to be adjusted using the arm's length standard—that is, to a price that unrelated parties would have set. The model treaty is widely accepted, but the way countries apply it can differ. However, worldwide support is strong for an approach to limit attempts by MNCs to reduce tax liability by setting transfer prices that differ from the arm's length standard.

The **arm's length standard** calls for setting transfer prices to reflect the price that unrelated parties acting independently would have set. The arm's length standard is applied in several different ways, but the three most widely used methods are (1) the comparable price method, (2) the resale price method, and (3) the cost plus method. The **comparable price method** is the most commonly used and the most preferred by tax authorities. It establishes an arm's length price by using the sales prices of similar products made by unrelated firms.[14]

The **resale price method** is used for distributors and marketing units when little value is added and no significant manufacturing operations exist. In this method, the transfer price is based on an appropriate markup using gross profits of unrelated firms selling similar products.

The **cost plus method** determines the transfer price based on the selling unit's cost plus a gross profit percentage determined by comparing the seller's sales to those of unrelated parties or by comparing unrelated parties' sales to those of other unrelated parties.

By keeping detailed records of the determination of cost, the management accountant can assist in determining the appropriate transfer price for international transfers of goods and services. The application of precise costing techniques, such as ABC (Chapter 5), would be particularly useful in terms of justifying a given transfer price to taxing authorities.

While it is true that there are limits to the transfer price charged in multinational transactions, it is also true that minimizing the total tax burden is a legitimate business objective. By setting a high transfer price for goods or services transferred to a unit operating in a relatively high-tax country, a company can reduce its total tax liability. Such a transfer price would increase the cost and thus reduce the income of the purchasing unit, thereby minimizing taxes for this unit. At the same time, the higher profits shown by the selling unit (as a result of the high transfer price) would be taxed at lower rates in the seller's home country. As demonstrated by the example that follows, international tax planning opportunities associated with a firm's transfer pricing process allow the firm to affect the "size of the pie."

Income Tax Planning Opportunities: International Transfer Pricing

To illustrate the tax planning opportunities associated with the setting of international transfer prices, refer to facts presented in Exhibit 19.11 and assume the following: (1) option 2 (i.e., all

[14] In this context, *unrelated* indicates that the firm has no common ownership interest.

transfers take place within HVC), (2) the x-chip product unit is located in South Korea, while the computer manufacturing unit is located in the United States; (3) the x-chip product unit incurs no fixed costs, and fixed costs for the computer manufacturing unit, per year, amount to $2,000,000; and (4) income tax rates are as follows: Korea, 40%, and the United States, 30%. Under these assumptions, the amount of operating income (i.e., *pretax* profits) shown under each of the three transfer pricing options, for both units and for HVC as a whole, is shown in Exhibit 19.12. The negotiated transfer price of $72.50 per unit was determined by taking a simple average of the market price per chip ($85) and the variable cost of the x-chip ($60). Thus, the highly condensed income statement presented in Exhibit 19.12 reflects the anticipated profit situation, *before tax and before customs/import duties,* for HVC as a whole.

In the preceding section, we saw that setting the appropriate transfer price (at $93 per chip) would ensure that, from HVC's perspective, a correct decision (between option 1 and option 2) would be made. It may seem from the data presented in Exhibit 19.12 that the choice of transfer price is irrelevant because the "bottom lines" are all the same. However, to this point we have left out of the exhibit the effect of one crucial factor: transnational differences in income tax rates. In HVC's case, the income tax differential that exists in Korea and the United States provides HVC with an ability, within limits, to maximize *after-tax* firmwide profits based on its choice of transfer price.

To illustrate, first focus on the bottom portion of Exhibit 19.12. What would the after-tax income statement look like for each division and for HVC as a whole given the assumed tax rates and under each of the three transfer pricing options? The relevant calculations are presented in Exhibit 19.13. As can be seen from this exhibit, both the total amount of taxes paid and the firmwide operating income after tax are affected by the choice of transfer price. We note, too, that the extent of this effect is a function of the difference in tax rates: The larger the disparity in tax rates, all else held constant, the greater the after-tax differences observed across transfer pricing options. In short, this is yet another example where the "size of the pie" for the firm as a whole is affected by the choice of transfer price.

Other International Considerations

In addition to income tax, there are other considerations that bear upon the transfer price decision in an international context. These include minimizing customs charges, using transfer prices to deal with currency restrictions of foreign countries, and dealing with the risk of expropriation of assets.

EXHIBIT 19.12 **HVC Unit and Total Operating Income (000s Omitted) under Alternative Transfer Prices**

	TRANSFER PRICING OPTIONS		
Volume = 150,000 units	Market Price ($85.00 per unit)	Variable Cost ($60.00 per unit)	Negotiated Price ($72.50 per unit)
x-Chip Production Division (Seller):			
Revenues	$ 12,750	$ 9,000	$ 10,875
Costs:			
Variable costs (Exhibit 19.11; $60 per unit)	9,000	9,000	9,000
Operating income	$ 3,750	$ -0-	$ 1,875
Computer Manufacturing Division (Buyer):			
Revenues (Exhibit 19.11; $850 per unit)	$127,500	$127,500	$127,500
Costs:			
Transferred-in costs (from x-chip product unit)	12,750	9,000	10,875
Variable costs (Exhibit 19.11; $650 per unit)	97,500	97,500	97,500
Fixed costs (assumed)	2,000	2,000	2,000
Operating income	$ 15,250	$ 19,000	$ 17,125
Combined Operating Income (HVC)	$ 19,000	$ 19,000	$ 19,000

Note: The combined contribution margin reflected in Exhibit 19.11 is $21,000,000 under all transfer pricing options (i.e., Option 2). To convert from contribution margin (Exhibit 19.11) to operating income (Exhibit 19.12), we are assuming that the computer manufacturing division of HVC incurs fixed costs of $2,000,000 per year. As such, firmwide operating income reflected in Exhibit 19.12 for each transfer pricing alternative is $19,000,000.

REAL-WORLD FOCUS   For Multinationals, Transfer Pricing Can Be Risky Business

Multinational companies often use transfer pricing to shift profits from units located in high-tax countries to units located in low-tax countries, allowing them to greatly reduce their total tax burden. Taxing authorities have taken notice, and many companies have been charged with subverting transfer pricing rules and using unreasonable and extreme assumptions and computations. Overreaching can be costly. In 2020, Fiat reached a settlement with the Italian Tax Agency (ITA) to pay €2.5 billion after the agency claimed that Fiat underestimated the value of its business by €5.1 billion when relocating its headquarters from Italy to the Netherlands. In 2019, Google agreed to a settlement of $481.5 million with the Australian Taxation Office for not paying taxes on sales made in Australia but run through a tax haven in Singapore. Apple is currently trying to overturn a decision made in 2016 by the EU to pay $15.6 billion in taxes and interest.

The risks associated with aggressive transfer pricing are high and seem to be getting higher. Many countries are working to protect their tax bases by writing stronger transfer pricing rules and increasing enforcement. The ITA has assessed over €30 billion of higher taxable profits claimed for transfer pricing adjustments in 2018 alone, while Australia has assembled a task force to audit tech companies and increase the taxes of digital filers.

Sources: S. Jewkes, "Fiat Reaches Settlement with Italy Tax Agency over Chrysler Value Claim," *Reuters,* February 7, 2020; E. Sylvers, "Fiat Chrysler Is Told to Pay $1.6 Billion in Italian Back Taxes," *The Wall Street Journal,* December 5, 2019; B. Butler, "Google to Pay $481.5m in Major Win for Australian Tax Office," *The Guardian,* December 17, 2019; J. White, "Transfer Pricing Cases to Watch in 2020," *International Tax Review,* January 30, 2020; A. Fossati, "Litigating in Italy: Transfer Pricing Dispute Resolution Evolves," *International Tax Review,* March 24, 2020.

EXHIBIT 19.13
HVC Unit and Total After-Tax Operating Income (000s omitted) and Income Tax Expense Based on Alternative Transfer Pricing Alternatives and Assumed Tax Rates

Volume = 150,000 units	Transfer Pricing Alternatives		
	Market Price ($85.00 per unit)	Variable Cost ($60.00 per unit)	Negotiated Price ($72.50 per unit)
x-Chip Production Division (Seller):			
Operating income (Exhibit 19.12)	$ 3,750	$ 0	$ 1,875
Less: Income taxes (@ 40%)	1,500	0	750
After-tax operating income	$ 2,250	$ 0	$ 1,125
Computer Manufacturing Division (Buyer):			
Operating income (Exhibit 19.12)	$15,250	$19,000	$17,125
Less: Income taxes (@ 30%)	4,575	5,700	5,138
After-tax operating income	$10,675	$13,300	$11,987
Combined (Firmwide) Amounts:			
Income tax expense	$ 6,075	$ 5,700	$ 5,888
After-tax operating income	$12,925	$13,300	$13,112

Risk of Expropriation

expropriation
A situation in which a government takes ownership and control of assets that a foreign investor has invested in that country.

Expropriation occurs when a government takes ownership and control of assets that a foreign investor has invested in that country. In managing the relationship with any one country, the management accountant attempts to find a strategic balance among sometimes conflicting objectives. For example, when a significant risk of expropriation exists, the firm can take appropriate actions such as limiting new investment or developing improved relationships with the foreign government (e.g., by actually paying higher taxes to that government via the transfer pricing decision).

Minimization of Customs Charges

The transfer price can affect the overall cost, including customs charges (i.e., tariffs and duties) imposed on goods imported from a nondomestic (i.e., foreign) unit. As such, issues related to these charges are similar to the income tax considerations discussed earlier. In order to reduce tariffs and customs duties, firms have incentives to lower the transfer prices for products imported into a country. Such charges should be expressed on an after-tax basis if the levies are deductible in determining taxable income in the country of import.

Currency Restrictions

As a foreign unit accumulates profits, a problem arises in some countries that limit the amount and/or timing of repatriation of these profits to the parent company. One way to deal with these restrictions is to set the transfer price so that profits accumulate at a relatively low rate. This issue therefore provides managers and the management accountant with additional planning opportunities in certain circumstances.

These international issues have become even more important because of the recent trend toward anti-globalization, as evidenced by the Brexit vote and the success of political parties and candidates who support more nationalistic policies on international trade. Given these developments, multinational companies need to be more informed and forward-looking than ever when establishing transfer pricing and sourcing policies. For example, supply chains that cross international boundaries may be disrupted if increased tariff and import costs make it harder for foreign units to supply needed parts.

Advance Pricing Agreements

advance pricing agreement (APA)

An agreement between the Internal Revenue Service (IRS) and a firm that establishes an agreed-upon transfer price.

An **advance pricing agreement (APA)** in the United States is an agreement between the Internal Revenue Service (IRS) and a firm that establishes an agreed-upon transfer price. The APA usually is obtained before the firm engages in the transfer. The APA program's goal is to resolve transfer pricing disputes in a timely manner and to avoid costly litigation. The program supplements the dispute resolution methods already in place: administrative (IRS), judicial, and treaty mechanisms.

Summary

Return on investment (ROI) and residual income (RI) are two of the most commonly used and well-understood measures for evaluating the short-term financial performance of investment centers.

ROI, which is defined as the ratio of operating income generated by an investment center to the level of investment in the investment center, has several disadvantages: a short-term focus, the difficulty in determining a unique measure for earnings and investment, and investment-disincentive effects.

RI is computed as the investment center's earnings for a period less a capital charge based on a minimum desired rate of return. RI solves some, but not all, of ROI's problems. For example, both have a short-term focus, both rely on accrual-based accounting numbers, and both focus solely on (short-term) financial performance.

The increased interest in the balanced scorecard (BSC) and in economic value added (EVA®) suggests that firms are adapting performance appraisal systems for investment centers to include more of a long-term strategic focus.

When an organization's business units exchange goods or services internally (i.e., between each other) and management desires to assess the financial performance of these units, a transfer price must be associated with the internal transfers. The management accountant can serve an important role by overseeing the objectives of transfer pricing: performance evaluation (of management and business units), tax minimization, management of foreign currencies and risks, and other strategic objectives. Common transfer pricing methods include variable cost, full cost, market value, and negotiated price. Cost-based transfer prices can be set either at actual or at standard cost (see Chapter 14). In setting the transfer price, management considers the availability and quality of outside supply, the internal selling division's capacity utilization, and the firm's strategic objectives in determining the proper transfer price. A general transfer pricing guideline specifies that the minimum transfer price to the selling division is the sum of incremental costs plus opportunity costs to the seller (if any). As was the case in the special order decision covered in Chapter 11, this rule provides a floor or minimum transfer price. Some companies use dual pricing, in which two separate prices are used to price an internal transfer.

Perhaps the most important objective in determining a transfer price for international transfers is minimizing the total tax burden. With the efforts of various international groups, each country monitors transfer prices used in international trade. The most common transfer pricing methods used for international trade include the comparable price method, the resale price method, and the cost plus method. A U.S. firm can determine the acceptability of its transfer pricing method by requesting what is called an advance pricing agreement (APA) from the IRS.

Key Terms

advance pricing agreement
  (APA), *851*
arm's length standard, *848*
asset turnover (AT), *828*
comparable price method, *848*
cost plus method, *848*
dual pricing, *843*
economic value added
  EVA®), *838*

expropriation, *850*
full cost method, *843*
gross book value (GBV), *833*
historical cost, *832*
liquidation value, *833*
market price method, *843*
negotiated price method, *843*
net book value (NBV), *832*

replacement cost, *833*
resale price method, *848*
residual income (RI), *836*
return on investment
  (ROI), *828*
return on sales (ROS), *828*
transfer pricing, *841*
variable cost method, *843*

Comments on Cost Management in Action

Transfer Pricing with New Profit Centers

A shift from a cost center to a profit center obviously changes how a manager leads the unit. The focus changes from providing goods and services at the lowest possible cost to ensuring that those activities are generating internal (and external) revenues in a way that maximizes the unit's profit. It's also more likely that the manager's compensation will include some pay-for-performance component based on profit. In other words, the manager needs to manage the unit like a business.

With respect to transfer pricing, managers who previously transferred goods and services to other internal units will now have to pay close attention to the prices at which those transfers take place. If the company's transfer pricing approach meets the objectives outlined in this chapter and aligns managers' incentives appropriately, this new focus can motivate more effective and efficient operations, as well as opening up new avenues for cost savings and new revenue sources. On the other hand, transfer pricing discussions could cause new friction with other unit managers, which could negatively affect company culture.

A shift to profit centers means that top management will need to be even more careful about establishing transfer pricing policies that align managers' incentives with the company's best interests. Establishing strict companywide policies (based on the framework and guidance provided in this chapter) may be the best approach because they remove uncertainty and help avoid interdepartmental disputes. However, rules-based transfer pricing centralizes the decision making over that activity, and top management must carefully consider the costs of abandoning decentralization when problems arise (or may arise). Allowing profit center managers to negotiate transfer prices preserves manager's autonomy and decision-making authority, but it does come with the disadvantages mentioned in the chapter: It can be time-consuming, it can be contentious, and the resulting profit measures may reflect managers' negotiation skills rather than their decision making or the actual operating effectiveness of the unit.

Top management may be best served by not imposing high pressure on newly formed profit centers, perhaps by reducing the strength of profit-based incentives for unit managers. Without such pressure, managers are likely to feel comfortable embracing their new roles, and their new interactions with other managers.

Sources: *CIO Journal*, "Top CIOs Hash Out Tech's Business Value," *The Wall Street Journal* (Online), May 22, 2017; J. Bacon, "How to Turn Marketing into a Revenue Generator," *Marketing Week* (Online), August 31, 2016, www.marketingweek .com/2016/08/31/how-to-turn-marketing-into-a-revenue-generator/.

Self-Study Problems

(For answers, please see Solutions.)

1. Return on Investment and Residual Income

Selected data from an investment center of IROL Inc. follow:

Sales	$8,000,000
Net book value of assets, beginning	2,500,000
Net book value of assets, ending	2,600,000
Net operating income	640,000
Minimum rate of return	12%

Required
1. Calculate return on sales (ROS), asset turnover (AT), and return on investment (ROI).
2. Calculate residual income (RI).

2. Transfer Pricing

Johnston Chemical Company manufactures a wide variety of industrial chemicals and adhesives. It purchases much of its raw material in bulk from other chemical companies. One chemical, T-Bar, is prepared in one of Johnston's own plants. T-Bar is shipped to other Johnston plants at a specified internal price.

The Johnston adhesive plant requires 10,000 barrels of T-Bar per month and can purchase it from an outside supplier for $150 per barrel. Johnston's T-Bar unit has a capacity of 20,000 barrels per month and is presently selling that amount to outside buyers at $165 per barrel. The difference between the T-Bar unit's price of $165 and the outside firm's T-Bar price of $150 is due to short-term pricing strategy only; the materials are equivalent in quality and functionality. The T-Bar unit's selling cost is $5 per barrel, and its variable cost of manufacturing is $90 per barrel.

Required

1. From the standpoint of the company as a whole, should the adhesive unit purchase T-Bar inside or outside the firm? Show calculations to support your answer.

2. Based on your answer in requirement 1, what is T-Bar's proper transfer price?

3. How would your answer to requirements 1 and 2 change, if at all, if the T-Bar unit had a capacity of 30,000 barrels per month?

The Student Resources section of Connect includes video tutorials for the Self-Study Problems.

Questions	**19-1** What is meant by the term *investment center*? How is the financial performance of investment centers measured?

19-2 What is return on investment (ROI), and how is it calculated?

19-3 What are the measurement issues to consider when using return on investment (ROI)?

19-4 What are the advantages and limitations of return on investment (ROI) as a performance measure?

19-5 What are the components of return on investment (ROI), and how is each component interpreted and used?

19-6 What are the advantages and limitations of residual income (RI) as a performance measure?

19-7 How does the concept of economic value added, EVA®, compare, as a measure of financial performance, to return on investment (ROI) and residual income (RI)?

19-8 What are the three methods most commonly used in international taxation to determine a transfer price acceptable to tax authorities? Explain each method briefly.

19-9 What is meant by the term *arm's length standard,* and for what is it used?

19-10 What does expropriation mean, and what is the role of transfer pricing in this regard?

Brief Exercises

[LO 19-1] **19-11** Smith Branded Apparel designs T-shirts for businesses and corporations. The accounting manager has presented the latest quarter's return on sales of 10% and asset turnover of 1.5. What is the company's current return on investment (ROI)?

[LO 19-1] **19-12** Williams Manufacturing uses scrap metal to produce various tools, such as drill bits, hammer heads, saw blades, and nails. The CEO has asked you to analyze the saw blades division to determine asset turnover for last quarter. You find that the saw blades division had an ROI of 20%, sales of $10 million, and operating profits of $1 million. What was the asset turnover rate for last quarter?

[LO 19-1] **19-13** Scott Healthcare provides a walk-in clinic for its patients and a pharmacy for any medication prescribed by the doctor. Last year, Scott generated total sales of $500,000 and $100,000 in profits. Scott also had average assets of $250,000 for the year. What are Scott Healthcare's return on sales (ROS), asset turnover (AT), and return on investment (ROI) for the year?

[LO 19-1] **19-14** Matthews Produce harvests and sells Florida oranges. Matthews has hired you to determine its return on investment (ROI) based on both net book value (NBV) and gross book value (GBV). Financial data for the company show that profits are $2 million, the NBV of operating assets is $10 million, and the GBV of these assets is $40 million. What is ROI based on NBV and based on GBV?

[LO 19-1] **19-15** Moore Money is a financial services firm specializing in fixed-income investments. You have been asked by the accounting manager to analyze the company's financial data from the last quarter. You find the firm had return on investment (ROI) of 15% and asset turnover of 0.5. What was the return on sales (ROS) for the quarter?

[LO 19-1] **19-16** King Mattresses sells both mattress sets and bed frames. Last quarter, total sales were $50,000 for mattress sets and $25,000 for bed frames. Return on investment (ROI) was 10% for both divisions, while asset turnover (AT) was 5 for mattress sets and 2 for bed frames. What was the amount of operating profit for each division?

[LO 19-1] **19-17** Using the data from Brief Exercise 19-16, compute King Mattresses's total return on sales (ROS) for the quarter.

[LO 19-2] **19-18** Foreman Publishing Company's income for the most recent quarter was $500,000, and the average net book value (NBV) of assets during the quarter was $1.5 million. If the company has a required rate of return of 15% on investment, what was the residual income (RI) for the quarter?

[LO 19-2]   19-19   Tinsley Plastics manufactures plastic bottles used for beverages and household cleaners. The average net book value (NBV) of assets during the quarter is estimated as $500,000. If the required rate of return is 10% on average assets and the firm wants to have residual income (RI) of $100,000 for this quarter, what must its profits be?

[LO 19-2]   19-20   Felton Co. produces rubber bands for commercial and home use. Felton reported $1 million residual income (RI) with $20 million net book value (NBV) of assets and $5 million in operating income for the year. What was the required rate of return?

Exercises

[LO 19-1]   19-21   **Return on Investment; Comparisons of Three Investment Centers (Divisions)**

Required   Fill in the blanks:

	Division		
	X	**Y**	**Z**
Sales	$1,500,000	$750,000	$ _____
Operating income	150,000	75,000	
Investment (assets)	600,000	_____	2,500,000
Return on sales	_____	_____	0.5%
Asset turnover	_____	_____	1.5
Return on investment	_____	1%	_____

[LO 19-1]   19-22   **Return on Investment; Different Measures for Total Assets; Spreadsheet Analysis**   Alex Chunn Inc. has the following financial data for 2022 for its three regional divisions:

		Historical Cost		Current Cost	
Region	**Operating Income**	**Net Book Value**	**Gross Book Value**	**Replacement Cost**	**Liquidation Value**
North Atlantic	$65,000	$250,000	$450,000	$990,000	$350,000
Mid Atlantic	40,000	290,000	310,000	380,000	445,000
South Atlantic	30,000	100,000	180,000	650,000	980,000

Required   Prepare an Excel spreadsheet that will calculate return on sales (ROS) for each division for 2022. The sales in the North Atlantic, Mid Atlantic, and South Atlantic regions are $2,350,000, $1,450,000, and $500,000, respectively. Calculate asset turnover (AT) and return on investment (ROI) for each of the four measures of investment.

[LO 19-1]   19-23   **Return on Investment; Return on Sales; Asset Turnover**   Liz Raiborn Inc. has the following financial results for the years 2022 through 2024 for its three regional divisions:

	2022	**2023**	**2024**
Revenue			
Southwest	$14,900	$22,000	$26,000
Midwest	6,700	7,000	7,200
Southeast	12,400	13,000	13,300
Total	$34,000	$42,000	$46,500
Net Operating Income			
Southwest	$ 1,100	$ 1,200	$ 1,350
Midwest	1,250	1,600	1,550
Southeast	1,000	1,200	1,600
Total	$ 3,350	$ 4,000	$ 4,500
Average Total Assets			
Southwest	$14,000	$14,200	$16,800
Midwest	4,700	4,200	4,200
Southeast	5,300	5,600	5,600
Total	$24,000	$24,000	$26,600

Required   Calculate return on sales (ROS), asset turnover (AT), and return on investment (ROI) for each division and also for the firm as a whole for each of the three years 2022, 2023, and 2024.

[LO 19-1]   19-24 **Target Sales Price; Return on Investment**   Schwenn Products, a bicycle manufacturer, uses normal volume as the basis for setting prices. That is, it sets prices on the basis of long-term volume predictions and then adjusts these prices only for large changes in pay rates or materials prices. You are given the following information:

Materials, wages, and other variable costs	$300 per unit
Fixed costs	$200,000 per year
Target return on investment (ROI)	25%
Normal volume	1,500 units per year
Investment (average total assets)	$1,000,000

Required

1. What sales price (to the nearest whole dollar) is needed to attain the 25% target ROI?
2. What ROI rates (to one decimal place) will be earned at sales volumes of 2,000 and 1,000 units, respectively, using the sales price you determined in requirement 1?

[LO 19-1]   19-25 **Return on Investment; Goal Congruence Issues**   As indicated in the chapter, return on investment (ROI) is well entrenched in business practice. However, its use can have negative incentive effects on managerial behavior. For example, assume you are the manager of an investment center and that your annual bonus is a function of achieved ROI for your division. You have the opportunity to invest in a project that would cost $500,000 and that would increase annual operating income of your division by $50,000. (This level of return is considered acceptable from top management's standpoint.) Currently, your division generates annual operating profits of approximately $600,000, on an asset base (i.e., level of investment) of $4,000,000.

Required

1. What is the current return on investment (ROI) being realized by your division (i.e., before considering the new investment)?
2. What would happen to the near-term ROI of your division after adding the effect of the new investment?
3. As manager of this division, given your incentive compensation plan, would you be motivated to make the new investment? Why or why not?
4. Can you offer any recommendations for improving the design of the incentive compensation plan under which you are working? That is, can you think of a plan that would result in increased alignment of your incentives with the goals of the company?

[LO 19-1, 19-2]   19-26 **Return on Investment and Residual Income**   Consider the following data (in millions) from Trident Financial Inc., which has two main divisions, mortgage loans and consumer loans:

	Mortgage Loans	Consumer Loans
Average total assets	$2,000	$20,000
Operating income	$ 400	$ 2,500
Return on investment (ROI)	20%	12.5%

Required

1. Based on ROI, which division is more successful? Why?
2. Trident uses residual income (RI) as a measure of the financial performance of its divisions. What is the RI (to the nearest whole dollar) for each division if the minimum desired rate of return is (a) 10%, (b) 15%, and (c) 20%? Which division is more successful under each of these rates?

[LO 19-1, 19-2, 19-3]   19-27 **Return on Investment; Residual Income; EVA**   Heather Smith Cosmetics (HSC) manufactures a variety of products and is organized into three divisions (investment centers): soap products, skin lotions, and hair products. Information about the most recent year's operations follows. The information includes the value of intangible assets, including research and development, patents, and other innovations that are not included on HSC's balance sheet. Were these intangibles to be included in the financial statements (as they are for EVA®), the increase in the balance sheet and the increase in after-tax operating income would be as given below:

Division	Operating Income	Average Total Assets	Value of Intangibles	Intangibles' Effect on Income
Soap products	$3,250,000	$60,000,000	$1,500,000	$1,000,000
Skin lotions	2,750,000	33,000,000	8,000,000	6,000,000
Hair products	5,000,000	55,000,000	1,000,000	700,000
Minimum desired rate of return	5.00%			
Cost of capital	4.00%			

Required

1. Calculate, to one decimal place, the return on investment (ROI) for each division.
2. Calculate, to the nearest whole dollar, the residual income (RI) for each division.
3. Calculate, to the nearest whole dollar, EVA® for each division and comment on your answers for ROI, RI, and EVA®.

[LO 19-2, 19-3]   19-28 **Economic Profit and Employee Productivity; Service Industries**   A paper published in the *Harvard Business Review* points out a new way to calculate economic profit that could be more appropriate for service firms and other people-intensive companies. Instead of focusing on investment and return on investment, the focus is on employee productivity, in terms of both generating revenues and reducing costs.

The approach is to first determine economic profit in the conventional way, except that we ignore taxes, so that economic profit is before tax, as follows:

$$\text{Economic profit} = \text{Operating profit} - \text{Capital charge}$$

Assume the following information for a hotel chain that wishes to adopt the new method. The firm has $100 million in operating profit, has $1 billion in investment, and uses a cost of capital rate of 5%, so the capital charge is $50 million and the economic profit is $50 million. Relevant calculations are contained in Part 1 of the following schedule:

Part 1: Economic Profit (in thousands, except cost of capital rate)	
Revenue	$ 500,000
Operating costs:	
Personnel costs	300,000
Other costs	100,000
Operating profit	$ 100,000
Operating profit before personnel costs (OPBP)	$ 400,000
Investment (capital)	$1,000,000
Cost of capital, rate	5%
Capital charge	$ 50,000
Economic profit = Operating profit − Capital charge	$ 50,000
Part 2: Economic Profit Calculated Using Employee Productivity	
Number of employees	10,000
Employee productivity:	
Operating profit before personnel cost per employee ($400,000 ÷ 10,000)	$ 40
Capital charge per employee ($50,000 ÷ 10,000)	5
Employee productivity	$ 35
Less personnel cost per employee ($300,000 ÷ 10,000)	30
Economic profit per employee = Productivity − Cost	$ 5
Total economic profit, all employees	$ 50,000
Note: All numbers in thousands except for number of employees	

The next step is to decompose economic profit using employee productivity. To do this, we first determine operating profit before personnel costs (OPBP):

$$\text{OPBP} = \text{Operating profit} + \text{Personnel costs}$$
$$\$400,000 = \$100,000 + \$300,000$$

Employee productivity can be determined by calculating OPBP less capital charge, per employee. For this example, because there are 10,000 employees, OPBP is $40,000 per employee and the capital charge is $5,000 per employee so that productivity is $35,000 per employee. The next step is to determine personnel cost per employee, $30,000, and subtract that from employee productivity to obtain economic profit per employee, $5,000 (i.e., $35,000 – $30,000). Total economic profit for all employees is thus $5,000 × 10,000, or $50 million, the same amount as determined in the conventional way. The value of the decomposition of economic profit into employee productivity and personnel costs per employee is that it provides measures that the hotel chain can benchmark to other hotel chains. It also provides a direct measure of the profit that is being generated per employee relative to the average personnel cost for each employee. Measures of revenue per employee and personnel cost per employee are widely used in the hospital, health and human services, and other people-oriented service industries.

Source: Felix Barber and Rainer Strack, "The Surprising Economics of the People Business," *Harvard Business Review,* June 2005, pp. 81–90.

Required Use the above approach and assume a chain of residential care facilities employs 15,000 people, has a cost of capital of 6%, and has the following information (000s):

Revenue	$ 600,000
Operating costs:	
Personnel costs	360,000
Other costs	150,000
Operating profit	$ 90,000
Investment	$1,000,000

Determine the productivity per employee, personnel costs per employee, and economic profit per employee.

[LO 19-1, 19-2, 19-3]

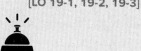

19-29 Return on Investment for Innovative Companies The Boston Consulting Group identified the world's 50 most innovative companies. The rankings are based on a survey of senior executives, as well as financial metrics such as total shareholder return (a measure that incorporates stock price change and dividends). The top five companies in the most recent rankings were Alphabet/Google, Amazon, Apple, Microsoft, and Samsung (**www.bcg.com/en-us/publications/2019/most-innovative-companies-innovation.aspx**).

Required What are the issues to consider in calculating the return on investment (ROI), residual income (RI), and economic value added (EVA®) for a highly innovative company?

[LO 19-4] **19-30 Transfer Pricing Issues** When transfer prices are based on actual cost, a supplying division often has no incentive to reduce cost. For example, a design change that would reduce the supplying division's manufacturing cost would benefit only downstream divisions if the transfer price is based on a markup over cost.

Required What can or should be done to provide the supplying division an incentive to reduce manufacturing costs when the transfer price is cost-based?

[LO 19-4] **19-31 General Transfer Pricing Rule** Scottsdale Manufacturing is organized into two divisions: Fabrication and Assembly. Components transferred between the two divisions are recorded at a predetermined transfer price. Standard variable manufacturing cost per unit in the Fabrication Division is $500. At the present time, this division is working to capacity. Fabrication estimates that the units it produces could be sold on the external market for $650. The product under consideration is viewed as a commodity-type product, with no differentiating features or characteristics.

Required
1. What roles are played by transfer prices? That is, why are transfer prices needed?
2. Use the general transfer pricing rule presented in the chapter to determine an appropriate transfer price. Why is the amount you calculated considered an appropriate transfer price?
3. What if the Fabrication Division had excess capacity? How would this change the indicated transfer price? Why is the amount you determined considered an appropriate transfer price?
4. Are there any downsides of using the general transfer pricing rule to determine the transfer price for internal transfers?

[LO 19-4] **19-32 Transfer Pricing; Decision Making** Truball Inc., which manufactures sports equipment, consists of several operating divisions. Division A has decided to go outside the company to buy materials because division B plans to increase its selling price for the same materials to $200. Information for division A and division B follows:

Outside price for materials	$150
Division A's annual purchases	10,000 units
Division B's variable costs per unit	$140
Division B's fixed costs, per year	$1,250,000
Division B's capacity utilization	100%

Required

1. What would be the net cost (or benefit) to the company of purchasing materials externally? Assume that division B cannot sell its materials to outside buyers.

2. Assume that division B can save $200,000 in fixed costs if it does not manufacture the material for division A. What would be the net cost (or benefit) of purchasing externally?

3. Assume the situation in requirement 1. If the outside market value for the materials drops $20, should division A purchase externally? Explain.

[LO 19-4]   19-33 **Transfer Pricing; Decision Making**   Using the facts from Exercise 19-32, assume that division B can sell 10,000 units outside the company for $215 per unit with variable marketing costs of $10.

Required   Should division B sell outside or to division A? Explain.

[LO 19-5]   19-34 **Transfer Pricing; International Taxation**   Crain Company has a manufacturing subsidiary in Singapore that produces high-end exercise equipment for U.S. consumers. The manufacturing subsidiary has total manufacturing costs of $1,500,000, plus general and administrative expenses of $350,000. The manufacturing unit sells the equipment for $2,500,000 to the U.S. marketing subsidiary, which sells it to the final consumer for an aggregate of $3,500,000. The sales subsidiary has total marketing, general, and administrative costs of $200,000. Assume that Singapore has a corporate tax rate of 17% and that the U.S. tax rate is 21%. Assume that no tax treaties or other special tax treatments apply.

Required   What is the effect on Crain Company's total corporate-level taxes if the manufacturing subsidiary raises its price to the sales subsidiary by 20%?

Problems

[LO 19-1]   19-35 **Return on Investment; Different Measures for Total Assets**   Ready Products Inc. operates two divisions, each with its own manufacturing facility. The accounting system reports the following data for 2022:

HEALTH CARE PRODUCTS DIVISION	
Income Statement	
For the Year Ended	
December 31, 2022	
Revenues	$600,000
Operating costs	470,000
Operating income	$130,000

COSMETICS DIVISION	
Income Statement	
For the Year Ended December 31, 2022	
Revenues	$600,000
Operating costs	400,000
Operating income	$200,000

Ready estimates the useful life of each manufacturing facility to be 15 years. As of the end of 2022, the plant for the health care division is 4 years old, while the manufacturing plant for the cosmetics division is 6 years old. Each plant had the same cost at the time of purchase, and both have useful lives of 15 years with no salvage value. The company uses straight-line depreciation and the depreciation charge is $70,000 per year for each division. The manufacturing facility is the only long-lived asset of either division. Current assets are $300,000 in each division.

An index of construction costs, replacement costs, and liquidation values for the manufacturing facilities for the period that Ready has been operating is as follows:

Year	Cost Index	Replacement Cost	Liquidation Value Health Care	Liquidation Value Cosmetics
2016	80	$1,000,000	$800,000	$ 800,000
2017	82	1,000,000	800,000	800,000
2018	84	1,100,000	700,000	700,000
2019	89	1,150,000	600,000	700,000
2020	94	1,200,000	600,000	800,000
2021	96	1,250,000	600,000	900,000
2022	100	1,300,000	500,000	1,000,000

Required

1. Compute return on investment (ROI) for each division using the historical cost of divisional assets (including current assets) as the investment base. Interpret the results.

2. Compute ROI for each division, incorporating current-cost estimates as follows:

   a. Gross book value (GBV) of long-lived assets plus book value of current assets.

   b. GBV of long-lived assets restated to current cost using the index of construction costs plus book value of current assets.

   c. Net book value (NBV) of long-lived assets restated to current cost using the index of construction costs plus book value of current assets.

   d. Current replacement cost of long-lived assets plus book value of current assets.

   e. Current liquidation value of long-lived assets plus book value of current assets.

3. Which of the measures calculated in requirement 2 would you choose to (a) evaluate the performance of each division manager and (b) decide which division is more profitable for the overall firm? What are the strategic advantages and disadvantages to the firm of each of the measures you selected?

[LO 19-1, 19-2] 19-36 **Return on Investment and Incentive/Goal Congruence Issues; Residual Income; Spreadsheet Application** Assume the purchase of new delivery trucks used in a product-delivery service. This equipment is needed to improve delivery service and respond to recent environmental goals embraced by the company. The cost of the new equipment is $1,200,000; the expected useful life of these assets is 5 years. Estimated salvage value at the end of 5 years is $0. The company will depreciate these assets over a 5-year period using straight-line depreciation. The anticipated increase in operating income (before depreciation deductions) attributable to the use of the new equipment is $360,000. Ignore taxes. Assume in all cases below that the proposed investment, on a discounted cash flow basis, is desirable (i.e., that its estimated net present value [NPV] is positive).

Required

1. Generate, using an Excel spreadsheet, a schedule of the year-by-year ROIs associated with this investment opportunity (use the SLN function in Excel to calculate the annual straight-line depreciation). For purposes of these calculations, define the investment base (denominator of the ROI ratio) as average net book value (NBV) of the assets during the year. What is the ROI in year 3 using net book value?

2. Generate a second schedule showing the year-by-year ROIs for this investment opportunity under the assumption that the denominator in the ROI calculation is defined as the gross book value of the assets to be acquired. What is the ROI in year 3 using gross book value?

3. Why do the results differ in requirements 1 and 2? What behavioral issue is associated with the use of the method used in requirement 1 compared to the method used in requirement 2?

4. What impact would the use of an accelerated depreciation method have on the conclusions in requirements 1 and 2? For example, prepare a new schedule of annual ROIs under the assumption that the double-declining-balance depreciation method is used. (Assume a switch to straight-line depreciation in year 4. Thus, the total depreciation charge over the 5-year period should be $1.2 million. Use the VDB function in Excel to calculate depreciation this way.)

5. Would the use of the residual income (RI) measure of financial performance eliminate the behavioral issue raised in requirement 4? Why or why not? For the methods specified in requirements 1, 2, and 4, show the year-by-year RIs for this investment, based on a weighted-average cost of capital (WACC) of 8%. For each of the four options (annual ROIs with NBV as the denominator; annual ROIs with GBV as the denominator; and annual ROIs for both scenarios repeated, assuming accelerated depreciation), base the imputed interest charge each year on a simple average of beginning-of-year and end-of-year asset values.

[LO 19-1]   19-37   **Return on Investment; Present Value Depreciation; Spreadsheet Application**   As indicated in the chapter, there are goal congruence problems associated with the use of return on investment (ROI) as an indicator of business unit financial performance. One such problem relates to the bias against accepting new investments because of the adverse effect on a business unit's ROI metric. Assume, for example, that the manager of a business unit can invest in a new, depreciable asset costing $75,000 and that this asset has a 3-year life with no salvage value. Cash inflows associated with this investment are projected to be as follows: $30,000, $35,000, and $43,200. (Ignore taxes.) This scenario leads to an estimated internal rate of return (IRR) of 19.44%. Assume that the minimum required rate of return is 15%.

Required

1. Demonstrate, using the IRR function in Excel, that the IRR on this proposed investment is indeed 19.44%.

2. Calculate the year-by-year ROI on this proposed investment. For this problem, use the beginning-of-year book value of the asset as the denominator of your calculation each year. Assume the asset will be depreciated using the straight-line method (you can use the SLN function in Excel to calculate the annual straight-line depreciation). What incentive effects can you anticipate based on the data you generated?

3. Recalculate the year-by-year ROI on this proposed investment, this time using present value depreciation (defined as the change in the present value of the asset during the period). Use the NPV function in Excel to calculate the present value of future cash inflows, and use the project's anticipated IRR (19.44%) as the discount factor in your calculations. As in requirement 2, define the denominator of your calculation as the beginning-of-year book value of the investment. (*Hint:* Your depreciation figures should be $15,417, $23,415, and $36,168, respectively, for years 1, 2, and 3.) Do the incentive effects you identified in requirement 2 change based on these calculations?

4. Calculate, to the nearest whole dollar, the residual income (RI) for each of the 3 years of the proposed investment. RI is defined as income after present value depreciation and after a capital charge assessed on the beginning-of-year book value of the asset. For these calculations, assume a 10% cost of capital (discount rate). Use the NPV function in Excel to estimate the NPV of the proposed investment. (*Hint:* Your answer should be approximately $13,655.) At a discount rate of 10%, determine the NPV of the RI figures you estimated. What is the potential value of using multiyear RI figures determined with present value depreciation?

[LO 19-1]   19-38   **Return on Investment and Human Capital; Strategy**   The authors of an article published in *Harvard Business Review* (Laurie Bassei and Daniel McMurrer, "Maximizing Your Return on People," *Harvard Business Review* (March 2007), p. 115-123) discuss how the concept of return on investment can be applied to the management of human resources. The authors note: "Globalization has left only one true path to profitability for firms operating in high-wage, developed nations: to base their competitive strategy on exceptional human capital management (HCM) . . . [M]anaging human capital by instinct and intuition becomes not only inadequate, but reckless. The most competitive companies will be those that manage their employees like the assets they are." Investments in HCM include programs such as leadership development, job design, and knowledge sharing. The authors of this article propose methods for measuring the contribution (returns) on investments in human capital so that these investments can be better managed. The methods consider the drivers of organizational performance in five categories: (a) leadership practices, (b) employee engagement, (c) knowledge accessibility, (d) workforce optimization, and (e) organizational learning capacity.

Required

1. How would you adapt management accounting systems such as those described in this chapter to guide and monitor investments in human capital?

2. The article was written in 2007, prior to Brexit and the trend toward economic nationalism that started in 2016. How do you imagine the authors would adapt (if at all) their comment on globalization quoted above given the events of 2016?

3. Which type of competitive strategy, cost leadership or differentiation, would most likely benefit from the focus on human capital management, and why?

[LO 19-1]   19-39   **Return on Investment; Corporate Wellness Programs**   What is the return on investment (ROI) of corporate wellness programs? What are the nonfinancial returns on such investments? The following article addresses the concept of return on investment for the wellness of the organization's workforce: Leonard L. Berry, Ann M. Mirabito, and William B. Baun, "What's the Hard Return on Employee Wellness Programs?," *Harvard Business Review*, December 2010, pp. 104–112, available at https://hbr.org/2010/12/whats-the-hard-return-on-employee-wellness-programs.

Required

1. How do the authors of this article define workplace wellness?

2. What evidence of financial returns on employee wellness programs is offered by the authors of this article?

3. According to the authors, what are some important nonfinancial performance indicators associated with corporate wellness programs?

4. What role could a management accountant play in the effective design and implementation of a corporate wellness program?

[LO 19-1] 19-40 **Return on Investment and Sustainability; Internet-Based Research** One of the three underlying precepts of sustainability is economic performance (balanced with social and environmental performance). This question pertains to the application of ROI as part of a performance-management system related to corporate sustainability. To answer the following questions, you'll have to search appropriate sites on the Internet.

Required

1. Define the term *corporate sustainability.*

2. What is the connection between the goal of corporate sustainability and the design of cost management systems?

3. Based on your research, what are some primary financial returns associated with corporate investments in sustainability projects?

4. Based on your research, provide at least five examples of relevant nonfinancial performance indicators associated with corporate sustainability projects.

[LO 19-1, 19-2] 19-41 **Return on Investment; Residual Income** Consolidated Industries is a diversified manufacturer with business units organized as divisions, including the Reigis Steel Division. Consolidated monitors its divisions on the basis of both unit contribution and return on investment (ROI), with investment defined as average operating assets employed. All investments in operating assets are expected to earn a minimum return of 9% before income taxes.

Reigis's cost of goods sold is considered to be entirely variable; however, its administrative expenses do not depend on volume. Selling expenses are a mixed cost with one-third attributed to sales volume. The 2022 operating statement for Reigis follows. The division's operating assets employed were $80,750,000 at November 30, 2022, unchanged from the year before.

REIGIS STEEL DIVISION
Operating Statement
For the Year Ended November 30, 2022
(000s omitted)

Sales revenue		$36,000
Less expenses:		
Cost of goods sold	$18,675	
Administrative expenses	4,000	
Selling expenses	2,700	25,375
Income from operations, before tax		$10,625

Required

1. Calculate Reigis Steel Division's unit contribution if it produced and sold 1,500,000 units during the year ended November 30, 2022.

2. Calculate the following performance measures for 2022 for Reigis:

a. Pretax ROI, based on average operating assets employed.

b. Residual income (RI), calculated on the basis of average operating assets employed.

3. Reigis management is presented the opportunity to invest in a project that would earn an ROI of 10%. Is Reigis likely to accept the project? Why or why not?

4. Identify several items that Reigis should control if it is to be fairly evaluated as a separate investment center within Consolidated Industries using either ROI or RI performance measures.

(CMA Adapted)

19-42   **Calculating Return on Investment and Residual Income; Comparing Results**   Blackwood Industries manufactures die machinery. To meet its expansion needs, it recently (2020) acquired one of its suppliers, Delta Steel. To maintain Delta's separate identity, Blackwood reports Delta's operations as an investment center. Blackwood monitors all of its investment centers on the basis of return on investment (ROI). Management bonuses are based on ROI, and all investment centers are expected to earn a minimum 10% return before income taxes.

Delta's ROI has ranged from 14% to 18% since 2020. The company recently had the opportunity for a new investment that would have yielded a 13% ROI. However, division management decided against the investment because it believed that the investment would decrease the division's overall ROI.

The 2022 operating statement for Delta follows. The division's operating assets were $16,000,000 at the end of 2022, a 6% increase over the 2021 year-end balance.

DELTA DIVISION
Operating Statement
For Year Ended December 31, 2022 (000s omitted)

Sales		$29,500
Cost of goods sold		19,920
Gross profit		9,580
Operating expenses:		
Administration	$2,808	
Selling	4,332	7,140
Operating income		$ 2,440

Required

1. Calculate the following performance measures for 2022 for the Delta division:

    a. Return on average investment in operating assets, to two decimal places.

    b. Residual income (RI), to the nearest whole dollar, calculated on the basis of average operating assets.

2. Which performance measure (ROI or RI) should Blackwood Industries use to provide the proper incentive for each division to act autonomously in the firm's best interests? Would Delta's management have been more likely to accept the capital investment opportunity if RI had been used as a performance measure instead of ROI? Explain.

3. What type of strategic performance measurement do you recommend for the Delta division? Explain.

19-43   **Residual Income; Performance Evaluation Time Horizon; Spreadsheet Application; Review of Chapter 12**   As referenced in the five-step process presented at the beginning of this chapter, one issue that confronts top management is selection of an appropriate time period for evaluating the financial performance of the company's investment centers. This problem demonstrates why, in conjunction with residual income (RI), it is desirable to evaluate financial performance over a multiyear period. The primary point is that, by doing so, top management is better able to align manager goals and incentives with organizational goals.

Assume, as covered in Chapter 12, that your company uses the net present value (NPV) method to evaluate capital investment opportunities. Generally speaking, this means that a long-term investment project will be undertaken if the present value of future net cash flows (after tax) is positive when discounted at the firm's weighted-average cost of capital (WACC).

The following facts pertain to an investment opportunity that is available to the manager of one of the investment centers in your company. Investment outlay cost, at time 0, is $800,000. This amount relates to an asset with a 5-year life, with no salvage value, that will be depreciated using the straight-line (SL) method. The investment is expected to increase cash inflows by $300,000 per year. Assume a discount rate of 10%, both for purposes of calculating NPV and for calculating annual residual income (RI) figures.

Required

1. Use Excel to prepare a schedule that contains annual cash-flow data, annual operating income amounts, and annual residual income (RI) figures. Use beginning-of-year net book values (NBV) to calculate RI. What is the estimated NPV of the proposed investment? What is the present value (PV) of the stream of expected RIs from this investment?

2. From a behavioral perspective, what is the primary implication of the analysis you conducted in requirement 1?

[LO 19-3]   19-44   **EVA® NOPAT and EVA® Capital: Operating Approach**   You are provided with the following financial statement information from Nimrod Inc. for its most recent fiscal year:

Statement of Financial Position (Balance Sheet)
End of Year (000s)

Assets	
Cash	$ 35
Net accounts receivable (A/R)	190
Inventory	190
Other current assets	95
Total current assets	$ 510
Property, plant, and equipment (net)	605
Other long-term assets	120
Total assets	$1,235
Liabilities and Stockholders' Equity	
Short-term debt (@ 10%)	$ 100
Accounts payable	150
Income taxes payable	20
Other current liabilities	200
Total current liabilities	$ 470
Long-term debt (8%)	150
Other long-term liabilities	120
Total liabilities	$ 740
Deferred income taxes	70
Common equity	425
Total liabilities and shareholders' equity	$1,235

The statement of income for the company for the year just ended is as follows:

Statement of Income
Most Recent Year (000s)

Net sales	$2,000
Cost of goods sold (COGS)	1,670
Gross margin	330
Less: SG&A costs	185
Depreciation	35
Other operating expenses	50
Total expenses	270
Net operating profit	60
Less: Interest expense	22
Plus: Other income	12
Income before tax	50
Less: Income tax (@ 40%)	20
Net profit after tax	$ 30

Assume a weighted-average cost of capital (WACC) of 10.7% and an income tax rate of 40%.

Required

1. Using the operating approach, prepare an estimate of EVA® NOPAT (to the nearest whole dollar). In addition to the preceding data, you discovered the following: increase during the year of the LIFO reserve, $2; and increase in deferred tax liability during the year, $5. (*Hint:* The amount of cash taxes paid on operating profit during the year is $25.)

2. What is the rationale for the various adjustments you made to the company's reported income statement?

3. Using the operating approach, prepare an estimate of EVA® capital (to the nearest whole dollar). In addition to the preceding information, you note the following: end-of-year value of the LIFO reserve, $10.

4. What is the rationale for the adjustments you made to reported balance sheet amounts in order to estimate EVA® capital?

5. Given the company's WACC, what is the estimated EVA® (to the nearest whole dollar) for the year?

6. How do you interpret the company's EVA® for the year?

[LO 19-3]   19-45 **EVA® NOPAT and EVA® Capital; Financing Approach**   Refer to Problem 19-44 for reported financial statement data for Nimrod Inc.

Required

1. Using the financing approach, prepare an estimate of EVA® NOPAT (to the nearest whole dollar). In addition to the preceding data, you discovered the following: increase during the year of the LIFO reserve, $2; and increase in deferred tax liability during the year, $5. (*Hint:* The amount of cash taxes paid on operating profit during the year is $25.)

2. What is the rationale for the various adjustments you made to the company's reported income statement?

3. Using the financing approach, prepare an estimate of EVA® capital (to the nearest whole dollar). In addition to the preceding information, you note the following: end-of-year value of the LIFO reserve, $10.

4. What is the rationale for the adjustments you made to reported balance sheet amounts in order to estimate EVA® capital?

5. Given the company's WACC, what is the estimated EVA® (to the nearest whole dollar) for the year?

6. How do you interpret the company's EVA® for the year?

[LO 19-3]   19-46 **EVA®; Shareholder Value Analysis and Sustainability; Internet-Based Research**   Increasing shareholder value is a key objective for many profit-seeking organizations. As indicated in the chapter, EVA® is meant to approximate economic income and, in this sense, can be viewed as a measure of shareholder value added by the firm during a period. Increasingly, managers are realizing that shareholder value is enhanced by creating value for employees, customers, suppliers, the community, and other stakeholders. This problem asks you to consider how EVA®, as a measure of economic value created during a period, can be used to guide and justify sustainability-related investments.

Required

1. How is economic value added (EVA®) for any accounting period estimated? How does this financial-performance metric differ from both conventional accounting income and residual income (RI)?

2. Given the definition of EVA® you provided in requirement 1, provide some thoughts as to how EVA® can be used as part of a comprehensive performance management system to assess and justify corporate investments in sustainability-related projects.

3. Search the internet to see whether you can identify an example of how an actual company used EVA® to support a sustainability-related investment project or program (i.e., one that dealt with social or environmental performance).

4. Explain how EVA®, as a financial performance metric, can be used as part of a larger strategic management system.

[LO 19-4]   19-47 **General Transfer Pricing Rule; Goal Congruence**   American Motors Inc. is divided, for performance evaluation purposes, into several divisions. The Automobile Division of American Motors purchases most of its transmission systems from another unit of the company. The Transmission Division's incremental cost for manufacturing a standard transmission is approximately $1,350 per unit. This division is currently working at 75% of capacity. The current market price for a standard transmission is approximately $1,875.

Required

1. Using the general transfer pricing rule presented in the chapter, what is the minimum price (to the nearest whole dollar) at which the Transmission Division would sell its output to the Automobile Division?

2. Suppose now that American Motors requires that whenever divisions with excess capacity sell their output internally to other divisions of the company, they must do so at the incremental cost of the supplying (producing) division. Evaluate this transfer pricing rule with respect to each of the following objectives: autonomy, goal congruence, performance evaluation of the divisions, and motivation/incentive effects.

3. If the two divisions of American Motors were to negotiate a transfer price, what are the lower and upper amounts (to the nearest whole dollar) of the likely range of prices?

4. Evaluate the use of a negotiated transfer price using the same objectives listed in requirement 2.

5. Which, in your opinion, is the preferable transfer pricing method—the one referenced in requirement 2 or the one referenced in requirement 3 (i.e., a negotiated price)? Why?

(CMA Adapted)

[LO 19-4] 19-48 **Transfer Pricing Methods** Mylar Corporation started as a single plant to produce its major components and then assembled its main product into electric motors. Mylar later expanded by developing outside markets for some components used in its motors. Eventually, the company reorganized into four manufacturing divisions: bearing, casing, switch, and motor. Each manufacturing division operates as an autonomous unit, and divisional performance is the basis for year-end bonuses.

Mylar's transfer pricing policy permits the manufacturing divisions to sell either externally or internally. The price for goods transferred between divisions is negotiated between the buying and selling divisions without any interference from top management.

Mylar's profits for the current year have dropped, although sales have increased, and the decreased profits can be traced almost entirely to the motor division. Jere Feldon, Mylar's chief financial officer, has learned that the motor division purchased switches for its motors from an outside supplier during the current year rather than buying them from the switch division, which is at capacity and has refused to sell to the motor division. The switch division can sell its entire output to outside customers at a price higher than the actual full (absorption) manufacturing cost, which has, in the past, served as the negotiated transfer price for transfers made to the motor division. The switch division would have sold to the motor division for the same price it received from outside buyers, but the motor division refused to meet that price. The motor division then had to purchase the switches from an outside supplier at an even higher price.

Jere is reviewing Mylar's transfer pricing policy because he believes that suboptimization has occurred. Although the switch division made the correct decision to maximize its division profit by not transferring the switches at actual full manufacturing cost, this was not necessarily in Mylar's best interest because of the price the motor division paid by going to an external supplier. The motor division has always been Mylar's largest division and has tended to dominate the smaller divisions. Jere has learned that the casing and bearing divisions are also resisting the motor division's expectation to use the actual full manufacturing cost as the negotiated price.

Jere has requested that the corporate accounting department study alternative transfer pricing methods to promote overall goal congruence, motivate divisional management performance, and optimize overall company performance. The three transfer pricing methods being considered follow. The one selected will be applied uniformly across all divisions.

- Standard full manufacturing cost plus an appropriate markup.
- Market selling price of the products being transferred.
- Outlay (out-of-pocket) costs incurred to the point of transfer plus opportunity cost to the seller, per unit.

Required
1. Discuss the following:
   a. The positive and negative motivational implications of employing a negotiated transfer-price system for goods exchanged between divisions.
   b. The motivational problems that can result from using actual full (absorption) manufacturing cost as a transfer price.
2. Discuss the motivational issues that could arise if Mylar Corporation decides to change from its current policy of negotiated transfer prices between divisions to a revised policy that would apply uniformly to all divisions.
3. Discuss the likely behavior of both buying and selling divisional managers for each of the three proposed transfer pricing methods listed earlier [i.e., standard full manufacturing cost plus an appropriate markup, market selling price of the item being transferred, and outlay (out-of-pocket) costs incurred to the point of transfer plus opportunity cost per unit], if it were adopted by Mylar.

(CMA Adapted)

[LO 19-4] 19-49 **Transfer Pricing; Decision Making** Phoenix Inc., a cellular communication company, has multiple business units, organized as divisions. Each division's management is compensated based on the division's operating income. Division A currently purchases cellular equipment from outside markets and uses it to produce communication systems. Division B produces similar cellular equipment that it sells to outside customers—but not to Division A at this time. Division A's manager approaches Division B's manager with a proposal to buy the equipment from Division B. If it produces the cellular equipment that Division A desires, Division B will incur variable manufacturing costs of $60 per unit.

Relevant Information about Division B

Sells 50,000 units of equipment to outside customers at $130 per unit

Operating capacity is currently 80%; the division can operate at 100%

Variable manufacturing costs are $70 per unit

Variable marketing costs are $8 per unit

Fixed manufacturing costs are $580,000

Income per Unit for Division A (assuming parts purchased externally, not internally from division B)

Sales revenue		$320
Manufacturing costs:		
Cellular equipment	80	
Other materials	10	
Fixed costs	40	
Total manufacturing costs		130
Gross margin		190
Marketing costs:		
Variable	35	
Fixed	15	
Total marketing costs		50
Operating income per unit		$140

Required

1. Division A proposes to buy 25,000 units from Division B at $75 per unit. What would be the effect (to the nearest whole dollar) of accepting this proposal on Division B's operating income? What would be the effect on the operating income of Phoenix Inc. as a whole?

2. Now suppose Division A could purchase from multiple suppliers and would accept *partial*shipment from Division B. How many units should Division B sell to Division A at $75 per unit, if any? What would be the effect on Division B's operating income (to the nearest whole dollar)? What would be the effect on the operating income of Phoenix Inc. as a whole?

3. What is the range of transfer prices over which the divisional managers might negotiate a final transfer price? Provide a rationale for the range you provide.

[LO 19-4]   19-50   **Transfer Pricing; Strategy**   Federated Manufacturing Inc. (FMI) produces electronic components in three divisions: industrial, commercial, and consumer products. The commercial products division annually purchases 10,000 units of part 23–6711, which the industrial division produces for use in manufacturing one of its own products. The commercial division is growing rapidly; it is expanding its production and now wants to increase its purchases of part 23–6711 to 15,000 units per year. The problem is that the industrial division is at full capacity. No new investment in the industrial division has been made for some years because top management sees little future growth in its products, so its capacity is unlikely to increase soon.

    The commercial division can buy part 23–6711 from Advanced Micro Inc. or from Admiral Electric, a customer of the industrial division now purchasing 650 units of part 88–461. The industrial division's sales to Admiral would not be affected by the commercial division's decision regarding part 23–6711.

Industrial Division:

Data on part 23–6711:	
Price to commercial division	$185
Variable manufacturing costs	155
Price to outside buyers	205
Data on part 88–461:	
Variable manufacturing costs	$ 65
Sales price	95

Other Suppliers of Part 23–6711:

Advance Micro Inc., price	$200
Admiral Electric, price	210

Required

1. What is FMI's unit cost (to the nearest penny) if the commercial division buys its additional 5,000 units of part 23–6711 from the industrial division? From FMI's perspective, from which supplier (industrial

division, Advance Micro Inc., or Admiral Electric) should the commercial division buy the additional units? If the sale were made internally, what would the correct transfer price be?

2. Assume that the industrial division's sales to Admiral will be canceled if the commercial division does not buy from Admiral. What would be FMI's unit costs (to the nearest penny) of (a) internal transfer and (b) purchasing from Admiral in this case? Would the correct transfer price change?

3. What are the strategic implications of your answer to requirement 1? How can FMI become more competitive in one or more of its divisions?

[LO 19-4] 19-51 **Strategy; Strategic Performance Measurement; Transfer Pricing** Ajax Consolidated has several divisions; however, only two of its divisions transfer products to other divisions. The mining division refines toldine, which it transfers to the metals division, where toldine is processed into an alloy and is sold to customers for $150 per unit. Ajax currently requires the mining division to transfer its total annual output of 400,000 units of toldine to the metals division at total (actual) manufacturing cost plus 10%. Unlimited quantities of toldine can be purchased and sold on the open market at $90 per unit. The mining division could sell all the toldine it produces at $90 per unit on the open market, but it would incur a variable selling cost of $5 per unit.

Brian Jones, the mining division's manager, is unhappy transferring the entire output of toldine to the metals division at 110% of cost. In a meeting with Ajax management, he said, "Why should my division be required to sell toldine to the metals division at less than market price? For the year just ended in May, the contribution margin on metals was more than $19 million on sales of 400,000 units while the mining division's contribution was just over $5 million on the transfer of the same number of units. My division is subsidizing the profitability of the metals division. We should be allowed to charge the market price for toldine when we transfer it to the metals division."

The following is the detailed unit cost structure for both the mining and metals divisions for the fiscal year ended May 31, 2022:

	Cost per Unit	
	Mining Division	**Metals Division**
Transfer price from mining division	—	$ 66
Direct material	$12	6
Direct labor	16	20
Manufacturing overhead	32*	25†
Total cost per unit	$60	$117

*Manufacturing overhead in the mining division is 25% fixed and 75% variable.
†Manufacturing overhead in the metals division is 60% fixed and 40% variable.

Required

1. Explain whether transfer prices based on cost are appropriate as a divisional performance measure and why.

2. Using the market price as the transfer price, determine (to the nearest whole dollar) the contribution margin of each of the two divisions for the year ended May 31, 2022.

3. If Ajax were to institute the use of negotiated transfer prices and allow divisions to buy and sell on the open market, determine the upper and lower amounts (to the nearest whole dollar) for toldine that both divisions would accept. Explain your answer.

4. Identify which of the three types of transfer prices—cost-based, market-based, or negotiated—is most likely to elicit desirable management behavior at Ajax and thus benefit overall operations. Explain your answer.

[LO 19-5] 19-52 **Transfer Pricing; Ethics** Zen Manufacturing, Inc., is a multinational firm with sales and manufacturing centers in 15 countries. One of its manufacturing divisions, in country X, sells a product to a retail division in country Y for $300,000 per unit. The division in country X has manufacturing costs of $150,000 for this product. The retail division in country Y sells the product to final customers for $450,000 per unit. Zen is considering adjusting its transfer prices to reduce its overall corporate tax liability.

Required

1. Assume that both country X and country Y have corporate income tax rates of 40% and that no special tax treaties or benefits apply to Zen. What would be the effect on Zen's total tax burden if the manufacturing unit raises its price from $300,000 to $360,000?

2. What would be the effect on Zen's total taxes if the manufacturing unit raised its price from $300,000 to $360,000 and the tax rates in countries X and Y are 20% and 40%, respectively?

3. Comment on any ethical issues you observe in this case.

[LO 19-5] 19-53 **Transfer Pricing—International Example** A subsidiary company located in country A purchases $100 worth of goods. It then repackages, exports, and sells those goods to the parent company, located in country B, for $200. The parent company sells the goods (to an external entity) for $300. Therefore, both entities have a $100 profit. Assume that the income tax rate in country A is 20%, while the tax rate in country B is 60%.

Required

1. Given the above facts and assumptions, what is the company's combined (i.e., worldwide) after-tax income for this transaction? (Show calculations.)

2. Consider now a transfer pricing approach in which the subsidiary sells the goods to the parent company for $280 and the parent company then sells the goods for $300. What is the revised worldwide (i.e., combined) after-tax profit for this transaction? (Show calculations.)

3. What is the effect of the transfer pricing decision when the income tax rates for the two countries in question are equal?

4. What limitations exist regarding the setting of transfer prices for multinational transfers?

[LO 19-5] 19-54 **Transfer Pricing; International Considerations; Strategy** As indicated in the chapter, determining the appropriate transfer price in a multinational setting is a very complex problem, with multiple strategic considerations. Consider as an example a U.S. company with a subsidiary in Italy and a subsidiary in Ireland. The Italian subsidiary produces a product at a cost of $1,000 per unit. This unit is then sold to the Irish subsidiary, which adds $100 of cost to each unit. The unit is then shipped to the U.S. parent company, which adds an additional $100 of cost to each unit. The unit is then sold to a U.S. customer for $2,000. Assume that the tax rate in Italy is 24%, the tax rate in Ireland is 12.5%, and the tax rate in the United States is 21%.

Required

1. Define the term *transfer price*. Why is transfer pricing strategically important to organizations?

2. What creates income tax planning opportunities when determining transfer prices in a multinational setting? Where could one go to obtain information regarding stated income tax rates for various countries?

3. Assume that the transfer price associated with the sale to the Irish subsidiary is $1,200 and that the transfer price for the sale to the U.S. parent company is $1,600. Under this situation, compute the income tax paid by each of the following: (a) the Italian subsidiary, (b) the Irish subsidiary, (c) the U.S. parent company, and (d) the consolidated entity (i.e., total tax paid)?

4. Assume now that the transfer price associated with the sale to the Irish subsidiary is $1,100, and that the transfer price for the sale to the U.S. parent company is $1,800. Under this situation, compute the income tax paid by each of the following: (a) the Italian subsidiary, (b) the Irish subsidiary, (c) the U.S. parent company, and (d) the consolidated entity (i.e., total tax paid)?

5. What considerations, including qualitative factors, bear on the transfer pricing decision in a multinational context?

Solutions to Self-Study Problems

1. Return on Investment and Residual Income

1. ROS = Operating income ÷ Sales
   = $640,000 ÷ $8,000,000
   = 0.08

   AT = Sales ÷ Average investment
       = $8,000,000 ÷ [($2,500,000 + $2,600,000) ÷ 2]
       = 3.137 times

   ROI = ROS × AT
       = 0.08 × 3.137
       = 25.1%

2. RI = Operating income − (Average investment × Minimum rate of return)
      = $640,000 − {[($2,500,000 + $2,600,000) ÷ 2] × 0.12}
      = $334,000

2. Transfer Pricing

1. Because the T-Bar unit is at full capacity and the contribution on outside sales of $70 (= $165 − $5 − $90) is higher than the $60 cost saving of inside production (= $150 − $90), the T-Bar unit should sell outside, and the adhesive unit should purchase T-Bar for $150 outside the firm.

2. From the standpoint of the company as a whole, the correct decision is induced if we appeal to the general transfer pricing rule. The minimum transfer price, from the firm's standpoint, is the sum of out-of-pocket costs of the T-Bar division ($90) plus the opportunity cost, if any, incurred because of an internal transfer ($70 = $165 − $90 − $5), or a total of $160. At this amount, the adhesive division will be motivated to purchase externally (at $150/unit), and the T-Bar unit will be indifferent between selling internally (contribution margin per unit = $160 − $90 = $70) and selling externally (contribution margin per unit = $165 − $90 − $5 = $70). Because of the latter, we say that $160 represents a minimum transfer price.

3. If the T-Bar unit has excess capacity, it can sell T-Bar both internally and externally. The correct transfer price is then the price that will cause the adhesive unit to purchase internally; that is, any price between variable cost of the seller ($90) and the outside market price to the adhesive unit ($150). The units might agree on a price by considering what is a fair return to each unit and in effect split the profit on the sale between them. The actual outcome of the negotiations for the transfer price depends on a number of factors, including the negotiation skills of the two managers.

Please visit Connect to access a narrated, animated tutorial for solving these problems.

Management Compensation, Business Analysis, and Business Valuation

After studying this chapter, you should be able to . . .

LO 20-1   Identify the strategic role of management compensation and the different types of compensation used in practice.

LO 20-2   Explain the three characteristics of a bonus plan: the base for determining performance, the compensation pool from which the bonus is funded, and the bonus payment options.

LO 20-3   Describe the role of tax planning and financial reporting in management compensation planning.

LO 20-4   Apply the different methods for business analysis and business valuation.

Shutterstock

"There's no praise to beat the sort you can put in your pocket."

Moliére, 17th century French playwright

In 2019, Bank of America Corp. approved a $26.5 million compensation package for its CEO, Brian Moynihan. Moynihan had led the bank back to high levels of both market and accounting measures of performance, after lagging behind rival banks for several years since the financial crisis of 2008. What was the performance? The bank's stock price increased by 40% during the year, and it reported record profits of $29.1 billion (after a one-time charge). An important feature is the components of Moynihan's total compensation contract: His base salary was $1.5 million, while the rest ($25 million) came in the form of restricted stock, much of which is locked until the bank meets certain future performance targets.[1]

Bank of America provides an example of an issue faced by virtually every company: how to compensate managers in a way that aligns their interests with those of firm owners (i.e., shareholders), motivates both short- and long-term performance, attracts and retains top talent, and can be explained and defended to shareholders and other public stakeholders who are likely to scrutinize executive compensation contracts. Meeting these multiple objectives can be an extremely difficult task. This chapter examines inputs and guidelines for management compensation, as well as tools for analyzing a firm's overall performance.

This chapter will also explain methods for estimating the economic value of the firm as a whole. We have emphasized strategy throughout the book. How do we quantitatively assess the firm's success in achieving its strategy and fairly compensate management for this success? Fundamentally, all measures of the firm's value are predictions of future performance—an assessment of the future value of the current ownership in the firm. Choosing a method for predicting future value is a difficult task, as Bill Barker, a writer for *The Motley Fool* (**www .fool.com**), says: "I don't think there is any method that anyone will think is the perfect one. If you ask 10 investors what the Holy Grail method would be, you'd get 10 different answers." In this spirit, we consider a number of different valuation methods in this chapter.

Part One: The Strategic Role of Management Compensation

LO 20-1

Identify the strategic role of management compensation and the different types of compensation used in practice.

Recruiting, motivating, rewarding, and retaining effective managers are critical to the success of all firms. Effective management compensation plans are an important and integral part of the determination of a strategic competitive advantage and are important concerns of the management accountant.

Types of Management Compensation

management compensation plans
Policies and procedures for compensating managers.

salary
A fixed payment for an employee.

bonus
Compensation based on the achievement of performance goals for a period.

benefits (perks)
Special benefits for the employee, such as automobile/parking, membership in a fitness club, tickets to entertainment events, and other extras paid for by the firm.

Management compensation plans are policies and procedures for compensating managers. Compensation includes one or more of the following: salary, bonus, and benefits. **Salary** is a fixed payment; a **bonus** is compensation based on the achievement of performance goals. **Benefits**, which are often also referred to as perks, may include a company automobile, parking, club membership, life insurance, medical benefits, tickets to special events, and other extras paid for by the firm.

Compensation can be paid currently (usually an annual amount paid monthly, twice a month, or weekly) or deferred to future years. Salary and benefits are typically awarded currently; bonuses are either paid currently or deferred, though a wide variety of plans are observed in practice.

The compensation plans for high-level managers are generally explained in the firm's proxy statements and must be approved by the shareholders. Base salary usually is an annual amount paid throughout the year, although it can also include predetermined future cash payments and/or stock awards. Perks are commonly awarded on an annual basis, although they can include future payments or benefits. Base salary and perks are negotiated when the manager is hired

---

[1] Ben Eisen, "Bank of America Keeps CEO's Pay at $26.5 Million," *The Wall Street Journal* (Online), February 7, 2020.

REAL-WORLD FOCUS SEC Disclosure and Executive Pay

Rules established by the Securities and Exchange Commission (SEC) require significant disclosure of executive pay by public companies, including total compensation, a breakdown showing cash versus stock compensation, and the payments that would be received if executives changed roles at the companies. The objective of these disclosures is to provide investors with a clearer and more complete understanding of the compensation of the firm's key executives.

In addition, the SEC has adopted a "say on pay" rule that requires companies to have nonbinding shareholder votes on executive pay. While companies can ignore the results of the vote, board members are likely to consider voter reaction when determining pay policies. In 2018, the average CEO compensation of S&P 500 companies went up 6 percent, but virtually every company that failed its "say on pay" vote (i.e., received less than 50% support) declared its intention to address the issue directly, usually by reducing overall pay or shifting more of the executive pay structure to variable compensation.

Sources: Theo Francis and Lakshmi Ketineni, "The WSJ CEO Pay Ranking," *The Wall Street Journal* (Online), May 16, 2019; Erin Lehr, "The Effects of Say on Pay Failures," Eqular Institute, October 3, 2019 (www.equilar.com/blogs/428-the-effects-of-say-on-pay-failures.html).

and when compensation contracts are reviewed and renewed. They are not commonly influenced by the manager's current performance, as is bonus pay. Recent studies of top executives at public companies show that bonus pay is the fastest-growing part of total compensation.

Strategic Role and Objectives of Management Compensation

The strategic role of management compensation has three aspects: (1) the strategic conditions facing the firm, (2) the effect of risk aversion on managers' decision making, and (3) certain ethical issues.

Designing Compensation for Existing Strategic Conditions

The compensation plan should be grounded in a strategic analysis of the firm: its competitive strengths and weaknesses and critical success factors. As the strategic conditions facing the firm change over time, the compensation plan should also change. For example, the firm's strategy changes as its products move through the different phases of the sales life cycle: product introduction, growth, maturity, and decline (Chapter 13). As a firm's product moves from the growth phase to the maturity phase, the firm's strategy also moves from product differentiation to cost leadership. When this happens, the compensation plan should change in response to the new strategy. Exhibit 20.1 illustrates how the mix of salary, bonus, and perks might change as the firm and its products move through different phases of the sales life cycle.

Note in Exhibit 20.1 that the mix of the three parts of total compensation changes as strategic conditions change. For example, in the mature phase of the product's life cycle, when competition is likely to be the highest and the firm is interested in maintaining an established market and controlling costs, a balanced compensation plan of competitive salary, bonus, and benefits is needed to attract, motivate, and retain the best managers. In contrast, during the growth phase, when the need for innovation and leadership is the greatest, the emphasis is on relatively large bonuses to effectively motivate managers. In effect, top management considers the specific strategic conditions facing the firm as a basic consideration in developing the compensation plan and making changes as strategic conditions change.

EXHIBIT 20.1
Compensation Plans Tailored for Different Strategic Conditions

Product Sales Life-Cycle Phase	Salary	Bonus	Benefits
Product introduction	High	Low	Low
Growth	Low	High	Competitive
Maturity	Competitive	Competitive	Competitive
Decline	High	Low	Competitive

Risk Aversion and Management Compensation

The manager's relative risk aversion can have an important effect on decision making (see Chapter 18). Risk aversion is the tendency to prefer decisions with predictable outcomes over those that are uncertain. It is a relatively common decision-making characteristic of managers. A risk averse manager is biased against decisions that have an uncertain outcome, even if the expected outcome is favorable.

For example, a risk averse manager might cancel a planned investment in new equipment that would reduce operating costs if there is a chance that nonoperating costs from installation problems, employee training needs, or other reasons might increase. In contrast, the firm's top management and shareholders might not see the risk of additional nonoperating costs as significant relative to the potential for a long-term reduction in operating costs. The difference in perspective comes about because a negative outcome of the decision is likely to have a larger and more direct impact on the manager's current bonus than on the firm as a whole (and therefore on top management and shareholders).

Compensation plans can manage risk aversion effectively by carefully choosing the mix of salary and bonus in total compensation. The higher the proportion of bonus in total compensation, the greater the incentive for the manager to avoid risky outcomes. To reduce the effect of risk aversion, a relatively large proportion of salary should be in total compensation, with a smaller portion in bonus. To determine the proper balance between salary and bonus, all three compensation objectives must be considered.

Ethical Issues

There is a common concern that executive pay is too high and that lower-level employees are not properly compensated relative to the very high salaries and bonuses of top executives, particularly during periods of corporate downsizing and decreasing earnings. High executive compensation is unjust, some argue, and compensation plans are unethical. Others point out that most executives are worth their high compensation because they bring far greater value to the firm than the cost of their compensation. Shareholders and bondholders who see their investments appreciate and attribute this to the executive are likely to see the compensation plans as just and ethical. For example, when Mark Hurd left as CEO of Hewlett-Packard (HP) in August 2010 (to become co-president and a director of a key rival, Oracle Corp.), HP's stock price began to fall relative to Oracle's, and as of May 2011, HP stock had fallen by more than 50 percent relative to Oracle stock. Some have called this the "Hurd effect," a measure of the value of Mark Hurd to HP. However, when Steven Mariano resigned as CEO of insurance company Patriot National Inc. in 2017, the stock price actually rose more than 12 percent.[2] For further discussion of ethics and executive compensation, see the Real-World Focus items in this chapter.

Sometimes the management compensation plan provides an incentive for unethical action. Notable examples include Kenneth Lay, CEO of Enron; Andrew Fastow, CFO of Enron; Scott Sullivan, CFO of WorldCom; and Dennis Kozlowski, CEO of Tyco International. Each of these executives was convicted of or admitted to illegal activities that harmed their companies and their shareholders. In all these cases, strong incentives to increase cash or stock-based compensation were present. Also, there is often evidence suggesting that top executives use inside information to time the exercise of their stock options. For example, Wells Fargo's former CEO, John Stumpf, exercised 1.5 million options in 2016, one month before U.S. regulators announced penalties over a fake accounts scandal that deeply harmed the bank (and its stock price).[3]

Objectives of Management Compensation

The firm's key objective is to develop management compensation plans that support its strategic objectives, as set forth by management and the owners. The objectives of management

---

[2] "The Mark Hurd Effect," *Bloomberg Businessweek,* May 16, 2011, p. 38; Keith Larsen, "Patriot National Sees Stock Price Rise after Mariano Resigns as CEO," *South Florida Business Journal* (Online), July 14, 2017.

[3] Stacy Cowley, "Wells Fargo Leaders Reaped Lavish Pay Even as Account Scandal Unfolded," *The New York Times* (Online), March 16, 2017. See also Eli Bartov and Partha Mahanram, "Private Information, Earnings Manipulations, and Executive Stock-Option Exercises," *The Accounting Review,* October 2004, pp. 889–920; Scott Patterson and Serena Ng, "Executives' Stock Deals Preceded Price Drops," *The Wall Street Journal,* June 4, 2009, p. C1.

compensation are therefore consistent with the three objectives of management control as defined in Chapter 18:

1. To motivate managers to exert a high level of effort to achieve the goals set by top management.
2. To provide incentive for managers, acting autonomously, to make decisions consistent with the goals set by top management.
3. To fairly reward managers for their effort and skill and the effectiveness of their decision making.

In Chapters 18 and 19, these objectives were used to develop performance measurement systems (e.g., cost, revenue, profit, and investment centers). In this chapter, the objectives are used to develop effective management compensation plans.

The first objective is to motivate managers to exert a high level of effort to achieve the firm's goals. A performance-based compensation plan is best for this purpose. For example, a bonus plan that rewards the manager for achieving particular goals is appropriate. The goals could be financial or nonfinancial, current or long-term.

The second objective is alignment: that is, to provide the appropriate incentive for managers to make decisions that are consistent with the firm's objectives. The firm's objectives are identified in the strategic competitive analysis from which its critical success factors (CSFs) are derived. CSFs include customer satisfaction, quality, service, product development, and innovation in production and distribution. Firms attend to CSFs by making them part of the manager's compensation.

For example, McDonald's rewards managers who improve the company's CSFs—quality, service, cleanliness, and value—in addition to the conventional financial performance measures (earnings, sales growth). International Paper Company includes nonfinancial indicators such as quality, safety, and minority employee development as factors in management compensation plans. Research has shown that successful firms with clear strategic goals specified in CSFs include these factors in their compensation plans.[4] The balanced scorecard can be a useful tool for developing compensation plans that incorporate the company's CSFs.

The third objective is to fairly determine the rewards earned by managers for their effort and skill and the effectiveness of their decision making. In developing compensation plans, the management accountant works with other financial professionals to achieve fairness by making the plan simple, clear, and consistent. Fairness also means that the plan focuses on the controllable aspects of the manager's performance. For example, compensation should not be affected by expenses that cannot be traced, at least somewhat directly, to the manager's unit.

Bonus Plans

LO 20-2

Explain the three characteristics of a bonus plan: the base for determining performance, the compensation pool from which the bonus is funded, and the bonus payment options.

> "As a general view, remuneration by fixed salaries does not in any class of functionaries produce the maximum amount of zeal."
>
> *John Stuart Mill, English philosopher and economist, 1806–1873*

As stated earlier, bonus compensation is the fastest-growing component of total compensation—and often the largest part. A wide variety of bonus pay plans can be categorized according to three key aspects:

* The **base of the compensation**—that is, how the bonus pay is determined. The three most common bases are (1) stock price; (2) cost, revenue, profit, or investment center–based performance; and (3) the balanced scorecard.

[4] C. Ittner and D. Larcker, "Total Quality Management and the Choice of Information and Reward Systems," *Journal of Accounting Research,* 1995 Supplement, pp. 1–34; R. Bushman, R. Indjejikian, and A. Smith, "CEO Compensation: The Role of Individual Performance Evaluation," *Journal of Accounting and Economics,* April 1996, pp. 161–193; Antonio Davila and Mahan Venkatachalam, "The Relevance of Non-financial Performance Measures for CEO Compensation: Evidence from the Airline Industry," *Review of Accounting Studies* 9 (2004), pp. 443–464.

- **Compensation pools**—that is, the source from which the bonus pay is funded. The two most common compensation pools are earnings in the manager's own SBU and the firm's total earnings.
- **Payment options**—that is, how the bonus is to be awarded. The two common options are cash and stock (typically common shares). The cash or stock can be either awarded currently or deferred to future years. Stock can be either awarded directly or granted in the form of stock options.

Bases for Bonus Compensation

The key objective in determining the base for compensation is to align managers' incentives with the strategic goals of the company. Bonus compensation can be determined on the basis of stock price, strategic performance measures (cost, revenue, profit, or investment center), or critical success factors identified in the balanced scorecard. For example, when the manager's unit is publicly held, its stock price is a relevant base. When stock price is used, the amount of the bonus could depend on the amount of the increase in stock price or on whether the stock price reaches a certain predetermined goal. When an accounting measure or CSF is used, the amount of the bonus can be determined in any one of three ways: by comparison of (1) current performance to that of prior years, (2) performance to a predetermined budget, or (3) the manager's performance to that of other managers. A limitation of the first two methods, comparison to prior years or to budget, is that the economic situation of the manager's unit may have changed significantly from the prior year or from the time the budget target was set, making the budget or prior-year amount an unfair basis for evaluation and compensation. A problem with the third method is that it does not take into account the different economic circumstances of the different managers, some of whom may be in units that are in favorable economic circumstances while others are not. The firm chooses its compensation plan to achieve the best balance of motivation and fairness from these options.

The choice of base follows from consideration of the compensation objectives, as outlined in Exhibit 20.2. A common choice is to use financial measures for cost, revenue, profit, or investment centers because they are often a good measure of economic performance; therefore, they are motivating and perceived to be fair. As many firms move to a more strategic

EXHIBIT 20.2 **Advantages and Disadvantages of Different Bonus Compensation Bases Relative to Compensation Objectives**

	Motivation	Right Decision	Fairness
Stock price	(+/−) Depends on whether stock and stock options are included in base pay and bonus (+) Aligns management compensation with shareholder interests	(+) Consistent with shareholder interests	(−) Might lack controllability
Strategic performance measures (cost, revenue, profit, and investment centers)	(+) Strongly motivating if noncontrollable factors are excluded	(+) Generally a good measure of economic performance (−) Typically has only a short-term focus (−) If bonus is very high, creates an incentive for inaccurate reporting	(+) Intuitive, clear, and easily understood (−) Measurement issues: differences in accounting conventions, cost allocation methods, and financing methods
Balanced scorecard (critical success factors)	(+) Strongly motivating if noncontrollable factors are excluded (+) Aligns management compensation with shareholder interests	(+) Consistent with management's strategy (−) Can be subject to inaccurate reporting of financial and nonfinancial measures	(+) If carefully defined and measured, CSFs are likely to be perceived as fair (−) Potential measurement issues, as above

Key: (+) means the base has a positive effect on the objective.
(−) means the base has a negative effect on the objective.

REAL-WORLD FOCUS   CEO Pay Ratio Disclosures

The Dodd-Frank Wall Street reform law included a new rule requiring U.S. companies to disclose a ratio comparing their CEO's salary with the median pay of the rest of the company's workforce. The rule's implicit objective is to help investors gauge the reasonableness of the CEO's compensation; many argue that a ratio that is too high could destroy firm value by indicating an overpaid CEO and/or damaging employee morale. However, a recent study finds that CEO pay ratios actually have a positive association with firm value and performance. Specifically, the authors find that a company with a CEO-to-worker pay ratio at the 85th percentile has a return on assets 13% higher than that of a firm at the median, with a similar difference in stock price performance. The study does not comment on the ethical or social justice implications of high CEO pay ratios, but it does suggest that high CEO pay reflects the true cost of attracting talented executives. As expected, the rule has both strong support and strong opposition.

Sources: David McCann, "Do High CEO Pay Ratios Harm Company Value?," CFO.com, July 11, 2017; Sarah N. Lynch, "U.S. Investors Fight to Preserve SEC Rule on CEO Pay Ratio," Reuters.com, March 22, 2017; Qiang Cheng, Tharinda Ranasinghe, and Sha Zhao, "Do High CEO Pay Ratios Destroy Firm Value?," Working paper, Singapore Management University, 2017.

approach to cost management, however, the use of CSFs and scorecard-based measures in compensation is likely to increase.

Once the base is chosen, the firm also must choose a method for calculating the amount of the bonus based on the actual level of performance relative to the target. The most common approach is a simple linear calculation—that is, the greater the amount that performance exceeds the target (prior year, budget, or that of other managers), the greater the amount of the bonus. For example, if the bonus formula is 10% of profit over budget, and actual and budgeted profit are $200,000 and $100,000, respectively, then the amount of the bonus would be $10\% \times (\$200,000 - \$100,000) = \$10,000$.

The base is likely to have multiple targets. As noted earlier (see "Strategic Role and Objectives of Management Compensation"), it is common to have management control systems with the balanced scorecard or some combination of financial and operating measures. In this case, there are multiple bases for the performance measurement. The issue then is to determine a weighting for the multiple measures. Which measures have the greatest priority? A common solution is to provide a numerical weight (as illustrated in many of the books and cases on the balanced scorecard), while a popular alternative is to have top management assign the priorities in a ranking or in a general way at the beginning of the period and then, at the end of the period (at the time of the performance evaluation), assess the overall performance of the manager by considering all of the performance measures simultaneously, without quantitative weights. This more subjective approach is favored by some who feel that top management needs the flexibility to apply their judgment to assess the overall performance of the manager across multiple dimensions.

Bonus Compensation Pools

unit-based pool
A basis for determining a bonus according to the performance of the manager's unit.

A manager's bonus can be determined by the so-called **unit-based pool** that is based on the performance of the manager's unit. For example, the bonus pool might be determined as the amount of the unit's earnings that are more than 5% of the investment in the unit. The appeal of the unit-based pool is the strong motivation for effective managers to perform and to receive rewards for their effort; the upside potential to the individual manager is very motivating.

firmwide pool
A basis for determining the bonus available to all managers through an amount set aside for this purpose.

Alternatively, the amount of bonus available to all managers is often a **firmwide pool** set aside for this purpose. A firmwide pool, for example, might be the amount of firmwide earnings that are more than 5% of firmwide investment. Each unit manager's bonus is then drawn from this common pool. As an example of a firmwide compensation pool, the investment banking firm Goldman Sachs bases its bonus pool on revenues.

When the bonus pool is unit based, the amount of the bonus for any one manager is independent of the performance of the other managers. In contrast, when a firmwide pool is used, each manager's bonus depends in some predetermined way on the firm's performance as a whole.

EXHIBIT 20.3 Advantages and Disadvantages of Different Bonus Pools Relative to Compensation Objectives

	Motivation	Right Decision	Fairness
Unit based	(+) Strong motivation for an effective manager—the upside potential (−) Unmotivating for manager of economically weaker units	(−) Provides the incentive for individual managers *not* to cooperate with and support other units when needed for the good of the firm	(−) Does not separate the performance of the unit from the manager's performance
Firmwide	(+) Helps to attract and retain good managers throughout the firm, even in economically weaker units (−) Not as strongly motivating as the unit-based pool	(+) Effort for the good of the overall firm is rewarded—motivates teamwork and sharing of assets among units	(+) Separates the performance of the manager from that of the unit (+) Can appear to be fairer to shareholders and others who are concerned that executive pay is too high

Key: (+) means the pool has a positive effect on the objective.
(−) means the pool has a negative effect on the objective.

The sharing arrangements vary widely, although a common arrangement is for all managers to share equally in the firmwide bonus pool. Generally, the firmwide pool provides an important incentive for coordination and cooperation among units within the firm because all managers share in the higher overall firm profits that result from cross-unit efforts. Moreover, those who think executive pay is too high often argue that pay linked to overall firm performance is preferable because all managers share in this success. We summarize the advantages and disadvantages of each approach to bonus pools in Exhibit 20.3.

Bonus Payment Options

In recent years, the use of different payment options for bonus compensation plans has greatly increased. As competition for top talent increases, firms are developing innovative ways to attract and retain the best executives.

The four most common payment options are:

1. **Current bonus** (cash and/or stock) based on current (usually annual) performance. This is the most common bonus form.
2. **Deferred bonus** (cash and/or stock) earned currently but not paid for two or more years. Deferred plans are used to avoid or delay taxes or to affect the manager's future total income stream in some desired way. This type of plan can also be used to retain key managers because deferred compensation is paid only if the manager stays with the firm.
3. **Stock options** confer the right to purchase stock at some future date at a predetermined price. Stock options are used to motivate managers to increase stock price for the benefit of the shareholders. Some firms require executives to own a significant amount of stock in the company.
4. **Performance shares** grant stock for achieving certain performance goals over two years or more.

Current and deferred bonus plans generally focus the manager's attention on short-term performance measures, most commonly on accounting earnings. In contrast, stock options and performance shares focus attention directly on shareholder value. See the advantages and disadvantages of the four plans in Exhibit 20.4.

As shown in Exhibit 20.4, all four bonus plans are subject to significant limitations, just as there are significant limitations to the responsibility accounting systems covered in Chapters 18 and 19. In particular, it is difficult to measure economic performance using one or even a few financial measures. Thus, it is difficult to align performance rewards with the desired motivation for managers. Moreover, bonus plans based on simple measures can be relatively easy for managers to manipulate—by making discretionary accounting changes, estimating

EXHIBIT 20.4   **Advantages and Disadvantages of Bonus Payment Options Relative to Compensation Objectives**

	Motivation	Alignment	Fairness
Current bonus	(+) Strong motivation for current performance; stronger motivation than deferred plans	(−) Short-term focus (−) Risk-averse manager avoids risky but potentially beneficial projects	(+/−) Depends on the clarity of the bonus arrangement and the consistency with which it is applied (−) Difficult to measure economic performance in one or a few financial measures (−) Simple measures are easily manipulated by managers
Deferred bonus	(+) Strong motivation for current performance, but not as strong as the current bonus plan because the reward is delayed (+) Tax advantages of deferred compensation (see next section)	Same as for current bonus	Same as for current bonus
Stock options	(+) Unlimited upside potential is highly motivating (−) Delay and uncertainty in reward reduce motivation	(+) Incentive to consider longer-term issues (+) Provide better risk incentives than for current or deferred bonus plans (+) Consistent with shareholder interests	(−) Uncontrollable factors affect stock price Same as for current bonus
Performance shares	Same as for stock options	(+) Incentive to consider long-term factors that affect stock price (+) Consistent with the firm's strategy, when critical success factors are used (+) Consistent with shareholder interests when earnings per share is used	(+/−) Depends on the clarity of the bonus arrangements and the consistency with which it is applied (−) Difficult to measure economic performance in one or a few financial measures (−) Simple measures are easily manipulated by managers

Key: (+) means the payment option has a positive effect on the objective.
    (−) means the payment option has a negative effect on the objective.

or timing transactions, and so on. Many have argued for multiple measures (as in a balanced scorecard) and longer-term payouts to better capture the relationship between economic performance and rewards. These are certainly useful approaches. Overall, designing effective compensation plans is a very challenging task.

Tax Planning and Financial Reporting

LO 20-3

Describe the role of tax planning and financial reporting in management compensation planning.

In addition to achieving the three main objectives of compensation plans, firms attempt to choose plans that reduce or avoid taxes for both the firm and the manager. By combining salary, bonus, and perks, accountants can maximize potential tax savings for the firm and delay or avoid taxes for the manager. For example, many perks (club memberships, company cars, entertainment) are deductible to reduce the firm's tax liability but are not considered income to the manager (and are therefore not taxed).

In contrast, although salary is a deductible business expense for the firm, it is taxable income for the manager. Bonus plans have a variety of tax effects, as outlined in Exhibit 20.5. Tax planning is complex and dynamic, and is therefore an integral part of compensation planning. Exhibit 20.5 suggests general relationships; a thorough coverage of tax planning is beyond the scope of this text.

REAL-WORLD FOCUS   Linking Performance to Pay

Companies are always looking for better ways to align the interests of shareholders, directors, and executives. A recent trend is to require executives and board members to hold significant shares of stock, and to own that stock for an extended period of time.

Comcast, for example, requires that high-level executives and board members do the following:

[M]aintain a significant ownership position in Comcast's shares of Class A or Class B common stock (collectively, "Comcast common stock"), as set forth in the applicable guidelines below . . .

Position	Guideline
Chief Executive Officer, President and Chairman of the Board of Directors	At least 10 times base salary
Corporate Division Vice Chairman; Corporate Division Senior Executive Vice Presidents; Non-executive employee directors	At least 3 times base salary
All other Section 16 executive officers	At least 1.5 times base salary

. . . employees subject to this Policy are prohibited from using any strategies or products (including derivative securities, such as put or call options, or short-selling techniques) to hedge against potential changes in the value of Comcast common stock. . . .

The idea is that payment in shares that must be held makes long-term stock performance the key form of performance-based compensation. This is attractive because long-term share prices reflect true value creation for stockholders and because they cannot be manipulated in the way that other metrics can. In fact, some experts believe board directors should only be compensated with stock.

Sources: Comcast Corporation, Employee Stock Ownership Policy, last revised February 18, 2020: **www.cmcsa.com/static-files/c8a2c6da-5acc-4c2c-8c63-bcacb7572aa9**; Stephen Wilmot, "How to Solve Problems of Misaligned Executive Pay," *The Wall Street Journal* (Online), July 5, 2017; Sanjai Bhagat, "Board Directors Should Be Paid Only in Equity," *Harvard Business Review* (Online), May 3, 2017.

Firms also attempt to design compensation plans that have a favorable effect on the firm's financial reports. For example, present accounting rules do not require current recognition of certain types of compensation, such as deferred compensation. A thorough coverage of financial reporting rules regarding management compensation is not attempted here. Exhibit 20.5 provides an overview of the issues.

EXHIBIT 20.5 **Tax and Financial Reporting Effects of Compensation Plans**

		Financial Statement Effect	Tax Effect* On the Firm	Tax Effect* On the Manager
Salary		Current expense	Current deduction	Currently taxed
Bonus	Current	Current expense	Current deduction	Currently taxed
	Deferred	Deferred expense	Deferred deduction	Deferred tax
	Stock options—nonqualified plans	Stock options must be expensed when granted (e.g., using an options pricing model) and the expense taken against current income	Deduction when expensed	Taxed as ordinary income when exercised
	Stock options—qualified plans	As above	No deduction	Taxed as capital gains when stock is sold if held 18 months from exercise date
	Performance shares	As above	Deferred deduction	Deferred tax
Perks	Certain retirement plans	Current expense	Current deduction	Deferred tax
	Other perks	Current expense	Current deduction (under the 2017 Tax Cuts and Jobs Act, the deductibility of certain perks is disallowed, and others are reduced)	Never taxed. The deduction for moving expenses is eliminated under the 2017 Tax Cuts and Jobs Act

*The tax law regarding deferred compensation has changed as a result of the American Jobs Creation Act of 2004. The law places restrictions on the deferral of taxes under these compensation plans.

Management Compensation in Service Firms

Although most compensation plans are used by manufacturing or merchandising firms, an increasing number of service firms, especially financial and professional service firms, are using these plans. A good example is the compensation plan for the architectural and engineering design firm Short-Elliott-Hendrickson Inc. (SEH).[5] SEH provides professional services in a variety of markets, each of which is organized as a profit center: airport planning, water resources, waste management, municipal services, structural engineering, architecture, and others. SEH has developed a compensation plan for managers of each profit center. The plan uses a balanced scorecard approach that focuses on three areas: (1) financial results, (2) client satisfaction, and (3) improvement in the process of developing and providing services. Management considers the financial results area to be the most important and has developed the following three criteria for evaluating managers and each profit center: profitability, efficiency, and collection of accounts receivable.

1. **Profitability** is measured by the profit multiplier, the ratio of net revenues to direct labor dollars.
2. **Efficiency** is measured by staff utilization, which is determined from the ratio of direct labor hours chargeable (to clients) to total hours worked less vacation and holiday time.
3. **Collection of accounts receivable** is measured by two ratios:
   a. The percentage of accounts receivable over 90 days, a measure of the ability to collect customer accounts.
   b. Average days of unbilled work outstanding, a measure of the ability to complete assignments and promptly bill for them.

As shown in Exhibit 20.6, SEH's compensation plan is based on three criteria and four measures (two measures for collection of accounts). Note that the Water Resources Group fell short of its target in each of the three areas with scores of 79% for the profit multiplier, 88% for staff utilization, and 92% and 89%, respectively, for the two measures of collection of accounts. The advantage of this compensation plan is that it clearly places responsibility for results on the three criteria that are important to SEH's strategy and is therefore consistent with the objectives of management compensation. The objectives of motivation and correct decision making are achieved because the managers of SEH's profit centers have clear, attainable goals consistent with the firm's strategy. The objective of fairness is achieved by focusing on ratios rather than total profits, which increases comparability among managers.

EXHIBIT 20.6   **Management Compensation Plan for the Water Resources Group of SEH Inc.**

1. Profit Multiplier (ratio: net revenues to direct labor dollars)		2. Staff Utilization (ratio: chargeable time to total time)		3. Collection of Accounts			
				Percentage of Accounts Receivable > 90 Days		Days Revenue Unbilled	
Actual	88%	Actual	79%	Actual	14%	Actual	50 days
Goal	95	Goal	83	Goal	10	Goal	45 days
Variance	7%	Variance	4%	Variance	4%	Variance	5 days
Multiply by weight of	3	Multiply by weight of	3	Multiply by weight of	2	Divide by goal	45 days
Weighted variance	21%	Weighted variance	12%	Weighted variance	8%	Percent variance	11%
Relative to	100	Relative to	100	Relative to	100	Relative to	100
Score	**79%**	**Score**	**88%**	**Score**	**92%**	**Score**	**89%**

[5] Mark Pederson and Gary A. Lidgerding, "Pay-for-Performance in a Service Firm," *Management Accounting,* November 1995, pp. 40–43. A similar balanced scorecard–based system, designed for public accounting firms, is described by Michael Hayes in "Pay for Performance," *Journal of Accountancy,* June 2002, pp. 24–28.

Many companies face hardships, cost pressures, and dipping stock prices even when the market as a whole is rising. What does a company do when its stock price falls and its executive stock options are no longer attractive? If the company does not move quickly, it can lose key executives to other employers that offer a more attractive compensation package. With the inevitable ups and downs of the stock market, companies are likely to face this problem at one point or another.

Required

What can/should a company do when its stock options "go bad"?

(Refer to Comments on Cost Management in Action at the end of the chapter.)

Part Two: Business Analysis and Business Valuation

LO 20-4

Apply the different methods for business analysis and business valuation.

The goal of strategic cost management is the success of the firm in maintaining competitive advantage, so it is critical to evaluate the firm's overall performance as well as the performance of individual managers. Business valuation is particularly important during times of business acquisition when analysts must assess values for acquired companies. Also, when companies fall short of their financial goals and see their market values fall, business valuation provides top management a means to assess the risk of takeover by a venture capital firm or other set of investors. We take a broad approach that includes both the process of evaluating a firm's overall performance and the process of determining an overall value for the firm. Ultimately, the objective of the firm's managers is to improve the overall value of the firm.

business analysis

Evaluates the firm's overall performance by using one or more of the following methods: balanced scorecard, financial ratio analysis, and economic value added.

Business analysis uses the balanced scorecard, financial ratio analysis, and/or economic value added as benchmarks to evaluate the firm's overall performance. In contrast, **business valuation** values the firm by estimating its total market value, which can then be compared to the market value for prior periods or for comparable firms.[6]

business valuation

Values the firm by estimating its total market value, which can be compared to the market value for prior periods or for comparable firms.

Business Analysis

Business analysis includes a set of tools used to evaluate the firm's competitiveness and financial performance. The objective is a comprehensive evaluation. Business analysis begins with a careful strategic and competitive analysis of the firm, including SWOT (strengths-weaknesses-opportunities-threats) analysis and strategic positioning analysis, tools that are explained in Chapters 1 and 2. Then we consider tools used to implement strategy, including the balanced scorecard. Finally, we move to financial ratios and other measures, including some that were used in Chapter 19 to measure the performance of individual SBU managers. We put all these tools together to complete a comprehensive business analysis of the firm.

Because business analysis for any company is comprehensive and extensive, we can only present a summary of some of the highlights of the analysis. We use an example of a firm that manufactures cleaning products, EasyKleen Company; summarized information for the firm is shown in Exhibit 20.7. The information includes the firm's balance sheet and income statement, additional financial information, the statement of operating cash flows, and calculation of free cash flow. The following shows a brief example of how the balanced scorecard, financial ratio analysis, and economic value added (EVA®) can be used for a business analysis of EasyKleen.

The Balanced Scorecard

The use of the balanced scorecard to evaluate the firm is similar to the use of critical success factors (CSFs) in evaluating and compensating the individual manager. When evaluating the firm using CSFs, the management accountant uses benchmarks from industry information and considers how the CSFs have changed from prior years. A favorable evaluation results

---

[6] A thorough presentation of business analysis and valuation goes beyond the scope of this text. The following text is an excellent reference: Krishna G. Palepu and Paul M. Healy, *Business Analysis and Valuation: Using Financial Statements,* 5th ed. (Mason, OH: South-Western, 2013).

EXHIBIT 20.7
Selected Financial Information

EASYKLEEN COMPANY Summary of Selected Financial Information For the Year Ended December 31,		
Financial Statements	**2022**	**2021**
Current assets		
Cash	$ 50,000	$ 70,000
Accounts receivable	100,000	80,000
Inventory	50,000	60,000
Total current assets	$ 200,000	$210,000
Long-lived assets	200,000	180,000
Total assets	$ 400,000	$390,000
Current liabilities	$ 50,000	$ 60,000
Long-term debt	150,000	200,000
Total liabilities	$ 200,000	$260,000
Shareholders' equity	200,000	130,000
Total liabilities and equity	$ 400,000	$390,000
Sales	$ 1,000,000 (50% are credit sales)	
Cost of sales	500,000	
Gross margin	$ 500,000	
Operating expenses	290,000	
Interest expense	10,000	
Income tax (50%)	100,000	
Net income	$ 100,000	
Additional Financial Information		
Depreciation expense	$ 30,000	
Capital expenditures	$ 50,000	
Dividends	$ 30,000	
Year-end share price	$ 16.25	
Number of outstanding shares	50,000	
Interest expense	$ 10,000 ($5,000 after-tax)	
Training expenses	$ 30,000 ($15,000 after-tax; 26 hours per employee)	
Quality defects	350 ppm (parts per million)	
Weighted-average cost of capital (WACC)	6%	
Cash Flow from Operations		
Net income	$ 100,000	
Depreciation expense	30,000	
Decrease (increase) in accounts receivable	(20,000)	
Decrease (increase) in inventory	10,000	
Increase (decrease) in current liabilities	(10,000)	
Total cash flow from operations	$ 110,000	
Free Cash Flow		
Cash flow from operations	$ 110,000	
Less: Capital expenditures	50,000	
Less: Dividends	30,000	
Free cash flow	$ 30,000	

when the CSFs are superior to the benchmarks and to prior years' performance. For example, assume that EasyKleen has three CSFs, one each from the three key performance categories:

1. Return on total assets (financial performance).
2. Number of quality defects (internal processes).
3. Number of training hours for plant workers (learning and growth).

A target level of performance is set for each CSF based on a study of the performance of the best firms in the industry. The benchmark is set at 90% of the best performance in the industry, and EasyKleen is evaluated on its overall performance, as illustrated in Exhibit 20.8.

EXHIBIT 20.8 Balanced Scorecard

		EASYKLEEN COMPANY Balanced Scorecard For the Year Ended December 31, 2022		
Category	**CSF**	**Target Performance**	**Actual Performance***	**Variance**
Financial performance	Return on total assets	22%	25.3%	3.3% (exceeded)
Internal processes	Quality defects	300 ppm	350 ppm	50 ppm (unmet)
Learning and growth	Training hours	32 hours per employee	26 hours per employee	6 hours (unmet)

*See Exhibit 20.9 for return on assets and Exhibit 20.7 for quality defects and training hours.

EasyKleen management sees from the balanced scorecard that the firm exceeded its goal in the financial area but fell short in both the operations and human resources areas. The scorecard is a guide for directing attention to achieving desired goals.

Financial Ratio Analysis

Financial ratio analysis uses financial statement ratios to evaluate the firm's performance. Two common categories of analysis include measures of liquidity and profitability. Liquidity refers to the firm's ability to pay its current operating expenses (usually for a year or less) and maturing debt. The six primary measures of liquidity are the accounts receivable turnover, the inventory turnover, the current ratio, the quick ratio (this is sometimes referred to as the acid-test ratio), the cash flow ratio, and the free cash flow ratio. The higher these ratios, the better the evaluation of the firm's liquidity. The four primary profitability ratios are gross margin percent, return on assets, return on equity, and earnings per share. The six liquidity ratios and four profitability ratios are explained in other finance and accounting texts and are not covered here. Instead, we show how each of the ratios is calculated for EasyKleen Company in Exhibit 20.9. The information is taken from Exhibit 20.7 and assumes that the benchmark level of performance is 90% of the best in the industry.

EXHIBIT 20.9 Financial Ratio Analysis

		EASYKLEEN COMPANY Financial Ratio Analysis For the Year Ended December 31, 2022		
Ratio	**Benchmark**	**Actual**	**Percent Achievement**
Liquidity Ratios			
Accounts receivable turnover (Credit sales/ Average receivables)	7	5.56 = $500,000 ÷ [($100,000 + $80,000) ÷ 2]	79% (unmet)
Inventory turnover (Cost of sales/Average inventory)	8	9.09 = $500,000 ÷ [($50,000 + $60,000) ÷ 2]	114% (met)
Current ratio (Current assets/Current liabilities)	2	4 = $200,000 ÷ $50,000	200% (met)
Quick ratio (Cash and receivables/Current liabilities)	1	3 = ($50,000 + $100,000) ÷ $50,000	300% (met)
Cash Flow Ratios			
Cash flow ratio (Cash flow from operations/ Current liabilities)	2.5	2.2 = $110,000 ÷ $50,000	88% (unmet)
Free cash flow ratio (Free cash flow/Current liabilities)	.5	.6 = $30,000 ÷ $50,000	120% (met)
Profitability Ratios			
Gross margin percent (Gross profit/Net sales)	35%	50% = $500,000 ÷ $1,000,000	143% (met)
Return on assets (Net income/Average total assets)	22%	25.3% = $100,000 ÷ [($400,000 + $390,000) ÷ 2]	115% (met)
Return on equity (Net income/Average shareholders' equity)	44%	60.6% = $100,000 ÷ [($200,000 + $130,000) ÷ 2]	138% (met)
Earnings per share (Net income/Weighted-average number of shares outstanding)	$2.15	$2.00 = $100,000 ÷ 50,000	93% (unmet)

As Exhibit 20.9 indicates, EasyKleen had a very good year financially. It met seven of its 10 goals. Profitability is the strongest area; it exceeded three of four ratios substantially; only the earnings per share target was unmet by a small margin. The liquidity goals were largely met, although receivables turnover and the cash flow ratio fell short. These results suggest a need to improve the collection of receivables, which would improve both of these ratios. Overall, the financial ratio analysis shows that EasyKleen performed quite well.

Economic Value Added

Economic value added (EVA®) is a customized measure of economic income, a business unit's income after taxes and other adjustments, minus a cost of capital charge (for the investments used in generating that income). The cost of capital is usually obtained by calculating a weighted average of the cost of the firm's two sources of funds, debt and equity. EVA® focuses managers' attention on creating value for shareholders. By earning higher profits than the firm's cost of capital, the firm increases its internal resources available for dividends and/ or to finance its continued growth, which increases stock price and adds shareholder value.

The calculation of EVA® is described fully in Chapter 19. Here we use a very simplified example in which the only adjustments to income are training expenses and interest expense and the only adjustment to invested capital is training expense. In effect, this example makes the simplifying assumptions that there are no "equity equivalents" such as deferred taxes, the firm uses FIFO for inventory, cost of goods sold equals the cash paid for inventory, and all operating expenses and taxes are paid in cash.

$$
\begin{aligned}
\text{EVA}^® = {} & \text{EVA}^® \text{ net income} - \left(\text{Cost of capital} \times \text{EVA}^® \text{ Invested capital}\right) \\
= {} & \text{Net income} + \text{Training expenses after tax} + \text{Interest expense after tax} \\
& - 0.06 \times (\text{Average total assets} + \text{Training expenses} - \text{Current liabilities}) \\
= {} & (\$100{,}000 + \$15{,}000 + \$5{,}000) - 0.06 \times [((\$400{,}000 + \$390{,}000) \div 2) \\
& + \$30{,}000 - \$50{,}000] \\
= {} & \$97{,}500
\end{aligned}
$$

The EVA® of $97,500 for EasyKleen is a positive value relative to net income and invested capital. It indicates the firm's strong profitability and, in particular, its significant contribution to shareholder value.[7]

Business Valuation

This section examines how to value the company at a single dollar figure. Some argue the value of the company and changes in its value are the most useful measures of the firm's success. Certainly these measures are relevant for the owners of the firm and interested investors. Management accountants with expertise in valuation tools and methods can provide a valuable service to their companies or clients. The AICPA administers the Accredited in Business Valuation (ABV) credential as a way for valuation professionals to distinguish themselves in the market for valuation services.

Initially, we take the approach of the owner, shareholder, or interested investor and calculate the value of the firm's shareholder equity. Later, we consider the broader question of what one would pay to purchase the entire company—debt, equity, and assets.

There are four approaches to measuring the value of shareholders' equity: the book value method, the market value method, the discounted cash flow method, and the multiples-based method. A fifth measure, enterprise value, estimates the acquisition value of a firm. The first and easiest to obtain is the book value of the firm's shareholders' equity from the balance sheet. For EasyKleen, the book value of equity is $200,000 in 2022. An advantage of the book value of equity measure is its clarity, accessibility, and objectivity. A limitation is that it reflects book values only and therefore does not reflect the market value of the firm's assets

---

[7] If the EVA® for future periods is projected and then the discounted value of each of these future EVA® values is taken, the sum is what is called market value added (MVA). MVA is an estimate of the difference between the market value of a company and the amount of invested capital. It is interpreted just as EVA® ; the difference is that it aggregates the net present value of all future projected EVA® amounts. MVA helps explain a company's market performance (and value) by linking it to projected returns on capital.

or liabilities and may not include key intangible assets. In many cases, the book value of the firm's equity is relatively small and undervalues the firm's equity.

A second approach is to obtain the market value of the firm's common equity directly from the current market value of the firm's shares. Here for simplicity we assume that all of EasyKleen's shareholders are common shareholders; there is no preferred stock.

The firm's market value is determined by multiplying the number of outstanding shares by the current market price of the shares. For EasyKleen Company, the value is:

$$\text{Number of shares} \times \text{Share price}$$
$$= 50{,}000 \times \$16.25 = \$812{,}500$$

The market value method has the advantage of providing a clear and objective measure of equity that reflects the current value of the company. This measure is often called the firm's *market capitalization.* For nonpublic firms, a relevant stock price is not available, and one of the other methods is needed to value the firm.[8]

The third method for obtaining the value of the firm is to obtain the present value of the firm's cash flows; this is called the *discounted cash flow (DCF) method.* It is one of the most commonly used methods in equity valuation. Economic and accounting theory indicate that the equity value of an investment should be the present value of future dividends from the investment, and the DCF method is the most consistent with that.

The Discounted Cash Flow Method

The discounted cash flow (DCF) method measures the firm's equity value as the discounted present value of its net cash flows. The DCF method is based on the same concepts used in Chapter 12 for capital-budgeting decisions. Cash flows a year or more into the future are discounted to consider the time value of money because cash flows in recent periods are more valuable than cash flows in distant periods.

There are four steps in the application of the DCF method:[9]

1. **Forecast free cash flows over a finite horizon (usually five years).** *Free cash flow* refers to cash flows available for investing and financing activities of the company and is calculated as operating cash flow less capital expenditures and dividends paid. For EasyKleen, free cash flow in 2022 is equal to $30,000. For this illustration, we assume that free cash flows will also be $30,000 in 2023 and will increase by $10,000 in each of the next four years. These cash flow assumptions are shown in Exhibit 20.10.

2. **Forecast free cash flows beyond the finite horizon, using some simplifying assumption.** For EasyKleen, we make the conservative forecast that free cash flows after 2027 will continue at the rate of $70,000 per year (the same as year 2027), and we also assume that these cash flows will continue indefinitely.

3. **Discount free cash flows at the weighted-average cost of capital (WACC), the firm's cost of capital weighted for both debt and equity.** The weighted-average cost of capital (WACC) for EasyKleen is given as 6%. The derivation of WACC is explained in Chapter 12 and is not duplicated here. The present value of free cash flows is determined using the WACC of 6%, as illustrated in Exhibit 20.10. The sum of the present values for the first five years is $205,700.

The present value of the cash flows for 2028 and beyond is determined using the discount factor for an annuity with a continuing life, which is the inverse of the discount rate $(1/0.06 = 16.667)$.[10] This gives a discounted value for these six-year-plus cash flows of $1,166,690. To discount this amount back from the beginning of 2028 to the present, we discount

---

[8] The valuation of privately held businesses is examined in David S. Jenkins and Gregory Kane, "A Contextual Analysis of Income- and Asset-Based Approaches to Private Equity Valuation," *The Accounting Review,* March 2006, pp. 19–35.

[9] The steps shown here are guided by the steps illustrated in the text by Palepu and Healy, *Business Analysis and Valuation: Using Financial Statements.*

[10] Typically, the firm's cash flows are assumed to continue indefinitely, and thus the discount factor for an annuity is used in perpetuity (continuing life). This assumption is consistent with the idea that the firm is an ongoing entity with little or no likelihood of bankruptcy. If a shorter period is desired, the appropriate discount factor from the annuity table can be used for the desired number of years. For example, if the desired period, after the planning period, is from the 6th year to the 20th year, the discount factor is found in the annuity table for 15 years (6 through 20), or 9.712. The factor 9.712 is then used in place of the factor 16.667 in the analysis in Exhibit 20.10.

EXHIBIT 20.10
DCF Valuation of EasyKleen Company

Years	Free Cash Flow	Present Value Factor (for 6%)	Present Value of Cash Flows
2023	$30,000	0.943	$ 28,290
2024	40,000	0.890	35,600
2025	50,000	0.840	42,000
2026	60,000	0.792	47,520
2027	70,000	0.747	52,290

Total present value of cash flows in the planning period ⟶ $ 205,700 (A)

| 2028+ | $70,000 | 16.667 | $1,166,690 (B) |

Total present value of 2028+ years' cash flows 0.747   871,517 (C) = (B) × 0.747

Plus: Marketable securities and investments   0 (D)

Less: Market value of debt (assumed = book value)   150,000 (E)

Value of the firm's equity $ 927,217 = (A) + (C) + (D) − (E)

$1,166,690 by the fifth year discount factor (0.747) to arrive at the discounted value of the continuing (six-year-plus) cash flows, $871,517.

4. **Calculate the value of equity.** To determine the firm's net valuation, we now add the discounted value of the planning period cash flows and the discounted value of the six-year-plus cash flows to the value of current nonoperating investments such as marketable securities, and we subtract the market value of long-term debt. The net valuation for the firm's equity is then $927,217. If the cash flow estimates are reliable, the DCF method provides a useful measure in determining the firm's value.

Multiples-Based Valuation

A common and easy-to-apply approach to valuing a business is to use a multiple of some financial measure—usually sales, earnings, or cash flow. For example, the earnings-based multiple computes value as the product of expected annual accounting earnings times a multiplier. The earnings multiplier is similar to the price-earnings (PE) ratio—that is, the ratio of stock price to earnings per share. The difference is that the earnings multiplier adjusts the PE ratio to recognize that future earnings should be discounted to determine the company's value. The earnings multiplier has important limitations. The accounting treatment of inventory, depreciation, and other important components of earnings might not be comparable to that of other firms in the industry. When earnings are not comparable, determining a relevant and useful multiplier is difficult.

If the earnings multiplier is not available for a given firm, an average or representative value is taken from the earnings multipliers of other firms in the industry. This multiplier can then be adjusted upward to recognize a firm with future profit potential not recognized in current earnings, or vice versa. Assume that the relevant earnings multiplier for EasyKleen is 8.5. Then the value of EasyKleen using this method is determined as follows:

$$\text{Earnings multiplier} \times \text{Earnings}$$
$$= 8.5 \times \$100,000 = \$850,000$$

The earnings multiplier is easy to apply and can provide a useful valuation of the firm, subject to the limitations noted. The sales-based multiple and the cash flow–based multiple are applied in a similar fashion. Multiples-based valuation is particularly relevant in estimating the value of small and medium-sized nonpublic companies.

In practice, the management accountant and analyst commonly use two or more of the valuation techniques and evaluate the assumptions in each to arrive at an overall valuation. In the case of EasyKleen, a valuation of approximately $900,000 is reasonable, given the range of measures obtained.

Enterprise Value

The methods we have considered thus far determine the value of the firm's equity. Enterprise value (EV) is another measure of what the market indicates the company is worth, but this time as an acquisition. In an acquisition, an acquirer would "buy" not only the firm's equity,

REAL-WORLD FOCUS   Relevance of the PE Ratio

The price-earnings ratio (PE) is the ratio of a company's stock price to current earnings per share (EPS). The numerator of this ratio, stock price, fluctuates often—sometimes dramatically—due to variation in numerous factors. A company's earnings also fluctuate, though usually not with the volatility of the stock price. The accompanying chart shows the PE ratio for the S&P 500 firms from 1910 to 2020. If you take a very long view, the price-earnings ratio for the S&P 500 has averaged about 17 over the last 110 years, with the lowest point in 1920 and the highest in 1999. Sometimes PE ratios will fall while earnings are holding steady; the market is indicating uncertainty about the sustainability of those earnings. At other times, the market shows "irrational exuberance" and PE ratios increase dramatically. A key take-away is that the price-earnings ratio will vary significantly as economic conditions change.

The ratio will differ significantly from industry to industry; as of early 2020, the highest PE ratios were in the insurance, oil and gas, and retail industries, while the lowest were in the energy and banking industries. Thus, investors should use caution when using the PE ratio in business valuation.

Sources: Data from Robert Shiller, Yale University (**www.multpl.com/shiller-pe/**), and Aswath Damodaran, New York University (**http://pages.stern.nyu.edu/~adamodar/New_Home_Page/datafile/pedata.html**).

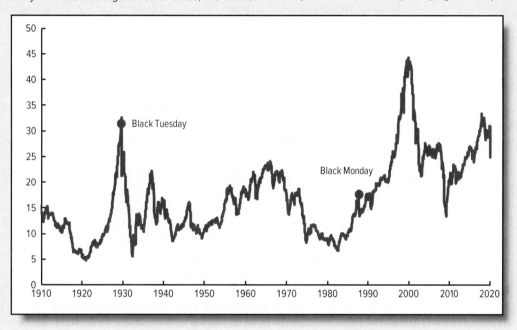

but also the firm's debt, cash, and cash equivalents. So EV is measured as the market value of the firm's equity (market capitalization) plus debt, and less cash (cash is subtracted because it is available after the acquisition to pay off debt or for other uses):

$$EV = \text{Market capitalization} + \text{Debt} - \text{Cash}$$

EV can obviously be used only for publicly traded companies, where market capitalization can be calculated. Where feasible, EV is a useful starting point for investors and shareholders when an acquisition is being considered.

An Illustration of the Five Steps of Strategic Decision Making in the Valuation of a Fashion Retailer

Arizona Sunrise Inc. (ASI) is a retailer of women's fashion clothing with 455 stores in the United States and 55 in Canada, an increase of 62 stores over the prior year. The company is growing quickly because of its unique fashion styles and the quality of its clothing. ASI products are priced at levels slightly higher than competitive brands, but production and selling costs are somewhat higher as well; thus sales have grown quickly, but earnings and cash flows have trailed behind. In some recent quarters, cash flow from operations has been low and, in some cases, even negative. Bettman PLC, a similar retailer located in London, is also known for its fashion-wise designs and product quality. Bettman has expressed an interest in buying ASI, both because of ASI's recent success and because the fall in the dollar relative to the British pound in recent years has effectively reduced the purchase cost in UK currency. Bettman would maintain the ASI brand name for at least a few years and at least initially would retain the local store management. In the longer term, Bettman's plan is to integrate the two product lines into a single global brand. Bettman plans to purchase ASI in a cash transaction but is not sure what value to place on ASI.

The Five Steps of Strategic Decision Making for Bettman

1. **Determine the strategic issues surrounding the problem.** Both firms involved in the case are differentiators based on quality and style. The key business issue is whether the combined firm will be more or less competitive than the separate firms. Bettman's plan to move the two firms to a larger, global brand could help the firm establish a presence globally, thereby improving its opportunity for further growth. The immediate issue is to determine the purchase price of ASI.

2. **Identify the alternative actions.** Bettman can use a variety of methods to value ASI, as described above: discounted cash flows, multiples of earnings, and enterprise value, among other methods.

3. **Obtain information and conduct analyses of the alternatives.** Bettman performs a discounted cash flow analysis based on ASI's projected free cash flow for the next five years and projects a value of $24 billion. A valuation based on the earnings multiple yields a smaller value of $14 billion, the current market value of ASI's equity is $16 billion, and the enterprise value is calculated to be $15 billion.

4. **Based on strategy and analysis, choose and implement the desired alternative.** The analysis produces a wide range of valuations, but a cluster of them is around $15 billion. Moreover, enterprise value is particularly appropriate for valuing a purchase because it takes into account ASI's debt and cash equivalents available to the purchaser. Bettman also considers the strategic advantages and disadvantages of the purchase and is persuaded to make an offer of $15 billion because the acquisition of ASI could help Bettman establish a stronger brand globally, thereby improving its opportunity for further growth and profitability.

5. **Provide an ongoing evaluation of the effectiveness of implementation in step 4.** If Bettman purchases ASI, it will need to complete the implementation through a plan for integrating the two businesses operationally, financially, and strategically. This will be a key management goal for the first few years after the acquisition. Bettman is required by international financial accounting standards to regularly assess the value of the acquisition, and if the value of the acquisition should fall, Bettman must write down the asset to the new fair market value.

Summary

In this chapter, we examine management compensation and the valuation of a business. The first part introduces the objectives and methods for compensating managers. The three principal objectives for management compensation, which follow directly from the objectives for management control, are the *motivation* of the manager, the *incentive* for proper decision making, and *fairness* to the manager.

The three main types of compensation are *salary, bonus,* and *benefits.* The bonus is the fastest-growing part of total compensation and often the largest part. The three important factors in the development of a bonus plan are the base for computing the bonus (cost, revenue, profit, investment center, stock price, and the balanced scorecard), the source of funding for the bonus (the business unit or the entire firm), and the payment options (current and deferred bonus, stock options, and performance shares). The development of an executive compensation plan is a complex process involving these three factors and the three types of compensation, as well as the objectives of management control.

Tax planning and financial reporting concerns are important in compensation planning because of management's desire to reduce taxes and report financial results favorably. Thus, accountants must consider taxes and financial reporting issues when they develop a compensation plan for managers.

Management compensation plans are used in service and not-for-profit organizations as well. The chapter illustrates an actual example for a professional services firm.

The second part of the chapter considers the valuation of the entire firm in contrast to the previous two chapters and the first part of this chapter, which focused on the individual manager. The valuation of the firm is important for investors and as one part of an overall assessment of the performance of top management. The common methods include the balanced scorecard, financial ratio analysis, and economic value added. Methods used to directly value a business include the market value method, the discounted cash flow method, the multiples-based method, and enterprise value.

Key Terms

benefits, *871*	firmwide pool, *876*	salary, *871*
bonus, *871*	management compensation	unit-based pool, *876*
business analysis, *881*	plans, *871*	
business valuation, *881*		

Comments on Cost Management in Action

When Good Options Go Bad

When a company's stock price falls and its executive stock options no longer look attractive, it has a number of choices. One is to simply reprice the options to a lower price that is more in keeping with the lower market price of the firm's stock. Another choice is to grant new options that have a lower exercise price to replace the old options.

A common way to reprice options is to backdate the options to a time when the stock price was somewhat lower; the result is that the exercise price is lower and the options are now again "in the money." Repricing options is legal as long as it is clearly communicated to shareholders and in the company's financial and tax reports. Illegal backdating has been identified at a number of large public companies and criminal penalties imposed. Because the legal issues regarding backdating were clarified in the Sarbanes–Oxley Act of 2002, instances of illegal backdating are now rare. A continuing issue, however, is the practice of timing stock option grants. *Spring-loading* is the term used to refer to the case in which grants are given prior to expected good news, while *bullet-dodging* refers to the practice of granting options after bad news. These practices are associated with an upward trend in stock prices after the grant date.

Another approach is to create stock option "exchanges" in which employees can trade underwater options for new options or restricted stock. This approach is easy to account for, lowers the risk to employees, and can benefit companies by reducing their compensation expenses (because companies are required to expense the value of outstanding options, even those that are underwater). Young technology firms that have recently gone public are the most likely to build such exchanges because of their need to use equity compensation to compete for top talent.

Some executives hedge their own stockholdings or stock options by buying "put" (right-to-sell) options on the firm's stock in the open market. If the stock price falls dramatically, the executive can still sell the stock or exercise the options at the relatively favorable ("put") price. This practice is very much like that engaged in by global firms to hedge their exposure to foreign exchange fluctuations. The problem with executives hedging their stock holdings and options is that it undermines the principle of pay for performance. Through hedging, the executive can effectively protect against a fall in the stock. Hedging reduces the risk of stock ownership and therefore reduces the incentive for executives to take steps to sustain the firm's stock price. Because of this, many firms (e.g., Comcast; see Real-World Focus on page 879) now prohibit such hedging activities by their executives, and the SEC has proposed a rule requiring the disclosure of hedging activities by employees.

Sources: Alix Stuart, "Companies Move to Reprice Employees' Stock Options," *The Wall Street Journal* (Online), September 13, 2016; Securities and Exchange Commission, "Proposed Rule: Disclosure of Hedging by Employees, Officers, and Directors," February 9, 2015: www.sec.gov/rules/proposed/2015/33-9723.pdf; Brian J. Hall and Thomas A. Knox, "Underwater Options and the Dynamics of Executive Pay-to-Performance Sensitivities," *Journal of Accounting Research,* May 2004, p. 365.

Self-Study Problems

(For answers, please see Solutions.)

1. Management Compensation Plan

Davis-Thompson-Howard & Associates (DTH) is a large consulting firm that specializes in the evaluation of governmental programs. The lawyers, accountants, engineers, and other specialists at DTH evaluate both the performance of existing programs and the success of potential new government programs. DTH obtains most of its consulting engagements by completing proposals in open bidding for the services desired by governmental agencies. The competition for these proposals has increased in recent years, and as a result, DTH's yield (the number of new engagements divided by proposals) has fallen from 49% a few years ago to only 26% in the most recent year. The firm's profitability has fallen as well. DTH has decided to study its management compensation plan as one step among the many it will take in attempting to return the firm to its previous level of profitability.

DTH has six regional offices, two located near Washington, DC, and the others near large metropolitan areas where most of its clients are located. Each office is headed by an office manager who is one of the firm's professional associates. The firm's services in these offices are classified into financial and operational audit services, educational evaluation, engineering consulting, and financial systems. The Washington offices tend to provide most of the financial and audit services, and the other offices offer their own mix of professional services. No two offices are alike because each has adapted to the needs of its regional client base. DTH's objective is to be among the three most competitive firms in its areas of service and to increase its revenues by at least 10% per year.

DTH's compensation plan awards each office a bonus based on (1) the increase in billings over the prior year and (2) the number of net new clients acquired in the current year. The office manager has the authority to divide the office bonus as appropriate, although these same two criteria are generally used to allocate it to the office professionals. Top management is not aware of any problems with the compensation plan; there have been no significant complaints.

One observation by the CEO might suggest a reason for the firm's decline in yield of proposals. It has been losing out particularly on large new contract proposals that require a large number of staff and a significant professional travel commitment. These are jobs for which it would be necessary to coordinate two or more DTH offices. The CEO notes that DTH has as many regional offices as most of its competitors, which now seem to be winning a larger share of these contracts.

Required Discuss the pros and cons of DTH's compensation plan. Is it consistent with the company's objectives and competitive environment?

2. Business Valuation

WebSmart is a relatively new Internet company that sells educational products on the web. The firm focuses on students preparing for college entrance exams. The key competitive advantage at WebSmart is its highly regarded publication, *Guide to Competitive Colleges,* which is sold widely in bookstores and on Amazon. com. The firm has grown rapidly and now is seeking additional venture capital investment to allow it to improve its operations and provide additional advertising and promotion. One of the venture capital firms that WebSmart approached has asked WebSmart to provide an estimate of the firm's value. Relevant financial information about WebSmart from the most recent financial statement follows. WebSmart owns no significant fixed assets but operates out of leased space. WebSmart management knows that the median stock price-to-sales multiple in the industry is approximately 7.

Total assets per most recent financial statements	$1,450,000
Total book value of equity, per most recent financial statements	1,200,000
Estimated market value of *Guide to Competitive Colleges*	1,350,000
Net income (loss)	(85,000)
Cash flow from operations	(165,000)
Total revenues	600,000

Required Develop an estimate of the value of WebSmart and explain your reasoning.

The Student Resources section of Connect includes video tutorials for the Self-Study Problems.

Questions

20-1 Identify and explain the three objectives of management compensation.

20-2 Explain the three types of management compensation.

20-3 Explain how a manager's risk aversion can affect decision making and how compensation plans should be designed to deal with risk aversion.

20-4 Explain how management compensation can provide an incentive to unethical behavior. What methods can be used to reduce the chance of unethical activities resulting from compensation plans?

20-5 From a financial reporting standpoint, what form of compensation is most desirable for the firm?

20-6 From a tax planning standpoint, what form of compensation is least desirable for the manager? For the firm?

20-7 List the three bases for bonus incentive plans; explain how they differ and how each achieves (or does not achieve) the three objectives of management compensation.

20-8 Identify and explain the six financial ratios used to evaluate liquidity as part of the firm's business analysis.

20-9 What are the two types of bonus pools for bonus incentive plans? How do they differ, and how does each achieve (or not achieve) the three objectives of management compensation?

20-10 List the four types of bonus payment options and explain how they differ. How does each achieve (or not achieve) the three objectives of management compensation?

20-11 Develop arguments to support your view as to whether executive pay in the United States is too high.

20-12 Explain the different business valuation methods. Which method do you think is superior? Why?

20-13 What type of management compensation is the fastest growing part of total compensation? Why do you think this is the case?

20-14 Why do you think it is important for a management accountant to be able to complete an evaluation of the firm that is separate from an evaluation of individual managers?

20-15 How does the firm's management compensation plan change over the life cycle of the firm's products?

Brief Exercises

[LO 20-1] 20-16 Which of the following is *not* one of the three key objectives of management compensation?
a. To motivate managers to work hard.
b. To reduce the taxes of the firm and the employee.
c. To provide an incentive for managers to make decisions that are in the best interest of the organization.
d. To determine fairly the rewards earned by managers.

[LO 20-3] 20-17 From a tax avoidance viewpoint, the best type of compensation is:
a. Salary: current deduction for firm and currently taxed to employee.
b. Deferred bonus: deferred tax for company, deferred deduction to employee.
c. Dividends: never taxed to firm or to the shareholder.
d. Perks: deduction for firm and not taxed to employee.

[LO 20-4] 20-18 Jamison Auto Parts produces replacement parts for automobiles. Last year, Jamison had EVA® net income of $200,000, cost of capital of 10%, and EVA® capital of $750,000. Determine the firm's economic value added (to the nearest whole dollar).

[LO 20-4] 20-19 Moore Heel is a shoe manufacturing company. Moore has hired you to value the company based on the discounted cash flow method. You have determined that the present value of the company's cash flows is $400,000, marketable securities total $150,000, and the market value of debt is $250,000. What is the estimated value of the firm?

[LO 20-4] 20-20 Smith Co. is a firm specializing in financial advice for retired individuals. After some analysis, you have determined that an earnings multiplier of 7 is appropriate for this type of business. Smith's most recent earnings totaled $250,000, and earnings per share was $4.50. What is the estimated value of the firm based on the earnings multiplier?

[LO 20-4] 20-21 Johnson Healthcare is a health care firm specializing in products for persons who are disabled. Johnson plans to maintain a 10% gross profit margin. After analyzing last year's data, you found that Johnson had gross profit of $250,000 and net sales of $1,500,000. What was the gross profit margin, and by what percentage did the firm achieve its goal?

[LO 20-4] 20-22 Sticky Fingers Inc. produces packing and masking tape. Last year's annual report has been compiled, and you are in charge of business analysis for the year. The company had a goal for inventory turnover of 6 for last year. The actual results were cost of goods sold of $400,000, beginning inventory of $50,000, and ending inventory of $70,000. What was the actual inventory turnover, and at what percent did the firm achieve its goal?

[LO 20-4] 20-23 Tinsley Inc. is an industry-leading cardboard manufacturer. You have been asked to determine a market value for the firm's equity. The firm has 100,000 shares outstanding, earnings per share of $2.50 last year, and a stock price of $25. What is the market value?

[LO 20-4] 20-24 The use of ratios and trends to assess the performance of a company is called:
a. Business analysis.
b. Financial analysis.
c. Business valuation.
d. Market valuation.

Exercises

[LO 20-1] 20-25 **Compensation; Strategy; Market Value** Jackson Supply Company is a publicly owned firm that serves the medical supply needs of hospitals and large medical practices in six southeastern states. The firm has grown significantly in recent years as the areas it serves have grown. Jackson has focused on customer service and has developed an excellent reputation for speed of delivery and overall quality of service. The company ensures that customer service is each manager's main focus by making it count for 50% of the management bonus. The firm measures specific indicators of customer service monthly; progress toward these measures as well as others is used to determine each manager's bonus. In the past several months, top management has noticed that although most managers are meeting or exceeding their customer service goals and receiving bonuses accordingly, the firm's stock price has been lagging while competitive firms' stock prices have been rising steadily.

Required What are the two most likely explanations for the problem facing Jackson Supply Company?

a. Measurement (the firm is not measuring customer service properly) and strategic causal linkage (customers are looking for other things before customer service).

b. Compensation (bonus payments are not high enough) and leadership (managers are not leading their units appropriately).

c. Economic forces (the economy is not strong enough for the firm's stock price to increase) and demand (health care needs are reduced due to more healthy living habits).

d. Advertising (the firm is not advertising effectively) and accounting (the firm's financial reporting does not conform with generally accepted accounting principles).

[LO 20-1] 20-26 **Evaluating an Incentive Pay Plan; Strategy** Anne-Marie Fox is the manager of a boat dealership. She has decided to reevaluate the compensation plan offered to her sales representatives to determine whether the plan encourages the dealership's success. The representatives are paid no salary, but they receive 20% of the sales price of every boat sold, and they have the authority to negotiate the boats' prices as far down as their wholesale cost if necessary.

Required Strategically, is this plan in the dealership's best interest, and why?

a. Yes, because the plan is likely to increase contribution margin.

b. No, because the plan is likely to reduce profits.

c. No, because the plan is likely to motivate illegal behavior.

d. Yes, because the plan is likely to increase profits.

[LO 20-1, 20-2] 20-27 **Alternative Compensation Plans; Strategy** ADM Inc., an electronics manufacturer, uses growth in earnings per share (EPS) as a guideline for evaluating executive performance. ADM executives receive a bonus of $5,000 for every penny increase in EPS for the year. This bonus is paid in addition to fixed salaries ranging from $500,000 to $900,000 annually. Cygnus Corporation, a computer components manufacturer, also uses EPS as an evaluation tool. Its executives receive a bonus equal to 40% of their salary for the year if the firm's EPS is in the top third of a list ranking the EPS for Cygnus and its 12 competitors.

Required

1. Why are companies such as ADM and Cygnus switching from stock option incentives to programs more like the ones described? What does the use of these plans by the two firms say about each firm's competitive strategy?

2. What are the weaknesses of incentive plans based on EPS?

[LO 20-1] 20-28 **Performance Evaluation and Risk Aversion** Jill Lewis is the office manager of PureBreds Inc. Her office has 30 employees whose collective job is to process applications by dog owners who want to register their pets with the firm. There is never a shortage of applications waiting to be processed, but random events beyond Lewis's control (e.g., employees out sick) cause fluctuations in the number of applications that her office can process. Jill is aware that it is important that the applications be processed quickly and accurately. Alex Zale, the district manager to whom Jill reports, bases his evaluation of Jill on the number of applications that are processed.

Required

1. If Jill is risk averse, how should Alex compensate her? Why?

a. Flat salary.

b. Straight commission based on the number of applications processed.

c. Flat salary with a bonus based on the number of applications processed.

d. Flat salary with a bonus based on the firm's earnings.

2. What is a disadvantage of an evaluation method that is based only on the number of processed applications?

3. List at least two ways that Alex could measure how accurately Jill's office is processing the applications.

[LO 20-1] **20-29 Performance Evaluation and Risk Aversion** Heartwood Furniture Corporation has a line of sofas marketed under the name NightTime Sleepers. Heartwood management is considering several compensation packages for Amy Johnson, NightTime's general manager. Amy's duties include making all investing and operating decisions for NightTime.

Required

1. Amy is risk neutral and prefers to receive the maximum reward for her hard work. Do you recommend compensation based on flat salary, an ROI-based bonus, or a combination of both?
   a. Flat salary.
   b. ROI-based bonus.
   c. Combination of flat salary and ROI-based bonus.
   d. None of the above.

2. If Amy does not make investing decisions for NightTime, is ROI still a good performance measure? If so, then explain why. If not, suggest an alternative.

3. Heartwood Furniture plans to evaluate Amy by comparing NightTime's ROI to the ROI of Stiles Furniture, which operates in a business environment similar to that of NightTime. Both companies have the same capabilities, but Stiles uses a significantly different manufacturing strategy than NightTime.
   a. Would evaluating Amy with this benchmark be fair?
   b. Would using residual income instead of ROI offer any advantages for Heartwood?

[LO 20-2] **20-30 Bonus Compensation** Ben Johnson is the manager of the jewelry department of a large chain of department stores. The department store has succeeded on the basis of customer service and quality of merchandise. As a manager, Ben is compensated with a salary of $200,000 and a bonus based on his unit's operating income. The bonus pool is 10% of company-wide operating income. When the unit's return on invested assets exceeds the rate of return of the whole company, the unit manager is included in the bonus pool, which is divided evenly among the managers who qualify for the bonus. In the current period, 25 managers qualified for the bonus, including Ben.

	Jewelry Department	Whole Company
Stock price	NA	$ 42
Operating income	$ 1,898,000	$ 16,500,000
Assets invested	$22,500,000	$287,500,000
Customer service	4	5
Quality of service	4	8
Total revenue	$ 3,500,000	$123,600,000

Required Based on the above information, what is the amount of total compensation for Ben (to the nearest whole dollar)?

[LO 20-2] **20-31 Bonus Compensation Base and Pool** There are three components to a bonus plan: the base of the bonus compensation (earnings, revenues, etc.), the bonus pool (firm- or unit-based), and the payment options (cash, stock options). It is common in many industries, including the financial services industry, to use a firmwide pool and revenue as the base for bonus compensation.

Required

1. What are some alternative bases for compensation pools, in addition to revenue?

2. What effect do you expect the use of revenues, rather than some other base, to have on both the motivation of managers and the total bonuses paid to managers? Comment on the effectiveness of the revenue base relative to other options for the bonus compensation base.

3. Explain the likely motivational effects of the use of the firmwide bonus plan for firms in the financial services industry.

4. Do you consider the firmwide revenue plan for bonus compensation to be a fair method for determining bonuses? Why or why not?

[LO 20-2] **20-32 Compensation and Trust; Ethics** Bill George, a Harvard Business School professor, notes the increasing lack of trust many now have for the executive compensation plans in place in many

corporations. He suggests six policies that, if followed by regulators and the compensation commit-
tees on corporate boards, would rebuild trust in corporate pay policies:

a. Provide full transparency for compensation policies and actual practices.

b. Create policies that reward long-term performance.

c. Reward executives for their performance, not the company's stock price.

d. Lengthen the time horizon for bonuses.

e. Use approaches that include qualitative measures like strategy implementation, research mile-
stones, and leadership development.

f. Boost fairness between executives and workers.

Required

1. Which of George's suggestions do you think are critical to rebuilding shareholders' and others' trust in
corporate compensation policies? Explain briefly.

2. Can you think of another suggestion for improving shareholders' trust in corporate executive pay policies and practices? Explain your choice(s) briefly.

[LO 20-2]   20-33 **Compensation at Nonpublic Companies** The executive compensation programs of the largest
public companies often include the types of equity-based compensation such as stock options and
performance shares described in this chapter. Smaller nonpublic companies often have the same
types of strategic goals and want to provide the same types of compensation plans but do not have
the equity types of compensation to offer because they do not have publicly traded stock.

Required:

1. What is the primary advantage of equity-based compensation such as stock options and performance
shares?

a. It is easier to administer than flat salary or performance-based cash payments.

b. Short-term stock prices cannot be influenced inappropriately by executives.

c. It aligns managers' incentives (to increase value) with those of the shareholders.

d. It is more consistent with generally accepted accounting procedures than other forms of compensation.

2. What types of compensation can nonpublic companies offer that would provide incentives similar to
those offered by equity-based compensation?

[LO 20-4]   20-34 **Business Analysis** Williams Company is a manufacturer of auto parts having the following financial
statements for 2021–2022.

Balance Sheet December 31,

	2022	2021
Cash	$ 260,000	$ 135,000
Accounts receivable	150,000	225,000
Inventory	385,000	175,000
Total current assets	$ 795,000	$ 535,000
Long-lived assets	1,640,000	1,500,000
Total assets	$2,435,000	$2,035,000
Current liabilities	$ 200,000	$ 175,000
Long-term debt	900,000	800,000
Shareholders' equity	1,335,000	1,060,000
Total debt and equity	$2,435,000	$2,035,000

Income Statement
For the Years Ended December 31

	2022	2021
Sales	$3,500,000	$3,600,000
Cost of sales	2,500,000	2,600,000
Gross margin	1,000,000	1,000,000
Operating expenses*	500,000	450,000
Operating income	500,000	550,000
Taxes	175,000	192,500
Net income	$ 325,000	$ 357,500

Cash Flow from Operations

	2022	2021
Net income	$ 325,000	$357,500
Plus depreciation expense	60,000	50,000
+ Decrease (− increase) in accounts receivable and inventory	(135,000)	−
+ Increase (− decrease) in current liabilities	25,000	−
Cash flow from operations	$ 275,000	$407,500

*Operating expenses include depreciation expense.

Additional financial information, including industry averages for 2022, where appropriate, includes:

	2022	2021	Industry 2022
Capital expenditures	$ 125,000	$ 100,000	
Income tax rate	35%	35%	35.0%
Depreciation expense	$ 60,000	$ 50,000	
Dividends	$ 50,000	$ 50,000	
Year-end stock price	$ 2.25	$ 2.75	25.00
Number of outstanding shares	1,800,000	1,800,000	
Sales multiplier			1.50
Free cash flow multiplier			18.00
Earnings multiplier			9.00
Cost of capital	5.0%	5.0%	
Accounts receivable turnover			11.10
Inventory turnover			10.50
Current ratio			2.30
Quick ratio			1.90
Cash flow from operations ratio			1.20
Free cash flow ratio			1.10
Gross margin percentage			30.0%
Return on assets (net book value)			20.0%
Return on equity			30.0%

Required   Calculate and interpret the financial ratios (see Exhibit 20.9) for Williams for both years. Because the calculation of many ratios requires the average balance in an account (e.g., average receivables is required in calculating receivables turnover), you may assume for simplicity that the balances in these accounts in 2021 are the same as those in 2020.

[LO 20-4]   20-35 **Business Valuation**   Refer to the information in Exercise 20-34.

Required:

1. Calculate free cash flow at Williams Company for each of the two years.
2. Develop a business valuation for Williams Company for 2022 using the following methods: (1) book value of equity, (2) market value of equity, (3) discounted cash flow (DCF), (4) enterprise value, and (5) all the multiples-based valuations for which there is an industry average multiplier. For the calculation of the DCF valuation, you may use the simplifying assumption that free cash flows will continue indefinitely at the amount in 2022.

[LO 20-4]   20-36 **Business Valuation**   Five different analysts have submitted valuations for a private technology firm that is the subject of a possible acquisition. The valuations are as follows:

Analyst	Valuation
1	$26,331,000
2	38,803,000
3	65,000,000
4	27,000,000
5	17,000,000

Required   The value of having multiple analysts' reports is that one can develop a range of possible valuations and select a final valuation estimate that seems appropriate. What estimated valuation would you choose for this technology company? Explain your reasoning.

[LO 20-4]   20-37 **Ratio Analysis** Consider the following balance sheet and income statement for Metro Eagle Outfitters, in condensed form, including some information from the cash flow statement:

Balance Sheet	2022	2021	2020
Cash and short-term investments	$ 630,992	$ 745,044	$ 734,693
Accounts receivable	46,321	40,310	36,721
Inventory	332,452	367,514	301,208
Other current assets	132,035	134,620	101,788
Total current assets	1,141,800	1,287,488	1,174,410
Long-lived assets	582,832	647,482	593,802
Total assets	$ 1,724,632	$1,934,970	$1,768,212
Current liabilities	$ 432,902	$ 405,401	$ 387,837
Total liabilities	503,445	517,786	417,141
Shareholders' equity	1,221,187	1,417,184	1,351,071
Total liabilities and equity	$ 1,724,632	$1,934,970	$1,768,212
Income Statement			
Sales	$ 3,475,802	$3,120,065	$2,945,294
Cost of sales	2,085,480	1,975,471	1,763,143
Gross margin	$ 1,390,322	$1,144,594	$1,182,151
Operating expenses	988,284	869,385	864,776
Earnings before interest and taxes	$ 402,038	$ 275,209	$ 317,375
Net income	$ 232,108	$ 151,705	$ 140,647
Interest paid in cash	80	182	161
Taxes paid in cash	142,009	99,756	45,737
Cash Flows			
Cash flow from operations	$ 499,671	$ 398,137	$ 380,416
Capital expenditures	93,939	89,466	75,904
Dividends	85,592	85,592	83,166

Required Calculate the following liquidity ratios for Metro Eagle in 2021 and 2022:

1. Inventory turnover.
2. Current ratio.
3. Quick ratio.
4. Cash flow ratio.

[LO 20-4]   20-38 **Ratio Analysis** Consider the following balance sheet and income statement for Yum! Brands Inc. (the company that operates Kentucky Fried Chicken and Pizza Hut), in condensed form, including some information from the cash flow statement:

	Yum! Brands Inc. (millions)		
	2019	2018	2017
Balance Sheet			
Cash and short-term investments	$ 743	$ 443	$ 1,723
Accounts receivable	623	597	575
Inventory	–	–	13
Other current assets	161	167	196
Long-lived assets	3,704	2,923	2,804
Total assets	5,231	4,130	5,311
Current liabilities	$1,541	$ 1,301	$ 1,512
Total liabilities	13,247	12,056	11,645
Shareholders' equity	(8,016)	(7,926)	(6,334)
Total liabilities and equity	$5,231	$ 4,130	$ 5,311
Income Statement			
Sales	$5,597	$ 5,688	$ 5,878
Cost of sales	1,235	1,634	2,954
Gross margin	$4,362	$ 4,054	$ 2,924
Earnings before interest and taxes	$1,859	$ 2,291	$ 2,719

	Yum! Brands Inc. (millions)		
	2019	**2018**	**2017**
Interest	486	452	445
Taxes	79	297	934
Net income	$1,294	$1,542	$1,340
Share price	$ 102	$ 92	$ 82
Earnings per share	4.23	4.80	3.86
Number of outstanding shares (millions)	300	306	332
Cash Flows			
Cash flow from operations	$1,315	$1,176	$1,030
Capital expenditures	196	234	318
Dividends	511	462	416

Required

1. Calculate the following ratios for Yum! Brands in 2019 and 2018. Round your calculations to 1 decimal place.

    a. Gross margin percent.

    b. Return on assets (ROA).

    c. Return on equity (ROE).

2. What unique information is provided by each of these profitability metrics?

3. Yum! Brands had negative equity in each of the three years reflected in the table, due to a massive stock repurchase that was approved and executed during 2016 (financed largely with new debt). What information does the ROE measure provide when equity is negative?

[LO 20-4] 20-39 **Business Valuation** Using the information in Exercise 20-38 for Yum! Brands, determine the estimated valuation of the company at the end of 2019 using each of the following three methods (round answers to the nearest whole dollar). Assume earnings and cash flows for the coming 10 years are equal to the earnings and cash flows in 2019. The appropriate free cash flow multiplier is 23.4.

    a. Market capitalization.

    b. Enterprise value.

    c. Free cash flow multiple.

Problems

[LO 20-2] 20-40 **Compensation; Net Present Value (see Chapter 12)** Kate's Candy Co. makes chewy chocolate candies at a plant in Winston-Salem, North Carolina. Steve Bishop, the production manager at this facility, installed a packaging machine last year at a cost of $500,000. This machine is expected to last for 10 more years with no residual value. Operating costs for the projected levels of production, before depreciation, are $100,000 annually.

Steve has just learned of a new packaging machine that would work much more efficiently in the production line. This machine would cost $580,000 installed, but the annual operating costs would be only $40,000 before depreciation. This machine would be depreciated over 10 years with no residual value. He could sell the current packaging machine this year for $250,000.

Steve has worked for Kate's Candy for 7 years. He plans to remain with the firm for about 2 more years, when he expects to become a vice president of operations at his father-in-law's company. Kate's Candy pays Steve a fixed salary with an annual bonus of 5% of net income for the year.

Assume that Kate's Candy uses straight-line depreciation and has a 10% required rate of return. Ignore income tax effects.

Required

1. What is the estimated net present value, to the nearest whole dollar, of purchasing the new machine? (*Note:* Use the NPV function in Excel.)

2. How much would Steve Bishop's compensation be increased or decreased by the investment?

3. What could Kate's Candy Co. do to reduce conflicts between the company's best interests and Steve Bishop's compensation?

[LO 20-1] 20-41 **Compensation; Benefits; Ethics** DuMelon Publishing Inc. is a nationwide company headquartered in Boston, Massachusetts. The firm's benefits are a significant element of employee compensation. All professional employees at DuMelon receive company-paid benefits, including medical insurance, term life insurance, and paid vacations and holidays. They also receive a set reimbursement amount of $250 per day maximum for travel expenses when they conduct business for DuMelon. DuMelon offers a 25% match for money the professionals deposit in the company-sponsored 401(k) plan.

These benefits vary, depending on the employee's salary and level in the company. For example, the amount of vacation days increases as a professional is promoted to higher levels. The maximum amount that can be contributed to the 401(k) plan also increases as the employee's salary increases, subject to an overall limitation provided by tax laws.

When a DuMelon employee attains the position of vice president of a function, such as operations or sales, that person qualifies for a special class of additional benefits: a company car, a larger office with decoration allowances, and access to the executive suite at the Boston office. (The executive suite features a dining room and lounge for the executives' use.) The perks also include total reimbursement for all business travel expenses.

Required

1. Explain the implications for employee behavior and performance of DuMelon's two levels of benefits for professional employees. Comment on any ethical issues.

2. Suppose the policy for benefits is not applied strictly at DuMelon. As a result, the following instances have occurred:

   a. The company has occasionally paid the travel expenses of vice presidents' spouses. Company policy is unclear as to whether this is allowed.

   b. Some vice presidents have special-ordered their company-provided vehicles, which costs the company, on average, an additional $23,000 for each car.

   c. Passes to the executive suite have been lent to other DuMelon professionals.

   d. Some of the vice presidents have offices that are much larger than those of other vice presidents. No apparent factors determine who gets the larger offices.

   How might these situations affect the behavior of vice presidents and other professionals at DuMelon? What are the underlying implications for cost control of benefits? Use specific examples when applicable.

[LO 20-2]   20-42   **Incentive Pay in the Hotel Industry**   Kristin Helmud is the general manager of Highland Inn, a local mid-priced hotel with 100 rooms. Her job objectives include providing resourceful and friendly service to the hotel's guests, maintaining an 80% occupancy rate, improving the average rate received per room to $88 from the current $85, achieving a savings of 5% on all hotel costs, and reducing energy use by 10% by carefully managing the use of heating and air conditioning in unused rooms and by carefully managing the onsite laundry facility, among other means. The hotel's owner, a partnership of seven people who own several hotels in the region, wants to structure Kristin's future compensation to objectively reward her for achieving these goals. In the past, she has been paid an annual salary of $72,000 with no incentive pay. The incentive plan the partners developed has each of the goals weighted as follows:

Measure	Percent of Total Responsibility
Occupancy rate (also reflects guest service quality)	20%
Operating within 95% of expense budget	30
Average room rate	30
Energy use	20
	100%

If Kristin achieves all of these goals, the partners determined that her performance should merit a bonus of $30,000. The partners also agree that her salary will need to be reduced to $60,000 because of the addition of the bonus.

The goal measures used to compensate Kristin are as follows:

Occupancy goal:	29,200 room-nights = 80% occupancy rate × 100 rooms × 365 days
Compensation:	20% weight × $30,000 target bonus = $6,000
	$6,000 ÷ 29,200 = $0.2055 per room-night
Expense goal:	5% savings
Compensation:	30% weight × $30,000 target bonus = $9,000
	$9,000 ÷ 5 = $1,800 for each percentage point saved
Room rate goal:	$3 rate increase
Compensation:	30% weight × $30,000 target bonus = $9,000
	$9,000 ÷ 300 = $30.00 for each cent increase
Energy use goal:	10% savings
Compensation:	20% weight × $30,000 target bonus = $6,000
	$6,000 ÷ 10 = $600 for each percentage point saved

Kristin's new compensation plan will thus pay her a $60,000 salary plus 20.55 cents per room-night sold plus $1,800 for each percentage point saved in the expense budget plus $30 for each cent increase in the average room rate plus $600 for each percentage point saved in energy use. The minimum potential compensation would be $60,000 and the maximum potential compensation for Kristin would be $60,000 + $30,000 = $90,000.

Required

1. Based on this plan, compute Kristin's total compensation if her performance results are:

   a. 30,000 room-nights, 5% saved, $3.00 rate increase, and 8% reduction in energy use.

   b. 25,000 room-nights, 3% saved, $1.15 rate increase, and 5% reduction in energy use.

   c. 28,000 room-nights, 0% saved, $1.00 rate increase, and 2% reduction in energy use.

2. Comment on the expected effectiveness of this plan (including sustainability). In what way, if at all, would you change the compensation weights?

[LO 20-2] 20-43 **Incentive Pay Formula Development** A restaurant manager has the following goals: (1) serve 300 customers per day and (2) achieve an average price per customer of $6.88. The restaurant is open 365 days per year. The two goals are equally important. The manager's salary is $68,000. The manager's incentive pay (i.e., bonus) should be $12,800 if both goals are achieved.

Required

1. Assuming the compensation function is linear, determine the following amounts in the contract:

   a. The rate per customer served, rounded to four decimal points.

   b. The rate per penny of average price per customer, rounded to four decimal points.

2. Independent of your answer to requirement 1, assume that the rate is $0.0763 per customer served and $11.4451 per penny of average price per customer. Calculate the manager's total compensation if the restaurant serves 280 customers per day at an average price of $6.75. Round your final answer to the nearest dollar.

[LO 20-2] 20-44 **Compensation Pools; Residual Income; Review of Chapter 19** McCoy Brands Inc. (MBI) is a retailer of consumer products. The company made two acquisitions in previous years to diversify its product lines. In 2020, MBI acquired a consumer electronics firm producing computers. MBI now (2022) has three divisions: Consumer Electronics, Office Supplies, and Computers. The following information (in thousands) presents operating revenue, operating income, and invested assets of the company over the last 3 years:

	Revenue	Income	Assets
Consumer Electronics			
2020	$155,780	$16,750	$84,550
2021	125,480	9,500	90,450
2022	90,950	5,700	92,450
Office Supplies			
2020	48,750	2,100	22,500
2021	45,660	2,340	21,900
2022	52,800	3,250	18,000
Computers			
2020	100,500	2,350	21,450
2021	95,400	1,650	22,550
2022	114,350	2,575	24,100

The number of executives covered by MBI's current compensation package follows:

	2020	2021	2022
Consumer Electronics	300	350	375
Office Supplies	40	40	37
Computers	120	140	185

The current compensation package is an annual bonus award. Senior executives share in the bonus pool, which is calculated as 10% of the company's annual residual income. *Residual income* is defined as operating income minus an interest charge of 6% of invested assets.

Required

1. Compute asset turnover, return on sales, and return on investment (ROI) for each division and for each year. Use year-end rather than average asset values. Round to 2 decimal places.

2. Use the ratios computed in requirement 1 to explain the differences in profitability of the three divisions.

3. Compute the total bonus amount to be paid during each year; also compute individual executive bonus amounts. Round to the nearest whole dollar.

4. If the bonuses were calculated by divisional residual income, what would the individual bonus amounts be? Round to the nearest whole dollar.

5. Discuss the advantages and disadvantages of basing the bonus on MBI's residual income compared to divisional residual income.

[LO 20-2]

20-45 **Compensation; Strategy** Digital Business Incorporated (DBI) is a worldwide manufacturing company that specializes in high technology products for the aerospace, automotive, and plastics industries. State-of-the-art technology and business innovation have been key to the firm's success over the last several years. DBI has 10 manufacturing plants in six foreign countries. Its products are sold worldwide through sales representatives and sales offices in 23 countries. Performance information from these plants and offices is received weekly and is summarized monthly at the Toronto headquarters.

The company's current bonus compensation plan focuses on giving rewards based on the utilization of capital within the company (i.e., management of inventory, collection of receivables, and use of physical assets). The board of directors is concerned, however, with the short-term focus of this plan.

Some employees believe that the company's current compensation plan does not reflect its stated goals of maintaining and enhancing its global position through innovative products.

Required Develop a bonus package that considers DBI's strategic goals and the global environment in which it operates.

[LO 20-2]

20-46 **Executive Compensation; Teams; Strategy; Ethics** Universal Air Inc. supplies instrumentation components to airplane manufacturers. Although only a few competitors are in this market, the competition is fierce.

Universal uses a traditional performance incentive plan to award middle-management bonuses on the basis of divisional profit. Recently, Charles Gross, chief executive officer, concluded that these objectives might be better served with new performance measures. On January 1, 2022, he assigned his executive team of top-level managers to develop these new measures.

The executive team conducted a customer survey. Although Universal has always prided itself on being on the technological forefront, the survey results indicated technology to be a low priority for customers, who were more concerned with product quality and customer service. As a result, the executive team developed 30 new criteria to measure middle-management performance and directed the controller to develop the necessary monthly reports and graphs to report on these new measures. Then the executive team announced to middle managers that these new indicators would be used to evaluate their performance. The managers were not enthusiastic and complained that some measures were influenced by the performance of other departments that they could not control. Over the next few months, customer complaints increased, and a major customer chose a competitor over Universal.

Upon seeing these results, Charles decided to review the new process. In a meeting with executive and middle managers, he emphasized that the new measures should help balance the company's performance between increased customer value and improved operating process efficiency. He set up two cross-functional teams of executives and middle managers to develop a second set of new measures: one to evaluate new product development and the other to evaluate the customer order and fulfillment process. Both teams are to focus on cost, quality, and scheduling time.

Richard Strong, quality inspection manager, is the brother-in-law of John Brogan, cost accounting manager. On June 1, John telephoned Sara Wiley, the purchasing manager at Magic Aircraft Manufacturing Inc., one of Universal's major customers. Brogan said, "Listen, Sara, we're jumping through all these hoops over here to measure performance, and management seems to be changing the measures every day. It was so easy before, getting a bonus based on the bottom line; now we have to worry about things out of our control based on how the customer perceives our performance. Would you do me a favor? If you have any complaints, please have your people call me directly so I can forward the complaint to the right person. All that really matters is for all of us to make money." In actuality, Richard was the only person to whom John reported the customer complaints that Sara offered.

Required

1. For Universal Air Inc. to remain competitive, should it implement the second set of new performance measures? Identify for the company:

   a. At least three customer value-added measures.

   b. At least three process-efficiency measures.

2. Identify at least three types of employee behaviors that Universal can expect by having middle management participate in the development of the second set of new performance measures.

3. Describe what executive management at Universal should do to ensure the effectiveness of the cross-functional teams.

4. Referring to the specific standards for ethical conduct by a management accountant (Chapter 1), consider whether John Brogan's behavior is unethical.

(CMA Adapted)

[LO 20-2]   20-47   **Compensation; Regression Analysis (see Chapter 8); Spreadsheet Application** Many people ask, "Are executives worth their very high pay?" As noted in the chapter, this is a difficult question to answer because the benefits an effective executive brings to the company are hard to measure. One thing we can do, however, is to see if *changes* in executive pay are correlated with changes in company performance. If pay increases when company performance increases, and vice versa, then this would be an indication that pay practices are aligned with the interests of shareholders. To study this question, we have data (from *The New York Times,* May 24, 2019) for 30 of the highest-paid chief executive officers (CEOs) in the United States in 2018 (these are not the 30 highest paid CEOs because some have been omitted due to insufficient data):

		% Change from 2017 to 2018	
CEO	**Company**	**Total Compensation**	**Total Return**
James Heppelmann	PTC	357%	89%
Fabrizio Freda	Estee Lauder	162%	50%
Richard Handler	Jefferies Financial Group	105%	−15%
Robert A. Iger	Disney	81%	20%
David M. Zaslav	Discovery	207%	11%
Robert A. Kotick	Activision	7%	−26%
Charles H. Robbins	Cisco	27%	38%
Lewis Bird III	At Home Group	2477%	−30%
James R. Murdoch	Twenty-First Century Fox	125%	77%
Joshua W. Sapan	AMC Networks	−30%	1%
Brian L. Roberts	Comcast	7%	−13%
Leonard S. Schleifer	Regeneron	0%	−1%
Stephen MacMillan	Hologic	275%	12%
Joseph M Hogan	Align Technology	256%	−6%
Daniel H. Schulman	Paypal	96%	14%
James Dimon	JPMorgan Chase	6%	−6%
Howard W. Lutnick	BGC Partners	89%	−36%
Shantanu Narayen	Adobe	29%	38%
Marc Benioff	Salesforce.com	510%	33%
Laurence D. Fink	BlackRock	−4%	−21%
Robert Greenberg	Sketchers U.S.A.	252%	−40%
James P. Gorman	Morgan Stanley	8%	−22%
Randall L. Stephenson	AT&T	1%	−21%
Satya Nadella	Microsoft	29%	45%
James M. Cracchiolo	Ameriprise Financial	11%	−36%
Michael L. Corbat	CitiGroup	36%	−28%
Reed Hastings	Netflix	48%	39%
Mary T. Barra	GM	0%	−15%
Marillyn A Hewson	Lockheed Martin	7%	−16%
Mark Zuckerberg	Facebook	148%	−26%

In the above table, the change in compensation is measured as the percentage change in total compensation from 2017 to 2018; total return (a measure of company performance) is measured by the percentage change in stock price plus dividends.

Required

1. Using the CORREL function in Excel, find the correlation between the change in executive pay and the change in shareholder return. Round your answer to 5 decimal places.

2. Using Excel, conduct regression analysis with the change in shareholder return as the dependent variable and the change in CEO pay as the independent variable. What is the *p*-value for the coefficient on the change in CEO pay? Round your answer to 5 decimal places.

3. Comment briefly on the findings. Does it appear that the change in CEO pay is significantly related to the change in company performance? Are there other considerations that could qualify your conclusions?

[LO 20-1]   20-48 **Compensation; Regression Analysis (see Chapter 8)**   A study of the airline industry examined whether performance on a selected nonfinancial measure was a significant predictor of CEO compensation. A sample of 35 firms was taken, and regression was conducted to determine the potential relationship between selected financial and nonfinancial independent variables and three dependent variables: (a) CEO cash compensation, (b) CEO compensation in the form of options granted during the year, and (c) total CEO compensation (a + b).

The independent variables were:

- Passenger load (PL), the proportion of seats filled to the seats available.
- Stock price return (RT), the increase in stock price plus dividends over the year relative to beginning of the year.
- Return on assets (ROA), income over total assets.
- Sales.
- Stock price volatility (V), the standard deviation of daily stock price changes in the company's stock price.
- CEO ownership (CEO), the percentage of the company's outstanding shares owned by the CEO.
- CEO tenure (CEO-T), the number of years the CEO has been on the job.
- Ratio of book value of the company to the market value of the company (BM).

The table below shows, for each dependent variable, the eight independent variables and their statistical significance (*p*-value) in each regression equation. For example, in the regression with cash compensation as the dependent variable (regression a), the PL variable is statistically significant at the 0.01 level, RT is statistically significant at the 0.01 level, and the ROA variable is not significant. The authors of the study hypothesized that there is a significant relationship between CEO compensation and passenger load.

	CEO Cash Compensation (a)*	CEO Option Compensation (b)*	Total CEO Compensation (a + b)*
Passenger load (PL)	0.01	NS	NS
Stock return (RT)†	0.01	0.01	0.01
Return on assets (ROA)	NS	NS	NS
Sales†	0.01	0.01	0.01
Stock price volatility (V)	NS	NS	0.05
CEO ownership % (CEO)†	0.01	0.01	0.01
CEO tenure (CEO-T)	0.01	NS	0.05
Book value to market value (BM)	NS	0.05	NS
R-squared	69.3%	11.0%	50.0%

*Dependent variables were transformed using the natural logarithm (a convenient process for transforming a highly skewed variable into a more normalized dataset).
†This variable had a statistically significant negative coefficient, indicating an inverse relationship with the dependent variable.
NS means that the variable is not statistically significant at $p = 0.05$ or less.

Required   Review the three regressions, and develop a brief explanation for each of the following:

1. Which of the three regressions would you most rely on? Why?

2. What do the regression results tell you about the relationships of the independent variables to the three dependent variables?

3. Were the authors of the study correct about their expectation regarding the PL variable?

4. How would you use this information in designing compensation plans for executives in the airline industry?

[LO 20-4]   20-49 **Business Analysis; Spreadsheet Application** Davidson Yachts is a small private company founded by two businesspeople who are friends and avid sailors. At present, they are interested in expanding the business and have asked you to review its financial statements.

Davidson Yachts sells approximately 100 to 150 sailboats each year, ranging from 14-foot din-ghies to 20-foot sailboats. Their sales prices range from $2,000 to more than $10,000. The company has a limited inventory of boats consisting primarily of one or two boats from each of the four manu-facturers that supply Davidson. The company also sells a variety of supplies and parts and performs different types of service. Most sales are on credit.

The company operates from a large building that has offices, storage, and sales space for some of the smaller sailboats. The larger sailboats are kept in a fenced area adjacent to the main building, and an ample parking area is nearby. This year, Davidson purchased a boat lift to haul boats. The lift has brought in revenues for boat repairs, hull painting, and related services, as well as the boat hauls.

The balance sheet and income statement for Davidson Yachts for 2017–2022 follow. The increase in net fixed assets in the recent 2 years is due to improvements in the building, paving of the parking area, and the purchase of the lift.

The company obtains its debt financing from two sources: (1) a small savings and loan for its short-term funds and (2) a larger commercial bank, also for short-term loans, but principally for long-term financing. The terms of the loan agreement with the bank include a restriction that Davidson's current ratio must remain higher than 1.5.

Required   Evaluate the liquidity and profitability of Davidson Yachts using selected financial ratios. Assess the company's overall profitability, liquidity, and desirability as an investment. Use a spreadsheet program like Excel to improve the speed and accuracy of your analysis.

DAVIDSON YACHTS COMPANY
Comparative Balance Sheet
December 31

	2017	2018	2019	2020	2021	2022
Cash	$ 23,260	$ 21,966	$ 18,735	$ 28,426	$ 43,692	$ 31,264
Accounts receivable	99,465	102,834	112,903	125,663	104,388	144,009
Allowance for bad debts	(9,304)	(8,786)	(8,824)	(11,266)	(7,282)	(12,506)
Inventory	35,009	56,784	61,792	67,884	58,994	96,774
Other current assets	11,894	12,894	9,024	11,006	18,923	22,903
Total current assets	$160,324	$185,692	$ 193,630	$221,713	$218,715	$282,444
Property and equipment	262,195	282,008	299,380	368,565	405,269	498,626
Accumulated depreciation	(65,984)	(93,442)	(122,892)	(158,099)	(187,227)	(227,307)
Total assets	$356,535	$374,258	$ 370,118	$432,179	$436,757	$553,763
Accounts payable	$ 82,635	$ 78,127	$ 63,346	$ 56,256	$ 40,189	$ 50,544
Taxes payable	11,630	10,983	11,780	14,083	3,738	16,132
Short-term loans	59,876	56,980	37,583	41,093	49,594	76,962
Accrued payroll payable	5,227	4,598	3,649	4,224	4,774	5,279
Total current liabilities	$159,368	$150,688	$ 116,358	$115,656	$ 98,295	$148,917
Long-term debt	158,173	172,388	179,490	214,997	229,471	262,258
Equity	38,994	51,182	74,270	101,526	108,991	142,588
Total liabilities and equity	$356,535	$374,258	$ 370,118	$ 432,179	$ 436,757	$553,763

DAVIDSON YACHTS COMPANY
Comparative Statement of Income and Operating Cash Flow
For the Years Ended December 31

	2017	2018	2019	2020	2021	2022
Sales	$767,580	$724,878	$777,480	$929,478	$764,610	$948,857
Returns and allowances	38,379	35,645	40,334	45,998	32,887	47,380
Cost of sales	473,908	441,298	458,015	545,778	453,669	530,597
Gross margin	$255,293	$247,935	$279,131	$337,702	$278,054	$370,880
Depreciation expense	$ 29,075	$ 27,458	$ 29,450	$ 35,207	$ 29,128	$ 40,080
Interest expense	18,597	19,557	20,998	21,475	24,889	28,993
Salaries and wages	81,923	73,664	77,846	95,764	92,903	101,447
Accounting and legal	9,304	8,786	9,323	11,834	13,108	11,380
Administration expense	79,666	75,234	80,693	96,469	87,995	97,441
Other expense	12,630	18,927	15,763	22,903	18,934	22,662
Total expense	$231,195	$223,626	$234,073	$283,652	$266,957	$302,003
Net income	$ 24,098	$ 24,309	$ 45,058	$ 54,050	$ 11,097	$ 68,877

DAVIDSON YACHTS COMPANY
Comparative Statement of Income and Operating Cash Flow
For the Years Ended December 31

	2017	2018	2019	2020	2021	2022
Cash flow from operations (adjustments to net income)						
Depreciation		$ 27,458	$ 29,450	$ 35,207	$ 29,128	$ 40,080
Decrease (increase) in receivables		(3,887)	(10,031)	(10,318)	17,291	(34,397)
Decrease (increase) in inventory		(21,775)	(5,008)	(6,092)	8,890	(37,780)
Decrease (increase) in other current assets		(1,000)	3,870	(1,982)	(7,917)	(3,980)
Increase (decrease) in current liabilities		(8,680)	(34,330)	(702)	(17,361)	50,622
		$ 16,425	$ 29,009	$ 70,163	$ 41,128	$ 83,422

[LO 20-4]   20-50 **Business Valuation** Refer to the information in Problem 20-49 for the Davidson Yachts Company.

Required

1. What is the valuation of Davidson Yachts Company using the book value of equity method?

2. What is the valuation of Davidson Yachts Company using the multiples-based method on earnings? Assume the industry average earnings multiple is 7. Use the median value of the most recent 3 years for earnings.

3. What is the valuation of Davidson Yachts Company using the mulitples-based method on operating cash flow? Assume the industry average multiple on operating cash flow is 5. Use the median value of the most recent 3 years for cash flow.

4. Compare and discuss the three valuations. Which of the methods would you use? Why?

[LO 20-4]   20-51 **Business Analysis** Brooks Plumbing Products Inc. (BPP) manufactures plumbing fixtures and other home improvement products that are sold in Home Depot and Walmart as well as hardware stores. BPP has a solid reputation for providing value products, good quality, and a good price. The company has been approached by an investment banking firm representing a third company, Garden Specialties Inc. (GSI), that is interested in acquiring BPP. The acquiring firm (GSI) is a retailer of garden supplies; it sees the potential synergies of the combined firm and is willing to pay BPP shareholders $38 cash per share for their stock, which is greater than the current stock price; the stock has traded at about $35 in recent months. Summary financial information about BPP follows.

Required   Evaluate BPP as a company using financial ratio analysis (including the liquidity, cash flow, and profitability ratios demonstrated in Exhibit 20.9). Because the calculation of some ratios requires the averaging of balances, you may assume for simplicity that the balances in 2020 are the same as those in 2021.

BROOKS PLUMBING PRODUCTS INC.
Selected Financial Information
For the Years Ended December 31

	2022	2021	2022 Industry Average
Cash	$ 79,919,778	$ 3,456,227	
Accounts receivable	56,778,465	87,294,771	
Inventory	39,665,416	59,883,645	
Long-lived assets			
Gross book value	167,278,377	143,778,377	
Net book value	100,620,809	95,887,302	
Replacement cost	170,587,409	188,465,338	
Liquidation value	68,734,002	67,335,209	
Current liabilities	119,045,766	120,995,274	
Long-term debt	31,997,364	37,885,302	
Shareholders' equity	125,941,338	87,641,369	
Capital expenditures	23,500,000	12,990,336	
Sales	667,534,771	638,776,465	

BROOKS PLUMBING PRODUCTS INC.
Selected Financial Information
For the Years Ended December 31

	2022	2021	2022 Industry Average
Cost of sales	498,657,788	477,491,001	
Operating expense*	102,667,355	134,765,229	
Income tax rate	38%	38%	38.0%
Depreciation expense	$ 18,766,493	$ 15,664,254	
Dividends	$ 2,750,000	$ 1,250,000	
Year-end stock price	$ 35.78	$ 22.99	
Number of outstanding shares	25,689,554	22,763,554	
Sales multiplier			1.40
Free cash flow multiplier			8.80
Earnings multiplier			13.50
Cost of capital	5.2%	5.2%	
Accounts receivable turnover			5.50
Inventory turnover			8.60
Current ratio			1.90
Quick ratio			1.10
Cash flow ratio			1.40
Free cash flow ratio			1.10
Gross margin percentage			33.0%
Return on assets (net book value)			19.0%
Return on equity			28.0%
Earnings per share			$2.33

*Operating expense includes depreciation expense.

[LO 20-4] 20-52 **Business Valuation** Refer to the information for Brooks Plumbing Products Inc. (BPP) in Problem 20-51.

Required (round all calculated answers to the nearest whole dollar)

1. What is the valuation of BPP (for 2022) using the market value method?
2. What is the valuation of BPP (for 2022) using the book value method?
3. What are the valuations of BPP (for 2022) using the multiples-based methods for sales, earnings, and free cash flow?
4. What is the estimated value for BPP using the discounted free cash flow method, assuming that the 2022 amount of free cash flow continues indefinitely?
5. Which of the methods would you use? Why?
6. Is the GSI offer a good one? Why or why not?
7. What would be the effect of sustainability issues, if any, in the acquisition of BPP by GSI?

[LO 20-4] 20-53 **Business Valuation** Read the article by Joel Litman and Mark L. Frigo titled "When Strategy and Valuation Meet," *Strategic Finance,* August 2004, pp. 31–39. The article provides a comprehensive discussion of how business strategy and business valuation are interrelated and provides five lessons based on an understanding of this interrelationship.

   The article is available at: http://sfmagazine.com/wp-content/uploads/sfarchive/2004/08/When-Strategy-and-Valuation-Meet-Five-Lessons-from-Return-Driven-Strategy.pdf.

Required

1. Explain briefly the different skills required by a business strategy expert and a business valuation expert.
2. Explain why a great product seldom ensures a great business.
3. Explain why being "different" is not central to strategy.
4. Explain the difference between a great company and a great stock.
5. Explain when and why growth is not necessarily a good thing.

Solutions to Self-
Study Problems

1. Management Compensation Plan

DTH's goal is to increase its business by at least 10% a year in a very competitive environment. The compensation plan is consistent with this goal because it rewards increases in revenues and new clients. It is likely, however, that under the current plan, each office is focusing only on the client base in its own region.

A problem occurs when DTH must make proposals that require joint cooperation and participation among two or more offices. The compensation plan does not have an incentive for cooperation. In fact, it could be a distraction and reduce the potential for a substantial bonus for any given office to develop a proposal for a large contract in which other offices might benefit. The cost of the proposal would be borne by the office, and the benefits would accrue to other offices as well as the originating office. The cost of the proposal for large contracts must therefore be shared among the offices in some way, or any one office will not have the incentive to spend the time and money necessary to develop a large proposal.

In addition to sharing the cost of the proposal, DTH should consider having a firmwide proposal development group for these large projects. The individual offices would then be charged for the cost of this group, perhaps in proportion to the fees received from large contracts in that office. Clearly, the firm is losing the larger contracts, and the compensation and proposal development plans must provide the needed incentive for each office to go after them aggressively.

Another alternative is to go to a firmwide compensation pool that would provide a direct and strong incentive for each office to cooperate in developing new business. A disadvantage of this approach is that it would reduce the motivation for each office to seek business in its own region because the revenues from these individual efforts would be shared firmwide.

Another issue concerning the current compensation plan is the office manager's discretion to divide the office bonus among the professionals in the office. Although no one has complained, a lower-level professional is unlikely to complain about the office manager's bonus decisions. The equity of this system should be reviewed to ensure that each office manager is using this discretion in a fair and appropriate way.

2. Business Valuation

Because WebSmart is a relatively new company currently showing losses and negative cash flows, the earnings-multiple and discounted cash flow approaches are not suitable. Moreover, because the company is not public, there is no current stock price. This leaves two possibilities: the book value of equity method and the revenue-multiple method. The book value of equity is given at $1,200,000. In contrast, the revenue multiple would estimate value at $4,200,000 = 7 \times $600,000. Alternatively, WebSmart could use projected revenues in the multiple calculation. Moreover, it could use projected cash flows in a cash flow multiple or discounted cash flow calculation because cash flow would presumably be positive in the coming years.

Also, the firm has an asset, the *Guide to Competitive Colleges,* which has a market value of $1,350,000, so any valuation should be higher than that figure. Overall, this is a difficult firm to value; the range from $1,350,000 to $4,200,000 is a very wide range. Also, there is significant uncertainty about future cash flows, which are critical to the overall valuation.

Please visit Connect to access a narrated, animated tutorial for solving these problems.

Glossary

A

abnormal spoilage   Waste in excess of what is expected to occur under normal operating conditions.

absolute quality conformance (robust quality approach)   Conformance that aims for all products or services to meet the quality target value *exactly,* with no variation.

accounting (book) rate of return (ARR)   A rate of return on a project measured as the ratio of some measure of accounting profit associated with the project to some measure of investment in the project.

activity   A specific task, action, or unit of work done.

activity analysis   The development of a detailed description of the specific activities performed in the firm's operations.

activity consumption cost driver   A measure of the demand placed on the resources by products, services, or customers.

activity-based budgeting (ABB)   A budgeting process that is based on activities and associated activity costs to support production and sales; an extension of the traditional form of activity-based costing (ABC).

activity-based costing (ABC)   A costing approach that assigns resource costs to cost objects based on activities performed for the cost objects.

activity-based management (ABM)   Uses activity analysis and activity-based costing to help managers identify the value of activities and to make strategic performance management decisions—adding and deleting products, adjusting process capacities, adjusting prices, removing costs and complexities, and more.

actual costing system   A costing process that uses actual costs incurred for direct materials, direct labor, and factory overhead.

actual factory overhead   Costs incurred in an accounting period for indirect materials, indirect labor, and other indirect production costs, including factory rent, insurance, property tax, depreciation, repairs and maintenance, power, light, heat, and employer payroll taxes for factory personnel.

advance pricing agreement (APA)   An agreement between the Internal Revenue Service (IRS) and a firm that establishes an agreed-upon transfer price.

allocation bases   The cost drivers used to allocate or assign costs to cost objects.

analysis of variance table   A table that separates the total variance of the dependent variable into both error and explained variance components.

analytic hierarchy process (AHP)   A multicriteria decision technique that can combine qualitative and quantitative factors in the overall evaluation of decision alternatives.

appraisal (detection) costs   Costs associated with detecting output that doesn't conform to quality standards.

arm's length standard   A transfer price set to reflect the price that unrelated parties acting independently would have set.

asset turnover (AT)   The amount of sales dollars generated per dollar of investment; measures the manager's ability to increase sales from a given level of investment.

authoritative standard   A standard determined solely or primarily by management.

average cost   The total cost of resources consumed (materials, labor, and overhead) divided by the units of output.

average cost method   A method that uses units of output to allocate costs to products.

average-risk projects   Projects that approximate the risk of the firm's existing assets and operations; the WACC (weighted-average cost of capital) is used in DCF (discounted cash flow) models to evaluate average-risk investment projects.

B

backflush costing   A method that charges current production costs (using standard costs) directly to Finished Goods Inventory without accounting for the flows in and out of Work-in-Process, or directly to Cost of Goods Sold without accounting for the flows in and out of WIP or Finished Goods.

balanced scorecard (BSC)   An accounting report that includes the firm's critical success factors in four areas: (1) financial performance, (2) customer satisfaction, (3) internal processes, and (4) learning and growth.

batch-level activity   An activity performed for each batch of products or services.

benchmarking   A process by which a firm identifies its critical success factors, studies the best practices of other firms (or other business units within a firm) for achieving these critical success factors, and then implements improvements in the firm's processes to match or beat the performance of those competitors.

benefits (perks)   Special benefits for the employee, such as automobile/parking, membership in a fitness club, tickets to entertainment events, and other extras paid for by the firm.

beta coefficient (β)   A measure of the sensitivity of a given stock's return to fluctuations in the overall market; the average beta of all stocks is 1.0; a beta coefficient greater than 1 implies greater sensitivity to market fluctuations, while a beta less than 1 implies lower sensitivity of return to fluctuations in the overall market.

bonus   Compensation based on the achievement of performance goals for a period.

breakeven after-tax cash flow   The minimum annual after-tax cash inflows needed for an investment project to be acceptable (in a present value sense).

breakeven point   The point at which total revenues equal total costs so that operating profit is zero.

budget   A detailed plan for the acquisition and use of financial and other resources over a specified period of time—for example, a year, a month, or a quarter.

budgetary slack   The difference between budgeted performance and expected performance; a "cushion" managers intentionally build into budgets to help ensure success in meeting the budget.

budgeted capacity utilization   The planned (forecasted) output for the coming period, usually a year.

budgeting   The process of preparing one or more budgets.

business analysis   Evaluates the firm's overall performance by using one or more of the following methods: balanced scorecard, financial ratio analysis, and economic value added.

business analytics (BA)   An approach to strategy implementation in which the management accountant uses data to understand and analyze business performance.

business process improvement (BPI)   A management method by which managers and workers commit to a program of continuous improvement in quality and other critical success factors.

business valuation   Values the firm by estimating its total market value, which can be compared to the market value for prior periods or for comparable firms.

by-products   Products in a joint production process whose total sales values are minor in comparison with the total sales value of all the joint products.

C

capital asset pricing model (CAPM)   Model that depicts the risk-return relationship for equity securities and that can be used to estimate the required rate of return on equity for a given company; a rate equal to the risk-free rate of return plus a risk premium measured as the product of β and the market-risk premium.

capital budget   A listing of approved investment projects as well as anticipated cash inflows and outflows associated with these projects for a given period.

capital budgeting   A process of identifying, evaluating, selecting, and controlling an organization's capital investments (i.e., its long-term projects and programs).

capital investment   A project that involves a large up-front expenditure of funds and expected future benefits over a number of years.

capital rationing   The case where investment capital for a given accounting period is limited—hence the need for these funds to be "rationed."

capital structure   The mix of debt and equity capital by which a company is financed.

cash budget   A schedule depicting the effects on cash of all budgeted activities.

cause-and-effect diagram   A diagram that organizes a chain of causes and effects to sort out root causes of an identified quality problem; also called a *"fish-bone" diagram.*

comparable price method   Establishes an arm's length transfer price by using the sales prices of similar products made by unrelated firms.

concurrent engineering   An engineering method that integrates product design with manufacturing and marketing throughout the product's life cycle; also called *simultaneous engineering.*

confidence interval (CI)   When using regression analysis to estimate costs, the CI refers to a range around the regression line

within which the management accountant can be confident the actual value of the predicted cost will likely fall.

constraints   Those activities or policies that slow the product's total manufacturing cycle time or limit throughput.

continuous improvement standard   A standard that gets progressively tighter over time.

contribution by profit center (CPC)   Measures profit after all traceable costs and is therefore a performance measure that is controllable by the profit center manager.

contribution income statement   In a contribution income statement, variable costs are subtracted from sales to get total contribution margin, from which fixed costs are subtracted, to yield the amount of operating profit for the period.

contribution margin per unit   The difference between the selling price per unit (p) and the variable cost per unit (v); a measure of the change in operating profit for each unit change in sales.

contribution margin ratio   The ratio of the contribution margin per unit to the selling price per unit, $(p - v) \div p$.

control   The set of procedures, tools, and systems that organizations use to reach their goals.

control chart   A graph that depicts successive observations of an operation (or cost) taken at constant intervals over a specified time.

controllable fixed costs   Fixed costs that the profit center manager can influence in approximately a year or less.

controllable margin   A margin determined by subtracting short-term controllable fixed costs from the contribution margin.

conversion cost   Direct labor and factory overhead combined into a single amount.

core competencies   Skills or competencies that the firm employs especially well.

correlation   Present when a given variable tends to change predictably in the same or opposite direction for a given change in the other, correlated variable.

cost   Incurred when a resource is used for some purpose.

cost allocation   The process of assigning indirect costs to cost pools and cost objects.

cost assignment   The process of assigning costs to cost pools or from cost pools to cost objects.

cost center   A firm's production or support unit that is evaluated on the basis of cost.

cost driver   A factor that causes or relates to a change in the total cost of an activity.

cost estimation   The development of a well-defined relationship between a cost object and its cost drivers for the purpose of predicting the cost.

cost leadership   A competitive strategy in which a firm outperforms competitors in producing products or services at the lowest cost.

cost life cycle   The sequence of activities within the firm that begins with research and development, followed by design, manufacturing, marketing/distribution, and customer service.

cost management   The development and use of cost management information.

cost management information   The information developed and used to implement the organization's strategy. It consists of financial information about costs and revenues and nonfinancial information about customer retention, productivity, quality, and other key success factors for the organization.

cost object Any product, service, customer, activity, or organizational unit to which costs are accumulated for some management purpose.

cost of goods manufactured The cost of goods that were finished and transferred out of the Work-in-Process Inventory account during a given period.

cost of goods sold The cost of the product transferred to the income statement when inventory is sold.

cost of quality (COQ) A comprehensive reporting framework for classification of quality-related costs.

cost plus method Within the context of transfer pricing, a method that determines the price based on the selling unit's cost plus a gross profit percentage determined by comparing the seller's sales to those of unrelated parties (or by comparing unrelated parties' sales to those of other unrelated parties).

cost pools The meaningful groups into which costs are collected.

cost tables Computer-based databases that include comprehensive information about the firm's cost drivers.

cost-volume-profit (CVP) analysis A short-term profit-planning model; a method for analyzing how various operating decisions and marketing decisions will affect short-term profit.

costing The process of accumulating, classifying, and assigning direct materials, direct labor, and factory overhead costs to products, services, or projects.

costs of conformance The sum of prevention costs and appraisal costs.

costs of nonconformance The sum of internal failure costs and external failure costs.

critical success factors (CSFs) Measures of those aspects of the firm's performance that are essential to its competitive advantage and therefore to its success.

cross-sectional regression A method of cost estimation for a particular cost object based on information on other cost objects and variables, where the information for all variables is taken from the same period of time.

currently attainable standard A level of performance that workers with proper training and experience can attain most of the time without having to exert extraordinary effort.

customer cost analysis Identifies cost activities and cost drivers related to servicing customers.

customer lifetime value (CLV) The net present value of estimated future profits from a given customer; in practice, a firm is likely to estimate this value over the next three to five years.

customer loyalty An indication of customer satisfaction, measured (for example) by repeat purchases or customer retention rates or by percentage growth in business with existing customers.

customer profitability analysis Identifies customer service activities, cost drivers, and the profitability of each individual customer or customer group.

customer response time (CRT) A measure of operating performance defined as the elapsed time between the time the customer places an order and the time the customer receives the order.

CVP graph A diagrammatic representation (expressed in units) of how revenues and total costs change over different levels of sales volume.

cycle time The amount of time between receipt of a customer order and shipment of the order.

D

death spiral effect Continual raising of selling prices in an attempt to recover fixed costs, in spite of successive decreases in demand; generally described as one of the dangers of cost-plus pricing.

decentralization A decision-making approach in which top management delegates a significant amount of decision authority and responsibility to subunit (SBU) managers.

degree of operating leverage (DOL) A measure, at any level of sales volume, of the sensitivity of operating profit to changes in volume; defined as the ratio of contribution margin to operating profit at any output level, Q.

degrees of freedom Represents the number of independent choices that can be made for each component of variance.

denominator activity level The output (activity) level used to establish the predetermined fixed overhead application rate; generally defined as *practical capacity;* also called the *denominator volume.*

denominator volume The output (activity) level used to calculate the predetermined fixed overhead application rate; generally defined as *practical capacity;* also called the *denominator activity level.*

dependent variable In cost estimation, the cost to be estimated.

design analysis A form of value engineering in which the design team prepares several possible designs of the product, each having similar features with different levels of both performance and cost.

design quality The extent to which actual product design matches customer expectations (for attributes, services, functionality, etc.).

differentiation A competitive strategy in which a firm succeeds by developing and maintaining a unique value for the product (or service) as perceived by consumers.

direct cost A cost that can be conveniently and economically traced directly to a cost pool or a cost object.

direct labor cost The labor used to manufacture the product or to provide the service.

direct labor efficiency variance The difference between the actual direct labor hours worked and the standard direct labor hours allowed for the units manufactured, multiplied by the standard wage rate per hour.

direct labor rate variance The difference between the actual and standard hourly wage rate multiplied by the actual direct labor hours worked during the period.

direct materials cost The cost of the materials in the product and a reasonable allowance for scrap and defective units.

direct materials flexible budget variance For each material, the difference between the total direct materials cost incurred and the flexible budget amount for this period's output.

direct materials price variance For each direct material, the difference between the actual and standard costs per unit of the material multiplied by the actual quantity of direct materials used (or purchased) during the period.

direct materials purchases budget A budget that shows the physical amount and cost of planned purchases of direct materials.

direct materials usage budget   A plan that shows the amount and budgeted cost of direct materials required for planned production.

direct materials usage variance   For each material, the difference between the actual direct material units used during the period and the number of standard units that should have been used for the output of the period, multiplied by the standard cost per unit of the direct material.

direct method   Service department cost allocation accomplished by using the service flows *only to production departments* and determining each production department's share of that service.

discount rate   A generic term that refers to the rate used for converting estimated future cash flows to a present-value basis.

discounted cash flow (DCF) models   Capital budgeting decision models that incorporate the present value of future after-tax cash flows.

discretionary-cost method   Used when costs are considered largely uncontrollable; an input-oriented approach that applies discretion at the planning stage.

dual allocation   A cost allocation method that separates fixed and variable costs and traces variable service department costs to the user departments; fixed costs are allocated based on either equal shares among departments or a predetermined budgeted proportion.

dual pricing   Involves the use of multiple prices for an internal transfer or cost allocation, one based on variable cost and one based on fixed cost.

dummy variable   Used in a regression model to represent the presence or absence of a condition.

Durbin-Watson (DW) statistic   The **Durbin-Watson (DW) statistic** is a measure of the extent of nonlinearity in the regression.

E

earnings management   The manipulation of reported income.

economic nationalism   The ideology that promotes domestic economic growth and opposes globalization, free trade, and immigration.

economic value added (EVA®)   A measure of financial performance designed to approximate an entity's *economic profit;* calculated most often as net operating profit after taxes (adjusted for accounting "distortions") less an imputed charge based on the level of invested capital.

employment contract   An agreement between the manager and top management, designed to provide incentives for the manager to act autonomously to achieve top management's objectives.

engineered-cost method   An output-oriented method that considers costs to be variable and, therefore, controllable.

enterprise resource planning (ERP)   The process by which a company manages and integrates key business processes (e.g., planning, purchasing, inventory, sales, marketing, finance, and human resources).

enterprise risk management (ERM)   A framework and process that firms use to manage the risks that could negatively or positively affect the company's competitiveness and success.

equivalent units   The number of units that could have been produced given the amount of work actually performed and

quantity of other production inputs used for both complete and partially complete units; used in conjunction with process costing.

executional cost drivers   Factors that the firm can manage in the short term to reduce costs such as workforce involvement, design of the production process, and supplier relationships.

expropriation   A situation in which a government takes ownership and control of assets that a foreign investor has invested in that country.

external failure costs   Costs associated with defective/poor-quality outputs detected after being delivered to the customer.

F

F-statistic   A measure of the statistical reliability of the regression.

facility-level activity   An activity performed to support operations in general (that is, an activity not related to volume of output, number of batches produced, or the support of individual products).

factory overhead   All the indirect manufacturing costs commonly combined into a single cost pool in a manufacturing firm.

factory overhead applied   The amount of overhead assigned to a cost object using a predetermined factory overhead rate.

FASB ASC 330-10-30   GAAP financial reporting guidance regarding the determination of overhead allocation rates and the treatment of abnormal idle-capacity variances.

FIFO method   A process costing method for calculating the current period's unit cost that includes only costs incurred and work performed during the current period

financial budgets   Budgets that identify and relate to sources and uses of funds for planned operations and capital expenditures.

financial control   The comparison of actual and budgeted financial results.

financial productivity   The ratio of output to the dollar amount of one or more input factors.

Finished Goods Inventory   The cost of goods that are ready for sale.

firmwide pool   A basis for determining the bonus available to all managers through an amount set aside for this purpose.

fixed cost   The portion of the total cost that, within the relevant range, does not change with a change in the quantity of a designated cost driver.

fixed overhead application rate   A term used for product-costing purposes; the rate at which fixed overhead cost is charged to production per unit of activity (or output).

fixed overhead production volume variance   The difference between budgeted (lump-sum) fixed overhead cost for the period and the standard fixed overhead cost applied to production (using the predetermined fixed overhead allocation rate); also called the *production volume variance* or the *denominator volume variance.*

fixed overhead spending (budget) variance   The difference between budgeted and actual fixed factory overhead costs for a period.

fixed-performance contract   An incentive compensation plan whereby compensation (reward) is a function of actual performance compared to a fixed (budgeted) target.

flexible budget   A budget that adjusts revenues and costs to reflect varying levels of output activity (i.e., different levels of volume and mix).

flexible budget variance   The difference between actual and flexible budget amounts on the income statement.

flow diagram   A flowchart of the work done that shows the sequence of processes and the amount of time required for each.

full cost method   A transfer price set equal to the variable cost of the selling unit, plus an allocated share of the selling unit's fixed costs, with or without a markup for profit.

full costing   A costing system in which all production costs (both fixed and variable) are included in the calculation of cost of sales. Full costing (also called absorption costing) is required by GAAP.

functional analysis   A type of value engineering in which the performance and cost of each major function or feature of the product is examined.

G

gaming the performance measure   Non-value-adding actions taken by managers to improve indicated performance.

goal congruence   The consistency among the goals of the firm, its subunits, and its employees. It is achieved when the manager acts independently in such a way as to simultaneously achieve personal objectives and those of top management.

goalpost conformance   Refers to a quality specification expressed as a specified range around a targeted performance level.

Grenzplankostenrechnung (GPK)   Detailed German cost accounting system, roughly translated as *flexible standard costing* or *Flexible Analytic Cost Planning and Accounting;* an extension of ABC.

gross book value (GBV)   An asset's historical (i.e., acquisition) cost without the reduction for accumulated depreciation.

group technology   A method of identifying similarities in the parts of products manufactured so the same part can be used in two or more products, thereby reducing costs.

H

high-low method   A method using algebra to determine a *unique* cost estimation line between representative high and low points in a given data set.

high-value-added activity   Something that, in the eyes of the consumer, adds value to a product or service.

histogram   A graphical representation of the frequency of attributes or events in a given set of data.

historical cost   In conjunction with measuring ROI or RI (residual income) of an investment center, a measure of investment equal to the book value of current assets plus the net book value (NBV) of long-lived assets.

hurdle rate   The minimum acceptable rate of return on an investment for capital budgeting purposes, also referred to as the *required rate of return;* for average-risk projects, the hurdle rate is defined as the weighted-average cost of capital (WACC).

I

ideal standard   A standard that reflects perfect implementation and maximum efficiency in every aspect of the operation.

idle capacity   The difference between the available capacity and the planned level of utilization.

idle capacity cost   The economic value of resources not utilized to produce products or provide services.

implementation error   A deviation from standard due to operator errors.

independent variable   A cost driver used to estimate the value of the dependent variable.

indirect cost   A cost that is not conveniently or economically traceable to a specific cost pool or cost object.

indirect labor cost   Labor costs associated with production that are not considered direct labor. Examples include supervision, quality control, inspection, purchasing and receiving, and other labor-related manufacturing support costs; a component of total manufacturing overhead.

indirect materials cost   The cost of materials used in manufacturing that are not part of the product or are not easily or economically traceable to the finished product; a component of total manufacturing overhead.

internal accounting controls   A set of policies and procedures that restrict and guide activities in the processing of financial data with the objective of preventing or detecting errors and fraudulent acts.

internal failure costs   Quality-related costs associated with defective processes or defective products detected before delivery to customers.

internal rate of return (IRR)   An estimate of the true (i.e., economic) rate of return on a proposed investment.

investment center   A business unit that includes in its financial-performance metric the level of assets (capital) employed by the unit as well as profit generated by that unit.

ISO 14000   A set of quality standards that address various aspects of environmental performance, including life-cycle analysis, communication, and auditing of environmental performance.

ISO 9000   A set of guidelines for quality management and quality standards developed by the International Organization for Standardization (ISO), located in Geneva, Switzerland.

J

job cost sheet   A cost sheet that records and summarizes the costs of direct materials, direct labor, and factory overhead for a particular job.

job costing   A product costing system that accumulates and assigns costs to specific jobs, customers, projects, or contracts.

joint costs   The cost of resources employed jointly in the production of two or more outputs; the cost cannot be directly assigned to any one of those outputs. Assignment is made through one or more consistent allocation procedures.

joint production costs   Costs incurred prior to the split-off point; common (i.e., indirect) costs.

joint production process   A process that yields multiple outputs from a common resource input.

joint products   Products from the same production process that have relatively substantial sales values.

just-in-time (JIT) manufacturing   A process in which production at any stage of the process does not take place until an order is received.

K

Kaizen budgeting   A budgeting approach that incorporates continuous improvement expectations in the budget.

L

lean accounting   The accounting technique that uses value streams to measure the financial benefits of a firm's progress in implementing lean manufacturing.

learning curve analysis   A systematic method for estimating costs when learning is present.

learning rate   The percentage by which average time (or total time) falls from previous levels as output doubles.

least squares regression   A cost-estimation method in which the variable and fixed cost coefficients are found by minimizing the sum of the squares of the estimation errors.

life-cycle costing   A method used to identify and monitor the costs of a product throughout its life cycle.

linear programming   A mathematical technique that can be used to solve constrained optimization problems, such as the optimum short-term product (or service) mix.

liquidation value   The estimated price that could be received from the sale of the assets of a business unit.

long-range plan   A plan that identifies actions required during the five- to seven-year period covered by the plan to attain the organization's strategic goals.

low-value-added activity   Consumes time, resources, or space but adds little in regard to satisfying customer needs.

M

management accounting   A profession that involves partnering in management decision making, devising planning and performance management systems, and providing expertise in financial reporting and control to assist management in the formulation and implementation of an organization's strategy.

management accounting and control system   An organization's core performance-measurement system.

management compensation plans   Policies and procedures for compensating managers.

management control   The system used by upper-level managers to evaluate the performance of mid-level managers.

manufacturing cells   A set of machines, typically laid out in the form of a semicircle, needed to produce a particular product or part.

manufacturing cycle efficiency (MCE)   The ratio of processing time to manufacturing cycle time.

manufacturing cycle efficiency (MCE)   A measure of operating performance in a manufacturing setting, defined as the ratio of processing time to total manufacturing time (or the ratio of value-added time to total time).

manufacturing cycle time   The time from the start of production to the shipment of the order.

margin of safety (MOS)   The amount of planned (or actual) sales above the breakeven point.

margin of safety (MOS) ratio   The margin of safety (in units or in dollars) divided by breakeven sales (in units or in dollars).

market price method   A transfer price set as the current price of the product (or service) in the external market.

market risk premium   The spread between the expected rate of return on a market portfolio of securities and the risk-free rate of return; represented as $(r_m - r_f)$, where r_m = return on a market portfolio of securities and r_f = risk-free rate of return.

market share variance   A comparison of the firm's actual market share to its budgeted market share and measurement of the effect of changes in the firm's market share on its total contribution margin and operating income.

market size variance   A measure of the effect of changes in the total market size on the firm's total contribution margin.

master budget   An aggregation of all subunit budgets into an integrated plan of action for the budget period.

master budget variance   The difference between actual operating income and the master budget operating income for the period.

materials inventory   Cost of the supply of materials used in the manufacturing process or to provide the service.

materials requisition   An online data entry or a source document used to request the release of materials into the production process.

materials usage ratio   The ratio of the quantity used to the quantity purchased.

mean absolute percentage error (MAPE)   A measure of cost-estimation accuracy, calculated as the mean (average) absolute percentage prediction error.

measurement errors   Incorrect numbers resulting from improper or inaccurate accounting systems or procedures.

merchandise purchases budget   A budget that shows the amount (and cost) of merchandise a firm plans to purchase during the budget period.

mixed cost   A cost that, within the relevant range, includes both variable and fixed cost components.

modeling error   A deviation from the standard because of the failure to include all relevant variables or because of the inclusion of wrong or irrelevant variables in the standard-setting process.

modified internal rate of return (MIRR)   The internal rate of return (IRR) of a capital investment adjusted to account for an assumed rate of return associated with interim project cash inflows.

Monte Carlo simulation (MCS)   An extension to scenario analysis in which a computer provides a distribution of possible outcomes—for example, project NPVs—based on repeated sampling from a distribution associated with one or more input variables in a decision model.

multicollinearity   The condition when two or more independent variables are highly correlated with each other.

multicriteria decision model   A model that includes more than one decision criterion.

multiple linear regression   Used to describe regression applications having two or more independent variables.

multistage ABC   The assignment of resource costs to certain activities that, in turn, are assigned to other activities before being assigned to the final cost objects.

N

negotiated price method The determination of a transfer price through a negotiation process and sometimes arbitration between units.

net book value (NBV) The original (acquisition) cost of a depreciable asset less accumulated depreciation to date on that asset.

net present value (NPV) The difference between the present value of future cash inflows and the present value of future cash outflows of an investment project.

net promoter score (NPS) A measure of customer satisfaction, defined as the difference between the percentage of customers classified as "promoters" and those classified as "detractors" (those not recommending the business plus those who are neutral).

net realizable value (NRV) The estimated sales value of the product at the split-off point; determined by subtracting the separable processing and selling costs beyond the split-off point from the ultimate sales value of the product.

net working capital For purposes of capital budgeting, current assets other than cash (CA − Cash) less current liabilities (CL).

non-DCF models Capital budgeting decision models that are not based on an analysis of the present value of future cash flows.

non-normal cash flows This involves a series of alternating cash flows, with a minimum of two sign changes (positive to negative, then negative to positive).

Nonconstant variance The condition when the variance of the errors is not constant over the range of the independent variable.

noncontrollable fixed costs Costs that are not controllable within a year's time, usually including facilities-related costs such as depreciation, taxes, and insurance.

normal capacity The expected average demand per year over an intermediate term—for example, the upcoming three to five years.

normal cash flows This involves one or more cash outflows followed by one or more cash inflows (or vice versa).

normal costing system A costing process that uses actual costs for direct materials and direct labor and applies factory overhead to various jobs using a predetermined application rate.

normal spoilage An unacceptable unit that occurs under efficient operating conditions; spoilage that is inherent in the manufacturing process.

O

operating budgets Plans for all phases of operation, including production, purchasing, personnel, and marketing budgets.

operating leverage The extent of fixed costs in an organization's cost structure.

operation costing A hybrid costing system that uses job costing to assign direct materials costs to jobs and process costing to assign conversion costs to products or services.

operational control The monitoring of short-term operating performance; takes place when mid-level managers monitor the activities of operating-level managers and employees.

operational productivity The ratio of output units to the number of units of an input factor.

opportunity cost The benefit lost when choosing one option precludes receiving the benefits from an alternative option.

order-filling costs Expenditures for freight, warehousing, packing and shipping, and collections.

order-getting costs Expenditures to advertise and promote the product.

outliers Unusual data points that strongly influence a regression analysis.

overapplied overhead The excess of applied overhead over actual factory overhead cost for a period.

overhead All the indirect costs commonly combined into a single cost pool; called factory overhead in a manufacturing firm.

overhead application A process of allocating overhead costs to cost objects.

overtime premium The *excess* wage rate per hour over the standard hourly wage rate.

P

***p*-value** Measures the risk that a particular independent variable has only a chance relationship to the dependent variable.

Pareto diagram A histogram of the frequency of factors contributing to a quality problem, ordered from the most to the least frequent.

partial productivity A productivity measure that focuses only on the relationship between one of the inputs and the output attained.

participative standard A method of establishing standards whereby employees affected by the standards participate in the development of those standards.

payback period The length of time (in years, months, etc.) required for the cumulative after-tax cash inflows from an investment to recover the initial investment outlay.

performance measurement A process that identifies and gathers information about the work performed and the results achieved by an individual, activity, process, or organizational unit as compared to preestablished criteria.

performance quality The extent to which the actual performance of the product matches (or is consistent with) design specifications of the product.

period costs All nonproduct expenditures for managing the firm and selling the product; also referred to as *selling, general, and administrative (SG&A) expenses.*

periodic inventory system A method that involves a count of inventory at the end of each accounting period to determine the ending balance in inventory.

perpetual inventory system A method that updates the finished goods inventory account for each purchase or sales transaction.

physical measure method A method that uses a physical measure such as pounds, gallons, yards, or units of volume produced at the split-off point to allocate the joint costs to joint products.

planning and decision making Budgeting and profit planning, cash flow management, and other decisions related to operations.

post audit An in-depth review of a completed capital investment project for the purpose of comparing its realized costs and benefits (both financial and nonfinancial) with the preinvestment estimates of these items.

practical capacity   Theoretical capacity reduced by normal output losses due to personal time, normal maintenance, and so on; the measure of capacity often recommended for estimating cost-driver rates under ABC and TDABC systems.

predatory pricing   Exists when a company has set prices below average variable cost and plans to raise prices later to recover the losses from the lower prices.

predetermined factory overhead rate   An estimated rate used to apply factory overhead cost to a cost object.

prediction error   A deviation from a standard because of an inaccurate estimation of the amounts for variables used in the standard-setting process.

preparation of financial statements   Requires management to comply with the financial reporting requirements of regulatory agencies.

present value (or discounted) payback period   The length of time required for the cumulative *present value* of after-tax cash inflows to recover the initial investment outlay.

present value (PV)   Future cash flows expressed in terms of current purchasing power; also referred to as time-adjusted value or current equivalent value.

prevention costs   Costs incurred to keep quality defects from occurring.

prime costs   The sum of direct materials and direct labor.

principal–agent model   A conceptual model that contains the key elements that contracts must have to achieve the desired objectives.

process map   A diagram that identifies each step in making a product or providing a service.

product costs   Only the costs necessary to complete the product (direct materials, direct labor, and factory overhead).

product-level activity   An activity performed to support the production of a specific type of product or service.

production budget   A budget showing planned output (production) for an upcoming period.

production cost report   A report that summarizes the physical units and equivalent units of a department, the costs incurred during the period, and the costs assigned to units completed and to units in ending Work-in-Process Inventories.

productivity   The ratio of output to input.

profit center   A business unit whose manager is responsible for revenues and expenses, but not the level of invested capital, in the unit.

profit-volume graph   Illustrates how the level of operating profit changes over different levels of sales volume, *Q*.

profitability index (PI)   A rate-of-return measure, defined as the ratio of the NPV of a project to the original investment outlay for the project; useful for project-selection purposes when capital funds are limited and therefore need to be rationed.

Q

quality   Defined as customer satisfaction with the total experience of a product or service. An overall measure of quality is the difference between customer expectations and actual performance of the product or service.

quality circle   A small group of employees from the same work area that meets regularly to identify and solve work-related problems and to implement and monitor solutions to these problems.

quality function deployment (QFD)   The integration of value engineering, marketing analysis, and target costing to assist in determining which components of the product should be targeted for redesign.

R

R-squared   A number between zero and one. Often it is described as a measure of the explanatory power of the regression; that is, the degree to which changes in the dependent variable can be explained by changes in the independent variable.

random variances   Variances beyond the control of management, either technically or financially.

real assets   Investments in both tangible property (e.g., a manufacturing facility) and intangible property (e.g., a new information system).

real options   Flexibilities and/or growth opportunities embedded in capital investment projects; can be contrasted with financial options, which are traded on an organized exchange.

reciprocal flows   The flow of services back and forth between service departments.

reciprocal method   A cost allocation method that considers all reciprocal flows between service departments through the use of simultaneous equations.

regression analysis   A statistical method for obtaining the unique cost-estimating equation that best fits a set of data points.

relative-performance (or relative-improvement) contracts   Contracts that reward managers for performance based on a comparison of actual results with specified benchmarks, not budgeted (fixed) targets; contrast with *fixed-performance contracts*.

relevant cost   A future cost that differs between and among decision alternatives; an avoidable cost.

relevant range   The range of the cost driver in which the actual value of the cost driver is expected to fall, and for which the relationship between the cost and the cost driver is assumed to be approximately linear.

replacement cost   The current cost to replace an asset at the current level of service and functionality of that asset.

resale price method   A transfer pricing method based on cost plus an appropriate markup based on gross profits of unrelated firms selling similar products.

residual income (RI)   A dollar amount equal to the income of a business unit less an imputed charge for the level of investment in the division.

resource   An economic element needed or consumed to perform activities.

resource capacity planning   Procedures used to ensure adequate but not excessive supply of capacity-related resources.

resource consumption accounting (RCA)   A comprehensive and fully integrated management accounting approach that provides management with decision support information based on an operational view of the organization.

resource consumption cost driver   A measure of the frequency and intensity of demand placed on a resource by an activity.

return on investment (ROI) A measure of profit divided by a measure of investment in a business unit.

return on sales (ROS) The amount of profit per sales dollar; measures the manager's ability to control expenses and increase revenues to improve profitability.

revenue center A business unit with responsibility for sales, defined either by product line or by geographic area, that focuses on the selling function.

revenue drivers The factors that affect sales volume, such as price changes, promotions, discounts, customer service, changes in product features, delivery dates, and other value-added factors.

rework The additional work that must be done to make a nonconforming good acceptable so that it can be sold in regular channels.

robust quality approach See *absolute quality conformance.*

rolling financial forecast A constant planning horizon with the use of regularly updated forecasts.

run chart A chart that shows trends in observations of a quality characteristic (or cost) over time.

S

salary A fixed payment for an employee.

sales budget A schedule showing forecasted sales, in units and dollars, for an upcoming period.

sales life cycle The sequence of phases in a product's or service's life in the market—from the introduction of the product or service to the market; to growth in sales; and finally to maturity, decline, and withdrawal from the market.

sales mix The relative proportion in which a company's products (or services) are sold.

sales mix variance The product of the difference between the actual and budgeted sales mix multiplied by the actual total number of units of all products sold and by the budgeted contribution margin per unit of the product.

sales quantity variance The product of three elements: (1) the difference between the budgeted and actual total sales quantity, (2) the budgeted sales mix of the product, and (3) the budgeted contribution margin per unit of the product. It measures the effect of the change in the number of units sold from the number of units budgeted to be sold.

sales value at split-off method A method that allocates joint costs to joint products on the basis of their relative sales values at the split-off point. Also known as the relative sales value method.

sales volume variance For each income statement item, the difference between the flexible budget amount for that item and the amount for that item reflected in the master budget for the period.

scenario analysis Simultaneous effect on a decision variable of interest of changing the values of a set of input factors; a special form of sensitivity analysis that is appropriate when the variables in a decision model are interrelated.

scrap Materials left over from the manufacture of a product that have little or no value.

selling price variance The difference between the total actual sales revenue for a period and the sales revenue in the flexible budget for the period.

sensitivity analysis The name for a variety of methods that examine how an amount changes if factors involved in predicting that amount change.

separable processing costs In a joint production process, costs incurred after the split-off point that are traceable to individual products.

service department A unit of the organization that performs one or more support tasks for production (also known as operating) departments.

simple linear regression Used to describe regression applications having a single independent variable.

Six Sigma An overall strategy to accelerate improvements and achieve unprecedented performance levels by focusing on characteristics that are critical to customers and identifying and eliminating causes of errors or defects in processes.

Solver An analytical tool available on the Data tab in Excel that can be used to solve linear programming (i.e., constrained-optimization) problems.

split-off point The point in a joint production process where products with individual identities emerge.

spoilage An unacceptable unit that is discarded or sold for disposal value.

standard cost The cost a firm should incur for a process or activity.

standard cost sheet A document that lists the standard costs of manufacturing and selling one unit of a product.

standard cost system An accounting system in which standard, not actual, costs flow through the formal accounting records.

standard error of the estimate (SE) A measure of the dispersion of the actual observations around the regression line; as such it provides a measure of the accuracy of the regression's estimates.

statistical control charts Charts that set control limits using a statistical procedure.

step cost A cost that varies with the cost driver, but in discrete steps within the relevant range; also called *semi-fixed cost.*

step method A cost allocation method that uses a sequence of steps in allocating service department costs to production departments.

strategic budget expenditures Planned spending on projects and initiatives that lead to long-term value and competitive advantage.

strategic business unit (SBU) A well-defined set of controllable operating activities over which an SBU manager is responsible.

strategic control system The processes an organization uses to monitor its progress in terms of accomplishing its strategic goals.

strategic management The development and implementation of a sustainable competitive position.

strategic performance measurement A system used by top management for the evaluation of SBU managers.

strategy A plan for using resources to achieve sustainable goals within a competitive environment.

strategy map A graphical representation of the organization's value proposition; used to depict the series of causes and effects embodied in the various perspectives of an organization's balanced scorecard.

structural cost drivers   Strategic plans and decisions that have a long-term effect with regard to issues such as scale, experience, technology, and complexity.

sunk costs   Costs that have been incurred in the past or committed for the future and are therefore irrelevant for decision-making purposes.

sustainability   The balancing of the company's short- and long-term goals in all three dimensions of performance—social, environmental, and financial.

SWOT analysis   A systematic procedure for identifying a firm's critical success factors: its internal strengths and weaknesses and its external opportunities and threats.

systematic variances   Variances that, until corrected, are likely to recur; also called *nonrandom variances.*

T

t-**value**   A measure of the reliability of each of the independent variables.

Taguchi quality loss function (QLF)   Depicts, in the form of a quadratic function, the relationship between quality costs and level of deviation from the target quality level or specification.

Takt time   The speed at which units must be manufactured to meet customer demand.

target costing   The desired cost for a product as determined on the basis of a given competitive price, so the product will earn a desired profit.

theoretical capacity   A measure of capacity (output or activity) that assumes 100% efficiency; maximum possible output (or activity).

theory of constraints (TOC)   An analysis of operations that improves profitability and cycle time by identifying the bottleneck in the operation and determining the most profitable product mix given the bottleneck.

throughput margin   A TOC measure of product profitability; it equals price less materials cost, including all purchased components and materials handling costs.

time ticket   A sheet showing the time an employee worked on each job, the pay rate, and the total cost chargeable to each job.

time-driven activity-based budgeting (TDABB)   A method of budget preparation used in conjunction with a time-driven activity-based cost (TDABC) system.

time-driven activity-based costing (TDABC)   The assignment of resource costs directly to cost objects using the cost per time unit of supplying the resource, rather than first assigning costs to activities and then from activities to cost objects.

time-series regression   The application of regression analysis to predict future amounts, using prior periods' data.

tolerance   An acceptable range of a quality characteristic, such as thickness (measured, e.g., in centimeters).

total contribution margin   The contribution margin per unit, $(p - v)$, multiplied by the number of units sold, Q.

total fixed overhead variance   The difference between actual fixed overhead costs for the period and the standard fixed overhead costs applied to production based on a standard fixed overhead application rate; also called *over- or underapplied fixed overhead* for the period; this variance can be broken down into a fixed overhead spending variance and a fixed overhead production volume variance.

total flexible budget variance   The difference between the flexible budget operating income and the actual operating income for the period.

total flexible budget variance for overhead   The difference between the total actual overhead cost for a period and the flexible budget for total overhead based on *output.*

total manufacturing cost   The sum of materials used, labor, and overhead for the period.

total overhead spending variance   The difference between actual factory overhead cost incurred during a period and the flexible budget for overhead based on inputs (i.e., based on actual direct labor hours worked during the period).

total productivity   A productivity measure that includes all input resources in computing the ratio of the output attained to the input resources consumed.

total quality management (TQM)   A method by which management develops policies and practices to ensure that the firm's products and services exceed customers' expectations.

total variable cost flexible budget variance   The difference between total variable cost incurred during a period and the total variable cost in the flexible budget for the period.

total variable overhead cost variance   The difference between actual variable overhead cost incurred and the standard variable overhead cost applied to production; also called *over- or underapplied variable overhead* for the period.

transfer pricing   The determination of an exchange price for a product or service when different business units within a firm exchange it; used to evaluate the financial performance of profit and investment centers.

transferred-in costs   The costs of work performed in the earlier departments that are transferred into the present department.

trend variable   A variable in a regression model that takes on values of 1, 2, 3, . . . for each period in sequence.

two-stage cost assignment   A procedure that assigns a firm's resource costs to cost pools and then to cost objects.

U

underapplied overhead   The amount by which actual factory overhead exceeds the factory overhead applied for a given accounting period.

unit cost   The total cost (materials, labor, and overhead) divided by the number of units of output.

unit-based pool   A basis for determining a bonus according to the performance of the manager's unit.

unit-level activity   An activity performed for each unit of the cost object.

units accounted for   The sum of the units transferred out and ending inventory units.

units to account for   The sum of the beginning inventory units and the number of units started during the period.

V

value activities   Firms in an industry perform activities to design, manufacture, and provide customer service.

value chain   An analytic tool firms use to identify the specific steps required to provide a product or service to the customer.

value engineering   Used in target costing to reduce product cost by analyzing the trade-offs between different types of product functionality and total product cost.

value stream A group of related products; useful for preparing profitability reports as part of lean accounting; all the activities required to create customer value for a family of products or services.

value-chain analysis A strategic analysis tool used to identify where value to customers can be increased or costs reduced, and to better understand the firm's linkages with suppliers, customers, and other firms in the industry.

variable cost A cost that changes in total in response to changes in one or more cost drivers.

variable cost method In transfer pricing, the transfer price equals the selling unit's variable cost, with or without a markup.

variable costing A costing system in which only variable production costs are included in the calculation of cost of sales. Under variable costing, fixed production costs are not included in inventory cost but are expensed in the period they are incurred.

variable overhead efficiency variance The difference between the flexible budget for variable overhead based on *inputs* (e.g., actual labor hours worked) and the flexible budget for variable overhead based on *outputs* (i.e., standard allowed labor hours for units produced).

variable overhead spending variance The difference between actual variable overhead cost incurred and the flexible budget for variable overhead based on *inputs* for the period (e.g., actual direct labor hours worked).

variances Differences between budgeted and actual amounts, for either financial or nonfinancial measures.

W

weighted-average contribution margin per unit An average per-unit contribution margin based on an assumed sales mix determined on the basis of physical units (not sales dollars).

weighted-average contribution margin ratio An average contribution margin ratio for a given sales mix based on sales dollars (not units).

weighted-average cost of capital (WACC) An average of a firm's (after-tax) cost of debt and equity capital in which each source of funds is proportionately weighted.

weighted-average method A method for calculating unit cost under process costing that includes all costs, both those incurred during the current period and those incurred in the prior period that are shown as the beginning Work-in-Process Inventory of the current period.

what-if analysis The calculation of an amount given different levels of a factor that influences that amount.

Work-in-Process Inventory An inventory account that contains all costs put into the manufacture of products that are started but not complete at the financial statement date.

Z

zero-base budgeting (ZBB) A budgeting process that requires managers to prepare budgets each period from a base of zero.

Index

Page numbers followed by *n* indicate notes.

Effective interest rate, 487n11

Efficiency, management compensation and, 880

eHarmony, 288

Eighme, J. E., 727n5

Einstein, Albert, 21

Eisen, Ben, 871n1

Eisenhower, Dwight D., 366

Electrolux, 548

Emett, Scott, 799, 799n

Employees. *See also* Management compensation
   avoid layoffs, 727
   laying off, 375

Employment contracts
   explanation of, 781
   risk aversion and, 781–782
   uncertainty and, 781

Empowerment, 748

End-of-period disposition of variances, 644–647

Engineered labor standards, 622

Ennis Inc. (EI), 132

Enron Corporation, 26, 36, 873

Enterprise resource management (ERM), 10–11, 652

Enterprise resource planning (ERP), 164, 799

Enterprise risk management (ERM), 17, 33

Enterprise value (EV), 884, 886–887

Environmental performance, 54, 720

Environmental responsibility, 603

Environmental, social, and governance (ESG) factors, 55, 56–57

Epstein, M. J., 54n2, 146n, 450n

Equipment maintenance costs, 735

Equity-equivalent (EE) adjustments, 840, 841

Equivalent units
   calculation of, 188, 190, 192–193
   conversion cost for, 188
   direct materials and, 188–189
   explanation of, 188
   in process costing system, 187–191

Errors
   aggregation, 119
   estimation, 284
   implementation, 653
   measurement, 120, 653
   modeling, 653
   in operational performance measurement, 653
   in overhead application, 120
   prediction, 653
   specification, 120

ESG. *See* Environmental, social, and governance (ESG) factors

Estimation error, 284

Ethical issues
   in cost allocation, 235–236
   management compensation and, 873

Ethical standards, for management accountants, 24–26, 36

Ethisphere Institute, 36

Euro, 43

European Union (EU), 8, 37, 43, 214, 604

European Union Circular Economy Programme, 214

EVA® capital, 840–841

Evaluation
   balanced scorecard and strategy map for, 798–800
   design of management control systems for, 783–785
   of financial performance of investment centers, 826–827
   performance, subjective, 792, 802
   variable costing *vs.* full costing for, 795–798

EVA® NOPAT, 840–841

Evans, J. R., 726n3, 728n6, 729n, 729n7, 737n

Evans, K., 344n

Ex ante evaluation, 784

Excel (Microsoft), 244, 246, 284n4, 290–291, 384, 385, 444n, 446–450, 492n18, 493n19, 551n5

Excess capacity, 153

Excessive relevant cost pricing, 432

Excessive short-term focus, 789

Exchange rates, 10, 43, 71

Execution
   balanced scorecard and, 51
   effects of competitive strategy on, 45
   strategy map and, 51
   in successful strategy, 43–45

Executional cost drivers, 87–88, 103

Exercise price, 495

Expected value analysis, 339

Expected value of perfect information (EVPI), 655

Expedia, 97

Expediting costs, 736

Experience, as structural cost driver, 86, 278

Ex post evaluation, 784

Expropriation, 850

External failure, 734, 736

External failure costs, 724, 732, 734, 735, 736, 738

External (customer-satisfaction) quality metrics, 740–741

External users, 4

ExxonMobil Corporation, 476, 847

EY, 88

F

Facility-level activities, 148, 336

Facility-level costs, 430

Factory overhead
   applying costs, 117
   cost drivers for, 116–117
   departmental overhead rates, 117–118
   explanation of, 80
   job costing and, 115–116
   in normal costing, 116–120
   potential errors in application and, 119–120
   as product cost in manufacturing, 89
   variance analysis for, 632–643

Factory overhead applied, 116

Factory overhead budget, 375, 377, 390

Factory overhead costs, 597

FASAB Standard Number 4, 157

FASB ASC 330-10-30, 636, 645, 646

Fast cycle time, 554

Fastow, Andrew, 873

Favoritism, as bias, 802

Fay, Rebecca, 446n

FCLT Global, 840

Featherstone, E., 477n7

Federal Accounting Standards Advisory Board (FASAB), 157

Federal Reserve Board, 33

Federal Trade Commission (FTC), 21–22

FedEx, 161, 167, 278

Feedback loops, 725

Ferreira, Nelson, 497n

FIFO method
   explanation of, 191
   in process costing, 195–200
   for process costing with multiple departments, 204–207
   weighted-average method compared with, 200–201

"Fighter brand," 561

Financial Accounting Standards Board (FASB), 6, 6n2, 22, 235

Financial budgets, 368

Financial control
   explanation of, 580
   short-term, 581–582

Financial control systems, 596